D1517891

A COURSEBOOK IN

INTERNATIONAL INTELLECTUAL PROPERTY

By

Doris Estelle Long
Professor of Law
The John Marshall Law School

Anthony D'Amato
Leighton Professor of Law
Northwestern University School of Law

AMERICAN CASEBOOK SERIES®

WEST
GROUP

ST. PAUL, MINN., 2000

ISBN 0–314–23076–9

 *TEXT IS PRINTED ON 10% POST
CONSUMER RECYCLED PAPER*

To Barb,
for bringing us together,
and
to Karen,
for putting up with the mess.

*

Preface and Acknowledgments

This Coursebook and its accompanying Documents Supplement are designed for a one-semester law school course in international intellectual property. As is typical with coursebooks of this kind, we have included somewhat more material than can comfortably be covered in one semester. This allows the professor to select topics according to his or her pedagogical needs. In particular, Parts X, XI and XII of this Coursebook explore specific problems in depth. Some, all, or none of these in-depth problems may be offered in a given semester. Also, Part I, which is a general view of US intellectual property law, may be skimmed or skipped depending on whether the students in the class have already taken one or more courses in US intellectual property.

We believe in being user-friendly. We've used easy-to-remember subject titles for cases and we've removed ellipses from edited case reports. Many provocative Notes and Questions are sprinkled throughout the Coursebook to help stimulate classroom discussion. We have added a unique website to update our Coursebook and Documents Supplement. Readers are invited to visit this site at www.long-damato.nwu.edu. Access to the site is free, courtesy of Northwestern University.

International intellectual property law is largely a matter of treaty regimes, reciprocal international legislation for the protection of literary and artistic works and scientific invention, and ownership issues that seem to come up in many countries as the global market works its accommodation with the rights of authors and inventors. We have selected cases from around the world that illustrate these recurring issues. In addition, we introduce "Controversies" as a companion to "Cases." A Controversy involves facts, issues, arguments, and a "decision" reached by a non-judicial body such as a legislature or by out-of-court settlement. When an intellectual property issue arises for the first time in the court of a particular country, references both to foreign cases and foreign controversies can be exceptionally persuasive in legal argument. We believe that practitioners of international intellectual property will increasingly use controversies in their legal research and briefs.

On the world stage there are analogues to domestic intellectual property rights that, in varying degrees, establish copyrights and patents, protect trade secrets, trade marks and industrial designs, and protect "neighboring rights" to these forms. In addition, international intellectual property law deals with a subject that has no domestic-law analogue, namely, the protection of cultural patrimony.

Our Coursebook grew out of our co-teaching a seminar at Northwestern University Law School on international intellectual property (also co-taught with Adjunct Professor William Streff, to whom we are indebted for his sharp insights), as well as Professor Long's regular courses in international intellectual property at The John Marshall Law School and Jiao Tung University in Shanghai. We are deeply indebted to our wonderful students who have contributed so much to our evolving thought on this vast subject. In particular, we are indebted to our summer research assistants on this project. One student, Isabella Rudes, who is now practicing law in Germany, contributed so much of her time and superb talent to this enterprise that she is our Virtual Co-Author. Our other summer research assistants, whose help we have been so fortunate to have, were Lisa Carroll, Salma Hammad, Matthew Weed, Adam von Poblitz, Sean Kahng, Chris Kohler, Laura MacFarland-Taylor, Tania Diklic, Julia Andrusiv, Craig Sandberg and Nathan Benditson. All of these marvelous colleagues have made it possible for us to search throughout the world for cases and materials that are not at all easy to track down on the internet.

We would also like to thank Pamela Seige and G. Brandon Bauer at West Group, our secretarial assistants Gwen Koenigsfeld, Malissa Strong, Eugene Limb, and especially Mary Finn and Chris Kotter. Miss Finn's exemplary help has been well beyond the call of duty. Thanks to Dean David Van Zandt of Northwestern Law School and Dean Robert Gilbert Johnston of The John Marshall Law School for their support and encouragement, and to Judd C. and Mary Morris Leighton who have generously contributed research funds for this project.

DORIS ESTELLE LONG
ANTHONY D'AMATO

REMINDER

For free updates of cases, controversies,

and documentary material, visit

www.long-damato.nwu.edu

Summary of Contents

*

Table of Contents

_____

Table of Cases
Sorted by Names of Parties

The principal cases are in bold type. Cases cited or discussed in the text are roman type. References are to pages. Cases cited in principal cases and within other quoted materials are not included.

Table of Cases
Sorted by Descriptive Names

The principal cases are in bold type. Cases cited or discussed in the text are roman type. References are to pages. Cases cited in principal cases and within other quoted materials are not included.

A COURSEBOOK IN

INTERNATIONAL INTELLECTUAL PROPERTY

*

International Intellectual Property Coursebook

INTRODUCTION: A TRIP BEGINS

To paraphrase a Chinese saying, the longest trip begins with a single step. And so I find myself sitting at my PC writing this Introduction. My name is Anthony D'Amato, and I am serving as co-editor with Professor Doris Estelle Long of your new coursebook on international intellectual property. As I write these words, I have a strong desire to own them—after all, they're my words, aren't they? Of course my purpose in writing these words is to share the ideas they express with you. Some people might say the writer isn't important; in order to make sense, words depend on the reader. But none of this post-modernist anti-formalist literary jargon for me; they're still my words. Just because you're reading them doesn't mean you own them. I mean, what's right is right, right?

What I'd like to do is simply rent my words and the ideas they may contain. You're the lessee, I'm the lessor (not spelled "lesser"). And this won't cost you any more money than you've already paid, because you paid your rent when you bought our coursebook. What's fair is fair.

Naturally, if there were no way that I could retain ownership of my words, then I'd have to throw in the towel. But society has provided me with a way to retain ownership. It's called copyright. Some years ago, when I started writing, I had to append a copyright notice to my work to protect my ownership of it. Nowadays I no longer have to do that. I can, but I don't have to. Just to be on the super-safe side, unnecessary though it is, I proceed to add a footnote to the end of this sentence.[1]

If you peeked at the bottom of this page, you noticed that I put in one of the symbols from the list of symbols in my computer program. It is the symbol ©. I could have used the word "Copyright" instead of the symbol, but hey, I rarely ever get the chance to use that list of symbols, so I jumped at the opportunity.

And thus, with the touch of the "Enter" key and the appropriate wait of a split cybersecond, my ownership of these very words is recorded, even though it was not necessary for me to enter this formal statement of copyright. And Congress has currently given me ownership

---

1. © 1999 Anthony D'Amato.

1

of these words for the rest of my life plus fifty years.[2] This means, with limited exceptions, you can only rent these words from me. The only way you could own them would be for me to sell them to you. But I'm not interested in selling, and I'm sure you're not interested in buying. Why buy when you can rent?

What "limited exceptions"? Now we're already thinking like lawyers. You can freely quote fifty words or so from this Introduction without getting permission from me, so long as you attribute the quote to me. Even if I object, you can do it. (Why would I object? Well, if you get a low grade in this course, and then try to get back at me by writing a nasty review of this book that quotes me out of context, I would like to stop you, but I can't.)

Is my ownership of these words recognized only in the United States? No—and here's our first peek into international intellectual property! I now own these words in most of the world. In 1989 the United States signed the Berne Convention, extending U.S. copyright protection through the Berne Convention to the vast majority of nations in the world.

I said that I owned the words, but I should be more careful. Of course I don't own the actual words, for the simple reason that I didn't create them. In fact if you think deeply about it or if you're a fan of Wittgenstein's philosophy, you'll see that it's impossible for a solitary individual to create any word. Suppose I now create a word: stenapt. What does it mean? I know, but you don't know. So then how can it be a word? A word is something that you and I both know the meaning of; a word, in short, is a vehicle for communication. But the so-called word "stenapt" is not really a word because it only has, as Wittgenstein would say, a "private meaning." A private meaning is a meaning that I know but you don't know.[3] (Unless you're a Scrabble fan and you guessed by playing with the letters.)

Copyright protection does not extend to individual words, even if the author invents them. It doesn't extend to titles.[4] It doesn't extend to parts of a word.[5] But if I don't own the actual words I've been writing, what do I own? Do I own the ideas behind them? No, because I can't copyright an idea.[6] But I can own my expression of those ideas. The form of words I have used to express my ideas is my property. And that's what gets copyrighted.

---

2. And NOT "whichever comes first"!

3. Wittgenstein goes on to say, of course, that there is no "meaning" in the notion of a "private meaning," but we don't have to get into that—not now, not here.

4. For example, Louisa May Alcott's book "little women" was made into a motion picture in 1933, in 1949, in 1978, and in 1994, all with the same title. (And two of them, the 1933 and 1949 versions, rank among the greatest movies of all time.)

5. At the time of Disney Inc.'s take-over of American Broadcasting Corp., one of my students, Ben Bass, remarked "Disney's purchase of ABC is just their first step in a nefarious plot to take over the entire alphabet."

6. If the idea is incorporated in a useful invention, I might be able to protect it by patenting it; but I still can't copyright it.

What is actually appearing on my computer screen as I write these words is not, strictly speaking, my expression of my ideas, but rather an electronic embodiment of that expression of ideas. Similarly, the book you are reading contains a hardcopy embodiment of my ideas. You can own the physical coursebook by buying it, and in so doing you own the physical pages in which my words appear as well as the ink-marks on those pages. You can highlight my words in shocking pink, you can ink out the ones you don't like, and in desperation you can rip out pages that you don't like. But you are only renting the expression of my ideas. That means, for example, that you can't photocopy this Introduction and sell or distribute it to others. If you did, you would be violating the U.S. Copyright laws and could be subject to civil or criminal prosecution. However, you could quote a paragraph or so of this Introduction without my permission through the "fair use" exception of the copyright laws mentioned earlier. Or if you're one of those rare students who doesn't like to write in or highlight books, you could photocopy my Introduction just for your own purpose of scribbling on the photocopy.

How does West Group, publisher of this book, get to sell you my copyrighted material? Everyone knows the answer to this: it is by a license agreement from me. West pays me a share of its revenue from sales, called a royalty. The license gives West various rights to print and sell this casebook in various specified countries and in various specified formats. However, I retained all motion picture and television serialization, sitcom and rerun rights throughout the world. I did so, frankly, because West never asked for them. Had they brought the matter up in the negotiations, they could have purchased all those subsidiary rights from me for one dollar. For all I know they considered the idea but decided that the price was too high.

IS INTELLECTUAL PROPERTY REALLY "PROPERTY"?

A year ago, after I had given a talk on international intellectual property, a person in the audience got up and said, "Professor D'Amato, you refer to copyrights and patents as 'property', but everyone know they're not really property, they're only temporary monopolies created by the government. How can you justify your use of the word property in this connection?"

I like good, fundamental, skeptical questions. And so, as an addict of the Socratic method, I replied by turning the question around: "The real question," I said, "is why do we call real estate 'property' when it is really the common heritage of mankind? Why should any individual 'own' land, or a house, or a car? Simply because they've bought them from someone else, who also had no right to own them? Shouldn't we reserve the word 'property' to things that individuals create, things that had never been in existence before a person invented them—things like original works of art or music, literature, and useful inventions? Isn't intellectual property the only genuine property?"

That was, near as I can remember it, my answer to the questioner from the audience. Let me add to it, here, a brief note on history. In the early millennia of human strivings known as the hunter-gatherer era, there was probably no concept of ownership of land. But as population increased and people began to domesticate wild plants and animals,[7] the ensuing horticultural and agricultural eras gave rise to exclusive claims to land. It was inevitable that if a farmer went to the trouble of planting and harvesting crops, he would claim exclusive right to the farmland he cultivated. (And thus the invention of the fence.)

Unfortunately the farmer, tied up in cultivating his crops, was a vulnerable person. So the rise of horticulture was accompanied by a rise in militarism and tyranny. The army would have a leader who would either proclaim himself or his friend emperor. The emperor would then levy taxes against the farmers to pay the army. Any farmer who resisted would face overwhelming military force. Thus the armies were very much like criminal gangs: they sold "government protection" to the farmers in return for "payments" which the government called "taxes." Farmers were typically taxed a half to two-thirds of their crops. As a result, enormous value in the form of food (and food that could be sold abroad) went into government coffers. Government leaders became immensely rich; they "paid off" the military in order to keep the army under control. The farmer class was continuously exploited (taxes were set at just the point to leave the farmers enough food to stay alive). Because ownership of the land was a cheap incentive to keep farmers working, emperor-tyrants by and large did not interfere with private land ownership. But in some countries the taxation was so onerous that farmers had to borrow money to pay taxes, putting up their land as collateral. Then if there was a bad season, the farmer lost the land to the lender. In many instances the lender was a rare prosperous farmer. In medieval Russia this process led to the creation of serfs—former farmers who lost their land and now had to work as farmhands on the large estates of the prosperous farmers.[8] (Only with the rise of democratic governments in the past few hundred years was the pattern of onerous taxation finally broken in most countries: give each farmer and farmhand the vote, and taxes will eventually be set at lower levels!)

You're probably wondering now why I'm going on like this about ancient history when the point seems to be a simple one—that early farmers made claims to the land they cultivated and those claims were by and large respected by governments (who were primarily interested in exploiting the product of the farmers' labors). My reason is that there is another lesson about early claims to property to be drawn from the same historical material, one that goes to the origins of intellectual property.

The early dictatorial governments were so successful in draining surplus value from the farmers that an elite leisure class was created— the ruler plus his or her family (usually large numbers of children), military leaders, religious leaders—though the total of all these folks was

---

7. For an interesting account, see Jared M. Diamond, Guns, Germs, and Steel (1998).

8. For a pathbreaking study of these macrosociological developments, see John

H. Kautsky, The Politics of Aristocratic Empires (1982).

not much more than one per cent of the population in most countries. This top immensely rich one per cent did no work and searched actively for amusements. Thus, from the ranks of the poor and dispossessed, came forth artisans, artists, story-tellers, poets, musicians, clowns, troubadours, jugglers—anxious to sell their amusements to the leisure class. (And thus the invention of "culture.")

The performing artists were lucky to get paid for reducing the boredom of the ruling class. They would not have dared to demand exclusive rights to their stories, paintings, songs, poems, or sculptures. Nor would it have occurred to the elites to give the artists property rights in their works. A story teller like Homer in ancient Greece might tell wondrous tales of the Iliad and the Odyssey, but he had no property rights in those stories even if he happened to be their author. Someone in the audience with a good memory and an even better oral delivery than Homer could repeat the same stories and draw the crowds away from Homer's recitations.

And through the centuries, artists never did muster the political clout to demand and get property rights in their works. An unforeseen interest group came to their rescue—book publishers. In the fifteenth century Johannes Gutenberg invented the printing press, making it possible to manufacture multiple copies of an author's work. If a book publisher had a best seller—the Bible, or a collection of poems or lyrics—then another publisher would buy a single copy of the book, set up his own type, and print multiple copies. Indeed it was easier for a publisher to wait and see which books would become hits, rather than spend money publishing an original book which might turn out to be a flop. After a while, there were a small number of successful publishers and a large number of would-be publishers waiting to rip off the next best seller. The successful publishers formed a guild and put pressure on the king or parliament to enact copyright protection. Different countries reacted at different times. England was one of the first to pass a copyright act (the Statute of Anne in 1710) [(It was listed in prior version)]; Spain took a lot longer, making it possible for Spanish publishers to rip off successful books originally published in England.

Since then, intellectual property has come a long way. The United States is a major exporter of licenses of intellectual property: movies, television shows and serials, books and magazines, computer software programs, and pharmaceuticals. Approximately half of the money brought into the United States from our trade with the rest of the world is presently attributable to these intellectual property rights. And the percentage grows every year. The creation of new intellectual property is something that the United States does very well. In the twenty-first century it is likely to be our most important product.

WHAT IS "INTERNATIONAL" ABOUT IT?

This is not a course in United States law of intellectual property—important as it is as a basic law-school course—but rather a course in international intellectual property. A skeptic might ask (I haven't gotten this particular question from the audience when I've spoken about international intellectual property, but I'm sure one will be asked some day): "Why should American law students study *international* intellectual property? Isn't it true that you just hire local counsel in a foreign country if you need to register or protect American intellectual property in that country—the same way that a foreign law firm will hire American lawyers if they have a problem regarding U.S. law?"

This is a serious question. It suggests that unless a course in International Intellectual Property can *add value* to the training of an American lawyer, it should have no significant place in the curriculum of an American law school. No one needs law-school training in how to place a phone call to counsel in another country.

Thus we must ask: What is the value added, if any, by a course in international intellectual property? Let's explore the issue by imagining that you are a young associate in a law firm. One of the partners comes by and tells you that one of the firm's clients, Cure–All Pharmaceuticals Inc., has received some intelligence that a start-up drug company in India is manufacturing and proceeding to rip off one of Cure–All's patented and very successful drugs, Spleenex. The CEO of Cure–All called the senior partner and read her the riot act. The partner adds that the law firm last year had the job of registering the Spleenex patent all over the world, but maybe we screwed up and forgot to register the patent in India, or maybe we didn't screw up and the patent was registered but India doesn't enforce these things or maybe the Indian drug company is proceeding illegally. Your job: get the facts and tell us how we can protect Cure–All's Spleenex patent in India.

The first call you make is to the associate in your law firm who supervised the international patenting of Spleenex. Right away you learn that it was not negligence on the part of the firm to fail to get an Indian patent for Spleenex, but rather no attempt was made. Why, you ask? Because India simply does not give patent protection to foreign pharmaceuticals. Instead, Indian firms reverse-engineer the foreign drugs and sell them in India. These firms are making a great deal of money ripping off foreign intellectual property in pharmaceuticals.

You recall that in law school you knew a graduate student from India. You get his number from the law school's alumni office and place a call to him in Bombay. He confirms the story: Indian drug companies are growing quite large from all the exploitation of foreign drug and are starting to do research and development on their own. He adds that in the near future the Indian companies may start to lobby the government of India to set up patenting for drugs so as to protect their own R & D. If they succeed, and then if India wants world-wide protection for its own inventions, India will be forced to give foreign inventors the same protection in India. But between now and when that day comes, Cure–All's foreign patent rights are worthless in India.

Do you give up and tell the senior partner that there's nothing we can do about India? No, because your job was to write a memo on how

Spleenex could be protected in India. In the practice of law, nothing is ever 100% sure or 0% sure. Everything in law, as in life, is a matter of cost/benefit. You wouldn't want to spend a million dollars to try to get an adverse judgment reversed if the chance of getting a reversal is 2% and the amount at stake is just two million dollars. Maybe protecting Spleenex in India—even if it were possible—would be too costly for any revenues that Cure–All might receive. But that decision is a business decision for Cure–All's board of directors to make. Your job is to outline an answer to the "how" question and leave the "whether" question to the client.

You discover, after some research, that India was one of the key opponents to establishing a world intellectual property regime under the auspices of GATT.[9] In the Uruguay Round of GATT negotiations in the 1990s, the famous TRIPS[10] agreement was set up.[11] India led the unsuccessful fight against TRIPS. India was especially opposed to intellectual property protection of pharmaceuticals. The argument India presented was that patent protection of needed medical products would place them beyond the reach of Indian consumers. (Does this argument strike you as economically sound? We'll be examining this question in this course.)

Despite its opposition to TRIPS, India signed on. But since then it has been dragging its feet about enacting patent reform in India to implement the TRIPS agreement. The U.S. filed a complaint with the WTO[12] alleging that India's failure to reform its patent legislation was a violation of TRIPS. The WTO panel heard arguments and held in favor of the U.S. position. As this coursebook goes to press, it is reported that India has agreed to revise its patent laws to bring them into conformity with TRIPS obligations.

You write, in your memorandum, that even if or when India reforms its patent laws, it might come too late to protect Spleenex. Well, perhaps India might make its laws retroactive, so as to cover Spleenex. But it is quite unlikely for any country to make its laws retroactive. Maybe India will give Spleenex patent protection from the time of the enactment of the legislation. But even then the damage is done, because Indian pharmaceutical companies are ripping off Spleenex and presumably will always be able to undercut Cure–All's prices (Cure–All has to pay transportation charges to get the drugs into India, and perhaps some export or import tariffs.)

Is there anything we can do for our client right now? Maybe we could bring a lawsuit against India, charging violation of TRIPS. Does the TRIPS agreement allow or contemplate such private lawsuits? Maybe we could sue the pharmaceutical companies in India that are ripping off Spleenex? If so, where would we bring these lawsuits? In the U.S.? In India? In some world court? In the WPO? Are there any

9. General Agreement on Trade and Tariffs.

10. Agreement on Trade–Related Aspects of Intellectual Property Rights.

11. If TRIPS is not familiar to you, soon it will be.

12. World Trade Organization (set up by Gatt; has authority over TRIPS).

precedents? How much would the litigation cost our client? What are the chances of success? Would litigation be cost-effective? Should we get some other pharmaceutical companies to join us and thus reduce our cost of litigation?

In writing your memo you are engaged in the practice of law. Your memo is informed by your knowledge of *international* intellectual property law. You need to know about the WPO, about TRIPS, about cross-country litigation, where to look for precedents, etc.

You're not going to find all the information you need on your computer. International intellectual property law is a rapidly growing field, and much of it is not available on the internet. Indeed, internet providers haven't even worked out the *questions* that you need to ask in handling an international intellectual property claim.

As I learned when I was a law student, learning the law is not about learning content; it's about learning what questions to ask. If you know the questions, then you have a foundation for guiding and maximizing your research efforts.

This exciting new course in International Intellectual Property Law is all about asking the right questions.

Part I

A WINDOW ON THE WORLD: U.S. INTELLECTUAL PROPERTY LAW

INTRODUCTION

A. WHAT DOES THE TERM "INTERNATIONAL INTELLECTUAL PROPERTY" MEAN?

An understanding of a concept as amorphous as "international intellectual property law" requires an understanding of what the term "intellectual property" entails. Intellectual property has been in existence nearly as long as human beings have sought to protect their creative or commercial output. The first recorded trademark may have existed 3500 years ago when potters placed markings on their jars to indicate craftsmanship. Despite its lengthy existence, there is no single international definition of what qualifies as "intellectual property" or what the standard bundle of rights should include. Nevertheless, most nations generally have agreed that the following forms may qualify as intellectual property:

1. patents,
2. trademarks,
3. copyright,
4. trade secrets, and;
5. industrial designs (also referred to as utility models).

Despite this general agreement on forms of intellectual property, there has been a broad discrepancy between nations regarding the weight that should be given to intellectual property protection.

The history of the development of international standards for protecting intellectual property largely reflects the history of the growth of trade and technology. As technology advanced in the fields affecting the creation of literary and artistic works, the subject matter for copyright protection similarly advanced. Early national copyright laws granted rights to authors of written literary works, charts and music. The

10

invention of photography, sound recordings, motion pictures and computer software required further refinements and expansion in the types of works protected under copyright law. Similarly, the development of patent law largely reflects technological advances in the areas of science and the useful arts.

Concurrently with the advance of technology in the areas of art and science, modes of transportation and communication media evolved from the oxcart to supersonic transports and from smoke signals to digital and internet communications. These developments provided an increasingly global marketplace for intellectual property-based products. The internationalization of the marketplace for such products in turn gave rise to growing concerns over the differing levels of protection of such products.

Countries which granted little or no protection to intellectual property became havens for counterfeit or pirated products. That piracy inevitably had an adverse economic impact on the intellectual property owner. In the 1970's the problem of world-wide counterfeiting became severe, affecting both local sales in the country where the pirated goods were manufactured and foreign sales since such products were increasingly exported to developed countries. As a result of these global piracy problems, developed countries renewed their efforts to increase international levels of intellectual property protection, especially because royalty income became an important factor in the balance of trade.

One of the reasons for the present international dispute over the scope of protection to be afforded intellectual property is the great difference between developed and developing nations regarding the perceived impact of such protection.

Today developed nations are perceived as possessing the majority of creators and inventors of intellectual property. The unauthorized use of intellectual property represents for these rights holders a serious financial loss. Current estimates place worldwide piracy losses of motion pictures, software and records at over $8 billion in 1998 alone. Developed countries, who suffer the greatest financial loss from these activities, advocate strong protection for intellectual property rights. They contend that, absent sufficient protection, creators can't recover the cost of their research and development. The result is lower production, fewer trading opportunities and higher costs to the consumer. Therefore, they argue, weak protection undermines the goal of free trade.

Developing countries, on the other hand, demand that all knowledge be treated as a "common heritage of mankind" and be made available free of charge to all nations as an act of developmental aid. They believe that the development of the Third World is in the interest of all nations. As developing countries possess scarce economic resources, they contend they cannot spend those resources to protect what are perceived to be foreign rights. Intellectual property is often seen as a means of dominating and exploiting the economic potential of the importing country. Paying for imports or royalties is thus seen as an economic burden which could foster a negative balance of trade. In the effort to determine what the international standard is or should be, the laws of the United States necessarily pay a role. They serve as a window to the world of intellectual property, through which international questions and issues can begin to be perceived. Like all windows, U.S. law may not accurately reflect the world. But its examination should provide a valuable insight into the nature of intellectual property as practiced by one of the oldest legal systems, as well as one of the leading exporters of technology to the global market today.

The efforts to develop international protection continue. The standard set in the U.S. for intellectual property protection cannot be ignored internationally. Therefore, intellectual property as it exists in the United States should serve as a window to the world and supply a basis for an understanding of the problems that arise in the process of trying to reach an international consensus in determining the precise nature, scope and protection of what we now call "intellectual property."

B. WHAT IS "INTELLECTUAL PROPERTY" UNDER U.S. LAW?

Intellectual property is the property right in an intangible asset—a right in the "product of the mind." Under U.S. law, intellectual property rights are largely are creatures of statute (with, perhaps, the rare exception of trade secrets). When the Constitutional Convention became aware of the need for protection, they gave Congress the power, in a rare example of providing a textual reason for one of its provisions, to promote the progress of science and useful arts, by securing for limited times to authors and inventors the exclusive right to their respective writings and discoveries.[1]

This provision, called the "Copyright and Patents Clause," provides a broad basis for both copyright and patent legislation. Copyright and patent laws were created and designed in the United States in order to increase the public's wealth of culture and knowledge, while granting certain rights to authors and inventors for a limited period of time. This clause reflects the economic philosophy that encouragement of individual effort by personal gain is the best way to advance the public welfare through the talents of authors and inventors.

In a similar way trademark rights developed to make sure that the trademark-owner obtains the necessary protection against copiers and free-riders who try to exploit consumer confusion to advance sales of their own goods or services. Even though such laws have been enacted by Congress using its broad Commerce Clause powers, federal trademark legislation is not based on so clear a grant of power as the Copyright Clause.

Protecting trade secrets generally serves the purpose of encouraging investment of labor and creativity, and of maintaining a standard of

---

1. Art. I, Section 8, Clause 8 of the U.S. Constitution. *See* Documents Supplement.

commercial ethics and morality in the marketplace. Trade secret law has developed largely as a product of the common law. Its principles have been codified under various state statutes modeled on the Uniform Trade Secrets Act. Only recently has Congress enacted federal trade secret statutes. Like federal trademark law, federal trade secret law, represented by the Economic Espionage Act, codified in 18 U.S.C. §§ 1831–1839, is based on the Constitutional grant of powers to issue legislation under the Commerce Clause. Since Congress has only recently entered the field, trade secrets largely remain a creature of state law. While treatment of trade secrets consequently varies on a state-by-state basis, many state laws reflect the concepts of protection codified by the Uniform Trade Secrets Act which in turn was strongly influenced by the Restatement of Torts Sections 757 and 758.

Industrial design itself is not a protected category of intellectual property in the U.S. It generally includes those design elements which are not subject to patent protection but have some degree of novelty and/or originality that warrants protection against unauthorized use. In the U.S. these designs either fall into one of the four existing categories of intellectual property such as design patents or trade dress or they are denied protection.

Chapter One

COPYRIGHTS

Origin and Purposes of the Copyright Law. Empowered by the U.S. Constitution Art. I, Sect. 8, Cl. 8 Congress created the Copyright Act of 1976 which states in Section 102:

"Copyright protection subsists, in accordance with this title, in *original works of authorship fixed in any tangible medium of expression*, now or later developed, from which they can be perceived, reproduced, or otherwise communicated, either directly or with the aid of a machine or device. Works of authorship include the following categories:

(1) literary works;

(2) musical works, including any accompanying words;

(3) dramatic works, including any accompanying music;

(4) pantomimes and choreographic works;

(5) pictorial, graphic, and sculptural works;

(6) motion pictures and other audiovisual works;

(7) sound recordings; and;

(8) architectural works.

In no case does the copyright protection for an original work of authorship extend to any idea, procedure, process, system, method of operation, concept, principle, or discovery, regardless of the form in which it is described, explained, illustrated, or embodied in such work." 17 U.S.C. § 102 (emphasis added).

The Role of Registration. Copyright under U.S. law is secured automatically upon creation.

No publication or registration or other action in the U.S. Copyright Office is required to secure copyright. Copyright is secured automatically when the work is created in tangible form for the first time.

Even though registration is not generally a requirement for protection, the copyright law provides several inducements or advantages to encourage copyright owners to seek registration. Among these advantages are the following:

- Registration establishes a public record of the copyright claim;
- Registration is ordinarily necessary before infringement suits may be filed in court by U.S. authors,
- If obtained before or within 5 years of publication, registration will establish prima facie proof in court of the validity of the copyright; and
- If registration is made within 3 months after publication of the work or prior to an infringement of the work, statutory damages and attorney's fees will be available to the copyright owner in court actions. Otherwise, only an award of actual damages and profits is available.

Registration may be made at any time within the life of the copyright. To assure that you have full legal rights for enforcement of your copyright you should file for registration within 3 months after your work is first published and be certain that all published copies carry a copyright notice.

Notice. Notice is no longer required to maintain copyright protection. However, proper notice may serve to eliminate certain defenses in a copyright infringement action, including, for example, innocent infringement.

Form of Notice for Visually Perceptible Copies

The notice for visually perceptible copies should contain all of the following three elements:

- The symbol comprising the letter C in a circle, the word "Copyright" or the abbreviation "C";
- The year of first publication of the work.
- The name of the owner of copyright in the work, or an abbreviation by which the name can be recognized, or a generally known alternative designation of the owner.

Form Of Notice For Sound Recordings

The copyright notice for sound recordings has somewhat different requirements. The notice should contain the following three elements:

- The symbol comprising the letter P in a circle;
- The year of first publication of the sound recording; and
- The name of the owner of copyright in the sound recording, or an abbreviation by which the name can be recognized, or a generally known alternative designation of the owner. If the producer of the sound recording is named on its labels or containers, and if no other name appears in conjunction with the notice, the producer's name shall be considered a part of the notice. The three elements

of the notice should ordinarily appear together on the copies or recordings.

A work created (fixed in tangible form for the first time) on or after January 1, 1978 is automatically protected from the moment of its creation, and is ordinarily given a term enduring for the author's life, plus an additional 50 years after the author's death.

A. WHAT ARE THE STATUTORY REQUIRE-MENTS FOR COPYRIGHT PROTECTION UNDER U.S. LAW?

THE TELEPHONE DIRECTORY CASE

FEIST PUBLICATIONS, INC. v. RURAL TELEPHONE SERVICE COMPANY

Supreme Court of the United States, 1991.
499 U.S. 340, 111 S.Ct. 1282.

JUSTICE O'CONNOR delivered the opinion of the Court.

This case requires us to clarify the extent of copyright protection available to telephone directory white pages.

Rural Telephone Service Company, Inc., is a certified public utility that provides telephone service to several communities in northwest Kansas. It is subject to a state regulation that requires all telephone companies operating in Kansas to issue annually an updated telephone directory. Accordingly, as a condition of its monopoly franchise, Rural publishes a typical telephone directory, consisting of white pages and yellow pages. The white pages list in alphabetical order the names of Rural's subscribers, together with their towns and telephone numbers. The yellow pages list Rural's business subscribers alphabetically by category and feature classified advertisements of various sizes. Rural distributes its directory free of charge to its subscribers, but earns revenue by selling yellow pages advertisements.

Feist Publications, Inc., is a publishing company that specializes in area-wide telephone directories. Unlike a typical directory, which covers only a particular calling area, Feist's area-wide directories cover a much larger geographical range, reducing the need to call directory assistance or consult multiple directories. The Feist directory that is the subject of this litigation covers 11 different telephone service areas in 15 counties and contains 46,878 white pages listings—compared to Rural's approximately 7,700 listings. Like Rural's directory, Feist's is distributed free of charge and includes both white pages and yellow pages. Feist and Rural compete vigorously for yellow pages advertising.

As the sole provider of telephone service in its service area, Rural obtains subscriber information quite easily. Persons desiring telephone service must apply to Rural and provide their names and addresses; Rural then assigns them a telephone number. Feist is not a telephone company, let alone one with monopoly status, and therefore lacks independent access to any subscriber information. To obtain white pages listings for its area-wide directory, Feist approached each of the 11 telephone companies operating in northwest Kansas and offered to pay for the right to use its white pages listings.

Of the 11 telephone companies, only Rural refused to license its listings to Feist. Rural's refusal created a problem for Feist, as omitting these listings would have left a gaping hole in its area-wide directory, rendering it less attractive to potential yellow pages advertisers.

Unable to license Rural's white pages listings, Feist used them without Rural's consent. Feist began by removing several thousand listings that fell outside the geographic range of its area-wide directory, then hired personnel to investigate the 4,935 that remained. These employees verified the data reported by Rural and sought to obtain additional information. As a result, a typical Feist listing includes the individual's street address; most of Rural's listings do not. Notwithstanding these additions, however, 1,309 of the 46,878 listings in Feist's 1983 directory were identical to listings in Rural's 1982–1983 white pages. App. 54 (§ 15–16),57. Four of these were fictitious listings that Rural had inserted into its directory to detect copying.

Rural sued for copyright infringement in the District Court for the District of Kansas taking the position that Feist, in compiling its own directory, could not use the information contained in Rural's white pages. Rural asserted that Feist's employees were obliged to travel door-to-door or conduct a telephone survey to discover the same information for themselves. Feist responded that such efforts were economically impractical and, in any event, unnecessary because the information copied was beyond the scope of copyright protection. The District Court granted summary judgment to Rural, explaining that "[c]ourts have consistently held that telephone directories are copyrightable" and citing a string of lower court decisions. We granted certiorari to determine whether the copyright in Rural's directory protects the names, towns, and telephone numbers copied by Feist.

This case concerns the interaction of two well-established propositions. The first is that facts are not copyrightable; the other, that compilations of facts generally are. Each of these propositions possesses an impeccable pedigree. That there can be no valid copyright in facts is universally understood. The most fundamental axiom of copyright law is that "[n]o author may copyright his ideas or the facts he narrates." *Harper & Row, Publishers, Inc. v. Nation Enterprises*, 471 U.S. 539, 556, 105 S.Ct. 2218, 2228, 85 L.Ed.2d 588 (1985). Rural wisely concedes this point, noting in its brief that "facts and discoveries, of course, are not themselves subject to copyright protection." At the same time, however, it is beyond dispute that compilations of facts are within the subject matter of copyright. Compilations were expressly mentioned in the Copyright Act of 1909, and again in the Copyright Act of 1976.

There is an undeniable tension between these two propositions. Many compilations consist of nothing but raw data—i.e., wholly factual information not accompanied by any original written expression. On what basis may one claim a copyright in such a work? Common sense tells us that 100 uncopyrightable facts do not magically change their status when gathered together in one place. Yet copyright law seems to contemplate that compilations that consist exclusively of facts are potentially within its scope.

The key to resolving the tension lies in understanding why facts are not copyrightable. The *sine qua non* of copyright is originality. To qualify for copyright protection, a work must be original to the author. *See Harper & Row, supra*, at 547-549, 105 S.Ct., at 2223-2224. Original, as the term is used in copyright, means only that the work was independently created by the author (as opposed to copied from other works), and that it possesses at least some minimal degree of creativity. To be sure, the requisite level of creativity is extremely low; even a slight amount will suffice. The vast majority of works make the grade quite easily, as they possess some creative spark, "no matter how crude, humble or obvious" it might be. Originality does not signify novelty; a work may be original even though it closely resembles other works so long as the similarity is fortuitous, not the result of copying. To illustrate, assume that two poets, each ignorant of the other, compose identical poems. Neither work is novel, yet both are original and, hence, copyrightable. *See Sheldon v. Metro-Goldwyn Pictures Corp.*, 81 F.2d 49, 54 (CA2 1936)

Originality is a constitutional requirement. The source of Congress' power to enact copyright laws is Article I, § 8, cl. 8, of the Constitution, which authorizes Congress to "secur[e] for limited Times to Authors ... the exclusive Right to their respective Writings." In two decisions from the late 19th century *The Trade–Mark Cases*, 100 U.S. 82, 25 L.Ed. 550 (1879); and *Burrow-Giles Lithographic Co. v. Sarony*, 111 U.S. 53, 4 S.Ct. 279, 28 L.Ed. 349 (1884)—this Court defined the crucial terms "authors" and "writings." In so doing, the Court made it unmistakably clear that these terms presuppose a degree of originality.

It is this bedrock principle of copyright that mandates the law's seemingly disparate treatment of facts and factual compilations. This is because facts do not owe their origin to an act of authorship. The distinction is one between creation and discovery: The first person to find and report a particular fact has not created the fact; he or she has merely discovered its existence. To borrow from *Burrow-Giles*, one who discovers a fact is not its "maker" or "originator." "The discoverer merely finds and records." Census takers, for example, do not "create" the population figures that emerge from their efforts; in a sense, they copy these figures from the world around them. Census data therefore do not trigger copyright because these data are not "original" in the constitutional sense. The same is true of all facts—scientific, historical, biographical, and news of the day. [T]hey may not be copyrighted and are part of the public domain available to every person. *Miller, supra*, at 1369.

Factual compilations, on the other hand, may possess the requisite originality. The compilation author typically chooses which facts to include, in what order to place them, and how to arrange the collected data so that they may be used effectively by readers. These choices as to selection and arrangement, so long as they are made independently by the compiler and entail a minimal degree of creativity, are sufficiently original that Congress may protect such compilations through the copyright laws. Thus, even a directory that contains absolutely no protectible written expression, only facts, meets the constitutional minimum for copyright protection if it features an original selection or arrangement.

This protection is subject to an important limitation. The mere fact that a work is copyrighted does not mean that every element of the work may be protected. Originality remains the *sine qua non* of copyright; accordingly, copyright protection may extend only to those components of a work that are original to the author. Thus, if the compilation author clothes facts with an original collocation of words, he or she may be able to claim a copyright in this written expression. Others may copy the underlying facts from the publication, but not the precise words used to present them. In *Harper & Row*, for example, we explained that President Ford could not prevent others from copying bare historical facts from his autobiography, *see* 471 U.S., at 556–557, 105 S.Ct. at 2228–2229, but that he could prevent others from copying his "subjective descriptions and portraits of public figures." *Id.*, at 563, 105 S.Ct., at 2232. Where the compilation author adds no written expression but rather lets the facts speak for themselves, the expressive element is more elusive. The only conceivable expression is the manner in which the compiler has selected and arranged the facts. Thus, if the selection and arrangement are original, these elements of the work are eligible for copyright protection.

This inevitably means that the copyright in a factual compilation is thin. Notwithstanding a valid copyright, a subsequent compiler remains free to use the facts contained in another's publication to aid in preparing a competing work, so long as the competing work does not feature the same selection and arrangement.

It may seem unfair that much of the fruit of the compiler's labor may be used by others without compensation. As Justice Brennan has correctly observed, however, this is not "some unforeseen byproduct of a statutory scheme." *Harper & Row*, 471 U.S., at 589, 105 S.Ct. at 2245 (dissenting opinion). It is, rather, "the essence of copyright," and a constitutional requirement. The primary objective of copyright is not to reward the labor of authors, but "[t]o promote the Progress of Science and useful Arts." Art. I, § 8, cl. 8. To this end, copyright assures authors the right to their original expression, but encourages others to build freely upon the ideas and information conveyed by a work. This principle, known as the idea/expression or fact/expression dichotomy, applies to all works of authorship. As applied to a factual compilation, assuming the absence of original written expression, only the compiler's selection and arrangement may be protected; the raw facts may be copied at will.

This result is neither unfair nor unfortunate. It is the means by which copyright advances the progress of science and art.

Courts developed a theory to justify the protection of factual compilations. Known alternatively as "sweat of the brow" or "industrious collection," the underlying notion was that copyright was a reward for the hard work that went into compiling facts.

The classic formulation of the doctrine appeared in *Jeweler's Circular Publishing Co.*, 281 F., at 88:

> "The right to copyright a book upon which one has expended labor in its preparation does not depend upon whether the materials which he has collected consist or not of matters which are publici juris, or whether such materials show literary skill or originality, either in thought or in language, or anything more than industrious collection. The man who goes through the streets of a town and puts down the names of each of the inhabitants, with their occupations and their street number, acquires material of which he is the author".

The "sweat of the brow" doctrine had numerous flaws, the most glaring being that it extended copyright protection in a compilation beyond selection and arrangement-the compiler's original contributions-to the facts themselves. Under the doctrine, the only defense to infringement was independent creation. A subsequent compiler was "not entitled to take one word of information previously published," but rather had to "independently wor[k] out the matter for himself, so as to arrive at the same result from the same common sources of information." *Id.*, at 88–89. "Sweat of the brow" courts thereby eschewed the most fundamental axiom of copyright law-that no one may copyright facts or ideas.

Not every selection, coordination, or arrangement will pass muster. This is plain from the statute. It states that, to merit protection, the facts must be selected, coordinated, or arranged "in such a way" as to render the work as a whole original. This implies that some "ways" will trigger copyright, but that others will not. See Patry 57, and n. 76. Otherwise, the phrase "in such a way" is meaningless and Congress should have defined "compilation" simply as "a work formed by the collection and assembly of preexisting materials or data that are selected, coordinated, or arranged." That Congress did not do so is dispositive. In accordance with *the established principle that a court should give effect, if possible, to every clause and word of a statute, Moskal v. United States,* 498 U.S. 103, 109–110, 111 S.Ct. 461, 466, 112 L.Ed.2d 449 (1990) we conclude that the statute envisions that there will be some fact-based works in which the selection, coordination, and arrangement are not sufficiently original to trigger copyright protection.

As discussed earlier, however, the originality requirement is not particularly stringent. A compiler may settle upon a selection or arrangement that others have used; novelty is not required.

Originality requires only that the author make the selection or arrangement independently (i.e., without copying that selection or arrangement from another work), and that it display some minimal level of creativity. Presumably, the vast majority of compilations will pass this test, but not all will. There remains a narrow category of works in which the creative spark is utterly lacking or so trivial as to be virtually nonexistent. *See generally Bleistein v. Donaldson Lithographing Co.*, 188 U.S. 239, 251, 23 S.Ct. 298, 300, 47 L.Ed. 460 (1903).

Even if a work qualifies as a copyrightable compilation, it receives only limited protection. This is the point of § 103 of the Act. Section 103 explains that "the subject matter of copyright ... includes compilations," § 103(a), but that copyright protects only the author's original contributions-not the facts or information conveyed:

> "The copyright in a compilation ... extends only to the material contributed by the author of such work, as distinguished from the preexisting material employed in the work, and does not imply any exclusive right in the preexisting material." § 103(b).

As § 103 makes clear, copyright is not a tool by which a compilation author may keep others from using the facts or data he or she has collected. "The most important point here is one that is commonly misunderstood today: copyright ... has no effect one way or the other on the copyright or public domain status of the preexisting material." H.R.Rep., at 57; S.Rep., at 55. The 1909 Act did not require, as "sweat of the brow" courts mistakenly assumed, that each subsequent compiler must start from scratch and is precluded from relying on research undertaken by another. *See, e.g., Jeweler's Circular Publishing Co.*, 281 F., at 88–89. Rather, the facts contained in existing works may be freely copied because copyright protects only the elements that owe their origin to the compiler-the selection, coordination, and arrangement of facts.

The 1976 revisions to the Copyright Act leave no doubt that originality, not "sweat of the brow," is the touchstone of copyright protection in directories and other fact-based works. Nor is there any doubt that the same was true under the 1909 Act. The 1976 revisions were a direct response to the Copyright Office's concern that many lower courts had misconstrued this basic principle, and Congress emphasized repeatedly that the purpose of the revisions was to clarify, not change, existing law. The revisions explain with painstaking clarity that copyright requires originality, § 102(a); that facts are never original, § 102(b); that the copyright in a compilation does not extend to the facts it contains, § 103(b); and that a compilation is copyrightable only to the extent that it features an original selection, coordination, or arrangement, § 101.

There is no doubt that Feist took from the white pages of Rural's directory a substantial amount of factual information. At a minimum, Feist copied the names, towns, and telephone numbers of 1,309 of Rural's subscribers. Not all copying, however, is copyright infringement. To establish infringement, two elements must be proven: (1) ownership of a valid copyright, and (2) copying of constituent elements of the work that are original. *See Harper & Row*, 471 U.S., at 548, 105 S.Ct., at 2224.The first element is not at issue here; Feist appears to concede that Rural's directory, considered as a whole, is subject to a valid copyright because it contains some foreword text, as well as original material in its yellow pages advertisements.

The selection, coordination, and arrangement of Rural's white pages do not satisfy the minimum constitutional standards for copyright protection. As mentioned at the outset, Rural's white pages are entirely typical. Persons desiring telephone service in Rural's service area fill out an application and Rural issues them a telephone number. In preparing its white pages, Rural simply takes the data provided by its subscribers and lists it alphabetically by surname. The end product is a garden-variety white pages directory, devoid of even the slightest trace of creativity.

Rural's selection of listings could not be more obvious: It publishes the most basic information-name, town, and telephone number-about each person who applies to it for telephone service. This is "selection" of a sort, but it lacks the modicum of creativity necessary to transform mere selection into copyrightable expression. Rural expended sufficient effort to make the white pages directory useful, but insufficient creativity to make it original.

We note in passing that the selection featured in Rural's white pages may also fail the originality requirement for another reason. Feist points out that Rural did not truly "select" to publish the names and telephone numbers of its subscribers; rather, it was required to do so by the Kansas Corporation Commission as part of its monopoly franchise .. Accordingly, one could plausibly conclude that this selection was dictated by state law, not by Rural.

Nor can Rural claim originality in its coordination and arrangement of facts. The white pages do nothing more than list Rural's subscribers in alphabetical order. This arrangement may, technically speaking, owe its origin to Rural; no one disputes that Rural undertook the task of alphabetizing the names itself. But there is nothing remotely creative about arranging names alphabetically in a white pages directory. It is an age-old practice, firmly rooted in tradition and so commonplace that it has come to be expected as a matter of course. It is not only unoriginal, it is practically inevitable. This time-honored tradition does not possess the minimal creative spark required by the Copyright Act and the Constitution.

We conclude that the names, towns, and telephone numbers copied by Feist were not original to Rural and therefore were not protected by the copyright in Rural's combined white and yellow pages directory. As a constitutional matter, copyright protects only those constituent elements of a work that possess more than a de minimis quantum of creativity. Rural's white pages, limited to basic subscriber information and ar-ranged alphabetically, fall short of the mark. As a statutory matter, 17 U.S.C. § 101 does not afford protection from copying to a collection of facts that are selected, coordinated, and arranged in a way that utterly lacks originality. Given that some works must fail, we cannot imagine a more likely candidate. Indeed, were we to hold that Rural's white pages pass muster, it is hard to believe that any collection of facts could fail.

Because Rural's white pages lack the requisite originality, Feist's use of the listings cannot constitute infringement. This decision should not be construed as demeaning Rural's efforts in compiling its directory, but rather as making clear that copyright rewards originality, not effort. As this court noted more than a century ago, "great praise may be due to the plaintiffs for their industry and enterprise in publishing this paper, yet the law does not contemplate their being rewarded in this way." *Baker v. Selden*, 101 U.S., at 105.

The judgment of the Court of Appeals is reversed.

Notes and Questions

1. The *Telephone Directory* case (Feist) is a notable case. It departs from the long followed "sweat of the brow" doctrine. Why does the Supreme Court reject the "sweat of the brow" doctrine? Why are "facts" themselves not a form of original expression?

2. What purpose is served by rejecting "sweat of the brow"? Shouldn't an author's labor in creating a factual compilation be rewarded? Why or why not?

3. Are originality and creativity the same thing? What constitutes creativity? Is creativity ultimately the threshold for determining "authorship" or is authorship a separate and separable prerequisite?

4. Was the holding in the *Telephone Directory* case correct? Was there maybe an aspect of the Rural telephone directory that contained a spark of creativity? Would that have made the work to any extent protectable? Is this holding also valid for an analysis of computer software? *See* Chapter 37, *infra. See also Computer Associates International v. Altai, Inc.*, 982 F.2d 693 (2d Cir.1992).

THE VIDEO GAME FIXATION CASE
STERN ELECTRONICS, INC. v. HAROLD KAUFMAN
United States Court of Appeals, Second Circuit, 1982.
669 F.2d 852.

NEWMAN, CIRCUIT JUDGE.

This appeal from the grant of a preliminary injunction concerns primarily the availability of copyright protection for the visual images electronically displayed by a coin-operated video game of the sort currently enjoying widespread popularity throughout the country. Omni Video Games, Inc., its distributor, and two of its officers appeal from an order entered May 22, 1981 in the District Court for the Eastern District of New York (Eugene H. Nickerson, Judge), preliminarily enjoining them from infringing the copyright of Stern Electronics, Inc. in the audiovisual work entitled "Scramble" and from making further use of the trademark "SCRAMBLE" in connection with electronic video games. Appellants contend that the visual images and accompanying sounds of the video game fail to satisfy the fixation and originality requirements of the Copyright Act, 17 U.S.C.App. § 102(a) (1976). We reject these contentions and affirm the preliminary injunction.

Video games like "Scramble" can roughly be described as computers programmed to create on a television screen cartoons in which some of the action is controlled by the player. In Stern's "Scramble," for example, the video screen displays a spaceship moving horizontally through six different scenes in which obstacles are encountered. With each scene the player faces increasing difficulty in traversing the course and scoring points. The first scene depicts mountainous terrain, missile bases, and fuel depots. The player controls the altitude and speed of the spaceship, decides when to release the ship's supply of bombs, and fires lasers that can destroy attacking missiles and aircraft. He attempts to bomb the missile bases (scoring points for success), bomb the fuel depots (increasing his own diminishing fuel supply with each hit), avoid the missiles being fired from the ground, and avoid crashing his ship into the mountains. And that is only scene one. In subsequent scenes the hazards include missile-firing enemy aircraft and tunnel-like airspaces. The scenes are in color, and the action is accompanied by battlefield sounds.

The game is built into a cabinet containing a cathode ray tube, a number of electronic circuit boards, a loudspeaker, and hand controls for the player. The electronic circuitry includes memory storage devices called PROMs, an acronym for "programmable read only memory."[2] The PROM stores the instructions and data from a computer program in such a way that when electric current passes through the circuitry, the interaction of the program stored in the PROM with the other components of the game produces the sights and sounds of the audiovisual display that the player sees and hears. The memory devices determine not only the appearance and movement of the images but also the variations in movement in response to the player's operation of the hand controls.

Stern manufactures amusement equipment, including video games, for distribution worldwide. In January 1981 at a London trade exhibit Stern became aware of "Scramble," an electronic video game developed in late 1980 by a Japanese corporation, Konami Industry Co., Ltd. The audiovisual display constituting what Stern alleges is the copyrightable work was first published in Japan on January 8, 1981. Stern secured an exclusive sub-license to distribute the "Scramble" game in North and

2. Memory devices of computers are generally either RAM (random access memory) or ROM (read only memory). RAM, used in most sophisticated computers, is a memory device in which stored information can be changed simply by writing in new information that replaces old information. The stored information in a ROM cannot be changed; it is imprinted into the ROM when the device is manufactured. A PROM is a ROM into which information can be imprinted (programmed) after manufacture; once the information is programmed in a PROM, it cannot be changed simply by writing in a new program.

South America from Konami's exclusive licensee, and began selling the game in the United States on March 17, 1981. Even in the fast-paced world of video games, "Scramble" quickly became a big success. Approximately 10,000 units were sold at about $2,000 each in the first two months for an initial sales volume of about $20 million.

On April 14, 1981, a Certificate of Copyright Registration for the audiovisual work "Scramble" was issued to Konami by the United States Copyright Office, and shortly thereafter documents were filed with the Copyright Office reflecting the license and sub-license to Stern. To satisfy the statutory requirement for deposit of copies of a work to be copyrighted, 17 U.S.C. § 408(b) (1976), Konami submitted video tape recordings of the "Scramble" game, both in its "attract mode" and in its "play mode."[3]

Omni alleges that, concurrently with Stern's sales of the "Scramble" game and even earlier, it was endeavoring to sell a line of video game products so constructed that each unit could be equipped for playing different games by substituting a PROM containing the program for a particular game. Omni contends that it planned to market this line of interchangeable games with the label "Scramble" affixed to the headboard of each unit; the name of the particular game was also to be prominently displayed. On December 1, 1980, Omni's president ordered ten silk screen nameplates bearing the name "Scramble." Between that date and March 17, 1981, the date of Stern's first sale of its "Scramble" game, Omni sold five units of video games bearing the name "Scramble" on the headboard. In April 1981 Omni began to sell a video game called "Scramble" that not only bears the same name as the "Scramble" game Stern was then marketing, but also is virtually identical in both sight and sound. It sold this copy of Stern's "Scramble" game, known in the trade as a "knock-off," for several hundred dollars less than Stern's game.

In challenging the preliminary injunction that bars distribution of its "Scramble" game, Omni does not dispute that Konami and its sub-licensee Stern are entitled to secure some copyright protection for their "Scramble" game. Omni contends that Konami was entitled to copyright only the written computer program that determines the sights and sounds of the game's audiovisual display. While that approach would have afforded some degree of protection, it would not have prevented a determined competitor from manufacturing a "knock-off" of "Scramble" that replicates precisely the sights and sounds of the game's audiovisual display. This could be done by writing a new computer program that would interact with the hardware components of a video game to produce on the screen the same images seen in "Scramble," accompanied by the same sounds. Such replication is possible because many different computer programs can produce the same "results," whether

---

3. "Attract Mode" Refers to the audiovisual display seen and heard by a prospective customer contemplating playing the game; the video screen displays some of the essential visual and sound characteristics of the game. "Play mode" refers to the audiovisual display seen and heard by a person playing the game.

those results are an analysis of financial records or a sequence of images and sounds. A program is simply "a set of statements (i.e., data) or instructions to be used directly or indirectly in a computer in order to bring about a certain result," Pub.L.No. 96–517, § 10(a), 94 Stat. 3015, 3028 (1980) (amending 17 U.S.C. § 101 (1976)). To take an elementary example, the result of displaying a "4" can be achieved by an instruction to add 2 and 2, subtract 3 from 7, or in a variety of other ways. Obviously, writing a new program to replicate the play of "Scramble" requires a sophisticated effort, but it is a manageable task.

To secure protection against the risk of a "knock-off" of "Scramble" based upon an original program, Konami eschewed registration of its program as a literary work and chose instead to register the sights and sounds of "Scramble" as an audiovisual work. *See* 17 U.S.C.App. § 102(a)(6) (1976). The Act defines "audiovisual works" as "works that consist of a series of related images which are intrinsically intended to be shown by the use of machines, or devices such as projectors, viewers, or electronic equipment, together with accompanying sounds, if any, regardless of the nature of the material objects, such as films or tapes, in which the works are embodied." 17 U.S.C.App. § 101 (1976). Omni contends that Konami is not entitled to secure a copyright in the sights and sounds of its "Scramble" game because the audiovisual work is neither "fixed in any tangible medium of expression" nor "original" within the meaning of § 102(a). Both contentions arise from the fact that the sequence of some of the images appearing on the screen during each play of the game will vary depending upon the actions taken by the player. For example, if he fails to avoid enemy fire, his spaceship will be destroyed; if he fails to destroy enough fuel depots, his own fuel supply will run out, and his spaceship will crash; if he succeeds in destroying missile sites and enemy planes, those images will disappear from the screen; and the precise course traveled by his spaceship will depend upon his adjustment of the craft's altitude and velocity.

If the content of the audiovisual display were not affected by the participation of the player, there would be no doubt that the display itself, and not merely the written computer program, would be eligible for copyright. The display satisfies the statutory definition of an original "audiovisual work," and the memory devices of the game satisfy the statutory requirement of a "copy" in which the work is "fixed."[4]

We agree with the District Court that the player's participation does not withdraw the audiovisual work from copyright eligibility. No doubt the entire sequence of all the sights and sounds of the game are different

4. In arguing that the permanent "imprinting" of the computer program in the game's memory devices satisfies the requirement of fixation in a tangible medium, Appellees direct our attention to the PROM, which contains, in electronically usable form, the computer program for the game. While the PROM device contains the program specifically written for the "Scramble" game, there are undoubtedly some items of program stored in memory devices located in other components of the game. Whether located in the PROM prepared for this particular game or elsewhere in the total assembly, all portions of the program, once stored in memory devices anywhere in the game, are fixed in a tangible medium within the meaning of the act.

each time the game is played, depending upon the route and speed the player selects for his spaceship and the timing and accuracy of his release of his craft's bombs and lasers. Nevertheless, many aspects of the sights and the sequence of their appearance remain constant during each play of the game. These include the appearance (shape, color, and size) of the player's spaceship, the enemy craft, the ground missile bases and fuel depots, and the terrain over which (and beneath which) the player's ship flies, as well as the sequence in which the missile bases, fuel depots, and terrain appears. Also constant are the sounds heard whenever the player successfully destroys an enemy craft or installation or fails to avoid an enemy missile or laser. It is true, as appellants contend, that some of these sights and sounds will not be seen and heard during each play of the game in the event that the player's spaceship is destroyed before the entire course is traversed. But the images remain fixed, capable of being seen and heard each time a player succeeds in keeping his spaceship aloft long enough to permit the appearances of all the images and sounds of a complete play of the game. The repetitive sequence of a substantial portion of the sights and sounds of the game qualifies for copyright protection as an audiovisual work.

Appellants' claim that the work lacks originality proceeds along two lines. Repeating their attack on fixation, they assert that each play of the game is an original work because of the player's participation. The videotape of a particular play of the game, they assert, secured protection only for that one "original" display. However, the repeated appearance of the same sequence of numerous sights and sounds in each play of the game defeats this branch of the argument. Attacking from the opposite flank, appellants contend that the audiovisual display contains no originality because all of its reappearing features are determined by the previously created computer program. This argument is also without merit. The visual and aural features of the audiovisual display are plainly original variations sufficient to render the display copyrightable even though the underlying written program has an independent existence and is itself eligible for copyright. Nor is copyright defeated because the audiovisual work and the computer program are both embodied in the same components of the game. The same thing occurs when an audiotape embodies both a musical composition and a sound recording. Moreover, the argument overlooks the sequence of the creative process. Someone first conceived what the audiovisual display would look like and sound like. Originality occurred at that point. Then the program was written. Finally, the program was imprinted into the memory devices so that, in operation with the components of the game, the sights and sounds could be seen and heard. The resulting display satisfies the requirement of an original work.

We need not decide at what point the repeating sequence of images would form too insubstantial a portion of an entire display to warrant a copyright, nor the somewhat related issue of whether a sequence of images (e.g., a spaceship shooting down an attacking plane) might contain so little in the way of particularized form of expression to be only an abstract idea portrayed in noncopyrightable form. *See Nichols v. Universal Pictures Corp.*, 45 F.2d 119, 121 (2d Cir.1930), cert. denied, 282 U.S. 902, 51 S.Ct. 216, 75 L.Ed. 795 (1931). Assessing the entire effect of the game as it appears and sounds, we conclude that its repetitive sequence of images is copyrightable as an audiovisual display.

The preliminary injunction is affirmed.

THE ZAPRUDER FILM CASE

TIME INCORPORATED v. BERNARD GEIS ASSOCIATES

United States District Court, S.D. New York, 1968.
293 F.Supp. 130.

WYATT, DISTRICT JUDGE.

When President Kennedy was killed in Dallas on November 22, 1963, Abraham Zapruder, a Dallas dress manufacturer, was by sheer happenstance at the scene taking home movie pictures with his camera. His film—an historic document and undoubtedly the most important photographic evidence concerning the fatal shots—was bought a few days later by Life; parts of the film were printed in several issues of the magazine. As to these issues and their contents (including, of course, the Zapruder pictures) and as to the film itself, Life has complied with all provisions of the Copyright Act (17 U.S.C. § 1 and following; the Act).

Defendant Thompson has written a book, 'Six Seconds in Dallas' (the Book), which is a study of the assassination. It is a serious, thoughtful and impressive analysis of the evidence.

This action was commenced on December 1, 1967. The complaint in a single count charges that certain frames of the Zapruder film were 'stolen surreptitiously' from Life by Thompson and that copies of these frames appear in the Book as published. The complaint avers that the conduct of defendants is an infringement of statutory copyrights, an unfair trade practice, and unfair competition.

While the word 'frame' with respect to motion picture film is generally understood, it may be advisable briefly to explain it. A motion picture consists of a series of photographs showing the objects in a scene in successive positions slightly changed. When the series is presented in rapid succession, the optical effect is of a picture in which the objects move. Each separate photograph in the series is called a 'frame'. Webster's Third New International Dictionary, pp. 902, 1475.

On November 22, Zapruder decided to make a motion picture film of the President passing by. He had an 8 millimeter color home movie camera with a "telephoto" lens.

The procession came into view and with the speed control at 'Run' (about 18 frames per second) Zapruder started his camera, not knowing the horror it would record. When the car came close to Zapruder, there were the sudden shots and the reactions of those in the car—all caught on Zapruder's color film.

On the same day—November 22—Zapruder had the original color film developed and three color copies made from the original film.

(There are about 480 frames in the Zapruder film, of which 140 show the immediate events of the shooting and 40 are relevant to the shots themselves. While working with the film, agents of the Secret Service or of the Federal Bureau of Investigation identified each frame with a number, beginning with '1' for the frame showing the lead motorcycles coming into view on Houston Street and continuing the numbers in sequence for the frames following; these numbers have since been used to identify the frames.)

On the same or the next day, Zapruder in his Dallas office turned over two copies of the film to the Secret Service, specifying that it was strictly for government use and not to be shown to newspapers or magazines because he expected to sell the film.

Life then negotiated with Zapruder and on November 25 by written agreement bought the original and all three copies of the film (two of which were noted as then in the possession of the Secret Service) and all rights therein, for $150,000 to be paid in yearly installments of $25,000.

In its next edition (cover date November 29, 1963) Life featured some 30 of the Zapruder frames, calling them a 'remarkable and exclusive series'. Doubtless because of time pressure, the frames were in black and white.

Life published on December 7, 1963 a special 'John F. Kennedy Memorial Edition'. This featured 9 enlarged Zapruder frames in color, telling how they came to be taken and how they recorded the tragic sequence 'with appalling clarity'.

President Johnson on November 29, 1963 appointed a Commission with Chief Justice Warren as Chairman (the Commission) to investigate the killing of President Kennedy. This Commission on September 24, 1964 submitted its lengthy report (the Warren Report) and all the evidence before it.

The Commission made extensive use of the Zapruder film, and placed great reliance on it, as evidence in the Report. Six of the Zapruder frames are shown in the body of the Report and some 160 Zapruder frames are included (in volume XVIII) in the Exhibits of the Commission printed and submitted with the Report.

At the request of the Commission and on February 25, 1964, Life took the original Zapruder film to Washington and showed it to representatives of the Commission, the FBI and the Secret Service.

Life then prepared for the Commission from the original film 3 sets of 35 millimeter color transparencies of those frames desired by the Commission, except for frames 207 through 212. It appears that these frames in the original had been accidentally damaged in handling. Life could not supply copies from the original of these frames, but the two copies of the Secret Service made from the original were available and one of these was marked in evidence as Exhibit 904 (V Report 178). Life also made available to the Commission for its use in Washington the copy in Life's possession made from the original film.

There appears to be no privilege for the United States to use copyrighted material without the consent of the owner. A statute (28 U.S.C. § 1498(b)) gives a remedy in the Court of Claims for copyright infringement by the United States. Another statute (17 U.S.C. § 8) provides that publication by the government of copyrighted material does not cause any 'abridgment' of the copyright and does not authorize 'any use of such copyright material without the consent of the copyright proprietor.'

Life did in fact consent to use by the Commission of the Zapruder film and to its reproduction in the Report, provided a usual notice of copyright was given. Apparently this proviso was disregarded by the Commission.

On or about June 22, Associates offered to pay Life a royalty equal to the profits from publication of the book in return for permission to use specified Zapruder frames in the Book. This offer was refused by Life.

Having failed to secure permission from Life to use the Zapruder pictures, Thompson and the other defendants (presumably with the advice of counsel) concluded that they would copy certain frames anyway. Doubtless having in mind the probability of an action for infringement, defendants did not reproduce photographically any Zapruder frames but employed an 'artist' to make copies in charcoal by means of a 'rendering' or 'sketch'. It is said that the artist was paid $1550.

Beginning November 18, 1967, Associates has been publishing and Random House, Inc. has been distributing the Book.

The Book relies heavily on the Zapruder pictures.

No Zapruder frame is reproduced in its entirety but whatever parts of any frame were considered significant by Thompson, these were reproduced.

Significant parts of 22 copyrighted frames are reproduced in the Book.

The so-called 'sketches' in the Book as listed above are in fact copies, as is readily apparent by comparison with the Zapruder frames involved, copies, as all of which have been submitted. The 'artist' has simply copied the original in charcoal with no creativity or originality whatever. The point is made clear by defendant Geis himself at the beginning of the Book in a 'Note'. While attempting to excuse the copying because the Zapruder film, as a 'crucial historical document', should not be 'sequestered from the eye through an accident of private ownership', Geis emphasizes how accurate the copies are. He says that they have been 'checked rigorously against the original sources', that is, the copyrighted pictures, so that 'their representation of the events is exact'. To illustrate how good the copies are, Geis points to a photographic reproduction of one of the Zapruder frames (No. 207) released by Life for publication in January, 1967. He then asks the reader to compare this original with the Book's 'charcoal sketch' and to be assured that 'all of the other sketches have been executed with the same care and fidelity'.

It is said for defendants that the pictures are simply records of what took place, without any 'elements' personal to Zapruder, and that 'news' cannot be the subject of copyright.

The Zapruder pictures are 'photographs' of an event. The Copyright Act provides (17 U.S.C. §§ 4, 5(j)) that 'Photographs' may be the subject matter of copyright. If this were all to be considered, it would seem clear that the pictures here were properly copyrighted because Congress has expressly made photographs the subject of copyright, without any limitation.

The copyright provision for photographs first appeared in an Act of July 8, 1870 which became Section 4952 of the Revised Statutes and is now Section 5(j) of Title 17 of the Code.

This provision first came before the Supreme Court in *Burrow-Giles Lithographic Co. v. Sarony*, 111 U.S. 53, 4 S.Ct. 279, 28 L.Ed. 349 (1884). The question was whether a studio photograph of Oscar Wilde could be the subject of copyright. It was assumed that Section 4952 applied to all photographs. The argument was made, however, that Congress could not constitutionally do so because photographs are not "writings" of which the photographers are "authors", as the quoted words are used in the Constitution (Art. I, § 8, cl. 8). The argument was that photographs were "merely mechanical" and involved no "novelty, invention or originality" (111 U.S. at 59, 4 S.Ct. at 279). The Supreme Court declined to say whether copyright could constitutionally be granted to "the ordinary production of a photograph." (111 U.S. at 59, 4 S.Ct. at 282). It found that the photograph in suit had involved the posing of the subject and a choice of costume, background, etc. The Court held that the photograph was a writing of which the photographer was the author and that the Congress could constitutionally make such photograph the subject of copyright. This left open whether an ordinary photograph of a real life object could constitutionally be a proper subject of copyright.

Judge Learned Hand believed that any photograph could be the subject of copyright because the Supreme Court had ruled that "no photograph, however simple, can be unaffected by the personal influence of the author, and no two will be absolutely alike". *Jewelers Circular Publishing Co. v. Keystone Pub. Co.*, 274 Fed. 932, 934 (S.D.N.Y.1921), affirmed 281 Fed. 83 (2d Cir.1922). Judge Hand in the same opinion said:

"under section 5(j) photographs are protected, without regard to the degree of 'personality' which enters into them. At least there has been no case since 1909 in which that has been held to be a condition. The suggestion that the Constitution might not include all photographs seems to me overstrained. Therefore, even if the cuts be deemed only photographs, which in these supposed cases they are, still I think that they and the illustrations made from them may be protected."

Mr. Justice Brandeis, in a dissenting opinion, stated: "The mere record of isolated happenings, whether in words or by photographs not involving artistic skill, are denied (copyright) protection." *International News Service v. Associated Press*, 248 U.S. 215, 254, 39 S.Ct. 68, 78, 63 L.Ed. 211 (1918; the .Associated Press. case). the "Associated Press" case).

The commentators, or at least most of them, have concluded that any photograph may be the subject of copyright.

There are very few decisions dealing with photographs of real life objects, apparently because their copyright protection has been assumed.

There is an interesting case in this Court some fifty years ago. The question was whether a photograph of a street scene showing the Public Library on Fifth Avenue could be the subject of copyright. The decision upheld the copyright, saying among other things (*Pagano v. Beseler Co.*, 234 Fed. 963, 964 (S.D.N.Y.1916)):

"It undoubtedly requires originality to determine just when to take the photograph, so as to bring out the proper setting for both animate and inanimate objects, with the adjunctive features of light, shade, position, etc."

Thus, if Zapruder had made his pictures at a point in time before the shooting, he would clearly have been entitled to copyright. On what principle can it be denied because of the tragic event it records?

The defendants argue that "news cannot be copyrighted" citing the *Associated Press* case and *National Tel. News Co. v. Western Union*, 119 Fed. 294 (7th Cir.1902).

Defendants are perfectly correct in their contention. A news event may not be copyrighted, as the cited cases hold. Life claims no copyright in the news element of the event but only in the particular form of record made by Zapruder.

It is said for defendants that aside from all else the Zapruder pictures could not be copyrighted because of the "doctrine" of a recent decision, *Morrissey v. Procter & Gamble Co.*, 379 F.2d 675 (1st Cir.1967). This "doctrine" is here invoked to avoid an "oligopoly of the facts of the assassination of President Kennedy."

The *Morrissey* case involved the rules of a sales promotion contest. The substance of the contest itself was found not to be copyrightable. It was also found that there was a very limited number of ways in which the rules could be expressed. If the rules were made the subject of copyright, then the uncopyrighted substance of the contest would be appropriated by the owner of the rules copyright. The Court declined to extend copyright protection to the rules.

Such a decision can have no possible application here. Life claims no copyright in the events at Dallas. They can be freely set forth in speech, in books, in pictures, in music, and in every other form of expression. All that Life claims is a copyright in the particular form of expression of the Zapruder film. If this be "oligopoly," it is specifically conferred by the Copyright Act and for any relief address must be to the Congress and not to this Court.

Life has a valid copyright in the Zapruder film.

Whether the use by defendants of the Zapruder pictures is a "fair use" is the most difficult issue in the case.

Unlike the owner of a patent (35 U.S.C. § 154), the owner of a copyright is not given by statute (17 U.S.C. § 1) any exclusive right to use the work. The word "use" does not appear in the statute. Whatever the significance of this omission may be, the copyright owner does have the exclusive right to "print, reprint, publish, copy and vend the copyrighted work."

Despite such exclusive rights, the courts have nonetheless recognized that copying or other appropriation of a copyrighted work will not entail liability if it is reasonable or "fair." The doctrine is entirely equitable and is so flexible as virtually to defy definition.

The earliest discussion of the principle was in 1841 by Mr. Justice Story at Circuit in *Folsom v. Marsh*, 9 Fed.Cas. p. 342, No. 4,901. The question arose over the copyright in certain letters of George Washington and was thus stated by Mr. Justice Story (9 Fed.Cas. at 348):

"The question, then, is, whether this is a justifiable use of the original materials, such as the law recognizes as no infringement of the copyright of the plaintiffs."

It was concluded that there was an invasion of the copyright and liability. The test of fair use was primarily the degree of injury to the plaintiff (9 Fed.Cas. at 348, 349):

"If so much is taken, that the value of the original is sensibly diminished, or the labors of the original author are substantially to an injurious extent appropriated by another, that is sufficient, in point of law, to constitute a piracy pro tanto. But if the defendants may take three hundred and nineteen letters, included in the plaintiffs' copyright, and exclusively belonging to them, there is no reason why another bookseller may not take other five hundred letters, and a third, one thousand letters, and so on, and thereby the plaintiffs' copyright be totally destroyed."

Section 107 of H.R. 2512 and of S. 597 [which was later codified in Section 107 of the 1976 Copyright Act, 17 U.S.C. § 107] is as follows:

"Limitations on exclusive rights: Fair Use

Notwithstanding the provisions of section 106, the fair use of a copyright work, including such use by reproduction in copies or phonorecords or by any other means specified by that section, for purposes such as criticism, comment, news reporting, teaching, scholarship, or research, is not an infringement of copyright. In determining whether the use made of a work in any particular case is a fair use, the factors to be considered shall include:

(1) the purpose and character of the use;

(2) the nature of the copyrighted work;

(3) the amount and substantiality of the portion used in relation to the copyrighted work as a whole; and

(4) the effect of the use upon the potential market for or value of the copyrighted work."

The Committee noted that any precise definition of fair use was impossible and said (at 32) that

"the endless variety of situations and combinations of circumstances that can arise in particular cases precludes the formulation of exact rules in the statute. We endorse the purpose and general scope of the judicial doctrine of fair use, as outlined earlier in this report, but there is no disposition to freeze the doctrine in the statute, especially during a period of rapid technological change. Beyond a very broad statutory explanation of what fair use is and some of the criteria applicable to it, the courts must be free to adapt the doctrine to particular situations on a case-by-case basis.

"Section 107, as revised by the committee, is intended to restate the present judicial doctrine of fair use, not to change, narrow, or enlarge it in any way." [Report of the Committee on the Judiciary, H. Rep. No. 83, 90th Cong., 1st Sess. 32 (1967)]

There is an initial reluctance to find any fair use by defendants because of the conduct of Thompson in making his copies and because of the deliberate appropriation in the Book, in defiance of the copyright owner. Fair use presupposes "good faith and fair dealing." On the other hand it was not the nighttime activities of Thompson which enabled defendants to reproduce copies of Zapruder frames in the Book. They could have secured such frames from the National Archives, or they could have used the reproductions in the Warren Report or in the issues of Life itself. Moreover, which hope by a defendant for commercial gain is not a significant factor in this Circuit, there is a strong point for defendants in their offer to surrender to Life all profits of Associates from the Book as royalty payment for a license to use the copyrighted

Zapruder frames. It is also a fair inference from the facts that defendants acted with the advice of counsel.

In determining the issue of fair use, the balance seems to be in favor of defendants.

There is a public interest in having the fullest information available on the murder of President Kennedy. Thompson did serious work on the subject and has a theory entitled to public consideration. While doubtless the theory could be explained with sketches of the type used at page 87 of the Book and in The Saturday Evening Post, the explanation actually made in the Book with copies is easier to understand. The Book is not bought because it contained the Zapruder pictures; the Book is bought because of the theory of Thompson and its explanation, supported by Zapruder pictures.

There seems little, if any, injury to plaintiff, the copyright owner. There is no competition between plaintiff and defendants. Plaintiff does not sell the Zapruder pictures as such and no market for the copyrighted work appears to be affected. Defendants do not publish a magazine. There are projects for use by plaintiff of the film in the future as a motion picture or in books, but the effect of the use of certain frames in the Book on such projects is speculative. It seems more reasonable to speculate that the Book would, if anything, enhance the value of the copyrighted work; it is difficult to see any decrease in its value.

The motion of plaintiff is denied.

Notes and Questions

1. Who is the author of the videogame in *Stern*? Of the film in *Zapruder*? What role does the player of a videogame or the subject of a live-action film play in creating the final work? Is this the kind of creative activity that U.S. copyright laws should protect?

2. How can a photograph be original, if it only shows what already exists and frames it onto film? Does it make a difference, if a photograph is taken from a painting or from another photograph? Could the second photograph still be "original"? And what if you photocopy the first picture or painting? Can there still be an original element?

3. What defines "originality"—the selection of the film, the camera, the lens, the motion, the angle from which it is taken? Or could it be that the originality lies in the idea to take this picture in the first place? Does this define authorship?

4. What defines "originality" in any interactive videogame or computer program? Is it the movement of the game piece, the options provided, the "plot line"? Which of these choices defines "authorship"?

5. For a case that discusses fair use in greater detail under current U.S. copyright law, *see* the *Hubbard Biography* case below.

B. WHAT ARE THE LIMITS OF COPYRIGHT PROTECTION UNDER U.S. LAW?
THE ACCOUNTING BOOK CASE
BAKER v. SELDEN

Supreme Court of the United States, 1879.
101 U.S. 99.

MR. JUSTICE BRADLEY delivered the opinion of the court.

Charles Selden in the year 1859 took the requisite steps for obtaining the copyright of a book, entitled "Selden's Condensed Ledger, or Bookkeeping Simplified," the object of which was to exhibit and explain a peculiar system of bookkeeping. In 1860 and 1861, he took the copyright of several other books, containing additions to and improvements upon the said system. The bill of complaint was filed against the defendant, Baker, for an alleged infringement of these copyrights. The latter, in his answer, denied that Selden was the author or designer of the books, and denied the infringement charged, and contends on the argument that the matter alleged to be infringed is not a lawful subject of copyright.

The book or series of books of which the complainant claims the copyright consists of an introductory essay explaining the system of bookkeeping referred to, to which are annexed certain forms or banks, consisting of ruled lines, and headings, illustrating the system and showing how it is to be used and carried out in practice. This system effects the same results as bookkeeping by double entry; but, by a peculiar arrangement of columns and headings, presents the entire operation, of a day, a week, or a month, on a single page, or on two pages facing each other, in an account book. The defendant uses a similar plan so far as results are concerned; but makes a different arrangement of the columns, and uses different headings. If the complainant's testator had the exclusive right to the use of the system explained in his book, it would be difficult to contend that the defendant does not infringe it, notwithstanding the difference in his form of arrangement; but if it be assumed that the system is open to public use, it seems to be equally difficult to contend that the books made and sold by the defendant are a violation of the copyright of the complainant's book considered merely as a book explanatory of the system. Where the truths of a science or the methods of an art are the common property of the whole world, any author has the right to express the one, or explain and use the other, in his own way. As an author, Selden explained the system in a particular way. It may be conceded that Baker makes and uses account books arranged on substantially the same system; but the proof fails to show that he has violated the copyright of Selden's book, regarding the latter merely as an explanatory work; or that he has infringed Selden's right in any way, unless the latter became entitled to an exclusive right in the system.

The evidence of the complainant is principally directed to the object of showing that Baker uses the same system as that which is explained and illustrated in Selden's books. It becomes important, therefore, to determine whether, in obtaining the copyright of his books, he secured the exclusive right to the use of the system or method of bookkeeping which the said books are intended to illustrate and explain. It is contended that he has secured such exclusive right, because no one can use the system without using substantially the same ruled lines and headings which he was appended to his books in illustration of it. In other words, it is contended that the ruled lines and headings, given to illustrate the system, are a part of the book, and, as such, are secured by the copyright; and that no one can make or use similar ruled lines and headings, or ruled lines and headings made and arranged on substantially the same system, without violating the copyright.

There is no doubt that a work on the subject of bookkeeping, though only explanatory of well-known systems, may be the subject of a copyright But there is a clear distinction between the book, as such, and the art which it is intended to illustrate. The mere statement of the proposition is so evident, that it requires hardly any argument to support it. The same distinction may be predicated of every other art as well as that of bookkeeping. A treatise on the composition and use of medicines, be they old or new; on the construction and use of ploughs, or watches, or churns; or on the mixture and application of colors for painting or dyeing; or on the mode of drawing lines to produce the effect of perspective-would be the subject of copyright; but no one would contend that the copyright of the treatise would give the exclusive right to the art or manufacture described therein. The copyright of the book, if not pirated from other works, would be valid without regard to the novelty, or want of novelty, of its subject matter. The novelty of the art or thing described or explained has nothing to do with the validity of the copyright. To give to the author of the book an exclusive property in the art described therein, when no examination of its novelty has ever been officially made, would be a surprise and a fraud upon the public. That is the province of letters-patent, not of copyright. The claim to an invention or discovery of an art or manufacture must be subjected to the examination of the Patent Office before an exclusive right therein can be obtained; and it can only be secured by a patent from the government.

The difference between the two things, letters-patent and copyright, may be illustrated by reference to the subjects just enumerated. Take the case of medicines. Certain mixtures are found to be of great value in the healing art. If the discoverer writes and publishes a book on the subject (as regular physicians generally do), he gains no exclusive right to the manufacture and sale of the medicine; he gives that to the public. If he desires to acquire such exclusive right, he must obtain a patent for the mixture as a new art, manufacture, or composition of matter. He may copyright his book, if he pleases; but that only secures to him the exclusive right of printing and publishing his book. So of all other inventions or discoveries.

The copyright of a book on perspective, no matter how many drawings and illustrations it may contain, gives no exclusive right to the modes of drawing described, though they may never have been known or used before. By publishing the book, without getting a patent for the art, the latter is given to the public. The fact that the art described in the book by illustrations of lines and figures which are reproduced in practice in the application of the art, makes no difference. Those illustrations are the mere language employed by the author to convey his ideas more clearly. Had he used words of description instead of diagrams (which merely stand in the place of words), there could not be the slightest doubt that others, applying the art to practical use, might lawfully draw the lines and diagrams which were in the author's mind, and which he thus described by words in his book.

The copyright of a work on mathematical science cannot give to the author an exclusive right to the methods of operation which he propounds, or to the diagrams which he employs to explain them, so as to prevent an engineer from using them whenever occasion requires. The very object of publishing a book on science or the useful arts is to communicate to the world the useful knowledge which it contains. But this object would be frustrated if the knowledge could not be used without incurring the guilt of piracy of the book. And where the art it teaches cannot be used without employing the methods and diagrams used to illustrate the book, or such as are similar to them, such methods and diagrams are to be considered as necessary incidents to the art, and given therewith to the public; not given for the purpose of publication in other works explanatory of the art, but for the purpose of practical application.

Of course, these observations are not intended to apply to ornamental designs, or pictorial illustrations addressed to the taste. Of these it may be said, that their form is their essence, and their object, the production of pleasure in their contemplation. This is their final end. They are as much the product of genius and the result of composition, as are the lines of the poet or the historian's period. On the other hand, the teachings of science and the rules and methods of useful art have their final end in application and use; and this application and use are what the public derive from the publication of a book which teaches them. But as embodied and taught in a literary composition or book, their essence consists only in their statement. This alone is what is secured by the copyright. The use by another of the same methods of statement, whether in words or illustrations, in a book published for teaching the art, would undoubtedly be an infringement of the copyright.

The use of the art is a totally different thing from a publication of the book explaining it. The copyright of a book on bookkeeping cannot secure the exclusive right to make, sell, and use account books prepared upon the plan set forth in such book. Whether the art might or might not have been patented, is a question which is not before us. It was not patented, and is open and free to the use of the public. And, of course, in using the art, the ruled lines and headings of accounts must necessarily be used as incident to it.

The conclusion to which we have come is, that blank account books are not the subject of copyright; and that the mere copyright of Selden's book did not confer upon him the exclusive right to make and use account books, ruled and arranged as designated by him and described and illustrated in said book.

The decree of the Circuit Court must be reversed, and the cause remanded with instructions to dismiss the complainant's bill; and it is so ordered.

Notes and Questions

1. Compare the accounting system in the *Accounting Book* case with the process for manufacturing steroids in the *Steroid Process* case in Chapter Two. Based on the information contained in the *Accounting Book* case, would the accounting system have met novelty requirements under U.S. patent law?

2. Would Baker's rights in his copyrighted book have been violated if, instead of copying the ledger pages to practice Baker's system, the defendant had reproduced the forms on canvas as a work of art? What if, instead of writing a book, Baker had painted his forms on canvas? Would these forms be protectable against unauthorized duplications?

THE HUBBARD BIOGRAPHY CASE
NEW ERA PUBLICATIONS INTERNATIONAL, APS v. CAROL PUBLISHING GROUP

United States Court of Appeals, Second Circuit, 1990.
904 F.2d 152.

FEINBERG, CIRCUIT JUDGE.

The biography at issue in this appeal is entitled *A Piece of Blue Sky: Scientology, Dianetics and L. Ron Hubbard Exposed*, and was written by Jonathan Caven–Atack. (We will refer to *A Piece of Blue Sky* as "the book" and to Caven–Atack as "the author.") The subject of the book is L. Ron Hubbard, the controversial founder of the Church of Scientology (the Church), who died in 1986.

As its title makes plain, the book is an unfavorable biography of Hubbard and a strong attack on Scientology; the author's purpose is to expose what he believes is the pernicious nature of the Church and the deceit that is the foundation of its teachings. The book paints a highly unflattering portrait of Hubbard as a thoroughgoing charlatan who lied relentlessly about his accomplishments. The author's attitude toward his subject can be gauged by his descriptions of Hubbard as "an arrogant, amoral egomaniac," "a paranoid, power hungry, petty sadist," and-perhaps ironically in light of the claims in this case-"an outright plagiarist."[5] The book quotes widely from Hubbard's works, using passages from Hubbard's writings both in the body of the text and at the beginning of many chapters. The author had a rich vein of material to mine, because Hubbard wrote prolifically on a wide variety of subjects, including science fiction, philosophy and religion. We are informed that Hubbard published nearly 600 fiction and non-fiction works during his lifetime, 111 of which are in print.

Plaintiff-appellee/cross-appellant New Era Publications International, ApS is the exclusive licensee of Hubbard's works. After learning that appellant Carol Publishing Group intended to publish the book, appellee sued appellant in the district court. The complaint sought, among other things, an injunction to stop publication of the book. Appellee subsequently moved for a temporary restraining order and a preliminary injunction; by stipulation, the proceedings for a permanent and for a preliminary injunction were later merged.

The district court granted a permanent injunction.

Appellant now appeals from the judgment granting an injunction, Appellant asserts that, contrary to the district court's view, all four fair use factors referred to in § 107 weigh in its favor, while appellee argues to the contrary. At the outset, we note that § 107 "requires a case-by-case determination whether a particular use is fair." *Harper & Row, Publishers, Inc. v. Nation Enterprises*, 471 U.S. 539, 549, 105 S.Ct. 2218, 2225, 85 L.Ed.2d 588 (1985). Furthermore, fair use is a mixed question of law and fact.

In addition, the structure of § 107 is significant. The section is entitled "Limitations on exclusive rights: Fair use," and the opening sentence makes clear that a "fair use ... is not an infringement of copyright." The same sentence furnishes examples of broad categories of fair use: "criticism, comment, news reporting, teaching ..., scholarship or research." The section then defines four non-exclusive factors to be considered in determining whether a particular use is fair.

As noted above, the book is an unfavorable biography. Section 107 provides that use of copyrighted materials for "purposes such as criticism, ... scholarship, or research, is not an infringement of copyright." Our cases establish that biographies in general, and critical biographies in particular, fit "comfortably within" these statutory categories "of uses illustrative of uses that can be fair."

Appellee contends that the book's use of Hubbard's works does not serve any fair use purpose, but was rather unnecessary appropriation of Hubbard's literary expression. We do not agree with this characterization. The author uses the quotations in part to convey the facts contained therein, and not for their expression. More importantly, even passages used for their expression are intended to convey the author's perception of Hubbard's hypocrisy and pomposity, qualities that may

5. We note here what should be obvious but nevertheless bears stating. We express no view of our own as to Hubbard, his teachings or the church. The unflattering characterizations are those of the author of the book. [Footnote by the court.]

best (or only) be revealed through direct quotation. The book "is not merely the product of 'the facile use of the scissors.' " Appellee points particularly to the 17 topic quotations that begin many of the chapters; while a few of these may arguably come close to the line separating critical study from appropriation, most do not. Indeed, even this border-line use appears to serve the author's purpose by juxtaposing the grandiose expression of the quotations with the banal (to the author) material contained in the body of the chapter. Moreover, the topic quotations sometimes serve to explain or to summarize matters discussed in the chapter.

We hold that factor one favors appellant.

The district court found that all of the works from which the author quoted had been published. Whether or not a work is published is critical to its nature under factor two, because "the scope of fair use is narrower with respect to unpublished works." *Harper & Row*, 471 U.S. at 564, 105 S.Ct. at 2232. Thus, "even substantial quotations might qualify as fair use in a review of a published work." *Harper & Row*, 471 U.S. at 564, 105 S.Ct. at 2232.

Furthermore, the scope of fair use is greater with respect to factual than non-factual works. While there is no bright-line test for distinguishing between these two categories, we have referred to the former as works that are "essentially factual in nature," or "primarily informational rather than creative." We have some hesitation in trying to characterize Hubbard's diverse body of writings as solely "factual" or "non-factual," but on balance, we believe that the quoted works-which deal with Hubbard's life, his views on religion, human relations, the Church, etc.-are more properly viewed as factual or informational.

Appellee is, of course, correct that there is no rule that one may copy with absolute impunity from a published work, regardless of the amount taken. Otherwise, the copyright law would be a nullity. Nevertheless, Hubbard's works have been published, and "[b]iographies, of course, are fundamentally personal histories and it is both reasonable and customary for biographers to refer to and utilize earlier works dealing with the subject of the work and occasionally to quote directly from such works." *Maxtone–Graham*, 803 F.2d at 1263.

We conclude that factor two favors appellant.

Factor three addresses the amount and substantiality of the portion used in relation to the copyrighted work, not to the allegedly infringing work. *Harper & Row*, 471 U.S. at 564–65, 105 S.Ct. at 2232–33. "There are no absolute rules as to how much of a copyrighted work may be copied and still be considered a fair use." *Maxtone-Graham*, 803 F.2d at 1263. This factor has both a quantitative and a qualitative component, so that courts have found that use was not fair where the quoted material formed a substantial percentage of the copyrighted work, *see, e.g., Salinger*, 811 F.2d at 98 (factor three favors copyright holder where one-third of 17 letters and 10% of 42 letters used) or where the quoted

material was "essentially the heart o" the copyrighted work. *Harper &
Row*, 471 U.S. at 565, 105 S.Ct. at 2233.

Here, the book uses overall a small percentage of Hubbard's works.
Appellant calculates that the book quotes only a minuscule amount of 25
of the 48 works that appellee claimed were infringed, 5–6% of 12 other
works and 8% or more of 11 works, each of the 11 being only a few pages
in length. In the context of quotation from published works, where a
greater amount of copying is allowed, this is not so much as to be unfair.

Nor is the use qualitatively unfair. Appellee asserts that "key
portions" of Hubbard's works are taken "in many cases." But the
district court found that the quotations in the book's text-which amount
to the bulk of the allegedly infringing passages-do not take essentially
the heart of Hubbard's works.

We find that factor three favors appellant.

Factor four of § 107 concerns the "effect of the use upon the
potential market for or value of the copyrighted work." According to the
Supreme Court, this "is undoubtedly the single most important element
of fair use." *Harper & Row*, 471 U.S. at 566, 105 S.Ct. at 2233. In
evaluating this factor, courts do not focus solely on the market for the
work itself, but also on the "harm to the market for derivative works."
Id. at 568, 105 S.Ct. at 2234.

Appellee argues strenuously that factor four favors it, asserting that
it intends to publish an authorized biography of Hubbard that will
include excerpts from all of his works, including material as yet unpublished, and that the book will discourage potential readers of the authorized biography by conveying the flavor of Hubbard's writings.

Even assuming that the book discourages potential purchasers of
the authorized biography, this is not necessarily actionable under the
copyright laws. Such potential buyers might be put off because the book
persuaded them (as it clearly hopes to) that Hubbard was a charlatan,
but the copyright laws do not protect against that sort of injury. Harm to
the market for a copyrighted work or its derivatives caused by a
"devastating critique" that "diminished sales by convincing the public
that the original work was of poor quality" is not "within the scope of
copyright protection." *Consumers Union*, 724 F.2d at 1051 (footnote
omitted). This is so because the critique and the copyrighted work serve
"fundamentally different functions, by virtue" of, among other things,
"their opposing viewpoints." *Maxtone-Graham*, 803 F.2d at 1264.
"Where the copy does not compete in any way with the original,"
copyright's central concern-"that creation will be discouraged if demand
can be undercut by copiers"-is absent. *Consumers Union*, 724 F.2d at
1051. Here, the purpose of the book is diametrically opposed to that of
the authorized biography; the former seeks to unmask Hubbard and the
Church, while the latter presumably will be designed to promote public
interest in Hubbard and the Church. Thus, even if the book ultimately
harms sales of the authorized biography, this would not result from
unfair infringement forbidden by the copyright laws, but rather from a

convincing work that effectively criticizes Hubbard, the very type of work that the Copyright Act was designed to protect and encourage.

We conclude that factor four favors appellant.

The factors enumerated in § 107 "are not meant to be exclusive," *Harper & Row*, 471 U.S. at 560, 105 S.Ct. at 2230, and we have looked to such additional considerations as "bad faith by the user of copyrighted material [that] suggests unfairness," *Maxtone-Graham*, 803 F.2d at 1264, or "prejudice suffered by [the alleged infringer] as the result of [the copyright holder's] unreasonable and inexcusable delay in bringing the action." New Era, 873 F.2d at 584. Although appellee argues that the book's use of passages from Hubbard's works was "predatory" rather than fair, we simply do not agree with this characterization, and find that there are no additional factors suggesting unfairness.

In sum, balancing all of the relevant factors, we believe that the present case presents a strong set of facts for invoking the fair use defense: The book is a critical biography, designed to educate the public about Hubbard, a public figure who sought public attention, albeit on his own terms; the book quotes from merely a small portion of Hubbard's works and from only those that have been published; and, it will cause no adverse impact protected by the copyright law on the market for Hubbard's writings. In these circumstances, we conclude that the book's use of passages from Hubbard's work is protected fair use.

Notes and Questions

1. The fair use doctrine seems at first sight to be a back door for allowing copyright infringement. The fair use doctrine explicitly permits some unauthorized use of copyrighted works. As the court recognized in *Wainright Securities*:

"The doctrine of "fair use" in copyright law creates a privilege in others to use the copyrighted material in a reasonable manner without the copyright owner's consent, notwithstanding the legal monopoly granted to the owner. The fair use doctrine offers means of balancing the exclusive rights of copyright holder with the copyright public's interest in dissemination of information affecting areas of universal concern, such as art, science and industry." *Wainright Securities, Inc. v. Wall Street Transcript Corporation* 558 F.2d 91 (2d Cir.1977), *cert. denied*, 434 U.S. 1014 (1978).

Should the factors set forth in Section 107, 17 U.S.C. § 107, be considered as an ultimate measuring stick for the determination of fair use? What other factors, if any, should be analyzed?

2. Should there be absolute categories of fair use, such as, for example, news reporting? What policy reason supports the grant of a license to use copyrighted materials, without the copyright owner's permission, *and* without compensation for such use?

3. *Unprotected Works.* Several categories of material are generally not eligible for statutory copyright protection. These include, among others:

- Works that have not been fixed in a tangible form of expression. For example: choreographic works which have not been noted or recorded or improvisational speeches or performances that have not been written or recorded.

- Titles, trademarks, names, short phrases, and slogans; familiar symbols or designs; mere variations of typographic ornamentation, lettering, or coloring; mere listings of ingredients or contents.

- Ideas, procedures, methods, systems, processes, concepts, principles, discoveries, or devices, as distinguished from a description, explanation or illustration.

- Works consisting entirely of information that is common property and containing no original authorship. For example: standard calendars, height and weight charts, tape measures and rules, and lists or tables taken from public documents or other common sources.

4. *Moral Rights.* US copyright law grants the author the economic right to control the exploitation of his work. Moral rights, by contrast, represent the non-economic right of an author to prohibit uses that are harmful to his reputation. Such moral right generally survives the transfer of any copyright in a work. US copyright law does not generally recognize moral rights with the exception of the Visual Artists Rights Act ("VARA"), codified at 17 U.S.C. § 106A. VARA grants an author the right to claim authorship and to "prevent any intentional distortion, mutilation, or other modification of [his] work which would be prejudicial to his ... honor or reputation." This moral right is limited to works of visual act. Is there a reason to distinguish between works of visual (versus literary) art with regard to protecting the author's reputation from distorting alterations?

Chapter Two

PATENTS: AN OVERVIEW

A. WHAT ARE THE STATUTORY REQUIREMENTS FOR PATENT PROTECTION UNDER U.S. LAW?

Origin and Purposes of Patents. A patent is a grant by the U.S. government, acting through the U.S. Patent and Trademark Office, to an inventor, conferring the right to exclude others for a limited time from making, using or selling the invention throughout the United States, its territories and possessions. The terms of the grant are set forth in a printed document in which the invention is fully described and the scope of the invention defined. U.S. patents run for a term of 20 years from the date they are granted for utility patents; and 14 years for design patents. Like copyrights, patents are granted to encourage the creation of new and useful inventions. Patents may be granted for inventions in any field of endeavour, including, without limitation, medicine, technology, engineering and pharmaceuticals.

Utility Patents. The Patent Act of 1953, 35 U.S.C. §§ 1–376, protects three types of inventions: utility patents, asexually reproduced plants, and design patents. Of these three the utility patent is the most frequent type granted and deserves the primary attention. In order to obtain a utility patent, an inventor must file an application for patent protection with the U.S. Patent and Trademark Office. This application must describe the patent fully enough to allow one skilled in the art to reproduce the invention; and must meet the statutory requirements of patentability under U.S. law.

Common Law. There is no common law protection for patents under U.S. law. Similarly, there are no state patent laws. Inventions may only protected if they meet statutory requirements under the Patent Act.

Statutory Requirements. The inventions that are patentable under U.S. law are described in Section 101:

> "Whoever invents or discovers any new and useful process, machine, manufacture, or composition of matter, or any new and

useful improvement thereof, may obtain a patent therefor, subject to the conditions and requirements of this title." (35 U.S.C. § 101)

Section 102 further defines the conditions for patentability by establishing the tests for novelty required under the statute:

A person shall be entitled to a patent unless:

a) the invention was known or used by others in this country, or patented or described in a printed publication in this or a foreign country, before the invention thereof by the applicant for patent, or

b) the invention was patented or described in a printed publication in this or a foreign country or in public use or on sale in this country, more than one year prior to the date of the application for patent in the United States, or

c) he has abandoned the invention, or

d) the invention was first patented or caused to be patented, or was the subject of an inventor's certificate, by the applicant or his legal representatives or assigns in a foreign country prior to the date of the application for patent in this country on an application for patent or inventor's certificate filed for than twelve months before the filing of the application in the United States, or

e) the invention was described in a patent granted on an application for patent by another filed in the United States before the invention thereof by the applicant for patent, or on an international application by another who has fulfilled the requirements of paragraphs (1), (2) and (4) of section 371(c) of this title before the invention thereof by the applicant for patent, or

f) he did not himself invent the subject matter sought to be patented, or

g) before the applicant's invention thereof the invention was made in this country by another who has not abandoned, suppressed, or concealed it. In determining priority of invention there shall be considered not only the respective dates of conception and reduction to practice of the invention, but also the reasonable diligence of one who was first to conceive and last to reduce to practice, from a time prior to conception by the other. (35 U.S.C. § 102)

Finally, Section 103(a) defines the conditions for establishing non-obviousness:

(a) A patent may not be obtained through the invention if not identically disclosed or described as set forth in section 102 of this title, if the differences between the subject matter sought to be patented and the prior art are such that the subject matter as a whole would have been obvious at the time the invention was made to a person having ordinary skill in the are to which the said matter pertains. (35 U.S.C. § 103(a))

Thus, under U.S. law, to obtain a utility patent, an invention must meet three statutory requirements. It must be novel, non-obvious, and useful. Inventions which fail any one of these tests are excluded from the limited legal monopoly which is the hallmark of U.S. patent law.

THE COMMERCIAL SUCCESS CASE
GRAHAM v. JOHN DEERE COMPANY

Supreme Court of the United States, 1966.
383 U.S. 1, 86 S.Ct. 684.

MR. JUSTICE CLARK delivered the opinion of the Court.

[This case] presents a conflict between two Circuits over the validity of a single patent on a 'Clamp for vibrating Shank Plows.' The invention, a combination of old mechanical elements, involves a device designed to absorb shock from plow shanks as they plow through rocky soil and thus to prevent damage to the plow. In 1955, the Fifth Circuit had held the patent valid under its rule that when a combination produces an 'old result in a cheaper and otherwise more advantageous way,' it is patentable. *Jeoffroy Mfg., Inc. v. Graham*, 219 F.2d 511, *cert. denied*, 350 U.S. 826. In 1964, the Eighth Circuit held, in the case at bar, that there was no new result in the patented combination and that the patent was, therefore, not valid. We granted certiorari. Although we have determined that neither Circuit applied the correct test, we conclude that the patent is invalid under Section 103 and, therefore, we affirm the judgment of the Eighth Circuit.

At the outset it must be remembered that the federal patent power stems from a specific constitutional provision which authorizes the Congress 'To promote the Progress of useful Arts, by securing for limited Times to Inventors the exclusive Right to their Discoveries.' Art. I, § 8, cl. 8. The clause is both a grant of power and a limitation. This qualified authority, unlike the power often exercised in the sixteenth and seventeenth centuries by the English Crown, is limited to the promotion of advances in the 'useful arts.' It was written against the backdrop of the practices-eventually curtailed by the Statute of Monopolies-of the Crown in granting monopolies to court favorites in goods or businesses which had long before been enjoyed by the public. The Congress in the exercise of the patent power may not overreach the restraints imposed by the stated constitutional purpose. Nor may it enlarge the patent monopoly without regard to the innovation, advancement or social benefit gained thereby. Moreover, Congress may not authorize the issuance of patents whose effects are to remove existent knowledge from the public domain, or to restrict free access to materials already available. Innovation, advancement, and things which add to the sum of useful knowledge are inherent requisites in a patent system which by constitutional command must 'promote the Progress of useful Arts.' This is the standard expressed in the Constitution and it may not be ignored. And it is in this light that patent validity 'requires reference to a standard written into the Constitution.' *Great A. & P. Tea Co.*, 340 U.S. at 154, 71 S.Ct. at 131 (concurring opinion).

Within the limits of the constitutional grant, the Congress may, of course, implement the stated purpose of the Framers by selecting the policy which in its judgment best effectuates the constitutional aim. This is but a corollary to the grant to Congress of any Article I power. Within the scope established by the Constitution, Congress may set out conditions and tests for patentability. It is the duty of the Commissioner of Patents and of the courts in the administration of the patent system to give effect to the constitutional standard by appropriate application, in each case, of the statutory scheme of the Congress.

Congress quickly responded to the bidding of the Constitution by enacting the Patent Act of 1790 during the second session of the First Congress. It created an agency in the Department of State headed by the Secretary of State, the Secretary of the Department of War and the Attorney General, any two of whom could issue a patent for a period not exceeding 14 years to any petitioner that 'hath invented or discovered any useful art, manufacture, or device, or any improvement therein not before known or used' if the board found that 'the invention or discovery (was) sufficiently useful and important.' 1 Stat. 110. This group, whose members administered the patent system along with their other public duties, was known by its own designation as 'Commissioners for the Promotion of Useful Arts.'

Thomas Jefferson, who as Secretary of State was a member of the group, was its moving spirit and might well be called the 'first administrator of our patent system.' He was not only an administrator of the patent system under the 1790 Act, but was also the author of the 1793 Patent Act. In addition, Jefferson was himself an inventor of great note. His unpatented improvements on plows, to mention but one line of his inventions, won acclaim and recognition on both sides of the Atlantic. Because of his active interest and influence in the early development of the patent system, Jefferson's views on the general nature of the limited patent monopoly under the Constitution, as well as his conclusions as to conditions for patentability under the statutory scheme, are worthy of note.

Jefferson, like other Americans, had an instinctive aversion to monopolies. It was a monopoly on tea that sparked the Revolution and Jefferson certainly did not favor an equivalent form of monopoly under the new government. His abhorrence of monopoly extended initially to patents as well. From France, he wrote to Madison (July 1788) urging a Bill of Rights provision restricting monopoly, and as against the argument that limited monopoly might serve to incite 'ingenuity,' he argued forcefully that 'the benefit even of limited monopolies is too doubtful to be opposed to that of their general suppression,' V Writings of Thomas Jefferson, at 47 (Ford ed., 1895).

His views ripened, however, and in another letter to Madison (Aug. 1789) after the drafting of the Bill of Rights, Jefferson stated that he would have been pleased by an express provision in this form:

"Art. 9. Monopolies may be allowed to persons for their own productions in literature, & their own inventions in the arts, for a term not exceeding ___ years, but for no longer term & no other purpose." Id., at 113.

And he later wrote:

"Certainly an inventor ought to be allowed a right to the benefit of his invention for some certain time. Nobody wishes more than I do that ingenuity should receive a liberal encouragement." Letter to Oliver Evans (May 1807), V Writings of Thomas Jefferson, at 75–76 (Washington ed.).

Jefferson's philosophy on the nature and purpose of the patent monopoly is expressed in a letter to Isaac McPherson (Aug. 1813), a portion of which we set out in the margin.[6] He rejected a natural-rights theory in intellectual property rights and clearly recognized the social and economic rationale of the patent system. The patent monopoly was not designed to secure to the inventor his natural right in his discoveries. Rather, it was a reward, an inducement, to bring forth new knowledge. The grant of an exclusive right to an invention was the creation of society–at odds with the inherent free nature of disclosed ideas–and was not to be freely given. Only inventions and discoveries which furthered human knowledge, and were new and useful, justified the special inducement of a limited private monopoly. Jefferson did not believe in granting patents for small details, obvious improvements, or frivolous devices. His writings evidence his insistence upon a high level of patentability.

As a member of the patent board for several years, Jefferson saw clearly the difficulty in "drawing a line between the things which are worth to the public the embarrassment of an exclusive patent, and those which are not." The board on which he served sought to draw such a

6. "Stable ownership is the gift of social law, and is given late in the progress of society. It would be curious then, if an idea, the fugitive fermentation of an individual brain, could, of natural right, be claimed in exclusive and stable property. If nature has made any one thing less susceptible than all others of exclusive property, it is the action of the thinking power called an idea, which an individual may exclusively possess as long as he keeps it to himself; but the moment it is divulged, it forces itself into the possession of every one, and the receiver cannot dispossess himself of it. Its peculiar character, too, is that no one possesses the less, because every other possesses the whole of it. He who receives an idea from me, receives instruction himself without lessening mine; as he who lights his taper at mine, receives light without darkening me. That ideas should freely spread from one to another over the globe, for the moral and mutual instruction of man, and improvement of his condition, seems to have been peculiarly and benevolently designed by nature, when she made them, like fire, expansible over all space, without lessening their density in any point, and like the air in which we breathe, move, and have our physical being, incapable of confinement or exclusive appropriation. Inventions then cannot, in nature, be a subject of property. society may give an exclusive right to the profits arising from them, as an encouragement to men to pursue ideas which may produce utility, but this may or may not be done, according to the will and convenience of the society, without claim or complaint from anybody." VI Writings of Thomas Jefferson, at 180–181 (Washington Ed.).

line and formulated several rules which are preserved in Jefferson's correspondence.[17] Despite the board's efforts, Jefferson saw "with what slow progress a system of general rules could be matured." Because of the "abundance" of cases and the fact that the investigations occupied "more time of the members of the board than they could spare from higher duties, the whole was turned over to the judiciary, to be matured into a system, under which every one might know when his actions were safe and lawful." Letter to McPherson, supra, at 181, 182. Apparently Congress agreed with Jefferson and the board that the courts should develop additional conditions for patentability. Although the Patent Act was amended, revised or codified some 50 times between 1790 and 1950, Congress steered clear of a statutory set of requirements other than the bare novelty and utility tests reformulated in Jefferson's draft of the 1793 Patent Act.

The difficulty of formulating conditions for patentability was heightened by the generality of the constitutional grant and the statutes implementing it, together with the underlying policy of the patent system that "the things which are worth to the public the embarrassment of an exclusive patent," as Jefferson put it, must outweigh the restrictive effect of the limited patent monopoly. The inherent problem was to develop some means of weeding out those inventions which would not be disclosed or devised but for the inducement of a patent.

This Court formulated a general condition of patentability in 1851 in *Hotchkiss,* 11 How. 248, 13 L.Ed. 683. The patent involved a mere substitution of materials—porcelain or clay for wood or metal in door-knobs—and the Court condemned it, holding:

> "(U)nless more ingenuity and skill were required than were possessed by an ordinary mechanic acquainted with the business, there was an absence of that degree of skill and ingenuity which constitute essential elements of every invention. In other words, the improvement is the work of the skilful mechanic, not that of the inventor." At p. 267.

Hotchkiss, by positing the condition that a patentable invention evidence more ingenuity and skill than that possessed by an ordinary mechanic acquainted with the business, merely distinguished between new and useful innovations that were capable of sustaining a patent and those that were not. The *Hotchkiss* test laid the cornerstone of the judicial evolution suggested by Jefferson and left to the courts by

---

17. "(a) Machine of Which We Are Possessed, Might Be Applied by Every Man to Any Use of Which It Is Susceptible." Letter to Isaac Mcpherson, Supra, at 181.

"(A) change of material should not give title to a patent. As the making a ploughshare of cast rather than of wrought iron; a comb of iron instead of horn or of ivory." Ibid.

"(A) mere change of form should give no right to a patent, as a high-quartered shoe instead of a low one; a round hat instead of a three-square; or a square bucket instead of a round one." Id., at 181–182.

"(A combined use of old implements.) A man has a right to use a saw, an axe, a plane separately; may he not combine their uses on the same piece of wood?" Letter to Oliver Evans, (Jan. 1814), VI Writings of Thomas Jefferson, at 298 (Washington ed.).

Congress. The language in the case, and in those which followed, gave birth to "invention" as a word of legal art signifying patentable inventions. Yet, as this Court has observed, "(t)he truth is, the word ('invention') cannot be defined in such manner as to afford any substantial aid in determining whether a particular device involves an exercise of the inventive faculty or not." *McClain v. Ortmayer*, 141 U.S. 419, 427, 12 S.Ct. 76, 78, 35 L.Ed. 800 (1891); *Great A. & P. Tea Co.*, 340 U.S., at 151, 71 S.Ct. at 129. Its use as a label brought about a large variety of opinions as to its meaning both in the Patent Office, in the courts, and at the bar. The *Hotchkiss* formulation, however, lies not in any label, but in its functional approach to questions of patentability. In practice, *Hotchkiss* has required a comparison between the subject matter of the patent, or patent application, and the background skill of the calling. It has been from this comparison that patentability was in each case determined.

The (1952 Patent) Act sets out the conditions of patentability in three sections. An analysis of the structure of these three sections indicates that patentability is dependent upon three explicit conditions: novelty and utility as articulated and defined in § 101 and § 102, and nonobviousness, the new statutory formulation, as set out in § 103. The first two sections, which trace closely the 1874 codification, express the "new and useful" tests which have always existed in the statutory scheme and, for our purposes here, need no clarification. The pivotal section around which the present controversy centers is § 103.

It is undisputed that this section was, for the first time, a statutory expression of an additional requirement for patentability, originally expressed in *Hotchkiss*. It also seems apparent that Congress intended by the last sentence of § 103 to abolish the test it believed this Court announced in the controversial phrase "flash of creative genius," used in *Cuno Engineering Corp. v. Automatic Devices Corp.*, 314 U.S. 84, 62 S.Ct. 37, 86 L.Ed. 58 (1941).

It is contended, however, by some of the parties and by several of the amici that the first sentence of § 103 was intended to sweep away judicial precedents and to lower the level of patentability. Others contend that the Congress intended to codify the essential purpose reflected in existing judicial precedents-the rejection of insignificant variations and innovations of a commonplace sort-and also to focus inquiries under § 103 upon nonobviousness, rather than upon "invention," as a means of achieving more stability and predictability in determining patentability and validity.

We believe that this legislative history, as well as other sources, shows that the revision was not intended by Congress to change the general level of patentable invention. We conclude that the section was intended merely as a codification of judicial precedents embracing the *Hotchkiss* condition, with congressional directions that inquiries into the obviousness of the subject matter sought to be patented are a prerequisite to patentability.

Approached in this light, the § 103 additional condition, when followed realistically, will permit a more practical test of patentability. The emphasis on non-obviousness is one of inquiry, not quality, and, as such, comports with the constitutional strictures.

While the ultimate question of patent validity is one of law, the § 103 condition, which is but one of three conditions, each of which must be satisfied, lends itself to several basic factual inquiries. Under § 103, the scope and content of the prior art are to be determined; differences between the prior art and the claims at issue are to be ascertained; and the level of ordinary skill in the pertinent art resolved. Against this background, the obviousness or nonobviousness of the subject matter is determined. Such secondary considerations as commercial success, long felt but unsolved needs, failure of others, etc., might be utilized to give light to the circumstances surrounding the origin of the subject matter sought to be patented. As indicia of obviousness or nonobviousness, these inquiries may have relevancy.

This is not to say, however, that there will not be difficulties in applying the nonobviousness test. What is obvious is not a question upon which there is likely to be uniformity of thought in every given factual context. The difficulties, however, are comparable to those encountered daily by the courts in such frames of reference as negligence and scienter, and should be amenable to a case-by-case development. We believe that strict observance of the requirements laid down here will result in that uniformity and definiteness which Congress called for in the 1952 Act.

While we have focused attention on the appropriate standard to be applied by the courts, it must be remembered that the primary responsibility for sifting out unpatentable material lies in the Patent Office. To await litigation is-for all practical purposes-to debilitate the patent system. We have observed a notorious difference between the standards applied by the Patent Office and by the courts. While many reasons can be adduced to explain the discrepancy, one may well be the free rein often exercised by Examiners in their use of the concept of "invention." In this connection we note that the Patent Office is confronted with a most difficult task. Almost 100,000 applications for patents are filed each year. Of these, about 50,000 are granted and the backlog now runs well over 200,000. 1965 Annual Report of the Commission of Patents 13—14. This is itself a compelling reason for the Commissioner to strictly adhere to the 1952 Act as interpreted here. This would, we believe, not only expedite disposition but bring about a closer concurrence between administrative and judicial precedent.

Although we conclude here that the inquiry which the Patent Office and the courts must make as to patentability must be beamed with greater intensity on the requirements of § 103, it bears repeating that we find no change in the general strictness with which the overall test is to be applied. We have been urged to find in § 103 a relaxed standard, supposedly a congressional reaction to the "increased standard" applied by this Court in its decisions over the last 20 or 30 years. The standard has remained invariable in this Court. Technology, however, has advanced-and with remarkable rapidity in the last 50 years. Moreover, the ambit of applicable art in given fields of science has widened by disciplines unheard of a half century ago. It is but an evenhanded application to require that those persons granted the benefit of a patent monopoly be charged with an awareness of these changed conditions. The same is true of the less technical, but still useful arts. He who seeks to build a better mousetrap today has a long path to tread before reaching the Patent Office.

Notes and Questions

1.   The name of the case is derived from another portion of the opinion which details the role that commercial success plays in the U.S. in determining patentability. For an excerpt of this portion of the opinion, see Chapter Eight.

2.   The Court in the *Commercial Success* case has developed a test that needs to have answered three questions of a factual nature before the non-obvious requirement can be examined:

a) What is the scope of the prior art?

b) What is the difference between the prior art and the patent application?

c) What is the extent of ordinary skill in the pertinent art at the time of examination of the patent application?

How do we decide what prior art is? How do we determine the person of "ordinary skill"? In determining the scope of the prior art and ordinary skill, is the examination limited to the United States? What if there are advances in science or technology in foreign countries?

3.   What is the main idea behind the non-obvious requirement?

4.   What is the difference between the novel and non-obviousness requirements? Both consider the issue of prior art. Is a work novel if a level of ordinary skill in the pertinent art is exceeded? If not, isn't the novelty requirement obsolete? Why do the courts continue to hang on to the novelty requirement when non-obviousness is also required?

THE STEROID PROCESS CASE
BRENNER v. MANSON
Supreme Court of the United States, 1966.
383 U.S. 519, 86 S.Ct. 1033.

MR. JUSTICE FORTAS delivered the opinion of the Court.

This case presents [the question] whether the practical utility of the compound produced by a chemical process is an essential element in establishing a prima facie case for the patentability of the process. The facts are as follows:

In December 1957, Howard Ringold and George Rosenkranz applied for a patent on an allegedly novel process for making certain known steroids.[8] They claimed priority as of December 17, 1956, the date on which they had filed for a Mexican patent. United States Patent No. 2,908,693 issued late in 1959.

In January 1960, respondent Manson, a chemist engaged in steroid research, filed an application to patent precisely the same process described by Ringold and Rosenkranz. He asserted that it was he who had discovered the process, and that he had done so before December 17, 1956. Accordingly, he requested that an "interference" be declared in order to try out the issue of priority between his claim and that of Ringold and Rosenkranz.[9]

Our starting point is the proposition, neither disputed nor disputable, that one may patent only that which is "useful." Suffice it to say that the concept of utility has maintained a central place in all of our patent legislation, beginning with the first patent law in 1790 and culminating in the present law's provision that

> "Whoever invents or discovers any new and useful process, machine, manufacture, or composition of matter, or any new and useful improvement thereof, may obtain a patent therefor, subject to the conditions and requirements of this title."

As is so often the case, however, a simple, everyday word can be pregnant with ambiguity when applied to the facts of life. That this is so is demonstrated by the present conflict between the Patent Office and the CCPA over how the test is to be applied to a chemical process which yields an already known product whose utility—other than as a possible object of scientific inquiry-has not yet been evidenced. It was not long ago that agency and court seemed of one mind on the question. In Application of *Bremner*, 182 F.2d 216, 217, 37 C.C.P.A. (Pat.) 1032, 1034, the court affirmed rejection by the Patent Office of both process and product claims. It noted that "no use for the products claimed to be developed by the processes had been shown in the specification." It held that "It was never intended that a patent be granted upon a product, or

---

8. The applicants described the products of their process as "2–Methyl Dihydrotestosterone Derivatives and esters thereof as well as 2–Methyl Dihydrotestosterone Derivatives having a c–17 lower Alkyl group. The products of the process of the present invention have a useful high anabolic-androgenic ratio and are especially valuable for treatment of those ailments where an anabolic or antiestrogenic effect together with a lesser androgenic effect is desired."

9. 35 U.S.C. § 135 (1964 Ed.) provides: "whenever an application is made for a patent which, in the opinion of the commissioner, would interfere with any pending application, or with any unexpired patent, he shall give notice thereof the question of priority of invention shall be determined by a board of patent interferences whose deci-

sion, if adverse to the claim of an applicant, shall constitute the final refusal by the patent office of the claims involved, and the commissioner may issue a patent to the applicant who is adjudged the prior inventor."

Patent Office Rule 204(b), 37 CFR § 1.204(b), provides: 'When the filing date or effective filing date of an applicant is subsequent to the filing date of a patentee, the applicant, before an interference will be declared, shall file an affidavit that he made the invention in controversy in this country, before the filing date of the patentee and, when required, the applicant shall file an affidavit setting forth facts which would prima facie entitle him to an award of priority relative to the filing date of the patentee."

a process producing a product, unless such product be useful." Nor was this new doctrine in the court.

The Patent Office has remained stead-fast in this view. The CCPA, however, has moved sharply away from *Bremner*. The trend began in Application of *Nelson*, 280 F.2d 172, 47 C.C.P.A. (Pat.) 1031. There, the court reversed the Patent Office's rejection of a claim on a process yielding chemical intermediates "useful to chemists doing research on steroids," despite the absence of evidence that any of the steroids thus ultimately produced were themselves "useful." The trend has accelerated, culminating in the present case where the court held it sufficient that a process produces the result intended and is not "detrimental to the public interest."

It is not remarkable that differences arise as to how the test of usefulness is to be applied to chemical processes. Even if we knew precisely what Congress meant in 1790 when it devised the "new and useful" phraseology and in subsequent re-enactments of the test, we should have difficulty in applying it in the context of contemporary chemistry where research is as comprehensive as man's grasp and where little or nothing is wholly beyond the pale of "utility"—if that word is given its broadest reach.

Respondent does not-at least in the first instance-rest upon the extreme proposition, advanced by the court below, that a novel chemical process is patentable so long as it yields the intended product and so long as the product is not itself "detrimental." Nor does he commit the outcome of his claim to the slightly more conventional proposition that any process is "useful' within the meaning of § 101 if it produces a compound whose potential usefulness is under investigation by serious scientific researchers, although he urges this position, too, as an alternative basis for affirming the decision of the CCPA. Rather, he begins with the much more orthodox argument that his process has a specific utility, which would entitle him to a declaration of interference even under the Patent Office's reading of § 101. The claim is that the supporting affidavits filed pursuant to Rule 204(b), by reference to Ringold's 1956 article, reveal that an adjacent homologue of the steroid yielded by his process has been demonstrated to have tumor-inhibiting effects in mice, and that this discloses the requisite utility. We do not accept any of these theories as an adequate basis for overriding the determination of the Patent Office that the "utility" requirement has not been met.

Even on the assumption that the process would be patentable were respondent to show that the steroid produced had a tumor-inhibiting effect in mice, we would not overrule the Patent Office finding that respondent has not made such a showing. The Patent Office held that, despite the reference to the adjacent homologue, respondent's papers did not disclose a sufficient likelihood that the steroid yielded by his process would have similar tumor-inhibiting characteristics. Indeed, respondent himself recognized that the presumption that adjacent homologues have the same utility has been challenged in the steroid field because of "a greater known unpredictability of compounds in that field." In these circumstances and in this technical area, we would not overturn the finding of the Primary Examiner, affirmed by the Board of Appeals and not challenged by the CCPA.

The second and third points of respondent's argument present issues of much importance. Is a chemical process "useful" within the meaning of § 101 either (1) because it works-i.e., produces the intended product? or (2) because the compound yielded belongs to a class of compounds now the subject of serious scientific investigation? These contentions present the basic problem for our adjudication.

In support of his plea that we attenuate the requirement of "utility," respondent relies upon Justice Story's well-known statement that a "useful' invention is one "which may be applied to a beneficial use in society, in contradistinction to an invention injurious to the morals, health, or good order of society, or frivolous and insignificant"-and upon the assertion that to do so would encourage inventors of new processes to publicize the event for the benefit of the entire scientific community, thus widening the search for uses and increasing the fund of scientific knowledge. Justice Story's language sheds little light on our subject. Narrowly read, it does no more than compel us to decide whether the invention in question is "frivolous and insignificant"-a query no easier of application than the one built into the statute. Read more broadly, so as to allow the patenting of any invention not positively harmful to society, it places such a special meaning on the word "useful" that we cannot accept it in the absence of evidence that Congress so intended. There are, after all, many things in this world which may not be considered "useful" but which, nevertheless are totally without a capacity for harm.

It is true, of course, that one of the purposes of the patent system is to encourage dissemination of information concerning discoveries and inventions. And it may be that inability to patent a process to some extent discourages disclosure and leads to greater secrecy than would otherwise be the case. The inventor of the process, or the corporate organization by which he is employed, has some incentive to keep the invention secret while uses for the product are searched out. However, in light of the highly developed art of drafting patent claims so that they disclose as little useful information as possible-while broadening the scope of the claim as widely as possible-the argument based upon the virtue of disclosure must be warily evaluated. Moreover, the pressure for secrecy is easily exaggerated, for if the inventor of a process cannot himself ascertain a "use' for that which his process yields, he has every incentive to make his invention known to those able to do so. Finally, how likely is disclosure of a patented process to spur research by others into the uses to which the product may be put? To the extent that the patentee has power to enforce his patent, there is little incentive for others to undertake a search for uses.

Whatever weight is attached to the value of encouraging disclosure and of inhibiting secrecy, we believe a more compelling consideration is that a process patent in the chemical field, which has not been developed and pointed to the degree of specific utility, creates a monopoly of knowledge which should be granted only if clearly commanded by the statute. Until the process claim has been reduced to production of a product shown to be useful, the metes and bounds of that monopoly are not capable of precise delineation. It may engross a vast, unknown, and perhaps unknowable area. Such a patent may confer power to block off whole areas of scientific development, without compensating benefit to the public. The basic quid pro quo contemplated by the Constitution and the Congress for granting a patent monopoly is the benefit derived by the public from an invention with substantial utility. Unless and until a process is refined and developed to this point-where specific benefit exists in currently available form-there is insufficient justification for permitting an applicant to engross what may prove to be a broad field.

These arguments for and against the patentability of a process which either has no known use or is useful only in the sense that it may be an object of scientific research would apply equally to the patenting of the product produced by the process. Respondent appears to concede that with respect to a product, as opposed to a process, Congress has struck the balance on the side of nonpatentability unless "utility" is shown. Indeed, the decisions of the CCPA are in accord with the view that a product may not be patented absent a showing of utility greater than any adduced in the present case. We find absolutely no warrant for the proposition that although Congress intended that no patent be granted on a chemical compound whose sole "utility" consists of its potential role as an object of use-testing, a different set of rules was meant to apply to the process which yielded the unpatentable product. That proposition seems to us little more than an attempt to evade the impact of the rules which concededly govern patentability of the product itself.

This is not to say that we mean to disparage the importance of contributions to the fund of scientific information short of the invention of something "useful," or that we are blind to the prospect that what now seems without "use" may tomorrow command the grateful attention of the public. But a patent is not a hunting license. It is not a reward for the search, but compensation for its successful conclusion. "(A) patent system must be related to the world of commerce rather than to the realm of philosophy."

The judgment of the CCPA is reversed.

Notes and Questions

1. How much reduction to practice is required before an invention is considered "useful"? For example, if Einstein had sought patent protection for his $E=mc^2$ theorem, would it qualify as useful? What would Einstein need to prove to show usefulness?

2. Is an invention which has no non-harmful purposes "useful"? Assume that the scientists who created the first atomic bomb sought patent protection and that the only known uses for the process were to create weapons of mass destruction. Would such process qualify as useful? Should it? *Compare Schultze v. Holtz*, 82 Fed.448 (C.C.N.D.Cal.1897) *with Whistler Corp. v. Autotronics, Inc.*, 14 U.S.P.Q. 2d 1885 (N.D.Tex.1988).

3. Would a process which might lead to isolating the HIV virus be protectable under the reasoning of the *Steroid Process* case?

4. Who would be harmed if a patent were granted for a chemical process that did not lead to a useful end product?

THE TV CONVERTER CASE

OAK INDUSTRIES, INC. v. ZENITH ELECTRONICS CORPORATION

United States District Court, N.D. Illinois, 1989.
726 F.Supp. 1525.

MORAN, District Judge.

[The patent at issue in this case, referred to as the "Mandell patent"] was issued on July 24, 1967 and expired in 1984. The Mandell patent claimed a method for eliminating direct interference on community antenna television (CATV) systems. This interference is caused by the small time difference in reception between the cable signal and the over-the-air VHF broadcast signal, and occurs when the broadcast signal is strong. Zenith produces devices called converters, which are capable of practicing the Mandell method, and sells such converters to cable operators. However, these converters also perform other functions such as expanding the number of channels that the subscriber may receive, providing subscribers with the ability to unscramble protected signals, thus allowing cable operators to scramble protected frequencies, and allowing cable operators to address and remotely control subscribers' programming.

Zenith converters apparently contain several electronic systems, such as a tuner, a detector, a decoder and a modulator. These systems are interconnected to perform multiple functions. In other words, the same circuitry that, for example, expands the number of channels that a subscriber may receive, also allows the subscriber to receive on cable an over-the-air VHF channel output on a channel not used by the over-the-air stations (such as channel 3 in Chicago). The use of the converter's electronic systems in this manner, when combined with the shielding inherent in the housing in the Zenith converters, allows subscribers-at least for the purposes of this motion-to directly infringe the Mandell method.

[The parties conceded that devices which anticipated the Mandell patent had been conceived by the Seattle Group prior to the conception date of the Mandell patent. They also conceded that Mandell's invention was "obvious" in light of a prior converter called the "David Do–All."

Thus, the only issues before the court were (1) whether the previously conceived invention had been abandoned, suppressed, or concealed (making it an inoperable bar to the Mandell patent's validity under Section 12(g); and (2) if not abandoned, suppressed or concealed, whether the inventions were publicly known or used thus barring Mandell's patent as lacking novelty (under Section 102(a)) or being obvious (under Section 103).]

To qualify as prior art under § 102(g)[a], a prior invention must be conceived and reduced to practice. Furthermore, the prior inventor must not have abandoned, suppressed or concealed the invention. There is no requirement under § 102(g) that the prior invention be known to the patentee or "to the art". Plaintiffs have conceded that the Davis and Crowe devices were completed prior to the Mandell conception date. Thus they are prior inventions and we need only determine if a material issue of fact exists concerning abandonment, concealment or suppression.

A court may find that an invention was abandoned, suppressed or concealed if within a reasonable time after the invention was reduced to practice the inventor took no steps to make the invention publicly known. Factors supporting a finding of abandonment, concealment or suppression include not filing a patent application, not publicly disseminating documents describing the invention, and not publicly using the invention. Most important, however, a court's conclusion of abandonment, suppression or concealment depends on the total facts of each case.

1. Abandonment

Abandonment means that the original inventor has voluntarily terminated any effort to exploit the invention. However, in order to preclude a § 102(g) defense, abandonment must occur prior to the time of the second invention. Thus Zenith must show that the Seattle Group did not abandon their invention prior to November 4, 1965.

Zenith points to evidence showing further work by one Wagner [and other members of the Seattle Group] as showing continued development after November 4. Defendant also claims that one or both of the devices were used in subscribers' homes for a four-to six-month period extending past November 4. Plaintiffs, on the other hand, claim that Wagner was only refining or improving [earlier] work, and further argue that as a matter of law any use in subscribers' homes terminated prior to November 4. Finally, plaintiffs contend that the Seattle Group's deliberate decision not to file a patent-based on the erroneous belief that the devices were unpatentable-is evidence of abandonment.

Although not filing a patent application within a reasonable time after reduction to practice may negate a § 102(g) defense, it is only one

a. A Author's Note: Section 102(G) prohibits patentability if another has previously conceived the invention and has not abandoned, suppressed or concealed her invention. *See* above.

factor. It appears that not filing or delaying the filing of a patent application may support a conclusion of suppression and concealment. However, it is not clear that failure to file a patent application would show abandonment. In fact, there simply is no requirement to file a patent application if a party is not seeking protection of the patent laws.

For example, there is ample evidence to show continued development by Wagner past November 4, 1965. In spite of this plaintiffs contend that Wagner's work only refined or improved on the Crowe device and thus did not excuse their failure to file a patent application. See *Lutzker v. Plet*, 843 F.2d 1364, 1367, 6 U.S.P.Q.2d 1370, 1372 (Fed.Cir.1988).[10] We do not believe Lutzker is applicable to our question of abandonment. Lutzker's activities were directed at commercialization and he made no changes in the construction of the apparatus during [a] 51–month delay. However, Wagner's work clearly differs in degree from what was done in Lutzker.

Wagner experimented with a different intermediate frequency than that used in the Crowe device (400 megahertz versus approximately 40 megahertz). Furthermore, Davis stated that the Crowe device needed further shielding because there were problems if the device was placed right over the television's local oscillator (Davis dep. at 40). Although some of Wagner's work was aimed at the channel expander function, we believe that it is reasonable to infer that Wagner's job included perfecting and improving on Crowe's work. Moreover, it is undisputed that Wagner's work continued past November 4, 1965.

We must also consider any use in subscribers' homes as evidence of non-abandonment. The development work alone clearly shows no abandonment. Brown's use of the devices for test purposes supports this conclusion, while failure to file a patent application does not really shed much light on the abandonment question.

2. Suppression and Concealment

Courts look to the policy behind § 102(g)—encouraging public disclosure of inventions—to determine suppression or concealment. We also note that courts have distinguished between deliberate concealment or suppression, and an inference of concealment or suppression based on an excessive delay in filing a patent application.

Zenith puts forward two arguments to show no suppression or concealment. First, Zenith contends that the converters were publicly used in subscribers' homes through November 4, 1965. Second, defendant claims that the converters were demonstrated to persons outside of the Seattle Group organization. Plaintiffs, however, argue that use of the converters in 30 or 40 homes does not show "steps ... taken to make the invention publicly known" because [the user] tried not to explain information about the converters. Plaintiffs also argue, as above, that

---

10. The full statement from *Lutzker* is that a delay in filing a patent application will not be excused where the improve-ments and refinements made are not disclosed in the final patent application. *Lutzker*, 843 F.2d at 1367, 6 U.S.P.Q.2d at 1372.

[such] use did not extend past November 4, 1965. Plaintiffs also note that the Seattle Group referred to their project as the "Manhattan project" because of the need to keep the work secret. Finally, plaintiffs reiterate that the Seattle Group never filed a patent application on any of their work.

a. Deliberate Suppression or Concealment

Plaintiffs argue that by characterizing the development work as the "Manhattan project" the Seattle Group intended to suppress and conceal any invention. Zenith counters that the reason for secrecy concerned the channel expander function of the converters and not the direct pickup interference function. However, if an invention was kept secret, the reason for the secrecy is irrelevant. We believe that the Seattle Group's characterization of the development work as the "Manhattan project" is evidence of an intent to keep the work secret. However, we must look at other factors because keeping a project secret does not necessarily mean we must conclude that the work is concealed or suppressed.

Although Zenith claims that use of the converters in 30 or 40 homes defeats a claim of concealment, plaintiffs argue that [such] actions were irrelevant because [the user] did not make the information about the invention known to others. We believe that in order to avoid a finding of suppression or concealment, Zenith need only show that the public enjoyed the use and benefits of the Seattle converters. A non-informing public use, as opposed to a secret public use, will defeat a claim of concealment, at least where the public benefits.

We do not believe use of the converters as test devices rises to the level of public use or benefit necessary to defeat an allegation of concealment under § 102(g). The converters were not "freely accessible to the public at large," so potential competitors could not discover the invention. [Such] use is also quite different from the sale of large quantities of products to the general public, which courts have found sufficient to show non-concealment and non-suppression.

Zenith is on firmer ground, however, in arguing that the Seattle Group's demonstration to outsiders of the converters precludes a finding of deliberate suppression and concealment. [Two witnesses testified to showing the converters to people outside the Seattle Group.] Although plaintiffs argue that these gentlemen could have been from other Seattle Group companies, or could have been subject to secrecy obligations, on this summary judgment motion we must give Zenith the benefit of reasonable inferences. Consequently, we infer that these visitors were outside the Seattle Group and not subject to secrecy obligations. Taking into account the inferences we must make, we believe there is sufficient evidence in these demonstrations for a jury to conclude, by clear and convincing evidence, that the Seattle Group did not intend to suppress or conceal the inventions.[11]

11. *Carboline Co. v. Mobil Oil Corp.*, 301 F.Supp. 141, 148, 163 U.S.P.Q. 273, 278–79 (N.D.Ill.1969), does not compel a different conclusion. In *Carboline*, an al-

Zenith also claims that the Davis or Crowe converters are prior art under § 102(a) because they were "known or used by others" prior to the date of conception of the Mandell method. Courts construe this phrase to mean that the public must have access to the knowledge of the prior art. *Carella v. Starlight Archery and Pro Line Co.*, 804 F.2d 135, 139, 231 U.S.P.Q. 644, 646–47, amended, 1 U.S.P.Q.2d 1209 (Fed.Cir. 1986) While there is no per se rule on the number of persons who must have knowledge of, or who used the prior invention, it appears that more than just a few persons must know or use the invention for it to be publicly known. However, where those skilled in the relevant art know of or use an invention, courts may infer the knowledge will become known to a sufficient number of people to become "public." Cf. *Carella*, 804 F.2d at 139, 231 U.S.P.Q. at 646 (to qualify as printed publication under § 102(a) a party should show accessibility and availability to those skilled in the art); *Refac*, 9 U.S.P.Q.2d at 1504 (publication must be accessible to those skilled in the art). Furthermore, the court may find a public use where there is a "non-secret use of a claimed process in the usual course of producing articles for commercial purposes".

Zenith argues that there was sufficient prior use or knowledge of the Davis or Crowe devices to qualify them as § 102(a) prior art because (1) converters were left in subscribers' homes overnight; (2) the converters were demonstrated to individuals other than those belonging to the Seattle Group; and (3) information on the converters was disclosed to [a person outside the Seattle Group]. Plaintiffs claim that none of these actions show public use or knowledge by clear and convincing evidence and reiterate that the Seattle Group called their development work the "Manhattan project" to hide the work from the public.

The requirements of public disclosure are greater for § 102(a) prior art. Consequently, we do not believe Zenith has met its burden to show overnight use of the converters qualifies them as § 102(a) prior art. See *Carella*, 804 F.2d at 138, 231 U.S.P.Q. at 646 (oral testimony of prior use or knowledge to be closely scrutinized and regarded suspiciously).

We also discussed [previously] the evidence concerning the demonstration of converters to others. The testimony of Brown and Davis refers to their demonstrating the converters to several people, at least some of whom were very knowledgeable in the electronics field, as well as at least one engineer involved with cable systems. For the purposes of this motion we must infer that the persons who saw the demonstration were skilled in the relevant art.

Davis also testified in the fall of 1965 that he explained to Hamlin how to make a converter. Although Hamlin did not corroborate Davis' statements, neither did he contradict them. Plaintiffs argue that Hamlin

leged prior inventor claimed to have disclosed his invention to 190 persons. The work was classified and none of the 190 persons testified at trial or was even named. Here, the work was not classified and davis named at least one person who saw a demonstration of the converters. We do not mean to imply that the deposition testimony available for this motion will allow zenith to prevail at trial. As we see in *Carboline*, more may be necessary.

never saw a converter prior to November 4, 1965 and, in any event, Hamlin, as a potential manufacturer, was under an obligation not to disclose confidential information.

While it is true that Davis could not recall if he showed Hamlin a converter, he stated that explaining how to make the device was sufficient to allow one to reproduce the converter. MacKenzie, however, did not know when he contacted Hamlin and it is also unclear what information MacKenzie gave him.

Overall, we believe a jury could find by clear and convincing evidence that information about the converters was publicly known prior to November 4. The testimony by Brown and Davis, together with reasonable inferences, supports this conclusion. We believe Davis' statements concerning the disclosure to Hamlin provides additional support. While we do not believe MacKenzie's discussion with Hamlin was a sufficient disclosure for the purposes of § 102(a), the overall evidence supports Zenith's position. We also are not convinced that under the circumstances of Davis' disclosure to Hamlin, Washington state law would impose on Hamlin an obligation of secrecy, because we believe it is questionable as to whether the information given to Hamlin by Davis was confidential. Finally, we reiterate that although characterizing converter development work as the "Manhattan project" is evidence of secrecy, this cannot overcome other evidence of public disclosure. Zenith need only show that a genuine issue of material fact exists to defeat plaintiffs' motion. We believe Zenith has met its burden.

Notes and Questions

1. The *TV Converter* case demonstrates that, under U.S. law, the quid pro quo for patent protection is full disclosure of an invention that is novel—that is not previously known or used. What test did the court establish for determining novelty? Must an inventor realize her invention is new? What evidence did the court consider in deciding the novelty of the inventions at issue in this case?

2. When does a prior case become public enough to qualify as anticipation sufficient to eliminate the novelty of an invention? For example, is conception alone sufficient to grant an inventor rights, or must she work to perfect her invention before such conception is given legal effect? *See, e.g., Rosaine v. National Lead Co.*, 218 F.2d 72 (5th Cir.), *cert. denied*, 349 U.S. 916 (1955).

3. The United States is one of the very few countries that limits patent protection to the first to invent. In most other countries there is a first-to-file system that grants a patent on the basis of who files the patent application first with the patent office. What public policy does the first-to-invent system fulfil?

4. Does a first-to-file system make more sense? What are the advantages of either system? Does the first-to-invent system avoid problems of proving who invented first? Does the first-to-file system harm the inventor who doesn't realize the extent of his invention? Which system do you believe is more equitable?

5. The purposes of the federal patent system are: first, to foster and reward invention; second, to promote disclosure of inventions, to stimulate further innovation, and to permit the public to practice the invention once the patent expires; and third to assure that the ideas in the public domain remain there for the free use of the public. *See generally Aronson v. Quick Point Pencil Co.*, 440 U.S. 257 (1979). How does the *TV Converter* case fulfil these goals? Are there other goals a patent system should entertain?

6. *Suppression and concealment.* Since disclosure of the invention is the trade-off that must be made by the inventor to obtain the 20 year monopoly grant under U.S. patent law, suppression or concealment may defeat an inventor's ability to obtain patent protection. In the *TV Converter* case, what evidence did the court examine to determine if the inventors had improperly concealed their inventions? Why should disclosure be required? What public purpose does this disclosure serve?

THE NAVAL ACCELERATOR CASE
UMC ELECTRONICS COMPANY v. UNITED STATES

United States Court of Appeals, Federal Circuit, 1987.
816 F.2d 647.

NIES, CIRCUIT JUDGE.

UMC Electronics Company brought this action, pursuant to 28 U.S.C. § 1498(a), to recover compensation for use of its patented invention by the United States. UMC is the owner of Patent No. 3,643,513, issued February 22, 1972, by assignment from the inventor Preston Weaver. The United States Claims Court, 8 Cl.Ct. 604, 228 USPQ 396 (1985), upheld the validity of all claims (1–4) but dismissed the complaint on the ground of no infringement or, more accurately, no use of the patented invention by the United States. Both parties appeal. We reverse the Claims Court's holding that the patented invention was not on sale within the meaning of 35 U.S.C. § 102(b).

The claimed invention is an aviation counting accelerometer (ACA), a device for sensing and for recording the number of times an aircraft has been subjected to predetermined levels of acceleration.[13] The sensor

---

13. The Patent Claims Read as Follows:

1. An accelerometer for counting the number of times each of a plurality of acceleration maneuvering loadings of predetermined magnitude of an aircraft occur, comprising means adapted to be mounted to an aircraft for sensing acceleration loading thereof, means providing a signal proportional to said accelerations, a plurality of sensing and storing means each responsive to an acceleration signal reaching a different predetermined value for sensing such signal and storing an indication of the value reached, a plurality of acceleration level recording means, timing means for timing a prede-termined cycle and furnishing a signal indicative of the end of said timing cycle, means responsive to an acceleration signal reaching a reference level for causing said timing means to initiate a timing cycle, means responsive to said end of cycle signal arranged to pass a signal from each of said sensing and storing means to an associated one of said recording means.

2. The accelerometer of claim 1 further including means for filtering high-frequency components from the signal waveform.

3. The accelerometer of claim 1 wherein said means for recording com-

component is mounted on the aircraft in a direction to measure acceleration loading and is connected electrically to the recorder component. Records produced by an ACA can indicate an aircraft's remaining useful life and show the need for structural inspection, overhaul, or rotation to less demanding service.

The patent application, which became the patent in this suit ('513) was filed on August 1, 1968. Under 35 U.S.C. § 102(b) the commercial exploitation and the state of development of the invention one year before the filing of the application for the subject invention are critical to resolution of the on-sale issue.

Prior to the late 1960's when UMC first entered this field, the U.S. Navy had procured ACA's from Maxson Electronics Company and from Giannini Controls Corporation. The Navy was dissatisfied with these ACA's because they sometimes recorded data that defied common sense, failed to count accelerations, or counted accelerations that never occurred. In 1966 the Navy contacted Preston Weaver, an employee of UMC, told him of the problems with existing ACA's and informed him of the Navy's interest in buying improved devices. Weaver designed an accelerometer, model UMC–A, and in late 1966, UMC was awarded a contract to supply the Navy with approximately 1600 units.

In early 1967, UMC concluded that its model UMC–A would not meet the Navy's performance specification required by its contract. Like the Maxson and Giannini ACA's, the UMC–A accelerometer utilized, as part of its sensor, an electromechanical transducer to mechanically generate signals that indicate levels of acceleration. Like the Maxson and Giannini devices, the UMC–A device sometimes counted and sometimes did not count the same acceleration load. The problem lay in the inherent frequency of the mass-spring system in the transducer. The devices could not distinguish between acceleration due to inflight maneuvers, which determines actual stress, and acceleration from other sources, e.g., windgusts or weapons release.

To prevent UMC from losing the ACA contract, Weaver began work to improve the sensor portion of an ACA and conceived his invention which uses an analog transducer in the sensor. An analog transducer electrically generates a varying signal (in contrast to the mechanically produced signal of prior devices) which can be filtered electronically to selectively remove the effects of superimposed vibrations. The Claims Court found that in April–May of 1967 Weaver built and tested an engineering prototype of his ACA containing a commercial analog transducer, a filter, a timing circuit and a voltage sensor that measured one

prises a plurality of counters, each counter arranged to be advanced by one of said sensing and storing means, said means for passing comprises a plurality of gates, each of said gates being arranged to apply an advance signal from one of said sensing and storing means to a respective one of said counters.

4. The accelerometer of claim 1 further including means for sensing when the signal exceeds said reference value, and disabling said sensing and storing means if the signal falls below said threshold value.

load level. UMC sought to modify the existing contract for ACA's to substitute an analog transducer for the electro-mechanical transducer specified in the contract, but was unsuccessful in negotiating a modification.

In late May, 1967, the Navy issued new specifications and in July, 1967, requested proposals from contractors to deliver ACA's built to the new specification (Mil–A–22145B). Technically, the request for proposals called separately for a certain number of sensor components of an ACA system and a certain number of recorders, the two units being compatible in combination. UMC responded to the request on July 27, 1967, the final date for making a proposal, with an offer to supply $1,668,743 worth of its improved ACA (hereinafter model UMC–B). UMC represented as part of its proposal that the sensor portion "has been constructed and tested in conjunction with voltage sensing and time controlled circuitry." In response to a Navy inquiry, on August 2, 1967, after the critical date, UMC submitted a technical proposal, which described the model UMC–B in detail and included test results and schematic drawings. On August 9, 1967, UMC gave a demonstration of its device to the Navy at the UMC facility.

In early 1968 the Navy canceled the request to which the above submission of UMC was directed, and in July 1968, it issued another. The latter request eventually led to a contract with Systron–Donner Corporation, which company has been providing the Navy with ACA's utilizing analog transducers since 1970.

In June, 1980, UMC filed the instant action against the United States seeking compensation (after attempting for a number of years to obtain compensation directly from the Navy) by reason of the Navy's alleged use of its invention in the Systron–Donner ACA's. The Claims Court upheld the validity of the patent claims, which were challenged by the government on a number of grounds, but found that the Systron–Donner ACA's did not fall within the scope of the claims. Both parties appeal: UMC asking for reversal of the Claims Court's finding of no infringement; the government seeking to have the claims in suit held invalid. Since we conclude that the Claims Court erred as a matter of law in holding that the claims of the '513 patent were not invalid under section 102(b), we need discuss only that issue in detail.

> (1) The complete invention claimed must have been embodied in or obvious in view of the thing offered for sale.... Complete readability of the claim on the thing offered is not required because whatever is published (or on sale) more than one year prior to the filing of a patent application becomes part of the prior art over which the claim must be patentable....

> (2) The invention must have been tested sufficiently to verify that it is operable and commercially marketable. This is simply another way of expressing the principle that an invention cannot be offered for sale until it is completed, which requires not merely its conception but its reduction to practice....

(3) Finally, the sale must be primarily for profit rather than for experimental purposes. . . .

Proceeding through the *Timely Products* requirements in reverse order, the Claims Court first noted that UMC had admitted that its offer to the Navy was for profit, not for experimentation. The court then found that the invention of the '513 patent had been reduced to practice before the critical date by Weaver's tests of the engineering prototype of the ACA in April–May, 1967, because Weaver admitted that as a result of those tests he was satisfied that his invention would serve its intended purpose. However, the court found the first requirement that the complete invention must be embodied in the thing offered for sale was not met because the engineering prototype did not include all elements of the claims. The court found that the evidence established that the inventor had not built a physical embodiment of the invention including all limitations of the claims before the critical date.

The court then construed the decision of this court in *Barmag Barmer Maschinenfabrik AG v. Murata Mach., Ltd.*, 731 F.2d 831, 221 USPQ 561 (Fed.Cir.1984). It interpreted *Barmag* as making an exception to the physical embodiment requirement where "commercial benefits outside the allowed time have been great." Because UMC "never produced its ACA," the court found it "reaped no commercial benefits." Based on those findings, the court held that the invention of the '513 patent was not on sale within the meaning of section 102(b). The court also held that the invention would not have been obvious from the prototype, which the court considered to be the thing offered for sale. This was error in the court's analysis, the prototype not being the thing offered for sale. The subject matter of the offer for sale is admittedly the claimed invention.

The government maintains that, properly interpreted, all three Timely Products requirements had been met, namely, (1) there was an offer to sell model UMC–B accelerometers which embodied the invention of the claims, (2) the invention had been reduced to practice, and (3) the offer to sell was for profit, not experimentation. Thus, per the government, the Claims Court erred as a matter of law in not holding the claims barred under section 102(b). UMC counters that because the inventor never built a physical embodiment containing all elements of the claims, the Claims Court erred in finding a reduction to practice of the invention, but that the court's error was cancelled out by its separate requirement for a physical embodiment.

As an initial matter, UMC is correct in pointing out the inconsistency between the Claims Court's conclusion that the claimed invention was "reduced to practice" before the critical date and its separate finding that no physical embodiment of the invention existed at that time. It is not sufficient for a reduction to practice that Weaver built and tested only a part of the later-claimed model UMC–B accelerometer. Under our precedent there cannot be a reduction to practice of the invention here without a physical embodiment which includes all limitations of the claim. Because the court found and the parties do not dispute that there was no physical embodiment containing all limitations of the claimed invention before the critical date, we conclude that the Claims Court erred in holding that there had been a reduction to practice.

The clarification of that issue, however, does not resolve the precise dispute here. Per the government, UMC's substantial attempted commercial exploitation of the claimed invention contravenes the policies of the on-sale bar despite the absence of a complete embodiment and, thus, raises an on-sale bar under section 102(b). On the other hand, UMC maintains that, as a matter of law, there is no on-sale bar unless the claimed invention had been reduced to practice before the critical date. Thus, we address first the issue whether reduction to practice of the claimed invention before the critical date is required to invoke the on-sale bar, and conclude, for reasons that follow, that reduction to practice is not always a requirement of the on-sale bar.[14] This leads to the issue whether there is an on-sale bar in this case. On the undisputed facts, we hold that the invention of the '513 patent was on sale within the meaning of section 102(b).

In *General Electric Co*, 654 F.2d at 61–64, 211 USPQ at 873–75, the Court of Claims, one of this court's predecessors, analyzed an on-sale bar issue by focusing on the policies underlying the bar to determine whether application of the bar would further those policies. Those policies were stated to be:

> First, there is a policy against removing inventions from the public which the public has justifiably come to believe are freely available to all as a consequence of prolonged sales activity. Next, there is a policy favoring prompt and widespread disclosure of new inventions to the public. The inventor is forced to file promptly or risk possible forfeiture of his invention [patent] rights due to prior sales. A third policy is to prevent the inventor from commercially exploiting the exclusivity of his invention substantially beyond the statutorily authorized 17–year period. The on-sale bar forces the inventor to choose between seeking patent protection promptly following sales activity or taking his chances with his competitors without the benefit of patent protection. The fourth and final identifiable policy is to give the inventor a reasonable amount of time following sales activity (set by statute as 1 year) to determine whether a patent is a worthwhile investment. This benefits the public because it tends to minimize the filing of inventions [sic] of only marginal public interest.

On the facts of that case, the court held that the policies were violated and that there was a reduction to practice before the critical date. The latter holding obviated the need to agree or disagree with a detailed analysis of the trial judge, who had concluded that reduction to practice was not "indispensable in every case".

---

14. The public use bar of section 102(b) implicates different considerations and nothing said here should be construed to encompass that part of the statute.

In *In re Foster*, 343 F.2d at 988, 145 USPQ at 173, that court held:

[S]ince the purpose of the statute has always been to require filing of the application within the prescribed period after the time the public came into possession of the invention, we cannot see that it makes any difference how it came into such possession, whether by a public use, a sale, a single patent or publication, or by combinations of one or more of the foregoing. In considering this principle, we assume, of course, that by these means the invention has become obvious to that segment of the "public" having ordinary skill in the art. Once this has happened, the purpose of the law is to give the inventor only a year within which to file and this would seem to be liberal treatment.

In view of all of the above considerations, we conclude that reduction to practice of the claimed invention has not been and should not be made an absolute requirement of the on-sale bar.

We hasten to add, however, that we do not intend to sanction attacks on patents on the ground that the inventor or another offered for sale, before the critical date, the mere concept of the invention. Nor should inventors be forced to rush into the Patent and Trademark Office prematurely. On the other hand, we reject UMC's position that as a matter of law no on-sale bar is possible unless the claimed invention has been reduced to practice in the interference sense.

The above conclusion does not lend itself to formulation into a set of precise requirements. However, we point out certain critical considerations in the on-sale determination and the respective burdens of proof which have already been established in our precedent. Thus, without question, the challenger has the burden of proving that there was a definite sale or offer to sell more than one year before the application for the subject patent, and that the subject matter of the sale or offer to sell fully anticipated the claimed invention or would have rendered the claimed invention obvious by its addition to the prior art. If these facts are established, the patent owner is called upon to come forward with an explanation of the circumstances surrounding what would otherwise appear to be commercialization outside the grace period. The possibilities of such circumstances cannot possibly be enumerated. If the inventor had merely a conception or was working towards development of that conception, it can be said there is not yet any "invention" which could be placed on sale. A sale made because the purchaser was participating in experimental testing creates no on-sale bar.

UMC made a definite offer to sell its later patented UMC–B accelerometer to the Navy more than one year prior to the date of the application for the patent in suit. In its bid, UMC specified a price of $404.00 for each sensor component of the ACA and $271.00 for the compatible recorder component. The total contract price was in excess of $1.6 million. This written offer which revealed use of the analog transducer in the ACA was supplied on July 27, 1967. UMC admits that the offer it made was for profit, not to conduct experiments.

UMC's activities evidence, at least prima facie, an attempt to commercialize the invention of the '513 patent by bidding on a large government contract more than one year prior to the filing of the underlying application and thereby to expand the grace period in contravention of the policies underlying the statute.

Countering the prima facie case, UMC offers only the purely technical objection that no complete embodiment of the invention existed at the time of the sale. In this case, that circumstance is unavailing when we look at the realities of the development of this invention. While UMC asserts that its improved ACA required further "development," as evidenced by its seeking a waiver of the liquidated damages provision in the RFP, that fact might weigh in UMC's favor if UMC had sought by convincing evidence to prove that the primary purpose of the sale was for experimental work. However, the contract was not a research and development contract, and UMC admits that the offer it made was for profit, not to conduct experimental work.

We do not attempt here to formulate a standard for determining when something less than a complete embodiment of the invention will suffice under the on-sale bar. However, the development of the subject invention was far beyond a mere conception. Much of the invention was embodied in tangible form. The prior art devices embodied each element of the claimed invention, save one, and that portion was available and had been sufficiently tested to demonstrate to the satisfaction of the inventor that the invention as ultimately claimed would work for its intended purpose. Thus, we conclude from the unchallenged facts with respect to the commercial activities of UMC, coupled with the extent to which the invention was developed, the substantial embodiment of the invention, the testing which was sufficient to satisfy the inventor that his later claimed invention would work, and the nature of the inventor's contribution to the art, that the claimed invention was on sale within the meaning of section 102(b).

Accordingly, we hold all claims of the '513 patent invalid.

Notes and Questions

1. Does the inventor in the *Naval Accelerator* case meet the novelty standard set forth in the *TV Converter* Case? Why not? What actions did the inventor take to make his invention lack novelty?

2. *Absolute Novelty.* In the *Naval Accelerator* case the court was concerned that the invention had been offered for sale too long before the patent application was filed. Under U.S. law, inventors are allowed a one-year grace period where they may disclose or use an invention in certain limited ways before losing their ability to obtain patent protection on the grounds of lack of novelty. These permitted uses are set forth in 35 U.S.C. § 102, and are often referred to as "statutory bars" to patentability. What is the benefit to allowing some disclosure of the invention, or some use, prior to requiring filing of a patent application? Is there a benefit if absolute novelty—*i.e.*, no use or disclosure prior to application—were required instead? Which system makes greater sense to you?

3.   What is the relationship between reduction to practice and the on-sale ban? Must an invention be totally commercialized to qualify as being "on-sale"? Do you agree with the court's decision regarding whether the accelerator was "novel"?

4.   *Public Use.* Public uses more than one year prior to filing a patent application eliminates novelty of the invention. However, experimental use, not designed to commercialize the invention, but to reduce it to practice, is acceptable. *See City of Elizabeth v. American Nicholson Pavement Company,* 97 U.S. 126 (1877). The question of when reduction to practice has been achieved is not always easy to determine. If one of the goals of U.S. patent law is to encourage the creation of new inventions, shouldn't inventors be allowed to perfect their inventions to assure the greatest economic return possible?

B.   WHAT TYPES OF INVENTIONS MAY QUALIFY FOR PATENT PROTECTION?

Design Patents. The previous cases you have read dealt with patent protection for inventions which were novel, non-obvious and *useful.* As noted previously, the patents granted such inventions are referred to as "utility patents." U.S. patent law also extends patent monopoly protection to certain qualified designs, and certain asexually reproduced plants. The design provisions are codified in sections 171–173 of the U.S. Patent Act, 35 U.S.C. §§ 171–173. The same novelty and non-obviousness requirements are imposed on designs as on inventions for which utility patents are sought. The only major difference between utility and design patents—other than the types of inventions covered—is that the requirement of usefulness for utility patents has been replaced by the requirement of "ornamentality" for design patents.

Thus, Section 171 provides: "Whoever invents any new, original and ornamental design for an article of manufacture may obtain a patent therefor, subject to the conditions and requirements of this title." 35 U.S.C. § 171.

THE FLASHLIGHT DESIGN CASE
BLACK & DECKER INC. v. PITTWAY CORPORATION

United States District Court, N.D. Illinois, 1986.
636 F.Supp. 1193.

SHADUR, DISTRICT JUDGE.

Black & Decker Inc. and Black & Decker (U.S.) Inc. (collectively "B & D," treated as a singular noun after this sentence) who hold patents for the design for rechargeable flashlights have sued Pittway Corporation ("Pittway") for patent infringement. Pittway now moves under Fed.R.Civ.P. ("Rule") 56 for summary judgment.

In early 1980 B & D decided to design a rechargeable flashlight, assigning that project to B & D employee Donald McCloskey. B & D wanted the flashlight design to resemble its Dustbuster cordless vacuum cleaner system, and McCloskey in fact used Dustbuster as a "reference" in developing a flashlight design.

On June 15, 1980 McCloskey prepared a drawing that substantially embodied the ultimately patented flashlight design. On July 10, 1981 B & D applied for its design patent. On January 31, 1984 U.S. Design Patent 272,476 ("Design Patent 476") issued to B & D, covering "[t]he ornamental design for a flashlight or similar article, as shown and described". B & D's "Spotliter" rechargeable flashlight embodies that design. B & D claims Pittway's "Ready–Lite" rechargeable flashlight infringes Design Patent 476.

Pittway also seeks summary judgment on the ground Design Patent 476 is invalid as "obvious" under Section 103:

A patent may not be obtained though the invention is not identically disclosed or described as set forth in section 102 of this title, if the differences between the subject matter sought to be patented and the prior art are such that the subject matter as a whole would have been obvious at the time the invention was made to a person having ordinary skill in the art to which said subject matter pertains.

That reference to "a person having ordinary skill in the art," in the field of design patents, has been taken to mean "the designer of ordinary capability who designs articles of the type presented in the application." *In re Nalbandian*, 661 F.2d at 1216.

B & D has failed to "set forth specific facts" controverting Pittway's submissions. Pittway has also established the obviousness of Design Patent 476 as a matter of law.

Litton Systems, Inc. v. Whirlpool Corp., 728 F.2d 1423, 1444 (Fed. Cir.1984) summarizes the legal standard of infringement in design patent cases:

More than one hundred years ago, the Supreme Court established a test for determining infringement of a design patent which, to this day, remains valid. *Gorham Co. v. White*, 81 U.S. (14 Wall.) 511, 20 L.Ed. 731 (1871). This test requires that "if, in the eye of an ordinary observer, giving such attention as a purchaser usually gives, two designs are substantially the same, if the resemblance is such as to deceive such an observer, inducing him to purchase one supposing it to be the other, the first one patented is infringed by the other." *Id.* at 528, 20 L.Ed. 731.

For a design patent to be infringed, however, no matter how similar two items look, "the accused device must appropriate the novelty in the patented device which distinguishes it from the prior art." *Sears, Roebuck & Co. v. Talge*, 140 F.2d 395, 396 (8th Cir.1944); *Horwitt v. Longines Wittnauer Watch Co.*, 388 F.Supp. 1257, 1263, 185 USPQ 123, 128 (S.D.N.Y.1975). That is, even though the court compares two items through the eyes of the ordinary observer, it must nevertheless, to find infringement, attribute their similarity to the novelty which distinguishes the patented device from the prior art.

Pittway argues its Ready–Lite does not transgress that standard and therefore does not infringe Design Patent 476.

Pittway and McCloskey concedes twelve differences exist between Ready–Lite and Spotliter:

(1) the "canted" or downward sloping joining of the head-to-handle in the RL30, which is not present in the Spotliter, the latter having a handle parallel to the reflector axis;

(2) the head of the Spotliter is much larger in proportion to its handle than is the RL30, the head of the RL30 being substantially smaller than the Spotliter's;

(3) a thicker, rounder handle on the RL30;

(4) the different angle of the head (10 to 15° of difference) when both the RL30 and the Spotliter are either resting on a horizontal surface or hand-held;

(5) the shoulder of the Spotliter angles back toward the handle, whereas the shoulder on the RL30 angles toward the front;

(6) the "on-off" switches are substantially different in size and shape, with the RL30's being about twice as long;

(7) the housings of the two units are different-the RL30 using a single molded part, whereas the Spotliter is a two-piece construction with visible screw openings and a visible mating line;

(8) the top of the RL30 handle is flat whereas the Spotliter's is rounded;

(9) the back of the RL30 handle is more slanted and does not have the retaining lip of the Spotliter;

(10) the RL30 does not have the Spotliter's adjustable wire bale, for angling the beam of light, or a finger recess in the housing to enable the bale to be gripped;

(11) the LED indicators are on opposite sides of the two units; and

(12) the RL30 bezel (front-most portion of the head) is square and of a uniform wall thickness, whereas the bezel of the Spotliter is sculptured and tapers toward the round lens opening.

A side-by-side photograph of Ready–Lite and Spotliter, facilitates an evaluation of those claimed differences, which have been confirmed by this Court's own physical inspection of Ready–Lite and Spotliter (in a literal application of the Gorham "eye of an ordinary observer" standard).

Perhaps no individual distinction would by itself justify a conclusion of noninfringement. However, the combination of those differences in Ready–Lite's design creates a distinct impression of an overall difference in appearance. In that respect, *Black & Decker, Inc. v. North American Philips Corp.*, 632 F.Supp. 185, 190–191, 228 U.S.P.Q. 659, 661 (D.Conn. 1986) (rejecting an infringement claim as to Dustbuster) might well have been written for this case:

> Plaintiffs also argue that comparison of the individual elements of the respective machines is impermissible. While the Gorham "eye" test anticipates that the court will make a judgment based on an overall impression of the products in issue and not compare individual components of a product [,] the court cannot avoid a consideration of the constituent elements of the machines, if only to use these elements as a point of reference for making a general comparison. Moreover, when the elemental differences are numerous and substantial, their combined effect causes the product in overall appearance to be distinct and different. The Court notes the differences between the constituent parts of the opposing designs not as determinative by themselves, but as part of the process of evaluating the overall appearances of the product. The Court would "have been deficient if it had not so specified the underlying reasons for its appraisal." *Tappan Co. v. General Motors Corp. and Halle Bros. Co., Inc.*, 380 F.2d 888, 891, 154 USPQ 561, 563 (6th Cir.1967).

Here B & D does not dispute the design differences identified by Pittway. Instead B & D says a factual issue as to infringement is created by its evidentiary submissions:

1.   a survey purporting to demonstrate that Ready–Lite and Spotliter appear confusingly similar to an ordinary observer; and

2.   two affidavits from B & D's Customer Service Manager Walter Biedermann purporting to establish actual instances of consumer confusion between Ready–Lite and Spotliter.

Like the rest of B & D's contentions, this one fails.

First, B & D's survey information does not surmount even the low threshold of Fed.R.Evid. 401's relevance definition.[27] B & D's survey "expert" first showed a number of people a printed advertisement displaying a variety of household products, including only one flashlight-B & D's Spotliter. Then the advertisement was removed from view, and the interviewees were asked to recall several of the products advertised. Those who remembered seeing a flashlight were then taken into a room with various household products on display, including only one flashlight-this time Pittway's Ready–Lite. At that point the respondents were asked which products on display they had earlier seen in the advertisement. According to B & D, 88% of those people incorrectly identified Pittway's Ready–Lite as the B & D Spotliter they had actually seen in the advertisement.

---

27. That Rule Reads: "Relevant evidence" means evidence having any tendency to make the existence of any fact that is of consequence to the determination of the action more probable or less probable than it would be without the evidence.

Just to describe that procedure shows how nonprobative it is of a confusing resemblance between Ready–Lite and Spotliter. It strongly resembles a card trick in which the magician forces on his subject the card he wants selected. *Black & Decker*, 228 U.S.P.Q. at 664, speaking of an identical survey conducted by B & D in litigation over its Dustbuster, articulated that criticism-only one of the survey's obvious flaws:

> The survey must be relevant "as to whether an ordinary shopper might be confused into buying [one product] when intending to buy [the other]." *Litton*, supra, 728 F.2d at 1447, 221 USPQ at 112. Plaintiffs' survey lacks relevancy, primarily because it lacks adequate control for the possibility of ambiguity and confusion in the questions to the respondents. The questions that were posed do not adequately distinguish between products and brand names. Since the NORELCO CLEAN UP MACHINE was the only hand held vacuum cleaner among the various household items on display, the only firm conclusion that can be drawn from the study is that the Black & Decker DUSTBUSTER and the NORELCO CLEAN UP MACHINE share several features in common. See *Litton*, supra, 728 F.2d at 1447, 221 USPQ at 112.

In the same way, B & D's survey here suggests only that the respondents identified both Ready–Lite and Spotliter as rechargeable flashlights.

[The court rejected the plaintiff's affidavits which referred to customer correspondence purportedly finding the two products confusingly similar on the grounds of hearsay.] Even were confusion between the products properly established, there is nothing at all to suggest the confusion stemmed from the patent-distinctive (that is, the allegedly "novel" or invented) part of B & D's design. That independently deprives the affidavits of any probative force, and it logically leads to the final phase of this opinion.

This Court's conclusion that Ready–Lite and Spotliter do not share the same overall design compels a finding of noninfringement under Gorham 's "eye" test. But the second paragraph previously quoted from *Litton*, 728 F.2d at 1444 also identifies a second and independent "point of novelty" standard for determining design patent noninfringement. That doctrine, under which the court must "attribute the [ ] similarity [between the two designs] to the novelty which distinguishes the patented device from the prior art," is of course simply an application of the general (and tautological) concept that only invention is entitled to patent-law protection. Except for such part of a design as is truly novel (and hence patentable), anyone is absolutely free to copy it, jot and tittle.

During discovery Pittway served an interrogatory on B & D designed to pinpoint the novel features of Design Patent 476. When B & D initially refused to answer that interrogatory, Magistrate James Balog ordered it to do so. B & D then identified just two features of Spotliter as novel:

1. a square-shaped head with a round lens and reflector blended into a single rearwardly-extending stick handle; and

2. a switch on top of the handle.

But Pittway's Ready–Lite incorporates neither of those features:

Thus B & D fails the "point of novelty" test as well. [16]

In sum on the infringement issue:

1. Pittway's Ready–Lite does not look sufficiently similar to B & D's Spotliter so as to confuse an ordinary observer.

2. Moreover and independently, Pittway's Ready–Lite has not appropriated the asserted novelty of Spotliter.

For each of those separate reasons, Pittway has not infringed Design Patent 476.

There is no genuine issue of material fact, and Pittway is entitled to a judgment as a matter of law, on B & D's Complaint. Design Patent 476 is neither valid nor infringed by Pittway's Ready–Lite. This action is dismissed.

Notes and Questions

1. What makes a design patent different from a utility patent? Is a work of designership well served with a design patent or is there another form of intellectual property which would provide a more appropriate means of protection?

2. In deciding infringement, the court considered the similarities of the two designs at issue. The issue of confusing similarity is also used to determine whether two trademarks or two trade dress designs are infringing. *See below*. What purpose is served by providing special patent protection to ornamental designs as opposed to relying solely on trademark protection?

3. U.S. design law provides a shorter term of protection for design patents. Utility patents are protected for a term of 20 years from the date of issuance of the patent, 35 U.S.C. § 151. By contrast, design patents are

---

16. In fairness, B & D was brought to the point of identifying "points of novelty" kicking and screaming. Its basic position has been that everything in Design Patent 476 is novel in its totality. And it must be recognized *Litton* approached the "point of novelty" inquiry (728 F.2d at 1444) after the court had already narrowed the scope of the design patent in that case in the course of holding it valid (id. at 1440–43). This opinion, which addresses noninfringement as an alternative defense (and must for that purpose also assume the patent's validity arguendo, though this court has ruled otherwise on the merits) cannot indulge the *Litton* luxury of limiting the patent claim. That factor does not appear to have been recognized by the District Court in *Black &*

Decker, 228 U.S.P.Q. at 662. There the district court really confused the "point of novelty" approach by impermissibly merging validity and infringement considerations (it rejected one acknowledged "point of similarity" because it found it "not a novel feature"—a factor relevant only in determining patent validity—and mistakenly relied on litton for that line of reasoning). In any event, candor here compels the acknowledgement that if B & D could have avoided being pinned down to identify the specific features it claimed as "novel," the spotliter might perhaps have survived the "point of novelty" test-but it could not pass the "eye" test in any event. That latter failure would remain just as fatal to B & D.

protected for a period of 14 years from the date of issuance, 35 U.S.C. § 173. What philosophy supports a shorter term for design patents?

4. Not every nation protects works of designership through design patents, even though most agree that there should be some form of protection for such designs. Design patents form part of a traditional form of intellectual property—the so-called industrial design. This form of protection is especially common in Europe and is recognized by various international intellectual property conventions, such as the Paris Convention for the Protection of Industrial Designs. This form of protection is also referred to sometimes as a "utility design." Industrial designs protect works of craftsmanship and designership that generally would not be eligible for protection as a patent or a trademark. To qualify for protection such design must contain some degree of novelty or originality, however, the degree of novelty or originality is generally lower than that required for a utility patent or a copyright. Design protection is the most controversial form of intellectual property, because the scope of protection varies greatly on a multinational basis. In Europe there is a new tendency towards broad Community-wide protection of industrial design that might even further separate the two fronts. Since 1993 there have been formal proposals for a Community–Design Regulation and a directive for the protection of industrial designs. These approaches seek to reach an EU-wide system of industrial design protection by harmonizing the requirements for its protection throughout Europe. And some believe that a regulation in Europe might stimulate a global approximation on the issue of industrial design. *See, e.g.,* Graeme B. Dinwoodie, *Federalized Functionalism: The Future of Design Protection in the European Union,* 24 AIPLA Q.J. 611 (1996).

Plant Patents. The final category of patentable inventions protected under U.S. patent laws are plant patents. Such patents are limited to asexually reproduced plants which represent "a distinct and new variety". Thus, under Section 161:

"Whoever invents or discovers and asexually reproduces any distinct and new variety of plant, including cultivated sports, mutants, hybrids, and newly found seedlings, other than an tuberpropagated plant or a plant found in an uncultivated state, may obtain a patent therefor, subject to the conditions and requirements of this title." Like design patents, the requirements of non-obviousness under Section 103 continues to apply to plant patents as well, 35 U.S.C. §§ 161, 103.

THE CHRYSANTHEMUM PLANT PATENT CASE

YODER BROTHERS, INC. v. CALIFORNIA-FLORIDA PLANT CORPORATION

United States Court of Appeals, Fifth Circuit, 1976.
537 F.2d 1347.

GOLDBERG, CIRCUIT JUDGE.

In this clash between two giants of the chrysanthemum business, we confront a myriad of antitrust and plant patent issues. Yoder Brothers (Yoder), plaintiff in the district court, sued, alleging infringement of twenty-one chrysanthemum plant patents by California–Florida Plant Corp. (CFPC) and California–Florida Plant Corp. of Florida (CFPCF) (sometimes referred to collectively as Cal–Florida). CFPC and CFPCF denied the infringement and filed antitrust counterclaims under sections 1 and 2 of the Sherman Act.

Chrysanthemums have been subject to intensive breeding efforts over the past thirty years; each individual specimen is a genetically unique complex organism. Several definitions of the term "variety" of chrysanthemum were offered at trial. Mr. Duffett, Yoder's head breeder, defined a variety as a group of individual plants which, on the basis of observation by skilled floriculturists and according to reasonable commercial tolerances, display identical characteristics under similar environments. Cal–Florida defined variety in its complaint as "a subspecies or class of chrysanthemums distinguishable from other subspecies or classes of chrysanthemums by distinct characteristics, such as color hue, shape and size of petal or blossom or any of them."

New varieties of chrysanthemums are developed in two major ways: by sexual reproduction and by mutagenic techniques. Sexual reproduction, the result of self or cross pollination, produces a genetically unique seedling, the characteristics of which are impossible to predict. Mutagenic techniques simply accelerate the natural rate of mutation in the chrysanthemum plant itself. A mutation was defined by Mr. Duffett as "a change in the number of chromosomes or a change in the chromosome position or a specific change in the genes within those chromosomes." Technically, only those mutations that first express themselves as bud variations are properly called "sports"; however, the word is used loosely in the industry as a general synonym for mutation, and we will so use it. Two types of sports can appear: spontaneous sports and radiation sports. The cells of all living things occasionally mutate, and spontaneous sports are simply the result of that process. Radiation sports, on the other hand, are induced artificially, through exposure to such things as gamma radiation from radioactive cobalt and X-rays. These techniques do nothing that could not occur in nature apart from speeding up the natural mutation process. Although most of the mutations induced by radiation are not commercially usable plants, a skilled breeder will select for further development those that display such desirable characteristics as fast response time, temperature tolerance, durability, size, and vigor.

After a breeder has successfully isolated a new variety, the only way he can preserve his creation is by means of asexual reproduction. In the case of chrysanthemums, the most common technique of asexual reproduction is the taking of cuttings from a stock plant. Cuttings, as defined in the Cal–Florida complaint, are "sections or parts of chrysanthemum plants which may be grown into mature plants for sale as cut flowers and/or potted plants or from which additional cuttings may be harvested." According to Yoder's suggested definition, cuttings are simply immature chrysanthemum plants. Since a cutting is genetically identical to the parent plant, it will develop into a plant whose characteristics match the parent's exactly, so long as the same environmental conditions obtain. A central fact of life in the chrysanthemum industry is the ease with which cuttings can be taken from parent plants: from one chrysanthemum, it is theoretically possible to develop an infinitely large stock, by taking cuttings, maturing some into flowered plants, taking more cuttings, and so on.

The issues in this litigation arose out of Yoder's breeding operations and its desire to secure a fair return from those efforts. Theoretically, once the first plant of a new variety is sold, it is impossible for a breeder ever again to be compensated for his efforts in developing it. As indicated above, anyone can take a cutting from that new plant, propagate a number of cuttings from the first cutting, and obtain an infinite supply of the plant. Even as a practical matter, the evidence at the trial suggested that it was relatively easy to obtain plant material of new varieties without the consent of the breeder.

Article I, section 8, clause 8 of the Constitution provided that Congress shall have the power:

> To promote the Progress of Science and useful Arts, by securing for limited Times to Authors and Inventors the exclusive Right to their respective Writings and Discoveries; . . .

Although the first legislation implementing this provision for mechanical inventions was passed in 1790 by the first Congress, 1 Stat. 109, Congress did not include plants within the clause's protection until 1930.

Since section 161 makes the general patent law applicable to plant patents except as otherwise provided, we take as our starting point the general requisites for patentability, and then apply them as well as we can to plants.

Normally, the three requirements for patentability are novelty, utility, and nonobviousness. *See, e. g., Graham v. John Deere Co.*, 383 U.S. 1 (1966). For plant patents, the requirement of distinctness replaces that of utility, and the additional requirement of asexual reproduction is introduced.

The concept of novelty refers to novelty of conception, rather than novelty of use; no single prior art structure can exist in which all of the elements serve substantially the same function. In *Beckman Instruments, Inc. v. Chemtronics, Inc.*, 5 Cir., 439 F.2d 1369, 1375, *cert. denied*, 1970, 400 U.S. 956, 91 S.Ct. 353–54, 27 L.Ed.2d 264, this Court said:

> (S)ection 102, which pertains to novelty, requires that the patentee be the original inventor of the object claimed in his patent, and also that the invention not have been known or used by others before his discovery of it. . . . Furthermore the prior art is to be considered as covering all uses to which it could have been put.

As applied to plants, the Patent Office Board of Appeals held that a "new" plant had to be one that literally had not existed before, rather than one that had existed in nature but was newly found, such as an exotic plant from a remote part of the earth.[30] *Ex parte Foster*, 90 U.S.P.Q. 16 (1951). In *Application of Greer*, Ct.Cust. & Pat.App.1973, 484 F.2d 488, the court indicated that the Board believed that novelty was to be determined by a detailed comparison with other known varieties.

The legislative history of the Plant Patent Act is of considerable assistance in defining "distinctness." The Senate Report said:

> (I)n order for the new variety to be distinct it must have characteristics clearly distinguishable from those of existing varieties and it is immaterial whether in the judgment of the Patent Office the new characteristics are inferior or superior to those of existing varieties. Experience has shown the absurdity of many views held as to the value of new varieties at the time of their creation.
>
> The characteristics that may distinguish a new variety would include, among others, those of habit; immunity from disease; or soil conditions; color of flower, leaf, fruit or stems; flavor; productivity, including ever-bearing qualities in case of fruits; storage qualities; perfume; form; and ease of asexual reproduction. Within any one of the above or other classes of characteristics the differences, which would suffice to make the variety a distinct variety, will necessarily be differences of degree.

S.Rep. 315, 71st Cong., 2d Sess. (1930). (Emphasis omitted.) A definition of "distinctness" as the aggregate of the plant's distinguishing characteristics seems to us a sensible and workable one.

The third requirement, nonobviousness, is the hardest to apply to plants, though we are bound to do so to the best of our ability. The traditional three part test for obviousness, as set out in *John Deere*, supra, inquires as to (1) the scope and content of the prior art, (2) the differences between the prior art and the claims at issue, and (3) the level of ordinary skill in the prior art. 383 U.S. at 17. Secondary characteristics such as commercial success, long felt but unsolved needs, and failure of others can be used to illuminate the circumstances surrounding the subject matter sought to be patented.

The Supreme Court has viewed the obviousness requirement of section 103 as Congress' articulation of the constitutional standard of invention. The obviousness requirement appears to presume that if the gap between the prior art and the claimed improvement is small, then an ordinary mechanic skilled in the art would have been able to create the improvement, thus leading to the conclusion that the improvement was obvious and a patentable invention not present. Section 103 requires the determination of obviousness *vel non* to be made with reference to the

---

30. In order for a plant to have "existed" before in nature, we think that it must have been capable of reproducing itself. Thus, we have concluded that the mere fact that a sport of a plant had appeared in the past would not be sufficient to preclude the patentability of the plant on novelty grounds, since each sport is a one-time phenomenon absent human intervention.

time the invention was made. See *Jacobson Bros., Inc. v. United States*, Ct.Cl.1975, 512 F.2d 1065, 1068. Obviousness, like the general question of patent validity, is ultimately a question of law, though factual inquiries are often necessary to its resolution.

Rephrasing the *John Deere* tests for the plant world, we might ask about (1) the characteristics of prior plants of the same general type, both patented and nonpatented, and (2) the differences between the prior plants and the claims at issue. We see no meaningful way to apply the third criterion to plants, *i. e.* the level of ordinary skill in the prior art. Criteria one and two are reminiscent of the "distinctness" requirement already in the Plant Patent Act. Thus, if we are to give obviousness an independent meaning, it must refer to something other than observable characteristics.

We think that the most promising approach toward the obviousness requirement for plant patents is reference to the underlying constitutional standard that it codifies namely, invention.

The general thrust of the "invention" requirement is to ensure that minor improvements will not be granted the protection of a seventeen year monopoly by the state. In the case of plants, to develop or discover a new variety that retains the desirable qualities of the parent stock and adds significant improvements, and to preserve the new specimen by asexually reproducing it constitutes no small feat.

This Court's case dealing with the patent on the chemical compound commonly known as the drug "Darvon," *Eli Lilly & Co. v. Generix Drug Sales, Inc.,* 5 Cir. 1972, 460 F.2d 1096, provides some insight into the problem of how to apply the "invention" requirement to a new and esoteric subject matter. The court first noted that

> (a)nalogical reasoning is necessarily restricted in many chemical patent cases because of the necessity for physiological experimentation before any use can be determined.

> In fact, such lack of predictability of useful result from the making of even the slightest variation in the atomic structure or spatial arrangement of a complex molecule ... deprives the instant claims of obviousness and anticipation of most of their vitality....

460 F.2d at 1101. The court resolved the apparent dilemma by looking to the therapeutic value of the new drug instead of to its chemical composition:

> (R)eason compels us to agree that novelty, usefulness and non-obviousness inhere in the true discovery that a chemical compound exhibits a new needed medicinal capability, even though it be closely related in structure to a known or patented drug. 460 F.2d at 1103.

The same kind of shift in focus would lead us to a more productive inquiry for plant patents. If the plant is a source of food, the ultimate question might be its nutritive content or its prolificacy. A medicinal plant might be judged by its increased or changed therapeutic value. Similarly, an ornamental plant would be judged by its increased beauty and desirability in relation to the other plants of its type, its usefulness in the industry, and how much of an improvement it represents over prior ornamental plants, taking all of its characteristics together.[18]

Before reaching the issues on appeal, we make a final comment about the requirement of asexual reproduction. It has been described as the "very essence" of the patent. Langrock, *Plant Patents Biological Necessities in Infringement Suits*, 41 J.Pat.Off.Soc. 787 (1959). Asexual reproduction is literally the only way that a breeder can be sure he has reproduced a plant identical in every respect to the parent. It is quite possible that infringement of a plant patent would occur only if stock obtained from one of the patented plants is used, given the extreme unlikelihood that any other plant could actually infringe. If the alleged infringer could somehow prove that he had developed the plant in question independently, then he would not be liable in damages or subject to an injunction for infringement. This example illustrates the extreme extent to which asexual reproduction is the heart of the present plant patent system: the whole key to the "invention" of a new plant is the discovery of new traits plus the foresight and appreciation to take the step of asexual reproduction.

During the trial, Cal–Florida offered as evidence certain documents showing that growers had found mutations on the Mandalay variety that were the same as the patented variety Glowing Mandalay, *i. e.* evidence that the sport Glowing Mandalay had recurred. Although Glowing Mandalay is no longer in the case, Cal–Florida later proffered similar evidence with respect to Gold Marble, Promenade, and Red Torch, which are three of the patents whose validity is challenged on appeal. Gold Marble, Promenade, and Red Torch are all sport patents, meaning that they first appeared as a sport of another plant, in contrast to seedling patents, which develop from seeds. Of the remaining four challenged patents, two were sport patents and two were seedling patents. Cal–Florida never proffered any sport recurrence evidence as to the other two sport patents, Mountain Sun and Southern Gold, nor did it offer any specific evidence attacking the seedling patents, Morocco and Mountain Snow. Since we find that the district court's ruling on the sport recurrence evidence did not preclude Cal–Florida from introducing other types of evidence to attack the validity of the patents, and since no sport recurrence evidence was introduced as to Mountain Sun and Southern Gold, we find no warrant on appeal to disturb the ruling that Mountain Sun, Southern Gold, Morocco, and Mountain Snow were valid and infringed. Plant patents, like others, enjoy a statutory presumption of validity that was not rebutted as to those four.

18. We suspect that part of our problem in applying patent concepts to the facts before us lies in the fact that we are dealing with ornamental plants. Beauty for its own sake is not often a goal of inventors indeed, even ornamental plant breeders might be more aptly described as seekers of beauty for profit. Nevertheless, the statute does not exempt ornamental plants, and so we are bound to treat them on a par with more "useful" botanical creations.

At the time the court rejected the sport return evidence for Glowing Mandalay, it made a ruling designed to apply to the rest of the trial with respect to that kind of evidence. That ruling is the focus of Cal–Florida's cross appeal on the plant patent validity point. Because of its importance, we set out the pertinent parts in some detail here:

It seems clear that it was the Congressional intent that a person who discovered an asexually reproduced variety of a new and distinct plant was entitled to a patent. It was not contemplated, apparently, that he invent, in the term that is used, or in the significance of that term, as we understand it, traditional concept of inventing a machine . . .

In any event, the issue presented here is a rather narrow one and it has some practical overtones.

The only possible probative value of the sport recurrence evidence would be to show that a sport of that particular size, shape, color, or other trait is predictable from a given variety of parent plant. Thus, we must first determine whether Congress intended predictability to negate the possibility of "invention." Next, if Congress considered that factor irrelevant, we must decide if the Constitution is offended by permitting patents on the kinds of sports that recur.[19]

Both the language of the statute and its legislative history persuade us that Congress did not intend to exclude the kind of mutation that might recur from the Act's protection. Instead, both Senate Report 315, 71st Cong., 2d Sess. (1930), on the original bill, and Senate Report 1937, 83d Cong., 2d Sess. (1954), on the 1954 amendment, speak generally about sports and mutations. The 1954 amendment was added to clarify Congress' intention that seedlings should be patentable, but in the process of describing the bill, the report states:

The enactment of this legislation will remove any doubt that the legislative intent of the Congress clearly means that sports, mutants, hybrids, and seedlings, discovered by persons engaged in agriculture or horticulture, should be patentable . . . S.Rep. 1937, *supra*.

Although we are willing to assume for purposes of this argument that some mutations may appear that would have been genetically impossible before i. e. that a fundamental change in the biochemical structure of the chromosome may take place by far the majority of mutations and sports of chrysanthemums are predictable to some extent for those skilled in the field. For example, the testimony at trial indicated that a yellow sport could be expected from a white chrysanthe-

---

19. In this discussion, we are concerned only with the "invention" or obviousness issue. As we have defined novelty, supra, the recurrence of a sport of a particular color would be irrelevant. Similarly, sport recurrence says nothing about the new plant's particular characteristics. The testimony at the trial amply established that Yoder's patented chrysanthemums were distinct to those skilled in the field i. e. those in the breeding business. We note that there is a distinction between looking to the opinion of persons in the industry to prove a feature of patentability and relying on commercial success to prove nonobviousness. Yoder's arguments relied on the former kind of evidence.

mum. Indeed, part of the skill required of a chrysanthemum breeder is to know what to look for and to take steps immediately to preserve it by asexual reproduction if the desired trait appears. Given that fact, we think that the purpose of the Plant Patent Act would be frustrated by a requirement that only those rare, never-before-seen, if not genetically impossible sports or mutations would be patentable. That purpose was "to afford agriculture, so far as practicable, the same opportunity to participate in the benefits of the patent system as has been given industry, and thus assist in placing agriculture on a basis of economic equality with industry." S.Rep. 315, *supra*. To make it significantly more difficult to obtain a plant patent than another type of patent would frustrate that purpose.

We therefore find that Congress did not intend to exclude the kind of sport that recurs frequently from the Plant Patent Act. That being the case, the district court correctly ruled that the evidence proffered by Cal–Florida was irrelevant, as a matter of statutory law.

The only way that the Constitution would be offended by permitting patents on recurring sports would be if such leniency indicated that no "invention" was present. We do not think that sport recurrence would negate invention, however. An infinite number of a certain sized sport could appear on a plant, but until someone recognized its uniqueness and difference and found that the traits could be preserved by asexual reproduction in commercial quantities, no patentable plant would exist. An objective judgment of the value of the sport's new and different characteristics, *i. e.* nutritive value, ornamental value, hardiness, longevity, etc. would not depend in any way on whether a similar sport had appeared in the past, or whether that particular sport was predictable. We therefore find no reason to disturb our approval of the district court's evidentiary ruling based on the constitutional standard of invention. As that standard applies to plant patents, the proffered evidence was irrelevant.

Viewing the evidence offered on the patent validity question as a whole, we find that Cal–Florida failed to rebut the statutory presumption of validity as to Gold Marble, Promenade, and Red Torch, as well as the other four discussed above. Thus, the lower court's finding of validity must be affirmed on this record.

On cross appeal, Cal–Florida asserts that the absence of flowering plants grown from the cuttings it had admittedly taken from Yoder's patented plants was fatal to Yoder's infringement counts. This is because the patent claim in each instance describes a mature flowering plant, and it is Cal–Florida's position that only another mature flowering plant could directly infringe. Yoder retorts that the Plant Patent Act provides that

> (i)n the case of a plant patent the grant shall be of the right to exclude others from asexually reproducing the plant or selling or using the plant so reproduced.

35 U.S.C. § 163. The district court ruled that the act of asexual reproduction was complete at the time the cutting was taken. Finally, the pretrial stipulations established that Cal–Florida had taken plant material, or cuttings, from Yoder's patented plants.

We agree with Yoder that it was not necessary to prove that the cuttings actually matured into flowered plants to show infringement. Under such a rule, it would be virtually impossible for a propagator-distributor directly to infringe a patent, despite the vital role he plays in dissemination of plant material. Furthermore, we think section 163 is plain in its statement that a patentee may exclude others from asexually reproducing, selling or using the plant. The negative inference to be drawn from this is that commission of one of those acts would constitute infringement. We therefore affirm the finding of infringement.

Notes and Questions

1. What is it that makes plants patentable? Where is the inventive spark? Especially, how can objects of nature be patented and others thus excluded from its benefits?

2. Normally, three requirements for patentability are novelty, utility and nonobviousness; however, for plant patents, the requirement of distinctness replaces that of utility and the additional requirement of asexual reproduction is introduced. Does the requirement of distinctiveness equal the utility requirement? Are the two comparable? Do they serve the same purpose?

3. Why isn't the discovery of a previously undiscovered plant enough to deserve patent protection?

4. Like utility patents, plant patents under U.S. law are granted a term of protection of 20 years from the date of issuance of the patent.

Chapter Three

TRADEMARKS

Origin and Purposes of Trademark Law. A trademark includes any word, name, symbol, or device or any combination thereof adopted and used by a manufacturer or seller to identify the source of the goods or services and distinguish them from those supplied by others. A service mark is a "trademark" that applies to services. Both of these types of mark are protected under the Lanham (Federal Trademark) Act, 15 U.S.C., §§ 1051–1127. Unlike patents and copyrights, trademarks are *not* exclusively a creature of federal statute. To the contrary, under U.S. law trademarks were first protected under state laws. The first federal trademark statute was not enacted until 1870. This statute was struck down in the *Trade–Mark Cases*, 100 U.S. 82 (1879), because Congress had based its power on the Patents and Copyrights Clause of the Constitution. The statute was re-enacted in 1881. Despite this relatively late entry, federal trademark law, and the principles developed under it, have come to dominate the U.S. field.

Other types of protected marks under U.S. law include certification marks—certifying the origin, materials, mode of manufacture, quality or other characteristics of a good or service—and collective marks—marks indicating membership in a union, association or other organization. *See* 15 U.S.C. § 1127.

The primary function of a trademark is to indicate origin. However, trademarks also serve to guarantee the quality of the goods or services so that the consumer may be confident in what he is purchasing. And, through advertising, it serves to create and maintain demand. Thus the holder of a trademark should be able to protect her investments from misappropriation through unauthorized third party use.

Acquisition and Loss of Rights. Rights in a trademark are acquired under U.S. law by use. Registration of a mark with the U.S. Patent and Trademark Office, consequently, is *not* required to gain rights to a trademark. Such registration, however, gains certain procedural advantages, including prima facie evidence of the trademark owner's exclusive right to use the mark through-out the United States as of the date of registration. Although an application to register a mark can be filed based on the owner's bona fide intention to use the mark, no U.S. owner can obtain a registration without first using the mark in interstate commerce in connection with the applied-for goods or services.

In choosing a trademark, the aim under U.S. law is to find a word, symbol or design or a combination of these which is not purely descriptive of the product or service concerned. A descriptive mark—or a common surname or geographical name—cannot, as a new mark, immediately qualify for registration because it lacks distinctiveness. Instead, the mark must be used in a sufficiently extensive manner to demonstrate that the mark has gained secondary meaning, in other words, that its primary significance to the public is as a source designator. Generic marks—those which consist of the common descriptive term for a good or service—can never be protected regardless of their length of use. An example of a generic mark is "pen" for a writing instrument, or multi-state bar exam for a multi-state examination to pass the bar.

Trademarks must be used properly to maintain the rights. A mark that becomes the generic name of a product is no longer treated as a trademark. Famous examples of lost trademarks are aspirin, nylon, yo-yo and cellophane. As noted earlier, registration of a trademark in the U.S. Patent and Trademark Office does not in itself create or establish any exclusive rights; it merely establishes certain rebuttable presumptions regarding the validity of the mark, and the owner's exclusive right to use it throughout the United States.

In order to be eligible for federal registration, a mark must be in use in interstate commerce. Since it is no longer necessary to use the mark prior to filing an application to register it, anyone can file an application by asserting a bona fide intent to use the mark. The application will then be fully examined and ruled upon, but the mark cannot be registered by a U.S. owner until actual use has occurred. This permits one to obtain a holding of registrability prior to an investment in labels, advertising, etc.

Trademarks can also be registered in individual states in which they are used. This is normally advisable when only local use of the mark is contemplated since the benefits of state registration are usually more limited than those available from a federal registration. In some instances, proceeding with both avenues of registration may be advisable.

Role of Registration. As noted above, registration of trademarks generally is not compulsory under U.S. law. Common law rights actually attach when a mark is first used in connection with the goods or services before the public. These trademark rights are enforceable, but are limited geographically to the actual area of use or reputation of the mark. Advantages of registrations include constructive notice to all subsequent parties of a claim to ownership throughout the U.S.

A. WHAT IS REQUIRED TO OBTAIN TRADEMARK RIGHTS UNDER U.S. LAW?

The term "trademark includes any word, name or symbol, or device, or any combination thereof:

1. used by a person, or;
2. which a person in bona fide intention to use in commerce and applies to register on the principal register established by this chapter,

to identify and distinguish his or her goods, including a unique product, from those manufactured or sold by others and to indicate the source of the goods, even if the source is unknown. (15 U.S.C. § 1127)

THE SAFARI CASE

ABERCROMBIE & FITCH COMPANY v. HUNTING WORLD INCORPORATED

United States Court of Appeals, Second Circuit, 1976.
537 F.2d 4.

FRIENDLY, CIRCUIT JUDGE.

This action in the District Court for the Southern District of New York by Abercrombie & Fitch Company (A&F), owner of well-known stores at Madison Avenue and 45th Street in New York City and seven places in other states against Hunting World, Incorporated (HW), operator of a competing store on East 53rd Street, is for infringement of some of A&F's registered trademarks using the word 'Safari'.

For many years A&F has used the mark 'Safari' on articles "exclusively offered and sold by it." Since 1936 it has used the mark on a variety of men's and women's outer garments. Its United States trademark registrations include:

Trademark	Number	Issued	Goods
Safari	358,781	7/26/38	Men's and Women's outer garments, including hats.
Safari Mills	125,531	5/20/19	Cotton Piece goods.
Safari	652,098	9/24/57	Men's and Women's outer garments, including shoes.
Safari	703,279	8/23/60	Woven cloth, sporting goods, apparel, etc.

A&F has spent large sums of money in advertising and promoting products identified with its mark 'Safari' and in policing its right in the mark, including the successful conduct of trademark infringement suits. HW, the complaint continued, has engaged in the retail marketing of sporting apparel including hats and shoes, some identified by use of 'Safari' alone or by expressions such as 'Minisafari' and 'Safariland'

The cases identify four different categories of terms with respect to trademark protection. Arrayed in an ascending order which roughly reflects their eligibility to trademark status and the degree of protection accorded, these classes are (1) generic, (2) descriptive, (3) suggestive, and (4) arbitrary or fanciful. The lines of demarcation, however, are not always bright. Moreover, the difficulties are compounded because a term that is in one category for a particular product may be in quite a different one for another,[34] because a term may shift from one category to another in light of differences in usage through time,[35] because a term may have one meaning to one group of users and a different one to others,[36] and because the same term may be put to different uses with respect to a single product. In various ways, all of these complications are involved in the instant case.

A generic term is one that refers, or has come to be understood as referring, to the genus of which the particular product is a species. At common law neither those terms which were generic nor those which were merely descriptive could become valid trademarks, see *Delaware & Hudson Canal Co. v. Clark*, 80 U.S. (13 Wall.) 311, 323, 20 L.Ed. 581 (1872) ("Nor can a generic name, or a name merely descriptive of an article or its qualities, ingredients, or characteristics, be employed as a trademark and the exclusive use of it be entitled to legal protection"). While the Lanham Act makes an important exception with respect to those merely descriptive terms which have acquired secondary meaning, see § 2(f), 15 U.S.C. § 1052(f), it offers no such exception for generic marks. The Act provides for the cancellation of a registered mark if at any time it "becomes the common descriptive name of an article or substance." This means that even proof of secondary meaning, by virtue of which some "merely descriptive" marks may be registered, cannot transform a generic term into a subject for trademark. As explained in *J. Kohnstam, Ltd. v. Louis Marx and Company*, 280 F.2d 437, 440, 47 CCPA 1080 (1960), no matter how much money and effort the user of a generic term has poured into promoting the sale of its merchandise and what success it has achieved in securing public identification, it cannot deprive competing manufacturers of the product of the right to call an article by its name. The pervasiveness of the principle is illustrated by a series of well known cases holding that when a suggestive or fanciful term has become generic as a result of a manufacturer's own advertising efforts, trademark protection will be denied save for those markets where the term still has not become generic and a secondary meaning has been shown to continue. A term may thus be generic in one market and descriptive or suggestive or fanciful in another.

---

34. To take a familiar example "Ivory" would be generic when used to describe a product made from the tusks of elephants but arbitrary as applied to soap.

35. *See, e. g., Haughton Elevator Co. v. Seeberger*, 85 U.S.P.Q. 80 (1950), in which the coined word 'Escalator', originally fanciful, or at the very least suggestive, was held to have become generic.

36. *See, e. g., Bayer Co. v. United Drug Co.*, 272 F. 505 (S.D.N.Y.1921).

The term which is descriptive but not generic stands on a better basis. Although § 2(e) of the Lanham Act, 15 U.S.C. § 1052, forbids the registration of a mark which, when applied to the goods of the applicant, is "merely descriptive," § 2(f) removes a considerable part of the sting by providing that "except as expressly excluded in paragraphs (a)-(d) of this section, nothing in this chapter shall prevent the registration of a mark used by the applicant which has become distinctive of the applicant's goods in commerce" and that the Commissioner may accept, as prima facie evidence that the mark has become distinctive, proof of substantially exclusive and continuous use of the mark applied to the applicant's goods for five years preceding the application. "Common descriptive name," as used in §§ 14(c) and 15(4), refers to generic terms applied to products and not to terms that are "merely descriptive." In the former case any claim to an exclusive right must be denied since this in effect would confer a monopoly not only of the mark but of the product by rendering a competitor unable effectively to name what it was endeavoring to sell. In the latter case the law strikes the balance, with respect to registration, between the hardships to a competitor in hampering the use of an appropriate word and those to the owner who, having invested money and energy to endow a word with the good will adhering to his enterprise, would be deprived of the fruits of his efforts.

The category of "suggestive" marks was spawned by the felt need to accord protection to marks that were neither exactly descriptive on the one hand nor truly fanciful on the other. [One] court has observed that:

> A term is suggestive if it requires imagination, thought and perception to reach a conclusion as to the nature of goods. A term is descriptive if it forthwith conveys an immediate idea of the ingredients, qualities or characteristics of the goods.

If a term is suggestive, it is entitled to registration without proof of secondary meaning. Moreover the decision of the Patent Office to register a mark without requiring proof of secondary meaning affords a rebuttable presumption that the mark is suggestive or arbitrary or fanciful rather than merely descriptive.

It need hardly be added that fanciful or arbitrary terms [37] enjoy all the rights accorded to suggestive terms as marks without the need of debating whether the term is "merely descriptive,"

We turn first to an analysis of A&F's trademarks to determine the scope of protection to which they are entitled.

It is common ground that A&F could not apply 'Safari' as a trademark for an expedition into the African wilderness. This would be a clear example of the use of 'Safari' as a generic term. What is perhaps

---

37. As terms of art, the distinctions between suggestive terms and fanciful or arbitrary terms may seem needlessly artificial. Of course, a common word may be used in a fanciful sense; indeed one might say that only a common word can be so used, since a coined word cannot first be put to a bizarre use. Nevertheless, the term "fanciful", as a classifying concept, is usually applied to words invented solely for their use as trademarks. When the same legal consequences attach to a common word, i. e., when it is applied in an unfamiliar way, the use is called "arbitrary."

less obvious is that a word may have more than one generic use. The word 'Safari' has become part of a family of generic terms which, although deriving no doubt from the original use of the word and reminiscent of its milieu, have come to be understood not as having to do with hunting in Africa, but as terms within the language referring to contemporary American fashion apparel. These terms name the components of the safari outfit well-known to the clothing industry and its customers: the 'Safari hat', a broad flat-brimmed hat with a single, large band; the 'Safari jacket', a belted bush jacket with patch pockets and a buttoned shoulder loop; when the jacket is accompanied by pants, the combination is called the 'Safari suit'. Typically these items are khaki-colored.

This outfit, and its components, were doubtless what Judge Ryan had in mind when he found that "the word 'safari' in connection with wearing apparel is widely used by the general public and people in the trade." The record abundantly supports the conclusion that many stores have advertised these items despite A&F's attempts to police its mark. In contrast, a search of the voluminous exhibits fails to disclose a single example of the use of 'Safari', by anyone other than A&F and HW, on merchandise for which A&F has registered 'Safari' except for the safari outfit and its components as described above.

What has been thus far established suffices to support the dismissal of the complaint with respect to many of the uses of 'Safari' by HW. Describing a publication as a "Safariland Newsletter", containing bulletins as to safari activity in Africa, was clearly a generic use which is nonenjoinable .. A&F also was not entitled to an injunction against HW's use of the word in advertising goods of the kind included in the safari outfit as described above. And if HW may advertise a hat of the kind worn on safaris as a safari hat, it may also advertise a similar hat with a smaller brim as a minisafari. Although the issue may be somewhat closer, the principle against giving trademark protection to a generic term also sustains the denial of an injunction against HW's use of 'Safariland' as a name of a portion of its store devoted at least in part to the sale of clothing as to which the term 'Safari' has become generic.

A&F stands on stronger ground with respect to HW's use of 'Camel Safari', 'Hippo Safari' and Chukka 'Safari' as names for boots imported from Africa. [T]here is no evidence that 'Safari' has become a generic term for boots. Since A&F's registration of 'Safari' for use on its shoes has become incontestable, it is immaterial (save for HW's contention of fraud which is later rejected) whether A&F's use of 'Safari' for boots was suggestive or "merely descriptive."

THE MEN'S SLACKS CASE

BLUE BELL, INC. v. FARAH MANUFACTURING COMPANY

United States Court of Appeals, Fifth Circuit, 1975.
508 F.2d 1260.

GEWIN, CIRCUIT JUDGE.

In the spring and summer of 1973 two prominent manufacturers of men's clothing created identical trademarks for goods substantially identical in appearance. Though the record offers no indication of bad faith in the design and adoption of the labels, both Farah Manufacturing Company (Farah) and Blue Bell, Inc. (Blue Bell) devised the mark "Time Out" for new lines of men's slacks and shirts. Both parties market their goods on a national scale, so they agree that joint utilization of the same trademark would confuse the buying public. Thus, the only question presented for our review is which party established prior use of the mark in trade. A response to that seemingly innocuous inquiry, however, requires us to define the chameleonic term "use" as it has developed in trademark law.

Farah conceived of the Time Out mark on May 16, after screening several possible titles for its new stretch menswear. Two days later the firm adopted an hourglass logo and authorized an extensive advertising campaign bearing the new insignia. Farah presented its fall line of clothing, including Time Out slacks, to sales personnel on June 5. In the meantime, patent counsel had given clearance for use of the mark after scrutiny of current federal registrations then on file. One of Farah's top executives demonstrated samples of the Time Out garments to large customers in Washington, D.C. and New York, though labels were not attached to the slacks at that time. Tags containing the new design were completed June 27. With favorable evaluations of marketing potential from all sides, Farah sent one pair of slacks bearing the Time Out mark to each of its twelve regional sales managers on July 3. Sales personnel paid for the pants, and the garments became their property in case of loss.

Following the July 3 shipment, regional managers showed the goods to customers the following week. Farah received several orders and production began. Further shipments of sample garments were mailed to the rest of the sales force on July 11 and 14. Merchandising efforts were fully operative by the end of the month. The first shipments to customers, however, occurred in September.

Blue Bell, on the other hand, was concerned with creating an entire new division of men's clothing, as an avenue to reaching the "upstairs" market. Though initially to be housed at the Hicks–Ponder plant in El Paso, the new division would eventually enjoy separate headquarters. On June 18 Blue Bell management arrived at the name Time Out to identify both its new division and its new line of men's sportswear. Like Farah, it received clearance for use of the mark from counsel. Like Farah, it inaugurated an advertising campaign. Unlike Farah, however, Blue Bell did not ship a dozen marked articles of the new line to its sales personnel. Instead, Blue Bell authorized the manufacture of several hundred labels bearing the words Time Out and its logo shaped like a referee's hands forming a T. When the labels were completed on June 29, the head of the embryonic division flew them to El Paso. He instructed shipping personnel to affix the new Time Out labels to slacks that already bore the "Mr. Hicks" trademark. The new tags, of varying sizes and colors, were randomly attached to the left hip pocket button of slacks and the left hip pocket of jeans. Thus, although no change occurred in the design or manufacture of the pants, on July 5 several hundred pair left El Paso with two tags.

Blue Bell made intermittent shipments of the doubly-labeled slacks thereafter, though the out-of-state customers who received the goods had ordered clothing of the Mr. Hicks variety. Production of the new Time Out merchandise began in the latter part of August, and Blue Bell held a sales meeting to present its fall designs from September 4–6. Sales personnel solicited numerous orders, though shipments of the garments were not scheduled until October.

By the end of October Farah had received orders for 204,403 items of Time Out sportswear, representing a retail sales value of over $2,750,-000. Blue Bell had received orders for 154,200 garments valued at over $900,000. Both parties had commenced extensive advertising campaigns for their respective Time Out sportswear.

Soon after discovering the similarity of their marks, Blue Bell sued Farah for common law trademark infringement and unfair competition, seeking to enjoin use of the Time Out trademark on men's clothing. Farah counter-claimed for similar injunctive relief. The district court found that Farah's July 3 shipment and sale constituted a valid use in trade, while Blue Bell's July 5 shipment was a mere "token" use insufficient at law to create trademark rights. While we affirm the result reached by the trial court as to Farah's priority of use, the legal grounds upon which we base our decision are somewhat different from those undergirding the district court's judgment.

A trademark is a symbol (word, name, device or combination thereof) adopted and used by a merchant to identify his goods and distinguish them from articles produced by others. Ownership of a mark requires a combination of both appropriation and use in trade. Thus, neither conception of the mark nor advertising alone establishes trademark rights at common law. Rather, ownership of a trademark accrues when goods bearing the mark are placed on the market. *Wallace & Co. v. Repetti*, 266 F. 307 (2d Cir.), *cert. denied*, 254 U.S. 639, 41 S.Ct. 13, 65 L.Ed. 451 (1920).

The exclusive right to a trademark belongs to one who first uses it in connection with specified goods. *McLean v. Fleming*, 96 U.S. 245, 24 L.Ed. 828 (1877). Such use need not have gained wide public recognition and even a single use in trade may sustain trademark rights if followed by continuous commercial utilization.

The initial question presented for review is whether Farah's sale and shipment of slacks to twelve regional managers constitutes a valid first use of the Time Out mark. Blue Bell claims the July 3 sale was merely an internal transaction insufficiently public to secure trademark ownership. After consideration of pertinent authorities, we agree.

Secret, undisclosed internal shipments are generally inadequate to support the denomination "use.' Trademark claims based upon shipments from a producer's plant to its sales office, and vice versa, have often been disallowed. Though none of the cited cases dealt with sales to intra-corporate personnel, we perceive that fact to be a distinction without a difference. The sales were not made to customers, but served as an accounting device to charge the salesmen with their cost in case of loss. The fact that some sales managers actively solicited accounts bolsters the good faith of Farah's intended use, but does not meet our essential objection: that the "sales' were not made to the public.

The primary, perhaps singular purpose of a trademark is to provide a means for the consumer to separate or distinguish one manufacturer's goods from those of another. Personnel within a corporation can identify an item by style number or other unique code. A trademark aids the public in selecting particular goods. As stated by the First Circuit:

> But to hold that a sale or sales are the sine qua non of a use sufficient to amount to an appropriation would be to read an unwarranted limitation into the statute, for so construed registration would have to be denied to any manufacturer who adopted a mark to distinguish or identify his product, and perhaps applied it thereon for years, if he should in practice lease his goods rather than sell them, as many manufacturers of machinery do. It seems to us that although evidence of sales is highly persuasive, the question of use adequate to establish appropriation remains one to be decided on the facts of each case, and that evidence showing, first, adoption, and, second, use in a way sufficiently public to identify or distinguish the marked goods in an appropriate segment of the public mind as those of the adopter of the mark, is competent to establish ownership . . .

New England Duplicating Co. v. Mendes, 190 F.2d 415, 418 (1st Cir. 1951)

Blue Bell's July 5 shipment failed to satisfy the prerequisites of a bona fide use in trade. Elementary tenets of trademark law require that labels or designs be affixed to the merchandise actually intended to bear the mark in commercial transactions. Furthermore, courts have recognized that the usefulness of a mark derives not only from its capacity to identify a certain manufacturer, but also from its ability to differentiate between different classes of goods produced by a single manufacturer. Here customers had ordered slacks of the Mr. Hicks species, and Mr. Hicks was the fanciful mark distinguishing these slacks from all others.

Blue Bell intended to use the Time Out mark on an entirely new line of men's sportswear, unique in style and cut, though none of the garments had yet been produced.

While goods may be identified by more than one trademark, the use of each mark must be bona fide. Mere adoption of a mark without bona fide use, in an attempt to reserve it for the future, will not create trademark rights. In the instant case Blue Bell's attachment of a secondary label to an older line of goods manifests a bad faith attempt to reserve a mark. We cannot countenance such activities as a valid use in trade. Blue Bell therefore did not acquire trademark rights by virtue of its July 5 shipment.

We thus hold that neither Farah's July 3 shipment nor Blue Bell's July 5 shipment sufficed to create rights in the Time Out mark. Based on a desire to secure ownership of the mark and superiority over a competitor, both claims of alleged use were chronologically premature. Essentially, they took a time out to litigate their differences too early in the game. The question thus becomes whether we should continue to stop the clock for a remand or make a final call from the appellate bench. While a remand to the district court for further factual development would not be improper in these circumstances, we believe the interests of judicial economy and the parties' desire to terminate the litigation demand that we decide, if possible, which manufacturer first used the mark in trade.

Careful examination of the record discloses that Farah shipped its first order of Time Out clothing to customers in September of 1973. Blue Bell, approximately one month behind its competitor at other relevant stages of development, did not mail its Time Out garments until at least October. Though sales to customers are not the sine qua non of trademark use, they are determinative in the instant case. These sales constituted the first point at which the public had a chance to associate Time Out with a particular line of sportswear. Therefore, Farah established priority of trademark use; it is entitled to a decree permanently enjoining Blue Bell from utilization of the Time Out trademark on men's garments.

The judgment of the trial court is affirmed.

Notes and Questions

1. What evidence did the court consider in deciding whether the various SAFARI marks at issue in *Abercrombie* were distinctive? Why should only distinctive marks be protected? What policy is served by this requirement?

2. What evidence would you consider in deciding whether the mark "Murphy Bed" for a pull-down bed concealed in a wall is generic? In deciding whether "XEROX" is generic for photocopy machines?

3. In the U.S., ownership of a trademark is determined by use, *not* registration. What advice would you give Blue Bell regarding the steps it

should take in the future to assure that it has prior rights to a mark it desires to adopt?

4. Would the following qualify as acceptable use under the *Men's Slacks* case—pre-manufacturing advertisements containing the mark, reputation based solely on foreign sales of slacks bearing the mark, offering slacks for sale at a trade show prior to manufacturing of any such slacks?

5. U.S. patent and copyright law is designed in part to encourage the creation of new inventions and new works. Is U.S. trademark law similarly designed to encourage the creation of new marks? What purposes does U.S. trademark law serve?

6. U.S. trademark law has been used to protect a wide variety of source designators, including word marks, symbols, logos, sounds, smell, color, packaging and container and product shapes. Regardless of the nature of the work sought to be protected, the touchstone for protection remains the distinctiveness of the mark and its use as a source designator.

B. WHAT ARE THE LIMITS OF TRADEMARK PROTECTION?

THE ASPIRIN CASE
BAYER CO. v. UNITED DRUG CO.

United States District Court, S.D. New York, 1921.
272 Fed. 505.

L. HAND, DISTRICT JUDGE

This is a suit in equity between the plaintiff, a New York corporation, and the defendant, a Massachusetts corporation, to enjoin infringement of the plaintiff's common-law trade-mark "Aspirin." The bill was filed in May, 1917, and alleged that the plaintiff or its predecessors had since 1899 been selling throughout the United States a drug known as "acetyl salicylic acid," to which they had given the artificial trade-mark "Aspirin;" that they had expended large sums of money in popularizing the trade-mark so adopted, which had thus become a synonym for the acetyl salicylic acid manufactured by them; that on May 5, 1899, the plaintiff's predecessor had registered this trade-mark in the United States, and that the plaintiff held both the common-law and the registered mark by proper assignments; that the value of the amount in controversy was more than $5,000; and that the defendant had infringed the mark by using the word "Aspirin" in the sale of acetyl salicylic acid. It prayed the usual injunction in such cases.

The facts shown upon the trial were in substance as follows: The predecessor of the plaintiff was a German corporation engaged in the manufacture of chemical products, among them the drug in question, which was its own invention. On August 1, 1898, it applied for a patent in the United States, and therein described the drug as "acetyl salicylic acid." This patent issued on February 27, 1900, and therefore expired 17 years thereafter. It was eventually sustained by the courts, and in theory should have given the plaintiff or its predecessors a monopoly of production. This, however, was not the case, at least for a long time, and probably not altogether at any time. Large quantities of it were surreptitiously introduced into this country and sold, and while the amounts are necessarily somewhat uncertain, the plaintiff showed that considerably more than 220 tons had in fact been imported, of which it is fair to presume that all or nearly all reached the eventual consumer. This represented a very substantial proportion of the drug manufactured and sold by the plaintiff itself or its predecessors. It is impossible to ascertain how much, if any, of this infringing drug was marketed under the name "Aspirin," but it is probable that little or none of it reached the retail druggists under that name.

The plaintiff called a number of retail druggists, who swore with substantial unanimity that they had never sold the infringing drug to the consumer under the name "Aspirin," and in many cases that the customers themselves asked for it as "Acetylo" or as "acetyl salicylic acid." In Europe, where the plaintiff's predecessor appears not to have enjoyed the benefit of a patent, the drug was manufactured in open competition, but the name "Aspirin" was uniformly respected as a trademark, other manufacturers selling either under the name mentioned in the patent or under artificial trade-marks invented by the manufacturers themselves.

The importation into this country by the plaintiff's predecessor began some time in the year 1899 and before the patent issued. At that time it was all sold in the form of powder, and for some years only to manufacturing chemists, retail druggists, or to physicians. The plaintiff's predecessor, however, did make it up into sample tablets, which it sent gratuitously to all or nearly all the physicians in the country in small quantities. It registered the name as a trade-mark on May 2, 1899. It advertised very largely in technical magazines, and in all its advertisements and on all its labels claimed the word "Aspirin" as its trade-mark. For example, this legend was commonly employed: "The word 'Aspirin' identifies it as the manufacture of" the plaintiff or its predecessors. None of these advertisements, however, were to the public at large, nor did any of the packages reach further than physicians, manufacturing chemists, or retail druggists. In its powder form it was only prescribed by physicians, except as now to be stated.

About 1904 the plaintiff's predecessor began to sell the powder in increasingly large quantities to wholesale manufacturing chemists, understanding that they would make it up into tablets to dispense to retail druggists in bottles containing 5,000, 1,000, 500, and 100 tablets. These chemists, who comprised nearly all the large houses in the country, sold the tablets to retailers under the name "Aspirin," and in no case did the name of the plaintiff or its predecessors appear upon the labels. Moreover, the manufacturing chemist in each case used his own name upon the bottle, e.g., "Aspirin, Squibb," or simply, "Aspirin," with his name or initials below. The tablets soon occupied by far the greater part of the field, the prescription by powder very largely decreasing in proportion, and remaining only in those cases in which a prescription required the drug as one ingredient. The tablet trade grew to very large proportions, amounting in the case of the defendant alone in two years to nearly 16,000,000 tablets, and in the case of Smith, Klein & French in nine years to about 6,000,000. The drug proving useful, the public in time thus acquired the habit of self-medication by means of it and bought it either by fives or dozens from the retail druggists, or in bottles of 50 or 100, and possibly in some instances even more. During this period the plaintiff or its predecessors continued its former policy of addressing only the drug trade or physicians, and the public continued to have no greater information than before of who was in fact manufacturing the drug under the name "Aspirin."

On November 30, 1918, an examiner of the Patent Office declared that the trade-mark was no longer valid and ordered its cancellation. From this decision no appeal was taken, and that feature of the case therefore falls out of consideration.

LEARNED HAND, District Judge (after stating the facts as above).

The single question, as I view it is merely one of fact: What do the buyers understand by the word for whose use the parties are contending? If they understand by it only the kind of goods sold, then, I take it, it makes no difference whatever what efforts the plaintiff has made to get them to understand more. He has failed, and he cannot say that, when the defendant uses the word, he is taking away customers who wanted to deal with him, however closely disguised he may be allowed to keep his identity. So here the question is whether the buyers merely understood that the word "Aspirin" meant this kind of drug, or whether it meant that and more than that; i.e., that it came from the same single, though, if one please, anonymous source from which they had got it before. Prima facie I should say, since the word is coined and means nothing by itself, that the defendant must show that it means only the kind of drug to which it applies. The fact that it was patented until 1917 is indeed a material circumstance, but it is not necessarily controlling.

In deciding that issue I cannot, however, approach the question formally, as the plaintiff wishes; as to say that there was a user before the patent, and therefore the patent could not forfeit this property right, or that there was never any intention to abandon the trade-mark and so it must have continued. No doubt it is convenient for many purposes to treat a trademark as property; yet we shall never, I think, keep clear in our ideas on this subject, unless we remember that relief always depends upon the idea that no man shall be allowed to mislead people into supposing that his goods are the plaintiff's, and that there can be no right or remedy until the plaintiff can show that at least presumptively this will result.

In the case at bar the evidence shows that there is a class of buyers to whom the word "Aspirin" has always signified the plaintiff, more specifically indeed than was necessary for its protection. I refer to manufacturing chemists, to physicians, and probably to retail druggists.

From 1899 it flooded the mails with assertions that "Aspirin" meant its own manufacture. This was done in pamphlets, advertisements in trade papers, on the packages and cartons, and by the gratuitous distribution of samples. True, after 1904 it abandoned the phrase "acetyl salicylic acid" for "monoaceticacidester of salicylicacid," but even that extraordinary collocation of letters was intelligible to these classes of buyers who, except possibly the more ignorant of the retail druggists, were measurably versed in the general jargon of pharmaceutical chemistry. Moreover, the drug continued to be generally known by the more tolerable phrase "acetyl salicylic acid," which also adequately described its chemical organization. As to these buyers the plaintiff has therefore, I think, made out a case at least to compel the addition of some distinguishing suffix, even though its monopoly had been more perfect than in fact it was.

The crux of this controversy, however, lies not in the use of the word to these buyers, but to the general consuming public, composed of all sorts of buyers from those somewhat acquainted with pharmaceutical terms to those who knew nothing of them. The only reasonable inference from the evidence is that these did not understand by the word anything more than a kind of drug to which for one reason or another they had become habituated. It is quite clear that while the drug was sold as powder this must have been so. It was dispensed substantially altogether on prescription during this period, and, although physicians appear to have used the terms, "Aspirin" or "acetyl salicylic acid" indifferently, it cannot be that such patients as read their prescriptions attributed to "Aspirin" any other meaning than as an ingredient in a general compound, to which faith and science might impart therapeutic virtue. Nor is there any evidence that such as may have seen both terms identified them as the same drug. I cannot speculate as to how many in fact did so. No packages could possibly have reached the consumer, nor was any advertising addressed to them; their only acquaintance with the word was as the name for a drug in whose curative properties they had got confidence.

In 1904, however, they began to get acquainted with it in a different way, for then all the larger manufacturing chemists began to make tablets, and the trade grew to extraordinary proportions. The consumer, as both sides agree, had long before the autumn of 1915 very largely abandoned consultation with physicians and assumed the right to drug himself as his own prudence and moderation might prescribe. In all cases-omitting for the moment the infringing product-the drug was sold in bottles labeled "Aspirin" with some indication of the name of the tablet maker, but none of the plaintiff. It is probable that by far the greater part of the tablets sold were in dozens or less, and that the bottles so labeled did not generally reach the hands of the consumer, but, even so, a not inconsiderable number of bottles of 100 were sold, and as to the rest they were sold only under the name "Aspirin." The consumer did not know and could not possibly know the manufacturer of the drug which he got, or whether one or more chemists made it in the United

States. He never heard the name "acetylsalicylic acid" as applied to it, and without some education could not possibly have kept it in his mind, if he had. So far as any means of information at all were open to him, they indicated that it was made by most large chemists indiscriminately.

This being the situation up to the autumn of 1915, the defendant seems to me to have effectually rebutted any presumption, which the coined word might carry.

The case, therefore, presents a situation in which, ignoring sporadic exceptions, the trade is divided into two classes, separated by vital differences. One, the manufacturing chemists, retail druggists, and physicians, has been educated to understand that "Aspirin" means the plaintiff's manufacture, and has recourse to another and an intelligible name for it, actually in use among them. The other, the consumers, the plaintiff has, consciously I must assume, allowed to acquaint themselves with the drug only by the name "Aspirin," and has not succeeded in advising that the word means the plaintiff at all. If the defendant is allowed to continue the use of the word of the first class, certainly without any condition, there is a chance that it may get customers away from the plaintiff by deception. On the other hand, if the plaintiff is allowed a monopoly of the word as against consumers, it will deprive the defendant, and the trade in general, of the right effectually to dispose of the drug by the only description which will be understood. It appears to me that the relief granted cannot in justice to either party disregard this division; each party has won, and each has lost.

The plaintiff argues that this is an innovation in the law. I think not. In two very recent cases the Supreme Court has taken the very point, though the division chanced to be territorial instead of arising from the facts of the market. In *Hanover Milling Co. v. Metcalf*, 240 U.S. 403, 36 Sup.Ct. 357, 60 L.Ed. 713, and *United Drug Co. v. Rectanus*, 248 U.S. 90, 39 Sup.Ct. 48, 63 L.Ed. 141, a trade-mark and a trade-name were refused protection, though valid elsewhere, in parts of the country where the buyers did not know that they signified the owner, and because they did not. Mr. Justice Pitney especially adverted to the basis upon which the whole law rests. "Cessit ratio, cessit lex." If the rule applies to vertical divisions of the demand, it must apply to horizontal. Of course, we must not attempt too fine an application of such divisions, one reason perhaps for Mr. Justice Holmes' concurring opinion in *Hanover Mills v. Metcalf, supra.* For example, in the case at bar it is impossible to provide for such rare retailers as may not, and such rare customers as may, know that "Aspirin" is a trade-mark. We can cut only so fine as our shears permit, and there will be ragged edges on either side.

Notes and Questions

1. On what basis did the court in the *Aspirin* case decide that the trademark ASPIRIN had become generic?

2. *Abandonment.* The court appeared to consider Bayer's failure to include its source of manufacture as an abandonment of its trademark rights. Under U.S. law, failure to control the quality of the goods sold bearing the mark may also lead to abandonment. *See Dawn Donut Co. v. Hart's Food Stores*, 267 F.2d 358 (2d Cir.1959). Similarly, failure to stop unauthorized third party users of infringing marks may qualify as an abandonment of exclusive rights to the mark. *See Illinois High School Ass'n v. GTE Vantage Inc.*, 99 F.3d 244 (7th Cir.1996). What policy is supported by removing the monopoly protection offered trademarks under these situations of "abandonment?"

3. *Token Use.* U.S. law no longer allows trademark rights to be gained or maintained on the basis of "token use." Instead, a mark must generally be used continuously in connection with the relevant goods or services. Copyright and patents have no such use requirements. What purposes are served by such requirements? What is the relationship between fame and use? For example, the mark "the Washington Senators" for a professional baseball team has not been used since the 1970's. Should a new professional baseball team be able to use the mark without the former mark owner's permission? *See, e.g., Major League Baseball Properties, Inc. v. Sed Non Olet Denarius, Ltd.*, 817 F.Supp. 1103 (S.D.N.Y.1993).

THE NEW KIDS 900 POLL CASE

THE NEW KIDS ON THE BLOCK v. NEWS AMERICA PUBLISHING, INC.

United States Court of Appeals, Ninth Circuit, 1992.
971 F.2d 302.

KOZINSKI, CIRCUIT JUDGE.

The individual plaintiffs perform professionally as The New Kids on the Block, reputedly one of today's hottest musical acts. This case requires us to weigh their rights in that name against the rights of others to use it in identifying the New Kids as the subjects of public opinion polls.

No longer are entertainers limited to their craft in marketing themselves to the public. This is the age of the multi-media publicity blitzkrieg: Trading on their popularity, many entertainers hawk posters, T-shirts, badges, coffee mugs and the like-handsomely supplementing their incomes while boosting their public images. The New Kids are no exception; the record in this case indicates there are more than 500 products or services bearing the New Kids trademark. Among these are services taking advantage of a recent development in telecommunications: 900 area code numbers, where the caller is charged a fee, a portion of which is paid to the call recipient. Fans can call various New Kids 900 numbers to listen to the New Kids talk about themselves, to listen to other fans talk about the New Kids, or to leave messages for the New Kids and other fans.

The defendants, two newspapers of national circulation, conducted separate polls of their readers seeking an answer to a pressing question:

Which one of the New Kids is the most popular? USA Today's announce-ment contained a picture of the New Kids and asked, "Who's the best on the block?" The announcement listed a 900 number for voting, noted that "any USA Today profits from this phone line will go to charity," and closed with the following:

New Kids on the Block are pop's hottest group. Which of the five is your fave? Or are they a turn off? ... Each call costs 50 cents. Results in Friday's Life section.

The Star's announcement, under a picture of the New Kids, went to the heart of the matter: "Now which kid is the sexiest?" The announce-ment, which appeared in the middle of a page containing a story on a New Kids concert, also stated:

Which of the New Kids on the Block would you most like to move next door? STAR wants to know which cool New Kid is the hottest with our readers.

Readers were directed to a 900 number to register their votes; each call cost 95 cents per minute.[24]

Fearing that the two newspapers were undermining their hegemony over their fans, the New Kids filed a shotgun complaint in federal court raising no fewer than ten claims: (1) common law trademark infringe-ment; (2) Lanham Act false advertising; (3) Lanham Act false designa-tion of origin; (4) Lanham Act unfair competition; (5) state trade name infringement; (6) state false advertising; (7) state unfair competition; (8) commercial misappropriation; (9) common-law misappropriation; and (10) intentional interference with prospective economic advantage. The two papers raised the First Amendment as a defense, on the theory that the polls were part and parcel of their "news-gathering activities." The district court granted summary judgment for defendants.

Since at least the middle ages, trademarks have served primarily to identify the source of goods and services, "to facilitate the tracing of 'false' or defective wares and the punishment of the offending crafts-man." The law has protected trademarks since the early seventeenth century, and the primary focus of trademark law has been misappropria-tion-the problem of one producer's placing his rival's mark on his own goods. The law of trademark infringement was imported from England into our legal system with its primary goal the prevention of unfair competition through misappropriated marks. Although an initial attempt at federal regulation was declared unconstitutional, trademarks have been covered by a comprehensive federal statutory scheme since the passage of the Lanham Act in 1946.

Throughout the development of trademark law, the purpose of trademarks remained constant and limited: Identification of the manu-

24. The USA Today poll generated less than $300 in revenues, all of which the newspaper donated to the Berklee College of Music. The star's poll generated about $1600.

facturer or sponsor of a good or the provider of a service.[25] And the wrong protected against was traditionally equally limited: Preventing producers from free-riding on their rivals' marks. Justice Story outlined the classic scenario a century and a half ago when he described a case of "unmitigated and designed infringement of the rights of the plaintiffs, for the purpose of defrauding the public and taking from the plaintiffs the fair earnings of their skill, labor and enterprise." *Taylor*, 23 F.Cas. at 744. The core protection of the Lanham Act remains faithful to this conception. See 15 U.S.C. § 1114 (prohibiting unauthorized use in commerce of registered marks). Indeed, this area of the law is generally referred to as "unfair competition"-unfair because, by using a rival's mark, the infringer capitalizes on the investment of time, money and resources of his competitor; unfair also because, by doing so, he obtains the consumer's hard-earned dollar through something akin to fraud.

A trademark is a limited property right in a particular word, phrase or symbol.[26] And although English is a language rich in imagery, we need not belabor the point that some words, phrases or symbols better convey their intended meanings than others. Indeed, the primary cost of recognizing property rights in trademarks is the removal of words from (or perhaps non-entrance into) our language. Thus, the holder of a trademark will be denied protection if it is (or becomes) generic, *i.e.*, if it does not relate exclusively to the trademark owner's product. This requirement allays fears that producers will deplete the stock of useful words by asserting exclusive rights in them. When a trademark comes to describe a class of goods rather than an individual product, the courts will hold as a matter of law that use of that mark does not imply sponsorship or endorsement of the product by the original holder.

A related problem arises when a trademark also describes a person, a place or an attribute of a product. If the trademark holder were allowed exclusive rights in such use, the language would be depleted in much the same way as if generic words were protectable. Thus trademark law recognizes a defense where the mark is used only "to describe the goods or services of [a] party, or their geographic origin." 15 U.S.C. § 1115(b)(4). "The 'fair-use' defense, in essence, forbids a trademark registrant to appropriate a descriptive term for his exclusive use and so prevent others from accurately describing a characteristic of their goods."

25. In economic terms, trademarks reduce consumer search costs by informing people that trademarked products come from the same source. The benefit of the brand name is analogous to that of designating individuals by last as well as first names, so that, instead of having to say "the Geoffrey who teaches constitutional law at the University of Chicago Law school—not the one who teaches corporations," you can say "Geoffrey Stone, not Geoffrey Miller." William M. Landes and Richard A. Posner, *Trademark Law: An Economic Perspective*, 30 J.L. & Econ. 265, 269 (1987).

26. Trademark protection, like other legal protections of property rights, guards against the overuse of resources while also providing incentives for the creation of new combinations of resources. *See G.S. Rasmussen & Assocs., Inc. v. Kalitta Flying Serv., Inc.*, 958 F.2d 896, 900 (9th Cir. 1992).

With many well-known trademarks, such as Jell–O, Scotch tape and Kleenex, there are equally informative non-trademark words describing the products (gelatin, cellophane tape and facial tissue). But sometimes there is no descriptive substitute, and a problem closely related to genericity and descriptiveness is presented when many goods and services are effectively identifiable only by their trademarks. For example, one might refer to "the two-time world champions" or "the professional basketball team from Chicago," but it's far simpler (and more likely to be understood) to refer to the Chicago Bulls. In such cases, use of the trademark does not imply sponsorship or endorsement of the product because the mark is used only to describe the thing, rather than to identify its source.

Indeed, it is often virtually impossible to refer to a particular product for purposes of comparison, criticism, point of reference or any other such purpose without using the mark.

A good example of this is *Volkswagenwerk Aktiengesellschaft v. Church*, 411 F.2d 350 (9th Cir.1969), where we held that *Volkswagen* could not prevent an automobile repair shop from using its mark. We recognized that in "advertising [the repair of Volkswagens, it] would be difficult, if not impossible, for [*Church*] to avoid altogether the use of the word 'Volkswagen' or its abbreviation 'VW,' which are the normal terms which, to the public at large, signify appellant's cars." Id. at 352. Church did not suggest to customers that he was part of the Volkswagen organization or that his repair shop was sponsored or authorized by VW; he merely used the words "Volkswagen" and "VW" to convey information about the types of cars he repaired. Therefore, his use of the Volkswagen trademark was not an infringing use.

Similarly, competitors may use a rival's trademark in advertising and other channels of communication if the use is not false or misleading. *See, e.g., Smith v. Chanel, Inc.*, 402 F.2d 562 (9th Cir.1968) (maker of imitation perfume may use original's trademark in promoting product).[27]

Cases like these are best understood as involving a non-trademark use of a mark-a use to which the infringement laws simply do not apply, just as videotaping television shows for private home use does not implicate the copyright holder's exclusive right to reproduction. Indeed, we may generalize a class of cases where the use of the trademark does not attempt to capitalize on consumer confusion or to appropriate the cachet of one product for a different one. Such nominative use of a mark-where the only word reasonably available to describe a particular thing

---

27. A trademark may even be used lawfully in a way that many people, including the trademark owner, may find offensive. Consider *Girl Scouts v. Personality Posters Mfg. Co.*, 304 F.Supp. 1228 (S.D.N.Y.1969): defendants published a poster showing "a smiling girl dressed in the well-known green uniform of the junior girl scouts, with her hands clasped above her protruding, clearly pregnant abdomen. The caveat 'be prepared' appears next to her hands." *Id.* at 1230. The court found no infringement: "[r]ational analysis of the situation does not indicate a likelihood that the public will believe that the Girl Scouts are the authors of the poster to which they understandably take such violent exception." *Id.* at 1231.

is pressed into service-lies outside the strictures of trademark law: Because it does *not* implicate the source-identification function that is the purpose of trademark, it does not constitute unfair competition; such use is fair because it does not imply sponsorship or endorsement by the trademark holder.

To be sure, this is not the classic fair use case where the defendant has used the plaintiff's mark to describe the defendant's own product. Here, the New Kids trademark is used to refer to the New Kids themselves. We therefore do not purport to alter the test applicable in the paradigmatic fair use case. If the defendant's use of the plaintiff's trademark refers to something other than the plaintiff's product, the traditional fair use inquiry will continue to govern. But, where the defendant uses a trademark to describe the plaintiff's product, rather than its own, we hold that a commercial user is entitled to a nominative fair use defense provided he meets the following three requirements: First, the product or service in question must be one not readily identifiable without use of the trademark; second, only so much of the mark or marks may be used as is reasonably necessary to identify the product or service; and third, the user must do nothing that would, in conjunction with the mark, suggest sponsorship or endorsement by the trademark holder.

The New Kids do not claim there was anything false or misleading about the newspapers' use of their mark. It is no more reasonably possible, however, to refer to the New Kids as an entity than it is to refer to the Chicago Bulls, Volkswagens or the Boston Marathon without using the trademark. Indeed, how could someone not conversant with the proper names of the individual New Kids talk about the group at all? While plaintiffs' trademark certainly deserves protection against copycats and those who falsely claim that the New Kids have endorsed or sponsored them, such protection does not extend to rendering newspaper articles, conversations, polls and comparative advertising impossible. The first nominative use requirement is therefore met.

Also met are the second and third requirements. Both The Star and USA Today reference the New Kids only to the extent necessary to identify them as the subject of the polls; they do not use the New Kids' distinctive logo or anything else that isn't needed to make the announcements intelligible to readers. Finally, nothing in the announcements suggests joint sponsorship or endorsement by the New Kids. The USA Today announcement implies quite the contrary by asking whether the New Kids might be "a turn off." The Star's poll is more effusive but says nothing that expressly or by fair implication connotes endorsement or joint sponsorship on the part of the New Kids.

The New Kids argue that, even if the newspapers are entitled to a nominative fair use defense for the announcements, they are not entitled to it for the polls themselves, which were money-making enterprises separate and apart from the newspapers' reporting businesses. According to plaintiffs, defendants could have minimized the intrusion into their rights by using an 800 number or asking readers to call in on normal telephone lines which would not have resulted in a profit to the newspapers based on the conduct of the polls themselves.

The New Kids see this as a crucial difference. The New Kids' argument in support of this distinction is not entirely implausible: They point out that their fans, like everyone else, have limited resources. Thus a dollar spent calling the newspapers' 900 lines to express loyalty to the New Kids may well be a dollar not spent on New Kids products and services, including the New Kids' own 900 numbers. In short, plaintiffs argue that a nominative fair use defense is inapplicable where the use in question competes directly with that of the trademark holder.

We reject this argument. While the New Kids have a limited property right in their name, that right does not entitle them to control their fans' use of their own money. Where, as here, the use does not imply sponsorship or endorsement, the fact that it is carried on for profit and in competition with the trademark holder's business is beside the point. Voting for their favorite New Kid may be, as plaintiffs point out, a way for fans to articulate their loyalty to the group, and this may diminish the resources available for products and services they sponsor. But the trademark laws do not give the New Kids the right to channel their fans' enthusiasm (and dollars) only into items licensed or authorized by them. The New Kids could not use the trademark laws to prevent the publication of an unauthorized group biography or to censor all parodies or satires, which use their name.[28] We fail to see a material difference between these examples and the use here.

Summary judgment was proper as to the first seven causes of action because they all hinge on a theory of implied endorsement; there was none here as the uses in question were purely nominative.

Notes and Questions

1. What purpose is served by allowing the plaintiff to use the NEW KIDS trademark? Is this the same purpose served by the fair use doctrine under copyright law?

2. What if, instead of a poll, the newspapers sold t-shirts that parodied the group and used the mark NEW KIDS? Would this "parody" use similarly be a fair one? Should it be?

THE ENJOY COCAINE CASE
THE COCA-COLA COMPANY
v. GEMINI RISING, INC.
United States District Court, E.D. New York, 1972.
346 F.Supp. 1183.

NEAHER, DISTRICT JUDGE.

The Coca–Cola Company brings this action to enjoin defendant from printing, distributing and selling commercially a poster which consists

---

28. Consider, for example, a cartoon which appeared in a recent edition of a humor magazine: the top panel depicts a man in medieval garb hanging a poster announcing a performance of "The New Kids on the Block" to an excited group of onlookers. The lower panel shows the five New Kids, drawn in caricature, hands tied behind their backs, kneeling before "The

of an exact blown-up reproduction of plaintiff's familiar "Coca–Cola" trademark and distinctive format except for the substitution of the script letters "ine" for "-Cola", so that the poster reads "Enjoy Cocaine."

Plaintiff is a Delaware corporation with its principal place of business in Atlanta, Georgia. Since prior to 1893 it has manufactured and sold a soft drink beverage under the trademark "Coca–Cola" and has continuously and extensively employed the trademark in connection with its business to the present time. Three federal trademark registrations pertaining to "Coca–Cola" have been obtained by plaintiff-No. 22,406 issued January 31, 1893, No. 47,189 issued October 31, 1905, and No. 238,145 issued January 31, 1928. Each registration statement specifies either "beverages" or "beverages and syrups" as the class of merchandise to which the trademark is appropriated. The registrations have been renewed from time to time and are currently in full force and effect. Two of them, Nos. 47,189 and 238,145, have become incontestable pursuant to the Lanham Act, 15 U.S.C. § 1051 et seq. The trademark is also registered in the State of New York.

Since the original registration in 1893 plaintiff has displayed the trademark "Coca–Cola" in distinctive stylized script lettering with the lower portion of the "C" in "Coca" extending under the remaining letters in the form of a curved dash. In the traditional print format, the word "Enjoy" appears above "Coca–Cola" and below it, the word "Trademark" followed by "R" in a circle. In more recent years a sweeping white curved band has been added below "Coca–Cola". The trademark as so described has been widely presented to the public in white lettering against a bright red background in advertising of all kinds, e. g., magazines, newspapers, billboards, display materials, television, truck panels and the like.[29]

Defendant is a New York corporation with its principal office and place of business in New York County. It is engaged in the business of creating, printing, distributing and selling commercially posters of various kinds. In November 1970 defendant "created" and began the sale of the poster which reproduces plaintiff's distinctive trademark and format as previously described. The poster is approximately two feet by three

---

Chopping Block" awaiting execution. Cracked #17 (inside back cover) (Aug. 1992). Cruel? No doubt—but easily within the realm of satire and parody.

29. Plaintiff states that in the past 40 years well over a half-billion dollars has been spent in media advertising for "Coca–Cola". Even before that vast expenditure, the trademark had become so widely known that the supreme court was moved to note: the name now characterizes a beverage to be had at almost any soda fountain. It means a single thing coming from a single source, and well known to the community. It hardly would be too much to say that the drink characterizes the name as much as the name the drink. *Coca-Cola Co. v. Koke Co.*, 254 U.S. 143, 146, 41 S.Ct. 113, 114, 65 L.Ed. 189 (1920). Indeed, "Coca–Cola" has been described as "one of the three most-recognized trademarks in the world. The other two are 'B.V.D.' and 'Singer'." *The Business Lawyer*, November 1971, at 309, n. 51.

feet in size and printed in the same white lettering on a bright red background as plaintiff employs.

Defendant admits it has sold over 100,000 copies of the "Enjoy Cocaine" poster throughout the United States since November 1970. A purchase of the poster was recently made in this district at a retail price of $2.00. It is a fair inference, therefore, that defendant is deriving substantial revenue from their sale.

Defendant filed the poster and a notice in the United States Copyright Office on May 4, 1971, and, following a copyright application, obtained a "Registration of Copyright" numbered K 94714 dated July 15, 1971. On February 8, 1972, upon learning of plaintiff's intention to bring this suit, defendant filed a changed copy of the poster with the United States Copyright Office. Defendant concedes that the new poster is in all respects the same as the former poster with one exception, *i. e.*, "Trade–Mark" has been changed to "Raid–Mark".

Defendant does not and could not seriously deny that it is deliberately imitating plaintiff's trademark in its "Enjoy Cocaine" poster. Although it contends that the word "Coca–Cola" as such does not appear anywhere on the poster one would have to be a visitor from another planet not to recognize immediately the familiar "Coca" in its stylized script and accompanying words, colors and design. Indeed, defendant's assertion that "the poster was intended to be a spoof, satirical, funny, and to have a meaning exactly the opposite of the word content" would be meaningless except in the context of an immediately recognizable association with the "Coca–Cola" trademark. This is buttressed by the only change made in the new poster, i. e., "Raid–Mark" in place of "Trade–Mark"—a clear indication of defendant's predatory intent, however humorous defendant considers it. But whether such an unauthorized use of plaintiff's trademark warrants injunctive relief in these novel circumstances is another matter, to which we now turn.

The record before the court, as already indicated, establishes beyond dispute plaintiff's ownership and registration of its widely known trademark, which is also the dominant element of its corporate trade name. There can be no question that the mark is valid and worthy of protection. "The mere fact of registration ... creates a strong presumption of validity, a presumption which in this case stands unrebutted by any of the evidence presented on behalf of defendant."

Defendant does not really challenge this. Its position is simply "that the protection of the trademark law does not extend to this particular situation, since there is no attempt by the defendant to sell merchandise similar to the plaintiff's; nor is there any reasonable likelihood, considering the nature of the poster, that anyone could or would be confused as to the origin of the poster; *i. e.*, that it was either published or authorized by the plaintiff."

Admittedly the parties are not in competition in the ordinary sense. "But recognition ... that [defendant is] not making infringing sales of a kind of goods that plaintiff sells under a trade mark, does not end the

matter." *Hobart Manufacturing Company v. Kitchen Aid Service, Inc.,*
260 F.Supp. 559, 561 (E.D.N.Y.1966). Here there is no question that
both are seeking to attract public attention and patronage for their
respective products by the graphic display of a distinctive and widely
known trademark. That trademark belongs to and is uniquely identified
with plaintiff and its products. Plaintiff's property right in its mark
clearly extends to its reproduction and publication in advertising and for
other promotional uses regarding its products. In this case defendant's
product-a simulated bill poster-is itself one of the common forms of
advertising utilized by plaintiff. Hence it is not surprising that plaintiff
has received "numerous communications from all over the country"
concerning defendant's poster-a clear indication of public identification
of the poster with plaintiff and strong confirmation of the public confusion which defendant contends does not exist.

Moreover, defendant's argument that no trespass infringing plaintiff's rights has been committed, because the protected words "Coca–
Cola" do not appear in its poster, is disingenuous to say the least.
Although "Coca–Cola" is missing, "Coca" is recognizably visible, albeit
changed into "Cocaine". It is precisely this change plaintiff claims as the
source of its grievance and likelihood of injury. Judicial notice may be
taken that cocaine is a narcotic drug possession of which for nonmedical
purposes is a felonious criminal offense against the laws of the United
States punishable by substantial prison terms and fines. *See* 21 U.S.C.
§§ 812, 841. The stringency of those laws reflects the national concern
that cocaine-far from being "enjoyable"-is part of the tragic drug problem currently afflicting this nation, and particularly its youth. To associate such a noxious substance as cocaine with plaintiff's wholesome
beverage as symbolized by its "Coca–Cola" trademark and format would
clearly have a tendency to impugn that product and injure plaintiff's
business reputation, as plaintiff contends.[30] In other words, to paraphrase Judge Dooling in *Hobart, supra,* while the argument "that
[defendant has] not used plaintiff's trademark precisely ... might have
force in other and innocent circumstances, on the facts it is altogether
clear that [defendant] here exactly and successfully trespassed on just
that area of unmistaken identifications of the word ["Coca–Cola"] with
plaintiff that did exist." 260 F.Supp. at 561.

Defendant nonetheless scoffs at the suggestion that the poster
"would confuse any person of average intelligence, or even (below
average intelligence)" and that its "very nature ... precludes anyone
from believing that it originates with the plaintiff." That is simply
defendant's self-serving *ipse dixit.* The appearance of defendant's name-
in relatively small lettering-on the poster does not meet plaintiff's
factual proof that some persons of apparently average intelligence did

30. That contention is not a flight of
fancy. The name "Coca–Cola" is derived
from the andean coca leaf plant and the
African Cola nut, extracts of which gave the
beverage its flavor. The coca leaf is the
source of cocaine. *See* Webster's Third New
International Dictionary. But as the Supreme Court pointed out in *Coca–Cola Co.
v. Koke Co., supra,* 254 U.S. 143, at 145–
146, 41 S.Ct. 113, there is no cocaine in
Coca–Cola.

attribute sponsorship to plaintiff and discontinued their use of Coca–Cola as an expression of resentment. Not only does visual comparison of defendant's poster with specimen advertising of plaintiff indicate the likelihood of such a mistaken attribution but recent so-called "pop art" novelty advertising utilized by plaintiff may have served to further the impression that defendant's poster was just another effort of that kind by plaintiff to publicize its product.[31]

At all events, in assessing the probability of confusion "[t]he standard to be employed is the ordinary purchaser, not the expert." And the ordinary purchaser consists of a "vast multitude which includes the ignorant, the unthinking and the credulous, who, in making purchases, do not stop to analyse, but are governed by appearances and general impressions." *Florence Mfg. Co. v. J. C. Dowd & Co.*, 178 F. 73, 75 (2 Cir.1910). Judged by that standard, plaintiff has made a sufficiently clear showing of a high probability of confusion resulting from defendant's use of the "Coca–Cola" trademark format in an advertising context.

A further apparently unanswered serious question relates to the applicability of § 368–d of the New York General Business Law, upon which plaintiff relies. That statute by its terms extends injunctive relief to cases of "[l]ikelihood of injury to business reputation or of dilution of the distinctive quality of a mark or trade name" without regard to the absence of competition or confusion.[50] Judge Lasker, moreover, found no evidence of any confusion, which is clearly not the case here, and all the more so if defendant's poster may be regarded as a "product" for that purpose-another of the unusual questions in this case. Finally, there are numerous New York cases granting injunctive relief to protect one's trade name or mark from another's imitation "in the absence of a threat of confusion as to the source or sponsorship of the goods or services." *Sullivan v. Ed Sullivan Radio & T. V.*, 1 A.D.2d 609, 152 N.Y.S.2d 227 (1st Dept.1956).

Plaintiff's motion for a preliminary injunction is granted on condition that it furnish security for any costs or damages of defendant in the amount of $25,000.

Notes and Questions

1. What is the mark which is allegedly being infringed—the Coca–Cola word mark or the Coca–Cola trade dress, composed of the words Coca–Cola,

31. Plaintiff has authorized the use of its logo trademark as a decorative fabric pattern for such clothing items as beach pants and shorts, beach hats, bowling shirts and blouses, sweatshirts, dungarees and aprons and on a variety of other articles in common use including jewelry, portfolios, pocket radios, Cigarette lighters, pens and pencils, playing cards, lamps and glasses. Affidavit of George M. Lawson, plaintiff's vice-president and general counsel.

50. § 368–D. Injury to business reputation; dilution likelihood of injury to business reputation or of dilution of the distinctive quality of a mark or trade name shall be a ground for injunctive relief in cases of infringement of a mark registered or not registered or in cases of unfair competition, notwithstanding the absence of competition between the parties or the absence of confusion as to the source of goods or services. Added L.1961, c. 583, eff. Sept. 1, 1961.

in white script on red background? Would the poster be infringing without the well-known red and white colors and script lettering?

2. *Trade Dress*. Trade dress has been defined as "involv[ing] the total image of a product and may include features such as size, shape, color or color combinations, texture, graphics or even particular sales techniques." *John H. Harland Co. v. Clarke Checks, Inc.*, 711 F.2d 966 (11th Cir. 1983). This type of mark presents special problems of distinctiveness where the trade dress at issue includes the shape or color of the product itself. *See, e.g., Qualitex Co. v. Jacobson Products Co.*, 514 U.S. 159 (1995); *Duraco Products Inc. v. Joy Plastic Enterprises Ltd.*, 40 F.3d 1431 (3d Cir.1994). What evidence would you require to demonstrate that the shape of a product, for example, the shape of a planter, qualifies as a source designator?

3. *Fame*. What role, if any, did the fame of the Coca–Cola mark play in the court's decision? Should a famous mark be granted a broader scope of protection?

4. *Likelihood of Confusion versus Dilution*. Under U.S. law, only the unauthorized use of marks which are likely to confuse consumers regarding the source or sponsorship of the goods or services at issue is prohibited. Courts consider a variety of factors to determine likely confusion; including the similarity of the marks, the similarity of the goods or services and the existence of actual confusion. *See, e.g., Polaroid Corp. v. Polarad Electronics Corp.*, 287 F.2d 492 (2d Cir.), *cert. denied*, 368 U.S. 820 (1961); *AMF Inc. v. Sleekcraft Boats* 599 F.2d 341 (9th Cir. 1979). Generally, to establish likely confusion, the marks must be used on goods which contain some competitive nexus. Thus, for example, the use of LEXUS for automobiles was held not likely to create confusion with the mark LEXIS for legal databases. *See Mead Data Central, Inc. v. Toyota Motor Sales*, 875 F.2d 1026 (2d Cir.1989). To broaden the scope of protection for certain famous and distinctive marks, Congress enacted the Federal Trademark Dilution Act, Pub. L. No. 104–98, 190 Stat. 985 (1995). This act added a new cause of action for the unauthorized use of a mark—dilution. Under current U.S. trademark law, dilution occurs either when an unauthorized use of a mark "blurs" the "distinctive nature of the mark" or "tarnishes it." Likelihood of confusion is *not* required. 15 U.S.C. §§ 1127, 1125(c).

5. *Tarnishment*. The harmfulness of "tarnishment" is that the registered mark is used in connection with a less qualitative or illegal product so that the buyer will have a negative association with the mark which will decrease the selling power of the product. Did the "Enjoy Cocaine" poster tarnish the COCA–COLA mark? How? Is there a relationship between fair use and dilution? For example, is it possible that a mark or name dilutes another mark but is still valid under the fair use doctrine? What about parodies? Should they qualify as a fair use? Consider the *Girl Scout Poster* case cited in footnote 12 of the *New Kids 900 Poll* case.

Chapter Four

TRADE SECRETS: AN OVERVIEW

A. WHAT ARE THE REQUIREMENTS FOR TRADE SECRET PROTECTION UNDER U.S. LAW?

Origins and purposes of trade secret law. Under 1996, no federal trade secret law existed. Consequently, under U.S. law trade secret protection has been largely a creature of state law. The absence of a federal statute in the area has led to a patchwork of decisions resulting in sometimes inconsistent decisions regarding the scope of protection to be afforded certain types of business information.

Despite this lack of identity, trade secret law has been largely influenced by Section 757 of The Restatement of Torts, and the Uniform Trade Secrets Act. Future developments in trade secret law will no doubt be derived from the Economic Espionage Act, 18 U.S.C. §§ 1831–1839, the first federal trade secret statute. Based on the Commerce Clause, this statute provides protection against the misappropriations of "all forms and types of financial, business, scientific, technical, economic or engineering information, including patterns, plans, compilations, procedures, programs or codes, whether tangible or intangible, and whether or how stored, compiled or memorialized physically, electronically, graphically, photographically or in writing" provided that such information meets two statutory requirements:

1. The owner has taken "reasonable measures" to keep the information secret, and;

2. The information "derives independent economic value, actual or potential, from not being generally know to, and not being readily ascertainable through proper means by, the public." 18 U.S.C. § 1839.

Generally, protectable trade secrets under U.S. law may consist of any formula, pattern, device or compilation of information which is used in one's business, and which gives a person an opportunity to obtain an advantage over competitors; it may be, *e.g.*, a formula, a chemical compound, a process of manufacturing, treating or preserving materials, a pattern for a machine or other device, or, in some instances, a list of customers. The scope of information protected will depend upon the secret nature of the information, efforts the owner has taken to maintain that secrecy, and, in certain states, the actual value of the trade secret to competitors.

Courts have widely adopted a six-factor test for determining whether information or an idea is a trade secret:

1) How widely is the information known outside the claimant's business? This first factor considers how well known the information is to the public or to others in the same business as the claimant. It is not necessary for the claimant to demonstrate that no outsiders know the information. Others may know of it so long as their numbers are not too great and they take measures to keep the information secret. Stated another way, the information must be "substantially secret."

2) Who within the claimant's company knows the idea or information? Under this factor the claimant/employer is permitted to disclose the information to employees and others connected with its business. However, it must exercise some reasonable precautions. For example, the claimant should limit disclosure to those employees who actually need to know the secret in order to perform their jobs, and restrict access by others. The claimant may be required to take some measures to ensure that those who know the secret retain it in confidence. (For example, it may be required to notify workers that the information is secret, have them sign confidentiality agreements, or review research papers to be presented by company researchers at conferences.) The extent of these measures will differ from case to case, depending on what is reasonable under the circumstances.

3) What measures has the claimant taken to ensure that the idea or information remains secret? The claimant should take reasonable precautions to ensure that the information remains a secret. It should anticipate ways in which others might be expected to obtain the information and take reasonable measures to prevent access. For example, if the secret can be ascertained by observing the production process in the claimant's factory, the claimant may be required to restrict public access to that part of the factory. However, the claimant will not be required to make unreasonable expenditures to protect secrecy.

4) How valuable is the information to the claimant and its competitors? The information must be valuable to the claimant and give it an advantage over competitors who do not have it. The value to the claimant must be commercial in nature. Religious or spiritual value, for example, generally will not suffice.

5) How much effort or money has the claimant expended in developing or acquiring the information? The greater the claimant's investment in developing the know-how, the more likely the know-how has real value to the claimant and to the public generally. The

greater the know-how's value, the greater the justification for providing protection as an incentive for its development.

6) How difficult would it be for others properly to acquire or duplicate the information? For example, has the idea or information ever been published, so that persons engaged in library research could find it? If so, it probably will not qualify as a trade secret. Another issue is whether the information (particularly a production process) could easily be ascertained by reverse engineering—that is, through examination or laboratory analysis of the finished product placed on the market. If it would be easy to learn the information by reverse engineering, it may not qualify as a trade secret. However, the fact that the information could be determined through complex reverse engineering in a laboratory generally will not destroy trade secret status if that was not the way in which the defendant discovered it.

Misappropriation. Unauthorized disclosure or use of a protected trade secret is generally actionable if the information has been obtained in an improper manner. The test for misappropriation has been strongly influenced by Section 757 of the Restatement of Torts which provides:

One who discloses or uses another's trade secret, without a privilege to do so, is liable to the other if

a) he discovered the trade secret by improper means, or

b) his disclosure or use constitutes a breach of confidence reposed in him by the other in disclosing the secret to him, or

c) he learned the secret from a third person with notice of the facts that it was a secret and that the third person discovered it by improper means or that the third person's disclosure of it was otherwise a breach of his duty to the other, or

d) he learned the secret with notice of the facts that it was a secret and that its disclosure was made to him by mistake.

The Uniform Trade Secrets Act similarly prohibits "actual or threatened misappropriation." Uniform Trade Secrets Act, § 2. It also defines "improper means" as including "theft, bribery, misrepresentation, breach or inducement of a breach of a duty to maintain secrecy, or espionage through electronic or other means," *Id.* at § 1.

Unlike the other forms of intellectual property, trade secrets do not require registration. To the contrary, secrecy (*not* disclosure) is the touchstone for trade secret protection under U.S. law.

Thus, Section 1831 of the Economic Espionage Act: "Whoever, intending or knowing that the offense will benefit any foreign government, foreign instrumentality, or foreign agent, knowingly—

(1) steals, or without authorization appropriates, takes, carries away, or conceals, or by fraud, artifice, or deception obtains a trade secret;

(2) without authorization copies, duplicates, sketches, draws, photographs, downloads, uploads, alters, destroys, photocopies, replicates, transmits, delivers, sends, mails, communicates, or conveys a trade secret;

(3) receives, buys, or possesses a trade secret, knowing the same to have been stolen or appropriated, obtained, or converted without authorization;

(4) attempts to commit any offense described in any of paragraphs (1) through (3); or

(5) conspires with one or more other persons to commit any offense described in any of paragraphs (1) through (3), and one or more of such persons do any act to effect the object of the conspiracy, shall, except as provided in subsection (b), be fined not more than $500,000 or imprisoned not more than 15 years, or both.

Organizations.—Any organization that commits any offense described in subsection (a) shall be fined not more than $10,000,000." Economic Espionage Act, 18 U.S.C. § 1831.

THE LIFE INSURANCE CASE
CYBERTEK COMPUTER PRODUCTS, INC. v. WHITFIELD ET AL.
California Superior Court, L.A. Co., 1977.
203 U.S.P.Q. 1020.

TITLE, SUPERIOR COURT JUDGE.

Very briefly, and by way of an overview without attempting to set forth the facts in any considerable detail, the dispute essentially arises out of the prior employment of defendant Whitfield by plaintiff, and his subsequent employment by defendant Tracor in the same field of endeavor. Plaintiff was formed in 1969 for the purpose of engaging in the business of furnishing computer related services to the life insurance industry. Defendant Whitfield was one of the founding officers of plaintiff, and had a substantial background and expertise in computer software, as specifically related to its use in the life insurance business. He purchased shares in plaintiff, and in his capacity as an employee of plaintiff, directly participated in the design and development of plaintiff's on-line new business computer system known as the Auto/Issue System, his responsibilities including the specific design of some major portions of the system. For a time he had management responsibility for this system, and subsequently was a senior analyst involved in its design, programming and testing.

In connection with his employment, defendant Whitfield executed an Employee Nondisclosure Agreement, dated December 2, 1970, which provided among other things that the techniques and methods relating to plaintiff's products were trade secrets and confidential, and that he would not at any time disclose to anyone outside of plaintiff any information about plaintiff's products which related to the design, use or development of such products. The agreement specifically made reference to the Auto/Issue System. He voluntarily terminated his employment and relationship with plaintiff on March 31, 1971, at which time he acknowledged in writing that he understood his agreement with plaintiff not to disclose confidential information, and that he had returned all confidential material to plaintiff. He thereafter did some consulting work for defendant Tracor between July and October, 1971, commenced full-time employment with said defendant on November 15, 1971, and ever since that time has remained in said defendant's employ. His duties with defendant Tracor have included responsibility for the development of an insurance on-line new business system, which would provide substantially the same capabilities as plaintiff's Auto/Issue System, and which was to be marketed in direct competition to plaintiff's Auto/Issue System.

Plaintiff developed its Auto/Issue System over a period of approximately two years, from November, 1969 through approximately November, 1971. Since that time it has been marketing the system. Defendant's similar system, which it has named Trac/70, has been substantially though not completely developed, but is nevertheless being marketed at the present time in competition with plaintiff's Auto/Issue System. It was stipulated by the parties that plaintiff and defendant Tracor have each expended in excess of $500,000 in the development of their respective systems.

It is plaintiff's contention that during defendant Whitfield's consultations and employment with defendant Tracor, he has been substantially and directly involved in the design of said defendant's Trac/70 System, in connection with which he has utilized and disclosed plaintiff's trade secrets and confidential information in violation of his duty to plaintiff, and in breach of his specific Nondisclosure Agreement with plaintiff. Both defendants deny any responsibility to plaintiff, and contend that the alleged trade secrets and confidential matter claimed by plaintiff are in fact not trade secrets or confidential, but rather are well known concepts in the computer industry, that they are, therefore, not confidential, and that defendant Whitfield has merely utilized his substantial degree of skill and experience in his employment by defendant Tracor which he had developed prior to his employment with plaintiff and which he has the right to so utilize.

Said nondisclosure agreement is not ideally drafted, and leaves some room for interpretation. Plaintiff concedes that it was not its intention to prohibit the disclosure of any and all information relating to its products, but only such information which would reasonably be deemed to be confidential or in the nature of a trade secret. The Court agrees with this interpretation, and finds that the parties intended by said agreement to prohibit defendant Whitfield from disclosing any information concerning its products which would reasonably be deemed confidential to the point where it should not be revealed to outsiders without some contractual control and limitations.

A fair reading of the cases would seem to indicate that considerable importance is placed upon the existence of such contracts, as compared to situations where no agreement exists between the employer and his former employee. While the existence or nonexistence of such a contract is not determinative, and relief may under some circumstances be granted even in the absence of a contract, the existence of a contract makes it more probable that the employer will be granted relief for breach of contract, and this may be so even if the confidential information, knowledge or technology, does not rise to the dignity of a trade secret.

The above observations of the Court must lead to the conclusion that if confidential matter relating to the Auto/Issue System was disclosed by defendant Whitfield to defendant Tracor, particularly if that confidential matter was in the nature of trade secrets, liability would have to be imposed.

Section 757 of the Restatement of Torts, Comment b, generally defines a trade secret as any formula, pattern, device or compilation of information which is used in one's business, and which gives him an opportunity to obtain an advantage over competitors who do not know or use it. In spite of this simple definition, it further states that an exact definition of a trade secret is not possible, and lists some factors to be considered in determining the existence or nonexistence of a trade secret. Briefly stated, these include the extent to which the information is known by others outside of the business or employees of the business, the extent of measures taken to guard the secrecy of the information, the value of the information, the effort and expense involved in developing it, and lastly the ease or difficulty with which the information could be properly acquired or duplicated by others. As to some of the latter factors, plaintiff clearly comes within their ambit, as the evidence is virtually uncontradicted that reasonably strict security measures were taken to guard the secrecy of the Auto/Issue System, in excess of $500,000 was expended by plaintiff to develop it, license fees of somewhere between $100,000 and $200,000 are charged plaintiff's customers for the right to use the system, and a formidable and expensive task is faced by any competitor who might desire to properly acquire or duplicate it. The serious conflict in the evidence arises, however, in connection with the factor dealing with the issue as to the extent to which the information is known to others outside of plaintiff's business. Defendants essentially contend that we are not dealing with trade secrets, nor for that matter even confidential matter to any degree, because all the alleged items are not secret or confidential information but rather consist of well known concepts in the computer and data processing industry, and consequently cannot by any stretch of the imagination be considered confidential or secret. This issue was joined in the traditional battle of the experts. The technical nature of their testimony would be mind boggling to the average lay person, as it was to the court. The Court has carefully considered all of the testimony, and has concluded that at least to some degree, defendants' position is correct in that some of the approaches utilized in the Auto/Issue System, standing separately, are general concepts known to experts in the computer industry. The cases indicate, and plaintiff concedes that general concepts are not protectible, *per se*, as trade secrets. However, the cases further indicate that while general concepts are not protectible, the specific implementation involving a particular combination of general concepts may well amount to a trade secret. The Court believes that while some of the concepts are general concepts not susceptible of protection, that the entire bundle or combination of these concepts as developed and utilized by plaintiff in its Auto/Issue System do constitute trade secrets which are protectible under the circumstances. As pointed out in the above mentioned Restatement of Torts, any information which provides a competitive advantage over competitors may well constitute a trade secret, and in the Court's view it is obvious that the combination of factors involved in the Auto/Issue System must give the plaintiff its protection under this doctrine.

The Court has considered the well recognized principle that where a defendant in a trade secret case claims independent development, that the burden then shifts to the defendant and places upon the defendant a heavy burden of persuasion to show that the production was a result of independent development and not from the use of information confidentially secured during the prior employment.

Looking to the evidence, it is not seriously controverted, and the Court finds that there are in fact substantial similarities in the Auto/Issue System and the Trac/70 System. Such similarity, while not determinative of the issue, is of obvious importance, and must be given weight. Granted that the systems are not identical, many cases indicate that such identity is not required, and that trade secrets need not be exactly copied in order to impose liability. Likewise, the conceded difference in terminology utilized in the systems is not significant.

Defendants have also argued that many of the similarities are purely coincidental, since there were relatively few options which every expert in the field would consider in arriving at methods of approach for a new business on-line system. However, plaintiff presented evidence to the effect that there were in fact significant design choices, and that similar choices utilized by defendants would, therefore, indicate copying rather than independent development. This again is a question of fact, and the Court accepts Dr. Gilbert's testimony to the effect that there were significant design choices, and not as indicated by defendants, choices only as to insignificant details. Furthermore, even if the Court resolves the conflict in the evidence regarding whether or not defendant Whitfield took away with him documentation concerning the Auto/Issue System in favor of defendant Whitfield, the cases are clear that documentation need not be taken in order to establish liability, since appropriation by memory alone is proscribed.

When the Court considers all of the above factors, and adds thereto the ingredient sustained by the evidence that defendant Whitfield had complete knowledge and understanding of plaintiff's system, and in addition supervised and oversaw the development of defendants' system, the Court concludes and finds that defendant Whitfield did disclose and utilize substantial aspects of plaintiff's Auto/Issue System in the development of the Trac/70 System.

Defendant Whitfield's liability having been established, the Court must finally determine whether defendant Tracor also has liability under the circumstances. The cases indicate, as does Section 757 of the Restatement of Torts, that a new employer may also be liable for misappropriation of trade secrets, provided that he utilizes the information with notice of the secret nature thereof and with notice that the employee has disclosed it in breach of his duty to the former employer. The evidence indicates that before any substantial development of the Trac/70 System was begun, defendant Whitfield had been placed on notice by plaintiff by letter concerning a possible trade secret violation, and defendant Tracor was apprised of said demand by defendant Whitfield. In addition, it is conceded by defendants that the instant lawsuit was actually filed before any substantial development of the Trac/70 system. Under these circumstances, the Court finds that defendant Tracor was on notice of the potential liability in this matter, and consequently the Court finds that defendant Tracor has liability herein along with defendant Whitfield.

Notes and Questions

1. Patents only protect information that has been publicly disclosed. By contrast, trade secrets are only protected if their secrecy is maintained. What policy supports encouraging secrecy over disclosure? What type of secrecy should be required? Reasonable secrecy or absolute secrecy?

2. What is the secret in the *Life Insurance* case? What steps would you advise Cybertek to take to protect its secrets?

3. What are the major differences between the Restatement of Torts and the Economic Espionage Act? Although Section 1831 of the Economic Espionage Act focuses on "espionage" acts by foreign agents, section 1831 also prohibits the theft of trade secrets "related to or included in a product that is produced for or placed in interstate or foreign commerce." Unlike its other federal counterparts (the Patent, Copyright, and Lanham Acts), the Economic Espionage Act does *not* provide for civil remedies by private parties. Instead, it is a criminal statute only. Consequently, civil protection for trade secrets remains an issue of state law.

4. *Term of Protection.* Unlike patents and copyrights which are protected by a limited monopoly, trade secrets remain protected for as long as they remain secret. Perhaps the most famous U.S. trade secret is the formula for Coca-Cola. It has remained a secret for over 100 years.

Part II

THE WORLD

Chapter Five

PRESENT PROBLEMS AND
FUTURE DISPUTES

In the 1800's, American and European consumers began to enjoy the fruits of a "global" market created by the colonial adventures of the major Western powers. Western European authors similarly looked forward to the expanded riches of a global readership. Scientists began to discover new cures; inventors began to create modern mechanical conveniences to permit greater leisure time, while companies began to advertise their new products using increasingly more famous marks. At the same time, instances of piracy and counterfeiting grew, leading to the first international efforts to establish a multinational accord for protecting the products of these new artistic, scientific and commercial ventures.

Concerns over international protection for so-called intellectual property rights have continued to grow. Nowadays, with the advent of the Internet, e-commerce and digital communications, the purported "global" marketplace of the 1800's has become a reality. Even the smallest domestic companies may sell their goods in international arenas. As the world has shrunk, the problems of international counterfeiting have grown larger. Films produced in the United States may be illegally reproduced in China, and sold in Russia. Just as industries have become global–so too has piracy. Companies which manufacture "counterfeit" drugs in Argentina, now invest in creating other counterfeit manufacturers in the Dominican Republic. Efforts to establish an international protection regime must do so in a world of differing economic, political, legal and cultural systems. Industrialized, technology-exporting countries seek enhanced protection for their "intellectual property rights." By contrast, emerging industrializing technology-importing countries seek little or no protection for what is perceived to qualify as the "common heritage of mankind," available to all. Even the philosophical bases for protecting the works of individual artists and inventors has come under increasing scrutiny.

The following controversies are designed to give you a brief overview of some of the more unusual problems which face intellectual property law in the international forum of the Twenty–First century. As you read these controversies, ask yourself whether intellectual property rights are involved and if so, how these controversies should be resolved. Remember, although you may have certain assumptions about the nature of traditional intellectual property rights (copyrights, patents, trademarks and trade secrets), these assumptions are derived from your experience with domestic intellectual property law. Such domestic laws reflect a country's political, economic, legal and cultural heritage, and may not accurately reflect the international standards established in a multinational, multi-cultural forum. Consequently, as you read the controversies below, ask yourself what solution you would recommend, and what assumptions about the nature of intellectual property rights underlie your decisions. It is these assumptions that we will explore in subsequent chapters to determine what applicability, if any, they have to international intellectual property rights in the Twenty–First century.

A. WHAT ARE THE PROBLEMS IN PROTECTING "INTELLECTUAL PROPERTY" IN TODAY'S MULTICULTURAL WORLD?

THE ZUNI AHAYU:DA CONTROVERSY

The Zuni pueblo in New Mexico struggled for many years for the return of their Ahayu:da, their twin gods of war that had been sold by single tribe members or stolen from their shrines in the pueblo since the late 1880's. Beginning in 1978, they started retrieving the Ahayu:da from museums, private art collectors, art galleries and auctions, and eventually secured the return of all the 69 Ahayu:da in the U.S. The Ahayu:da are cylindrical carved wooden idols about two to three feet tall that show Uyuyemi and Maia'sewi, the two twin gods of war. They are carved by the Bear and the Deer Clan once a year. Then they are placed in outdoor shrines, so that, with their potentially destructive powers, they can protect the tribe. They are purposely exposed to the elements so that they can do their job as religious objects and must remain in the same place until they fully decay to nourish and replenish the earth. The worship of these gods ensures the tribe's pursuit of happiness and successful future and are therefore essential to the spiritual well being of the tribe. By the 1970's, the Zuni had determined that the imbalance and violent occurrences, such as earthquakes, that the world has faced in this century, is due to the fact that the Ahayu:da were not in their proper place. They therefore approached, among others, the Smithsonian Institute to request the repatriation of these war gods. The negotiations with the Smithsonian Institute were the most intensive and lasted over nine years. They serve as an excellent paradigm for the issues involved in such repatriation.

The Zuni argued that once the figures are placed in the shrine no one has the right to remove them, as they have to stay and decay. The Ahayu:da are, if owned by anyone, communally owned, so that if sold by one Zuni or stolen, they were always wrongfully removed since the tribe as a whole never authorized the removal. During lengthy negotiations the Zuni tried to explain the value of these war gods to the tribe hoping that this alone would persuade the Smithsonian Institute and others to repatriate the Ahayu:da.

The Smithsonian, on the other hand, as many other museums, was concerned that the return of the Ahayu:da would violate its trust as a public institution, having to preserve the collection for all the people, and would set an unfortunate precedent that could ultimately result in the loss of much of its collection. The Smithsonian believed it had acquired the Ahayu:da legally and was concerned about returning such valuable artifacts without guarantees that they would be protected against theft or eventual destruction in an outdoor shrine.

Even though there was no legal precedent, given the religious nature of the objects, the Smithsonian decided they were communally owned by the tribe as a whole. Once placed in the shrine they could not legally be removed. Consequently, any Ahayu:da not in the shrine was considered stolen and subject to recovery pursuant to 18 U.S.C. § 1163 (which made it a federal crime to possess stolen tribal property). The Zuni wanted the war gods to be repatriated on the basis that any object produced by the Zuni is an object that belongs to them as a whole. The Smithsonian, however, rejected this rationale. In addition, as a counterpart to the voluntary repatriation of the Ahayu:da, the Smithsonian expected the Zuni to install a high security facility around the shrine in the pueblo to protect the Ahayu:da from theft while meeting the religious requirement that the shrine be exposed to the elements.

The negotiations and the eventual return of the Ahayu:da were seen as a great advancement for the repatriation of sacred objects. But such praise may be premature. First of all, despite the fact that the negotiations lasted over nine years, there was no agreement on the reason for the return of these sacred objects. Secondly, the Zuni did not secure the repatriation on the basis of moral or religious issues, but on the idea of communal ownership, which it was forced to prove. The return of the Ahayu:da represented only the second time that the Smithsonian has returned artifacts to an Indian tribe. And the Smithsonian did not fully acknowledge the ownership of the Ahay:da by the Zuni pueblo, because it did not leave the Zuni free to treat their figures anyway they wanted to, but expected safety measures as defined by the Smithsonian.

The Ahayu:da controversy nonetheless has resulted in a drastic change in policy concerning Native American artifacts. In 1990, the U.S. took legislative action for the repatriation of artifacts, passing the Native American Graves Protection and Repatriation Act (Public Law 101–601), also known as NAGPRA. Section 5 of the NAGPRA requires all museums receiving federal funds to inventory holdings of cultural property and human remains of Native Americans, while Section 7 mandates repatriation of all such items, with limited exceptions, in consultation with Native American organizations. In a single act almost an entire category of cultural property is to be returned to source peoples. The Smithsonian, though, is excluded from the NAGPRA. A similar federal repatriation law was passed only for the Smithsonian in 1989 (Public Law 101–185), but it does not mention the repatriation of sacred objects. However, the Smithsonian's Departments of Anthropology and National Museum of Natural History have publicly stated their intention to embrace the spirit and the intent of the NAGPRA, broadening its mandate to include consideration of the repatriation of sacred objects by the Smithsonian as well. Although the NAGPRA only applies to federally funded institutions within the U.S., 34 states have passed additional laws to fill perceived gaps in coverage in the NAGPRA legislation. Consequently, the NAGPRA has set a precedent with museum authorities throughout the U.S. and on an international level as well.

Notes and Questions

1.   Are the Ahayu:da governed by copyright? If so, who is the holder of such copyright–the artist or the tribe?

2.   Could an individual Zuni create an Ahuyu:da and sell it to the Smithsonian for display without violating the tribe's rights? What if an artist who was not Zuni created such a sculpture and mass marketed it? Should these actions violate international intellectual property rights? Who has the right to control the distribution of works utilizing elements of native culture?

THE AUSTRALIAN MORNING STAR POLE CONTROVERSY

In Australia there have also been serious problems concerning the protection of Aboriginal cultural patrimony from destruction or distortion. In *Yumbulul v. Reserve Bank of Australia (21 I.P.R. 481)*, Yumbulul, an Aboriginal artist created, with the permission of his clan, "Morning Star Poles." The Morning Star Pole is made of wood, carved in a particular way, painted and adorned with feathers and string. These Poles are said to have the power to "take the spirit of the dead to the Morning Star, which will return them to their ancestral home". The Pole may only be carved by an artist that has undergone various initiation and revelatory ceremonies which teach the artist the important cultural meanings behind the artistic works. The artist must then obtain permission to carve them and to sell every single pole created. Ultimately the Aborigines own the Morning Star Poles and what they stand for as a community. They only allow the sale of these items because they believe that the sanctity of the Pole is not damaged by the sale. However, they screen who may buy the Poles and only permit such limited sales to educate Non–Aborigines regarding their culture.

Yumbulul has been selling the Morning Star Poles for ten years to museums and craft shops before this case came to court in 1991. In 1986 Yumbulul had created a Morning Star Pole that was going to be displayed in the Australian Museum of Sydney. An interest subsequently developed in using the Pole for a commemorative Australian bank note commissioned by the Reserve Bank of Australia. Yumbulul signed a licensing agreement for the reproduction of the Morning Star Pole on the bank note. The clan though did not give their approval and opposed this display of their art. At trial Yumbulul argued that his permission could only go as far as the permission of the clan. As the clan had not authorized the reproduction, he could not effectively contract away these rights. The Australian Court considered the role of Australian copyright law in protecting Aboriginal rights, but ultimately decided such laws were currently unavailing.

There have been some efforts to take the cultural patrimony of the Aborigines into account. The Australian legislature passed the Aboriginal and Torres Strait Islander Heritage Protection Act of 1994, which is supposed to protect against theft or vandalizing of Aboriginal cultural property. It has broad language and might be applicable to commercial use of an Aboriginal object such as the Morning Star Pole as it speaks of protection against an object being "used or treated in a manner inconsistent with Aboriginal tradition." But it is not clear if the Australian Courts will extend this prohibition to cover commercial uses. Thus, the Aborigines have to rely either on more responsible contracting or on strict inalienability of their works. Gradually reports have been produced by the Australian government that reflect an awareness of the need to respect and value the contributions of Aboriginal traditions and culture in the overall society.

Notes and Questions

1. Is there a similarity between the communal ownership rights of the Zuni and the Aborigines in Australia? What are the differences?

2. Should the degree of communal ownership be tied to the importance of the works to the clan? If the objects are communally owned should they be inalienable?

3. If the artist consents to a particular use of his work, does copyright law recognize a communal veto over such works? Should it?

4. Assume your client has uncovered a rare tomb in Africa that contains the remains of an ancient culture. Your client wants to reproduce some of the artifacts for sale. The descendants of the tribe that originally constructed the tomb object to the commercialization of what they consider to be religious artifacts. Are any intellectual property rights of these descendants adversely affected by the proposed commercialization?

THE AIDS DRUGS CONTROVERSY

No one can dispute that the AIDS epidemic raised one of the most serious global health problems of the latter part of the Twentieth Century. In 1999, 90% as new HIV infections occurred in developing countries. Medical treatments designed to combat the disease were estimated to cost approximately $15,000 per patient per year. For cash-starved countries, whose typical budget is $10 per person per year, that cost is prohibitive.

One of the factors that contributes to the high cost of new drug treatments is the role of patent protection in controlling the distribution of such new drugs. The Agreement on Trade–Related Aspects of Intellectual Property Rights (TRIPS), administered by the World Trade Organization (WTO), requires all signatory countries to grant patent protection to novel and non-obvious pharmaceutical products. Such patent protection permits drug companies to control access to their patented drugs, and, according to developing countries, charge supra monopolistic prices. Drug companies respond that such prices are necessary to re-coop research and development costs, and to permit future research.

In response, some countries such as India and Argentina refuse to extend patent protection to pharmaceuticals. Others take advantage of an apparent loophole in Article 31 of the Agreement on Trade Related Aspects of Intellectual Property Rights (TRIPS) to grant compulsory licenses "in the case of national emergency" so long as royalty fees ("adequate remuneration") are paid. Still others permit the importation of grey market (parallel imports) of drugs from other countries, thus circumventing higher prices set by patent holders in certain areas.

South Africa in 1998 passed a law that gave the Ministry of Health the discretion to authorize compulsory licensing and parallel importation of pharmaceuticals in cases where the need for the drugs has reached a "critical" capacity. The law has been challenged by a consortium of over 40 drug companies. With nearly 3.5 million of its 40 million citizens HIV infected, South Africa's attempt to "circumvent" its patent regime has led to heated debates over the role of patent protection in the medical community.

A similar struggle over patent rights to pharmaceuticals is occurring in Thailand. In the 1980's, Thailand's refusal to extend patent protection to pharmaceuticals led to threatened trade sanctions by the United States. Patent protection remains problematic. Yet the existence of a local manufacturing base has resulted in lower drug prices.

Patent owners contend that lack of patent protection will ultimately result in a lack of sufficient revenues (or desire) to fuel new drug research. Moreover, the lack of quality control over the production of "generic" (non-patent protected) drugs may result in the distribution of unefficacious (and, in certain instances, harmful) products. In Argentina, which currently does not protect pharmaceuticals under patent laws, 18 different varieties of "Viagra" are being manufactured and sold. Some are potent, but many others are not.

By contrast, developing countries point to the crushing cost of medical care and the lower prices which naturally result from the greater competition created by a non-existent, or ineffective drug patent regime. In Thailand, Flicanazole, an antibiotic used to fight a fatal form of meningitis that accompanies AIDS cost $7.36 a tablet. After local manufacture began, the price dropped to $1 per tablet.

Notes and Questions

1. Are there types of inventions which should be subject to lower international protection standards due to their health, safety or technological significance?

2. Is there any way to balance the competing international concerns reflected in the controversy without eviscerating patent protection for pharmaceuticals?

3. What qualifies as a "national emergency" to warrant compulsory licensing under Article 31 of TRIPS? A growing rate of HIV infection? The threat of famine due to poor crop fertilization methods? High levels of air pollution due to poor air filtering technology? Poor living conditions due to lack of electricity?

THE VIDEO PIRACY CONTROVERSY

In December 1997, the blockbuster film *Titanic* opened in Hong Kong, with Chinese subtitles. Despite the existence of a Chinese language translation, the film was not scheduled for theatrical release in the People's Republic of China until April 1, 1998. By the time the movie was officially released, it was estimated that a majority of the people who desired to see the film had already done so—on pirated video discs.

The unlawful reproduction and distribution of copyrighted movies on counterfeit video cassettes and video discs is a world-wide problem. The Motion Picture Association of America (MPAA) estimates that in 1998, video piracy resulted in over $1,799,500,000,000 in lost profits world-wide.

Such wide spread piracy is the result of several factors. First is the widespread availability and ease of reproduction techniques. Such reproduction techniques are relatively inexpensive and mobile—allowing counterfeiters to easily move their "factories" when law enforcement threatens. Because of the low cost, the price of such counterfeit products is much cheaper than lawfully produced. Second, because piracy provides jobs and local manufacturing businesses, many law enforcement officials are hesitant to spend money enforcing anti-piracy laws. In some instances, government officials own the larger factories, making law enforcement less likely. Finally, despite newly established, international enforcement standards under TRIPS, many laws remain largely unenforced—with only minimal fines imposed. Consequently, video piracy becomes a relatively low risk, low cost, but highly lucrative, criminal enterprise.

Copyright owners loudly decry the lack of vigorous enforcement—citing lost income and diminishing profit returns. Such decreasing returns may have a profound effect on the film industry, particularly for indie productions, or nascent domestic film studios which rely on profits to fuel future films. By contrast, pirates cite the need for an inexpensive alternative to escalating ticket and legitimate video prices. They contend that they are filling a need—artificially—created by the very copyright owners who then decline to fill that need, either by delayed release dates or artificially high prices.

They further point to pro-economic benefits of pirating activities. Such benefits, IP owners claim, should be balanced against the revenues lost in uncollected taxes and the potential corruption of the legal process that arises from unenforced laws.

Notes and Questions

1. If piracy is so widespread, should efforts to enforce IP laws be abandoned so valuable resources can be spent on other matters, such as violent crime? How would you allocate such resources?

2. What benefits does a developing country receive by enforcing intellectual property rights?

3. One suggested solution to the problem of video piracy has been the world-wide roll-out of a film on the same day, at variable prices to reflect regional economic variations. Is there a down-side to this practice? What if, instead of films, we were dealing with music piracy? Would regional pricing variations to take into account lower standards of living (and, therefore, lesser amounts of disposable income) solve the problem of global piracy? What are the problems that arise in such pricing schemes for distributed goods?

THE GERMAN INTERNET PORNOGRAPHY CONTROVERSY

The Internet revolutionized international communications and commerce in the latter part of the Twentieth Century. It also posed new problems in enforcing intellectual property rights in a digitized global environment. Given the rapid, international dissemination of material placed on the Internet, and the relatively inexpensive cost of securing a personal web page, even the smallest company has the potential for global dissemination of digitized information via the Internet. As a result, the Internet has served as a primary battleground against music, video and computer piracy. Because information uploaded (placed on the Internet) in one country can potentially be viewed and copied (downloaded) anywhere in the world that access to a web server exists, infringement has gone global and (virtually) instantaneous. Policing becomes impossible as web pages multiply exponentially each day. In 1999 it was estimated that the Internet had over 42 million domain sites, and that a new web page is created every 17 seconds.

Because of the widespread proliferation of web sites, content control has become a critical international issue. Specifically the proper balance between domestic censorship concerns, and international access to information is hotly debated.

Like many countries, Germany has enacted a series of laws aimed at regulating the distribution of pornographic and hate speech materials. Under the Information and Communications Act (ICA), making public racist or pornographic materials is a criminal offense, even if the material is lawfully created abroad. Commentators suggested that the ICA would not apply to the Internet. Nevertheless, in April 1997, the general manager for CompuServe in Germany was indicted on 13 counts for distributing on-line pornography and illegal materials, including Nazi texts. The material in question had not been placed online by the manager or CompuServe. To the contrary, CompuServe had only served as the source provider. The manager was convicted and given a two-year suspended sentence. CompuServe blocked the offending sites from access in Germany.

Other countries have prohibited access to religiously offensive materials, to materials which criticize government practices, and to materials which "harm social order" (defined in cultural or political terms). Both the efficacy of blocking technologies and the appropriateness of imposing legal liability on ISP's for the actions of their end users has been hotly debated. To date, no international accord has been reached.

Notes and Questions

1. What if the material at issue in the German CompuServe case was created and uploaded in the United States, and was legal in that country? Should Germany be able to penalize the ISP for the distribution of this information inside Germany, even though the ISP has no notice of the content of this material?

2. Assume that the material at issue was not pornographic, but was illegal because it infringed German copyright law. Assume further that the material was uploaded in Japan, where copyright protection had expired. Could the copyright owner sue the Japanese "creator" of the infringing material in Germany? What restrictions, if any, would you place on an IP owner's ability to sue for Internet infringement in any jurisdiction where the web page is received?

Part III

SOURCES AND POLICIES OF INTERNATIONAL INTELLECTUAL PROPERTY LAW

Chapter Six

GENERAL INTRODUCTION

A. WHERE DO WE "FIND" INTERNATIONAL INTELLECTUAL PROPERTY LAW?

There is no one single source of "international intellectual property law." Instead, the standards that currently exist for the international recognition, protection and enforcement of so-called "intellectual property rights" are derived from a multitude of international sources, including multilateral treaties, regional harmonization directives, key decisions from recognized courts of high standards such as the Court of Justice of the European Community and the U.S. Supreme Court, and international custom and practice as illustrated by the domestic laws of the leading developed nations.

Laws are modified over time to reflect the changing needs of society and the culture that created it. As the world has developed from an agricultural to an industrial to a global economy, intellectual property laws have changed to keep pace with the increasingly sophisticated demands of the global commercial society. Such rapid changes have been the hallmark of intellectual property protection in the latter part of the Twentieth Century. As you will discover, the growth of intellectual property protection historically has been tied to the growth of technology. Thus, for example, the need for copyright protection was not recognized until after technology had developed the printing press. With Gutenberg's invention in the 14th Century, an author's words could be commodified and a publishing industry could develop. The development of this industry gave rise to the grant of "patents" for publishing guilds in the 15th and 16th Centuries, which ultimately gave rise to the first copyright statute in Great Britain to protect an author's rights.

With the advent of the global marketplace of the latter Twentieth Century the battles for technological protection have expanded beyond national boundaries to encompass international disputes.

The significance of international property protection on a global scale is perhaps most clearly demonstrated by the number of multinational negotiations that have focused on the problem of IPR ("intellectual property rights") protection during the latter part of the Twentieth

Century. Although the first significant effort at establishing an international protection regime for intellectual property occurred in the latter part of the Nineteenth Century with the establishment of the Berne Convention for the Protection of Literary and Artistic Works, the number of multinational agreements in the area multiplied as the market expanded into a global one. During the last twenty years of the Twentieth Century, multinational regimes covering such critical issues as intellectual property as an item of trade, the protection of copyright in a digital environment, the protection of performance rights, databases, computer software, and satellite broadcasting rights first saw the light of day. Debates over these and other issues regarding the protection of intellectual property are no longer merely debates over the ownership of private property rights. Instead IPR has become an integral part of the debates over some of the most critical issues facing the international community today, including environmental protection, wealth transfer, sustainable economic development and the protection of indigenous culture against the ravages of consumerism. Furthermore, with the collapse of the Soviet Union and the discrediting of Marxism, unbridled capitalism has taken over the world. The demand for new products, new inventions, new comforts is matched only by the efforts of inventors and producers to protect their rights of invention and production.

At its most fundamental level, debates over the nature of intellectual property and the scope of protection to be afforded any particular form reflect the culture, heritage, and political and economic philosophy of a given nation. Before international consensus regarding, for example, what rights a director should be given to protect her film from unauthorized distribution performance or adaptation, some agreement regarding the general purpose behind such protection must be reached. As you review the cases below, ask yourself what purpose the proposed intellectual property rights protection scheme is designed to serve and what philosophy is behind the court's decision. Then consider whether you would reach a similar result. If not, why not?

A FIVE–CENT LECTURE ON THE LAW OF TREATIES

Anthony D'Amato

If you know the law of contracts, you already know a lot about the international law of treaties. But there are some important differences. Here's a quick nickel tour of treaty law with an emphasis on the differences.

The word "treaty" is no more important than the word "contract." A treaty can also be called a convention, an agreement, a protocol, or the like. A treaty is "signed" when the authorized representatives of the various states, which intend to be parties to the treaty, sign it. But a treaty only "comes into force" when it is ratified. What happens is that the signed document goes back to the various governments, who then undertake a formal ratification process. In the United States, although a

U.S. ambassador can sign a treaty, it doesn't become binding on the United States until it is signed by the President with the consent of two-thirds of the Senate (the House of Representatives has no formal role in treaty-making).

A treaty that is signed but not yet ratified nevertheless has some legal clout. If an ambassador signs a treaty, then the ambassador's home state cannot act in such a way as to defeat the "object and purpose" of the treaty. This and many other specificities of treaty law can be found in the Vienna Convention on the Law of Treaties of 1969.[1]

A "reservation" to a treaty occurs when a state party to a treaty does not accept all of the treaty's provisions. For example, a state may wish to ratify the Convention on the Rights of the Child without accepting the definition of a child as a person under 18 years of age. So it may ratify the treaty with the "reservation" that, as far as it is concerned, a child is only a person under 16 years of age.[2] However, the right to make reservations is not unlimited. First and most importantly, the treaty itself may prohibit reservations as to some or all of its provisions. The Rights of the Child Convention does not prohibit reservations as to the age definition of "child"; if it did, then a country would be faced with only two alternatives: ratify the treaty with the definition of "child" intact, or don't ratify the treaty. The third way out—ratification with reservation—would be prohibited by the treaty itself. Secondly, a state may not become party to a treaty if its reservation is incompatible with the object and purpose of the treaty. International courts can resolve the question of incompatability with respect to particular treaties. Thirdly, any reservation that a state makes to a treaty operates reciprocally. For example, if State A reserves the definition of "child" to someone under 16 years of age, then that definition is modified for State A as well as for all the other parties in their dealings with State A. Thus, State A cannot complain if State B treats a person in State B as an adult if that person is 17 years old. We must note, however, that although State A's reservation applies to and for State A, it doesn't change the legal relations for the other parties. Thus, A's reservation has no relevance to a dispute under the treaty between B and C. B and C remain bound by the 18–year definition vis-a-vis each other.

In international intellectual property treaties, the concept of reservations can become extremely difficult to apply among states which become parties to a treaty in widely separated points of time. For example, what is the effect of a revision of the language of a treaty in 1940 when State A ratified the treaty with reservations in 1930 and State B ratified the treaty with reservations in 1950? This question has not been definitively answered, but the basic principles of reservations

1. 8 Int'l Law Materials 679 (1969).

2. The United States objects to the Rights of the Child Convention on this point, because the Convention prohibits capital punishment of children. The United States wishes to preserve the right to execute juveniles between 16 and 18 years of age.

I've given in the previous paragraph still apply as a first cut to this kind of problem.

A final major topic in the law of treaties is the idea of "change of circumstances."

If at the time of the ratification of the treaty the parties based their agreement on the existence of certain essential facts and circumstances, and those essential circumstances later change in a manner that radically transforms the extent of obligations still to be performed under the treaty, then that change of circumstances can allow a party to get out of its obligations under the treaty. Of course, the party wishing to get out of the treaty cannot do so if it itself created the change of circumstances. And in any event, under international treaty law, "change of circumstances" does not apply to treaties establishing an international boundary between states.

You can get some idea of the doctrine of change of circumstances under treaty law if you've studied "relational contracts" (as opposed to "discrete contracts") in your contracts class. Nearly all treaties are "relational"; they are meant to apply over a long period of time. But, as in all other aspects of international treaty law, a knowledge of contract law only gets you up to a point. Many lawyers encountering treaties for the first time have made the major mistake of assuming that all they need to know is contract law.

B. DOES INTELLECTUAL PROPERTY FAVOR THE "HAVE" NATIONS?

As noted above, from the initial preparatory work prior to the September 1986 Declaration commencing the Uruguay Round, many developing countries, including Brazil and India, hotly contested the ability or propriety of GATT to establish substantive norms in the area of intellectual property protection. The position of these developing countries was that if there was any need for the development of international norms in, for example, the copyright area, WIPO was the proper forum. Part of the reluctance to use GATT as a forum for addressing the desirability of new or additional international standards for intellectual property protection derived from the perception of many of these countries that GATT was primarily a forum for the "have" nations. Thus, many developing countries were concerned that their needs would not be given sufficient consideration in the GATT arena. Furthermore, to the extent that international norms might be required, these countries believed that the Berne Convention, with its emphasis on national treatment, had already dealt with the issue and that any changes which might be required should be dealt with only by WIPO, which had responsibility for overseeing the Convention. As an East German representative indicated in support for a statement by Cuba on behalf of the "Group of 77" challenging the use of GATT to address intellectual property issues:

The strong international links between economy, science, technology and culture do not exclude other organizations or agreements in their activities to be concerned with the problems of implementing intellectual property rights. However, for legal certainty and comprehensiveness, the competence of WIPO and its direct participation should be maintained since the solution of these problems belongs to the scope of its duties.

By contrast, the developed countries, including the United States, were strongly dissatisfied with efforts to resolve existing copyright issues under WIPO auspices. While developing countries saw WIPO as a generally hospitable forum for their concerns, many developed countries considered it to be indifferent to their needs at best and hostile at worst, in view of renewed efforts by some developing countries to use WIPO to lessen the level of protection established under the Berne Convention. The developed countries perceived GATT as providing a forum where an international consensus could be reached regarding the scope of protection for works not covered by the Berne Convention—including software and computer databases—outside the potentially politicized open meetings required by WIPO. Finally, developed countries sought to rectify a perceived lack of adequate enforcement mechanisms under the Berne Convention. Although Article 33 of the Berne Convention provides that disputes can be brought before the International Court of Justice, at the time of the Uruguay Round negotiations not one dispute had been referred to that court in over forty-five years. Because WIPO had no other enforcement procedures for assuring that a member's laws complied with Berne's agreed-upon minimums, the developed countries sought to establish an enforcement mechanism under GATT which would force full compliance by all member countries.

Much of the debate regarding GATT versus WIPO jurisdiction was largely resolved by 1987, when WIPO was granted observer status in GATT negotiations on TRIPS. Debates regarding the balance to be struck between Berne Convention and non-Berne Convention issues of copyright protection, however, continued to be infected by this underlying jurisdictional debate.

Notes and Questions

1. *The Effect of Intangibility.* Unlike land, cars, televisions sets and other forms of "property" over which people are granted rights, intellectual property is considered an "intangible" property right. Consequently, the use, whether authorized or not, of a particular form of intellectual property does not result in the physical diminution or destruction of the intellectual property right itself. This argument has often been used by developing countries to support their failure to enforce intellectual property rights; they contend that the intellectual property owner is not harmed by the manufacture and sale of infringing goods. The argument is made that the owner is still entitled to make as many lawful copies as she desires. Furthermore, since pirated goods are often sold at prices far below market value, no actual harm has occurred because the purchasers of pirated goods could not have

afforded to buy the legitimate version. Does the following argument throw any light on this issue?

One striking difference between intellectual property and most other forms of property is the fact that the majority of works of art, once produced, can be reproduced an infinite number of times at little cost. Arguably, therefore, the harm to the copyright holder, when her work is "stolen'" through reproduction, is not as great as the harm to other property owners. If I steal your car, then I have stolen all your investment in the car, and you are without transportation. But if I steal your artistic expression by copying your novel, then you have not lost either the original of the novel itself or the right to charge others for the right to copy. From a different perspective, the loss of the car can be considered less serious than the reproduction of the novel. The car is essentially fungible—if you are covered by insurance, then it can be easily replaced. The novel, on the hand, is unique.

Another feature of intellectual property is the fact that it is difficult to prevent unauthorized uses—it is much easier to copy a book than to steal a car. This fact creates a concern economists call the "free rider" problem. They argue that when a good can be used easily by people who have not paid for it, these people will become "free riders" at the expense of those who did pay for the good. Linda J. Lacey, *Of Bread And Roses And Copyrights,* 1989 Duke L.J. 1532 (1989)

2. Common Heritage of Mankind. Under the Universal Declaration of the Rights of Peoples, "Scientific and technical progress, being part of the common heritage of mankind, every people has the right to participate in it." (Article 9). The Declaration goes on to state: "Every people has the right to make use of the common heritage of mankind, such as the high seas, the sea-bed and outer space." Does intellectual property fit within the definition "common heritage" under Article 9? If you believe it does fit within this definition, what right of "participation" should be granted all nations?

3. What limitations would you put on the types of intellectual property that should be considered the "common heritage of mankind"?

4. Should a vaccine to prevent AIDS be considered the "common heritage of mankind"? Should the Mona Lisa? Should technology that eliminates particulates from emissions to reduce air pollution?

5. The Universal Declaration of the Rights of Peoples is only one of numerous international human rights declarations that concern the protection of intellectual property. Article 27 of the Universal Declaration of Human Rights states:

1. Everyone has the right freely to participate in the cultural life of the community, to enjoy the arts and to share in scientific advancement and its benefits.

2. Everyone has the right to the protection of the moral and material interests resulting from any scientific, literary or artistic production of which he is the author.

This language also appears in Article 13 of the American Declaration of the Rights and Duties of Man, and in Article 14 of the Protocol to the American Convention of Human Rights in the Area of Economic, Social and Cultural Rights.

6. *Sustainable Development.* At an international conference designed to address the international problems of environmental protection and the biosphere held in Rio de Janeiro in 1992, Fidel Castro, in a speech that was praised by many Third World, developing nations, examined the relationship between intellectual property protection, economic development and environmental impact. He stated:

> Today more than ever, the underdeveloped countries urgently need access to knowledge, to scientific and technological development. This is not only because it would allow them to solve infinite economic, social and ecological problems, but because, in the current stage of capitalist development, scientific knowledge plays a principal role in the accumulation of capital. Through the possibilities presented by the modern development of modern biotechnology, the genetic resources of the underdeveloped world have gained extraordinary value. In fact, the possession and control of genetic resources constitutes a new way of plundering the Third World, which has become the main objective of those transnational corporations involved in this field.

> The privatization boom, together with the need to maximize profit, are having a growing impact on the new mechanisms for controlling copyrights of biotechnological advances, and even on the control of the national heritage of the underdeveloped countries. Attempts are being made to impose a patent system on the underdeveloped countries which does not recognize the right of these countries to enjoy the profits made. Due to the fragility of the ecosystems of the underdeveloped nations and the lack of resources available for them to confront the deterioration of the environment, the transfer of environmentally sound technology is an essential component of sustainable development. As a consequence of the profound transformations brought about by the current scientific and technological resolutions, there have been significant changes in the corporate strategies of transnational companies. These corporate strategies promote the formation of strategic alliances among firms in the developed nations in order to confront the rising costs of research and development and to guarantee greater protection of copyrights. This lessens the transfer of technology to the Third World.

> These new corporate strategies have met with strong support from the industrialized nations. In effect, the governments of these countries, particularly that of the United States, have pushed strongly in the Uruguay Round for stricter and more uniform norms regarding the protection of intellectual property rights.

> The establishment of these kinds of protective measures would result in rising costs for imported technology, especially in the industries that make intensive use of patented procedures. This entails additional demands for financial resources in the underdeveloped nations, which must be taken into account where new agreements and protocols are signed for the protection of the environment.

Fidel Castro, Tomorrow Is Too Late: Development and the Environmental Arises in the Third World at 32–40 (Ocean Press 1993).

This speech was praised by developing nations as an accurate reflection of their concerns and needs. What response would you make if you represented a developed country?

7. *The Problem of Language.* Notice that in the speech by Fidel Castro he refers to all intellectual property rights as "copyright." Yet some of his concerns regarding intellectual property protection regimes involve not copyright protection for expressive works, but patent protection for scientific inventions and discoveries. One of the problems in dialogues regarding international intellectual property rights is the absence of agreement on the precise scope of rights that should be protected under each particular intellectual property form. As you will see in the materials below, before nations can agree on whether intellectual property rights should be granted for a particular patent, copyright or trade secret, they must first agree on what exactly is meant by the terms "patent" or "copyright." The answer to that question is not always readily apparent.

Chapter Seven

COPYRIGHTS UNDER INTERNATIONAL LAW

A. WHAT WORKS SHOULD QUALIFY FOR INTERNATIONAL COPYRIGHT PROTECTION?

The Software Protection Controversy

The latter part of the 20th Century has seen an explosion in technology that has exponentially expanded both the access to, and the value of, information. Between computerization of inventory, the ubiquitous development of electronic scanners for every purpose from inventory control to security, the widespread availability of home (or personal) computers and the ready access to the Internet and its digitized bonanza of information, we have become an age that has greater access to more varied sources of information than ever before.

Although the development of the Information Age cannot be traced to one individual factor, it appears indisputable that it could not have developed quite so rapidly without the development of computer hardware from the mainframes of the 1970's to the personal computer revolution of the 1980's. With the increased availability of personal computers came the need to create new software to fill growing consumer demand. Computerization has invaded every aspect of life, from home communications, to global business negotiations over the Internet, to increasing mechanization for industrial manufacturing. It is an international phenomenon. Yet as the desirability and market for computer software burgeoned the legal problem of the scope of protection to be afforded this latest technological advance has proven a daunting one.

While the earliest developments in software technology might have been protected as new and useful inventions under existing patent regimes, their basis in algorithms and other abstract ideas initially precluded such protection. *See, e.g. Parker v. Flook*, 437 U.S. 584 (1978); *Gottschalk v. Benson*, 409 U.S. 63 (1972). Given the critical market role of computer software, efforts have been made to "fill the gap" in protection by applying copyright laws. This has lead to worldwide concern about the application of intellectual property laws designed primarily for the print medium to the new digital environment of computer software and the Internet.

One of the most pressing problems today is the extent to which copyright protection should be used to protect computer technology and works contained in the digital environment of the Internet. As you read the following excerpts ask yourself whether copyright, which originally protected artistic, literary and musical works, is the proper mechanism to use to protect such works of technology as computer software and the digitized communications that form the information backbone of the Internet. Should copyright be limited to works of "fine art" or of "high artistic endeavor"? Or can it be used to protect such mundane works as maps, computer programs and digitized photographs for clip art programs? If copyright should only be used to encourage the creation of useful (artistically valuable) works, whose definition of "art" should apply? Since current international standards for copyright protection requires that most works be protected for the life of the author plus an additional fifty years, is it appropriate to grant such lengthy terms of protection to a computer software whose "shelf-life" for usefulness may be limited to, at most, five years?

B. ART OR INDUSTRY: WHAT ARE THE LIMITS OF COPYRIGHT PROTECTION?

THE ANTI–DISCRIMINATION CASE

GEORGE BLEISTEIN v. DONALDSON LITHOGRAPHING COMPANY

Supreme Court of the United States, 1903
188 U.S. 239, 23 S.Ct. 298

Mr. Justice Holmes delivered the opinion of the court.

This case comes here from the United States circuit court of appeals for the sixth circuit by writ of error. It is an action brought by the plaintiffs in error to recover the penalties prescribed for infringements of copyrights. The alleged infringements consisted in the copying in reduced form of three chromolithographs prepared by employees of the plaintiffs for advertisements of a circus owned by one Wallace. Each of the three contained a portrait of Wallace in the corner, and lettering bearing some slight relation to the scheme of decoration, indicating the subject of the design and the fact that the reality was to be seen at the circus. One of the designs was of an ordinary ballet, one of a number of men and women, described as the Stirk family, performing on bicycles, and one of groups of men and women whitened to represent statues. The circuit court directed a verdict for the defendant on the ground that the chromolithographs were not within the protection of the copyright law, and this ruling was sustained by the circuit court of appeals.

There was evidence warranting the inference that the designs belonged to the plaintiffs, they having been produced by persons employed and paid by the plaintiffs in their establishment to make those very things. It fairly might be found, also, that the copyrights were taken out in the proper names.

Finally, there was evidence that the pictures were copyrighted before publication.

We shall do no more than mention the suggestion that painting and engraving, unless for a mechanical end, are not among the useful arts, the progress of which Congress is empowered by the Constitution to promote. The Constitution does not limit the useful to that which satisfies immediate bodily needs. *Burrow-Giles Lithographic Co. v. Sarony*, 111 U.S. 53, 28 L.Ed. 349, 4 Sup.Ct.Rep. 279. It is obvious also that the plaintiff's case is not affected by the fact, if it be one, that the pictures represent actual groups—visible things. They seem from the testimony to have been composed from hints or description, not from sight of a performance. But even if they had been drawn from the life, that fact would not deprive them of protection. The opposite proposition would mean that a portrait by Velasquez or Whistler was common property because others might try their hand on the same face. Others are free to copy the original. They are not free to copy the copy. The copy is the personal reaction of an individual upon nature. Personality always contains something unique. It expresses its singularity even in handwriting, and a very modest grade of art has in it something irreducible, which is one man's alone. That something he may copyright unless there is a restriction in the words of the act.

If there is a restriction it is not to be found in the limited pretensions of these particular works. The least pretentious picture has more originality in it than directories and the like, which may be copyrighted. We assume that the construction of Rev. Stat. 4952 (U. S. Comp. Stat. 1901, p. 3406), allowing a copyright to the "author, designer, or proprietor ... of any engraving, cut, print ... [or] chromo' is affected by the act of 1874 (U. S. Comp. Stat. 1901, p. 3412). That section provides that, "in the construction of this act, the words 'engraving,' 'cut,' and 'print' shall be applied only to pictorial illustrations or works connected with the fine arts." We see no reason for taking the words "connected with the fine arts" as qualifying anything except the word "works," but it would not change our decision if we should assume further that they also qualified "pictorial illustrations," as the defendant contends.

These chromolithographs are "pictorial illustrations." The word "illustrations' does not mean that they must illustrate the text of a book, and that the etchings of Rembrandt or Muller's engraving of the Madonna di San Sisto could not be protected today if any man were able to produce them. Again, the act, however construed, does not mean that ordinary posters are not good enough to be considered within its scope.

The antithesis to "illustrations or works connected with the fine arts" is not works of little merit or of humble degree, or illustrations addressed to the less educated classes; it is "prints or labels designed to be used for any other articles of manufacture." Certainly works are not the less connected with the fine arts because their pictorial quality attracts the crowd, and therefore gives them a real use—if use means to increase trade and to help to make money. A picture is none the less a picture, and none the less a subject of copyright, that it is used for an advertisement. And if pictures may be used to advertise soap, or the theatre, or monthly magazines, as they are, they may be used to advertise a circus. Of course, the ballet is as legitimate a subject for illustration as any other. A rule cannot be laid down that would excommunicate the paintings of Degas.

Finally, the special adaptation of these pictures to the advertisement of the Wallace shows does not prevent a copyright. That may be a circumstance for the jury to consider in determining the extent of Mr. Wallace's rights, but it is not a bar. Moreover, on the evidence, such prints are used by less pretentious exhibitions when those for whom they were prepared have given them up.

It would be a dangerous undertaking for persons trained only to the law to constitute themselves final judges of the worth of pictorial illustrations, outside of the narrowest and most obvious limits. At the one extreme, some works of genius would be sure to miss appreciation. Their very novelty would make them repulsive until the public had learned the new language in which their author spoke. It may be more than doubted, for instance, whether the etchings of Goya or the paintings of Manet would have been sure of protection when seen for the first time. At the other end, copyright would be denied to pictures which appealed to a public less educated than the judge. Yet if they command the interest of any public, they have a commercial value—it would be bold to say that they have not an aesthetic and educational value—and the taste of any public is not to be treated with contempt. It is an ultimate fact for the moment, whatever may be our hopes for a change. That these pictures had their worth and their success is sufficiently shown by the desire to reproduce them without regard to the plaintiffs' rights. We are of opinion that there was evidence that the plaintiffs have rights entitled to the protection of the law.

The judgment of the Circuit Court of Appeals is reversed; the judgment of the Circuit Court is also reversed and the cause remanded to that court with directions to set aside the verdict and grant a new trial.

MR. JUSTICE HARLAN, dissenting:

Judges Lurton, Day, and Severens, of the circuit court of appeals, concurred in affirming the judgment of the district court. Their views were thus expressed in an opinion delivered by Judge Lurton: "What we hold is this: That if a chromo, lithograph, or other print, engraving, or picture has no other use than that of a mere advertisement, and no value aside from this function, it would not be promotive of the useful arts, within the meaning of the constitutional provision, to protect the 'author' in the exclusive use thereof, and the copyright statute should not be construed as including such a publication, if any other construction is admissible. If a mere label simply designating or describing an article to which it is attached, and which has no value separated from the article, does not come within the constitutional clause upon the subject of copyright, it must follow that a pictorial illustration designed and useful only as an advertisement, and having no intrinsic value other than its function as an advertisement, must be equally without the obvious meaning of the Constitution. It must have some connection with the fine arts to give it intrinsic value, and that it shall have is the meaning which we attach to the act of June 18, 1874 (U. S. Comp. Stat. 1901, p. 3411), amending the provisions of the copyright law. We are unable to discover anything useful or meritorious in the design copyrighted by the plaintiffs in error other than as an advertisement of acts to be done or exhibited to the public in Wallace's show. No evidence, aside from the deductions which are to be drawn from the prints themselves, was offered to show that these designs had any original artistic qualities. The jury could not reasonably have found merit or value aside from the purely business object of advertising a show, and the instruction to find for the defendant was not error. ... The judgment must be affirmed."*Courier Lithographing Co. v. Donaldson Lithographing Co.*, 44 C.C.A. 296, 104 F. 993, 996.

I entirely concur in these views, and therefore dissent from the opinion and judgment of this court. The clause of the Constitution giving Congress power to promote the progress of science and useful arts, by securing for limited terms to authors and inventors the exclusive right to their respective works and discoveries, does not, as I think, embrace a mere advertisement of a circus.

Mr. Justice McKenna authorizes me to say that he also dissents.

Notes and Questions

1. *Protecting Useful Works.* Copyright laws are generally used to protect literary, artistic and musical works. U.S. copyright law is based on the Congressional grant of authority found in Article 1 of the U.S. Constitution: "Congress shall have the power ... To promote the Progress of Science and *useful Arts*, by securing for limited Times to Authors and Inventors the exclusive Right to their respective Writings and Discoveries ..."

What would you consider to be a "useful Art"? Is a critically acclaimed novel "useful"? Is a scientific article? Should usefulness be judged on the basic of public appeal or its role in public instruction? How did the court in the *Anti-Discrimination* case define a "useful Art"?

2. If, as in the *Anti-Discrimination* case, advertising is protected under copyright law, what role should trademark law play in the protection of corporate symbols? Can a corporate symbol which contains a graphic element, such as Mickey Mouse or the Rolex crown be protected under copyright law as a "useful Art"? Should it be?

3. *The Role of Artistry.* Is there a policy reason for limiting protection under copyright to "artistic" expression such as those represented by novels, music and paintings? The first recorded copyright statute was the Statute of Anne, enacted in Great Britain in 1710 and entitled "An Act for the Encouragement of Learning by Vesting the Copies of Printed Books in the Authors or Purchasers of such copies..." It protected "printed books and other writings." [8 Anne, ch.19 (1710)(Eng)]. Even the first significant multinational treaty concerning copyright protection, The Berne Convention, enacted in 1886, protected "artistic, literary and musical" works. (Article 2.) The problem arises, however, from the never ceasing progress of technology. If a realistic painting of a waterfall qualifies as an "artistic work," does a photograph of the same waterfall also qualify? Does a digital reconstruction of the waterfall from publicly available clip art qualify? What about a trademark for beer featuring as part of its logo a photograph of the waterfall?

4. Justice Holmes suggests that courts should not discriminate between works of art that they perceive to be artistic and those that seem to be less so. This anti-discrimination rule is one of the early tenets of U.S. copyright law, although it appears to be honored more in the breach than in its enforcement. *Compare Alva Studios, Inc. v. Winninger,* 177 F.Supp. 265 (S.D.N.Y.1959)(protection extended to scaled-down reproduction of Rodin's statue *The Hand of God* because the work required "great skill and ingenuity" to "produce a scale reduction of a great work with exactitude") *with L. Batlin & Son, Inc. v. Snyder,* 536 F.2d 486 (2d Cir.1976), *cert. denied,* 429 U.S. 857 (1976) (plastic model of an antique cast iron "Uncle Sam" bank denied copyright protection because "the plastic version is not, and was scarcely meticulously produced to be an exactly faithful reproduction.").

5. In Great Britain, by contrast, the absence of any level of artistry or aesthetic appeal may preclude protection under copyright law. What if the useful article is the design of a child's toy that is used for building toy houses? Should copyright protection depend on whether the structure in question has some level of demonstrated artistic appeal? See *Interlego A.G. v. Tyco Indus., Inc.,* [1987] 1 App. Cas. 217, 241 (P.C. 1988) (appeal taken from H.K.) (under U.K. law, "originality" requires some artistic element). Should some degree of "artistic" expression by required internationally for copyright protection to attach? If no "artistic" element is required, how do you prevent the first author of a functional language for a computer software program from gaining a monopoly under copyright which would essentially prohibit anyone else from using the same language? *See, e.g.,* Lloyd L. Weinreb, *Copyright for Functional Expression,* 111 Harv. L. Rev. 1149 (1998).

6. U.S. copyright law does not extend protection to "useful articles" which are defined under Section 101 of the 1976 Copyright Act, as amended, as "an article having an intrinsic utilitarian function that is not merely to portray the appearance of the article or to convey information." 17 U.S.C. § 101. Despite the prohibition of copyright protection for "useful" articles, U.S. copyright law *does* permit protection of pictorial, sculptural or graphic designs which may have useful aspects "only if, and to the extent that, such design incorporates pictorial, graphic, or sculptural features that can be

identified separately from, and are capable of existing independently of, the utilitarian aspects of the article." 17 U.S.C. § 101.

7. Great Britain similarly declines to extend protection to "features of shape, configuration, pattern or ornament applied to an article by any industrial process or means, being features which in the finished article appeal to and are judged solely by the eye, but does not include features of shape or configuration which are dictated solely by the function which the article to be made in that shape or configuration has to perform." United Kingdom Registered Designs Act of 1949, Section 1(3). Under Paragraph 8(2) of Schedule 7 to the Copyright Act 1956: "Copyright shall not subsist by virtue of this Act in any artistic work made before the commencement of section 10 which, at the time when the work was made, constituted a design capable of registration under the Registered Designs Act 1949 ... and was used, or intended to be used, as a model or pattern to be multiplied by any industrial process." United Kingdom Copyright Act of 1956, Schedule 7, Para. 8(2). [*Interlego Ag v. Tyco Industries, Inc., Et Al.*, [1989] 1 AC 217, [1988] 3 All ER 949, [1988] 3 WLR 678, [1988] RPC 343].

8. The problem of determining whether a particular work is a "useful article" whose protection falls outside the scope of copyright is a difficult one. For example, is a marble sculpture of a naked female torso a useful article? Does it become a useful article if the same sculpture is made out of plastic and used to display clothes for sale in a store? *See Carol Barnhart Inc. v. Economy Cover Corp.*, 773 F.2d 411 (2d Cir.1985) (denying protection for human torso mannequins because they did not demonstrate sufficient "conceptual separability" from their utilitarian aspects).

9. Would a software program qualify as a "useful article"? Does it matter what the purpose of the software is? For example, would an operating system be "useful" but a video game protected? To what extent should copyright protection internationally be limited to works which demonstrate some modicum of artistry or creativity?

THE BICYCLE RACK CASE

BRANDIR INTERNATIONAL, INC v. CASCADE PACIFIC LUMBER CO

United States Court of Appeals, Second Circuit, 1987
834 F.2d 1142

OAKES, CIRCUIT JUDGE.

In passing the Copyright Act of 1976 Congress attempted to distinguish between protectable "works of applied art" and "industrial designs not subject to copyright protection." The courts, however, have had difficulty framing tests by which the fine line establishing what is and what is not copyrightable can be drawn. Once again we are called upon to draw such a line, this time in a case involving the "RIBBON Rack," a bicycle rack made of bent tubing that is said to have originated from a wire sculpture.

The statutory definition of "pictorial, graphic, and sculptural works" states that "the design of a useful article, as defined in this section, shall be considered a pictorial, graphic, or sculptural work only if, and only to the extent that, such design incorporates pictorial, graphic, or sculptural features that can be identified separately from, and are capable of existing independently of, the utilitarian aspects of the article." 17 U.S.C. § 101.[3] The legislative history added gloss on the criteria of separate identity and independent existence in saying:

On the other hand, although the shape of an industrial product may be aesthetically satisfying and valuable, the Committee's intention is not to offer it copyright protection under the bill. Unless the shape of an automobile, airplane, ladies' dress, food processor, television set, or any other industrial product contains some element that, physically or conceptually, can be identified as separable from the utilitarian aspects of that article, the design would not be copyrighted under the bill.

As courts and commentators have come to realize, however, the line Congress attempted to draw between copyrightable art and noncopyrightable design "was neither clear nor new." One aspect of the distinction that has drawn considerable attention is the reference in the House Report to "physically or conceptually "separable elements. [I]n *Kieselstein-Cord v. Accessories by Pearl, Inc.*, 632 F.2d 989, 993 (2d Cir.1980), this court accepted the idea that copyrightability can adhere in the "conceptual" separation of an artistic element. Indeed, the court went on to find such conceptual separation in reference to ornate belt buckles that could be and were worn separately as jewelry.

In *Carol Barnhart Inc. v. Economy Cover Corp.*, 773 F.2d 411 (2d Cir.1985), a divided panel of this circuit affirmed a district court grant of summary judgment of noncopyrightability of four life-sized, anatomically correct human torso forms. *Carol Barnhart* distinguished *Kieselstein-Cord*, but it surely did not overrule it. The distinction made was that the ornamented surfaces of the Kieselstein–Cord belt buckles "were not in any respect required by their utilitarian functions," but the features claimed to be aesthetic or artistic in the *Carol Barnhart* forms were "inextricably intertwined with the utilitarian feature, the display of clothes." 773 F.2d at 419.

"Conceptual separability" is thus alive and well, at least in this circuit. The problem, however, is determining exactly what it is and how it is to be applied. Judge Newman's illuminating discussion in dissent in *Carol Barnhart, see* 773 F.2d at 419–24, proposed a test that aesthetic features are conceptually separable if "the article ... stimulate[s] in the mind of the beholder a concept that is separate from the concept evoked by its utilitarian function." *Id.* at 422.

Perhaps the differences between the majority and the dissent in Carol Barnhart might have been resolved had they had before them the Denicola article on Applied Art and Industrial Design: A Suggested

---

3. The statute also defines "useful article" as one "having an intrinsic utilitarian function that is not merely to portray the appearance of the article or to convey infor- mation. An article that is normally a part of a useful article is considered a 'useful article.' " 17 U.S.C. § 101.

Approach to Copyright in Useful Articles, [67 Minn.L.Rev. 707 (1983)]. There, Professor Denicola points out that although the Copyright Act of 1976 was an effort " 'to draw as clear a line as possible,' "in truth "there is no line, but merely a spectrum of forms and shapes responsive in varying degrees to utilitarian concerns." 67 Minn.L.Rev. at 741. Denicola argues that "the statutory directive requires a distinction between works of industrial design and works whose origins lie outside the design process, despite the utilitarian environment in which they appear." He views the statutory limitation of copyrightability as "an attempt to identify elements whose form and appearance reflect the unconstrained perspective of the artist," such features not being the product of industrial design. *Id*. at 742. "Copyrightability, therefore, should turn on the relationship between the proffered work and the process of industrial design." *Id*. at 741. He suggests that "the dominant characteristic of industrial design is the influence of nonaesthetic, utilitarian concerns" and hence concludes that copyrightability "ultimately should depend on the extent to which the work reflects artistic expression uninhibited by functional considerations." To state the Denicola test in the language of conceptual separability, if design elements reflect a merger of aesthetic and functional considerations, the artistic aspects of a work cannot be said to be conceptually separable from the utilitarian elements. Conversely, where design elements can be identified as reflecting the designer's artistic judgment exercised independently of functional influences, conceptual separability exists.

We believe that Professor Denicola's approach provides the best test for conceptual separability and, accordingly, adopt it here for several reasons. First, the approach is consistent with the holdings of our previous cases. In *Kieselstein–Cord*, for example, the artistic aspects of the belt buckles reflected purely aesthetic choices, independent of the buckles' function, while in *Carol Barnhart* the distinctive features of the torsos—the accurate anatomical design and the sculpted shirts and collars—showed clearly the influence of functional concerns. Though the torsos bore artistic features, it was evident that the designer incorporated those features to further the usefulness of the torsos as mannequins. Second, the test's emphasis on the influence of utilitarian concerns in the design process may help, as Denicola notes, to "alleviate the de facto discrimination against nonrepresentational art that has regrettably accompanied much of the current analysis." Id. at 745. Finally, and perhaps most importantly, we think Denicola's test will not be too difficult to administer in practice. The work itself will continue to give "mute testimony" of its origins. In addition, the parties will be required to present evidence relating to the design process and the nature of the work, with the trier of fact making the determination whether the aesthetic design elements are significantly influenced by functional considerations.

Turning now to the facts of this case, we note first that Brandir contends, and its chief owner David Levine testified, that the original design of the RIBBON Rack stemmed from wire sculptures that Levine had created, each formed from one continuous undulating piece of wire. These sculptures were, he said, created and displayed in his home as a means of personal expression, but apparently were never sold or displayed elsewhere. He also created a wire sculpture in the shape of a bicycle and states that he did not give any thought to the utilitarian application of any of his sculptures until he accidentally juxtaposed the bicycle sculpture with one of the self-standing wire sculptures. It was not until November 1978 that Levine seriously began pursuing the utilitarian application of his sculptures, when a friend, G. Duff Bailey, a bicycle buff and author of numerous articles about urban cycling, was at Levine's home and informed him that the sculptures would make excellent bicycle racks, permitting bicycles to be parked under the overloops as well as on top of the underloops. Following this meeting, Levine met several times with Bailey and others, completing the designs for the RIBBON Rack by the use of a vacuum cleaner hose, and submitting his drawings to a fabricator complete with dimensions. The Brandir RIBBON Rack began being nationally advertised and promoted for sale in September 1979.

In November 1982 Levine discovered that another company, Cascade Pacific Lumber Co., was selling a similar product. Thereafter, beginning in December 1982, a copyright notice was placed on all RIBBON Racks before shipment and on December 10, 1982, five copyright applications for registration were submitted to the Copyright Office. The Copyright Office refused registration by letter, stating that the RIBBON Rack did not contain any element that was "capable of independent existence as a copyrightable pictorial, graphic or sculptural work apart from the shape of the useful article." An appeal to the Copyright Office was denied by letter dated March 23, 1983, refusing registration on the above ground and alternatively on the ground that the design lacked originality, consisting of "nothing more than a familiar public domain symbol." In February 1984, after the denial of the second appeal of the examiner's decision, Brandir sent letters to customers enclosing copyright notices to be placed on racks sold prior to December 1982.

Applying Professor Denicola's test to the RIBBON Rack, we find that the rack is not copyrightable. It seems clear that the form of the rack is influenced in significant measure by utilitarian concerns and thus any aesthetic elements cannot be said to be conceptually separable from the utilitarian elements. This is true even though the sculptures which inspired the RIBBON Rack may well have been—the issue of originality aside—copyrightable.

Brandir argues correctly that a copyrighted work of art does not lose its protected status merely because it subsequently is put to a functional use.

Had Brandir merely adopted one of the existing sculptures as a bicycle rack, neither the application to a utilitarian end nor commercialization of that use would have caused the object to forfeit its copyrighted status. Comparison of the RIBBON Rack with the earlier sculptures, however, reveals that while the rack may have been derived in part from one of more "works of art," it is in its final form essentially a product of industrial design. In creating the RIBBON Rack, the designer has clearly adapted the original aesthetic elements to accommodate and further a utilitarian purpose. These altered design features of the RIBBON Rack, including the spacesaving, open design achieved by widening the upper loops to permit parking under as well as over the rack's curves, the straightened vertical elements that allow in- and above-ground installation of the rack, the ability to fit all types of bicycles and mopeds, and the heavy-gauged tubular construction of rustproof galvanized steel, are all features that combine to make for a safe, secure, and maintenance-free system of parking bicycles and mopeds. Its undulating shape is said in Progressive Architecture, January 1982, to permit double the storage of conventional bicycle racks. Moreover, the rack is manufactured from 2 3/8 inch standard steam pipe that is bent into form, the six-inch radius of the bends evidently resulting from bending the pipe according to a standard formula that yields bends having a radius equal to three times the nominal internal diameter of the pipe.

Brandir argues that its RIBBON Rack can and should be characterized as a sculptural work of art within the minimalist art movement. Minimalist sculpture's most outstanding feature is said to be its clarity and simplicity, in that it often takes the form of geometric shapes, lines, and forms that are pure and free of ornamentation and void of association. As Brandir's expert put it, "The meaning is to be found in, within, around and outside the work of art, allowing the artistic sensation to be experienced as well as intellectualized." People who use Foley Square in New York City see in the form of minimalist art the "Tilted Arc," which is on the plaza at 26 Federal Plaza. Numerous museums have had exhibitions of such art, and the school of minimalist art has many admirers.

It is unnecessary to determine whether to the art world the RIBBON Rack properly would be considered an example of minimalist sculpture. The result under the copyright statute is not changed. Using the test we have adopted, it is not enough that, to paraphrase Judge Newman, the rack may stimulate in the mind of the reasonable observer a concept separate from the bicycle rack concept. While the RIBBON Rack may be worthy of admiration for its aesthetic qualities alone, it remains nonetheless the product of industrial design. Form and function are inextricably intertwined in the rack, its ultimate design being as much the result of utilitarian pressures as aesthetic choices. Indeed, the visually pleasing proportions and symmetricality of the rack represent design changes made in response to functional concerns. Judging from the awards the rack has received, it would seem in fact that Brandir has achieved with the RIBBON Rack the highest goal of modern industrial design, that is, the harmonious fusion of function and aesthetics. Thus there remains no artistic element of the RIBBON Rack that can be identified as separate and "capable of existing independently, of, the utilitarian aspects of the article." Accordingly, we must affirm on the copyright claim.

Judgment affirmed as to the copyright claim; reversed and remanded as to the trademark and unfair competition claims.

WINTER, CIRCUIT JUDGE

I respectfully dissent from the majority's discussion and disposition of the copyright claim.

My colleagues, applying an adaptation of Professor Denicola's test, hold that the aesthetic elements of the design of a useful article are not conceptually separable from its utilitarian aspects if "[f]orm and function are inextricably intertwined" in the article, and "its ultimate design [is] as much the result of utilitarian pressures as aesthetic choices." Applying that test to the instant matter, they observe that the dispositive fact is that "in creating the Ribbon Rack, [Levine] has clearly adapted the original aesthetic elements to accommodate and further a utilitarian purpose." (emphasis added). The grounds of my disagreement are that: (1) my colleagues' adaptation of Professor Denicola's test diminishes the statutory concept of "conceptual separability" to the vanishing point; and (2) their focus on the process or sequence followed by the particular designer makes copyright protection depend upon largely fortuitous circumstances concerning the creation of the design in issue.

With regard to "conceptual separability," my colleagues deserve considerable credit for their efforts to reconcile *Carol Barnhart Inc.* with *Kieselstein–Cord*. In my view, these cases are not reconcilable. *Carol Barnhart* paid only lip service to the fact that the "conceptual separability" of an article's aesthetic utilitarian aspects may render the design of a "useful article" a copyrightable "sculptural work." 17 U.S.C. ? 101 (1982). Actually, the *Carol Barnhart* majority applied a test of physical separability. They thus stated:

"What distinguishes [the *Kieselstein–Cord*] buckles from the *Barnhart* forms is that the ornamented surfaces of the buckles were not in any respect required by their utilitarian functions; the artistic and aesthetic features could thus be conceived of as having been added to, or superimposed upon, an otherwise utilitarian article. The unique artistic design was wholly unnecessary to performance of the utilitarian function. In the case of the *Barnhart* forms, on the other hand, the features claimed to be aesthetic or artistic, e.g., the life-size configuration of the breasts and the width of the shoulders are inextricably intertwined with the utilitarian feature, the display of clothes. 773 F.2d at 419 (emphasis added). In contrast, *Kieselstein–Cord* focused on the fact that the belt buckles at issue could be perceived as objects other than belt buckles:

"We see in appellant's belt buckles conceptually separable sculptural elements, as apparently have the buckles' wearers who have used them as ornamentation for parts of the body other than the waist." 632 F.2d at 993.

My colleagues' adaptation of the *Denicola* test tracks the *Carol Barnhart* approach, whereas I would adopt that taken in *Kieselstein–Cord*, which allows for the copyrightability of the aesthetic elements of useful articles even if those elements simultaneously perform utilitarian functions. The latter approach received its fullest elaboration in Judge Newman's dissent in *Carol Barnhart*, where he explained that "[f]or the [artistic] design features to be 'conceptually separate' from the utilitarian aspects of the useful article that embodies the design, the article must stimulate in the mind of the beholder a concept that is separate from the concept evoked by its utilitarian function." 773 F.2d at 422 (Newman, J., dissenting).

In other words, the relevant question is whether the design of a useful article, however intertwined with the article's utilitarian aspects, causes an ordinary reasonable observer to perceive an aesthetic concept not related to the article's use. The answer to this question is clear in the instant case because any reasonable observer would easily view the Ribbon Rack as an ornamental sculpture. Indeed, there is evidence of actual confusion over whether it is strictly ornamental in the refusal of a building manager to accept delivery until assured by the buyer that the Ribbon Rack was in fact a bicycle rack. Moreover, Brandir has received a request to use the Ribbon Rack as environmental sculpture, and has offered testimony of art experts who claim that the Ribbon Rack may be valued solely for its artistic features. As one of those experts observed: "If one were to place a Ribbon Rack on an island without access, or in a park and surround the work with a barrier, . . . its status as a work of art would be beyond dispute."

My colleagues also allow too much to turn upon the process or sequence of design followed by the designer of the Ribbon Rack. They thus suggest that copyright protection would have been accorded "had Brandir merely adopted . . . as a bicycle rack" an enlarged version of one of David Levine's original sculptures rather than one that had wider upper loops and straightened vertical elements. I cannot agree that copyright protection for the Ribbon Rack turns on whether Levine serendipitously chose the final design of the Ribbon Rack during his initial sculptural musings or whether the original design had to be slightly modified to accommodate bicycles. Copyright protection, which is intended to generate incentives for designers by according property rights in their creations, should not turn on purely fortuitous events. For that reason, the Copyright Act expressly states that the legal test is how the final article is perceived, not how it was developed through various stages. It thus states in pertinent part:

> the design of a useful article . . . shall be considered a . . . sculptural work only if, and only to the extent that, such design incorporates . . . sculptural features that can be identified separately from, and are capable of existing independently of, the utilitarian aspects of the article. 17 U.S.C. § 101 (1982) (emphasis added).

I therefore dissent from the decision so far as it relates to copyrightability.

THE LEGO TOY CASE

INTERLEGO AG v. TYCO INDUSTRIES INC.

Privy Council [Appeal From The Court Of Appeal Of Hong Kong], 1988, [1989]
1 AC 217, [1988] 3 All ER 949, [1988] 3 WLR 678, [1988] RPC 343.

Lord Oliver of Aylmerton:

The plaintiff appellant in this appeal is one of a group of companies engaged in the manufacture and sale of what must be one of the most universally known and used children's toys in this century. "Lego" is a system of model-building consisting in the main of plastic brick-shape blocks (although there are other shapes) so designed that they are capable of being joined together so as to form a stable structure but one which is capable of being disassembled without damage to the constituent elements. This is accomplished by providing on the upper surface of each block one or more cylindrical studs or knobs which are so spaced and designed as to fit tightly into the base of another similar block, such base being hollow and furnished with a shirt and tubes positioned so as to bear upon the studs and hold them in position. The system was originally designed by a Mr. Hilary Page who marketed it under the trade-name "Kiddicraft." It was the subject matter of United Kingdom patents which expired in 1954 and 1959 respectively.

The plaintiff is a Swiss company holding the intellectual property rights of the group which was originally founded by a Mr Christiansen and has its headquarters in Denmark. It will be convenient to refer to the plaintiff and the group to which it belongs as "Lego."

In addition to the ordinary range of Lego bricks, Lego also devised a system of model-building designed for small children and marketed under the name "Duplo." This consisted broadly of a large-scale Lego, the block being substantially larger than Lego bricks so that they could be easily handled by smaller children. They operated in the same way, the blocks being held together by studs on the lower block bearing on the skirt of the upper block. They were so designed and proportioned that they could also be used in conjunction with blocks from the Lego range.

Although other manufacturers have attempted to launch and market competing products operating on broadly similar principles, none has achieved anything like the success of the Lego and Duplo ranges which, for the past 30 years or more, have completely dominated the market in children's model-building systems.

The first defendants, Tyco Industries Inc., are a United States corporation established some 50 years ago. They carry on a successful business of toy manufacturers with factories in the United States and Hong Kong. The second defendant is the Hong Kong subsidiary of the first defendants and they can conveniently be referred to together as

"Tyco." In 1983 Tyco resolved to break into the model building market. They concluded, no doubt correctly, that the dominance of Lego in that market was such that no model-building system could be successfully marketed unless it was so designed as to be compatible and capable of being combined with Lego. Lego's patents and designs in the United States had, by this time, expired by effluxion of time and Tyco were advised that there was nothing to prevent them from manufacturing and marketing model-building elements which were precise copies of the principal Lego elements. They accordingly purchased examples of these elements in the United States and in Hong Kong in 1983, and it is common ground that they copied elements of the old design which form the core of the Lego system. They also manufactured elements of their own design which were so proportioned and devised as to conform with the basic dimension of the Lego system. It should be emphasised that there was nothing underhand about this. Tyco exhibited the prototypes of their modular elements at the New York Toy Fair in February 1984 and informed Lego representatives of what they were proposing to do, that is to say, to manufacture and sell a model-making system openly advertised as looking like Lego, working like Lego, and capable of combination with Lego but sold at a competitive price. It was part of Tyco's marketing strategy that some or all of the modular units should be manufactured in Hong Kong and an open letter dated 25 May 1984 was addressed by their attorneys to Lego setting out what they proposed to do. As a result of this Lego instituted proceedings in Hong Kong for infringement of copyright and it is from those proceedings that the present appeal arises. Lego claim that in producing, by a process of what is called "reverse engineering," what are, in all essential features, replicas of Lego and Duplo construction units, Tyco have infringed Lego's copyright in the design drawings from which the Lego and Duplo units were manufactured. It is not suggested nor could it be suggested that Tyco ever had or even saw the design drawings themselves. Their elements were made simply by measuring and reproducing the configuration of the three-dimensional Lego elements.

Section 10 of the Act of 1956 contains a code for regulating the extent and subsistence of copyright in relation to an artistic work where a design corresponding to such work is applied industrially. Paragraph 8(1) of Schedule 7 to the Act, however, provides that the section is not to apply to artistic works made before the commencement of the section, that is to say, in the instant case, 1 January 1973. Paragraph 8(2) is in the following terms:

> "Copyright shall not subsist by virtue of this Act in any artistic work made before the commencement of section 10 which, at the time when the work was made, constituted a design capable of registration under the Registered Designs Act 1949, or under the enactments repealed by that Act, and was used, or intended to be used, as a model or pattern to be multiplied by any industrial process."

The United Kingdom Registered Designs Act 1949 was not extended to Hong Kong in exactly the same way as the Act of 1956, but the United Kingdom Designs (Protection) Ordinance (Laws of Hong Kong, 1964 rev, c 44) provides that, subject to certain provisions which are immaterial for present purposes, the registered holder of a design in the United Kingdom is to enjoy, in Hong Kong, the same privileges and rights as if the United Kingdom certificate of registration had been issued with an extension to Hong Kong. Thus, for practical purposes, the parallel rights conferred by the Acts of 1949 and 1956 are both extended to Hong Kong. The questions raised by Lego's appeal are, therefore, first, whether the pre–1973 drawings constituted, as the Court of appeal held, "designs" as defined by the Act of 1949 and were thus excluded from the ambit of copyright by the provisions of paragraph 8(2) of Schedule 7 to the Act of 1956 and secondly whether, assuming that they constituted "designs" as defined, they were "capable of registration" inasmuch as, in Lego's contention, they lacked the essential quality of novelty without which a design cannot properly be registered under the Act of 1949.

Prior to the Act of 1911 there was no single provision covering the various forms of artistic copyright. Engravings and prints were protected by a number of 18th century statutes, works of sculpture by the Sculpture Copyright Act 1814 and paintings, drawings and photographs by the Fine Arts Copyright Act 1862, under which registration was necessary before the copyright could be enforced. Moreover, the concept of infringement by three-dimensional reproduction of two-dimensional works had not yet been developed. The philosophy behind the concept of artistic copyright during the 19th century was that it was not conceived of as a protection for purely industrial designs. These were provided with their own code of protection in the form of a series of statutes from 1842 onwards, finally consolidated in the Patents, Designs and Trade Marks Act 1883, which provided for registered designs not merely a protection against copying but a short term monopoly consisting of an exclusive right to make use of the design. These provisions were amended and re-enacted in the Patents and Designs Act 1907. Immediately before the commencement of the Copyright Act 1911, therefore, the protection of a design applied industrially to the manufacturer of artifacts was to be found only in the Patents and Designs Act 1907 and the provisions of section 22(1) of the Act of 1911 were clearly intended to exclude such designs from the scope of artistic copyright, the various forms of which were, for the first time, brought under a single umbrella.

In these proceedings Lego base their monopoly on copyright asserted not for the bricks but for the uninspired and uninspiring engineering drawings of bricks. By attributing new periods of copyright protection to every minor alteration in the form of a brick which is recorded in such a drawing they seek to obtain, effectively, a perpetual monopoly. In *In re Coco–Cola Co* [1986] 1 WLR 695, 697, the House of Lords drew attention to the undesirable practice of seeking to expand the boundaries of intellectual property rights beyond the purposes for which they were created in order to obtain an unintended and undeserving monopoly. These proceedings are a further illustration of that undesirable practice.

Tyco do not deny that the bricks which they have manufactured and marketed were produced as a result of "reverse engineering" from the 1983 Lego bricks. It is thus not in issue that Tyco have, indirectly, copied the drawings from which those bricks were manufactured, those drawings having been produced after 1 January 1973. There are some subsidiary issues relating to particular articles, but the main burden of the appeal is directed to two issues, *viz*: (1) Are the post–1972 drawings, which substantially reproduce the salient features of the pre–1973 drawings, entitled to copyright as original artistic works? (2) If so, has Tyco, in manufacturing its products (which display significant differences from the post–1973 drawings) copied a substantial part of those drawings and thus infringed Lego's copyright?

Engineering drawings are no doubt "artistic works" within the broad meaning of that expression in the Copyright Act 1956 but it has to be remembered that they are essentially no more then manufacturing instructions for a three-dimensional artifact. Their claim to artistic copyright rests solely upon the fact that they are drawings and not upon the technical significance of the instructions by which they can be interpreted which are frequently represented only by conventional symbols or figures. In the nature of things the original drawings come to be reproduced, probably many times, and updated from time to time as minor modifications are made in design or methods of manufacture. To accord an independent artistic copyright to every such reproduction would be to enable the period of artistic copyright in what is, essentially, the same work to be extended indefinitely. Thus the primary question on Tyco's appeal can be expressed in this way: can Lego, having enjoyed a monopoly for the full permitted period of patent and design protection in reliance upon drawings in which no copyright any longer subsists, continue their monopoly for yet a further, more extensive period by re-drawing the same designs with a number of minor alterations and claiming a fresh copyright in the re-drawn designs?

Section 3(2) of the Copyright Act 1956 provides that "Copyright shall subsist, subject to the provisions of this Act, in every original artistic work which is unpublished ... and 'artistic work' is defined in subsection (1) of the same section as meaning 'irrespective of artistic quality ... paintings, sculptures, drawings, engravings and photographs.' 'Drawing' includes 'any diagram, map, chart or plan:' section 48(1). Not altogether surprisingly there is no statutory definition of the word 'originality' but there is a classical statement of what is comprised in the concept of originality in the context of copyright in the judgment of Peterson J *in University of London Press Ltd. v. University Tutorial Press Ltd.* [1916] 2 Ch. 601, 608–609:

> "The word 'original' does not in this connection mean that the work must be the expression of original or inventive thought. Copyright Acts are not concerned with the originality of ideas, but

with the expression of thought, and, in the case of 'literary work,' with the expression of thought in print or writing. The originality which is required relates to the expression of the thought. But the Act does not require that the expression must be in an original or novel form, but that the work must not be copied from another work—that it should originate from the author.''

Originality in the context of literary copyright has been said in several well known cases to depend upon the degree of skill, labour and judgment involved in preparing a compilation. *Macmillan & Co. Ltd. v. Cooper*, 40 TLR 186 was such a case. Skill, labour or judgment merely in the process of copying cannot confer originality.

A well executed tracing is the result of much labour and skill but remains what it is, a tracing. Moreover, it must be borne in mind that the Copyright Act 1956 confers protection on an original work for a generous period. The prolongation of the period of statutory protection by periodic reproduction of the original work with minor alterations is an operation which requires to be scrutinised with some caution to ensure that that for which protection is claimed really is an original artistic work.

The other important consideration which has also to be borne in mind in any case of three-dimensional copying by reverse engineering is that the plaintiff's claim to protection in the case of a non-patented industrial article not registered under the Registered Designs Act 1949 rests solely upon artistic copyright, that is to say, upon the visual image in the form of a drawing of the article from which that which is claimed to be an infringement is produced. It does not rest upon the copyright owner's inventiveness or method of working, upon the confidentiality of his instructions to his engineering or production staff or upon his literary copyright in any written communication of those instructions. Essentially artistic copyright is concerned with visual image.

The essence of an artistic work (to adopt the words of Whitford J in a judgment delivered in *Rose Plastics GmbH v. William Beckett & Co. (Plastics) Ltd.* (unreported), 2 July 1987, of which their Lordships have seen only an approved transcript)is that which is ''visually significant;'' and Mr. Jacob asks, forensically, what is there in the 1976 drawings which is visually significant and which was not contained in and directly copied from the 1968 drawings? With deference to the Court of Appeal and accepting both the importance of and the skill involved in producing the design information transmitted to the mould makers by the revised figures substituted on the drawing, their Lordships can see no alteration of any visual significance such as to entitle the drawing, as a drawing, to be described as original.

In the argument before their Lordships the 2 X 4 brick was taken as the exemplar because, it was said, there was no significant distinction between that case and the other bricks in the Lego range. In deference to the argument of Mr. Rogers and to the judgment of Clough JA, where the items were dealt with individually, these items should be briefly considered. It will be convenient to take first three elements which were treated by Clough JA (in the part of his judgment omitted from [1987] FSR 409) as broadly following the same pattern. These are: (i) The 1 X 2 brick. The drawing from which the 1983 version of this was manufactured was also produced in 1976. Again it was admittedly copied from a 1968 drawing via an intermediate drawing produced in 1972. It is drawn to a different scale but it was accepted in the evidence that scale was of no materiality. Apart from small differences in tolerance and in the width of the central pin, which are indicated by the insertion of revised figures, there is no significant variation from the 1968 drawing. (ii) The one knob brick. There is no visual difference between the 1968 and 1976 drawings, the only modifications being in tolerance and an increase in the inside width from 4.83 mm to 4.84 mm. (iii) The 1 X 4 brick. This again was based on a 1976 drawing derived from a drawing in 1968. The 1976 drawing, although drawn to a scale of 5 to 1 instead of 2 to 1 appears, to all intents and purposes, to be merely a scaled-up version of the 1968 drawing with a small variation in dimension and tolerance indicated by figures and the addition of a one degree taper on the internal pins. Again, this is merely the 1968 drawing reproduced and adapted to illustrate new manufacturing and design instructions.

In relation to these three elements, all of which were drawn by the same draftswoman, Hanne Fabrin, the considerations which led Clough JA to hold that they were original drawings entitled to copyright, although clearly copied in each case from the 1968 original, were (i) the technical skill of Miss Fabrin and the time taken by her in producing the copy, (ii) the technical skill of Mr. Pucek in instructing her in the dimensions and tolerances to be shown on the drawings and (iii) in the case of the 1 X 4 brick, the fact that the middle cross-sectional view was enlarged and that a second cross-sectional view shown in the 1968 version was omitted. For the reasons already given, their Lordships cannot agree that these three matters were sufficient to establish originality in the drawings as artistic works.

There remains, therefore, to be dealt with only a point raised by Mr Jacob and determined by the Court of Appeal in Lego's favour in relation to section 9(8) of the Act of 1956. This arised in relation to two further items in the Lego range, namely the Duplo 6 X 12 base-plate and the trailer wheel. Section 9(8) provides:

> "The making of an object of any description which is in three dimensions shall not be taken to infringe the copyright in an artistic work in two dimensions, if the object would not appear, to persons who are not experts in relation to objects of that description, to be a reproduction of the artistic work."

It is not in dispute that the original wheel proposed to be manufactured by Tyco would have been an infringement of Lego's drawing. It was, however, modified to incorporate certain alterations which make it less like the Lego wheel. Both the trial judge and the Court of Appeal found that the modified version was a substantial reproduction of the

Lego drawing and granted an injunction in respect of it. There are obvious differences on casual inspection. The Tyco wheel has a different wall thickness, it has no radius on the inside and there is a different design of axle entry. Similarly in relation to the base-plate, Tyco have produced a version which is smaller in size than the Duplo plate and incorporates certain differences in the number of connectors to the tubes. Additionally, the knobs are not hollowed out as the Lego ones. It is clear, however, that Tyco produced their base-plate simply by taking a section of the Duplo plate and copying the appropriate dimensions from it and the question is not whether the end products display differences, but whether the finished article would, to the non-expert, appear to be a reproduction of Lego's drawings. The defence under section 9(8) in a case of acknowledged copying is notoriously difficult to establish, for it starts from a position that the object does in fact reproduce a substantial part of the drawing, the only question being whether it would appear to the non-expert that it does. The trial judge was clearly of the opinion that both elements did appear to reproduce the Lego drawings and, it seems, so were Clough and Fuad JJA, though Huggins V–P entertained some doubts. Their Lordships, having inspected the articles and the drawings, agree with the trial judge that the defence is not made out in relation to these two articles.

In the result their Lordships will humbly advise Her Majesty that Lego's appeal should be dismissed and that Tyco's cross-appeal should be allowed in respect of all the elements enumerated in schedule B. Lego must pay Tyco's costs both before the Board and in the courts below.

DISPOSITION:

Appeal dismissed. Judgment accordingly.

THE PHOTOCOPY CASE
THE REJECT SHOP PLC v. ROBERT MANNERS

Queen's Bench, High Court of Justice, 1995.
[1995] Fleet Street Reports, vol. 22, p. 870.

LEGATT, L.J.

[The defendant appealed its conviction for infringement of copyright in various designs created by Robert Manners for use originally in the form of hand made titles. Manners had produced the designs by creating a series of drawings, selecting a drawing, photocopying that drawing and then laminating on the tile. At issue was whether the photocopies qualified as "original" works whose copyright could be infringed by the defendant's unauthorized reproduction.]

The first question, for present purposes, is whether copyright subsisted in the relevant work. It is particularly to be noted that the relevant work identified by the summonses, as accepted by the parties before the magistrates, as well as in this court, was not Mr. Manners' drawings which indisputably were original but the so-called "final images", that is to say the photocopies in the second of the forms in which photocopies were produced, namely as a distorted photocopy or, as I have indicated, an enlargement of the previous photocopy.

On behalf of Mr. Manners, Mr. Garnett, Q.C. first submits that the production of the second form of photocopy was the culmination of a creative process or what he termed "the end of one continuous chain". His submission was that as a computer may sometimes be, and as exemplified in one of the decided cases, so in this case the photocopier was but a tool in the production of the final image. The photocopier (and this is the essence of Mr. Garnett's submission) was a tool to create an artistic work. The question is whether the photocopier was, indeed, part of the evolution of the artistic work, or whether, on the other hand, it was merely part of the manufacturing process by while tiles bearing the pattern or design produced by Mr. Manners were translated from his original drawings.

Mr. Garnett scorned the defendant's approach in this matter, characterising as a game their identification of the final image as being that which was copied, and the attempt to designate it as something other than an original work in itself or viewed as part of a continuous chain which he submitted constituted the artistic work in question.

He cited the case of *LA Gear Inc. v. High–Tech Sports Plc* [1992] F.S.R. 121. That was a case in which what was copied was a drawing for a man's shoe, and the question was whether the drawing relied upon could be said to be the drawing from which the copy was made for the purposes of an Order 14 judgment. Mr. Garnett relied upon a passage in the judgment of Nourse L.J., at page 136, where he said:

> "At this point Mr. Purvis raised a novel and disturbing argument. He said that if Miss McKinstry, in preparing drawing 1, had produced one or more preliminary versions, the copyright would exist not in the finished product, drawing 1, but in the original version. Accordingly, submitted Mr. Purvis, since it was said that there was more than one drawing and since it was not shown that drawing 1 was the original version, it was arguable that there was no originality in drawing 1."

Pausing there, I stress the word "arguable". It was used because the court was concerned, as I have indicated, with the question of whether summary judgment had rightly been signed. The Lord Justice continued:

> "That argument must be firmly rejected. What the Copyright Acts require is that the work should be the original work of its author. If, in the course of producing a finished drawing, the author produces one or more preliminary versions, the finished product does not cease to be his original work simply because he adapts it with minor variations, or even if he simply copies it, from an earlier version. Each drawing having been made by him, each is his original work. It would be an extraordinary state of affairs if the law were otherwise. Indeed, it might have far-reaching consequences on other artistic and literary works, for example on the manuscripts of books

and plays. We were told that there was no authority in point. I agree
with Mr. Baldwin that the principle is so obvious that it needs no
authority to support it. Accordingly, there being no reason to doubt
the evidence of Miss McKinstry that drawing I was her original
work, I think it very clear indeed that there is no possibility of a
different finding being made at trial."

Thus the court came to the clear and unsurprising conclusion on the
facts of that case that drawing one represented a culmination of the
endeavours of the person concerned and that was, therefore, correctly
identified (rather than any of the intermediate stages in course of its
production) as being the copyright work—the work, that is, in which
copyright subsisted and of which infringement was alleged.

Mr. Garnett argues that artistic work in the production of a final
work would constitute part of that final work, and so-called underlying
or intermediate works are to be regarded as part of a totality which is
itself infringed.

As I understood him, for the purposes of his argument, individual
parts of the final work are necessarily to be regarded as part of a totality
which is itself infringed.

He invited us to accept, from one of the passages that I have read of
the case stated, that the Magistrate had identified the production of a
final image as part of, or the culmination of a continuous process, and he
urged us to treat the classic case of *Interlego AG v. Tyco Industries Inc.*,
[1989] A.C. 217 as being a special case involving a manifest abuse which
was recognised as such by the Privy Council. The case was concerned
with engineering drawings of the well-known toy bricks used in the Lego
kits which are familiar to many. In that case the copyright in the
relevant drawings had expired and the manufacturers thereupon sought
to reproduce the original drawings by a process of inking in and adding
certain explanatory written material. They, therefore, claimed copyright
in the revised form of the drawings.

Delivering the opinion of the Board, Lord Oliver of Aylmerton, at
page 262H, (([1988]) R.P.C. 343 at 371) said this:

> "Take the simplest case of artistic copyright, a painting or a
> photograph. It takes great skill, judgment and labour to produce a
> good copy by painting or to produce an enlarged photograph from a
> positive print, but no one would reasonably contend that the copy of
> painting or enlargement was an "original" artistic work in which
> the copier is entitled to claim copyright. Skill, labour or judgment
> merely in the process of copying cannot confer originality."

After remarking that here is no more reason for denying originality
to the depiction of a three-dimensional prototype than there is for
denying originality to the depiction in two-dimensional form of any other
physical object his Lordship continued:

> "It by no means follows, however, that that which is an exact and
> literal reproduction in two-dimensional form of an existing two-

dimensional work becomes an original work simply because the process of copying it involves the application of skill and labour. There must in addition be some element of material alteration or embellishment which suffices to make the totality of the work an original work. Of course, even a relatively small alteration or addition quantitatively may, if material, suffice or convert that which is substantially copied from an earlier work into an original work. Whether it does so or not is a question of degree having regard to the quality rather than the quantity of the addition. But copying, *per se*, however much skill or labour may be devoted to the process, cannot make an original work. A well executed tracing is the result of much labour and skill but remains what it is, a tracing. Moreover it must be borne in mind that the Copyright Act 1956 confers protection on an original work for a generous period. The prolongation of the period of statutory protection by periodic reproduction of the original work with minor alterations is an operation which requires to be scrutinised with some caution to ensure that that for which protection is claimed really is an original artistic work."

In the result their Lordships held that Lego was not entitled to copyright in the more modern form of the drawings. That case, characterised by Mr. Garnett as, in effect, an abuse by the copyright holders is to be distinguished from the present, because there was not there the same consideration, as there is here, of the identification of a stage in the continuous process, upon which he relies.

In my judgment it is important not to be confused by the fact that the final image could be said to have been an intermediate stage in the production of the final work, namely the tile. It does not help the respondent to view the final image as a stage in the production of the final work, if only because he did not rely upon copyright in the final work, that is to say in the tile itself. What he established copyright in were the drawings and the magistrate so found. To make good infringement, not of the drawings but of the final image, he therefore had to show that he had expended artistic skill and labour in the production of the final image. However, in truth, the final image was not a stage in the production of the artistic work but it was a stage in the manufacturing process.

In my judgment the photocopying by Mr Manners of his drawings did not result in a depiction substantially different from the drawings themselves. He devoted to the copying of them no such skill and labour as conferred originality of an artistic character. The process was wholly mechanical and there is nothing to suggest that enlargement was for any purpose of that kind. There was, in short, no evidence before the magistrate of the exercise in the production of what he called the "distorted photocopies" of any relevant skill and labour whatever. It follows that the final images were not original works and so no copyright could subsist in them.

I would allow the appeal and set aside the appellant's convictions on all five summonses.

Notes and Questions

1. In WHAT IS ART (1898), Tolstoy described art as follows: "Art is not a handicraft, it is the transmission of feelings the artist has experienced." Does this definition of "art" apply when determining what qualifies as an "artistic work" for purposes of copyright protection? Should it?

2. What purpose is served by requiring more than an expenditure of labor in producing a work to be protected under copyright? Who should be the judge of whether such work demonstrates "artistry"? Is there artistry in selecting an arrangement of facts to be included in a directory? In the description of a manufacturing process? In the creation of a scientific article for a medical journal?

3. Where would you draw the line between copyright and "useful," non-artistic articles? Do you agree with the lines drawn in the previous cases? What if a person used digital manipulation to "create" a "new" photograph by blending the works of two other authors? Is this manipulation alone "artistry"?

C.   WHAT IMPACT DOES TECHNOLOGY HAVE ON ORIGINALITY?

THE OSCAR WILDE PHOTO CASE
BURROW–GILES LITHOGRAPHIC CO. v. SARONY

Supreme Court of the United States, 1884.
111 U.S. 53, 4 S.Ct. 279.

MILLER, J.

This is a writ of error to the circuit court for the southern district of New York. Plaintiff is a lithographer, and defendant a photographer, with large business in those lines in the city of New York. The suit was commenced by an action at law in which Sarony was plaintiff and the lithographic company was defendant, the plaintiff charging the defendant with violating his copyright in regard to a photograph, the title of which is "Oscar Wilde, No. 18." A jury being waived, the court made a finding of facts on which a judgment in favor of the plaintiff was rendered for the sum of $600 for the plates and 85,000 copies sold and exposed to sale, and $10 for copies found in his possession, as penalties under section 4965 of the Revised Statutes. Among the finding of facts made by the court the following presents the principal question raised by the assignment of errors in the case:

That the plaintiff, about the month of January, 1882, under an agreement with Oscar Wilde, became and was the author, inventor, designer, and proprietor of the photograph in suit, the title of which is "Oscar Wilde, No. 18," being the number used to designate this particular photograph and of the negative thereof; that the same is a useful, new, harmonious, characteristic, and graceful picture, and that said plaintiff made the same at his place of business in said city of New York, and within the United States, entirely from his own original mental conception, to which he gave visible form by posing the said Oscar Wilde in front of the camera, selecting and arranging the costume, draperies, and other various accessories in said photograph, arranging the subject so as to present graceful outlines, arranging and disposing the light and shade, suggesting and evoking the desired expression, and from such disposition, arrangement, or representation, made entirely by the plaintiff, he produced the picture in suit, Exhibit A, April 14, 1882, and that the terms 'author,' 'inventor,' and 'designer,' as used in the art of photography and in the complaint, mean the person who so produced the photograph."

Other findings leave no doubt that plaintiff had taken all the steps required by the act of congress to obtain copyright of this photograph.

The eighth section of the first article of the constitution is the great repository of the powers of congress, and by the eight clause of that section congress is authorized "to promote the progress of science and useful arts, by securing, for limited times to authors and inventors the exclusive right to their respective writings and discoveries." The argument here is that a photograph is not a writing nor the production of an author. Under the acts of Congress designed to give effect to this section, the persons who are to be benefited are divided into two classes— authors and inventors. The monopoly which is granted to the former is called a copyright; that given to the latter, letters patent, or, in the familiar language of the present day, patent-right. We have then copyright and patent-right, and it is the first of these under which plaintiff asserts a claim for relief. It is insisted, in argument, that a photograph being a reproduction, on paper, of the exact features of some natural object, or of some person, is not a writing of which the producer is the author. Section 4952 of the Revised Statutes places photographs in the same class as things which may be copyrighted with "books, maps, charts, dramatic or musical compositions, engravings, cuts, prints, paintings, drawings, statues, statuary, and models or designs intended to be perfected as works of the fine arts." "According to the practice of legislation in England and America, the copyright is confined to the exclusive right secured to the author or proprietor of a writing or drawing which may be multiplied by the arts of printing in any of its branches."

The construction placed upon the constitution by the first act of 1790 and the act of 1802, by the men who were contemporary with its formation, many of whom were members of the convention which framed it, is of itself entitled to very great weight, and when it is remembered that the rights thus established have not been disputed during a period of nearly a century, it is almost conclusive. Unless, therefore, photographs can be distinguished in the classification of this point from the maps, charts, designs, engravings, etchings, cuts, and other prints, it is difficult to see why congress cannot make them the subject of copyright as well as the others. These statutes certainly answer the objection that books only, or writing, in the limited sense of a book and its author, are within the constitutional provision. Both these words are susceptible of a more enlarged definition than this. An author in that sense is "he to whom anything owes its origin; originator; maker; one who completes a work of science or literature." So, also, no one would now claim that the word "writing" in this clause of the constitution, though the only word used as to subjects in regard to which authors are to be secured, is limited to the actual script of the author, and excludes books and all other printed matter. By writings in that clause is meant the literary productions of those authors, and Congress very properly has declared these to include all forms of writing, printing, engravings, etchings, etc., by which the ideas in the mind of the author are given visible expression. The only reason why photographs were not included in the extended list in the act of 1802 is, probably, that they did not exist, as photography, as an art, was then unknown, and the scientific principle on which it rests, and the chemicals and machinery by which it is operated, have all been discovered long since that statute was enacted. Nor is it supposed that the framers of the constitution did not understand the nature of copyright and the objects to which it was commonly applied, for copyright, as the exclusive right of a man to the production of his own genius or intellect, existed in England at that time.

We entertain no doubt that the constitution is broad enough to cover an act authorizing copyright of photographs, so far as they are representatives of original intellectual conceptions of the author.

But it is said that an engraving, a painting, a print, does embody the intellectual conception of its author, in which there is novelty, invention, originality, and therefore comes within the purpose of the constitution in securing its exclusive use or sale to its author, while a photograph is the mere mechanical reproduction of the physical features or outlines of some object, animate or inanimate, and involves no originality of thought or any novelty in the intellectual operation connected with its visible reproduction in shape of a picture. That while the effect of light on the prepared plate may have been a discovery in the production of these pictures, and patents could properly be obtained for the combination of the chemicals, for their application to the paper or other surface, for all the machinery by which the light reflected from the object was thrown on the prepared plate, and for all the improvements in this machinery, and in the materials, the remainder of the process is merely mechanical, with no place for novelty, invention, or originality. It is simply the manual operation, by the use of these instruments and preparations, of transferring to the plate the visible representation of some existing object, the accuracy of this representation being its highest merit. This may be true in regard to the ordinary production of a photograph, and that in such case a copyright is no protection. On the question as thus stated we decide nothing.

In regard, however, to the kindred subject of patents for invention, they cannot, by law, be issued to the inventor until the novelty, the utility, and the actual discovery or invention by the claimant have been established by proof before the commissioner of patents; and when he has secured such a patent, and undertakes to obtain redress for a violation of his right in a court of law, the question of invention, of novelty, of originality is always open to examination. Our copyright system has no such provision for previous examination by a proper tribunal as to the originality of the book, map, or other matter offered for copyright. A deposit of two copies of the article or work with the Librarian of Congress, with the name of the author and its title page, is all that is necessary to secure a copyright. It is therefore much more important that when the supposed author sues for a violation of his copyright, the existence of those facts of originality, of intellectual production, of thought, and conception on the part of the author should be proved than in the case of a patent-right. In the case before us we think this has been done.

The third finding of facts says, in regard to the photograph in question, that it is a "useful, new, harmonious, characteristic, and graceful picture, and that plaintiff made the same entirely from his own original mental conception, to which he gave visible form by posing the said Oscar Wilde in front of the camera, selecting and arranging the costume, draperies, and other various accessories in said photograph, arranging the subject so as to present graceful outlines, arranging and disposing the light and shade, suggesting and evoking the desired expression, and from such disposition, arrangement, or representation, made entirely by plaintiff, he produced the picture in suit." These findings, we think, show this photograph to be an original work of art, the product of plaintiff's intellectual invention, of which plaintiff is the author, and of a class of inventions for which the constitution intended that congress should secure to him the exclusive right to use, publish, and sell.

The judgment of the circuit court [in the plaintiff's favor] is accordingly affirmed.

Notes and Questions

1. *The Problem of Communication Technology.* At the time of the *Oscar Wilde Photo* case, photography was already a well-established communications technology. Yet the same problem of the treatment of new advances in the communications arts under copyright law reasserted itself with the development of sound recordings, motions pictures, satellite, cable and television broadcasts, computer software and, most recently, digital communications over the Internet. Are there any general principles which the courts in the *Oscar Wilde Photo* case and the *Anti-Discrimination* case used that can be applied to determine whether new works based on new technological breakthroughs in communications media should be subject to copyright treatment?

2. *The Definition of Originality.* One of the critical issues in the protection of copyrighted works under U.S. law is whether the work in question contains sufficient "original" expression to qualify. Under U.S. law

copyright protection resides in "original works of authorship fixed in a tangible medium of expression . . ." (17 U.S.C. § 102.)

3. In Germany copyright protection is given to the "personal intellectual creations" of authors of original literary, scientific or artistic work.

4. In France under the 1957 Act, the "intellectual works" (oeuvres de l'esprit) of an author are protected "regardless of their nature, form of expression, merit or destination." (French Intellectual Property Code, Art. L–112–1, Article 1).

5. The People's Republic of China protects "works of literature, art, natural science, social science, engineering technology and the like which are expressed in the following forms: written works, oral works, musical, dramatic, quyi and choreographic works, works of fine art and photographic works, cinematographic, television and videographic works; drawings of engineering designs and product designs, and descriptions thereof; maps, sketches and other graphic works; computer software; [and] other works as provided for in laws and administrative regulations." (Chinese Copyright Law of 1990, Article 3).

6. Canada provides copyright protection "in every original literary, dramatic, musical and artistic work . . ." (Copyright Act, R.S.C. 1985, c C–42, § 5.)

7. Japan provides copyright protection for "works" ("chosakubutsu") which are "creative expressions of thought or sentiment which falls within the literary, scientific, artistic or musical domain." (Chosaku-ken Ho Law No 48, 1970, Art 2, para. 1, item 1 (as reported in *Doing Business in Japan*, Part 16.08 (Matthew Bender & Co., Inc. 1998)).

8. In Great Britain copyright is a "property right" which subsists in "original literary, dramatic, musical or artistic works, sound recordings, films, broadcasts or cable programs, and the typographical arrangement of published editions." (UK Copyright, Designs and Patents Act of 1998, (c 48), Section 1)

9. Under Russian laws, copyright "shall extend to the works of science, literature and the arts that are the result of creative activity, irrespective of the purposes or merits of such works, and the methods of expressing the same." (Law of the Russian Federation on Copyright and Neighboring Rights of 1993, Article 6).

10. Would the Wilde photograph qualify as a protected work under these statutes? What if instead of a photograph that could be hung on the wall, the Wilde photograph was instead digitized so that it could be uploaded onto the Internet. Would the person who created the digitized version have added enough "original expression" to warrant protection under these statutes?

11. *Berne Convention.* The Berne Convention undoubtedly qualifies as one of the most important multinational treaties concerning international copyright standards. Originally enacted in 1886, the Berne Convention established minimum substantive standards for the protection of author's rights. It requires member countries to protect "the rights of authors in their literary and artistic works." Article 2 defines "literary and artistic works" as follows:

The expression "literary and artistic works" shall include every production in the literary, scientific and artistic domain, whatever may be the mode or form of its expression, such as books, pamphlets and other writings; lectures, addresses, sermons and other works of the same nature; dramatic or dramatic-musical works; choreographic works and entertainments in dumb show; musical compositions with or without words; cinematographic works to which are assimilated works expressed by a process analogous to cinematography; works of drawing, painting, architecture, sculpture, engraving and lithography; photographic works to which are assimilated works expressed by a process analogous to photography; works of applied art; illustrations, maps, plans, sketches and three-dimensional works relative to geography, topography, architecture or science.

This definition has been adopted as a part of the Agreement on Trade Related Aspects of Intellectual Property Rights (TRIPS) and applies to all TRIPS member nations, regardless of whether they are signatories of the Berne Convention. (TRIPS, Article 9.)

12. Although the definition of a "literary" or "artistic" work under Berne appears broad, does computer software fall within its scope? Does a computer database composed solely of factual information? Does an anonymous poem written during the Middle Ages and transmitted over the Internet?

THE FUNCTIONAL TERMINAL CASE

AMP INCORPORATED v. UTILUX PROPRIETARY LIMITED

House Of Lords, 1971.
[1972] RPC 103, [1971] FSR 572.

LORD REID:

The respondents manufacture electrical apparatus including terminals which are used to facilitate the assembly of electrical apparatus. Hoover manufacture large numbers of washing machines each of which contains fairly elaborate electrical apparatus. They thought that the use of terminals would help them and they consulted the respondents. The respondents found that none of their existing range was exactly suitable and as Hoovers would need many millions of these small articles they designed a new terminal to meet Hoover's requirements. Then it occurred to them that the design of this new terminal could be registered under the Registered Designs Act |107Œ 1949, so they had it registered in 1960. In 1966 one of their representatives saw exhibited for sale by the appellants on a stand at a technical exhibition a terminal which appeared to be an exact copy of their terminal. So they immediately raised an action against the appellants on the ground of infringement of their registered design. In their defence the appellants pleaded that the respondent's registration was invalid on a number of grounds, and sought rectification of the register by cancellation of the respondents' design.

The registered design consists of five sketches of the terminal from different angles together with the statement "the novelty resides in the shape or configuration of the article as shewn in the representations". If it is desired to make a good electrical connection between two wires without having to solder them, one wire is attached to a plug or male terminal and the other is attached by crimping to one end of this terminal, being held by ears in a conductor channel. At the other end of this terminal is a receptacle so made and shaped that the male terminal is inserted and firmly held. Everything except the insertion of the male terminal is done cheaply and rapidly by automatic or semi-automatic machinery. A large number of different terminals made by different manufacturers were exhibited. No two are alike in appearance but as they all serve the same purpose there is great similarity between them. All this was explored in great detail in the evidence but I do not think it necessary to set out farther facts because in the end the case turns in my view on the proper construction of the definition of "design" in the 1949 Act.

"Design" is defined by section 1(3):

"In this Act the expression 'design' means features of shape, configuration, pattern or ornament applied to an article by any industrial process or means, being features which in the finished article appeal to and are judged solely by the eye, but does not include a method or principle of construction or features of shape or configuration which are dictated solely by the function which the article to be made in that shape or configuration has to perform."

There had been protection of new or original designs against infringement in a succession of statutes for over a century before 1949. The present definition dates in part from 1919 and in part from 1949. I get little assistance from the way in which it has evolved. It remains obscure in several respects. Before considering its terms I would enquire what is the problem and what is the apparent policy of the legislation.

Those who wish to purchase an article for use are often influenced in their choice not only by practical efficiency but by appearance. Common experience shews that not all are influenced in the same way. Some look for artistic merit. Some are attracted by a design which is strange or bizarre. Many simply choose the article which catches their eye. Whatever the reason may be one article with a particular design may sell better than one without it: then it is profitable to use the design. And much thought, time and expense may have been incurred in finding a design which will increase sales.

Parliament has been concerned to see that the originator of a profitable design is not deprived of his reward by others applying it to their goods. But it has not given protection under the 1949 Act to everything which could be called a design. To be protected the design must come within the definition.

The definition includes features of shape, configuration, pattern or ornament. We are not concerned with pattern or ornament. Configuration may have a meaning slightly different from shape: no point is made of that in this case. The first requirement is that the shape is "applied" by an industrial process. "Applied" is an appropriate word for pattern or ornament but is an awkward word with regard to shape. The idea must be that there can be two articles similar in every respect except shape, and that the novel feature of shape which is the design has been added to the article by making it in the new shape instead of in some other shape which is not novel.

Then there come the words "being features which in the finished article appeal to and are judged solely by the eye". This must be intended to be a limitation of the foregoing generality. The eye must be the eye of the customer if I am right in holding that the policy of the Act was to preserve to the owner of the design the commercial value resulting from customers preferring the appearance of articles which have the design to that of those which do not have it. So the design must be one which appeals to the eye of some customers. And the words "judged solely by the eye" must be intended to exclude cases where a customer might choose an article of that shape not because of its appearance but because he thought that the shape made it more useful to him.

In the case of finished articles sold to members of the public for use by them I doubt whether this limitation is of much importance. The onus is on the person who attacks the validity of the registration of a design. So he would have to shew on a balance of probability that an article with the design would have no greater appeal by reason of its appearance to any member of the public than an article which did not have this design. Looking to the great variety of popular tastes this would seem an almost impossible burden to discharge.

No doubt in the great majority of cases which the Act will protect the designer had visual appeal in mind when composing his design. But it could well be that a designer who only thought of practical efficiency in fact has produced a design which does appeal to the eye. He would not be denied protection because that was not his object when he composed the design.

I would allow this appeal.

Lord Morris of Borth-y-Gest:

Mr. Collier very fairly acknowledged that no sort of artistic conception was involved in what they devised. All that they set out to do was to produce "the terminal that would do the job". He agreed that customers who bought electric terminals did not buy "on appearance but on performance and delivery and price". What Hoovers wanted was something "that would do the job for them". The terminals would have to be of the "flag" type, and would have to fit within the space available and would have to have a conductor channel capable of accommodating the three sizes of insulation diameters of the conductor wires.

I turn then to a consideration of section 1 of the Act. By subsection (1) it is provided that a "design" may be registered. It may be registered in respect of an article (or set of articles). An "article" (see section 44) means any article of manufacture and includes any part of an article if that part is made and sold separately.

The question is raised as to the sense in which the features in a finished article are to appeal to and are to be judged solely by the eye. I think that it is clear that the particular feature which is in question or under consideration must be seen when the finished article is seen. But the words of the definition point, in my view, to considerations other than that of merely being visible. The phrases "appeal to" and "judged solely by the eye" denote features which will or may influence choice or selection. They eye concerned will be the eye, not of the court, but of the person who may be deciding whether or not to acquire the finished article possessing the feature in question. This does not mean that the "appeal" or the attraction must be to an aesthetic or artistic sense—though in some cases it may be. The features may be such that they gain the favour of or appeal to some while meeting with the disfavour of others. Beyond being merely visible the feature must have some individual characteristic. It must be calculated to attract the attention of the beholder.

The expression "design" does not include a method or principle of construction or features of shape or configuration which are dictated solely by the function which the article to be made in that shape or configuration has to perform. There is no room for doubt as to the functions that the terminals when made would have to perform. Was their devising governed solely by the consideration that they must perform those functions? On the facts of this case I think it is clear that that was the sole consideration which actuated Mr. Collier. I would not, however, exclude from possible validity for registration a case where someone set out to produce an article that would perform a particular function but where in producing it he added or applied (by any industrial process or means) some feature of shape that was additional to or supplementary to what was functionally needed, with the result that in the finished article there was a feature that appealed to the eye. There might, then, be a feature of shape which was not solely dictated by or governed by the consideration that the article should do what it was required to do. In the present case the terminal was simply devised so that it should "do the job." It was to perform the function that was defined by Hoover's requirements. The terminal is I think to be considered as and looked at as a unit. But if its constituent parts are considered I think that on the evidence each one was solely devised so that it should correctly perform its own particular function. There was nothing extra. There was nothing that could be regarded as any kind of embellishment. First and last and all the time the key-note was functional success. The terminals, unseen in the machines for which they were required (save by those who make or service the machines), had only to pass the test of being able to perform their functions. They would be judged by performance and not by appearance.

It was argued on behalf of AMP that as there could be variations of shape in terminals that would successfully do what was required of them then the "features of shape" would not have been "dictated solely" by the function which the terminals would have to perform. In my view, this contention is not sound. If there are alternative features of shape but if each one is "dictated solely" by the function which is to be performed by the article then each one would be excluded from the expression "design".

There will often be cases where there will be variations in the form or shape of what may be devised for the performance of some function. There may be what could be called trade variations. I take the expression from the judgment of Simonds J. in a case (*Infields Ltd. v. Rosen* (1939) 56 R.P.C. 163) which had relation to a thumb groove in a spring clip: the learned judge said (at page 182):

> "the difference, where you require a grip, between slotting and grooving and dimpling, whatever the word may be, really amounts to no more than an ordinary trade variation, in order to secure the proper functioning of the device with which you are dealing."

In the features of shape of the terminals in the present case there was neither the purpose nor the result of making an appeal to the eye: the features of shape were adopted only because of functional requirements: they were dictated solely by the function which terminals to be made in that shape would have to perform.

I would allow the appeal.

Judgment: Lord Pearson

The first statutory reference to an appeal to the eye and judgment by the eye is to be found in section 19 of the Patents and Designs Act, 1919. This section also contains for the first time express exclusion of a mode or principle of construction and of a mere mechanical device. The full terms of the definition in this section are as follows:

> " 'Design' means only the features of shape, configuration, pattern or ornament applied to any article by any industrial process or means, whether manual, mechanical or chemical, separate or combined, which in the finished article appeal to and are judged solely by the eye; but does not include any more or principle of construction or anything which is in substance a mere mechanical device."

From this point onwards the phrase "which in the finished article appeal to and are judged solely by the eye" has been a statutory phrase to be interpreted is its statutory context and not necessarily having quite the same meaning as in the judgments from which the language was derived. The phrase is naturally to be read as importing some limitation of the expression "features of shape, configuration, pattern or ornament". Not all such features constitute a design. It is not reasonable to suppose that the only limitation is that the features are visible in the finished article. If that had been the intention, it could have been expressed much more simply. The emphasis is on external appearance, but not every external appearance of any article constitutes a design. There must be in some way a special, peculiar, distinctive, significant or striking appearance—something which catches the eye and in this sense appeal to the eye. The phrase was interpreted in this way by Lord Avonside in *G.A. Harvey & Co. (London) Ltd. v. Secure Fittings Ltd.* [1966] R.P.C. 515. Lord Avonside said in the *G.A. Harvey* case (*supra*) at pages 517–8:

> "There is no doubt that the design is to be applied to an article. The judge of the design is the eye and the eye alone and the eye it must appeal. The design to appeal must be noticeable and have some perceptible appearance of an individual character. Where, as in the present instance, the design is for a shape or configuration of the article as a whole, the only effective application of the design rests in making an article of that shape or configuration. In that situation, in order to achieve application of design to an article, the article produced must be such as appeals to the eye as possessing, by reason of its shape or configuration, features which distinguish it from others of its type and class. There can be 'a unit comprising in combination cold and hot water tanks' which is functional and basic in that it comprises only these elements which are essential for its operation for its purpose, an 'article' without 'design'. Where design is claimed as in this case the initial question is whether or not the making of the article in the chosen shape or configuration results in the production of an article which displays to the eye features different from those of the basic or fundamental 'unit', and alteration or embellishment of that 'unit'."

The article in respect of which the design is registered is called a "terminal", but in fact it forms an electric connection between two electric conductors. Theoretically the terminal could be of any size, so long as the registered design was applied to it, and could be made of any metal which is a good conductor of electricity, but as it was in fact devised and produced in very large numbers for incorporation in a particular machine—the Hoover Keymatic washing machine—it is a small piece of electric equipment, made of phosphor bronze, having a maximum length of about three-quarters of an inch, a maximum width of about five-eighths of an inch and a maximum height of about one quarter of an inch. A small article may have a striking appearance, but this one does not. On being merely looked at, it does not make any appeal to the eye. It has no feature of shape or configuration which is special, peculiar, distinctive, significant or striking. There is nothing in its appearance which catches the eye. It is not intended to be looked at: it is to form part of the interior mechanism of the washing machine, and would not normally be seen by anyone, except a maintenance engineer. If it had any eye appeal, that would be wasted, but I do not think it has any. An experienced electrical engineer, if he examined it carefully before it was incorporated in a machine, might be able to envisage it in operation and form some provisional opinion as to its probable efficiency when tested in operation. But he would be judging it by the mind for efficiency, not by the eye for appearance. In my view, the registered design could be held to be invalid on the ground that it fails to comply with the positive statutory requirement mentioned above.

The design has no feature of shape or configuration which appeals to the eye.

I would allow the appeal.

Notes and Questions

1. Compare the court's treatment of originality and artistry in the *Functional Terminal* case with the *Lego Toy* case. Why doesn't the court consider whether the terminals in the *Functional Terminal* case are artistic?

2. What is the dividing line that the court establishes between copyright and design models in the above cases? Should protection extend to protect "useful" elements such as the design of an electric terminal? Under which theory—copyright, design protection or patents?

3. Do you agree with the court's decision that the existence of alternative designs does not make plaintiff's terminal design non-functional? *Compare* this decision *with Sunbeam Products Inc. v. West Bend Co.*, 39 U.S.P.Q. 2d 1545 (S.D.Miss.1996), *aff'd*, 123 F.3d 246, 44 U.S. P.Q. 2d 1161 (5th Cir. 1997) (U.S. court protects shape of mixer in part due to existence of alternative designs).

THE ANODE DRAWINGS CASE
THE DURIRON COMPANY INCORPORATED
v. HUGH JENNINGS & CO. LTD.

Chancery Division, 1982.
[1984] F.S.R. 1.

HARMAN J.

In this matter Mr. Lunzer moves for injunctions to restrain the defendant company from reproducing drawings, with a number given, in any material form and selling or offering by way of trade, etc., any tubular anodes which are substantial reproductions of the plaintiffs tubular anodes or the aforesaid drawings thereof.

The plaintiff company is a substantial American concern who make and claim to have, in broad terms, invented objects called tubular anodes which are used very largely in the oil industry, and also in some other industries for the protection of structures from corrosion by salt in the sea, acids or salt in the ground or indeed any other form of material which may attack a structure made of metal whether it be iron or some other and different form of metal structure.

The defendant company, Hugh Jennings & Company Limited, is an iron founder in a reasonably modest way of business in the north-east of

England. The claim is a claim in copyright. It is claimed by the Duriron Company that they have copyright in certain drawings of what I would have called until now "pipes" . The drawings are of the most jejune and simple character. They are expressly not to scale. They are six in number. They start with a drawing made by someone called Tsocaris. This is dated 5th April 1972. The drawing has, as drawn upon it, a representation which even the lay eye like mine can see is meant to be a pipe. An overall measurement of 84 inches is shown but no other measurement of any sort. The drawing is not to scale.

The drawing consists of firm lines showing the external limits of the object drawn, dotted lines showing the internal limits of them, a line which has a couple of breaks in it which I think is the centre line of the object and in the middle a conventional representation of an object longer in size than the drawing itself would indicate with a twisted cut away showing the internal appearance of what would be a pipe in the form of two extremely pointed ovals. That drawing is the drawing for which copyright is claimed.

The drawing sheet has written on it a series of other matters including a table in the top left hand corner giving sizes from 2 to 5A; an A and a B, which by reference to the drawing can be seen to be references to measurements on different sizes of tube, A being the internal diameter and B being the external diameter; patent numbers; an area in square inches; and, a column for weight on which only one item is completed, pipe 5 which is specified as 110 lbs. Upon the drawing is also written in the top left "material Duriron alloy code D51" and a description, "Anode–NJA-tubular." The drawing as so described is in its design qualities jejune in the extreme, if indeed there is any design quality to be seen in it. The description of the differing sizes of pipe is a description which is obviously of interest but does not appear to be something which is based upon or is integral to the design of the pipe.

[In an affidavit, one witness claimed:] "An anode serves its purpose by being just a lump of metal buried for years under the ground. Its shape is almost immaterial (save, as *e.g.* I have already shown that a tubular shape is better than a solid cylinder)." He explains that a tube has a very much larger surface area than a solid cylinder and consequently has far greater, what I will call unscientifically, communication with the surrounding matter in which it is buried than a solid cylinder could do. The important phrase is "Its shape is almost immaterial".

He goes on to say: "What does matter to the designer or the prospective purchaser of a cathodic protection system is that there should be available to him accurate performance data in relation to the anodes which he proposes to use. Thus, I emphsise that given adequate performance data, it does not matter whether the anodes are tubular, triangular or square in cross-section, or whether they are of any particular size or shape. What does matter ... is that whatever the size or shape, it has been tried and tested to an extent sufficient for there to be available to the designer of the cathodic protection system data to establish the performance of the anodes." He goes on to refer to the United States patents which are referred to on the drawings I have already referred to. He refers to attempts to get an English patent and the abandonment of that patent attempt due to publication in this country of an article by Mr. McKinney which disclosed the invention in the United Kingdom and thereby made the matter incapable of patent protection. For that one may indeed sympathise with the plaintiffs who plainly had invented something of value, worked hard on it and have produced a step which might well, although I have nothing to do with patent decisions in this court, have been a step of novelty and one quite sufficient to warrant patent protection being given. They lost the chance of that valuable right by an inadvertent step and deserve sympathy for their loss.

It is notable that Mr. Dailey at no time says that the plaintiffs have copied the design. He says that they have used and have based themselves upon the plaintiff's work, have used the benefit of the research data which have been known in the industry. None of that has anything to do with the design, in the sense of shape, size or configuration, of these tubular anodes as shown in the drawings. It is also notable, as he says, that the plaintiff's tubular anodes were originally made in about 1971 by engineers using existing centrifugal casting machines and those anodes were made and tested. He does not say that there was any drawing made, any design of the pipe as an anode made, before the original tubular anodes were made and tested. The original tubular anodes were made on what were, and I think it is an inevitable inference from the way that Mr. Dailey puts it, ordinary standard centrifugal casting machines used for the making of pipes, the external dimensions of which would be fixed by the moulds and the internal dimensions by the quantity of material injected, the weight of it, the speed of rotation and such other matters. In no sense does he say that the drawings were made and from those designs the anodes were produced.

As I have observed, the drawings themselves are of the simplest possible quality. None the less, copyright can exist in a very simple drawing and that factor by itself would not disable them from copyright. But, it does not seem to me that these drawings are not to scale, not accurate in their form because, as is pointed out in the evidence, the extremely pointed nature of the internal pipe would produce (what is not in fact the case) an oval internal pipe. That is certainly not so; the pipes are cylindrical internally and externally. The whole of the drawing is not capable of being more than a very rough representation of a pipe, a pipe of varying sizes. It seems to me that given that it was not drawn for the purpose of making the first anode but is produced after the event, and is so inaccurate a representation, the drawing is not an original artistic work as defined by the section. It seems to me that no originality exists at all in the drawing of the pipe which is merely a rough representation not to scale and which could be drawn in any textbook by anybody without any element of originality at all.

Thus I find on this evidence that the drawings are not the originals from which the plaintiff's first tubular anodes were made; and on the design of which, after experimentation to provide data, all subsequent anodes were based. The drawings are simply representations of existing objects. In 1972 Mr. Tsocaris drew the anode put before him. He did not make a design; he reproduced an existing object and he did so with an inaccuracy as to shape and not to scale. That is not in my judgment an original artistic work.

The originality in this matter, which is no doubt substantial, real and important, lies in the nature of the material used, Duriron originally and Durichlor later, and the fact that it is now known in the industry due to the work and endeavour of the plaintiff company that tubes of these dimensions in that material will have certain cathodic protection effects. None of that is dependent upon the design; none of that is to do with the drawing; all of that is appropriate to matters which would go to patent protection, this being an invention, but that protection is unfortunately not available to the plaintiff in this country. It therefore seems to me that this motion never gets off the ground at all because, as I understand it, there is no proper claim to copyright which could be likely to succeed at trial in this case.

I do not base myself on the fact that the design is simple. It has been shown in the Armstrong case that the drawing of a bar could be the subject of protection in copyright. I base it upon the proposition that this drawing is not the origin or the design or the thing from which the making of the tubular anodes originated. They originated from the standard work, standard pipes, a special form of allow and a lengthy experiment to discover what particular proportions of width, internal and external diameter giving different square inch areas of superficial exposure would be of what value in particular circumstances. It seems to me that this is an attempt to use the law of copyright to obtain protection for something which certainly would have warranted protection in a different form had there not been the accident of prior publication. I cannot believe that the law of copyright could or should be brought into this field. Consider the duration of copyright. It could last for the life of the designer and 50 years. Compare that with something like a patent where there is a monopoly for a period of 14 years or maybe by extension 21 years. The art in this matter lies, it seems to me, in the knowledge of the effects of materials having this exposure in protecting structures, not in the design which seems, according to Mr. Dailey's own evidence, to be really wholly immaterial. One could have drawn triangular anodes. One could have drawn rectangular tubular anodes. Any form or shape would do. There is nothing in the design, using that word as being what one would consider a designer sitting down to make something, to adapt it for a particular purpose, would find difficult or worth original work. There seems to me to be no originality in it so far as design, properly so called, so far as the drawing which is the subject of copyright, is itself concerned.

Notes and Questions

1. If Duriron had drawn the anode pipes before their physical construction, would such drawings have been protectable under copyright? Should they be?

2. Can a drawing be too simple to be copyright-protected because it lacks originality or artistic elements?

3. Given the extended nature of copyright protection–a minimum term of the life of the author plus 50 years–should copyright protection be extended to potentially useful or functional designs? To charts of information? Under what circumstances?

4. Would you extend copyright protection to the photograph in the *Oscar Wilde Photo* case? The electrical terminals in the *Functional Terminal* case? The anodes in the *Anode Drawing* case? Why or why not? What goals should copyright law encourage? Artistry? Creativity? Anything else?

5. *Utility Models and Designs.* Industrial designs, also referred to as "utility models" or "utility designs" are the fifth type of intellectual property that may be protected internationally. "Industrial designs" generally include those designs not subject to patent protection, but having some degree of novelty or originality that warrants protection against unauthorized use. The standards for novelty or originality of an industrial design are generally lower than for a patent or copyright. *See generally* TRIPS, Article 25(a) (members to protect "independently created industrial designs that are new or original"). *See also* Christine Fellner, Industrial Design Law (1995), Hector L. MacQueen, Copyright, Competition and Industrial Design (2d ed. 1995); Guy Tritton, Intellectual Property in Europe ch. 5 (1996). In the United States, design protection is generally granted under design patents, copyrights or trade dress. For a short criticism of the usefulness of design protection, *see* Ruth Gana, *Prospects for Developing Countries under the TRIPS Agreement*, 29 Vand. J. Transnat'l L. 735 (1996).

6. If a design is not patentable, (such as in the *Anode Drawings* case), should it still be protected under design model or copyright laws? What requirements would you impose before such protection attached? What goals does such protection achieve?

7. Under Article 6bis of the Berne Convention an author must be granted the non-economic (moral) right to "object to any distortion, mutilation, or other derogatory action ... which would be prejudicial to his honor or reputation." What impact should the level of artistry have on the scope of moral rights in a work? Can a photograph be distorted with less harm to the author's reputation than a painting?

Chapter Eight

PATENTS UNDER INTERNATIONAL LAW

A. WHAT INVENTIONS SHOULD QUALIFY FOR INTERNATIONAL PATENT PROTECTION?
THE CLONED SHEEP PATENT CONTROVERSY

In February 1997, a Scottish scientist Dr. Ian Wilmut claimed to have cloned a living sheep "Dolly" from the cells of an adult sheep. Cloning generally means that cells or genes are duplicated from a single cell, all of which are identical to the original cell. Although scientists had been cloning animal, plant and other organism cells and genes for over 20 years, no one had claimed to be able to clone an adult animal from the cells of another adult animal. Dr. Witmut's discovery has given rise to numerous efforts to duplicate his experiment.

Cloning techniques have already led to the development of break-through medicines, diagnostic tools and vaccines to treat such varied health problems as heart attack, hemophilia, anemia, various cancers, hepatitis and other diseases. Cloning technology has already proven invaluable in understanding early cell growth and is expected to contribute to the diagnosis, treatment and cure of various diseases, including cancer and AIDS. Clearly among the possible uses for Dr. Wilmut's cloning technology is the cloning of a human child using the DNA of an adult donor. For the international scientific and intellectual property communities, the legality of such actions, and the scope of possible protection for the results of such endeavors, are among the most hotly debated topics.

The question of international protection for the results of human DNA cloning presents one of the most cutting edge issue in the arena of international intellectual property protection. Should patent protection be extended to the product of a successful human DNA cloning experiment? If the result of such experimentation should *not* be protected, should the process utilized be entitled to patent protection? Would your answer change if such cloning could be used to eradicate AIDS or Ebola fever? If you object to the protection of cloning of human DNA on moral grounds, should such grounds play a role in establishing international standards? If so, whose morality should apply?

B. THE GOALS OF INTERNATIONAL PROTECTION: ENCOURAGING THE PROGRESS OF SCIENCE OR MANUFACTURE?

THE RASTERIZER CASE
IN RE KURIAPPAN P. ALAPPAT

U.S. Court of Appeals, Federal Circuit, 1994
33 F.3d 1526.

RICH, J.

[Kurian Alappat had developed a method for creating a smooth waveform display in a digital oscilloscope. His invention (referred to as a rasterizer) used a mathematical equation for determining the intensity at which a particular pixel (spot on the screen) is to be illuminated. The Patent Office had rejected the inventor's application because the claimed subject matter as a whole was a mathematical formula which represented nothing more than a "law of nature" which could not be patented under U.S. law.]

The plain and unambiguous meaning of § 101 is that any new and useful process, machine, manufacture, or composition of matter, or any new and useful improvement thereof, may be patented if it meets the requirements for patentability set forth in Title 35, such as those found in §§ 102, 103, and 112. The use of the expansive term "any" in § 101 represents Congress's intent not to place any restrictions on the subject matter for which a patent may be obtained beyond those specifically recited in § 101 and the other parts of Title 35. Indeed, the Supreme Court has acknowledged that Congress intended § 101 to extend to "anything under the sun that is made by man." *Diamond v. Chakrabarty*, 447 U.S. 303, 309, 100 S.Ct. 2204, 2208, 65 L.Ed.2d 144 (1980), quoting S.Rep. No. 1979, 82nd Cong., 2nd Sess., 5 (1952).

Despite the apparent sweep of § 101, the Supreme Court has held that certain categories of subject matter are not entitled to patent protection. In *Diamond v. Diehr*, 450 U.S. 175, 101 S.Ct. 1048, 67 L.Ed.2d 155 (1981), its most recent case addressing § 101, the Supreme Court explained that there are three categories of subject matter for which one may not obtain patent protection, namely "laws of nature, natural phenomena, and abstract ideas." Of relevance to this case, the Supreme Court also has held that certain mathematical subject matter is not, standing alone, entitled to patent protection. *See Diehr*, 450 U.S. 175, 101 S.Ct. 1048. A close analysis of *Diehr* and others reveals that the Supreme Court never intended to create an overly broad, fourth category of subject matter excluded from § 101. Rather, at the core of the Court's analysis in each of these cases lies an attempt by the Court to explain a rather straightforward concept, namely, that certain types of mathematical subject matter, standing alone, represent nothing more than abstract ideas until reduced to some type of practical application, and thus that subject matter is not, in and of itself, entitled to patent protection.

Diehr also demands that the focus in any statutory subject matter analysis be on the claim as a whole. Indeed, the Supreme Court stated in *Diehr*:

[W]hen a claim containing a mathematical formula [mathematical equation, mathematical algorithm, or the like] implements or applies that formula [equation, algorithm, or the like] in a structure or process which, when considered as a whole, is performing a function which the patent laws were designed to protect (e.g., transforming or reducing an article to a different state or thing), then the claim satisfies the requirements of § 101. *Diehr*, 450 U.S. at 192, 101 S.Ct. at 1059–60 (emphasis added)

Given the foregoing, the proper inquiry in dealing with the so called mathematical subject matter exception to § 101 alleged herein is to see whether the claimed subject matter as a whole is a disembodied mathematical concept, whether categorized as a mathematical formula, mathematical equation, mathematical algorithm, or the like, which in essence represents nothing more than a "law of nature," "natural phenomenon," or "abstract idea." If so, Diehr precludes the patenting of that subject matter. That is not the case here.

Although many, or arguably even all, of the means elements recited in claim 15 represent circuitry elements that perform mathematical calculations, which is essentially true of all digital electrical circuits, the claimed invention as a whole is directed to a combination of interrelated elements which combine to form a machine for converting discrete waveform data samples into anti-aliased pixel illumination intensity data to be displayed on a display means. This is not a disembodied mathematical concept which may be characterized as an "abstract idea," but rather a specific machine to produce a useful, concrete, and tangible result.

Under the Board majority's reasoning, a programmed general purpose computer could never be viewed as patentable subject matter under § 101. This reasoning is without basis in the law. The Supreme Court has never held that a programmed computer may never be entitled to patent protection. Indeed, the *Benson* court specifically stated that its decision therein did not preclude "a patent for any program servicing a computer." *Benson*, 409 U.S. at 71, 93 S.Ct. at 257. Consequently, a computer operating pursuant to software may represent patentable subject matter, provided, of course, that the claimed subject matter meets all of the other requirements of Title 35. In any case, a computer, like a rasterizer, is apparatus not mathematics.

For the foregoing reasons, the appealed decision of the Board affirming the examiner's rejection is Reversed.

ARCHER, CHIEF JUDGE, dissenting in part:

Alappat has arranged known circuit elements to accomplish nothing other than the solving of a particular mathematical equation represented in the mind of the reader of his patent application. Losing sight of the forest for the structure of the trees, the majority today holds that any claim reciting a precise arrangement of structure satisfies 35 U.S.C. § 101. As I shall demonstrate, the rationale that leads to this conclusion and the majority's holding that Alappat's rasterizer represents the invention of a machine are illogical, inconsistent with precedent and with sound principles of patent law, and will have untold consequences.

The Patent Clause of the Constitution empowers the Congress to "promote the Progress of . . . useful Arts, by securing for limited Times to . . . Inventors the exclusive right to their . . . Discoveries." U.S. Const. art. I, 8, cl. 8. Congress has implemented this limited grant of power in 35 U.S.C. § 101 by enumerating certain subject matter, the invention or discovery of which may entitle one to a patent: "Whoever invents or discovers any new and useful process, machine, manufacture, or composition of matter, or any new and useful improvement thereof, may obtain a patent therefor, subject to the conditions and requirements of this title." 35 U.S.C. § 101 (1988). The terms used in § 101 have been used for over two hundred years—since the beginnings of American patent law—to define the extent of the subject matter of patentable invention. Coexistent with the usage of these terms has been the rule that a person cannot obtain a patent for the discovery of an abstract idea, principle or force, law of nature, or natural phenomenon, but rather must invent or discover a practical "application" to a useful end.

Patent law rewards persons for inventing technologically useful applications, instead of for philosophizing unapplied research and theory.

Additionally, unapplied research, abstract ideas, and theory continue to be the "basic tools of scientific and technological work," which persons are free to trade in and to build upon in the pursuit of among other things useful inventions.[4] Even after a patent has been awarded for a new, useful, and non-obvious practical application of an idea, others may learn from the underlying ideas, theories, and principles to legitimately "design around" the patentee's useful application.

The requirement of the patent law that an invention or discovery reside in the application of an abstract idea, law of nature, principle, or natural phenomenon is embodied in the language of 35 U.S.C. § 101. A patent can be awarded to one who "invents or discovers" something within the enumerated classes of subject matter—"process," "machine," "manufacture," "composition of matter." These terms may not be read in a strict literal sense entirely divorced from the context of the patent

---

4. Even Sir Isaac Newton, who is credited with among other things the formulation of differential calculus, conceded that he traded in prior ideas, stating, "If I have seen further, it is by standing upon the shoulders of Giants."

law. Rather they must be read as incorporating the longstanding and well-established limitation that the claimed invention or discovery must reside in a practical application.

In addition to the basic principles embodied in the language of § 101, the section has a pragmatic aspect. That subject matter must be new (§ 102) and non-obvious (§ 103) in order to be patentable is of course a separate requirement for patentability, and does not determine whether the applicant's purported invention or discovery is within § 101. Section 101 must be satisfied before any of the other provisions apply, and in this way § 101 lays the predicate for the other provisions of the patent law. When considering that the patent law does not allow patents merely for the discovery of ideas, principles, and laws of nature, ask whether, were it not so, the other provisions of the patent law could be applied at all. If Einstein could have obtained a patent for his discovery that the energy of an object at rest equals its mass times the speed of light squared, how would his discovery be meaningfully judged for nonobviousness, the sine qua non of patentable invention?[5] When is the abstract idea "reduced to practice" as opposed to being "conceived"? What conduct amounts to the "infringement" of another's idea?

Consider for example the discovery or creation of music, a new song. Music of course is not patentable subject matter; a composer cannot obtain exclusive patent rights for the original creation of a musical composition. But now suppose the new melody is recorded on a compact disc. In such case, the particular musical composition will define an arrangement of minute pits in the surface of the compact disc material, and therefore will define its specific structure. Alternatively suppose the music is recorded on the rolls of a player piano or a music box.

Through the expedient of putting his music on known structure, can a composer now claim as his invention the structure of a compact disc or player piano roll containing the melody he discovered and obtain a patent therefor? The answer must be no. The composer admittedly has invented or discovered nothing but music. The discovery of music does not become patentable subject matter simply because there is an arbitrary claim to some structure.

And if a claim to a compact disc or piano roll containing a newly discovered song were regarded as a "manufacture" and within § 101 simply because of the specific physical structure of the compact disc, the "practical effect" would be the granting of a patent for a discovery in music. Where the music is new, the precise structure of the disc or roll would be novel under § 102. Because the patent law cannot examine music for "nonobviousness," the Patent and Trademark Office could not make a showing of obviousness under § 103. The result would well be the award of a patent for the discovery of music. The majority's simplistic approach of looking only to whether the claim reads on structure and

---

5. *See Graham*, 383 U.S. at 9, 86 S.Ct. at 689, 148 U.S.PQ at 464 (nonobviousness "draw[s] a line between the things which are worth to the public the embarrassment of an exclusive patent, and those which are not") (quoting Thomas Jefferson).

ignoring the claimed invention or discovery for which a patent is sought will result in the awarding of patents for discoveries well beyond the scope of the patent law.

Patent cases involving the distinction between idea or principle may involve subtle distinctions. Section 101 embodies the very soul of the intangible nature of invention. Without particular claimed subject matter in mind, it is impossible to generalize with bright line rules the dividing line between what is in substance the invention or discovery of a useful application within § 101 versus merely the discovery of an abstract idea or law of nature or principle outside § 101. Each case presenting a question under § 101 must be decided individually based upon the particular subject matter at issue. There are however answers in every § 101 case. But they are found by applying precedent and principles of patent law to the particular claimed subject matter at issue.

Discoveries and inventions in the field of digital electronics are analyzed according to the aforementioned principles as any other subject matter. Digital electronics, including so-called general purpose digital computers, often call into play § 101 because digital electronic devices "operate[ ] on data expressed in digits, solving a problem by doing arithmetic as a person would do it by head and hand." *Gottschalk v. Benson*, 409 U.S. 63 (1972). Like the discovery of a law of nature, abstract idea, or principle, the discovery of mathematic functions, relationships, operations, or algorithms does not entitle a person to a patent therefor. It does not matter how "original," "inventive," or "useful" the mathematics might be in the ordinary sense of those words.

Every case involving a § 101 issue must begin with this question: What, if anything, is it that the applicant for a patent "invented or discovered"? To resolve this inquiry, the patent or patent application must be reviewed and the subject matter claimed as the invention or discovery "must be considered as a whole."

In considering claimed subject matter for eligibility under § 101, it must be determined whether a scientific principle, law of nature, idea, or mental process, which may be represented by a mathematical algorithm, is included in the subject matter claimed as the invention or discovery. When the claimed invention or discovery includes a mathematical formula (or scientific principle or phenomenon of nature), an inquiry must be made into whether the claim is seeking patent protection for that formula in the abstract, or whether the claim containing a mathematical formula implements or applies that formula in a structure or process which, when considered as a whole, is performing a function which the patent laws were designed to protect,

Thus the dispositive issue is not whether the claim recites on its face something more physical than just abstract mathematics. The dispositive issue is whether the invention or discovery for which an award of patent is sought is more than just a discovery in abstract mathematics. Where the invention or discovery is only of mathematics, the invention or discovery is not the "kind" of discovery the patent law was designed to protect and even the most narrowly drawn claim must fail. To come within the purview of § 101 and the patent law, a mathematical formula or operation must be applied in an invention of a type set forth in 35 U.S.C. § 101.

The Supreme Court has held that a claimed invention may represent merely the discovery of a law of nature and be outside the patent law, even though the claim entirely recites a specific and complete structure. See *Funk Bros. Seed Co.*, 333 U.S. at 130 (claim to species of bacteria represented discovery of law of nature and was outside § 101). The Supreme Court has also held that a claimed process may be non-statutory even if it implements a principle in a "specific fashion." *Flook*, 437 U.S. at 593. And the Supreme Court has held that a claimed invention may represent the discovery of mathematics alone and be outside § 101 even though the claim recites specific structural limitations. *E.g., Benson*, 409 U.S. at 64.

Getting back to the music analogy, Alappat is like a composer who claims his song on a compact disc, and then argues that the compact disc is equivalent to a player piano or a music box with the song on a roll or even sheet music because they all represent the same song. The composer is thus clearly asking for (and getting from the majority) a patent for the discovery of a song and a patent covering every physical manifestation of the song.

In any event, even if a programmed general purpose computer is "equivalent" to the rasterizer, it cannot be deemed to be within § 101 by simply reasoning as does the majority that it is a "new machine." Alappat posits that a "programmed digital computer becomes a special purpose digital computer to perform the function specified by the software. The special purpose computer can be implemented likewise by digital components, or even by analog components." The majority casually agrees that a "general purpose computer in effect becomes a special purpose computer once it is programmed to perform particular functions from program software." One cannot, however, just call a programmed computer a "new machine" without going through the § 101 analysis required by the trilogy of Supreme Court decisions. Whether or not subject matter is a "new machine" within § 101 is precisely the same question as whether or not the subject matter satisfies the § 101 analysis I have described.

A known circuit containing a light bulb, battery, and switch is not a new machine when the switch is opened and closed to recite a new story in Morse code, because the invention or discovery is merely a new story, which is nonstatutory subject matter. An old stereo playing a new song on a compact disc is not a new machine because the invention or discovery is merely a new song, which is nonstatutory subject matter. The perforated rolls of a player piano are parts of a machine which, when duly applied and properly operated in connection with the mechanism to which they are adapted, produce musical tones in harmonious combination. Yet a player piano playing Chopin's scales does not become a "new machine" when it spins a roll to play Brahms' lullaby. The distinction between the piano before and after different rolls are inserted resides not in the piano's changing quality as a "machine" but only in the changing melodies being played by the one machine. The only invention by the creator of a roll that is new because of its music is the new music. Because the patent law does not examine musical compositions to determine their relation to those that have gone before, the distinction between new and old music can never qualify for patent protection.[6]

It is not the computer—the machine qua computer—that performs the mathematic function, but, rather, the mathematic function is attained only through use of the general-purpose computer. The general-purpose digital computer is itself a total and self-complete machine entity. Versatility in electronic data processing is its endowment, its reason for being, its stock in trade.

A programmed general purpose digital computer alleged to be patentable subject matter because of the program presents an independent § 101 inquiry that is not resolved simply by calling the structure a "new machine."

Finally, a claim formally to a general purpose computer running a certain program cannot be deemed to satisfy § 101 simply because the computer is a physical, tangible device. It is illogical to say that although a claim to a newly discovered mathematical operation to be performed by a computer is merely a nonstatutory discovery of mathematics, a claim to any computer performing that same mathematics is a statutory invention or discovery. Our precedent has rejected reasoning that way.

The majority's holding is dangerous in the following way. First, it reasons that one can obtain a patent for a discovery in mathematics as long as some structure is formally recited on the face of the claim. Under this aspect of the holding, many of the requirements for patentability other than "newness," such as nonobviousness, make no sense and cannot be meaningfully applied. Thus, mathematical patents will be easier to obtain than other patents. Moreover, the patent law will now engage in the charade wherein claims directed to a particular method of calculating numbers (for use in a computer) are unpatentable, but claims directed to a computer (performing a particular method of calculating numbers) are patentable.

Second, the majority accepts the argument that all digital electronic circuitry is statutory subject matter when it performs a mathematical operation, and it is all equivalent when the particular mathematical operation is the same. Under this aspect, the mathematical patents will create an enormous scope of technological exclusivity. The lack of

6. Of course, a player piano itself could be a new machine, for example in relation to a music box, and, likewise, a player piano capable because of design of improved piano-playing might also be a new machine. *E.g., Aeolian Co. v. Schubert Piano Co.*, 261 F. 178 (2d Cir.1919). In such cases, the invention or discovery is the quality of the structure of the piano—its mode of operation—and not the particular piece of music being played.

meaningful examination and the breadth of exclusive rights conferred by patents for discoveries of bare mathematical operations are repugnant to Congress's careful statutory scheme for the promotion of the useful arts.

As the player piano playing new music is not the stuff of patent law, neither is the mathematics that is Alappat's "rasterizer." Alappat's claimed discovery is outside 35 U.S.C. § 101, and for this reason I would affirm the board's rejection. I dissent from the majority's decision on the merits to the contrary.

THE PATENTED BACTERIA CASE
DIAMOND v. CHAKRABARTY

United States Supreme Court, 1980.
447 U.S. 303, 100 S.Ct. 2204.

MR. CHIEF JUSTICE BURGER delivered the opinion of the Court.

We granted certiorari to determine whether a live, human-made micro-organism is patentable subject matter under 35 U.S.C. § 101.

In 1972, respondent Chakrabarty, a microbiologist, filed a patent application, assigned to the General Electric Co. The application asserted 36 claims related to Chakrabarty's invention of "a bacterium from the genus Pseudomonas containing therein at least two stable energy-generating plasmids, each of said plasmids providing a separate hydrocarbon degradative pathway." This human-made, genetically engineered bacterium is capable of breaking down multiple components of crude oil. Because of this property, which is possessed by no naturally occurring bacteria, Chakrabarty's invention is believed to have significant value for the treatment of oil spills.

Chakrabarty's patent claims were of three types: first, process claims for the method of producing the bacteria; second, claims for an inoculum comprised of a carrier material floating on water, such as straw, and the new bacteria; and third, claims to the bacteria themselves. The patent examiner allowed the claims falling into the first two categories, but rejected claims for the bacteria. His decision rested on two grounds: (1) that micro-organisms are "products of nature," and (2) that as living things they are not patentable subject matter under 35 U.S.C. § 101.

The relevant legislative history ... supports a broad construction. The Patent Act of 1793, authored by Thomas Jefferson, defined statutory subject matter as "any new and useful art, machine, manufacture, or composition of matter, or any new or useful improvement [thereof]." Act of Feb. 21, 1793, § 1, 1 Stat. 319. The Act embodied Jefferson's philosophy that "ingenuity should receive a liberal encouragement." 5 Writings of Thomas Jefferson 75–76 (Washington ed. 1871). *See Graham v. John Deere Co.*, 383 U.S. 1, 7–10, 86 S.Ct. 684, 688–690, 15 L.Ed.2d 545 (1966). Subsequent patent statutes in 1836, 1870, and 1874 employed this same broad language. In 1952, when the patent laws were recodified, Congress replaced the word "art" with "process," but otherwise left Jefferson's language intact. The Committee Reports accompanying the 1952 Act inform us that Congress intended statutory subject matter to "include anything under the sun that is made by man." S.Rep.No.1979, 82d Cong., 2d Sess., 5 (1952); H.R.Rep.No.1923, 82d Cong., 2d Sess., 6 (1952).[7]

This is not to suggest that § 101 has no limits or that it embraces every discovery. The laws of nature, physical phenomena, and abstract ideas have been held not patentable. *See Parker v. Flook*, 437 U.S. 584, 98 S.Ct. 2522, 57 L.Ed.2d 451 (1978); *Gottschalk v. Benson*, 409 U.S. 63, 67, 93 S.Ct. 253, 255, 34 L.Ed.2d 273 (1972); *Funk Brothers Seed Co. v. Kalo Inoculant Co.*, 333 U.S. 127, 130, 68 S.Ct. 440, 441, 92 L.Ed. 588 (1948). Thus, a new mineral discovered in the earth or a new plant found in the wild is not patentable subject matter. Likewise, Einstein could not patent his celebrated law that $E=mc^2$; nor could Newton have patented the law of gravity. Such discoveries are "manifestations of . . . nature, free to all men and reserved exclusively to none." *Funk, supra*, 333 U.S., at 130, 68 S.Ct., at 441.

Judged in this light, respondent's micro-organism plainly qualifies as patentable subject matter. His claim is not to a hitherto unknown natural phenomenon, but to a nonnaturally occurring manufacture or composition of mattera product of human ingenuity "having a distinctive name, character [and] use." The point is underscored dramatically by comparison of the invention here with that in Funk. There, the patentee had discovered that there existed in nature certain species of root-nodule bacteria which did not exert a mutually inhibitive effect on each other. He used that discovery to produce a mixed culture capable of inoculating the seeds of leguminous plants. Concluding that the patentee had discovered "only some of the handiwork of nature," the Court ruled the product nonpatentable:

> "Each of the species of root-nodule bacteria contained in the package infects the same group of leguminous plants which it always infected. No species acquires a different use. The combination of species produces no new bacteria, no change in the six species of bacteria, and no enlargement of the range of their utility. Each species has the same effect it always had. The bacteria perform in their natural way. Their use in combination does not improve in any way their natural functioning. They serve the ends nature originally provided and act quite independently of any effort of the patentee." 333 U.S., at 131, 68 S.Ct., at 442.

Here, by contrast, the patentee has produced a new bacterium with markedly different characteristics from any found in nature and one having the potential for significant utility. His discovery is not nature's

---

7. This same language was employed by P. J. Federico, a principal draftsman of the 1952 recodification, in his testimony regarding that legislation: "[U]nder section 101 a person may have invented a machine or a manufacture, which may include anything under the sun that is made by man." Hearings on H.R. 3760 before Subcommittee No. 3 of the House Committee on the Judiciary, 82d Cong., 1st Sess., 37 (1951).

handiwork, but his own; accordingly it is patentable subject matter under § 101.

The petitioner's second argument is that micro-organisms cannot qualify as patentable subject matter until Congress expressly authorizes such protection. His position rests on the fact that genetic technology was unforeseen when Congress enacted § 101. From this it is argued that resolution of the patentability of inventions such as respondent's should be left to Congress. The legislative process, the petitioner argues, is best equipped to weigh the competing economic, social, and scientific considerations involved, and to determine whether living organisms produced by genetic engineering should receive patent protection. In support of this position, the petitioner relies on our recent holding in *Parker v. Flook*, 437 U.S. 584, 98 S.Ct. 2522, 57 L.Ed.2d 451 (1978), and the statement that the judiciary "must proceed cautiously when . . . asked to extend patent rights into areas wholly unforeseen by Congress." *Id.*, at 596, 98 S.Ct. at 2529.

It is, of course, correct that Congress, not the courts, must define the limits of patentability; but it is equally true that once Congress has spoken it is "the province and duty of the judicial department to say what the law is." *Marbury v. Madison*, 1 Cranch 137, 177, 2 L.Ed. 60 (1803). Congress has performed its constitutional role in defining patentable subject matter in § 101; we perform ours in construing the language Congress has employed. In so doing, our obligation is to take statutes as we find them, guided, if ambiguity appears, by the legislative history and statutory purpose. Here, we perceive no ambiguity. The subject-matter provisions of the patent law have been cast in broad terms to fulfill the constitutional and statutory goal of promoting "the Progress of Science and the useful Arts" with all that means for the social and economic benefits envisioned by Jefferson. Broad general language is not necessarily ambiguous when congressional objectives require broad terms.

Nothing in *Flook* is to the contrary. That case applied our prior precedents to determine that a "claim for an improved method of calculation, even when tied to a specific end use, is unpatentable subject matter under § 101." 437 U.S., at 595, n. 18, 98 S.Ct., at 2528, n. 18. The Court carefully scrutinized the claim at issue to determine whether it was precluded from patent protection under "the principles underlying the prohibition against patents for 'ideas' or phenomena of nature." Id., at 593, 98 S.Ct. at 2527. We have done that here. *Flook* did not announce a new principle that inventions in areas not contemplated by Congress when the patent laws were enacted are unpatentable per se.

To read that concept into *Flook* would frustrate the purposes of the patent law. This Court frequently has observed that a statute is not to be confined to the "particular application[s] . . . contemplated by the legislators." *Barr v. United States*, 324 U.S. 83, 90, 65 S.Ct. 522, 525, 89 L.Ed. 765 (1945). This is especially true in the field of patent law. A rule that unanticipated inventions are without protection would conflict with the core concept of the patent law that anticipation undermines patentability. Mr. Justice Douglas reminded that the inventions most benefiting mankind are those that "push back the frontiers of chemistry, physics, and the like." *Great A. & P. Tea Co. v. Supermarket Corp.*, 340 U.S. 147, 154, 71 S.Ct. 127, 131, 95 L.Ed. 162 (1950) (concurring opinion). Congress employed broad general language in drafting § 101 precisely because such inventions are often unforeseeable.[8]

To buttress his argument, the petitioner, with the support of amicus, points to grave risks that may be generated by research endeavors such as respondent's. The briefs present a gruesome parade of horribles. Scientists, among them Nobel laureates, are quoted suggesting that genetic research may pose a serious threat to the human race, or, at the very least, that the dangers are far too substantial to permit such research to proceed apace at this time. We are told that genetic research and related technological developments may spread pollution and disease, that it may result in a loss of genetic diversity, and that its practice may tend to depreciate the value of human life. These arguments are forcefully, even passionately, presented; they remind us that, at times, human ingenuity seems unable to control fully the forces it creates—that with Hamlet, it is sometimes better "to bear those ills we have than fly to others that we know not of."

It is argued that this Court should weigh these potential hazards in considering whether respondent's invention is patentable subject matter under § 101. We disagree. The grant or denial of patents on microorganisms is not likely to put an end to genetic research or to its attendant risks. The large amount of research that has already occurred when no researcher had sure knowledge that patent protection would be available suggests that legislative or judicial fiat as to patentability will not deter the scientific mind from probing into the unknown any more than Canute could command the tides. Whether respondent's claims are patentable may determine whether research efforts are accelerated by the hope of reward or slowed by want of incentives, but that is all.

What is more important is that we are without competence to entertain these arguments—either to brush them aside as fantasies generated by fear of the unknown, or to act on them. The choice we are urged to make is a matter of high policy for resolution within the legislative process after the kind of investigation, examination, and study that legislative bodies can provide and courts cannot. That process involves the balancing of competing values and interests, which in our democratic system is the business of elected representatives. Whatever their validity, the contentions now pressed on us should be addressed to

---

8. Even an abbreviated list of patented inventions underscores the point: telegraph (Morse, No. 1,647); telephone (Bell, No. 174,465); electric lamp (Edison, No. 223,-898); airplane (the Wrights, No. 821,393); transistor (Bardeen & Brattain, No. 2,524,-035); neutronic reactor (Fermi & Szilard, No. 2,708,656); laser (Schawlow & Townes, No. 2,929,922). See generally Revolutionary Ideas, Patents & Progress in America, United States Patent and Trademark Office (1976).

the political branches of the Government, the Congress and the Executive, and not to the courts. [9]

We have emphasized in the recent past that "[o]ur individual appraisal of the wisdom or unwisdom of a particular [legislative] course . . . is to be put aside in the process of interpreting a statute." *TVA v. Hill*, 437 U.S., at 194, 98 S.Ct., at 2302. Our task, rather, is the narrow one of determining what Congress meant by the words it used in the statute; once that is done our powers are exhausted. Congress is free to amend § 101 so as to exclude from patent protection organisms produced by genetic engineering. *Cf.* 42 U.S.C. § 2181(a), (exempting from patent protection inventions "useful solely in the utilization of special nuclear material or atomic energy in an atomic weapon."). Or it may chose to craft a statute specifically designed for such living things. But, until Congress takes such action, this Court must construe the language of § 101 as it is. The language of that section fairly embraces respondent's invention.

Accordingly, the judgment of the Court of Customs and Patent Appeals is affirmed.

MR. JUSTICE BRENNAN, with whom MR. JUSTICE WHITE, MR. JUSTICE MARSHALL, and MR. JUSTICE POWELL join, dissenting.

I agree with the Court that the question before us is a narrow one. Neither the future of scientific research, nor even, the ability of respondent Chakrabarty to reap some monopoly profits from his pioneering work, is at stake. Patents on the processes by which he has produced and employed the new living organism are not contested. The only question we need decide is whether Congress, exercising its authority under Art. I, § 8, of the Constitution, intended that he be able to secure a monopoly on the living organism itself, no matter how produced or how used. Because I believe the Court has misread the applicable legislation, I dissent.

The patent laws attempt to reconcile this Nation's deep-seated antipathy to monopolies with the need to encourage progress. Given the complexity and legislative nature of this delicate task, we must be careful to extend patent protection no further than Congress has provided. In particular, were there an absence of legislative direction, the courts should leave to Congress the decisions whether and how far to extend the patent privilege into areas where the common understanding has been that patents are not available.

In this case, however, we do not confront a complete legislative vacuum. The sweeping language of the Patent Act of 1793, as re-enacted

---

9. We are not to be understood as suggesting that the political branches have been laggard in the consideration of the problems related to genetic research and technology. They have already taken action. In 1976, for example, the National Institutes of Health released guidelines for NIH-sponsored genetic research which established conditions under which such research could be performed. 41 Fed.Reg. 27902. In 1978 those guidelines were revised and relaxed. 43 Fed.Reg. 60080, 60108, 60134. And Committees of the Congress have held extensive hearings on these matters.

in 1952, is not the last pronouncement Congress has made in this area. In 1930 Congress enacted the Plant Patent Act affording patent protection to developers of certain asexually reproduced plants. In 1970 Congress enacted the Plant Variety Protection Act to extend protection to certain new plant varieties capable of sexual reproduction. Thus, we are not dealing—as the Court would have it—with the routine problem of "unanticipated inventions." Ante, at 2211. In these two Acts Congress has addressed the general problem of patenting animate inventions and has chosen carefully limited language granting protection to some kinds of discoveries, but specifically excluding others. These Acts strongly evidence a congressional limitation that excludes bacteria from patentability.[10]

First, the Acts evidence Congress' understanding, at least since 1930, that § 101 does not include living organisms. If newly developed living organisms not naturally occurring had been patentable under § 101, the plants included in the scope of the 1930 and 1970 Acts could have been patented without new legislation. Those plants, like the bacteria involved in this case, were new varieties not naturally occurring. Although the Court rejects this line of argument, it does not explain why the Acts were necessary unless to correct a pre-existing situation. I cannot share the Court's implicit assumption that Congress was engaged in either idle exercises or mere correction of the public record when it enacted the 1930 and 1970 Acts. And Congress certainly thought it was doing something significant. The Committee Reports contain expansive prose about the previously unavailable benefits to be derived from extending patent protection to plants. Because Congress thought it had to legislate in order to make agricultural "human-made inventions" patentable and because the legislation Congress enacted is limited, it follows that Congress never meant to make items outside the scope of the legislation patentable.

Second, the 1970 Act clearly indicates that Congress has included bacteria within the focus of its legislative concern, but not within the scope of patent protection. Congress specifically excluded bacteria from the coverage of the 1970 Act. 7 U.S.C. § 2402(a). The Court's attempts to supply explanations for this explicit exclusion ring hollow. It is true that there is no mention in the legislative history of the exclusion, but that does not give us license to invent reasons. The fact is that Congress, assuming that animate objects as to which it had not specifically legislated could not be patented, excluded bacteria from the set of patentable organisms.

---

10. But even if I agreed with the Court that the 1930 and 1970 Acts were not dispositive, I would dissent. The caveat of *Parker v. Flook*, 437 U.S. 584, 596, 98 S.Ct. 2522, 2529, 57 L.Ed.2d 451 (1978), an admonition to "proceed cautiously when we are asked to extend patent rights into areas wholly unforeseen by Congress," therefore becomes pertinent. I should think the necessity for caution is that much greater when we are asked to extend patent rights into areas Congress has foreseen and considered but has not resolved.

The Court protests that its holding today is dictated by the broad language of § 101, which cannot "be confined to the 'particular application [s] ... contemplated by the legislators.'" Ante, at 2211, quoting *Barr v. United States*, 324 U.S. 83, 90, 65 S.Ct. 522, 525, 89 L.Ed. 765 (1945). But as I have shown, the Court's decision does not follow the unavoidable implications of the statute. Rather, it extends the patent system to cover living material even though Congress plainly has legislated in the belief that § 101 does not encompass living organisms. It is the role of Congress, not this Court, to broaden or narrow the reach of the patent laws. This is especially true where, as here, the composition sought to be patented uniquely implicates matters of public concern.

THE HARVARD MOUSE CASE

IN RE PRESIDENT AND FELLOWS OF HARVARD COLLEGE, EXAMINING DIVISION OF THE EUROPEAN PATENT OFFICE

European Patent Office 1992.
1992 Official Journal EPO 588.

[In April 1988, 2 inventors obtained a U.S. Patent for a new breed of genetically altered mice in which half of the females develop cancer. The mice were potentially useful in cancer research. The inventors also sought a European Patent for their invention. In eventually deciding to grant the application, the European Patent Office attached the following comments:]

The development of new technologies is normally afflicted with new risks; this is an experience mankind has made many times in the past. The experience has also shown that these risks should not generally lead to a negative attitude vis-à-vis new technologies but rather to a careful weighing up of the risks on the one hand and the positive aspects on the other and that the result of this consideration should be the determining factor in whether a new technology should be used or not. If higher life forms are involved in the new technology it is not only the risk which must be considered but also the possible harm which is done to such higher life forms. This leads one to the question of morality. Inventions which are made in connection with new technology and which are to be patented under the EPC have to satisfy the requirements of Article 53(a) EPC. This means that for each individual invention the question of morality has to be examined and possible detrimental effects and risks have to be weighed and balanced against the merits and advantages aimed at. From the previous items it follows that biotechnological inventions and particularly inventions relating to genetic engineering are not in general excluded from patent protection.

(4) In the case at hand three different interests are involved and require balancing: there is a basic interest of mankind to remedy widespread and dangerous diseases, on the other hand the environment has to be protected against the uncontrolled dissemination of unwanted

genes and, moreover, cruelty to animals has to be avoided. The latter two aspects may well justify regarding an invention as immoral and therefore unacceptable unless the advantages, i.e. the benefit to mankind, outweigh the negative aspects. The following considerations particularly apply:

(i) The present invention's usefulness to mankind cannot be denied. Cancer is one of the most frequent causes of death in many countries of the world and also causes severe suffering. Any contribution to the development of new and improved human anti-cancer treatments is therefore a benefit to mankind and must be regarded as valuable and highly welcome by everybody. Legislation in Contracting States allows animal testing under certain restrictions and subject to administrative approval.

(ii) The Applicant has pointed out that the use of the animals according to the invention gives rise to a smaller number of animals being required when compared to the number of animals needed in corresponding conventional testing. Accordingly, the present invention contributes to a reduction of the overall extent of animal suffering.

(iii) Another question to be considered in this connection is whether there exist alternatives to animal testing in the given context which are as reliable as the animal tests and which are therefore accepted by health authorities. In this respect it is noteworthy to take into account what the scientific community thinks about animal testing procedures in cancer research and this is well reflected in an overview article by A. Berns in "Current Biology," Volume 1, Number 1/1991, p. 28, who concludes that onco-mice are a powerful tool with which co-operating genes in tumorigenesis can be identified. Thus it is clear that in cancer research animal test models are at present considered indispensable.

(iv) In respect of "possible risks to the environment" the Division has considered the purpose of the present invention and the risk which may be associated by practicing the invention in the purpose-limited way. Obviously, the purpose of the present invention is to provide animal test models which are to be used exclusively in the laboratory under controlled conditions by qualified staff. No release is intended into the general environment. Therefore the risk of an uncontrolled release is practically limited to intentional misuse or blatant ignorance on the part of the laboratory personnel carrying out the tests. There mere fact that such uncontrollable acts are conceivable cannot be a major determinant for deciding whether a patent should be granted or not.

Exclusion from patentability cannot be justified merely because a technology is dangerous. There are many examples of inventions the patentability of which has never been questioned which cannot be used without severe security measures. For example work with certain pathogens is allowed under very limited conditions only and release of the material into the environment must be excluded by appropriate measures: patentable inventions may nevertheless arise from such work.

(v) In the overall balance the Examining Division concludes that the present invention cannot be considered immoral or contrary to public order. The provision of a type of test animal useful in cancer research and giving rise to a reduction in the amount of testing on animals together with a low risk connected with the handling of the animals by qualified staff can generally be regarded as beneficial to mankind. A patent should therefore not be denied for the present invention on the grounds of Article 53(a) EPC.

Notes and Questions

1. *Technology and International Protection.* The growth of technology presents constant problems in developing readily predictable protection standards for the products of intellectual labor. At the domestic level is the problem of who should determine whether new technology is covered by existing protection schemes—the courts, by applying existing standards, or should any such protection await legislative action. At the international level, the problem arises how to develop international standards to protect new technologies. Should international treaties be read broadly to include within their coverage technology that was never anticipated at the time the treaty was established, or should such new advances be covered only by new treaties? *See, e.g.,* Shira Perlmutter, *Future Directions in International Copyright,* 16 Cardozo Arts & Ert. LJ 369 (1998); Michael L. Doane, *TRIPS and International Intellectual Property Protection in an Age of Advancing Technology,* 9 Am U.J. Int'l L. & Pol'y 465 (1994); Niva Elkin–Koren, *Cyberlaw and Social Change: A Democratic Approach to Copyright Law in Cyberspace,* 14 Cardozo Arts & Ert. L.J. 369 (1998); Pamela Samuelson, et al, *A Manifesto Concerning the Legal Protection of Computer Programs,* 94 Colum. L. Rev. 2308 (1994). ITAA Discussion Paper: "Intellectual Property Protection in Cyberspace: Towards a New Consensus" 1996 WL 710185, 12–12–96 WLN 13241.

2. Which opinion in the *Patent Bacteria* case do you agree with—the majority or the dissent? Why? What if the bacteria in the *Patent Bacteria* case were the best method for cleaning up oil spills? Should one company be given a monopoly over its use? Should it be allowed to obtain whatever level of compensation it can obtain based on solely on market demand?

3. In the *Patent Bacteria* case the issue of patent protection for the process of creating the bacteria was not at issue. Should a different rule apply to patenting the processes that create bacteria, as opposed to patenting the bacteria itself?

4. What moral considerations are raised by the patenting of bacteria and transgenic mice? Should courts consider such issues in deciding patentability?

5. Do the *Patent Bacteria* and *Rasterizer* cases provide guidance for determining what the position of the U.S. courts would be if your client were to seek protection for the results of human DNA cloning? What arguments against such protection could you anticipate based on these two cases? How would you respond to the morality concerns of the *Harvard Mouse* case?

6. What should be the goals of patent protection according to these decisions? Are such goals furthered by the extension of patent protection to

the products of human cloning? Are they furthered by extending protection to the *process* of cloning human DNA?

7. *International Protection For Genetically Engineered Organisms.* The *Patented Bacteria* case was only the first in a long line of U.S. cases that have gradually extended protection for "non-naturally occurring non-human multicellular organisms" to include a variety of animals. The first U.S. animal patent was issued in 1988 and covered the genetically altered mouse to be used for cancer research, which was the subject of the *Harvard Mouse* case. (U.S. Patent No. 4,736,866.) Such protection, however, has been criticized. *See, e.g.,* Thomas Moga, *Transgenic Animals as Intellectual Property (or the Patented Mouse that Roared),* 76 J. Pat Off. Soc. 511(1994); *Worms, Mice, Cows & Pigs: The Importance of Animal Patents in Developing Countries,* Elisabeth T. Jozwiak, 14 Nw.J. Int'l L. & Bus. 620 (1994). The issue of patent protection for genetically engineered organisms remains hotly debated in Europe, as well. *See, e.g.,* Richard Ford, *The Morality of Biotech Patents: Differing Legal Obligations in Europe?,* 19 EUR. INTELL PROP REV 315 (1997); Cynthia M. Mo, *Building a Better Mousetrap: Patenting Biotechnology in The Europeon Community,* 3 Duke J Comp & Int'l L.J. 173 (1992); Ann Lawton, *Regulating Genetic Destiny: A Comparative Study of Legal Constraints in Europe and the United States;* 11 Emory L. Rev. 365 (1997); Carrie F. Walter, *Beyond the Harvard Mouse: Current Patent Practice and the Necessity of Clear Guidelines in Biotechnology Patent Law,* 73 Ind. L. J. 1025 (1998).

8. *Patent Protection for Software.* Should patent protection be extended to computer software internationally? The European Patent Convention in Article 52(2) explicitly places "programs for computers," "mathematical methods" and "presentations of information" outside the scope of patent protection. But despite this apparent prohibition the European Patent Office has granted patents to a wide variety of computer-related inventions. *See, e.g,* Computer–Related Invention/VICOM, 1987 OJ EPO 14 (1986). Japan has also granted patent rights to computer related inventions. *See, e.g., Protection of Computer Software,* Doing Business in Japan Part 6.5.10 (Matthew Bender & Co. 1998); Dennis S. Karyata, *Copyright Protection of Computer Software in the United States and Japan,* EUR. Intell. Prop. Rev. 231 (1991). For a further discussion of international software protection, see Chapter 36.

9. *Patent Protection for DNA Sequences.* The identification and isolation of human DNA sequences have also resulted in the grant of patent rights. *See, e.g.,* U.S. Patent No. 4, 994, 371 (sequence of human factor IX)(February 9, 1991). Some critics fear that such patent rights may have an adverse effect on the availability and cost of resultant medical uses. Thus, for example, if one person is given a monopoly over the isolation of a DNA strain that later turns out to be necessary in the cure for cancer, that person, theoretically may be able to charge monopolistic prices for the use of such cures. Furthermore, since no one can "use" a patented product without the patentee's permission, the patent owner might be able theoretically to prevent future research in the area if he refuses to grant permission to competitors to utilize his patent for such purposes. What role, if any, should these concerns play in the establishment of an international patent regime?

10. *Morality and Protection*. The United Kingdom Patent Act of 1977 provided in Section 13 (a): "[A] patent shall not be granted for an invention the publication or exploitation of which would be generally expected to encourage offensive, immoral or anti-social behavior." What standards should be used to consider "offensive, immoral or anti-social behavior"? Community standards? Cultural ones? Global ones? Should countries be allowed to deny protection for reasons other than efficacy or economic efficiency? *Compare with* TRIPS at Article 2 (permitting members to exclude from patentability inventions "the prevention within their territory of the commercial exploitation of which it is necessary to protect *ordre public.*").

11. How should a determination of harm be made? For example, assuming reduction to practice, and proof of more than theoretical application, could the invention of the process for atomic energy have been denied patentability because its use could lead to the "harmful" creation of the atom bomb? How direct must the correlation be between harm and the invention be to permit protection under *public ordre* doctrines?

THE PATENT SYSTEM AND COMPETITIVE POLICY

Donald F. Turner, 44 New York University. Law. Rev. 450 (1969).

No one knows that the magnitude of underinvestment in the production of knowledge would be in the absence of special rewards, because it is fairly certain that a large amount of invention and innovation would take place in any event. Much research, as in universities and similar institutions, is relatively unaffected by the profit motive. Moreover, both economic analysis and empirical study indicate that a good deal of the research and other inventive and innovative activities of business enterprises would go on without special rewards of any kind. In many situations, this is a matter of competitive necessity; he who lags in invention and innovation will find himself driven from the market. Even without benefit of statutory protection, the inventor and innovator will often, if not usually, benefit from a head start, full imitation lagging well behind. And in many of our imperfectly competitive markets, price competition may simply not be vigorous enough to prevent the inventor or innovator from recovering his developmental costs.

There is no doubt that the patent system, be giving a monopoly to the holder of a patentable invention and thus increasing the realizable reward for successful inventive activity, produces a substantial amount of invention and innovation that would not otherwise take place. There is also little doubt that the patent system evokes disclosure of some new knowledge that would otherwise remain secret, or at least remain secret be in fact very great: it has been contended that patents are often granted without full disclosure of all that must be known to make effective use of the invention; and it is also contended that in many areas patents are sought only for inventions that cannot be kept concealed anyway. But the patent system must make some net contribution to disclosure for the simple reason that it could hardly cause anyone to conceal what he would disclose if the patent system did not exist.

Offsetting these benefits, however, are several significant costs. The first is the cost of having a patent system: the cost of administering it, the cost of patent litigation, and the cost of trying to figure out whether one has a patentable invention and whether one's activity infringes the patents of others. The second cost, and a substantial one, is underutilization of all the new patentable knowledge what would have been produced without a patent system. Generally speaking, the marginal cost of using new knowledge, once produced, is zero. Ideally, therefore, it should be freely available without cost to anyone for whom it has any positive value at all. By its very nature, of course, the patent monopoly restricts the use of new knowledge well below the social ideal, because even if its use is made generally available by licensing, it comes only at a price. Third, the patent system has contributed to the creation and perpetuation of monopoly power of dimensions and duration well beyond that intrinsic to the patents themselves. Fourth, the patent system often leads competitors of patent holders to invest resources in duplicating research, *i.e.*, to find noninfringing ways of obtaining the same or nearly the same result. Fifth, the patent system has adverse effects on inventive activity in two respects. It tends to inhibit research in areas heavily hedged in by existing patents; the existence of large numbers of patents in a particular field reduces the likelihood of coming up with noninfringing results that can be profited from—in short, it reduces the probable rewards from inventive activity in that area. In addition, existing patents tend to increase the cost of solving any given research problem by shutting off those avenues of solution that would entail infringement.

Finally, the patent system would appear to worsen, rather than improve, the allocation of research resources as between applied research on the one hand and basic research on the other. As we have noted, unless there are special inducements, underinvestment in basic research is likely to be much less likely than applied research to produce what the law will call "invention." Thus, the patent system will tend to divert research resources away from basic research. This effect would not be a clear loss if the patent system so increased the total resources devoted to research that the resources spent on basic research, though relatively less, were absolutely greater. But even if this were so, the patent system obviously is not the ideal system for incentives in that it does not allocate research resources in the most beneficial way.

Can these adverse effects of the patent system, as we have known it, be reduced or eliminated by appropriate statutory revisions? I see no way of eliminating the loss caused by underutilization of new patentable knowledge that would have been produced without patent protection, for there is simply no feasible way of determining precisely or even crudely what those cases are. The underutilization cost could be reduced by requiring compulsory licensing at reasonable royalties, but could by no means be eliminated, for any positive royalty excludes uses of less value than the royalty price.

Compulsory licensing would also reduce, though not eliminate, the contribution of the patent system to monopoly power, to wasteful duplicating research, to the devotion of resources to obtaining blocking patents, and the inhibitions on research imposed by patents in being. But compulsory licensing of course raises problems of its own. Arguably, it might so reduce the potential rewards of patents as to materially affect the patent incentive to inventive activity. Related to that problem, but involving more, compulsory licensing requires a determination of what is a "reasonable" royalty, a question for which there is simply no happy answer.

Finally, I see no practical way within the patent system itself for eliminating the probable bias against basic research. The solution would have to lie in some revision of the definition of patentable invention. But surely it would be intolerable to give a patent on most of the fundamental ideas that rise from basic research.

I believe this last consideration also demonstrates how unpersuasive the moral defense of the patent system is. Even if we assume that in an ideal world society should pay each creator of a new idea its full economic value, the impossibility of devising any workable scheme for doing so leaves no moral ground for paying some but not others—particularly when it is the fundamental discovery (and such important innovations in business methods as the assembly line, the self-service supermarket, and computerization) that typically must go substantially underrewarded.

But a moment's reflection leads us to question the proposition that were it possible, society should feel a moral obligation to compel all who use an idea to pay monetary tribute to its creator. On this point, I can do no better than to quote Professor Rahl:

> In most of the important fields of human activity it is not usually considered wrong to imitate valuable things, ideas and methods. The more acceptable to society the thing is, the more others are encouraged to imitate it. Education is founded upon this premise, as is progress in science, art, literature, music, and government.

> We have but to look around us to see that our "dynamic" economy is one which thrives upon and requires rapid imitation of innovated trade values.

> [W]e cannot have a general rule against copying of published trade values and at the same time have an effective system of competition. Although competition has many definitions and descriptions, it is clear to all that it cannot exist without the availability of reasonably close alternative for the satisfaction of economic wants.

It is not freedom of competition which requires apology. It is its absence.

Notes and Questions

1. *Economic Impact of Protection.* The economic impact of patent protection has been well-documented. Thus, for example, in the early 1990's,

Thailand became the subject of U.S. concern for its failure to protect pharmaceutical products under its patent laws. In 1991 the U.S. identified Thailand as a priority country under Section 301 for its failure to protect pharmaceuticals and began to apply diplomatic pressure to cause Thailand to change its laws. Thai nationals strongly objected to U.S. interference in what they perceived to be a domestic issue. Furthermore, they were concerned about the potential monopoly effect such patent grants would have upon drug availability. Moreover, there was concerned that patent protection would necessarily increase the cost of such drugs, to the detriment of the Thai people.

Although the dispute eventually ended with the Thai government agreeing to change its laws to meet U.S. demands, the issues regarding the protection of such basic products as drugs, medical techniques and agricultural products remains hotly contested. Most recently, the U.S. sought sanctions against India in the World Trade Organization for its failure to provide patent protection for pharmaceutical products. For a good discussion of the Thai dispute and its ultimate effect on the Thai government, see D'Amato & Long, International Intellectual Property Law Anthology, 59–61 (Anderson Pub. 1996).

2. Disagreements over the patentability of the products of biotechnology have not been limited to the economic impact of granting patent protection to pharmaceutical or agricultural products. To the contrary, they have renewed old concerns that the developed nations may be using the biota of the developing countries as their own personal source for raw materials much as the old colonial masters of the 18th and 19th Centuries plundered the "New World" for the raw materials needed to fuel their industrial growth. *See* Chapter Forty.

3. What role should these concerns play in the decision to protect newly emerging forms of technology in the area of biogenetics and biochemistry on an international basis?

4. The U.S. has already recognized that patent protection can be extended to segments of DNA that can be isolated and used in medical detection and treatment of certain diseases. Is there a difference in nature between patenting human DNA versus patenting human DNA cloning? If not, hasn't the issue of patenting the product of human DNA cloning already been decided in the U.S.? What implications should such a decision have on international protection standards for the products of human DNA cloning?

C. WHAT IS A "WORTHY" INVENTION?
THE COMMERCIAL SUCCESS CASE
GRAHAM v. JOHN DEERE COMPANY

United States Supreme Court, 1966
383 U.S. 1, 86 S.Ct. 684.

Mr. Justice Clark

[The petitioners sued infringement of a U.S. patent for a "clamp for vibrating shank plows." A conflict between the circuits arose over the validity of the patent. For a more detailed discussion of the case and the philosophy behind U.S. patent law, see Chapter Three.]

At the outset it must be remembered that the federal patent power stems from a specific constitutional provision which authorizes the Congress 'To promote the Progress of useful Arts, by securing for limited Times to Inventors the exclusive Right to their Discoveries.' Art. I, s 8, cl. 8. The clause is both a grant of power and a limitation. The Congress in the exercise of the patent power may not overreach the restraints imposed by the stated constitutional purpose. Nor may it enlarge the patent monopoly without regard to the innovation, advancement or social benefit gained thereby. Moreover, Congress may not authorize the issuance of patents whose effects are to remove existent knowledge from the public domain, or to restrict free access to materials already available. Innovation, advancement, and things which add to the sum of useful knowledge are inherent requisites in a patent system which by constitutional command must 'promote the Progress of useful Arts.' This is the standard expressed in the Constitution and it may not be ignored.

This Court formulated a general condition of patentability in 1851 in *Hotchkiss v. Greenwood*, 11 How. 248, 13 L.Ed. 683. The patent involved a mere substitution of materials—porcelain or clay for wood or metal in doorknobs—and the Court condemned it, holding:

'(U)nless more ingenuity and skill were required than were possessed by an ordinary mechanic acquainted with the business, there was an absence of that degree of skill and ingenuity which constitute essential elements of every invention. In other words, the improvement is the work of the skillful mechanic, not that of the inventor.' At p. 267.

Hotchkiss, by positing the condition that a patentable invention evidence more ingenuity and skill than that possessed by an ordinary mechanic acquainted with the business, merely distinguished between new and useful innovations that were capable of sustaining a patent and those that were not. The language in the [*Hotchkiss*] case, and in those which followed, gave birth to 'invention' as a word of legal art signifying patentable inventions. In practice, *Hotchkiss* has required a comparison between the subject matter of the patent, or patent application, and the background skill of the calling. It has been from this comparison that patentability was in each case determined.

The 1952 Patent Act sets out the conditions of patentability [In § 103, it provides;]

Sections 103. Conditions for patentability; non-obvious subject matter [:]

'A patent may not be obtained though the invention is not identically disclosed or described as set forth in section 102 of this title, if the differences between the subject matter sought to be patented and the prior art are such that the subject matter as a whole would have been obvious at the time the invention was made to a person having ordinary skill in the art to which said subject matter pertains. Patentability shall not be negatived by the manner in which the invention was made.'

'Section 103, for the first time in our statute, provides a condition which exists in the law and has existed for more than 100 years, but only by reason of decisions of the courts. An invention which has been made, and which is new in the sense that the same thing has not been made before, may still not be patentable if the difference between the new thing and what was known before is not considered sufficiently great to warrant a patent.

Under § 103, the scope and content of the prior art are to be determined; differences between the prior art and the claims at issue are to be ascertained; and the level of ordinary skill in the pertinent art resolved. Against his background, the obviousness or nonobviousness of the subject matter is determined. Such secondary considerations as commercial success, long felt but unsolved needs, failure of others, etc. might be utilized to give light to the circumstances surrounding the origin of the subject matter sought to be patented. As indicia of obviousness or nonobviousness , these inquiries may have relevancy.

Notes and Questions

1. *International Non–Obviousness.* The requirement of nonobviousness discussed by the court in the *Commercial Success* case has been recognized as an international standard for patent protection, although the precise meaning of non-obviousness, as well as the tests to be applied vary from country to country. *See, e.g.,* Joanna Schmidt–Szalewski, *Nonobviousness as a Requirement of Patentablility in French Law*, 23 Int'l Rev. Indus Prop & Copyright 725 (1992); David J. Abraham, *Shinpo-Sei: Japanese Invention Step Meets U.S. Non–Obviousness*, 77 J. Pat & Trademark Off. Soc'y 528 (1995).

2. The requirement of non-obviousness has been adopted by the most recent multinational treaty to address international patent protection—The Agreement on Trade Related Aspects of Intellectual Property Rights (TRIPS). Under Article 27 of TRIPS, member nations must grant patent protection to "any inventions, whether products or processes, in all fields of technology, provided that they are new, involve an inventive step and are capable of industrial application." Footnote 5 of TRIPS defines these terms as being synonymous with "non-obvious" and "useful" respectively.

3. *International Novelty.* In addition to the requirement of non-obviousness, TRIPS also requires that an invention be "new." This requirement is also reflected in U.S. law and its requirement of "novelty" before a patent will issue. To qualify as a "novel" invention under U.S. law, the invention cannot be "known or used" "in the U.S." 35 U.S.C. § 102. It cannot be published or patented anywhere in the world; it cannot be in public use in the U.S. more than one year prior to the date of its U.S. application, and it cannot be abandoned or suppressed. *See generally* Chapter Two.

4. The United States basically provides a one-year "grace period" for novelty assessments. So long as the subject matter of the invention has not been disclosed within one year of the application date, the invention will not

be considered unpatentable for want of novelty. Consequently, an inventor may discover a new drug which will cure the common cold. He may publish his findings in a scientific journal before he files for a patent application and his published article will not be considered unpatentable for lack of novelty. Internationally, however, the inventor's actions may preclude patent protection. While the U.S. allows a one-year grace period for novelty findings, other countries require absolute novelty. Any publication, even those by the inventor, may serve to preclude a finding of sufficient novelty to permit protection.

5. *TRIPS.* The most recent, and in the authors' view, the most significant, multinational treaty concerning intellectual property rights is The Agreement on Trade Related Aspects of Intellectual Property Rights (TRIPS). The result of nearly seven years of multinational negotiations during the Uruguay Round of GATT, TRIPS represents the views of over 120 nations regarding the minimum substantive standards of protection for intellectual property. Although TRIPS has been criticized as representing the triumph (once again) of developed nations over developing countries, it undoubtedly stands as the single most important development in international intellectual property since the establishment of the Berne and Paris Conventions in the late 1880's. The sheer number of adherents in the world's community alone to this treaty would ensure its importance. But significantly, TRIPS not only established international minimum standards of protection in the arena of intellectual property law, it established minimum international standards for the enforcement of such rights.

In the area of patent protection, as noted above, TRIPS required that patent protection be extended to inventions "in all fields of technology" and further required that patent rights be extended only to those inventions which are "new," "involve an inventive step," and are "capable of industrial application." Among the rights that foreign and domestic patent owners must be granted under TRIPS is a twenty year minimum term of protection from the date of the application, the right to prohibit the unauthorized use of a patented process, and the unauthorized "making, using, offering for sale, selling or importing" of a patented product or of a product created directly by a patented process. For a detailed examination of TRIPS, see Part V, A Trip Through Trips.

Does the protection of the product of human DNA cloning qualify as patentable subject matter under TRIPS? Must it be patented even if a country objects to such cloning on moral, ethical, religious or cultural grounds?

6. *Permissible Variations.* Although TRIPS arguably established an international definition for patents, no two countries have the identical patent laws, although many share certain fundamental concepts regarding the types of inventions which should be protected. The broad language of the treaty allows for variation based on domestic needs and views.

7. The United States defines a patentable invention as "any new and useful process, machine, manufacture or composition of matter or any new and useful improvement thereof may obtain a patent thereunder..." , which meets the statutory obligations of non-obviousness. (35 U.S.C. § 101.)

8.   Great Britain protects an invention which is "new," "involves an inventive step" (similar to the U.S. non-obvious requirement) and "is capable of an industrial application." (Patents Act of 1977, (c37) Section 1.)

9.   The People's Republic of China protects inventions that "possesses novelty, inventiveness and practical applicability." (Patent Laws of China (of 1984), Article 22.)

10.   Japan protects "any highly advanced creation of technical idea making use of a law of nature (Shizen Losoku)" which meet requirements of novelty, non-obviousness, and the ability to be "utilized in industry." (Patent Act (Tokkyo Mo)) Law No 121, 1959, Arts 2 and 29 (as reported in Doing Business in Japan, Part 6, 2.01 (Matthew Bender & Co. 1998))

11.   Russia currently requires that an invention be "novel, possess an inventive legal, and is industrially applicable." (Russian Patent Law of 1992, Article 4(1)).

12.   Egypt protects "original works within the field of literature, art and science, whatever their type, mode of expression, [or] extent of purpose." (Law Relating to the Protection of Copyright, Article 1.)

13.   Do these variations meet TRIPS requirements for patentability? Do they all require the identical protection for the identical invention? For example, based on their statutory language are pharmaceutical products protectable under these standards? Is a new hybrid brand of wheat that has an exceptionally short growing season? Is human DNA cloning?

14.   *Permissible Exclusions from Protection.* Despite its profound effect in establishing international standards of protection, even TRIPS acknowledges that countries may have other over-riding concerns that require the denial of protection where such denial is in the country's self interest. Article 27 (2) provides:

> Members may exclude from patentability inventions, the prevention within their territory of the commercial exploitation of which necessary to protect *ordre public* or morality, including to protect human, animal or plant life or health or to avoid serious prejudice to the environment, provided that such exclusion is not made merely because the exploitation is prohibited by their law.

Article 27(3) further provides:

> Members may also exclude from patentability (a) diagnostic, therapeutic and surgical methods for the treatment of humans or animals, (b) plants and animals other than micro-organisms, and essentially biological processes, for the production of plants or animals other than non-biological and microbiological processes.

May a country decide to exclude protection for pharmaceutical products under Article 27 on the grounds that its economic development requires that all drugs be produced within the country? Could it deny protection to human DNA cloning on *public ordre* grounds?

15.   If you represented a client country who wanted to exclude from protection any pharmaceutical products that cured Ebola fever, what arguments would you make to bring such exclusion within the permissible scope of Article 27?

16.   Should the exclusions granted under Article 27 be read broadly or narrowly? Does your answer depend on whether you are examining the issue from the perspective of a developed or developing country?

THE YEAR 2000 CONTROVERSY

The United States Patent and Trademark Office recently issued a patent for a solution to the "Year 2000" or "Turn of the Century" Problem for Computers. Computer software at that time was unable to handle date-based information for the next century, because it only recognized two date digits, thus the Year 2001 would have to be written as 01, which would make the computer believe it is the Year 1901. This problem began with the creation of the first generation of computers. They were not able to store the amount of memory needed to build a four-digit year format. Consequently, only a two digit system was used.

At the end of the Twentieth Century, software developers were desperately looking for the ultimate solution to the Y2K problem without having to rewrite the entire computer software program. Firms were created solely to find a solution, such as, for example, the "Turn of the Century Solution, Inc."

On February 4, 1997 the Turn of the Century Solution, Inc. as an owner by assignment through the inventor Harvey Alter, obtained U.S. Patent No. 5,600,836 for a "system and method for processing date-dependent information which spans one or two centuries." It solved the problem by a "time change interface" to shift dates.[11] And there are other inventors that have tried to come up with even a better solution, the last one being a German computer specialist who has thought of a method of placing just a comma before the two digits, potentially creating a three digit system.

Since patent laws are designed to strive to increase the public's wealth of culture and knowledge while granting certain rights to inventors for a limited period of time, does the patenting of such solutions give inventors an unlimited right? Every computer software owner in the late 1990's faced the "Turn of the Century" problem. In the Year 2000 everyone arguably needed this patented solution. Once everybody owns the solution, the patent will have been fully exploited. Given the potentially world-wide impact of the Turn of the Century solution, should this solution be protected? If not, would this lack of protection lead to a disadvantage for the "public's wealth of information"?

Problem

Your client has developed a new surgical technique for open heart surgery. This technique requires the use of both special surgical scalpels, made from a new alloy that allows them to maintain extreme sharpness so that they cut more surely and quickly through human tissue, and a special

---

11.   For further details see Patent Pro-   (1998).
files, 13 NO. 10 Computer L. Strategist 8

cutting technique that allows the heart to be treated through only a small incision. According to the documentation your client has provided, the special alloy has been used previously for kitchen knives, but none has used the alloy for medical scalpels. He also tells you that *he published* five months ago a paper in the *European Medical Journal* that completely disclosed his new methodology. Although the client has conducted numerous tests to prove the effectiveness of his methodology, he claims the speed of the maneuvers makes the technique dangerous for all but the most talented surgeons. Others claim the client's techniques make open heart surgery more efficient, less costly, and, therefore readily available to more potential patients. The client wants to obtain world wide patent rights for his methodology and the scalpels. What problems do you foresee in attempting to obtain patent protection internationally?

Chapter Nine

THE INTERFACE BETWEEN COPY-RIGHT AND PATENTS UNDER INTERNATIONAL LAW

A. SHOULD COPYRIGHT BE USED TO PROTECT COMPUTER SOFTWARE?

THE APPLE SOFTWARE CASE

APPLE COMPUTER, INC. v. FRANKLIN COMPUTER CORPORATION

United States Court of Appeals, Third Circuit, 1983.
714 F.2d 1240.

SLOVITER, CIRCUIT JUDGE.

Apple, one of the computer industry leaders, manufactures and markets personal computers (microcomputers), related peripheral equipment such as disk drives (peripherals), and computer programs (software). ... Franklin, the defendant below, manufactures and sells the ACE 100 personal computer and at the time of the hearing employed about 75 people and had sold fewer than 1,000 computers. The ACE 100 was designed to be "Apple compatible," so that peripheral equipment and software developed for use with the Apple II computer could be used in conjunction with the ACE 100. Franklin's copying of Apple's operating system computer programs in an effort to achieve such compatibility precipitated this suit.

Like all computers both the Apple II and ACE 100 have a central processing unit (CPU) which is the integrated circuit that executes programs. In lay terms, the CPU does the work it is instructed to do. Those instructions are contained on computer programs.

There are three levels of computer language in which computer programs may be written. High level language, such as the commonly used BASIC or FORTRAN, uses English words and symbols, and is relatively easy to learn and understand (e.g., "GO TO 40" tells the computer to skip intervening steps and go to the step at line 40). A somewhat lower level language is assembly language, which consists of alphanumeric labels (e.g., "ADC" means "add with carry"). Statements in high level language, and apparently also statements in assembly language, are referred to as written in "source code." The third, or lowest level computer language, is machine language, a binary language using two symbols, 0 and 1, to indicate an open or closed switch (e.g., "01101001" means, to the Apple, add two numbers and save the result). Statements in machine language are referred to as written in "object code."

The CPU can only follow instructions written in object code. However, programs are usually written in source code which is more intelligible to humans. Programs written in source code can be converted or translated by a "compiler" program into object code for use by the computer. Programs are generally distributed only in their object code version stored on a memory device...

Computer programs can be categorized by function as either application programs or operating system programs. Application programs usually perform a specific task for the computer user, such as word processing, checkbook balancing, or playing a game. In contrast, operating system programs generally manage the internal functions of the computer or facilitate use of application programs. The parties agree that the fourteen computer programs at issue in this suit are operating system programs.

Franklin did not dispute that it copied the Apple programs. Its witness admitted copying each of the works in suit from the Apple programs. Its factual defense was directed to its contention that it was not feasible for Franklin to write its own operating system programs.

Franklin's principal defense at the preliminary injunction hearing and before us is primarily a legal one, directed to its contention that the Apple operating system programs are not capable of copyright protection.

Under the law, two primary requirements must be satisfied in order for a work to constitute copyrightable subject matter—it must be an "original wor[k] of authorship" and must be "fixed in [a] tangible medium of expression." 17 U.S.C. § 102(a).

Although section 102(a) does not expressly list computer programs as works of authorship, the legislative history suggests that programs were considered copyrightable as literary works. The 1980 amendments added a definition of a computer program:

A "computer program" is a set of statements or instructions to be used directly or indirectly in a computer in order to bring about a certain result. 17 U.S.C. § 101.

We turn to the heart of Franklin's position on appeal which is that computer operating system programs, as distinguished from application programs, are not the proper subject of copyright "regardless of the language or medium in which they are fixed." Brief of Appellee. Franklin contends that operating system programs are per se excluded from copyright protection.

Franklin argues that an operating system program is either a "process", "system", or "method of operation" and hence uncopyrightable. Franklin correctly notes that underlying section 102(b) is the distinction which must be made between property subject to the patent law, which protects discoveries, and that subject to copyright law, which protects the writings describing such discoveries. However, Franklin's argument misapplies that distinction in this case. Apple does not seek to copyright the method which instructs the computer to perform its operating functions but only the instructions themselves. The method would be protected, if at all, by the patent law, an issue as yet unresolved.

Franklin argues that the operating systems cannot be copyrighted because they are "purely utilitarian works" and that Apple is seeking to block the use of the art embodied in its operating systems. This argument stems from the following dictum in *Baker v. Selden* 101 U.S. 99 (1880):

"The very object of publishing a book on science or the useful arts is to communicate to the world the useful knowledge which it contains. But this object would be frustrated if the knowledge could not be used without incurring the guilt of piracy of the book. And where the art it teaches cannot be used without employing the methods and diagrams used to illustrate the book, or such as are similar to them, such methods and diagrams are to be considered as necessary incidents to the art, and given therewith to the public; not given for the purpose of publication in other works explanatory of the art, but for the purpose of practical application." 101 U.S. at 103.

Although a literal construction of this language could support Franklin's reading that precludes copyrightability if the copyright work is put to a utilitarian use, that interpretation has been rejected by a later Supreme Court decision. In *Mazer v. Stein*, 347 U.S. 201, 218 (1954), the Court stated: "We find nothing in the copyright statute to support the argument that the intended use or use in industry of an article eligible for copyright bars or invalidates its registration. We do not read such a limitation into the copyright law."

Franklin's other challenge to copyright of operating system programs relies on the line which is drawn between ideas and their expression.

"Just as a patent affords protection only to the means of reducing an inventive idea to practice, so the copyright law protects the means of expressing an idea; and it is as near the whole truth as generalization can usually reach that, if the same idea can be expressed in a plurality of totally different manners, a plurality of copyrights may result, and no infringement will exist." [*Dymow v. Bolton*, 11 F.2d 690, 691 (2d Cir. 1926)]

We focus on whether the idea is capable of various modes of expression. If other programs can be written or created which perform the same function as an Apple's operating system program, then that program is an expression of the idea and hence copyrightable. In essence, this inquiry is no different than that made to determine whether the expression and idea have merged, which has been stated to occur where there are no or few other ways of expressing a particular idea.

Franklin's contentions that operating system programs are per se not copyrightable is unpersuasive. Since we believe that the district court's decision on the preliminary injunction was, to a large part, influenced by an erroneous view of the availability of copyright for operating system programs, we must reverse the denial of the preliminary injunction and remand for reconsideration.

Notes and Questions

1.   Compare the treatment of the court in the *Apple Software* case of idea/expression with *Computer Associates International, Inc. v. Altai, Inc.*, 126 F.3d 365 (2d Cir.1997). Are they in agreement?

2.   *Inconsistent Treatment for Software.* Despite the relatively early determination under U.S. law that software is subject to copyright protection, internationally the protection of software remained subject to inconsistent treatment. Until 1995 many countries declined to protect software under copyright laws and instead erected sui generis schemes that often posed difficult barriers to software protection, by requiring (*inter alia*) registration or recordation of user licenses before protection would attach. In 1994 TRIPS at least appears to have resolved part of the issue by including computer software as a literary work. Article 10 of TRIPS states:

Computer programs, whether in source code or object code, shall be protected as literary works under the Berne Convention.

This provision, however, does not prohibit requiring a degree of creativity or originality before protection attaches. It also does not address the critical issue of whether certain types of computer programs or certain aspects of computer programs may fall outside the scope of copyright protection because they represent functional or utilitarian language. Thus, the problem of which aspects of a computer program qualify as protectable expression and which qualify as unprotected "ideas" remains unresolved internationally.

3.   *Determining Expression.* If copyright only extends to "expression" what qualifies as an unprotected "idea"? Is a chronology of historical events a protectable directory or unprotected facts? What if the chronology is translated from Sanskrit? Does that change its degree of protection? What if the chronology is part of computer database available on the Internet? Does a change in medium create a new work that may be subject to protection?

What if instead of a chronology of historical fact, the work is a digitized version of the Mona Lisa? Does the digitized version contain protectable expression?

4. *Artistic Style.* The closer a work is to the traditional conception of a literary or artistic work, the easier it ought to be to determine whether the work contains copyright protectable expression which has been infringed. Nevertheless, even an artist's style may have an impact on the degree of protection afforded under copyright. In *Franklin Mint Corporation v. National Wildlife Art Exchange, Inc.*, 575 F.2d 62 (3d Cir.1978), the court had to decide whether two paintings of the same subject matter painted by different artists were infringing. In reaching its conclusion of non-infringement, the court discussed the nature of copyright protection and artistic style. It stated: "Precision in marking the boundary between the unprotected idea and the protected expression, however, is rarely possible. [I]n the world of fine art, the ease with which a copyright may be delineated may depend on the artist's style. A painter like Monet when dwelling upon impressions created by light on the facade of the Rouen Cathedral is apt to create a work which can make infringement attempts difficult. On the other hand, an artist who produces a rendition with photograph-like clarity and accuracy may be hard pressed to prove unlawful copying by another who uses the same subject matter and the same technique. A copyright in that circumstance may be termed "weak," since the expression and the subject matter converge. In contrast, in the impressionist's work the lay observer will be able to differentiate more readily between the reality of subject matter and subjective effect of the artist's work. The limitations imposed upon the artist by convention are also factors which must be considered. A scientific drawing of a bird must necessarily be more similar to another of the same nature than it would be to an abstract version of the creature in flight.

"The 'copying' proscribed by copyright law, therefore, means more than tracing the original, line by line. To some extent it includes the appropriation of the artist's thought in creating his own form of expression. There was testimony on the tendency of some painters to return to certain basic themes time and time again. Winslow Homer's schoolboys, Monet's facade of Rouen Cathedral, and Bingham's flatboat characters were cited. Franklin Mint relied upon these examples of 'variations on a theme' as appropriate examples of the freedom which must be extended to artists to utilize basic subject matter more than once. National vigorously objects to the use of such a concept as being contrary to the theory of copyright. We do not find the phrase objectionable, however, because a 'variation' probably is not a copy and if a 'theme' is equated with an 'idea,' it may not be monopolized. We conceive of 'variation on a theme,' therefore, as another way of saying that an 'idea' may not be copyrighted and only its 'expression' may be protected."

This problem of determining where style ends and copyright protection begins becomes even more pronounced when the subject of protection reflects longstanding artistic or cultural tastes.

B.   WHERE IS THE BOUNDARY BETWEEN PATENTABLE "IDEAS" AND COPY-RIGHTABLE "EXPRESSION"?

THE CHROMOLITHOGRAPH CASE
ALFRED BELL & CO. v. CATALDA FINE ARTS, INC.

United States Court of Appeals, Second Circuit, 1951.
191 F.2d 99.

Thus legislators peculiarly familiar with the purpose of the Constitutional grant by statute, imposed far less exacting standards in the case of copyrights. They authorized the copyrighting of a mere map which, patently, calls for no considerable uniqueness. They exacted far more from an inventor. And, while they demanded that an official should be satisfied as to the character of an invention before a patent issued, they made no such demand in respect of a copyright. In 1884, in *Burrow-Giles Lithographic Co. v. Sarony*, 111 U.S. 53, 57, 4 S.Ct. 279, 28 L.Ed. 349, the Supreme Court, adverting to these facts said: "The construction placed upon the constitution by the first act of 1790 and the act of 1802, by the men who were contemporary with its formation, many of whom were members of the convention which framed it, is of itself entitled to very great weight, and when it is remembered that the rights thus established have not been disputed during a period of nearly a century, it is almost conclusive.' Accordingly, the Constitution, as so interpreted, recognizes that the standards for patents and copyrights are basically different.

The defendants' contention apparently results from the ambiguity of the word "original". It may mean startling, novel or unusual, a marked departure from the past. Obviously this is not what is meant when one speaks of "the original package," or the "original bill," or (in connection with the "best evidence" rule) an "original" document; none of those things is highly unusual in creativeness. "Original" in reference to a copyrighted work means that the particular work "owes its origin" to the "author." No large measure of novelty is necessary. Said the Supreme Court in *Baker v. Selden*, 101 U.S. 99, 102–103, 25 L.Ed. 841: "The copyright of the book, if not pirated from other works, would be valid without regard to the novelty, or want of novelty, of its subject-matter. The novelty of the art or thing described or explained has nothing to do with the validity of the copyright. To give to the author of the book an exclusive property in the art described therein, when no examination of its novelty has ever been officially made, would be a surprise and a fraud upon the public. That is the province of letters-patent, not of copyright. The claim to an invention or discovery of an art or manufacture must be subjected to the examination of the Patent Office before an exclusive right therein can be obtained; and it can only be secured by a patent from the government. The difference between the two things, letters-patent and copyright, may be illustrated by reference to the subjects just enumerated. Take the case of medicines. Certain mixtures are found to be of great value in the healing art.

"If the discoverer writes and publishes a book on the subject (as regular physicians generally do), he gains no exclusive right to the manufacture and sale of the medicine; he gives that to the public. If he desires to acquire such exclusive right, he must obtain a patent for the mixture as a new art, manufacture, or composition of matter. He may copyright his book, if he pleases; but that only secures to him the exclusive right of printing and publishing his book. So of all other inventions or discoveries."

In *Bleistein v. Donaldson Lithographing Co.*, 188 U.S. 239, 23 S.Ct. 298, 47 L.Ed. 460, the Supreme Court cited with approval *Henderson v. Tompkins, C.C.*, 60 F. 758, where it was said, 60 F.at page 764: "There is a very broad distinction between what is implied in the word "author," found in the constitution, and the word "inventor." The latter carries an implication which excludes the results of only ordinary skill, while nothing of this is necessarily involved in the former. Indeed, the statutes themselves make broad distinctions on this point. So much as relates to copyrights is expressed, so far as this particular is concerned, by the mere words, "author, inventor, designer or proprietor," with such aid as may be derived from the words "written, composed or made". But a multitude of books rest safely under copyright, which show only ordinary skill and diligence in their preparation. Compilations are noticeable examples of this fact. With reference to this subject, the courts have not undertaken to assume the functions of critics, or to measure carefully the degree of originality, or literary skill or training involved." It is clear, then, that nothing in the Constitution commands that copyrighted matter be strikingly unique or novel. Accordingly, we were not ignoring the Constitution when we stated that a "copy of something in the public domain" will support a copyright if it is a "distinguishable variation"; or when we rejected the contention that "like a patent, a copyrighted work must be not only original, but new", adding, "That is not the law as is obvious in the case of maps or compendia, where later works will necessarily be anticipated." All that is needed to satisfy both the Constitution and the statute is that the "author" contributed something more than a "merely trivial" variation, something recognizably "his own." Originality in this context "means little more than a prohibition of actual copying." No matter how poor artistically the "author's" addition, it is enough if it be his own.

On that account, we have often distinguished between the limited protection accorded a copyright owner and the extensive protection granted a patent owner. So we have held that "independent reproduction of a copyrighted work is not infringement", whereas it is vis a vis a patent. Correlative with the greater immunity of a patentee is the doctrine of anticipation which does not apply to copyrights: The alleged inventor is chargeable with full knowledge of all the prior art, although in fact he may be utterly ignorant of it. The "author" is entitled to a copyright if he independently contrived a work completely identical with what went before; similarly, although he obtains a valid copyright, he has no right to prevent another from publishing a work identical with his, if not copied from his. A patentee, unlike a copyrightee, must not merely produce something "original"; he must also be "the first inventor or discoverer." "Hence it is possible to have a plurality of valid copyrights directed to closely identical or even identical works. Moreover, none of them, if independently arrived at without copying, will constitute an infringement of the copyright of the others."

Notes and Questions

1. *Patent or Copyright?* The lesser protection which the court in the *Chromolithograph* case refers to is the lesser standard of protection which copyright is supposedly granted under U.S. law. Although the term of copyright protection is longer than for patents (life of the author plus 50 years, versus 20 years), only "original expression" is protected under copyright law. A third party is not prohibited from using the ideas contained in the work; only from using the protected expression contained in that work. *See, e.g.,* 17 U.S.C. § 106. *See generally Kregos v. Associated Press,* 937 F.2d 700 (2d Cir.1991); *CCC Information Services v. Maclean Hunter Market Reports, Inc.,* 44 F.3d 61 (2d Cir.1994).

By contrast, patent law precludes third parties from making, using or selling the patented invention. Thus, if an inventor obtains a patent for a quick growing brand of hybrid wheat, he can prevent others from growing that wheat without his permission. If the inventor had merely written about his ideas for creating a new brand of hybrid wheat, however, his expression would be protected under copyright law, but the practice of his ideas would not be. Consequently, although patents generally last for shorter periods of time, they may at least theoretically have a greater monopolistic effect on the covered invention than a copyright would grant.

2. Although patent grants for inventions were recorded as early as Venice during the Middle Ages, copyright was actually the first intellectual property right to be protected by statute. In 1710 Great Britain enacted the Statute of Anne, which extended protection to published books and other written works "for the Encouragement of Learning, by Vesting the Copies of Printed Books in the Authors or Purchasers of such copies..." Under present international standards, most copyrighted works are protected for the life of the author plus fifty years. *See* Berne Convention at Article 7. By contrast, patent protection is generally granted for a term of 20 years from the date of application for the patent. *See* TRIPS at Art. 33. Thus, the decision to protect a work under copyright could have a profound impact on the degree or scope of protection afforded the work in question.

THE PROGRAM FORMAT CONTROVERSY

Anthony Martino and Claire Miskin, "The price is not right".
141 New Law Journal, 813 (Butterworth, 1991).

The issue whether formats should be entitled to protection under [British] copyright law has recently generated a good deal of heat and not much light. In a letter to The Independent on January 16 this year,

Peter Smith (Thames Television) and others ask whether "[t]he creators of these ... programmes have the right to expect the law to protect them from international thieves who steal original programme formats for financial gain". They answer their own question thus: "It is the Government's duty to provide the legal framework within which business may be conducted fairly and efficiently. There is no reason to exclude the inventors of original TV formats from that remit ..." Some intellectual property lawyers and their clients ... believe and would have the rest of us believe that for every jot, scrap and tittle of creation, there exists and ought to exist—somewhere, somehow—an available regime of legal protection. ...

Format protection is the latest bee in the intellectual property lawyer's bonnet. ...

Format originators are looking for a right in the nature of copyright—or at least, something very much like it. See, for example, *Fink v. Goodson–Todman Enterprises, Inc.*, 9 Cal. App. 3d 996 (1970), in which the California Court of Appeal found that common law copyright could afford relief if the allegedly copied ideas were novel and concrete. The court recognized that it was extending the copyright doctrine into an "uncertain middle ground" by finding rights in format ideas, as opposed merely to the expression of those ideas. *Ibid* at 1016. ... Their argument runs something like this: originators and producers of formats and format works respectively, invest time, skill, labor and money in creating a product, only to find that once their work has been unveiled, they have no power to evict those who would trespass upon it. Of course, they might be able to enjoin an imitator from exploitation should he mislead the public as to the work's provenance, but we have to accept that the action for passing off is, at least for the time being, practically worthless. Before we forget to mention it, the format originators have one more point to make: we have witnessed a proliferation of formats with resulting increased trade in spin-offs from them, the pace of which the law has unmatched. So what, we ask? The failure or otherwise of the law to keep abreast of increasing commercial ingenuity (or depravity, depending on your point of view), begs the question whether formats confront us with an unmet need.

So why do they want copyright protection? Easy: copyright is a property right. A property right is a legally enforceable power to exclude others from using a resource, without the need to contract with them.

Why they shouldn't have it?

Property rights confer valuable economic benefits. The absence of property rights would lead to the inefficient use of "scarce" resources. (Scarce resources are all resources which are not so plentiful that unlimited use may be made of them by everyone.) Investment will not take place in the absence of property protection and those who use scarce resources will not take into account the external costs of that use.

To illustrate: suppose that all property rights have been abolished. A farmer plants corn, fertilizes it and erects scarecrows. No sooner is the corn ready to be picked, than his neighbor takes it away for his own use. Assuming that defensive measures are not feasible, after a few such incidents, society will shift from the cultivation of land to methods of subsistence involving less preparatory investment—for example, hunting. Again, assume that there are no property rights. In this instance we shall take as an example a natural pasture. If the "owner" cannot exclude others from using his pasture there will be overgrazing. Pasturing additional cows will impose a cost on all of the farmers because the cows will have to graze more in order to find enough to eat, thereby reducing their weight and their value. These costs will be ignored by the farmers.

The problem would disappear if someone owned the pasture. The owner would charge each farmer for use of the land and the level of the charge would include the cost he imposes on the other farmers by pasturing additional cows, because the cost reduces the value of the pasture to the other farmers and therefore the price they are willing to pay the owner for its use.

Economic efficiency therefore demands that scarce resources should be the subject of ownership and that their owners should be able to exclude others. Economic efficiency also demands that property be freely transferable. If the owner of farmland is a bad farmer, his land would be more productive in the hands of someone who could farm it effectively.

So much for the benefits of property rights. Property rights also impose costs. We shall look first at the cost of protection and enforcement. Intellectual property is a particularly costly form of property to protect. Whereas land may be fenced off against trespassers and perhaps recorded in a land registry, an idea cannot be seen or traced in its descent. Whilst these factors indicate that intellectual property is deserving not only of protection, but of a sophisticated regime of protection, they also caution that the cost of protection may exceed the benefits.

Another cost of property rights is the social cost of restricting the use of property when it has a "public good" character. In the case of farmland, adding a user will impose costs on the existing users. However, no one person's hearing or viewing of a musical performance precludes another from enjoying the same performance. As such, musical performance rights—like any other intellectual property rights—exhibit the characteristic of a public good. In contrast to private goods, which may be consumed by only one person at a time, public goods may be consumed by any number of persons simultaneously. The marginal cost of additional consumption is zero.

To illustrate: the classic example of a private good, and one much beloved of economists, is an apple. If you take a bite of my apple, there is less of that apple left for me to consume. In addition, the same musical composition is often used in the production of sheet music and sound recordings, as well as in television, radio and live performances. Thus, a huge stock of compositions have no economic cost for present use. The cost of creating them has been incurred in the past (sunk), owing to the demands of users other than, say, radio. Therefore the marginal cost of licensing the performing rights in compositions to television companies is zero. When the marginal cost of using a resource is zero, excluding someone from using it creates a deadweight loss, in addition to the cost of enforcing exclusion.

Finally, intellectual property rights sometimes create serious problems of what economists characterize as "rent seeking". Take the example of a sunken ship whose salvage value is £1,000,000, while the cost of salvage is only £100,000. The potential gain to the salvor is £900,000 if a property right in the sunken ship can be acquired. The problem is that the competition from other sources to acquire the property right in the sunken ship may erode all or most of the potential rents, thus transforming them into social costs. Intellectual property often creates serious problems of rent seeking, because the resource is continuously created or discovered rather than being already owned. Like the sunken ship, it is waiting to be invented.

Let us now apply the foregoing analysis to formats. A major economic disadvantage of the absence of property rights is disregard of external costs. It is tempting therefore to conclude that overexploitation of a format will cause it to diminish in value in the same way as an overgrazed pasture. Users will not take into account the problem of overuse. Unlike the pasture, however, there will always be a certain supply of existing and newly created formats. From the point of view of the format originator, overuse of his format is costly; but from the point of view of the user and society at large, the cost is small since a plentiful supply of alternative resources exists. The cost of investment in a substitute format may be small compared to the expected benefit.

The ideas or concepts underlying a format or format work are for the most part "obvious". Why do you suppose that an invention, to be patentable, must not be obvious? The reason is clear. "Obviousness" implies a low cost of discovery and development and therefore a large potential gap between value and cost—a large opportunity to obtain economic rents. Patents are granted early in order to head off costly development work. The limited duration of patents limits rent seeking by putting a ceiling on the expected value of the patent. It also reflects the high cost of tracing an idea over a long period of time in which it may have become embodied in a great variety of inventions.

Lastly, does it really make sense to grant someone a sole and despotic dominion over commonplace ideas? Trademark law has a few lessons to offer here. No one can appropriate exclusively unto himself a generic designation. The effect of allowing a word processor manufacturer to register as a trademark the words word processor, or WP, would deprive his competitors of the very words they need to announce to buyers their arrival in the marketplace. It is not difficult to see the chilling effect which copyright protection would have on the format market. In these circumstances, insofar as it is appropriate to extend protection to formats, it makes more sense to accord to format originators not a property right, but what Calabresi and Melamed designate a "liability entitlement". (Calabresi and Melamed, 85 Harv L Rev 1089 (1972)).

Broadly, a person has a liability entitlement where another is freely able to destroy the entitlement so long as he or see is willing to pay an objectively determined value for it. The advantage of a liability entitlement, as against a property entitlement is that it allows for optimal adjustments to changing values.

The transaction costs of acquiring the right to use a format simply exceed the value of the right. A liability rule—of which the action for passing off is an example—would reallocate the use of formats in accordance with their value.

Notes and Questions

1. What role, if any, should economics play in the determination of copyright protection levels worldwide?

2. *The Problem of Piracy.* In recent years the pirating of software in developing countries has been widely reported by the media. In 1995 China and the U.S. nearly entered into a trade war over China's purported failure to protect intellectual property rights. It is estimated that the U.S. software industry loses over $800 million to $1 billion per year (38 Ariz. L. Rev 1081) to piracy in China alone. *See, e.g.,* Glenn R. Butterton, *Pirates, Dragons and U.S. Intellectual Property Rights in China: Problems and Prospects of Chinese Enforcement,* 38 Ariz. L. Rev. 1081 (1996). On the other hand, consumers in China claim that the price of software is too high and that they must either purchase the pirated software which is sold at a price they can afford or do without. It is estimated that Microsoft earns over $650 million a year in sales of its WINDOWS® operating system. Should international law establish a formula for maximum return on investment, after which copyright protection is eliminated for a particular product or category of works (such as software)?

3. Are there instances where third parties ought to be able to use copyright protected works without the copyright owner's permission? For example, what if a country has decided that, for purposes of national security, it wants to develop its domestic automotive industry. In order to modernize, the country must be able to use software owned by a third party, who refuses to license the software because it is concerned that the licensee nation does not provide adequate protection for intellectual property rights. Should the licensee country be able to use the software anyway? What if, instead of refusing to license the software, the owner merely demands a royalty that the developing country believes is exorbitant. Should it be able to use the software without paying the asked for royalty? Is it acceptable if the licensee country merely pays the owner what it considers to be reasonable compensation?

4. Is economic encouragement of labor the only reason to grant protection to copyrighted works? Put another way, would Tolstoy have written War and Peace without copyright protection? Would Gone with the Wind have been filmed without such protection? Would Bill Gates have developed

Microsoft WINDOWS® without such protection? On the other hand, didn't Homer write The Iliad and The Odyssey well before copyright protection was even conceived?

THE CIRCUIT DIAGRAM CASE

ANACON CORPORATION LIMITED v. ENVIRONMENTAL RESEARCH TECHNOLOGY LIMITED

Chancery Division, 1994.
[1994] FSR 659.

JACOB, J.

In this action the plaintiffs, Anacon Corporation Limited and John Nelo Jones, sue a company called Environmental Research Technology Limited and a Mr. Brian Richmond. We have just reached the fourth day of the trial and in the morning Mr. Richmond indicated through his counsel that he had settled with the plaintiffs and I made an appropriate Tomlin Order, certain undertakings being given to the court.

That leaves the position of the company Environmental Research Technology, which I shall call ERT. That company is currently in liquidation, having been restored to the register pursuant to an application by the plaintiffs, The liquidator has consented to an order permitting the action to be pursued, but the company does not appear. However, the company did put in a defence, originally a joint defence with Mr. Richmond. Accordingly the plaintiff has to prove its case.

The plaintiffs' claimed in its amended statement of claim, (the liquidator consented to the amendment) that it owned the copyright to three classes of work concerned with an electronic dust meter analyser. The three classes of work are, first, a computer program; secondly, some engineering drawings for hardware; and, thirdly, some circuit diagrams. I have heard the evidence, which indeed was to some extent contested while Mr. Richmond was still contesting the action. I am satisfied that the plaintiffs' claim as against the defendant company is good so far as the claim in relation to copyright in the software and in the drawings for the hardware is concerned.

However, the position in relation to the circuit diagrams gave me more concern. I think I should explain why. The circuit diagrams concerned are a series of pieces of paper upon which in the usual schematic way circuit diagrams are indicated. I am quite prepared to accept that the various pieces of paper should be read effectively as one. The circuit diagram as I shall call it in the singular in future, is a conventional type of circuit diagram. The components, resistors, transistors, capacitors and so on, are shown by the conventional symbols for these components. Against each is a written piece of information indicating the appropriate rating or whatever on that particular component. The plaintiffs' circuit board, made using that circuit diagram, looks nothing like it. All the various components indicated in the circuit diagram are connected together topologically but not visually in the way shown in the circuit diagram.

On the evidence I infer that the defendant company took the plaintiffs' circuit as it was laid out on a circuit board and made at least what is called a "net list". A net list is a list of all the components in a circuit and in relation to each component what other components it is connected to and, if necessary, where. These days one can feed a net list into a computer and it will produce a circuit diagram and probably also a scheme for making a printed circuit board. So the defendants' circuit boards were made using information derived from the plaintiffs' original circuit diagram. I am satisfied that the creation of the plaintiffs' circuit diagram itself involved original work, original work not only in devising the circuit but sufficient original work to create a copyright work, namely the circuit diagram. The work was done before the present Copyright Design and Patents Act, 1988 came into force but, nonetheless, copyright subsists in the diagram by virtue of that Act. However, by paragraph 5(1) it must be shown that copyright subsisted in the circuit diagram before the coming into force of this Act, namely by virtue of the provisions of the Copyright Act, 1956.

Mr. Whittle says, first of all, that the circuit diagram is an artistic work. So far I agree. He says it has three visual aspects: first of all what components are shown on the page albeit by the use of conventional symbols, secondly, where on the page and, thirdly, how they are connected together. He says that the defendants have in their net list, additionally in their circuit, taken what is shown on the page, how it is connected, but not where on the page. Hence the fact that the circuit looks quite different visually. He says that is quite enough to amount to reproduction of a substantial part of the circuit diagram. After all, that is what the diagram is for and surely one should take into account what the diagram is for in considering what is a substantial part of it. I do not agree and I do not do so because the essential nature of a graphic work, as the present Act calls it, is that it is a thing to be looked at in some manner or other. It is to be looked at in itself. I believe that the essence of the reasoning in *Interlego AG v. Tyco Industries Ltd* [1988] RPC 343 at 373 is that what matters in relation to artistic works, particularly drawings, is that which is "visually significant." In the context of that case it was that which was visually significant by way of changes from earlier drawings which was being considered, the issue being whether there was originality. But the phrase "visually significant" arose in an infringement case. I cannot see why that which matters from the point of view of originality does not matter equally from the point of view of infringement. So Mr. Whittle's argument on the basis that the circuit diagram is an artistic work fails because the alleged infringement simply does not look like the artistic work. Yes, it was made using information contained in the artistic work, but that is not enough.

Mr. Whittle puts his case in an alternative way. He says: "Well, if one looks at the circuit diagram it is more than just visual information, it is in fact technical information containing a lot of writing—a lot of writing altogether—against each component being the information as to what it is, and an indication in visual form of what other component each component is connected to." He says, in effect, that the circuit diagram is a list of components together with information as to how they are connected together. Thus, he says, not only is it an artistic work, it is also a literary work. Under the present Act—and the provisions are no different in this regard from the old Act—a literary work means any work, other than dramatic or musical work, which is written and includes a table or compilation. He points out that by the definition Section 178:

> " 'writing' includes any form of notation or code, whether by hand or otherwise and regardless of the method by which or medium in or on what it is recorded and 'written' shall be construed accordingly."

So, he says, that any information you write down is a literary work, that this circuit diagram has lots of writing on it, that some of it may be written in code, (eg a resistor) symbol—but so what? He says that it follows that there is here at least a table or compilation, the latter being a compilation of parts. The fact that it is scattered about between pieces of paper and joined up by lines does not stop it being a literary work.

I think he is right in this. My first thought was that it would be absurd to regard a circuit diagram as a literary work, but the more one thinks about the ambit of that expression, as used in the Act, the more one is driven to the conclusion that provided it is all written down and contains information which can be read by somebody, as opposed to appreciated simply with the eye, the more one sees that that is just what it is. Similarly musical notation is written down, but needs expressly to be taken out of the definition of "literary work". But that which is not expressly taken out remains within it. What one has here is electrical engineer's notation.

Thus it is, in my judgment, that when the defendants came to make their net list they reproduced the information which is the literary work contained in the circuit diagram.

Whether they did so in relation to the circuits themselves is not that important as far as Mr. Whittle is concerned. There is an argument for saying that the literary work is reproduced in the circuits themselves, not because of the presence of the components in the circuits, but because in relation to each of the components there is also a written or coded indication of what it is. So that one can read the circuit as well as use it. I prefer not to decide whether the circuit infringes however and Mr. Whittle did not ask me to.

Indeed I would have preferred not to have decided this circuit diagram point in any way at all in the absence of argument on the other side. It may well be that in some subsequent case where the matter is fully argued a different view might be taken. But on the arguments of Mr. Whittle that is how I so hold. The consequence is that the action succeeds against the company defendant in relation to all the matters claimed against them in the amended statement of claim. That includes proof of the acts of infringement, not only by reason of sale to a company called Hoval Farrar Limited, but also the sales to the Ford Motor Company.

Notes and Questions

1. What dividing line does the court draw between patents and copyrights? Do you agree?

2. Should the functional nature of the information contained in the circuit diagram preclude its protection under copyright law? Compare the *Circuit Diagram* Case with *Computer Associates International, Inc. v. Altai, Inc.*, 893 F.2d 26 (2d Cir.1990).

3. Should the information contained in the diagrams be subject to patent protection?

4. Given the extended nature of copyright protection—a minimum term usually of the life of the author plus 50 years—should copyright protection be extended to potentially useful or functional designs, charts or information? Should they be protected under patent law, which provides for a shorter period of protection?

5. Should technological advances be protected at all, or should they be freely available to all to assure even greater advances?

Problem

Your client has developed a new software program that assists in the computer generation of architectural drawings for high stress bridges. He used the program to generate a drawing for a new-style joint for a high-suspension bridge. The joint is currently being used with your client's permission in the construction of a new suspension bridge across the Thames. Your client has recently discovered that another company is using the joint to build a bridge in New York City. Your client claims that she developed the program to fill a long-felt need in the construction industry for computer-assisted design (CAD) of high-stress bridge and truss joints. Although other designs exist, your client insists that her design is the most clean, most strong, most easy to use. Your client wants to protect both her computer program, and the drawings and joints that are developed by the program. What problems do you foresee in attempting to obtain international protection for your client's software and joint design? Can you preclude use of the design by the company in New York City if the design was developed using a lawful copy of the software? Using an unlawful copy?

Chapter Ten

TRADEMARKS UNDER INTERNATIONAL LAW

A. WHEN DOES A PRODUCT NAME BECOME PROPERTY?

THE DOMAIN NAME CONTROVERSY

With the development of the Internet, companies are increasingly turning to the Web to advertise and market their products. Under traditional trademark doctrines, a mark is placed directly on the goods or in advertisement for the services rendered under the mark. Thus, COCA COLA® appears on the containers for soda, CITIBANK® appears on bank signs and on ads for banking and financial services and WEST® appears on textbooks. It is easy for consumers to identify the goods or services which the mark signifies. What about the goods or services represented by a domain name? Are they as easily discernible? For example, if you went to the web cite http://www.westgroup.com you would locate the West Group web page. That page displays a variety of information about desktop legal research tools, west clips and jump cites to other West Group cites. But how would you describe the services being offered under the "Westgroup.com" web cite? Internet information services? Legal research services? Are these the same types of services for which service mark protection has traditionally been granted? Some scholars contend that a web page cite or domain name does not really serve a trademark function at all. Instead, it is merely an address for a web page, and, therefore, unworthy of trademark protection. *See* Kenneth L. Port, *The "Unnatural" Expansion of Trademark Rights: Is a Federal Dilution Statute Necessary?* 18 Seton Hall Legis. J. 433 (1994); Gary W. Hamilton, *Trademarks on the Internet: Confusion, Collusion or Dilution?*, 4 Tex Intell. Prop. L. J. 1 (1995); Carl Oppedahl, *Remedies in Domain Name Lawsuits: How is a Domain Name Like a Cow?*, 15 J. Marshall J. Computer & Info L 437 (1997); Dan L. Burk, *Trademarks Along the Infobahn: A First Look at the Emerging Law of Cybermarks,* 1 Rich. J.L. & Tech. 1 (1995).

Even if web cites qualify as a "service" for which trade mark or source designation protection may exist, how should such domain names be distributed internationally? Under traditional trademark doctrines, the same mark may be used on a variety of unrelated goods, by unrelated partied generally without giving rise to trademark confusion. Thus, ACME may be used by both a moving company (for its toys) without causing harm under traditional trademark doctrines. The differences in the goods and the channels of trade and distribution would generally be considered sufficient to avoid confusion. Consequently use of a trademark by one company, does not preclude its adoption and use on unrelated, non-confusing goods and services.

Domain names, used as the location of a web cite on the Internet (such as Westlaw.com), by their very nature arguably can only be used by *one* user. Does "Allied.com" represent the web page of the furniture moving company or the toy company? What if there is a local company in Argentina called "Allied" which manufactures high quality leather goods? Which of the three should obtain rights to the domain name Allied.com? The first to apply? The first to use the domain name? If the first to apply is given rights, cybersquatters may end up with the rights. If the first to use is given rights, companies located in developing countries may be effectively precluded from obtaining web cites under their own marks (because they will have been used by the rest of the world).

In 1996, the IAHC proposed establishing seven new first tier generic domain names. They are:

.web	.firm	.nom
.shop	.arts	
.info	.rec	

Does this resolve the *Allied* conflict described above in a satisfactory matter? Are domain names the types of "symbols" that should be protected under international trademark regimes, or is a sui generis method desirable?

A. WHAT ARE THE VALUES REPRESENTED BY A TRADEMARK?
THE RED SHOES CASE
MISHAWAKA RUBBER & WOOLEN MFG. CO. v. S. S. KRESGE CO.

United States Supreme Court, 1942.
316 U.S. 203, 62 S.Ct. 1022.

MR. JUSTICE FRANKFURTER delivered the opinion of the Court.

The petitioner, which manufactures and sells shoes and rubber heels, employs a trade-mark, registered under the Trade–Mark Act of 1905, 33 Stat. 724, 15 U.S.C. § 81 et seq., 15 U.S.C.A. § 81 et seq., consisting of a red circular plug embedded in the center of a heel. The heels were not sold separately but were attached to shoes made by the petitioner. It has spent considerable sums of money in seeking to gain the favor of the consuming public by promoting the mark as assurance of a desirable product. The respondent sold heels not made by the petitioner but bearing a mark described by the District Court as "a circular plug of red or reddish color so closely resembling that of the plaintiff (petitioner) that it is difficult to distinguish the products sold by the defendant from the plaintiff's products." The heels sold by the respondent were inferior in quality to those made by the petitioner, and "this tended to destroy the good will created by the plaintiff in the manufacture of its superior product." Although there was no evidence that particular purchasers were actually deceived into believing that the heels sold by the respondent were manufactured by the petitioner, the District Court found that there was a "reasonable likelihood" that some purchases might have been induced by the purchaser's belief that he was obtaining the petitioner's product. "The ordinary purchaser having become familiar with the plaintiff's trade-mark, would naturally be led to believe that the heels marketed by the defendant were the product of the plaintiff company." Concluding that the petitioner's mark had thus been infringed, the Court enjoined future infringement and also ordered that the respondent account to the petitioner for profits made from sales "to purchasers who were induced to buy because they believed the heels to be those of plaintiff and which sales plaintiff would otherwise have made."

The protection of trade-marks is the law's recognition of the psychological function of symbols. If it is true that we live by symbols, it is no less true that we purchase goods by them. A trade-mark is a merchandising short-cut which induces a purchaser to select what he wants, or what he has been led to believe he wants. The owner of a mark exploits this human propensity by making every effort to impregnate the atmosphere of the market with the drawing power of a congenial symbol. Whatever the means employed, the aim is the same-to convey through the mark, in the minds of potential customers, the desirability of the commodity upon which it appears. Once this is attained, the trade-mark owner has something of value. If another poaches upon the commercial magnetism of the symbol he has created, the owner can obtain legal redress.

The "right to be protected against an unwarranted use of the registered mark has been made a statutory right" by [the Trade–Mark Act]. Section 19 of the Act provides that "upon a decree being rendered in any such case for wrongful use of a trade-mark the complainant shall be entitled to recover, in addition to the profits to be accounted for by the defendant, the damages the complainant has sustained thereby, and the court shall assess the same or cause the same to be assessed under its direction; and in assessing profits the plaintiff shall be required to prove defendant's sales only; defendant must prove all elements of cost which are claimed." 33 Stat. 724, 729; 15 U.S.C. § 99, 15 U.S.C.A. § 99. Infringement and damage having been found, the Act requires the trademark owner to prove only the sales of articles bearing the infringing mark. Although the award of profits is designed to make the plaintiff whole for losses which the infringer has caused by taking what did not belong to him, Congress did not put upon the despoiled the burden—as often as not impossible to sustain—of showing that but for the defendant's unlawful use of the mark, particular customers would have purchased the plaintiff's goods.

If it can be shown that the infringement had no relation to profits made by the defendant, that some purchasers bought goods bearing the infringing mark because of the defendant's recommendation or his reputation or for any reason other than a response to the diffused appeal of the plaintiff's symbol, the burden of showing this is upon the poacher. The plaintiff of course is not entitled to profits demonstrably not attributable to the unlawful use of his mark. The burden is the infringer's to prove that his infringement had no cash value in sales made by him. If he does not do so, the profits made on sales of goods bearing the infringing mark properly belong to the owner of the mark. There may well be a windfall to the trade-mark owner where it is impossible to isolate the profits which are attributable to the use of the infringing mark. But to hold otherwise would give the windfall to the wrongdoer. In the absence of his proving the contrary, it promotes honesty and comports with experience to assume that the wrongdoer who makes profits from the sales of goods bearing a mark belonging to another was enabled to do so because he was drawing upon the good will generated by that mark. And one who makes profits derived from the unlawful appropriation of a mark belonging to another cannot relieve himself of his obligation to restore the profits to their rightful owner merely by showing that the latter did not choose to use the mark in the particular manner employed by the wrongdoer.

Reversed.

THE TRADE–MARK CASES
UNITED STATES v. STEFFENS; UNITED STATES v. WITTEMANN; UNITED STATES v. JOHNSON

United States Supreme Court, 1879.
100 U.S. 82.

MR. JUSTICE MILLER delivered the opinion of the court.

The three cases whose titles stand at the head of this opinion are criminal prosecutions for violations of what is known as the trade-mark legislation of Congress. The first two are indictments in the southern district of New York, and the last is an information in the southern district of Ohio. In all of them the judges of the circuit courts in which they are pending have certified to a difference of opinion on what is substantially the same question; namely, are the acts of Congress on the subject of trade-marks founded on any rightful authority in the Constitution of the United States?

The entire legislation of Congress in regard to trade-marks is of very recent origin.

As the first and only attempt by Congress to regulate the right of trade-marks is to be found in the act of July 8, 1870, entitled "An Act to revise, consolidate, and amend the statutes relating to patents and copyrights,' terms which have long since become technical, as referring, the one to inventions and the other to the writings of authors, it is a reasonable inference that this part of the statute also was, in the opinion of Congress, an exercise of the power found in [the Patents and Copyright] clause of the Constitution

Any attempt to identify the essential characteristics of a trade-mark with inventions and discoveries in the arts and sciences, or with the writings of authors, will show that the effort is surrounded with insurmountable difficulties.

The ordinary trade-mark has no necessary relation to invention or discovery. The trade-mark recognized by the common law is generally the growth of a considerable period of use, rather than a sudden invention. It is often the result of accident rather than design, and when under the act of Congress it is sought to establish it by registration, neither originality, invention, discovery, science, nor art is in any way essential to the right conferred by that act. If we should endeavor to classify it under the head of writings of authors, the objections are equally strong. In this, as in regard to inventions, originality is required. And while the word writings may be liberally construed, as it has been, to include original designs for engravings, prints, & c., it is only such as are original, and are founded in the creative powers of the mind. The writings which are to be protected are the fruits of intellectual labor, embodied in the form of books, prints, engravings, and the like. The trade-mark may be, and generally is, the adoption of something already in existence as the distinctive symbol of the party using it. At common law the exclusive right to it grows out of its use, and not its mere adoption. By the act of Congress this exclusive right attaches upon registration. But in neither case does it depend upon novelty, invention, discovery, or any work of the brain. It requires no fancy or imagination, no genius, no laborious thought. It is simply founded on priority of appropriation. We look in vain in the statute for any other qualification or condition. If the symbol, however plain, simple, old, or well-known, has been first appropriated by the claimant as his distinctive trade-mark, he may by registration secure the right to its exclusive use. While such legislation may be a judicious aid to the common law on the subject of trade-marks, and may be within the competency of legislatures whose general powers embrace that class of subjects, we are unable to see any such power in the constitutional provision concerning authors and inventors, and their writings and discoveries.

Notes and Questions

1. Do you agree with the court in *The Trademark Cases* that the creation of trademarks requires little if any "intellectual" labor? If the

purpose of trademark laws is *not* to encourage the expenditure of intellectual labor in creating the trademark, what is its purpose? Should the originality of a trademark play any role in its protection under international standards?

2. *Creativity*. Although the creation of a trademark clearly requires at least some modicum of creativity, trademarks have long suffered from being considered less intellectually desirable than copyrights or patents. This second-class status may be devolved in part from the plainly commercial nature of the property involved. An artist may write a novel for his own personal pleasure, a scientist may invent a new formula for paint for the same reason, but a trademark is only created to be used in marketing a particular product or service. It is this source designating function and *not* the intellectual labor involved in creating the trademark that is protected under international standards.

3. *Image Advertising and Brand Names*. One of the problems with trademarks internationally is their perceived role in encouraging consumers in developing countries to spend their money on famous brand names, when a less-expensive local brand will do as well. Thus, for example, given the choice among two soft drinks, LONG'S COLA and COCA–COLA®, consumers may buy COCA–COLA® even when LONG'S COLA is cheaper and would cure a person's thirst as well as COCA–COLA®. Part of the selection of COCA–COLA® over LONG'S COLA may be the result of a taste preference by consumers, but another psychological reason for the choice is the desire to demonstrate sophistication and the ability to afford the "finer" (Western) things in life. This image role of trademarks has been strongly condemned by some countries. *See, e.g.*, Mitchell M. Wong, *The Aesthetic Functionality Doctrine and the Law of Trade–Dress Protection*, 83 Cornell L. Rev. 1116. (1998). *See generally* Joan Meyers–Levy, *The Influence of a Brand Name's Association Set Size and Word Frequency on Brand Memory*, 16 J. Consumer Res. 197 (1989); Thomas D. Drescher, *The Transformation and Evolution of Trademarks From Signals to Symbols to Myth*, 82 Trademark Rep. 301 (1992). In order to "combat" such "harm," some countries required that foreign marks be licensed to local companies. Others required that the local name appear alongside the more famous brand name to help develop brand identification. Thus, in this hypothetical, Long's would be allowed to call its product "Long's Coca Cola." What impact does such joint use have on the name-recognition or psychological impact of the COCA–COLA® trademark? Is there any benefit to the foreign trademark owner from such local use?

4. COCA–COLA®, MCDONALD'S®, PIZZA HUT®, KENTUCKY FRIED CHICKEN® are world-renowned trademarks that represent billions of dollars of investment in advertising for their respective companies. One of the greatest challenges for intellectual property owners in the latter days of the Twentieth Century is assuring the continued viability of these trademarks in the global marketplace. As more and more companies compete in the provision of goods and services internationally, each strives to develop a recognizable trademark that will encourage consumers to select that company's products over those of a competitor. Advertising increasingly focuses on "image" encouraging consumers to buy a particular product because it is the choice of the young, the wealthy or the sophisticated. In many instances the only difference between products be may the brand name under which it is sold. As marketing techniques become more sophisticated, companies are

seeking to distinguish their goods on the basis of the sounds they make (a HARLEY DAVIDSON® motorcycle), their smell (the plumeria smell of Clarke's yarn), their product configuration (the Grecian urn of Duraco), their marketing techniques (the "adoption" papers for CABBAGE PATCH® dolls) and just about any other feature that could be used to distinguish a company's goods from those of another. As companies attempt to stretch the boundaries of trademarks, conflicts inevitably arise regarding the role of trademark protection in a global economy.

THE COKE BOTTLE CASE
IN RE COCA–COLA CO'S APPLICATIONS

House Of Lords, 1986.
[1986] 2 All ER 274, [1986] 1 WLR 695, [1986] FSR 472, [1986] RPC 421.

LORD TEMPLEMAN.

[Coca–Cola sought to register its "classic" bottle as a trademark. The application was denied on the grounds that trademark protection did not extend to containers.]

My Lords, this is another attempt to expand on the boundaries of intellectual property and to convert a protective law into a source of monopoly. The attempt to use the Copyright Act 1956 for this purpose failed recently in British Leyland Motor Corp. Ltd. v. Armstrong Patents Co. Ltd. [1986] 1 All ER 850, [1986] 2 WLR 400.

Since the early 1920s the appellant, the Coca–Cola Co, has sold in the United Kingdom a non-alcoholic beverage under the name 'Coca-Cola' contained in bottles of a distinctive shape.

The Patents Act 1977 and its predecessors conferred on the inventor of a registered novel product the right for a period, now 20 years, to control the use of the invention. The Coca–Cola bottle is not a novel product. The Copyright Act 1956 and its predecessors conferred on the author of an original artistic work the right for the life of the author and 50 years thereafter to control the reproduction of the work. The Coca–Cola bottle is not an artistic work. The Registered Designs Act 1949 and its predecessor, the Patents and Designs Act 1907, conferred on the author of a registered design the right for 15 years to control the use of the design. By § 1(3) of the 1949 Act "design" means:

> "features of shape, configuration, pattern or ornament applied to an article by any industrial process or means, being features which in the finished article appeal to and are judged solely by the eye ..."

The shape of the Coca–Cola bottle was accepted as a design and was registered under the 1907 Act. The effect of this registration expired in 1940 since when any rival manufacturer has been free to use the design of the Coca–Cola bottle.

The Coca–Cola Co now claims that during and since the period of protection for the Coca–Cola bottle under the 1907 Act the Coca–Cola Co has been entitled to a monopoly in the Coca–Cola bottle as a trade mark. The application of the Coca–Cola Co to register the Coca–Cola bottle as a trade mark has been rejected by the hearing officer, by Falconer J, and by the Court of Appeal (Lawton, Browne–Wilkinson LJJ and Sir Denis Buckley) ([1985] FSR 315). The Coca–Cola Co, undeterred by this formidable display of judicial unanimity, now appeals with the leave of the House.

The 1938 Act confers on the proprietor of a registered trade mark the exclusive right in perpetuity, subject to payment of fees and the observance of certain conditions not here relevant, to the use of a trade mark which is distinctive. By § 9(2) of the 1938 Act "distinctive" means "adapted, in relation to the goods in respect of which a trade mark is registered or proposed to be registered, to distinguish goods with which the proprietor of the trade mark is or may be connected in the course of trade from goods in the case of which no such connection subsists."

I assume, without deciding, that the Coca–Cola bottle is distinctive of a bottle containing the Coca–Cola beverage purveyed by the Coca–Cola Co. The application by the Coca–Cola Co is for the registration of the Coca–Cola bottle with its distinctive shape as a trade mark in respect of non-alcoholic beverages.

It is not sufficient for the Coca–Cola bottle to be distinctive. The Coca–Cola Co must succeed in the startling proposition that the bottle is a trade mark. If so, then any other container or any article of a distinctive shape is capable of being a trade mark. This raises the spectre of a total and perpetual monopoly in containers and articles achieved by means of the 1938 Act. Once the container or article has become associated with the manufacturer and distinctiveness has been established, with or without the help of the monopolies created by the Patents Act, the Registered Designs Act or the Copyright Act, the perpetual trade mark monopoly in the container or article can be achieved. In my opinion the 1938 Act was not intended to confer on the manufacturer of a container or on the manufacturer of an article a statutory monopoly on the ground that the manufacturer has in the eyes of the public established a connection between the shape of the container or article and the manufacturer. A rival manufacturer must be free to sell any container or article of similar shape provided the container or article is labelled or packaged in a manner which avoids confusion as to the origin of the goods in the container or the origin of the article. The Registrar of Trade Marks has always taken the view that the function of trade mark legislation is to protect the mark but not the article which is marked. I agree. By § 68(1) of the Act of 1938: "mark" includes a device, brand, heading, label, ticket, name, signature, word, letter, numeral, or any combination thereof. "Trade mark" means. "A mark used or proposed to be used in relation to goods for the purpose of indicating, or so as to indicate, a connection in the course of trade between the goods and some person having

> the right either as proprietor or as registered user to use the mark, whether with or without any indication of the identity of that person."

The word "mark" both in its normal meaning and in its statutory definition is apt only to describe something which distinguishes goods rather that the goods themselves. A bottle is a container not a mark. The distinction between a mark and the thing which is marked is supported by authority. In *Re James's Trade Mark, James v. Soulby* (1886) 33 Ch. D 392, the plaintiffs sold black lead in the form of a dome and in other shapes. Their products were impressed with the representation of a dome and their labels carried a picture of a black dome. The plaintiffs were allowed to register the representation or picture of a black dome as their trade mark. Similarly, the Coca–Cola Co has been allowed to register a line drawing of a Coca–Cola bottle as a trade mark. But, dealing with the article itself, in *Re James's Trade Mark* Lindley LJ said (at 395):

> "A mark must be something distinct from the thing being marked. The thing itself cannot be a mark of itself, but here we have got the thing and we have got a mark on the thing, and the question is, whether that mark on the thing is or is not a distinctive mark within the meaning of the Act. Of course the plaintiffs' in this case have no monopoly in black lead of this shape. Anybody may make black lead of this shape provided he does not mark it as the plaintiffs mark theirs, and provided he does not pass it off as the plaintiffs' black lead. There is no monopoly in the shape, and I cannot help thinking that that has not been sufficiently kept in mind. What the plaintiffs have registered is a brand, a mark like a dome intended to represent a dome."

In the course of argument counsel for the Coca–Cola Co relied on the decision of this House in *Smith Kline and French Laboratories Ltd. v. Sterling–Winthrop Group Ltd.* [1975] 2 All ER 578, [1975] 1 WLR 914. In that case the plaintiffs were allowed to register 10 distinctive colour combinations as trade marks for drugs sold in pellet form within capsules. One typical example was:

> "The trade mark consists of a maroon colour applied to one half of the capsule at one end, and the other half being colourless and transparent, and yellow, blue and white colours being each applied to a substantial number of pellets so that each pellet is of one colour only.' ([1975] 2 All ER 578 at 581, [1975] 1 WLR 914 at 916)

The Smith Kline case only related to the colour of goods and has no application to the goods themselves or to a container for goods. A colour combination may tend to an undesirable monopoly in colours but does not create an undesirable monopoly in goods or containers. I do not consider that the Smith Kline case is of assistance to the Coca–Cola Co. I would accordingly dismiss this appeal.

Notes and Questions

1. Do you agree with the House of Lord's decision in the *Coke Bottle* case? Do you think consumers recognized that the Coca–Cola bottle was a source designator? Would it make a difference if the company developed the bottle shape specifically to serve as a trademark? What if the evidence proved that the shape of the Coca–Cola bottle was the most effective shape for ensuring a long shelf-life for carbonated beverages? Should this have any impact on the decision whether to grant trademark protection to the bottle shape?

2. Problems arise when the purported "trade dress" feature also serves a functional or aesthetic purpose. Thus, for example, if a company has developed a uniquely shaped spray bottle for its cleaning products, should it be able to prohibit others from using the container's shape on the basis that the shape is a trademark for the product? What if the shape qualifies for patent protection because of its useful design? Can a patent owner later claim protection for his patented design because it has become a trademark for his product?

3. *Paris Convention.* Although trademarks have been in existence for thousands of years (the first reported trademark may well have been the marks found on pottery created 3500 years ago), their international protection remains inconsistent. The first significant multinational treaty dealing with trademark issues, the Paris Convention, was adopted in 1883. Despite this early recognition of the importance of establishing an international protection regime for trademarks, the Convention itself did not even define the primary features of a trademark. To the contrary, it dealt almost exclusively with international registration issues. No multinational treaty definition of trademarks was established until the adoption of TRIPS in the 1990's.

4. *TRIPS.* TRIPS defines a trademark as "any sign or any combination of signs, capable of distinguishing the goods or services of one undertaking from those of other undertakings." (Article 15) Must the Coca–Cola bottle design be protected under the TRIPS definition of a trademark?

5. Must a mark which consists of three musical tones (a sound mark) be protected under TRIPS? What about a mark that is composed of the shape of the product itself? What about a domain name (the name of a web page cite on the Internet)?

6. The United States defines a trademark as "any word, name, symbol or device, or any combination thereof used by a person ... to identify and distinguish his or her goods, including a unique product, from those manufactured or sold by others and to indicate the source of the goods, even if that source is unknown" (15 U.S.C. § 1127.)

7. Great Britain defines a trademark as: "any sign capable of being represented graphically which is capable of distinguishing goods or services of one undertaking from those of other undertakings" (Trade Marks Act 1994, ch. 26 § 1(1)).

8. China defines a trademark as: "Any word, device, or their combination that is [also] distinctive so as to be distinguishable." (China Trademark Law of 1993, Article 7.)

9. Japan defines a trademark as: "letters, figures or symbols or three dimensional shapes or any combination of these including their combination with colors. . . . used by a person in respect of the goods it manufactures, certifies or sells as a part of its business or used by a person in respect of the services it offers or certifies as a part of its business." (Trademark Law No. 68 of 1997, as amended).

10. Egypt defines a trademark as "names assuming distinctive shapes, signatures, words, letters, numerals, designs, symbols, signboards, stamps, seals, vignettes, embossed engravings, and any other mark or any combination thereof, used or proposed to be used, either for distinguishing the products of any industrial, agricultural, forest or mining venture or any other goods, or for indicating the origin, quality, category, guarantee, method of preparation or performance of services." (The Republic of Egypt Trademark Law (No. 57 of 1939), Article 1).

11. Russia defines a trademark as "designations capable of distinguishing accordingly the goods and services of legal or natural persons from similar goods and services . . . of other legal or natural persons." (Law of the Russian Federation Trademarks of 1992, Article 1).

12. Do these definitions comply with the minimum substantive requirements of the TRIPS agreement? Would a sound mark, product shape or domain name fall within the scope of protection of these statutes? Should it as a matter of policy?

THE GRECIAN URN CASE
DURACO PRODUCTS, INC. v. JOY PLASTIC ENTERPRISES, LTD.

United States Court of Appeals, Third Circuit, 1994.
40 F.3d 1431.

BECKER, CIRCUIT JUDGE.

[Plaintiff Duraco Products claimed the defendant had infringed its trade dress in its plastic planters molded in the shape of Grecian urns. In denying relief, the court was critical of efforts to extend trademark protection to product (as opposed to container) configurations.]

"Trade dress" originally referred to the packaging or displays associated with trademarked goods. That principle of trade dress law grounded in design protection has since been extended to the design of a product itself.

The Lanham Act protection of product configurations extends to "the total image of a product, including features such as size, shape, color or color combinations, texture, graphics, or even particular sales techniques." *Computer Care v. Service Sys. Enters., Inc.*, 982 F.2d 1063, 1067 (7th Cir.1992).

In this case we deal exclusively with trade dress said to inhere in the product itself, rather than trade dress alleged in a product's packaging. Because the legal doctrines in these two very different situations will substantially diverge in various incidents, we will employ the designation "product configuration" to refer to trade dress alleged in the product itself, whether in a specific feature or in some combination or arrangement of features, and to distinguish that type of trade dress from "product packaging."

Duraco argues that the design of its Grecian Classics planters is inherently distinctive because it is "suggestive." Duraco borrows the term "suggestive" from trademark law, as trademarks have long been classified according to whether they are generic, descriptive, suggestive, arbitrary, or fanciful. In trademark law, marks belonging to the latter three categories of the taxonomy-suggestive, arbitrary, or fanciful-are deemed inherently distinctive and are automatically entitled to protection. Marks falling within the first category—generic marks—are never subject to trademark protection, because to tolerate their monopolization would preclude competitors from accurately and efficiently describing their products and hence unduly hobble them in competition. The marks falling within the remaining category—descriptive—acquire distinctiveness only if they come to identify and distinguish the producer's goods, i.e., if they acquire secondary meaning. To have acquired secondary meaning, "in the minds of the public, the primary significance of a product feature or term [must be] to identify the source of the product rather than the product itself." *Inwood Labs., Inc. v. Ives Labs., Inc.*, 456 U.S. 844, 851 n. 11, 102 S.Ct. 2182, 2187 n. 11, 72 L.Ed.2d 606 (1982) (dicta).

[U]nlike product packaging, a product configuration differs fundamentally from a product's trademark, insofar as it is not a symbol according to which one can relate the signifier (the trademark, or perhaps the packaging) to the signified (the product). Being constitutive of the product itself and thus having no such dialectical relationship to the product, the product's configuration cannot be said to be "suggestive" or "descriptive" of the product, or "arbitrary" or "fanciful" in relation to it. The very basis for the trademark taxonomy—the descriptive relationship between the mark and the product, along with the degree to which the mark describes the product—is unsuited for application to the product itself.

Moreover, insofar as consumer motivation to purchase a product will much more likely be predicated on an appreciation of a product's features than on an appreciation of a product's name, assuming no secondary meaning attached to either, one cannot automatically conclude from a product feature or configuration—as one can from a product's arbitrary name, for example—that, to a consumer, it functions primarily to denote the product's source. As Judge Nies wrote, concurring in *In re DC Comics, Inc.*, 689 F.2d 1042, 1050–51 (C.C.P.A.1982):

> There are different considerations where one seeks protection of a product design itself, and I have found no precedent in decisions of this court, or others, which recognizes the protectability of any product design as a trademark for that product without proof of distinctiveness, that is, distinctiveness as an indication of origin, not simply that it is a distinctive design in the sense of being unusual.

The semantics, in referring to a design as "distinctive," impedes clarity in analysis. Descriptive designations are not presumed to function as indications of origin immediately upon first use, unlike arbitrary word marks or arbitrary logo designs, but rather must be used from some period of time before acquiring the status of a trademark.

Thus, a fanciful or arbitrary mark, having had no established meaning prior to its adoption as a trademark and serving no apparent purpose other than to identify (signify) the source, is legally presumed to achieve customer recognition and association immediately upon its adoption and use. In contrast, a product configuration can not generally give rise to a similar presumption, as consumers usually appreciate a product's configuration for its contribution to the inherent appeal of the product, not (in the absence of secondary meaning) its signifying function. If one felt compelled to apply the trademark taxonomy, one could at best say that a product configuration is descriptive of (because identical with) the product itself. This case illustrates the point rather clearly: whether or not the Grecian Classics are "suggestive" of a marble construction or anything else, we think it quite improbable that a consumer upon seeing Joy's plastic planter in a store would reasonably associate its specific configuration with a particular source, even if the consumer had repeatedly before seen a Duraco plastic planter.

Accordingly, for all the aforementioned considerations, we conclude that the trademark taxonomy, carefully and precisely crafted through a long succession of cases to accommodate the particularities of trademarks, does not fit the quite different considerations applicable to product configurations.

Congress has repeatedly chosen not to protect designs unless they meet certain strict requirements. We believe that courts should exercise restraint so as not to undermine Congress's repeated determinations not to afford virtually perpetual protection to product configurations with an expansive construction of section 43(a). What Congress has, for the great span of this century, been unwilling to do, should not be effected by the judiciary.

Thus Duraco's suggestion, that the capacity of the product's configuration to distinguish the plaintiff's goods from others suffices to establish inherent distinctiveness, is grossly overinclusive. It is also circular: clearly any perceptible product feature or combination or arrangement of features can distinguish goods, and perhaps is likely to do so if, as a rule, nobody else were allowed to copy it. That is, provided that no one besides the originator is allowed to use a particular feature, it would be difficult to conjure up any perceptible feature that users can train upon that is not capable of distinguishing the originator's goods from those of others. For example, even the basic design of a light bulb is "capable of identifying a particular source of the product," assuming that only one manufacturer produces the basic design, a fact which would be assured, of course, if the design were protected against copying.

Duraco's proposal to treat any product feature or configuration as inherently distinctive if it were merely capable of identifying the source of the product would therefore eviscerate the requirement for showing secondary meaning.

In any event, the analysis appropriate for a product's packaging, is not necessarily appropriate for a product's configuration. Product packaging designs, like trademarks, often share membership in a practically inexhaustible set of distinct but approximately equivalent variations, and an exclusive right to a particular overall presentation generally does not substantially hinder competition in the packaged good, the item in which a consumer has a basic interest. A product configuration, contrariwise, commonly has finite competitive variations that, on the whole, are equally acceptable to consumers. Moreover, because of consumers' common abundant experience with similar goods being sold in differing packaging, a consumer is substantially more likely to trust a product's packaging, rather than its configuration, as an indicium of source.

It is not ipso facto "unfair competition," we believe, for one boldly to copy a competitor's product; it is only "unfair competition" to trade off another's good will and in the process dupe consumers into mistaking one's products for another's. A proper approach to inherent distinctiveness must distinguish between nonfunctional but desirable designs—which, absent secondary meaning, unfair competition law has no interest in precluding others from copying—and nonfunctional designs representing to consumers the source of the goods—which unfair competition law does and should forbid others from copying.

For a product configuration to have the capacity to distinguish goods in a consumer's mind—the first prerequisite for inherent distinctiveness—it must be unusual and memorable. It must partake of a unique, individualized appearance, so that a consumer informed of all the options available in the market could reasonably rely on it to identify a source.

Moreover, unless the trade dress is memorable—that is, striking or unusual in appearance, or prominently displayed on the product packaging, or otherwise somehow apt to be impressed upon the minds of consumers, so that it is likely to be actually and distinctly remembered—it cannot serve as a designator of origin. Thus, for example, designs customary in the industry can not be inherently distinctive (nor for that matter can they acquire secondary meaning).

But the uniqueness of a product configuration is not enough by itself to make the configuration inherently distinctive. To be inherently distinctive, a product configuration must also be conceptually separable from the product, so that a consumer will recognize its symbolic (signifying) character. This requirement ensures that consumers unaware of any association of the product with a manufacturer (i.e., where a configuration has no secondary meaning) will not become confused about whether a particular configuration may be trusted as an indicium of origin. To be conceptually separable, the product configuration must be recognizable by the consumer "as an indicium of source, rather than a decorative symbol or pattern.... " *Stuart Hall*, 31 U.S.P.Q.2d at 1471, 1994 WL 228939 at *4 (internal quotation marks omitted).

As with trademarks, an inherently protectable product configuration must, at least conceptually, be "something other than, and separate from, the merchandise." *Davis v. Davis*, 27 F. 490, 492 (C.C.Mass.1886). That is, the configuration for which protection is sought must not appear to the consumer as a mere component, or the essence, of the product gestalt, but rather must appear as something attached (in a conceptual sense) to function in actuality as a source designator—it must appear to the consumer to act as an independent signifier of origin rather than as a component of the good.

Third, to be inherently distinctive, it must be likely that the product configuration will primarily serve as a designator of the source of the product. If the configuration itself, separate from the product, is likely to serve some substantial purpose other than as a designation of origin— that is, besides to set it apart from other sources' products in consumers' minds—then it cannot be inherently distinctive, but must acquire secondary meaning before becoming entitled to protection against copying.

We acknowledge that, to a large extent, how courts resolve the inherent distinctiveness inquiry could, theoretically at least, cause a snowballing effect. If product configurations are easily protected, consumers might learn to rely on configurations as source designators; if protection is rare, consumers will disregard product configurations as source designators, and no confusion will result. But partial protection, if not carefully circumscribed, may eventually cause even greater consumer confusion, as consumers will face difficulties determining what features are legitimate source designators (because inherently distinctive) and which are not. The narrow test that we adopt encourages consumers to rely on a product's configuration as a source designator only when it rather plainly serves an identifying function.

Notes and Questions

1. In the *Grecian Urn* case, the court demonstrated a marked hostility toward the protection of product designs under trademark law. Is there any difference between a product design, such as the Grecian urn planter in this case and a container design such as the Coca–Cola bottle that would warrant different treatment?

2. What if the evidence demonstrated that a Grecian urn design is common in Greece but has never been used in Lesotho? Should the design in the *Grecian Urn* case qualify for protection in Lethoso as a trademark, even if it is not protectable in Greece? What if this design were world renown? Should this fact have an impact on its protection internationally?

3. *Fame.* Article 6*bis* of the Paris Convention requires members to "refuse or to cancel the registration, and to prohibit the use, of a trademark which constitutes a reproduction, an imitation, or a translation, liable to create confusion, of a mark considered by the competent authority of the country of registration or use to be *well known* in that country..." What

evidence would you supply to demonstrate the your client's Grecian urn design was "well-known"? What if your client had never used the Grecian urn mark in a particular country? Would that preclude its protection as a "well-known" mark? For a further discussion of the problem of protecting "famous" marks internationally, *see* Part VII.

C. WHERE DO YOU DRAW THE LINE BE-TWEEN PATENTABLE INVENTIONS AND TRADEMARKABLE DESIGNS?

THE FAN CONFIGURATION CASE

VORNADO AIR CIRCULATION SYSTEMS, INC., v. DURACRAFT CORPORATION

United States Circuit Court of Appeals, Tenth Circuit, 1995.
58 F.3d 1498.

ANDERSON, CIRCUIT JUDGE.

This case presents an issue of first impression in our circuit concerning the intersection of the Patent Act and the Lanham Trade–Mark Act. We must decide whether a product configuration is entitled to trade dress protection when it is or has been a significant inventive component of an invention covered by a utility patent.

After expiration of any patents or copyrights on an invention, that invention normally passes into the public domain and can be freely copied by anyone. The district court found, however, that because the spiral structure of the household fan grill in question is "nonfunctional," a status largely determined by the availability of enough alternative grill designs so that other fan manufacturers can effectively compete without it, the grill can serve as trade dress. The court held that the grill could be protected under Lanham Act section 43(a) against copying by competitors, because that copying was likely to confuse consumers.

The court's injunction effectively prevents defendant Duracraft Corp. from ever practicing the full invention embodied in the patented fans of plaintiff Vornado Air Circulation Systems, Inc., after Vornado's utility patents expire. For the reasons discussed below, we find this result to be untenable. We hold that although a product configuration must be nonfunctional in order to be protected as trade dress under section 43(a), not every nonfunctional configuration is eligible for that protection. Where a product configuration is a significant inventive component of an invention covered by a utility patent, so that without it the invention cannot fairly be said to be the same invention, patent policy dictates that it enter into the public domain when the utility patents on the fans expire. To ensure that result, it cannot receive trade dress protection under section 43(a). The district court's order is reversed.

The product configurations at issue in this case are two household fan grills with spiral—or arcuate—vanes, produced by the plaintiff, Vornado, and the defendant, Duracraft.

The idea of using a spiral grill on a fan is not new. An arcuate vane structure for propellers "applicable to ventilators and the like" was reflected in expired U.S. Patent No. 1,062,258, a utility patent issued May 20, 1913, to G.A. Schlotter, and arcuate vanes were incorporated into a household fan guard as early as 1936, as shown by expired U.S. Patent No. 2,110,994, a utility patent issued to J.H. Cohen.

Vornado began selling its fans with spiral grills in November 1988, at a time when it was the only fan company using that type of grill. On January 9, 1989, Vornado's founders, Donald J. Moore and Michael C. Coup, applied for a utility patent on their ducted fan with a spiral grill. They asserted, among other things, that their spiral grill produced an optimum air flow, although their own tests had shown that it performed about the same as the more common straight radial grill, and later tests suggested that some other grills worked better in some respects.

Their patent application claimed a fan with multiple features, including the spiral grill. The inventive aspect of Vornado's spiral grill was that the point of maximum lateral spacing between the curved vanes was moved inboard from the grill's outer radius, so that it was at the impeller blade's point of maximum power. Vornado emphasizes that its fan grill was not patentable by itself because a spiral grill per se was already in the public domain as "prior art," a patent law term for what was already known from previous patents or other sources.

On May 22, 1990, Messrs. Moore and Coup were issued a utility patent. They subsequently applied for and on February 22, 1994, were granted a reissue patent expanding their claims, including those that involved the arcuate-shaped grill vane structure.

Vornado advertised its grill as the "Patented AirTensity Grill," although the company had no separate patent on the grill. Between January 1989 and August 1990, Vornado sold about 135,000 fans. In its advertising, the company touted the grill as a "true achievement in aerodynamic efficiency," "the result of determinant ergonomic design," with "unique AirTensity vortex action," accomplishing "a high degree of safety and functionality."

In August 1990, Duracraft began offering an inexpensive electric household fan called the Model DT–7 "Turbo Fan." The grill on Duracraft's Turbo Fan incorporated a spiral vane structure that was copied from Vornado's considerably more expensive fan models but was purposely designed not to infringe Vornado's patent. Apart from its look-alike grill and some aspects of the fan blade design, the Turbo Fan differed significantly from Vornado's fans in its overall configuration, its base and duct structure, its center knob, neon colors, packaging, labeling, and price. The box in which the Turbo Fan came had a circle cut out of the front so that the grill design showed through and was emphasized when the fan was displayed in its box.

By November 1992, Duracraft had sold nearly one million Turbo Fans in the United States. The Turbo Fan was the company's second-largest-selling household fan product.

Section 43(a) of the Lanham Act, 15 U.S.C. 1125(a), provides a federal cause of action for unprivileged imitation, including trade dress infringement. Trade dress features are those comprising a product's look or image.

A plaintiff in a trade dress infringement case must make two showings. First, the plaintiff must show either (a) that its product's trade dress features (or feature) are inherently distinctive because their intrinsic nature is such as to "almost automatically tell a customer that they refer to a brand," or (b) that the trade dress has become distinctive through acquisition of secondary meaning, so that its primary significance in the minds of potential consumers is no longer as an indicator of something about the product itself but as an indicator of its source or brand. Second, a plaintiff must show that potential customers are likely to be confused by the defendant's trade dress into thinking that the defendant is affiliated, connected or associated with the plaintiff or that the defendant's goods originated with, or are sponsored or approved by the plaintiff. *See* 15 U.S.C. 1125(a).

The producer of an allegedly infringing product may defend by showing that what the plaintiff is claiming as its trade dress is functional, and therefore that all competitors must be permitted to copy it in their own products, regardless of any producer-identifying capacity it may possess.

[P]atent law creates a federal right to copy and use product features that are in the public domain, whether under an expired patent or for lack of patentability in the first place.

When asked to balance the concerns of patent law against those of unfair competition law with respect to the copying of product shapes, the Supreme Court has ruled repeatedly over the years that the right to copy must prevail. Applying the common law of unfair competition, the Court held in Kellogg that it was not unfair competition for Kellogg Co. to copy National Biscuit Co.'s pillow-shaped shredded wheat cereal after invalidation of the design patent for the cereal shape and expiration of the utility patents for the machines to make it, where Kellogg had made reasonable efforts to distinguish its product by using a different carton, label, company name, and biscuit size. *See Kellogg,* 305 U.S. at 119–22. In *Singer,* the Court reached the same conclusion regarding the defendant's copying of Singer sewing machines after their patents had expired. *See Singer,* 163 U.S. at 185–202.

Despite what appears to be a widespread perception that product configurations covered by utility patents are automatically functional for Lanham Act purposes, the district court in our case ably demonstrated that this is not so. Configurations can simultaneously be patentably useful, novel, and nonobvious and also nonfunctional, in trade dress parlance. To obtain a utility patent, an inventor need only show that an invention is 1) useful in the sense of serving some identified, beneficial purpose, and then—much more difficult to prove—that it is 2) novel, i.e., not previously known, and 3) nonobvious, or sufficiently inventive, in light of prior art. *See* 35 U.S.C. §§ 101–103.

Functionality, by contrast, has been defined both by our circuit, and more recently by the Supreme Court, in terms of competitive need. *See Qualitex,* 115 S. Ct. at 1304–07; *Hartford,* 846 F.2d at 1272–74; *Brunswick,* 832 F.2d at 519; *see also* Restatement (Third) of Unfair Competition 17 & cmts. a & b (1995). If competitors need to be able to use a particular configuration in order to make an equally competitive product, it is functional, but if they do not, it may be nonfunctional. The availability of equally satisfactory alternatives for a particular feature, and not its inherent usefulness, is often the fulcrum on which Lanham Act functionality analysis turns.

Given that the functionality doctrine does not eliminate overlap between the Patent Act and the Lanham Act, we must decide whether Vornado is right that this doctrine nevertheless should be used to limit patent law's public domain.

Except to the extent that Congress has clearly indicated which of two statutes it wishes to prevail in the event of a conflict, we must interpret and apply them in a way that preserves the purposes of both and fosters harmony between them. Where, as here, both cannot apply, we look to their fundamental purposes to choose which one must give way.

First, patent law seeks to foster and reward invention; second, it promotes disclosure of inventions to stimulate further innovation and to permit the public to practice the invention once the patent expires; third, the stringent requirements for patent protection seek to assure that ideas in the public domain remain there for the free use of the public.

Vornado suggests that no patent law purpose is served by allowing copying of product configurations that are not necessary to competition. We cannot agree. We find no support in the Patent Act itself or its application for the proposition that the patent goals are limited to enhancing competition, at least in the direct sense. To the contrary, patents operate by temporarily reducing competition. They create monopolies to reward inventors who invent " 'things which are worth to the public the embarrassment of an exclusive patent.' " *Graham v. John Deere Co.,* 383 U.S. 1, 9, 15 L. Ed. 2d 545, 86 S. Ct. 684 (1966) (quoting Thomas Jefferson, author of the 1793 Patent Act). Although competition ultimately may be enhanced by the increased product supply that results from operation of the patent law, the system's more obvious objective is to give the public the benefits of technological progress.

In this respect, it is significant that the framers of the patent system did not require an inventor to demonstrate an invention's superiority to existing products in order to qualify for a patent. That they did not do so tells us that the patent system seeks not only superior inventions but also a multiplicity of inventions. A variety of choices is more likely to satisfy the desires of a greater number of consumers than is a single set of products deemed "optimal" in some average sense by patent examiners and/or judges. And the ability to intermingle and extrapolate from many inventors' solutions to the same problem is more likely to lead to further technological advances than is a single, linear approach seeking to advance one "superior" line of research and development. We conclude that patent law seeks the invention and the passing into the public domain of even what trade dress law would consider nonfunctional inventions.

Allowing an inventor both patent and trade dress protection in a configuration would not necessarily inhibit invention directly. Quite the opposite, this double benefit would probably increase an inventor's direct incentives to pursue an idea. But the inventor's supply of ideas itself and freedom to experiment with them might diminish if the inventor had to do a competitive market analysis before adopting useful features from others' inventions once their patents expired. *See Bonito Boats,* 489 U.S. at 161–62 (stating that federal patent scheme allows public to ascertain status of intellectual property embodied in a manufacture or design, and "the public may rely upon the lack of notice in exploiting shapes and designs accessible to all").

The core concepts of trademark protection are that consumers not be confused, misled, or deceived as to whose product they are buying, that sellers' goodwill—or investment in their reputation for quality—be protected, and that competition thereby be enhanced. *See Park 'N Fly, Inc. v. Dollar Park and Fly, Inc.,* 469 U.S. 189, 198, 83 L. Ed. 2d 582, 105 S. Ct. 658 (1985). "The protection of trademarks and trade dress under 43(a) serves the same statutory purpose of preventing deception and unfair competition." *Two Pesos,* 112 S. Ct. at 2760. Because trademarks promote competition and product quality, "Congress determined that 'a sound public policy requires that trademarks should receive nationally the greatest protection that can be given them." *Park 'N Fly,* 469 U.S. at 193 (quoting S. Rep. No. 1333, 79th Cong., 2d Sess. 6 (1946), reprinted in 1946 U.S.C.C.S. 1274, 1277); *see also* 15 U.S.C. 1127.

The degree to which a producer's goodwill will be harmed by the copying of product configurations correlates with the degree of consumer confusion as to source or sponsorship that is likely to result from the copying. We do not doubt that at least some consumers are likely to ignore product labels, names, and packaging and look only to the design of product features to tell one brand from another. These consumers are likely to be confused by similar product designs, and to the degree that this confusion is tolerated, the goals of the Lanham Act will be undermined.

We recognize also that consumer confusion resulting from the copying of product features is, in some measure, a self-fulfilling prophecy. To the degree that useful product configurations are protected as identifiers, consumers will come to rely on them for that purpose, but if copying is allowed, they will depend less on product shapes and more on labels and packaging.

We conclude that protecting against that degree of consumer confusion that may arise from the copying of configurations that are significant parts of patented inventions is, at best, a peripheral concern of section 43(a) of the Lanham Act.

Given, then, that core patent principles will be significantly undermined if we do not allow the copying in question, and peripheral Lanham Act protections will be denied if we do, our answer seems clear.

We hold that where a disputed product configuration is part of a claim in a utility patent, and the configuration is a described, significant inventive aspect of the invention, *see* 35 U.S.C. 112, so that without it the invention could not fairly be said to be the same invention, patent law prevents its protection as trade dress, even if the configuration is nonfunctional.

REVERSED

Notes and Questions

1. In order to qualify for protection internationally a mark must be distinctive. It must be capable of helping the consumers distinguish one good or service from those of another. Is the patented shape of the Vornado fan capable of distinguishing Vornado's goods? If so, on what basis did the court deny protection? How can a feature be both non-functional and yet incapable of serving as a source designator? The correctness of the Vornado decision, and the balance it strikes between patents and trademarks has been hotly debated. *See, e.g.* Andrea Falk, *Harmonization of the Patent Act and Federal Trade Dress Law*, 21 J. Corp L. 827 (1996); Graeme B. Dinwoodie, *Reconceptualizing The Inherent Distinctiveness of Product Design Trade Dress*, 75 No. Car. L. Rev. 741 (1997), Manotti L. Jenkins, *A Request to the High Court: Don't Let the Patent Laws Be Distracted by a Flashy Trade Dress*, 15 J. Marshall J. Computer & Info L. 323 (1997); Tom Bell, *Virtual Trade Dress: A Very Real Problem*, 56 Md. L. Rev. 384 (1992).

2. What about the balance between trademark and copyright law? For example, in 1928 Walt Disney created the first cartoon featuring a "Mickey Mouse" like character who appeared in an animated film called *Steamboat Willie*. This film has since entered the public domain. Could your client use the Steamboat Willie character as a trademark for her line of cartoon books for children? *See Frederick Warne & Co. v. Book Sales, Inc.*, 481 F.Supp. 1191 (S.D.N.Y.1979).

Problem

Your client has developed an ergonomically correct cell phone that can be grasped comfortably within the hand. He applied two months ago for a U.S. utility patent for the shape of the cell phone based upon its ergonomic utility in reducing joint stress and cramped muscles. His patent attorney has advised him he has a 90% chance of receiving a U.S. utility patent. Currently your client plans on manufacturing the cell phones in several neon bright colors which he intends to advertise with the slogan "The Phone That Feels as Great as It Looks." Your client wants to develop a "total protection package" for his cell phone design, including a web page advertising the benefits of its ergonomically correct phone. What methods should he use to protect his invention internationally? What problems do you foresee?

Chapter Eleven

TRADE SECRETS UNDER INTERNATIONAL LAW

A. THE NATURE OF TRADE SECRETS: WHEN SHOULD SECRECY BE ENCOURAGED? THE VW CONTROVERSY

Technology is accelerating at such a rapid pace that companies that are not engaged in constant efforts to improve their products or services often find themselves outstripped by their competitors. Increasingly, the problem of industrial espionage, or more specifically the theft of confidential business information, has become an issue of international concern. A recent report by the FBI estimated that almost two dozen foreign governments have established clandestine means for the illegal acquisition of U.S. industrial secrets. *See* Douglas Pasternak & Gordon Wilkin, *The Lure of the Steal: America's Allies are Grabbing U.S. Technology, Washington is Worried*, U.S. News & World Report (March 4, 1996). In addition to the increase in industrial espionage, commercial espionage is also on the rise. Such "espionage" may include such diverse acts as breaking and entering into safes and other secured areas to steal confidential formulas, and hacking into computers to obtain secret information, to the more mundane but no less troublesome hiring of a competitor's employees to utilize their knowledge of their former employer's business practices. Recently, the hiring by Volkswagen in Germany of a former officer and chief development official of GM lead to international headlines and lawsuits in two countries over the violation of trade secret agreements and misappropriation on valuable commercial information.

The dispute between GM and VW stemmed from the 1993 departure of one of GM's top managers, Jose Ignacio Lopez de Arriortua, and his subsequent hiring by VW, one of GM's principal competitors. As the company's head of purchasing of automobile parts, Lopez was widely credited with developing a strategy to obtain better prices from the suppliers, thereby adding significantly to GM's profitability. Shortly after the success of this buying strategy became known, Lopez joined VW, allegedly taking with him several other GM managers. In a complaint filed in the United States, GM alleged that Lopez took thousands of pages of trade secrets, ranging from the price manufacturers paid for parts to GM's secret plans for a more efficient manufacturing plant.

While the civil suit was pending in the U.S., public prosecutors in Darmstadt, Germany indicted Lopez and three former GM managers who had also joined VW with Lopez. The prosecutors did not indict VW or any of its senior officials. The indictment in Germany signals a significant development in the arena of international trade secret protection since it demonstrates a willingness to get involved in trade secret protection, even if it is against a domestic company. As one author has noted, however, the protection of trade secrets in the context of employment situations, particularly where the employee formerly worked for a competitor, raises complex legal issues. In *GM-VW Action Brings Clarity to Legal Issues* appearing in the January 24, 1997 issue of Eurowatch, Morgan Chu offered the following hypothetical: "Let's say there are two companies, Lockheed and Boeing, who are developing stealth radar technology. Lockheed has already spent hundreds of millions of dollar researching this technology. One of those engineers working on the project has been with the company for ten years. He's making $70,000, but he would like to live in the Seattle area. So he approaches Boeing and is hired. Now Boeing hasn't hired this guy to put in rivets. It wants the stealth technology. So soon after the engineer is hired, he finds himself sitting in a meeting room as his peers consider whether or not to conduct a $2 million experiment, one that Lockheed has already tried. He knows it won't work. Does he say anything?" Volunteering such information may be a violation of his fiduciary duty to his former employer or a breach of an outstanding duty of confidentiality.

What relief, if any, should be awarded to Lockheed to prevent such unauthorized disclosures? How do you balance the right of an employee to pursue his career and the need to protect an employer's sensitive information? The answers to these questions continue to cause problems internationally.

THE TV FORMAT CASE
DE MAUDSLEY v. PALUMBO

Chancery Division, 1995.
[1996] FSR 447.

Knox, J.

In this action the plaintiff Mr. Ray Andrew de Maudsley ("Mr. de Maudsley") seeks against all the defendants an inquiry as to damages and an injunction restraining breaches of Mr. de Maudsley's confidence in his idea for an all night dance club whether by using that idea of disclosing it to others. The defendants consist of three natural persons and two companies. The three natural persons are Mr. James Rudolph

Palumbo ("Mr. Palumbo") Mr. Humphrey Vlademar Waterhouse ("Mr. Waterhouse") and Mr. Justin Charles Berkmann ("Mr. Berkmann"). Of the two defendant companies one, Dance Studio UK Ltd ("Dance Studio UK"), has been ordered to be wound up compulsorily on December 9,1992 and has not been represented whereas the other, Danceclub Ltd ("Danceclub"), is still in existence and was represented by Mr. Neish of Counsel who also appeared for the three natural defendants.

The action hinges primarily upon what transpired at a supper party at Mr. Palumbo's flat on November 1, 1989 when he provided a meal for Mr. de Maudsley and Miss Lisa Smalley with whom Mr. Palumbo was at that stage having an intimate relationship which did not last long into the New Year of 1990. Miss Smalley was at the time residing in the same flat as Mr. de Maudsley but not on the basis of any such intimate relationship. Put very shortly, Mr. de Maudsley's case is that during that supper party he revealed to Mr. Palumbo his idea for a night club of a novel nature and that Mr. Palumbo was so impressed by its possibilities that he offered to Mr. de Maudsley to fund it or arrange for its financing and that this offer was accepted. This agreement was, it is claimed, elaborated over the following weeks, notably so as to include Mr. Waterhouse and Mr. Berkmann as participants in the project for the proposed nightclub on terms that the four of them, Mr. de Maudsley, Mr. Palumbo, Mr. Waterhouse and Mr. Berkmann would through the medium of a company to be acquired share the profits of the intended business in equal shares. Over a year and three-quarters later in September 1991 a nightclub Ministry of Sound ("Ministry of Sound") was opened by Dance Studio Ltd UK of which Mr. Palumbo owned half the issued shares and in which none of Mr. de Maudsley, Mr. Waterhouse or Mr. Berkmann was a shareholder but Mr. Waterhouse and Mr. Berkmann were involved in different capacities whereas Mr. de Maudsley had no beneficial involvement of any significance.

[I]t is claimed that all the defendants other than Danceclub are guilty of breach of confidence in having opened and operated through Dance Studios UK the nightclub Ministry of Sound which it is said incorporated all of Mr. de Maudsley's ideas which he communicated to Mr. Palumbo at the supper party on November 1, 1989 without Mr. de Maudsley's licence, and that the disclosure of those ideas without Mr. de Maudsley's licence constitutes an actionable breach of confidence. Danceclub's involvement is that it took over the nightclub Ministry of Sound on the liquidation of Dance Studio UK and continues to run it and it is claimed that this involves a further breach of confidence in that the transfer to it of a business incorporating Mr. de Maudsley's idea was effected without Mr. de Maudsley's licence.

Nearer to the case before me are those dealing with the boundaries of copyright where breach of confidence has mitigated the well-established principle in copyright law that there is no copyright in ideas or information. For example, a series of cases, of which *Gilbert v. Star Newspaper Co. Ltd.* (1894) 11 TLR 4 is one, has established that the courts will protect the plot and dramatic ideas in plays which remain unpublished in written form so that no breach of copyright is threatened but the material has come to the defendant in circumstances giving rise to a duty of confidence. Another related class of case concerns the duty of confidence which arises when a prospective inventor submits his ideas to a person in a commercial context with a view to its exploitation by that person. Thus in *Seager v. Copydex Limited* [1967] 1 WLR 923 the plaintiff, an inventor, who had patented a form of carpet grip, negotiated with the defendants for its manufacture by them but no contract resulted from those negotiations. During the negotiations the plaintiff revealed another form of grip which he had thought of but was not the subject of patent protection. The defendants were held liable in damages for breach of confidence in having subconsciously copied the unpatented grip which had been revealed to them in confidence.

[T]he principles stated by Megarry J regarding the necessary elements for an action for breach of confidence are highly significant and have often been adopted and applied since. He said in *Coco v. AN Clark (Engineers) Ltd.* [1969] RPC 41 at p 47:

> In my judgment, three elements are normally required if, apart from contract, a case of breach of confidence is to succeed. First, the information itself, in the words of Lord Greene MR in the *Saltman* case [*Saltman Engineering Co. Ltd. v. Campbell Engineering* (1948) 65 RPC 203] on p. 215 must "have the necessary quality of confidence about it". Secondly, that information must have been imparted in circumstances importing an obligation of confidence. Thirdly, there must be an unauthorised use of that information to the detriment of the party communicating it.

With regard to the first element he said this also on p. 47:

> First, the information must be of a confidential nature. As Lord Greene said in the *Saltman* case at page 215, "something which is public property and public knowledge" cannot per se provide any foundation for proceedings for breach of confidence. However confidential the circumstances of communication, there can be no breach of confidence in revealing to others something which is already common knowledge. But this must not be taken too far. Something that has been constructed solely from materials in the public domain may possess the necessary quality of confidentiality: for something new and confidential may have been brought into being by the application of the skill and ingenuity of the human brain. Novelty depends on the thing itself, and not upon the quality of its constituent parts. Indeed, often the more striking the novelty, the more commonplace its components ... whether it is described as originality or novelty or ingenuity or otherwise, I think there must be some product of the human brain which suffices to confer a confidential nature upon the information:

The latter passage contains a second echo of what Lord Greene MR said in the *Saltman* case at p. 215 when he said:

It is perfectly possible to have a confidential document, be it a formula, a plan, a sketch, or something of that kind which is the result of work done by the maker upon materials which may be available for the use of anybody: but what makes it confidential is the fact that the maker of the document has used his brain and thus produced a result which can only be produced by somebody who goes through the same process.

The principle involved has also been applied in the world of theatre and entertainment in circumstances where there is no tangible finished product in the sense of a detailed written script. Mr. de Maudsley relied upon two authorities concerning ideas for a television programme. The first was *Talbot v General Television Corporation Pty. Ltd.* [1981] RPC 1. In this case the plaintiff had prepared a written submission, to be used in negotiations with television networks, which set out in some detail an idea for a television series consisting of programmes illustrating the lives of real millionaires (in Australian dollars) and examining how they had achieved this and their lifestyles.

Having set out the arguments of counsel on either side, which included a submission on behalf of the defendant that there is no property in an idea, [Harris, J.] dealt with the question whether the idea or concept of the plaintiff was sufficiently developed to constitute confidential information. In relation to that he said at page 9:

Without deciding that it is always necessary for a plaintiff to go that far, I am satisfied that where a concept or idea has been developed to the stage where the plaintiff had developed his concept, it is capable of being the subject of a confidential communication. The plaintiff had developed his concept so that it could be seen to be a concept which had at least some attractiveness as a television programme and to be something which was capable of being realised as an actuality.

He also held that the plaintiff's concept, although dealing with a familiar phenomenon, could not be treated as public knowledge and therefore not confidential, saying at page 9:

I am satisfied that what was called the "commercial twist" or the particular slant, of the plaintiff's concept (or idea) does give it a quality which takes it out of the realm of public knowledge.

As the court in *Fraser v. Thames Television Ltd.* [1984] QB 44 recognized:

I accept that to be capable of protection the idea must be sufficiently developed, so that it would be seen to be a concept that has at least some attractiveness for a television programme and which is capable of being realised as an actuality: see per Harris J. in Talbot v. General Television Corporation Pty. Ltd. [1981] RPC 1, 9, lines 20–22. But I do not think this requirement necessitates in every case a full synopsis. In some cases the nature of the idea may require extensive development of this kind in order to meet the criteria. But in others the criteria may be met by a short unelaborated statement of an idea.

Unquestionably, of course, the idea must have some significant element of originality not already in the realm of public knowledge. The originality may consist in a significant twist or slant to a well known concept (*Talbot's* case). This is, I think, by analogy, consistent with the statements in *Saltman Engineering Co. Ltd. v. Campbell Engineering Co. Ltd.* (1948) 65 RPC 203 and *Coco v. AN Clark (Engineers) Ltd.* [1969] RPC 41, that novelty in the industrial field can be derived from the application of human ingenuity to well known concepts.

This of course does not mean that every stray mention of an idea by one person to another is protected. To succeed in his claim the plaintiff must establish not only that the occasion of communication was confidential, but also that the content of the idea was clearly identifiable, original, of potential commercial attractiveness and capable of being realised in actuality. With these limitations, I consider there is no basis for Mr. Harman's fears that authors' freedom to develop ideas will be unduly stultified.

The following points emerge from this decision. First, it is not essential in order to constitute confidential information for the material to be in writing or other permanent form. Secondly, it is essential for the material to have at least some attractiveness to an end user and be capable of being realised "as an actuality", by which I understand to be meant as a finished product in the relevant medium. The requirement for it to have some attractiveness does not with all due respect seem to me to advance matters very much if only because if that element is missing it is hardly likely to be appropriated. It is the other element of being capable of being realised as a finished product which is significant for my purposes. This seems to me to be an element which can be traced back to Lord Greene MR's reference in the *Saltman* case to the maker of the product, in that case a document, having used his brain and produced a result which can only be produced by somebody who goes through the same process. That connotes a mental process and a product of the mental process which can properly be described as a result. There is a significant difference between that concept and an aspiration the flavour of which can be captured in the phrase "Wouldn't it be great if . . . ".

Before the status of confidential information can be achieved by a concept or an idea it is necessary to have gone far beyond identifying a desirable goal. A considerable degree of particularity in a definite product needs to be shown to be the result of the mental process in question. That does not of course exclude simplicity.

The third and last observation to be made regarding Fraser's case is that the existence of a trade or industry practice to treat the type of information in issue as confidential played a significant part in Hirst J's decision that the plaintiffs' idea constituted confidential information.

Mr. Neish summarised the requirements for a literary, creative or entertainment industry idea to achieve the status of confidential information as follows. Basing himself on what Hirst J. said in *Fraser v. Thames Television*, above, he said that the idea must

(1) contain some significant element of originality;

(2) be clearly identifiable (as an idea of the confider);

(3) be of potential commercial attractiveness;

(4) be sufficiently well developed to be capable of actual realisation.

Subject to what I have said above I accept that formulation.

The idea upon which Mr. de Maudsley's claim to breach of confidence was based was pleaded on his behalf to have five features, which, as the statement of claim was originally drafted, were alleged to be individually original, but by amendment were only claimed to be original as a combination. Those features were as follows:

(a) the club would operate all night long, but unlike existing all-night dance clubs, would so operate legally;

(b) it would be big and the decor for the debut would be novel and would be of "high tech industrial" warehouse style;

(c) the club would incorporate separate areas for dancing, for resting and socialising and a "VIP lounge";

(d) the separate enclosed dance area within the club would be of an acoustic design ensuring excellent sound quality, light and atmosphere with no leakage of its elements beyond this environment;

(e) top disc jockeys from the United Kingdom and around the world would appear at the club.

In relation to those features my conclusions regarding the three elements quoted above from Megarry J. in *Coco v. AN Clark (Engineers) Ltd.* required to establish a breach of confidence are as follows. The elements it will be recalled are:

(i) the information must have the necessary quality of confidence;

(ii) the information must have been imparted in circumstances importing an obligation of confidence;

(iii) there must have been an authorised use of that information.

In my view this action fails on all three elements. As regards the second element, communication in circumstances importing an obligation of confidence, on the facts regarding the supper party on November 1, 1989, as I have found them, there are two insuperable objections. The first is that the occasion was a social, and not a business one. Nothing was said, even on Mr. de Maudsley's evidence, to take the occasion out of the social, and put it into a business sphere. Secondly, again even on Mr. de Maudsley's evidence, he deliberately refrained from mentioning confidentiality. As he himself said, this was "because I did not want to blow the deal there and then". That involves his appreciation that there was at least a risk of Mr. Palumbo not agreeing to do what Mr. de Maudsley wanted him to do, produce or procure money in large quantities, if the information was stated to be confidential. It is quite impossible to infer an obligation of confidence in such circumstances. Also on this aspect, there was no evidence of any trade or professional practice. The nearest that the evidence came to this was Mr. Berkmann's evidence that he would not have expected Mr. Palumbo and Mr. Waterhouse to go off and do the project with others after the initial meeting in November 1989.

Turning to the other two elements my finding as regards the five features relied upon by Mr. de Maudsley are as follows:

(a) The all night long legal operation was novel. Such evidence as there was of other legal all night clubs was either very old, dating back to the 1960s, or very specialised, namely a club limited to night club staff after other night clubs had closed. But I do not accept that so general and vague an idea is sufficiently elaborated to constitute confidential information.

(b) Size is far too vague to qualify and indeed lacks novelty. The individual high-tech decor is also in my judgment too vague to qualify although it might well have qualified on novelty alone.

(c) Separate areas for dancing, resting and socialising including a VIP lounge fail both on grounds of novelty, for the concept was not novel, and of vagueness, but primarily on the former ground.

(d) Separate enclosed acoustically designed dancing area fails because that was not what Mr. de Maudsley had worked out by November 1, 1989. The acoustic enclosed area was the product of the later meeting with Mr. Andrews and his partner. Mr. de Maudsley's original idea was that there should be privacy for the dancers, without any technical acoustic element for he had no acoustic knowledge or experience. As such that idea of Mr. de Maudsley was in my view too vague to constitute confidential information.

(e) The idea of having high quality disc jockeys of far flung provenance is far too vague to constitute confidential information. The point hardly needs elaboration.

The claim to originality in relation to the combination of the five features must also fail, partly because quite significant parts of the claimed five features were not in fact part of Mr. de Maudsley's idea and partly because a combination of features which were not individually novel does not automatically become novel by being added together.

So far as the use of Mr. de Maudsley's idea is concerned, I am satisfied that the extent to which it was used, namely an all-night legal club with separate dancing area from the other areas, such as the VIP lounge and bars, would not be sufficient to constitute unauthorised use for the purposes of breach of confidence because the club Ministry of Sound was as it opened, a substantially different club principally in that it was primarily based on Paradise Garage rather than Mr. de Maudsley's idea. There were very important features which formed no part of Mr. de Maudsley's idea, notably lack of alcohol and limitation to over 21–year-olds and the American sound system and some features of Mr. de Maudsley's idea, notably industrial high-tech decor, were not present in Ministry of Sound.

For all these reasons this action fails but the fact remains that Mr. de Maudsley was in my view rather shabbily treated in that he was encouraged to think that he would be part of the enterprise but was only told that this would not be so, long after Mr. Palumbo and Mr. Waterhouse had decided, almost certainly justifiably because of Mr. de Maudsley's rather difficult character and limited abilities, that he would not be included in their project. It is the fact that it was Mr. de Maudsley who sowed the original seed in Mr. Palumbo's mind and he has in the event got very little indeed out of it. It would have been preferable for him to have been told a great deal earlier and more clearly that he was being dropped, as dropped he was. However that is not a matter which supports either of his two claims to breach of contract or breach of confidence. It does go some way to explain his being disgruntled.

The action will be dismissed.

Notes and Questions

1. Where did the courts draw the line between protectable ideas and publicly available ones in the *TV Format* case?

2. Can parties agree to keep information secret which would not otherwise qualify for protection? Should courts uphold such agreements even if disclosure of the secret information would be in the public interest?

3. What requirements would you impose to establish protectable confidential information? Why?

B. WHAT MUST AN OWNER DO TO PROTECT ITS "SECRETS"?

THE AERIAL PHOTOGRAPHY CASE

E.I. DUPONT DENEMOURS & COMPANY v. ROLFE CHRISTOPHER

United States Court of Appeals, Fifth Circuit, 1970.
431 F.2d 1012.

GOLDBERG, CIRCUIT JUDGE.

This is a case of industrial espionage in which an airplane is the cloak and a camera the dagger. The defendants-appellants, Rolfe and Gary Christopher, are photographers in Beaumont, Texas. The Christophers were hired by an unknown third party to take aerial photographs of new construction at the Beaumont plant of E. I. duPont deNemours & Company, Inc. Sixteen photographs of the DuPont facility were taken from the air on March 19, 1969, and these photographs were later developed and delivered to the third party.

DuPont employees apparently noticed the airplane on March 19 and immediately began an investigation to determine why the craft was circling over the plant. By that afternoon the investigation had disclosed that the craft was involved in a photographic expedition and that the Christophers were the photographers. DuPont contacted the Christophers that same afternoon and asked them to reveal the name of the person or corporation requesting the photographs. The Christophers refused to disclose this information, giving as their reason the client's desire to remain anonymous.

Having reached a dead end in the investigation, DuPont subsequently filed suit against the Christophers, alleging that the Christophers had wrongfully obtained photographs revealing DuPont's trade secrets which they then sold to the undisclosed third party. DuPont contended that it had developed a highly secret but unpatented process for producing methanol, a process which gave DuPont a competitive advantage over other producers. This process, DuPont alleged, was a trade secret developed after much expensive and time-consuming research, and a secret which the company had taken special precautions to safeguard. The area photographed by the Christophers was the plant designed to produce methanol by this secret process, and because the plant was still under construction parts of the process were exposed to view from directly above the construction area. Photographs of that area, DuPont alleged, would enable a skilled person to deduce the secret process for making methanol. DuPont thus contended that the Christophers had wrongfully appropriated DuPont trade secrets by taking the photographs and delivering them to the undisclosed third party. In its suit DuPont asked for damages to cover the loss it had already sustained as a result of the wrongful disclosure of the trade secret and sought temporary and permanent injunctions prohibiting any further circulation of the photographs already taken and prohibiting any additional photographing of the methanol plant.

This is a case of first impression, for the Texas courts have not faced this precise factual issue. The only question involved in this interlocutory appeal is whether DuPont has asserted a claim upon which relief can be granted. The Christophers argued both at trial and before this court that they committed no 'actionable wrong' in photographing the DuPont facility and passing these photographs on to their client because they conducted all of their activities in public airspace, violated no government aviation standard, did not breach any confidential relation, and did not engage in any fraudulent or illegal conduct. In short, the Christophers argue that for an appropriation of trade secrets to be wrongful there must be a trespass, other illegal conduct, or breach of a confidential relationship. We disagree.

It is true, as the Christophers assert, that the previous trade secret cases have contained one or more of these elements. However, we do not think that the Texas courts would limit the trade secret protection exclusively to these elements. On the contrary, in *Hyde Corporation v. Huffines*, 1958, 158 Tex. 566, 314 S.W.2d 763, the Texas Supreme Court specifically adopted the rule found in the Restatement of Torts which provides:

> 'One who discloses or uses another's trade secret, without a privilege to do so, is liable to the other if (a) he discovered the secret by improper means, or (b) his disclosure or use constitutes a breach of confidence reposed in him by the other in disclosing the secret to him .' (Restatement of Torts § 757 (1939)).

Thus, although the previous cases have dealt with a breach of a confidential relationship, a trespass, or other illegal conduct, the rule is much broader than the cases heretofore encountered. Not limiting itself to specific wrongs, Texas adopted subsection (a) of the Restatement which recognizes a cause of action for the discovery of a trade secret by any 'improper' means.

The question remaining, therefore, is whether aerial photography of plant construction is an improper means of obtaining another's trade secret. We conclude that it is and that the Texas courts would so hold. The Supreme Court of that state has declared that 'the undoubted tendency of the law has been to recognize and enforce higher standards of commercial morality in the business world.' *Hyde Corporation v. Huffines*, supra 314 S.W.2d at 773. That court has quoted with approval articles indicating that the proper means of gaining possession of a competitor's secret process is 'through inspection and analysis' of the product in order to create a duplicate. *K & G Tool & Service Co. v. G & G Fishing Tool Service*, 1958, 158 Tex. 594, 314 S.W.2d 782, 783, 788. Later another Texas court explained:

> 'The means by which the discovery is made may be obvious, and the experimentation leading from known factors to presently unknown results may be simple and lying in the public domain. But these facts do not destroy the value of the discovery and will not advantage a competitor who by unfair means obtains the knowledge without paying the price expended by the discoverer.' *Brown v. Fowler*, Tex.Civ.App.1958, 316 S.W.2d 111, 114.

We think, therefore, that the Texas rule is clear. One may use his competitor's secret process if he discovers the process by reverse engineering applied to the finished product; one may use a competitor's process if he discovers it by his own independent research; but one may not avoid these labors by taking the process from the discoverer without his permission at a time when he is taking reasonable precautions to maintain its secrecy. To obtain knowledge of a process without spending the time and money to discover it independently is improper unless the holder voluntarily discloses it or fails to take reasonable precautions to ensure its secrecy.

In the instant case the Christophers deliberately flew over the DuPont plant to get pictures of a process which DuPont had attempted to keep secret. The Christophers delivered their pictures to a third party who was certainly aware of the means by which they had been acquired and who may be planning to use the information contained therein to manufacture methanol by the DuPont process. The third party has a right to use this process only if he obtains this knowledge through his own research efforts, but thus far all information indicates that the third party has gained this knowledge solely by taking it from DuPont at a time when DuPont was making reasonable efforts to preserve its secrecy. In such a situation DuPont has a valid cause of action to prohibit the Christophers from improperly discovering its trade secret and to prohibit the undisclosed third party from using the improperly obtained information.

We note that this view is in perfect accord with the position taken by the authors of the Restatement. In commenting on improper means of discovery the savants of the Restatement said:

> 'f. Improper means of discovery. The discovery of another's trade secret by improper means subjects the actor to liability independently of the harm to the interest in the secret. Thus, if one uses physical force to take a secret formula from another's pocket, or breaks into another's office to steal the formula, his conduct is wrongful and subjects him to liability apart from the rule stated in this Section. Such conduct is also an improper means of procuring the secret under this rule. But means may be improper under this rule even though they do not cause any other harm than that to the interest in the trade secret. Examples of such means are fraudulent misrepresentations to induce disclosure, tapping of telephone wires, eavesdropping or other espionage. A complete catalogue of improper means is not possible. In general they are means which fall below the generally accepted standards of commercial morality and reasonable conduct.' Restatement of Torts 757, comment f at 10 (1939).

In taking this position we realize that industrial espionage of the sort here perpetrated has become a popular sport in some segments of our industrial community. However, our devotion to free wheeling industrial competition must not force us into accepting the law of the jungle as the standard of morality expected in our commercial relations. Our tolerance of the espionage game must cease when the protections required to prevent another's spying cost so much that the spirit of inventiveness is dampened. Commercial privacy must be protected from espionage which could not have been reasonably anticipated or prevented. We do not mean to imply, however, that everything not in plain view is within the protected vale, nor that all information obtained through every extra optical extension is forbidden. Indeed, for our industrial competition to remain healthy there must be breathing room for observing a competing industrialist. A competitor can and must shop his competition for pricing and examine his products for quality, components, and methods of manufacture. Perhaps ordinary fences and roofs must be built to shut out incursive eyes, but we need not require the discoverer of a trade secret to guard against the unanticipated, the undetectable, or the unpreventable methods of espionage now available.

In the instant case DuPont was in the midst of constructing a plant. Although after construction the finished plant would have protected much of the process from view, during the period of construction the trade secret was exposed to view from the air. To require DuPont to put a roof over the unfinished plant to guard its secret would impose an enormous expense to prevent nothing more than a school boy's trick. We introduce here no new or radical ethic since our ethos has never given moral sanction to piracy. The market place must not deviate far from our mores. We should not require a person or corporation to take unreasonable precautions to prevent another from doing that which he ought not do in the first place. Reasonable precautions against predatory eyes we may require, but an impenetrable fortress is an unreasonable requirement, and we are not disposed to burden industrial inventors with such a duty in order to protect the fruits of their efforts. 'Improper' will always be a word of many nuances, determined by time, place, and circumstances. We therefore need not proclaim a catalogue of commercial improprieties. Clearly, however, one of its commandments does say 'thou shall not appropriate a trade secret through deviousness under circumstances in which countervailing defenses are not reasonably available.'

Having concluded that aerial photography, from whatever altitude, is an improper method of discovering the trade secrets exposed during construction of the DuPont plant, we need not worry about whether the flight pattern chosen by the Christophers violated any federal aviation regulations. Regardless of whether the flight was legal or illegal in that sense, the espionage was an improper means of discovering DuPont's trade secret.

The decision of the trial court is affirmed and the case remanded to that court for proceedings on the merits.

Notes and Questions

1. Are there additional steps which duPont could have taken to protect its secret manufacturing processes? For example, couldn't duPont have simply built a temporary roof over the site to avoid the problem? Is this reasonable? What if the factory site had been surrounded by tall buildings? Would some sort of temporary roof have been reasonable in those circumstances?

2. *Reverse Engineering.* What steps could a competitor legitimately have taken to discover duPont's trade secret processes? Would the Christophers have been liable to duPont if they had taken photographs of the plant while on a tour of the plant where photography was not prohibited? Would the Christophers have been liable to duPont if they had hired an employee of duPont to take photographs of the plant and the employee had a confidentiality agreement that prohibited him from disclosing trade secrets?

3. *Definitional Issues.* Unlike the other traditional forms of intellectual property, trade secret protection has had a difficult period of adjustment. Until 1994, no international treaty had specifically addressed the international protection of confidential information. Even in those countries like the

United States and Great Britain where trade secrets have had a relatively long history of protection, no single definition of what qualifies as a trade secret has emerged. For example, is a customer list a trade secret? Does it matter if the list could be reconstructed by simply following a delivery truck and taking note of the location of the deliveries? What balance should be struck between healthy competition and protecting business confidential information?

4. *International Standards*. The Paris Convention prohibits "unfair methods of competition" under Article 10*bis* but did not expressly mention trade secrets or confidential information as one of the methods to be protected. Is using an airplane to take pictures of the interior of a competitors new factory "unfair"? Is using sophisticated telephoto camera equipment to achieve the same result "unfair"? What goals are achieved if businesses are encouraged (by providing trade secret protection) to keep business secrets?

5.   The first express mention of trade secret protection in a significant multinational treaty appeared in Article 1711 of the North American Free Trade Agreement. It provided:

Each Party shall provide the legal means for any person to prevent trade secrets from being disclosed to, acquired by, or used by others without the consent of the person lawfully in control of the information in a manner contrary to honest commercial practices, in so far as:

(a) the information is secret in the sense that it is not, as a body or in the precise configuration and assembly of its components generally known among or readily accessible to persons that normally deal with the kind of information in question;

(b) the information has actual or potential commercial value because it is secret; and

(c) the person lawfully in control of the information has taken reasonable steps under the circumstances to keep it secret.

6.   This tri-partite test is largely reflected in Article 39 of TRIPS which states:

(1) In the course of ensuring effective protection against unfair competition as provided in Article 10*bis* of the Paris Convention, Members shall protect undisclosed information in accordance with paragraph 2 . . .

(2) Natural and legal persons shall have the possibility of preventing information lawfully within their control from being disclosed to, or acquired by, or used by others without their consent in a manner contrary to honest commercial practices so long as such information :

(a)is secret in the sense that it is not, as a body or in the precise configuration and assembly of its components generally known among or readily accessible to persons within the circles that normally deal with the kind of information in question;

(b)has commercial value because it is secret; and

(c)has been subject to reasonable steps under the circumstances by the person lawfully in control of the information to keep it secret.

7. Would duPont's secret manufacturing process qualify as a trade secret under NAFTA? Under TRIPS?

8. What if duPont had not yet used its manufacturing process that it had not yet developed "commercial value"? Must it still be protected as a trade secret under NAFTA? Under TRIPS?

9. The United States defines a trade secret generally as "all forms and types of financial, business, scientific, technical, economic, or engineering information, including patterns, plans, compilations, procedures, programs, or codes ... if the owner thereof has taken reasonable measure to keep such information secret, and the information derives independent economic value, actual or potential, from not being generally known to, and not being readily ascertainable through the proper means by, the public ... " (18 U.S.C § 1839.)

10. Great Britain protects information used in trade or business, where the owner limits dissemination because the disclosure to a competitor would result in significant harm to the owner. (Simon Mehigan, *United Kingdom* in World Wide Trade Secrets Law § 3.201(2)(1997))

11. China defines a trade secret as "technical information" and "operational information" that must meet the following conditions. 1) not known already to the public 2) the owner is able to derive economic gain from such information; 3) it is useful and 4) the owner has adopted measures to protect the information. (Unfair Competition Law, Art. 1)

12. Japan defines a trade secret as "technical or business information," which is "useful or valuable for production, marketing and other business activities," is "kept secret," (meaning that the owner has taken active steps to insure secrecy) and "is not publicly known." (Unfair Competition Prevention Act, art.1 et seq.)

13. Mexico defines a "trade secret" as "any information having industrial utility that is kept in confidential fashion, regarding which sufficient means or systems have been undertaken to preserve its confidential nature and limit access thereto" and "relates the nature, characteristics or purposes of products, production methods or processes, the means and forms of distribution or trade, or the rendering of services." (as reported in Manuel A. Gomez–Maqueo, *Analysis of Mexico's New Industrial Property Law*, 42 Pat. Trademark & Copyright J. 383 (1991))

14. Do these definitions comply with the minimum substantive requirements of the TRIPS agreement? Would duPont's secret processes be protectable under these definitions? Is a customer list required to be protected? Are future advertising or product development plans?

15. *Fixation.* Many countries such as Mexico and the European Union require that the secret be fixed in a tangible medium of expression to be protected. This can create practical problems in adequately defining the trade secret when it is being described in a licensing or disclosure agreement.

C. WHERE SHOULD WE DRAW THE LINE BE-TWEEN ENCOURAGING SECRECY AND PER-MITTING UNFETTERED COMPETITION?

THE PEPSI EMPLOYEE CASE

PEPSICO, INC. v. WILLIAM E. REDMOND, JR., AND THE QUAKER OATS COMPANY

United States Court of Appeals, Seventh Circuit, 1995.
54 F.3d 1262.

FLAUM, CIRCUIT JUDGE

Plaintiff PepsiCo, Inc., sought a preliminary injunction against defendants William Redmond and the Quaker Oats Company to prevent Redmond, a former PepsiCo employee, from divulging PepsiCo trade secrets and confidential information in his new job with Quaker and from assuming any duties with Quaker relating to beverage pricing, marketing, and distribution. The district court agreed with PepsiCo and granted the injunction. We now affirm that decision.

The facts of this case lay against a backdrop of fierce beverage-industry competition between Quaker and PepsiCo, especially in "sports drinks"[12] and "new age drinks."[13] Quaker's sports drink, "Gatorade," is the dominant brand in its market niche. PepsiCo introduced its Gatorade rival, "All Sport," in March and April of 1994, but sales of All Sport lag far behind those of Gatorade. Quaker also has the lead in the new-age-drink category. Although PepsiCo has entered the market through joint ventures with the Thomas J. Lipton Company and Ocean Spray Cran-berries, Inc., Quaker purchased Snapple Beverage Corp., a large new-age-drink maker, in late 1994. PepsiCo's products have about half of Snapple's market share. Both companies see 1995 as an important year for their products: PepsiCo has developed extensive plans to increase its market presence, while Quaker is trying to solidify its lead by integrat-ing Gatorade and Snapple distribution. Meanwhile, PepsiCo and Quaker each face strong competition from Coca Cola Co., which has its own sports drink, "PowerAde," and which introduced its own Snapple-rival, "Fruitopia," in 1994, as well as from independent beverage producers.

William Redmond, Jr., worked for PepsiCo in its Pepsi–Cola North America division ("PCNA") from 1984 to 1994. Redmond became the General Manager of the Northern California Business Unit in June, 1993, and was promoted one year later to General Manager of the business unit covering all of California, a unit having annual revenues of more than 500 million dollars and representing twenty percent of PCNA's profit for all of the United States.

---

12. Sports drinks are also called "iso-tonics," implying that they contain the same salt concentration as human blood, and "electrolytes," implying that the sub-stances contained in the drink have dissoci-ated into ions.

13. "New age drink" is a catch-all cate-gory for non-carbonated soft drinks and in-cludes such beverages as ready-to-drink tea products and fruit drinks. Sports drinks may also fall under the new-age-drink head-ing.

Redmond's relatively high-level position at PCNA gave him access to inside information and trade secrets. Redmond, like other PepsiCo management employees, had signed a confidentiality agreement with PepsiCo. That agreement stated in relevant part that he w[ould] not disclose at any time, to anyone other than officers or employees of [PepsiCo], or make use of, confidential information relating to the business of [PepsiCo] ... obtained while in the employ of [PepsiCo], which shall not be generally known or available to the public or recognized as standard practices.

Donald Uzzi, who had left PepsiCo in the beginning of 1994 to become the head of Quaker's Gatorade division, began courting Redmond for Quaker in May, 1994. Redmond met in Chicago with Quaker officers in August, 1994, and on October 20, 1994, Quaker, through Uzzi, offered Redmond the position of Vice President–On Premise Sales for Gatorade. Redmond did not then accept the offer but continued to negotiate for more money. Throughout this time, Redmond kept his dealings with Quaker secret from his employers at PCNA.

On November 8, 1994, Uzzi extended Redmond a written offer for the position of Vice President–Field Operations for Gatorade and Redmond accepted. Later that same day, Redmond called William Bensyl, the Senior Vice President of Human Resources for PCNA, and told him that he had an offer from Quaker to become the Chief Operating Officer of the combined Gatorade and Snapple company but had not yet accepted it. Redmond also asked whether he should, in light of the offer, carry out his plans to make calls upon certain PCNA customers. Bensyl told Redmond to make the visits.

Redmond also misstated his situation to a number of his PCNA colleagues, including Craig Weatherup, PCNA's President and Chief Executive Officer, and Brenda Barnes, PCNA's Chief Operating Officer and Redmond's immediate superior. As with Bensyl, Redmond told them that he had been offered the position of Chief Operating Officer at Gatorade and that he was leaning "60/40" in favor of accepting the new position.

On November 10, 1994, Redmond met with Barnes and told her that he had decided to accept the Quaker offer and was resigning from PCNA. Barnes immediately took Redmond to Bensyl, who told Redmond that PepsiCo was considering legal action against him.

True to its word, PepsiCo filed this diversity suit on November 16, 1994, seeking a temporary restraining order to enjoin Redmond from assuming his duties at Quaker and to prevent him from disclosing trade secrets or confidential information to his new employer. The district court granted PepsiCo's request that same day but dissolved the order sua sponte two days later, after determining that PepsiCo had failed to meet its burden of establishing that it would suffer irreparable harm. The court found that PepsiCo's fears about Redmond were based upon a mistaken understanding of his new position at Quaker and that the likelihood that Redmond would improperly reveal any confidential information did not "rise above mere speculation."

From November 23, 1994, to December 1, 1994, the district court conducted a preliminary injunction hearing on the same matter. At the hearing, PepsiCo offered evidence of a number of trade secrets and confidential information it desired protected and to which Redmond was privy. First, it identified PCNA's "Strategic Plan," an annually revised document that contains PCNA's plans to compete, its financial goals, and its strategies for manufacturing, production, marketing, packaging, and distribution for the coming three years. Strategic Plans are developed by Weatherup and his staff with input from PCNA's general managers, including Redmond, and are considered highly confidential. The Strategic Plan derives much of its value from the fact that it is secret and competitors cannot anticipate PCNA's next moves. PCNA managers received the most recent Strategic Plan at a meeting in July, 1994, a meeting Redmond attended. PCNA also presented information at the meeting regarding its plans for Lipton ready-to-drink teas and for All Sport for 1995 and beyond, including new flavors and package sizes.

Second, PepsiCo pointed to PCNA's Annual Operating Plan ("AOP") as a trade secret. The AOP is a national plan for a given year and guides PCNA's financial goals, marketing plans, promotional event calendars, growth expectations, and operational changes in that year. The AOP, which is implemented by PCNA unit General Managers, including Redmond, contains specific information regarding all PCNA initiatives for the forthcoming year. The AOP bears a label that reads "Private and Confidential–Do Not Reproduce" and is considered highly confidential by PCNA managers.

In particular, the AOP contains important and sensitive information about "pricing architecture"—how PCNA prices its products in the marketplace. Pricing architecture covers both a national pricing approach and specific price points for given areas. Pricing architecture also encompasses PCNA's objectives for All Sport and its new age drinks with reference to trade channels, package sizes and other characteristics of both the products and the customers at which the products are aimed. Additionally, PCNA's pricing architecture outlines PCNA's customer development agreements. These agreements between PCNA and retailers provide for the retailer's participation in certain merchandising activities for PCNA products. As with other information contained in the AOP, pricing architecture is highly confidential and would be extremely valuable to a competitor. Knowing PCNA's pricing architecture would allow a competitor to anticipate PCNA's pricing moves and underbid PCNA strategically whenever and wherever the competitor so desired. PepsiCo introduced evidence that Redmond had detailed knowledge of PCNA's pricing architecture and that he was aware of and had been involved in preparing PCNA's customer development agreements with PCNA's California and California-based national customers. Indeed, PepsiCo showed that Redmond, as the General Manager for California, would have been responsible for implementing the pricing architecture guidelines for his business unit.

PepsiCo also showed that Redmond had intimate knowledge of PCNA "attack plans" for specific markets. Pursuant to these plans, PCNA dedicates extra funds to supporting its brands against other brands in selected markets. To use a hypothetical example, PCNA might budget an additional $500,000 to spend in Chicago at a particular time to help All Sport close its market gap with Gatorade. Testimony and documents demonstrated Redmond's awareness of these plans and his participation in drafting some of them.

Finally, PepsiCo offered evidence of PCNA trade secrets regarding innovations in its selling and delivery systems. Under this plan, PCNA is testing a new delivery system that could give PCNA an advantage over its competitors in negotiations with retailers over shelf space and merchandising. Redmond has knowledge of this secret because PCNA, which has invested over a million dollars in developing the system during the past two years, is testing the pilot program in California.

Having shown Redmond's intimate knowledge of PCNA's plans for 1995, PepsiCo argued that Redmond would inevitably disclose that information to Quaker in his new position, at which he would have substantial input as to Gatorade and Snapple pricing, costs, margins, distribution systems, products, packaging and marketing, and could give Quaker an unfair advantage in its upcoming skirmishes with PepsiCo. Redmond and Quaker countered that Redmond's primary initial duties at Quaker as Vice President–Field Operations would be to integrate Gatorade and Snapple distribution and then to manage that distribution as well as the promotion, marketing and sales of these products. Redmond asserted that the integration would be conducted according to a pre-existing plan and that his special knowledge of PCNA strategies would be irrelevant. This irrelevance would derive not only from the fact that Redmond would be implementing preexisting plans but also from the fact that PCNA and Quaker distribute their products in entirely different ways: PCNA's distribution system is vertically integrated (i.e., PCNA owns the system) and delivers its product directly to retailers, while Quaker ships its product to wholesalers and customer warehouses and relies on independent distributors.

The defendants also pointed out that Redmond had signed a confidentiality agreement with Quaker preventing him from disclosing "any confidential information belonging to others," as well as the Quaker Code of Ethics, which prohibits employees from engaging in "illegal or improper acts to acquire a competitor's trade secrets." Redmond additionally promised at the hearing that should he be faced with a situation at Quaker that might involve the use or disclosure of PCNA information, he would seek advice from Quaker's in-house counsel and would refrain from making the decision.

PepsiCo responded to the defendants' representations by pointing out that the evidence did not show that Redmond would simply be implementing a business plan already in place. On the contrary, as of November, 1994, the plan to integrate Gatorade and Snapple distribution consisted of a single distributorship agreement and a two-page "contract terms summary." Such a basic plan would not lend itself to widespread application among the over 300 independent Snapple distributors. Since the integration process would likely face resistance from Snapple distributors and Quaker had no scheme to deal with this probability, Redmond, as the person in charge of the integration, would likely have a great deal of influence on the process.

PepsiCo further argued that Snapple's 1995 marketing and promotion plans had not necessarily been completed prior to Redmond's joining Quaker, that Uzzi disagreed with portions of the Snapple plans, and that the plans were open to re-evaluation. Uzzi testified that the plan for integrating Gatorade and Snapple distribution is something that would happen in the future. Redmond would therefore likely have input in remaking these plans, and if he did, he would inevitably be making decisions with PCNA's strategic plans and 1995 AOP in mind. Moreover, PepsiCo continued, diverging testimony made it difficult to know exactly what Redmond would be doing at Quaker.

Redmond described his job as "managing the entire sales effort of Gatorade at the field level, possibly including strategic planning," and at least at one point considered his job to be equivalent to that of a Chief Operating Officer. Uzzi, on the other hand, characterized Redmond's position as "primarily and initially to restructure and integrate our—the distribution systems for Snapple and for Gatorade, as per our distribution plan" and then to "execute marketing, promotion and sales plans in the marketplace." Uzzi also denied having given Redmond detailed information about any business plans, while Redmond described such a plan in depth in an affidavit and said that he received the information from Uzzi. Thus, PepsiCo asserted, Redmond would have a high position in the Gatorade hierarchy, and PCNA trade secrets and confidential information would necessarily influence his decisions. Even if Redmond could somehow refrain from relying on this information, as he promised he would, his actions in leaving PCNA, Uzzi's actions in hiring Redmond, and the varying testimony regarding Redmond's new responsibilities, made Redmond's assurances to PepsiCo less than comforting.

On December 15, 1994, the district court issued an order enjoining Redmond from assuming his position at Quaker through May, 1995, and permanently from using or disclosing any secrets or confidential information. This appeal followed.

The Illinois Trade Secrets Act ("ITSA"), which governs the trade secret issues in this case, provides that a court may enjoin the "actual or threatened misappropriation" of a trade secret. 765 ILCS 1065/3(a). A party seeking an injunction must therefore prove both the existence of a trade secret and the misappropriation. The defendants' appeal focuses solely on misappropriation; although the defendants only reluctantly refer to PepsiCo's marketing and distribution plans as trade secrets, they do not seriously contest that this information falls under the ITSA.[14]

The question of threatened or inevitable misappropriation in this case lies at the heart of a basic tension in trade secret law. Trade secret law serves to protect "standards of commercial morality" and "encourage [ ] invention and innovation" while maintaining "the public interest in having free and open competition in the manufacture and sale of unpatented goods." [2 Melvin F. Jaeger, Trade Secrets Law IL.01C7] at IL–7 to 8Cclark Boardman Callaghan, rev, ed 1994)] Yet that same law should not prevent workers from pursuing their livelihoods when they leave their current positions. It has been said that federal age discrimination law does not guarantee tenure for older employees. Similarly, trade secret law does not provide a reserve clause for solicitous employers.

This tension is particularly exacerbated when a plaintiff sues to prevent not the actual misappropriation of trade secrets but the mere threat that it will occur. While the ITSA plainly permits a court to enjoin the threat of misappropriation of trade secrets, there is little law in Illinois or in this circuit establishing what constitutes threatened or inevitable misappropriation.[15] Indeed, there are only two cases in this circuit that address the issue: *Teradyne, Inc. v. Clear Communications Corp.*, 707 F.Supp. 353 (N.D.Ill.1989), and *AMP Inc. v. Fleischhacker*, 823 F.2d 1199 (7th Cir.1987).

In *Teradyne*, Teradyne alleged that a competitor, Clear Communications, had lured employees away from Teradyne and intended to employ them in the same field. In an insightful opinion, Judge Zagel observed that "[t]hreatened misappropriation can be enjoined under Illinois law" where there is a "high degree of probability of inevitable and immediate ... use of ... trade secrets." Teradyne, 707 F.Supp. at 356. Judge Zagel held, however, that Teradyne's complaint failed to state a claim because Teradyne did not allege "that defendants have in fact threatened to use Teradyne's secrets or that they will inevitably do so." Teradyne's claims would have passed Rule 12(b)(6) muster had they properly alleged inevitable disclosure, including a statement that Clear intended to use Teradyne's trade secrets or that the former Teradyne employees had

---

14. Under the ITSA, trade secret "means information, including but not limited to, technical or non-technical data, a formula, pattern, compilation, program, device, method, technique, drawing, process, financial data, or list of actual or potential customers that: (1) is sufficiently secret to derive economic value, actual or potential, from not generally being known to other persons who can obtain economic value from its disclosure or use; and (2) is the subject of efforts that are reasonable under the circumstances to maintain its secrecy or confidentiality." 765 ILCS 1065/2(d). Although pre-ITSA Illinois case law had somewhat muddled the question, the ITSA "was

specifically drafted to overcome any confusion, and return Illinois to its earlier, more stable situation, where important confidential business information is protectable under trade secret law." 2 Jager, supra, ? IL.05 at IL–14.1.

15. The ITSA definition of misappropriation relevant to this discussion is "the disclosure or use of a trade secret of a person without express or implied consent by another person who ... at the time of disclosure or use, . knew or had reason to know that the knowledge of the trade secret was ... acquired under circumstances giving rise to a duty to maintain its secrecy...." 765 ILCS 1065/2(b).

disavowed their confidentiality agreements with Teradyne, or an allegation that Clear could not operate without Teradyne's secrets. However, [t]he defendants' claimed acts, working for Teradyne, knowing its business, leaving its business, hiring employees from Teradyne and entering the same field (though in a market not yet serviced by Teradyne) do not state a claim of threatened misappropriation. All that is alleged, at bottom, is that defendants could misuse plaintiff's secrets, and plaintiffs fear they will. This is not enough. It may be that little more is needed, but falling a little short is still falling short.

In *AMP*, we affirmed the denial of a preliminary injunction on the grounds that the plaintiff AMP had failed to show either the existence of any trade secrets or the likelihood that defendant Fleischhacker, a former AMP employee, would compromise those secrets or any other confidential business information. AMP, which produced electrical and electronic connection devices, argued that Fleishhacker's new position at AMP's competitor would inevitably lead him to compromise AMP's trade secrets regarding the manufacture of connectors. AMP, 823 F.2d at 1207. In rejecting that argument, we emphasized that the mere fact that a person assumed a similar position at a competitor does not, without more, make it "inevitable that he will use or disclose ... trade secret information" so as to "demonstrate irreparable injury." [*AMP*, 823 F.2d at 1207.]

The ITSA mostly codifies rather than modifies the common law doctrine that preceded it.

The ITSA, *Teradyne*, and *AMP* lead to the same conclusion: a plaintiff may prove a claim of trade secret misappropriation by demonstrating that defendant's new employment will inevitably lead him to rely on the plaintiff's trade secrets.

Admittedly, PepsiCo has not brought a traditional trade secret case, in which a former employee has knowledge of a special manufacturing process or customer list and can give a competitor an unfair advantage by transferring the technology or customers to that competitor. PepsiCo has not contended that Quaker has stolen the All Sport formula or its list of distributors. Rather PepsiCo has asserted that Redmond cannot help but rely on PCNA trade secrets as he helps plot Gatorade and Snapple's new course, and that these secrets will enable Quaker to achieve a substantial advantage by knowing exactly how PCNA will price, distribute, and market its sports drinks and new age drinks and being able to respond strategically. This type of trade secret problem may arise less often, but it nevertheless falls within the realm of trade secret protection under the present circumstances.

PepsiCo finds itself in the position of a coach, one of whose players has left, playbook in hand, to join the opposing team before the big game. Quaker and Redmond's protestations that their distribution systems and plans are entirely different from PCNA's are thus not really responsive.

The district court also concluded from the evidence that Uzzi's actions in hiring Redmond and Redmond's actions in pursuing and accepting his new job demonstrated a lack of candor on their part and proof of their willingness to misuse PCNA trade secrets, findings Quaker and Redmond vigorously challenge.

The facts of the case do not ineluctably dictate the district court's conclusion. Redmond's ambiguous behavior toward his PepsiCo superiors might have been nothing more than an attempt to gain leverage in employment negotiations. The discrepancy between Redmond's and Uzzi's comprehension of what Redmond's job would entail may well have been a simple misunderstanding. The court also pointed out that Quaker, through Uzzi, seemed to express an unnatural interest in hiring PCNA employees: all three of the people interviewed for the position Redmond ultimately accepted worked at PCNA. Uzzi may well have focused on recruiting PCNA employees because he knew they were good and not because of their confidential knowledge. Nonetheless, the district court, after listening to the witnesses, determined otherwise. That conclusion was not an abuse of discretion.

Thus, when we couple the demonstrated inevitability that Redmond would rely on PCNA trade secrets in his new job at Quaker with the district court's reluctance to believe that Redmond would refrain from disclosing these secrets in his new position (or that Quaker would ensure Redmond did not disclose them), we conclude that the district court correctly decided that PepsiCo demonstrated a likelihood of success on its statutory claim of trade secret misappropriation.

For the foregoing reasons, we affirm the district court's order enjoining Redmond from assuming his responsibilities at Quaker through May, 1995, and preventing him forever from disclosing PCNA trade secrets and confidential information.

Affirmed.

THE CUSTOMER LIST CASE
STRATEGICAL SOLUTIONS LIMITED (T/A CANNON HILL CONSULTING) AND ANOTHER v. ROBINSON AND OTHERS
Chancery Division, 1997.

WALKER, J:

The plaintiffs are two associated companies, Strategic Solutions Limited (t/a Cannon Hill Consulting) and Cannon Hill Consulting Limited. The directors and shareholders of both companies are Mr. William Hall and Mr. David Oxley. The two companies are so closely associated that I can, for most purposes, refer to them together as 'CHC'.

The first defendant, Mr. Mark Robinson, worked for CHC—though as an independent contractor rather than as an employee and through the medium of the second defendant—between June and December 1996. On 18 December he sent a fax to CHC, with very little notice or warning, stating that he would no longer work for it.

The second and third defendants, Latitude Consulting Limited (Latitude) and Selkirk Associates Limited (Selkirk) are companies owned and run by Mr. Robinson and his wife, Mrs. Annika Robinson. The companies have, confusingly, exchanged names and I will refer to them by their present names. Mrs. Robinson is qualified as a chartered accountant, a point I shall have to come back to.

The fourth defendant, Mr. Xerxes Hodivala, is a long-standing colleague of Mr. Robinson. They worked together for some years at Oracle Corporation (UK) Limited, a United Kingdom subsidiary of Oracle Corporation, the world's second-largest software company. Mr. Hodivala was employed by CHC (though without any written contract being signed by him) on 4 November 1996. He gave notice to leave his employment on 30 December 1996, and left the next day. The fifth defendant, Mr. Nicholas Garnett, became an employee (with a written contract) at about the end of October 1996 and gave notice on 23 September, to expire on 21 January this year

The essential facts, so far as I can sift them out from the mass of paper, are that CHC has been in business run by Mr. Hall and Mr. Oxley since about 1994. Its business is that of providing consulting services in the field of business information technology. CHC supplied either its employees, or self-employed contractors engaged by it, to assist clients in designing, installing, adapting and updating computer software particularly suitable for that client's special business needs. CHC's biggest client is the Legal Aid Board which is, as is well known to lawyers, engaged on a major programme of reorganising its use of information technology.

Oracle licenses out various software packages, some highly specialised and sophisticated. The most important—for present purposes—is 'OLAP', which is an on-line analytical processing system. This is a versatile information-technology tool which licensees can adapt and apply to meet the particular needs of their clients.

In June 1996 CHC had very few employees (as opposed to independent contractors) working for it. Mr. Robinson engaged several employees of CHC, including Mr. Hodivala, Mr. Garnett, Mr. Mark Cherry, Mr. Sean Hoban and Mr. Anthony Woods. All these men, except Mr. Woods, had worked for Oracle and had at different times worked with, but in positions subordinate to, Mr. Robinson. One result of their recruitment was that a substantial part of CHC's employees had stronger personal loyalties to Mr. Robinson than they had to Mr. Hall or Mr. Oxley.

During the period of about six months when Mr. Robinson worked for CHC he had considerable success in obtaining new clients for CHC, very largely through contacts which he had had at Oracle. This brought valuable new work for CHC and justified the expansion of CHC's employed staff, though Mr. Hall says that Mr. Robinson acted without authority in some of the terms of employment that he negotiated. I can readily understand that Mr. Robinson did, in a general way, regard this business generated by him as being his clients and Mr. Hodivala and others as being his team. The fact is however that Mr. Robinson's job title was as CHC's sales and marketing manager. His job purpose was 'to promote and sell CHC's business and technical services and products, both to existing marketing segments and entering new target markets', and for this CHC was paying him L2,000 a week plus 20% net of the profit from business generated by Mr. Robinson.

It was CHC, not Mr. Robinson, who was paying the employees whom Mr. Robinson had hired. Mr. Roy Lemon, who appears for all the defendants, accepted that Mr. Hodivala and Mr. Garnett, as employees, owed a duty of fidelity to CHC. He accepted that Mr. Robinson, as an independent contractor operating through his own company, owed a sort of duty of fidelity to CHC. One of the main issues before me is to form a provisional view for interlocutory purposes as to the nature of this duty of fidelity and to see what interlocutory relief, if any, may be appropriate to prevent Mr. Robinson obtaining any unfair advantage from any breach of duty without being permanently disabled from earning his living by the use of his undoubted talents.

There is some evidence, which is for the most part disputed by Mr. Robinson, of his having copied numerous disks at CHC's premises during the first part of December 1996. Mr. Robinson accepts that he copied a number of CVs. What is beyond dispute—because it was revealed on the execution of the Anton Piller orders and the subsequent investigation of what was on Mr. Robinson's computer and Psion organiser—is that on his leaving CHC Mr. Robinson had, and retained, on his computer a large quantity of material which related either to the internal organisation and working of CHC's business or to work which CHC had undertaken or hoped to undertake for clients or prospective clients of CHC. Mr. Robinson's evidence dismissed this material as out-of-date or worthless, but I find that part of his evidence implausible.

There is compelling evidence—principally in the form of e-mail messages transcribed under the Anton Piller orders—that while working out their notice, Mr. Hoban and Mr. Cherry, but not Mr. Garnett, devoted much of their time and energies to communicating with Mr. Robinson and Mr. Hodivala and letting them know what was happening at CHC's offices. These messages were sometimes accompanied by vulgar insults directed at Mr. Hall and Mr. Oxley.

Mr. Lemon submitted to me that standards in the computer software industry should be judged by those of an active modern industry in which job changes are frequent, as with certain jobs in the City of London. That may not, in view of recent events concerning the Co-operative Wholesale Society, be an entirely happy comparison. The more frequent job changes are, the more important it is that the court should not depart from upholding the basic duty of fidelity that any employee—high paid or low paid—owes to his or her employer. In *Wessex Dairies v.*

Smith [1935] 23 KB page 85, Greer LJ said that an employee's obligation to protect his master's interests lasts until the last hour of his service.

It seems to me that both Mr. Robinson and Mr. Hodivala were under a duty not to appropriate for themselves information belonging to CHC, either during the time when they were working there or during the period after they had left, but Mr. Hoban and Mr. Cherry remained as their Fifth Column within CHC.

It is submitted that the relevant information was information which did not belong to CHC, but was which in the individual defendants' heads. But as Norse LJ said in *Roger Bullivant Ltd. v. Ellis* [1987] FSR 172, [1987] IRLR 491 at page 495 of the latter report):

> "Having made deliberate and unlawful use of the plaintiffs' property, he cannot complain if he finds that the eye of the law is unable to distinguish between those who he could, had he chose, have contacted lawfully and those whom he could not. In my judgment it is of the highest importance that the principle of *Robb v. Green* (1895) 2 QB 315 which, let it be said, is one of no more than fair and honourable dealing, should be steadfastly maintained."

The reference to *Robb v. Green* is of interest because it shows how deep are the roots of this principle as to the duty of fidelity and how the principle grows out of breach of trust and confidence, as well as breach of contract. In *Robb v. Green*, Kay LJ quoted what had been said by Turner V–C as long ago as 1851 in *Morison v. Moat* (1851) 199 ER 241:

> ". . . The true question is whether, under the circumstances of this case, the Court ought to interpose by injunction, upon the ground of breach of faith or of contract. That the Court has exercised jurisdiction in cases of this nature does not, I think, admit of any question. Different grounds have indeed been assigned for the exercise of that jurisdiction. In some cases it has been referred to property, in others to contract; and in others, again, it has been treated as founded upon trust or confidence—meaning, as I conceive, that the Court fastens the obligation on the conscience of the party, and enforces it against him in the same manner as it enforces against a party to whom a benefit is given the obligation of performing a promise on the faith of which the benefit has been conferred; but, upon whatever grounds the jurisdiction is founded, the authorities have no doubt as to the exercise of it."

Mr. Lemon relies on the well known case of *Printers & Finishers v. Holloway* [1964] 3 All ER 731, [1965] 1 WLR 1, as regards the skills and experience which trained employees carry in their heads and submits that Mr. Robinson's and Mr. Hoban's client contacts were equivalent to their tools of trade.

The client connection of much less highly paid employees—hairdressers and milk roundsmen—was regarded as part of the employer's goodwill in cases such as *Home Counties Dairies Ltd. v. Skilton* [1970] 1 All ER 1227, [1970] 1 WLR 526 and *Marion White Ltd. v. Francis* [1972]

3 All ER 857, [1972] 1 WLR 1423. Note the clear contrast in the latter case which Buckley LJ made, at page 863 of the latter report, between 'the employee's personality and skill' and 'the employer's goodwill'.

The court should not in my view impose less demanding standards on more highly paid workers.

There are two principal points to be settled, which interact together: the period appropriate to neutralise the springboard advantage and the identification—whether by name or by description—of clients or possible clients of CHC in relation to which these defendants should be restrained, it being common ground that if any injunctive relief is to be granted, should, as to its length, be on the lines of what May LJ said in *Roger Bullivant v. Ellis* at page 482:

> "... That an injunction restraining a company from making unlawful use of confidential information may or will drive it into liquidation is of itself *nihil ad rem*, provided that the *American Cyanamid* tests can be satisfied; cf. the *Potters-Ballotini Ltd. v. Weston–Baker* [1977] RPC 202) Such a consideration does, however, emphasise the necessity of ensuring that any interim injunction of the nature that we have to consider in this appeal runs for no longer than is necessary properly to protect a plaintiff in the respect I have referred to, and that once this is achieved the continuance of the injunction is not allowed to prejudice legitimate competition by a defendant."

As to the identification of the companies or other bodies affected, there are obvious difficulties about a descriptive formula because CHC's client base was changing rapidly during (and because of) Mr. Robinson's activity during his six months with CHC.

A list of names would achieve the greatest certainty, and a defendant who is enjoined should know as certainly as possible what it is he is forbidden to do; but its compilation is, in the circumstances of this case, difficult and almost bound to have a rather arbitrary element. It should include CHC's regular and old-established clients and their inclusion will—if the defendants are not interested in the Legal Aid Board or anyone else of that sort—cause no hardship. It should include clients whom Mr. Robinson had successfully introduced during his period with CHC. It should also, it seems to me, include clients who Mr. Robinson was attempting to introduce, especially where there is evidence that he then slowed down his recruitment efforts or took preliminary action with a view to diverting them to his own business. It should not, in my judgment, include Oracle or any of its divisions, departments or subsidiaries, because Oracle is, in the context, not so much a client as a wholesale source or supplier of possible clients. The longer the list is, the shorter the period that is appropriate.

In my judgment certainty is of the highest importance in this case, even at the risk of some arbitrariness, and a fairly wide but precise prohibition for a relatively short period will best achieve the ends of justice. I shall, therefore, grant an injunction against the first four defendants prohibiting them until six months from the execution of the Anton Piller order—that is until 12th August, 1997—from soliciting or providing any business services either directly or through the medium of any other contractor to any company or organisation which (a) is designated as a 'partner' on the list headed 'CHC Progress Report References', in exhibit WH/2, including the names (out of alphabetical order) at the end, but excluding any company, department or division within Oracle; (b) designated as a client in that list, including the names out of alphabetical order at the end, but not including those designated as 'associate potentials' (except under (c) below); and, (c) Miller Freeman, Ford (UK) and Carlsberg Tetley.

The defendants may write to these companies—in the form of a letter which should be approved by the plaintiffs' solicitors—informing them of the injunction; such a letter should not contain anything that could be construed as canvassing for work at the end of the injunction period.

Notes and Questions

1. In the *Pepsi Employee* case the court based its grant of injunctive relief on a theory of trade secret protection. What theory did the court use to protect the customer contacts in the *Customer List* case?

2. How long should injunctive relief last in a case of trade secret misappropriation by a former employee? What facts would you consider in establishing an acceptable period of time?

3. Does the court's decision in the *Pepsi Employee* case effectively preclude Redmond from pursuing his chosen profession? Does the court's decision in the *Customer List* case preclude Robinson from pursuing his chosen profession? How do courts distinguish between secret information which belongs to the company and an individual's talent or skills? For example, if Microsoft hired a college graduate and trained them in the "Microsoft way of doing business", could Microsoft lawfully preclude that employee from working for another competitor for the rest of his career? Where should the boundary be drawn between an employee's right to earn a living and an employer's right to protect its valuable secrets?

4. *Term of Protection.* What if Redmond had been hired by a PepsiCo competitor in another country? Should PepsiCo be able to prevent such foreign competition? How long should a trade secret last? The formula for Coca–Cola has remained a secret for over 100 years. Theoretically, a trade secret should remain protectable so long as reasonable steps are taken to protect its confidential nature. Nevertheless, the licensing of such secret information, even where continued confidentiality is required may result in the loss of the trade secret. Thus, for example, the European Union's regulation on know-how licensing limits protection to "technical information [which] is secret, substantial and identified in any appropriate form" and further limits any protection for such information to a period of ten years from the date the information is first licensed anywhere in the European Union. Commission Regulation 556/89 on the Application of Article 85 (3) of the Treaty to Certain Categories of Know–How Licensing Agreements, 1989 O.J. 7 at Art. 1 cl. (7).

THE SWISS DRUG CASE
ADAMS v. COMMISSION OF THE EUROPEAN COMMUNITIES

European Court Of Justice, 1985.
[1986] 1 QB 138, [1986] 2 WLR 367, [1986] FSR 617.

MR. Advocate General Mancini delivered the following opinion.

1. In its judgment of 13 February 1979 in Hoffmann–La Roche & Co AG v Commission of the European Communities (Case 85/76), [1979] ECR 461, 552, para 125, the court stated for the first time:

> "By prohibiting the abuse of a dominant position within the market ... article 86 [of the EEC Treaty] ... covers not only abuse which may directly prejudice consumers but also abuse which indirectly prejudices them by impairing the effective competitive structure as envisaged by article 3(f).

The court thus recognised that the Swiss multinational's conduct in the market in vitamins for use in the pharmaceutical and food industries could adversely affect both competition and intro-Community trade and that it was therefore necessary to put an end to and penalise that conduct.

Although I am not in possession of precise information, I am convinced that that judgment contributed greatly to the liberation of the European market in vitamins (products of fundamental importance for the physical welfare of modern man and in modern economic life) from the monopolistic straitjacket in which it had languished for years, and enabled that market to breathe once again the invigorating air of freedom.

Someone, therefore, had the right idea in suggesting to the Commission of the European Communities, early in 1973, that it should investigate the hidden and almost inaccessible recesses of a commercial empire founded for the most part on unlawful rules and clauses. In a "personal and confidential" letter sent on 25 February to Mr. Borschette, then the Commissioner for Competition, that person expressly asked the Commission to take action against Hoffmann–La Roche (hereinafter referred to as "Roche") for infringement of article 86 of the EEC Treaty. The role and the activity of that undertaking on the world market in vitamins were described in detail and an equally thorough account was provided of the anti-competitive measures which it applied and imposed. The letter concluded:

> "I request you not to let my name be connected with this matter. However, I remain at your entire disposal for further information, as well as documentary evidence about every point which I have raised in this letter. Furthermore, I am prepared to discuss any point with your assistants or yourself at any time, and if necessary I am prepared to fly to Belgium or Rome for this purpose.

Additionally, after I leave Roche around July 1973 I would be prepared even to appear before any court to give sworn evidence on my statements. I trust to hear from you soon to know in what direction I can be of further help . . .''

The author of that letter was, therefore, employed by the Swiss company. Today his name is well known: Stanley George Adams, a Maltese national and director of the International Affairs Division of Hoffmann–La Roche at Basle. In fact, Mr. Adams's identity as the Commission's informant in the vitamins case was not a secret for long. It was certainly no longer secret after 31 December 1974, when he was arrested at the Swiss–Italian border by the Swiss authorities and, on the basis of a complaint laid by Roche, charged with the criminal offences of disclosure of business information and breach of business confidentiality under articles 273 and 162 of the Swiss Penal Code. That was the beginning of the former Roche employee of a long calvery. On 21 March 1975, he was released on bail of SF 25,000 and on 1 July 1976, after a trial in which certain sittings were held in camera, he was sentenced in absentia by the criminal court of Basle to one year's imprisonment (suspended) and prohibited from entering Switzerland for a period of five years. He appealed against that judgment to the Court of Appeal and then to the Bundesgericht (the Federal Supreme Court), Lausanne. However, the conviction at first instance was upheld and in due course became definitive.

I am well aware that that brief account does not cover all the aspects of the Adams affair. However, I do not think that it is necessary to set down here all the events (frequently painful and sometimes tragic) which followed his first contact by letter with the Commission. By an application (Case 145/83) lodged on 18 July 1983, he asked the court to find the Commission liable in respect of certain acts and omissions which brought about the disclosure of his identity and to order it to pay damages for the injury which he subsequently suffered. In addition, Mr. Adams accuses the Commission of a breach of the duty, which it had assumed voluntarily, to advise his lawyers as to the possibility of laying a complaint against Switzerland for infringement of the European Convention on Human Rights, articles 6 and 10. I therefore intend to consider only those facts which, according to Mr. Adams, give rise to that liability and only in order to establish whether and to what extent the Commission's conduct must be considered unlawful and constitutes the cause of the injury for which Mr. Adams claims damages.

5. As regards the breach of a duty of confidentiality, Mr. Adams claims that his relationship with the Commission was from the beginning confidential. In his view that is clear both from the wording of his first letter and the tenor of the discussions which he had with officials from DG IV during the meeting of 9 April 1973. If only for that reason the Commission was under a duty not to disclose his name.

The Commission, on the other hand, contends that once Mr. Adams left his employment with Roche, it was no longer bound by any duty of confidentiality. Mr. Adams himself placed that limit on the Commission's obligation by writing in his first letter that once he had resigned from Roche he would not hesitate to give evidence before any court. How is it possible, asks the Commission, to give evidence in court without disclosing one's personal particulars? Moreover, when he left Basle, Mr. Adams did not even bother to leave the officials from DG IV his new address. He thus showed that he was completely indifferent to any subsequent developments in the investigation and the possibility that his name might be implicated.

As I have stated under point 2, Mr. Adams denies that last contention and states that he communicated to Mr. Carisi his address in Italy. However, his main argument is based on different grounds. He claims that the Commission misunderstood him. When he wrote "I would be prepared ... to give ... evidence," he in no way intended to put an end to the Commission's obligation by renouncing the anonymity which he had insisted on. What he meant was that he would be prepared to reveal his identity (but by his own decision and on his own initiative) once the investigation had been terminated and a case had been brought before the court. In other words, only he could decide how and when he would make his public appearance.

The two views are therefore diametrically opposed. In my opinion the second is more convincing, although it is expressed in terms which are perhaps too rigid. However, even that view does not take us very far if it is accepted that, until 31 December 1974 (in other words until the beginning of the chain of events giving rise to the injury for which Mr. Adams claims compensation), the Commission did not openly reveal the name of its informant.

Indeed prudence, care and, if necessary, discretion are among the fundamental requirements for administrative activity. Although it was free to use the documents entrusted to it how and when in considered appropriate, the Commission could not disregard those requirement. The point, then, is this: can it be said that the Commission complied with those requirements? Did the methods chosen by it to obtain from Roche the evidence which it needed and the measures taken to put those methods into practice correspond to the conduct of a reasonable and responsible man in a similar situation, or that of, as the Romans used to say, a "bonus paterfamilias?"

Mr. Adams is convinced that they did not. In his view, to show the "Management Information" memorandum to the directors of the Belgian and French subsidiaries was an act which was, at least, imprudent because it enabled Roche to establish that, in all probability, he must have been the source of the information. The Commission takes an entirely different view. It contends that, quite apart from not having given in instructions, Mr. Adams failed to warn it that to disclose those particular documents would be to run the risk of revealing their source. Moreover, the officials charged with the investigation chose to show the "most anonymous" documents and endeavoured to make them unrecognisable by removing anything which might facilitate the search for the informant. Clearly no one can say whether their precautions were successful. However, it is significant that in its complaint Roche justified its suspicions of Mr. Adams by reference to his bad relationship with his superiors and to circumstances concerning information which was never in the Commission's possession.

Mr. Adams reproaches the Commission with not having informed him of it in time and, in particular, with not having warned him of the serious risks which he would run if he re-entered Switzerland. Thus the Commission had "fallen short of exercising the standard of care" which is required for administrative action and that failure had "aggravated" the damage sustained by him as a result of the "breach of professional confidentiality."

To protect the informant by preserving his anonymity is not an end in itself but serves in particular to prevent reprisals from the party damaged by his information. [T]he duty of confidentiality incumbent on the Commission did not cease upon the Community inspectors' visit to the subsidiaries in Paris and Brussels. The Commission therefore was under a duty to ensure that that visit did not produce results which were different from those intended by it and, in particular, that it did not have unfavourable consequences for Mr. Adams. However, such consequences (reprisals in the form of criminal proceedings with the possibility of arrest and conviction) were indeed threatened by Dr. Alder in the course of a meeting which was itself one of the result of that visit. The inference which may be drawn is clear. The Commission should have taken all the necessary measures, in accordance with the normal standard of care, to prevent such threats from becoming a reality.

Instead, the Commission remained inactive and that inactivity cannot be justified. Even if Dr. Alder's attitude may have suggested that he was "bluffing," the stakes were such that it should have "seen" the cards in his hand to find out whether they really were weak. It should not have been too difficult for the lawyers of the DG IV to verify the existence of provisions contained in a code which is certainly to be found in the Commission's library and to determine the exact scope of those provisions simply by researching the case law on the subject. I would add that the content of those provisions is not very different from that of various provisions which are still in force in the legal orders of certain member states (for example article 623 of the Italian Penal Code). If they had thought of all that and if they had taken action accordingly, those lawyers would have reached the conclusion that Dr. Alder had indeed tried to intimidate them but that he was far from bluffing; in fact, he held some very strong cards.

There remains the argument concerning the impossibility of tracing Mr. Adams. Clearly I do not deny that, after leaving his employment, Mr. Adams displayed no interest in the inquiry and provided only occasional and notably vague indications as to his Italian schemes. He maintains, however, that in November 1973 he telephoned Mr. Carisi and gave him his address, precisely in order to enable the Commission to remain in contact with him. It is entirely probable that that is what happened. As we know, Mr. Carisi did not appear at the preparatory inquiry. Other officials, and in particular Mr. Schlieder, nevertheless recall a telephone call from Mr. Adams. They can say nothing of what was said, but in view of when it was made (in the period immediately following his departure from Roche) and the place from which it came (certainly Italy), it is difficult to see what purpose it served except to communicate his address to the Commission.

It is in any event indisputable that the Commission did not even try to find Mr. Adams, although it had plenty of time to do so (it must not be forgotten that Mr. Pappalardo replied to Dr. Alder's second question almost one month after the discussion!). In my view, that is enough to justify the conclusion that the Commission's conduct did not conform to the ordinary standard of care. It therefore constitutes wrongful conduct giving rise to non-contractual liability.

JUDGMENT:

As regards the existence of a duty of confidentiality it must be pointed out that article 214 of the EEC Treaty lays down an obligation, in particular for the members and the servants of the institutions of the Community:

> "not to disclose information of the kind covered by the obligation of professional secrecy, in particular information about undertakings, their business relations or their cost components."

Although that provision primarily refers to information gathered from undertakings, the expression "in particular" shows that the principle in question is a general one which applies also to information supplied by natural persons, if that information is "of a kind" that is confidential. That is particularly so in the case of information supplied on a purely voluntary basis, but accompanied by a request for confidentiality in order to protect the informant's anonymity. An institution which accepts such information is bound to comply with such a condition.

As regards the case before the court, it is quite clear from Mr. Adams's letter of 25 February 1973 that he requested the Commission not to reveal his identity. It cannot therefore be denied that the Commission was bound by a duty of confidentiality towards Mr. Adams in that respect. In fact the parties disagree not so much as to the existence of such a duty but as to whether the Commission was bound by a duty of confidentiality after Mr. Adams had left his employment with Roche.

In that respect it must be pointed out that Mr. Adams did not qualify his request by indicating a period upon the expiry of which the Commission would be released from its duty of confidentiality regarding the identity of its informant. No such indication can be inferred from the fact that Mr. Adams was prepared to appear before any court after he had left Roche. The giving of evidence before a court implies that the witness has been duly summoned, that he is under a duty to answer the questions put to him, and is, in return, entitled to all the guarantees provided by a judicial procedure. Mr. Adams's offer to confirm the accuracy of his information under such conditions cannot therefore be interpreted as a general statement releasing the Commission from its duty of confidentiality. Nor can any such intention be inferred from Mr. Adams's subsequent conduct.

It must therefore be stated that the Commission was under a duty to keep Mr. Adams's identity secret even after he had left his employer.

Of the events mentioned by Mr. Adams, the only occasion on which the Commission directly revealed the identity of its informant was the telephone conversation between Mr. Schlieder and Dr. Alder at the beginning of February 1975. However, that conversation took place after Mr. Adams had caused an anonymous letter to be sent to the Commission informing it of his detention and seeking its help. It is difficult to see how the Commission could have acted on that request without confirming, at least by implication, that Mr. Adams was in fact its informant. Moreover, it transpired subsequently that at that time Mr. Adams had already admitted to the Swiss police that he had given information, at least orally, to the Commission and it is clear from the decisions of the Swiss courts that the confirmation of that fact by Mr. Schlieder did not have a decisive bearing on Mr. Adams's conviction. The disclosure of Mr. Adams's identity at that time and in those circumstances cannot be regarded as constituting a breach of the duty of confidentiality which could give rise to the Commission's liability vis-a-vis Mr. Adams.

On the other hand, it is clear that the handing over of the edited photocopies to members of the staff of the Roche subsidiaries enabled Roche to identify Mr. Adams as the main suspect in the complaint which it lodged with the Swiss Public Prosecutor's Office. It was therefore that handing over of the documents which led to Mr. Adams's arrest and which in addition supplied the police and the Swiss courts with substantial evidence against him.

It appears from the documents before the court that the Commission was fully aware of the risk that the handing over to Roche of the photocopies supplied by Mr. Adams might reveal the informant's identity to the company. For that reason the Commission officials first attempted to obtain other copies of the documents in question from the Roche subsidiaries in Paris and Brussels. When that attempt failed, the Commission prepared new copies of the documents which it considered were the least likely to lead to the discovery of Mr. Adams's identity and it took care to remove from those copies any indication which it considered might reveal the source of the documents. However, since it was not familiar with Roche's practices regarding the distribution of the documents in question within the company, the Commission could not be sure that those precautions were sufficient to eliminate all risk of Mr. Adams's being identified by means of the copies handed over to Roche.

The Commission was therefore, in any event, imprudent in handing over those copies to Roche without having consulted Mr. Adams.

It is not, however, necessary to decide whether, in view of the situation at the time and in particular of the information in the Commission's possession, the handing over of the documents is sufficient to give rise to the Commission's liability regarding the consequences of Mr. Adams's being identified as the informant. Although the Commission was not necessarily aware, when those documents were handed over, of the gravity of the risk to which it was exposing Mr. Adams, Dr. Alder's visit on 8 November 1974, on the other hand, provided it with all the necessary information in that respect. Following that visit the Commission knew that Roche was determined to discover how the Commission had come into possession of the documents in question and that it was preparing to lay a complaint against the informant under article 273 of the Swiss Penal Code, the contents of which Dr. Alder even took care to explain. The Commission also knew that there was a possibility of obtaining from Roche, in return for the disclosure of the informant's identity, an undertaking not to take action against him. It could not, however, pursue that possibility without Mr. Adams's consent.

In those circumstances it was not at all sufficient for the Commission merely to take the view that it was unlikely that Mr. Adams would be identified, that he was probably never going to return to Switzerland and that, in any event, the Swiss authorities did not intend to institute criminal proceedings against him. On the contrary, the Commission was under a duty to take every possible step to warn Mr. Adams, thereby enabling him to make his own arrangements in the light of the information given by Dr. Alder, and to consult him as to the approach to be adopted in relation to Dr. Alder's proposals.

Although Mr. Adams had not left any precise address making it possible for the Commission to contact him easily, in his letter of 25 February 1973 he had indicated his intention of setting up his own meat business in Italy, near Rome. Even in the absence of other indications, that information would have enabled the Commission to make inquiries with a view to discovering where Mr. Adams was staying. It is common ground that the Commission did not even attempt to find Mr. Adams, although it allowed almost one month to elapse before communicating to Dr. Alder its final refusal to discuss the origin of the documents in its possession, a refusal which was followed by the lodging of Roche's complaint at the Swiss Public Prosecutor's Office.

It must therefore be concluded that, by failing to make all reasonable efforts to pass on to Mr. Adams the information which was available to it following Dr. Alder's visit of 8 November 1974, even though the communication of that information might have prevented, or at least limited, the damage which was likely to result from the discovery of Mr. Adams's identity by means of the documents which it had handed over to Roche, the Commission has incurred liability towards Mr. Adams in respect of that damage.

It must therefore be concluded that in principle the Community is bound to make good the damage resulting from the discovery of Mr. Adams's identity by means of the documents handed over to Roche by the Commission. It must, however, be recognised that the extent of the Commission's liability is diminished by reason of Mr. Adams's own negligence. Mr. Adams failed to inform the Commission that it was possible to infer his identity as the informant from the documents themselves, although he was in the best position to appreciate and to avert that risk. Nor did he ask the Commission to keep him informed of the progress of the investigation of Roche, and in particular of any use that might be made of the documents for that purpose. Lastly, he went back to Switzerland without attempting to make any inquiries in that respect, although he must have been aware of the risks to which his conduct towards his former employer had exposed him with regard to Swiss legislation.

Consequently, Mr. Adams himself contributed significantly to the damage which he suffered. In assessing the conduct of the Commission on the one hand and that of Mr. Adams on the other, the court considers it equitable to apportion responsibility for that damage equally between the two parties.

It follows from all the foregoing considerations that the Commission must be ordered to compensate Mr. Adams to the extent of one half of the damage suffered by him as a result of the fact that he was identified as the source of information regarding Roche's anti-competitive practices. For the rest, however, the application must be dismissed. The amount of the damages is to be determined by agreement between the parties or, failing such agreement, by the court.

On those grounds, the court as an interlocutory decision, hereby (1) orders the Commission to compensate Mr. Adams to the extent of one half of the damage suffered by him as a result of the fact that he was identified as the source of information which led the Commission to impose a fine on his former employer, the Swiss company Hoffmann–La–Roche, for certain anti-competitive practices; (2) for the rest, dismisses the application; (3) orders the parties to inform the court within 9 months from delivery of this judgment of the amount of damages arrived at by agreement; (4) orders that, in the absence of agreement, the parties shall transmit to the court within the same period a statement of their views with supporting figures; and (5) reserves the costs.

Notes and Questions

1. *Preventing Unfairness.* As noted previously, the international basis for trade secret protection, at least according to TRIPS, is *not* an individual owner's private property right in the trade secret. It is the "unfairness" or "dishonesty" in using the secret information that requires remedy. The unfair competition basis for trade secret protection has a limiting effect on the scope of protection afforded such secrets. Since the owner does not have a property interest per se in her trade secret, she is only allowed to prohibit "unfair" uses. Thus, for example, a trade secret owner cannot prohibit use

of the trade secret by competitors where the secret has been discovered through lawful means. Where trade secret protection is based on unfair competition concerns, reverse engineering would not be illegal in the absence of a contractual arrangement forbidding such actions. Consequently, a trade secret owner's "property" right is only so good as its ability to withstand reverse engineering.

2. *Reverse Engineering.* It is not always clear which efforts qualify internationally as legal efforts to reverse engineer a trade secret. Assume that your client is a joint venture that manufactures and distributes cough syrup. Your client has discovered that that one of its competitors has developed a drug which will cure a cold. The drug in unable to be patented so that the formula is only protected by trade secret. Under the *Aerial Photography* and *Pepsi Employee* cases, which of the following acts (if any) could your client lawfully do to obtain the competitor's trade secret formula:

A. Have an employee buy the drug over the counter and reverse engineer it?

B. Hire someone to break into the competitor's offices and steal the formula?

C. If the drug is a prescription drug, have an employee pretend to be ill in order to buy the drug and reverse engineer it?

Under TRIPS which of these acts, if any, must be prohibited? What test should be used to determine if an action is "contrary to honest commercial practices"? What role should societal standards of "commercial morality" play in making this determination? Whose moral norms should be utilized? Developed countries? Western countries? Developing countries?

3. *Economic Espionage.* Increasingly nations have treated the theft or misappropriation of trade secrets as a criminal matter—a type of "economic espionage" punishable by criminal fines and penalties. In the *Swiss Drug* case what balance did the court strike between protection confidential information and Swiss criminal trade laws? Should the reason for Adams' disclosure of Hoffman–Roche's confidential information have been treated as a complete defense to the criminal charges? What if such information had led to an investigation, but no finding of a violation, by the Commission? Would your answer be the same?

Problem

For the past five years, your client has been the head of international marketing for a computer software company specializing in high end video games. As part of his duties, your client has been actively involved in developing marketing plans for his company's next generation of video games—virtual reality. He has worked closely with the tech team to assure a user-friendly design and to develop a cutting edge advertising campaign, combining video, TV and print promotions. Your client has gained fame for his previous marketing campaign which combined video giveaways with sweepstakes tickets for trips to the fantasy lands contained in the games. Your client has been approached by his employer's biggest competitor. He claims this competitor is ready to launch a virtual reality game next year—a full year before his current employer. He is excited about marketing cutting edge technology internationally but feels guilty because "everything I know

about international marketing of videogames I learned from my employer."
What guidance would you give regarding your client's ability to work for the
competitor? What risks does he run?

EXERCISE

How would you define "intellectual property"? Some have suggested
that a broad definition for such "property" is "products of the mind."
Make a list of the attributes that such products must have to qualify as
protectable property. For example, would you include unexpressed ideas
under the rubric of protectable property? If not then one of the attributes on your list would be "tangible form," and there might be "disclosure." As you make your list of attributes, ask yourself what each
attribute contributes to make a product of the mind worthy of protection
from unauthorized use by others. Once you have created your list of
attributes, draft a definition of intellectual property that would appear in
a multinational treaty. Be prepared to defend your language.

Part IV

THE TRIP TO TRIPS

The manufacturing and sale of counterfeit and pirated goods is a recurring global problem. Similar to the treatment of other recurring international problems, countries have attempted to avoid recurring disputes over IP issues through bilateral and multinational treaties. Since the 19th Century, countries have used bilateral and multilateral treaty approaches to reduce multinational disputes over intellectual property rights and enforcement. The negotiation of these treaties has often required extensive "horse-trading" as each country or block of interests attempts to achieve treaty language which reflects its own particular interests. Probably the most extensive IP treaty negotiations to date, in terms of length and issues addressed, were those which resulted in the TRIPS Agreement. Initial negotiations regarding the inclusion of TRIPS as part of the Uruguay Round of GATT began in 1986, yet the treaty itself was not finally acceded to until 1994. The history of these eight year negotiations, which you will be examining in this chapter, help highlight the complicated problems that arise when countries of differing histories and culture attempt to reach accord on issues involving international intellectual property protection.

As you may have already guessed from the brief glimpses you have taken of the TRIPS treaty, including its preamble and definitional sections, TRIPS built on earlier multinational treaties to develop its standards. These earlier treaties included the Berne Convention for the Protection of Literary and Artistic Works and the Paris Convention for the Protection of Industrial Property, and arose from the problems of the Nineteenth Century and the Romantic literary traditions of that Century. As you examine these treaties, ask yourself to what extent their proposed solutions remain viable in today's digital, highly technology-oriented, global marketplace. Are there other, newer solutions that should be resolved to solve the "problem" of global piracy? Are there even other definitions of "piracy" that ought to be adopted to take into account the concerns of less developed countries?

Chapter Twelve

TREATY REGIMES

A. WHEN ARE TREATY REGIMES A USEFUL SOLUTION TO INTERNATIONAL PROBLEMS?

THE DOMAIN NAME CONTROVERSY– A POSSIBLE SOLUTION?

Because of its global reach, and the ease with which information can be reproduced and disseminated, the Internet often serves as a focal point for many of the emerging international intellectual property protection issues. Information uploaded (copied) on to the "Net" in the United States, is readily accessible in, for example, India and can be easily reproduced and downloaded. One of the issues of emerging concern directly related to the Internet and its operations is the use and control of domain names. A domain name is the shorthand address for a particular page or site on the web. It is often used in searches by Internet users who are seeking information regarding the site. Thus, for example, the Domain Name for the West Publishing Company is West-law.com.

Since the Internet is international in nature, a problem arises when more than one company in the world wants to use the same name for its website. One way to resolve such a dispute is for the companies involved to reach a private settlement. Where the parties fail to reach such a settlement, however, the problem becomes a legal issue whose result may differ depending on the domestic law applied to the problem.

Given both the global scope of the problem and its recurring nature, one method for resolving the issue may be to develop an international treaty regime to resolve the problem. Developing such a regime, however, may pose its own unique set of problems. For example, should the regime be a bilateral one, between the home countries of the affected companies, or a multilateral one, attempting to reach an accord among diverse nations? What are the benefits of such an approach? What are the limitations? How can such accords be enforced?

Review A Five Cent Lecture on Treaties in Chapter Six.

Notes and Questions

1. Treaty regimes currently fall into two broad categories–bilateral and multilateral. Bilateral treaties are negotiated between two countries and generally reflect single issue concerns between such countries. Multilateral treaties, on the other hand, are negotiated between several countries and, depending on the number of countries which are signatories to the treaty, may reflect the accord of numerous countries of different philosophical, cultural, historical and political backgrounds. Much of international intellectual property law is governed by multilateral treaties. These treaties govern such diverse topics as registration procedures for obtaining intellectual property rights (such as the Patent Cooperation Treaty), the minimum protection standards to be granted a foreign intellectual property owner under domestic law (such as the Berne Convention) or the minimum enforcement procedures to be provided to intellectual property owners (such as TRIPS). Multinational treaties may also be regional in nature, such as the North American Free Trade Agreement (governing diverse issues such as free trade zones between the United States, Canada and Mexico, and intellectual property protection) or the Banjul Protocol (governing trademark registration issues among members of the African Regional Industrial Property Organization (ARIPO)).

2. Perhaps the most important multinational treaty of the latter part of the Twentieth Century was the Agreement on Trade Related Aspects of Intellectual Property Rights (TRIPS), first signed by over 111 countries on April 15, 1994. TRIPS, however, was built upon several earlier multinational treaties which laid the foundation for the minimum substantive standards contained in this seminal treaty. Among the most important precursors which you will be studying in Part IV are the Paris Convention for the Protection of Industrial Property and the Berne Convention for the Protection of Literary and Artistic Works. These two multilateral treaty regimes are over 100 years old. They have been revised countless times to reflect international demands for clearer or more expanded protection as a result of technological or commercial demands.

3. For a good overview of some of the issues faced in the interpretation and enforcement of multinational treaty regimes affecting intellectual property rights, see D'Amato and Long, International intellectual property anthology, Chapter Eight (Anderson Publishing 1996).

EXERCISES

1. Select a country other than the United States. You are to represent that country's interest in negotiating with your class mates a proposed multilateral treaty for the protection of non-copyright protectable databases and other collections of information. The draft treaty is set forth below. Develop your negotiating strategy. Is your country in need of protection for its database industry? Is it in favor of such protection? Opposed to it? What changes, if any, would your country desire before it would agree to sign a database treaty? Which countries would your

country consider as allies in its fight regarding the issues which would be raised in any negotiations regarding the proposed database treaty? Prepare a negotiating position paper that reflects your opinion on these matters.

2. Based on the position paper you have developed, negotiate the treaty set forth below. Under the rules of engagement you are allowed to contact other countries to develop voting blocks for your position. You must reflect your countries needs and you must continue to negotiate until you have reached agreement with a majority of your class mates regarding the terms of the Database Treaty.

3. Review the results of your negotiations efforts. What issues proved problematical in obtaining agreement with other countries? How specific is the language which you eventually agreed to in the negotiated treaty? Does the treaty resolve all of your country's concerns over database protection? What "loopholes" remain? What compromises were you forced to make in order to attain agreement? The results of these exercises reflect some of the "real world" problems that occur when countries attempt to negotiate multinational intellectual property treaty regimes.

4. Keep a copy of the final treaty. As we discover the problems of lack of clarity and harmonization in subsequent chapters, ask yourself to what extent your own negotiated treaty reflects these international problems.

DRAFT TREATY ON DATABASE PROTECTION

(1) Whereas databases are at present not sufficiently protected in all Member States by existing legislation;

(2) Whereas copyright remains an appropriate form of exclusive right for authors who have created databases;

(3) Whereas databases are a vital tool in the development of an information market;

HAVE ADOPTED THIS TREATY

Article 1

Scope

1. This Treaty concerns the legal protection of databases in any form.

2. For the purposes of this Treaty, 'database shall mean a collection of independent works, data or other materials arranged in a systematic or methodical way and individually accessible by electronic or other means.

Article 2

Database authorship

The author of a database shall be the natural person or group of natural persons who created the database who shall own the economic rights in such database.

Article 3

Object of protection

1. Member States shall provide for a right for the maker of a database which shows that there has been qualitatively and/or quantitatively a substantial investment in either the obtaining, verification or presentation of the contents to prevent extraction and/or re-utilization of the whole or of a substantial part, evaluated qualitatively and/or quantitatively, of the contents of that database.

2. For the purposes of this Chapter:

(a) 'extraction shall mean the permanent or temporary transfer of all or a substantial part of the contents of a database to another medium by any means or in any form;

(b) 're-utilization shall mean any form of making available to the public all or a substantial part of the contents of a database by the distribution of copies, by renting, by on-line or other forms of transmission.

3. The right referred to in paragraph 1 may be transferred, assigned or granted under contractual licence.

4. The right provided for in paragraph 1 shall apply irrespective of the eligibility of that database or its contents for protection by copyright or by other rights.

5. The repeated and systematic extraction and/or re-utilization of insubstantial parts of the contents of the database implying acts which conflict with a normal exploitation of that database or which unreasonably prejudice the legitimate interests of the maker of the database shall not be permitted.

Article 4

Term of protection

1. The right provided for in Article 2 shall run from the date of completion of the making of the database. It shall expire fifteen years from the first of January of the year following the date of completion.

2. In the case of a database which is made available to the public in whatever manner before expiry of the period provided for in paragraph 1, the term of protection by that right shall expire fifteen years from the first of January of the year following the date when the database was first made available to the public.

3. Any substantial change, evaluated qualitatively or quantitatively, to the contents of a database, including any substantial change resulting from the accumulation of successive additions, deletions or alterations, which would result in the database being considered to be a substantial new investment, evaluated qualitatively or quantitatively, shall qualify the database resulting from that investment for its own term of protection.

Article 5

Beneficiaries of protection under the sui generis right

The right provided for in Article 7 shall apply to database whose makers or right holders are nationals of a Member State or who have their habitual residence in the territory of the Community.

Article 6

Remedies

Member States shall provide appropriate remedies in respect of infringements of the rights provided for in this Directive.

Article 7

Final provisions

Member States shall bring into force the laws, regulations and administrative provisions necessary to comply with this Directive before 1 January 2010.

B. CAN PROTECTION BASED ON "NATIONAL TREATMENT" UNDER DOMESTIC LAWS RESOLVE THE GLOBAL PIRACY PROBLEM?

Read the following treaty provisions from the Supplement: The Berne Convention, Article 5; The Paris Convention, Article 2; TRIPS, Article 1(3)

NEW DYNAMICS IN INTERNATIONAL COPYRIGHT

Paul Edward Geller, 16 Columbia–VLA Journal of Law & The Arts 461 (1992).

The building blocks of international copyright seem to be territorial. In the past, these building blocks have always been nation-states, which concluded copyright treaties, these states have had to protect foreign works against acts of infringement localized within their territories.

The classic dynamics of international copyright started to gather momentum some five hundred years ago. Three types of classic processes followed each other in time; first, the impetus given by the print media to copyright lawmaking; second, the decentralization of copyright interests; and, third, the emergence of international copyright.

The first classic process commenced in the fifteenth century. The printing press was introduced into Europe, and the church and kings sought to control the rising book trade. They gave publishers, in capitals such as Paris and London, state-protected monopolies to print and sell books the censors had approved. These monopolies were territorial: royal authorities—or, publishers, by powers delegated from the sovereign—policed these monopolies on national territories. Tensions arose, however, as print shops opened throughout the provinces, books were increasingly smuggled across borders, and the growing reading public also sought better access to printed works.

The second classic process, the decentralization of copyright interests, hit its stride in the eighteenth century. Control of the dissemination of works was shifted from centers of royal power, outward to individual authors and publishers. These parties were granted copyright as a private right, exploitable throughout the national marketplace and enforceable by any court on civil suit. Ultimately, neither the state nor copyright owners but the public buying books or theater tickets in this marketplace decided which works were to gain the widest dissemination. Note also that the first copyright law, the Statute of Anne of 1709, was enacted at the very moment England and Scotland were being joined into a common market.

The third classic process, internationalization, began to take effect in the mid-nineteenth century. Books moved easily between the many countries of Europe sharing close borders. These countries began to cover Europe with a complicated web of bilateral treaties in order to protect the works of their respective nationals abroad. These treaties varied greatly, and authors, publishers and lawyers soon began to ask how to make more uniform law to govern the growing international market for works. Some proposed that all countries adopt the same copyright code at once, but a more modest proposal prevailed: simply conclude one copyright treaty, binding as many countries as possible, to compel the same choice of laws in cases of foreign works. This process culminated in 1886, when ten countries, seven of them European, established the Berne Convention.

The Berne Convention began what one commentator has called the "dissolution of the territoriality" of copyright.[1] Under the Berne principle of national treatment, the law of each Berne country applies when copyright in a Berne-protected work is infringed on its national territory. A court can easily localize the distribution of pirate copies or unauthorized theatrical performances in a given country. The court choosing law pursuant to the Berne Convention, however, need not sit within the territory of the country whose law it is to apply. For example, a court in the United States asserted jurisdiction to apply the Berne choice of law to infringement taking place in Latin America.[2]

In the Twentieth Century, the media have been changing radically, setting new and continuing dynamics into motion.

First, the dominance of the print media gave way to a proliferation of other media. Second, as if in a kaleidoscope, copyright interests have been regrouping. New media have led copyright interests into turbulent regroupings. Performing artists acquired new importance with the ad-

---

1. Gyorgy Boytha, Fragen Der Entstehung Des Internationalen Urheberrechts in Wohes Kommt Das Urheberrecht Und Wohin Geht Es? 181, 182 (Robert Dittrich Ed. 1988).

2. *London Film Prods. Ltd. v. Intercontinental Communications, Inc.*, 580 F. Supp. 47 (S.D.N.Y.1984).

vent of sound recording and motion pictures. Thus, Enrico Caruso became the first singer heard by fans, not merely in local concert halls, but in recordings sold worldwide. Enterprises specialized in different, competing media have lobbied for legal provisions serving their respective, conflicting interests.

Third, internationally, under the pressure of new media and interests, copyright itself has begun to splinter into diverse rights. In response to these pressures, each Berne revision has introduced new minimum rights, such as the rights to control broadcasting and cable retransmission in Article 11bis and reproduction in Article 9 of the Paris Act. The Rome Convention has instituted neighboring rights, not only to satisfy performing artists reaching worldwide audiences, but also sound-recording producers and broadcasting organizations.

This splintering of copyright threatens to undermine the Berne principle of national treatment for coordinating rights. For example, the Austrian copyright law imposed a levy on blank-tape cassettes to fund a royalty for the home recording of works. Austro–Mechana, an Austrian collecting society administering the levy, however, drew out over half of all such levies to finance programs that benefited only national authors, irrespective of foreign claims to share in all the levies. The German collecting society, GEMA, challenged that construction of the law, and the High Court of Austria reasoned that the "controlling principle of national treatment in the law of the international copyright conventions" precluded Austrian national law from allowing such a "one-sided discrimination against foreign citizens."[3] More subtle devices have been used to undercut national treatment elsewhere: for example, in France, the 1985 Act instituted so-called neighboring rights for audiovisual producers, while specifying that holders of these rights are entitled to receive their distinct portion of blank-tape royalties. Of course, since no convention provides for national treatment relative to such so-called neighboring rights for audiovisual producers, this portion of the blank-tape royalties may be withheld from foreign claimants. More subtly yet, the local procedures of collecting societies sometimes have unintended consequences on the flow of copyright monies due to foreign claimants. Compounding these problems, there is great uncertainty concerning who owns splintering rights from country to country.[4]

At the threshold of the twenty-first century, more recent dynamics have been putting radically new stresses on the Berne system.

3. Judgment of July 14, 1987 (About the "Einbehaltungs Verpflichtung" Decision) Obersten Gerichtshof 1988 Gewerblicher Rechtsschutz Und Urheberrecht Internationaler Teil (Grur Int) 365, 368.

4. Not all countries vest the same economic rights in the same parties worldwide, and many countries have developed their own rules concerning copyright transfers.

No systematic International Instrument guides the courts in tracing out chain of title from original owners to ultimate transferees of rights effective from country to country. Furthermore, while some countries have systems for putting copyright transfers on the public record, not all countries do, and no treaty instrument regulates the worldwide effect of such recordation.

The first of these recent processes is political and legal. European nation-states, with their respective colonial empires, formed the Berne Union in 1886. European countries also played important roles in revising the Berne Convention repeatedly in this century. At present, however, these countries no longer need the Berne Union to stabilize legal conditions in the European media market. The reason is simple: the European Community has begun to function as a supra-national lawmaking authority in the field of copyright in Europe. Indeed, the Court of First Instance of the European Communities has recently declared that Berne provisions need not apply as between E.C. member countries if they conflict with E.C. law on point.

The second recent process represents a revolution in media trends. The media, once proliferating, are now being reconsolidated into tele-communication networks.

Works will continue to be available, albeit with decreasing frequency, both as hard copies obtained on the marketplace and as performances seen and heard in theaters or concert halls. But there will be less and less need to clutter up our files and shelves with printed matter, tapes or discs, or to make photocopies or recordings from books or broadcasts. We will simply receive works on demand in digital form from more or less centralized data bases, through more or less centralized telecommunication networks. The works will then be played back on high-fidelity and high-definition multimedia monitors. There will accordingly be a decreasing need to buy, rent or make hard copies. We have to ask what the consequences will be for international copyright.

The third recent process involves a shift from private to public international law, as well as to supranational law. The Berne Convention is above all an instrument of private international law, assuring private parties of rights in literary and artistic works. To have effect, these rights must be vindicated in national courts, to which private parties may have recourse in copyright disputes with other private parties. The GATT, by contrast, is essentially an instrument of public international law: it governs disputes between public entities, notably nation-states, and has procedures to adjudicate such disputes and to sanction states for violating its rules. European Community law is supranational: E.C. directives and judicial rulings may bind private parties or E.C. member states, eventually preempting national laws.

Think, for example, of Article 11bis of the Berne Convention. It is at the heart of the debate on the issue which has stretched the notion of territoriality to the breaking point: What country's law localizes acts of satellite broadcasting? One proposed resolution of this issue, I believe, illustrates how more powerful media drive us beyond the classically territorial framework of the private international law of copyright. The European Community is considering a proposed directive which defines acts of satellite communication to be subject to the law of the place where a work-carrying broadcast is uplinked to a satellite. At the same time, it is argued, since the directive would harmonize the applicable laws throughout the Community, no significant choice-of-law issues would arise within any satellite footprint inside the Community. Thus the entire question of how to localize infringing acts territory by territory seems to be mooted by recourse to supranational law.

Consider this issue of territoriality more broadly. A book or a theatrical performance exists at a given point on this earth. By contrast, a work may arise and be virtually accessible at all points throughout a telecommunication network worldwide. Suppose that I collaborate by telephone, facsimile transmission or modem with a team of coauthors scattered over five continents in creating a work. Suppose, further, that our work is stored without our authorization in a data bank for release into a worldwide telecommunication network, accessible in all those continents at once. Suppose, finally, that the work is improperly indexed in the data bank and that authorship is not properly attributed to the members of the creative team. Would it make sense to localize this work in any one country of origin or to localize its infringing storage or misattribution in any one protecting country? Indeed, in this case, creation and infringement quite simply take place throughout the network, across territorial boundaries.

As the Berne principle of national treatment is undercut, there is the clear risk of increasing the "Balkanization" of international copyright. That is, an increasing variety of copyright claims could be differently handled as between different pairs of countries.

In truth, international copyright now has to deal with more comprehensive telecommunication networks that transcend national territories. Only the European Community is now elaborating non-territorial copyright regimes for such networks.

The difficulty, however, is deeper. The Berne Union was Eurocentric from the start, in part because of European colonial dominance in the nineteenth century. Europe, with its many borders confined in a small space, also provided a microcosm of the world, in which to try out a territorial organized system of international copyright. In uniting, Europe now provides a new laboratory in which to experiment with supranational copyright schemes. For a variety of reasons, however, its models may well diverge from those more appropriately adopted in other environments.

We will, I believe, soon find ourselves faced with the following three options: first, adopt the new European models, if only for lack of anything better; second, adopt divergent schemes, thereby fracturing international copyright; or, third, develop a more comprehensive regime for copyright in the world at large. Such a regime could further bolster, or even in some cases supplant, national treatment with an even more comprehensive set of minimum rights. In any event, the media are making any territorial regime, with all its accompanying habits of thought, increasingly obsolete.

Notes and Questions

1. *The Meaning of National Treatment.* Do the provisions dealing with national treatment require that the country in which the infringing act is occurring apply a particular standard to determine infringement? Or do they simply require that the country apply the same rules to foreign authors and creators that they apply to domestic (national) ones?

2. Does national treatment assure a uniform international standard of enforcement? For example, can a country simply refuse to grant any patent protection for *any* new inventions regardless of who the inventor is and still be in compliance with Article 3 of the Paris Convention?

3. In examining the shortcomings of the national treatment approach, Jean Dettmann stated:

Shortcomings of applying [national treatment] become obvious if the applicable municipal laws are themselves insufficient. For example, the Paris Convention grants each signatory country the right to determine what is patentable. This means that each country creates its own specific intellectual property regime. Thus, countries with the res communis ideology have flexibility under the Paris Convention to enact very limited or even no laws recognizing patentability. Consequently, [national treatment] creates a disparate level of protection in different countries. It does not ensure substantive equivalence. Thus, according to [national treatment] principles, a country with a high level of protection must grant this higher protection even to foreigners of countries with a lower level of protection. However, when citizens from the country with a higher level of protection visit the country with a lower level of protection, they must settle for the lower protection of that country. In many situations, [national treatment] only provides a foreigner with inadequate protection from the host country's municipal laws. Thus, municipal law coupled with [national treatment] does not offer an effective solution to the distortions of intellectual property trade.

(Jean M. Dettmann, *GATT: An Opportunity for an Intellectual Property Rights Solution,* 4 Transnational Lawyer 347 (1991)).

4. Are the concerns expressed by Ms. Dettmann realistic ones? Do you perceive additional or different problems with a national treatment approach in today's global, digital environment? As you examine substantive standards of the TRIPS agreement below, ask yourself whether TRIPS has resolved some of these shortcomings. For a more detailed discussion of the problems of national treatment and territoriality, see Anthony D'Amato and Doris Estelle Long, INTERNATIONAL INTELLECTUAL PROPERTY ANTHOLOGY, Chapter Seven (Anderson Publishing Co., 1996).

5. *The Problem of Satellite Broadcasting.* Article 11 *bis* of the Berne Convention provides:

(1) Authors of literary and artistic works shall enjoy the exclusive right of authorizing:

(i) the broadcasting of their works or the communication thereof to the public by any other means of wireless diffusion of signs, sounds or images;

(ii) any communication to the public by wire or by rebroadcasting of the broadcast of the work, when this communication is made by an organization other than the original one;

(iii) the public communication by loudspeaker or any other analogous instrument transmitting, by signs, sounds or images, the broadcast of the work.

(2) It shall be a matter for legislation in the countries of the Union to determine the conditions under which the rights mentioned in the preceding paragraph may be exercised, but these conditions shall apply only in the countries where they have been prescribed. They shall not in any circumstances be prejudicial to the moral rights of the author, nor to his right to obtain equitable remuneration which, in the absence of agreement, shall be fixed by competent authority.

(3) In the absence of any contrary stipulation, permission granted in accordance with paragraph (1) of this Article shall not imply permission to record, by means of instruments recording sounds or images, the work broadcast. It shall, however, be a matter for legislation in the countries of the Union to determine the regulations for ephemeral recordings made by a broadcasting organization by means of its own facilities and used for its own broadcasts. The preservation of these recordings in official archives may, on the ground of their exceptional documentary character, be authorized by such legislation.

6. Does this Article give guidance as to which country's laws govern a dispute over an allegedly unauthorized satellite broadcast of a copyrighted film? For example, what if your client were a U.S. film producer? The copyrighted film in question was created wholly in the United States. It was authorized for television broadcast in Russia. An unauthorized copy of the film is uplinked in Russia to a satellite. As a result of the uplink, the film is available for viewing in Hungary, Czechoslovakia and the Ukraine as a part of the satellite's footprint (its broadcast reception area).

Your client has discovered that the film was downlinked in Czechoslovakia and received by an unknown number of viewers in that country. Your client wants to sue to enforce her rights. Where should she bring suit? In Russia, where the film was uplinked without authorization? In Czechoslovakia, where it was downlinked? In the U.S., where the copyright owner is?

Regardless of where you decide to bring suit, whose domestic laws should govern in determining if the satellite broadcast, including its reception, is lawful? Does national treatment resolve these issues? We will be revisiting the problem of cross-border enforcement in Part VIII.

7. *Reciprocity.* In addition to the concept of national treatment, many early multinational treaty regimes utilized the concept of reciprocity for certain rights. Thus, under Article 13 of The Berne Convention, each member is given the right to "impose for itself reservations and conditions on the exclusive right granted to the author of a musical work, ... to authorize the sound recording of that musical work; ... but all such reservations and conditions shall apply only in the countries which have imposed them and shall not, in any circumstances, be prejudicial to the

rights of these authors to obtain equitable remuneration which, in the absence of an agreement, shall be fixed by competent authority.''

8. Reciprocity basically means that the domestic country must grant a foreign creator rights under its laws only if the creator's home country grants authors equivalent rights. One of the most prevalent examples of reciprocity exists in connection with rental rights for copyrighted videos and sound recordings. In the 1980's and early 1990's several European countries had compulsory licensing regimes for the rental of video tapes and sound recordings. Such provisions required collective rights societies to distribute the royalties obtained pursuant to these compulsory licensing schemes to the native authors and/or copyright owners of the songs or movies so utilized. Foreign authors and rights holders were also given the right to their share of the royalties, but only if their home countries provided for similar royalties for foreign authors. Since the United States did not have a similar compulsory rights scheme, U.S. authors were not entitled to a share in the royalties.

What are the shortcomings of requiring reciprocity as opposed to national treatment? Are there any reasons why a country might favor a reciprocity scheme *over* one of national treatment?

9. The inequality of the reciprocal rights scheme discussed above was strongly criticized and eventually resulted in Articles 11 and 14 of TRIPS as a compromise. Article 11 of TRIPS states in pertinent part:

> In respect of at least computer programs and cinematographic works, a Member shall provide authors and their successors in title the right to authorize or to prohibit the commercial rental to the public of originals or copies of their copyright works. A Member shall be excepted from this obligation in respect of cinematographic works unless such rental has led to widespread copying of such works which is materially impairing the exclusive right of reproduction conferred in that Member on authors and their successors in title. In respect of computer programs, this obligation does not apply to rentals where the program itself is not the essential object of the rental.

Article 14(4) of TRIPS further provides:

> The provisions of Article 11 in respect of computer programs shall apply mutatis mutandis to producers of phonograms and any other right holders in phonograms as determined in a Member's law. If on 15 April 1994 a Member has in force a system of equitable remuneration of right holders in respect of the rental of phonograms, it may maintain such system provided that the commercial rental of phonograms is not giving rise to the material impairment of the exclusive rights of reproduction of right holders.

10. Have Articles 11 and 14(4) eliminated all requirements of reciprocity for domestic compulsory rental licensing schemes? What are the limitations imposed on any such reciprocity? Do these limitations resolve the shortcomings you identified above?

11. For a discussion of the rental rights issue and various compulsory licensing schemes, see generally, John M. Kernochan, *Ownership and Control of Intellectual Property Rights in Motion Pictures and Audiovisual Works: Contractual and Practical Aspects—Response of the United States to*

the ALAI Questionnaire, 20 COLUM.-VLA J.L. & ARTS 379 (1996); SCOTT M. MARTIN, *THE BERNE CONVENTION AND THE U.S. COMPULSORY LICENSE FOR JUKEBOXES: WHY THE SONG COULD NOT REMAIN THE SAME,* 37 J. COPYRIGHT SOC'Y U.S.A 262 (1990); ROBERT MERGES, *CONTRACTING INTO LIABILITY RULES INTELLECTUAL PROPERTY RIGHTS AND COLLECTIVE RIGHTS ORGANIZATIONS,* 84 CAL. L. REV. 1293 (1996).

12. *Territoriality.* Although Professor Geller discusses the territorial nature of copyrights, similar territorial concerns exist with regard to patents and trademarks. As you saw previously, no invention is subject to patent protection unless it has been granted by the domestic authorities. Similarly, with the exception of famous marks discussed in Part VII, most trademarks are only subject to protection if they have been registered or used in the domestic country. For a further discussion of the impact of territoriality on international IP protection schemes, see Curtis A. Bradley, *Territorial Intellectual Property Rights In an Age of Globalism,* 37 Va. J. Int'l L. 505 (1997); Thomas F. Cotter, *Owning What Doesn't Exist, Where It Doesn't Exist: Rethinking Two Doctrines From the Common Law of Trademarks,* 1995 U. Ill. L. Rev. 487 (1995); Robert S. Smith, *The Unresolved Tension Between Trademark Protection and Free Movement of Goods in the European Community,* 3 Duke J. Corp. & Int'l L. 89 (1992); William Jay Gross, *The Territorial Scope of Trademark Rights,* 44 U. Miami L. Rev. 1075 (1990).

C. ARE THERE STEPS BEYOND NATIONAL TREATMENT THAT CAN RESOLVE INTERNATIONAL PROBLEMS?

Given the limitations that exist in a multinational or bilateral treaty that requires solely national treatment or reciprocity, the international community soon sought a broader basis for understanding. Thus, both the Berne Convention and the Paris Convention went beyond simply requiring signatory countries to provide national treatment to foreign creators and inventors. Instead, each treaty sought to establish minimum standards of protection for the covered intellectual property rights. These standards helped to establish an international standard of protection that has undergone, and is still undergoing, revision as technology and international economic and cultural trends require adjustments.

As you examine the standards set forth in the Berne and Paris Conventions, and in other significant multinational intellectual property treaties, such as TRIPS and the WIPO Copyright Treaty in future chapters, ask yourself whether the standards reflect a particular cultural or economic bias. Do the standards meet the purported goals of the treaties as set forth in their preambles? And, perhaps most importantly, are these standards workable in today's digital, global marketplace?

Chapter Thirteen

COPYRIGHT UNDER THE BERNE CONVENTION

A. HOW DID THE BERNE CONVENTION "INTERNATIONALIZE" COPYRIGHT?

THE BERNE CONVENTION: ITS HISTORY AND ITS KEY ROLE IN THE FUTURE

Peter Burger, 3 J.L. & Tech. 1 (1988).

On September 27, 1858, the Congress of Authors and Artists held its first meeting in Brussels. The Congress was truly international in nature, with participants from many different countries[5] representing many different interests.[6] The participants passed five resolutions supporting greater international protection of authors' rights.[7] The Congress met twice more, in 1861 and 1877, and each time adopted resolutions asking governments to join together in passing legislation for the international protection of authors.

A new International Association, initially comprised only of authors and presided over by Victor Hugo, convened in 1878 and adopted five resolutions that eventually became the foundation for the original Berne Convention of 1886. In 1882, the International Association, later named

---

5. The Countries Represented Were Belgium, Canada, Denmark, France, Germany, Great Britain, Italy, the Netherlands, Portugal, Russia, Spain, Sweden, Norway, Switzerland, and the United States.

6. More than three hundred persons attended the meeting. Included in that number were 62 authors, 54 delegates of literary societies, 40 members of political assemblies, 29 lawyers, 29 librarians and printers, 24 artists, 21 economists and 16 journalists.

7. The Resolutions Were:

(1) That the principle of international recognition of copyright in favor of authors must be made part of the legislation of all civilized countries.

(2) This principle must be admitted regardless of reciprocity.

(3) The assimilation of foreign to national authors [national treatment] must be absolute and complete.

(4) Foreign authors should not be required to comply with any particular formalities for the recognition and protection of their rights, provided they have complied with the formalities required in the country where publication first took place.

(5) It is desirable that all countries adopt uniform legislation for the protection of literary and artistic works.

L'Association Litteraire et Artistique Internationale (ALAI), agreed that the only way to achieve its goal of increased international copyright protection would be to form a Union for the protection of literary property. Consequently, the International Association called a meeting in 1883 of all parties interested in creating such a Union. The meeting convened in Berne, Switzerland, where the participants drafted a treaty consisting of ten articles, the most important of which provided for national treatment and the absence of formalities as a prerequisite for copyright protection. Following general approval of the draft treaty, the Swiss government invited various governments to meet in Berne on September 8, 1884, for the purpose of forming an international copyright Union.

Eleven nations responded affirmatively to the Swiss government's invitation to meet in Berne. The countries broke down into essentially three groups. The first group was comprised of those nations that favored a codified international law of copyright—a universal law. At the opposite end of the spectrum were those countries that wanted as little unification and as much national independence as possible. Moreover, they wanted the copyright treaty to be built on a reciprocity foundation. The final group of countries occupied a middle position. They favored a codified law of international copyright, but desired some domestic flexibility on issues such as the translation right and the term of protection. Rather than adopting universal protection all at once, these countries wished to move slowly toward the goal of international copyright unification.

Of the three groups present at the 1884 Berne Conference, it was the middle group, representing those countries which preferred some common legislation along with some provisions reserved for national law, that emerged as the mainstream.

The Berne Convention of 1886. The basic structure of the Berne Convention has remained relatively unchanged throughout each of the five revisions and two additional acts; the scope of authors' rights has, however, increased markedly. The original Convention provided an explicit, but not exclusive, list of works to be protected. The Convention also defined the conditions for protection, known as points of attachment, and specified rules governing the term of protection. Subsequent conferences have amended each of these provisions in order to increase the scope of authors' rights.

The Convention also established the concept of authors' exclusive rights, which functioned as minimum standards that all member countries were required to recognize. The translation right was the first exclusive right established by the 1886 Convention.[8]

Although the Convention's primary focus was on the author, most contracting states agreed that in certain circumstances authors' rights

---

8. The exclusive right to make or authorize translations was limited to ten years after publication of the work.

had to be limited in order to assure public access to important information. The Convention, therefore, defined the situations in which a contracting state could permit certain works to be reproduced without the authors' express authorization. Many of these situations dealt with news of the day, newspaper articles or articles of political discussion. The Convention also allowed individual countries to create exceptions for the use of literary or artistic works in publications of a scientific or educational nature. These provisions have been both expanded and narrowed during Berne's subsequent revisions.

The Substantive Provisions of the Berne Convention of 1886. Article 1 of the Berne Convention unequivocally stated that the Union was formed for the protection of the rights of authors. This focus was indicative of the continental European, droit d'auteur countries' influence in drafting the Convention.

The basic strategy of the Convention was to establish certain minimum standards which all contracting countries were required to recognize and later to expand these minimum requirements to achieve the ultimate objective of a uniform international law of copyright. Individual countries could give foreign authors greater protection than required by the Convention, but in no case could they give less protection. The purpose and strategy of the Convention has not changed since the 1886 Convention.

The fundamental principle of the Berne Convention was, and continues to be, national treatment. Under the national treatment concept, Berne signatories grant authors who are nationals of other Berne countries the same protection they accord to their own nationals. National treatment is significant because it ensures nondiscriminatory treatment for authors in all contracting states.

Brussels Revision Conference of 1948. The Brussels revision created significant improvements in the substantive rights of authors. After unsuccessful attempts at both the Berlin conference of 1908 and the Rome conference of 1928, the Brussels conferees succeeded in enacting a life-plus-fifty-year term of protection as a minimum Berne requirement. In all Union states, therefore, an author could expect a minimum term of protection of life plus fifty years after death for almost all enumerated works. Union states could grant longer terms of protection within their domestic legislation. They could also limit the term of protection for foreign authors to the term granted in the foreign authors' country of origin if that term was shorter than in the Union country where protection was sought.

The life-plus-fifty-year term of protection did not apply to photographic works, works of applied art, and cinematographic works. The term of protection for these works was governed by the law of the country where protection was sought, but could not exceed the term granted in the country of origin of the work. The term of protection for pseudonymous works became fifty years after the date of publication of the work unless the pseudonym left no doubt as to the author's identity.

If an author's identity became known, the author would receive the life-plus-fifty-year term of protection.

The Brussels conferees also strengthened the authors' moral right. Under the 1928 Rome revision, an author's moral right was guaranteed during his or her lifetime; contracting states were not bound to recognize the moral right after the author's death. Under the 1948 Brussels Convention, the contracting states were required to recognize the moral right for the whole term of copyright, in most cases fifty years after death, if the legislation of the individual Union countries so permitted. The conferees did not require all Union countries to recognize the moral right after an author's death, because in some countries moral right was not protected under copyright law; rather, it was protected under alternative legislation or common law. Under the common law of torts in Great Britain, for example, authors could only maintain a tort action during their lifetime. Great Britain, therefore, could not agree to a Convention rule that would establish protection of the moral right beyond the author's death. Thus, it remained each individual contracting state's choice to extend the moral right past the author's lifetime, making the amendment rather insignificant in terms of effect. The amendment did, however, indicate the direction which Union members wanted the right to take at a subsequent revision conference.

Since the original Convention of 1886, authors had the exclusive right to authorize the public representation of dramatic or dramatico-musical works and the public performance of musical works only if the country in which protection was sought recognized those rights. In other words, the right of public representation and performance was not a minimum right under the Convention; an author would only benefit if the Union state in which protection was sought recognized the right.

Under the Brussels revision, the contracting states agreed to make the right of public performance and representation a minimum right. Consequently, authors of dramatic, dramatico-musical, or musical works enjoyed the exclusive right to authorize public presentations and performances of their works. The right of public performance was not subjected to a compulsory license. However, if the public performance were achieved through broadcast or through the playing of a recording of a musical work, the compulsory licenses established under the broadcasting and recording rights would apply to the public performance. In these situations, an author's work could be publicly performed absent express authorization, but no contracting state could enact a compulsory license that would be prejudicial to the author's moral right or to the author's right to receive just remuneration.

The advances made in Brussels were significant and they secured a solid level of international protection for authors which endured until the Stockholm revision in 1967.

Stockholm Revision Conference Of 1967. Almost twenty years after the Brussels conference in 1948, the Berne Union members convened in Stockholm, once again with the intention of making substantive and structural improvements to the Convention. Although the contracting states made significant improvements in authors' rights and improved the Union's infrastructure, those results were almost destroyed by a conflict that the Union had never before confronted.

The problem emanated from the new composition of member states. Many of the Berne Union's fifty-nine members were developing countries that had achieved their independence in the post-World War II years. These developing countries needed literary and artistic resources from developed countries and, as a result, demanded special concessions from the developed countries such as compulsory licenses for translation and broadcasts and shorter terms of protection. In response to those demands, the contracting states drafted a protocol for the benefit of developing countries. The conferees also agreed to tie the substantive changes in Articles 1 through 20 of the Stockholm Convention to the protocol, thus making it impossible to accept the substantive changes without the protocol. The developing country protocol was very controversial. Its compulsory license provisions and shortened terms of protection significantly weakened the rights of authors, rights that had been hard-won over Berne's five previous revisions.

Authors and publishers in the developed countries so opposed the protocol that they were willing to forego the substantive and structural improvements made in the Stockholm Convention in order to avoid enactment of the protocol's concessionary provisions. As a result, the Stockholm Convention did not receive the minimum number of ratifications necessary to enter into force.

Aside from Stockholm's developing country controversy, one other significant event occurred in Stockholm. The contracting states agreed to the formation of the World Intellectual Property Organization. WIPO's formation was achieved through a separate treaty; thus, the Union's inability to ratify the Stockholm revision did not affect WIPO's establishment.

The Stockholm revision significantly broadened the conditions for protection of non-Union authors by adopting a second point of attachment to accompany the previous requirement enacted in the 1886 Convention. Under previous Conventions, protection for non-Union authors was dependent on first or simultaneous publication in one of the Union countries. This was referred to as the "geographical criterion." The geographical criterion still exists, but is now accompanied by the "personal criterion," which provides that authors who are nationals or habitual residents of a Union country are protected in all Union countries no matter where first publication occurs. This protection also applies to unpublished works.

The Stockholm conferees also strengthened the Convention's moral right provisions. Under the original moral right provision, enacted at the Rome Revision Conference in 1928, contracting states were required to recognize the moral right until the author's death. At the Brussels Revision Conference, the contracting states strengthened the right somewhat by encouraging Union members to extend the moral right past the authors' death. Finally, at Stockholm, the conferees required Union members to recognize the authors' moral right after death for at least as long as the author's economic right was protected.

The conferees enacted one exception to the new moral right: "those countries whose legislation, at the moment of their ratification of or accession to this Act, does not provide for the protection after death of the author of all the rights set out in the preceding paragraph may provide that some of these rights may, after his death, cease to be maintained." This exception resulted from a compromise with Great Britain and other Anglo–American copyright countries that, like the United States, do not recognize the moral right under their copyright laws, but provide equivalent protection under other common laws. For example, in many countries the moral right is protected under the common law of defamation, which usually permits the maintenance of a suit only during the author's lifetime.

Notes and Questions

1.   Many of the historical developments of the Berne Convention reflect the growing challenges of technological development. What are some of the current technological advances that you believe international copyright law should address? What role should copyright play in regulating Internet content? In protecting computer technology?

2.   One of the key debates in the area of copyright is the extent to which key computer technology should be subject to international protection. Although the situation is slowly changing, most software is currently created and owned by individuals and companies located in developed countries. These creators and owners have insisted that copyright protection should be extended to such creations to encourage future development and assure an adequate economic return on such creators and owners research and development costs. By contrast, developing countries insist that heightened protection for such fundamental building blocks of technology places them at a disadvantage in their efforts to become equal players in the global marketplace. Such protection, they argue, increases the cost of necessary software beyond the limited economic means of their citizens and industry. Should computer software and other technology based developments be subject to international copyright protection? If so, what limitations, if any, would you place on the rights granted to the copyright owner of such program? Can those limitations be handled most effectively by an international treaty regime? If copyright protection should *not* be extended to such technology based products, what type of protection should be afforded to these products?

Read the following Articles of The Berne Convention from the Supplement: 2, 2bis, 3, 4, 5(2), 6bis, 7, 7bis.

Notes and Questions

1. Does the Berne Convention define the elements required to qualify as a copyright protectable work? What are they?

2. Could a country which is a signatory to the Berne Convention refuse to grant copyright protection to a novel written by an identifiable author without violating treaty obligations? Could it refuse grant copyright protection to the public domain elements in a song without violating treaty obligations? Could it refuse to grant moral rights protection to the identifiable author of a computer program without violating treaty obligations?

3. Article 1 through Article 19 of the Berne Convention establish the minimum substantive enforcement standards for copyrights under the Convention. Do these provisions establish a minimum term of protection for copyright? Do they establish the minimum rights that an author or artist must be granted to control the exploitation of her work? Do they establish the legal standards for determining if such rights have been exploited?

4. In its Copyright Directive of 1993, the European Union established a term of protection for copyright of the life of the author plus *seventy* years. Is this Directive in violation of treaty obligations under the Berne Convention?

5. *U.S. Accession.* Prior to 1989 the United States was *not* a signatory to the Berne Convention. U.S. opposition to the Berne Convention was based largely on opposition to two provisions of the Convention; Article 6bis (the moral rights *provision*), and Article 5(2)(requiring the elimination of all formalities for copyright protection to attach). Consequently, the United States became a signatory to, and one of the main supporters of the Universal Copyright Convention (UCC), which allowed countries to impose registration, notice and other formalities on the recognition of copyright under domestic law. For a further discussion of the relationship between the UCC and Berne, in the wake of U.S. accession to the Berne Convention, *see generally* J.H. Reichman, *Goldstein on Copyright Law: A Realist's Approach to a Technological Age*, 43 Stan. L. Rev. 943 (1991); Thomas P. Arden, *The Questionable Utility of Copyright Notice*, 24 Loy. U. Chi. L. J. 259 (1993); Susan Stanton, *Development of the Berne International Copyright Convention and Implications of United States Adherence*, 13 Hous. J. Int'l L. 149 (1990).

6. Review the definitions of copyright set forth in Chapter Five in the Notes and Questions. Are these definitions in compliance with the Berne Convention?

B. WHAT FAIR USE EXCEPTIONS SHOULD BE GRANTED FOR COPYRIGHTED WORKS UNDER INTERNATIONAL LAWS?

Read the following Articles from the Berne Convention from the Supplement: 5(1), 8, 9, 10, 10bis, 11, 11bis, 11ter, 12, 13, 14, 14bis.

Notes and Questions

1. What are the minimum rights which must be granted to an author of a play under the Berne Convention? To the author of a poem? To the author of a musical composition?

2. *The Problem of Authorship.* The Berne Convention requires that copyright protection be granted to the "author" of the covered work. Does the Convention define who the author of a work is? For example, assume that your client has been hired by a movie company to write an original screenplay. Your client's screenplay is later turned into a movie with Steven Spielberg as the director. Who is the "author" of the screenplay? Who is the "author" of the movie? If the Berne Convention does not establish a minimum definition for authorship, then how does a court in a signatory country determine who may exercise control over the exploitation of the work? Which "author" may enforce moral rights in the work?

3. Assume that you represent CNN who provides an international cable news service which is broadcast throughout the world. Your client has obtained a video tape which shows a high government official taking a bribe. Is that videotape subject to copyright protection under Article 2 of the Berne Convention? If it is, does the Berne Convention impose an absolute requirement that *a signatory country require* your client to obtain permission from the copyright owner before broadcasting segments of this videotape?

THE NATIVITY CASE

COMMUNITY FOR CREATIVE NON–VIOLENCE
v. JAMES EARL REID

United States Supreme Court, 1989.
490 U.S. 730, 109 S.Ct. 2166.

JUSTICE MARSHALL delivered the opinion of the Court.

In this case, an artist and the organization that hired him to produce a sculpture contest the ownership of the copyright in that work. To resolve this dispute, we must construe the "work made for hire" provisions of the Copyright Act of 1976 (Act or 1976 Act), 17 U.S.C. §§ 101 and 201(b), and in particular, the provision in § 101, which defines as a "work made for hire" a "work prepared by an employee within the scope of his or her employment" (hereinafter § 101(1)).

Petitioners are the Community for Creative Non–Violence (CCNV), a nonprofit unincorporated association dedicated to eliminating homelessness in America, and Mitch Snyder, a member and trustee of CCNV. In the fall of 1985, CCNV decided to participate in the annual Christmastime Pageant of Peace in Washington, D.C., by sponsoring a display to dramatize the plight of the homeless. As the District Court recounted:

"Snyder and fellow CCNV members conceived the idea for the nature of the display: a sculpture of a modern Nativity scene in which, in lieu of the traditional Holy Family, the two adult figures and the infant would appear as contemporary homeless people huddled on a streetside steam grate. The family was to be black (most of the homeless in

Washington being black); the figures were to be life-sized, and the steam grate would be positioned atop a platform 'pedestal,' or base, within which special-effects equipment would be enclosed to emit simulated 'steam' through the grid to swirl about the figures. They also settled upon a title for the work—Third World America'—and a legend for the pedestal: 'and still there is no room at the inn.' " 652 F.Supp. 1453, 1454 (DC 1987).

Snyder made inquiries to locate an artist to produce the sculpture. He was referred to respondent James Earl Reid, a Baltimore, Maryland, sculptor. In the course of two telephone calls, Reid agreed to sculpt the three human figures. CCNV agreed to make the steam grate and pedestal for the statue. Reid proposed that the work be cast in bronze, at a total cost of approximately $100,000 and taking six to eight months to complete. Snyder rejected that proposal because CCNV did not have sufficient funds, and because the statue had to be completed by December 12 to be included in the pageant. Reid then suggested, and Snyder agreed, that the sculpture would be made of a material known as "Design Cast 62," a synthetic substance that could meet CCNV's monetary and time constraints, could be tinted to resemble bronze, and could withstand the elements. The parties agreed that the project would cost no more than $15,000, not including Reid's services, which he offered to donate. The parties did not sign a written agreement. Neither party mentioned copyright.

After Reid received an advance of $3,000, he made several sketches of figures in various poses. At Snyder's request, Reid sent CCNV a sketch of a proposed sculpture showing the family in a creche like setting: the mother seated, cradling a baby in her lap; the father standing behind her, bending over her shoulder to touch the baby's foot. Reid testified that Snyder asked for the sketch to use in raising funds for the sculpture. Snyder testified that it was also for his approval. Reid sought a black family to serve as a model for the sculpture. Upon Snyder's suggestion, Reid visited a family living at CCNV's Washington shelter but decided that only their newly born child was a suitable model. While Reid was in Washington, Snyder took him to see homeless people living on the streets. Snyder pointed out that they tended to recline on steam grates, rather than sit or stand, in order to warm their bodies. From that time on, Reid's sketches contained only reclining figures.

Throughout November and the first two weeks of December 1985, Reid worked exclusively on the statue, assisted at various times by a dozen different people who were paid with funds provided in installments by CCNV. On a number of occasions, CCNV members visited Reid to check on his progress and to coordinate CCNV's construction of the base. CCNV rejected Reid's proposal to use suitcases or shopping bags to hold the family's personal belongings, insisting instead on a shopping cart. Reid and CCNV members did not discuss copyright ownership on any of these visits.

On December 24, 1985, 12 days after the agreed-upon date, Reid delivered the completed statue to Washington. There it was joined to the steam grate and pedestal prepared by CCNV and placed on display near the site of the pageant. Snyder paid Reid the final installment of the $15,000. The statue remained on display for a month. In late January 1986, CCNV members returned it to Reid's studio in Baltimore for minor repairs. Several weeks later, Snyder began making plans to take the statue on a tour of several cities to raise money for the homeless. Reid objected, contending that the Design Cast 62 material was not strong enough to withstand the ambitious itinerary. He urged CCNV to cast the statue in bronze at a cost of $35,000, or to create a master mold at a cost of $5,000. Snyder declined to spend more of CCNV's money on the project.

In March 1986, Snyder asked Reid to return the sculpture. Reid refused. He then filed a certificate of copyright registration for "Third World America" in his name and announced plans to take the sculpture on a more modest tour than the one CCNV had proposed. Snyder, acting in his capacity as CCNV's trustee, immediately filed a competing certificate of copyright registration.

Snyder and CCNV then commenced this action against Reid and his photographer, Ronald Purtee, seeking return of the sculpture and a determination of copyright ownership. The District Court granted a preliminary injunction, ordering the sculpture's return. After a 2–day bench trial, the District Court declared that "Third World America" was a "work made for hire" under § 101 of the Copyright Act and that Snyder, as trustee for CCNV, was the exclusive owner of the copyright in the sculpture. 652 F.Supp., at 1457. The court reasoned that Reid had been an "employee" of CCNV within the meaning of § 101(1) because CCNV was the motivating force in the statue's production. Snyder and other CCNV members, the court explained, "conceived the idea of a contemporary Nativity scene to contrast with the national celebration of the season," and "directed enough of [Reid's] effort to assure that, in the end, he had produced what they, not he, wanted." *Id.*, at 1456.

The Court of Appeals for the District of Columbia Circuit reversed and remanded, holding that Reid owned the copyright because "Third World America" was not a work for hire. Adopting what it termed the "literal interpretation" of the Act as articulated by the Fifth Circuit in *Easter Seal Society for Crippled Children & Adults of Louisiana, Inc. v. Playboy Enterprises*, 815 F.2d 323, 329 (1987), *cert. denied*, 485 U.S. 981, 108 S.Ct. 1280, 99 L.Ed.2d 491 (1988), the court read § 101 as creating "a simple dichotomy in fact between employees and independent contractors." 270 U.S.App.D.C., at 33, 846 F.2d, at 1492. Because, under agency law, Reid was an independent contractor, the court concluded that the work was not "prepared by an employee" under § 101(1). Nor was the sculpture a "work made for hire" under the second subsection of § 101 (hereinafter § 101(2)): sculpture is not one of the nine categories of works enumerated in that subsection, and the parties had not agreed in writing that the sculpture would be a work for hire. The court suggested that the sculpture nevertheless may have been jointly authored by CCNV and Reid, and remanded for a determination whether the sculpture is indeed a joint work under the Act.

We granted certiorari to resolve a conflict among the Courts of Appeals over the proper construction of the "work made for hire" provisions of the Act.[9] We now affirm.

The Copyright Act of 1976 provides that copyright ownership "vests initially in the author or authors of the work." 17 U.S.C. § 201(a). As a general rule, the author is the party who actually creates the work, that is, the person who translates an idea into a fixed, tangible expression entitled to copyright protection. The Act carves out an important exception, however, for "works made for hire." If the work is for hire, "the employer or other person for whom the work was prepared is considered the author" and owns the copyright, unless there is a written agreement to the contrary. § 201(b). Classifying a work as "made for hire" determines not only the initial ownership of its copyright, but also the copyright's duration, § 302(c), and the owners' renewal rights, § 304(a), termination rights, § 203(a), and right to import certain goods bearing the copyright, § 601(b)(1). The contours of the work for hire doctrine therefore carry profound significance for freelance creators—including artists, writers, photographers, designers, composers, and computer programmers—and for the publishing, advertising, music, and other industries which commission their works.

Section 101 of the 1976 Act provides that a work is "for hire" under two sets of circumstances:

> "(1) a work prepared by an employee within the scope of his or her employment; or

> (2) a work specially ordered or commissioned for use as a contribution to a collective work, as a part of a motion picture or other audiovisual work, as a translation, as a supplementary work, as a compilation, as an instructional text, as a test, as answer material for a test, or as an atlas, if the parties expressly agree in a written instrument signed by them that the work shall be considered a work made for hire."

The dispositive inquiry in this case therefore is whether "Third World America" is "a work prepared by an employee within the scope of his or her employment" under § 101(1). The Act does not define these terms. In the absence of such guidance, four interpretations have emerged. The first holds that a work is prepared by an

9. *Compare Easter Seal Society for Crippled Children & Adults of Louisiana, Inc. v. Playboy Enterprises*, 815 F.2d 323 (C.A.5 1987) (agency law determines who is an employee under § 101), cert. denied, 485 U.S. 981, 108 S.Ct. 1280, 99 L.Ed.2d 491 (1988), *with Brunswick Beacon, Inc. v. Schock–Hopchas Publishing Co.*, 810 F.2d 410 (C.A.4 1987) (supervision and control standard determines who is an employee under § 101); *Evans Newton, Inc. v. Chicago Systems Software*, 793 F.2d 889 (CA7) (same), cert. denied, 479 U.S. 949, 107 S.Ct. 434, 93 L.Ed.2d 383 (1986); and *Aldon Accessories Ltd. v. Spiegel, Inc.*, 738 F.2d 548 (CA2) (same), cert. denied, 469 U.S. 982, 105 S.Ct. 387, 83 L.Ed.2d 321 (1984).

employee whenever the hiring party retains the right to control the product. Petitioners take this view. A second, and closely related, view is that a work is prepared by an employee under § 101(1) when the hiring party has actually wielded control with respect to the creation of a particular work. A third view is that the term "employee" within § 101(1) carries its common-law agency law meaning. This view was endorsed by the Fifth Circuit in *Easter Seal Society for Crippled Children & Adults of Louisiana, Inc. v. Playboy Enterprises*, 815 F.2d 323 (1987), and by the Court of Appeals below. Finally, respondent and numerous amici curiae contend that the term "employee" only refers to "formal, salaried" employees.

The Act nowhere defines the terms "employee" or "scope of employment." It is, however, well established that "[w]here Congress uses terms that have accumulated settled meaning under the common law, a court must infer, unless the statute otherwise dictates, that Congress means to incorporate the established meaning of these terms." In the past, when Congress has used the term "employee" without defining it, we have concluded that Congress intended to describe the conventional master-servant relationship as understood by common-law agency doctrine. Nothing in the text of the work for hire provisions indicates that Congress used the words "employee" and "employment" to describe anything other than " 'the conventional relation of employer and employe.' On the contrary, Congress' intent to incorporate the agency law definition is suggested by § 101(1)'s use of the term, "scope of employment," a widely used term of art in agency law. *See* Restatement (Second) of Agency § 228 (1958) (hereinafter Restatement).

In past cases of statutory interpretation, when we have concluded that Congress intended terms such as "employee," "employer," and "scope of employment" to be understood in light of agency law, we have relied on the general common law of agency, rather than on the law of any particular State, to give meaning to these terms. Establishment of a federal rule of agency, rather than reliance on state agency law, is particularly appropriate here given the Act's express objective of creating national, uniform copyright law by broadly pre-empting state statutory and common-law copyright regulation. See 17 U.S.C. § 301(a). We thus agree with the Court of Appeals that the term "employee" should be understood in light of the general common law of agency. In contrast, neither test proposed by petitioners is consistent with the text of the Act. The exclusive focus of the right to control the product test on the relationship between the hiring party and the product clashes with the language of § 101(1), which focuses on the relationship between the hired and hiring parties. The right to control the product test also would distort the meaning of the ensuing subsection, § 101(2). Section 101 plainly creates two distinct ways in which a work can be deemed for hire: one for works prepared by employees, the other for those specially ordered or commissioned works which fall within one of the nine enumerated categories and are the subject of a written agreement. The right to control the product test ignores this dichotomy by transforming into a work for hire under § 101(1) any "specially ordered or commissioned" work that is subject to the supervision and control of the hiring party. Because a party who hires a "specially ordered or commissioned" work by definition has a right to specify the characteristics of the product desired, at the time the commission is accepted, and frequently until it is completed, the right to control the product test would mean that many works that could satisfy § 101(2) would already have been deemed works for hire under § 101(1). Petitioners' interpretation is particularly hard to square with § 101(2)'s enumeration of the nine specific categories of specially ordered or commissioned works eligible to be works for hire, e.g., "a contribution to a collective work," "a part of a motion picture," and "answer material for a test." The unifying feature of these works is that they are usually prepared at the instance, direction, and risk of a publisher or producer. By their very nature, therefore, these types of works would be works by an employee under petitioners' right to control the product test.

The actual control test, articulated by the Second Circuit in *Aldon Accessories*, fares only marginally better when measured against the language and structure of § 101. Under this test, independent contractors who are so controlled and supervised in the creation of a particular work are deemed "employees" under § 101(1). Thus work for hire status under § 101(1) depends on a hiring party's actual control of, rather than right to control, the product. *Aldon Accessories*, 738 F.2d, at 552. Under the actual control test, a work for hire could arise under § 101(2), but not under § 101(1), where a party commissions, but does not actually control, a product which falls into one of the nine enumerated categories. Nonetheless, we agree with the Court of Appeals for the Fifth Circuit that "[t]here is simply no way to milk the 'actual control' test of *Aldon Accessories* from the language of the statute." *Easter Seal Society*, 815 F.2d, at 334. Section 101 clearly delineates between works prepared by an employee and commissioned works. Sound though other distinctions might be as a matter of copyright policy, there is no statutory support for an additional dichotomy between commissioned works that are actually controlled and supervised by the hiring party and those that are not. We therefore conclude that the language and structure of § 101 of the Act do not support either the right to control the product or the actual control approaches. The structure of § 101 indicates that a work for hire can arise through one of two mutually exclusive means, one for employees and one for independent contractors, and ordinary canons of statutory interpretation indicate that the classification of a particular hired party should be made with reference to agency law.

In sum, we must reject petitioners' argument. Transforming a commissioned work into a work by an employee on the basis of the hiring party's right to control, or actual control of, the work is inconsistent with the language, structure, and legislative history of the work for hire provisions. To determine whether a work is for hire under the Act, a court first should ascertain, using principles of general common law of agency, whether the work was prepared by an employee or an independent contractor. After making this determination, the court can apply the appropriate subsection of § 101.

We turn, finally, to an application of § 101 to Reid's production of "Third World America." In determining whether a hired party is an employee under the general common law of agency, we consider the hiring party's right to control the manner and means by which the product is accomplished. Among the other factors relevant to this inquiry are the skill required; the source of the instrumentalities and tools; the location of the work; the duration of the relationship between the parties; whether the hiring party has the right to assign additional projects to the hired party; the extent of the hired party's discretion over when and how long to work; the method of payment; the hired party's role in hiring and paying assistants; whether the work is part of the regular business of the hiring party; whether the hiring party is in business; the provision of employee benefits; and the tax treatment of the hired party. *See* Restatement § 220(2) (setting forth a nonexhaustive list of factors relevant to determining whether a hired party is an employee). No one of these factors is determinative.

Examining the circumstances of this case in light of these factors, we agree with the Court of Appeals that Reid was not an employee of CCNV but an independent contractor. True, CCNV members directed enough of Reid's work to ensure that he produced a sculpture that met their specifications. But the extent of control the hiring party exercises over the details of the product is not dispositive. Indeed, all the other circumstances weigh heavily against finding an employment relationship. Reid is a sculptor, a skilled occupation. Reid supplied his own tools. He worked in his own studio in Baltimore, making daily supervision of his activities from Washington practicably impossible. Reid was retained for less than two months, a relatively short period of time. During and after this time, CCNV had no right to assign additional projects to Reid. Apart from the deadline for completing the sculpture, Reid had absolute freedom to decide when and how long to work. CCNV paid Reid $15,000, a sum dependent on "completion of a specific job, a method by which independent contractors are often compensated." Reid had total discretion in hiring and paying assistants. "Creating sculptures was hardly 'regular business' for CCNV." Indeed, CCNV is not a business at all. Finally, CCNV did not pay payroll or Social Security taxes, provide any employee benefits, or contribute to unemployment insurance or workers' compensation funds.

Because Reid was an independent contractor, whether "Third World America" is a work for hire depends on whether it satisfies the terms of § 101(2). This petitioners concede it cannot do. Thus, CCNV is not the author of "Third World America" by virtue of the work for hire provisions of the Act. However, as the Court of Appeals made clear, CCNV nevertheless may be a joint author of the sculpture if, on remand, the District Court determines that CCNV and Reid prepared the work "with the intention that their contributions be merged into inseparable or interdependent parts of a unitary whole." 17 U.S.C. § 101. In that case, CCNV and Reid would be co-owners of the copyright in the work. See § 201(a).

For the aforestated reasons, we affirm the judgment of the Court of Appeals for the District of Columbia Circuit.

Notes and Questions

1. Is the test for determining authorship used in the *Nativity* case in compliance with the substantive provisions of the Berne Convention? What if the court had determined that CCNV was the author of the work because CCNV had exercised adequate control over the work? Would this decision also be in accordance with the requirements of the Berne Convention?

2. The question of authorship, and in particular the determination of who qualifies as an author in a potential work for hire situation, has not been treated consistently. Thus, under U.S. law, copyright in works created by "employees" which have been created "within the scope of employment" automatically belong to the employer, absent on agreement to the contrary, and without the need for additional compensation. 17 U.S.C. §§ 101, 201. The employee has no right to control subsequent use of the created work, moral rights are considered transferred to the employer.

In the UK, the employer is similarly granted the copyright interest in works made by an "employee" "in the course of his employment." UK Copyright Designs and Patent Act of 1988, Section 87(2). By contrast, in France, the creator of the work owns an "exclusive incorporeal property right in the work, effective against all persons," including his employer. French Copyright Law Art 1 (3). Courts have interpreted the provision as giving the employer the economic rights under an employment contract, but the employee retains the non-transferable moral rights in the work. German law also adheres to the basic principle that only natural persons are authors. Thus, employees retain both economic and moral rights in their works absent agreements to the contrary. Greece similarly vests copyright in the author-employee; the employer may only obtain rights through a subsequent transfer.

3. What impact, if any, does such differential treatment on employee's rights have on the development of a uniform international copyright protection standard? For a brief overview of some of the differing European treatments of the work for hire issue, see Robert A. Jacobs, *Work For Hire and the Moral Right Dilemma in the European Community: A U.S. Perspective*, 16 B.C. Int'l & Comp. L. Rev. 29 (1993); Colleen Creamer Fielkow, *Clashing Rights under the United States Copyright Law: Harmonizing an Employer's Economic Right with the Artist–Employee's Moral Right in a Work Made for Hire*, 7 DePaul–LCA J. Art. & Ent. L. 218 (1997); R. Scott Miller, Jr., *Photography and the Work-for-Hire Doctrine*, 1 Tex. Weslayan L. Rev. 81 (1996).

4. Which approach would you advocate for an international standard of authorship? Does your standard take into account the competing philosophies of authorship examined in Chapter Seven (economic versus moral (personality) rights)? How do you reconcile your treatment of work for hire with the moral rights standards required under Article 6*bis* of the Berne Convention?

THE DENNY VIDEO CASE

LOS ANGELES NEWS SERVICE
v. KCAL–TV CHANNEL 9

United States Court of Appeals, Ninth Circuit, 1997.
108 F.3d 1119.

RYMER, CIRCUIT JUDGE.

Los Angeles News Service (LANS) shot the Reginald Denny beating from its helicopter. Its videotape was copyrighted and licensed to the media. KCAL–TV used it, without a license. LANS sued for copyright infringement, but the district court granted summary judgment in KCAL's favor, holding that its telecasts of LANS's videotape were exempted from liability under the "fair use" doctrine. 17 U.S.C. § 107. We see the balance of fair use factors differently, and reverse.

Los Angeles News Service (LANS) is an independent news organization that provides news stories, photographs, audiovisual works and other services to the news media. When rioting broke out in Los Angeles on April 29, 1992, in the aftermath of the Rodney King verdict, LANS's helicopter hovered above the intersection of Florence and Normandie where Reginald Denny was beaten. Markika Tur's camera captured the incident from overhead. It was broadcast "live" on KCOP, a LANS licensee, and by tape later that evening. Other stations broadcast the Videotape as well, before it was broadcast by KCAL. KCAL asked LANS for a license, which LANS refused, but KCAL obtained a copy of the tape from another station and broadcast it a number of times on April 30 and thereafter on its commercially sponsored news programs.

The district court held that the doctrine of fair use exempts KCAL from liability based on undisputed facts that the Denny Videotape is a unique and newsworthy videotape of significant public interest and concern; KCAL used portions of the tape in its newscasts for purposes of news reporting; and LANS failed to identify any sale or license or potential sale or license that it lost due to KCAL's conduct. Accordingly, it granted summary judgment in KCAL's favor. LANS moved for reconsideration based on evidence that it had lost at least one sale as a result of KCAL's unlicensed use of the Denny tape and that KCAL had other footage of the beating available to it. The district court denied the motion, and LANS timely appealed.

" 'Fair use is a mixed question of law and fact.' If there are no genuine issues of material fact, or if, even after resolving all issues in favor of the opposing party, a reasonable trier of fact can reach only one conclusion, a court may conclude as a matter of law whether the challenged use qualifies as a fair use of the copyrighted work." *Hustler Magazine, Inc. v. Moral Majority, Inc.*, 796 F.2d 1148, 1150 (9th Cir. 1986) (quoting *Harper & Row Publishers, Inc. v. Nation Enterprises*, 471 U.S. 539, 559, 105 S.Ct. 2218, 2230, 85 L.Ed.2d 588 (1985).

LANS argues that the district court inappropriately resolved the fair use factors because KCAL's use was nontransformative, commercial, and improper; it interfered with LANS's ability to control the initial dissemination of the Denny tape; the use was substantial even though KCAL broadcast only 30 seconds of the four minute, 40 second Videotape because it was the heart of the work; and it had a serious effect on the potential market for LANS's copyrighted work because KCAL's unauthorized commercial broadcasts competed directly with LANS's authorized licensees.

KCAL, on the other hand, focuses on the factual nature of the Videotape and its use for news reporting purposes. It challenges LANS's view that its use was nontransformative, noting that both the Supreme Court and this circuit have recognized that news reporting is a productive use. KCAL also emphasizes that the Videotape had been published before KCAL ever used it. Further, it points out, only a small portion of the total amount of LANS's tape was used, and even then, only enough for KCAL to carry out its news reporting function of reporting on the riots. Moreover, KCAL submits, its use of the Videotape did not diminish the potential sale of the work or interfere with its marketability because LANS entered into more than a dozen licenses for the Videotape after KCAL used it. Rather, its use for news reporting purposes enabled the public to understand what the rioters did to Denny, and thus did not replace any demand for the original work. Finally, KCAL maintains that the Videotape is unique because the Videotape itself is part of the news event. For this reason, First Amendment considerations reinforce the conclusion that KCAL's use was fair.

As KCAL undeniably used LANS's copyrighted work without permission, we turn to whether its use was fair. This requires us to balance the non-exclusive factors set out in 17 U.S.C. § 107.[10]

Purpose and character of use. Even though the fact that KCAL was reporting news weighs heavily in its favor (§ 107 itself gives news reporting as an example), the fact that LANS and KCAL are both in the business of gathering and selling news cuts the other way. LANS does work that its licensees choose not to do for themselves, for example, operating its own helicopter with news crew aboard, and gets paid for licensing its coverage of news to the media. By the same token, KCAL is a for-profit company that is engaged in a commercial enterprise that also gathers, and then (indirectly) "sells" news. It, therefore, "stands to profit from exploitation of the copyrighted material without paying the customary price." *Harper & Row*, 471 U.S. at 562, 105 S.Ct. at 2231.

---

10. Section 107 provides in relevant part: notwithstanding the provisions of sections 106 and 106a, the fair use of a copyrighted work for purposes such as news reporting, is not an infringement of copyright. In determining whether the use made of a work in any particular case is a fair use the factors to be considered shall include: (1) the purpose and character of the use, including whether such use is of a commercial nature or is for nonprofit educational purposes; (2) the nature of the copyrighted work; (3) the amount and substantiality of the portion used in relation to the copyrighted work as a whole; and (4) the effect of the use upon the potential market for or value of the copyrighted work.

"[N]ewscasts are commercially supported by advertisers, who pass the cost of sponsorship on to those who purchase their products." Note, *Who Can Use Yesterday's News?: Video Monitoring and the Fair Use Doctrine*, 81 Geo.L.J. 2345, 2345 n. 2 (1993). Thus, KCAL competes with other stations for advertising dollars, which are in turn dependent upon KCAL's viewership. The fact that KCAL used LANS's copyrighted footage free of charge, rather than paying LANS or someone else for the footage, or investing in its own helicopter and crew to obtain the footage itself, at least raises an inference that its articulated purpose of reporting the news was mixed with the actual purpose of doing so by using the best version—whether or not it meant riding LANS's (or some other station's) copyrighted coattails. While this did not serve to supplant the copyright holder's commercially valuable right of first publication as The Nation did in Harper & Row by scooping the hardcover and Time abstracts of President Ford's memoirs, we cannot say that KCAL's use of the Denny tape had neither the effect nor purpose of depriving LANS of its also valuable right of licensing its original videotape which creatively captured the Denny beating in a way that no one else did.

On the other hand, there is a forceful argument that the LANS tape of the Denny beating itself became a news item shortly after it was published because its view was so extraordinary. To the extent that KCAL ran the tape as a news story, this would weigh in its favor. However, this factor does not weigh nearly so heavily as it might otherwise since there is no evidence that KCAL used the tape in this way. It did not attribute the tape to LANS, and so far as the record discloses, aired it as if it were KCAL's own rather than, for example, indicating that the best tape of the beating had been made by a LANS helicopter crew. Instead, the tape was simply used as part of KCAL's coverage of the riots. Although KCAL apparently ran its own voice-over, it does not appear to have added anything new or transformative to what made the LANS work valuable—a clear, visual recording of the beating itself.

While the fact that KCAL had requested a license but had been refused one is not dispositive, "the propriety of the defendant's conduct" is relevant to the character of the use at least to the extent that it may knowingly have exploited a purloined work for free that could have been obtained for a fee. Nothing in this record suggests that KCAL requested a license "in a good faith effort to avoid this litigation." KCAL obtained a copy of the tape from another station, directly copied the original, superimposed its logo on the LANS footage, and used it for the same purpose for which it would have been used had it been paid for.

Nature of the copyrighted work. The Denny beating tape is informational and factual and news; each characteristic strongly favors KCAL. Likewise the fact that the tape was published before its use by KCAL. Although the Videotape is not without creative aspect in that it is the result of Tur's skills with a camera, still this factor makes it a great deal easier to find fair use. Therefore, this factor weighs substantially in KCAL's favor.

Amount and substantiality of what was used. While a small amount of the entire Videotape was used, it was all that mattered. As we said of the defendant Audio Video Reporting Services in *Los Angeles News Service v. Tullo*, which provided a video "news clipping" service by monitoring television news programs, recording them on videotape and selling copies to interested individuals and businesses, "[a]lthough AVRS copied only a small part of the raw footage shot by LANS, it was the most valuable part of that footage. In preparing a newscast, a television station selects the most effective and illustrative shots from the raw footage available. Thus the news programs AVRS copied included what LANS's customers thought was the best of the LANS footageits 'heart.'" *Id.* at 798. Here, as there, this factor weighs against KCAL, for "the fact that a substantial portion of the infringing work was copied verbatim is evidence of the qualitative value of the copied material, both to the originator and to the plagiarist who seeks to profit from marketing someone else's copyrighted expression."

Effect on the market. This case doesn't fit neatly into a traditional niche, because "news" isn't normally thought of as having a secondary market. " 'Copying a news broadcast may have a stronger claim to fair use than copying a motion picture' because the potential market for copies of news broadcasts is not as great as that for copies of movies." Also, LANS's tape had been licensed—and published—before KCAL's use, and was licensed after its use. To that extent, this factor weighs in favor of KCAL. At the same time, KCAL's stated purpose was to use the tape as "news" and it was a potential (and in the past was an actual) licensee or consumer of LANS's product; there is evidence that, given what LANS and KCAL do, KCAL's use of LANS's works for free, without a license, would destroy LANS's original, and primary market. Just as we recognized in *Los Angeles News Service v. Tullo* that customers might choose to buy raw footage from LANS if they couldn't buy it from AVRS, *Tullo*, 973 F.2d at 799, KCAL was ready to buy from LANS if it could, but went elsewhere when it couldn't. Were this to happen more broadly, it no doubt would adversely affect LANS's creative incentives. All told, this weighs against a finding of fair use.

In sum, KCAL's use of LANS's copyrighted tape was arguably in the public interest because it was a percipient recording of a newsworthy event. However, KCAL's use was commercial and came in the wake of LANS's refusal of a license. Although KCAL explains that it used the tape because it recorded news of considerable significance from the best perspective of any witness, there is no evidence that alternatives were not available (albeit from a less desirable vantage point). Also, while the tape had been licensed and published before KCAL's use, it is not obvious that there was no impact on the market for first publication rights as KCAL itself requested a license. There is no dispute that KCAL used the heart of the tape. Under these circumstances, we cannot say that fair use is the only reasonable conclusion a trier of fact could reach in this case. We therefore reverse and remand for further proceedings.

REVERSED AND REMANDED.

THE WORLD CUP BROADCAST CASE
BBC v. BRITISH SATELLITE BROADCASTING

Chancery Division, 1991.
[1991] 3 W.L.R. 174.

SCOTT J.

This is an action for breach of copyright brought by the BBC against British Satellite Broadcasting ("BSB"), the previous name of the company now known as British Sky Broadcasting Ltd. The action is based on the use made by BSB of the BBC's broadcasts of international football matches played in Italy in June and July 1990 in the course of the World Cup finals. The BBC transmitted in the United Kingdom live broadcasts of a number of the World Cup matches. In doing so the BBC acquired copyright in the broadcasts. The BBC, as the copyright owner, became entitled under the Act, subject to certain important exceptions, to the exclusive right to make copies of the copyright work and to broadcast the copyright work.

Under section 17 of the [1988 Copyright] Act the copying of a copyright work is an act restricted by copyright. Under section 20 the broadcasting of a copyright work is an act restricted by the copyright. Section 16(3) of the Act provides:

> "References in this Part to the doing of an act restricted by the copyright in a work are to the doing of it—(a) in relation to the work as a whole or any substantial part of it, and (b) either directly or indirectly; and it is immaterial whether any intervening acts themselves infringe copyright."

In July 1987 BSB was awarded by the Independent Broadcasting Authority ("IBA") a 15–year franchise to transmit, via satellite, television programmes to the United Kingdom. For the purpose of doing so BSB established five separate specialist channels each directed to a specific audience. This action is concerned only with the sports channel. The sports channel, as its name indicates, was devoted almost exclusively to sport. It was aimed at persons with a particular interest in sport. One of the regular programmes appearing on the sports channel was the Sportsdesk programme. This programme is described by Mr. Hunter, the then managing director of the sports channel, in this way:

> "The sports channel has its own regularly scheduled sports news programme, Sportsdesk. Sportsdesk is transmitted at 18.00, 19.30, (previously 22.30), and 24.00 each day. There is an additional programme on Saturday and Sunday at 13.00. Each edition of Sportsdesk throughout the day is updated, as is the case with the regularly scheduled news bulletins which do not concentrate on sports events. The Sportsdesk programme is approximately half an hour duration and it concentrates on sports news, results and information. It is followed immediately by one of BSB's news bulle-

tins summarising the general news of the day (world events, politics, etc). In weekday afternoons at about 13.25 and 16.00 BSB also broadcasts between three to four minutes of sports news headlines on the sports channel."

Over the period of the World Cup finals in Italy the Sportsdesk programmes included reports of the results of the World Cup matches. These reports were accompanied by films showing prominent features of the matches. The films were taken from the BBC's live broadcasts. The BBC contends that this use by BSB of its broadcasts represented a breach of copyright. The BBC sues accordingly for an injunction and damages.

Various issues are raised by the pleadings, but before me the parties have concentrated on the one issue that matters. BSB accepts that the BBC has copyright in its World Cup broadcasts. It accepts that the use it has made of those broadcasts would, prima facie, have represented an infringement of copyright. But it relies as a defence on section 30(2) of the Act of 1988. Section 30 is in these terms:

"(1) Fair dealing with a work for the purpose of criticism or review, of that or another work or of a performance of a work, does not infringe any copyright in the work provided that it is accompanied by a sufficient acknowledgement.

2) Fair dealing with a work (other than a photograph) for the purpose of reporting current events does not infringe any copyright in the work provided that (subject to subsection (3)) it is accompanied by a sufficient acknowledgement. (3) No acknowledgement is required in connection with the reporting of current events by means of a sound recording, film, broadcast or cable programme."

BSB contends that its use of the BBC's World Cup broadcasts was "fair dealing ... for the purpose of reporting current events." It therefore denies that its use of the broadcasts was an infringement of copyright.

There appears to be no reported case in which the scope of the fair dealing defence "for the purpose of reporting current events" has been considered.

There are a number of features of the excerpts taken from the BBC broadcasts that I should mention: (i) The duration of the excerpts, save for the so-called "menu" excerpts, varied between 14 seconds and 37 seconds. (ii) The menu excerpts were very short excerpts lasting only four or five seconds each, shown with other menu items of the start of the news programme in order, presumably, to excite the interest of the viewer and to tempt him or her to watch the whole of the programme. (iii) Each excerpt was shown in successive news programmes over roughly the 24 hours following the match. Thus, for example, the Egypt v. Holland excerpt was shown on 12 June in the 10.30 pm and midnight Sportsdesk programmes, and on 13 June in a 5.30 pm programme—in place of the normal 6 pm programme—and in the 7.30 programme. So, omitting the menus, the excerpts were shown four times. So was the Argentina v. Brazil excerpt. The Argentina v. Romania excerpt was shown twice. The Brazil v. Sweden excerpt was shown only once. Most of the excerpts from the other matches were shown three times. All of this ignores the menus. (iv) Each excerpt concentrated on one or two significant happenings from the match in question. The scoring of a goal or a near miss were obvious choices. In most cases, but not in every case, a slow motion replay of the significant happening was also shown. Sometimes the replay showed the incident from a different camera angle. Since the menu usually consisted of a fleeting glimpse of the same significant happening, there were often three recordings in one Sportsdesk programme of the same incident—first in the menu, then in the main news report, and, finally, in the slow motion replay. The replays were taken from the replays which formed part of the BBC's live broadcasts. (v) The broadcasting of each excerpt was accompanied by a verbal report of the incident being shown and of the match as a whole. (vi) In the Brazil v. Sweden report the excerpt showed not only the goal scored by Brazil, but also the celebratory shuffle performed by the Brazilian goal scorer after he had scored. (vii) The Egypt v. Holland report on 13 June, the match having been played in the afternoon of 12 June, included reference not only to the result, a draw, but also to the effect of the result on the odds being offered by the bookmakers about Egypt's chances of winning the World Cup (viii) One of the commentators, whose voice accompanied some of the Sportsdesk World Cup news reports, was a well known professional, or ex-professional, footballer, Andy Gray. This is apparently regarded by the BBC as significantly detracting from the status of the reports as genuine news reports. (ix) Each excerpt was accompanied by an acknowledgement of the source of the film. The acknowledgements were given when the main excerpts were shown. They did not appear on the menus.

There is no longer an absolute monopoly to which a proprietor of broadcasting copyright is entitled. Parliament has eroded that monopoly by permitting fair dealing with the copyright work for the purpose of reporting current events. There is no justification for limiting the statutory defence so as to apply only to reporting current events in a general news programme.

The use made by BSB in its Sportsdesk programmes of excerpts from the BBC's live broadcasts took place necessarily after the broadcasts had been transmitted, but took place before the BBC's or the ITV's World Cup review programmes had taken place. It was suggested by Mr. Rayner James that thereby the audience appeal of the review programmes would have been reduced. I regard this suggestion as fanciful. If anything, the BSB news reports, with their use of the excerpts, would have been likely in my opinion to have whetted the appetite of the football enthusiast. In any event the reporting of current events must be done promptly. Football matches, even important ones, very quickly cease to be current events. To have required BSB to postpone its use of the material until after the material had been used in the BBC's or in

ITV's World Cup review programmes would in practice have barred the use of the material as an adjunct to the reporting of the World Cup matches as current events. If BSB was to use the material at all, it had to be used promptly.

As I have earlier in this judgment remarked, my impression when I viewed the videos of the Sportsdesk news programmes was that the use made of the BBC material was fair dealing for the purpose of reporting the results of the World Cup matches. These were news reports. They were not programmes of football analysis or of review. The use of the BBC material was short, was pertinent to the news reporting character of the programme, and was accompanied by an attribution to the BBC. The evidence I heard and the argument addressed to me after my viewing of the videos confirmed my initial impression. I do not regard this in any sense as a borderline case. The use of the BBC material falls, in. my judgment, fairly and squarely within section 30(2) of the Act of 1988.

I therefore dismiss this action.

Notes and Questions

1. News reporting is identified as one of the potential fair uses that may be exempted from protection under Article 10bis of the Berne Convention. What are other potential exempted uses? Must a signatory nation exempt all of the identified uses or does it have discretion in this matter?

2. If you were the judge in the *Denny Video* case on remand, based on the factual information provided in the above reported excerpt, would you decide the accused use qualified as a fair one?

3. What limitations, if any, does the Berne Convention put on the exercise of a fair use exemption? Have these limitations been complied with under U.S. law, according to the above excerpt?

4. What if instead of broadcasting a video tape of a riot, the television station had read over the air, without permission, the first chapter of a book that is currently listed as number one of the New York Times Best Seller Non–Fiction list? Would that act qualify as an excused fair use under the *Denny Video* case? Under the *World Cup Broadcast* case? Under the Berne Convention?

5. If a use is considered "fair," should the author be allowed to challenge it as a violation of her moral rights in the work?

6. For a further discussion of fair use and its role as a tool of censorship and government taking, see Chapter Thirty–Three.

Chapter Fourteen

PATENTS UNDER THE PARIS CONVENTION

A. DID THE PARIS CONVENTION PROVIDE A WORKABLE SOLUTION TO THE INTERNATIONAL PATENTING DILEMMA?

The protection of pharmaceutical products has been a topic of heated debate internationally between developed and developing countries. Developed countries, who are perceived as being the primary discoverers of new drugs to treat various medical illnesses, contend that patent protection should be extended internationally to assure recovery of their high research and development costs. By contrast, developing countries contend that patent protection raises the cost of much needed medical treatment, perhaps beyond the means of their people. Consequently, products that relate directly to the health or safety of the general populace, they contend, should not be subject to patent protection. Are there limitations to the rights that should be extended to pharmaceutical products internationally? What would those limitations be? For example, should the owners of patents for pharmaceutical products be given the same rights as those for a new video disc player? Can international treaty regimes be structured to take account of these limitations? How?

THE HISTORY OF THE PATENT HARMONIZATION TREATY: ECONOMIC SELF–INTEREST AS AN INFLUENCE
R. Carl Moy, 26 J. Marshall L. Rev. 457 (1993).

The Paris Convention for the Protection of Industrial Property was first concluded in 1883. Since its inception, the Convention has been revised six times, the last revision occurring in 1967 at Stockholm. Concurrent with the latest revision was the establishment of WIPO, which assumed responsibility from the United International Bureau for the Protection of Intellectual Property (BIRPI) for the performance of the administrative tasks of the Paris Union.

The national patent systems that existed prior to the Paris Convention often contained widely varying legal rules. The United States, for example, examined patent applications substantively, while many European countries did not. Most countries published the technical disclosures of patent applications upon grant, some held the disclosures in secret until after the patent expired, while still others published the disclosure immediately upon filing. Generally speaking, the variation between national provisions at the time appears to have been substantially larger than exists today.

These variations in national patent practices created procedural obstacles to the international assertion of patent rights. In those countries that published patent disclosures immediately upon filing, for example, the mere act of applying for patent disclosed the invention publicly. At the same time, other countries conditioned patentability on absolute novelty worldwide. Applying for a patent in one country could thus create an absolute barrier to obtaining a valid patent in another.

These procedural obstacles to patenting generally appear to have arisen inadvertently. There also existed at this time, however, another category of obstacles that national governments had erected purposefully. The obstacles in this second category were essentially protectionist. By the late 1800s European and United States scholars had explored the economics of patenting extensively. As explained below, many granting sovereigns had begun to manipulate their national patent laws to enrich themselves in relation to their trading partners.

Patent systems are large-scale governmental intrusions into the free-market economy. They involve manipulating social costs and benefits to increase the national wealth. Perhaps the most significant cost of such systems is the higher prices imposed on consumers of the patented advance. If the patented technology has some economic value the patent owner is able to impose single-source pricing on its a price that is higher than would exist in a truly competitive market.

Patent systems exist because this social cost of higher prices is presumed to result in an increased pace of invention. Higher prices transfer increased amounts of money from consumers of the patented technology to producers. Knowing this, inventors will strive to invent patentable technology more vigorously. Some will succeed who otherwise would have failed. The sophistication of the country's industrial base thus increases, and new technology becomes available to consumers. According to the presumption, the social benefits of this increased rate of invention are large enough to more than offset the costs of patenting.

In a purely domestic economy the national effects of these costs and benefits are linked together relatively tightly. Each unit of increased cost imposed on domestic consumers provides a unit of increased revenue to domestic industry. Evaluating such a patent system therefore involves, in large part, estimating the amount of increased invention that will actually result from a given increase in expected revenue. In addition, the increased resources diverted to a domestic patent owner are not wholly lost to the domestic economy. Rather, the domestic patent owner generally will reinvest all or a part of those resources, thereby mitigating the cost of patenting to some degree.

International patenting, on the other hand, de-couples the national effects of patenting. Assume that an inventor exploits the advance through patenting, not in his or her own country, but in a foreign country. In that situation industry domestic to the inventor's own country receives increased profits from patenting, but domestic consumers do not pay the associated higher prices. Instead, the higher prices are imposed on consumers in the foreign country. International patent transactions therefore reallocate wealth away from the granting country and into the country of the patent owner.

Prior to the Paris Convention many countries had acted on this basic economic truth. Their national laws included numerous, varied provisions that curtailed the domestic patent rights of foreign nationals. Some countries, for example, had adopted compulsory-licensing provisions. By their very nature, compulsory licenses lower the cost of the patented advance closer to multiple-source pricing. In addition, if the compulsory license is given to a domestic entity a portion of the foreign trade is prevented outright. Both these mechanisms reduce the amount of wealth that flows out of the country into the hands of the foreign patent owner.

Another type of protectionist provision motivated by the same economic calculation was the widespread presence of national working requirements. Generally, these provisions required patent owners to supply domestic demand for the patented technology through domestic production. The failure to do so resulted in the patent becoming invalid or unenforceable. Facially neutral with regard to nationality, working requirements had an obviously greater, purposeful impact on patent owners who were foreign. In essence, foreign patentees were required to either abandon their patent rights or behave as if they were domestic entities.

In addition to increased prices, patents impose another social cost that is relevant to international patenting: they retard further research in the patented technology. Patents commonly dominate inventions that remain to be discovered and patented themselves. Once a patent issues, therefore, every person other than the patent owner has a reduced expectation of return from further research in the areas of technology that the patent dominates. Rationally, then, researchers will reduce their inventive efforts in technology that is dominated by another's patent. If competition spurs the speed of research, this reduction in competition will slow industrial development over time. The issue in a purely domestic economy is optimally balancing the initial incentive to the original patent owner with the detriment to future researchers.

With international patenting, however, the problem becomes more complex. The teachings of an issued patent can travel beyond the borders of the granting sovereign and into other countries. Corresponding patent rights in such other countries may, or may not, exist. In countries where they do not, the public learns of the advance and yet is free from the economic impediment of dominating patent rights. Technological development therefore continues unabated. In countries where dominant patent rights do exist, in contrast, only the holder of the dominant patent is fully motivated to continue researching. Over time, this risks reducing the industrial sophistication of the patenting country in comparison to that of the non-patenting country.

These economic considerations spurred a number of countries to act during the early period of international patenting. Primary among those actions were national provisions that caused domestic patents to expire as soon as any corresponding foreign patent expired. In operation, these provisions freed domestic industry from the constraining effects of patenting as soon as the industry in another country became free.

In total, these various protectionist provisions inflicted immense difficulties on patent owners. Often, one simply could not obtain patent rights in a foreign country. Even if a foreign patent could be obtained, many times its continued existence depended on the patent owner rapidly initiating manufacture in that foreign country. This could be disadvantageous for many different reasons.

Prior to the Paris Convention essentially no international agreements addressed the obstacles to international patenting set out in the preceding section. Instead, patent owners who wished to assert patent rights in foreign countries were forced to rely on their own resources. As a practical matter, they were forced to restrict the number of countries in which they sought patent protection.

In 1883, a decade-long process of negotiation culminated in a number of countries signing the Paris Convention. Although the creation of the convention was an act of international diplomacy, the participants in the negotiations included not only representatives of national governments, but representatives of industrial interests as well. It appears, in fact, that the negotiations began primarily at the insistence of industrial interests.

The Paris Convention addressed a portion of the obstacles to international patenting. At the same time, other obstacles remained unresolved. This partial failure raises an immediate question: Why was agreement on those issues not reached? Many causes doubtlessly contributed. At the same time, however, the pattern of successes and failures suggests that the different economic interests of the various parties to the negotiations was a significant cause. In particular, agreement appears to have been possible only where the economic interests of national government and industry coincided.

It is axiomatic that the interests of national government will tend to be national in scope. With regard to patenting, these interests will include the full range of social costs and benefits of a patent system: the potential benefits of an increased rate of innovation, for example, as well as the costs of higher consumer prices, the costs of administering the patent system, and the costs borne by other endeavors from whom the increased resources spent on patenting have been diverted.

This focus on both the costs and the benefits of patenting should also hold true with regard to transactions of international patenting. A national government will be concerned with the increased incentive that patent rights in foreign countries bestow upon its domestic industry. Government will also be concerned with the domestic costs of awarding patents to foreigners: the loss of national wealth from importation of patented goods, and the potential stunting of domestic industry via international patenting that is uneven.

Industry's view of patenting, in contrast, is potentially quite different. Industry will be concerned with how patenting affects its own, private interests. Those interests will in all likelihood be very different from the interests of society as a whole. For example, patent systems rely entirely on the incentive of increased profits to spur innovative activity. Patenting therefore bestows large private benefits on industry. At the same time, the social costs of patenting are generally spread throughout society. They therefore impose private costs on industry to a much lesser degree.

This observation is very significant. Unless one views inventors as entitled to monopoly profits naturally, patent systems must be seen as societal mechanisms for providing an optimal amount of incentive to invent. To determine that amount of incentive, one must consider more than industry's narrow, private interests. The result of that broader calculation need not coincide with industry's preferences. Thus, society can prefer rules of patent law that industry would not choose. Stated conversely, industry can prefer rules of patent law that are adverse to society. The differences of position between the two groups should be systematic.

For the same reasons, industry and national governments should also have systematically different interests with regard to international patenting. If they behave rationally according to economic criteria, national governments will be interested in obtaining agreements that maximize the wealth of their individual countries. These will be agreements whose operation bestows on the particular national economy both large benefits and small costs from international patenting. Industry, in contrast, will seek the private benefits of increased international patenting but will be relatively unconcerned with any associated social costs. In particular, industry will be largely unconcerned with whether a disproportionate share of such costs falls on any particular national economy, including that of its own country.

In essence, because the parties to an international sale of a patented item each belong to a different national economy, their private costs and gains become social costs and gains for the countries involved. For example, where a national of the country under consideration holds a foreign patent, the sale of goods under that patent transfers wealth out of the foreign country into the hands of the patent-owning national. The national's private gain is thus a social gain for the national's own country. Conversely, where a country has granted one of its patents to a foreigner, the domestic sale of goods under the patent impoverishes domestic consumers and enriches the foreign patentee. The consumer's private cost is thus a social cost to the granting country. The outlook of national government differs from that of its patent-owning industry because the nation participates in both import and export transactions, while industry is largely preoccupied with exports.

The structure of the Paris Convention is consistent with the operation of these economic interests. Foreign patenting, for example, is crucial to the objectives of both industry and national government. Patents provide the market power that yields increased profits to industry. If such increased profits are to be had on foreign sales, industry must obtain foreign patents. Those same increased profits on foreign sales, moreover, appear to be the major mechanism by which countries enrich themselves through international patenting. National government is thus interested in seeing its citizens obtain as many foreign patents as possible. Additionally, foreign patents are needed to constrain the industrial development of competing countries while an advance is subject to domestic patent rights.

For these reasons, one would expect easy agreement in the Paris Convention to increase the general availability of foreign patenting. The interests of national governments are more or less the same on this particular issue. In addition, the self interests of national governments and industry generally coincide.

The original text of the Paris Convention shows such easy agreement on this issue through the concept of foreign priority:

> Any one who shall have regularly deposited an application for a patent of invention in one of the contracting States, shall enjoy for the purpose of making the deposit in the other States a right of priority under the periods hereinafter determined.

> In consequence, the deposit subsequently made in one of the other States of the Union, before the expiration of [this] period cannot be invalidated by acts performed in the interval, especially by another deposit, by the publication of the invention or by its working by a third party.

As a result of this provision, an inventor could establish a date of filing in all member countries via an initial filing in a single country. The act of applying for patent rights on the same invention in several foreign countries was therefore made much easier.

As to protectionist provisions, the economic interests of national government and patent owners appear to diverge. National government is critically interested in retaining the freedom to impose protectionist provisions. By definition, these provisions reduce the outflow of national wealth to foreign patentees. They are an important means of minimizing the domestic costs of international patenting.

Industry, in contrast, will be generally opposed to protectionist provisions. Protectionist provisions reduce the market power of industry's foreign patents. Industry will therefore object to their presence in the patent systems of foreign countries and will seek their abolition. In addition, because others pay the private costs of increased patents on imports, industry has little reason to favor protectionist provisions in the domestic patent system of its own country.

Under an economic analysis, therefore, patent-owning industry will seek broad prohibitions against protectionist measures. In contrast, each national government will seek to preserve at least those protectionist provisions that operate to the country's own net benefit. Based upon these fundamentally different interests one would expect difficulty in achieving any agreement to eradicate protectionist provisions generally.

The historical course of negotiations over the Paris Convention is consistent with this analysis as well. The original text of the Paris Convention contained conspicuously little with regard to the two most widespread protectionist measures, working requirements and compulsory licenses:

> The introduction by the patentee into countries where the patent has been granted, of articles manufactured in any other of the States of the Union, shall not entail forfeiture.

> The patentee, however, shall be subject to the obligation of working his patent conformably to the laws of the country into which he has introduced the patented articles.

The text did require signatories to permit importation. At the same time, it specifically allowed the continued existence of national working requirements generally. It did not mention compulsory licenses at all.

In addition to the principle of foreign priority, the Paris Convention also adopted the principle of national treatment. "The subjects or citizens of each of the contracting States shall enjoy, in all other States of the Union, so far as concerns patents for inventions the advantages that the respective laws thereof at present accord, or shall thereafter accord to subjects or citizens." Stated simply, national treatment requires each government to apply the same provisions to both its own citizens and foreign nationals. It has been described, along with the principle of foreign priority, as a fundamental tenet of the Convention.

The Paris Union's agreement to provide for national treatment stands in apparent opposition to the economic analysis suggested in this article. At least in theory, national treatment prevents governments from employing the most effective tool for reducing the domestic cost of international patenting: expressly denying domestic patent rights to foreign inventors. In addition, the Paris Union consciously selected national treatment over the competing principle of reciprocity. Under reciprocity, each government need award to foreign inventors only those patent rights that the foreign inventor's own government awards to non-nationals. Reciprocity would thus seem a favorite of national governments: under it, the cost of awarding domestic patents to foreigners is tied directly to the benefits that domestic industry receives from patenting in foreign markets.

What, then, does the Paris Union's selection of national treatment imply? Does it invalidate the assertion that economic self-interest explains the Paris Convention's substantive provisions? More broadly, does it show the Paris Union to have adopted an internationalist, free-trade approach to foreign patenting?

When examined carefully, the adoption of national treatment probably does not support these suppositions. Reasons completely apart from a free-trade rationale can cause government to favor national treatment over reciprocity. A country applying reciprocity, for example, must be expert in the patent laws of every foreign country. Reciprocity thus risks large administrative costs.

In addition, a deeper examination shows that national treatment still permits government many forms of protectionist behavior in patenting. Still possible, for example, are provisions that are facially neutral with regard to nationality, but which impact foreigners disproportionately. Working requirements and compulsory licenses are examples of two such provisions; the restrictions in United States law against proof of invention by foreign activities are another.

Another, more subtle type of protectionist provision permitted under national treatment involves reducing the domestic costs of patenting generally. The loss of domestic wealth to foreign patentees can occur only when domestic patenting results in valuable rights. Thus, government can reduce the outflow of wealth to foreigners by simply reducing the economic value of the domestic patent rights that are available. Indeed, the loss can be reduced to zero by refusing to grant domestic patents altogether.

The Swiss patent system provides a historical example of a national government employing this latter technique. Switzerland progressed through the industrial revolution without a patent system. The economic rationale behind this decision was sound: without domestic patents Swiss consumers paid no increased prices for new technology. Switzerland thus minimized the outflow of its wealth to importers. Indeed, refusing to issue patents removed all the social costs of patenting from the domestic Swiss economy. At the same time, Switzerland continued to receive most of the benefits of patenting. True, Swiss industry could not expect patent profits from introducing new technology into the domestic Swiss economy. The absence of domestic patents, however, gave Swiss industry free access to all the new technology that others developed. In addition, Swiss industry held patents in foreign countries, thus earning patent profits from exports and receiving an incentive to invent in that way. In fact, because the Swiss economy was small, the incentive that Swiss industry received from patented exports was arguably greater than the incentive that dominating the domestic Swiss economy via patenting might have supplied.

National treatment provided no obstacle to this strategy. The original Paris Convention did not commit its members to provide any minimum rights to patentees. Thus Switzerland could, and in fact did, adhere to the Paris Convention even though it had no patent system whatsoever. Its denial of patent rights equally to domestic nationals and foreigners satisfied the requirement of national treatment. Additionally, adhering to the Paris Convention guaranteed Swiss inventors national treatment from foreign governments, thereby ensuring Swiss industry access to patent profits on its exports. In fact, Switzerland did not find it in her interest to enact a national patent system until Germany threatened her with retaliatory tariff action.

Subsequent negotiations to revise the Paris Convention have continued to follow this pattern. It has been increasingly possible to harmonize the procedural requirements of patenting. At the same time, agreement to limit the use of national patent provisions for protectionist purposes has not progressed very far. The Paris Union has repeatedly revisited the issues of working requirements and compulsory licensing since 1883. The resulting provisions place very few restrictions on national governments that wish to use these mechanisms. Compulsory licenses can be granted as soon as three years after the patent issues. The patent can be revoked for failure to work two years thereafter. Perhaps more significant, even today the Paris Convention contains virtually no requirements that national governments grant any other minimum rights to patent holders. Indeed, the Convention still does not even require that national governments enact patent systems at all.

Notes and Questions

1.   What does Professor Moy see as the economic conflict posed between a domestic and international patent regime? Do you agree with his analysis?

2.   What do you perceive as the benefits of international as opposed to domestic standards for patent protection? What are the problems?

3.   Are protectionist measures such as working requirements outdated in today's global economy? Should they be eliminated to assure a robust international patent regime or do they serve to protect the interests of less developed countries?

4.   What if trade secret protection for various products, such as pharmaceutical or agricultural products were used instead of patent protection? Would such a scheme resolve some of the economic conflicts identified above? Or would it simply present new problems?

Read the following Articles from the Paris Convention from the Supplement: 1(2–4), 4, 4bis.

THE PRIORITY ANTICIPATION CASE
ANESTHETIC SUPPLIES PTY. LTD.

In the Federal Court of Australia New South Wales
District, Registry General Division, 1992.
No. N G156 of 1992; Fed No. 811.

GUMMOW, J.

At the trial of this proceeding the applicant alleged infringement of each of claims 1, 3, 6, 7, 8, 9 and 11 of standard patent no. 560360 ("the Patent") for an invention entitled "device for treating snoring sickness". The applicant is the present registered proprietor of the Patent. It was incorporated on 29 May 1989. The inventor, who was the applicant for grant, was Professor C E Sullivan. Professor Sullivan is Professor of Medicine at the University of Sydney, and has an international reputation for research in the field of respiratory medicine and sleep disorders.

Obstructive sleep apnoea ("OSA") is a syndrome associated with an extreme form of snoring in which the sufferer chokes on his or her tongue and soft palate repeatedly whilst asleep. In an article published in 1981 in "The Lancet", Professor Sullivan and 3 members of his unit in the Faculty of Medicine at the University discussed OSA. Professor Sullivan's experiments with patients, leading eventually to the conclusions expressed in this paper, had commenced in June 1980. The authors said that OSA was a common disorder particularly in middle aged overweight males. They continued:

> "The underlying problem is sleep-induced occlusion of the oropharyngeal airway, which results in multiple apnoeic episodes during sleep. There is severe fragmentation of sleep, and as the disease progresses over months or years, greater degrees of asphyxia occur; the duration of apnoea frequently exceeds two minutes and the arterial haemoglobin oxygen saturation falls below 50%. Remarkably, the patient may be unaware of his nightly struggle for breath. Rather, his major symptoms are those of excessive daytime sleepiness and snoring. The nocturnal asphyxia eventually causes a variety of clinical presentations including cardiac arrhythmias, pulmonary hypertension and right heart failure, systemic hypertension, severe morning headache, intellectual and personality changes, and polycythaemia. The only effective treatment now available is a tracheostomy which is left open at night. This immediately results in disappearance of the excessive daytime sleepiness; and the life threatening complications of hypoxaemia, such as arrhythmias and cor pulmonale, improve dramatically within days. In patients who do not have any of the immediately life-threatening complications, a decision to do a tracheostomy is invariably difficult, despite the knowledge that the disease is progressive. We describe here a method which has prevented upper airway occlusion for an entire night of sleep in each of five patients with severe obstructive sleep apnoea."

In the summary of their paper the authors state:

" Five patients with severe obstructive sleep apnoea were treated with continuous positive airway pressure (CPAP) applied via a comfortable nose mask through the nares. Low levels of pressure (range 4.5—10 cm H20) completely prevented upper airway occlusion during sleep in each patient and allowed an entire night of uninterrupted sleep. Continuous positive airway pressure applied in this manner provides a pneumatic splint for the nasopharyngeal airway and is a safe, simple treatment for the obstructive sleep apnoea syndrome."

Professor Zwillich is a distinguished expert from the United States with extensive clinical experience. He is Professor of Medicine at Pennsylvania State University. He was called by the applicant. Before he read "The Lancet" article, it had never occurred to him to apply CPAP therapy to patients suffering from OSA. His evidence is that the result of Professor Sullivan's work has been to revolutionise treatment of OSA, because of the simplicity, safety, efficacy and high degree of acceptability of the CPAP therapy. There are also advantages of relatively low cost and of long term "at home" treatment of patients away from hospital. Professor Zwillich himself has effectively treated large numbers of patients who otherwise might have remained untreated.

In addition to denying infringement of any of the claims relied upon by the applicant, the respondent, by its cross claim, seeks revocation of the Patent. The attack on validity, as presented at the trial, was directed to those claims in respect of which the applicant pressed its case as to infringement. Various grounds of invalidity were relied upon by the respondent.

First it is said that there is lack of novelty by reason of certain prior publications and prior user. The strength of the case on novelty depends upon which of the possible priority dates are held for the claims by the applicant is made good. The applicant concedes that it must lose on the issue of novelty if the relevant date is 17 December 1985 [the date applicant amended its application]. However the applicant contends that this is not the relevant date because, within the meaning of § . 159A of the 1952 Act, the amended claims did not claim new matter "in substance" first disclosed in the specification as a result of amendment of the specification in 1985. Further, the applicant contends, and the respondent denies, that within the meaning of sub-s. 45(2) of the 1952 Act, the claims of the complete specification were "fairly based on matter disclosed in the provisional specification". The result would follow that the priority date of those claims is the date, not of lodgement of the complete specification (23 April 1982), but the date of lodgement of the provisional specification (24 April 1981).

In final address, counsel for the applicant conceded that it was vital for his client's case to establish fair basing upon matter disclosed in the provisional specification and thereby to make good the priority date of 24 April 1981. This was because of the disclosure in the article published in the issue of "The Lancet" dated April 18, 1981. The disclosure there would provide an anticipation of the claims of the Patent if the earliest priority date is that of the lodgment of the complete specification, 23 April 1982. (Whilst the issue of "the Lancet" bears the date April 18, 1981, that is to say before the date of lodgment of the provisional specification on 24 April 1981, it was submitted that I should find (and I do find), that "the Lancet" was not published in Australia until after 24 April 1981.

So far as relevant, § 40 of the 1952 Act provides:

"40(1) A complete specification

(a) shall fully describe the invention, including the best method of performing the invention which is known to the applicant; and;

(b) shall end with a claim or claims defining the invention.

(2) The claim or claims shall be clear and succinct and shall be fairly based on the matter described in the specification."

The practical application by Professor Sullivan of his apparatus has been modified from time to time and the preferred form of the apparatus has changed. That which is now marketed by both sides to this litigation differs from the proffered embodiment disclosed in the drawings to the complete specification, in particular by the use of 1 not 2 tubes respectively for the supply to and expiration of air by the patient. This will be important in dealing with an issue as to "best method" and, upon the question of infringement of claim 11, with an argument as to the use in the respondent's devices of mechanical equivalents.

The evidence indicates that the use of the "one tube" apparatus rather than the "two tube" apparatus has distinct advantages, for example, by assisting the plaintiff to sleep with his or her head in various positions whilst the apparatus is in operation. The evidence also indicates that the "one tube" apparatus was not known to Professor Sullivan as the best method of performing the invention on the international filing date, 23 April 1982. That date is the priority date by reference to which, for example, issues of anticipation and obviousness of the claims are assessed under § . 100 of the 1952 Act. On its face, § . 40 would suggest that the complete specification should include the best method of performing the invention known to the applicant when lodging the complete specification.

On the other hand, the respondent contends that the relevant date for the disclosure of the best method is the date of publication. In the present case, as I indicated earlier in these reasons, that is 4 November 1982. The respondent contends, and the applicant denies, that at that date the best method known to Professor Sullivan involved use of the "one tube" apparatus, whereas only the "two tube" apparatus is described in the complete specification.

In re-examination Professor Sullivan said that he could not remember the details sufficiently to say whether in April 1982 he was using with patients the "one tube" method. He had agreed in cross-examination that "at the end of 1982" his preferred method was the "one tube" system. But, taken as a whole, Professor Sullivan's oral evidence, including the manner in which it was given by him, gave me the firm impression that he had no specific recollection of dates when they were not supported by contemporary records or by memorable events such as the presentation of papers at learned conferences.

In May 1982, after the priority date, Professor Sullivan presented a paper at the annual meeting of the American Thoracic Society. The learned journal which published the paper received it in its original form on 13 September 1982 and in a revised form on 4 January 1983. That was well after 4 November 1982, the publication date and that contended for by the respondent as the relevant date for disclosure of the best method. In figure 2 in the paper as published there appears a drawing of the apparatus using the "two tube" system for the provision of nasal CPAP. In the body of the paper it is said that it was this apparatus which was used to supply nasal CPAP to the patients whose treatment is discussed in the paper.

On 20 July 1983 Professor Sullivan attended and presented material at the 4th International Congress of Sleep Research at Bologna. He was embarrassed at not having a Paper ready for presentation on that occasion. He later wrote his paper, with other co-authors from his team, and the paper was submitted almost 9 months after the conference. It was published in 1984. It gives what is described as a preliminary account of the results of home CPAP treatment to 35 patients, with detailed information being given of the treatment of 5 patients over periods of up to 5 or 6 months. It is said that a number of methods of nasal CPAP were used. A description is given both of the "two tube" and the "one tube" method, the latter being described as "the latest method of applying nasal CPAP in the home." This is consistent with Professor Sullivan's oral evidence that over an indeterminate period he and his team "were transitioning between two and one tube" and that whilst eventually they did change over "I couldn't describe it as quickly."

Upon consideration of the evidence as a whole, I find that the respondent has not discharged to the necessary degree its burden of showing that by 4 November 1982, more than 6 months before the Bologna conference, the best method known to Professor Sullivan was the "one tube" method.

In the light of that finding it is unnecessary to determine the issue of law which, if decided favourably to the applicant would have the effect of moving the relevant date back to the international filing date, namely 24 April 1982. If the matter is assessed from that date, of course, the position of the applicant on the evidence as to this issue becomes even stronger. In the circumstances, I should express my views on the point.

Section 36 of the Patents Act 1903 ("the 1903 Act") stated:

"36. A complete specification must fully describe and ascertain the invention and the manner in which it is to be performed, and must end with a distinct statement of the invention claimed."

This provision followed sub-§§ . 5(4), (5) of the British Patents, Designs and Trade Marks Act 1883 (UK). Express provision as to disclosure of best method was not introduced into British legislation until the insertion in 1932 (by the Patents and Designs Act 1932 (UK), of para. (j) in sub-s. 25(2) of the Patents and Designs Act 1907 (UK). This expressly provided that the patent might be revoked if the complete specification did not disclose the best method known to the applicant "at the time when the specification was left at the Patent Office" must be disclosed.

In the United Kingdom the position appears to be that a specification must be sufficient at the date of publication, that it cannot subsequently be rendered as insufficient, and that sufficiency at the date of publication is enough, whatever may have been the position at the date of filing. It has been said that there is good reason for saying that sufficiency at the date of publication is enough, for until then, no addressee of the specification can be puzzled or mislead by the insufficiency of the directions for putting the alleged invention into practice

The adequacy of the disclosure should be judged by reference to the time from which dated the monopoly granted the applicant in exchange for the disclosure. In the present case that is the international filing date, 23 April 1982. This is the date from which the term of the patent runs.

I turn to consider the alleged paper anticipations. In address, counsel for the respondent limited his case to 3 articles published in foreign learned journals, which were received in Australia before the priority date. Further articles had been relied upon in the Particulars of Objections. The 3 articles were identified as those by Arp (published 1969), Kattwinkel (published 1973) and Wung (published 1975). These articles related to research conducted in the United States.

All three articles are concerned with the use of CPAP devices in pediatric medicine, in particular for the treatment of RDS and apnoea of prematurity in premature and full term infants. Before the priority date Professor Sullivan had been aware of this use of CPAP devices but he did not consider it could have relevance in treating the adult sleep disorder OSA. This was because of differences in aetiology of RDS in neonates and apnoea of prematurity, compared with the aetiology of OSA.

RDS was thought to be caused by a lack of a surface active agent (or surfactant) in immature lungs, something which caused them to collapse. Physical inability of the lungs was not seen to be the cause. The aetiology of apnoea of prematurity was thought to be caused by failure in the central nervous system to maintain the neurological responses required for breathing.

In this field of pediatric medicine, CPAP was not used for the purpose of maintaining the opening of the upper airways. This was not thought, and still is not thought, to be a cause of RDS or of apnoea of prematurity or to be relevant to the treatment thereof. CPAP here was used not to create any form of "air splint" of the upper airways, but to maintain lung volume so as to prevent lung collapse until the lungs of the infant could function unassisted. OSA was not a syndrome which, in 1981, was observed in neonates.

The Arp article had been read by Professor Sullivan before April 1981. It is entitled "A New Approach to Ventilatory Support of Infants with Respiratory Distress Syndrome." It contains the following passage: "The mask consists of a plastic shell slightly larger than the infant's nose. It is filled with a soft, quick-setting, denture-lining material which molds itself exactly to the nasal contours with 10 to 15 seconds of intermittent pressure to the infant's moistened nose. The shells are fabricated from dental acrylic and are made in various sizes. An exhaust port in the end of the mask is closed, during delivery to the infant of a preselected volume of air-oxygen mixture, by inflating a rubber diaphragm. The diaphragm is deflated at the end of a delivery phase of the respirator to allow the infant to exhale freely...."

A critical factor is the lack of any means providing resistance to air flow so as to maintain pressure during the breathing cycle. Nevertheless, the respondent submits that there is no reason to believe that such a mask could not have been used successfully to apply nasal CPAP to keep open the upper airways of a patient suffering with OSA rather than an infant with RDS who required resuscitation. The evidence does not show that the apparatus described in the Arp article could have been so used. In any event, it would have to be shown that the article contained "clear and unmistakable directions" so to use the apparatus: *Flour Oxidizing Company Ltd. v. Carr and Co. Ltd.* (1908) 25 RPC 428 at 457–9. Plainly that is not the case with the Arp article.

The Kattwinkle article is entitled "A Device for Administration of Continuous Positive Airway Pressure by the Nasal Route." This article also deals with the treatment of RDS in very young infants. Again, the pediatric CPAP treatment with which this article is concerned was not directed to keeping open the upper airways by maintenance of air pressure slightly greater than atmospheric during inspiration, as claimed in the Patent. Professor Sullivan's evidence was that the pressure upon the upper airways to infants to whom pediatric CPAP was administered in accordance with the discussion in this article (and the Wung article) is not required to be greater than atmospheric pressure at all times throughout the breathing cycle of the patient. This is not the result of any neglect or failing on the part of the authors of these articles. Rather, it is because the pediatric CPAP with which they are concerned involves the use of intermittent positive pressure ventilation (IPPV) administered to infants by means of a nasal mask. The purpose of IPPV is to provide a mechanical aid to inspiration by the infant. The objective is to increase lung volume by synchronisation of the mechanical aid to the spontaneous inspiratory efforts of the infant, rather than to maintain the opening of the upper airways.

In addition, the Wung article entitled "A New Device for CPAP by Nasal Route" does not disclose the use of a nose mask. It teaches the use of nasal cannulae (or small tubes) which are inserted into the nostrils of the infant suffering with RDS. Thus an essential integer of claim 1 is omitted. In the end, the respondent appeared not to rely upon this disclosure as an anticipation.

I should refer also, for the sake of completeness, to an article "Upper Airway Patency in the Human Infant: Influence of Airway Pressure and Posture". This was published in 1980 in the United States and was described in evidence as the Wilson and Thach article. Professor Sullivan had read this article before April 1981. It describes a number of experiments conducted on the corpses of dead infants to establish whether there is a connection between airway pressure and posture on airway patency. No airflow was involved in the normal sense of breathing, the pressures being applied in a static manner involving no air flow. Pressurised air was supplied from a syringe into a short tube inserted into one nostril of the dead infant. The other nostril and the mouth were taped closed and the oesophagus was tied off. Thus there was no nose mask, and no apparatus for administering nasal CPAP as claimed in claim 1 of Patent.

None of these articles is a disclosure amounting to an anticipation, in the sense of the authorities, of claim 1 of the Patent.

Notes and Questions

1.   Does the Paris Convention contain a definition of what qualifies as a patented invention? Could a country which is a signatory to the Paris Convention refuse to grant patent protection to pharmaceuticals without violating treaty obligations? Must a signatory to the Paris Convention grant a patent to an invention which is considers to be obvious, even though a patent has been granted by both the United States and Japan?

2.   Does the Paris Convention resolve the "problem" of inconsistent novelty requirements (novelty versus *absolute* novelty) identified above? Did the court in the *Priority Anticipation* case apply an absolute novelty standard? How did it select the date for deciding novelty?

3.   Articles 1 through Article 5*quater* of the Paris Convention establish the minimum substantive enforcement standards for patent rights. (Other rights covered by the Paris Convention include trademarks, and utility designs. They are discussed in greater detail below.) Review these provisions. Do they establish a minimum term of protection for patent rights? Do they establish a minimum list of rights to be granted a patent owner, such as the right to control the manufacture, use or sale of a product containing or using the patented invention? Do they establish minimum substantive requirements for protection–such as novelty or inventive step? The failure to provide these minimum terms led to inconsistent treatment of patent rights internationally, increasing the cost of protection globally and creating a demand for a regime that would "correct" these problems.

4.   *Priority*. One of the most significant provisions of the Paris Conventions is the priority registration provision of Article 4. The one year priority requirement is absolute. Thus, if you are representing a client which has developed a potentially patentable invention for a new chemical plant growth formula, one of the issues you must face is how best to protect those interests internationally. In order to take advantage of the priority provision, what is the first step that you should take: file a patent application in the inventor's domicile country, file a patent application in the United States, or file a patent application in the countries your client identifies as key markets for its patented invention?

5.   Assume that you have properly filed a patent application in your client's domiciliary country of Japan. You have also filed patent applications in the United States and the countries of the European Union. If all of these applications are filed within the one year priority period granted under the Paris Convention, does such timely filing alone guarantee that your client's applications for a patent will be granted in all countries? Why or why not?

6.   What role did priority play in the *Priority Anticipation* case?

7.   The Paris Convention is only one of numerous international treaties which establish registration procedures and guidelines for obtaining intellectual property rights. Among other treaties which establish such procedures are the Patent Cooperation Treaty and the Trademark Registration Treaty. For a more detailed discussion of such treaties, see Part VI.

8.   Review the definitions of patentable inventions set forth in the Notes and Questions in Chapter Eight. Are these definitions in compliance with the Paris Convention? What is the minimum definition of a patentable invention according to the Paris Convention? What are the minimum rights that are granted a patent owner under the Convention? As you can see from your answer to these questions, the Paris Convention established few true substantive standards for patents. It was not until the 1990's with the entry into force of TRIPS that many of the loopholes of the Paris Convention were closed. For a closer analysis of these issues, *see* Part V, A Trip Through TRIPS.

Chapter Fifteen

TRADEMARKS UNDER THE PARIS CONVENTION

A. DID THE PARIS CONVENTION RESOLVE THE PROBLEMS OF INTERNATIONAL PROTECTION FOR TRADEMARKS?

Read the following Articles from The Paris Convention from the Supplement: 6, 6bis, 6ter, 6quinquies, 6sexies, 7, 7bis, 8, 9.

Notes and Questions

1. *The Problem of Definitions.* If you had to develop a definition of a protectable trademark based on the Paris Convention, what would its attributes be? Does the Paris Convention provide a category of protected "marks" similar to Article 2 of the Berne Convention for protected "works"?

2. Could a country which is a signatory to the Paris Convention refuse to grant trademark protection to generic marks without violating treaty obligations? Could it refuse to grant protection to a mark which is a parody of the portrait of a high government official? Must a signatory to the Paris Convention grant trademark rights to an invention which it considers to be non-distinctive, even though trademark registration has already been granted by both the United States and Japan?

3. Article 6 through Article 10*ter* of the Paris Convention establish the minimum substantive enforcement standards for trademark rights. Do these provisions establish a minimum term of protection for trademark rights? Do they establish a minimum list of rights to be granted a trademark owner, such as the right to control the use of a confusingly similar mark on non-identical goods?

4. *Priority Registration.* One of the most significant provisions of the Paris Convention is the priority registration provision of Article 4. The six months priority requirement is absolute. Thus, if you are representing a client which has developed a potentially protectable trade mark for its new virtual reality game, one of the issues you must face is how best to protect those interests internationally. In order to take advantage of the priority provision, what is the first step that you should take: file a trademark application in the inventor's domicile country, file a application in the

United States, or file an application in the countries your client identifies as key markets for its software invention?

5.   Assume that you have properly filed a trademark application in your client's domiciliary country of Japan. You have also filed trademark applications in the United States and the countries of the European Union. If all of these applications are filed within the six month priority period granted under the Paris Convention, does such timely filing alone guarantee that your client's applications for a trademark will be granted in all countries? Why or why not?

6.   *The Problem of Service Mark Protection.* Does the Paris Convention require registration of a service mark (one that is used to identify and distinguish services as opposed to goods)? What if your client is a fast food franchisor, such as McDonald's or Kentucky Fried Chicken? Assume that your client wants to develop a chain of restaurants in Greece that features hot dogs and hamburgers, "American style" and that Greece does not allow the registration of service marks. One way to protect your client's mark may be to register it for related products, such as for hot dogs and hamburgers. Sometimes, however, such registration may not be considered sufficient. *See, e.g.,* Kenneth L. Port, *Protection of Famous Trademarks in Japan and the United States*, 15 Wis. Int'l L. J. 259 (1997).

7.   *Other Registration Treaties.* The Paris Convention is only one of numerous international treaties which establish registration procedures and guidelines for obtaining trademark rights. Among other treaties which establish such procedures are the Madrid Protocol and the Trademark Registration Treaty. For a more detailed discussion of such treaties, see Part VI.

8.   Review the definitions of trademarks set forth in Chapter Ten in the Notes and Questions. Are these definitions in compliance with the Paris Convention? What is the minimum definition of a protected trademark according to the Paris Convention? What are the minimum rights that are granted a trademark owner under the Convention? As you can see from your answer to these questions, similar to its treatment of patents, the Paris Convention established relatively few true substantive standards for trademarks. It was not until the 1990's with the entry into force of TRIPS that many of the loopholes of the Paris Convention were closed. For a closer analysis of this issues, *see* Part V, A Trip Through TRIPS.

B.   WHAT IS THE STANDARD FOR TRADE-MARK PROTECTION: LIKELY CONFUSION OR ASSOCIATION?

THE JAPANESE NOODLE CASE
WAGAMAMA v. CITY CENTRE RESTAURANTS PLC

Chancery Division, 1995.
[1995] FSR 713.

LADDIE, J.

This is an action for registered trade mark infringement and passing off. The plaintiff company, Wagamama Limited, owns and operates a restaurant under the name WAGAMAMA. It is also the proprietor of three registered trade marks. Each mark consists of the word WAGAMA-MA. These registrations are in classes 32, 33 and 42 and cover a range of services and goods including restaurant services, catering services, beer, alcoholic and non-alcoholic drinks and mineral water. In this action nothing turns on the precise goods covered by the registrations nor is the validity of any of the registrations in issue.

The majority of the shares in the plaintiff company are owned by its managing director, Alan Takwai Yau. He came to England from Hong Kong and decided to open a restaurant which fused Japanese cuisine and western health consciousness. The restaurant was to serve high quality food but at reasonable prices. The result was the opening of WAGAMA-MA restaurant in Streatham Street, London, WC1 in April 1992. It is described by Mr. Yau as a Japanese-style noodle bar. Its decor is minimalist. It contains long simple tables at which customers are seated at long simple benches.

The name was chosen in the following manner. In 1989 Mr. Yau's sister had a Japanese flat mate. Mr. Yau did not understand any Japanese but Japanese visitors used the word "Wagamama". He remembered it and subsequently found out that it meant selfishness or wilfulness. He thought that the word would be suitable for his restaurant. It is not in dispute between the parties that the word WAGAMAMA has no meaning to the overwhelming majority of the population in England.

WAGAMAMA has been very successful. I was told that the plaintiff has engaged in very little advertising, a mere L24,000 in three years, but the fame of its restaurant has spread. It has received considerable press coverage, much of it very favourable. It has been reviewed in a wide variety of publications including Homes & Gardens, Evening Standard Magazine, The Times, London Student, City Limits, Time Out, The Daily Telegraph, Tatler, Cosmopolitan, The Independent, The Guardian, the Sunday Times and many others. WAGAMAMA has also been featured on a number of television programmes. It has received a number of awards including The Independent Restaurant of the Year award in 1992 and the Time Out Budget Meal of the Year award in 1993. An indication of WAGAMAMA's success is that customers are prepared to queue out into the street and wait for up to half-an-hour before they get a table.

The plaintiff also sells a book called WAGAMAMA: The Way of the Noodle which was first published in November 1994. Some 7,000 of these books have been sold not only to people from all over the United Kingdom but also from many other countries in Europe and further afield. The plaintiff also sells T-shirts bearing its name. About 100 of them are sold each week.

It is not in dispute that the plaintiff owns a significant reputation in its mark WAGAMAMA, at least in relation to its business of running an inexpensive Japanese-style noodle bar. The success of the first restaurant is such that a second much larger restaurant is in the course of development. It also will be located in central London.

The reputation of WAGAMAMA has not only attracted customers, it has also attracted businessmen, a number of whom have asked in vain for franchises.

The defendant is also in the restaurant business. It, or its wholly owned subsidiaries, run a number of restaurant chains. These are operated under the following brand names: Adams Rib, Filling Stations, Nacho's Mexican Restaurants, Garfunkel's Restaurants, Chiquito's Mexican Restaurants, Caffe' Uno and Deep Pan Pizza. The published accounts record that in the year ended December 31 1993 the defendant had a turnover in excess of L95 million with profits before taxation of in excess of L12.5 million. It was intending to open 10 new restaurants in 1994 and up to 20 restaurants a year in subsequent years.

In late 1993 the defendant decided to develop another branded restaurant chain. In the words used by the defendant's witnesses, this was to be an American theme restaurant with Indian decor and food. Mr. Fysh, who appeared for the plaintiff, described it as having a decor evoking the atmosphere of an up station Indian Civil Service club of the Raj which had been recently visited by a wealthy and benevolent American. The name eventually chosen for this new chain was RAJAMAMA. The first restaurant bearing this name was opened at the very end of April 1995.

The present proceedings were commenced with great expedition. Announcements of the opening of the defendant's restaurant appeared in the press on about April 7. A letter before action was sent on April 18. Following a rebuff dated April 21 there was an opposed application for ex parte relief on April 26. The writ was issued on the same day. The plaintiff also served a notice of motion seeking full interlocutory relief. However on seeing the defendant's evidence and realizing what its exposure would be under a cross-undertaking in damages, the plaintiff did not pursue that relief. Instead directions were sought for a speedy trial. The trial, which included cross-examination of witnesses, took place in mid-July. By the commencement of the trial, the defendant's restaurant had been trading for less than three months. There is no evidence before the court of how many customers it has so far attracted or the extent of any advertising, if any, it has undertaken.

As I have mentioned, at the time of the writ, the name used by the defendant was RAJAMAMA. However, as a result of the commencement of this action and in response to the application for interlocutory relief, the defendant decided to change the restaurant fascias and menus so that its brand name is now RAJA MAMA'S. That is the name it intends to continue to use. The plaintiff argues that whether the defendant uses RAJAMAMA (one word) or RAJA MAMA'S (two words) this will constitute infringement of its registered trademarks and passing off.

It is convenient to consider the issue of trademark infringement first. This part of the case raises an important question of law: what acts now constitute an infringement of a registered trade mark?

1.   Trade Mark Infringement: The statutory framework

Infringement in this action is to be determined in accordance with the Trade Marks Act 1994 (the 1994 Act). This provides at section 10, as far as material to this case, as follows:

10.(1) A person infringes a registered trade mark if he uses in the course of trade a sign which is identical with the trade mark in relation to goods or services which are identical with those for which it is registered.

(2) A person infringes a registered trade mark if he uses in the course of trade a sign where because—

(a) the sign is identical with the trade mark and is used in relation to goods or services similar to those for which the trade mark is registered, or

(b) the sign is similar to the trade mark and is used in relation to goods or services identical with or similar to those for which the trade mark is registered, there exists a likelihood of confusion on the part of the public, which includes the likelihood of association with the trade mark.

These provisions are new to our law. Prior to the 1994 Act, infringement of a registered trade mark was covered by the Trade Marks Act 1938 (the 1938 Act). The equivalent section in the latter Act was section 4 which, in so far as material, provided:

4.(1) Subject to the provisions of this section, and of sections seven and eight of this Act, the registration (whether before or after the commencement of this Act) of a person in Part A of the register as proprietor of a trade mark (other than a certification trade mark) in respect of any goods shall, if valid, give or be deemed to have given to that person the exclusive right to the use of the trade mark in relation to those goods and, without prejudice to the generality of the foregoing words, that right shall be deemed to be infringed by any person who, not being the proprietor of the trade mark or a registered user thereof using by way of the permitted use, uses a mark identical with it or so nearly resembling it as to be likely to deceive or cause confusion, in the course of trade, in relation to any goods in respect of which it is registered, and in such manner as to render the use of the mark likely to be taken either—

(a) as being used as a trade mark; or

(b) in a case in which the use is use upon goods or in physical relation thereto or in an advertising circular or other advertisement issued to the public, as importing a reference to some person having the right either as proprietor or as registered user to use the trade mark or to goods with which such a person as aforesaid is connected in the course of trade.

In 1984 the words "a mark identical with it or so nearly resembling it as to be likely to deceive or cause confusion" were removed from section 4(1) and the words "a mark identical with or nearly resembling it" were added after "in the course of trade". These alterations were not thought to have effected any significant alteration to British trade mark law.

1. INFRINGEMENT UNDER THE 1938 ACT

Under the 1938 Act, to find infringement the court compared the mark as registered with the mark as used by the alleged infringer. In essence the court would determine whether, as a result of similarities between the marks, goods or services bearing the alleged infringer's mark were likely to be thought to be derived from or connected with the proprietor of the registered mark. In determining whether the marks were too similar the court would bear in mind imperfect recollection and would also consider whether the "idea" of or principal impact conveyed by the marks were so similar that confusion was likely. Furthermore the test was essentially practical in the sense that the court would not consider just what the marks looked like but also what they sounded like. If, in accordance with these principles, the marks were too similar, usually infringement would be found even if in the market place the infringer took steps to prevent confusion in fact occurring—for example by putting disclaimers on his goods. Indeed the proprietor might not have used his registered mark at all so confusion in the market place would be impossible, yet he could succeed in infringement proceedings at least until the mark was removed from the register for non-use. To this extent therefore, a registered trade mark created a monopoly which might sometimes go beyond what was strictly necessary to protect the proprietor's goods and his reputation. Nevertheless the confusion which was looked for was confusion as to source or origin of the goods. It was enough that the similarity of the marks would make a customer believe that the alleged infringer's goods were associated with the proprietor's goods or services, for example that they were an extension of the range of goods made by the proprietor. However even in these cases, the association had to be an association as to source or origin. In this action this type of confusion as to source has been referred to by both parties as "classic infringement".

2. INFRINGEMENT UNDER THE 1994 ACT

There is no dispute between the parties that such classic infringement by confusion as to the source or origin of goods or services will also constitute an infringement under section 10 of the 1994 Act. The plaintiff alleges that there is such classic infringement in this case. That is a matter to which I will return later. However the plaintiff goes further. It says that section 10 of the 1994 Act, particularly section 10(2), covers confusion in a much broader sense. It is said that the registered proprietor can prevent mere association between the marks. It is argued that there will now be infringement if, on seeing the defendant's mark, the registered mark would be "called to mind" by a customer even if there is no possibility of the customer being under any misapprehension as to the origin of the goods. This is a new concept to those steeped in British trade mark law.

To illustrate his point, Mr. Fysh referred to a number of witness statements. In these various members of the public said inter alia that on hearing the name RAJAMAMA their first thoughts were of WAGA-MAMA because the names sound similar. Mr. Fysh said that even if their evidence had stopped there that sort of association without any more indicates trade mark infringement. He said that this was so even if the customer would have no doubt when considering just the trade marks that they are similar but unconnected. This type of association in which there is no confusion as to origin but the infringing mark "brings to mind" the registered one, I shall refer to in this judgment as "non-origin association".

Mr. Fysh pointed to the fact that the words "the likelihood of association with the trade mark" in our Act are taken from Article 5(1) of the 1988 Directive. That Article is in the following terms:

> The registered trade mark shall confer on the proprietor exclusive rights therein. The proprietor shall be entitled to prevent all third parties not having his consent from using in the course of trade—
>
> (a) any sign which is identical with the trade mark in relation to goods or services which are identical with those for which the trade mark is registered,
>
> (b) any sign where, because of its identity with, or similarity to, the trade mark and the identity or similarity of the goods or services covered by the trade mark and the sign, there exists a likelihood of confusion on the part of the public, which includes the likelihood of association between the sign and the trade mark.

The words "which includes the likelihood of association between the sign and the trade mark" in the Directive are said to be derived from Benelux trade mark law where they cover non-origin association. There-fore Mr. Fysh says that the words must be treated as having the same meaning in the 1994 Act as they do in Benelux law. There are three arguments which he deploys in support of this. First he says that a document exists which indicates that the words in the Directive were intended to have the meaning for which he contends. Secondly he says that whether or not any document exists which so indicates, it is a matter of common knowledge that the words were inserted in the Directive for this purpose. Thirdly he says that the Directive was supposed to introduce a new era of trade mark law harmony in the European Union. Since the Benelux courts have construed their equiva-lent trade mark law derived from the Directive to cover non-origin association, the British courts should do likewise both as a matter of comity and to help deliver the harmony which the Directive hoped to secure.

Since none of the arguments on construction put forward by the plaintiff is acceptable, it is necessary to approach the Directive and the 1994 Act from first principles.

Monopolies are the antithesis of competition. Intellectual property rights such as patents, trade marks and copyright can create barriers to trade within a country. They can create barriers to trade between countries. Differences between the laws of Member States of the European Union may add further obstructions to inter-state trade because what is permissible under the law of one Member State may be prohibited under the law of its neighbor. However, both at the domestic level and at the international level monopolies can be tolerated or even encouraged if they assist the development of commerce in some other way. Patent monopolies are the classic example. A valid patent may prevent competitors from entering a given field of commerce for up to 20 years. But this is a price which society, through its legislators, has agreed to pay to secure the increased investment in research and development which it is hoped patent monopolies will encourage. The important factor to bear in mind is that what justifies the monopoly is not the monopoly itself but the extent to which it gives, or is hoped to give, a benefit to commerce which compensates for the temporary restraint on competition. The monopoly is an adjunct to, and is designed to promote, commerce. This is central to the western system of commerce. Monopolies are the exception, not the rule. *Marsden v. Saville Street Co.* (1878) LR 3 Ex D 203. They need to be justified. As long ago as 1615 in this country it was said that the effect of an unjustified monopoly was "to take away free trade, which is the birthright of every subject" (*The Clothworkers of Ipswich* (1615) Godbolt 252).

Trade marks have historically been used to protect the trade with which they are associated. A good summary of their function is to be found in the speech of the Advocate General in *SA CNL–SUCAL NV v. HAG GF AG*, [1990] 3 CMLR 571 (HAG II). He said at 583:

Like patents, trade marks find their justification in a harmonious dove-tailing between public and private interests. Whereas patents reward the creativity of the inventor and thus stimulate scientific progress, trade marks reward the manufacturer who consistently produces high-quality goods and they thus stimulate economic progress. Without trade mark protection there would be little incentive for manufacturers to develop new products or to maintain the quality of existing ones. Trade marks are able to achieve that effect because they act as a guarantee, to the consumer, that all goods bearing a particular mark have been produced by, or under the control of, the same manufacturer and are therefore likely to be of similar quality. The guarantee of quality offered by a trade mark is not of course absolute, for the manufacturer is at liberty to vary the quality; however, he does so at his own risk and he—not his competitors—will suffer the consequences if he allows the quality to decline. Thus, although trade marks do not provide any form of legal guarantee of quality the absence of which may have misled some to underestimate their significance—they do in economic terms provide such a guarantee, which is acted upon daily by consumers.

A trade mark can only fulfill that role if it is exclusive. Once the proprietor is forced to share the mark with a competitor, he loses control over the goodwill associated with the mark. The reputation of his own goods will be harmed if the competitor sells inferior goods. From the consumer's point of view, equally undesirable consequences will ensue, because the clarity of the signal transmitted by the trade mark will be impaired. The consumer will be confused and misled.

Similarly in THE LAW OF INTELLECTUAL PROPERTY (1984) Ricketson stated:

> The primary function of a trade mark, traditionally, has been to identify the commercial or trade origin of the goods (or services) to which it is applied. This, of course, is of central importance to a trader as the mark then indicates to the market that these goods are his, even if he is not personally identified, and it becomes the focus for his growing goodwill or reputation in that market (page 603).

That the primary function of trade marks is to indicate origin of goods or services has also been accepted by the European Court of Justice. In *HAG II* the court said at 608:

> Consequently, as the Court has stated on many occasions, the specific subject-matter of a trade mark right is to grant the owner the right to use the mark for the first marketing of a product and, in this way, to protect him against competitors who would like to abuse the position and reputation of the mark by selling products to which the mark has been improperly affixed. To determine the exact effect of this exclusive right which is granted to the owner of the mark, it is necessary to take account of the essential function of the mark, which is to give the consumer or final user a guarantee of the identity of the origin of the marked product by enabling him to distinguish, without any possible confusion, that product from others of a different provenance: see Case 102/77, Hoffman–La Roche and Case 3/78, Centrafarm v. American Home Products.

Under these circumstances the essential function of the mark would be compromised if the owner of the right could not exercise his option under national law to prevent the importation of the similar product under a name likely to be confused with his own mark because, in this situation, consumers would no longer be able to identify with certainty the origin of the marked product and the bad quality of a product for which he is in no way responsible could be attributed to the owner of the right.

As mentioned above, there are two possible constructions which may be placed on Article 5 of the 1988 Directive and section 10(2) of the 1994 Act. The rights of the proprietor against alleged infringers may be limited to classic infringement which includes association as to origin or, following the Benelux route, it could cover not only classic infringement but also non-origin association. In my view, the former construction is to be preferred. If the broader scope were to be adopted, the Directive and our Act would be creating a new type of monopoly not related to the proprietor's trade but in the trade mark itself. Such a monopoly could be likened to a quasi-copyright in the mark. However, unlike copyright, there would be no fixed duration for the right and it would be a true monopoly effective against copyist and non-copyist alike. I can see nothing in the terms of the Directive (or our Act), or in any secondary material which I could legitimately take into account, which would lead me to assume that this was its objective. On the contrary, the preamble to the Directive seems to point in the opposite direction since it states:

Whereas the protection afforded by the registered trade mark, the function of which is in particular to guarantee the trade mark as an indication of origin,

Furthermore there appears to be little commercial justification for any such extension of trade mark rights. If it had been the intention to make the directive identical with Benelux law on this important issue it could have said so. Indeed, in view of the fact that to have done so would have been significantly to expand trade mark rights and thereby significantly restrict the freedom of traders to compete, I would have expected any such expansion to have been stated in clear and unambiguous words so that traders throughout the European Union would be able to appreciate that their legislators had created a new broad monopoly. As it is, no such clear and unambiguous words have been used and the language of the Directive and the 1994 Act is consistent with the rights being restricted to classical infringement.

It follows that this Court cannot follow the route adopted by the Benelux courts on this issue. This is regrettable since one of the main objectives of the 1988 Directive was to avoid differences in scope of trade mark rights which could lead to barriers to inter-state trade. Nevertheless the natural inclination to come to a conclusion which would further harmony on this issue is not so strong that I am prepared to agree that a new millstone round the neck of traders has been created when that is not my view. If the plaintiff is to succeed in its case of trade mark infringement it must do so on the classic grounds.

Notes and Questions

1. The court in the *Japanese Noodle* case later determined that the plaintiff had proven a case of classic infringement. Do you agree? If you represented the plaintiff, which test would you want the court to apply to determine infringement: "classic" or "non-origin association"?

2. Does the Paris Convention require that likely confusion be determined on "classic grounds" or on "non-origin association" grounds?

3. Assume that your client is Kentucky Fried Chicken who has decided to open a chain of fast food restaurants in Indonesia under the well-known KFC® mark. After establishing its first restaurant in Jakarta, your client

discovers that a second comer is using the name "Kentucky Chicken". Is the "Kentucky Chicken" mark infringing under a classic test? Under a non-origin association test? Are there instances where the selection of a classic infringement test over a non-origin association test could result in a lesser scope of protection?

4. *Harmonization.* As the court in the *Japanese Noodle* case recognized, harmonization of laws is one of the goals of the European Union Directive on Trademark Harmonization. If Great Britain and Belgium apply a different test for determining infringement, have the laws truly been harmonized? For the text of EU Directive, see Supplement. Does harmonization require identical treatment or something less?

C. SHOULD A FAMOUS MARK BE SUBJECT TO SPECIAL INTERNATIONAL PROTECTION?

THE McDONALD'S CONTROVERSY

South Africa, India Secures U.S. Marks.
Michael I. Davis, The National Law Journal, Oct. 28, 1996.

Last fall, when McDonald's Corp. lost its claim to a well-known mark in South Africa, it seemed a terrible blow to U.S. corporations seeking to do business in Commonwealth countries.

Recently, however, the highest appeals court in South Africa reversed this decision.[11]

On Aug. 27, the Appellate Division of the Supreme Court of South Africa ruled in a unanimous decision that McDonald's was entitled to protection as a "well-known trademark" under the relevant provisions of the new trademarks law, and that the various McDonald's Corp. marks remain valid and registered in South Africa. These marks had been the subject of an attack by two local South African companies.

The appeals court reversed the decision of the lower court that had denied this status to the McDonald's mark and in addition had ordered the cancellation of various McDonald's trademark registrations on the grounds of nonuse. The high court thus restored to validity more than 52 registrations McDonald's Corp. had obtained in South Africa, and it enjoined the respondents, two local South African companies, from using any of the McDonald's trademarks.

In the McDonald's case, the lower court had been presented with survey evidence and extensive evidence on affidavit, as to the recognition of the McDonald's mark in South Africa. McDonald's wanted to show that its mark had acquired the status of a well-known mark in South Africa, despite the absence of actual use in the jurisdiction during the years of apartheid policies and U.S. sanctions.

11. Author's note: for an excerpted version of this appellate decision, *See* Chapter Twenty–Seven.

The new South African Trademarks Act—which came into force May 1, 1993, during the course of the proceedings—contains a provision that establishes statutory protection for well-known trademarks. In order to qualify for such recognition, the mark must be well known in South Africa as being that of a national of a Paris Convention country or of a person or entity domiciled in, or having a real and effective industrial or commercial establishment in, a Paris Convention country. The statute explicitly states that protection is to be granted whether or not the trademark owner "carries on business or has any goodwill" in South Africa itself.

The lower court held that in order for a mark to gain well-known status under the statute, it was necessary for McDonald's to show that the public not only would regard the mark as well known in South Africa, but also would be aware that McDonald's had met the other conditions expressed in the statute–for example, that it had a commercial establishment in a Paris Convention country.

1.   Well Known to All Sectors

During the course of the proceedings, McDonald's Corp. commenced operations in South Africa through a franchisee, thus commencing use of the McDonald's marks there.

Additionally the lower court had held that for the mark to qualify as well known, McDonald's would need to establish that its mark was well known to all sectors of the public in South Africa. In the view of the lower court. McDonald's had failed to meet either burden.

Thus, in reaching the decision that the mark was not shown to have been well known, the lower court rejected the survey evidence offered by McDonald's, holding it to be inadmissible as hearsay evidence, and found McDonald's remaining evidence to be unpersuasive.

The appeals court rejected the legal analysis of the lower court as well as its evaluation of the evidence offered. In regard to the finding that the public would need to have knowledge of the domicile or commercial establishment of the trademark owner and that its country of origin was a Convention country, the appeals court held that such an interpretation would render the provision a "dead letter," commenting that "it is difficult to imagine any mark, however well known, in respect of which such facts would be common knowledge." In considering the manner in which the provision granting protection to well-known marks should be interpreted, the appeals court ruled that it should look to prior decisions in South Africa and the United Kingdom, which had denied relief to owners of marks that were admittedly shown to be well known, but whose owners did not have a local business or local goodwill. These decisions arose in claims based on passing off, the only remedy previously available in the United Kingdom and South Africa in circumstances in which a claim of statutory trademark infringement could not be brought.

Focusing on the wording of the new South African act, which extends protection to a trademark owner whether or not such owner "carries on business or has any goodwill in the Republic," the court concluded that the statute was intended to grant protection on essentially the same basis as in prior passing-off cases, but without the requirement of proof of a local business or goodwill.

The appeals court also disagreed with the lower court's holding that the mark would need to be known by all sectors of the public. The appeals court applied the criteria established in the passing-off cases and found that awareness of the mark had to be ascertained with regard to the relevant sector of the population.

The appeals court was thus prepared to consider the evidence presented regarding the international marketing of the McDonald's business, the spillover of advertising into South Africa and the knowledge of the mark that would have been gained by South Africans who traveled abroad. Furthermore evidence of "spontaneous acts" by South Africans, such as forwarding requests to McDonald's to establish local franchises, impressed the court as significant evidence of local reputation.

In addition, the court noted as probative of local recognition of the mark the zeal with which the defendants had pursued the McDonald's name, stating that "intrinsically the word McDonald's has not attractive force [sic] Had it not been for the reputation it had acquired over the years nobody would wish to appropriate it. It is therefore significant that [the defendants] have gone to considerable trouble and expense to obtain control over the McDonald's marks."

The court also held that the survey evidence was receivable in evidence and was clearly persuasive as showing awareness among the sector of the public that would be likely patrons of McDonald's restaurants. Although conceding that the basic evidence contained in the surveys—namely, statements of respondents who were nonwitnesses—technically was hearsay, the appeals court held that the specific exceptions governing the admission of such evidence in the local statute permitted acceptance of the evidence offered by McDonald's.

The court was of the view that the surveys had been properly conducted following the criteria set forth in the statute. It also noted that the defendants had been given a full opportunity to check the results of the surveys but had failed to challenge their correctness. The court found that the evidence established that the McDonald's marks were known to a substantial number of people who were interested in its goods and services, so McDonald's Corp. had met its burden.

The defendants had pressed claims that the McDonald's registered marks should be canceled because of nonuse, an issue that had occupied a great deal of the record and argument in the lower court and which had been decided against McDonald's Corp., resulting in orders that McDonald's registrations should be canceled. The appeals court found that despite the absence of use of the registered marks, it had discretion as to whether to order their cancellation.

Having found the marks to have gained well-known status, the appeals court reversed the cancellation by the lower court, commenting that it did not need to enter into a detailed examination of the facts since the defendants were by its ruling enjoined from using the marks.

By so holding, the appeals court avoided dealing with the issue, which still remains undecided, as to the criteria relevant to protecting trademarks that were not used during the period when the apartheid policies of the South African government were in force and foreign companies were affected by U.S. sanctions and other influences against doing business in South Africa. There has thus been no pronouncement by the appellate court on the nature of the evidence that might justify nonuse during this era.

2. PRACTICAL APPROACH

The appeals court ruling is significant in that it demonstrates a practical, businesslike approach to the assessment of trademark rights and signals a willingness to protect the legitimate interests of international trademark owners. Because the new South African trademarks law includes various provisions—in addition to the well-known-trademarks provision—aimed at modernizing South Africa's trademark system, it is to be anticipated that other courts and administrative agencies will adopt a similar practical approach in interpreting other provisions of the new law that deal with enhanced registration rights and expanded protection against infringement.

From the perspective of foreign trademark owners, the shock caused by the lower court's decision to cancel the McDonald's trademarks to the benefit of local parties who sought to misappropriate McDonald's fame has been dispelled. The decision should help South Africa attract investments from owners of well-known marks as part of the process of building a post-apartheid regime.

Apart from the significance of the case in its interpretation of the well-known-marks provision, it is noteworthy that the appeals court approved the use of survey evidence. Previously, such evidence had been rejected or treated with considerable reserve by courts in South Africa as well as in the United Kingdom.

It will be interesting to observe whether the United Kingdom and other Commonwealth courts in the future follow the approach of the South African courts.

Notes and Questions

1. South Africa is not the only country where McDonald's has had trouble protecting its mark against local rivals. To the contrary, McDonald's has faced initially challenges to its marks in countries such as Japan and Scotland.

2. *"Well-known" Marks*. Does Article 6bis define the characteristics that are required to qualify as a "well-known" mark, subject to protection without registration? For example, must a mark be used in a country in

order to be well-known there? Or is it sufficient if the mark is simply recognized by a significant number of people in the country?

3.   If local recognition is sufficient, which people must "recognize" the mark? Is it sufficient if people who travel abroad recognize the mark or should a significant percentage of local potential consumers recognize the mark? How would you determine who these "potential consumers" are?

4.   The split in the lower and circuit court decisions in the South African case was based in part on the types of use and knowledge that would demonstrate that a mark is a well-known one. Among the types of evidence that were presented by McDonald's to establish that its mark was well-known were:

1.   Details of its worldwide operations, the end of 1993. including the operation of nearly 14,000 McDonald's restaurants in over 70 countries by

2.   An annual turnover of over $23 billion;

3.   An annual advertising expenditure of $900 million;

4.   Sponsorship of sporting events such as the Soccer World Cups in Italy and the United States;

5.   An affidavit stating that over 240 interested parties had inquired about opening a McDonald's franchise in South Africa;

6.   Market surveys to measure the public recognition of the McDonald's trademark in South Africa among a survey audience defined as white males and females, aged 16 years and older living in selected higher income suburbs and cities.

Which of these types of evidence do you believe is the most persuasive? The least persuasive? Why? What other types of evidence would be useful in deciding whether a mark is well-known?

5.   For a further discussion of the role of fame in establishing intellectual property rights internationally, see Part VII.

6.   *Territoriality.* One of the problems in deciding how much "special" protection should be afforded a "famous" or "well-known" mark derives from the initially "territorial" nature of a trademark. Most trademarks do not become globally "famous" the minute they are used (although the instantaneous nature of fame due to satellite broadcasts, cable and the Internet may be changing this "truism" of the business world). Instead, most trademarks develop a local reputation which is then spread through advertising, business expansion (including franchises) and word of mouth. Such territorial beginnings assure that some conflict will arise as geographically separate uses collide in the global market place. The problem remains in deciding whose territorial rights survive.

Chapter Sixteen

TRADE SECRETS UNDER THE
PARIS CONVENTION

A. ARE TRADE SECRETS PROTECTABLE
UNDER IP TREATY REGIMES?

Read the following Article from The Paris Convention from the Supplement: 10bis.

Notes and Questions

1. *The Definitional Problem.* Are trade secrets included within the scope of protection afforded against acts of competition "against unfair competition," under Article 10bis?

2. If so, what is their scope of protection? For example, does Article 10bis establish the minimum standards required to protect "trade secrets"? What types of information must be protected to comply with Paris Convention requirements of promoting "honest commercial practices"? Must the information be absolutely secret, or only reasonably so?

3. Du Pont has spent $5,000,000 developing a new synthetic that is impenetrable to most bullets and yet transparent enough to see through. The company's attorney has advised Du Pont that neither the synthetic product, nor the process for creating it, qualifies for patent protection. Du Pont has made no public disclosure of its new process for creating the synthetic. It has, however, sold windshields made out of the synthetic to one car manufacturer to test its usefulness as a bullet proof windshield. The manufacturer in its written agreement with Du Pont has agreed to keep the existence of the new synthetic secret until authorized to disclose it by Du Pont, and to conduct safety tests on the windshield. Without Du Pont's knowledge, the manufacturer conducts tests on the windshield to reverse-engineer it. As a result of these tests, the manufacturer discovers the formula for the synthetic. Has the car manufacturer violated the "honest commercial practices" standard referred to in Article 10bis?

GUIDE TO THE APPLICATION OF THE PARIS CONVENTION FOR THE PROTECTION OF INDUSTRIAL PROPERTY (BIRPI 1968)

G.M.C. Bodenhauser.

(a) The original Convention of 1883 did not contain any specific provision concerning the repression of unfair competition. In view of the fact that such repression was not even enumerated amongst the subjects of industrial property concerning which "national treatment" must be granted to persons entitled to the benefits of the Convention, the Additional Act, adopted by the Revision Conference of Brussels in 1900, introduced the latter principle with respect to unfair competition in a newly inserted Article 10bis. The Revision Conference of Washington in 1911 went a step further, in introducing into the said Article the obligation for all member States to assure to nationals of the Union effective protection against unfair competition. This obligation was strengthened, and a definition and examples of acts of unfair competition were included in the Article by the Revision Conference of The Hague in 1925. The Revision Conference of London in 1934 improved these provision, and the Revision Conference of Lisbon in 1958 added a further example of acts of unfair competition (paragraph (3)3).

(b) The various countries of the Union have different concepts of what is to be understood by *"unfair competition."* Several acts are considered to be acts of unfair competition in one or more countries, but not—or only in special circumstances—in other countries. In giving effective protection against unfair competition, each country may itself determine which acts come under this category, provided, however, that paragraphs (2) and (3) of the Article under consideration are complied with.

(c) The provision defines acts of unfair competition as *any act of competition as any act of competition contrary to honest practices in industrial or commercial matters*.

What is to be understood by *"competition"* will be determined in each country according to its own concepts: countries may extend the notion of acts of unfair competition to acts which are not competitive in a narrow sense, that is, within the same branch of industry or trade, but which unduly profit from a reputation established in another branch of industry or trade and thereby weaken such reputation.

Any act of competition will have to be considered unfair if it is contrary to *honest practices in industrial or commercial matters*. This criterion is not limited to honest practices existing in the country where protection against unfair competition is sought. The judicial or administrative authorities of such country will therefore also have to take into account honest practices established in international trade.

If a judicial or administrative authority of the country where protection is sought finds that an act complained of is contrary to honest practices in industrial or commercial matters, it will be obliged to hold such act to be an act of unfair competition and to apply the sanctions and remedies provided by its national law. A wide variety of acts may correspond to the above criterion.

(d) Paragraph (3) of the Article under consideration gives examples of acts which are particularly to be regarded as acts of unfair competition and must therefore be prohibited. This provision again contains common legislation for all countries of the Union and must either be accepted as part of their domestic legislation or be directly applied by their judicial or administrative authorities. The enumeration of examples given of acts of unfair competition is not limitative and constitutes only a minimum.

(e) The first example given of acts which must be regarded as acts of unfair competition relates to all acts of such a nature as to create *confusion* by any means whatever with the *establishment*, the *goods*, or the *industrial* or *commercial activities*, of a *competitor*. Such confusion can be created by the use of identical or similar trademarks or trade names and will then frequently be prohibited by special legislation concerning those subjects. If this is not the case, acts creating confusion by those means must be prohibited as acts of unfair competition. This is also true for other means by which similar confusion can be created, such as the form of packages, titles of publicity, references to the seat or other particulars of an enterprise, etc. It is immaterial whether those acts committed in good faith, although good faith may have an influence on the sanctions to be applied.

(f) The second example of acts which must be regarded as acts of unfair competition relates to *false allegations* in the *course of trade* of such a nature as to *discredit* the *establishment*, the *goods*, or the *industrial* or *commercial activities*, of a *competitor*. The mere fact of discrediting a competitor by untrue allegations which would discredit his business, goods or services, even without injurious intention on the part of the person making the allegations, is sufficient for the application of this provision. It has been left to the domestic legislation or case law of each country to decide whether, and under what circumstances, discrediting allegations which are not strictly *untrue* may also constitute acts of unfair competition.

(g) The third example of acts of unfair competition concerns *misleading allegations* but, this time, not particularly regarding the goods of a competitor—such allegations being generally covered by the preceding item—but concerning the *goods of the person who makes the allegations*. The provision under examination applies to all *indications* or *allegations* the use of which, *in the course of trade*, is liable to *mislead the public* as to the *nature*, the *manufacturing process*, the *characteristics*, the *suitability* for their *purpose*, or the *quantity*, of the goods concerned. It does not relate to similar indications or allegations as to the *origin* or *source* of the goods or the *identity of the producer*, his *establishment* or his *industrial or commercial activities*. As to such acts, in so far as they are not covered by Article 10 of the Convention, national legislations or case law will determine whether they are acts contrary to honest practices in industrial or commercial matters and for that reason must be deemed to be acts of unfair competition.

Notes and Questions

1. G.M.C. Bodenhauser was the unofficial reporter for the Paris Convention Revision in the late 1960's. His commentary serves as an unofficial "legislative history" for the Convention. Does the commentary on Article 10bis identify the nature of the rights sought to be protected against "unfair competition"? Does it answer the questions posed above?

2. *Property Right or Competition Privilege.* Assuming that trade secrets qualify for protection under Article 10bis, what is the basis for such protection? Are trade secrets a branch of unfair competition law whose scope of protection is directly related to the "fairness" of the restraint against unfettered (and unregulated) competition? If so, then the owner of such trade secret has no "property" right to its use. Such use could then be broadly regulated in accordance only with a society's view of what is required to encourage competition?

By contrast, if trade secrets qualify as "property" then by definition a government's ability to regulate such property (or, more precisely, to refuse to regulate such property by permitting its uncontrolled use by others) becomes more problematic. Does Article 10bis require treatment of trade secrets as a "property" right? Does it prohibit such treatment? *See, e.g.,* Elissa Safer, *Protecting Trade Secrets in a World Without Borders,* 27 Colo. Lawyer 67 (April 1998); Robert L. Tucker, *Industrial Espionage as Unfair Competition,* 28 U. of Toledo L. Rev. 245 (1998); Damon L. Boyd, *Trade Secret Doctrines of the NAFTA Countries: The Sources of Law, The Remedies Available, and Suggestions for Improvement,* 14 Ariz. J. of Comp. & Int'l L. 879 (1997).

B. WHITHER INTELLECTUAL PROPERTY?

The Paris and Berne Conventions represented landmark developments in global efforts to establish intellectual property treaty regimes. Although each significantly advanced the goal of international protection, they also left significant gaps in protection, patents, trademarks, and trade secrets suffered from definitional gaps, and a failure to define clearly the minimum rights that IP owners could rely on internationally. Copyrights, fared better but suffered from the absence of global consensus over the application of Berne terminology to new technological advances, including satellite broadcasts and the new digital technology. All recognized forms of intellectual property suffered from inconsistent enforcement standards. Indeed the problem of global piracy, fueled in part by the absence of sanctions for countries who failed to enforce IP laws in accordance with treaty obligations, began to appear as an issue in international *trade* negotiations in the 1970's. The increased importance of technology as an item of trade, the failure of other for a—such as

WIPO—to provide workable solutions to international IP conflicts, and the growing gap between alleged and actual compliance with Berne and Paris Convention treaty obligations contributed to the series of events that became "THE SOLUTION" to the problem—the Agreement on Trade Related Aspects of Intellectual Property Rights.

Part V

A TRIP THROUGH TRIPS

The adoption, in April 1994, by over 118 countries of the Agreement on Trade Related Aspects of Intellectual Property Rights ranks as one of the most significant developments in international intellectual property law of the Twentieth Century. Indeed, there are many that rank TRIPS as *the* most important development. There is no question that the post-TRIPS world is a different place. TRIPS provides a forum for continuing international attention to the issues of IPR. For the first time in the history of international intellectual property relations, TRIPS (administered by the WTO) has provided potentially powerful international sanctioning tools for assuring compliance with TRIPS obligations. It has codified as an international standard, adoption of the rule of law for intellectual property legal regimes. It has served to fill many of the gaps in definition that previous multinational regimes left vacant. And last, but by no means its least important achievement, TRIPS has established a minimum enforcement norm that *requires* countries to provide minimum procedural safeguards to assure enforceability of the minimum rights required under the treaty. These enforcement provisions, combined with the sanctioning power of the World Trade Organization (WTO), for treaty violation, promise to re-work the face of international intellectual property law.

Despite these noteworthy achievements, TRIPS did not resolve all disputes regarding the nature of intellectual property. The effect of digitation on copyright, the protection of data, and the recognition of commutarian rights in selected works of indigenous cultures are among a few of the issues which remained unresolved at the time TRIPS was finally signed.

Chapter Seventeen

THE PHILOSOPHY OF TRIPS

A. TRIPS—GAP FILLER, GREAT LEAP FORWARD, OR JUST ANOTHER SET OF PROBLEMS?

COPYRIGHT AND THE URUGUAY ROUND AGREEMENTS: A NEW ERA OF PROTECTION OR AN ILLUSORY PROMISE?
Doris Estelle Long, AIPLA Q.J. 531 (1994).

II. A SHORT HISTORY OF THE URUGUAY ROUND NEGOTIATIONS

Article XX of the GATT specifically permits measures "necessary to secure compliance with laws or regulations including those relating to the protection of patents, trademarks, and copyrights and the prevention of deceptive practices." Despite this early recognition that the failure to protect [intellectual property] adequately might have an impact on trade, until the Ministerial Declaration of September 20, 1986 ("September 1986 Declaration" or "Declaration"), GATT had played only a small role in the development of international [*IP*] protection norms. In the September 1986 Declaration, which officially launched the Uruguay Round of the Multilateral Trade Negotiations, the Ministers identified "trade related aspects of intellectual property rights, including trade in counterfeit good" as one of the subjects for negotiation. The disputes that led to the inclusion of TRIPS as a formal GATT negotiating subject for the Uruguay Round foreshadowed the problems that would bedevil subsequent negotiations.

A. *Uruguay Round Preparatory Work: A Preview Of Future Problems.*

Interest by certain developed countries in using GATT as a forum to address intellectual property issues arose primarily as a result of the perceived inability of existing international conventions to resolve the global trade problems posed by an explosion in international trafficking of counterfeit products can be directly attributed to, inter alia, the advent of new technology which made such counterfeiting cheaper and, therefore, more economically feasible, and the absence of an effective international mechanism for requiring other nations to prohibit the

357

manufacture, importation, or sale of such counterfeit goods. Although such counterfeit and pirated goods could, and often did, include copyrighted works, most early efforts against such illicit traffic focused on the need to prohibit the trafficking in counterfeit trademarked goods. Over time, however, efforts to utilize GATT to prohibit trademark counterfeiting expanded to include copyright under the umbrella of rights for which a GATT solution to infringement was sought. The perceived adverse economic impact from this illicit international traffic led the United States and other developed countries to conclude that the absence of a workable international trademark protection mechanism could and did have a direct distorting impact on trade.

During the Tokyo Round, the United States spearheaded an unsuccessful effort to negotiate an anti-counterfeiting code prohibiting the importation of counterfeit trademarked products. Although no agreement was reached prior to the end of the Tokyo Round, the negotiations set the stage for renewed efforts during the next round to use GATT to combat international trademark counterfeiting. In 1982, after meeting to establish an agenda for topics to be addressed after the Tokyo Round, the United States submitted a formal proposal advocating further negotiations regarding the adoption of a model anti-counterfeiting code under GATT auspices. The negative reaction of the developing nations to this relatively limited proposal presaged later conflicts regarding the propriety of utilizing GATT to address copyright protection issues. In particular, Brazil and India (who later spearheaded much of the developing countries' opposition to TRIPS) decried any attempt to include the protection of intangible intellectual property rights under GATT.

This early challenge to GATT jurisdiction for intellectual property matters was never wholly defeated or effectively resolved prior to the start of the Uruguay Round. In fact, when the United States tabled a proposal with the Preparatory Committee seeking to include all intellectual property rights (including copyright) within GATT negotiations, the debate between the developed and developing countries regarding the jurisdictional scope of GATT gained renewed vigor. The developing countries considered the inclusion of copyright protection among the issues proposed for inclusion in the Uruguay Round particularly inappropriate given the intangible nature of the rights sought to be protected. The developing countries contended that GATT's jurisdiction was limited solely to the trade impact of tangible goods, and insisted that the World Intellectual Property Organization ("WPO") had exclusive jurisdiction over issues regarding substantive intellectual property rights. Formal negotiations failed to resolve the conflict. Eventually, a proposal by the Swiss and Columbian representatives, which represented the views of only forty delegates, served as the basis for the September 1986 Declaration formally launching the TRIPS negotiations. Given the lack of uniformity regarding even the desirability of including intellectual property rights as a GATT topic, the issuance of the September 1986 Declaration only served as the opening volley in lengthy, divisive debates regarding GATT's proper role in regulating intellectual property.

B. The Ministerial Declaration: The Formal Debate Begins

intellectual property rights' as a negotiating topic "[I] order to ensure that measures and procedures to enforce intellectual property rights do not themselves become barriers to legitimate trade." The Declaration emphasized that the purpose of the negotiations was to "clarify GATT provisions and elaborate as appropriate new rules and disciplines" to reduce any "distortions and impediments to international trade." Such negotiations were intended to "develop a multilateral framework of principles, rules and disciplines dealing with international trade in counterfeit goods, taking into account work already undertaken in the GATT." Reflecting the failure to resolve the earlier-expressed concerns of the developing countries regarding the role which GATT initiatives should play in the area, the September 1986 Declaration stated that all negotiations regarding trade related aspects of intellectual property law were to be "without prejudice to other complementary initiatives that may be taken in WIPO and elsewhere to deal with these matters." The Negotiating Plan for TRIPS, established January 28, 1987, exhibited the continuing debate regarding the propriety of GATT jurisdiction.

The first formal proposal for achieving the negotiating ends under the Negotiating Plan was submitted by the United States on October 19, 1987, and reflected the U.S. view that intellectual property rights protected under GATT should include more than protection against trademark counterfeiting. While not abandoning the issue of protection against trademark counterfeiting nor under GATT auspices, the U.S. proposal sought the establishment of agreed-upon minimum substantive ms under GATT for the protection of all types of intellectual property, including copyright. The United States believed that such norms would serve as an effective deterrent to trade distortions caused by the infringement of intellectual property rights, and proposed that such norms be based on existing international conventions. In order to assist nations in harmonizing their national intellectual property laws with such agreed-upon international standards, the United States further proposed that parties to the agreement provide technical assistance to such countries.

The initial U.S. proposal received relatively little support. By the end of 1989, proposals had been submitted by seventeen nations and negotiating groups, including the Nordic States, Canada, Switzerland, Australia, Austria, New Zealand, Hong Kong, The Republic of Korea, Brazil, Peru, India, the European Community, Thailand, Mexico, Japan, and Bangladesh. The proposals were as varied as the interest of the proposing parties. However, the major disagreements among the various participants primarily concerned two issues: the jurisdictional role of GATT in the development of international intellectual property norms and procedures and the impact of such norms and procedures on the ability of developing countries to compete effectively in the world market. These fundamental disputes existed at the beginning of the Uruguay Round and formed the backdrop against which all subsequent TRIPS negotiations occurred. The compromises achieved in resolving these disputes are largely responsible for the concerns examined in this Article regarding the effectiveness of the TRIPS Agreement. In order to appreciate fully the decisions reached during the Uruguay Round, it is necessary to understand the broad economic, political and philosophical concerns underlying this debate.

C. The Jurisdictional Debate—GATT Or WIPO?

As noted above, from the initial preparatory work prior to the September 1986 Declaration commencing the Uruguay Round, many developing countries, including Brazil and India, hotly contested the ability or propriety of GATT to establish substantive norms in the area of intellectual property protection. The position of these developing countries was that if there was any need for the development of international norms in, for example, the copyright area, WIPO was the proper forum. Part of the reluctance to use GATT as a forum for addressing the desirability of new or additional international standards for intellectual property protection derived from the perception of many of these countries that GATT was primarily a forum for the "have" nations. Thus, many developing countries were concerned that their needs would not be given sufficient consideration in the GATT arena. Furthermore, to the extent that international norms might be required, these countries believed that the Berne Convention, with its emphasis on national treatment, had already dealt with the issue and that any changes which might be required should be dealt with only by WIPO, which had responsibility for overseeing the Convention. As an East German representative indicated in support for a statement by Cuba on behalf of the "Group of 77" challenging the use of GATT to address intellectual property issues: The strong international links between economy, science, technology and culture do not exclude other organizations or agreements in their activities to be concerned with the problems of implementing intellectual property rights However, for legal certainty and comprehensiveness, the competence of WIPO auspices. While developing countries saw WIPO as a generally hospitable forum for their concerns, many developed countries considered it to be indifferent to their needs at best and hostile at worst, in view of renewed efforts by some developing countries to use WIPO to lessen the level of protection established under the Berne Convention. The developed countries perceived GATT as providing a forum where an international consensus could be reached regarding the scope of protection for works not covered by the Berne Convention—including software and computer databases—outside the potentially politicized open meetings required by WIPO. Finally, developed countries sought to rectify a perceived lack of adequate enforcement mechanisms under the Berne Convention.

Although Article 33 of the Berne Convention provides that disputes can be brought before the International Court of Justice at the time of the Uruguay Round negotiations not one dispute had been brought in over forty-five years. Because WIPO had no other enforcement procedures for assuring that a member's laws complied with Berne's agreed-upon minimums, the developed countries sought to establish an enforcement mechanism under GATT which would force full compliance by all member countries. Much of the debate regarding GATT versus WIPO jurisdiction was largely resolved by 1987, when WIPO was granted observer status in GATT negotiations on TRIPS. Debates regarding the balance to be struck between Berne Convention and non-Berne Convention issues of copyright protection, however, continued to be infected by this underlying jurisdictional debate.

Notes and Questions

1.   The General Agreement on Trade and Tariffs (GATT) was strictly a trade agreement, dealing with such issues as border tariffs and non-tariff barriers to trade. Initial focus on trade aspects of intellectual property during the latter stages of the Tokyo Round and the early aspects of the Uruguay Round focused solely on the issue of counterfeit and pirated *goods* (as opposed to *rights*). Subsequent negotiations resulted in a broader view of what qualifies as a *trade related* aspect of intellectual property rights.

2.   As you review the substantive standards established under TRIPS, ask yourself whether these standards are limited to issues of intellectual property as a trade item or whether TRIPS goes beyond this potentially narrow focus.

B.   HAS TRIPS ESTABLISHED A STRICTLY PRIVATE RIGHTS REGIME?

TRIPS
PREAMBLE (EXCERPTED)

Recognizing that intellectual property rights are private rights;

Recognizing the underlying public policy objectives of national systems for the protection of intellectual property, including developmental and technological objectives;

Recognizing also the special needs of the least-developed country Members in respect of maximum flexibility in the domestic implementation of laws and regulations in order to enable them to create a sound and viable technological base;

Hereby agree as follows: * * *

THE TRIPS AGREEMENT: IMPERIALISTIC, OUTDATED, AND OVERPROTECTIVE
Marcia A. Hamilton, 29 Vand. J. Transnat'l L. 613 (1996).

The WTO/GATT Agreement involving Trade–Related Aspects of Intellectual Property Rights (Agreement or TRIPS) is a lot more than its moniker reveals. Far from being limited to trade relations, correcting the international balance of trade, or lowering customs trade barriers, TRIPS attempts to remake international copyright law in the image of Western copyright law. If TRIPS is successful across the breathtaking sweep of signatory countries, it will be one of the most effective vehicles of Western imperialism in history. Moreover, the Agreement will have achieved this goal under the heading "trade-related," which makes it appear as though it is simply business. To understand TRIPS, it is important to embrace an interdisciplinary approach, to widen the copyright lens to include culture, politics, and human rights. Despite its broad sweep and its unstated aspirations, TRIPS arrives on the scene already outdated. TRIPS reached fruition at the same time that the on-line era became irrevocable. Yet it makes no concession, not even a nod, to the fact that a significant portion of the international intellectual property market will soon be conducted on-line. This silence could transform a troubling treaty into a weapon of extortion by the publishing industry, which has already succeeded in crafting TRIPS as a blunt instrument for copyright protection. While the corporeal universe has permitted Western societies to receive and copy large numbers of copyrighted works for free—through libraries, commercial browsing, personal lending, and copyright doctrines such as the first sale doctrine, fair use, and the idea/expression dichotomy, the on-line era raises the possibility that the publishing industry can track every minuscule use of a work and thereby turn the free use zone into a new opportunity for profit. TRIPS' silence threatens to make it both outdated and overprotective.

II.   COPYRIGHT NORMS AND FREEDOM IMPERIALISM

The cultural underpinnings of existing copyright law require a reevaluation to assess their appropriateness and usefulness in building a universal copyright scheme. The subject of the AALS Symposium, the TRIPS Agreement, is the first giant step toward globalization of intellectual property rights. Globalization introduces a new level of complexity into copyright law and creates a need for more creative ways of understanding and justifying rights protected by copyright. The United States is no longer negotiating primarily with European countries that share a similar moral and religious heritage and economic understandings. Now, the United States is also dealing with the Eastern countries as well as with the world's developing countries. Therefore, focus on copyright must extend beyond markets and trade issues to interdisciplinary understandings. Cultural views on human effort and reward are particularly important. With 117 signatory countries from around the world, TRIPS is ambitious to say the least. It is also old-fashioned, Western-style imperialism. One commentator describes the TRIPS Agreement as "impolite." This description is too polite. Despite its innocuous name, TRIPS does not merely further trade relations between these many countries. Rather, TRIPS imposes a Western intellectual property system across-the-board—which is to say that it imposes presuppositions about human value, effort, and reward. And it has appeared without serious public debate over its latent political mission. It is not surprising that there might be uneven compliance across the world even after so many countries signed the TRIPS Agreement. Intellectual property is nothing more than a socially-recognized, but imaginary, set of fences and gates. People must believe in it for it to be effective. To believe in the Western version of copyright rights, one must first accept some version of the following canon:

1.   Individualism: Individual human creative effort is valuable.

2.   Reward: Society should single out original products of expression by granting their owners proprietary rights over them. Reward is determined according to the qualities of the product; mere effort is not sufficient to deserve such reward.

3.   Commodification: Products should be capable of being disassociated from their producers and sent through the stream of commerce. In other words, product creators need not be the product's owners or distributors. Indeed, in the interest of achieving the greatest distribution of copyrighted goods worldwide, creators probably should not be the primary distributors.

By strongly supporting the TRIPS Agreement, the United State—which is to say U.S. publishers—is exporting and imposing Protestant-based capitalism. The United States is also endorsing the imposition of a revolution-tending construct of the person. Individualism, as captured in the Western intellectual property system, is the *sine qua non* for a society to recognize and honor personal liberty. TIPS is nothing less than freedom imperialism. Whether such imperialism is a good idea involves difficult questions of political, sociological, and legal import that are better served by later contemplation.

Notes and Questions

1.   Assume your client is a world-renown botanist and explorer. While cruising down the Amazon, she discovers a plant that is unknown to all but a small tribe of indigenous people living in that section of the rain-forest. The plant is known by these people for its ability to cure a wasting disease which the explorer recognizes as the local term for cancer. The botanist takes the plant back with her, reduces the seeds to their essential elements through a well-known scientific process, and discovers an active ingredient which, after substantial clinical testing, is proven to be an effective agent to retard the growth of certain cancerous tumors.

Under a private rights regime, would the explorer be entitled to a patent for discovering the plant? (*See* Article 29 of TRIPS for the definition of a patentable invention.)

2.   Would the local tribe be entitled to a patent for their cure using this plant?

3.   Would the explorer be entitled to a patent for her distillation of the active ingredient?

4.   Assume the explorer has been granted a patent for the distilled product. Because of the difficulty of cultivating the plant, the company that has purchased the patent rights decides to harvest the plants from the rainforest. The company enters into a written agreement with the tribal head (enforceable under domestic laws), agreeing to pay the head $1,000 for the perpetual right to harvest the plants in the portion of the jungle owned, controlled or inhabited by the tribe. The drug is so effective that the

company earns back its investment in full in the first year of production. Have the indigenous people contributed "knowledge" for which compensation should be provided, beyond the $1,000 paid for the harvest right for the plants? Does the purported private rights scheme of TRIPS require or even permit the protection of indigenous knowledge or culture?

5.   As you examine the rights regime established under TRIPS, consider the extent to which TRIPS has provided guidance in resolving the issue of compensation for the knowledge and artistry of indigenous peoples. *See* Part XII for more in-depth discussion of these issues.

C.   DOES TRIPS MERELY INCORPORATE PRIOR STANDARDS OR DOES IT ESTABLISH NEW ONES?

Read the following Articles from TRIPS from the Supplement: 2, 9.

Notes and Questions

1.   Does incorporation of, for example, Berne Convention standards, mean that copyright protection under Berne and TRIPS are identical? For example, consider the question of fair use. Compare Article 10 of the Berne Convention and Article 13 of TRIPS below:

Berne: Article 10 (1)

It shall be permissible to make quotations from a work which has already been lawfully made available to the public, provided, that their making is compatible with fair practice, and their extent does not exceed that justified by the purpose, including quotations from newspaper articles and periodicals in the form of press summaries.

TRIPS

Article 13

Members shall confine limitations or exceptions to exclusive rights to certain special cases which do not conflict with a normal exploitation of the work and do not unreasonably prejudice the legitimate interests of the right holder.

2.   Is being "compatible with fair practice" and not exceeding uses "justified by their purpose" the same as not "conflicting with a normal exploitation of the work" and not "unreasonably prejudicing the legitimate interests of the right holder"? Do the different words contained in the two treaties evidence an intent to establish a different standard for determining the acceptable limits of a fair use exception? If they do establish different standards, which one appears facially tougher to meet than the other?

3.   As examined more fully in Chapter Thirty–Three, many countries provide that use of copyrighted works for news reporting privileges is considered fair. The ABC Broadcasting Company has filmed, in its totality, the 3 minute performance by a hot new performance artist. The performance consists of the artist walking onto the stage, pouring

chocolate over her body and announcing "I am One with the Rage." ABC broadcasts the entire performance in its daily "Newsmakers" slot. When the artist sues for infringement of her copyrighted choreography, ABC defends on the basis of domestic law that states "Any use of a copyrighted work for purposes of legitimate news reporting shall qualify as a fair use for which no compensation is owed to the copyright owner." Does this statute violate Article 10(1) of the Berne Convention? Is the rebroadcast of the entire performance in accordance with "fair practices."? *See Zacchini v. Scripps–Howard Broadcasting Co.*, 433 U.S. 562 (1977).

4. What are the "legitimate interests" of the performance artist? Does the rebroadcast of her performance prejudice those rights, or does it help promote her act?

5. What if, instead of merely showing the performance, ABC showed clips interspersed with comments by an art critic on her performance? Does this use meet the non-interference with "normal exploitation" requirement of TRIPS?

6. To what extent may countries consider other international standards in interpreting their obligations under TRIPS? For example, in deciding what is "normal exploitation," should courts consider rights granted owners under other international treaties, such as for example, NAFTA (North American Free Trade Agreement) or the WIPO Copyright Treaty? *See, e.g.*, Neil W. Netanel, *The Next Round: The Impact of the WIPO Copyright Treaty on TRIPS Dispute Settlement*, 37 Va. J. Int'l L. 441 (1998).

INDIA DRUG PATENT CONTROVERSY

The Report of the Panel on India—Patent Protection for Pharmaceutical
And Agricultural Chemical Products, WT/DS50/R (September 5, 1997)

[Although India was a signatory to TRIPS, it had not enacted legislation designed to grant patents to pharmaceuticals. The United States filed a complaint with the WTO alleging, inter alia, that India's failure to craft legislation designed to permit patent protection for qualifying pharmaceuticals violated India's duties under TRIPS. India defended, in part, on the grounds that Article 65 granted it a five year grace period in which to develop complying legislation. The United States disagreed, contending that Article 65 required legislation to be in place so that it would be in compliance immediately upon the termination of the grace period.]

Interpretation of the TRIPS Agreement

Before examining specific measures in dispute, we first deal with a general interpretative issue, namely standards applicable to interpretation of the TRIPS Agreement. In the first instance, Article 3.2 of the DSU directs panels to clarify the provisions of the covered agreements, including the TRIPS Agreement, "in accordance with customary rules of interpretation of public international law." As a number of recent panel reports and Appellate Body reports have pointed out, customary rules of interpretation of public international law are embodied in the text of the 1969 Vienna Convention on the Law of Treaties ("Vienna Convention"). Article 31 (1) of the Vienna Convention provides:

> "A treaty shall be interpreted in good faith accordance with the ordinary meaning to be given to the terms of the treaty in their context and in the light of its object and purpose."

Accordingly, the TRIPS Agreement must be interpreted in good faith in light of (I) the ordinary meaning of its terms, (ii) the context and (iii) is object and purpose. In our view, good faith interpretation requires the protection of legitimate expectations derived from the protection of intellectual property rights provided for in the Agreement. A similar view has also been taken in the Underwear panel report:

> "The relevant provisions [of the Agreement of Textiles and Clothing] have to be interpreted in good faith. Based upon the wording, the context and the overall purpose of the Agreement, exporting Members can legitimately expect that market access and investments made would not be frustrated by importing Members taking improper recourse to such action."[1]

Second, we must bear in mind that the TRIPS Agreement, the entire text of which was newly negotiated in the Uruguay Round and occupies a relatively self-contained, *sui generis* status in the WTO Agreement, nevertheless is an integral part of the WTO system, which itself builds upon the experience over nearly half a century under the General Agreement on Tariffs and Trade 1947 ("GATT 1947"). Indeed, Article XVI:1 of the WTO Agreement provides:

> "Except as otherwise provided under this Agreement or the Multilateral Trade Agreements, the WTO shall be guided by the decisions, procedures and customary practices followed by the CONTRACTING PARTIES to GATT 1947 and the bodies established in the framework of GATT 1947."

Since the TRIPS Agreement is one of the Multilateral Trade Agreements, we must be guided by the jurisprudence established under GATT 1947 in interpreting the provisions of the TRIPS Agreement unless there is a contrary provision. As the Appellate Body indicated in the *Japan-Alcoholic Beverages* case, adopted panel reports "create legitimate expectations among WTO Members, and, therefore, should be taken into account where they are relevant to any dispute."[2] Indeed, in light of the fact that the TRIPS Agreement was negotiated as a part of the overall balance of concessions in the Uruguay Round, it would be inappropriate not to apply the same principles in interpreting the TRIPS Agreement as

---

1. Panel Report on "United States—restrictions on Imports of Cotton and Manmade Fibre Underwear," Adopted on 25 February 1997, Wt/ds24/r, Para. 7.20

2. Appellate Body Report on "Japan—taxes on Alcoholic Beverages," Adopted on 1 November 1996, Wt/ds8/ab/r, Wt/ds10/ab/r, Wt/ds13/ab/r, Page 14

those applicable to the interpretation of other parts of the WTO Agreement.

The protection of legitimate expectations of Members regarding the conditions of competition is a well-established GATT principle, which derives in part from Article XXIII, the basic dispute settlement provisions of GATT (and the WTO).[3] Regarding Article III of GATT, the panel on *Italian Agricultural Machinery* stated that "the intent of the drafters was to provide equal conditions of competition once goods had been cleared through customs."[4] This principle was later elaborated by the *Superfund* panel, which stated that "[t]he general prohibition of quantitative restrictions under Article XI and the national treatment obligation of Article III have the same rationale, namely to protect expectations of the contracting parties as to the competitive relationship between their products and those of the other contracting parties as to the competitive relationship between their products and those of the other contracting parties."[5] The panel on *Section 337*, which dealt with issues involving protection of intellectual property at the border, also reached similar conclusions.[6]

The protection of legitimate expectations is central to creating security and predictability in the multilateral trading system. In this connection, we note that disciplines formed under GATT 1947 (so-called GATT *acquis*) were primarily directed at the treatment of the goods of other countries, while rules under the TRIPS Agreement mainly deal with the treatment of nationals of other WTO Members. While this calls for the concept of the protection of legitimate expectations to apply in the TRIPS areas to the competitive relationship between a Member's own nationals and those of other Members (rather than between domestically produced goods and the goods of other Members, as in the goods area), it does not in our view make inapplicable the underlying principle. The Preamble to the TRIPS Agreement, which recognizes the need for new rules and disciplines concerning "the applicability of the basic principles of GATT 1994," provides a useful context in this regard.

In conclusion, we find that, when interpreting the test of the TRIPS Agreement, the legitimate expectations of WTO Members concerning the TRIPS Agreement must be taken into account, as well as standards of interpretation developed in past panel reports in the GATT framework, in particular those laying down the principle of the protection of conditions of competition flowing from multilateral trade agreements.

3. We note in this regard that Article 64 of the trips agreement (on dispute settlement) provides for the application of Article XXIII of GATT1994, as elaborated by the DSU, to the settlement of disputes under the trips agreement.

4. Panel report on "Italian Discrimination Against Imported Agricultural Machinery," Adopted on 23 October 1958, Bisd 7S/60, Para. 12–13

5. Panel report on "United States–taxes on Petroleum and Certain Imported Substances," Adopted on 17 June 1987, Bisd 34S/136, Para. 5.2.2

6. Panel report on "United States–section 337 of the Tariff Act of 1930," Adopted on 7 November 1989, Bisd 36S/345, Para.5.13

Notes and Questions

1. In determining what were the "legitimate expectations" of the contracting parties to be protected, whose expectations should be considered? Those of the developed countries? Does it matter?

2. Does the Report preclude the consideration of other multinational treaties in deciding the scope of obligations imposed under TRIPS? Could a country rely on the meaning of "fair use" under the WIPO Copyright Treaty in deciding the scope of normal exploitation allowed under Article 13 of TRIPS?

3. The WIPO Copyright Treaty was adopted December 1996, after TRIPS. Article 10 of the WIPO Treaty permits limitations and exceptions to the granted rights "in certain special cases that do not conflict with a normal exploitation of the work and do not unreasonably prejudice the legitimate interests of the author" (Article 10(1)). The Treaty goes on to confine limitations or exceptions "when applying the Berne Convention ... to rights provided for therein to certain special cases that do not conflict with a normal exploitation of the work and do not unreasonably prejudice the legitimate interests of the author." (Article 10(2)) Despite the different fora for TRIPS and the WIPO Copyright Treaty, international standards for protection exceptions, such as fair use, appear to be coalescing. By contrast, the treatment of moral rights may be diverging. Under Article 6bis of the Berne Convention, moral rights protection must be granted authors of copyrighted works. Article 9 of TRIPS, however, expressly excludes incorporation of Article 6bis. Can a signatory to both treaties deny moral rights protection for a cinematographic work without violating its treaty obligations? Would colorization of a black and white film by the copyright owner, without the director's consent, violate the author's moral rights under Berne? Under TRIPS? For an excellent discussion of the moral rights dilemma, *see generally* D'Amato & Long, Chapter 6, INTERNATIONAL INTELLECTUAL PROPERTY LAW ANTHOLOGY (Anderson Publishing 1995).

Chapter Eighteen

COPYRIGHT UNDER TRIPS

A. DID TRIPS BRING COPYRIGHT PROTECTION UNDER BERNE UP TO DATE?

Read the following Articles from TRIPS from the Supplement: 9, 10.

Notes and Questions

1. Do computer programs fit within previous Berne Convention definitions of a copyright protectable work? (*See* Article 2) Is there something unique about computer programs that require different treatment than that generally provided works under copyright law? *See, e.g.*, Pamela Samuelson, et al, *A Manifesto Concerning the Legal Protection of Computer Programs*, 94 Colum. L. Rev. 2308 (1994). Can a signatory to TRIPS provide for *sui generis* protection without violating its treaty obligations? Can it provide *sui generis* protection as an additional form of protection?

2. *Computer Databases.* The issue regarding the inclusion of computer databases among the enumerated defined categories of the Berne Convention was one of the more bitter North–North debates during the Uruguay Round. What was the compromise reached between the competing parties? Under Article 10, must computer databases be protected under copyright law, or are only some databases to be so protected? If so, which ones?

3. Does TRIPS define the test to be applied to determine whether a database contains the required "intellectual creativity"? Is "intellectual creativity" the same as originality or does it require some degree of novelty or artistry?

4. For an in-depth discussion of database protection, see Chapter Thirty–Eight.

Review the *Telephone Directory* case (Feist) in Chapter One.

Notes and Questions

1. *Sweat of the Brow.* Would the white pages at issue qualify as containing "intellectual creativity," under Article 10 of TRIPS?

2. Are all compilations and factual databases excluded from copyright protection under the court's analysis in the *Telephone Directory* case?

3. Done and Overton have spent over $1 million creating a database composed of the e-mail addresses for every company with corporate head-quarters located in the United States which make over $1,000,000 annual gross income. To create the database, Done and Overton have used a competitor's corporate database to obtain the names of all companies which earn over $1,000,000 annual gross income. It then searched on line to obtain Internet addresses for these companies and verified the addresses. The database was sold on a searchable computer disc, with the companies listed in alphabetical order. Done and Overton expect to spend another $100,000 updating and correcting the database. Is this database subject to copyright protection under the *Telephone Directory* case?

4. What advice would you give Done and Overton about protecting their database internationally?

THE EC DATABASE DIRECTIVE

DIRECTIVE 96/9/EC OF THE EUROPEAN PARLIAMENT AND OF THE COUNCIL OF 11 MARCH 1996 ON THE LEGAL PROTECTION OF DATABASES

THE EUROPEAN PARLIAMENT AND THE COUNCIL OF THE EUROPEAN UNION,

(1) Whereas databases are at present not sufficiently protected in all Member States by existing legislation; whereas such protection, where it exists, has different attributes;

(2) Whereas such differences in the legal protection of databases offered by the legislation of the Member States have direct negative effects on the functioning of the internal market as regards databases and in particular on the freedom of natural and legal persons to provide on-line database goods and services on the basis of harmonized legal arrangements throughout the Community; whereas such differences could well become more pronounced as Member States introduce new legislation in this field, which is now taking on an increasingly international dimension;

(4) Whereas copyright protection for databases exists in varying forms in the Member States according to legislation or case-law, and whereas, if differences in legislation in the scope and conditions of protection remain between the Member States, such unharmonized intellectual property rights can have the effect of preventing the free movement of goods or services within the Community;

(5) Whereas copyright remains an appropriate form of exclusive right for authors who have created databases;

(11) Whereas there is at present a very great imbalance in the level of investment in the database sector both as between the Member States

and between the Community and the world's largest database-producing third countries;

(12) Whereas such an investment in modern information storage and processing systems will not take place within the Community unless a stable and uniform legal protection regime is introduced for the protection of the rights of makers of databases;

(13) Whereas this Directive protects collections, sometimes called "compilations" of works, data or other materials which are arranged, stored and accessed by means which include electronic, electromagnetic or electro-optical processes or analogous processes;

(18) Whereas this Directive is without prejudice to the freedom of authors to decide whether, or in what manner, they will allow their works to be included in a database, in particular whether or not the authorization given is exclusive; whereas the protection of databases by the sui generis right is without prejudice to existing rights over their contents, and whereas in particular where an author or the holder of a related right permits some of his works or subject matter to be included in a database pursuant to a non-exclusive agreement, a third party may make use of those works or subject matter subject to the required consent of the author or of the holder of the related right without the sui generis right of the maker of the database being invoked to prevent him doing so, on condition that those works or subject matter are neither extracted from the database nor re-utilized on the basis thereof;

(29) Whereas the arrangements applicable to databases created by employees are left to the discretion of the Member States; whereas, therefore nothing in this Directive prevents Member States from stipulating in their legislation that where a database is created by an employee in the execution of his duties or following the instructions given by his employer, the employer exclusively shall be entitled to exercise all economic rights in the database so created, unless otherwise provided by contract;

(42) Whereas the special right to prevent unauthorized extraction and/or re-utilization relates to acts by the user which go beyond his legitimate rights and thereby harm the investment; whereas the right to prohibit extraction and/or re-utilization of all or a substantial part of the contents relates not only to the manufacture of a parasitical competing product but also to any user who, through his acts, causes significant detriment, evaluated qualitatively or quantitatively, to the investment;

(44) Whereas, when on-screen display of the contents of a database necessitates the permanent or temporary transfer of all or a substantial part of such contents to another medium, that act should be subject to authorization by the rightholder;

(45) Whereas the right to prevent unauthorized extraction and/or re-utilization does not in any way constitute an extension of copyright protection to mere facts or data;

HAVE ADOPTED THIS DIRECTIVE:

Article 1

Scope

1. This Directive concerns the legal protection of databases in any form.

2. For the purposes of this Directive, "database" shall mean a collection of independent works, data or other materials arranged in a systematic or methodical way and individually accessible by electronic or other means.

3. Protection under this Directive shall not apply to computer programs used in the making or operation of databases accessible by electronic means.

Article 3

Object of protection

1. In accordance with this Directive, databases which, by reason of the selection or arrangement of their contents, constitute the author's own intellectual creation shall be protected as such by copyright. No other criteria shall be applied to determine their eligibility for that protection.

2. The copyright protection of databases provided for by this Directive shall not extend to their contents and shall be without prejudice to any rights subsisting in those contents themselves.

Article 4

Database authorship

1. The author of a database shall be the natural person or group of natural persons who created the base or, where the legislation of the Member States so permits, the legal person designated as the rightholder by that legislation.

2. Where collective works are recognized by the legislation of a Member State, the economic rights shall be owned by the person holding the copyright.

3. In respect of a database created by a group of natural persons jointly, the exclusive rights shall be owned jointly.

Article 5

Restricted acts

In respect of the expression of the database which is protectable by copyright, the author of a database shall have the exclusive right to carry out or to authorize:

(a) temporary or permanent reproduction by any means and in any form, in whole or in part;

(b) translation, adaptation, arrangement and any other alteration;

(c) any form of distribution to the public of the database or of copies thereof. The first sale in the Community of a copy of the database by the rightholder or with his consent shall exhaust the right to control resale of that copy within the Community;

(d) any communication, display or performance to the public;

(e) any reproduction, distribution, communication, display or performance to the public of the results of the acts referred to in (b).

Article 6

Exceptions to restricted acts

1.   The performance by the lawful user of a database or of a copy thereof of any of the acts listed in Article 5 which is necessary for the purposes of access to the contents of the databases and normal use of the contents by the lawful user shall not require the authorization of the author of the database. Where the lawful user is authorized to use only part of the database, this provision shall apply only to that part.

2.   Member States shall have the option of providing for limitations on the rights set out in Article 5 in the following cases:

(a) in the case of reproduction for private purposes of a non-electronic database;

(b) where there is use for the sole purpose of illustration for teaching or scientific research, as long as the source is indicated and to the extent justified by the non-commercial purpose to be achieved;

(c) where there is use for the purposes of public security or for the purposes of an administrative or judicial procedure;

(d) where other exceptions to copyright which are traditionally authorized under national law are involved, without prejudice to points (a), (b) and (c).

3.   In accordance with the Berne Convention for the protection of Literary and Artistic Works, this Article may not be interpreted in such a way as to allow its application to be used in a manner which unreasonably prejudices the rightholder's legitimate interests or conflicts with normal exploitation of the database.

Article 7

Object of protection

1.   Member States shall provide for a right for the maker of a database which shows that there has been qualitatively and/or quantitatively a substantial investment in either the obtaining, verification or presentation of the contents to prevent extraction and/or re-utilization of the whole or of a substantial part, evaluated qualitatively and/or quantitatively, of the contents of that database.

2.   For the purposes of this Chapter:

(a) "extraction" shall mean the permanent or temporary transfer of all or a substantial part of the contents of a database to another medium by any means or in any form;

(b) "re-utilization" shall mean any form of making available to the public all or a substantial part of the contents of a database by the distribution of copies, by renting, by on-line or other forms of transmission. The first sale of a copy of a database within the Community by the rightholder or with his consent shall exhaust the right to control resale of that copy within the Community;

Public lending is not an act of extraction or re-utilization.

3.   The right referred to in paragraph 1 may be transferred, assigned or granted under contractual license.

4.   The right provided for in paragraph 1 shall apply irrespective of the eligibility of that database for protection by copyright or by other rights. Moreover, it shall apply irrespective of eligibility of the contents of that database for protection by copyright or by other rights. Protection of databases under the right provided for in paragraph 1 shall be without prejudice to rights existing in respect of their contents.

5.   The repeated and systematic extraction and/or re-utilization of insubstantial parts of the contents of the database implying acts which conflict with a normal exploitation of that database or which unreasonably prejudice the legitimate interests of the maker of the database shall not be permitted.

Article 8

Rights and obligations of lawful users

1.   The maker of a database which is made available to the public in whatever manner may not prevent a lawful user of the database from extracting and/or re-utilizing insubstantial parts of its contents, evaluated qualitatively and/or quantitatively, for any purposes whatsoever. Where the lawful user is authorized to extract and/or re-utilize only part of the database, this paragraph shall apply only to that part.

2.   A lawful user of a database which is made available to the public in whatever manner may not perform acts which conflict with normal exploitation of the database or unreasonably prejudice the legitimate interests of the maker of the database.

3.   A lawful user of a database which is made available to the public in any manner may not cause prejudice to the holder of a copyright or related right in respect of the works or subject matter contained in the database.

Article 9

Exceptions to the *sui generis* right

Member States may stipulate that lawful users of a database which is made available to the public in whatever manner may, without the authorization of its maker, extract or re-utilize a substantial part of its contents:

(a) in the case of extraction for private purposes of the contents of a non-electronic database;

(b) in the case of extraction for the purposes of illustration for teaching or scientific research, as long as the source is indicated and to the extent justified by the non-commercial purpose to be achieved;

(c) in the case of extraction and/or re-utilization for the purposes of public security or an administrative or judicial procedure.

Article 10

Term of protection

1. The right provided for in Article 7 shall run from the date of completion of the making of the database. It shall expire fifteen years from the first of January of the year following the date of completion.

2. In the case of a database which is made available to the public in whatever manner before expiry of the period provided for in paragraph 1, the term of protection by that right shall expire fifteen years from the first of January of the year following the date when the database was first made available to the public.

3. Any substantial change, evaluated qualitatively or quantitatively, to the contents of a database, including any substantial change resulting from the accumulation of successive additions, deletions or alterations, which would result in the database being considered to be a substantial new investment, evaluated qualitatively or quantitatively, shall qualify the database resulting from that investment for its own term of protection.

Article 11

Beneficiaries of protection under the *sui generis* right

1. The right provided for in Article 7 shall apply to database whose makers or rightholders are nationals of a Member State or who have their habitual residence in the territory of the Community.

2. Paragraph 1 shall also apply to companies and firms formed in accordance with the law of a Member State and having their registered office, central administration or principal place of business within the Community; however, where such a company or firm has only its registered office in the territory of the Community, its operations must be genuinely linked on an ongoing basis with the economy of a Member State.

3. Agreements extending the right provided for in Article 7 to databases made in third countries and falling outside the provisions of paragraphs 1 and 2 shall be concluded by the Council acting on a proposal from the Commission. The term of any protection extended to

databases by virtue of that procedure shall not exceed that available pursuant to Article 10.

Article 12

Remedies

Member States shall provide appropriate remedies in respect of infringements of the rights provided for in this Directive.

Notes and Questions

1. *Sui generis protection.* The *Telephone Directory (Feist)* case is often cited as rejecting the "sweat of the brow" doctrine for protection. Does the Database Directive similarly reject labor (without creativity) as a basis for protecting products of the mind?

2. Would the database in the *Telephone Directory* case be protectable under the Database Directive if it were owned by a European company?

3. Under Article 7, how much money must a company spend to qualify as making a "substantial investment"? Is there a quantitative limit or is it a qualitative one? For example, is it sufficient if a company spends only $1,000 to create a database but the database itself is highly commercially successful because it fills a long felt need for information?

4. What is the philosophical basis for extending intellectual property type protection to unoriginal collections of facts? Is it to reward labor? To encourage creativity?

5. The Database Directive had a profound effect on the international community. After its adoption, The World Intellectual Property Organization circulated a Draft Database Directive modeled on the EC Directive. Like the EC Directive, the Draft Treaty granted database owners the right to control the use of the material comprising its database. For a further examination of the Draft Treaty, see Chapter Thirty–Eight.

6. Done and Overton, owner of a protected database of email addresses for U.S. corporations earning $1,000,000 + annual gross income, discover that an end user has been using their database to create an on-line directory of U.S. corporations earning $5,000,000 in gross profits. Done and Overton estimate that the end user has copied approximately 40% of their database. Does the end user's use of Done and Overton's database without authorization violate the Directive?

7. What if the end user was a reporter for a financial magazine that accessed the database to get information for the articles she writes. The reporter estimates that she has used the database approximately 60 times in the last three months and has probably reviewed about 30% of the entries. Does this use violate the Directive?

8. *Clinical Data.* Drug companies must create and assemble *clinical data* in order to obtain necessary governmental approvals to market their medical products and devices. Such clinical data consists of factual reports regarding effectiveness, bioequivalency, and side effects, in both lab and human testing. Does such data qualify as a protectable compilation under Article 10 of TRIPS? Does it qualify as protectable under the EC Directive?

Should such information be protected internationally? (*See* TRIPS Article 39 discussed below)

9. For a further discussion of international efforts to protect databases or other factual compilations, see Chapter Thirty–Eight.

Read the following Articles from TRIPS from the Supplement: 11, 12, 13.

Notes and Questions

1. Rental rights were one of the most hardly fought battles during the Uruguay Round Negotiations. Many European and Asian countries have compensatory licensing schemes which permit distribution of royalties charged for compulsory licensing rights only to authors whose countries provide for reciprocal rights. The United States was concerned over the loss of control over rental income by its copyright owners and fought hard for Article 11. Does Article 11 preclude compulsory licensing schemes for rentals for all copyrighted works?

2. How would you demonstrate that a video rental rights program was "materially impairing the exclusive right of reproduction" of the copyright owner? What evidence would you introduce? Would it make a difference if many people in the country in question had access to video cassette recorders? What if there were a technological solution that would preclude unauthorized copying but the copyright owner did not use it because of cost concerns? Would such evidence preclude a finding of material impairment?

3. The last sentence of Article 11 regarding the need for computer programs to be "the essential object of the rental" was added to exclude from coverage the rental of cars, videos, stereos and other items which include computer chips. Section 109 of the 1976 U.S. Copyright Act similarly excludes from the general right of purchasers of legitimate copyrighted works to rent such works without the copyright owner's permission sound recordings and computer programs "embodied in a machine or product and which cannot be copied during the ordinary operation or use of the machine or product." 17 U.S.C. § 109 (b)(1)(B). Section 109 also excludes computer programs which are "embodied in or used in conjunction with a limited purpose computer that is designed for playing video games and may be designed for other purposes." *Id.*

4. For a further discussion of fair use under TRIPS and other compulsory licensing issues, see Chapter Thirty–Three.

Chapter Nineteen

PATENTS UNDER TRIPS

A. DID PATENT PROTECTION UNDER TRIPS FILL ALL THE GAPS IN TREATMENT?

Read the following Articles from TRIPS from the Supplement: 27, 29.

Notes and Questions

1. As you may recall, in examining the Paris Convention, we discovered that the Convention did not clearly define what was meant by the term "patent" or more specifically, what types of inventions are required to be granted patent protection internationally. Has TRIPS solved some of the loophole problems that you identified for the Paris Convention? For example, could a country which is a signatory to TRIPS refuse to grant patent protection to pharmaceuticals without violating treaty obligations?

2. India has long objected to the protection of pharmaceutical products by patent. Part of its objection is based on economics. Quite simply, if patent protection is granted, then the cost of manufacture of protected products will increase because the patent owner must be paid a royalty for the use of her patent. India signed the TRIPS Agreement, but refused to extend patent protection to pharmaceutical products on national interest grounds. Can India continue to refuse to protect pharmaceuticals and not be in violation of its treaty obligations under TRIPS? *See, e.g.*, Martin J. Adelman, *Prospects And Limits Of The Patent Provision In The Trips Agreement: The Case Of India.* 29 Vand. J. Transnat'l L. 507 (1996). For a discussion of the sanctioning mechanisms that may be brought to bear if India is found to be in violation of treaty obligations under TRIPS, see below.

3. Must a signatory country provide protection to a new surgical technique for conducting open heart bypass surgery? Is there some difference in nature between pharmaceutical products and surgical techniques that would permit or require their different treatment internationally?

4. Footnote 5 of TRIPS provides "For the purposes of this Article, the terms 'inventive step' and 'capable of industrial application' may be deemed for a member to be synonymous with the terms 'non-obvious' and 'useful' respectively." Does TRIPS identify what the test for "non-obviousness" should be on an international level?

THE BIOTECH CONTROVERSY
OF SEEDS AND SHAMANS: THE APPROPRIATION OF THE SCIENTIFIC AND TECHNICAL KNOWLEDGE OF INDIGENOUS AND LOCAL COMMUNITIES

Naomi Roht–Arriaza 17 Mich. J. Int'l L. 919 (1996).

I. THE SCIENTIFIC AND TECHNICAL KNOWLEDGE OF INDIGENOUS AND LOCAL COMMUNITIES

Indigenous and local communities have a long history of using plants for almost all needs, including food, shelter, clothing, and medicine. Common remedies used today were often first developed by healers prior to contract with industrial societies. Yet, although many of today's drugs and cosmetics originated from the stewardship and knowledge of indigenous and local communities, that knowledge remains unrecognized and unvalued until appropriated from those communities by Western corporations or institutions. To cite a few examples:

The well-known cure for malaria, quinine, comes from the bark of the Peruvian cinchona tree. Andean indigenous groups used quinine as a cure for fevers, supposedly learning of the bark's powers while observing feverish jaguars eating it.

The rosy periwinkle plant, unique to Madagascar, has been found to contain properties that combat certain cancers. The anti-cancer drugs vincristine and vinblastine have been developed from the periwinkle, resulting in $100 million in annual sales for Eli Lilly and virtually nothing for Madagascar.

For thousands of years, indigenous farmers in India have used the leaves and seeds of the neem tree as a natural insecticide. Juice from the tree has also been used to prevent scabies and other skin disorders. Villagers still scrub their teeth with neem twigs.

Several patents have now been granted in the United States and other industrialized countries for products based on the neem plant. The U.S.-based multinational corporation, W.R. Grace, which received a patent for an insecticide based on the active ingredient in neem, has stated that it does not plan to compensate anyone in India for providing the knowledge that underlies its neem-based product. Corporate Vice–President Martin B. Sherwin has dismissed the Indian people's discovery and development of the plant's uses as "folk medicine."

The University of California and Lucky Biotech, a Japanese corporation, were recently granted a patent for the sweetening proteins naturally derived from two African plants, katempfe and the serendipity berry. These plants have long been used by African peoples for their sweetening properties. Thaumatin, the substance that makes katempfe sweet, is 2,000 times sweeter than sugar yet calorie-free. Although any transgenic plant containing the derived sweetening proteins would be covered by the patent, no arrangements have been made to return part of the benefits to the African communities.

A barley gene that confers resistance to the yellow-dwarf virus is the product of centuries of breeding and cultivation by Ethiopian farmers. U.S. farmers and scientists who patented this barley variety receive substantial profits from its current cultivation in the U.S., but the Ethiopian farming communities that originally developed the variety receive nothing.

In 1990, scientist Sally Fox of California received a U.S. patent for colored cotton. This patent is economically significant because multinational corporations, such as Levi Strauss and Esprit, want environmentally friendly materials like naturally colored cotton for their clothes. Unfortunately, credit for the "invention" of colored cotton does not go to its true developers. The seed for Sally Fox's patented cotton came from a United States Department of Agriculture collection obtained by Dr. Gus Hyer during his travels in Latin America. Colored cotton resulted from centuries of breeding and cultivation by Latin American indigenous groups. Even now, 15,000 indigenous farmers grow colored cotton, and over 50,000 indigenous women still spin and weave it. Fox's patent directs all profits to her, not these indigenous inventors and cultivators.

II.   Mechanisms of Appropriation: What Counts as Valuable Knowledge?

Perhaps the most prevalent and insidious form of appropriation of indigenous knowledge and resources has been the construction of conceptual and legal categories of valuable knowledge and resources that systematically exclude the knowledge and resources of local communities, farmers, and indigenous peoples. This construction of exclusion takes several forms. First, Western science characterizes certain natural materials that indigenous and local communities have cared for, preserved, improved, and developed as mere "wild" species or, at the most, as "primitive species" (commonly known as "landraces.)" Formal, scientific systems of innovation and research have therefore, at least until recently, denigrated and denied the value of indigenous and subsistence farmers' informal systems of knowledge-transmission and innovation. Second, while the products of formal knowledge systems have been protected as "property," those of informal, traditional systems have been tagged the freely available "common heritage of humanity." In particular, patentability under current intellectual property law is systematically biased against the innovations and knowledge of indigenous and farmers' communities. Finally, the products of indigenous and local communities' knowledge have been detached from their ecological and sociocultural base through removal and preservation in Northern-dominated ex situ collections and projects, while the knowledge underlying the products attains merely anthropological interest. Thus Western science and industry treat the living knowledge of existing indigenous and local communities as "quaint," "quackery," or "quits,"

More importantly, to a large extent these tangible resources exist in their current form thanks to the applied knowledge of indigenous and local communities, a knowledge uniquely gained from conserving and often improving resources for specific purposes. For these communities, the differences between intellectual, cultural, and material property are artificial, are part of the communities' heritage: "Heritage" is everything that belongs to the distinct identity of a people and which is theirs to share, if they wish, with other peoples. It includes all of those things which international law regards as the creative production of human thought and craftsmanship, such as songs, stories, scientific knowledge and artworks. It also includes inheritances from the past and from nature, such as human remains, the natural features of the landscape, and naturally-occurring species of plants and animals with which a people has long been connected. Furthermore, for indigenous communities, their heritage does not consist of mere economic rights over things but of a bundle of relationships with the animals, plants, and places involved. One of the main mechanisms of appropriation has been precisely the separation of what is considered knowledge from what is considered a physical resource. Ending appropriation requires viewing them together.

Western science has been largely unable to recognize or value the role of indigenous and local farming communities because the innovators themselves have been invisible, the forms of transmission of knowledge incomprehensible, and the purpose of the work has differed from that of much formal science. Thus the indigenous farmer's work of testing, comparing, and breeding "folk" varieties of seed is usually not recognized as "plant breeding" by Western researchers. Performed in fields over the centuries rather than in laboratories over a few years, the indigenous farmer's plant breeding is necessarily highly specific to the local environment. That the resulting farmers' varieties or landraces are known as "primitive" is perhaps the clearest expression of the cultural biases inherent in the distinctions of Western science.

Western researchers often fail to appreciate innovative indigenous farming practices because the innovators or "plant breeders" are peasant women. Women in many parts of the world play key roles in seed selection, vegetative propagation, and livestock management-all central to preserving and fomenting diversity. Often, their work of breeding and management takes place in kitchen gardens for domestic consumption rather than in outlying fields worked for income. This work may or may not be recognized within the local communities, where women often lack visibility and power, but it is clearly unrecognized by Western-style farmers, extension agents, and researchers visiting from afar.

Western researchers also fail to recognize the role of indigenous and traditional farmers in plant breeding and selection because the farmers share their knowledge in ways incomprehensible to Western science. Indigenous and traditional peoples transmit much knowledge about the qualities and uses of plants, animals, or soils for medicinal purposes may also be dismissed because the corresponding maladies or diseases are described in ways that integrate the physical, mental, and spiritual and so are alien to Western researchers. Such knowledge is easily dismissed as folklore, superstition, old wives' tales, or the quaint remnants of dying cultures. Similarly, questions asked by Western researchers may elicit confusing or meaningless responses because they do not correspond to the classification of phenomena used by the indigenous or local people. Such responses are therefore discounted and the respondents classified as backwards and ignorant.

Moreover, Western researchers may also overlook traditional farmers' role in plant breeding and selection because many of the useful genetic characteristics of plants are found not in "domesticated" varieties but in those related varieties that are not cultivated. Western researchers label these species, which can be found in the environs of indigenous and traditional farming communities, wild or semi-wild. Western researchers consider these species to have ended up in underdeveloped areas by luck or natural bounty. Yet it is now becoming clear that almost all the different types of species to be found in and around traditional rural communities have been nurtured or developed by local people. Far from being "wild," these partner or "associated" species are often an integrated part of farming or forest farming systems.

Many indigenous and local communities draw a significant share of their resources from these partner species and make little distinction between wild and cultivated foods. Similarly, many indigenous and traditional communities have conserved and protected wild plants known to have medicinal qualities without formally cultivating them. These communities also recognized the value of other wild plants ad microorganisms and protected wild plants known to have medicinal qualities without formally cultivating them. These communities also recognized the value of other wild plants and microorganisms and protected them indirectly, through preservation and improvement of the local ecosystems of which they form a part. Yet, because these plants are not cultivated in ways that are obvious to visiting Western researchers, they are deemed to exist independently of human intervention. As such, they are free for the taking.

Much of the recent debate about appropriation of the scientific and technical knowledge of indigenous and local peoples has centered on the role of intellectual property rights in recognizing formal, but not informal, innovation. Such rights, generally expressed through patents, have historically served to provide financial rewards to those appropriating indigenous knowledge and its products, while denying such rewards to the communities whose knowledge is appropriated.

The aim of the patent system is to encourage innovation by providing an inventor with a time-limited monopoly over her invention. In exchange, she must fully and publicly describe it and thereby make it available to others. Patents may be granted for products or processes. They are generally granted on a national level, and each State may usually decide what to exclude from patenting. Under the recently revised General Agreement on Tariffs and Trade (GATT 1994), however, all members of the World Trade Organization (WTO) must provide "effective" protection of intellectual property rights, including those in living matter.

1. Novelty or Newness

Patentable inventions must be novel or new. Most indigenous and local knowledge, however, is collective and is passed down from generation to generation. It builds on prior knowledge in an organic, accretive way that makes it difficult to single out a certain individual inventor or inventive origin in time. In those cases where it is not widely held, as in the case of medicinal knowledge held by shamans, the accretion and transmission of knowledge from generation to generation would invalidate it on novelty grounds.

The novelty requirement means that inventors must seek a patent at the earliest possible moment; if they do not, they cannot later "catch up." Those whose inventions are now known cannot retroactively apply for patent protection. Indigenous and traditional communities that had no practical opportunity to participate in the development of world intellectual property systems and that are only now beginning to debate and to demand a place in those systems, albeit with much disagreement about that place, are frozen out.

2. Nonobviousness or the Inventive Step

The TRIPS agreement requires that patentable items "involve an inventive step," while U.S. law expresses the same requirement through the term, "nonobvious". The test to determine if an invention is obvious is whether a person skilled in the field would, with all of the prior art available, see the inventions as obvious. If the inventor merely examines all prior knowledge and follows the next logical step to solve a problem, then she has not overcome the nonobviousness requirement. In cases dealing with chemical compounds, when the prior art suggests that a compound might display certain properties, applicants for a patent must rebut a presumption of obviousness. One method is to show that the compound displays "unexpectedly improved properties." Since plant-based genetic materials are simply biochemical compounds, the purification or isolation of the genetic material must be accompanied by proof that the transformed product demonstrates "unexpected properties." Clearly, proving the "unexpected properties" of many indigenous and informal innovations would be tremendously difficult; the prior knowledge of a plant's medicinal effects, for instance, would categorize any unprocessed, indigenous use of the plant as obvious. Indigenous and local communities, moreover, possess neither the means nor any inherent reason to "improve" compounds in order to satisfy the nonobviousness requirement.

Notes and Questions

1. Does TRIPS allow a definition of non-obviousness that would permit protection of the native discoveries identified above? To qualify as non-obvious, under U.S. law an invention must not be obvious to an ordinary person skilled in the art. *See also* 35 U.S.C. § 102. *See generally Graham v. John Deere Co.*, 383 U.S. 1 (1966). Would native knowledge qualify as non-obvious?

2. In *Hodosh v. Block Drug Co.*, 786 F.2d 1136 (Fed.Cir.1986) a 2,000 year old Chinese text which discussed medicinal uses of Saltpeter was cited against a U.S. invention using potassium nitrate in toothpaste. Similarly, the grant of a U.S. patent for the wound healing properties of turmeric's was denied after the Indian Council of Scientific and Industrial Research challenged the grant on the basis of the long-standing knowledge of turmeric healing properties by certain indigenous peoples in India.

3. In 1998, the U.S. Patent Office granted a new method of doing business to a company called Priceline. The patent covered the method of conducting a "name your own price" auction for airline tickets sold through the Internet. Is this method of conducting electronic commerce sufficiently different from other forms of electronic commerce so that it qualifies as a non-obvious invention? Is there a difference between technical knowledge regarding the Internet and tribal knowledge regarding the healing properties of turmeric so that one deserves international protection and the other does not?

4. Chinese Patent law defines the test for non-obviousness (which it calls "inventiveness") as "compared with the technology existing before the date of filing the invention has prominent substantive features and represents a notable progress." (Article 22)

5. Russian Patent law considers an invention "to have an inventive level, if it is evident to a specialist that an invention does not come from the technological level." (Article 4) The statute defines the "level of technology" as including "any information which had become universally available before the invention priority date." (Article 4)

6. UK Patent law requires an "inventive step" which occurs "if it is not obvious to a person skilled in the art, having regard to any matter which forms part of the state of the art." (Patents Act of 1977, § 3). "The state of the art" is defined by statute as "comprising all matter (whether a product, a process, information about either, or anything else) which has at any time before the priority date of that invention been made available to the public (whether in the United Kingdom or elsewhere) by written or oral description, by use or in any other way."

7. Do any of these definitions of inventiveness or non-obviousness permit the consideration of indigenous knowledge to eliminate obviousness? Do they *require* such elimination?

B. DID TRIPS CLARIFY THE RIGHTS EXERCISED BY PATENT OWNERS INTERNATIONALLY?

THE NEW ZEALAND LEUKEMIA PATENT CASE

WELCOME FOUNDATION

In the Court of Appeal of New Zealand, 1982.
[1983] Fsr 593.

COOKE, J.

The case raises the fundamental question whether a patent may be granted in New Zealand for a method of treatment of disease or illness in human beings. The Wellcome Foundation claims primarily a patent for a method of treating or preventing meningeal leukaemia or neoplasms in the brain of man or other mammals by the use of known compounds (such as methodichlorophen and ethodichlorophen, known respectively as metorprine and etoprine) which have been used in the past for treating malaria. The discovery or invention claimed is essentially that they are notably capable of crossing the blood-brain barrier and concentrating within the brain.

The Assistant Commissioner declined to proceed with the application on the ground that the claims were not patentable, as in his view they did not relate to a manner of new manufacture as defined in the Patents Act 1953, § 2, as interpreted over the years.

We gave the Commissioner leave to appeal at this stage. One of our reasons was that in *The Upjohn Company (Robert's) Application* [1977] RPC 94 the Court of Appeal in England dealing with a case at a similar stage held it to be well established that a method of treatment of a human ailment with a known substance is not capable of being an invention under the same statute law as still applies in New Zealand. They accordingly held that the Comptroller of Patents was correct in this respect to refuse the patent there applied for. Delivering the judgment of the court, Russell, LJ concluded by saying that if the law was to be changed, it must be for the legislature.

In giving leave to appeal we said that the result would not necessarily be the same in New Zealand. Notwithstanding the respect which we always have for English authority, particularly of course at appellate level, we have certainly not approached the far-reaching arguments that we have heard in the frame of mind that we would automatically follow the *Upjohn* case.

The Statute of Monopolies of 1623 declared monopolies void, but section 6 provided:

"VI. Provided also, and be it declared and enacted, that any declaration before mentioned shall not extend to any letters patents and grants of privilege for the term of 14 years or under, hereafter to be made, of the sole working or making of any manner of new manufactures within this Realm, to the true and first inventor and inventors of such manufactures, which others at the time of making such letters patents and grants shall not use, so as also they be not contrary to the law or mischievous to the State, by raising prices of commodities at home or hurt of trade, or generally inconvenient . . ."

That is still the basis of New Zealand patent law because it is incorporated by reference in the definition of "invention" in the Patents Act 1953. "Manner of new manufacture" is an expression having no ordinary meaning today. It is commonplace that the scope of the idea can only be ascertained by seeing how the law has evolved in the decided cases, and that the trend has been to broaden the scope gradually. But it is also clear that until the decision of Davison CJ no court in the Commonwealth had treated it as extending to a method of treatment of human illness or disease. As recognized in the *Upjohn* case it had been understood in the United Kingdom for more than 60 years that such methods were not patentable, although there was apparently no House of Lords or Court of Appeal authority to that effect. Courts in England and Australia have indicated doubts as to whether the limitation is logical, but the decision now under appeal is the first to take the step of repudiating it.

There was a time when it was thought that if a process was to be patentable it had to have relation in some way, directly or indirectly, to the production of a vendible article or marketable commodity. That was one ground on which two members of the Court of Appeal in *Maeder v. "Ronda" Ladies' Hairdressing Salon* [1943] NZLR 122 at 176–177, 202–203, Myers, CJ. and Johnston, J. held against a claim to a process for permanent waving of hair growing on the human head. However, that limitation, unless construed very liberally indeed, is out of line with subsequent case law in England. And also in Australia.

I respectfully think a deep-seated sense that the art of the physician or the surgeon in alleviating human suffering does not belong to the area of economic endeavour or trade and commerce.

The practical aspect of that idea is well put by an Israeli judge, Kahn J in *The Wellcome Foundation Ltd v. Plantex Ltd* [1974] RPC 514 at 539:

"Notwithstanding the important reasons for doing away with any distinction between a therapeutic treatment of the human body and other patentable subject matter. I am not ready to agree with my honourable colleague, Witkon J, that we are called upon now to construe the Patents Ordinance in this sense. There exist grave reasons against the creation of a monopoly by this sense. There exists grave reasons against the creation of a monopoly by a patent in respect of medical treatment. We are confronted here with saving human life or alleviating human suffering and one should take great care lest a restriction on the freedom of action of those who treat, caused by patents, should affect human life or health. This also was the view of the Israeli legislature who laid down in section 7 of the Patents Act 1967 that no patent shall be granted for methods of therapeutic treatment of the human body.

Of course on both humanitarian and economic grounds the search for medical advance is to be encouraged. The award of limited monopolies is a standard way of helping to compensate for the expense of research. And I respectfully agree that the discovery of new properties or uses of known pharmaceutical drugs does merit encouragement. In a broad sense, however, the discovery of a new drug is different from the discovery of new uses for an old one. It is not absurd that the law should reflect this distinction.

Ultimately therefore resolution of the present issue is a balancing exercise. Kahn J explicitly approached the Israeli case already cited in that way. That case was concerned with Israeli law as it stood before their 1967 Act. After the passage in his judgment already quoted he explained how section 7 of that Act introduced a restriction common to the patent laws of various European countries: an express provision that no patent shall be granted for methods of therapeutic treatment of the human body, which, however, is not to prevent a grant for an invention whereby a known substance not before used in human therapy is so used for the first time:

> "It appears to me that the approach which underlies the proposal for a European Patent ... is a fair compromise between opposing interests which are, on the one hand, the need to encourage research in connection with drug manufacture and, on the other hand, the need not unduly to restrict the activities of those who engage in the therapy of humans. I believe that we shall not do injustice to the spirit of our era and to recent developments in the world as regards the policy in respect of the grant of patents, if we do not abolish outright the prohibition by which no patents are granted on methods of therapeutic treatment of the human body, but rather preserve this prohibition in a restricted scope even in respect of matters to which the Patents Ordinance still applies. It is therefore my conclusion that an invention by which a known substance, a known composition or a known device is used for the therapeutic treatment of the human body is patentable. However, where a substance, composition or device has already been used for the therapeutic treatment of the human body or where it is obvious on the basis of existing knowledge that they are capable of so being used for the therapeutic treatment of humans, no patent is to be granted to an inventor who discovers a new and until then unknown use for medical treatment. For example, it is possible to grant a patent to an inventor who discovers that a known substance which had been used in the food industry and for which it was not known that it can serve for curing humans, is suitable for the treatment of intestinal diseases; against this, no patent will be granted to an inventor who

discovered that a medicine used for the treatment of the kidneys can also serve for the treatment of mental diseases."

In England the *Upjohn* case was decided in March 1975. It is conceivable that the Court of Appeal were not unmindful of the pendency of new legislation. In line with the European laws mentioned by Kahn J the effect in the United Kingdom of the Patents Act 1977, § 2(6) and 4(2) is that an invention comprising a method of treatment of the human or animal body by surgery of therapy or of diagnosis practised on the human body is not to be taken to be capable of industrial application and is therefore not patentable. There may, however, be a claim to a substance or composition or use in such methods. The fact that the substance or composition has been previously known or used does not prevent the invention from being taken to be new if the use of the substance or composition in any such method of treatment does not form part of the state of the art. This is said to allow claims of the type "compound X for use in the treatment of diabetes" provided that no prior use of or suggestion to use X as a pharmaceutical is known.

It is noteworthy too that, although Canadian patent legislation has its own distinctive history and differs in its details from that of England and New Zealand, the Supreme Court of Canada reached the result that the discovery that a known adhesive substance can be used for bonding human tissue does not give rise to a valid claim: *Tennessee Eastman Co. v. Commissioner of Patents* (1972) 33 DLR (3d) 459.

By contrast it appears from materials put before us by counsel for the respondent (for whose help, as always in these difficult patent cases, we express gratitude) that other views, rather more favourable to industrial enterprise, have been taken in the United States and (recently) the Federal Republic of Germany. A ruling American decision is still apparently *Ex parte Scherer*, 103 U.S.PQ 107, a majority decision of the U.S. Patent Office Board of Appeals in 1954 on a method of injecting fluids into the human body by a high pressure jet.

"Methods of diagnosis or treatment, including a regimen of drug therapy, are deemed statutory processes, even though one or more steps thereof are performed upon a human or other living organism. To be patentable the method must be new. Although the analgesic properties of aspirin have long been recognized, it is only recently that the effectiveness of aspirin in preventing heart attacks has been established. If the dosages of aspirin and the intervals of its administration to ward off a heart attack are the same as that for which aspirin has been taken as an analgesic, such is but the discovery of a heretofore unrecognized benefit which however meritorious would not be patentable as the method itself is old." [Rosenberg, Patent Law Fundamentals (1982)]

And the Federal Supreme Court of West Germany, overruling on this point the Federal Patent Court and the German Patent Office, appears to have held in the *Sitosterylglycoside* case, [1982] GRUR 548, that the surprising effectiveness in the treatment of an illness of a previously known active ingredient may ground a use claim to a patent, though not a composition claim.

The current variations in national patent laws bring out that this is the class of problems for which no one can say that any particular resolution is necessarily right. In all the circumstances I think, in agreement with the other members of the court, and with the measure of regret already mentioned, that we should resist any temptation to break new ground. If the practice of not granting patents for methods of treating human illness or disease's to be altered or modified, it is best left to Parliament.

McMULLIN, J.

The granting of patents in New Zealand is governed by the Patents Act 1953. Part of section 2(1) and all of section 51(1) of the Act are relevant. They provide:

"2. (1): "Invention" means any manner of new manufacture the subject of letters patent and grant of privilege within section 6 of the Statute of Monopolies and any new method or process of testing applicable to the improvement or control of manufacture, and includes an alleged invention.

51. (1): Without prejudice to the foregoing provisions of this Act, where a patent is in force in respect of:

(a) A substance capable of being used as food or medicine or in the production of food or medicine; or

(b) A process for producing such a substance as aforesaid; or

(c) Any invention capable of being used as or as part of a surgical or curative device, the Commissioner shall, on application made to him by any person interested, order the grant to the applicant of a licence under the patent on such terms as he thinks fit, unless it appears to him that there are good reasons for refusing the application."

There is much to be said for developing the law to allow of the grant of patents for methods of treatment of human illness by the putting of known compounds to new therapeutic uses. Human suffering may thereby be alleviated to the greater good of mankind. In the fields covered by this case research may be encouraged by the knowledge that what is discovered or invented will be protected from competition and assured of a reward. But there is another side to the picture. The grant of a patent is the grant of a monopoly. In recognition of this feature the patents legislation aims to balance the desirability of encouraging and protecting technological advances against the restrictions, impediments and even abuse which may result from monopolies. A shift in emphasis which favours one interest will probably be achieved only at the expense of the other. Whether, and to what extent, any significant innovative movement is justifiable is, I think, not a matter for the courts.

Patent law is a rather artificial, highly complex and somewhat refined subject. It involves scientific and commercial features outside everyday experience and the knowledge of the courts. Therefore, any major thrust should be left to Parliament.

In the United Kingdom it was thought necessary to establish a committee to examine the patent system and law in the light of the increasing need for international collaboration in patent matters and in particular of the United Kingdom Government's intention to ratify the Council of Europe Convention on Patent Laws. This last consideration is of no present relevance but it would be idle to ignore the international aspects of patents particularly when disease and its treatment have no national barriers.

For these reasons I think that on the present state of the law a patent should not be granted in the present case. Whether methods of treatment of the kind contemplated should be patentable should be left to the Legislature. I would therefore allow the appeal.

APPENDIX:

Extract from "The British Patent System—Report of the Committee to Examine the Patent System and Patent Law—Chairman MAL Banks Esq." (July 1970, Cmnd 4407).

The new use of known substances

237.   Broadly speaking, the present position is that, in most fields, the use of a known substance is not necessarily excluded from patentability provided it is a manufacturing use. The use of such substances in the agricultural field was not considered patentable before the Swift and NRDC cases, but patents have since been granted for such inventions. Their validity, however, remains doubtful in the absence of an authoritative decision by the Court. This doubt would be removed if, as we have proposed, it was made clear that agricultural processes would be considered as patentable.

238.   A process consisting of using a known compound for treating a human being medically has never been held to be patentable because the Courts have consistently expressed the opinion that a process for medical treatment of human beings is not a proper subject for a patent monopoly. It has been represented to us that lack of patent protection in this field has resulted in insufficient research and development effort being put into discovery whether chemical compounds used for the treatment of one disease could be effective in the treatment of a different one. Examples were given of drugs where this was found to be the case. The proposal that the present law should be changed in this respect made it clear that there would have to be adequate safeguards for medical staff and patients so that their actions would not constitute infringement of the patent. A claim would, however, lie against a supplier of the article with specific instruments for its use.

239.   Since new chemical compounds, processes for making such compounds and even known compounds presented in a different form are already patentable, the only type of invention which would be

patentable under the proposal would be a known compound in a known form which could be used against a disease for which it was not previously thought to be effective. The extension of patent protection in this way would result, in effect, in patents for the treatment of human beings, since a claim for such an invention would have to specify the condition against which the compound was effective and to include instructions for its use. This would not, in our view, be desirable.

240.   The majority of other countries do not grant patents for a new medical use of a known substance. An exception is France and it is sometimes said that the United States grants such patents. The position in the United States is, however, not altogether clear, but it appears that what can be done is to obtain patent protection for a new but structurally obvious substance on the basis of a new but not obvious use or property. We also have some doubt whether the grant of patents for new medical uses for known substances would accord with the requirement of the Strasbourg Convention that patents should be granted for inventions susceptible of "industrial application." We do not, therefore, recommend that processes for treating human beings with known substances should be added to the list of inclusions.

Notes and Questions

1.   Does Article 27 of TRIPS require protection of Wellcome's new treatment?

2.   *Reliance on Outside Authorities.* What decisions were discussed by the judges in the *New Zealand Leukemia Patent* case? What role did the decisions of other countries play in the court's decision? To what extent should courts consider international law in interpreting the scope of domestic intellectual property laws?

3.   Compare the courts' treatment of economic and moral issues in the *New Zealand Leukemia Patent* case and in the *Harvard Mouse* case in Chapter Eight. Do you agree with the decisions reached in these cases? Are there other "moral" issues that courts could consider in deciding to grant protection to new inventions? For example, assuming novelty and non-obviousness, could a country deny protection to a process for creating atomic energy on the grounds that such process could also be used to create weapons of mass destruction? Would such denial violate TRIPS?

Read the following Articles from TRIPS from the Supplement: 33,28,30.

Notes and Questions

1.   Does TRIPS establish a minimum term of protection for patent rights?

2.   In response to TRIPS, the U.S. revised its patent laws to grant patent holders a 20 year term of protection, beginning from the date of grant of the application. *See* 35 U.S. C. § 254. Is this provision in accordance with TRIPS requirements?

3. UK patent law provides for a 20 year patent term as of the date of application. Is this in accordance with TRIPS requirements?

4. If Company A applies for a patent for the same invention on the same day in both the U.S. and the UK, assuming the applications are granted, will the invention be subject to the same period of protection? As a matter of international protection standards, should countries be required to grant the identical term of protection to patented inventions? What are the benefits of such a system? What are its disadvantages?

5. Does TRIPS establish a minimum list of rights to be granted a patent owner, such as the right to control the manufacture, use or sale of a product containing or using the patented invention? Are these rights broader than the rights granted under the Paris Convention?

6. As you will discover later in this course, many countries require that a patented invention be practiced or "worked" in the granting country. Failure to do so may result in the inventor being required by law to grant a compulsory license to companies willing to work the invention. Is such "working" requirement permitted under TRIPS? Is the grant of a compulsory license to meet such working requirement permitted under TRIPS? Must the licensor under such a compulsory license pay a royalty to the patent owner under TRIPS standards, or can the compulsory license be royalty-free?

7. For a discussion of the multinational patent application and registration procedures, see Part VI.

Chapter Twenty

TRADEMARKS UNDER TRIPS

A. DID TRIPS FILL IN THE GAPS FOR TRADEMARK PROTECTION UNDER PARIS?

Read the following Article from TRIPS from the Supplement: 15.

THE FRENCH CELLOPHANE CASE

SOCIETE LA CELLOPHANE v. JEAN VILMAIN & CIE

Cour De Cassation, 1996.
[1967] FSR 538.

NOTE: CELLOPHANE is also a registered trade mark in the United Kingdom.

The Court:

1. From the findings of the judgment appealed against (Court of Nancy [1st Chamber] 12 June 1963) it emerges that La Societe la Cellophane is the owner of the trade mark CELLOPHANE by reason of an assignment to it in 1922 by La Societe Blanchisserie et Teinturerie de Thaon. The trade mark was originally registered on 25 March 1912 at the registry of the Epinal Commercial Court to cover "sheets of cellulose produced by regenerating and transforming viscose and all products made such sheet". La Societe La Cellophane intervened in the action brought by Jean Vilmain et Cie against Goasdoue, Le Moal et Cie in connection with the supply of bags of a cellulose material manufactured by La Societe La Cellulose de Conde, known as CELCOSA. La Societe La Cellophane sought to have a judgment of the Epinal Commercial Court of the 13 November 1960 reversed on the points which concerned its interests. This judgment held that the word CELLOPHANE is a generic term and that therefore Jean Vilmain et Cie had delivered goods in conformity with contract when it supplied Goasdoue, Le Moal et Cie with sheets of a cellulose material manufactured by La Societe La Cellulose de Conde (known as CELCOSA) and not by La Societe La Cellophane.

The first ground of appeal against the judgment of the court of Nancy is that the court found that the word CELLOPHANE was made up of the root "cello", referring to the substance's being derived from cellulose, and the suffix "phane" (from the greek "phanos") referring to its transparency, but nevertheless held that the word was an invented term with no descriptive force. It is objected that the court reached this conclusion on the grounds that the word was a new one, and was neither a generic term denoting the class of products to which the goods covered by the trade mark belong, nor an adjective which merely described the substance's appearance and composition. Therefore, says the appellant, in the first place the court of Nancy must have failed to draw the correct conclusions from its findings, and in fact contradicted itself in holding that the word CELLOPHANE which refers to the composition and transparency of the cellulose derivative, has no descriptive force. Secondly, they argue that even a new word can be descriptive if its elements merely refer to a product's main characteristics or chemical composition, though it may not be an adjective nor denote the class to which the product belongs. The court of Nancy is therefore clearly wrong, according to the appellant, in finding that the trade mark was not of a descriptive character for the sole reason that it was considering a new word, w which was not an adjective and did not denote the class of products to which CELLOPHANE belonged.

But in fact the court of Nancy, without contradicting itself in any way, analysed the etymological meanings of the root and suffix of CELLOPHANE which refer respectively to the substance's chemical composition and to one of its properties, and then went on to decide that their combination constituted a new word. After holding that this word is neither an adjective in the French language, nor a generic term for the products intended to be covered by the registration of the trade mark the court declared that the word is an invented term, and we find that it was correct in doing so. The appellant's first ground of appeal fails therefore.

2. The second ground of appeal is that the judgment appealed against found that the product in dispute could have been given no other name than CELLOPHANE in the ordinary way, but decided that the name CELLOPHANE was not a generic term. This it did on the grounds that an inventor or those claiming through him cannot be prevented from protecting the name he has given to a new product even after the expiry of the patents protecting its manufacture by registering it as a trade mark, and cannot be deprived of his rights by general use of the name by the public unless he has renounced them. The appellant argues, in the first place that when the name given to a patented product by the inventor becomes its only name as a result of common usage, it becomes the generic term for the product, even without the inventor's consent, and cannot be claimed exclusively as a trade mark once the patent has expired. Secondly, it is said that the court of Nancy, having decided that no generic name has been found since the invention of the product known as CELLOPHANE, other than the word CELLOPHANE itself,

could not hold without contradicting itself that the word is not the generic name for the product.

But, as appears from the judgment appealed against, it has not been established that sheets of regenerated cellulose were known to the public as CELLOPHANE before the registration of the trade mark. The court of Nancy held correctly that periodic renewal of the registration is sufficient to prove the intention of the person who registered the trade mark to preserve his rights in it, and that this is especially so where, as here, the company owning the trade mark has incorporated it into its firm name. The court could therefore conclude from these findings without any self contradiction that there is little significance in the fact that the inventor, (who was the agent of the registering company) used this word CELLOPHANE to describe the product protected by a patent which was not made public until over a year after the registration of the trade mark. Likewise the court was entitled to hold that it was irrelevant that no other ordinary name could have been used to describe the product. Finally the court was correct in holding that any use which may have been made of the term in current administrative and scientific language after registration of the trade mark cannot affect the rights of La Societe La Cellophane, which has taken every precaution to prevent wrongful use of it occurring in commerce and leading to the sort of confusion on which Jean Vilmain et Cie have relied. The second ground of appeal therefore fails.

For these reasons the court dismisses the appeal against the judgment of the court of Nancy of 12 June 1963.

DISPOSITION:

Appeal dismissed.

THE CANADIAN THERMOS CASE
ALADDIN INDUSTRIES v. CANADIAN THERMOS PRODUCTS LTD.

Exchequer Court of Canada, 1969.
57 C.P.R. 230, 1969 CPR Lexis 141.

KERR, J.

These proceedings were initiated by an originating notice of motion dated August 17, 1964, for the expungement of the following trade mark registrations:

No. 50/12223, dated September 12, 1907, THERMOS;

Newfoundland No. 264, dated January 8, 1908, THERMOS;

No. 245/52994, dated September 12, 1931, SUPER THERMOS, and

No. 118,050 dated May 13, 1960, THERMOS.

The applicant and the respondent company are competitors in the manufacture and sale of their products in Canada, principally vacuum-insulated bottles used to keep liquids and foods hot or cold or at the temperature they had when put in the bottle. The main feature of such a bottle is its "filler", a double-walled glass container from which the air between the walls has been evacuated. The fillers have protective casings, corks or closures of various kinds and other improvements. Its forerunner was Sir James Dewar's vacuum flask of about 1893. Terms used by the public and in the trade to describe the bottles include "thermos"; "thermos bottle"; "vacuum bottle"; "vacuumware", and "bouteille isolante". The applicant contends that "thermos" and "thermos bottle" are generic and descriptive terms in Canada for such bottles and are synonymous with "vacuum bottle".

(1) The applicant is a Canadian federal company [Aladdin Industries (Canada) Ltd.] with its head office at Toronto, Ontario. It deals in many wares including vacuum bottles.

(2) The Respondent, Canadian Thermos Products Limited, is a Canadian federal company with its head office at Scarborough, Ontario. It deals in many wares including vacuum bottles.

(3) The Respondent, Canadian Thermos Products Limited, is the registered owner of the word 'THERMOS' as a trade mark under the registrations above set forth.

(4) The said word 'THERMOS' as of the date hereof does not express or define any right of the Respondent, Canadian Thermos Products Limited, thereto, being generic and descriptive of vacuum bottles.

The particulars of the grounds upon which expungement of the trade marks is sought run to 49 pages. They are mainly as follows:

A. The word 'thermos' has been generic and descriptive in Canada of vacuum bottles since prior to the date of application for trade mark registration No. 50/12223, being already in the Oxford English Dictionary at that time.

B. The word 'thermos', whether used alone or with such words as 'bottle', 'jug', 'flask', 'jar' or 'bouteille', is both, in English and French, the name of the wares in connection with which it is used or is clearly descriptive or deceptively misdescriptive, both in English and French, of the character or quality of wares in association with which it is used, such character or quality being that such wares will keep liquids hot or cold for extended periods of time.

C. Vacuum bottles are generally known and have been generally known for the last sixty years in Canada by the name 'thermos'.

D. The word 'thermos' appears in the following dictionaries and encyclopedias. Throughout the Particulars, libraries where each work may be found are indicated. [And then the names of 19.8 dictionaries and encyclopedias are given, and in these and other particulars giving the names of books, the libraries in Canada where the books are found are also named.]

E.   The word 'thermos' has been used generically and descriptively by the following authors of scientific books and textbooks, all of which are well known and used in Canada, and considered authoritative: [134 Books].

F.   References to the word 'thermos' as generic and descriptive are to be found in the following works by philologists widely read and considered authoritative in Canada: [5 Books].

G.   The word 'thermos' has been used generically and descriptively in the following works which are well known in Canada and considered authoritative in their respective fields: [15 Books].

H.   The word 'thermos' has been used generically and descriptively by the following authors in the works hereinafter set forth, all of which have or have had wide Canadian circulation: [34 Books].

I.   The works listed in paragraphs D, E, F, G and H above are to be found in a great many libraries (public and private) in addition to those indicated, as well as in schools, colleges, universities and other educational institutions and in homes throughout Canada. Their language in either English or French and in particular their use of the word 'thermos' is that of English-speaking and French-speaking Canadians respectively.

L.   The word 'thermos' has been used generically and descriptively in the following articles which have appeared in newspapers published in Canada or, where published elsewhere, widely circulated in Canada: [39 Articles].

M.   The word 'thermos' has been used generically and descriptively in numerous obituaries concerning the death of Sir James Dewar which have appeared in newspapers published in Canada: [28 Newspapers].

N.   The word 'thermos' has been used generically and descriptively in magazines published in Canada or, where published elsewhere, widely circulated in Canada: [84 Magazines].

O.   The word 'thermos' has been used generically and descriptively in the Canadian patent Literature in the face of Rule 28 under the Patent Act which prohibits the use of trade marks in patent specifications, except in unusual circumstances, or unless identified as such, and in the face of the constant practice of the Patent Office not to allow the use of trade marks in patent claims. The applicant will rely on the following documents: [11 patent documents].

T.   The word 'thermos' has been used generically and descriptively on innumerable occasions by the Respondent Canadian Thermos Products Limited itself in its advertisements, correspondence both internal and external and otherwise ... The Respondent's corporate name, prior to its change in 1960, involved a generic and descriptive use of the word 'thermos', such name being 'Canadian Thermos Bottle Co. Limited.'

In looking at the use of the word "thermos" in dictionaries one must bear in mind that the word is registered as a trade mark in

England, the United States, France and many other countries, and that when it appears in a dictionary published in one of those countries it may indicate only the meaning and usage of the word there, which may not be the same as in Canada. However, dictionaries and books that are used and read in Canada, no matter where published, have an influence on the use of words in Canada.

Dictionaries and books of reference do not always reflect accurately the true meaning of words. Many of them have a preface which explains the use of capitals, trade mark designations and other indications of the meaning or use of the words in the dictionary. However, the Courts may refer to dictionaries. The Judicial Committee of the Privy Council said in *Coca-Cola Co. of Canada Ltd. v. Pepsi–Cola Co. of Canada Ltd.*, 1 C.P.R. 293 at p. 299, [1942] 2 D.L.R. 657, 2 Fox Pat. C. 143:

While questions may sometimes arise as to the extent to which a Court may inform itself by reference to dictionaries, there can, their Lordships think, be no doubt that dictionaries may properly be referred to in order to ascertain not only the meaning of a word, but also the use to which the thing (if it be a thing) denoted by the word is commonly put.

Much information as to the use by the respondent of its trade mark THERMOS and its course of conduct is found in the evidence of Mr. Parker, its president, who has been with the company ever since 1935, and in catalogues, price lists, advertisements and other documents emanating from the respondent and put in evidence. I will reproduce some pages of the catalogues, for they speak for themselves better than any description I can give.

Exhibit C1 is an example of numerous "Directions for Use sent out by the respondent with its bottles. It is undated; Parker said it was prior to 1985. It contains the following paragraph:

What is a THERMOS Bottle?

A THERMOS Brand Bottle is a vacuum bottle manufactured by Thermos Bottle Company Limited. 'THERMOS' is a coined word—a registered trade mark belonging exclusively to Thermos Bottle Company, Limited, in Canada. If the Vacuum product is not marked 'THERMOS', it simply is not THERMOS brand ware, and cannot be advertised or sold as such.

The respondent has made substantial efforts, in greater measure during the past 30 years than previously, to impress upon the public that THERMOS is a registered trade mark and should not be used otherwise. These efforts increased considerably after it became apparent that there was a growing tendency to use the word in a generic sense.

The applicant says that by then the word had fallen into public domain and the respondent's efforts were too little and too late to retrieve it or to reverse the trend of its use as a generic word. The respondent says that, in any event, its trade mark was and is distinctive of its wares, whether or not the word is used by some persons in a generic sense.

The word "thermos" appears to have originated in Germany, about 1905, from a Greek word meaning hot or warm. But when it was originated and when it was first registered as a trade mark in Canada in 1907, such a derivation would have been known by few persons other than classicists and persons familiar with the Greek language, and in my opinion, it was a now and freshly coined fancy word which would not convey any obvious meaning to ordinary persons in Canada.

I am not convinced that on a question whether in Canada a particular word is a generic or descriptive word in the English or French languages, or as to what its meaning is (other than technical words and words having special meaning in a profession, trade, etc.), a Judge must decide the question solely on the evidence which is adduced and cannot use his own knowledge of the word and of the way persons use and respond to it in conversation in ordinary society. If I were to use my own knowledge and experience respecting the use of the word "thermos" in conversation, it would support my conclusion above stated. However, as I have the impression that counsel's view was that my findings should be based upon the evidence adduced, I have endeavoured to make my findings solely on that evidence and inferences therefrom, without being influenced by any personally subjective feelings I may have.

As of the date the proceedings were commenced an appreciable portion of the population in Canada knew and recognized the respondent's trade mark THERMOS and its significance, and that to them it was distinctive of the respondent's vacuum bottles. They were influenced, no doubt, by the 20,000,000 (Parker's figure) of the respondent's bottles bearing the trade mark which were sold in Canada in the period 1935–64 in competition with imported and other bottles, and by the extensive advertising by the respondent and by the millions of "directions for use", etc., in connection with the respondent's bottles and trade mark, which reached the public and purchasers of vacuum bottles. I think there can be little doubt that trade marks used in connection with articles sold in large volume over a long period usually have a reputation associated with them. The catalogue sales figures referred to in the Kingdon–Johnson correspondence show that the purchasers who had a choice of brand name bottles chose the THERMOS brand in preference to the other brands.

It is my opinion, also, that many of the public are aware of the dual use and meaning of the word "thermos" and that they use it in its generic sense or in its trade mark sense, as the case may be, as circumstances may call for. In day-to-day conversation such persons may use the word in a generic sense without adding "brand" or "vacuum bottle", and without having in mind a bottle of a particular manufacturer; but when they go to a store to buy a vacuum bottle they will have in mind that the name THERMOS on a bottle has a significance which distinguishes bottles made by the respondent and sold under that brand name from bottles bearing some other brand or no brand. They may have had experience with vacuum bottles or have been induced to regard bottles bearing the word "thermos" as bottles warranted by a reputable maker, although they do not know the manufacturer by name—people often look for brand name goods without knowing the name of the manufacturer.

Having concluded that the word "thermos" has come into common use as a generic word, in speech and in writing, I must go on to determine whether for that reason the respondent's registration of it should be expunged, as being not distinctive, notwithstanding that it is distinctive to a significant portion of the people who sell or buy vacuum bottles. The words of Maclean, J., in *Bayer Co. Ltd. v. American Druggists' Syndicate Ltd.*, [1994] S.C.R. 558, in reference to the situation in that case, are pertinent here. He said at p. 598:

> The same section of the public, in Canada, would no doubt to-day, identify aspirin as the Bayer production of acetyl salicylic acid and, to that extent at least, the word aspirin does not denote the name of the article. It was through the sale of acetyl salicylic acid in tablet form under the name of 'Aspirin' first by manufacturing chemists and later by the Bayer Company itself, that the public began to purchase direct from retail druggists, instead of through the physician's prescription. Owing to this fact, possibly another section of the public, consumers of aspirin, gradually came to identify that word as the name of the article. But all this has occurred in recent years. Much advertising has brought this about and produced the strange situation, if the respondents' contention be sound, that the more successful the manufacturer of a product, identified by some registered word mark, is in inducing the public to consume his product, the nearer he approaches the end of the user of his trade mark even though originally it was a proper entry. The implications from such a state of the law are considerable and serious, and even with statutory authority existing to expunge trade-marks in such a condition of facts, one can readily perceive the difficulties in justly resolving the many complex issues which might arise.

Although the word "thermos" is now commonly used in a descriptive sense, I do not regard it as a merely descriptive word, in the sense that "shredded wheat" or "cellular cloth" were said to be merely descriptive. A descriptive word can be distinctive when used in certain circumstances.

It is also recognized, at least in our neighbour, the United States, that a word registered as a trade mark may in fact retain its significance as a trade mark even after it has become publici juris and has become a part of the public domain as a generic descriptive designation for the class or type of goods. In 1962, in *American Thermos Products Co. v. Aladdin Industries Inc.*, 207 F.Supp. 9, 134 U.S.P.Q. 98, the United States District Court, District of Connecticut, found, on the evidence before it, that the word "thermos" had become a generic descriptive word in the English language as used in the United States and had become a part of the public domain, but that there is an appreciable, though minority, segment of the consumer public which knows, recognizes and uses the trade mark THERMOS and, therefore, to eliminate confusion and the possibility of deceit of such consumers, the Court decreed that the generic use of the word "thermos" by Aladdin Industries Inc., in its literature and advertising and on its labels would be subject to certain restrictions and limitations set forth in the decision. The Court declared the THERMOS trade marks there in question to be valid, except that they will not be infringed by the generic and descriptive use of the word "thermos" when used in accordance with the provisions of the decision.

The applicant contends that the continued registration of the word "thermos" as a trade mark puts it at a competitive disadvantage vis-a-vis the respondent, for prospective purchasers of vacuum bottles may and do ask for a "thermos" and they are consequently sold a THERMOS brand bottle, rather than an "Aladdin" brand bottle, even when they use the word in a generic sense and are not seeking only a THERMOS brand bottle or a bottle of a particular manufacturer.

There is the question whether the average purchasers of vacuum bottles, acting with normal caution, would be likely to be misled or confused if the respondent's trade marks are expunged and if, in consequence, bottles of the respondent's competitors, including imported bottles, are then marked and sold as "thermos" bottles without explanation, qualification or distinction. Might such purchasers be misled into buying those other bottles, thinking that they are buying the respondent's bottles? Vacuum bottles are inexpensive articles sold from shelves, across the counter and through mail-order catalogues. I would not expect purchasers to exercise as much care in buying a vacuum bottle as in buying a more expensive article. Bottles of various origins look much alike. Ordinary persons might not look for the manufacturer's name. If the label says that it is a thermos bottle, they might assume that it is a bottle made by the same manufacturer whose bottles have carried the trade mark and the manufacturer's warranties, and that replacement parts would be obtainable if needed.

I have come to the conclusion that expungement of the respondent's trade mark would involve the risk above mentioned and that the risk is sufficiently serious to override the disadvantage under which the applicant is labouring in not having the use of the word "thermos" in its business. The word is not the only apt or practical term. The applicant has the term "vacuum bottle". I agree that it is not used as frequently as "thermos".

The application to expunge the respondent's trade marks is dismissed with costs.

Application dismissed.

Notes and Questions

1. What are the key characteristics of a trademark under TRIPS? Would a computer icon which always appears at the beginning of a program qualify as a protectable mark under TRIPS? Must these marks be protected under TRIPS or is their protection discretionary?

2. *Visual Perception.* TRIPS sets a minimum standard that requires the protection for signs that are "visually perceptible." This appears to be a narrower criterion that the graphic representation requirement of the Trademark Directive of the European Union or the United States. Under the TRIPS standard would the Harley Davidson motorcycle engine sound mark have to be protected?

3. *Distinctiveness.* TRIPS allows signatories to require acquired distinctiveness where a "sign" is not inherently distinctive. Generic marks can never be protected because they can never become distinctive. Neither TRIPS nor the Paris Convention, however, sets forth the criteria for deciding when a mark is generic. Consequently, although a mark such as *MC DONALD'S*® or *COCA-COLA*® might be globally famous, it is possible that no mark may be globally generic.

4. What evidence did the courts in the *Canadian Thermos* and the *French Cellophane* cases consider to determine genericness? What test did they apply? To what extent should courts consider whether a mark is generic in its own language in deciding trademark distinctiveness?

5. Would an international register of generic marks resolve these problems? Who would maintain such a register? More importantly, who would determine genericness?

Read the following Articles from TRIPS from the Supplement: 22, 23.

Notes and Questions

1. Many wines are grown from vines that have been imported from other countries. If your client had imported vines from Bourgogne (Burgundy) for its California vineyard, would its use of the term "Burgundy," if permitted by domestic law, violate TRIPS?

2. Are there geographic indicators other than those for wines and spirits which should be considered internationally protected, such as Cuban cigars, Puerto Rican rum, Roquefort cheese, Ceylon tea, Waterford crystal, or Swiss chocolates? Or are these terms generic marks which should be available for *use* by all?

3. Article 1(2) of the Paris Convention includes "indications of source or appellations of origin" as an example of "industrial property" to be protected. Articles 9 and 10 of the Paris Convention provide for the seizure of goods "in cases of direct or indirect use of a false indication of the source of the goods." Conceivably, a false geographic origin should qualify as a "false indication of source" subject to seizure.

4. The term "geographic indications" in Article 23 of TRIPS seems to encompass both "indications of source" and "appellations of origin." "Indi-

cations of source" has been defined as including "any expression or sign used to indicate that a product or service originates in a country, region or specific place." "Appellations of origin" means the geographical name of a country region or specific place which serves to designate a product originating therein the characteristic qualities of which are due exclusively or essentially to the geographical environment." Ludwig Bauemer (1991) *The International Protection of Geographical Indications* WIPO Symposium on the International Protection of Geographical Indications at 24 (reprinted in Frederick W. Mostert), FAMOUS AND WELL-KNOWN MARKS at 102 n.2 (Sweet & Maxwell 1997).

What is the difference between a trademark and a geographical indication? For example, if I use the trademark for *PARIS NIGHTS* for perfume, could another manufacturer of French perfume use the mark? If PARIS is considered a geographical indicator, could other manufacturers use the term for their French perfume?

5.　Are there other designations that indicate a geographical origin but are not composed of a geographical name? For example, OUZO? GRAPPA? Are these terms protected as geographical indicators for wine under Article 23 of TRIPS?

6.　The European Union has numerous directives and regulations designed to prohibit the misleading use of geographic designators. Thus, the "Wine Regulation," Council Regulation (EEC) No. 2392/89 of July 24, 1989, for the Description and Presentation of Wines and Grape Musts, requires that the description and presentation likely to cause confusion or are likely to be misleading are addressed "with respect to, inter alia, their origin." Regulation at Article 10(1). The Foodstuffs Regulation, Council Regulation (EEC) No. 2081/92 of July 14, 1992, the Protection of Geographical Indications and Designations of Origin for Agricultural products and Foodstuffs, provides for a registration system for geographical indicators for foodstuffs and agricultural products (excluding wines and spirits).

7.　In addition to TRIPS, there are numerous treaties that similarly prohibit the use of false or misleading geographic indicators. Among the most significant are: the Pan American Convention for Trademark and Commercial Protection (Article 23); the Central American Convention for the Protection of Industrial Property (Articles 74–75); the Mercosur Protocol (Protocol of Harmonization of Rules Regarding Intellectual Property within Mercosur in the Area of Trademarks, Indications of Source and Denominations of Origin). (Article 19); the Cartagena Agreement (Andean Pact) (Articles 129–142)(which sets up a registration system for appellations of origin and stipulates that unauthorized use of such appellation "shall be considered as a sanctionable act of unfair competition") (Article 131); and NAFTA (North American Free Trade Agreement)(Article 1712). For a good discussion of the international protection of famous geographic indicators see Frederick W. Mosert, *Protection of Famous and Well Known Geographical Indications*, Famous and Well-Known Marks, 102–123 (Sweet & Maxwell 1997).

THE ELDERFLOWERS CHAMPAGNE CASE
TAITTINGER v. ALLBEV LTD.

Court of Appeal (Civil Division), 1993.
[1994] 4 All ER 75, [1993] FSR 641, 12 TR L 165.

GIBSON, LJ.

Elderflower Champagne is the name given by the defendants to a beverage which they first marketed in October 1991 and is now widely available from health food shops as well as from retail outlets from which both alcoholic and non-alcoholic drinks are sold, for example: Sainsbury. The first defendant, Allbev Ltd, a producer and wholesaler of mainly non-alcoholic drinks but also of some wines, produces Elderflower Champagne and the second defendant, a partnership Between Dr Guy Woodall and his wife Mrs Sheila Woodall trading as Thorncroft Vineyard, advertises, markets, distributes and sells it wholesale. It is sold in two sizes of bottle, of 75cl and 25cl. Most of its sales are of the larger size bottle, the attractive get-up of which makes it look like a champagne bottle. But it is not a product of the Champagne district of France; it is not made from the grape and it is non-alcoholic. It is a drink made from elderflowers, sugar, citric acid and lemons to which carbonated water is added.

The use by the defendants of the word "champagne came to the attention of the champagne producers of France. In the last three decades no group had been more vigorous than the champenois in asserting their rights. No less than sixty-four instances were given in evidence of steps taken in England since 1960 to ensure that the name of champagne is only used commercially to refer to wine from the Champagne district of France. In February 1992 proceedings were commenced, initially only by the first plaintiff, Taittinger, against Allbev Ltd. Taittinger, one of the great champagne houses, sues in a representative capacity for all who produce wine in Champagne and ship such wines to England and Wales.

The plaintiffs sued both in passing off and in assertion of a right under Council Regulation 823/87 (as amended), laying down special provisions relating to quality wines produced in specified regions of the European Community. They sought permanent injunctions and also applied for an interlocutory injunction restraining the defendants from using the word "champagne" in relation to "Elderflower Champagne." Mr. Robert Reid, QC, sitting as a deputy judge of the Chancery Division, on 15 April 1992, would have granted an injunction against passing off until trial but for an undertaking to the like effect being offered to the court and accepted. ([1992] FSR 647). The drink continued to be sold but without the word champagne as part of its name on the label.

The plaintiffs say that they are entitled to permanent injunctions against the defendants both in passing off.

The Facts

The word "champagne" is distinctive of a sparkling alcoholic wine produced in, and only in, Champagne. It is usually sold in a green 75cl bottle with a dimpled bottom and a mushroom-shaped cork held down with wire, the cork and neck being covered in foil. The style of the label will vary from make to make but the label often shows the name of the champagne in a cursive script with the name "champagne" in block letters underneath. Champagne is a quality drink, associated in the minds of the public with celebratory occasions, and it retails in the United Kingdom from about £7.50 upwards.

Elderflower Champagne retails at about £2.45 a 75cl bottle. It is marketed, in that form, in a bottle of approximately the size, colour and shape usually associated with champagne, although the glass appears to be thinner and the defendants say that the bottle is purchased from a cider bottle manufacturer. It is corked with a mushroom-shaped cork, but unlike a champagne cork which has to be of a shape that requires compression to insert into the neck of the champagne bottle, the Elderflower Champagne cork is reusable. The cork is also wired, though unlike that for a champagne cork, the wire appears unnecessary for a bottle containing not fermented but carbonated liquid. At the time of the trial, save for bottles sold to Sainsbury, there was no foil over the wired cork and neck. For bottles sold to Sainsbury, at Sainsbury's request, foil covered the wired cork and neck, and the foil used by the defendants bore the emblem of a bunch of grapes on two sides of the neck and on the top but at a time when the word "Champagne" was deleted from the label. Since then foil without that emblem has been used on bottles sold to Sainsbury. There is a front label headed "Thorncroft" on a gold background. Below that there are various words printed on a white background. At the top there is the word "Traditional" in small print. Underneath there is the prominent word "Elderflower" in a large cursive script and beneath that in smaller but distinct block letters is the word "Champagne." The word "Champagne" was deleted after Mr. Reid's ruling in April 1992 but after the trial "Champagne" has reappeared on the label but in a cursive script like "Elderflower." Below that the words "The Natural Non Alcoholic Sparkling Refreshment" are printed in yet smaller print. Representations of small white flowers are shown on a green background surrounding the white central area of the label. The back label reads:

> Elderflower Champagne is a delightfully refreshing traditional drink with a provenance dating back to the middle ages. The distinctive flavour of fresh elderflowers, reminiscent of lychees and muscat grapes, imparts to it a length and body more commonly found in wine than soft drinks. Elderflowers also have a reputation for warding off colds and flus, and for cooling and cleansing the system. Serve chilled and refrigerate after opening.

The ingredients (which I have already stated) are given and at the bottom of the label is "Thorncroft Vineyard" with its address. We have been told that the word "Vineyard" no longer appears on the bottle label. The 25cl bottle has the same labels but a screw cap.

The suggestion that the defendants' "Elderflower Champagne" is a traditional drink with a provenance dating back to the middle ages seems to me on the evidence to be a creative interpretation of what was known to Dr Woodall. Whilst there is a seventeenth century literary reference to an infusion of elderflowers in small ale, the earliest publication containing a recipe for homemade "elderflower champagne" that was produced in evidence was dated 1949; further, the fizzy drink to which the published recipes refer depended on fermentation for its fizz, was mildly alcoholic and used white wine vinegar and no carbonated water. However the judge himself expressed that the defendants' product might be regarded as a modern type of "elderflower champagne" produced commercially. Certainly there is no evidence of any commercial sales of "elderflower champagne" until the defendants' product was marketed.

Dr Woodall is the moving spirit among the defendants. He formed Allbev Ltd to produce the elderflower cordial that he decided to produce first on a commercial scale. When that venture prospered, other "hedgerow" products were made and in 1989 he decided to expand the range of elderflower drinks to Elderflower Champagne. His evidence was that he knew of a drink called "elderflower champagne" from his grandmother and from recipe books and he was most keen to retain the traditional name, but he positively did not want people to believe that the product was alcoholic.

Passing off

The authoritative modern formulation of what constitutes the tort of passing off is contained in *Erven Warnink BV v. Townend & Sons* (Hull) [1979] AC 731 ("the Advocaat case"). In that case, Lord Diplock identified five characteristics which must be present in order to create a valid cause of action for passing off:

(1) a misrepresentation (2) made by a trader in the course of trade, (3) to prospective customers of his or ultimate consumers of goods or services supplied by him, (4) which is calculated to injure the business or goodwill of another trader (in the sense that this is a reasonably foreseeable consequence) and (5) which causes actual damage to a business or goodwill of the trader by whom the action is brought or (in a quia timet action) will probably do so; [1979] AC 731 at 742.

Lord Diplock pointed out that even if all five characteristics are present, it does not follow that the court is bound to conclude that there has been an actionable wrong; but he held that all those characteristics were present in the Advocaat case and that as there was no exceptional feature which justified on grounds of public policy withholding a remedy, an injunction would lie.

Lord Diplock in the Advocaat case specifically approved the extension to the law of passing off made by Danckwerts J in *J Bollinger v.*

Costa Brava Wine Co. Ltd. [1960] Ch 262. That case first recognised that there could be goodwill attaching to the name "champagne" which was shared by a large number of traders using that name as distinctive of their wines and which could be protected in a passing off action against traders who had no goodwill in that way but sought to make use of the reputation and goodwill of champagne. At the trial, Danckwerts J in Bollinger v. Costa Brava Wine Co. Ltd. (No 2) [1961] 1 WLR 277 held, on evidence to which the judge in the present case likened the evidence put before him, that champagne was distinctive of the wine produced in Champagne, that a substantial portion of the public, being "persons whose life or education has not taught them much about the nature, and production of wine, but who from time to time want to purchase champagne, as the wine with the great reputation," was likely to be misled by the misrepresentation constituted by the description by the defendant in that case of its wine as "Spanish champagne" and that it was a deliberate case of passing off which should be restrained by an injunction.

The judge below found:

There is the simple unworldly man who has in mind a family celebration and knows that champagne is a drink for celebrations. He may know nothing of elderflower champagne as an old cottage drink. Seeing "Elderflower" on the label with below the name "Champagne" he may well suppose that he is buying champagne. Since the simple man I have in mind will know little of champagne prices, he is likely to suppose that he has found champagne at a price of L2.45. I do not mean that I now refer to any majority part of the public or even to any substantial section of the public, but to my mind there must be many members of the public who would suppose that the defendants' "Elderflower" is champagne. Thus it is that I find it established that the defendants' misrepresentation is a misrepresentation that is calculated to deceive.

This, therefore, is a plain finding of fact by the judge that many members of the public who are prospective purchasers of champagne would be deceived into thinking that the defendants' product was champagne. In my judgment there was evidence before the judge from which he could properly reach that conclusion.

Moreover, when the case is tried in an atmosphere of educated persons, many of whom are well acquainted with the qualities of various wines, it may seem absurd that persons should be deceived by what may appear to be a transparent impersonation.

Nevertheless, he held that a substantial portion of the public would be misled. It is right not to base any test on whether a moron in a hurry would be confused, but it is proper to take into account the ignorant and unwary.

But in my judgment the real injury to the champagne houses' goodwill comes under a different head. Mr. Sparrow had argued that if the defendants continued to market their product, there would take place a blurring or erosion of the uniqueness that now attends the word "champagne," so that the exclusive reputation of the champagne houses would be debased. He put this even more forcefully before us. He submitted that if the defendants are allowed to continue to call their product Elderflower Champagne, the effect would be to demolish the distinctiveness of the word "champagne," and that would inevitably damage the goodwill of the champagne houses.

In *Wineworths Ltd. v. CIVC* [1992] 2 NZLR 327 at 341, the sale of Australian sparkling wine under the name champagne was held to constitute passing off. The New Zealand Court of Appeal upheld the decision of Jeffries J who had held in *CIVC v. Wineworths* [1991] 2 NZLR 432 at 450: "By using the word champagne on the label the defendant is deceptively encroaching on the reputation and goodwill of the plaintiffs." Jeffries J had no doubt that if relief was not granted the plaintiffs would most certainly suffer damage if the word was used on all or any sparkling wine sold in New Zealand. He thought the ordinary purchaser in New Zealand without special knowledge on wines was likely to be misled. Gault J said (at p 343):

> I find the issue of damage or likely damage to the goodwill with which the name "Champagne" is associated equally obvious in light of the finding that there is in fact an established goodwill in New Zealand. I have no doubt that erosion of the distinctiveness of a name or mark is a form of damage to the goodwill of the business with which the name is connected. There is no clearer example of this than the debasing of the name "Champagne" in Australia as a result of its use by local wine makers.

By parity of reasoning it seems to me no less obvious that erosion of the distinctiveness of the name champagne in this country is a form of damage to the goodwill of the business of the champagne houses. There are undoubtedly factual points of distinction between the New Zealand case and the present case, as Mr. Isaacs has pointed out, and he placed particular reliance on the fact that in the New Zealand case, as well as in *Bollinger v. Costa Brava Wine Co. Ltd.* (No 2), the court held that there was a deliberate attempt to take advantage of the name champagne, whereas in the present case the judge found no such specific intention. In general it is no doubt easier to infer damage when a fraudulent intention is established. But that fact does not appear to have played any part in the reasoning on this particular point either of Jeffries J or of Sir Robin Cooke P, who ([1992] 2 NZLR 327 at 332) thought the case exemplified the principle that a tendency to impair distinctiveness might lead to an inference of damage to goodwill. It seems to me inevitable that if the defendants, with their not insignificant trade as a supplier of drinks to Sainsbury and other retail outlets, are permitted to use the name Elderflower Champagne, the goodwill in the distinctive name champagne will be eroded with serious adverse consequences for the champagne houses.

In my judgment, therefore, the fifth characteristic identified in the Advocaat case is established. I can see no exceptional feature to this case which would justify on grounds of public policy withholding from the champagne houses the ordinary remedy of an injunction to restrain passing off. I would therefore grant an injunction to restrain the defendant from selling, offering for sale, distributing and describing, whether in advertisements or on labels or in any other way, any beverages, not being wine produced in Champagne, under or by reference to the word champagne. That injunction, I would emphasize, does not prevent the sale of the defendants' product, provided it is not called champagne.

JUDGMENT BY SIR THOMAS BINGHAM

The plaintiff's first task in a passing off action is to prove an established commercial reputation distinctively attached to his goods or his services. That was not in issue in this case. The judge held:

The word champagne is distinctive exclusively of a sparkling wine that is produced in the Champagne district of France as shown on a map that was produced. It is admitted that a valuable reputation and goodwill has been built up in the name Champagne, such goodwill being part of the trading assets of the first plaintiff and those represented by the first plaintiff.

In the United Kingdom, and throughout most of the world, that distinctiveness has been tenaciously and vigilantly protected by the Champagne houses. The nature, origin or source and composition of a bottle of Champagne are accordingly clear. I shall use the noun "Champagne" with a capital C to refer, and refer only, to the first plaintiffs' distinctive product.

Most, if not all, commercial products convey a statement as to what they are. The first issue in this case is as to the statement conveyed by the defendants' product. The plaintiffs' case is very clear. They say that the product is represented to be Champagne. They rely, first and foremost, on the label which so describes the contents of the bottle. They also rely, but to a lesser extent, on the appearance of the bottle, particularly the use of green glass, the use of a mushroom-shaped cork and a wire retaining device (which of course have a specific function in the case of champagne but are unnecessary with a product such as this where there is no pressure to withstand) and, in the case of bottles sold through Sainsbury's, the use of gold foil to enclose the neck of the bottle, the cork and the wire retaining device.

The defendants' case is equally clear. That product is not, they say, represented to be Champagne but "Elderflower Champagne," a traditional English country drink unrelated to Champagne. They contend that any suggested association with champagne is negatived by this description, by the statement that the drink is non-alcoholic, by the label indicating that the cork is resealable, by the use of the English trade-name Thorncroft, by the absence of any reference to France, by the text of the label on the back of the bottle and by the price, a small fraction of the price of the cheapest Champagne, at which the product is sold.

The effect on the plaintiffs' reputation will in my view be nil or minimal. I say that because those who buy Elderflower Champagne in the belief that it is champagne make up the very small section of the public that I have referred to above; and that consideration is coupled with the fact that the defendants' activities are on a small scale (as compared with those represented by the plaintiffs). Furthermore, there was no indication of any likely large scale enlargement of the defendants' operation. Since the plaintiffs do not establish a likelihood of substantial damage the passing off claim fails.

Plainly, those with any knowledge of wine will not buy the defendants' product instead of Champagne. It is also hard to imagine anyone buying the defendants' product instead of Champagne for a celebratory occasion for which he would otherwise buy Champagne. Even on those sporting occasions when the consumer's intention is not so much to drink the contents of the bottle as to spray it around, the defendants' product would be unsuitable as the bottle would not, even if shaken, produce the necessary head. Like the judge, I do not think the defendants' product would reduce the first plaintiffs' sales in any significant and direct way. But that is not, as it seems to me, the end of the matter. The first plaintiffs' reputation and goodwill in the description Champagne derive not only from the quality of their wine and its glamorous associations, but also from the very singularity and exclusiveness of the description, the absence of qualifying epithets and imitative descriptions. Any product which is not Champagne but is allowed to describe itself as such must inevitably, in my view, erode the singularity and exclusiveness of the description Champagne and so cause the first plaintiffs damage of an insidious but serious kind. The amount of damage which the defendants' product would cause would of course depend on the size of the defendants' operation. That is not negligible now, and it could become much bigger. But I cannot see, despite the defendants' argument to the contrary, any rational basis upon which, if the defendants' product were allowed to be marketed under its present description, any other fruit cordial diluted with carbonated water could not be similarly marketed so as to incorporate the description champagne. The damage to the first plaintiffs would then be incalculable but severe.

Differing as I do from the judge on the damage issue, but agreeing with him on the other passing off issues, I would allow the plaintiffs' appeal and grant appropriate injunctive relief. This conclusion is not in my view offensive to the common sense or the fairness of the situation. The defendants are plainly very anxious to describe their product as "Elderflower Champagne" rather than as "Elderflower" (the description used while the interlocutory injunction was in force) or some variant such as "Elderflower Sparkling Drink." Why? Because a reference to champagne imports nuances of quality and celebration, a sense of something privileged and special. But this is the reputation which the Champagne houses have built up over the years, and in which they have a property right. It is not in my view unfair to deny the defendants the opportunity to exploit, share or (in the vernacular) cash in on that reputation, which they have done nothing to establish. It would be very unfair to allow them to do so if the consequence was, as I am satisfied it would be, to debase and cheapen that very reputation.

DISPOSITION:

Appeal allowed with costs in Court of Appeal and below; application for leave to appeal to the House of Lords refused.

Notes and Questions

1. *Co-Existence.* Miguel Torres, SA has used the TORRES trademark for generations for its Spanish wine and has registered the mark in diverse countries. In 1989 a new wine region called TORRES VEDRAS was officially recognized in Portugal. Does TRIPS require that Miguel Torres SA cease using the TORRES mark for urne which is *not* grown in the TORRES VEDRAS region? *See* Peter Weiss, *U.S.TA World Trademark Synposium*, 82 Trademark Reporter 1009 (1992).

2. The issue of protecting geographic indicators for wines and spirits has become a fight between the "Old World" and the "New." "Old World" countries such as France and Germany have taken the position that such indicators are part of their national heritage which should receive absolute protection. The "New World," by contrast, view such terms as protectable *only if* they have achieved a source designating reputation in the country of sale or manufacture. *See, e.g.*, J. Thomas McCarthy & Veronica Colby Devitt, *Protection of Geographic Denominations: Domestic and International*, 69 Trademark Reporter 199 (1994). TRIPS represents a partial victory of the "Old" over the "New."

3. Under the reasoning of the *Elderflower Champagne* case, could a well-know couture house describe its perfume as "the Champagne of Perfumes," without violating the geographic indicators protection of the *Champagne* designator for wine? Would such use violate Article 23 of TRIPS?

4. If the product in the *Elderflowers Champagne* case had been a sparkling beverage with all the qualities of Champagne but created using grapes from California, would the plaintiff's passing off claim have succeeded? Would such use violate Article 23 of TRIPS?

5. Which party should be protected against confusion in the marketplace? The sophisticate? The naive?

6. Does the TRIPS definition of a trademark resolve the issue of what qualifies as a distinctive mark? For example, assume that your client wishes to register the term Le Sorbet in the United States for a frozen ice desert. Your investigation has revealed that the term Le Sorbet in France is considered the common descriptive term for this frozen ice dessert. Should the mark LA SORBET be registrable? What if your client tells you that it tried unsuccessfully to register its LE SORBET mark in France and was refused on ground of genericness? Does this refusal preclude protection in

any other country? For a case which raised similar problems in the United States, see *In re Le Sorbet, Inc.*, 228 U.S.P.Q. 27 (plaintiff AB 1985); *Donald F. Duncan, Inc. v. Royal Tops Manufacturing Co.*, 343 F.2d 655 (7th Cir. 1965).

B. DID TRIPS CLARIFY THE RIGHTS EXERCISED BY TRADEMARK OWNERS INTERNATIONALLY?

Read the following Articles from TRIPS from the Supplement: 16, 17, 18, 20, 21.

Notes and Questions

1. *Minimum Substantive Rights*. Does TRIPS establish a minimum term of protection for trademark rights? Does it establish a minimum list of rights to be granted a trademark owner, such as the right to control the use of a confusingly similar mark on non-identical goods?

2. Review the *Japanese Noodle* case in Chapter Fifteen. Do the TRIPS articles above answer the question whether trademark infringement should be determined on the basis of associative or classical infringement?

3. Heavenly Cookies, Co., has been manufacturing and selling to retail grocery stores their HEAVENLY COOKIES cookie dough in Canada and the United States. The company discovers a chain of retail bakeries doing business in Ottawa, Canada, called "Heavenly Cookies." The bakeries started using the mark *after* the cookie company. If Canada's trademark laws are identical to TRIPS, would the cookie company be able to stop the restaurant on grounds of trademark infringement?

4. Heavenly Cookies decides to expand into Great Britain but discovers there is a chain of restaurants located through-out London called HEAVEN'S COOKIES, which specializes in all types of baked desserts. Assuming for purposes of this problem that Great Britain's trademark laws are identical to TRIPS, would the cookie company be able to stop the restaurant's prior use of the HEAVEN'S COOKIES mark?

5. Prior to TRIPS, some countries imposed registered user requirements that actually served as a compulsory license for foreign marks sought to be registered. Can a country impose such a requirement under TRIPS without violating its obligations? Could a country impose a "working" requirement similar to the working requirement imposed by some countries in connection with the grant of patent rights?

C. HAS TRIPS CLARIFIED THE PROTECTION FOR FAMOUS MARKS?

Read the following Articles from TRIPS from the Supplement: 16(2 & 3).

THE DUFF BEER CASE

TWENTIETH CENTURY FOX FILM CORPORATION v. THE SOUTH AUSTRALIAN BREWING CO. LTD.

Federal Court of Australia, New South Wales
District Registry, General Division, 1996.
No. Ng 155 of 1996.

TAMBERLIN, J.

NATURE OF THE APPLICATION. This application is brought by Twentieth Century Fox Film Corporation ("Fox") and Matt Groening Productions Inc ("Groening"), (which I shall refer to collectively as "the producers") to restrain the South Australian Brewing Co Ltd ("SAB-CO") and Lion Nathan Australia Pty Ltd ("Lion"), (which I shall refer to collectively as "the breweries") from promoting or dealing with any product in the form of a can, (the "breweries' can") with the wording, get-up and name. The basis of the claim is that such activities are said to constitute deceptive conduct and breach the Trade Practices Act 1974 (Cth) ("the Act"), and also to falsely pass off the breweries' can and product as being associated with "The Simpsons" television series.

Groening and Fox are United States Corporations, organized and existing under that Law. Groening is owned by Fox. Groening is the employer of Matt Groening who is the creator of the characters, stories and titles which comprise the animated television series, known as "The Simpsons". Fox is the maker and producer of "The Simpsons" television series. The central characters of "The Simpsons" comprise a somewhat dysfunctional family. "Homer Simpson", the father, is a world famous and well-recognized television character. "Homer" is married to "Marge". They have three children, a son "Bart", his younger sister "Lisa", and an infant "Maggie". "Homer" is also given a father and two formidable sisters-in-law, Selma and Patty, to fill out the family tree.

Each member of the family has a strong and distinctive image, character traits, habits, and levels of intelligence. "Homer" and "Bart" (unlike the female family members), could not be described as endowed with much intelligence, taste or common sense. "Homer" is depicted as inept and bumbling but good natured. His preferred drink is "Duff Beer". His attachment to this beer is a prominent characteristic of his fictional personality. He is regularly depicted clutching or consuming this beer, on occasions, in copious quantities. It is fair to say that the beer and its consumption are not shown in a favourable light.

In 1989, Matt Groening conceived the name "Duff" as the name of an imaginary beer which would be associated particularly with "Homer" and also with his "bar-fly" friends and associates. Depictions and references to "Duff beer" pervade many of the animated cartoon episodes, which comprise the series. The evidence is that "Duff Beer" appears in nearly all episodes of the series broadcast in Australia up to April 1996, with varying degrees of prominence. These appearances range from the common scenario of "Homer" going to the refrigerator to pull out a can of "Duff Beer", to "Homer" and his friends sitting in "Moe's Bar" ordering "Duff Beer". There is one whole episode substantially devoted to the theme of "Duff Beer" ("Duffless") and the name "Duff" features prominently and repeatedly in another 22 minute episode, "Selma's Choice". "Duff Beer" is assigned an important role in the series viewed as a whole.

The series was first screened on television in Australia on 10 February 1991, and has been regularly broadcast and repeated nationally since that date during prime time through to the present.

In addition to the publicity generated in relation to the "The Simpsons", since 1989 Fox has licensed the use of the characters' names and images which appear in the series for use on, and in relation to, a wide range of merchandise, which has been extensively promoted and sold throughout Australia. The merchandise comprises T-shirts, caps, sweat shirts, tank tops, ceramic mugs, trading cards, greeting cards, mouse pads, swim wear and canvas show bags to mention only a few. It is proposed to license and market boxer shorts and other goods depicting characters from the series.

Licensed merchandise relating specifically to "Duff Beer" and sold prior to the hearing date include T–Shirts and caps marketed by "Top Heavy Pty Ltd". The merchandise contains references to copyright and to the reserved rights of Groening or Twentieth Century Fox.

In Australia and New Zealand, "Duff Beer" caps sold over 900 units between October 1995 and April 1996. T-shirts showing "Duff Beer" have been sold during various periods between January 1995 through to April 1996 in Australia and New Zealand, in the order of 24,000.

In addition, comics of "The Simpsons" have been sold in Australia since June 1994. One of these comics entitled "The Amazing Colossal Homer!", a story about "Duff Beer" and the "Duff Brewery" was sold in Australia from 22 June to 27 July 1994. Approximately 15,900 copies were sold. Another comic relating to "Duff Beer" was sold from 24 January to 21 February 1996. Approximately 26,300 copies were distributed to retailers. The 1996 "Simpsons' Diary" which contained nine specific references to "Duff Beer' has been sold throughout Australia since 30 November 1995, and is still on sale. Fifty thousand of these have been distributed to retailers.

The inroads made by the series into consumer consciousness has therefore taken place at many levels and in many different ways.

The producers claim, and I accept, that the series has acquired substantial goodwill and reputation in Australia in relation to the characters, names and images appearing in "The Simpsons" including the name "Duff Beer".

In about November 1995, the breweries launched and promoted a beer, using the name "Duff Beer" in the get-up and style depicted above as the breweries' can.

The producers say that by manufacturing, promoting and selling beer under and by reference to the name "Duff Beer", the breweries have represented that the product is made with the permission of the producers, when the true position is that no such license or permission has been granted.

The producers also allege that the breweries adopted the name "Duff Beer" and the get-up and style in the knowledge and for the reason that the name "Duff Beer" had acquired a substantial reputation as a consequence of its association with "The Simpsons" and that the breweries intended to exploit that reputation in relation to their beer product.

Fox has consistently refused to grant licenses to parties who have sought to use "The Simpsons" in connection with alcohol and tobacco products, or other substances considered detrimental to children.

The transcripts generally support the existence of a strong and immediate connection in many instances between "Duff Beer" and "The Simpsons".

It is well settled that a word which has an ordinary dictionary meaning can become distinctive of a particular trader as well as having its primary dictionary denotation. The tort of passing off is wide enough to include descriptive material such as slogans or visual images which television advertising campaigns might lead the market to associate a trader with a product. The test is whether, for example, a product has derived a distinctive character which the market recognizes. In the present, the word "Duff" cannot be said to be descriptive of the beer's qualities but even if it were descriptive, a secondary distinctive meaning might in some circumstances be established.

Once a secondary meaning is established, the fact that there may be a descriptive dictionary meaning will not of itself defeat a claim for passing off. The relevant question is whether the use of the word or name will convey the secondary meaning to consumers.

The name or word under consideration does not have to be associated with goods manufactured by the trader. In *Radio Corporation Pty Ltd. v. Disney* (1937) 57 CLR 448 (the Mickey Mouse Case) at 453, Latham CJ in relation to the names "Mickey Mouse" and "Minnie Mouse" considered that these were: "so closely associated in the public mind, with Walter E Disney and his activities, that the use of either the names or the figures in connection with any goods at once suggests that the goods are 'in some way or other' connected with Disney."

So that, a name without an image may be sufficient to suggest an "association".

Character merchandising has been recognized as attracting the protection of the law in a number of recent cases. In *Fido Dido Inc. v.*

Venture Stores (Retailers) Pty Ltd (1988) 16 IPR 365, Foster J said at 371:

> "With some hesitation, I have come to the view that IT IS REASONABLE IN THIS DAY AND AGE TO ASSUME A STATE OF KNOWLEDGE IN THE BUYING PUBLIC THAT CHARACTERS APPEAR IN CHARACTER MERCHANDISING AS A RESULT OF SOME SYSTEM OF AT LEAST SPONSORSHIP OR APPROVAL BY A CHARACTER HIMSELF in the case of a living person, or the owner of a character in the case where it is inanimate." (Emphasis added)

In this case, it is clear that the name "Duff" has acquired a powerful secondary meaning when used in the collocation "Duff Beer".

An examination of the dictionary meanings of the word "duff" is not particularly helpful. The word is used in relation to golf to refer to striking a ball clumsily or failing to play a shot. The word "duffer", which is perhaps more relevant, connotes a plodding, stupid or incompetent person. However, in my view it would be artificial in the extreme to suggest that consumers would be attracted by the concept of "Duff" on the basis of its dictionary meaning. Indeed, one of the expert advertising research reports specifically advised against using other dictionary meanings of the word "duff" when it advised:

> "Our attempts to portray Duff as a brand without any association with the Simpsons (by using alternative meanings from the Dictionary) also doesn't work as it removes the brand from its source of current franchise and its fun positioning"

The word "Duff" does not describe the contents of the product nor on the evidence does it conjure up connotations of being "fun", "cool" or "trendy". These key attractive features arise from the association with "The Simpsons" and not from any literal dictionary meaning of the word "duff."

The applicants submit that there is a vast gulf between the prominence given to "The Simpsons" names and images when compared to the prominence given to "Duff Beer". An unusual aspect of this case, is that it concerns not a fictional "character" as such, but a "make-believe" product, namely the fictional "Duff Beer" which is coupled with a character, a background institution, ("Duff Brewery"), and also with the associated advertising signs, posters and images of the beer, which play an important role in the series. These features form part of the fictional "environment" in which the stories are played out. It plays a background role as part of the fictional world which the characters inhabit. No doubt, the assignation of the name "Duff" to the product was designed to achieve a more believable specific fictional effect than to have an anonymous generic "beer" can and it serves to endow the characters with more focused identifiable "human" traits.

The evidence shows that the use of the "Duff Beer" name on the breweries' can is sufficient to invest the beer in the minds of consumers with many of the associations of "The Simpsons". Accordingly, in my view, the principles which apply to character image or title association are equally applicable to the name of a product which features in the program, in this instance, "Duff Beer".

There is no need to reinforce the name with an image of any character or any other title or description or indeed any reference to the words "The Simpsons". To paraphrase the words of Dixon J in the Disney case, supra at 457, the breweries, in using the name "Duff Beer", are making use of an element which belongs to "the reputation and fame" of Matt Groening's creations to create the association.

On a literal reading of § 52 of the Act, the deliberate creation by the breweries of an association by use of the name "Duff" between the breweries' beer can with "The Simpsons" program, in circumstances where there is no association and indeed, where such an association is contrary to the express policy of the producers, amounts to misleading and deceptive conduct. There is no necessity to demonstrate that the viewer or consumer must think in specific terms of permission or allowance in order to constitute deceptive conduct. The intentional use of the name "Duff Beer" which produces the false association is sufficient, in my view. As indicated above, I am satisfied on the balance of probabilities that consumers are in fact likely to assume sanction, permission or allowance on the part of the producers. This is not caused by any erroneous assumption on their part, but by the deceptive conduct of the breweries.

It is submitted by the breweries that steps were taken to ensure that there would be no suggestion to consumers that the product was manufactured or sold with the license or permission of the applicants.

It is important to note that there is no disclaimer to consumers on the can, or in the retail advertising or promotional material, to the effect that the beer is not that referred to in "The Simpsons" program. An express disclaimer, can if sufficiently prominent, destroy any suggestion of association between a character and the product under consideration. For example, in the *Maybelline* case, the controlling consideration was, that across the top of the picture in large and striking letters were the words "OLIVIA? NO, MAYBELLINE!" Given this express statement it would be difficult to assert any relevant association between "Maybelline" and Olivia Newton–John.

The steps which are said to have been taken to disassociate the "Duff Beer" from "The Simpsons" in the present case include ensuring that the words "The Simpsons" were not referred to on the can and the design, colour and get-up of the yellow can was said to be quite different from that featured in "The Simpsons". Nor did the image of any "Simpsons" character appear on the can.

Consideration of the letters sent to Swan Liquor Retailers and other retailers in Western Australia, South Australia and Victoria indicate the "tongue-in-cheek" nature of the attempts at "disassociation". A circular letter sent to retailers contains the following note:

"Oh and (to be serious for a moment) yes we're aware of the fact that another 'Duff Beer' features in "The Simpson's" TV show. Please note Homer's favourite drop is a completely separate, fictitious product. We would encourage you not to use "Simpson's" imagery or logos in supporting "Duff Beer" as these are not owned by us and in doing so you may run the risk of infringing legal copyright."

There is a notable lack of any attempt to drive this message home to the "consuming public".

These letters indicate a view, on the part of the breweries, that if "The Simpsons" image or title appeared on the can, there was a real risk of infringing copyright. Far from indicating a disassociation, these letters relied on by the brewery, reinforce the conclusion that the beer was intended to be marketed with a keen awareness of the existence of "The Simpson" program and of the force of "The Simpsons" association.

There has been a misrepresentation as to the association of the goods with "The Simpsons", made by breweries in the course of trade, to prospective customers or ultimate consumers. It is reasonably foreseeable that the business or goodwill of "The Simpsons" and their licensing and merchandising rights could be adversely affected, particularly in the light of the policy in relation to alcohol promotion. If the product is permitted to be marketed it will probably cause actual damage to the producers. There will be loss of licensing fees.

My conclusion is that the breweries have engaged in a course of conduct calculated to achieve and exploit a strong association between their use of the name "Duff Beer" and "The Simpsons", which in fact is deceptive, while at the same time, hoping to avoid legal liability. In fact, their hope of avoiding legal liability were not realized in that they have breached the Act and the charge of passing off has also been made out.

ORDER:

As the present hearing was limited to the question of liability, I direct the applicants to bring in Short Minutes of Order to give effect to these reasons and also draft directions in order to progress the further hearing in relation to relief sought

Notes and Questions

1. Compare Article 16 of TRIPS with Article 6*bis* of the Paris Convention. What additions did TRIPS make to the scope of marks to be protected as a well-known mark under the Paris Convention?

2. What evidence does Article 16 specify must be considered in deciding whether a mark is well-known? What evidence did the court in the *Duff Beer* case consider in deciding the fame of the mark? Do you agree that Duff Beer qualifies as a famous *mark*?

3. Some countries such as the United States and Great Britain have used Article 6*bis* of the Paris Convention (and its TRIPS clarifications) as a

basis for supporting the international adoption of a minimum dilution standard. For a further discussion of fame and dilution, see Part VII.

4. *Non-competing Goods.* One of the most troublesome aspects of protecting famous marks is the problem of deciding how broad such protection should be. Clearly a junior user of a famous mark on similar goods violates Article 6bis (as amended by TRIPS). But does the use of a famous mark on non-similar, non-competing goods similarly violate Article 6bis? Only if the famous mark is registered? This is a narrower scope of protection than under U.S. law (*see* 15 U.S.C. § 1125(c)(dilution protection for well-known marks regardless of registration)) or under the European Union ("marks having a reputation protected against unauthorized use on non-similar goods").

Chapter Twenty–One

TRADE SECRETS UNDER TRIPS

A. HAS TRIPS ESTABLISHED A WORKABLE REGIME FOR TRADE SECRET PROTECTION?

Read the following Article from TRIPS from the Supplement: 39.

Notes and Questions

1. What are the characteristics that "undisclosed information" must contain to be protected under Article 39?

2. How do you determine whether information "has commercial value because it is secret"? Must the information already be valuable or is potential commercial value sufficient? For example, the Food Group, Inc., is researching the potential value of ginger as a food preservative. Its R & D department has just begun conducting tests using a newly distilled extract of ginger. Its lab personnel report that the tests look "promising" but it is still too soon to tell whether the extract actually will increase the shelf-life of food, without altering its taste. A competitor has lured one of Food Corps's lab technicians to disclose the confidential extraction process for ginger, in violation of his confidentiality agreement. The domestic laws of Food Corp's principal place of business, and corporate headquarters, is identical to Article 39 of TRIPS. Do Food Corp's distillation process and efforts to use a ginger extract as a preservative qualify as "having commercial value"? Or must the process have resulted in a marketable form before it can be protected?

3. In 1996, the United States enacted the Economic Espionage Act (EEA) which criminalized the theft of certain trade secrets. It defined a trade secret as "all forms and all types of financial, business, scientific, technical, economic, or engineering information whether tangible or intangible if the information derives independent economic value, actual or potential, from not being generally known to, and not being readily ascertainable through proper means by, the public." 18 U.S.C. § 1839(3). Is the test of "independent economic value" set forth in the EEA in accordance with Article 39? Is it broader than the minimum standards established under TRIPS? Would the ginger extraction process qualify as a protectable trade secret under the EEA?

4. Review the trade secret definitions set forth in Chapter Eleven in Notes and Questions. Are these in accordance with TRIPS requirements? Which, if any, are broader than the minimum required protection standards?

5. In Footnote 10, TRIPS defines "a manner contrary to honest commercial practices" as meaning "at least practices such as breach of contract, breach of confidence and inducement to breach, and includes the acquisition of undisclosed information by third parties who knew, or were grossly negligent in failing to know, that such practices were involved in the acquisition." What if your client obtained a confidential encryption key from a freely accessible Internet web site? Would use of this key for your client's commercial purposes qualify as "contrary to honest commercial practices" as that term is defined under TRIPS? Under Article 10*bis* of the Paris Convention?

6. Eli Drug has developed a new anti-cancer drug using turmeric as the active ingredient. Eli Drug has filed patent applications in its major global markets and has completed clinical testing of the drug. Eli estimates that it has spent approximately $5,000,000 in research, development and testing of the new drug. In accordance with the domestic laws of various countries, Eli has submitted its clinical data to specified government agencies for approval prior to marketing the new drug. Six months after Eli receives government approval, the government of Eli's major overseas market approves a generic drug, using Eli's own test data to speed its review process. Did use of this test data violate the government's treaty obligations under TRIPS? If you represented Eli Drug what steps could you take to protect its clinical data on a global basis?

THE BAD BROTHER CASE

LANCASHIRE FIRES LIMITED v. SA LYONS & COMPANY LIMITED AND OTHERS

Court of Appeal (Civil Division), 1996.
[1997] IRLR 113, [1996] FSR 629.

SIR THOMAS BINGHAM

The plaintiff manufactures gas fires and related products at a small factory in Blackburn. In particular it manufactures artificial coals and logs and other components for use in gas fires. The managing director and moving spirit of the plaintiff is Mr. Jim Wright, who began trading under the name "Lancashire Fires" some 12 years ago and incorporated the company nine years ago. He had run a shop selling gas fires and developed a fire of his own in a workshop behind the shop.

Jim Wright's younger brother is the second defendant Arthur Wright. Until 1992 Arthur Wright had his own plumbing and heating business in which he had at one time employed Jim. This business failed and Arthur Wright was employed by the plaintiff as "New Projects Manager" in about October 1992.

As new projects manager of the plaintiff from about October 1992 onwards, Arthur Wright carried out a variety of tasks, generally concerned with the repair and improvement of the plaintiff's building and plant. Although he had no staff directly reporting to him, he had unrestricted access to all parts of the factory and became very familiar with the processes involved in producing the artificial components already referred to. When it was decided to supply these components to other manufacturers, Arthur Wright was given the specific task of supervising the expansion (in three phases) of the plaintiff's plant for that purpose. During this period the plaintiff was improving and refining the process which it had been licensed by Arthur Corry to use. It was found in practice that the process was capable of producing very realistic and good quality components, but it had a number of drawbacks, one of which was that it did not lend itself to mass production. The plaintiff accordingly made a number of changes to the process, substantially altering the nature of the mould, and enabling the components to be produced in much larger quantities.

The plaintiff had developed some outlets for the sale of its products in Canada through an agent named Ray Wood. In November 1993 representatives of a major Canadian company called Lennox Industries (Canada) Limited visited the plaintiff's factory. There had been discussion of a possibility that the plaintiff might manufacture gas fires for Lennox, but in the event it was unable to meet Lennox's requirements within the stipulated timescale.

By about this time, Arthur Wright had begun to form the plan of setting up on his own account. He met the Lennox representatives briefly on their visit to the plaintiff's factory, and in January 1994 contacted Lennox by fax to inquire whether it could provide some financial assistance for research and development of a prototype automated plant. He took the opportunity of a short holiday to visit Lennox in Canada. This resulted in an agreement dated February 8, 1994 under which Lennox provided an interest free loan of up to L12,000 in stages linked to the development of Arthur Wright's process. The loan was to be to SA Lyons & Co which was the trading name adopted by Arthur Wright. Under the written agreement signed by Arthur Wright, Lyons was to enter into a mutually acceptable agreement to sell ceramic components relating to the decorative gas fire industry to Lennox, on an exclusive basis, in North America.

Arthur Wright was still employed by the plaintiff and had given his brother Jim no indication of his intention. However, in May 1994 Jim Wright heard from a supplier that Arthur was setting up his own business at Albert Mill. He visited the site and was able to see enough to suggest that steps were in hand to set up a business of a similar nature to the plaintiff's. He confronted his brother who admitted he had decided to leave the plaintiff and go into business on his own. He resigned on May 18, 1994 and went to work full-time at Albert Mill. His evidence was that despite working very intensively and for long hours he continued to have problems in perfecting his process design. But a visit to Lennox in Canada in August 1994 gave him new impetus, and his process was ready for production in January 1995.

In *Faccenda Chicken Limited v. Fowler* [1984] ICR 589 at 598 ([1985] FSR 105 at 114.), Goulding, J. identified three classes of information which an employee might acquire in the course of his service:

> First there is information which, because of its trivial character or its easy accessibility from public sources of information, cannot be regarded by reasonable persons or by the law as confidential at all. The servant is at liberty to impart it during his service or afterwards to anyone he pleases, even his master's competitor.

This class is uncontroversial. The law of confidence does not apply to it. The second class comprises information which the servant must treat as confidential (either because he is expressly told it is confidential, or because from its character it obviously is so) but which once learned necessarily remains in the servant's head and becomes part of his own skill and knowledge applied in the course of his master's business. So long as the employment continues, he cannot otherwise use or disclose such information without infidelity and therefore breach of contract. But when he is no longer in the same service, the law allows him to use his full skill and knowledge for his own benefit in competition with his former master; . . . If an employer wants to protect information of this kind, he can do so by an express stipulation restraining the servant from competing with him (within reasonable limits of time and space) after the termination of his employment.

There is in this passage an echo of what Bennett J said in *United Indigo Chemical Company Limited v. Robinson* (1932) 49 RPC 178 at 187:

> In those circumstances it seems to me to be almost impossible, in justice to the servant, to restrain him when he leaves his master's employment from using—not disclosing—information which he could not help acquiring. It seems to me that to try to restrain him by injunction from using knowledge, which in that way has become his own, is to try to do something which the Court really has no power to do, or rather has no power to enforce the injunction if one could be granted . . . That is really what the plaintiffs are trying to do here . They are trying to stop the defendant from using after he has left the plaintiffs' service knowledge, skill and experience which as a result of his service have become his own.

In *Faccenda*, Goulding J held that the information in issue in the case fell within this second class. It was argued on appeal that no such special class existed: [1987] Ch 117 at 122–123. ([1986] FSR 291 at 301–302.). The Court of Appeal rejected this argument. It held (at page 135) ([1986] FSR 291 at 302–303.):

> (2) In the absence of any express term, the obligations of the employee in respect of the use and disclosure of information are the subject of implied terms.

(3) While the employee remains in the employment of the employer the obligations are included in the implied term which imposes a duty of good faith or fidelity on the employee.

On one point the Court of Appeal did differ from Goulding, J. At page 137 ([1986] FSR 291 at 304.) it said:

> We must therefore express our respectful disagreement with the passage in Goulding J's judgment at [1984] ICR 589, 599E, where he suggested that an employer can protect the use of information in his second category, even though it does not include either a trade secret or its equivalent, by means of a restrictive covenant. As Lord Parker of Waddington made clear in *Herbert Morris Ltd. v. Saxelby* [1916] 1 AC 688, 709, in a passage to which Mr. Dehn drew our attention, a restrictive covenant will not be enforced unless the protection sought is reasonably necessary to protect a trade secret or to prevent some personal influence over customers being abused in order to entice them away.

In our view the circumstances in which a restrictive covenant would be appropriate and could be successfully invoked emerge very clearly from the words used by Cross J in *Printers & Finishers Ltd. v. Holloway* [1965] 1 WLR 1, 6 [[1965] RPC 239 at 256] (in a passage quoted later in his judgment by Goulding J [1984] ICR 589, 601):

> "If [the managing director] is right in thinking that there are features in his process which can fairly be regarded as trade secrets and which his employees will inevitably carry away with them in their heads, then the proper way for the plaintiffs to protect themselves would be by exacting covenants from their employees restricting their field of activity after they have left their employment, not by asking the court to extend the general equitable doctrine to prevent breaking confidence beyond all reasonable bounds."

The third class identified by Goulding J (at page 600) ([1985] FSR 105 at 115.) was:

> "specific trade secrets so confidential that, even though they may necessarily have been learned by heart, and even though the servant may have left the service, they cannot lawfully be used for anyone's benefit but the master's. An example is the secret process which was the subject matter of *Amber Size and Chemical Company Limited v. Menzel* [1913] 2 Ch 239.

The characteristics of information falling within this class were classically described by Lord Greene MR in *Saltman Engineering Co Limited v. Campbell Engineering Co. Limited* (1948) 65 RPC 203 at 215:

> The information, to be confidential, must, I apprehend, apart from contract, have the necessary quality of confidence about it, namely, it must not be something which is public property and public knowledge. On the other hand, it is perfectly possible to have a confidential document, be it a formula, a plan, a sketch, or something of that kind, which is the result of work done by the

maker upon materials which may be available for the use of anybody: but what makes it confidential is the fact that the maker of
the document has used his brain and thus produced a result which
can only be produced by somebody who goes through the same
process.

The mere fact that the confidential information is not embodied
in a document but is carried away by the employee in his head is
not, of course, of itself a reason against the granting of an injunction
to prevent its use or disclosure by him. If the information in
question can fairly be regarded as a separate part of the employee's
stock of knowledge which a man of ordinary honesty and intelligence would recognize to be the property of his old employer, and
not his own to do as he likes with, then the court, if it thinks that
there is a danger of the information being used or disclosed by the
ex-employee to the detriment of the old employer, will do what it can
to prevent that result by granting an injunction.

In my judgment, three elements are normally required if, apart from
contract, a case of breach of confidence is to succeed. First, the information itself, in the words of Lord Greene, MR in the Saltman case on page
215, must "have the necessary quality of confidence about it". Secondly,
that information must have been imparted in circumstances importing
an obligation of confidence. Thirdly, there must be an unauthorized use
of that information to the detriment of the party communicating it. I
must briefly examine each of these requirements in turn.

In *Fuccenda Chicken* (at page 137) the Court of Appeal drew
attention to some of the matters which must be considered in determining whether any particular item of information falls within the implied
term of a contract of employment so as to prevent its use or disclosure
by an employee after his employment has ceased. Those matters included: the nature of the employment; the nature of the information itself;
the steps (if any) taken by the employer to impress on the employee the
confidentiality of the information; and the ease or difficulty of isolating
the information in question from other information which the employee
is free to use or disclose. We have no doubt that these are all very
relevant matters to consider. In the ordinary way, the nearer an employee is to the inner counsels of an employer, the more likely he is to gain
access to truly confidential information. The nature of the information
itself is also important: to be capable of protection, information must be
defined with some degree of precision: and an employer will have great
difficulty in obtaining protection for his business methods and practices.
If an employer impresses the confidentiality of certain information on
his employee, that is an indication of the employer's belief that the
information is confidential, a fact which is not irrelevant. But much will
depend on the circumstances. These may be such as to show that
information is, or is being treated as, confidential; and it would be
unrealistic to expect a small and informal organization to adopt the same
business disciplines as a larger and more bureaucratic concern. It is plain
that if an employer is to succeed in protecting information as confiden-

tial, he must succeed in showing that it does not form part of an employee's own stock of knowledge, skill and experience. The distinction between information in Goulding, J.'s class 2 and information in his class 3 may often on the facts be very hard to draw, but ultimately the court must judge whether an ex-employee has illegitimately used the confidential information which forms part of the stock-in-trade of his former employer either for his own benefit or to the detriment of the former employer, or whether he has simply used his own professional expertise, gained in whole or in part during his former employment.

The defendants challenged the view that the details of the Lancashire Fires' process were in any sense confidential or a trade secret. This challenge was put in different ways. First, it was said, the processes were well known to the practitioners in this field, and therefore to be regarded as in the public domain. Secondly, it was said that they could be readily ascertained by a form of "reverse engineering" from a study of the products themselves. Thirdly, it was said that Mr. Jim Wright did not in fact prevent visitors to the factory from seeing what was going on, and indeed allowed photographs to be taken for two articles in the press.

I do not accept this challenge. Certainly the basic processes for making ceramic components from ceramic fibres are well documented. However, there was no evidence that the refinements which Lancashire Fires had introduced into the system, and which impressed Mr. Alfred Wright [the plaintiff's expert witness], are so documented or widely known. It is possible that they have been replicated in individual companies here or abroad, but that does not put them in the "public domain" in the sense that is used in the cases.

There was some discussion about the purpose of a stack of shelves, erected by Arthur, which Jim Wright said acted as a security screen. I do not find it necessary to resolve that point. It seems to me that anyone who was going to gain anything from an inspection of the plant would have needed to know what to look for. The evidence shows that Jim Wright was careful with certain competitors to limit their view of particular parts of the plant, and on occasions to stop operations while the visit took place. On the other hand, other visitors, whom for whatever reason he did not regard as a threat had freer access. Similarly, the two newspaper photographs were set up under supervision, and did not give away any secrets about the nature and use of the moulds. An intelligent reader would have been able to infer that he had devised a novel process using vacuum technology. But the precise details of that process would not have been apparent.

Similarly, I have no doubt that employees understood that parts of the process were to be treated as confidential. The employees who gave evidence of steps taken to shield information from the "competitors", clearly understood that this was because Jim Wright did not want his processes widely known among that group of people, even though they did not know precisely who the "competitors" were. Arthur Wright was also aware of steps taken to protect information from competitors, although he recalls some visits where no such steps were taken. He was privy to much more detailed information than other employees about the working of the system, and he does not suggest that he would have felt free to divulge the material to outsiders while he was employed with Lancashire Fires. I have no doubt that, during the course of his employment, he was under an obligation of confidence in relation to the detailed workings of the process, particularly relating to the moulds.

The subjective view of the owner cannot be decisive. There must be something which is not only objectively a trade secret, but which was known, or ought to have been known, to both parties to be so. The normal presumption is that information which the employee has obtained in the ordinary course of his employment, without specific steps such as memorizing particular documents, is information which he is free to take away and use in alternative employment.

Applying that approach to the present case, I am not satisfied that there was any information used by Arthur Wright after his departure from Lancashire Fires other than information which he acquired in the ordinary course of his employment at Lancashire Fires. Nor am I satisfied that it was ever made clear to him that there was a specific part of the process, relating to the moulds, which was to be treated in a different category from the remainder. There was nothing in the laboratory books or in any of the other contemporary documentation which suggests that he was put into a particular position of confidence, either expressly or impliedly, in relation to that aspect. Even when Jim Wright became aware of the activities which led to his enforced departure in May 1994, nothing appears to have been said to suggest that Jim Wright was asserting a right to limit the use of any particular information. His concern was direct competition by his brother, in the precise field in which he was engaged, but, in the absence of a covenant against competition. He had no power to restrain that. Of course, the fact that he was dealing with his brother may help to explain why no such covenant had been obtained. It may also suggest that Arthur Wright was in breach of his moral obligations as a brother. However, I do not think that that affects the legal position. In fact, no specific covenants had been obtained from any other employees of Lancashire Fires up until that time. Subsequently employees were made to sign specific covenants. The precise terms and effect of those covenants are not relevant to the issues before me.

We think that the judge took too strict a view of the degree of precision to be required of an employer in defining and pointing out what he seeks to protect as a trade secret. In this respect we allow the appeal and will grant injunctions against Arthur Wright.

Applying these principles and having regard to Arthur Wright's position in the plaintiff, the judge was in our view plainly right to conclude that there was a breach of the duty of fidelity. Arthur Wright was not simply seeking employment with a competitor or taking preliminary steps to set up his own business. His activities at Albert Mill and his dealings with Lennox, already described, placed him well on the wrong side of the line. Indeed, any employee with technical knowledge and experience can expect to have his spare time activities in the field in which his employers operate carefully scrutinized in this context.

Arthur Wright's cross-appeal will be dismissed.

DISPOSITION:

Plaintiff's appeal allowed. Injunctions granted against all three defendants in terms sought in the statement of claim.

Notes and Questions

1. To what extent did the "dishonesty" of a former employee affect the court's decision in the *Bad Brother* case? In order to demonstrate "dishonesty," how specific must an employee's knowledge be of the confidential nature of the information he is learning?

2. If Wright had entered into a non-competition agreement with his brother, would this fact make the plaintiff's case for misappropriation easier? Or should it be irrelevant?

3. The European Directive on Know–How Licensing limits protection for confidential information to "business and technical information." Would the trade secrets in the *Bad Brother* case fit within this category? Would the trade secrets in the *Aerial Photography* case in Chapter Eleven?

4. Does Article 39 require a broader scope of undisclosed information to be protected than "business information"?

5. Does Article 39 clarify whether trade secrets are protected as a property right or as a problem of unfair competition? Would there be a difference in the treatment of trade secrets if they were considered property?

6. Are the principles set forth in the *Bad Brother* and *Aerial Photography* cases in accordance with Article 39 of TRIPS?

Chapter Twenty-Two

ENFORCEMENT UNDER TRIPS

A. HAS TRIPS GIVEN THE WTO THE POWER TO ENFORCE INTERNATIONAL WILL?

Read the following Article from TRIPS from the Supplement: 41(1 & 2).

Notes and Questions

1. *The Development of Minimum Standards.* One of the most important developments in international protection may well be the minimum enforcement standards set down by TRIPS. For the first time international protection moved beyond simply specifying substantive standards and actually required the enforcement by signatory countries of the minimum rights required to be granted under a multinational intellectual property treaty. Does Article 41 specify whether such enforcement must be done through judicial proceedings? Could a country meet its obligations by establishing administrative enforcement mechanisms?

2. What are the minimum enforcement standards that you believe a country should provide in order to ensure "fair and equitable" procedures? What relief should be available? Who should judge the case? An impartial judiciary or one interested in the case? If you represented the defendant of what minimum procedural rights would you want to be assured?

3. Because TRIPS is under the auspices of the WTO, signatories who fail to meet their obligations are subject to WTO sanctioning power, which includes the imposition of trade sanctions. The threat of this trade remedy helped encourage signatory countries, including Japan, the European Union and the United States, to change their laws to comply with the minimum requirements of TRIPS.

B. ARE EQUITABLE PROCEDURES ASSURED UNDER TRIPS?

Read the following Articles from TRIPS from the Supplement: 41(2–5), 42–50, 63.

Notes and Questions

1. *Rule of Law.* Perhaps the greatest advance in international protection by TRIPS was the establishment of a rule of law regime for the enforcement of intellectual property rights. Transparency, rights determinations via an unbiased proceeding and the right to provisional relief based on known evidence all require a legal system that is predictable and fair. These minimal requirements for justice have begun an international revolution, not simply for intellectual property protection, but for other areas of law as well.

2. What rights must a country grant a plaintiff challenging the alleged infringement of its intellectual property rights under TRIPS?

3. What right must a defendant be granted under TRIPS?

4. If you were a plaintiff, what rights would you want in a proceeding abroad to protect your rights? Have all of these rights been required under TRIPS? What rights, if any, are missing?

5. Your U.S. client has begun distributing its well-known local beer, Triplex, in Mexico. The initial product launch has been so successful across the border that your client has discovered counterfeit products being sold in Mexico City. What relief would you want to obtain for your client in Mexico in a trademark infringement action against this counterfeiter? Is such relief required under TRIPS?

6. Assume that you have obtained a seizure of purportedly infringing Triple XXX beer in Mexico. It turns out the information was false, and all seized products were lawful. What remedies would you expect to be available to the defendant for the wrongful seizure? Are such remedies required under TRIPS?

Read the following Article from TRIPS from the Supplement: 61.

THE GREEK TELEVISION COMPLAINT

ENFORCEMENT OF INTELLECTUAL PROPERTY RIGHTS FOR MOTION PICTURES AND TELEVISION PROGRAMS

World Trade Organization, 1998.

Request for Consultations by the United States

The following communication, dated 30 April 1998, from the Permanent Mission of the United States to the Permanent Delegation of the European Commission and to the Dispute Settlement Body, is circulated in accordance with Article 4.4 of the DSU.

My authorities have instructed me to request consultations with the European Communities pursuant to Article 4 of the Understanding on Rules and Procedures Governing the Settlement of Disputes (DSU) and Article 64 of the Agreement on Trade–Related Aspects of Intellectual Property Rights (TRIPS) (to the extent it incorporates by reference

Article XXIII of the General Agreement on Tariffs and Trade 1994) regarding the enforcement of intellectual property rights in Greece.

The TRIPS Agreement applied to developed Members of the WTO, such as the European Communities, as of 1 January 1996. Such Members are obligated to comply with the provisions of Part III of the TRIPS Agreement regarding the enforcement of intellectual property rights, among other obligations.

A significant number of television stations in Greece regularly broadcast copyrighted motion pictures and television programs without the authorization of copyright owners. Effective remedies against copyright infringement do not appear to be provided or enforced in Greece with respect to these unauthorized broadcasts. Copyrights owned by U.S. nationals have been infringed in this manner repeatedly, and continue to be infringed, despite efforts by U.S. right holders to prevent such infringement and to pursue their rights in Greece. This situation appears to be inconsistent with the obligations of Members under Articles 41 and 61 of the TRIPS Agreement.

We look forward to receiving your reply to the present request and to fixing a mutually convenient date for consultations.

THE SWEDISH REMEDIES COMPLAINT

MEASURES AFFECTING THE ENFORCEMENT OF INTELLECTUAL PROPERTY RIGHTS
World Trade Organization, 1998.

Request for Consultations by the United States

The following communication, dated 28 May 1997, from the Permanent Mission of the United States to the Permanent Mission of Sweden and to the Dispute Settlement Body, is circulated in accordance with Article 4.4 of the DSU.

My authorities have instructed me to request consultations with the Government of Sweden pursuant of Article 4 of the Understanding on Rules and Procedures Governing the Settlement of Disputes (DSU) and Article 64 of the Agreement on Trade–Related Aspects of Intellectual Property Rights (TRIPS) (to the extent it incorporates by reference Article XXII of the General Agreement on Tariffs and Trade 1994) regarding the making available of provisional measures under Swedish law.

The TRIPS Agreement obligates all Members of the World Trade Organization to make provisional measures available in the context of civil proceedings involving intellectual property rights. In light of Sweden's status as a developed country, the TRIPS Agreement applied to it on 1 January 1996.

Sweden does not appear to make available provisional measures in the context of civil proceedings involving intellectual property rights. As such, Swedish law would appear to be inconsistent in its obligations under the TRIPS Agreement, including but not necessarily limited to TRIPS Agreement Articles 50, 63 and 65.

We look forward to receiving your reply to the present request and to fixing a mutually convenient date for consultations.

Notes and Questions

1. Does TRIPS specify whether enforcement must be through civil or criminal laws?

2. What are the limitations on required criminal procedures? Do they apply for all IP forms?

3. What rights has Greece purportedly failed to provide in violation of its treaty obligations under TRIPS? What steps should it take to correct these failures?

4. What rights has Sweden purportedly failed to provide in violation of its treaty obligations under TRIPS? What steps should it take to correct these failures?

5. How much time should Greece and Sweden be allowed to correct their failures? For an update on the current status of these proceedings, see http://www.wto.org.

6. *Corruption.* Many countries which have poor legal protection mechanisms for IP rights have serious problems with corruption of the judicial process. For example, in the late 1990's China had a severe problem in enforcing intellectual property laws against the unauthorized reproduction and sale of CD ROM sound recordings by foreign musicians. Efforts to seize such recordings, and to block the manufacture of the pirated works, were often hampered by the reported ownership of such factories by the People's Liberation Army. What solution does TRIPS propose to resolve this problem?

7. Solutions Plus has developed a state of the art computer assisted design program for medical diagnosis. Solutions Plus sells its CAD–MED program for $460. It estimates that for each program sold it earns a gross profit of $300 and a net profit of $220. Solutions Plus had discovered that its CAD–MED program is being illegally manufactured in Hong Kong. Its private investigators have discovered copies of the game being sold for $4 in Beijing and Shanghai. Solutions Plus has further discovered that approximately 2,000 copies of the counterfeit software have been sold. Solutions Plus has hired you to help stop these infringing acts. Develop a plan of action.

8. If China provides for "damages adequate to compensate the copyright holder for the injury suffered" (in accordance with Article 45 of TRIPS) which should be the appropriate basis for recovery? The counterfeiter's profits? The copyright owner's lost profits based on the counterfeiter's retail sales price? The copyright owner's lost profits based on its own retail sales price? Or a statutory damage amount based on the average income of a laborer in China? How would you decide what the appropriate international standard should be?

9. TRIPS also contains detailed minimum border control measures. *See* TRIPS Article 51.

C. DOES TRIPS ESTABLISH AN EFFECTIVE MECHANISM FOR ASSURING COMPLIANCE WITH TREATY OBLIGATIONS?

Read the Understanding on Rules and Procedures Governing the Settlement of Disputes from the Supplement.

Notes and Questions

1. One of the most unique aspects of TRIPS was the existence of a dispute resolution mechanism under the WTO. What is the governing philosophy of the dispute resolution mechanism—hard fought "combat by trial"? Mediation? Mutually acceptable settlements?

2. What special rules or special treatments are established under the Understanding for developing countries? What is the purpose for these special rules?

3. Among the sanctions that can be imposed under WTO mechanisms is the suspension of most favored nation treatment. Such suspension can result in the imposition of higher tariffs on the imports of the accused country. These trade sanctions may pose a sufficient economic penalty to assure compliance with TRIPS obligations but may be limited in effectiveness to those countries with significant exports.

COMPLAINTS BEFORE THE WTO AS OF NOVEMBER 1998

Pending Caps

(37)(a) European Communities—Enforcement of Intellectual Property Rights for Motion Pictures and Television Programs, complaint by the United States (WT/DS124/1). This request, dated 30 April 1998, is in respect of the lack of enforcement of intellectual property rights in Greece. The U.S. claims that a significant number of TV stations in Greece regularly broadcast copyrighted motion pictures and television programs without the authorization of copyright owners. The U.S. contends that effective remedies against copyright infringement do not appear to be provided or enforced in Greece in respect of these broadcasts. The U.S. alleges a violation of Articles 41 and 61 of the TRIPS Agreement.

(36)(b) Greece—Enforcement of Intellectual Property Rights for Motion Pictures and Television Programs, complaint by the United States (WT/DS125/1). This request, dated 30 April 1998, is in respect of the same measures raised against the EC above (DS124).

(29) Canada—Patent Protection of Pharmaceutical Products, complaint by the European Communities (WT/DS114/1). This request, dated 19 December 1997, is in respect of the alleged lack of protection of

inventions by Canada in the area of pharmaceuticals under the relevant provisions of the Canadian implementing legislation (in particular the Patent Act). The EC contends that Canada's legislation is not compatible with its obligations under the TRIPS Agreement, because it does not provide for the full protection of patented pharmaceutical inventions for the entire duration of the term of protection envisaged by Articles 27.1, 28 and 33 of the TRIPS Agreement.

(17) Sweden—Measures Affecting the Enforcement of Intellectual Property Rights, complaint by the United States (WT/DS86/1). This request, dated 28 May 1997, is in respect of Sweden's alleged failure to make provisional measures available in the context of civil proceedings involving intellectual property rights. The U.S. contends that this failure violates Sweden's obligations under Articles 50, 63 and 65 of the TRIPS Agreement.

(16) Denmark—Measures Affecting the Enforcement of Intellectual Property Rights, complaint by the United States (WT/DS83/1). This request, dated 14 May 1997, is in respect of Denmark's alleged failure to make provisional measures available in the context of civil proceedings involving intellectual property rights. The U.S. contends that this failure violates Denmark's obligations under Articles 50, 63 and 65 of the TRIPS Agreement.

(15)(a) Ireland—Measures Affecting the Grant of Copyright and Neighbouring Rights, complaint by the United States (WT/DS82/1). This request, dated 14 May 1997, is in respect Ireland's alleged failure to grant copyright and neighbouring rights under its law. The U.S. contends that this failure violates Ireland's obligations under Articles 9–14, 63, 65 and 70 of the TRIPS Agreement. On 9 January 1998, the United States requested the establishment of a panel.

(15)(b) European Communities—Measures Affecting the Grant of Copyright and Neighbouring Rights, complaint by the United States (WT/DS115/1). This request, dated 6 January 1998, raises exactly the same measures as in 16(a) above in respect of Ireland but makes the complaint to the EC. On 9 January 1998, the United States requested the establishment of a panel.

COMPLETED CASES

(8) India—Patent Protection for Pharmaceutical and Agricultural Chemical Products, complaint by the United States (WT/DS50). This request, dated 2 July 1996, concerns the alleged absence of patent protection for pharmaceutical and agricultural chemical products in India. Violations of the TRIPS Agreement Articles 27, 65 and 70 are claimed. The United States requested the establishment of a panel on 7 November 1996. The DSB established a panel at its meeting on 20 November 1996. The Panel found that India has not complied with its obligations under Article 70.8(a) or Article 63(1) and (2) of the TRIPS Agreement by failing to establish a mechanism that adequately preserves novelty and priority in respect of applications for product patents for pharmaceutical and agricultural chemical inventions, and was also not in

compliance with Article 70.9 of the TRIPS Agreement by failing to establish a system for the grant of exclusive marketing rights. The report of the Panel was circulated on 5 September 1997. On 15 October 1997, India notified its intention to appeal certain issues of law and legal interpretations developed by the Panel. The Appellate Body upheld, with modifications, the Panel's findings on Articles 70.8 and 70.9, but ruled that Article 63(1) was not within the Panel's terms of reference. The report of the Appellate Body was circulated to Members on 19 December 1997. The Appellate Body report and the Panel report, as modified by the Appellate Body, were adopted by the DSB on 16 January 1998. At the DSB meeting of 22 April 1998, the parties announced that they had agreed on an implementation period of 15 months.

Settled or Inactive Cases

(16) Pakistan—Patent Protection for Pharmaceutical and Agricultural Chemical Products, complaint by the United States (WT/DS36). In its request for consultations dated 30 April 1996, the United States claimed that the absence in Pakistan of (i) either patent protection for pharmaceutical and agricultural chemical products or a system to permit the filing of applications for patents on these products and (ii) a system to grant exclusive marketing rights in such products, violates TRIPS Agreement Articles 27, 65 and 70. On 4 July 1996, the United States requested the establishment of a panel. The DSB considered the request at its meeting on 16 July 1996, but did not establish a panel due to Pakistan's objection. At the DSB meeting on 25 February 1997, both parties informed the DSB that they had reached a mutually agreed solution to the dispute and that the terms of the agreement were being drawn up, and would be communicated to the DSB once finalized. On 28 February 1997, the terms of the agreement were communicated to the Secretariat.

(15)(a) Japan—Measures Concerning Sound Recordings, complaint by the United States (WT/DS28). This request, dated 9 February 1996, is the first WTO dispute settlement case involving the TRIPS Agreement. The United States claims that Japan's copyright regime for the protection of intellectual property in sound recordings is inconsistent with, inter alia, the TRIPS Agreement Article 14 (protection of performers, producers of phonograms and broadcasting organizations). On January 24 1997, both parties informed the DSB that they had reached a mutually satisfactory solution to the dispute.

(15)(b) Japan—Measures Concerning Sound Recordings, complaint by the European Communities (WT/DS42). This request for consultations, dated 24 May 1996, concerns the intellectual property protection of sound recordings under GATT Article XXII:1. Violations of Articles 14.6 and 70.2 of the TRIPS Agreement are alleged. Earlier, the United States requested consultations with Japan on the same issue (WT/DS28), in which the EC joined. On 7 November 1997, both parties notified a mutually agreed solution.

(12) Portugal—Patent Protection under the Industrial Property Act, complaint by the United States (WT/DS37). This request for consultations dated 30 April 1996, concerned Portugal's term of patent protection under its Industrial Property Act. The U.S. claimed that the provisions in that Act with respect to existing patents were inconsistent with Portugal's obligations under the TRIPS Agreement. Violations under Articles 33, 65 and 70 were alleged. On 3 October 1996, both parties notified a mutually agreed solution to the DSB.

Notes and Questions

1. As you can see from the above list of complaints filed as of November 1998 with the WTO involving intellectual property protection issues, many complaints are settled before they reach the final adjudication phase. The threat of TRIPS sanctions has also served to assure resolution of complaints through independent bilateral negotiations.

2. Select one of the cases above and research the impact of the WTO Dispute Resolution mechanism on the alleged violation. Did the threat of sanctions have a measurable impact in eliminating the violation? How effective was the sanctioning mechanism?

3. *Special rules for developing and least developed countries.* The Dispute Settlement mechanism of TRIPS is only one example of the special treatment afforded developing and least developed countries. Articles 65 and 66 of TRIPS similarly provides for specialized treatment of non-developed countries. They provide for "grace periods" before TRIPS obligations are triggered.

These articles provide for the following specialized "grace periods":

TRIPS

Article 65

1. Subject to the provisions of paragraphs 2, 3 and 4, no Member shall be obliged to apply the provisions of this Agreement before the expiry of a general period of one year following the date of entry into force of the WTO Agreement.

2. A developing country Member is entitled to delay for a further period of four years the date of application, as defined in paragraph 1, of the provisions of this Agreement other than Articles 3, 4 and 5.

4. To the extent that a developing country Member is obliged by this Agreement to extend product patent protection to areas of technology not so protectable in its territory on the general date of application of this Agreement for that Member, as defined in paragraph 2, it may delay the application of the provisions on product patents of Section 5 of Part II to such areas of technology for an additional period of five years.

5. A Member availing itself of a transitional period under paragraphs 1, 2, 3 or 4 shall ensure that any changes in its laws, regulations and practice made during that period do not result in a lesser degree of consistency with the provisions of this Agreement.

TRIPS

Article 66

1. In view of the special needs and requirements of least-developed country Members, their economic, financial and administrative constraints, and their need for flexibility to create a viable technological base, such Members shall not be required to apply the provisions of this Agreement, other than Articles 3, 4 and 5, for a period of 10 years from the date of application as defined under paragraph 1 of Article 65. The Council for TRIPS shall, upon duly motivated request by a least-developed country Member, accord extensions of this period.

4. What policies support the granting of differential grace periods? Do the time periods granted provide sufficient time for countries to comply with their TRIPS obligations?

5. *Technical assistance.* To assist developing countries, TRIPS imposes certain obligations of "technical assistance" on developed countries. Thus, Articles 66 and 67 specifically state:

TRIPS

Article 66

2. Developed country Members shall provide incentives to enterprises and institutions in their territories for the purpose of promoting and encouraging technology transfer to least-developed country Members in order to enable them to create a sound and viable technological base.

TRIPS

Article 67

In order to facilitate the implementation of this Agreement, developed country Members shall provide, on request and on mutually agreed terms and conditions, technical and financial cooperation in favour of developing and least-developed country Members. Such cooperation shall include assistance in the preparation of laws and regulations on the protection and enforcement of intellectual property rights as well as on the prevention of their abuse, and shall include support regarding the establishment or reinforcement of domestic offices and agencies relevant to these matters, including the training of personnel.

In addition to the duty to provide "technical assistance" to less-developed countries, Article 66 also requires that incentives be provided by developed countries to encourage the transfer of necessary technology to less-developed countries.

6. Despite the grant of special treatment for "developing" and "least developed" countries, TRIPS does not provide a definition or standard for determining which countries fall within which categories.

7. What categories (developed, developing or least developed) do the following countries fall within?

United States

Cuba

Japan

China

South Korea

Ukraine

Czech Republic

Argentina

Brazil

Can a country change category? Given the special treatment granted lesser developed countries under TRIPS, the determination of status may have a significant impact on a country's obligations.

8. TRIPS also provides for a special grace period for countries who are converting from a non-market to a market economy (such as the members of the former Soviet Union):

TRIPS
Article 65

3. Any other Member which is in the process of transformation from a centrally-planned into a market, free-enterprise economy and which is undertaking structural reform of its intellectual property system and facing special problems in the preparation and implementation of intellectual property laws and regulations, may also benefit from a period of delay as foreseen in paragraph 2.

9. May a country like China (assuming it is a developing country) obtain an expanded grace period by combining categories? For example, may it obtain a grace period of four years for being a non-market economy *plus* an additional four years for being a developing country? May a country obtain an additional grace period if it fails to enact complying laws within the original time-frame?

11. In the absence of clearly delineated standards in TRIPS, countries have disagreed over the precise meaning of the grace period granted under TRIPS. In 1997, India, in response to a complaint for sanctions filed by the U.S. with the WTO for India's failure to establish a mechanism for recording pharmaceutical patents, alleged that such system did not have to be in place until *after* the grace year period (ie 2000). The Appellate Board of the WTO Dispute Resolution Body disagreed. In its first Appellate Decision the Board reasoned as follows:

Article 70.9 of the TRIPS Agreement reads:

Where a product is the subject of a patent application in a Member in accordance with paragraph 8(a), exclusive marketing rights shall be granted, notwithstanding the provisions of Part VI, for a period of five years after obtaining marketing approval in that Member or until a product patent is granted or rejected in that Member, whichever period is shorter, provided that, subsequent to the entry into force of the WTO Agreement, a patent application has been filed and a patent granted for that product in another Member and marketing approval obtained in such other Member.

With respect to Article 70.9, the Panel found:

Based on customary rules of treaty interpretation, we have reached the conclusion that under Article 70.9 there must be a mechanism ready for the grant of exclusive marketing rights at any time subsequent to the date of entry into force of the WTO Agreement. Panel Report, para. 7.60.

India argues that Article 70.9 establishes an obligation to grant exclusive marketing rights for a product that is the subject of a patent application under Article 70.8(a) after all the other conditions specified in Article 70.9 have been fulfilled. India's appellant's submission, p. 19. India asserts that there are many provisions in the TRIPS Agreement that, unlike Article 70.9, explicitly oblige Members to change their domestic laws to authorize their domestic authorities to take certain action before the need to take such action actually arises. Ibid.; for example, India asserts that according to Articles 42–48 of the TRIPS Agreement, the judicial authorities of Members "shall have the authority" to grant certain rights. Article 51 obliges Members to "adopt procedures" to enable right holders to prevent the release of counterfeited or pirated products from customs. Article 39.2 requires Members to give natural and legal persons "the possibility of preventing" the disclosure of information. According to Article 25.1 "Members shall provide for the protection" of certain industrial designs and Article 22.2 obliges Members to "provide the legal means for interested parties to prevent" certain misuses of geographical indications. India further asserts that a comparison of the terms of Article 70.9 with those of Article 27 according to which "patents shall be available" for inventions is revealing. India maintains that the Panel's interpretation of Article 70.9 has the consequence that the transitional arrangements in Article 65 allow developing country Members to postpone legislative changes in all fields of technology except the most "sensitive" ones, pharmaceutical and agricultural chemical products. India claims that the Panel turned an obligation to take action in the future into an obligation to take action immediately. India's appellant's submission, p. 21. India's arguments must be examined in the light of Article XVI:4 of the WTO Agreement, which requires that:

Each Member shall ensure the conformity of its laws, regulations and administrative procedures with its obligations as provided in the annexed Agreements.

Moreover, India acknowledged before the Panel and in this appeal that, under Indian law, it is necessary to enact legislation in order to grant exclusive marketing rights in compliance with the provisions of Article 70.9. This was already implied in the Ordinance, which contained detailed provisions for the grant of exclusive marketing rights in India effective 1 January 1995. However, with the expiry of the Ordinance on 26 March 1995, no legal basis remained, and with the failure to enact the Patents (Amendment) Bill 1995 due to the dissolution of Parliament on 10 May 1996, no legal basis currently exists, for the grant of exclusive marketing rights in India. India notified the Council for TRIPS of the promulgation of the Ordinance pursuant to Article 63.2 of the TRIPS Agreement IP/N/1/IND/1, 8 March 1995. , but has failed as yet to notify the Council for TRIPS that the Ordinance has expired.

Given India's admissions that legislation is necessary in order to grant exclusive marketing rights in compliance with Article 70.9 and that it does not currently have such legislation, the issue for us to consider in this appeal is whether a failure to have in place a mechanism ready for the grant of exclusive marketing rights, effective as from the date of entry into force of the WTO Agreement, constitutes a violation of India's obligations under Article 70.9 of the TRIPS Agreement.

By its terms, Article 70.9 applies only in situations where a product patent application is filed under Article 70.8(a). Like Article 70.8(a), Article 70.9 applies "notwithstanding the provisions of Part VI". Article 70.9 specifically refers to Article 70.8(a), and they operate in tandem to provide a package of rights and obligations that apply during the transitional periods contemplated in Article 65. It is obvious, therefore, that both Article 70.8(a) and Article 70.9 are intended to apply as from the date of entry into force of the WTO Agreement.

India has an obligation to implement the provisions of Article 70.9 of the TRIPS Agreement effective as from the date of entry into force of the WTO Agreement, that is, 1 January 1995. India concedes that legislation is needed to implement this obligation. India has not enacted such legislation. To give meaning and effect to the rights and obligations under Article 70.9 of the TRIPS Agreement, such legislation should have been in effect since 1 January 1995.

For these reasons, we agree with the Panel that India should have had a mechanism in place to provide for the grant of exclusive marketing rights effective as from the date of entry into force of the WTO Agreement, and, therefore, we agree with the Panel that India is in violation of Article 70.9 of the TRIPS Agreement.

12. For an earlier portion of the panel report describing the interpretation methodology used by the panel, see Chapter Seventeen.

D. IS TRIPS THE "FINAL WORD" FOR INTERNATIONAL STANDARDS FOR PROTECTING INTELLECTUAL PROPERTY RIGHTS?

The simple answer to this question is "No." No sooner had the ink dried on the WTO Agreement (and TRIPS Annex), then developed nations began clamoring for strengthened protection in areas that they felt had been over-looked or ignored. Developing countries similarly began to question the efficacy of TRIPS, particularly where the protection of their indigenous knowledge and culture were concerned.

Finally, WIPO, having attended the Uruguay Round Negotiations as an invited observer, stepped once more to the forefront of international IP protection by circulating proposed draft multilateral treaties concerning digital copyright, performance and sound recording rights, and database protection. These efforts led to the adoption of the WIPO Copyright Treaty and the WIPO Performance Rights Treaty in December 1996. For a further discussion of these treaties see Chapter Thirty–Six.

WIPO is also serving as a forum for on-going discussions regarding such diverse issues as famous mark protection, domain name registration, industrial design protection, and the protection of the cultural heritage of indigenous peoples.

In addition to these substantive treaties, as you will see in the following chapters, there are countless multinational and regional treaty regimes that establish minimum standards for the registration of diverse intellectual property rights.

Part VI

REGISTRATION, USE AND THE PROCESS FOR FORMAL PROTECTION OF RIGHTS

Many forms of intellectual property—including patents, trademarks and industrial designs—require registration before that owner is granted a property right in his creation or discovery. Even though early multinational treaty regimes such as The Paris Convention required national treatment, burdensome registration procedures can become a severe impediment to the recognition of a foreign owner's rights. Thus, for example, requiring notarization, legalization or attestation of documents may result in additional costs and delay in registration. Requiring special pleading forms or special user agreements may similarly delay registration or add burdensome costs domestic applicants do not have to bear.

The first efforts to resolve this problem were directed to designing uniform registration *procedures*. One such early effort was the Paris Convention, which established a right of priority of application date for trademarks and patents. This approach was later expanded into uniform application procedures, such as in the Patent Cooperation Treaty and the Trademark Registration Treaty. Later efforts have been directed toward devising a uniform registration *system*. For example, even though under the Patent Cooperation Treaty, application requirements for applicants of signatory countries are identical, an applicant must still prosecute her application in each country. Such individualize prosecution requires the securing of local counsel, the payment of local fees and compliance with local substantive requirements that are not in violation of substantive international treaty obligations. If, however, a uniform registration system existed, ideally, one could file a single application with a single institution who could grant a registration that would be recognized and enforced in all designated countries. To a certain extent, the Community Trademark in the European Union represents such a single registration system.

The problem with establishing a uniform registration system is separating issues of sovereignty and the right to determine local substantive requirements for a grant of property rights with the need for a uniform system of registration. As you read the following sections, ask yourself why registration or notice or other formalities should be required before granting a property right to an intellectual creation? Are there benefits in requiring such registration? And perhaps, most importantly, what attributes should a *workable* international registration system possess?

Chapter Twenty–Three

COPYRIGHTS UNDER INTERNATIONAL LAW

A. WHAT ARE THE FORMAL REQUIREMENTS FOR OBTAINING INTERNATIONAL COPYRIGHT PROTECTION?

Prior to its accession to the Berne Convention, U.S. copyright protection terms were limited to a 28 year period, renewable for an additional 28 years upon the filing of the appropriate documentation with the U.S. Copyright Office, including an application for registration. U.S. law also imposed stringent copyright registration and notice requirements. Many foreign authors' works failed to achieve copyright protection in the United States because they did not meet U.S. formality requirements. Many old U.S. movies similarly failed to achieve copyright renewal status as a result of their failure to comply with complicated U.S. regulations.

Failure to achieve copyright status resulted in the dedication of countless foreign and U.S. films to the public, available for use without compensation to the author. As a result, movie distributors began to produce and distribute cheaply priced copies of these films on videocassettes. Advertisers began to use film clips from these public domain films, also without compensation. In 1989 the U.S. finally acceded to the Berne Convention which precludes requiring any registration formalities and specifies a life plus 50 term of protection for most protected works. What happens to the works that were placed in the public domain prior to U.S. accession for failure to comply with U.S. formalities? Should they be granted renewed copyright status? Should they remain in the public domain? What if the works were no longer protected in their home country (or country of origin)? Should this have any impact on their protection in the United States? How should an international protection regime treat the problem of differing periods of protection between nations?

Read the following from the Supplement: The Berne Convention, Article 5, Universal Copyright Convention, Article III.

THE ROBOT TOYS CASE

HASBRO BRADLEY, INC. v. SPARKLE TOYS, INC.

United States Court of Appeals, Second Circuit, 1985.
780 F.2d 189.

FRIENDLY, CIRCUIT JUDGE.

The companies involved in this copyright case in the District Court for the Southern District of New York are Takara Co., Ltd. ("Takara"), a Japanese company that designed the toys here in question; plaintiff Hasbro Bradley, Inc. ("Hasbro"), a large American toy manufacturer and seller that acquired Takara's rights to United States copyrights for the toys; and defendant Sparkle Toys, Inc. ("Sparkle"), a smaller American toy manufacturer and seller that copied the toys in Asia from models manufactured by Takara which did not carry the copyright notice required by § 401 of the Copyright Act of 1976 (the "Act"), 17 U.S.C. § 101 *et seq.*, and by Article III(1) of the Revised Universal Copyright Convention (U.C.C.), 25 U.S.T. 1341 (1971), to which the United States and Japan are parties. The appeal, by Sparkle, is from an order of Judge Broderick entered April 29, 1985, granting Hasbro a preliminary injunction prohibiting Sparkle from "distributing, selling, marketing, promoting, advertising, imitating or exploiting, in this country, its toys, formerly denoted 'Trans Robot,' which are in violation of plaintiff's registered copyrights in the sculptural embodiments of its 'Topspin' and 'Twin Twist' toys."

"Topspin" and "Twin Twist" (the "toys") are part of Hasbro's "The Transformers" series of changeable robotic action figures. The sculptural expressions of the toys are original designs of Takara, which manufactures "The Transformers" for Hasbro. Takara authored the designs in the summer of 1983 and by the end of November had completed molds for manufacturing the toys. These molds did not contain a copyright notice. Takara avers that the omission was due to the facts that Japanese law does not recognize copyright in toy products and that Takara was unaware that American law does recognize copyright in such works but requires notice, even on copies of the work distributed outside the United States, for copyright protection to be claimed inside the United States. Production of the unmarked toys began in December 1983 and ended in February 1984. Between January and March, approximately 213,000 of the unmarked toys were sold; thereafter, sales were minor and were made only to remove inventory. Whether the unmarked toys were sold only in Asia or some of them were sold as well in the United States is in dispute.

Hasbro was shown the toys by Takara in June 1984 and decided to adopt them into "The Transformers" series. In the course of modifying the toys to meet Hasbro's specifications, Takara designed new molds that contained a copyright notice; at the same time, it added a copyright notice to its old molds. Takara avers that after August 1984 no toys using molds that did not contain a copyright notice were manufactured for sale anywhere in the world. Hasbro has widely distributed the toys in the United States, beginning in January 1985. Sparkle does not dispute that all of the toys sold in this country by Hasbro have born copyright notice.

Sometime in June 1984, Takara orally granted Hasbro the exclusive right to import and sell the toys in the United States and assigned to Hasbro the United States copyrights in the designs of the toys, including the right to apply for copyright registration. A written confirmation of assignment was executed as of November 12, 1984. Hasbro applied to register copyrights in the United States in both sculptural expressions of each toy on November 29, 1984, listing Takara as the "author" and itself as the "copyright claimant" by virtue of the assignment from Takara. Certificates of registration were granted effective December 3, 1984.

The settled law of this circuit is that a preliminary injunction may be granted only upon a showing of "(a) irreparable harm and (b) either (1) likelihood of success on the merits or (2) sufficiently serious questions going to the merits to make them a fair ground for litigation and a balance of hardships tipping decidedly toward the party requesting the preliminary relief." Irreparable harm may ordinarily be presumed from copyright infringement. *Wainwright Securities, Inc. v. Wall Street Transcript Corp.*, 558 F.2d 91, 94 (2 Cir.1977), *cert. denied* 434 U.S. 1014, 98 S.Ct. 730, 54 L.Ed.2d 759 (1978). A *prima facie* case of copyright infringement consists of proof that the plaintiff owns a valid copyright and the defendant has engaged in unauthorized copying. Since Sparkle admits to unauthorized copying, the only issue before us in reviewing the grant of the preliminary injunction is whether Hasbro's copyrights for the toys are valid. Under § 410(c) of the Act, Hasbro's certificates of copyright registration are *prima facie* evidence that the copyrights are valid, shifting to Sparkle the burden of proving the contrary. Sparkle attempts to meet this burden with various lines of argument, all stemming from the fact that the toys were initially sold by Takara without copyright notice.

Sparkle's most basic position is that sale of the unmarked toys by Takara in Japan injected the designs into the public domain. If the designs were truly in the public domain, Hasbro could have enjoyed no copyrights in the toys, and Sparkle's copying would have been permissible.

There is no dispute that the toys here at issue were originally designed by Takara in June 1983. Since the toys were authored by a Japanese national and first "published" (*i.e.* sold) in Japan, they enjoyed copyright protection under United States law from the moment they were created, by virtue of both § 104(b) of the Act and Article II(1) of the U.C.C.[4]

---

4. Section 104(B) of the act reads, in pertinent part: The works specified by sec-tions 102 and 103, when published, are subject to protection under this title if(1) on

As previously stated, there is also no dispute that before the assignment of Takara's copyrights to Hasbro approximately 213,000 of the toys were sold, mostly in Japan, without copyright notice. This omission of notice from toys sold by Takara or with its authority outside the United States violated § 401(a) of the Act, which requires: Whenever a work protected under this title is published in the United States or elsewhere by authority of the copyright owner, a notice of copyright as provided by this section shall be placed on all publicly distributed copies from which the work can be visually perceived, either directly or with the aid of a machine or device.

This does not mean, however, that the Takara designs were immediately thrust into the public domain. The Act explicitly provides in § 405(a) that the omission of notice from copies of a protected work may be excused or cured under certain circumstances, in which case the copyright is valid from the moment the work was created, just as if no omission had occurred.

It is not contended that the omission of notice from the toys could have been excused under either subsections (1) or (3) of § 405(a); rather, reliance is placed on subsection (2). In effect, § 405(a)(2) allows a person who publishes a copyrightable work without notice to hold a kind of incipient copyright in the work for five years thereafter: if the omission is cured in that time through registration and the exercise of "a reasonable effort to add notice to all copies that are distributed to the public in the United States after the omission has been discovered," the copyright is perfected and valid retroactively for the entire period after cure; if the omission is not cured in that time, the incipient copyright never achieves enforceability.

There is no dispute that Takara had not cured the omission of notice from the toys under § 405(a)(2) before assigning to Hasbro in June 1984 "the entire right, title and interest to any copyrights on the DESIGNS for the United States of America." Hasbro's copyrights initially had only such validity as Takara's. As shown above, Takara's violation of the notice requirement left Hasbro with only an incipient copyright, subject to cure.

The issue thus becomes whether Hasbro has cured Takara's omission of notice under § 405(a)(2). There is no question that Hasbro, as Takara's assignee, is permitted to effect cure through its own efforts. Not disputing this, Sparkle argues that Hasbro cannot effect cure under § 405(a)(2) because Takara's omission of notice was deliberate.

the date of first publication, one or more of the authors is a national or domiciliary of the United States, or is a national, domiciliary, or sovereign authority of a foreign nation that is a party to a copyright treaty to which the United States is also a party; or (2) the work is first published in the United States or in a foreign nation that, on the date of first publication, is a party to the universal Copyright Convention; Article II(1) of the U.C.C. reads: Published works of nationals of any Contracting State and works first published in that state shall enjoy in each other contracting State the same protection as that other State accords to works of its nationals first published in its own territory, as well as the protection specially granted by this Convention.

We conclude that the omission of notice from the toys, even if deliberate on Takara's part, was subject to cure under § 405(a)(2), and we pass on to the question whether Hasbro in fact effectuated cure.

There is no dispute that Hasbro validly registered its copyrights in the Takara designs within five years of publication of the unmarked toys, thus satisfying one of the two requirements for cure under § 405(a)(2). Sparkle admits also that Hasbro has affixed notice to all of the toys since sold under its authority in the United States and elsewhere. It argues, however, that Hasbro did not make "a reasonable effort" to affix notice to toys from the unmarked batch initially produced by Takara and thus failed to satisfy the second requirement of § 405(a)(2). Hasbro asserts that this was unnecessary: that its obligations under § 405(a)(2) are limited to unmarked toys distributed to the public in the United States by its own authority as the "copyright owner" and, insofar as we have previously concluded that this phrase includes Takara, to unmarked toys so distributed by Takara before the assignment.

We are not prepared to endorse this. The introductory words to § 405(a) indeed speak of copies "publicly distributed by authority of the copyright owner." However, as we have held above, the sales of unmarked toys by Takara in Japan before the assignment of the copyright fall within this phrase. In the absence of any prohibition on resale of these toys in the United States, the purchasers were free to sell them here. To be sure, the requirement of § 405(a)(2) to add notice is limited to copies "that are distributed to the public in the United States," but it seems significant that Congress did not here repeat the words "by authority of the copyright owner."

We are content, however, to leave undecided the question whether Hasbro would be obligated under § 405(a)(2) to make a reasonable effort to affix notice even with respect to unmarked toys distributed in the United States by persons other than itself or Takara. At this juncture, Sparkle has yet to produce credible evidence that any of the unmarked toys have been publicly distributed in the United States at all, let alone evidence of who distributed them. Whether any unmarked toys were introduced into the United States and, if so, who introduced them and what efforts to mark them would be reasonable are questions that can be resolved at trial when Hasbro seeks a permanent injunction.

Notes and Questions

1.   Patents must be applied for before they are granted protection. Why aren't copyrights subject to similar international registration requirements? Is there something unique about copyrighted works that makes registration unnecessary?

2.   What goals do copyright registration and notice provisions serve?

3.   The Uniform Copyright Convention (U.C.C.) was largely developed in response to U.S. refusals to accede to the Berne Convention. With U.S. accession to Berne, the significance of the U.C.C. has waned. Some countries,

however, remain signatories to the U.C.C., and have not yet acceded to the Berne Convention or TRIPS. Thus, compliance with the notice provisions under the U.C.C. for internationally distributed works may be a useful precaution.

4. Under the Berne Convention, may the United States continue to impose the notice requirements discussed in the *Robot Toys* case without violating its treaty obligations?

5. Must Hasbro correct notice deficiencies abroad to protect its U.S. copyright? What steps must it take?

6. Subsequent to U.S. accession to the Berne Convention, U.S. copyright laws were revised to eliminate the notice provisions of Section 405 for all works first distributed subsequent to March 1, 1989 (post-accession).

7. *Continuing Registration Requirements.* Although the Berne Convention under Article 5 mandates that no formal qualification requirements be imposed on the works of foreign nationals for protection to attach, it does not preclude a country's requiring more stringent formalities for its own citizens' works. Thus, although under U.S. law registration is *not* required for a foreign national to obtain copyright protection for his works, U.S. citizens must still record their claim of copyright with the U.S. Copyright Office prior to filing suit to enforce their copyright. 17 U.S.C. § 401.

8. *Retroactivity.* Prior to acceding to the Berne Convention in 1989, the U.S. had placed various works into the public domain for their failure to comply with U.S. notice and/or registration requirements. Having acceded to Berne, are these works now removed from the public domain? If so, what rights, if any, should parties who used such works prior to their removal from the public domain have to continue using such works? The U.S., through legislation, decreed that all foreign works placed in the public domain as a result of lack of compliance with U.S. formalities would be restored to copyright protected status for the term of their remaining copyright term. The Copyright Restoration Act provides:

(1) Copyright subsists, in accordance with this section, in restored works, and vests automatically on the date of restoration.

(2) Any work in which copyright is restored under this section shall subsist for the remainder of the term of copyright that the work would have otherwise been granted in the United States if the work never entered the public domain in the United States.

(3) Ownership of restored copyright. A restored work vests initially in the author or initial rightholder of the work as determined by the law of the source country of the work.

(4) Filing of notice of intent to enforce restored copyright against reliance parties. On or after the date of restoration, any person who owns a copyright in a restored work or an exclusive right therein may file with the Copyright Office a notice of intent to enforce that person's copyright or exclusive right or may serve such a notice directly on a reliance party. Acceptance of a notice by the Copyright Office is effective as to any reliance parties but shall not create a presumption of the validity of any of the facts stated therein. Service on a reliance party is effective as to that reliance party and any other reliance parties with

actual knowledge of such service and of the contents of that notice. (17 U.S.C. § 104A)

Was the enactment of this statute mandated under Berne?

Problem

Your client Sophisticated Games has developed a software program that turns any computer screen into a virtual reality monitor. Sophisticated Games is ready to send the program for beta testing in the United States. If the game proves as successful as it anticipates, Sophisticated plans to market the game in the U.S., Canada, Australia, the United Kingdom, and Japan. What steps would you recommend the client take to protect its copyright in the Game? What notices, if any, should it provide on its software? On the packaging? On any documentation provided with the game?

Chapter Twenty–Four

PATENTS UNDER INTERNATIONAL LAW: THE FIRST TO FILE CONTROVERSY

The image of the mad scientist working in his basement to create the Frankenstein monster is a potent one in Western literature. The reality is that a great many inventions and scientific discoveries are made, not by engineers and research scientists employed by well-endowed corporations and research institutions, but by single individuals with a better idea. The problem is that the small inventor may not have the money to capitalize his invention, including the money or access to legal counsel to file applications internationally to protect his rights. Can an international patent registration system meet its obvious goals of administrative efficiency and predictability while still providing protection for small inventors?

What if, as a matter of culture and history, one country has always valued the role of the creative genius, the single inventor slaving away to create a better mousetrap? In order to continue to encourage such small inventors, the laws of this country provide that patent rights are granted to the first person that invents a protected device. Other countries grant patent rights to the first person to file a patent invention, in order to promote administrative efficiency and order. How should the international community deal with this conflict? Is it really simply a question of procedural rules or is there a substantive component to this issue? Where do you draw the line between substance and procedure in establishing an international registration system?

Most countries today base patent rights on the date an application for patent registration is filed in the country in which patent protection is sought. Thus, for example, if two people have created the same patentable invention, the first one to file for patent protection is generally entitled to the patent.

By contrast, in the United States patent rights go to the first to invent. Thus, in the United States, if Inventor A first comes up with the idea for a patentable invention (conception) and works diligently to reduce the idea to practice, even if Inventor B files a patent application before Inventor A, Inventor A has the right to sole ownership of the patent. In fact, if Inventor A has the right to challenge Inventor's B ownership of the patent, even *after* the Patent Office has issued the Patent. Although registration procedures have been proposed in the U.S. which would alter the first-to-invent model, such legislation has been strongly (and, to date, successfully) challenged.

A. WHAT ARE THE FORMAL REQUIREMENTS FOR OBTAINING PATENT PROTECTION INTERNATIONALLY?

No country grants patent rights without registration of the protected invention. Furthermore, since novelty is a recognized international requirement (*See, e.g.*, Article 27 of TRIPS), failure to apply for patent protection within a narrow time frame (upon creation in countries that require absolute novelty, one year from the time of first publication or public use of the invention in countries like the U.S. that grant a grace period) precludes protection in that country. One of the greatest problems facing a patent owner is the potentially staggering costs of registering his invention in every country where he anticipates commercializing the invention. International efforts to facilitate international registration of patents has generally taken one of two forms—multinational treaties establishing uniform registration *procedures* and multinational treaties establishing uniform registration *standards*. The second category of protection has been difficult to achieve in light of both economic and national sovereignty concerns.

U.S. PATENT 5,816,267
Oct. 6, 1998.

BARRETTE COMBINED WITH A COMB

INVENTOR: Chou, Kuo–Hua, No. 17, Alley 10, Lane 118, Su–Wei Rd., Wu–Ku Hsiang, Taipei County, China (Taiwan)

APPL–N0: 880,872

FILED: Jun. 23, 1997

ABSTRACT

A barrette combined with a comb is provided that includes an elongated base plate having a retainer unit at one end and two upright lugs bilaterally disposed at an opposite end. A clamping plate is included that has a fixed end pivoted to the upright lugs of the base plate and a free end formed with a coupling that is adapted for coupling to the retainer unit of the base plate. A comb strip is also included that is pivotally coupled to the retainer unit of the base plate. The comb strip has longitudinal rows of teeth and is displaceable between a first position, in which the comb strip is closed on the base plate and retained thereto by the clamping plate, and a second position in which the cob strip is extended out of the base plate and secured in the extended position by the clamping plate for cleaning and smoothing the hair.

BACKGROUND OF THE INVENTION

The present invention relates to barrettes for holding a woman's hair, and more particularly to such a barrette which can be arranged into the form of a hairbrush for cleaning and smoothing the hair.

A regular barrette is generally comprised of an elongated, smoothly arched base plate having two upright lugs bilaterally disposed at one end and a retainer unit disposed at an opposite end, and an arched clamping plate having a fixed end pivoted to the upright lugs of the base plate and a free end releasably secured to the retainer unit of the base plate. The arched clamping plate has two longitudinal slots disposed in parallel and defining an arched springy strip there between. When in use, the free end of the clamping plate is secured to the retainer unit of the base plate, permitting the hair to be retained between the clamping plate and the base plate and held down by the arched springy strip of the clamping plate. This structure of barrette has drawbacks. Because engagement position between the free end of the clamping plate and the retainer unit of the base plate is not adjustable, the clamping force of the clamping plate cannot be adjusted subject to the volume of hair to be clamped. Another drawback of this structure of barrette is that the hair tends to be stretched or damaged when closing or opening the clamping plate. Furthermore, this structure of barrette can only be used for holding the hair, it cannot be used for hairbrush means for cleaning or smoothing the hair.

SUMMARY OF THE INVENTION

The present invention has been accomplished under the circumstances in view. It is one object of the present invention to provide a barrette which can be conveniently adjusted subject to the volume of hair to be clamped. It is another object of the present invention to provide a barrette which can be arranged into the form of a hairbrush for cleaning and smoothing the hair. According to one aspect of the present invention, the barrette comprises an elongated base plate having a retainer unit at one end and two upright lugs bilaterally disposed at an opposite end, and a clamping plate having a fixed end pivoted to the upright lugs of the base plate and a free end made with coupling means adapted for securing to the retainer unit of the base plate, wherein a comb strip is coupled to the retainer unit of the base plate and set between a first position in which the comb strip is closed on the base plate and retained thereto by the clamping plate, and a second position in which the comb strip is extended out of the base plate and secured in the extended position by the clamping plate for cleaning and smoothing the hair, the comb strip comprising two horizontal pivot rods bilaterally disposed at a fixed end thereof and respectively pivoted to the retainer unit of the base plate, two shoulders bilaterally disposed at a free end thereof which are forced into engagement between the upright lugs of the base plate when the comb strip is turned to the first position, and longitudinal rows of teeth raised between its fixed end and free end for cleaning and smoothing the hair. According to another aspect of the present invention, the retainer unit of the base plate comprises two hooked retaining strips having vertically spaced hooked portions adapted for adjustably securing the coupling means of the free end of the clamping plate to hold down the hair by a proper clamping force.

CLAIMS: What the invention claimed is:

1.   A combined barrette and comb, comprising:

a longitudinally extended base plate having a retainer unit formed on a first end thereof and a pair of spaced upright lugs formed on an opposing second end of said base plate, said retaining unit including a pair of hooked retaining strips respectively extending from a pair of upright finger strips;

a clamping plate having one end pivotally coupled to said base plate between said upright lugs and an opening formed in an opposing end for releasable coupling with said pair of hooked retaining strips; and,

a comb strip having longitudinal rows of teeth extending from one side thereof and being of sufficient length to comb a user's hair, said comb strip having a first end pivotally coupled to said retainer unit and a second end extending to said pair of upright lugs when said comb strip is in a first position overlaying said base plate, said comb strip being maintained in said first position by said clamping plate being disposed in overlaying relationship and engaged by said pair of hooked retaining strips, said comb strip having a coupling hole formed there through adjacent said first end thereof for releasable coupling with said pair of hooked retaining strips when said comb strip is rotated into a second position wherein said comb strip extends from said base plate.

Notes and Questions

1.   Although patents are often sought to protect important or complicated technological developments, as the above patent demonstrates, patents can be granted for low-tech developments such as improvements in barrette technology as well.

2.   What are the claims covered by the patent in question?

3.   Do the specifications clarify the claims or add to them in any way?

4.   Who is the inventor of the invention? Has the patent been assigned?

5.   Under U.S. law, the "best mode" of the invention must be disclosed. (*See* 35 U.S.C. § 112). How would you determine whether the barrette patent meets these requirements?

6.   *The Role Of Patents In Protecting Inventions.* The precise claims in the patent play a pre-eminent role in determining the scope of protection to be afforded the invention in question. Regardless of how the inventor personally describes his invention, the actual invention lies in the claims and specifications set forth in the issued patent registration—sometimes referred

to as the "patent grant" or "letters patent." Consequently, the drafting of patent claims in the application may be among the most significant acts taken to protect the inventor's rights internationally.

7.   As you examine the international procedures established to govern the grant of patent rights, ask yourself whether the barrette patent meets these requirements. What changes would you be required to make (if any) to assure compliance with the various treaty requirements discussed below?

B. WHAT PROCEDURES ARE REQUIRED UNDER THE PATENT COOPERATION TREATY?

Read the following Articles from The Patent Cooperation Treaty from the Supplement: 3, 5, 6, 11, 15, 27.

Notes and Questions

1.   The Patent Cooperation Treaty was entered into force on January 24, 1978. It is a special agreement under the Paris Union and is currently administered by the WIPO. The International Bureau of WIPO is responsible for transmitting the application and International Search Report on prior art to all member countries which the applicant has designated. Upon provision of a translation and payment of the necessary registration fees, the application will be converted into a national application. Regulations have been adopted which further clarify the requirements of the PCT. Thus, for example, Rule 9 specifies that an international application under the PCT "shall not contain expressions or drawing contrary to morality or to public order" or "statements disparaging the products or processes of any particular person other than the applicant or the merits or validity of applications or patents of any such person." The rule further provides that "mere comparisons with the prior act shall not be considered disparaging *per se.*" The regulations clarify the requirement a description of the invention of a "drawing" and "claims" under Articles 5, 6 and 7 of the PCT, respectively.

2.   *Procedure v. Substance.* The Patent Cooperation Treaty does not contain a substantive definition of a patent similar to Article 27 of TRIPS. Its only definition of a covered patent is in Article 2(i) which states: "references to a 'patent' shall be construed as references to patents for inventions, inventors' certificates, utility certificates, utility models, patents or certificates of addition." Does the Patent Cooperation Treaty establish any minimum substantive requirements for the grant of a patent? For example, could a country require absolute novelty without violating its obligations under the Patent Cooperation Treaty?

3.   Review Articles 2 and 27–34 of TRIPS which establish the minimum substantive standards for patent protection under the treaty. Do any of these articles specify the procedures to be used to register the patent in question? If so, does the Patent Cooperation Treaty satisfy these requirements? Does it satisfy the minimum substantive requirements of Articles 4 and 5 of the Paris Convention?

4. *The "National" Aspects of the PCT.* Does the Patent Cooperation Treaty provide for an international patent grant upon the filing of a single application? For example, assume that your client has created a new software that results in universal platform compatibility. She has indicated that she intends to market this software in North America, Asia and Europe. You file an application on her behalf under the Patent Cooperation Treaty and designate 10 countries for patent protection. Assuming that your application is successfully filed, is your client guaranteed patent protection in all ten countries?

5. What if the United States issues a final refusal because it finds your client's invention to be obvious? Does the United States' failure to afford your client patentability preclude patent protection in the other ten countries? What if the United States is the home or domiciliary country for your client? Does the domiciliary country's failure to afford protection preclude the grant of patent rights by other countries?

6. The Patent Cooperation Treaty is open to any country that is a signatory to the Paris Convention and has become one of the most important treaties for international patent registration. Compare its requirements and treatment of the problem of international registration with the European Patent Convention discussed below.

7. In addition to the Patent Cooperation Treaty, there are numerous other multinational treaties that deal with patent registration issues for particular types of inventions.

8. *Microorganisms.* The Budapest Treaty on the International Recognition of the Deposit of Microorganisms for the Purposes of Patent Procedure, for example, was entered into force to establish procedures for depositing microorganisms in connection with patent applications. Because of their specialized nature, microorganisms often cannot be properly disclosed by a simple written statement. The Budapest Treaty provides for the establishment of international depository authorities who accept the deposit of microorganism samples in connection with patent applications and who agree to abide by certain regulations regarding the storage, testing and providing of samples to appropriate requesting authorities. The Treaty is administered by the International Bureau of the World Intellectual Property Organization (WIPO).

9. *Plant Varieties.* The International Convention for the Protection of New Varieties of Plants (UPOV) goes beyond simply establishing registration procedures for a particular type of invention–in this case, breeder plant varieties. Instead, it establishes minimum substantive standards for the protection of such plants. Like the Paris Convention, which did not cover botanical plant varieties, UPOV requires national treatment and establishes certain minimum substantive requirements, including granting a "special title of protection" or "patent" recognizing a plant breeder's right to protection for qualified new plant varieties. Applicants are given a one year priority filing period similar to that granted utility patents under the Paris Convention. For a discussion of the potential impact of plant patents on the issue of the protection of flora and fauna in developing countries, see Part XII.

10. *Patent Classification*. The Strasbourg Agreement Concerning International Patent Classification establishes a uniform classification system for patents which aids in creating a uniform basis for international patent searches. The classification system established under the Agreement divides patents into 114 classes, with over 46,000 groups and subgroups. It is administered by WIPO's International Bureau.

11. *International Searching*. Each application under the PCT is subject to an international prior art search by an "International Searching Authority" (ISA). The ISA is usually a national patent office or an institution like the European Patent Office. The ISA will draw up an international search report (ISR) and send it to the applicant and the WIPO. The ISA must consider published international PCT patent applications and patents, published regional applications for patents and inventors' certificates, and published regional patents and inventors' certificates. It must also consider non-patent literature and the following "national patent documents":

> patents issued in and after 1920, and patent applications published in and after 1920, by France, Germany, Japan, the former Soviet Union, Switzerland, the United Kingdom and the United States of America; inventors' certificates issued by the Soviet Union, published applications for and utility certificates issued by France, and patents issued by, and published applications published in, every other country after 1920 that are in English, French, German or Spanish so long as the national Patent Office of the country in question sorts such documents and places them at the disposal of the ISA. (Rule 34 Regulations under the Patent Cooperation Treaty).

ABSTRACT OF A PCT PATENT APPLICATION BACK PACK FRAME CONVERTIBLE TO CHAIR

WO9727776A2.

Inventor: COLGAN, Ken, 11748 Welby Way, North Hollywood, CA 91604, United States of America

Application No.: WO1997U.S.0001530

Priority: U.S.1996008596573

Designated Countries: AL, AM, AT, AU, AZ, BA, BB, BG, BR, BY, CA, CH, CN, CU, CZ, DE, DK, EE, ES, FI, GB, GE, HU, IL, IS, JP, KE, KG, KP, KR, KZ, LC, LK, LR, LS, LT, LU, LV, MD, MG, MK, MN, MW, MX, NO, NZ, PL, PT, RO, RU, SD, SE, SG, SI, SK, TJ, TM, TR, TT, UA, UG, UZ, VN, YU, European patent: AT, BE, CH, DE, DK, ES, FI, FR, GB, GR, IE, IT, LU, MC, NL, PT, SE, OAPI patent: BF, BJ, CF, CG, CI, CM, GA, GN, ML, MR, NE, SN, TD, TG, ARIPO patent: KE, LS, MW, SD, SZ, UG

Abstract: This invention relates to back pack frames which are convertible to chairs. This invention includes a back pack frame interconnected to a mutually independent set of generally lightweight seat and rear leg attachments that allow the user to quickly convert a back pack into a secure, comfortable chair, and to conversely quickly convert the chair into a back pack. The attachments include seat and rear leg frames. The seat frame is connected to the front side of the back pack frame and the rear leg frame is connected to the back side of the back pack frame. The frames are operably connected to independently move from a first closed back pack position and a second open chair position. In the back pack position, the frame members are disposed generally parallel to each other. The seat and rear leg frames are in general alignment with the front and back sides of the back pack frame. In the chair position, the back pack frame provides the chair back and front legs. The seat frame extends outward from the front side of the back pack frame to provide the seat of the chair. The rear leg frame extends outwardly from the back side of the back pack frame to provide the rear legs of the chair. The back pack, seat and rear leg frames are capable of a unitary, self contained arrangement.

The seat and rear leg frames are also selectively demountable for storage purposes in the back pack position. The seat frame may include a seat cover.

Notes and Questions

1.   What is the subject of the applied-for invention? Does it facially qualify as patentable subject matter under TRIPS and the PCT?

2.   What is the home country or country of origin of the invention?

3.   Has the invention been granted patent protection in any country at the time o f the PCT application?

4.   Is the applicant seeking priority treatment? Based on which country?

5.   What additional information would you need in order to complete the PCT application contained in the Supplement for this invention?

6.   What additional information would you need in order to advise the inventor whether his invention would be patentable in all of the designated countries?

C.   WHAT ARE THE PROCEDURES FOR REGISTERING AN INVENTION UNDER THE EUROPEAN PATENT CONVENTION?

Read the following Articles from the European Patent Convention (EPC) from the Supplement: 52–54, 66, 56, 57, 62–65, 71, 83, 84.

Notes and Questions

1.   The European Patent Convention (EPC) was entered into force in 1977. Only those countries which are members of the European Union may accede to the EPC, however, any natural or legal person, regardless of nationality or place of residence may file an application for a European Patent. The EPC is administered by the European Patent Office and the Administrative Council, which is composed of representatives of European Union member states and oversees the European Patent Office. All applications under the EPC must be submitted to the European Patent Office.

2. *Substance v. Procedure.* Does the European Patent Convention establish any minimum substance requirements for the grant of a patent? For example, could a country require absolute novelty without violating its obligations under the European Patent Convention?

3. Does the European Patent Convention provide for an international patent grant upon the filing of a single application? For example, assume that your client, who is domiciled in France, has created a new software that results in universal platform compatibility. She has indicated that she intends to market this software throughout Europe. You file an application on her behalf under the European Patent Convention and designate 10 countries for patent protection. Assuming that your application is successfully filed, is your client guaranteed a patent registration in all ten countries? Compare your answer with the results obtained under the Patent Cooperation Treaty.

4. Under Article 64, if the European Patent Office grants the patent, as of its date of publication, the European Patent is treated as if it were granted as a national patent in each designated country. Infringement, however, is dealt with under the national laws of each country. (Article 64(3)).

5. Once a European Patent issues, it can only be revoked if the patent does not cover patentable subject matter, if the invention is not adequately disclosed, if the patent granted exceeds the scope of the application or if the proprietor of the patent is not entitled to it. (Article 138).

6. The European Patent Office may be a designated office under the Patent Cooperation Treaty. Thus, an applicant of a non-European Union member country can obtain a European Patent by requesting a European Patent in his application.

7. What if Spain refuses to enforce your client's patent because under Spanish law it would be considered obvious? Would this ground of invalidity serve to invalidate the European Patent under the Convention? If yes, would invalidity under Spanish law preclude patent protection in the other nine countries? What if, under English law, the law of the client's home or domiciliary country, your client's patent is considered invalid due to lack of novelty? Would England's failure to protect your client's invention preclude the grant of patent rights by other countries? Compare your answers with the results obtained under the Patent Cooperation Treaty above.

8. For a more complete discussion of European Patent Convention requirements, *see generally* Guy Tritton, INTELLECTUAL PROPERTY IN EUROPE (Sweet & Maxwell 1996).

9. A client interested in obtaining international protection for its invention in a member country of the European Union has three options: file a national application; file an application under the European Patent Convention or file an application under the PCT. Each path has different advantages and disadvantages, based primarily on cost, time for prosecution and scope of protection. *See generally* Guy Tritton, INTELLECTUAL PROPERTY IN EUROPE, §§ 2.217–2.218 (Sweet & Maxwell 1996).

10. Some foreign attorneys recommend that where protection is sought in several European countries it may be preferable to make national filings,

examine the national search reports, and (if encouraging) file an international application under the PCT, designating the EPO as the International Search Authority and International Preliminary Examining authority. This route provides a high degree of flexibility. *See, e.g., Helmut Sonn, "National Patents, EPC or PCT: Which Route to Choose?"* Patent World (April 1990); Guy Tritton, *supra.*

11. *Eurasian Patents.* The European Patent Treaty is not the only treaty which attempts to establish a regional patent application system. The Eurasian Patent Convention establishes a Eurasian Patent Organization whose official language is Russian and which consists of a Eurasian Patent Office and an Administrative Council, made up of officials of the member states and charged with administering the Eurasian Patent Office. Similar to the European Patent Convention, the Eurasian Patent Convention allows for the grant of a Eurasian Patent, based on a substantive examination. The validity of the patent, and its infringement is determined by the national laws of each member state. Where the Eurasian Patent is denied, the applicant may convert the application into a national filing in the designated countries. Current members of the Convention include many of the former members of the Soviet Union, including the Russian Federation, Krygyzstan and Turkmenistan.

D. WHAT INTERNATIONAL REGISTRATION PROBLEMS ARE CAUSED BY THE U.S. BEST MODE REQUIREMENT?

THE M16 RIFLE CASE
CHRISTIANSON v. COLT INDUSTRIES OPERATING CORP.

U.S. Court of Appeals, Seventh Circuit, 1989.
870 F.2d 1292 (7th Cir.), *cert. denied*, 493 U.S. 822, 110 S.Ct. 81 (1989).

Christianson challenged the sufficiency of the inventor's disclosure of its patent for improvements on M–16 rifles parts. He claimed that the Colt's patent was invalid because it failed to disclose the specifications and tolerances necessary to make the newly patented parts interchangeable with existing M–16 rifles. This interchangeability, Christianson claimed, was the best mode of the invention required to be disclosed under Section 112. The court rejected Christianson's claim. The court found that interchangeability was not a covered claim of plaintiff's patent. It stated:

"The best mode requirement assures that inventors do not conceal the best mode known to them when they file a patent application, but the 'best mode' is that of practicing the *claimed* invention." *It has nothing to do with mass production or sales to customers having particular requirements.* (Emphasis in original; citation omitted) In this case, interchangeability with M–16 parts appears nowhere as a limitation in any claim ... Thus, the *best mode* for making and using and carrying out the *claimed inventions* does not entail or involve either the M–16 rifle or interchangeability [aspects arguably necessary for commercialization of the invention]. The "best mode" for making and using the claimed parts relates to their use in *a* rifle, any rifle.

THE AZEOTROPING CASE

GLAXO INC. v. NOVOPHARM LTD

U.S. Court of Appeals, Federal Circuit, 1995.
52 F.3d 1043.

Glaxo was the owner of a U.S. patent for a specific crystalline form of the compound ranitidine hydrochloride which it marketed as an anti-ulcer medication under the brand name Zantac. The patent disclosed "Form 1" of the compound. "Form 2" of the compound had better filtration and drying properties. It had poor flow properties though. These flow properties were overcome by a novel azeotroping process (a technique for separating chemical mixtures) that also was not disclosed in the patent. The defendant claimed Glaxo's failure to disclose the azeotroping process used to create Form 2 (which Glaxo had decided to commercialize because of its improved properties) violated the duty to provide the specification that "set[s] forth the best mode contemplated by the inventor of carrying out his invention." 35 U.S.C. § 112. Glaxo defended on the basis that the inventor of the invention did not know of the azeotroping of the compound or its benefits and, therefore, did not consider this the best mode of his invention. Evidence introduced by Glaxo established that the inventor was not involved in commercialization decisions. It is unclear whether Glaxo purposefully walled-off the inventor to keep knowledge of the azeotroping method from the inventor to avoid its disclosure under best mode requirements.

The best mode of carrying out an invention; indeed if there is one, to be disclosed is "that 'contemplated by the inventor.' This requirement it should be noted, is not absolute, since it only requires disclosure of the best mode contemplated by the inventor, presumably at the time of filing the application. The best mode requirement lies at the heart of the statutory *quid pro quo* of the patent system. In fact, as we have previously stated, the sole purpose of the best mode requirement "is to restrain inventors from applying for patents while at the same time concealing from the public the preferred embodiments of *their inventions* which *they* have in face conceived." *Chemcast Corp. v. Arco Indus. Corp.*, 913 F.2d 923 (Fed.Cir.1990). The best mode inquiry focuses on the inventor's state of mind at the time he filed his application, raising a subjective factual question The specificity of disclosure required to comply with the best mode requirement must be determined by the knowledge of facts within the possession of the inventor at the time of filing the application."

Given the focus on the knowledge of the inventor, the court held that the absence of knowledge of the azeotroping process by the inventor precluded its required disclosure.

[T]he practical reality is that inventors in most every corporate scenario cannot know all of the technology in which their employers are engaged. Therefore, whether intentionally or not, inventors will be effectively isolated from research no matter how relevant it is to the field in which they are working. Separating scenarios in which employers unintentionally isolate inventors from relevant research from instances in which employers deliberately set out to screen inventors from research would ignore the very words of § 112 Congress specifically limited the best mode required to that contemplated by the inventor.

THE GASKET CASE
CHEMCAST CORP. v. ARCO INDUS. CORP.

U.S. Court of Appeals, Federal Court, 1990.
913 F.2d 923.

The '879 patent claims a sealing member in the form of a grommet or plug button that is designed to seal an opening in, for example, a sheet metal.

Chemcast and its competitor Arco Industries Corporation were both engaged in the manufacture and sale of sealing members such as grommets, gaskets, and plug buttons, which are designed to seal openings in sheet metal and are used in the automobile industry. An Ex-Arco employee Phillip L. Rubright founded Chemcast in 1973 and subsequently conceived of and designed specifically for Oldsmobile, a Chemcast customer, a dual durometer grommet. He filed a patent application together with an assignment of invention to Chemcast in January of 1976. The patent issued in April of 1978. Chemcast later sued Arco Industries for patent infringment. Arco claimed that the grommet patent was invalid for failure to disclose the best mode of the invention. In analyzing the defendant's claims, the court reaffirmed the subjective nature of the analysis, stating:

> Failure to comply with the best mode requirement amounts to concealing the preferred mode contemplated by the applicant at the time of filing. *See Hybritech Inc. v. Monoclonal Antibodies*, Inc., 802 F.2d 1367, 1384–85, 231 U.S.PQ 81, 94 (Fed.Cir.1986), *cert. denied*, [480 U.S. 947, 107 S.Ct. 1606, 94 L.Ed.2d 792] (1987). In order for a district court to conclude that the best mode requirement is not satisfied, the focus must be that the inventor knew of, *i.e.*, "contemplated," and concealed a better mode than he disclosed. *Id* . The focus for a best mode analysis is not simply on whether the patent discloses the most suitable material for carrying out the claimed invention. The best mode inquiry focuses on the inventor's state of mind as of the time he filed his application—a subjective, factual question. But this focus is not exclusive. Our statements that "there is no objective standard by which to judge the adequacy of a best mode disclosure," and that "only evidence of concealment (acciden-

tal or intentional) is to be considered," *In re Sherwood*, 613 F.2d 809, 816, 204 U.S.PQ 537, 544 (CCPA 1980), assumed that both the level of skill in the art and the scope of the claimed invention were additional, objective metes and bounds of a best mode disclosure. Of necessity, the disclosure required by section 112 is directed to those skilled in the art. Therefore, one must consider the level of skill in the relevant art in determining whether a specification discloses the best mode. We have consistently recognized that whether a best mode disclosure is adequate, that is, whether the inventor concealed a better mode of practicing his invention than he disclosed, is a function of not only what the inventor knew but also how one skilled in the art would have understood his disclosure. *See, e.g., Dana Corp.*, 860 F.2d at 418, 8 U.S.PQ2d at 1696 (best mode requirement violated because inventor failed to disclose whether to use specific surface treatment that he knew was necessary to the satisfactory performance of his invention, even though how to perform the treatment itself was known in the art. "Dana's argument that the best mode requirement may be met solely by reference to what was known in the prior art is incorrect.") (emphasis added), *Spectra-Physics*, 827 F.2d at 1536, 3 U.S.PQ2d at 1745 (best mode violated where inventors of laser failed to disclose details of their preferred TiCuSil brazing method which were not contained in the prior art and were "contrary to criteria for the use of TiCuSil as contained in the literature."); *W.L. Gore*, 721 F.2d at 1556, 220 U.S.PQ at 316 (no best mode violation where inventor did not disclose the only mode of calculating stretch rate that he used, because that "mode would have been employed by those of ordinary skill in the art at the time the application was filed. As indicated, Dr. Gore's disclosure must be examined for § 112 compliance in light of knowledge extant in the art on his application filing date."); *Sherwood*, 613 F.2d at 816, 204 U.S.PQ at 544 (no best mode violation where specification disclosed underlying concepts and mathematical equations that, together with "the menial tools known to all who practice the art," would yield the contemplated best mode digital computer program, even though "the inventor had more information in his possession concerning his contemplated best mode than he disclosed in the specification."). Thus, the level of skill in the art is a relevant and necessary consideration in assessing the adequacy of a best mode disclosure. The other objective limitation on the extent of the disclosure required to comply with the best mode requirement is, of course, the scope of the claimed invention.

In short, a proper best mode analysis has two components. The first is whether, at the time the inventor filed his patent application, he knew of a mode of practicing his claimed invention that he considered to be better than any other. This part of the inquiry is wholly subjective, and resolves whether the inventor must disclose any facts in addition to those sufficient for enablement. If the inventor in fact contemplated such a preferred mode, the second part of the analysis compares what he knew with what he disclosed—is the disclosure adequate to enable one skilled in the art to practice the best mode or, in other words, has the inventor "concealed" his preferred mode from the "public"? Assessing the adequacy of the disclosure, as opposed to its necessity, is largely an objective inquiry that depends upon the scope of the claimed invention and the level of skill in the art.

THE CLEANING SOLUTION CASE
RANDOMEX INC. v. SCOPUS CORP.

United States Court of Appeals, Federal Circuit, 1988.
849 F.2d 585.

[The holder of a U.S. patent for a portable apparatus for cleaning computer disks brought an infringement action against competitor. The defendant claimed that Randomex had failed to meet the best mode requirements of Section 112, because it had not disclosed its trade secret formula for the cleaner solution which it recommended as the best mode for practicing the invention. The defendant claimed that the simple naming of its commercially available product was insufficient.]

The court disagreed, stating:

Although a trade name alone may be inappropriate in a best mode disclosure when suitable substitutes are unavailable, here, commercial substitutes were readily available in the prior art and the trade. The failure to disclose its cleaning fluid formula was, as the inventor and president of Randomex admitted, merely a public relations attempt to generate sales for its cleaning fluid. It disclosed the best mode of practicing its claimed invention using in conjunction with it a non-residue detergent solution.

[To support its finding the court cited the fact that the patent did not claim or add anything to the prior art with respect to the cleaning fluid to be used.

In an interesting footnote, the court clarified the scope of disclosure required to meet U.S. best mode requirements, stating:]

For example if one should invent a new and improved internal combustion engine, the best mode requirement would require a patentee to divulge the fuel on which it would run best. This patentee, however, would not be required to disclose the formula for refining gasoline or any other petroleum product. Every requirement is met if the patentee truthfully stated that the engine ran smoothly and powerfully on Brand X super-premium lead free "or equal." Making engines and refining petroleum are different arts, and the person skilled in the art of making engines would probably buy the suggested gasoline. But if the hypothetical maker or user of the engine did not want to use the Brand X super-premium, he would then explore the "or equal" alternative of the patent disclosure. Practically speaking, he would not buy a test tube of Brand X gasoline and reverse engineer it to determine how Brand X refined it. He would ask dealers what other brands of gasoline are available that, in their view, would do for the patented engine what Brand X did. The user is not driven by lawyer's ideology. He is a person who elects practical means to accomplish practical ends.

Notes and Questions

1. What purposes are identified as being served by the "best mode" requirement under U.S. law? Do the decisions in the above cases further those purposes?

2. Are these purposes different from those met by enablement requirements under the Patent Cooperation Treaty?

3. U.S. law differentiates best mode from its enablement requirement. To meet the U.S. enablement requirement the patentee must provide sufficient information so as "to enable any person skilled in the art to which it pertains, or with which it is most nearly connected to make and use the same." 35 U.S.C. § 112. As the court in *Spectra-Physics Inc. v. Coherent, Inc.*, 827 F.2d 1524 (Fed.Cir.), *cert. denied*, 484 U.S. 954 (1987), explained: "Enablement looks to placing the subject matter of the claims generally in the possession of the public. If, however, the applicant develops specific instrumentalities or techniques which are recognized at the time of filing as the best way of carrying out the invention, then the best mode requirement imposes an obligation to disclose that information to the public as well." The court in the *Azeotroping* case contrasted the enablement and best mode requirements, stating: "The enablement requirement looks to the objective knowledge of one of ordinary skill in the at, while the best mode inquiry is a subjective, factual one, looking to the state of mind of the inventor."

4. Review the application requirements of the Patent Cooperation Treaty. Does the Treaty require the applicant to disclose the "best mode" of his invention? Can the U.S. require foreign applicants to disclose the best mode without violating its obligations under the Patent Cooperation Treaty?

5. Failure to disclose the best mode under U.S. patent law results in a substantive refusal of patent protection. It also results in denial of an application date. In representing a foreign client who intends to file a U.S. patent application, failure to meet best mode requirements in a Patent Cooperation Treaty application for an international patent precludes reliance on this international application for a U.S. patent.

6. *Trade Secrets*. One of the greatest problems internationally with the best mode requirement under U.S. law is that such disclosures arguably necessitate the disclosure of trade secrets related to the invention, with no ability to maintain the secret. Thus, inventors may be forced to decide between patent protection in the U.S. and maintenance of valuable trade secretes.

7. What goals are furthered (if any) by the best mode requirement that are *not* already met by the enablement requirement? Are these goals valuable enough to be extended to all patent registration systems through a treaty?

8.   Are the best mode goals you have identified met by the line drawn in the *Azeotroping* case which allows companies to wall off knowledge from their research departments to protect commercialization secrets from exposure?

E.   WHAT SPECIAL PROBLEMS ARE POSED BY DIFFERING "REGISTRATION" REQUIREMENTS?

THE WINDSURFER PATENT CASE
WINDSURFING INTERNATIONAL v. TABUR MARINE

Court of Appeal, 1985, R.P.C.

The defendant challenged plaintiff's patent for a "wind-propelled vehicle" on the grounds of lack of an inventive step (obviousness). Defendant claimed that an article by a Mr. Darby which first appeared in a U.S. publication and was later republished in the U.K to 600 members of the Amateur Yacht Research Society, made plaintiff's invention obvious to one who was skilled in the relevant art.

The article disclosed a sailboard with an instayed sail attached to a spar held by the user and inserted into a hollow socket in a mast step mounted on the sailboard. The sail was a square one. The patent claimed a triangular sail ("Bermuda rig"). The court found the article qualified as valid prior art, but rejected defendant's non-obviousness claim:

We agree, of course, that one must not assume that the skilled man, casting his experienced eye over [the prior art at issue], would at once be fixed with the knowledge that here was something which had a great commercial future which he must bend every effort to develop and improve, but he must at least be assumed to appreciate and understand the free-sail concept taught by [the purported prior art reference] and to consider in the light of his knowledge and experience, whether it will work and how it will work. One has, in our judgment, to postulate a person who comes to [the prior art reference] knowing of the advantages of a Bermuda rig over a square rig and who is at least sufficiently interested to read the article and consider how the vehicle described would work on water.

THE FOAM FOOTBALL CASE
ODDZON PRODUCTS, INC. v. JUST TOYS, INC.

U.S. Court of Appeals, Federal Circuit, 1997.
122 F.3d 1396.

Plaintiff owned a design patent for a foam football-shaped ball with a tail and fin structure sold under the Vortex brand name. Defendant challenged the plaintiff's patent as obvious on the basis of two confidential ball designs which had been disclosed to the inventor as which "inspired" him. The plaintiff claimed that such non-public information could not qualify as prior art. The Court disagreed. It acknowledged the public nature of prior art generally, stating:

> "The patent laws have not generally recognized as prior art that which is not accessible to the public. It has been a basic principle of patent law, subject to minor exceptions that prior art is 'technology already available to the public.' It is available, in legal theory at least, when it is described in the world's accessible literature, including patents, or has been probably known or in public use or sale 'in this country.' That is the real meaning of 'prior art' in legal theory—it is knowledge that is available, including what would be obvious from it, at a given time, to a person of ordinary skill in the art." (citing *Kimberly-Clark Corp. v. Johnson & Johnson*, 745 F.2d 1437 (Fed.Cir.1984))

Despite these requirements, secret art which has been disclosed to the inventor, and which is not held in common ownership (such as by members of teams involved in research) qualifies as prior art which may make an invention obvious.

THE PORTABLE TOILET CASE
THETFORD CORP v. FIAMMA

Court of Justice of the European Communities, 1988.
[1990] Ch 339, [1989] 2 All ER 801, [1990] 1 WLR 1394.

The Judge Rapporteur (Giacinto Bosco) presented the following report for the hearing.

I. Facts and Procedure

In two actions for patent infringement, Thetford Corp, which is the owner of two United Kingdom patents relating to inventions for portable toilets, is suing Fiamma SpA, a manufacturer of such toilets in Italy, and Fiamma UK (hereinafter referred to as "Fiamma"), which imports them into the United Kingdom. Fiamma has no licence from Thetford Corp in Italy, the United Kingdom or anywhere else. According to the documents before the court, the products in question are not patented in any other member state of the EEC.

Before the Patents Court Fiamma denied the patent infringement and argued that Thetford Corp's patent was void on the grounds of lack of novelty and lack of inventive step.

By way of preliminary the Court of Appeal states that for the purpose of deciding the questions of law posed it is necessary to assume that

    (a) patent 235 is a valid patent under United Kingdom law,

    (b) patent 235 would be invalid under the laws of other member states, except possibly Ireland, because of the seven cited patent specifications published more than 50 years before the priority date but excluded from consideration in the United Kingdom under § 50 of the Patents Act 1949,

(c) the exclusion of 50–year-old specifications under § 50 of the 1949 Act does not apply to patents granted under the Patents Act 1977,

(d) the plaintiffs have not sought to obtain any corresponding patent in any other member state and (e) the alleged infringing articles were manufactured in Italy and imported and sold in the United Kingdom.

The court put a written question to the United Kingdom and the Commission on the 50–year rule under the Patents Act 1949.

II. WRITTEN OBSERVATIONS SUBMITTED TO THE COURT

The first question: Thetford Corp and another, the plaintiffs in the main proceedings (hereinafter referred to as Thetford), argue in the first place that it is well established in Community law that patents granted under the national laws of member states constitute "industrial or commercial property" within the meaning of art. 36 of the Treaty.

Although steps have been taken towards the harmonisation of patent law in the EEC, that objective had not been achieved when the patent in question was granted and still has not been achieved today. Consequently, the existence and the validity of patents must depend on the national law under which they were granted.

The patent in question was properly granted under the national law of the United Kingdom, and the fact that the invention may not be patented or patentable in other member states is not material. It would not be practically possible to consider the validity or the enforceability of every patent by reference not only to the national law of the member state granting it, but also by reference to the national laws of the other member states. Even if such an inquiry were feasible, the question would arise in the event of inconsistency between the laws of two or more member states as to which should benefit from the provisions of art 36 and which should not. As at the date when the patent in question was applied for, the laws of the member states differed widely, in particular with regard to the "novelty of a patent application."

The United Kingdom maintains, first, that under the [Paris] Convention for the Protection of Industrial Property, a patent can be recognised as such regardless of the detailed criteria adopted by the national law for determining validity.

The legislation applicable at the time when the patent in question was granted, namely the Patents Act 1949, provided that any document relied on as depriving an invention of novelty must be published in the United Kingdom, and any patent specification must additionally be less than 50 years old. The reasons for that concept of "relative novelty', which was introduced by the Patents Act 1902, lie in the fact that it was considered that the requirement of absolute novelty was not necessarily in the public interest. In particular, a very old document lodged at the

Patent Office "should not be used to defeat a meritorious contribution to the industry of the country."

Second, the existence of a national patent right is not affected by Community rules and, at the present stage of development of Community law, the criteria according to which a member state grants patent rights are a matter for the national law of that member state. In the present case, the criteria followed by a member state for granting a national patent affect the existence of national patent rights, which, according to the case law of the court, is a matter for the national law. Community law merely requires that the measure go no further than is justified by the protection of the interest in question. That is not the case as regards the protection given by United Kingdom law to a patent issued under the circumstances described by the Court of Appeal.

The Commission, therefore, suggests that the first question should be answered as follows:

"In the present state of development of Community law, national patent legislation is not incompatible with arts 30 and 36 of the EEC Treaty merely because it provides that a patent may be granted in respect of an invention, and such a patent may not be revoked, even though the invention is described in a patent specification filed more than 50 years earlier."

Fiamma argues essentially that the court's case law with regard to the application of art 36 to patents cannot be relied on in this instance. The previous decisions of the court relate to inventions, characterised by the fact that they were new and involved an inventive step. On the other hand, the Thetford patent is in respect of matter which was made available to the public many years ago. The patent is in respect of "insubstantial" subject matter which Thetford has not sought to protect or enforce in other member states of the EEC. The effect of the patent is therefore to isolate the United Kingdom from the rest of the EEC, where the products in question may be freely manufactured and sold.

Fiamma argues, in particular, that it is not enough that a national law calls a particular right a "patent" for it necessarily to follow that "industrial or commercial property" is involved. On the contrary, regard must be had to whether the right in question has the "minimum characteristics" of a patent and can therefore derogate from the fundamental principle of the free movement of goods. The question therefore arises as to what is the "area of discretion" available to national patent laws in the present state of development of Community law. Fiamma identifies the following three tests which, in its view, should be applied to delimit that discretion: (i) the greater the steps which have been taken towards harmonisation, the smaller the area of discretion must be (ii) whilst it is true that at present Community law has not yet laid down an exhaustive regime and hence the procedures for obtaining a national patent are a matter for national laws, those procedures must nevertheless fall within the limits which are necessary to give effect to the requirements of the free movement of goods (iii) certain matters are fundamental to particular industrial property rights (for example, the rule that patents should be granted only for inventions). In relation thereto, the area of discretion should be smaller than that which is justified in the case of procedural rules.

On the basis of those three tests, Fiamma reaches the conclusion that the patent in question is outside the area of discretion, since it is in the field of patents that the most progress has been made towards harmonisation (the Convention on the Unification of Certain Points of Substantive Law on Patents for Invention (Strasbourg, 27 November 1963 TS 70 (1980) Cmnd 8002) the Convention on the Grant of European Patents (the European Patent Convention) (Munich, 5 October 1973 TS 20 (1978) Cmnd 7090) the Convention for the Patent for the Common Market (the Community Patent Convention) (Luxembourg, 15 December 1975 EC 18 (1976) Cmnd 6553), which is not yet in force, and the resolution annexed to the latter) "novelty" is the fundamental requirement of a patent. Neither of the conventions places a restriction on which published documents form part of the state of the art the justification for the 50–year rule in the Patents Act 1949 was probably administrative convenience (to ease the burden of the examination of patents). It therefore offers no justification for preventing those alleged to have infringed the patent from relying on all relevant material which has been published.

Fiamma therefore proposes that the court should answer the first question as follows:

> "It is an essential requirement of a patent that it be granted in respect of novel subject matter. Therefore, it is not justified to grant relief which will have the effect of restricting imports from another member state in respect of a patent granted in the circumstances set out in the first question asked by the Court of Appeal."

III.   ANSWERS TO QUESTION PUT BY THE COURT

The court asked the United Kingdom and the Commission to provide additional explanations of the rationale of the principle of "relative novelty" in the light of the written observations submitted to the court.

In its answer, the Commission acknowledges that the precise reason for the existence of the 50–year rule is more complex and less satisfactory as regards art 36 of the EEC Treaty than it suggested in its written observations.

In particular, the Commission considers that an aspect of the 50–year rule is contrary to arts 30 and 36, namely the provision whereby use or publication of an invention outside the United Kingdom during the 50 years prior to the lodging of the application would not defeat the claim to novelty. The effect of that requirement, since abolished by the Patents Act 1977, was that it allowed a patent to be obtained in the United Kingdom in respect of an invention which was freely used or published in another member state at the time of the application but not if it was used or published in the United Kingdom at that time.

Although there is nothing in this case to suggest that the invention in question was used or published in another member state during the 50 years preceding the grant of the patent, the Commission considers that the court should make it clear that it is not justified to limit the examination to use or publication in the United Kingdom to the exclusion of use or publication in other member states.

The United Kingdom traces the history of the principle of "relative novelty" and points out that prior to 1902 the Patent Office did not examine patent applications for novelty. By enacting the recommendations of the Committee of Inquiry chaired by Sir Edward Fry (Report on the Patent Acts (Cd 506, 530) (1901)), the Patents Act 1902 provided for the examination of applications for prior publication in the specification of United Kingdom patents less than 50 years old. It laid down that an invention is not to be taken as anticipated by reason only of its publication in a specification of a United Kingdom patent more than 50 years old.

The 50–year limitation seems to have been adopted for practical reasons connected with the cost of searches at the Patent Office. Also, it was considered that obsolete patents which had never been worked and never published except in patent specifications should not be available as anticipations, since they had provided no public utility.

Lastly, the United Kingdom emphasises that the rule in question applied only to inventions published in patent specifications. If an invention had been used, however long ago that use had taken place, it was grounds for invalidating the patent.

21. In view of the foregoing considerations, the answer to the national court's first question must be that, in the present state of Community law, art 36 must be interpreted as not precluding the application of a member state's legislation on patents which provides that a patent granted for an invention may not be declared invalid by reason only of the fact that the invention in question appears in a patent specification filed more than 50 years previously.

Notes and Questions

1. Does the definition of patentable subject matter in the *Portable Toilet* case meet the definition of obviousness or novelty under the PCT or EPC? Does the exclusion of certain documents from the consideration of patentability meet the goals of patent protection as discussed in the previous disclosure and enablement cases you have considered?

2. Issues of best mode, obviousness and novelty are primarily issues of substantive law. They become an issue of registration and formalities, however, because the failure to meet such substantive requirements results in the denial of registration. Is the test of obviousness identical in the above cases? Do any of these cases violate TRIPS standards? Do they violate PCT standards?

3. Does either the Patent Cooperation Treaty or the European Patent Convention require the applicant to demonstrate non-obviousness in order to

obtain the patent? Do they establish an identical test for determining obviousness? For example, under each of these treaties, which of the following may be considered prior art for purposes of obviousness (or inventive step) determinations:

- a patent granted in 1930 in France

- an article about a related invention published in Turkish

- an article about an invention in an analogous field published in English in a magazine of limited circulation

- a doctoral dissertation contained in a university library in Germany

- a confidential oral disclosure made to a small group of researchers (but *not* the inventor)

4. Which of the above described prior art would be *excluded* from consideration under the rationale of the above cases?

PATENT PROTECTION AND THE FIRST TO FILE DEBATE

Doris Estelle Long, International Intellectual Property
Law Anthology (Anderson Publishing 1996)

One of the key international debates in the area of intellectual property protection concerns the role recordation formalities play in deciding the existence of domestic patent rights. While nations generally agree that, unlike trademarks and copyrights, patents arise only upon compliance with registration formalities, the scope of such formalities is hotly debated.

While all nations which presently grant patent protection premise such protection upon the filing of an acceptable application, the scope of review varies significantly. Some countries, such as Japan, publish pending patent applications and permit third parties to oppose the applied-for patent. By contrast, in the United States, patent applications remain confidential until after the patent is granted. No opportunity for third party oppositions (except for interference proceedings) exists under U.S. law. Furthermore, if the application is denied, the file remains closed to the public. Thus, unsuccessful applicants in the U.S. retain the option of protecting their inventions as potential trade secrets.

Perhaps the greatest difference in the treatment of registration formalities lies in the impact a successful application has on the rights of prior inventors of similar inventors. In most countries, the first to file a successful patent application obtains the patent. Only two countries—the United States and the Philippines—grant patent rights on the basis of the first to invent. Thus, the first to file a patent application in the U.S. only obtains the patent if the invention falls within the subject matter of patentable matter, if the applicant complies with all patent formalities *and* if there is no prior inventor who has conceived of the invention prior to the applicant's date of first conception. By premising patent protection on the inventor's status as first-to-invent, the United States has rejected the relatively easy administrability of a first-to-file system and has added a level of insecurity in the value of an issued patent that does not exist in those countries where compliance with registration formalities alone determines ownership.

Notes and Questions

1.　As a general rule, it is easier to obtain international consensus on procedural issues rather than substantive ones. Substantive issues, such as who is entitled to obtain patent protection, are often perceived as involving issues of national sovereignty. As noted earlier, only the United States relies upon a first to invent basis for awarding patent ownership rights. Is this a procedural or substantive issue? What are the benefits to using a first to file system? What are the disadvantages?

2.　Efforts in the United States to establish a first to file regime have met with strong opposition on policy and philosophical grounds. Which argument offered in the above article did you find persuasive? Why?

3.　One of the key issues we have been endeavoring to determine is what international standards, if any, exist for the recognition, protection and enforcement of intellectual property rights. If every country, except the United States, used the first to file rule for patent ownership, does that make first to file an international standard? If so, should the United States be required to follow such international rule?

THE MULTI–THREAD CASE

MARTIN GARDNER REIFFIN v. MICROSOFT CORPORATION

United States District Court, N.D. California, 1998.
48 U.S.P.Q.2D 1274.

WALKER, J.

Plaintiff Martin Gardner Reiffin brings this action claiming patent infringement against defendant Microsoft Corporation. Reiffin claims that he owns a patent on a form of computer technology called multi-threading. In essence, computers with multi-threading capabilities can switch between tasks with such rapidity that they appear to be performing two or more tasks at once. For example, a computer with multi-threading capabilities can run a word processing program that appears to be receiving data (*i.e.*, words) at the same time it is spell-checking those words. In actuality, the computer's processor (CPU) is switching from one task to the other by quickly processing keystroke threads, then spell-check threads, then keystroke threads and so on.

Reiffin claims that several of Microsoft's software applications make unlawful use of his patented multi-threading technology. Reiffin has moved for a temporary restraining order and a preliminary injunction enjoining Microsoft from distributing Windows 98 and other products that allegedly infringe Reiffin's patents.

In response to Microsoft's charges that Reiffin has strategically amended his claims in order to benefit from the inventions of others via a "submarine patent, "Reiffin claims that there is nothing unlawful about such a strategy. To support this argument, Reiffin selectively quotes the following language from Kingsdown to the court:

It should be made clear at the outset of the present discussion that there is nothing improper, illegal or inequitable in filing a patent application for the purpose of obtaining a right to exclude a known competitor's product from the market; nor is it in any manner improper to amend or insert claims intended to cover a competitor's product [that] the applicant's attorney has learned about during the prosecution of a patent application. Reiffin Opp Mem at 15 (quoting *Kingsdown Medical Consultants Ltd. v. Hollister, Inc.*, 863 F.2d 867 (Fed.Cir.1988). In the very next sentence of the Kingsdown opinion, however, the Federal Circuit cautioned that "any such amendment or insertion must comply with all statutes and regulations, of course." *Kingsdown (Id)*.

[The court subsequently granted Microsoft's motion for summary judgment on the basis that it had not infringed the plaintiff's patent because Microsoft's technology did not contain four required elements of plaintiff's invention.]

THE SUBMARINE PATENT CASE
DISCOVISION ASSOCS. v. DISC MFG.

U.S. District Court of Delaware, 1997.
42 U.S.P.Q.2D 1749.

In describing the nature of a "submarine patent" the court offered the following definition:

"Patents that remain "submerged" during a long *ex parte* examination process and then "surface" upon the grant of the patent have been labeled "submarine patents. "A patent application may have a long examination period due to delays by the PTO and/or from continuation applications. A holder of a "submarine patent" may be able to demand high royalties from nonpatent holders who invested and used the technology not knowing that a patent would later be granted."

SYMPOSIUM: EARLY PATENT PUBLICATION: A BOON OR BANE? A DISCUSSION ON THE LEGAL AND ECONOMIC EFFECTS OF PUBLISHING PATENT APPLICATIONS AFTER EIGHTEEN MONTHS OF FILING

16 Cardozo Arts & Ent LJ 601 (1998).

HERBERT WAMSLEY:

Finally, let me go back to certainty, and to a topic that is my favorite. It is called submarine patents—it is a controversial area. I submit to you that one of the reasons we need eighteen-month publication of patent applications is to drive a few more nails in the coffin of submarine patents.[73] Those are patent applications that have been submerged in the PTO for ten years, twenty years, thirty years, and in some cases forty years, before they became patents.

According to research conducted by IPO, there is an epidemic of submarine patents since the mid-eighties. According to research we did this summer, we identified 320 cases of patents that were granted between 1971 and 1996 that met a list of criteria including: pending in the PTO from the earliest effective filing date for at least fifteen years, were under secrecy order, and were refiled at least twice. Of those 320 applications, the great bulk of them were issued after 1985. A substantial number of those applications were pending in the Office more than twenty years. And about five for more than forty years.[75] This kind of uncertainty, in many of these cases, resulted in technology being kept secret for all of those years. In all of those cases, keeping secret until the end what the scope of the claims was going to be, caused a lot of dislocation, a lot of unnecessary expense, and a lot of litigation for U.S. industry. A giant nail was driven into the coffin of submarine patents by the change of the law in 1995, which changed the patent term from seventeen years from the date of grant to twenty years from the date of filing.[76]

The thing that drove that change was the need to get rid of submarine patents. But we also need the eighteen-month publication law, because there is still, under the existing practice, the opportunity for gamesmanship by keeping the scope of claims confidential for ten years and then springing it on the U.S. industry. That's something we need to get rid of and eighteen-month publication will put that problem to rest. Thank you.

Douglas Wyatt:

The basic problem with the eighteen-month publication is that it is a disincentive to inventors. It is a weakening of the powerful patent system that we have here in the United States. If you consider each side of the argument separately, they are closely in balance, but weigh against each other. But, when you put it in the bill that includes this eighteen-month publication legislation, it weighs towards weakening the

---

73. Submarine patents are patent applications that have been delayed in the PTO for a number of years by the patentee, before the application finally issues into a patent. *See generally* Bernard Wysocki, Jr., *Royalty Rewards: How Patent Lawsuits Make a Quiet Engineer Rich and Controversial*, Wall St. J., Apr. 9, 1997, at a1 (discussing the effects of "submarine" patents). George Selden is credited with pioneering submarine patents, when his patent, related to a gasoline driven vehicle, surfaced in 1895 from an application that had been filed 16 years earlier. *See also Patent Term*

and Publication Reform Act of 1994: hearing on Bill S. 1854 Before the Senate Comm. of Judiciary, 103d Cong. (1994) (statement of Harold C. Wegner, Prof. of Law at George Washington Univ. Nat'l Law Ctr).

75. For instance, Jerome Lemelson received a patent in 1994, for an application that he had filed on December 24, 1954. *See* Jerome Lemelson, U.S. Patent 5,351,078, Issued Sept. 27, 1994; *See Also* Teresa Riordan, *Patents*, N.Y. Times, Apr. 4, 1994, at D4.

76. *See* 35 U.S.C. 154(a)(2) (1994).

American patent system. Now, let me give you some background, so you know why we are here.

When I first started in this business, nobody cared about patents. Intellectual property was a backwater area of practicing law.

Patents have become extremely important. Patent litigation has mushroomed—particularly in jury trials. One of the famous people who made money out of suing on patents is Jerry Lemelson. Some of you may have seen articles on the front page of the Wall Street Journal, where Jerry and his lawyer Jerry Hosier from Chicago, are sitting on their multi-million-dollar mansion out in Aspen, overlooking the skiers, talking about the next suit they're going to file. They've got hundreds of millions of dollars in filing patent applications on submarine patents.

Let me tell you about Jerry Lemelson twenty years ago. My partner, Eliot Gerber, tried a case down here for Jerry. One of his first cases, in the Southern District of New York, with Judge McMahon. You people are too young to know anything about Judge McMahon. If you could try a case before Judge McMahon, you could try a case anywhere. He was the toughest judge that ever came down the pike. Well, Eliot Gerber won the case for Jerry Lemelson. The patent was found valid and infringed, and damages awarded. Then it went up on appeal. We went around and asked: what are the chances of the Second Circuit upholding this decision? What came back almost universally was zero as an answer.

Today, if that patent went up before the Court of Appeals for the Federal Circuit, his chances of winning would probably be 70 or 80%, if not higher. So the world has changed and the interest in intellectual property has increased dramatically because of it. We have a U.S. culture that is different than cultures in other countries. We have individualism, stronger here than anywhere else. It is part of the nature of our system. [15]It is part of the immigrants who came here. Their attitudes were that the individual counts; he is very important. Now, in this fight, there's been a lot of what people call Japan-bashing. There should not be any, since Japan has a wonderful system, a system that has adapted to their culture. The same thing with the Europeans, which is adapted to their culture. Neither in Japan nor in Europe, with perhaps the exception of Germany, are patents as important as they are here. In the United States, if you go into the courtroom with a patent of a small inventor against a large corporation, let me tell you, that large corporation is shaking in its boots because juries are pro-patent. Anyone who has ever done a jury study—and I have done a number of them: we do ten or fifteen test juries on a case before we go to trial—will find that juries are just overwhelmingly pro-patent for the individual inventor.

---

15. Unlike any other country in the world, we have an economy and a patent system that rewards the individual. Independent inventors are responsible for most of the breakthrough technology in the U.S. they account for most of the patentable technology in the world.

They are the reason the U.S. produces the vast majority of Nobel Prizewinners in Science. *See Hearings on Patent Bills* S. 507 and H.R. 400.

In my view, the eighteen-month publication rule is a disincentive to the inventive process that we have here in our tremendously entrepreneurial culture. If an entrepreneur can get some venture capital together, and get a decent patent behind his product, he can really go places. The patent can help cut into the market of someone who already dominates a market. Now, if you're going to publish in eighteen months, you are cutting the legs out from under those people who want to start up a new business, because you cannot start a new business in eighteen months; it is at least a five-year project. There are many benefits in eighteen-month publication, and there are many arguments favoring it. But, when you balance the pros and cons, the eighteen—month publication is a disincentive to what we have here in this country: a wonderfully strong patent system.

Mr. Wamsley mentioned submarine patents earlier. I submit that submarine patents are no longer a problem. I know how difficult submarine patents can be. I wound up on the other side of a Jerry Lemelson case. He sued General Electric Corporation ("GE")—this is in the early nineties—for his robot patents. The robot patent was filed back in the early fifties. So here I was looking at a patent that was in effect forty years later. And GE has robots all over. This was a gun to our head. How could we go back and find prior art to a patent that was forty years old? It was a difficult problem. But that problem has been eliminated. To me, it is a red herring to argue that the eighteen-month publication has anything, whatsoever, to do with eliminating submarine patents. Your patent is now good for twenty years from the day you file it. If it issues in a year, you have it for nineteen years. If it issues in three years, you have it for seventeen years. Thus, while submarine patents used to be an argument for the eighteen-month publication rule before we had the twenty-year rule, they are not anymore.

I admit that in the old system, it was true that an eighteen-month publication rule would help eliminate the problems with a submarine patent. To say today that, just because a patent is going to be published in eighteen months, you are going to know what the claims are, is incorrect. You can still have a patent that takes ten years to get out of the patent office for one reason or another, and the public will not necessarily know what the scope of those claims are. If the application is published, you will know what it says in the specification, but not in the claims. The claims are the term, the metes and bounds, of what the invention is. So I do not find that publication will allow one to learn about potential claims by others.

Let me just say in conclusion that this is an argument that is painful. Because, on one hand, the large U.S. companies, who seek to promote this legislation, do wonderful things for our economy. It is generally in their interest to have eighteen-month publication, and I understand that. But, you have to balance that against what eighteen-month publication does to the incentive to go out and invent and invest in new businesses and new products by the smaller entities.

PATENTS: AN INVENTOR WINS, BUT ISN'T HAPPY
Edmund L. Andrews, The New York Times, § 1, page 36 (Dec. 14, 1991)

Having just won his second big patent battle against the automobile industry, Robert W. Kearns is well on the way to becoming a very rich man. One would think the inventor of the intermittent windshield wiper might finally be at peace.

Mr. Kearns's device, which sweeps the windshield of light rain or mist every few seconds, has become a common auto fixture, and his long struggle against the industry has resulted in victory against Ford and this week against Chrysler. But Mr. Kearns still feels the patents system has failed. It is not just that he feels the payments he has received are far less than he had argued were fair compensation. The bigger issue, he said, is lost time.

A patent is valid for only 17 years [under current U.S. patent law, a patent is now valid for 20 years], and the windshield wiper case was so convoluted that Mr. Kearns did not win his first court victory until several years after the last of his patents had already expired. Thus, while the law entitles him to collect back royalties, Mr. Kearns argues that he has nevertheless been deprived of the opportunity to fullfill his real goal: to start his own business and become a manufacturer.

OFTEN-FORGOTTEN ISSUE

Although some experts disagree with Mr. Kearns, he raises a potentially important issue that is often forgotten because attention in patent disputes usually focuses simply on money.

On the money front, Mr. Kearns has won some victories. Indeed, after years of lonely, grueling courtroom struggle, Mr. Kearns, a 64–year-old engineer, has now largely vindicated himself as the inventor of the intermittent windshield wiper. His victory last year against the Ford Motor Company, led to a $10.2 million payment from Ford to settle claims. This week's decision by a Federal jury that the Chrysler Corporation had infringed his patents, makes it likely that Chrysler will also have to pay him millions of dollars.

And that is just the beginning. Mr. Kearns has sued more than 15 other car-makers around the world, all of which are scheduled to be tried on roughly the same issues in the same courtroom.

Hard as it may be for others to believe, however, Mr. Kearns is not happy. "All my friends are saying 'You won,' "he said after the Chrysler decision. "In truth, I lost."

DEPRIVED OF TRUE PATENT

In effect, Mr. Kearns argues, the lengthy litigation has deprived him of holding a true patent, which gives an inventor the exclusive right to make, use or sell an invention in the United States. The key to a patent, he said, is the right to exclude anybody else from using one's invention, a right that makes it possible to raise money from investors to start a business from scratch. But because courtroom challenges from car companies cast a doubt on his patents for their entire lifetimes, Mr. Kearns argues that the courts left him with a much weaker right to enter licensing agreements with car manufacturers.

Notes and Questions

1. Most countries provide for publication of patent applications within approximately 18 months of their filing. Some countries, such as Japan, allow an applicant to avoid publication by limiting publication to those applications for which review is requested. If an applicant decides he wants to avoid publication, he can simply fail to request review within the application time period. His application lapses, but his invention remains unpublished.

2. What are the benefits of publishing patent applications before the patent issues, as opposed to after it issues (which occurs in the United States)? Are there disadvantages?

3. Under U.S. law, patent applications remain secret until and unless a patent issues. Thus, an applicant of a denied patent under U.S. law, might still be able to protect her invention under trade secret law. Consequently, a decision to file a patent application, or even proceed to review of that application, does not result in a public dedication of the invention if that invention is denied patent protection. Compare this benefit with the harm of submarine patents. Where would you strike the balance between these two? Is there another method for resolving the "problem" of submarine patents that does not require publication of all pending applications?

Problem

You represent Low Tech International who specializes in the development and worldwide patenting of mechanical inventions which improve the small issues of everyday life. One of Low Tech's researchers, in the course of his employment, has created a barrette in the shape of a hair brush for cleaning and smoothing the hair. Unlike previous barrettes, this one does not damage the hair and is fully functional as both a barrette and mini-hairbrush.

Low Tech has advised you that it would like to obtain patent protection for its barrette in Europe, the U.S., Canada and Latin America. Draft a patent application using the PCT application form provided in the supplement. What additional information, if any, would you need? For information regarding prior art for this invention, *see* U.S. Patent No.5,816,267.

Chapter Twenty–Five

TRADEMARKS UNDER INTERNATIONAL LAW

A. WHAT ARE THE FORMAL REQUIREMENTS FOR OBTAINING INTERNATIONAL TRADEMARK PROTECTION?

Trademarks perhaps more than any other form of intellectual property rely upon language and meaning for their right to protection. No one in the United States would think of obtaining trademark rights in the word "PEN" for a writing device that uses ink. It is the common descriptive, or generic term for the writing instrument and, therefore, lacks the distinctiveness trademarks must have to distinguish are producer's goods from another. But what if you called your product "Le Pen"? Is it now protectable since "Le Pen" has no English equivalent? What if you were selling your writing instruments in France and used "Pen"? Is it protectable since the French word for "pen" is "La plume."?

One of the most difficult tasks facing a trademark owner in today's global marketplace is developing a global trademark that takes into account the language and culture of diverse countries. Stories are legion about trademark owners who failed to consider such issues at their peril–such as the care company that named its new care Nova and sold the care in Mexico to dismal results. The reason for such poor sales performance? "Nova" in Spanish means "It won't go."

Not only must a trademark owner chose his mark carefully, he must also determine the most effective method for registering his mark. As the international community struggles to develop an efficient international trademark registration system, the problem of meaning has to be dealt with. For example, what if your client has developed a new mark "XYZT" for gizmos. Your client applies for registration of his trademark in the U.S., the UK, Japan, and France and Germany. In American English XYZT has no special meaning, but in England it is slang expression for an obscene act, in Japan, its translation is "gizmo" and in

France it means "your friendly helper." Can an international registration system be developed that would take these issues into consideration or must trademarks be treated like patents on a country-by-country basis?

Read the following Articles from The Madrid Agreement from the Supplement: 1, 3, 4, 6.

Notes and Questions

1. Does the Madrid Agreement establish a solitary registration system for trademarks? For example, if you filed an application under the Madrid System and designated UK, France, Germany, and Italy as countries for which you were seeking registration, would registration in one country guarantee registration in all of them? Does a refusal to register a mark in one country preclude registration in the others? What if the country which refuses registration is your client's home country?

2. Does the Madrid Agreement define the qualities of a registerable trademark? Does the Madrid Agreement specify what the test for genericness is?

3. Could a signatory to the Madrid Agreement refuse to register your client's distinctive product shape as a trademark without violating the treaty?

4. The Madrid Agreement is administered by the World Intellectual Property Organization. To qualify for registration (through a single application) in covered countries, the mark must be *registered* in an adherent to the Agreement, and that country must be the country of origin of domicile or of "a real and effective industrial or commercial establishment of the applicant." Applications must be filed with the International Bureau in Geneva, Switzerland where it is entered in the International Register of the Bureau and noticed to all Madrid member countries designated by the applicant. Each designated country has a period of 12 months in which to reject the application or file a "provisional objection" to obtain further time to examine the mark.

5. Registrations under the Madrid Agreement are limited to the goods and services designated in the "home" registration. Thus, if the home designation seeks to register the mark "Long's Cola" for "beverages," registration for Long's Cola for t-shirts in another country, based on the Madrid filing, would be denied.

Read the following Articles from the Madrid Protocol in the Supplement: 2, 3, 3bis, 3ter, 4bis, 5, 6, 7(1).

Notes and Questions

1. Does the Madrid Protocol establish a solitary registration system for trademarks? For example, if you filed an application under the Madrid System and designated UK, France, Germany, and Italy as countries on which you were seeking registration, would registration in one country under the Protocol guarantee registration in all of them? Does a refusal to register a mark in one country preclude registration in the others? What if the country which refuses registration is your client's home country?

2. Does the Madrid Protocol define the qualities of a registerable trademark? Does the Madrid Agreement specify what the test for genericness is?

3. Could a signatory to the Madrid Protocol refuse to register your client's distinctive product shape as a trademark without violating the treaty?

4. Like the Madrid Agreement, the Protocol is administered by the World Intellectual Property Organization. To qualify for registration (through a single application) in covered countries, the mark must be *registered* in an adherent to the Protocol or Agreement, and that country must be the country of origin of domicile or of "a real and effective industrial or commercial establishment of the applicant." Applications must be filed with the International Bureau in Geneva, Switzerland where it is entered in the International Register of the Bureau and noticed to all member countries designated by the applicant. Each designated country has a period of 12 months in which to reject the application or file a "provisional objection" to obtain further time to examine the mark.

6. *Central Attack.* One of the key problems of the Madrid Agreement was the "central attack" provisions of Article 6. Under Article 6 if trademark registration was denied or subsequently canceled, for whatever reason, all of the registrant's applications and registrations relying on the same domestic application were canceled. Thus, a successful attack on the "central mark" resulted in loss of rights for *all* registrations based on the canceled mark. The Protocol was designed in part to correct this problem. What solution does it use?

7. Under the Madrid Agreement, applications must be based on a previously registered mark in the applicant's home country. Under the Protocol, a registration is *not* required. Instead, registration may be based on a home *application*. If the application fails within the first five years, the applicant may reapply for registration on an individual basis in each previously designated foreign jurisdiction. Such "converted" applications, will be given the priority date of the original application. The Protocol also allows for transformation in the event of a "central attack."

8. Some of the benefits of a streamlined registration system is efficiency, avoidance of needless duplication of effort, and reduction in costs. Does the transformation system of the Protocol achieve these goals in the event of a successful "central attack"?

Read the following Articles from The Trademark Law Treaty (TLT) from the Supplement: 2, 3.

Notes and Questions

1. Does the TLT create a solitary registration system?

2. Does the TLT describe the qualities of a registrable trademark?

3. Could a new hologram mark for credit card services be registered under the TLT?

4. Are all marks required to be protected under Article 16 of TRIPS governed by the registration procedures of the TLT?

5. Is the TLT more similar to the PCT or the EPC? Why?

6. *Special Treatment for Foreign Marks.* One of the key differences in domestic trademark systems is the role that use and registration play in developing protectable rights in a mark. Under U.S. law, as you saw in Chapter Three, no U.S. owned mark can be registered without evidence of its use in interstate commerce in connection with the applicable goods or services. By contrast, foreign marks may be registered *without* use, so long as applications for registration are based upon a foreign registered mark. Does this treatment violate the principle of National Treatment?

7. *Classification.* The TLT specifies the use of the Nice Classification System for all marks filed under the its procedures. The Nice Classification System is a worldwide classification agreement established under the Nice Agreement Concerning the International Classification of Goods and Services for the Purposes of the Registration of Mark. The Nice Agreement established 42 classes for trademarks and service marks.

8. The Locarno Agreement Establishing an International Classification for Industrial Designs establishes a similar classification system for industrial designs. Locarno does not contain the same classification categories as Nice. Thus, "foodstuffs" are categorized as Class 1 under the Locarno Agreement, but they are categorized as Class 30 under the Nice System.

9. *Misleading Indicators.* The Agreement of Madrid for the Prevention of False or Misleading Indications of Source on Goods requires seizure or import prohibition against all goods bearing a false or misleading source (geographic) indicator. Originally established to correct a limitation in Article 10 of the Paris Convention, which only prohibited the use of a false source indicator if fraudulent intent could be proven, the agreement has become less significant since the Paris Convention was modified in 1958 to remove the intent requirement. Each member country may determine which geographic indicators it considers generic. (Compare Article 4 of this Agreement with Article 23 of TRIPS)

10. *Appellations of Origin.* The Lisbon Agreement for the Protection of Appellations of Origin protects appellations of origin which it defines as "the geographical name of a country, region or locality, which serves to designate a product originating therein, the quality and characteristics of which are due exclusively or essentially to the geographical environment." (Article 2) Under the Lisbon Agreement, such appellations may not be used even if their use does *not* confuse the general public. To qualify for protection, the appellation of origin must be registered with the International Bureau of WIPO.

FACILITATING TRADEMARK REGISTRATION ABROAD: THE IMPLICATIONS OF U.S. RATIFICATION OF THE MADRID PROTOCOL

Roger E. Schechter, 25 Geo. Wash. J. Int'l L. & Econ. 419 (1992).

Unlike the Madrid Agreement–which requires a home country registration–the Protocol will allow international registration to be predicated on a home country application. Thus, under the Protocol a U.S. firm need not delay the pursuit of protection abroad until the U.S. PTO completes its sometimes lengthy *ex parte* review and until all risk of a domestic opposition passes. Rather, it could proceed at once to secure registrations abroad, with the significant advantage of a much earlier priority date in any contest with another claimant for the same mark. In addition, since U.S. firms can now at least file an application in advance of use (although U.S. registration will not issue until proof of use is provided), the Protocol will permit U.S. firms to obtain an early priority date for trademarks whose use is contemplated in foreign markets.

A second major innovation of the Protocol is its substantial elimination of the central attack features of the Agreement. Under Article 9 *quinquies* of the Protocol, should the home country registration be successfully challenged or otherwise deemed invalid, the mark owners have three months to convert any previously obtained extension registrations into national registrations–something that was not possible under the original Madrid Agreement. Such a prospect for conversion effectively severs the connection between the extension registration and the home country registration and would permit free exploitation, licensing, or transfer of foreign trademark rights, without any concern that an eleventh hour challenge in the U.S. PTO or in the U.S. court system could subvert foreign rights.

Thirdly, the Protocol is responsive to many of the administrative problems traditionally cited as obstacles to U.S. adherence to the original version of the Madrid Agreement. For instance, under the Protocol, English would become a working language of the Madrid Union. This should both speed up use of the system by U.S. firms and reduce costs associated with translation. Similarly, the Protocol provides that national offices will have eighteen months within which to refuse a registration predicated on a Madrid filing, rather than the twelve months provided for in the original Madrid Agreement. That expanded time frame makes it more likely that Madrid filings can be examined in ordinary course without pushing U.S. domestic filing "to the back of the line" or necessitating the expense of hiring numerous additional examiners. In addition, the draft regulations under the Protocol contemplate a revised fee structure that will effectively permit national offices–such as the U.S. PTO–to charge international registrants fees comparable to those charged to domestic firms. This goes a long way toward insuring that domestic applicants are not subsidizing firms based abroad who utilize the Madrid system.

With these changes in the system, it might seem that U.S. adherence is an all but foregone conclusion. There are, however, some additional issues which are a continuing cause for concern on the part of the U.S. PTO and U.S. trademark owners.

Perhaps the biggest sticking point with the Protocol involves the "intent-to-use" requirement imposed by U.S. law on foreign trademark applicants. Under Section 44(d) of the Lanham Act, certain foreign parties may file a trademark application in the U.S. PTO, and if the U.S. application is filed within six months of the date of a prior foreign application, the applicant is given a U.S. filing date equivalent to the date of its foreign application. A Section 44(d) application, however, must be accompanied by a declaration by the applicant of a bona fide intention to use the mark in U.S. domestic commerce. Foreign applicants can also rely on a previously issued foreign registration as a basis for a U.S. trademark registration, but, once again, the statute requires that they affirm their *bona fide* intent to use the mark in the United States before the registration will issue.

Congress added a requirement that foreign applicants allege an intent to use the mark in the United States when it amended the Lanham Act to permit pre-use application by domestic firms. The requirement reflected notions of equity. Just as domestic firms are obliged to make an "intent-to-use" declaration when they file an application prior to using a mark in the United States, these provisions subject foreign applicants to the same requirement. In the eyes of many U.S. trademark owners, U.S. law still gives foreign applicants preferential treatment, since they may obtain a U.S. registration without ever having used the mark in the United States, while no such possibility exists for a U.S. firm.

These features of U.S. law raise a number of interrelated questions. First, if the United States acceded to the Madrid Protocol, could it require foreign firms using the Protocol to make a declaration of intention to use when seeking U.S. trademark protection? The Protocol itself is silent on the point, and without an affirmative resolution of the issue, U.S. adherence is considerably less likely.

A related question is whether foreign firms filing under the Protocol to seek extension registrations in the United States will be granted U.S. registration solely on the strength of their declaration of an intent to use in the future, or whether an affidavit of actual use will be required? As noted, the current U.S. system requires proof of use before a registration will issue to a domestic U.S. firm, in addition to such a firm's declaration of an intention to use the mark in the future. On the other hand, foreign applicants under Section 44 routinely receive U.S. registrations without any proof of actual use in the United States, provided they have made the required declaration. Thus, the issue is whether to treat applications under the Madrid Protocol as more like domestic applications or Section 44 applications.

It would appear from the text of the Protocol that no proof of actual use can be required of foreign applicants utilizing the Madrid Protocol. Thus, if the United States adheres to the Protocol, it would seem to have little choice in the matter. Representatives of the U.S. PTO have indicated, in negotiating sessions surrounding the drafting of the implementing regulations, that they cannot insist upon proof of actual use for applications submitted under the Madrid system. Instead, they plan to treat the applications comparably to applications under Section 44. This, of course, does not dispose of the normative question of whether such treatment is warranted.

Permitting registration of marks without proof that they are in actual use once again raises the specter of a U.S. firm experiencing enhanced difficulty in locating a suitable mark because of "clutter" on the U.S. register in the form of Madrid Protocol registrations that are not actually being used in the U.S. market. Under the current system—with no U.S. participation in the Madrid Union—the expense to a foreign firm of proceeding under Section 44 gives some added assurance that its declaration of an intent-to-use is probably grounded in fact. Why else would such a firm bother to retain U.S. trademark counsel and pursue the application? This helps minimize the "clutter" problem because most registrations that ultimately issue to applicants under Section 44 probably relate to marks that are being used in the United States. Because registration under the Madrid Protocol will be appreciably less complicated and expensive, presumably many more firms will take advantage of the procedure, and, despite a declaration of intent-to-use in the United States, they may ultimately never exploit the mark in actual sales. Nonetheless, the marks will be unavailable to domestic firms.

Concerns about "deadwood" or "clutter" on the register may, however, be overstated. There is no reason to assume that foreign firms will commonly make false declarations of their intentions concerning the U.S. market. Moreover, registrants under the Madrid system would still be subject to post-registration requirements under the Lanham Act. Specifically, they will be required to attest, under oath, five years after registration, that the mark is still being used. While this is a far from perfect method of keeping the register current, it does provide some assurance that problems will remain within manageable bounds. On balance, then, this feature of the Protocol should not be an obstacle to U.S. adherence.

Another potential problem left unresolved by the Protocol concerns the specificity with which applicants must identify the goods and/or services on which the mark is or will be used. Under U.S. practice, a fairly detailed specification is required, and much of the application process is often devoted to narrowing the description of goods for which protection is claimed until the PTO is satisfied. This contrasts with the more relaxed practice in many other nations. In many nations, trademark applicants are permitted to seek registration of a mark for broad categories of goods even though the mark may only actually be used on a single narrow product line.

U.S. firms may discover that the asymmetrical practices concerning the description of goods make the Madrid scheme less attractive. United States firms can, of course, only avail themselves of the advantages of the Protocol after filing a U.S. application. That application will typically contain a narrow description of goods so as to comply with the traditional U.S. practices in this regard. The U.S. firm will be bound by that description when it then uses the Protocol to extend registration to twenty or more other countries. If that same U.S. firm filed separate applications in the national offices of those other countries, it might be able to claim a much broader description of goods.

Another key issue bearing on adherence to the Madrid Protocol concerns the effect it will have on the ability of U.S. firms to "clear" marks in the future.

This problem, however, is intrinsic to any system of international trademark cooperation, regardless of the details.

Trademarks serve not only the interests of trading companies, but also the interests of consumers. As many scholars have noted, trademarks reduce search costs for consumers by giving them a swift and inexpensive way to relocate goods that they have previously purchased and enjoyed. Trademark infringement is universally condemned not only because it harms honest merchants, but also because it makes it difficult for consumers to make informed choices in the market place.

As the century draws to a close, consumers are more mobile than ever. Because such individuals associate a brand name with a particular set of product attributes, having that brand name signal those attributes throughout the world is becoming increasingly logical and important. The U.S. citizen living in Egypt benefits if he or she can assume that the "CREST" name on a tube of toothpaste on sale in Egypt signifies a toothpaste with the same attributes as the one on sale in Chicago. A French citizen living in New York similarly benefits if he or she can assume the same thing about the French brand "FLUROCARIL."

Although an expanded system of international trademark registration may increase processing and application costs, and although it may make the clearance of new marks more difficult for U.S. firms, ultimately an expanded system of trademark registration will make the location of desirable goods easier for consumers the world over. And that, after all, is a primary purpose of trademark law. This consumer recognition factor, perhaps more than any other, counsels in favor of speedy adherence to the new Madrid Protocol.

THE OLYMPIANS TRADE MARK CASE
CANADIAN SCHENLEY DISTILLERS LTD. v. MOLSON CO. LTD.

Trade Marks Opposition Board, 1978.
47 C.P.R. 2D 137.

METCALFE, J.

The applicant sought to register the trade marks THE OLYMPIANS & Design and LES OLYMPIENS & Design for use in association with brewed alcoholic beverages. The opponent based its opposition on grounds of registrability, entitlement and distinctiveness by reason of its prior use and registration of OLYMPIC in association with distilled alcoholic beverages. The opponent's evidence was directed to the labels used in association with its wares and the extent of use of its trade mark.

In the matter of oppositions by Canadian Schenley Distillers Ltd. To application Nos. 373,099 THE OLYMPIANS & Design and 373,101 LES OLYMPIENS & Design.

The applicant filed application Nos. 373,099 and 373,101 on March 6, 1974, to register the trade marks shown below for use in association with wares described as brewed alcoholic beverages. The applications were based on intention to use the trade marks in Canada.

The allegations of the opponent in the statements of opposition, all generally denied by the applicant, are as follows:

1. Under the provisions of § . 37(2)(b) of the Trade Marks Act and s. 12(1)(d) the trade marks of the applicant are not registrable in view of opponent's registration for the trade mark OLYMPIC, registered May 14, 1971, No. 176175, for use in association with distilled alcoholic beverages.

The evidence of the opponent is the affidavit of Anton F. Lambrecht, senior vice-president-administration, according to whom the opponent first became interested in using the word "olympic" as a trade mark in association with distilled alcoholic beverages in 1970 and eventually registered the mark. The opponent has used the trade mark OLYMPIC in Canada in association with distilled alcoholic beverages.

Copies of invoices attached to the affidavit as exs. B, C and D show that in each of the three years 1971, 1973 and 1974, the opponent sold a case of 25oz. bottles of olympic whisky to the Liquor Control Board in the Province of Quebec, in 1971 to Regie des Alcools du Quebec and in 1973 and 1974 to Societe des Alcools du Quebec. At the time of the affidavit, October 16, 1974, the opponent had been actively considering variations in the shape of its product container and in the labelling. Several variations are represented in ex. E and a physical exhibit that is included as ex. F carries a two-piece label that is represented below and is made up of a small circular upper label illustrating a discus thrower and a representation of the five-ring Olympic symbol and below that a second label carrying the trade mark OLYMPIC, the word Schenley together with a fanciful leaf design and miscellaneous reading matter:

The affiant concludes the affidavit by stating that both whisky and beer are alcoholic beverages, that production and sale are regulated by federal and provincial governments and that the products move through similar channels of trade.

The applicant's evidence is the affidavit of James R. Taylor, vice-president, marketing, of Molson Breweries of Canada Limited, a wholly owned subsidiary of the applicant. Taylor states that he has never seen whisky or any other distilled alcoholic beverage sold or offered for sale or advertised in Canada by the opponent under the trade mark OLYMPIC, that the brewing and distilling industries in Canada are independent of one another and that as far as he is aware there are no distillers in the brewing business and no brewers in the distilling business.

As evidence in reply the opponent submitted the affidavits of Elizabeth Pederson, John F. Griffiths, Vivian Gustafson, Gary Bacon, Pierre Leduc and Charles Mahoney, all of whom are unanimous in stating that they do not know whether any of the beer manufacturing companies in

Canada have a financial interest in any company manufacturing or selling distilled alcoholic beverages. None of the affiants explains the source of that rather sweeping generalization.

The applications are based on intention to use while in the case of the opponent the Lambrecht affidavit refers to use of the trade mark OLYMPIC in Canada in association with distilled alcoholic beverages. In support of that statement three invoices are supplied as exhibits which have already been described. In my opinion the sale in each of the three years of a single case of opponent's olympic whisky to the Quebec Liquor Control Board falls outside the area prescribed by the statement in § . 4(1) of the Trade Marks Act "in the normal course of trade". In the unreported decision of Thurlow, A.C.J., on behalf of the Federal Court of Canada, Trial Division, dated December 12, 1977, 38 C.P.R. (2d) 60] in reference to *American Distilling Co. v. Canadian Schenley Distilleries Ltd.*, the trade mark under review being the respondent Schenley's registered trade mark AMIGO, the Registrar having decided to amend but not to expunge the registration. The decision includes the following information beginning at p. 1 of the transcript, p. 61 C.P.R.:

On February 9, 1977, Schenley filed an affidavit, the body of which read as follows:

I, A.F. Lambrecht, of the City of Montreal, Province of Quebec,

Canada, make oath and say as follows:

1.   THAT I am Senior Vice–President, Administration of Canadian Schenley Distilleries Ltd., the owner of the trade mark AMIGO and registration thereof in the Trade Marks Office under number 157,360 and as such I have knowledge of the facts hereinafter set forth.

2.   THAT attached to this my affidavit and identified as "Exhibit A" is a carbon copy of an invoice no. 18851 from the registrant herein, Canadian Schenley Distilleries Ltd., to Societe des Alcools du Quebec, relating to the sale of an alcoholic beverage namely "rum" under the trade mark AMIGO, which invoice is dated December 29, 1976.

The invoice copy exhibited lists as one of three items which are its subject matter, one case of AMIGO Rum.

In respect of that evidence Mr. Justice Thurlow concludes in part as follows, p. 4 of the transcript, pp. 62–3 C.P.R.:

The affidavit is more remarkable for what is not in it than for what is there. It does not say that the mark is or ever was in use as a trade mark, or that it was ever used to distinguish Schenley rum from the rum of others or that it was ever so used in the normal course of trade. Nor does it relate facts from which such user ought to be inferred. If it had said that the trade mark was in use in the normal course of trade in association with Schenley rum, the citation of one instance of a sale, even though it was a sale after the date of the § . 44 notice, and the exhibition of a copy of an invoice relating to such sale, might have lent some support. By itself, however, the single sale as described is not direct evidence of the material fact, that is, use in association with rum in the normal course of trade, and any evidentiary value it has depends on the inference to be drawn from it. It is to be noted that it is not stated in the affidavit that the single sale cited was a sale in the normal course of trade.

According to the invoices the total quantity of opponent's Olympic whisky sold to the Liquor Control Board of the Province of Quebec presumably for resale through the years 1971, 1973 and 1974, was no more than four "British proof gallons". Without drawing any conclusions as to the extent of the liquor business in this country and without attempting to estimate the per capita consumption of rye whisky I feel certain that the merchandising of no more than a few gallons of a distilled alcoholic beverage in this country over a period of four years is not use in the normal course of trade as envisaged by the provisions of § 4 of the Act. As a matter of fact that which Lambrecht points to as use of the trade mark OLYMPIC in association with the wares in this country is in reality no use at all and far from the volume of use that would be required to develop for the opponent in terms of his olympic whisky product a reputation for those goods in this country. On the question of reputation the following statement appears in Fox, *Canadian Law of Trade Marks and Unfair Competition*, 3rd ed. (1972), p. 246:

As already noted, the onus of showing that confusion is unlikely lies upon the applicant; nevertheless where an opponent relies on the reputation established by his alleged conflicting mark, the onus lies on the opponent to adduce evidence from which such reputation invoked can reasonably be inferred. Before an objection based on prior use of a confusing trade mark or trade name under § 16 can be sustained, it is necessary for an opponent to establish a reputation in trade in connection with a trading style, device or mark of some character, before the tribunal or court will proceed to consider whether, having regard to that reputation, the possibility of confusion upon reasonable user of the mark applied for will arise.

As for the respective wares they are as far as I am concerned of the same general class, that being the decision reached by Gibson, J., *in Carling Breweries Ltd. v. Registrar of Trade Marks* (1972), 8 C.P.R. (2d) 247, where he concluded at p. 251 that the alcoholic beverage industry is one industry. The wares being similar, the respective services, businesses and trades would also be similar.

Finally, with respect to the degree of resemblance, while there is a family resemblance between the mere words "olympic" and "olympians" or "olympiens" the marks as totalities as noted above, on the basis of imperfect recollection and first impression, are not confusingly similar.

Summing up, it has been found that the trade marks of the applicant, LES OLYMPIENS & Design and THE OLYMPIANS & Design, are not confusingly similar to the registered trade mark OLYMPIC of the opponent, that the respective wares, though not identical, are of the same general class, that the use to which opponent's trade mark has been shown to have been subjected is not use "in the normal course of trade" so that the mark cannot be deemed to have been used in association with the wares and hence has not been used within the meaning of § 4 of the Trade Marks Act, the use referred to in opponent's evidence being nothing more than an insignificant or token use.

Those being my conclusions it follows that the trade marks of the applicant are distinctive.

The oppositions are rejected under the authority of § . 37(8) of the Trade Marks Act.

Notes and Questions

1.   What role should use play in determining whether a company is entitled to register or own a mark internationally? Does the TRT, the Madrid Agreement or the Madrid Protocol require use before rights to a mark attach? Do any of them prohibit requiring use of a mark before ownership rights attach?

2.   Some countries, such as Austria, Hungary, the Czech Republic and Poland, base ownership of a trademark on who is the first to file for registration (as opposed to who is the first to use the mark). Some of these countries, however, permit prior domestic users of the mark to challenge the registration of the mark. What are the benefits of a first to file system for trademark protection? What are the problems inherent in such a system?

3.   Under Section 44 of the Lanham Act, 15 U.S.C. § 1126, foreign applied-for or registered marks may be registered without use. However, an application to register a foreign mark is not granted automatic registration status. To the contrary, Section 42 of the Lanham Act specifically provides "that only foreign marks which are 'eligible.'" It further provides that registration in the U.S. of any foreign registration is "independent of the registration in the country of origin, and the duration, validity or transfer in the United States of such registration shall be governed by the provisions of this chapter." (15 U.S.C. §§ 1127(e) and (f).) Thus, for example, the U.S. Trademark Office may require an applicant to narrow its description of goods or services, or to disclaim exclusive rights to descriptive portions of a composite mark, or may even refuse registration on the grounds that the mark is (e.g.) generic, scandalous or deceptive. See 15 U.S.C. § 1052.

4.   Do these provisions violate U.S. treaty obligations under the Trademark Law Treaty?

5.   Would they violate U.S. obligations under the Madrid Protocol, if the U.S. were a signatory to that treaty?

6.   The Madrid Agreement and Protocol and the Trademark Registration Treaty are designed to streamline registration procedures. They do not, however, provide a solitary registration system. The Community Trademark is a notable exception. Recipients of a Community Trademark may obtain exclusive rights to their mark throughout the European Union (subject to the rights of prior users). For a further discussion of the Community Trademark, see Chapter Forty.

7.   There are also numerous regional trademark registration systems designed to facilitate trademark registration procedures in a particular

region, including the Andean Pact (for certain Latin American countries) and Banjul Protocol (for certain African countries).

Problem

Your client Croissants DeLuxe is domiciled in France (which has acceded to the Madrid Union and Protocol, the Paris Convention and the TLT). It has obtained a registration in France for the mark CROISSANTS DELUXE for baked goods in International Class 30. It filed an application four months ago for PUR DELITE for baked breads. Croissants DeLuxe has sold its goods only in France but expects to expand its sales into the United Kingdom, Italy, the United States, Canada and Japan. It has hired you to protect its trademarks internationally. What steps would you recommend the client take? What additional information will you need to protect its marks? What problems, if any, do you foresee? Review the Application Forms in the Supplement for guidance.

Chapter Twenty–Six

TRADE SECRETS UNDER INTERNATIONAL LAW

A. WHAT FORMALITIES ARE REQUIRED TO PROTECT TRADE SECRETS INTERNATIONALLY?

There are no formal registration requirements for protecting trade secrets. Nevertheless, where trade secrets (or "confidential information") is licensed for use, in order to be protected, the trade secret may need to be precisely identified and described. Thus, for example, in the European Union, the license of "know-how" must be "identified" in order to fall within the scope of EC Directive on Know–How Licensing. This Directive provides a block exemption from the antitrust prohibitions of certain practices for Article 85(3) for licenses of secret "business and technical information." The term "identified" is defined under the Directive as "described or recorded in such a manner as to make it possible to verify that it fulfills the criteria of secrecy and substantiability and to ensure that the licensee is not unduly restricted in his exploitation of his own technology." (Article 1) "Substantiality" requires that the know-how be competitively "useful" and be information "of importance for the whole or a significant part" of a manufacturing process; product or service (or its development) (Id.) This identification requirement may necessitate a relatively detailed disclosure of the trade secret either in the written license agreement or in some documentary form attached to it. See EC Know–How Directive in Supplement.

Part VII

CAN FAME ALONE CREATE RIGHTS?

In the global marketplace, celebrity is readily translated into market share. Famous actors lend their names and faces to products and services throughout the world. Multinational companies, such as, McDonald's and Kentucky Fried Chicken open franchises in other countries. WINDOWS® software by Microsoft becomes an industry standard in developing countries, and merchandise bearing the logos of sports teams such as the CHICAGO BULLS® is sold through-out the world.

"Fame" can be obtained in a variety of ways. Notoriety, accomplishments in one's chosen profession, advertisements and word of mouth are only a few ways in which a mark, a person, a work or a product can become famous. In today's globalized economy, the difficulty is determining when "fame" requires special protection.

For example, few would dispute that at least in its home country (the United States), the mark BURGER KING® is famous for is hamburgers. Due to long use, a great sales volume of hamburgers, a large number of franchised fast food restaurants through out the country bearing the mark and extensive advertising, the mark has become well-known. But is BURGER KING® famous in Canada or Mexico (which border the home country)? More importantly, if it is famous, should it be protected against an unauthorized use by a third party in these countries, even if the BURGER KING® mark has not been registered or used in these countries?

What about an advertiser who uses an ELVIS PRESLEY impersonator to sell its liquor, or a digitized photo of Fred Astaire to sell its vacuum cleaners without permission? Should the commercialization of a public figure's image or personality be protected? Even after the figure is dead?

As you examine the issue of "fame" in its various contexts, ask yourself whether fame alone (however you choose to measure it) should give an intellectual property owner superior rights.

494

Chapter Twenty–Seven

FAMOUS TRADEMARKS

A. WHAT SPECIAL PROTECTION EXISTS FOR A FAMOUS MARK?

Read the following Articles from the Supplement: Paris Convention, Article 6bis, TRIPS, Article 16.

Notes and Questions

1. What are the qualities a mark must possess in order to qualify as "well-known" under Article 6bis? Must it be used in a country to be well-known, or is it sufficient if it is simply advertised in the country? Can a mark be "well known" through reputation alone?

2. Does Article 6bis explain which segment of the population must recognize the mark in order for it to be famous? Must the mark be well-known among the public at large or only to the trade circle in which the relevant goods or services circulate?

3. Does Article 16 of TRIPS clarify which segment of the public must know the mark? For example, if both the plaintiff and defendant are using the marks on similar or identical goods, the proper segment would most likely be potential users of both plaintiff's and defendant's goods. But what if the marks are used on non-competing goods? Whose segment becomes the proper one to consider? The plaintiff's? The defendant's? Both? The answer may depend upon whether the "commercial magnetism" of the mark is great enough to attract plaintiff's potential customers to the defendant's goods. Thus, in an opposition in the UK to registration of the mark VOGUE DESSOU.S. for undergarments, by the owner of the mark VOGUE for magazines, the hearing officer recognized that overlapping purchasers might be confused regarding the relationship between the marks. He stated: "The evidence indicates that VOGUE has a massive reputation in association with ladies' fashion clothing. I could well imagine that a percentage of such readers, if they encountered clothing being sold under the mark VOGUE DESSOU.S. would assume a connection with VOGUE magazine, perhaps by way of a licensing agreement, when this is in fact not the case." Application by Vogue Brassiere, Inc.; Opposition by Conde Nast Publications 29 December 1995 (reported in Frederick W. Mostert, FAMOUS AND WELL-KNOWN MARKS p. 28 n. 38 (Butterworths 1997)).

4. Survey evidence is often helpful in proving fame. Countries may differ, however, regarding the percentage of potential consumers who must know the mark. Thus, for example, in Germany, different percentages are required depending on the level of protection sought. Consequently, under the Court's rationale in *Avon* (German Federal Supreme Court, 21 March 1991 [1991] GRUR 863), if a survey demonstrates 80% of the public knows the mark, the mark is "famous." By contrast, if the survey indicates only 40% know the mark, it is "well-known." *Dimple* (German Federal Supreme Court, 29 November 1984 [1985] GRUR 550). Not all countries, however, accept survey evidence to prove renown.

5. *Defensive Registrations.* Some countries such as Japan allow defensive registration of a "widely recognized" mark to cover goods or services other than those listed in the original registration. No use on such goods or services is usually required. Under Japanese law, to qualify for defensive registration, the mark must be "widely recognized by consumers" (hiroku ninshiki sareta); there must be an apprehension of confusion (kondo no osore) if the mark were used on such goods or services. According to the *Guidelines for Examination of Trademarks* published by the Japanese Patent Office. The degree of fame of a work is determined by reference to the following factors:

1. Duration and area of use; the range of goods on which the mark is used;

2. Extent of advertisement used or other methods of publicizing the mark;

3. The amount of recognition the mark already enjoys within the Patent Office.

These requirements have been strictly applied. Recently the Japanese Patent Office denied a defensive mark registration for the SCOTCH trademark. The mark had been registered for tape and other adhesives. The applicant CM Corporation sought a defensive registration to prevent its use on kitchen utensils and other kitchen products. The Japanese Trademark Examiner denied the application on the grounds that the registered mark was in upper case, and the use of SCOTCH on other products was in lower case letters. The Tokyo High Court reversed, holding that the appropriate standard must include an analysis of the effect of the mark in the marketplace. If consumers would preclude the two marks identified the same source, the mark should be registered. *See generally,* Kenneth L. Port, JAPANESE TRADEMARK JURISPRUDENCE (Kluwer Law International (1998)).

6. Which of these marks is "famous"?

McDonald's for hamburgers

Budweiser for beer

Haier for air conditioners

Smirnoff for vodka

Lego for toys

How would you decide? What information would you need to determine if the mark were famous in the U.S.? In Argentina? In Russia? In China?

B. HOW DOES A MARK BECOME "FAMOUS"?

Despite the territorial nature of trademarks, it is undisputed that some marks have become so well-known they have a global reputation. Marks such as COCA–COLA®, MICROSOFT® and MCDONALD'S® seem to have reputations that have spread into every corner of the known world. But the reality is that there are still countries that have not yet experienced these consumer luxuries. Are these marks so famous that they deserve protection even in countries where the goods are not sold or advertised? If such protection does *not* exist, why establish the special protection for "well-known" marks under Article 6*bis* of the Paris Convention? These issues remain hard-fought, often invoking concerns over national pride and sovereignty.

THE BUD–VAR CASE
ANHEUSER–BUSCH v. BUDEJOVICKY BUDVAR NARODNI PODNIK

Chancery Division, 1998.
[1998] RPC 669.

RIMER J.

Connoisseurs of beer will have known for at least the last 20 years that an unelaborated request for a "Budweiser" beer in a bar, restaurant or shop in the United Kingdom may perhaps have resulted in the production of one or other of two different beers. One is the "Budweiser" beer produced by the American brewery, Anheuser–Busch Inc ("AB"). The other is the "Budweiser Budvar" beer produced by the Czech company, Budejovicky Budvar Narodni Podnik ("BB"). The use by both companies of the word "Budweiser" in relation to their beers is a feature which has an inevitable potential for at least some degree of confusion between their products, although the beers themselves, as well as the labels on their bottles and cans, are very different.

This potential for confusion has led to litigation between AB and BB. The matter before me is a further round in it. The first round was an action commenced in 1979 by which AB sued BB to restrain it from using the word "Budweiser" in relation to any beer other than AB's, a claim which was met with a counterclaim by BB seeking like relief against AB. Whitford J dismissed both claim and counterclaim. AB appealed to the Court of Appeal, which dismissed its appeal. The proceedings are reported as *Anheuser-Busch Inc. v. Budejovicky Budvar NP* (trading as Budweiser Budvar Brewery) and Others [1984] FSR 413 ("the passing off action").

The second round concerned an appeal by AB against BB's successful application under the Trade Marks Act 1938 to register "BUD" (a contraction of Budweiser) as a trade mark. Walton J dismissed the appeal and upheld the registration. The proceedings are reported as *BUD Trade Mark* [1988] RPC 535 ("the Bud proceedings").

The matter before me arises out of four further applications under the 1938 Act to register trade marks, three by AB and one by BB. The dates, numbers and nature of AB's applications are: (i) 11 December 1979, No 1,125,449, for the mark BUDWEISER for "Beer, ale and porter"; (ii) 12 June 1980, No 1,135,251, for a label mark for "Lager beer", bearing (*inter alia*) the words BUDWEISER, PREMIUM BEER; and (iii) 22 October 1981, No 1,163,438, for a label mark for "Beer", bearing (*inter alia*) the words BUDWEISER, KING OF BEERS. All applications were made in Class 32. BB filed oppositions to them on 3 February 1988.

On 28 June 1989 BB filed application No 1,389,680 to register the mark BUDWEISER in Class 32 for "Beer, ale and porter malt beverages, all included in Class 32 but not including any such goods for supply to, or sale in, the United States of America's Embassy and PX [postal exchange] stores in the United Kingdom." AB filed its opposition to it on 24 August 1990.

On 30 July 1997, Mr. Naharkness, the Assistant Registrar of Trade Marks, acting for the Registrar of Trade Marks, held that all four marks should proceed to registration.

On 29 August 1997 AB appealed against that decision in so far as it allowed BB's application. On 27 August 1997 BB appealed against it in so far as it allowed AB's applications.

BB is the successor of a brewing enterprise established in 1895 and carries on its business from a brewery established in Ceske Budejovice in the Czech Republic. That town was formerly in the Austro–Hungarian empire and was known to its German inhabitants as Budweiser. It has a history of brewing going back many centuries. BB has for many years used the name BUDWEISER in connection with its beer.

AB's brewing business was founded in Missouri in the nineteenth century and it has also used the trade name BUDWEISER for its beer. It has done so since about 1875. The choice of name was inspired by the method of brewing adopted in Budweiser, but the name has always been used by AB as a trade name and not as signifying a geographical origin. BB started selling its Budweiser beer in the United Kingdom in significant quantities in about 1973. The labels on its bottles bore the prominent words BUDWEISER BUDVAR. Since about 1967 BB's style of labelling had and has given more prominence to the word BUDWEISER, which was and is underlined by a rearward extension of the "R". "Var" is Czech for "brew" so that "Budvar" means "Bud brew". By midsummer of 1979 BB had sold in excess of 1,000,000 bottles in the UK.

Before 1974, AB had exported none of its Budweiser beer to the United Kingdom for commercial sale. Such sales only started in 1974, and between then and 1979 its UK sales were only on a small scale, totalling only some 240,000 cans. The main outlets for it were American-style restaurants, clubs or foodstores, with AB's first sales on the open market in the UK being only in about 1976. However, from at least 1962 to 1973 substantial quantities of AB's beer had been imported for use and sale in U.S. military and diplomatic establishments in the United Kingdom. They were available for purchase, duty free, by serving Americans and also by British employees of American service establishments, but they were not available for general purchase. BUDWEISER was well known to United States citizens and visitors as a trade mark for beer. References to the American product, both by customers and by AB in its advertising material, were sometimes abbreviated to BUD. AB also used the phrase "King of Beers" on the labelling and advertising of its Budweiser beer.

The labels on AB' s and BB' s respective cans and bottles were very distinctive, as were the beers they contained. Nevertheless, by 1979, when the writ in the passing off action was issued, both Budweiser beers were competing in the UK market and it is not surprising that the use of the common name led to the crossclaims made in that action.

Walton J referred, at [1988] RPC 535, 548, to the fact that it was inevitable that a certain amount of confusion arose from two beers in this country both called Budweiser, but added that:

> "The evidence demonstrates that the two beers are of somewhat different qualities and nobody who orders the one, knowing what he is going to get, would be satisfied when he received the other. The confusion would be at once apparent."

He referred to the fact that the drinkers of both types of beer referred to them as "BUD" and used that contraction to demand the beer. He referred to the passing off action and summarised its outcome as follows, namely that:

> "The result—which may be said to be a somewhat unexpected one—was that the Court of Appeal held that both of them were entitled to use the name 'Budweiser' and neither could prevent the other from doing that. In the action AB had asked for an injunction on the ground of passing off in relation to the use of the word BUD as against BB and that, in the course of the action, failed also. So we have the comparatively rare situation of two bodies each being entitled to use 'Budweiser' in respect of their own beers and neither being able to complain of the use of that word by the other one."

AB's case is that it alone has used the mark BUDWEISER simpliciter in relation to its beer products; it contends that BB has only used the word BUDWEISER in relation to its own products as part of a composite mark on its bottles and cans which includes the word BUDVAR: BB's beer brands are, and always have been, known as Budvar Budweiser or Budweiser Budvar. Each company failed in the passing off action to prevent the other's use of the word Budweiser, so that AB has no continuing complaint about the use by BB of the word Budweiser as part of its composite mark. Its argument, however, is that BB is not entitled to close yet further the narrow distinguishing gap still existing between the two marks by abandoning the word Budvar and asserting proprietorship of the right, which only AB has enjoyed, of using the mark Budweiser by itself.

AB relies primarily on § 11 (tendency to deceive or cause confusion), 12(1) (close resemblance to the trade marks covered by AB's own earlier three applications) and 17 (unjustified claim to proprietorship) of the 1938 Act. As well as setting out those sections, I should also set out § 10, 19 and 21. In relation to trade marks for goods, these sections provide, so far as is material, as follows:

"Capability of distinguishing requisite for registration in Part B

10.-(1) In order for a trade mark to be registrable in Part B of the register it must be capable, in relation to the goods in respect of which it is registered or proposed to be registered, of distinguishing goods with which the proprietor of the trade mark is or may be connected in the course of trade from goods in the case of which no such connection subsists, either generally or, where the trade mark is registered or proposed to be registered subject to limitations, in relation to use within the extent of the registration.

(2) In determining whether a trade mark is capable of distinguishing as aforesaid the tribunal may have regard to the extent to which–

(a) the trade mark is inherently capable of distinguishing as aforesaid; and

(b) by reason of the use of the trade mark or of any other circumstances, the trade mark is in fact capable of distinguishing as aforesaid.

Prohibition of registration of deceptive, etc., matter 11. It shall not be lawful to register as a trade mark or part of a trade mark any matter the use of which would, by reason of its being likely to deceive or cause confusion or otherwise, be disentitled to protection in a court of justice, or would be contrary to law or morality, or any scandalous design.

Prohibition of registration of identical and resembling trade marks.

12.-(1) Subject to the provisions of subsection (2) of this section, no trade mark shall be registered in respect of any goods or description of goods that is identical with or nearly resembles a mark belonging to a different proprietor and already on the register in respect of–

(a) the same goods,

(b) the same description of goods, or

(c) services or a description of services which are associated with those goods or goods of that description.

(2) In case of honest concurrent use, or of other special circumstances which in the opinion of the Court or the Registrar make it proper so to do, the Court or the Registrar may permit the registration by more than one proprietor in respect of–

(a) the same goods,

(b) the same description of goods or

(c) goods and services or descriptions of goods and services which are associated with each other, of marks that are identical or nearly resemble each other, subject to such conditions and limitations, if any, as the Court or Registrar, as the case may be, may think it right to impose.

(3) Where separate applications are made by different persons to be registered as proprietors respectively of marks that are identical or nearly resemble each other, in respect of–

(a) the same goods,

(b) the same description of goods, or

(c) goods and services or descriptions of goods and services which are associated with each other, the Registrar may refuse to register any of them until their rights have been determined by the Court, or have been settled by agreement in a manner approved by him or on an appeal (which may be brought either to the Board of Trade or to the Court at the option of the appellant) by the Board or the Court, as the case may be."

Mr. Hobbs submits, first, that BB's application fails to surmount the § 11 hurdle. The central factual plank on which he rests his submissions is that BB's beer has been marketed for many years under the composite Budweiser Budvar mark. BB's bottle and neck labels are in evidence and those two words are prominent on all of them, usually in script form. The use of the word Budweiser by BB as part of its composite mark is already confusing, but no complaint is made of that. If, however, BB is permitted to use the mark Budweiser alone, as AB does, it will simply serve to increase the likelihood of deception or confusion. Mr. Hobbs submits that the law does not willingly countenance the removal of distinguishing additions from a trader's mark or name where such removal is liable to increase the risk of deception or confusion. He referred me to *My Kinda Town Ltd. v. Soll and Another* [1983] RPC 407, at 425, where Oliver LJ said:

> "The question to be asked is, no doubt, in all cases the same—is the get-up, or the method of training, or the use of a particular trading name by the defendants calculated to lead to the belief that their business is the plaintiff's business? But it becomes an extraordinarily difficult question to answer where there is already a substantial potentiality for confusion of the two businesses simply by reason of their being engaged in the same trade. That does not mean, of course, that a defendant is legitimately entitled to build on and increase that potentiality in such a way that confusion becomes worse confounded, but it does mean that where evidence of actual confusion is tendered it has to be approached—as indeed it was here by the learned judge—with the caveat that there may well be reasons why it occurs which involve no question of legal liability at all."

As to § 17, Mr. Hobbs accepts that BB can claim proprietorship of the composite mark Budweiser Budvar, but he says that it cannot claim proprietorship of the mark Budweiser by itself. That is to usurp AB's title, which has been built up and acquired over long use. For like reasons, he submits that BB cannot satisfy § 21(1) in relation to the Budweiser element of its composite mark.

Mr. Kitchin's argument in support of the registrar's decision in respect of BB's application is that, although the parties have disputed the right to use the word Budweiser, and also its contraction BUD, the outcome is that the Court of Appeal in the passing off action concluded that both AB and BB must live together as proprietors of the mark Budweiser; and Walton J in the Bud proceedings decided that both parties were entitled to registration of the mark BUD. The registrar in the present case arrived at his conclusion in relation to all four applications before him on the basis that the earlier decisions of the courts had concluded that both parties could claim to be proprietors of the mark Budweiser and that it followed that all four marks should proceed to registration. Mr. Kitchin submits that the registrar was correct. Although BB has appealed against the registrar's decision in respect of the AB applications, Mr. Kitchin's primary position is that both appeals should be dismissed and that the decisions on all four applications should be upheld. His secondary submission is that, if only one side is entitled to registration of the mark Budweiser, then it is BB.

Subsection 12(2) provides that honest concurrent use or other special circumstances may allow registration of conflicting marks, within the tribunal's discretion. The main matters for consideration when subsection 12(2) is invoked were laid down by Lord Tomlin in Pirie's Trade Mark [1933] 50 RPC 147 at 159. They are:

i.   The extent of, use in time and quantity and the area of the trade.

ii.   The degree of confusion likely to ensue from the resemblance of the marks, which is, to a large extent, indicative of the measure of public inconvenience.

iii.   The honesty of the concurrent use.

iv.   whether any instances of confusion have been proved.

v.   The relative inconvenience which would be caused if the mark in suit were registered, subject if necessary to any conditions and limitations."

Turning to this case, Mr. Kitchin submitted that AB's objections to BB's registration are not made out. He emphasised the unusual and special circumstances of the case. He submitted that BB had made use of the word Budweiser both on its own and as part of the composite name Budweiser Budvar since 1973, and he referred to the prominence given to the word Budweiser on the BB labels. He submitted that it was established in the passing off case, and accepted by the Court of Appeal, that from about 1973 to 1979 (the date of the first of AB's applications) BB's beer was advertised and sold under and by reference to the name Budweiser, that it was demanded by its customers and ordered under that name and that it was evidently known by that name. He pointed out, as was also accepted by the Court of Appeal, that by 1979 BB had established a reputation and right to use the mark Budweiser in the UK and had made substantial commercial use of the name Budweiser in the open UK market, and that its use of such name in that market probably preceded AB's use of it there. Walton J's decision established BB's right to register the word BUD as a trade mark. That was a contraction of Budweiser, so that the right to register Budweiser as a trade mark must be a fortiori in the light of the decision of the Court of Appeal.

As to the position since the passing off action, Mr. Kitchin submitted that the evidence shows that from 1979 to 1992 (the latest date covered by the evidence) BB continued to conduct its business in a like manner and on an increasing scale.

As to the use made of the word Budweiser alone in relation to BB's beer, Miss Zilkha exhibits promotional material used in the 1970s and up to 1983 in which BB's beer was referred to simply as Budweiser lager. She exhibits some promotional material used by BB in the middle 1980s at a beer festival, which also refers to BB's beer simply as Budweiser, which Mr. Kitchin submits is a plain example of trade mark use of the word Budweiser alone. On 2 January 1990 Andrew Barr wrote an article in the Evening Standard which referred to both of AB's and BB's beers, and referred to BB's version simply as Budweiser. In 1988 the Daily Mirror World Beer Guide included an article about BB's beer, which referred to it as "The original Budweiser—or Budweiser Budbar to give it its full name ..." and also referred to it as "the Czech Budweiser" in contrast to "the American Budweiser". On 23 December 1989, The Grocer included an article referring to BB's beers, the title to which was "Czechoslovak Budweiser Multipack". A Courage advertisement in 1984/5 for BB's beer included a picture with a rondel in a prominent position at the top bearing the single word Budweiser. Miss Zilkha exhibits a menu from a chain of brasseries which refers to BB's beer simply as Budweiser. There is also some evidence from Mr. Cozens, who has run an off-licence since 1985. He says that the most popular beer he sells is Budweiser Budvar, that over 50% of his customers refer to it simply as Budweiser, with the next two most common modes of reference being either Bud or Czech Bud. Mr. Carlisle, who has run a wine bar since 1984, also sells Budweiser Budvar. He deposes that most of his customers refer to it as Bud or Budweiser, without any qualification, although sometimes they refer to it as Czech Bud or Czech Budweiser. Mr. Carlisle says that he used to order the beer from his supplier simply by using the name Budweiser. Anne Lo, of Ken Lols Memories of China, a restaurant at Chelsea Harbour, says that the restaurant supplies Budweiser Budvar, and that its customers normally refer to it as Budweiser without qualification, although its wine list describes the beer as "Budweiser Budvar (Czechoslovakia)". Miss Lo deposes that she too orders the beer simply under the name Budweiser.

Mr. Kitchin submits that there will be no risk of passing off by BB if it is allowed registration of Budweiser as a trade mark, since there is no suggestion that BB would use the mark in any manner likely to increase the existing degree of confusion between the two beers. To allow BB's application will not be to entitle it use of the mark Budweiser in any way which is misleading, nor will it affect AB's common law rights. AB's and BB's respective labels have always distinguished their respective beers in the past and there is no basis for any inference that that is going to change in the future. The use by BB of the mark Budweiser will not necessarily result in any increased confusion. It all depends how it is done. Equally, the use by AB of the mark Budweiser is capable of being more confusing than it has in the past, but the practicalities are that AB will use its mark in a way which does not increase that confusion. But if BB's registration is not allowed and AB's registrations are, then BB's traders and customers will be at serious risk, since the evidence is that certain of them are and have been in the habit of referring to BB's beer merely as Budweiser. In such event, if they continue such habit, they would, on the face of it, be infringing AB's registered mark and could be faced with the threat or the reality of proceedings. Mr. Kitchin submits that such a consequence would be an unfair one, involving giving AB an unjust advantage over BB as compared with the position which it has previously enjoyed.

In his reply, Mr. Hobbs submitted that BB's declared intentions as to a non-confusing use of the mark Budweiser were irrelevant. He says that the normal and fair use contemplated of a mark is a use in the way in which marks of this sort are normally used on bottles and cans. BB is not offering to submit to any limitations, conditions or restrictions controlling its use of the mark. It is claiming a monopoly in the single word Budweiser. He says that the evidence shows that its beer has always been described and held out as Budweiser Budvar, whereas BB is now, in effect, claiming a right to call it Budweiser. BB's submissions amount to an argument that the Budvar element of the name of its beer is almost an irrelevance. Mr. Hobbs argues, however, that Budvar has always been prominent on BB' s labels and must have been there for a purpose. He says that it has a trade mark significance as part of the composite name Budweiser Budvar. He submitted that the evidence relied on by Mr. Kitchin as supporting trade references to BB's beer simply as Budweiser was too slender to support the submission Mr. Kitchin sought to found upon it.

If AB did not exist, and BB's pattern and history of trading had been exactly the same as it has been, I cannot think that there could be any difficulty under § 17 and/or 21, or under any other provision of the 1938 Act, in allowing BB's application for the registration which it seeks. Mr. Hobbs accepted as much at the opening of his submissions. That being so, it appears to me that the only real question is whether AB has raised an objection under § 11 or, if it has, whether that objection should be overridden under § 12(2). In my judgment, the § 11 objection is not made out, because this is a case where BB's right to use the name Budweiser concurrently with AB has been established by the decision in the passing off action. If, however, I am wrong in that, then I consider that this is a case where there has for long been an honest concurrent use by both AB and BB of the mark Budweiser; and that the unusual circumstances of this case, including in particular the use by BB's traders and customers of the word Budweiser to refer to its beer, are anyway sufficiently special to justify any § 11 objection being overridden under § 12(2).

In my judgment, the assistant registrar's conclusion on BB's application was correct and I dismiss AB's appeal against his decision. Mr. Kitchin made plain that, despite BB's appeal against the decision on AB's applications, BB's primary position is that both sides' applications should be allowed to proceed and that both appeals should be dismissed. I agree that BB's appeal against the AB applications should also be dismissed. With regard to those applications too, I consider that no § 11 objection is made out by BB; alternatively, that the registrations should be permitted under § 12(2).

DISPOSITION:

Appeals dismissed.

Notes and Questions

1. Which of the two marks qualifies as a "famous" or "well-known" mark under Article 6bis?

2. If the court had considered the question of protection of a famous mark, would the court have reached a different decision?

3. If you were representing the American Budweiser company in this matter, what advice would you give about resolving the dispute with the Czech Budvar company?

4. If this dispute occurred in the United States, with the same facts, would the court have reached the same decision?

THE SOUTH AFRICAN McDONALD'S CASE

McDONALD'S CORPORATION v. JOBURGERS DRIVE-INN RESTAURANT (PTY)

In the Supreme Court of South Africa, 1996.
Case No 547/95, 1996.

GROSSKOPF, JA

This is a dispute about the use and continued registration of the appellant's trade marks. The appellant, to which I shall refer to as McDonald's, is a corporation incorporated in the state of Delaware in the United States of America. It is one of the largest franchisers of fast food restaurants in the world, if not the largest. It first commenced business in the United States of America in 1955 and has carried on business internationally since 1971. It operates its own restaurants and also franchises others to do so. It sells hamburgers and other fast foods. The McDONALD'S trade mark is widely used in relation to restaurants owned by McDonald's as well as those that are franchised.

McDonald's obtained registration of its trade marks in South Africa in 1968, 1974, 1979, 1980, 1984 and 1985. It is now the registered proprietor of fifty-two marks. Of these, twenty-seven consist of or incorporate the word "McDONALD" or "McDONALD'S". Also used is the letter "M" in the form of so-called golden arches, with or without the word "McDONALD'S". Others consist of the words BIG MAC, EGG McMUFFIN and McMUFFIN. There are also two clown devices. The trade marks are registered in respect of goods, mainly in classes 29 and 30, and for services in class 42.

When the present proceedings commenced, McDonald's had not traded in South Africa nor, we may assume for present purposes, had it used any of its trade marks here.

Joburgers Drive–Inn Restaurant (Pty) Limited ("Joburgers") is a South African company with its principal place of business in Johannesburg. Its managing director is Mr. George Sombonos. Mr. Sombonos has been engaged in the fast food industry since 1968. In 1979 he registered a company called Golden Fried Chicken (Pty) Limited ("Chicken Licken"). He holds 90% of the shares in the company and is its managing director. In 1979 Chicken Licken applied for the registration of a number of trade marks, including CHICKEN LICKEN. Since then it has franchised the Chicken Licken business so that today there are more than 177 stores throughout South Africa. Mr. Sombonos says that Chicken Licken is the biggest fried chicken fast food franchise chain in the world not having its origins in the United States of America.

During 1992 Mr. Sombonos on behalf of Joburgers decided to establish fast food outlets and restaurants using the trade marks McDONALD'S, BIG MAC and the golden arches design. In 1993 Mr. Sombonos applied for the registration of these and some other McDonald's marks. At the same time he applied to the Registrar of Trade Marks in terms of Section 36(1)(a) and (b) of the Trade Marks Act, No. 62 of 1963 ("the old Act") for the expungement of the trade marks which are held by McDonald's. McDonald's opposed these applications and filed its counter-statements in the expungement applications during August 1993. During the same period McDonald's applied again for the registration of all the trade marks in its name.

On 29 August 1993 there appeared an article in the Sunday Times newspaper reading *inter alia* as follows:

> "Big Macs may soon be eaten all over South Africa, but not because American hamburger giant McDonald's is entering the market. Nor will they be on sale before judgment in which could be SA's biggest trade mark battle.

> Chicken Licken franchise owner George Sombonos plans to start his own national McDonald's hamburger chain. Sites have been chosen and an advertising campaign is being prepared.

> Mr. Sombonos' lawyer Shaun Ryan of Ryans Attorneys, says the first restaurant will open in Johannesburg "as soon as physically possible".

> The chain will serve McMuffins and Big Mac burgers.

Restaurants will also be decorated with a large M device similar to two joined arches."

In response to this article McDonald's wrote through its attorneys to Joburgers' attorney *inter alia* as follows:

"We are instructed that the intended use of McDonald's trade marks [which were listed in an annexure to the letter] constitutes an infringement of our client's trade mark rights. Your client has unequivocally expressed a clear intention to use such trade marks.

We have been instructed to demand as we hereby do that your client unequivocally undertake that it will not use our client's registered trade marks or any other marks which are deceptively or confusingly similar to our client's registered trade marks."

Failing an undertaking as demanded in this letter McDonald's threatened legal proceedings.

Joburgers' reply was uncompromising. It read, *inter alia*,

"We are aware that your client is the Registrant for the trade marks listed in the Annexure to your letter. Your client is not the Proprietor of these trade marks. The true proprietor of the subject matter of these registrations is Joburgers Drive–Inn Restaurant (Pty) Limited. You may take it that it is our client's intention to both use and register its trade marks in the Republic of South Africa. Your client is invited to take legal proceedings as threatened."

On 23 September 1993 McDonald's launched an urgent application against Joburgers in the Transvaal Provincial Division for relief on the grounds of infringement of its trade marks, passing off and unlawful competition. I shall refer to this application as the Joburgers application. On 28 September 1993 Swart J granted an order by agreement, the relevant part of which read as follows :

"The respondent undertakes pending the determination of this application and the proposed counter-application, not to infringe the applicant's registered trade marks which undertaking is made an order of court."

On 1 May 1995 the Trade Marks Act, No. 194 of 1993 ("the new Act") came into force. Section 35 of the new Act provides for the protection of "well-known" trade marks emanating from certain foreign countries. On 20 June 1995 McDonald's brought an application against Joburgers under Sec. 35 of the new Act. It claimed that all 52 of its trade marks were well-known marks in terms of the section, and sought an order that Joburgers be interdicted and restrained from imitating, reproducing or transmitting those marks in the Republic of South Africa. I shall call this the "well-known marks application".

Sec. 71 of the new Act repealed the old Act. However, Sec. 3(2) of the new Act provides that all applications and proceedings commenced under the repealed Act shall be dealt with in accordance with the provisions of that Act as if it had not been repealed. The Joburgers application must therefore be dealt with in accordance with the old Act. The well-known marks applications, on the other hand, must be decided according to the new Act.

The three applications were heard together by Southwood J. He found in favour of Joburgers. Accordingly, in the Joburgers application, the application by McDonald's for an interdict was dismissed and Joburgers' counter-application for expungement granted; and the well-known marks application by McDonald's was refused. In all cases appropriate costs orders were made.

With the leave of the court a quo McDonald's now appeals against these orders.

For convenience I start with the well-known marks application. Sec 35 of the new Act reads as follows:

"(1) References in this Act to a trade mark which is entitled to protection under the Paris Convention as a well-known trade mark, are to a mark which is well known in the Republic as being the mark of—

(a) a person who is a national of a convention country; or

(b) a person who is domiciled in, or has a real and effective industrial or commercial establishment in, a convention country, whether or not such person carries on business, or has any goodwill, in the Republic.

(2) A reference in this Act to the proprietor of such a mark shall be construed accordingly.

(3) The proprietor of a trade mark which is entitled to protection under the Paris Convention as a well-known trade mark is entitled to restrain the use in the Republic of a trade mark which constitutes, or the essential part of which constitutes, a reproduction, imitation or translation of the well-known trade mark in relation to goods or services which are identical or similar to the goods or services in respect of which the trade mark is well known and where the use is likely to cause deception or confusion."

There was a large area of agreement between the parties about the meaning and application of this section. Thus it was common cause that McDonald's in fact is a person such as is described in paragraphs (a) and (b) of sub-section (1). The parties were also agreed on what it is that has to be "well known" in the Republic. In this regard the court a quo had said :

> "It is not sufficient that the mark simply be well-known in the Republic. It must be established that the mark is well-known as the mark of a person who is (a) a national of, or (b) is domiciled in, or (c) has a real and effective industrial or commercial establishment in, a convention country: *i.e.* it must also be well known that there is a connection between the mark and some person falling in categories (a), (b) or (c)."

This seems to suggest that the section only applies if what is well known is not only the mark itself but also the nationality, domicile, or place of business of the mark's owner, and moreover the fact that the relevant country is a convention country. Before us counsel were *ad idem* that such an interpretation could not be supported. If it were correct the section would be a dead letter. It is difficult to imagine any mark, however well known, in respect of which such further facts would be common knowledge. The parties accordingly accepted (I think correctly) that it would be enough for a plaintiff to prove that the mark is well known as a mark which has its origin in some foreign country, provided that as a fact the proprietor of the mark is a person falling within subsection (1)(a) or (b).

The essential dispute between the parties was what level of awareness in the public mind is required for a mark to qualify as "well-known" in terms of section 35. In this regard it is useful to look at the background to the section.

The Paris Convention, to which reference is made in Sec. 35, is the Paris Convention on the Protection of Industrial Property of 20 March 1883 as revised or amended from time to time (sec 2 of the Act). For present purposes art 6bis(1) of the Convention is apposite. Its relevant portion read as follows:

> "The countries of the Union undertake, ex officio if their legislation so permits, or at the request of an interested party, to refuse or to cancel the registration, and to prohibit the use, of a trade mark which constitutes a reproduction, an imitation, or a translation, liable to create confusion, of a mark considered by the competent authority of the country of registration or use to be well-known in that country as being already the mark of a person entitled to the benefits of this Convention and used for identical or similar goods."

Although art 6bis was inserted into the convention as far back as 1925, neither Britain nor South Africa gave legislative effect to it until recently—South Africa in sec 35 of the new Act, and Britain in sec 56 of the Trade Marks Act, 1994 (42 & 43 Elizabeth 2 C. 26). The two sections are very similar. Section 35(1) and (2) of the new Act, in particular, is, for practical purposes, identical to sec 56(1) of the British Act, save for the substitution of "the Republic" for "the United Kingdom" wherever it appears. The reason why Britain did not legislate earlier was that previously it claimed to be honouring the article by means of its common law of passing off. See Richard C Abnett, AIPPI : Famous Trade Marks Require a New Legal Weapon, Trademark World, Dec 1990/Jan 1991, p. 23.

The protection granted to foreign marks by the law of passing off was limited, however, by the requirement that a plaintiff had to establish a goodwill in the country. In a well known passage from *The Commissioners of Inland Revenue v. Muller & Co's Margarine Ltd*

[1901] AC 217 (HL) at 223–4 Lord Macnaghten defined goodwill as follows:

> "It is a thing very easy to describe, very difficult to define. It is the benefit and advantage of the good name, reputation, and connection of a business. It is the attractive force which brings in custom. It is the one thing which distinguishes an old-established business from a new business at its first start. The goodwill of a business must emanate from a particular centre or source. However widely extended or diffused its influence may be, goodwill is worth nothing unless it has power of attraction sufficient to bring customers home to the source from which it emanates. For my part, I think that if there is one attribute common to all cases of goodwill it is the attribute of locality. For goodwill has no independent existence. It cannot subsist by itself. It must be attached to a business. Destroy the business, and the goodwill perishes with it, though elements remain which may perhaps be gathered up and be revived again." (Emphasis added)

The "attribute of locality" mentioned in this passage led to a result described as follows in Kerly's LAW OF TRADE MARKS AND TRADE NAMES, 12th ed (1986) p 358 para 16–18 :

> "Since an essential ingredient of passing-off is damage to goodwill, he, *i.e*, the plaintiff in an action founded on passing-off in the United Kingdom] must show that he had in this country not merely a reputation but also a goodwill capable of being damaged. Goodwill, however, is local; it is situated where the business is. Thus a foreign plaintiff may have a reputation in this country—from travellers on the one hand, or periodicals of international circulation, for instance, on the other—yet still fail in an action for passing-off because he has here no business and so no goodwill. Such cases have been not uncommon in recent years, and have caused considerable difficulty."

Examples of such cases are *Alain Bernardin et Compagnie v. Pavilion Properties Ltd* [1967] RPC 581 (the "Crazy Horse" case*)*, *The Athletes Foot Marketing Associates Inc v. Cobra Sports Ltd and Another* [1980] RPC 343 (Ch) and *Anheuser-Busch Inc. v. Budejovicky Budvar NP* (trading as Budweiser Budvar Brewery) and Others [1984] FSR 413 (CA).

In the *Alain Bernardin* case the plaintiff was the proprietor and operator of a bar and cabaret in Paris known as the "Crazy Horse Saloon". The bar had been continuously and extensively publicised in the United Kingdom for sixteen years. The defendant commenced a place of entertainment in London under the name of "Crazy Horse Saloon" and issued an advertisement stating "Crazy Horse Saloon comes to London". The plaintiff applied for an interlocutory injunction against the defendant on the grounds of passing-off. The application was refused. The court stated (at 584 lines 30–47):

"That a trader cannot acquire goodwill in this country without some sort of user in this country. I do not think that the mere sending into this country by a foreign trader of advertisements advertising his establishment abroad could fairly be treated as user in this country. If that were so, the range of the action of passing-off would be extended far beyond anything which has hitherto been treated as its proper scope. That observation applies I think particularly to such establishments as hotels and even more to restaurants. It may well be that the owner of a foreign hotel or restaurant acquires in this country a reputation for the name of his hotel or restaurant in a wide sense, that the travel agents or other persons to whom he sends advertisements know of his establishment. Again he may acquire a reputation in a wide sense in the sense of returning travellers speaking highly of that establishment, but it seems to me that those matters, although they may represent reputation in some wide sense, fall far short of user in this country and are not sufficient to establish reputation in the sense material for the purpose of a passing-off action. It is very clear that in such circumstances the foreign trader has not acquired anything which in law could be described as goodwill in this country."

In the *Athletes Foot* case the plaintiffs carried on in the United States of America and elsewhere, but not in Great Britain, an extensive business in which they granted franchises to independent stores to sell footwear for athletes under the name "The Athlete's Foot". During 1978 and 1979 they had taken steps to secure a franchise agreement for the United Kingdom and a prospective franchisee had gone so far as to order goods and stationery with a view to establishing a chain of stores under the name "The Athlete's Foot". However no franchise contract had been concluded and no sales had in fact been made under that name. There was nevertheless an awareness of the plaintiffs' trade name and trading activities in a substantial section of the public in England as a result of over-spill publicity through American journals circulating there.

In the Anheuser–Busch case the plaintiffs and their predecessors were brewers of beer in the United States of America. Their beer had been sold since 1875 under the "Budweiser" trade mark. The first defendants were from 1895 brewers of beer in Ceske Budejovice, a town in Czechoslovakia formerly known by its German name of Budweis. In sales in Europe the first defendants used the word "Budweiser" in relation to their beer.

On appeal it was accepted that the plaintiffs' Budweiser beer enjoyed a significant reputation among members of the public in the United Kingdom as a result of visits to the United States and spill-over advertising. Such reputation was, however, not enough. What was required was a goodwill in the United Kingdom, which could not exist without a business there. This was expressed by Oliver L J as follows (p 470):

"Mr. Kentridge argues that once a goodwill exists it is for the owner of the goodwill to choose when and how he will go into the market with his product. But this, with respect, begs the question, because it assumes the existence of the goodwill apart from the market, and that, as it seems to me, is to confuse goodwill, which cannot exist in a vacuum, with mere reputation which may, no doubt, and frequently does, exist without any supporting local business, but which does not by itself constitute a property which the law protects."

And O'Connor L J said (at p 471),

"As a result of the plaintiffs' enormous business in the U.S.A. expanded by ever increasing advertising, I am in no doubt that the evidence showed that the plaintiffs' Budweiser beer enjoyed a significant reputation among members of the public in this country. That is not sufficient to found an action for passing off. It is the goodwill of a business carried on in this country that can be protected, not the reputation—goodwill if you like—of a business carried on in another country."

On the facts the Court of Appeal held that the activities of the plaintiffs in the United Kingdom did not amount to the carrying on of a business there.

Whether the above cases were right or wrong, they demonstrate that the courts in this country and the United Kingdom have in fact not protected the owners of foreign trade marks who did not have a goodwill within the country. To that extent the common law of passing off has not been sufficient to constitute compliance with art 6bis of the Paris Convention.

It seems clear that sec 35 of the new Act and the corresponding provision in the United Kingdom were intended to remedy this lack. Thus sec 35(1) pertinently extends protection to the owner of a foreign mark "whether or not such person carries on business, or has any goodwill, in the Republic". And the type of protection which is granted by sub-sec (3) is typical of that which is available under the common law of passing off; a prohibition on the use of the mark in relation to goods or services in respect of which the mark is well known and where the use is likely to cause deception or confusion.

It is against this background that the expressions "well-known trade mark" and "well known in the Republic" must be interpreted. Counsel for McDonald's contended that the legislature intended to impose no more than the ordinary requirement for passing off actions, namely that the reputation must extend to a substantial number of members of the public or persons in the trade in question.

Of course, the mere fact that the legislature intended to provide some protection for a foreign trader who does not have a goodwill or a business inside the country does not necessarily mean that such protection must be coterminous with that afforded to local businessmen. It is accordingly conceivable that, in order to receive protection, the foreigner might have to prove a greater public awareness of his mark than is required of a local businessman claiming a remedy against passing off. And, indeed, the respondents argued that the legislature in giving protection only to well-known marks, did impose a higher standard. On the ordinary meaning of language, so the argument went, a mark is well known in the Republic only when known to a large part of the population as a whole.

This argument raises two questions, namely

(a) must the mark be well-known to all sectors of the populations; and

(b) whatever the relevant sector of the population may be, what degree of awareness within that sector is required before a mark can properly be described as well-known.

The answer to question (a) is, I think, clear. Section 35 of the new Act was intended to provide a practical solution to the problems of foreign businessmen whose marks were known in South Africa but who did not have a business here. The South African population is a diverse one in many respects. There are wide differences in income, education, cultural values, interests, tastes, personal life styles, recreational activities, etc. This was obviously known to the legislature when it passed the new Act. If protection is granted only to marks which are known (not to say well-known) to every segment of the population (or even to most segments of the population) there must be very few marks, if any, which could pass the test. The legislation would therefore not achieve its desired purpose. Moreover, there would not appear to be any point in imposing such a rigorous requirement. In argument we were referred as example to a mark which might be very well known to all persons interested in golf. Why should it be relevant, when deciding whether or not to protect such a mark, that non-golfers might never had heard of it? I consider therefore that a mark is well-known in the Republic if it is well-known to persons interested in the goods or services to which the mark relates.

The next question then is : how well should it be known to such persons? (question (b) above). On behalf of McDonald's it was argued that the test in this regard is qualitative and not a quantitative one. The question is not, it was argued, how many of the relevant persons know the mark, but how profound the knowledge of the mark is among those who do know it. In my view this argument is untenable. I suppose that knowledge of a mark could be so vague or superficial as hardly to count as knowledge at all, but apart from that I would not have thought that there would normally be great differences in the degree of knowledge of the mark by members of the public, or that such differences, if they existed, would be of any relevance. In the present context the important practical question is not whether a few people know the mark well but rather whether sufficient persons know it well enough to entitle it to protection against deception or confusion.

How many people are sufficient? The only guideline provided by the legislature lies in the expression "well-known". This is in itself so vague as hardly to provide any assistance at all. It is certainly capable of bearing the meaning urged upon us by counsel for McDonald's, namely a substantial number as used in the law of passing off generally. In this regard the judge a quo commented that if it was the object of the subsection to require knowledge only of a substantial number of persons, "it is strange that this was not simply stated to be the requirement instead of merely adopting the terminology of section (sic) 6bis (1) of the Paris Convention". With respect, I do not agree. The purpose of the legislature clearly was to give legislative force to article 6bis of the Paris Convention. To this end it was natural to repeat the language of the Convention, leaving it to the courts to give practical effect to the vague expressions used.

On behalf of the respondents it was contended that a greater extent of public knowledge is required. The difficulty here is one of definition and practical application. If a substantial number is not sufficient, what is? To require one hundred percent would clearly be excessive, but how must less would suffice? Seventy-five percent, fifty percent? What logical basis is there for laying down any such requirement? And how does one prove any such arbitrary percentage?

It seems to me that McDonald's contention must be sustained. The legislature intended to extend the protection of a passing off action to foreign businessmen who did not have a business or enjoy a goodwill inside the country provided their marks were well-known in the Republic. It seems logical to accept that the degree of knowledge of the marks that is required would be similar to that protected in the existing law of passing off. The concept of a substantial number of persons is well established. It provides a practical and flexible criterion which is consistent with the terms of the statute. No feasible alternative has been suggested.

I turn now to the evidence concerning the extent to which the McDonald's trade marks are known in the Republic. As I have stated earlier, McDonald's is one of the largest, if not the largest, franchiser of fast food restaurants in the world. At the end of 1993 there were 13 993 McDonald's restaurants spread over 70 countries. The annual turnover of McDonald's restaurants amounts to some $23 587 million. McDonald's trade marks are used extensively in relation to its own restaurants as well as to those that are franchised. The level of advertising and promotion which has been carried out by McDonald's, its subsidiaries, affiliates and franchisees in relation to McDonald's restaurants exceeds the sum of $900 million annually. Their international marketing campaigns have included sponsorship of the 1984 Los Angeles and 1992 Barcelona Olympics. McDonald's has also been a sponsor of the 1990 soccer World Cup Tournament in Italy and the 1994 World Cup Soccer Tournament in the United States of America. Mr. Paul R Duncan, the vice president and general counsel of McDonald's, stated on affidavit that, in view of the vast scale of his organisation's operations, the

McDonald's trade marks are in all probability some of the best known trade marks in the world. This was not denied. Although there was no evidence on the extent to which the advertising outside South Africa spilled over into this country through printed publications and television, it must, in all probability, be quite extensive. In addition the McDonald's trade marks would be known to many South Africans who have travelled abroad. This again would not be an insignificant number.

Spontaneous acts by South Africans have confirmed that there is a general level of knowledge in this country about the operations of McDonald's. Thus McDonald's disclosed that, between 1975 and 1993 it received 242 requests from South Africans to conclude franchising agreements. Some of these applicants were prominent companies. For reasons which are not relevant at present, none of these applications were acceded to.

The conduct of Joburgers in the present case confirms the reputation attaching to the McDonald's mark. Intrinsically the word McDonald has no attractive force. It is a fairly common surname. Had it not been for the reputation it has acquired over the years nobody would wish to appropriate it. It is therefore significant that Joburgers have gone to considerable trouble and expense to obtain control over the McDonald's marks. Joburgers announced its intention of operating under the name McDonald's in a provocative manner through an article in the Sunday Times which was bound to stimulate legal action against it. It may be noted in passing that the article in the Sunday Times, which is quoted above, itself clearly presupposes that its readers would be aware of McDonald's, its business, products and marks.

The basic theory of market research is that from a given representative sample of the consumer public it is possible to project, by means of acceptable mathematical methods, results of such sampling to a general population or "universe" within certain statistical limits. In other words, the researcher first determines the class of persons (or universe) which is sought to be tested, and then questions individuals from that universe. The confidence that one has in a projection from the samples to the universe varies according to the number of persons interviewed in the survey, the sampling technique used and the level of response.

During September 1993 Mr. Corder was instructed to conduct a market survey on behalf of McDonald's. He was informed that the objectives of the study were to establish awareness of the name McDonald's, to measure recognition of the McDonald's trade marks, to ascertain the association of McDonald's with certain products or types of business undertakings, and to establish the awareness of McDonald's hamburgers. The method used by him was the conducting of personal interviews using a structured questionnaire and interviewing aids. The interviewing aids consisted of two text show cards and one colour picture show card featuring the main McDonald's trade marks. Copies of the questionnaires and show cards were before the Court.

The universe for the survey was defined as white adult males and females, aged 16 years and over, living in houses in high income suburbs of Pretoria, Verwoerdburg, Johannesburg, Bedfordview, Randburg and Sandton. A sample of 202 persons was taken. The fieldwork was conducted from 7 December to 24 December 1993 by trained interviewers under the supervision of field supervisors. Twenty-one percent of the interviews were back checked in order to ensure reliability. Affidavits of supervisors and interviewers were filed to confirm their actions. Mr. Corder, who was in overall control, also confirmed that the survey was properly conducted. The relevant conclusions were set out as follows :

> "A large majority of respondents were aware of the name McDonald's, and/or the McDonald's logos/trademarks (77%). More than half had heard of both McDonald's, and knew the logos/trademarks too (57%).

Most respondents spontaneously associated McDonald's with hamburgers, knew of "McDonald's Hamburgers" (80%).

The results indicate that the majority of white adults, aged 16 and over, living in households in high income suburbs of Johannesburg and Pretoria are aware of the McDonald's brand name, and associate McDonald's with hamburgers."

During January and February 1995 a similar survey was conducted among white males and females, aged 16 years and over, living in selected higher income suburbs of Durban. The conclusions were stated as follows:

> "A large majority of respondents were aware of the name McDonald's, and/or the McDonald's logos/trade marks (90%). More than half had heard of both McDonald's, and also knew the logos/trade marks (52%).

Most respondents spontaneously associated McDonald's with hamburgers, or knew of McDonald's Hamburgers (87%).

The results indicate that the majority of white adults, aged 16 and over, living in the higher income Durban suburbs of Broadway, Essenwood, Morningside and Musgrave are aware of the McDonald's brand name, and associate McDonald's with hamburgers.

As I have said above, I consider that it would be enough for McDonald's to show that its marks are known to a substantial number of persons who are interested in the goods or services provided by it. On behalf of McDonald's it was contended, correctly in my view, that there are two categories of such persons—potential customers and potential franchisees. Potential customers would cover a wide field. It would include all persons who like fast food of this type and have the money to buy it. Since the cost is not high there would be many such people. Potential franchisees would be a smaller group, namely persons who can finance and run a McDonald's franchise, or consider that they can.

The evidence adduced by McDonald's leads, in my view, to the inference that its marks, and particularly the mark McDONALD'S, are well known amongst the more affluent people in the country. People who travel, watch television, and who read local and foreign publications, are likely to know about it. They would have seen McDonald's outlets in other countries, and seen or heard its advertisements there or its spillover here in foreign journals, television shows, etc. Although the extent of such spillover has not been quantified it must be substantial. Moreover, as has been shown, McDonald's has also received publicity in the local media. The market survey evidence specifically related to two groups of adult white persons living in relatively affluent suburbs of Gauteng and KwaZulu Natal. It is reasonable to suppose that much the same results would be achieved elsewhere among persons of all races who have a similar financial and social background. These are also the type of people who would have heard about McDonald's and its marks from Collins, or who would have discussed these matters with him, or would have written to McDonald's to solicit a franchise agreement.

By the same token, people who are poor, do not travel abroad, do not read foreign publications or, possibly do not read at all, and are not exposed to television, are likely not to have heard of McDonald's or its marks. It is accordingly not surprising that market surveys commissioned by Joburgers showed a low awareness of McDonald's and its marks among black persons generally.

These conclusions must be applied to the relevant categories among the public. Potential franchisees, I consider, would be the type of persons who would almost without exception have heard of McDonald's and know its marks. Among potential customers the level of awareness would be lower. Many people who would be interested in buying a hamburger would not have heard of McDonald's. However, a certain degree of financial well-being is required for the purchase of prepared food. Extremely poor people are not likely to patronise McDonald's establishments. Of the persons who are likely to do so, at least a substantial portion must be of the category who would probably have heard of McDonald's and know its marks, or some of them. This inference is supported by the zeal shown by Joburgers to appropriate these marks for themselves.

I consider therefore that at least a substantial portion of persons who would be interested in the goods or services provided by McDonald's know its name, which is also its principal trade mark. At least this mark is in my view well-known for the purposes of sec. 35 of the new Act. Since McDonald's has not in fact carried on business in South Africa, people who know its mark will also know it as a foreign (and, more particularly, American) business. It almost goes without saying that if the McDonald's mark is used as contemplated by Joburgers in relation to the same type of fast food business as that conducted by McDonald's, it would cause deception or confusion within the meaning of sec. 35(3) of the new Act. In the result McDonald's has in my view satisfied all the requirements of this sub-section.

In the result the following order is made: In the well-known marks application (case number 11700/95): The Respondents are hereby interdicted and restrained, with costs, from imitating, reproducing or translating in the Republic of South Africa any of the Applicant's trade marks in which the word McDONALD or McDONALD'S appears.

Notes and Questions

1. What evidence did the court consider in deciding whether the McDonald's mark was famous? Do you agree with its decision?

2. What role did the treatment of famous marks in other countries play in the court's decision?

3. Is the court's decision in accordance with the requirements of Article 6bis of the Paris Convention? With Article 16 of TRIPS?

4. For a short article discussing in detail the appellate history of this case, see Chapter Fifteen.

THE RUSSIAN VODKA CONTROVERSY
SMIRNOFF AND SMIRNOV BATTLE IT OUT IN RUSSIA'S VODKA WARS

www.cnn.com. November 28, 1997 St.Petersburg, Russia.
To some, it might be a question of spelling.
To Russians, it's Smirnoff vs. Smirnov.

The U.S.-based distiller Heublein manufactures Smirnoff, and sells its vodka in 142 countries worldwide.

Smirnov, meanwhile, is made in Russia by a company called "The Trading House of the Heirs of the P.A. Smirnov."

The companies are locked in a five-year legal battle over the right to use the renowned name of the czarist-era Pyotr Smirnov in their trademarks.

Boris Smirnov, Pyotr's great-grandson, heads the modern-day Russian company. He contends the American Smirnoff is "just a bunch of letters."

> "First of all, Russia is the motherland of all vodka. Second, we use the real Smirnov recipe, which is very important, to refine vodka in the Russian way with Russian technology," he says. "And of course, you need a Russian soul to make Russian vodka."

Boris Smirnov started his company only six years ago. Last year, he moved his operation to a factory outside of Moscow.

Business, he says, is booming. A year ago, the factory produced 200,000 bottles per month. This year, production jumped to 2.5 million a month.

Heublein, meanwhile, has been producing vodka since the 1930s. The U.S. company says it bought the Smirnoff name from a businessman who obtained the rights from the founder's son. Although most of its vodka is made in Connecticut, it also uses a Russian factory in St. Petersburg.

The Russian Smirnov won the first legal skirmishes. Heublein was barred from importing and selling its vodka in Russia.

Heublein, however, appealed the decision, and it has never gone into effect. Now the Russian supreme court is considering the matter. Until it is settled, each company is trying to persuade the Russian consumer that it is the real thing.

The U.S. Smirnoff is advertising its "Russian character," while the Russian Smirnov claims that Russians can "taste" the difference.

Russians, for one, seem undecided. One consumer praises Smirnov for being "homemade," while another claims Smirnoff tastes better.

As the Russian say, "To each according to his own taste."

THE FRENCH RESTAURANT CASE
MAXIM'S LTD v. DYE

Chancery Division, 1997.
[1978] 2 All ER 55, [1977] 1 WLR 1155, [1977] CMLR 410, [1977] FSR 364.

GRAHAM, J.

These proceedings arise out of an action by the plaintiff to restrain the defendant from, *inter alia*, operating at 13/14 The Walk, Norwich, a restaurant under the name "Maxim's" and from passing off the defendant's said restaurant business in that city as that of the plaintiff's well-known restaurant business of the same name in Paris or as a business connected therewith.

The plaintiff is an English company first registered in 1907 and has since that date owned the world famous Parisian restaurant known as 'Maxim's'. The plaintiff's business enjoys an extensive fame and goodwill and the name Maxim's is taken by the public in this country as referring to the said business. The plaintiff has its registered office in this country. Its restaurant in Paris is extensively patronised by persons resident in England and on past occasions some of such persons have written direct from England to the restaurant to book a table. The goodwill is not confined to the city of Paris but extends to many countries of the world including this country. In the past the plaintiff has obtained decisions in many countries and in particular in the United States of America and Switzerland against persons trying to set up restaurants under the name Maxim's in such countries. Furthermore, in or about June 1970 a restaurant named Maxim's was opened at 13/14 The Walk, Norwich, that is the same address at which the defendant now trades, by a company named Norwich (Maxim's) Ltd. In an action in the High Court of Justice, Chancery Division, between the present plaintiff and that company, the latter undertook, *inter alia*, not to operate any restaurant under the name Maxim's after 30th December 1973 and that they would obliterate permanently the name Maxim's on the premises. On such and other undertakings the action was stayed. In or about December 1975 the defendant opened a restaurant at 13/14 The Walk, Norwich, under the name Maxim's as to which the following facts must be taken to be proved. There was a sign over the entrance bearing the word "Maxim's" and one at the entrance bearing the words "The New Maxim's". The menu cards were headed "The New Maxim's Late Night Restaurant", the premises are furnished in an Edwardian style red plush and brass rail decor with framed French cartoons by Toulouse Lautrec and like well-known left-bank artists so as to give a period French atmosphere to the establishment.

As a result of the foregoing, the defendant's business is calculated to cause loss and damage to the plaintiff and the defendant threatens and intends to persist in the conduct complained of unless restrained. The defendant has refused to desist in spite of being asked in writing to do so and on or about 4th January 1977 by telephone she claimed she was entitled to call her restaurant Maxim's because she had registered the name at the registry of business names. Notwithstanding that it was explained to her that such registration did not confer any right to use the name, the defendant had not at the date of the statement of claim changed such name. The defendant's restaurant is run to a much lower standard than the plaintiff's genuine restaurant Maxim's and the conduct of the defendant is calculated to injure the goodwill and reputation of the plaintiff.

True, the plaintiff is an English company but it is clear it has not and never has had any business in this country. Nevertheless I am bound on the statement of claim to hold that as a fact the plaintiff has a reputation in this country by virtue of its restaurant in Paris. If it is in law correct to say that a plaintiff cannot establish that he has goodwill in England which will be protected by our courts without actually showing that he has a business in England, then of course that is the end of the matter and the plaintiff cannot recover here, but in my judgment that is not the law.

The argument based on community law may be stated in the following propositions on the assumption that confusing similarity between the names of the plaintiff and defendant is proved. (1) The proprietor of a business carried on in a limited part of England, e g, the London area, is entitled to bring a passing-off action against a person carrying on a business outside the London area provided the former's reputation extends to the area of the latter. This is an accepted principle of English law based on earlier precedent. (2) It follows that the proprietor of a business carried on in France (but not in England even though its reputation extends to England) is not entitled to bring a passing-off action against a business carried on in England. (3) If proposition (2) is correct it follows that English law discriminates between businesses in different member states of the community on the basis of their location, e.g. if reputation in England is proved and the business from which it is derived is situated in England then passing-off relief will be given but if the business from which it is derived is situated in France it will not be given. Thus English law will permit damage to be done to the reputation of a business situated in France which it will forbid if the business is situated in England. If such is the effect of English law it will obstruct or make more difficult the provision in England by an existing French company or business of services similar to those it is providing in France. (4) If the above were correct, it would follow that the prohibitions of English law which make it so (a) though they may be prohibitions or restrictions relating to industrial property also "constitute a means of arbitrary discrimination or disguised restriction on trade between Member States" contrary to art 36 of the EEC Treaty, (b) tend to distort competition contrary to art 3(f) of the treaty and are incompatible with the spirit of the treaty as set forth in the preamble since they are an obstacle to ensuring fair competition, (c) constitute a restriction on the free supply of services within the community contrary to art 59 of the treaty, which reads as follows:

> Restrictions on freedom to provide services within the Community shall be progressively abolished during the transitional period in respect of nationals of Member States who are established in a State of the Community other than that of the person for whom the services are intended.

The denial of legal protection against damage to reputation and trade connection to a person purely on the ground that his business is established exclusively, for example, in France although he has a famous reputation in England is an instance of a requirement imposed on him which, making it as it does more difficult for him to conduct his business, is prohibited by art 59. There ought to be no requirement that he must trade in England in order to prevent his reputation there being tarnished or stolen. If, in fact, it is permissible for a third party to steal his reputation and start a business ahead of him under the same name in England, it may be very difficult, if not impossible, for him to start trading in England when, as he may, he later decides to do so.

I see no reason why the reality of the reputation in the United Kingdom should not be protected and I believe that our courts could properly be regarded as being out of touch with reality if they have not the power to protect such goodwill. I think that they always have had such power and, even if they did not, have it in the past they have it now by reason of community law, which since accession is part of our law.

Notes and Questions

1.   Can a mark ever become well-known if goods bearing the mark are not sold in the country in question?

2.   What factors other than use should be considered in deciding whether a mark is famous?

3.   The Paris Convention and TRIPS are not the only international documents which establish criteria for determining when a mark is well-

known or famous. Article 84 of Decision 344 of the Cartagena Agreement (Andean Pact) requires that "due account" be taken of the following criteria in deciding whether a mark is well known:

(a) the extent to which it is known to the consuming public as the distinguishing mark of the goods or services for which it was granted registration;

(b) the scale and scope of dissemination and advertising or promotion of the mark;

(c) the age of the mark and the constancy of its use;

(d) analysis of the production and marketing of the goods identified by the mark.

4. The Canadian Trade-mark Act by contrast requires use of a mark "in association with wares or services" before it is deemed to be "made known." Such marked goods or services must either be distributed in Canada or advertised in "any printed publication circulated in Canada in the ordinary course of commerce among potential dealers in or users of the wares or services" or in radio broadcasts "ordinarily received in Canada by potential dealers in or users of the wares or services. The mark must further 'become well-known' in Canada 'by reason of the distribution or advertising.'" R.S.C. 1985, Chap. T–13, § 5.

5. A variety of terms are used to refer to "well-known" marks including "notorious," "famous," "highly renowned" and "highly reputed." Among the benefits that may be extended to a well-known mark is protection even if the mark is not registered in the country of the infringement, or if the mark is registered, protection against unauthorized use on goods or services that do not compete with those contained in the registration.

6. The EC Trademark Harmonization Directive also provides that a mark that "has a reputation in the Community" may be used to invalidate the use of a mark "identical with, or similar to" it "where the mark is 'well-known' under Article 6*bis* of the Paris Convention *and* where its use 'without due cause would take unfair advantage of, or be detrimental to, the distinctive character or the repute of the earlier Community trademark.' (§ 3) Under the Directive, junior users of marks 'having a reputation' on non-competing goods or services may be prohibited."

7. *First to File.* Japan, among other countries, provides trademark rights to the first to file. In 1966, before McDonald's Corporation opened its first restaurant in Japan (but after the name McDonald's had become known in Japan as the name of an American restaurant,) KK Maru–Shin Foods obtained Japanese trademark registrations for a variety of marks, including *MacBurger* in a design that featured a yellow arch. Because of KK Marushin Food's prior registration, it took McDonald's Corporation over 10 years and millions of dollars to stop KK Marushin's use of its admittedly famous mark.

INDIA'S COURTS INCREASE PROTECTIONS
FOR FOREIGN TRADEMARKS

Dara P. Mehta & Sharad D. Abhyankar, IP Worldwide
(November 1997/December 1997).

For many years, foreign trademarks had a rough time in India.

The nadir came under the Foreign Exchange Regulation Act, 1973. This statute not only imposed stringent restrictions on the use of foreign brand names in India, it prohibited any type of payment (direct or indirect) for the use of foreign brand names in India.

Owners of foreign brand names were forced to use devious methods to circumvent the statute. One method was to use in India joint or "double-barreled" marks such as "Leher Pepsi," "Hero Honda," or "Maruti Suzuki."

Then, in July 1991, a watershed change began in India's economic policies. Under the New Industrial Policy, the government began to look favorably on foreign trade and investment. Soon—in May 1992—the government of India introduced a non-legislative policy change permitting the use of foreign brand names in India.

But there remained another difficulty for foreign trademark owners. The common law rule in India was that a trademark owner could prove his goodwill in a mark only by proving actual sales of relevant branded goods in India. Transnational reputation by itself could not protect a mark in India.

Three court decisions have recently changed this part of the common law—and owners of foreign marks should be pleased.

BITING INTO APPLE

The 1991 case of *Apple Computer Inc. vs. Apple Leasing and Industries*, Delhi offered the Delhi High Court the opportunity to review whether reputation by itself was sufficient to create protectable goodwill in India. The court indicated that—despite some earlier precedents— reputation should be entitled to protection under the Indian law of passing off.

The plaintiff in this case had been exporting and marketing its computer parts in India since 1977. It had applied for the registration of its APPLE word mark and the APPLE logo (a color drawing of an apple with a bite taken out of it). The mark and logo were extensively advertised in relation to plaintiff's services.

In 1986, plaintiff became aware that the defendant was adopting the corporate name "Apple Leasing and Computer Ltd." and was issuing advertisements regarding its proposed sale of securities. In January 1986, plaintiff sent a notice to defendant calling upon defendant to cease and desist from using "Apple" as part of its corporate name and representing that it was associated or connected with the plaintiff.

The parties met and tried to negotiate the matter, but no agreement was reached. In September, 1986, defendant changed its corporate name to "Apple Leasing and Industries Ltd."

In 1988, defendant advertised its services under the name "Apple Computer Education" and prominently used the marks APPLE COMPUTER, APPLE and the plaintiff's logo of a half-bitten apple.

Plaintiff again sent a cease and desist letter. Defendant then claimed the exclusive right to use the word "Apple" as a trademark and as part of its trading style in India.

Plaintiff filed a suit in the Delhi High Court, claiming that, *inter alia*, defendant's use of the words "Apple Computer" constituted passing off. Defendant replied that plaintiff was not entitled to injunctive relief.

Defendant also argued that a passing off action is maintainable only if the plaintiff proves it is entitled to protectable goodwill—and such goodwill can exist only if the plaintiff carries on business on in India. In this case, plaintiff itself was not carrying on business in India; its products were distributed in India through authorized third parties. Since plaintiff did not do business in India, the passing off action should be dismissed.

THE OLD RULE

The *Athlete's Foot Marketing Inc. v. Cobra Sports* [(1980) RPC 343] supported the defendant's position. In that case, the plaintiff was a U.S. retailer that was not carrying on any business in England. It had, however, licensed the mark ATHLETE'S FOOT to independent stores in England that were engaged in the business of selling athletic footwear.

The English court refused to issue the injunction requested by plaintiff, primarily because (i) plaintiff did not carry on any business in England, (ii) there had been no sales of any goods in the UK under the mark ATHLETE'S FOOT, and (iii) evidence had not been produced to prove that any sales had been made outside England to visitors from the UK of any goods bearing the mark ATHLETE'S FOOT.

Finally, there was the famous Budweiser case [*Anheuser-Busch, Inc. v. Budejovicky BudvarNP (1984) F.S.R. 413*]. In that case, a U.S. company's passing off action was dismissed by an English court, because the company had insufficient goodwill in the UK. The company sold more than five million cases of BUDWEISER beer in England, but only on U.S. military bases. Some of this beer was consumed by British subjects, but the English court ruled that the sale and consumption of this beer was insufficient to establish goodwill in England.

BYE, BYE BUDWEISER

The Delhi High Court did not approve of the principle laid down in England in the *Budweiser* case and stated that many Indian courts had deviated from the hard-line view taken in *Budweiser*.

The Delhi High Court approvingly mentioned the unreported judgment of a division bench of the Bombay High Court in *Yardley & Co. v.*

Kamal Trading Co.[Appeal No. 1116 of 1987]. In that case, Yardley & Co. was an English company which had sought to enjoin defendant, Kamal Trading Co., from manufacturing, selling, offering for sale, or otherwise dealing in toothbrushes and similar goods bearing the trade mark YARDLEY, or any other trademark deceptively similar thereto so as to pass off, or as would be likely to pass off the defendant's goods for those of the plaintiff.

The trial court had followed the principle in *Budweiser* and declined to grant this injunction because plaintiff's goods had not been available in India after 1958 because of import restrictions.

The plaintiff appealed to a Division Bench of the Bombay High Court, which had stated that, in its opinion, the view taken in *Budweiser* was not correct and that plaintiff's goodwill in India was not extinguished merely because its goods had not been available in the country for "some duration" (in this case was more than 25 years).

The Division Bench noted that the only explanation which could be given by counsel for Kamal Trading Company on why it had used the word "Yardley" was that it was a well known word and had acquired a reputation in India. The court said, "that is exactly what the plaintiffs are claiming, and that is why they complained that the defendants are passing off the goods by using the plaintiff's reputation." The Division Bench granted the injunction sought by the plaintiff.

In *Apple*, the Delhi High Court observed that the courts in New Zealand, Australia, Canada, and India had all deviated from the principle decided in *Budweiser*. The high court was therefore inclined to accept the views of those other courts as the more appropriate.

The Delhi High Court also noted the huge exchange of information which currently prevails between various countries of the world including the movement of newspapers, magazines, video, motion pictures, and people.

The court acknowledged that there is a new legal trend that upholds product reputation, per se. In addition, there is a trend to prevent public deception, whether deliberate or innocent. The court stated that India had a great need to catch up with more advanced countries in terms of legal protections, and therefore it was all the more necessary to prevent public deception whether innocent or deliberate. Such deception should be restrained by injunction, and the court therefore granted an interim injunction against the defendant.

The Supreme Court says

The rationale of *Apple* has been confirmed and expanded by the Supreme Court of India in its 1996 decision, *N.R .. Dongre vs. Whirlpool Corp* [Reported in Ahuja's Intellectual Property Cases, vol 2 p.7].

Whirlpool Corporation, U.S.A made and sold washing machines around the world. The company had registered the trademark WHIRLPOOL in more than 65 countries and had registered the mark in India between 1937 and 1977 in classes 7, 9, and 11. The Indian registration was not renewed after 1977 due to import restrictions imposed by the Indian government.

N.R. Dongre operated two companies that manufactured washing machines in India. In 1986, Dongre applied for registration of the trademark WHIRLPOOL. Whirlpool Corporation filed an opposition, but the Indian trademark registration was granted to the defendants.

Whirlpool Corporation subsequently filed a suit in the Delhi Court, alleging a passing off of its trademark WHIRLPOOL. The trial Judge of that court, recognizing the transborder reputation of the mark, granted a temporary injunction restraining Dongre from using WHIRLPOOL on its goods.

Dongre appealed. The injunction was upheld by the Division Bench of the Delhi High Court [Reported in Ahuja;s Intellectual Property Cases, vol 2 p.7].

Although Whirlpool Corporation no longer owned the Indian registration of WHIRLPOOL, the high court noted that Whirlpool Corporation continued to trade its products in India, though on a limited scale.9 More importantly, the court found that the WHIRLPOOL mark was also known to potential Indian customers by extensive advertisements in magazines circulating in India; the Whirlpool Corporation was entitled to the benefit of the mark's transborder reputation.

Dongre appealed one last time. The injunction was again upheld, this time by the Supreme Court of India.

The Supreme Court held that Dongre's adoption of the WHIRLPOOL mark was prima facie dishonest and that the non-renewal of the mark by Whirlpool Corporation did not establish its abandonment. Of particular importance, the court ruled that the WHIRLPOOL mark had a transborder reputation in India and that advertising was equivalent to use. The court stated that, "In view of the prior use of the mark by [Whirlpool Corporation] and its transborder reputation extending to India, the trade mark WHIRLPOOL gives an indication of the origin of the goods as emanating from or relating to the Whirlpool Corporation."

This ruling is binding authority in India that well-known foreign marks are entitled to protection under the law of passing off.

THE LATEST DEVELOPMENT

In August 1997, the Delhi High Court delivered a judgement reinforcing the protection of foreign brand names. The court restrained an Indian company from using the internationally renown trademarks SYNTHES and AO/ASIF.

The Swiss owner of these trademarks, Mathys Ltd. Bettlach, had registered the SYNTHES mark in India and abroad, but had registered the AO/ASIF mark only in countries other than India.

The Swiss owner had licenced the marks in India to Rob Mathys (India) Private Limited Company. After the license was ended, this

Indian company continued to use the marks without the authority or approval of the Swiss proprietor.

A trial court enjoined the Indian company from using the marks, and the Delhi High Court confirmed the injunction. The High Court observed that, "We must readily support decisions which seek to promote commercial morality and discourage unethical trade practices."

This judgment should go a long way to allay the fears of foreign trademark owners who wish to license their marks in India for a limited period of time.

Notes and Questions

1.   Compare the treatment of famous foreign marks in India with their treatment in South Africa in the *South African McDonald's* case. Are there significant differences in their treatment? Based on these cases, how do you think the Russian courts will treat the Smirnoff dispute? How would you decide the case?

THE JAPANESE CLOTHING CASE
PERSON'S CO., LTD. v. CATHERINE CHRISTMAN

United States Court of Appeals, The Federal Circuit, 1990.
900 F.2d 1565.

SMITH, SENIOR CIRCUIT JUDGE.

Person's Co., Ltd. appeals from the decision of the Patent and Trademark Office Trademark Trial and Appeal Board (Board) which granted summary judgment in favor of Larry Christman and ordered the cancellation of appellant's registration for the mark "PERSON'S" for various apparel items. Appellant Person's Co. seeks cancellation of Christman's registration for the mark "PERSON'S" for wearing apparel on the following grounds: likelihood of confusion based on its prior foreign use, abandonment, and unfair competition within the meaning of the Paris Convention. We affirm the Board's decision.

The facts pertinent to this appeal are as follows: In 1977, Takaya Iwasaki first applied a stylized logo bearing the name "PERSON'S" to clothing in his native Japan. Two years later Iwasaki formed Person's Co., Ltd., a Japanese corporation, to market and distribute the clothing items in retail stores located in Japan.

In 1981, Larry Christman, a U.S. citizen and employee of a sportswear wholesaler, visited a Person's Co. retail store while on a business trip to Japan. Christman purchased several clothing items bearing the "PERSON'S" logo and returned with them to the United States. After consulting with legal counsel and being advised that no one had yet established a claim to the logo in the United States, Christman developed designs for his own "PERSON'S" brand sportswear line based on appellant's products he had purchased in Japan. In February 1982, Christman contracted with a clothing manufacturer to produce clothing articles with the "PERSON'S" logo attached. These clothing items were sold, beginning in April 1982, to sportswear retailers in the northwestern United States. Christman formed Team Concepts, Ltd., a Washington corporation, in May 1983 to continue merchandising his sportswear line, which had expanded to include additional articles such as shoulder bags. All the sportswear marketed by Team Concepts bore either the mark "PERSON'S" or a copy of appellant's globe logo; many of the clothing styles were apparently copied directly from appellant's designs.

In April 1983, Christman filed an application for U.S. trademark registration in an effort to protect the "PERSON'S" mark. Christman believed himself to be the exclusive owner of the right to use and register the mark in the United States and apparently had no knowledge that appellant soon intended to introduce its similar sportswear line under the identical mark in the U.S. market. Christman's registration issued in September 1984 for use on wearing apparel.

In the interim between Christman's first sale and the issuance of his registration, Person's Co., Ltd. became a well known and highly respected force in the Japanese fashion industry. The company, which had previously sold garments under the "PERSON'S" mark only in Japan, began implementing its plan to sell goods under this mark in the United States. According to Mr. Iwasaki, purchases by buyers for resale in the United States occurred as early as November 1982. This was some seven months subsequent to Christman's first sales in the United States. Person's Co. filed an application for U.S. trademark registration in the following year, and, in 1985, engaged an export trading company to introduce its goods into the U.S. market. The registration for the mark "PERSON'S" issued in August 1985 for use on luggage, clothing and accessories. After recording U.S. sales near 4 million dollars in 1985, Person's Co. granted California distributor Zip Zone International a license to manufacture and sell goods under the "PERSON'S" mark in the United States.

In early 1986, appellant's advertising in the U.S. became known to Christman and both parties became aware of confusion in the marketplace. Person's Co. initiated an action to cancel Christman's registration on the following grounds: (1) likelihood of confusion; (2) abandonment; and (3) unfair competition within the meaning of the Paris Convention. Christman counterclaimed and asserted prior use and likelihood of confusion as grounds for cancellation of the Person's Co. registration.

The Board held in its opinion on reconsideration that Christman had not adopted the mark in bad faith despite his appropriation of a mark in use by appellant in a foreign country. The Board adopted the view that copying a mark in use in a foreign country is not in bad faith unless the foreign mark is famous in the United States or the copying is undertaken for the purpose of interfering with the prior user's planned expansion into the United States. Person's Co. appeals and requests that this court direct the Board to enter summary judgment in its favor.

In the present case, appellant Person's Co. relies on its use of the mark in Japan in an attempt to support its claim for priority in the

United States. Such foreign use has no effect on U.S. commerce and cannot form the basis for a holding that appellant has priority here. The concept of territoriality is basic to trademark law; trademark rights exist in each country solely according to that country's statutory scheme. Christman was the first to use the mark in United States commerce and the first to obtain a federal registration thereon. Appellant has no basis upon which to claim priority and is the junior user under these facts.

Appellant vigorously asserts that Christman's adoption and use of the mark in the United States subsequent to Person's Co.'s adoption in Japan is tainted with "bad faith" and that the priority in the United States obtained thereby is insufficient to establish rights superior to those arising from Person's Co.'s prior adoption in a foreign country.

The Person's Co. had no goodwill in the United States and the "PERSON'S" mark had no reputation here. Appellant's argument ignores the territorial nature of trademark rights.

Appellant next asserts that Christman's knowledge of its prior use of the mark in Japan should preclude his acquisition of superior trademark rights in the United States. The Board found that, at the time of registration, Christman was not aware of appellant's intention to enter the U.S. clothing and accessories market in the future. Christman obtained a trademark search on the "PERSON'S" mark and an opinion of competent counsel that the mark was "available" in the United States. Since Appellant had taken no steps to secure registration of the mark in the United States, Christman was aware of no basis for Person's Co. to assert superior rights to use and registration here. Appellant would have us infer bad faith adoption because of Christman's awareness of its use of the mark in Japan, but an inference of bad faith requires something more than mere knowledge of prior use of a similar mark in a foreign country.

As the Board noted below, Christman's prior use in U.S. commerce cannot be discounted solely because he was aware of appellant's use of the mark in Japan. While adoption of a mark with knowledge of a prior actual user in U.S. commerce may give rise to cognizable equities as between the parties, no such equities may be based upon knowledge of a similar mark's existence or on a problematical intent to use such a similar mark in the future. Knowledge of a foreign use does not preclude good faith adoption and use in the United States. While there is some case law supporting a finding of bad faith where (1) the foreign mark is famous here[23] or (2) the use is a nominal one made solely to block the prior foreign user's planned expansion into the United States,[24] as the Board correctly found, neither of these circumstances is present in this case.

---

23. *See, E.g., Vaudable v. Montmartre, Inc.,* 20 Misc. 2d 757, 193 N.Y.S. 2d 332, 123 U.S.P.Q. 357 (N.Y.Sup.Ct.1959); *Mother's Restaurants, Inc. v. Mother's Other Kitchen, Inc.,* 218 U.S.P.Q. 1046 (TTAB 198).

24. See Davidoff Extension, S.A. v. Davidoff Int'l., 221 U.S.P.Q. 465 (S.D.Fla. 1983).

We agree with the Board's conclusion that Christman's adoption and use of the mark were in good faith. Christman's adoption of the mark occurred at a time when appellant had not yet entered U.S. commerce; therefore, no prior user was in place to give Christman notice of appellant's potential U.S. rights. Christman's conduct in appropriating and using appellant's mark in a market where he believed the Japanese manufacturer did not compete can hardly be considered unscrupulous commercial conduct. Christman adopted the trademark being used by appellant in Japan, but appellant has not identified any aspect of U.S. trademark law violated by such action. Trademark rights under the Lanham Act arise solely out of use of the mark in U.S. commerce or from ownership of a foreign registration thereon; "the law pertaining to registration of trademarks does not regulate all aspects of business morality." When the law has been crafted with the clarity of crystal, it also has the qualities of a glass slipper: it cannot be shoe-horned onto facts it does not fit, no matter how appealing they might appear.

Appellant next claims that Christman's adoption and use of the "PERSON'S" mark in the United States constitutes unfair competition under Articles 6 bis and 10 bis of the Paris Convention. It is well settled that the Trademark Trial and Appeal Board cannot adjudicate unfair competition issues in a cancellation or opposition proceeding. The Board's function is to determine whether there is a right to secure or to maintain a registration.

In *United Drug Co. v. Rectanus Co.*, [248 U.S. 90 (1918)] the Supreme Court of the United States determined that "there is no such thing as property in a trademark except as a right appurtenant to an established business or trade in connection with which the mark is employed. Its function is simply to designate the goods as the product of a particular trader and to protect his goodwill against the sale of another's product as his; and it is not the subject of property except in connection with an existing business." [*Id.* at 97.] In the present case, appellant failed to secure protection for its mark through use in U.S. commerce; therefore, no established business or product line was in place from which trademark rights could arise. Christman was the first to use the mark in U.S. commerce. This first use was not tainted with bad faith by Christman's mere knowledge of appellant's prior foreign use, so the Board's conclusion on the issue of priority was correct. Accordingly, the grant of summary judgment was entirely in order, and the Board's decision is affirmed.

Notes and Questions

1. Do you agree with the court's decision that the U.S. company's adoption of the PERSON's mark was in good faith? Would you reach a different conclusion if the mark had been GIVENCHY (a French clothing designer)? Why or why not?

2. The court in the *Japanese Clothing* case refused to consider the principles established under Article 6*bis* of the Paris Convention. Based on the evidence contained in this case, would you consider PERSON'S famous

under Article 6*bis*? What additional evidence, if any, would you place into evidence to prove the Japanese mark was famous?

THE BAYER ASPIRIN CASE

STERLING DRUG, INC. v. BAYER AG, BAYER USA INC., AND MILES, INC.

United States Court of Appeals, the Second Circuit, 1994.
14 F.3d 733.

NEWMAN, CHIEF JUDGE.

This appeal primarily concerns the permissible scope of an injunction issued to protect American trademark rights against infringement by a foreign corporation. The context of the dispute is the name and mark "Bayer" in which both an American corporation, Sterling Drug Inc. ("Sterling"), and a German corporation, Bayer AG, hold rights.

At the turn of the century, the rights to the "Bayer" name and mark in the United States were owned by Bayer AG. It lost those rights during World War I when Bayer AG's United States subsidiary, The Bayer Company, Inc., was seized by the United States Alien Property Custodian. In 1918, Sterling acquired rights to the "Bayer" name and mark by purchasing The Bayer Company from the Alien Property Custodian. That acquisition precipitated decades of controversy between Sterling and Bayer AG, marked by a series of lawsuits and agreements.

Sterling is a Delaware corporation with its principal place of business in New York. Sterling manufactures and sells prescription drugs and over-the-counter ("OTC") medicines, as well as home and personal care products. Ever since purchasing The Bayer Company, Sterling (which was itself acquired by the Eastman Kodak Company in 1988 and, since this lawsuit began, has changed its name to Sterling Winthrop, Inc.) has sold aspirin and related products in the United States under the "Bayer" trademark. Sterling's total sales in 1989 were $1.6 billion, of which $125 million was attributable to aspirin and related products using the "Bayer" trademark. Over the last five years, Sterling has spent approximately $50 million a year in promoting and advertising its "Bayer" trademark and products.

Bayer AG, founded in Germany some 125 years ago by Friedrich Bayer, is a large multinational corporation headquartered in Leverkusen, Germany, with worldwide sales in 1990 of $25.7 billion. The United States is Bayer AG's largest single market. In the United States, Bayer AG owns Miles, Inc., a pharmaceutical company, and Mobay Corporation, a chemical company. Bayer AG also owns Bayer USA Inc., a Delaware corporation, which is the subject of much of the pending controversy. Since the initiation of this lawsuit, Bayer USA and Mobay have been merged into Miles, and Bayer AG no longer uses "Bayer" as part of the name of any subsidiary in the United States.

1. THE AGREEMENTS

In 1955, Bayer AG brought suit against Sterling in an ultimately unsuccessful effort to regain the right to use the "Bayer" mark in the United States. *See Farbenfabriken Bayer A.G. v. Sterling Drug, Inc.*, 307 F.2d 210 (3d Cir.1962), *cert. denied*, 372 U.S. 929, 9 L. Ed. 2d 733, 83 S. Ct. 872 (1963).

Following this decision, Sterling and Bayer AG signed a contract in 1964 governing Bayer AG's use of the Bayer mark in the United States. The 1964 Agreement prohibited Bayer AG from using the Bayer name "in connection with Aspirin or other analgesics ... [or] in the course of trade in any other goods." 1964 Agreement P 1, 2. The Agreement recognized an exception that allowed Bayer AG to use its full name (then "Farbenfabriken Bayer A.G.") in packaging inserts for consumer goods including pharmaceutical products. The Agreement also permitted Bayer AG to use its full name for nonpharmaceutical and non-consumer goods, as long as it did not advertise them on radio or television.

In 1970, Bayer AG and Sterling signed another agreement, this time dealing with the use of the "Bayer" name and mark in all countries other than the United States and Cuba. Under this agreement, in return for a payment of $2.8 million, Sterling recognized Bayer AG's exclusive rights in the "Bayer" name and mark everywhere except the United States, Canada, and some Caribbean nations. In Canada, the parties agreed to concurrent use of the "Bayer" name, while in some Caribbean countries, Sterling was granted exclusive rights to the "Bayer" name and mark.

Following execution of the 1986 Agreement, defendants began to make extensive use of the "Bayer" name and mark. Bayer AG began by obtaining federal registrations for the "Bayer" mark for industrial and agricultural chemicals and related products. It advertised these products in trade journals. In accordance with the 1986 Agreement, it renamed Rhinechem "Bayer USA Inc." During 1987 and 1988, Bayer USA conducted a corporate "image" campaign, placing a total of 67 advertisements in the Wall Street Journal, Forbes, Fortune, Business Week, and the "Business World" section of the Sunday New York Times. The advertisements introduced Bayer USA as the "highest-ranked new company on the Fortune 500," and described Bayer USA as a "group of progressive, dynamic, forward-looking companies like Miles Laboratories and Mobay Corporation." The advertisements observed that Bayer USA's "businesses range from chemical to health and life sciences to imaging and graphic information systems." Miles also distributed press releases that identified it as "the healthcare company of Bayer USA Inc." Bayer AG sponsored at least three international medical symposia held in the United States. Bayer AG used its name freely in these symposia, including it in the literature printed for the events, and sometimes even incorporating it into the name of the symposium, as, for example, in "(Bayer AG Centenary Symposium: Perspectives in Anti-infective Therapy")".

This case differs from the usual Lanham Act case, in which a senior user contends that a junior user is using the mark to sell goods based on the misperception that they originate with the senior user. Sterling's complaint is not only that consumers might believe that Bayer AG's goods actually come from Sterling, but also that defendants' use of the "Bayer" mark might confuse consumers into believing that Sterling's Bayer aspirin is actually defendants' product. Sterling also protests that Bayer AG's use of the "Bayer" mark has created confusion about the relationship between Sterling and Bayer AG.

Bayer AG contends that the District Court clearly erred in finding that Bayer AG's and Sterling's products compete. Bayer AG argues that Sterling and Bayer do not use the "Bayer" mark in labeling or advertising any competing products. While it is true that Bayer AG did not use the "Bayer" mark in labeling or advertising any competing products, it did extensively seek to associate Miles, Inc., its health care division, with "Bayer U.S.A."

Considering Sterling's survey evidence of actual confusion, the strength of its mark, the fact that Bayer AG uses a mark that is "virtually identical" to Sterling's mark, and the competition between Sterling's Bayer AG's products, we hold that Sterling has shown a likelihood of confusion arising from Bayer AG's use of the "Bayer" name and mark.

Bayer AG argues that regardless of any confusion arising from its use of the "Bayer" mark, it did not violate Sterling's trademark rights because it held rights to "concurrent use" of the mark. As part of the 1986 Agreement, Bayer AG had purchased the rights to use the mark for non-consumer, non-pharmaceutical products. Bayer AG accordingly sought and obtained registrations, two on the principal register and one on the supplemental register, from the Patent and Trademark Office ("PTO") for the "Bayer" mark for use on industrial and chemical products.

The fact that Bayer AG has obtained registration from the PTO for a trademark held by a prior user does not incontrovertibly establish its rights to the mark. If a second user's use of the mark creates a likelihood of confusion, a prior user can obtain a cancellation of the second user's registration. *See, e.g., Southern Enterprises, Inc. v. Burger King of Florida, Inc.*, 57 C.C.P.A. 826, 419 F.2d 460 (C.C.P.A. 1970) (cancelling "Whoppaburger" registration because of likelihood of confusion with Burger King's "Whopper" trademark). Even if the second user's registration has become "incontestable," 15 U.S.C. § 1065 (1988), it can still be challenged if the second user is using the mark in a manner that misrepresents the source of goods. *See* 15 U.S.C. §§ 1064(3), 1065 (1988).

When the PTO approved Bayer AG's registration applications, its findings of no likelihood of confusion were based on Bayer AG's claims regarding its intended use of the mark. The PTO accordingly granted Bayer AG registrations for certain products for "all industrial use" or for "sale to commercial users in the field of agriculture and not for sale to lawn, garden or household consumers" (registrations 1,482,868 (Apr. 5, 1988), 1,484,862 (Apr. 19, 1988), and 1,531,469 (Mar. 21 1989)). While the PTO may have been correct that confusion would not have been likely if Bayer AG had restricted its use of the mark within these bounds, that determination does not apply where Bayer AG's use of the mark has far exceeded the scope of its registrations. Bayer AG was entitled to no favorable presumption in this trademark infringement suit on the question of likelihood of confusion because it had obtained registrations in the United States for the "Bayer" mark for certain industrial uses.

Having concluded that Bayer AG did violate Sterling's contract and trademark rights, we now turn to the question of relief. The District Court broadly enjoined Bayer AG or its subsidiaries from using the "Bayer" name or mark in:

> any product, institutional or company-identifying advertisement or promotional materials published or reasonably likely to be disseminated in the United States" (para. 1(g)(i));

> any employment notice published or reasonably likely to be distributed within the United States (para. 1(g)(ii));

> any radio or television broadcast . . . or other electronic means of mass communication received through one or more stations, channels or services, or by subscribers, within the United States (para. 1(g)(iv)); or

> any news release or informational materials distributed, or reasonably likely to be distributed, within the United States, or at any press conference held, or reasonably likely to be reported on, within the United States." (para. 1(g)(vi))

The Court allowed a few narrow exceptions to these prohibitions. Under the injunction, Bayer AG may use the mark in advertisements or employment notices (1) in foreign print publications that have a U.S. circulation of 5,000 or less; and (2) in trade publications when the advertisements or employment notices refer only to non-pharmaceutical, non-consumer products or pharmaceutical intermediates or ingredients. With perhaps a nod towards corporate disclosure requirements, the District Court also allowed Bayer AG to use the mark in not more than two press releases a year exclusively concerning extraordinary events involving Bayer AG, such as changes in corporate control." The Court allowed an exception for press conferences held abroad and attended primarily by foreign journalists if (1) such press conferences were not conducted in English; (2) the subject of the conference did not include "any discovery, invention, activity, event, product or service within the United States"; or (3) the conferences related exclusively to Bayer AG's worldwide activities, without any special prominence given to either health care matters or Bayer AG's activities within the United States. The Court allowed the same three exceptions for press releases as long as the releases indicated that the information was "Not for Distribution or Release in the United States."[6] The Court also allowed Bayer AG to use the mark in press releases exclusively concerning non-pharmaceutical, non-consumer products or pharmaceutical intermediates and ingredients, as long as these releases are disseminated only to print trade publications. Notwithstanding these exceptions, Bayer AG contends that the "extraterritorial injunctive provisions impair the ability of one of Europe's largest corporations to conduct its everyday business in its home country and around the world."

It is well-established that United States courts have jurisdiction to enforce the Lanham Act extraterritorially in order to prevent harm to United States commerce. The Supreme Court divined such a Congressional intent to project the Act extraterritorially in *Steele v. Bulova Watch Co., Inc.*, 344 U.S. 280, 97 L. Ed. 319, 73 S. Ct. 252 (1952). In that leading case, the Court applied the Act to prevent a U.S. citizen from selling fake "Bulova" watches in Mexico on the ground that his use of the "Bulova" name diverted sales in Mexico and the United States from the American trademark holder. But courts have also recognized limits on the application of the Lanham Act beyond our borders. In *Vanity Fair Mills, Inc. v. T. Eaton Co.*, 234 F.2d 633 (2d Cir.), *cert. denied*, 352 U.S. 871, 1 L. Ed. 2d 76, 77 S. Ct. 96 (1956), an American clothing manufacturer that sold women's underwear in the U.S. and Canada using its "Vanity Fair" trademark sought to enjoin a Canadian retailer from selling women's undergarments using the same mark in Canada. We dismissed the claims against the defendant because it was a Canadian corporation using a mark to which it held presumably valid trademark rights in Canada.

We oblige the District Court to frame more carefully the scope of its injunction in light of the concurrent rights of the parties. "In establishing the parameters of injunctive relief in the case of lawful concurrent users, a court must take account of the realities of the marketplace." Restatement of the Law of Unfair Competition, Tentative Draft No. 335 cmt. f (1991) (approved 1993). In today's global economy, where a foreign TV advertisement might be available by satellite to U.S. households, not every activity of a foreign corporation with any tendency to create some confusion among American consumers can be prohibited by the extraterritorial reach of a District Court's injunction.

Upon remand, the District Court may grant an extraterritorial injunction carefully crafted to prohibit only those foreign uses of the mark by Bayer AG that are likely to have significant trademark-impairing effects on United States commerce. If the Court finds that Bayer AG's use of the mark abroad carries such significant effects in the United States, the District Court may require Bayer AG to take appropriate precautions against using the mark in international media in ways that might create confusion among United States consumers as to the

6. Even these narrow exceptions for press conferences are further conditioned by the requirement that Bayer AG has to instruct the attending journalists not to use the "Bayer" name in the United States in connection with the subject matter of the press conference.

source of "Bayer" pharmaceutical products in the United States. It might be appropriate, to take examples offered by appellee, to prevent Bayer AG from placing a full-page "Bayer" advertisement in the U.S. edition of a foreign magazine or newspaper, or inviting representatives of the U.S. press to an offshore briefing in which Bayer AG distributed materials describing "Bayer's" analgesics products for publication in the U.S. On the other hand, it might be inappropriate, to take examples offered by *the amicus curiae*, to leave the injunction so broad as to ban the announcement of new medical research in Lancet, or an employment notice in Handelsblatt, or a press conference in England to publicize a new over-the-counter remedy developed in the United States, or sponsorship of a German soccer team if that team might appear, wearing "Bayer" jerseys, on a television broadcast carried by an American sports cable channel.

Where, as in the instant case, both parties have legitimate interests, consideration of those interests must receive especially sensitive accommodation in the international context. While Bayer AG suggests that we must accept these conflicts as the unavoidable result of an international community of nations in which each nation exercises the power to grant trademark rights, we prefer to allow the District Court to fashion an appropriately limited injunction with only those extraterritorial provisions reasonably necessary to protect against significant trademark-impairing effects on American commerce.

Paragraph 1(e) of the injunction prohibits Bayer AG from identifying itself by using the "Bayer" mark in the United States, subject to only a few limited exceptions. Bayer AG urges us to vacate this provision as unnecessary to achieve the goals of the Lanham Act or to vindicate Sterling's contract rights. Bayer AG apprehends that this provision would proscribe a host of ordinary business activities:

Literal compliance with this remarkable provision would, for example, bar an executive of Bayer AG from identifying his business affiliation in a telephone call to a Miles employee, to a government official or to another company's executive during a business trip. Defendants could not register securities or make acquisitions in the U.S., since doing so would require identifying Bayer AG as the ultimate parent of the U.S. subsidiaries in a variety of legally required communications, including disclosures under U.S. securities laws. Defendants could not deal with U.S. banks, investment advisors or insurers, or access the U.S. capital markets—all of which require complete information about the corporate structure and finances of a customer's or borrower's affiliates. Indeed, if enforced to its absurd literal limits, paragraph 1(e) would make the filing of this brief—and the retention of U.S. counsel and their work on Bayer's behalf—punishable as a contempt of court.

The Lanham Act does not require a total ban on the use of a mark by an infringing junior user. To the contrary, the Lanham Act demands that injunctive relief be " 'no broader than necessary to cure the effects of the harm caused.' " A near total ban on Bayer AG's use of the mark is not necessary to protect Sterling's trademark. Nor do we find any provision in the parties' agreements that requires Bayer AG to refrain from using the mark in communicating with investors or subsidiaries. The District Court should redraw this provision of the injunction to accommodate Bayer AG's global business interest in raising capital and communicating with its subsidiaries.

We vacate the remedial injunction and remand for entry of a modified injunction.

THE ORKIN BUG CASE

ORKIN EXTERMINATING CO. v. PESTCO CO. OF CANADA LTD.

Ontario Court of Appeal, 1995.
5 C.P.R. 3d 433

MORDEN, J.A.

This is a passing-off action in which Orkin Exterminating Company, Inc., an American company which does not carry on business in Canada, was granted an injunction against the defendants restraining them from using in Canada its trade name Orkin Exterminating Company and the trade marks ORKIN and ORKIN in a logo (called ORKIN & Design) and, also, judgment for nominal damages of $1,000. The defendant, the Pestco Company of Canada Limited, which carries on business in the Metropolitan Toronto area, and its president and manager, the defendant Emanuel Valder, appeal from this judgment.

It can be said at the outset that Orkin and Pestco are in the same business, that of providing pest control and exterminating services to residential and commercial customers. Orkin, and its predecessors, have been carrying on business in the United States since 1901, and the name Orkin has been associated with the business since that time. The founder of the business was Otto Orkin. The name Orkin Exterminating Company, Inc., as already indicated, is the company's corporate name and trading style and has been used by it and its predecessor since the 1920s. The Orkin logo, which is a red diamond with "Orkin" in capital letters inside it, has been used in connection with the company's business as the primary trade mark and logo of the business since the 1930s.

Orkin is now, and at all times material to this proceeding has been, one of the largest pest control companies in the world. It is highly regarded by its customers, which include Canadian customers, for the "excellent" and dependable service which it provides.

Orkin spent substantial sums of money advertising its name, logo and business in the United States through radio, television, newspapers and billboards.

As far as Orkin's reputation in Canada is concerned the following matters may be noted. Canadians travelling in the United States are exposed to Orkin's extensive advertising and use of its trade marks in that country. There was evidence adduced that millions of Canadians travel in the United States every year, particularly in the southern vacation states, where Orkin's operations are extensive. Canadians in Canada are exposed to Orkin's advertising and articles appearing in American publications which circulate here. Examples of publications in which such articles and advertisements have appeared are: Fortune, 1952; Newsweek, 1964; Business Week, 1964; Time, 1964; United States News and World Report, 1964; Supermarket News, 1975, 1977 and 1978; and National Geographic, 1977.

Mr. Geiger estimated that over the past three or five years, thousands of Canadians have used Orkin services on a regular basis in connection with property owned or rented by them in the United States. Some of these received the bills for the service at their homes in Canada. Advertising material accompanied the bills.

Orkin provides services to companies which have operations in Canada including Burger King, McDonald's, Coca–Cola, Howard Johnson, Ponderosa, Sheraton Hotels and Hilton Hotels as well as carriers such as Delta, Eastern and United Airlines and Amtrak.

Orkin's international reputation in the pest control field resulted in the Canadian government seeking its advice as a consultant respecting the control of pests for the Exposition in Montreal in the mid–1970s.

Orkin advertises extensively in the United States by signs on its trucks and logos on the uniforms of its servicemen, in magazines and on billboards, by radio and television. Canadians travelling in the United States see its trucks, servicemen and billboards. At home they read American magazines and see and hear Orkin advertising on radio and television, which is broadcast from American stations but received in Canada. The only advertising Orkin has had done in Canada is some radio advertising in Windsor, but that was admittedly for the Detroit market.

I have already mentioned Orkin's Canadian customers. Eight of them from the Toronto area gave evidence with respect to their familiarity with Orkin, its business and the Orkin name and trade marks. They all said that if they were to see the Orkin name or logo in use in Canada they would assume that they represented the Orkin company with which they were familiar or some business that was affiliated with it.

In 1976 Pestco filed an application in Canada under the Trade Marks Act, R.S.C. 1970, c. T–10, indicating that it proposed to use the identical logo that Orkin had used since the 1930s. Mr. Valder admitted that he took the design from one of Orkin's brochures. Also in 1976 Pestco began using the Orkin logo on invoices which it sent to customers after performing services for them under the Pestco name. Orkin and Pestco became involved in opposition proceedings in the Canadian Trade Marks Office. It was during these proceedings, which are still pending, that Orkin was informed for the first time that Pestco had been using the Orkin name since 1967. In 1978 Pestco applied under the Trade

Marks Act to register the name, Orkin, alone. Shortly after it found out about Pestco's use of its name, Orkin commenced this action.

Apart from the use of "Orkin Exterminating Company" in the telephone directories, Pestco made no public use of the name. Specifically, the name was never used on Pestco's brochures, business cards, contracts, invoices, letter-head, signs, uniforms or trucks. In fact, Pestco has conducted all of its business under the trade name "Pestco" and its own name "The Pestco Company of Canada Limited". All of its contracts, letterhead, business cards, brochures, uniforms, and signs on its trucks prominently display the name "Pestco". It also uses a logo in connection with all of its business. It is a horizontal oval with "Pestco" in capital letters inside it. It appears on all of Pestco's brochures, business cards, contracts, letter-head, uniforms and trucks.

Pestco has never actually carried on business under the name "Orkin Exterminating Company". This "company" has no assets, no employees, and no bank account. It has never entered into any contracts, nor has it ever had any income. "Orkin Exterminating Company" is listed by the appellants in the telephone book as nothing more than a name. In fact, Mr. Valder admitted in evidence that it was just a name in the telephone directory used to attract the attention of potential customers.

In 1976, as indicated earlier in these reasons, Pestco began to place the Orkin logo, the red diamond with "Orkin" in it, on its invoices along with "The Pestco Company of Canada Limited" and the Pestco logo. Mr. Valder knew that it was the logo that had been used by Orkin in the United States. It was taken from an Orkin brochure. Also, as I have said, in 1976, Pestco filed a trade mark application in Canada indicating that it proposed to use this logo. The Pestco invoices carrying the logo are seen by customers after services have been performed under the Pestco name.

A plaintiff does not have to be in direct competition with the defendant to suffer injury from the use of its trade name by the defendant. If the plaintiff's trade name has a reputation in the defendant's jurisdiction, such that the public associates it with services provided by the plaintiff, then the defendant's use of it means that the plaintiff has lost control over the impact of its trade name in the defendant's jurisdiction. The practical consequence of this is that the plaintiff is then vulnerable to losing the Ontario customers it now has as well as prospective Ontario customers, with respect to services provided in the United States. Also, it can result in Orkin being prevented from using its trade name in Ontario when it expands its business into Ontario.

I need not, and do not, say that the defendant's bad faith alone will confer a cause of action on a foreign plaintiff but it surely must be a relevant factor to take into account in adjusting competing interests. The significance of a defendant's state of mind has for some time been an important factor with respect to several different torts: see Ames, "How

Far an Act May be a Tort because of the Wrongful Motive of the Actor", 18 Harv. L. Rev. 411 (1905).

I should say a word about the term "goodwill". Pestco strongly argued, as I have indicated, that a plaintiff's goodwill cannot exist outside the area where it carries on business. That this reflects the "meaning" of goodwill has been affirmed in several cases, the most recent of which is *Anheuser-Busch Inc. v. Budejovicky Budvar N.P.* (trading as Budweiser Budvar Brewery) et al., [1984] F.S.R. 413 (Eng. C.A.).

Generally, the facts which must be proven are that the trademark owner has an established reputation in the subject country, the local infringer has usurped the trademark in bad faith, and deception of the public is likely to occur. The theories for recognizing such protection vary slightly from country to country although common threads run throughout the decisions. (Hoffman and Brownstone, *"Protection of Trademark Rights Acquired by International Reputation without use or Registration"*, 71 The Trademark Reporter 1 at pp. 1–2 and 4 (1981).)

In each case the issue is whether, in the territory in which the actor's designation is used, there are or are likely to be a considerable number of prospective purchasers of the goods or services in connection with which the trademark and the designation are used, who are likely to be confused or misled by the actor's designation. (American Law Institute, RESTATEMENT OF THE LAW, TORTS, Tentative Draft No. 8 (1963), at p. 113).

Orkin concedes that the competing rights of the parties have to be determined as of 1967, when Pestco started using the Orkin name in Ontario, In 1967 Orkin's reputation in Ontario, based on its customers in Ontario and advertising of various kinds was, in the circumstances, of sufficient strength to make Orkin's rights superior to those of Pestco. Its reputation has grown steadily since 1967.

What are the circumstances? A very cogent circumstance is Pestco's decision in 1967 to use the Orkin name in Ontario. This is evidence from which it may be inferred that the name Orkin had commercial value at that time in Ontario.

A further circumstance which I think is important is the way in which Pestco used Orkin's name. Not only was it dishonest because it was intended to deceive customers into thinking that there was some connection with Orkin, it was also not a bona fide use in that no real steps were taken to create in the public mind any association between "Orkin" and Pestco. The only public use of "Orkin" to attract business was that in the telephone directories and even this use was not one which connected the name with Pestco but rather merely served as a trap for the unwary customer who, after being initially attracted by the name Orkin Exterminating Company in the directory, was thereafter served by Pestco. The evidence given by Mr. Valder on cross-examination made Pestco's position clear in this regard:

Q. The name Pestco is both part of your corporate name and the trademark of your company?

A. Yes.

Q. You have a registered trademark for the name Pestco in a design?

A. Yes.

Q. This is the name and the trademark which appears on all of your literature and brochures and business cards?

A. Yes.

Q. This is also the name that you want your customers to see as being your name and as identifying your business?

A. Yes.

Q. Orkin is just a name you use to get people's attention in the telephone directory; is that correct?

A. Yes.

Q. You don't advertise the name. You don't have business cards or uniforms or trucks with the name Orkin on them?

A. No. I said earlier I think we did advertise the name in a small home directory, but I couldn't swear to that. I couldn't recall.

The trial judge was right in finding that Pestco: "During the time it used the name 'Orkin Exterminating Company', the defendant Pestco did not create any significant amount of goodwill for that name or for the diamond logo." This, in fact, is an understatement. For all practical purposes Pestco has always carried on its business under the Pestco name and logo. In short, from the very beginning of Pestco's use of Orkin in Ontario it could not be said that Orkin meant one thing in the United States market and an entirely different thing in Ontario.

In the light of all these considerations, I am satisfied that from the beginning of its "use" of Orkin in 1967 Pestco acquired no rights against Orkin and that in 1967 Orkin, if it had known of the misappropriation, could have obtained an injunction against Pestco to protect its rights in Ontario. Orkin's rights, because of its steadily increasing reputation in Ontario, were even more solidly based in 1976 when Pestco began to use the Orkin logo.

Notes and Questions

1. Your client has operated a fast food franchise in Paraguay under the mark *McDonald's*. The mark has never been used in the country or registered there by the U.S. owner of the MCDONALD'S® mark. The user admits that he was aware of the MCDONALD'S mark. Under the rationale applied by the U.S. Court in the *Japanese Clothing* case, would McDonald's be able to stop such use?

2. Compare your answer above with the court's decision in Paraguay where the lower court's decision to cancel the registrations was upheld. The court inferred bad faith from the worldwide use and reputation of the

plaintiff's marks. *See* Hugo Berkemeyer, TRADEMARK WORLD 10–11 (Feb. 1993).

3.   What role did international uses of BAYER have upon the court's decision in *Sterling Drugs*? Did the court's resolution of the issue appropriately reflect the realities of the global marketplace? What changes, if any, would you make in the court's injunction? What about potential confusion in Germany? Does the court's order consider the potential confusion that might arise in Germany from the American company's use of BAYER? Should it?

4.   Another "famous" mark connected with the Bayer companies is "ASPIRIN." This mark has been registered in various countries, including Spain and Canada. It has been denied registration as a generic mark in the United States. Can a famous mark be denied protection without violating the principles of Article 6*bis*?

5.   Compare the development of competing marks in the *Japanese Clothing* and *Bayer Aspirin* cases. These represent two common methods by which conflicting "famous" marks may develop. The *Budvar* case represents another common fact pattern. What steps should multinational corporations take when selling their rights in the same mark to different companies in different countries in order to avoid the problems in the *Bayer Aspirin* case? For a similar problem of marks initially owned by the same company, see the Russian Vodka controversy, above.

6.   *Bad Faith*. Under Article 6bis there is no time limit for canceling a mark registered in bad faith. G.H.C. Bodehausen in his GUIDE TO THE APPLICATION OF THE PARIS CONVENTION FOR THE PROTECTION OF INDUSTRIAL PROPERTY (1967) stated: "Bad faith will normally exist when the person who registers or uses the conflicting mark knew of the well-known mark and presumably intended to profit from the possible confusion between that mark and the one he has registered or used." But is knowledge of the prior mark alone sufficient, or must predatory intent be proven? Do the Paris Convention or TRIPS establish a standard for answering this question?

7.   What test did the court in the *Bug* case apply to decide the issue of bad faith adoption? Was bad faith alone sufficient?

8.   Bad faith is also considered a significant factor in countries such as Benelux, Brazil, France, Germany, India, Israel, Peru, Singapore, the United Kingdom, and Venezuela. *See generally* Frederick W. Mostert, FAMOUS AND WELL KNOWN MARKS (Butterworth's 1997).

9.   *Trade names*. Under Article 12(1) of the Paris Convention, "trade names" are specifically recognized as a form of "industrial property." Article 8 requires member countries to protect trade names "without the obligation of filing or registration, whether or not it forms part of a trademark." *See also* The Cartagena Agreement at Article 128; the Pan American Convention at Article 14. *But see* Central American Convention, Article 50 (requires registration for trade names to be protected). Consequently, most nations require proof that the trade name is well-known if it is *not* registered. The owner of a well-known trade name may wish to register his trade name to gain the benefit of protection without proof of registration be extended under most domestic laws. Some countries, however, may require that a company do business or be domiciled there for its trade name to be registrable. In those countries, it may be preferable to register the trade name as a trademark or service mark where possible.

Chapter Twenty-Eight

ENFORCEMENT

A. HOW BROAD IS THE SCOPE OF PROTECTION AFFORDED A FAMOUS MARK?

THE NIKE COSMETICS CASE

NIKE (IRELAND) LTD v. NETWORK MANAGEMENT LTD

Chancery Division, 1994.

JACOB, J.

To my mind this is a very plain case. The plaintiffs are two companies within the Nike Group of companies, the parent company of both plaintiffs being an American company. Nike is, amongst the young and those interested in sports and sports wear, a household name. The sales in the United Kingdom alone in 1994 of Nike goods amounted to 116 million. Sales commenced in the early 1980s. By 1983 they were 6.6 million and have grown at a remarkable rate since.

The goods of the plaintiffs are sports clothes, sports shoes, bags and leisure wear. As is now commonly the practice, the owner of a goodwill, particularly in things like sports clothes, is likely to try and branch out into other fields. Other well-known sportswear brands have expanded into the field of cosmetics, particularly Slazenger, Puma and Adidas.

The plaintiffs say they have a large and substantial goodwill for their sports shoes, bags and leisure wear. They say that if the word "Nike" appears on perfumes, aftershave and so on, particularly products aimed at the young and sporty, the consumers will assume that the goods are connected with the plaintiffs. I think the plaintiffs are very likely to establish that at trial—so likely that there is no arguable defence to that. It may be that if there was qualification of the word "Nike" in some way, it would be possible to avoid deception of the public, but it would have to be a very effective qualification indeed.

The first defendants are a company called Network Management Ltd, a UK distributor of perfumes, after-shave and the like, products sometimes called "toiletries". The second and third defendants are Spanish concerns who have inherited the trademark "Nike" in Spain for cosmetics. They have registrations in Spain and in other countries in class 3 of the international classification system, the class covering toiletries. They also have a registration in this country for toiletries. Not surprisingly, it is under attack by Nike of America. The actual company holding the trademarks is the first plaintiff Nike (Ireland) Ltd.

Recently, the first defendants began the distribution of the Spanish company's goods in this country. They are marked simply "Nike". At an earlier stage there was a plan to mark them "Nike Sport"; the third defendant, now called "Nike Cosmetics", was originally called "Nike Sport Cosmetics".

It is submitted in the first place on behalf of the defendants that there is no passing off. What is said is that it is not accepted that the plaintiffs' reputation extends to cosmetics and fragrances. That, to my mind, misses the point. The plaintiffs' reputation is generated by their sales of sports wear and is the first element of a passing off action.

The next element of the passing off action is deception. The plaintiffs say that the defendants use of "Nike" will deceive the public. I think that is very likely. This is not a case where I think there might be some members of the public who would not be deceived. In my judgment most members of the public would be deceived.

The third element of passing off is damage to goodwill or to the plaintiffs' business. It is true that the plaintiffs will not actually lose sales of toiletries because they do not make any, but there is a real and very substantial risk or danger, in my judgment, of damage to their goodwill. If most of the sales of these defendants' Nike products are assumed or taken by the public to be the products of or connected with the plaintiffs, then plainly the plaintiffs' reputation and goodwill is moved into the hands of the defendants.

Mr. Morcom says that there would be an arbitrary discrimination and a disguised restriction on trade between Member States if the defendants are stopped here. He says that the plaintiffs have entered the Spanish market with their goods and the plaintiffs have consented to co-existence with the defendants in Spain; and that therefore somehow or other it is arbitrary not to have co-existence in this country. But that point falls down at the place where Mr. Morcom's proposition of fact is stated. The plaintiffs have not consented to co-existence in Spain. They may have to put up with it, but there is no question of an agreement of any kind. It may well be under National law that in some parts of the Community two trademarks may run side by side. We have a doctrine in this country of honest concurrent use which may allow some marks to be used side by side. But it by no means follows that they can be used side by side throughout the Community. All would depend on special local circumstances. I do not think there is anything in this point.

I therefore have come to the conclusion that there is in fact no triable defence. I have done so without making any finding of fraud. No allegation of fraud is made in the pleadings and it would not be proper for me to do so. I cannot help but observe, however, that the defendants' sales strategy uses such phrases as "Nike will help to grow the market on its name alone", "the Nike name is perceived as volume prestige"; "the Nike perceived position is premium but accessible"; and, in an advertisement to the trade, "an instantly recognisable and successful name".

In the result, the plaintiffs' application succeeds. Whether the form of order they seek is right, or whether they should have a form of injunction which permits the defendants to distinguish (if they can), is a matter upon which I will hear counsel.

DISPOSITION:

Judgment accordingly.

THE McSLEEP CASE
QUALITY INNS INTERNATIONAL, INC.
v. McDONALD'S CORPORATION

United States District Court, District of Maryland, 1988.
695 F.Supp. 198.

NIEMEYER, UNITED STATES DISTRICT JUDGE

On September 21, 1987, Quality Inns International, Inc. announced a new chain of economy hotels to be marketed under the name "McSleep Inn." The response of McDonald's Corporation was immediate. It demanded by letter sent three days later that Quality International not use the name "McSleep" because it infringed on McDonald's family of marks that are characterized by the use of the prefix "Mc" combined with a generic word. Five days later, on September 29, 1987, Quality International filed this action seeking a declaratory judgment that the mark "McSleep Inn" (1) does not infringe McDonald's federally registered trademarks in violation of 15 U.S.C. § 1114; (2) does not constitute a false designation of origin or a false description or representation of services as being associated with or originating with McDonald's in violation of 15 U.S.C. § 1125(a); and (3) does not infringe or violate any common law rights that McDonald's may have to its marks.

Quality International is a Delaware corporation with its principal offices in Silver Spring, Maryland. It is engaged in the lodging business, particularly in inns, hotels, suites, and resorts. Since 1981 it has been the fastest growing hotel franchise chain in the United States and is now the third largest franchiser of hotels both in terms of hotels and rooms available. Its sales for 1987 were over $56 million.

Having no product to compete in the economy segment, Quality International designed a concept for a hotel with a smaller basic room which would rent for between $20 and $29 per night. Each room would have a queen size bed, plush carpeting, color TV, and a contiguous bathroom. There would be no conference rooms, food or other amenities on the premises, except a swimming pool in certain geographical areas. These economy hotels would all be of new construction and a consistent architecture. The name selected by Mr. Hazard for this product was "McSleep Inn." The first McSleep Inn is scheduled to open in December, 1988.

McDonald's Corporation is a Delaware corporation with its principal offices in Oak Brook, Illinois. Founded by Ray A. Kroc, it opened its first restaurant in April, 1955, in Des Plaines, Illinois. It is now the largest fast food business in the world, with over 10,000 restaurants in 45 countries and over $14 billion in sales annually.

McDonald's has achieved an extremely high awareness in the minds of the American public. It claims that when asked to name a fast food restaurant, 90 percent of the public will name McDonald's. The recognition of Ronald McDonald by children between the ages of two and eight is 100 percent, a figure matched only by Santa Claus.

In 1977, McDonald's began advertising a fanciful language called "McLanguage" that featured the formulation of words by combining the "Mc" prefix with a variety of nouns and adjectives. In television advertising viewed by the Court, Ronald McDonald is shown teaching children how to formulate "Mc" words, and he used words such as McService, McPrice, McFries and McBest.

In a consistent vein McDonald's has coined "Mc" words for many of its products and services. McChicken, Chicken McNuggets, Egg McMuffin or Sausage McMuffin, McD.L.T., McHappy Day, McFortune Cookie, McFeast, McCola, McPizza, McSnack are but some of the many. It has obtained trademark registrations for all of these.

McDonald's marks are not limited to the fast food area, and it has obtained registrations for the use of marks in other areas as well. In the areas of children's clothing, it owns McKids; in interstate travel plazas, McStop; in job programs, McJobs; in computer software, McClass; in ground shuttle transportation, McShuttle. It calls its own hotel at its home offices in Oak Brook, Illinois, McLodge.

McSleep is aimed at the entire travel market. Like McDonald's, it is acceptable for the upscale traveler who wants only a good night's sleep and for the economy traveler who wants to save money.

The owner of a mark who has developed a reputation and identity with a mark through his products, service, marketing, and presence in the market, has an interest in protecting the business and reputation for which the mark stands, not only at the present time in the current markets in which he does business, but for future times and in related markets that the development of his business might naturally take him. *Yale Electric Corp. v. Robertson*, 26 F.2d 972 (2d Cir.1928); *McDonald's Corp. v. McBagel's, Inc.*, 649 F. Supp. 1268 (S.D.N.Y.1986). The extent to which he may protect this interest relates directly to the strength of his mark. While one mark may not enjoy the strength of identity to preclude use of a junior mark in a related field or neighboring market, another may enjoy such recognition that confusion might result outside his own field or beyond the markets in which he does business. *See, e.g. Maier Brewing Co. v. Fleischmann Distilling Corp.*, 390 F.2d 117 (9th Cir.), *cert. denied*, 391 U.S. 966, 20 L. Ed. 2d 879, 88 S. Ct. 2037, 157 U.S.P.Q. 720 (1968) (beer vs. scotch); *Cook Chemical Co. v. Cook Paint & Varnish Co.*, 185 F.2d 365 (8th Cir.1950) (paint vs. insecticide*); Carling Brewing Co., Inc. v. Philip Morris, Inc.*, 277 F. Supp. 326 (N.D.Ga.1967) (beer vs. tobacco); *Esquire, Inc. v. Maira*, 101 F. Supp. 398 (M.D.Pa.1951) (magazine vs. clothing store). The measurement of this strength is revealed by evidence demonstrating a likelihood of confusion. The relationship of these two factors, strength and confusion, operates such that evidence of strength of a mark is perhaps the most significant factor in predicting the likelihood of confusion. On the other hand, evidence of the likelihood of confusion in a related field or neighboring market, or even in a competitive market, defines the scope of a mark's enforcement and therefore is the measurement of its strength. Variations on the weight of evidence on these two aspects, i.e., the strength of the mark and the likelihood of confusion, will determine whether one mark will preclude the use of a later adopted and used mark.

Accordingly, a mark may enjoy such strength that it may be enforced in related fields or neighboring markets, whether they are product markets or territorial markets. Or, stated obversely, the likelihood of confusion in related fields or neighboring markets will demonstrate the strength of the mark. Thus, a mark is not to be confined formulistically to a classification established by the Patent and Trademark Office or by lines of market competition. A mark is the identity of a corporation, a product or a service, and to the extent goodwill attaches, it knows no boundaries. Its reach is its strength. Where the public is confused and attributes a source, product, or service incorrectly, the owner of the mark, even though not a competitor, may experience damage to his reputation and goodwill. Both of these may have more meaning to the owner than immediate profits in the marketplace because they represent the potential for long range future profits.

On the other hand, two marks that serve to identify products in two unrelated markets may very well coexist without confusion in the public's eye. Thus Notre Dame brand imported french cheese has been permitted to coexist with Notre Dame University; Bulova watches with Bulova shoes; Alligator raincoats with Alligator cigarettes; "This Bud's for you" in beer commercials with the same phrase used by a florist; White House tea and coffee with White House milk; Blue Shield medical care plan with Blue Shield mattresses; Family Circle magazine with Family Circle department store; Ole' cigars with Ole' tequila; and Sunkist fruits with Sunkist bakery products. The list continues.

It cannot be overlooked, however, that a close affinity of markets for two different products or services can create in the public perception a belief or expectation that one would be expected to go into the other. This belief or expectation becomes a factor in explaining confusion that may be shown between two products that do not compete with each other. Thus, the relatedness of markets in which the competing marks are used is relevant to the likelihood-of-confusion issue.

McDonald's golden arches and the McDonald's logo rank among the strongest marks, enjoying instant recognition among virtually all members of our society. McDonald's spends almost a billion dollars each year on marketing and advertising, a sum which increases steadily with its sales, which are at $14 billion. While the fact that McDonald's is the largest single brand advertiser in the United States could alone lead to the conclusion of the strong public awareness of its marks, the evidence showed affirmatively that awareness was virtually universal, to the point where a journalist could allude to McDonald's, without using its name, by coining words as "McLaw," "McPaper," and "McFashion."

In recent years, McDonald's began to focus on a long distance travel market, defined by customers traveling on the road who are more than 30 miles from home when they use the service. Pursuing this market, McDonald's took over numerous tollway restaurants and converted them to McDonald's restaurants. After the first year of conversion, the increased sales at all of the restaurants that were converted averaged over three times the previous year's sales, and indeed the sale of gas at the neighboring gas station increased significantly, although not as much. McDonald's attributes these successes to its recognition.

The evidence established that there are many third-party uses. McHappy and McDonuts are used for baked goods and doughnuts in Ohio and the midwest area. McMaid is used for maid service franchising in various midwestern states. McDivots is used for golf accessories in the Colorado area. McFranchise is used for management consulting in the northeast. McMoose is used in Heritage Park on the east coast. McWest is used for contracting. McSports is used for a sports store in a strip shopping center. McPrint is used for franchised printing in the New York area. McQuick is used for quick change lubrications in the midwest area, mostly Indiana. McBud is a florist in the midwest.

Prior to 1984, McCrory's used McBurger, McCheddar, and McCheese for various hamburger sandwiches. These uses were phased out pursuant to an agreement with McDonald's, and McCrory's retained only Captain Mac's restaurant. Likewise, McAuto is used for computer data by McDonnell Douglas, but it, too, is being phased out. McJeans has been used to label wholesale jeans, but not at retail. McDuck is used in connection with greeting cards in a small business which has $3,000 in advertising per year. McTavern is used to name a lounge and deli in Indiana. There were other uses, but most of them are not significant in terms of market, product, advertising, or public awareness. Still other names use the prefix "Mac," instead of "Mc." While McDonald's has the well-known marks "Big Mac" and "Mac Attack," no formulated mark using a prefix "Mac" plus a generic word was brought to the Court's attention.

There are four of these third-party uses which the Court considers significant: McQuick for franchised oil change operations in the midwest,

McPrint for franchised printing shops in the New York area, McHappy for baked goods in the midwest, and McMaid for the franchising of maid service in the Chicago area. In these instances, the uses were franchised for use at multiple locations, and they must be considered when examining the strength and enforceability of McDonald's marks in this case.

The Court can point to no evidence that public awareness of McDonald's family of marks and their attribution of source to McDonald's has been lessened by the third-party uses. The more important question, and probably the only relevant one, is whether third-party uses are so prevalent that the public would not likely confuse McSleep Inn with McDonald's. The Court found no evidence to suggest impact by third-party uses on this question of confusion. The central question for resolution in this litigation is whether the use of McSleep Inn is likely to cause confusion so that an appreciable number of the public attribute the product and services of McSleep Inn to McDonald's.

With the announcement of McSleep Inn, the questions from the press and the industry as to whether Quality International would be infringing on the marks of McDonald's were instantaneous. The message directed to Quality International by reporters and potential customers was "what will McDonald's think?" The association was immediate and unambiguous.

It is true that mere association may not amount to confusion. It is one thing to say that a use brings McDonald's to mind, but without confusion that McDonald's is behind the product or service, and quite another to conclude that an appreciable number of typical consumers are likely to become actually confused. In the former case, there will be no trademark violation since trademark law does not protect words alone. Unlike a copyright, mere reproduction of a trademark is not an infringement. Thus, a non-confusing parody of a famous mark ("Jordache" vs. "Lardashe") would not be trademark infringement because the owner of the mark "does not own in gross the penumbral customer awareness of its name, nor the fallout from its advertising." *Jordache Enterprises, Inc. v. Hogg Wyld, Ltd.*, 625 F. Supp. 48, 56 (D.N.M.1985), aff'd, 828 F.2d 1482 (10th Cir.1987). As Justice Holmes said:

What new rights does the trademark confer? It does not confer a right to prohibit the use of the word or words. It is not a copyright. A trademark only gives the right to prohibit the use of it so far as to protect the owner's goodwill against the sale of another's product as his. When the mark is used in a way that does not deceive the public we see no such sanctity in the word as to prevent its being used to tell the truth. It is not taboo. *Prestonettes, Inc. v. Coty*, 264 U.S. 359, 360, 68 L. Ed. 731, 44 S. Ct. 350 (1924) (citations omitted).

It can be argued persuasively, however, that in this case the level of association reaches a level so great that confusion is likely to result. The question could well be asked: "With so much suggestion of or association with McDonald's, could it be true that perhaps McDonald's is a sponsor of McSleep Inns?"

The confusion caused by the name is not mitigated to an acceptable level by the distinctive uses of the logo, facilities and advertising. Even use of the clarifying language "by Quality International" and the substantial use of its corporate signature does not avoid the likelihood of confusion in this case. Quality International's own survey evidence shows that even with all the mitigating factors, which were clearly depicted (more clearly than would be the case in real life) in a rendering of a McSleep Inn, still 16% to 20% of the public would continue to believe that it was sponsored by McDonald's. Projected across the 144 million people who are considered to be the potential audience for McSleep Inn, well over 20 million would be likely to be confused. This is not an insubstantial number.

The Court concludes that the name McSleep is so similar to the McDonald's family of marks that in whatever clothing it is dressed, the public will persist in perceiving some connection with McDonald's. The marketing hook, as Mr. Hazard observed, is the name McSleep, which would be "instantly recognized." So long as the word McSleep is used, the infringement occurs. This holding, however, would not preclude a name such as "Sleep–Inn," for it is not the logo or the word "sleep" that causes the problem; it is the use of the fancifully coined word, McSleep.

The intent to trade on the goodwill or reputation of another projects as does a missile to its target. In the absence of evidence of actual confusion, a Court may conclude, therefore, that the intended infringement would hit its target; certainly the infringer should not be the one to complain that it did not.

The Court finds that Mr. Hazard hoped that Quality International would become the "McDonald's of lodging." He believed, though mistakenly, that because he was in the lodging business and McDonald's was in the fast food business, he was free to borrow, and expected that the confusion that would result would benefit his product. He wanted instant recognition, an image of consistency, quality, and value, all at the courtesy of McDonald's.

There is a universe of names to select from and he combined "Mc" plus the generic word "sleep," a combination that he knew McDonald's invented and which had no meaning except to associate a product or service with McDonald's. Despite his protestations, which the Court concludes were too vigorous, the Court finds that Mr. Hazard had McDonald's in mind in the selection of the name and planned to use the name as the marketing hook—a reputation instantly understood by the public and a prophesy which Quality International intended to fulfill.

Perhaps he had a good faith belief he could use the name legally and truly intended, after adopting it, to try to distinguish it from McDonald's. But its use was not available.

For the reasons given the Court finds and concludes that (1) McDonald's is entitled to enforce its family of marks that are characterized by the combination of the prefix "Mc" with a generic word; (2) the name McSleep Inn is likely to cause an appreciable number of the public to be confused by believing that McSleep Inn is sponsored, associated, affiliated, connected, or endorsed by McDonald's; and (3) the adoption and use by Quality International of the name McSleep Inn was a deliberate attempt to benefit by the good will and reputation of McDonald's. Therefore, the Court will find trademark infringement, unfair competition, and dilution under the Illinois statute (Ill. Rev. Stat. Ch. 140, § 22).

THE WEDGWOOD RESTAURANT CASE
WEDGWOOD PLC v. THERA HOLDINGS LTD.

Trade Marks Opposition Board, 1987.
18 C.P.R. 3D 201

Martin, J.

On March 26, 1984, the applicant, Thera Holdings Ltd., filed an application to register the trade mark WEDGWOOD based on proposed use in Canada in association with the following services:

Hotel and restaurant services namely providing lodgings, convention facilities and conference facilities, and servicing food and beverages through dining room, restaurant, cocktail lounge, catering, banqueting and room service facilities.

The application was advertised for opposition purposes on October 10, 1984.

The opponent, Wedgwood plc, filed a statement of opposition on January 7, 1985, a copy of which was forwarded to the applicant on January 25, 1985. The first ground of opposition is that the applied for trade mark is not registrable pursuant to the provisions of § 12(1)(d) of the Trade Mark Act, R.S.C. 1970, c. T–10, in that it is confusing with the opponent's trade mark WEDGWOOD registered under No. 58/14229 in association with "chinaware, earthenware, stoneware, jasper, porcelain, tiles, pottery and other like articles" and with the opponent's trade mark WEDGWOOD & Design registered under No. 263/56518 for "chinaware".

There have been substantial sales in Canada of the opponent's Wedgwood products. In fact, the agent for the applicant conceded that the opponent's trade mark WEDGWOOD is a "very famous" mark in respect of such wares.

In considering the issue of confusion in the present case, I have given particular consideration to the decision of Mr. Justice Cattanach in *Conde Nast Publications Inc. v. Gozlan Brothers Ltd.* (1980), 49 C.P.R. (2d) 250 (Fed. Ct. T.D.) involving an appeal from an opposition by the owner of the trade mark VOGUE for a publication for women's fashions to an application for the identical trade mark for use in association with costume jewellery. Mr. Justice Cattanach allowed the appeal from the original rejection of the opposition notwithstanding that the Hearing Officer felt obliged to find no confusion in view of the specific wording of

§ 6(2) of the Act even though he did find some potential connection between the marks of the parties. As stated by Mr. Justice Cattanach at p. 254 of the reported decision:

"The Hearing Officer by finding as a fact, as he did, that the public infer that the use of 'Vogue' as a trade mark in respect of costume jewellery by the respondent was approved, licensed or sponsored by the appellant or that there was some like business connection between the appellant and the respondent recognizes as a fact that 'people's minds will be put in a state of doubt or uncertainty.' "

"That being so there is no longer a reason for the Hearing Officer to have limited the cause of the doubt or uncertainty to the conjecture that cause may have been the business connections of which he made mention but it would have been logical to extend that cause to include the inference, from the concurrent use of the trade mark VOGUE by the appellant and the respondent, that appellant had embarked upon the manufacture or sale of costume jewellery."

Likewise, in the present case, the fact that the opponent's trade mark is a "very famous" mark, the fact that the marks of the parties are virtually identical and the fact that **fair use** of the applicant's mark could be made by using it on the tableware in its proposed restaurants suggest the possibility that potential patrons of the applicant's hotels and restaurants would assume that the owner of the WEDWOOD trade mark had, in some way, approved, licensed or sponsored the applicant's use of its mark. In other words, I consider that the opponent has made out its case that the public may, in fact, assume that the opponent had commenced to use, licence or otherwise employ its trade mark WEDG-WOOD in the hotel and restaurant business.

The applicant's position is that the opponent's trade mark is so well known for china, dinnerware and the like that no one would confuse it with the same or a similar mark used for unrelated wares or services.

In applying the test for confusion, I have considered that it is a matter of first impression and imperfect recollection. Furthermore, I have considered that the onus is on the applicant to show no reasonable likelihood of confusion. As noted above, the opponent has made out its case. This is not to say that, as a matter of fact, people will assume a connection between the applicant's proposed services and the opponent. Rather, the conclusion that follows is that the opponent's evidence suggests such a connection may be made and the applicant has done nothing to counter that suggestion. Since the onus is on the applicant to show no reasonable likelihood of confusion, the opponent's first ground of opposition based on its registered trade mark WEDGWOOD is successful.

In view of the above, I refuse the applicant's application.

Notes and Questions

1. What evidence did the court in the *McSleep* case use to determine if the mark had "fame"?

2. The North American Free Trade Agreement requires courts take account of the knowledge of the trademark "in the relevant sector of the public, including knowledge in the Party's territory obtained as a result of the promotion of the trademark," (Article 1708(6)). Article 1708(6) goes on to provide: "No Party may require that the reputation of the trademark extend beyond the sector of the public that normally deals with the relevant goods or services." Which, if any, of the cases you have considered reject this provision?

3. Although the *McSleep* case did not deal with a famous foreign mark, it contains a useful listing of the factors courts consider in deciding whether unauthorized use of a mark on a non-competing good or service causes a likelihood of confusion. Does this test represent the classic test mentioned in the *Japanese Noodle* case in Chapter Fifteen?

4. How similar must products be to create a likelihood of confusion with a famous mark? Would the following be considered confusing:

> MICROSOFT for computer software and clothing
>
> COKE for soda and tractors
>
> PEPSI for soda and clothing
>
> APPLE for computers and sound recordings
>
> HALSTON for perfume and furniture

What factors did you consider in reaching your conclusion?

5. In *United Artists v. Pink Panther Beauty Corporation*, 67 C.P.R. (3d)216 [Canada], in deciding whether PINK PANTHER for hair care and beauty products infringed THE PINK PANTHER for phonograph records, motion pictures, film leasing and entertainment services the court rejected an automatic assumption of confusion. Instead it stressed that differences in goods and services should be no less important in deciding likelihood of confusion where the mark is famous.

6. Would the use of *McSleep, Nike* and *Wedgwood* in the above cases meet the test of the EC Directive that use of the mark "takes unfair advantage of" the repute of the McDonald's/Nike/Wedgwood mark? Is such use "detrimental to the distinctive character of" the McDonald's/Nike/Wedgwood mark? While the courts in the above cases generally consider whether use of a mark causes likelihood of confusion with the "famous" mark, the test of "detriment to distinctiveness" is usually treated as a dilution matter. Does Article 6*bis* require use of likelihood of confusion or dilution to determine whether the use or registration of the challenged mark violates Article 6*bis*? For a more detailed discussion of dilution, see below. For a more detailed discussion of the EC Trademark Harmonization Directive, see Chapter Thirty–Nine.

7. *Geographic Indicators*. Many geographical indicators such as COGNAC, DARJEELING, HAVANA and EVIAN are famous. Their protection internationally has been extremely difficult since some countries treat geographic indicators as protectable trademarks, while others consider them generic terms (and, therefore, unenforceable). Under Article 23 of TRIPS only geographic indicators for wine and cheese are recognized as entitled to global protection. Recently, experts have recommended that consideration be

given to protecting geographic indicators internationally as collective or certification marks. *See, e.g., U.S.A World Trademark Symposium*, 82 Trademark Reporter 998 (1992).

8. Even where a famous mark is used in a country, it is increasingly difficult to prohibit the use of a similar mark in a foreign country on noncompeting goods. In *United Artists Corporation v. Pink Panther Beauty Corporation*, as noted above, the Canadian Federal Court of Appeal declined to prohibit the registration of the PINK PANTHER mark for a variety of hair care and beauty products, even though the PINK PANTHER mark used by United Artists in the marketing of phonographic records, motion picture films, and related entertainment services was widely known in Canada. Despite the mark's broad reputation, the Federal Court of Appeal found that the "gaping divergence in the nature of the wares and in the nature of the trade" was not "a fissure but a chasm." The court rejected United Artists' argument that the general trend of corporate diversification would lead a consumer to assume UA had expanded into the beauty products market.

B. DOES FAME MAKE CONFUSION IRRELEVANT?

DAWNING ACCEPTANCE OF THE DILUTION RATIONALE FOR TRADEMARK–TRADE IDENTITY PROTECTION

Beverly W. Pattishall, 74 TMR 289 (1984).

In 1927, the late Frank I. Schechter urged that the only rational basis for trademark protection lay in proscribing the "gradual whittling away or dispersion of the identity and hold upon the public mind of the mark or name by its use upon non-competing goods."[1] Schechter never actually referred to his theory as one protecting against "dilution," but rather as a basis providing "preservation of the uniqueness of a trademark." He argued that "uniqueness or singularity" is the essential trademark right and also that the right to preservation of the trademark's uniqueness or singularity amounted to a property right belonging to the trademark owner, but only in the cases of coined or unique marks.

Prior to Schechter's radical, new rationale for trademark protection, a few decisions had afforded relief, ostensibly under the traditional likelihood of confusion rationale, against what really amounted to diluting rather than confusing use of famous marks on widely diverse goods.[4] The first of a series of the so-called "anti-dilution" statutes espousing Schechter's thesis was not enacted until twenty years later. During the succeeding thirty-six years, there followed a steadily expanding legislative endorsement of the concept by an additional twenty-one states. The

---

1. Frank I. Schechter, *The Rational Basis of Trademark Protection*, 40 Harv L.Rev 813, 825 (1927) *Reprinted* in 22 TM Bull 139, 152 (1927), and 60 TMR 334 342 (1970).

4. The German *Odol* Case, supra note 2 (mouthwash and various steel products);

Wall v. Rolls–Royce of America, 4 F2d 333 (C.A.3 1925) (United States radio tubes case); *Eastman Kodak Co. v. Kodak Cycle Co.*, 15 RPC 105 (1898) (British bicycles case).

courts with a few exceptions, however, failed to follow that lead. Even a half-century after Schechter, the statutes, or basic provisions of them, were being widely ignored or curiously misconstrued and emasculated by the courts.

Much of the prolonged difficulty encountered by the dilution rationale seems to have derived from the sharp difference between its basic concept and that of the confusion of source rationale. The historical or traditional confusion of source torts of trademark infringement and trade identity unfair competition sound in deceit. Their talisman and test is a likelihood of confusion or deception as to source with the goods or services of the prior user. The facts of these cases take many forms, but the unitary rationale for all is the right to protection from confusion of identity. Their essential guideline and limit is that whatever identifies as to source is entitled to protection against a likelihood of confusion, but only to the extent it identifies and only to the extent confusion is likely.

Dilution results when use of a mark by others generates awareness that the mark no longer signifies anything unique, singular or particular, but instead may (or does) denominate several varying items from varying sources. In short, when use of the same or similar marks by others has caused a mark to become less distinctive than before, it has been diluted.

The tort of trademark or trade name dilution sounds not in deceit but in trespass and is a wrong damaging to an incorporeal property right in the sanctity of whatever distinguishing quality may be associated with one's mark or name. The right is to be protected against any trespass likely to diminish or destroy the distinguishing quality of that mark or name. The guideline and limit for protection against dilution is to protect the distinctive quality of that which is distinctive to the extent it is likely to be diluted or threatened with dilution.

The market place, where trademarks are in action today, is a multimedia, mass merchandising one. The marketing revolution of the past three decades has permanently shifted consumer product distribution from the "hand to hand" methods that prevailed even into the 1950s to the fast tracks of media motivated, self-service and semi self-service distribution. This applies not only for small, consumable and portable goods, but also for heavy appliances and similar items, even automobiles. The number of product brands and images now competing for a few instants of awareness by the consumer increases annually.

These pervasive changes have generated a dramatically increased need for realistic, effective and prompt protection of the enormous "commercial magnetism" values rapidly derived from the identifying use of marks and names in the complex and turbulent market place where billions of dollars are involved in purchaser choices every day. The need for the traditional protection against confusion of source remains and, indeed, is increasing. The need for effective protection against dilution, however, seems to have become acute. Happily, the dawn of acceptance for a legal rationale affording such protection also seems to have arrived.

[Review the *Red Shoes* case in Chapter Ten regarding commercial magnetism]

EC TRADEMARK HARMONIZATION DIRECTIVE

Article 5(2)

Any Member State may also provide that the proprietor shall be entitled to prevent all third parties not having his consent from using in the course of trade any sign which is identical with, or similar to, the trademark in relation to the goods or services which are not similar to those for which the trade mark is registered, where the latter has a reputation in the Member State and where use of that sign without due cause takes unfair advantage of, or is detrimental to, the distinctive character or repute of the trademark.

Review the *Enjoy Cocaine* case in Chapter Three.

THE DIMPLE SOAP CASE
DIMPLE

Decision of the Federal Supreme Court, 1984.
Case No. I ZR 158/82.

The first plaintiff is a society whose function, according to Sec. 2(1) of its bylaws, is "the promotion and protection of the common interests of the liquor industry in the Federal Republic of Germany and West Berlin through the voluntary association of its members involved in this industry."

The second plaintiff manufactures the whisky brands "Haig's" and "Dimple" and distributes them in Germany. It owns the mark No. 409717 "Dimple", applied for in 1929, and registered for the classification "wines, beers, ales, stouts and liquor."

Defendant who has been listed in the trade register since 1976, is engaged in the production and sale of cosmetic, chemical, pharmaceutical, and dietetic products, as well as the import and export of various merchandise. On December 22, 1976, it applied for the word mark "Dimple" for the following goods: "detergents and bleaches; scouring, polishing, grease-removal, and grinding agents; soaps; perfumes, essential oils, body and beauty care products, hair tonics; dentifrices." On August 29, 1977, the word mark "Dimple" was registered under No, 962138. Defendant intends to use it for a line of men's cosmetics.

Plaintiffs asserted that the mark "Dimple" represents a famous, world-renowned mark whose promotional power defendant intends to exploit to its advantage in an unfair and misleading manner. Plaintiffs feel that a considerable segment of the public would assume the alcohol used by defendant to be "Dimple" whisky; also, they expect a more than insignificant segment to assume that defendant's "Dimple" products originate from the second plaintiff and that, at the very least, there is an interrelationship between the two manufacturers so that defendant's use of the mark "Dimple" amounts to a kind of quality guarantee. It is common knowledge, according to plaintiffs, that lately, some manufacturers have begun utilizing their known marks for goods heretofore unrelated to their product line (*e.g.* "Dunhill" for ties, scarves, etc.). Finally, a more than insignificant segment of the population—plaintiffs further claim—is misled to believe that defendant's products originate from an English-speaking country, in particular, the United Kingdom.

Plaintiffs requested that defendant be ordered:

1. to agree that its registered trademark No. 962138 "Dimple" be cancelled and to file a declaration with the German Patent Office to this effect;

2. to refrain, under penalty of the law, from selling or distributing detergents and bleaches, scouring, polishing, grease-removal, and grinding agents, perfumes, essential oils, body and beauty care products, hair tonics, or dentifrices under the mark "Dimple".

It is true that this Court, even in its more recent decisions has adhered to the requirement of an actual competitive relationship between the party benefiting from, and the party affected by, an infringing act, while this requirement has been repeatedly questioned in the literature. However, in the interest of effective individual protection under competition law, this Court has not been applying strict requirements to the existence of such a competitive relationship and, in particular, has stated repeatedly that it does not require that the involved firms be in the same business, nor necessarily that the sale of a certain product is impeded by another. Rather, it is sufficient that the infringer, through its infringing act, actually competes with the affected party in some manner. This could happen, for instance, if the infringer implies status equality in so many words or by visual image to associate itself with another product's reputation and prestige, seeking to exploit the same for the sale of its (dissimilar and non-competing) products. In these cases, the infringing acts from the basis of a competitive relationship in terms of commercial exploitation of the reputation and prestige of the affected product which may satisfy the existing requirements if commercial exploitation of this reputation is possible also on the part of its owner. Whether and how the owner implements such an exploitation is of no consequence; the only prerequisite is that the reputation be so outstanding that its commercially meaningful exploitation is conceivable.

These principles are applicable to the case at bar. While this case does not entail an association with the reputation of another product through words or visual images, it does involve an exploitation of a trademark's reputation, which was earned in connection with a certain product, by the use of an identical trademark.

As the Court of Appeals established without legal error, the mark "Dimple" enjoys a reputation which satisfies the stated requirements.

The Court of Appeals has established that the mark "Dimple"—representing considerable individuality and undisputed uniqueness in Germany, where the meaning of the English word is largely unknown—is used for a brand of whisky which exhibits outstanding quality due to long-term aging, falls into the higher-priced category, and possesses the image of an exclusive mark which is enhanced by the unusual shape of the bottle.

This good reputation, established as a fact without legal error, definitely lends itself to independent commercial utilization, and especially so in connection with the cosmetic products primarily at issue in this case. For, it is especially that circle of consumers, which is familiar with the mark "Dimple" and therefore associates it with high quality, as the Court of Appeals established, *i.e.* especially the circle of consumers who actually but and drink whisky with some regularity—which is also likely to buy better cosmetics, particularly men's cosmetics like those which defendant intends to market under the identical mark. Moreover, this circle of consumer—regardless of the question concerning the accuracy of the Court of Appeals' estimate—appears sufficiently large to allow for commercial exploitation of the trademark's reputation; for, even if the estimate should not be acceptable without certain reservations, the assumption of an at least considerable popularity of the mark "Dimple", even at the time of defendant's application for registration, would not be contrary to experience. Even this assumption, however, would still establish the existence of a commercially exploitable circle of such potential buyers of (men's) cosmetics, who associate "Dimple" with high quality.

The Court of Appeals considered the defendant's actions to have been *contra bonos mores* from an objective as well as subjective point of view. With reference to the concept of immorality pursuant to Sec. 1, Act Against Unfair Competition, this is without legal error insofar as it refers to registration of the mark "Dimple" for soaps, perfumes, essential oils, body and beauty care products, hair tonics and dentifrices, as well as the intended use of the mark for a line of men's cosmetics.

With this type of product—as established by the Court of Appeals without legal error—transference of the reputation of a whisky trademark by the consumer is quite conceivable. To this extent, defendant's use of the designation is to be viewed as an exploitation of the mark's reputation in the promotion of defendant's own products which is considered to be *contra bonos mores*. The courts have repeatedly held that it constitutes an act of unfair competition to associate the quality of one's goods or services with that of prestigious competitive products for the purpose of exploiting the good reputation of a competitor's goods or services in order to enhance one's promotional efforts. That the defendant acted deliberately in this regard, *i.e.* was fully aware of the pertinent circumstances, was likewise established without legal error by the Court of Appeals, which pointed out the simultaneous application for registration of the mark "Dimple."

Consequently, the second plaintiff's claim for injunctive relief and—since even the application for registration of the mark was filed with the intention o funfair association and therefore carries the stigma of unfair competition—also the claim for its cancellation, prove to be justified pursuant to Sec. 1, Act Against Unfair Competition, insofar as there claims refer to the cancellation and cessation of use of the mark "Dimple" for the aforementioned products.

By contrast, a more far-reaching claim of the second plaintiff, *i.e.* for cancellations and/or cessation of use of the mark "Dimple" also in connection with detergents and bleaches, scouring, polishing, grease-removal, and grinding agents, cannot be derived from Sec. 1,Act Against Unfair Competition, nor from Sec. 826, Civil Code or Sec. 11(3), Trademark Act.

The Court of Appeals ruled out the possibility of a transference of notions of quality-which the consumer harbors in connection with the whisky brand "Dimple"—to these products. This ruling is not legally questionable in view of the great disparity in all respects between these products and whisky—as also established by the Court of Appeals in this regard—and to that extent precludes any claims from the viewpoints of misleading the consumer and unfair exploitation of a mark's reputation.

Furthermore, a claim for cancellation and for injunctive relief with regard to these products is also not justified because—as the Court of Appeals assumed—the use of the mark for these products allegedly would detract from the promotional power of the heretofore unique mark "Dimple" and also inflict upon it a negative image.

It is true that the possibility of such interference in case of actual use of the mark for these products cannot be entirely precluded and that a claim for injunctive relief under competition law would, in that case, be conceivable under certain circumstances. However, the mere registration o f the mark for such products—so widely divergent from the product whisky—cannot in itself be considered unfair interference with the promotional power and/or the "image" of the mark "Dimple", and certainly not an immoral injury in the sense of Sec. 826, Civil Code.

Notes and Questions

1. What is the harm caused by the unauthorized use of the marks in the *Dimple* and *Enjoy Cocaine* cases? Is there any likelihood that consumers would be confused about the affiliation between the producers of the goods at issue?

2. *Commercial Magnetism.* How does a mark develop "commercial magnetism" or "reputation"? Must a mark be famous to have commercial magnetism? How should fame be determined? What factors should be considered?

3. Did the court in the *Enjoy Cocaine* case base its decision on the likelihood of confusion or dilution? What role did the "fame" of the Coca-Cola mark play in the court's decision?

4. Did the court in the *Soap* case base its decision on likelihood of confusion or dilution? Do you agree with the different treatment for claims for registration/injunctive relief?

5. Consider the earlier cases in Part VII. Would the result in those case have been different if the doctrine of dilution had been considered?

6. U.S. Federal Dilution Act Section 43(c) of the (U.S.) Lanham Act prohibits the dilution of "famous" marks. It provides:

(1) The owner of a famous mark shall be entitled, subject to the principles of equity and upon such terms as the court deems reasonable, to an injunction against another person's commercial use in commerce of a mark or trade name, if such use begins after the mark has become famous and causes dilution of the distinctive quality of the mark, and to obtain such other relief as is provided in this subsection. In determining whether a mark is distinctive and famous, a court may consider factors such as, but not limited to:

(A) the degree of inherent or acquired distinctiveness of the mark;

(B) the duration and extent of use of the mark in connection with the goods or services with which the mark is used;

(C) the duration and extent of advertising and publicity of the mark;

(D) the geographical extent of the trading area in which the mark is used;

(E) the channels of trade for the goods or services with which the mark is used;

(F) the degree of recognition of the mark in the trading areas and channels of trade used by the marks' owner and the person against whom the injunction is sought;

(G) the nature and extent of use of the same or similar marks by third parties; and

(H) whether the mark was registered under the Act of March 3, 1881, or the Act of February 20, 1905, or on the principal register.

(2) In an action brought under this subsection, the owner of the famous mark shall be entitled only to injunctive relief unless the person against whom the injunction is sought willfully intended to trade on the owner's reputation or to cause dilution of the famous mark. If such willful intent is proven, the owner of the famous mark shall also be entitled to the remedies set forth in sections 35(a) and 36, subject to the discretion of the court and the principles of equity.

(4) The following shall not be actionable under this section:

(A) Fair use of a famous mark by another person in comparative commercial advertising or promotion to identify the competing goods or services of the owner of the famous mark.

(B) Noncommercial use of a mark.

(C) All forms of news reporting and news commentary.

This statute was enacted prior to the *Enjoy Cocaine* case. If the case were brought today under Section 43(c) would the court reach the same result?

7. One of the grounds in support of the enactment of the Federal Trademark Dilution Act was the need for dilution protection to meet U.S. obligations under TRIPS. *See* Statement of Senator Orren Hatch in support of the Federal Trademark Dilution Act, Cong. Rec. § 19310 (12/29/95). Is dilution protection required under Article 6bis? What purpose does dilution serve that is not met by a likelihood of confusion test? Compare the results in the *McSleep* and *Enjoy Cocaine* cases. Is dilution necessary to provide protection for famous marks? In what circumstances?

8. In Germany, a company began to use the mark MARS and the slogan "Mars Gives Energy for Sex–Sport and Play" in connection with the sale of joke condoms. The owner of the MARS mark for candy (and of the slogan "Mars Gives Energy for Work, Sport and Play") successfully sued for tarnishment of the distinctiveness and repute of its mark. The court determined that the unauthorized use of the "known" mark MARS presented a concrete risk of transferring a negative image to the mark by evoking prejudicial associations. Do you agree with the court's decision? Why? What result would the court reach under Section 43(c) if it were presented with the same act situation as in *Mars*?

9. Section 22 of the Canadian Trade-marks Act, R.S.C. 1985, Chap. T–13 has been applied to prohibit the dilution of certain marks. It states: "No person shall use a trademark registered by another person in a manner that is likely to have the effect of depreciating the value of the good will attaching thereto." Canadian courts have interpreted the "depreciation" elements as including tarnishment. In *Clairol International Corp. and Clairol Inc. of Canada v. Thomas Supply and Equipment Ltd.*, [1968] Ex CR 552, the court stated "Depreciation of the value of goodwill occurs whether it arises through reduction of the esteem in which the mark itself is held or through the direct persuasion and enticing of customers who could otherwise be expected to buy goods bearing the trade mark."

10. "4711" has been widely used as perfume in Germany and has become well-known. A sewer company uses the number 4711 on its tank trucks (which tend to have an unsavory odor). The number 4711 is their telephone number. Should such use be precluded? On what grounds?

Problem

Your client represents the estate of the Princess Diana of Wales. It was discovered that countless merchandisers are using the likeness of the Princess in selling various items from China to posters to t-shirts. What steps can you take under international trademark law to prevent such uses. Does the image of the Princess qualify as a famous mark? Does her name? Under what circumstances?

C. CAN FAME GIVE A PARTY PROPERTY RIGHTS BEYOND THOSE GRANTED UNDER TRADITIONAL INTELLECTUAL PROPERTY LAW DOCTRINES?

THE VANNA WHITE CASE

VANNA WHITE v. SAMSUNG ELECTRONICS AMERICA, INC.

United States Court of Appeals, Ninth Circuit, 1993.
989 F.2d 1512.

DISSENT BY JUDGE KOZINSKI.

Saddam Hussein wants to keep advertisers from using his picture in unflattering contexts. Clint Eastwood doesn't want tabloids to write about him. Rudolf Valentino's heirs want to control his film biography. The Girl Scouts don't want their image soiled by association with certain activities.[4] George Lucas wants to keep Strategic Defense Initiative fans from calling it "Star Wars."[5] Pepsico doesn't want singers to use the word "Pepsi" in their songs.[6] Guy Lombardo wants an exclusive property right to ads that show big bands playing on New Year's Eve. Uri Geller thinks he should be paid for ads showing psychics bending metal through telekinesis. Paul Prudhomme, that household name, thinks the same about ads featuring corpulent bearded chefs. And scads of copyright holders see purple when their creations are made fun of.

Trademarks are often reflected in the mirror of our popular culture. *See* Truman Capote, Breakfast at Tiffany's (1958); Kurt Vonnegut, Jr., Breakfast of Champions (1973); Tom Wolfe, The Electric Kool–Aid Acid Test (1968) (which, incidentally, includes a chapter on the Hell's Angels); Larry Niven, Man of Steel, Woman of Kleenex in All the Myriad Ways (1971); Looking for Mr. Goodbar (1977); The Coca–Cola Kid (1985) (using Coca–Cola as a metaphor for American commercialism); The Kentucky Fried Movie (1977); Harley Davidson and the Marlboro Man (1991); The Wonder Years (ABC 1988–present) ("Wonder Years" was a slogan of Wonder Bread); Tim Rice & Andrew Lloyd Webber, Joseph and the Amazing Technicolor Dream Coat (musical).

Something very dangerous is going on here. Private property, including intellectual property, is essential to our way of life. It provides an

---

4. *Girl Scouts v. Personality Posters Mfg.*, 304 F. Supp. 1228 (S.D.N.Y.1969) (poster of a pregnant girl in a Girl Scout uniform with the caption "Be Prepared").

5. *Lucasfilm Ltd. v. High Frontier*, 622 F. Supp. 931 (D.D.C.1985).

6. Pepsico Inc. claimed the lyrics and packaging of grunge rocker Tad Doyle's "Jack Pepsi" song were "offensive to [it] and [are] likely to offend [its] customers," in part because they "associate [Pepsico] and its Pepsi marks with intoxication and

drunk driving." Russell, Doyle Leaves Pepsi Thirsty for Compensation, Billboard, June 15, 1991, at 43. Conversely, the Hell's Angels recently sued Marvel Comics to keep it from publishing a comic book called "Hell's Angel," starring a character of the same name. Marvel settled by paying $35,000 to charity and promising never to use the name "Hell's Angel" again in connection with any of its publications. Marvel, Hell's Angels Settle Trademark Suit, L.A. Daily J., Feb. 2, 1993, § II, at 1.

incentive for investment and innovation; it stimulates the flourishing of our culture; it protects the moral entitlements of people to the fruits of their labors. But reducing too much to private property can be bad medicine. Private land, for instance, is far more useful if separated from other private land by public streets, roads and highways. Public parks, utility rights-of-way and sewers reduce the amount of land in private hands, but vastly enhance the value of the property that remains.

So too it is with intellectual property. Overprotecting intellectual property is as harmful as underprotecting it. Creativity is impossible without a rich public domain. Nothing today, likely nothing since we tamed fire, is genuinely new: Culture, like science and technology, grows by accretion, each new creator building on the works of those who came before. Overprotection stifles the very creative forces it's supposed to nurture.

The panel's opinion is a classic case of overprotection. Concerned about what it sees as a wrong done to Vanna White, the panel majority erects a property right of remarkable and dangerous breadth: Under the majority's opinion, it's now a tort for advertisers to remind the public of a celebrity. Not to use a celebrity's name, voice, signature or likeness; not to imply the celebrity endorses a product; but simply to evoke the celebrity's image in the public's mind. This Orwellian notion withdraws far more from the public domain than prudence and common sense allow. It conflicts with the Copyright Act and the Copyright Clause. It raises serious First Amendment problems. It's bad law, and it deserves a long, hard second look.

Samsung ran an ad campaign promoting its consumer electronics. Each ad depicted a Samsung product and a humorous prediction: One showed a raw steak with the caption "Revealed to be health food. 2010 A.D." Another showed Morton Downey, Jr. in front of an American flag with the caption "Presidential candidate. 2008 A.D." n12 The ads were meant to convey—humorously—that Samsung products would still be in use twenty years from now.

The ad that spawned this litigation starred a robot dressed in a wig, gown and jewelry reminiscent of Vanna White's hair and dress; the robot was posed next to a Wheel-of-Fortune-like game board. The caption read "Longest-running game show. 2012 A.D." The gag here, I take it, was that Samsung would still be around when White had been replaced by a robot.

Perhaps failing to see the humor, White sued, alleging Samsung infringed her right of publicity by "appropriating" her "identity." Under California law, White has the exclusive right to use her name, likeness, signature and voice for commercial purposes. Cal. Civ. Code § 3344(a); Eastwood v. Superior Court, 149 Cal. App. 3d 409, 417, 198 Cal. Rptr. 342, 347 (1983). But Samsung didn't use her name, voice or signature, and it certainly didn't use her likeness. The ad just wouldn't have been funny had it depicted White or someone who resembled her—the whole joke was that the game show host(ess) was a robot, not a real person. No one seeing the ad could have thought this was supposed to be White in 2012.

The district judge quite reasonably held that, because Samsung didn't use White's name, likeness, voice or signature, it didn't violate her right of publicity. Not so, says the panel majority: The California right of publicity can't possibly be limited to name and likeness. If it were, the majority reasons, a "clever advertising strategist" could avoid using White's name or likeness but nevertheless remind people of her with impunity, "effectively eviscerating" her rights. To prevent this "evisceration," the panel majority holds that the right of publicity must extend beyond name and likeness, to any "appropriation" of White's "identity"—anything that "evokes" her personality. 971F.2d at 1398–99.

But what does "evisceration" mean in intellectual property law? Intellectual property rights aren't like some constitutional rights, absolute guarantees protected against all kinds of interference, subtle as well as blatant. They cast no penumbras, emit no emanations: The very point of intellectual property laws is that they protect only against certain specific kinds of appropriation. I can't publish unauthorized copies of, say, Presumed Innocent; I can't make a movie out of it. But I'm perfectly free to write a book about an idealistic young prosecutor on trial for a crime he didn't commit. So what if I got the idea from Presumed Innocent? So what if it reminds readers of the original? Have I "eviscerated" Scott Turow's intellectual property rights? Certainly not. All creators draw in part on the work of those who came before, referring to it, building on it, poking fun at it; we call this creativity, not piracy.

The majority isn't, in fact, preventing the "evisceration" of Vanna White's existing rights; it's creating a new and much broader property right, a right unknown in California law. It's replacing the existing balance between the interests of the celebrity and those of the public by a different balance, one substantially more favorable to the celebrity. Instead of having an exclusive right in her name, likeness, signature or voice, every famous person now has an exclusive right to anything that reminds the viewer of her. After all, that's all Samsung did: It used an inanimate object to remind people of White, to "evoke her identity." 971 F.2d at 1399.

Consider how sweeping this new right is. What is it about the ad that makes people think of White? It's not the robot's wig, clothes or jewelry; there must be ten million blond women (many of them quasi-famous) who wear dresses and jewelry like White's. It's that the robot is posed near the "Wheel of Fortune" game board. Remove the game board from the ad, and no one would think of Vanna White. But once you include the game board, anybody standing beside it—a brunette woman, a man wearing women's clothes, a monkey in a wig and gown—would evoke White's image, precisely the way the robot did. It's the "Wheel of Fortune" set, not the robot's face or dress or jewelry that evokes White's image. The panel is giving White an exclusive right not in what she looks like or who she is, but in what she does for a living.[18]

This is entirely the wrong place to strike the balance. Intellectual property rights aren't free: They're imposed at the expense of future creators and of the public at large. Where would we be if Charles Lindbergh had an exclusive right in the concept of a heroic solo aviator? If Arthur Conan Doyle had gotten a copyright in the idea of the detective story, or Albert Einstein had patented the theory of relativity? If every author and celebrity had been given the right to keep people from mocking them or their work? Surely this would have made the world poorer, not richer, culturally as well as economically.

This is why intellectual property law is full of careful balances between what's set aside for the owner and what's left in the public domain for the rest of us: The relatively short life of patents; the longer, but finite, life of copyrights; copyright's idea-expression dichotomy; the fair use doctrine; the prohibition on copyrighting facts; the compulsory license of television broadcasts and musical compositions; federal pre-emption of overbroad state intellectual property laws; the nominative use doctrine in trademark law; the right to make soundalike recordings. All of these diminish an intellectual property owner's rights. All let the public use something created by someone else. But all are necessary to maintain a free environment in which creative genius can flourish.

The intellectual property right created by the panel here has none of these essential limitations.

Moreover, consider the moral dimension, about which the panel majority seems to have gotten so exercised. Saying Samsung "appropriated" something of White's begs the question: Should White have the exclusive right to something as broad and amorphous as her "identity"? Samsung's ad didn't simply copy White's schtick—like all parody, it created something new. True, Samsung did it to make money, but White does whatever she does to make money, too; the majority talks of "the difference between fun and profit," 971 F.2d at 1401, but in the entertainment industry fun is profit. Why is Vanna White's right to exclusive for-profit use of her persona—a persona that might not even be her own creation, but that of a writer, director or producer—superior to Samsung's right to profit by creating its own inventions? Why should

---

18. Once the right of publicity is extended beyond specific physical characteristics, this will become a recurring problem: Outside name, likeness and voice, the one thing that most reliably reminds the public of someone are the actions or roles they're famous for. A commercial with an astronaut setting foot on the moon would evoke the image of Neil Armstrong. Any masked man on horseback would remind people (over a certain age) of Clayton Moore. And any number of songs—"My Way," "Yellow Sub-marine," "Like a Virgin," "Beat It," "Michael, Row the Boat Ashore," to name only a few—instantly evoke an image of the person or group who made them famous, regardless of who is singing. *See also Carlos V. Lozano, West Loses Lawsuit Over Batman TV Commercial,* L.A. Times, Jan. 18, 1990, at B3 (Adam West sues over Batman-Like character in commercial); *Nurmi v. Peterson,* 10 U.S.P.Q.2d 1775 (C.D.Cal. 1989) (1950s tv movie hostess "Vampira" sues 1980s tv hostess "Elvira").

she have such absolute rights to control the conduct of others, unlimited by the idea-expression dichotomy or by the fair use doctrine?

For better or worse, we are the Court of Appeals for the Hollywood Circuit. Millions of people toil in the shadow of the law we make, and much of their livelihood is made possible by the existence of intellectual property rights. But much of their livelihood—and much of the vibrancy of our culture—also depends on the existence of other intangible rights: The right to draw ideas from a rich and varied public domain, and the right to mock, for profit as well as fun, the cultural icons of our time.

In the name of avoiding the "evisceration" of a celebrity's rights in her image, the majority diminishes the rights of copyright holders and the public at large. In the name of fostering creativity, the majority suppresses it. Vanna White and those like her have been given something they never had before, and they've been given it at our expense. I cannot agree.

THE VELVET ELVIS CASE

ELVIS PRESLEY ENTERPRISES, INC. v. BARRY CAPECE

United States District Court, S.D. Texas, 1996.
950 F.Supp. 783.

GILMORE, DISTRICT JUDGE

Elvis Presley Enterprises ("EPE") is a Tennessee corporation formed in 1981 under the terms of a testamentary trust created by Elvis Presley ("Presley"). EPE is the assignee and registrant of all trademarks, copyrights, and publicity rights belonging to the Presley estate, including over a dozen United States federal trademark registrations and common law trademarks of Presley's name and likeness. None of these marks, however, are registered service marks for use in the restaurant and tavern business. EPE's exclusive rights are marketed through a licensing program which grants licensees the right to manufacture and sell Elvis Presley merchandise worldwide. Products range from t-shirts to juke boxes. Merchandise sales have generated over $20 million dollars in revenue in the last five years and account for the largest percentage of EPE's annual earnings. In addition, EPE operates a mail order business and several retail stores at Graceland, the Elvis Presley home in Memphis, Tennessee, including two restaurants and an ice cream parlor. EPE recently announced plans to open an Elvis Presley night club in 1997 on Beale Street in Memphis and is also currently exploring the possibility of opening similar establishments throughout the world.

In April of 1991, Barry Capece ("Capece") opened a nightclub on Kipling Street in Houston, Texas named "The Velvet Elvis." The name, "The Velvet Elvis," referring to one of the more coveted velvet paintings, was selected for the powerful association it immediately invokes with a time when lava lamps, velvet paintings, and bell bottoms were popular. Capece intended the bar to parody an era remembered for its sensationalism and transient desire for flashiness. By taking bad, albeit once widely popular, art and accentuating it with gallery lights and by showcasing decor which mocks society's idolization of less than scrupulous celebrities, Capece ridiculed a culture's obsession with the fleeting and unimportant. His biting criticism provides his patrons with a constant reminder not to take themselves nor the world they live in too seriously.

Plaintiff claims that the focal point of the bar's name, decor, and advertisements is Elvis Presley. To protect its exclusive right to license the commercial use of Elvis Presley's name, image, and likeness, Plaintiff filed suit against the Velvet, Ltd., Audley, Inc., and Capece, as owner of "The Velvet Elvis" service mark, on April 21, 1995. Plaintiff sued Defendants for unfair competition, trademark infringement, and dilution, under both the common law and the Lanham Act, 15 U.S.C. § 1051 et seq. (1994), and for infringement of its common law and corresponding statutory right of publicity. Plaintiff seeks injunctive relief, an accounting for profits, attorneys fees, costs, and an Order to the Commissioner of Trademarks to cancel Capece's registration for "The Velvet Elvis."

Even though Plaintiff's widely recognized Elvis Presley trademarks are deserving of protection, this fact alone does not support a finding of confusion. Defendants' use of the service mark "The Velvet Elvis" when combined with the bar's gaudy decor form an integral part of Defendants' parody of the faddish, eclectic bars of the sixties. The phrase "velvet Elvis" has a meaning in American pop culture that is greater than the name, image, or likeness of Elvis Presley. The phrase symbolizes tacky, "cheesy," velvet art, including, but not limited to velvet Elvis paintings. Here, the image of Elvis, conjured up by way of velvet paintings, has transcended into an iconoclastic form of art that has a specific meaning in our culture, which surpasses the identity of the man represented in the painting. That image is confirmed upon entering the bar. Plaintiff's own witnesses testified that despite their thoughts about the bar's name, they immediately realized the tacky bar they had just encountered was in no way associated or affiliated with EPE. The humorous jab at the trends of the sixties is almost overpowering and readily apparent with one quick look around a lounge cluttered with tasteless art, long strand beads, and a lighted disco ball conspicuously hung from the ceiling. The customer's recognition and appreciation of Defendants' parody decreases the probability of confusion that would otherwise result from use of a trade name which partially incorporates a relatively strong mark. Thus, the Court finds that while Plaintiff's mark is entitled to protection, it is doubtful that its inclusion within the name "The Velvet Elvis" will mislead consumers into believing that the bar is affiliated or somehow associated with EPE. Nor will customers mistake "The Velvet Elvis" for an EPE owned or sponsored business because Elvis related items are used in the bar's decor. This factor therefore weighs against finding a likelihood of confusion exists both with respect to Defendants' use of "The Velvet Elvis" service mark and Elvis memorabilia as bar decor.

After reviewing the evidence presented, the Court concludes that Defendants' service mark, "The Velvet Elvis," as currently used, and Defendants' use of Elvis memorabilia as bar decor does not create a likelihood of customer confusion under either the Lanham Act or the common law. Accordingly, the Court finds this aspect of Plaintiff's infringement claim to be without merit.

Tarnishment generally arises when "a plaintiff's trademark is linked to products of shoddy quality, or is portrayed in an unwholesome or unsavory context likely to evoke unflattering thoughts about the owner's product." The threat of tarnishment occurs when the reputation and goodwill of the plaintiff's trademark is connected with products that "conjure associations that clash with the associations generated by the owner's lawful use of the mark." *L.L. Bean*, 811 F.2d at 31. Generally, tarnishment has been found in cases where a distinctive mark is depicted in a context of sexual activity, obscenity, or illegal activity, *see Dallas Cowboys Cheerleaders, Inc. v. Pussycat Cinema, Ltd.*, 604 F.2d 200, 205 (2d Cir.1979) (Dallas Cowboy Cheerleader uniforms used in sexually depraved movie); *Coca-Cola Co. v. Gemini Rising, Inc.*, 346 F. Supp. 1183, 1189 (E.D.N.Y.) (Coca–Cola logo used in poster stated "Enjoy Cocaine"); *Pillsbury Co. v. Milky Way Productions, Inc.*, 8 Media L. Rep. 1016, 215 U.S.P.Q. 124, 135 (N.D.Ga.1981) (Pillsbury dough boy depicted engaging in sexual intercourse). Courts have also found tarnishment to occur even though the plaintiff's mark was not portrayed in an unwholesome manner but have done so only in cases involving identical or almost identical trade names, *see Steinway & Sons v. Robert Demars & Friends*, 210 U.S.P.Q. 954, 961 (C.D.Cal.1981) (Steinway pianos tarnished by Stein–Way clip-on beverage can handles), or cases where alterations of a mark are "made by a competitor with both an incentive to diminish the favorable attributes of the mark and ample opportunity to promote its products in ways that make no significant alteration." *Deere*, 41 F.3d at 45.

This Court has already determined that the marks in dispute are not sufficiently similar to constitute tarnishment on this basis. Further, because the parties are not currently in direct competition nor were they when "The Velvet Elvis" opened, the Court also finds that Defendants' parody does not ridicule Plaintiff's mark for the purpose of promoting its own competitive product. Plaintiff bases its tarnishment claim on the unsupported assumption that Defendants' use of the Elvis name in association with a tacky bar that indiscriminately displays explicit and almost pornographic paintings of nude women has tainted the wholesome image of Elvis and EPE sponsored products and services. The Court finds, however, without any evidence to the contrary, that nude portraits hung in a bar for the purpose of mocking the tasteless decor of the sixties does not inspire negative or unsavory images of Elvis or Elvis related products or services in the minds of EPE customers. Furthermore, the nude pictures and the bar's intentional tackiness are an

obvious part of the parody and are associated, to the extent any association is made, for purposes of the parody only, rather than for creating a
permanent derogatory connection in the public's mind between the two
businesses. Although "The Velvet Elvis" might be considered by some
customers to be in poor taste, the Court is convinced that it is not likely
to prompt an unsavory or unwholesome association in consumers minds
with the "Elvis" or "Elvis Presley" trademarks. Absent such a showing,
a tarnishment claim cannot be sustained.

Plaintiff claims that Defendants' use of the name, image, likeness,
and other indicia of Elvis for the purposes of trade constitutes an
appropriation of Elvis Presley's right of publicity. As owner of the
exclusive rights in the identity of Elvis, Plaintiff seeks redress for a
violation of its common law right as well as its corresponding statutory
rights under either Tennessee or Texas law.

The right of publicity has been defined as the "inherent right of
every human being to control the commercial use of his or her identity"
and prevent the exploitation of any aspect of their persona without
permission. McCarthy, *supra*, § 28.01[2][a]. It is considered a property
right and is descendible as an asset of the estate upon an individual's
death. Publicity rights do not have a "likelihood of confusion" requirement and are more expansive than any statutory or common law right to
protection against trademark infringement. To violate a plaintiff's right
of publicity, however, the defendant must employ an aspect of persona in
a manner that symbolizes or identifies the plaintiff, such as the use of a
name, nickname, voice, picture, achievements, performing style, distinctive characteristics or other indicia closely associated with a person.

Under Texas law a person is specifically prohibited from using:
without the written consent of a person who may exercise the property
right, a deceased individual's name, voice, signature, photograph, or
likeness in any manner, including: (1) in connection with products,
merchandise or goods; or (2) for purpose of advertising, selling, or
soliciting the purchase of products, merchandise, goods or services.

TEX. PROP. CODE § 26.011 (Vernon 1984 & Supp. 1996). A prima
facie case requires proof that (1) the defendant has appropriated another's identity and (2) is using it for trade or commercial benefit.

Plaintiff claims that Defendants have violated its publicity rights by
using the Elvis name as part of its service mark, by promoting its bar
services through ads containing pictures or using the image or likeness
of Elvis, by making reference to Elvis on its dinner menu, and by using
Elvis memorabilia as bar decor. In essence, the Plaintiffs complaint is
that "The Velvet Elvis" is simply a disguised attempt at capitalizing on
the identity of Elvis Presley.

Use of Elvis memorabilia as decor does not amount to any violation
as it is not intended for the purpose of advertising, selling, or soliciting
the purchase of products, merchandise, goods or services. in other words,
the function of the memorabilia is not to promote a product or capitalize
on the personality of Elvis himself but rather to recreate an era of which

Elvis was a public part. In fact, with the exception of the now infamous velvet Elvis portrait, Defendants have removed most of the Elvis related objects with no apparent effect on the bar's message or success. Likewise, the Court finds the menu's use of the expression "King of Dive Bars" and its incorporation of peanut butter and banana sandwiches as a menu item are not actionable. While it may be true that Elvis enjoyed peanut butter and banana sandwiches, this fact alone will not support a claim for violation of the Plaintiff's right of publicity. To trigger infringement the plaintiff must be clearly identifiable from use of the item or phrase in question. *McFarland v. Miller*, 14 F.3d 912, 920 (3d. Cir.1994) (recognizing that without identification, the right of publicity is worthless); see also McCarthy, *supra*, § 28.01[4]. Such is not the case here.

Additionally, the Court finds Defendants' use of the service mark, "The Velvet Elvis," does not amount to an unauthorized commercial exploitation of the identity of Elvis Presley. The service mark represents an art form reflective of an era that Elvis helped to shape. "The velvet Elvis" became a coined phrase for the art of velvet paintings and was adopted by Defendants for this reason—not because of its identification with Elvis Presley. Elvis's association with velvet paintings was not a product of his own doing nor can it be considered a part of the character or personality of Elvis that Plaintiff has the right to control. Unlike "Here's Johnny," this phrase is not the thumbprint, work product, or tangible expression of Elvis Presley's celebrity identity. The mere association of a phrase or expression with a celebrity without the intent or effect of exploiting his identity or persona is insufficient cause for a violation of publicity rights.

Notes and Questions

1. On appeal the court found that defendants' use of the VELVET ELVIS mark infringed plaintiff's trademark rights. It stated "The Defendants' parody of the faddish bars of the sixties does not require the use of EPE's marks because it does not target Elvis Presley; therefore, the necessity to use the marks significantly decreases and does not justify the use." It went on to find that the "persuasiveness of EPE's marks across the spectrum of products and the success and proliferation of entertainment and music-themed restaurants like Planet Hollywood and Hard Rock Café support a likelihood of confusion." Which decision do you believe reflects more appropriately the protections to be afforded famous marks internationally?

2. *Right of Publicity*. Increasingly, the issue of international protection for publicity rights is gaining greater prominence. As merchandising efforts spread to a wider variety of goods, and celebrity becomes global, greater efforts are expended to protect rights beyond those generally granted under traditional trademark doctrines. Consider the adverse consequences of celebrity in the following cases. Do you agree with the balance struck between publicity and "property" rights by the courts in these cases? How broad should publicity rights be? Limited to commercial exploitation? Should they last beyond the celebrity's lifetime? For how long?

THE TARZAN TRADEMARK CASE
IN RE TARZAN TRADE MARK

Supreme Court of Judicature Court of Appeal, 1970.
[1970] RPC 450, [1970] FSR 245.

SALMON, L.J.

In November 1965, the applicants, an American company called Banner Productions Inc., applied to register the name TARZAN as a trade mark in Part A, alternatively in Part B, of the register in respect of films prepared for exhibition and magnetic tape recordings.

The first question to consider is whether TARZAN at the date of the application was an invented word. Undoubtedly, many years before November 1965, an author called Edgar Rice Burroughs did invent the word and wrote many stories about a ficitious character whom he called Tarzan. The question is, however, whether in November 1965 TARZAN could be correctly described as an invented word.

The case against the applicant was that, although Mr. Burroughs had originally invented the word, by November 1965 it had passed into the language and had indeed become a household word.

We have been referred to Webster's International Dictionary. In the second edition, "Tarzan" is described as a character of a series of stories by Edgar Rice Burroughs. He is described as "a white man of prodigious strength and chivalrous instincts reared by African apes". In the third and latest edition he is described as "a hero of adventure stories of Edgar Rice Burroughs, a strong agile person of heroic proportions and bearing".

In my view, the learned judge's conclusion that the word "Tarzan" had passed into the language and was well-known by every adult, and indeed by most children, is quite incapable of attack.

The learned Judge said that it was not of course necessary that the applicant should invent the word. Indeed, that is right. It was not fatal to the application that the word had been invented many years before the application was made. For example, if a word was invented, say, in 1925, and had not passed into the language, it would still remain an invented word in 1965. The trouble facing Mr. Burrell is that it seems quite plain that the word TARZAN had by 1965 passed into the language.

The next point is whether the word had a direct reference to the character or quality of the goods in respect of which it was sought to register it. I asked Mr. Burrell during the course of his argument if he could think of a more direct reference to the character of a film dealing with some exploits of Tarzan than the description that it was a "Tarzan" film. This was a question which Mr. Burrell, despite his wide experience and ingenuity, was quite unable to answer. Indeed, it seems plain that such a film could not better be described or referred to than as a "Tarzan" film. The learned judge so found. I agree with him, and Mr. Burrell's second point accordingly fails also.

I do not think that there is anything about the word TARZAN which would make it inherently incapable of distinguishing the applicants' goods in any circumstances at any future time. On the other hand, there is no evidence of use or any other circumstance which makes the mark now in fact capable of distinguishing the applicants' goods.

EDMUND DAVIES, L.J.

Whether the word or words sought to be registered as a trade mark can be regarded as "invented" within the meaning of section 9(1)(c) of the Trade Marks Act 1938, is primarily a question of fact. Furthermore, the answer to the question depends on the facts existing at the date when registration is sought. What answer was called for in the present case? Although undoubtedly originally an invented word, has TARZAN long ago become too well-known to be any longer so regarded, as Lindley, L.J. asked regarding the word TRILBY in Holt's Trade Mark (1896) 13 R.P.C. 118 at 121?

The learned judge answered that question in this way:

> "It is quite clear that in the present case by the time of registration here the word 'Tarzan' to the ordinary member of the English-speaking public had acquired a very definite meaning and quite clearly referred to the character in Edgar Rice Burroughs novels. There is no doubt that this character is extremely well-known as having been portrayed on films and generally is a person, although fictitious, who is well-known to the public. In these circumstances, I do not see how it can properly be said that the word is an invented word at the date of the registrations."

> "Since 1962 the applicants have been solely and exclusively entitled by virtue of a number of agreements made from time to time with Edgar Rice Burroughs Inc. to produce films, records and merchandise for distribution throughout the world, including the United Kingdom, centred on the fictional character 'Tarzan'." In these circumstances, I, like the learned trial judge, have some difficulty in thinking up a "reference to the character or quality of the goods" which could be clearer or more direct.

In the light of the affidavit evidence, Mr. Burrell has submitted that, as the applicants are in certain respects exclusive licensees, no-one else could make TARZAN films or toys. From this he argues that the word TARZAN "is in fact adapted to distinguish" the applicants' goods from all others. What is there about the word TARZAN which entitles it to be regarded as "inherently adapted to distinguish" the applicants' goods? In *WELDMESH Trade Mark* [1966] R.P.C. 200 at228, Harman, L.J. said, "By 'inherently adapted' I take the Act to mean adapted of itself, standing on its own feet". Respectfully adopting that interpretation. I do not find any inherently distinctive quality in the word TARZAN which points to the applicants' goods rather than to those of any other trader.

Certainly, I am not satisfied that, in answering the question as he did, the learned judge was in error.

Nor do I think that error is shown in the rejection of registration in Part B. Graham, J. held that "the mark is at present not shown to be capable of distinguishing the goods of the applicants", but was careful to add, "I am not to be taken as saying that no application in Part B on proof of user of the mark in practice could not be successful at a later date." This seems to me to apply correctly the test propounded by Lloyd–Jacob, J. and approved of by the Court of Appeal in the WELDMESH case, that the phrase "capable of distinguishing" in section 10(1) emphasised that, in spite of the absence of a sufficient distinguishing characteristic in the mark itself, that distinctiveness can be acquired by appropriate user, thereby overcoming a negative quality in the mark. This could happen to the present applicants who, in time, may cogently submit that TARZAN has acquired distinctiveness. Whether that will prove to be so remains to be seen, but in the light of circumstances existing at the time of application I do not consider that the learned trial judge is shown to have come to an erroneous conclusion regarding Part B registration either.

THE ELVISLY YOURS CASE
RE ELVIS PRESLEY TRADE MARKS

Chancery Division, 1997, [1997].
RPC 543.

JUSTICE LADDIE

On 26 January 1989 Elvis Presley Enterprises Inc ("Enterprises") of Presley Boulevard, Memphis, Tennessee in the United States of America applied to register three trade marks under the provisions of the Trade Marks Act 1938. The first, numbered 1371624, is for a manuscript version of the name "ELVIS A PRESLEY". This mark was referred to before me as the "signature mark". The second mark, numbered 1371627, is for the word "ELVIS" *simpliciter* and the third, number B1371627, is for the words "ELVIS PRESLEY" *simpliciter*. All three marks are sought to be registered for the following specification of goods;

> "Toilet preparations, perfumes, eau de colognes; preparations for the hair and teeth; soaps, bath and shower preparations; deodorants, anti-perspirants and cosmetics; all included in Class 3."

On 16 June 1991 all three were opposed by Mr. Sid David Shaw. Amongst the grounds of objection raised by Mr. Shaw were those of lack of distinctiveness under sections 9 and 10 of the 1938 Act and deceptiveness under section 11 and under section 12 as a result of an alleged conflict with a trade mark registration of his own.

Mr. Shaw has traded under the name "ELVISLY YOURS" since the late 1970's. In 1982 he formed a trading company called Elvisly Yours

Limited. Mr. Shaw is the proprietor of the registered trade mark "ELVISLY YOURS" also in Class 3 for a wide specification of goods, including toiletries, soaps, perfumes, cosmetics and shampoos. The validity of that registration has not been challenged in these proceedings. Mr. Shaw has traded in a wide range of products which bear the whole or parts of Elvis Presley's name or likeness. He has sold his products not only in the United Kingdom but also abroad. Mr. Shaw asserts, and it is not denied, that Elvisly Yours was the exclusive supplier of Elvis Presley souvenirs to Graceland in August 1982. It appears that Enterprises and Mr. Shaw have been in litigation in the U.S.A which effectively resulted in Mr. Shaw being injuncted from carrying on trade in Elvis Presley memorabilia in that country.

Although the arguments before me have ranged over a considerable area, at their heart are two crucial issues; (a) can anyone claim the exclusive right under the 1938 Act to use the names Elvis and Elvis Presley or the signature as a trade mark for a range of common retail products and, if so, (b) who?

There is nothing akin to a copyright in a name. This has been part of our common law for a long time. In *Du Boulay v. Du Boulay* (1869) LR 2 PC 430 the Privy Council said;

> "In this country we do not recognise the absolute right of a person to a particular name to the extent of entitling him to prevent the assumption of that name by a stranger. The mere assumption of a name, which is the patronymic of a family, by a Stranger who had never before been called by that name, whatever cause of annoyance it may be to the family, is a grievance for which our Law affords no redress."

Even if Elvis Presley was still alive, he would not be entitled to stop a fan from naming his son, his dog or goldfish, his car or his house "Elvis" or "Elvis Presley" simply by reason of the fact that it was the name given to him at birth by his parents. To stop the use of the whole or part of his name by another he would need to show that as a result of such use, the other person is invading some legally recognised right.

Just as Elvis Presley did not own his name so as to be able to prevent all and any uses of it by third parties, so Enterprises can have no greater rights. Similarly, Elvis Presley did not own his appearance. For example, during his life he could not prevent a fan from having a tattoo put on his chest or a drawing on his car which looked like the musician simply on the basis that it was his appearance which was depicted. For the same reason under our law, Enterprises does not own the likeness of Elvis Presley. No doubt it can prevent the reproduction of the drawings and photographs of him in which it owns copyright, but it has no right to prevent the reproduction or exploitation of any of the myriad of photographs, including press photographs, and drawings in which it does not own the copyright simply by reason of the fact that they contain or depict a likeness of Elvis Presley. Nor could it complain if a fan commissioned a sculptor to create a life-size statue of the musician in a characteristic pose and then erected it in his garden. It can only complain if the reproduction or use of the likeness results in the infringement of some recognised legal right which it does own.

At the date of application, Elvis Presley had been dead for more than 10 years but his fame continued to exist on a large scale. There were at the date of application, and still are, many people in this country who wish to acquire recordings of his songs and films and a wide variety of domestic articles bearing his likeness and/or his name. It is not in dispute that there is a large market in Elvis Presley memorabilia. It has kept Mr. Shaw in business for more than 18 years. This judgment does not deal with what Elvis Presley could have obtained by way of trade mark registration if he had applied for such rights during his life. In particular it should not be assumed that I accept Mr. Prescott's assertion that there is "no doubt" that Elvis Presley would be entitled to registration of his own name. That is a proposition which is beset with difficulties but which does not arise for resolution on this appeal.

It seems to me that Mr. Meade was right when he said that the word ELVIS had very low inherent distinctiveness. Not only is this a well known given name, it also will be taken by many members of the public to refer back to Elvis Presley. This accords with the view expressed by Mr. Tuck:

"To me, therefore, the name Elvis means Elvis Presley."

The classification of goods for which Enterprises seeks registration covers a wide range of small value products which can carry the image of Elvis Presley.

The more a mark has come to describe the goods to which it is to be applied or to indicate some quality of those goods, the less it is inherently adapted to carry out the trade mark function of distinguishing the trade origin of the proprietor's goods from the origin of similar goods from other sources. This is consistent with Mr. Meade's argument that the more famous Elvis Presley is, the less inherently distinctive are the words "Elvis" and "Presley". They are peculiarly suitable for use on the wide range of products sold as Elvis Presley memorabilia. He therefore does not contest but adopts Enterprises' assertion that "Elvis is about as famous a name as could be, made famous by the efforts of Elvis Presley. Why else do members of the public wish to purchase Elvis merchandise?" Just as members of the public will go to see a Tarzan film because it is about Tarzan, so they will purchase Elvis merchandise because it carries the name or likeness of Elvis and not because it comes from a particular source. There is no reason why Mr. Shaw or anyone else for that matter should not sell memorabilia and momentoes of Elvis Presley, including products embellished with pictures of him, and such traders are likely, in the ordinary course of their business and without any improper motive, to desire to use the name Elvis or Elvis Presley upon or in connection with their own such goods.

Mr. Prescott argued that this was not the correct approach to adopt in the late 1990's. He said I should take judicial notice of the fact that markets have changed since the days of the *Tarzan* case. There is more public awareness of character merchandising now. Therefore cases such as *Tarzan* which were lost in the 1970's would succeed now.

Mr. Prescott suggested that the public's awareness of merchandising practices means that they will always assume that products of famous personalities or fictitious characters come from a particular "genuine" source. By "genuine source" I assume that he meant, in the case of a dead human, either his estate or someone with "rights" granted by his estate. In the case of fictitious characters perhaps "genuine" refers to the creator or his successors.

I am quite unable to accept that proposition. It may be that in some cases a plaintiff in a passing off action or an applicant for a registered trade mark will be able to show that to be the case. But I am not willing to assume that that is the public perception generally. On the contrary, my own experience suggests that such an assumption would be false. When people buy a toy of a well known character because it depicts that character, I have no reason to believe that they care one way or the other who made, sold or licensed it. When a fan buys a poster or a cup bearing an image of his star, he is buying a likeness, not a product from a particular source. Similarly the purchaser of any one of the myriad of cheap souvenirs of the royal wedding bearing pictures of Prince Charles and Diana, Princess of Wales, wants momentoes with likenesses. He is likely to be indifferent as to the source. Of course it is possible that, as a result of the peculiarities of the way goods are marketed or advertised, an inference of association with a particular trader may be possible to draw. This may be the case when the proprietor's products bear the word "Official". But that does not mean that absent that word members of the public would draw any such inference.

It follows that I have come to the conclusion that there is very little inherent distinctiveness in the mark "ELVIS".

For the above reasons I have come to the conclusion that the "ELVIS" mark is not a distinctive mark within the requirements of section 9 of the 1938 Act.

I will allow the appeal in relation to all three applications.

Notes and Questions

1. Did the courts in the *Tarzan* and the *Elvisly Yours* cases give appropriate deference to the "fame" of the marks at issue? What about the knowledge of most consumers about the widespread practices of celebrity merchandising nowadays? Did the court give appropriate deference to this issue?

2. Compare the treatment of ELVIS marks in the *Velvet Elvis* and *Elvisly Yours* cases. What problems do these cases present for owners of the ELVIS PRESLEY marks? Are these decisions aberrations or do they demonstrate a lesson on mistakes to avoid in policing the rights of celebrities?

3.   Would it have made a difference in these cases if the "marks" had been portraits or photographs of Elvis Presley instead of his name or signature? Would the same reasoning apply?

4.   If you were buying a t-shirt with a photograph of Marilyn Monroe, would you assume that it had been authorized by her estate and that the photograph served as a source designator? What if instead of a photograph of Marilyn Monroe, the t-shirt bore a photograph of a COCA–COLA bottle? Would you assume that the Coca–Cola company had authorized the use of the photograph? Does trademark protection depend on a consumer's knowledge of authorization? Should it?

5.   Can a mark become so famous it loses its distinctiveness? Should it be possible (from a philosophical basis) to be "too famous"?

6.   Do the decisions in the *Tarzan* and *Elvisly Yours* cases violate Article *6bis* of the Paris Convention?

7.   Can fame result in the loss of rights of other forms of intellectual property? For example, can a copyright protectable work become so famous that others should be allowed to use it as part of the common heritage of mankind? What about copyright protected works that relate to technology, such as computer software? Consider *Lotus Development Corp. v. Borland International Inc.* 49 F.3d 807 (1st Cir 1995), *aff'd per curiam*, 516 U.S. 1167 (1996).

8.   Fame may also arise as a result of the celebrity of a given person or character. With the recent death of Princess Diana of Wales, concern about balancing the right of privacy with the public's right of access to famous people has once again become an issue of international concern. How should the balance be struck between a property right in an individual celebrity's name or likeness and free speech or newsreporting? Do you agree with the lines the courts drew in these situations? Do any of these "marks" qualify as "famous" under Article *6bis*? Should they?

Part VIII

INTERNATIONAL ENFORCEMENT AND REMEDIES

Piracy of copyrighted works has been a problem almost since the invention of the printing press. Many developed nations today have relied at least in part on pirating activities in their early stages of industrial development. Even the United States, which is generally perceived as a stalwart defender of intellectual property rights, in its infancy built its publishing industry at least in part on the pirated works of foreign authors—particularly those of Great Britain. The longstanding nature of the global piracy problem, however, does *not* mean that the problem has remained static or that a certain level of piracy is inevitable and, therefore, acceptable, among the international community (although this latter point is certainly open to debate). Technological advances—which have simultaneously reduced both the time and money needed to engage in piracy—coupled with an increasingly globalized marketplace have made the problem of global piracy an issue of growing divisiveness between developed and developing nations.

The latter part of the Twentieth Century has seen a burgeoning international accord on the fundamental rights granted intellectual property owners.

Despite the existence of minimum international standards for the recognition of intellectual property rights, represented *inter alia* by TRIPS, the Berne Convention, the Patent Cooperation Treaty and the Madrid Union, *enforcement* of those rights remains problematic. In the last decade of the Twentieth Century, industry analysts estimated that lack of enforcement of copyright in computer software alone resulted in hundreds of billions of lost revenues each year. Some developing countries, such as China and Russia, experienced counterfeiting levels of over 90% for IP-based products such as computer software, sound recordings and video discs and cassettes of theatrically-released movies. Lack of enforcement did not result from a single factor. Instead, absence of the rule of law, corruption, lack of efficient judicial enforcement mechanisms, fiscal concerns, and local culture and prejudices all contributed toward a global pirating problem that at times seemed insurmountable.

578

The first major international efforts at combatting this lack of enforcement were directed toward developing an anti-Counterfeiting Code under the auspices of GATT in the late 1970's. First proposed toward the end of the Tokyo Round of Negotiations, the impetus for this Code laid the groundwork for what eventually became the TRIPS Agreement, established during the Uruguay Round of GATT and currently administered by the World Trade Organization (WTO). TRIPS became the first significant multinational IP treaty to establish minimum standards for the *procedures* used to *enforce* intellectual property rights. Backed by the sanctioning power of the WTO, these standards gave rise to concerted efforts by signatory nations (and by non-signatory nations who wished to join the WTO) to perfect their legal systems to meet TRIPS minimum enforcement standards.

Despite the development of these initial minimum enforcement standards, international enforcement mechanisms remain problematic at best. Just as there is no one global culture, there is similarly no single legal mechanism for enforcing intellectual property rights. As you will discover in your readings, international enforcement problems bear certain global similarities. Blanket solutions, however, have generally proven ineffectual. As you examine some of the problems currently faced by IP owners seeking to enforce their rights internationally, ask yourself what workable international enforcement standards are possible in a global environment composed of civil law, common law, rule of virtue, rule of man, and rule of law countries.

Chapter Twenty-Nine

OVERVIEW

A. IF LAWS EXIST, CAN ENFORCEMENT BE FAR BEHIND?

ESTIMATES OF 1995 U.S. LOSSES DUE TO FOREIGN PIRACY AND LEVELS OF FOREIGN PIRACY

Study by the International Intellectual Property Alliance.

Piracy inflicts heavy damage to national economies. Piracy creates a hostile environment for local authors, composers, programmers, publishers and producers in which they cannot be properly rewarded with a return on their investments of creativity, intellect or capital. As local creators are discouraged from creative endeavors, national economies are deprived of tax revenues and revenues and jobs resulting from infrastructure that supports these industries, *e.g.* local distributors, retail, advertising etc. Cultural and technological development is also stunted. Copyright piracy is also a trade barrier.

International firms and investors cannot do business in countries where their copyrighted products are not protected by adequate copyright laws or where enforcement agencies or courts are ineffective.

How Are Piracy Losses Estimated?

The estimated trade losses due to piracy are calculated by IIPA's member associations. These associations estimate losses by using such information as legitimate sales of copyrighted products, sales of hardware (such as VCRs and personal computers), and the estimated sales of unauthorized products. IIPAs member associations gather and compile this information through their staff, representatives and agents worldwide.

The piracy loss figures significantly underestimate the overall impact of piracy because they quantify only the losses suffered by U.S.-based copyright industries, not those inflicted on local creators, publishers and distributors in each country and on third countries creators and companies. Pirate production for export is included in the loss figure for the country of manufacture, not the country of ultimate sale. For example, the recording and music industries report losses estimated at $60 million from sales in Russia of Chinese and Bulgarian CDs. This total is included in the China and Bulgaria loss numbers for recordings and music. As noted, losses to the motion picture industry reflects losses in the home video market and do not include often extensive losses from TV, cable and other piracy involving unauthorized exhibition of audio visual products.

WHAT ARE PIRACY LEVELS?

Piracy levels estimated by IIPA member associations represent the share of a country's market that consists of pirate materials. For example, the business applications piracy level in Thailand is 82%, which means that more than eight of every ten copies of business applications in use in Thailand are pirate products.

Piracy levels provide a more valuable indicator of the scope of a country's piracy problem than piracy losses standing alone. For example, in some countries, piracy levels may be as low as three or four percent indicating that the legal structure and enforcement activities in these countries are relatively effective against piracy. Yet, because of the size of those markets, the loss numbers may be sizable.

Piracy levels present a much clearer picture of the nature and effectiveness of the enforcement climate or the adequacy of copyright legislation. For example, any country with an audio and video piracy rate in excess of twenty-five percent or a software piracy rate in excess of forty percent has unmistakably failed to structure its copyright laws or enforcement system to deal adequately with piracy.

The IIPA and its member organizations focus their efforts on countries where piracy levels run rampant because of inadequate copyright laws and/or a lack of enforcement. For more information on copyright piracy losses and levels, and on the methodology, see www. iipa.org.

WORLDWIDE SOFTWARE PIRACY LOSSES ESTIMATED AT $11.4 BILLION IN 1997
Report by the Software Business Alliance.

STUDY FINDS FOUR IN EVERY TEN BUSINESS APPLICATIONS IS PIRATE COPY

June 16, 1998—Washington, D.C.—The results of a third independent study on global software piracy were released today by the Business Software Alliance (BSA) and the Software Publishers Association (SPA), the two leading trade associations of the software industry. The study estimates that, of the 574 million new business software applications installed globally during 1997, 228 million applications—or four in every ten—were pirated. This represents an increase of two million more new applications being pirated than in 1996.

GLOBAL OVERVIEW

Revenue losses to the worldwide software industry due to piracy were estimated at $11.4 billion. This is a reversal of the 16 percent decrease in estimated losses between 1995 and 1996 that were generally attributed to lower software prices. North America, Asia and Western Europe accounted for the majority (84%) of revenue losses. The top ten countries with the highest dollar losses due to software piracy are (in ranking order) the United States, China, Japan, Korea, Germany, France, Brazil, Italy, Canada and the United Kingdom. Total losses for these countries are $7.8 billion, or 68% of worldwide losses.

REGIONAL SUMMARIES

Asia: Asia continues to be the region with the greatest dollar losses, which totaled $3.9 billion in 1997, up from $3.7 billion in 1996. This increase results from a three percent increase in the number of new business software installations, coupled with a trend toward piracy of more sophisticated and costly applications. The countries with the highest rates were Vietnam (98%), China (96%) and Indonesia (93%). Countries with the highest dollar losses were China ($1.4 billion), Japan ($752 million) and Korea ($582 million).

Eastern Europe: Although dollar losses in Eastern Europe seem relatively low compared to other regions ($561 million in 1997), Eastern Europe continues to be the region with the highest piracy rate. Nearly eight out of ten applications were pirated in 1997. With an overall regional rate of 77% representing only a 3% decline from the previous year—the countries with the highest piracy rates were Bulgaria (93%), the CIS—less Russia (92%), and Russia (89%). Countries with the highest dollar losses in Eastern Europe were Russia ($251 million), Poland ($107 million) and the Czech Republic ($51 million).

Western Europe: The largest dollar losses to software piracy occurred in Germany ($509 million), France ($408 million) and the UK ($335 million). The highest piracy rates were in Greece (73%), Ireland (65%) and Spain (59%). The average piracy rate in Western Europe declined by four percentage points, to 39%.

Latin America: Countries with the largest revenue losses include Brazil ($395 million), Mexico ($133 million) and Argentina ($105 million). These three countries represent 69% of the region's dollar losses, corresponding to the 65% of the business software market these countries represent. While the piracy rate in Latin America declined by six percentage points, more than six out of every ten applications were pirated in the region during 1997 with an overall regional piracy rate of 62%. The countries with the highest piracy rates were El Salvador (89%—still the highest in the region), Bolivia (88%) and Paraguay (87%).

Middle East and Africa: At 65%, this region had the second highest regional piracy rate in the world, even after a 9% decline from 1996. South Africa, Turkey and Israel represent 49% of the monetary losses in the region.

North America: At $3.1 billion, losses to software piracy in North America represent 27% of worldwide losses. The U.S. accounted for $2.7 billion of the North American losses, up from $2.3 billion in 1996. The dollar losses reflect a 28% piracy rate, coupled with a market that represents 43% of the business software in use worldwide.

"This survey shocks the conscience, further illustrating that fighting piracy needs to be elevated to a higher priority. For example, while the average 'inventory shrinkage' (losses from shoplifting and other sources) for the U.S. retail sector is less than 2 percent, the software industry loses 27 percent in the U.S. while worldwide losses average an alarming 40 percent. These losses have serious negative implications well beyond the industry, stealing jobs and hurting customers," said Robert Holleyman, president & CEO of the Business Software Alliance.

"Software piracy continues unabated, and even more sobering is the realization that piracy of educational and entertainment software costs uncounted billions more," said Ken Wasch, president of the Software Publishers Association. "We call on governments around the world to ratify the WIPO Copyright Treaty, which would provide much-needed remedies against software piracy tools, and to rededicate themselves to fighting piracy by and through enforcement and education."

Jointly commissioned by BSA and SPA, this study—like the first two—was conducted by International Planning and Research (IPR). The IPR study evaluated sales data and market information for 82 countries in the six major world regions, and was based on 26 different business applications. Today's study compares 1997 piracy rates to losses in 1994, 1995, and 1996. The complete text—including charts, graphs and methodology—of the 1997 Global Software Piracy Report can be accessed at www.bsa.org or www.spa.org.

Notes and Questions

1. Based on the BSA report excerpted above, which countries appear to pose the greatest threat of piracy? Do these countries share any similarities?

2. Which countries appear to pose the least threat of piracy? Do these countries share any similarities?

3. Although reports by IP owners regarding piracy focus on lost income to the IP owners, does piracy represent lost income to the country where the pirating occurred? For instance, what effects could piracy have on the domestic government's ability to earn revenue through taxation?

4. Pick a country listed in the BSA report and determine whether its piracy levels have risen or fallen. What factors explain the change (if any)?

5. Review the IIAP's methodology for determining levels of piracy. What assumptions are contained in these figures? What effect do these assumptions have on the accuracy of the data contained in this report?

6. Given that piracy is a problem in virtually every country, is piracy inevitable? If so, should a certain level be considered acceptable or at least tolerated?

ROMANIA—INTELLECTUAL PROPERTY: NEW LAW OFFERS COPYRIGHT PROTECTION FOR SOFTWARE

Mark A. Meyer, Information Access Company 1997.

INTRODUCTION

Although Romania constitutes Eastern Europe's second-largest market after Poland, it consistently ranks at the bottom of the barrel when it comes to the use of computers and computer-related products. For example, there are only 200,000 computers in use amongst a population of over 23 million people. That's one computer for every 115 inhabitants. In Romania, only $1.50 per person is spent on computer products. Despite a doubling of the market since 1993, Romania appears not much more attractive to executives in the computer industry. Major software manufacturers, such as Microsoft, have only recently opened up subsidiary offices in the country despite having been established in the rest of Eastern Europe for years. Other computer companies, such as IBM, have been present in Romania since 1995, but not in a significant way.

Romania remains terra incognita to the foreign software industry (75 percent of which is controlled by U.S. companies) for justifiable reasons: the country has been a haven for software pirates for years. The Business Software Alliance ("BSA"), a global industry watchdog, estimates that roughly 93 percent of software used in Romania is pirated; roughly on a par with figures for China, Vietnam, El Salvador, Indonesia and Bulgaria. Until the enactment of Romania's 1996 Copyright Law, Romanian law offered little in the way of protection for software developers. Furthermore, penalties for counterfeiting were relatively small and foreigners trying to take action against software piracy had to do so under local laws since Romania is not a signatory to international conventions covering the recording of copyright material. Even where Romanian legislation provided copyright protection, judicial prejudice against intellectual property rights, procedural inefficiencies in the court system and a dearth of intellectual property attorneys, contributed to a de facto non-recognition of intellectual property rights in Romania.

THE PIRACY PREDICAMENT AND ITS COST

Under such legal indifference, pirating prospered as Microsoft and other foreign and software manufacturers stayed out of the Romanian market. Domestic software developers and manufacturers also suffered. One consequence of software piracy, and one reason why it deters many would-be investors from a particular market, is the long-term effect that piracy has on the process of reinvestment and new product development.

Romania is, by no means, unique to the existence of software piracy and its costs. Nevertheless, the problem is more pronounced in Romania than in many countries of Eastern Europe. Along with the phenomenon of piracy, Romanian society also shares a disproportionate amount of its costs. However, with the country's new Copyright Law (the "Law"), which took effect in June 1996, the situation promises to change.

BRIGHTER DAYS AHEAD: THE 1996 COPYRIGHT LAW

The present Law attempts to modernize the current protective regime and bring it closer to current European Union and World Trade Organization standards. Most copyrighted works normally protected under the laws of EU countries are covered under the Law. Primary works in, among other things, the literary, scientific, artistic, musical, and architectural fields, produced directly by the author, are covered, as are their adaptations, annotations, translations, and anthologies by secondary authors. Databases and other compilations are also protected.

Computer software is given specific protection as a literary work, although the Law does not specifically refer to multimedia works. Protection extends to "any form of expression of a program, application programs and operating systems, regardless of the language used, either in the source or object code, preliminary design material, as well as manuals." Protection, however, does not extend to "ideas, processes, functioning methods, mathematical concepts and principles on which any element of a computer program is based, including those on which computer interfaces are based."

The Law permits a variety of moral and economic rights over copyright material, particularly the right to produce and authorize: (1) the temporary or permanent reproduction of a program in whole or in part, (2) any translation, adaptation, arrangement and any other changes made to a particular program; as well as, (3) the reproduction of the result of these operations. Holders of a copyright may also authorize the distribution, sale or rental of originals or copies of software. Assignment of the right to use software by a particular author does not imply the transfer of a copyright. An agreement to use computer software grants a non-exclusive right to use the product, but a designated user cannot then yield such right to another person.

Limitations to the right of an author include the making of archival or backup copies by an authorized user, so long as the copy is necessary to ensure the proper use of the program. An authorized user may also decompose a software program "for the purpose of determining the ideas and principles on which any element of the computer program is based during any loading, displaying, conversion, transmission or storage of the program." In either case, such rights may not prejudice the copyright holder's right to exploit the work. Other copyright limitations referred to in Chapter 6 of the Law, such as the right to copy a work for a user's "normal circle of family and acquaintances," or for non-profit educational objectives, as well as other limitations, do not apply to computer programs.

Software copyright generally extends to the author of the particular program. However, copyright for software developed by employees within the scope of their employment belongs to the employer in the absence of a contrary agreement. Copyright protection for collective works are usually granted, jointly, to the co-authors. In general, copyright protection is free of formalities and is extended for a term lasting the life of the author plus 50 years. Direct protection, however, extends only to software published in Romania, or published in Romania within 30 days of publication elsewhere. The author must be a Romanian citizen, resident or must maintain an office in the country, in order to receive copyright protection under the Law. Software protected under foreign copyrights must be covered by international or bilateral agreements to which Romania is a signatory. In the absence of such agreements, recognition of foreign-owned copyrights is based on the principal of reciprocity on a country-specific basis.

ENFORCEMENT

The Law provides for tough criminal sanctions for violators of copyright protections, such as prison terms of up to 3 years plus fines of up to 7 million lei. The Courts are also given the right to order the confiscation and destruction of illegal copies of protected software, and the equipment used to make such copies. Injunctions are available in civil cases where copyright infringement is about to take place but has not yet occurred.

The Law also foresees the establishment of a Romanian Copyright Office ("RCO") whose function will be analogous to the State Office for Patents and Trademarks. It is hoped that the RCO staff, in association with the police, court and customs officials will perform on-the-spot investigations of vendors selling protected works in the country.

PRACTICAL CONSIDERATIONS

Proper legal protection is only part of the picture. Along with the introduction of legislation, institutions and concepts needed to make the Law work must also be thought out. First, it will be necessary to distinguish between "professional pirates" who actively violate the Law, and "passive violators" of the Law, most of whom constitute individual, business or institutional users who purchase unauthorized versions of software programs, either because they are unaware that such purchases constitute illegal acts, or because they are not in a financial position to lay down the considerable investment that adherence to the Law requires. The distinction is important because while police measures may be efficacious against "professional pirates," similar measures may be unfeasible or politically undesirable against "passive violators." In a country where the majority of state institutions and private businesses use pirated software, a more graduated approach to enforcement, coupled with educational programs and the commensurate development of an authorized software market may constitute a better course of action.

Judges, prosecutors and police officials must also receive appropriate training so that they may conduct proper investigations and eventual prosecutions of software piracy. The enforcement of software copyright legislation implies an understanding of technical complexities, legal concepts and the use of computers and related products which is virtually non-existent amongst Romanian officials. As a positive development, the European PHARE Program has already begun to finance training programs which will assist institutional training and coordination. The continued funding of such programs by the Romanian government and the international community is central to the success of the country's anti-piracy efforts.

In light of Romania's institutional deficiencies, cooperation between official law enforcement and special interest groups within the software industry is particularly necessary. Because such groups are made up of companies and individuals having extensive knowledge of the industry and of the various forms in which software piracy appears, their efforts can be channeled into anti-piracy campaigns according to the nature, motive, and frequency of the particular pirating activity. Recent reports that Microsoft Romania, in association with Dayna, Oracle, Novell, and others, intends to form a Romanian arm of the BSA, which will monitor and prosecute software piracy in the country, as a positive first step. Finally, educational programs which serve to alert end-users of the advantages of using authorized software may lessen the demand for pirated products. The worldwide BSA organization publishes a Guide to Software Management which provides detailed guidelines by which corporate users may recognize and prevent installation, distribution, and use of illegally obtained copies of software programs. Such publications are extremely useful in Romania, where many users are innocent infringers, and may otherwise be convinced that the technical and legal advantages of using legally obtained software products outweigh the additional price.

FROM THE DARK AGES TO THE INFORMATION AGE

Appropriate legislation and the development of effective educational and law enforcement institutions have provided some success in the continuing fight against software piracy in Western Europe. On the other hand, even Romania's neighbors, most notably Hungary, Poland, Slovakia and the Czech Republic, have enjoyed a lower incidence of software piracy since having passed comprehensive laws and treaties protecting computer software. The introduction of Romania's Copyright Law takes into account the scope of protection recognized as de minimis in the international community and will help weave Romania into the fabric of international copyright and neighboring rights legislation.

Piracy does more than ruin data banks and company reputations. The aim of proper copyright legislation should be to balance the interests of developers, users, and licensees in relation to the use, copying, translation, development, and duplication of software programs. Failure to strike an appropriate balance by providing inadequate protection to the rights of authors in computer programs stifles innovation within the industry and discourages software publishers from entering into potentially lucrative markets. The global software industry has grown over 269 percent over the last 10 years, has generated almost $60 billion in yearly revenues, and currently employs over 600,000 people worldwide. Romania simply cannot afford to do without it. Its absence would deprive

Romania of investment capital and access to software needed to run Romania's institutions and industries into the 21st century.

Notes and Questions

1. Is the enactment of strong laws sufficient to assure adequate enforcement of intellectual property rights? What other steps are required to assure that such rights are enforced? Is a strong judicial system—one that is unbiased and staffed by trained individuals—sufficient?

2. Do Romania's copyright laws as described in the above article comply with Berne and TRIPS requirements?

3. Your client, Business Software Inc., is considering expanding its marketing efforts into Romania. Business Software presently markets under non-exclusive licensing arrangements business applications software for accounting, word processing and spreadsheet applications. What advice would you give regarding the legal risks involved? What steps could Business Software take to improve its changes of protecting its investments in Romania?

4. If enforcement, at least in the initial stages, is always problematic, why should a developing country like Romania bother enacting domestic intellectual property legislation?

IN INDIA, IP FALLS ON HARD TIMES

Pravin Anand, IP Worldwide (May/June 1998).

Many in India are calling it a national calamity. Politicians, voters, and the media are demanding that the government take immediate action.

The supposed "calamity" is a decision taken far away, at the U.S. patent office. On February 12, [1998] according to the popular press, the U.S. PTO granted a patent on basmati rice to a U.S. multinational company.

The U.S. PTO, in fact, did nothing of the sort. But the truth has gotten lost amidst public controversy. The result has been yet another major blow to the Indian public's support of IP rights.

This controversy is part of a larger movement against IP rights in India. For the past three years, these rights have come under attack from many sides. Government officials and legislators, judges and police, counterfeiters and ordinary citizens—all are undermining the IP rights that are supposed to be protected under law.

How has this come about? And what does it mean for the future of IP rights in the world's largest democracy?

It is not new for political powerful groups in India to oppose IP rights. In the past, however, these groups were relatively small and concerned only with patent rights.

Indian courts have come to recognize and enforce the IP rights of foreign companies, even when the issues have been in "gray areas" of the law; and even when this meant ruling against large and powerful Indian defendants. Some rulings may even surpass the rights given to IP owners in developed countries.

In the last two years, the police have made over 50 arrests for violations of copyrights in software. Many arrests have also been made for infringements of film and music industry copyrights. Huge quantities of pirated software, cassettes, CD–ROMs, music CDS and duplicating machines have been seized.

In over 100 enforcement actions, Anton Piller Orders (5) have been granted and huge quantities of infringing goods—such as counterfeit Levis jeans, Kit Kat chocolates, Horlicks biscuits, Sony electronic equipment, Crocin tablets—have been seized from cities all over the country.

The Business Software Alliance has sent out over 100 cease and desist letters to top Indian companies, banks, public sector undertakings, etc., alleging end-user piracy of computer software. This has resulted in large scale purchases of legitimate software.

In every area of IP rights—be it trademarks, copyrights, or patents—wrongdoers were either in trouble or knew that they soon would be. But as the strength of IP rights grew, it produced a backlash, and other groups joined the IDMA's fight against IP rights.

COUNTER-REVOLUTION BEGINS

The backlash began when some sought to extend patent rights to plant varieties. Farmers expressed concern, and pundits spoke of the indigenous people's right to control their traditional genetic resources. These people were joined by others who feared that the growth of multinational corporations in India would harm domestic industry. As a result of these groups' political might, India has not joined the UPOV Convention (6) or enacted laws to grant patent rights in plants.

Over the past three years, as the protections have increased for all types of IP rights, the opposition has no longer been directed solely to patent laws. For the first time, there has also been a major reaction against trademark and copyright protections.

Places known for piracy and counterfeiting have developed strong trade associations. For example, software raids in Nehru Place in Delhi strengthened the computer association, which started to fight back at every raid. Members of the association have developed an effective network of communications to warn each other of raids; they have, for instance, put informants in parking lots, police stations, and even in courts.

The raids against counterfeit trademark jeans in Gandhi Nagar have produced the Gandhi Nagar Association, which has also strongly resisted enforcement efforts. On several occasions the Association even manhandled senior officials of the Delhi High Court and forcibly taken back a good part of the seized property.

Other, more legitimate businesses are also working together to fight against IP rights. For instance, India's pharmaceutical companies have formed the National Working Group on Patent Laws. This Institute works to counter the growth and enforcement of IP rights.

Government Hostility to IP

Many legislators, police, and judges have also turned against IP rights. Members of Parliament, for instance, have created a forum for reexamining IP rights and the implications of TRIPS.

Many police have been influenced to believe that the owners of IP rights are large, multinational companies that are trying to bully legitimate Indian traders. This has definitely harmed efforts to enforce the country's IP laws. For example, some police have displayed printed lists of their enforcement priorities that do not indicate protecting IP rights is a priority.

In some areas, the police are known to act in ways that leak information to infringers. This can have devastating effects on enforcement. At Brigade Road at Bangalore, many software pirates are concentrated within a few hundred yards. But if the pirates know when a raid is coming, the pirates simply refuse to sell infringing goods to decoy customers, and the enforcement efforts come to naught.

Groups of judges have begun resisting the enforcement of IP rights. The judges assert technical grounds, such as lack of jurisdiction or a party's failure to pay court fees, even where these technicalities are clearly satisfied. Practicing IP lawyers can see this trend and are frustrated by it, but they have been unable to change the judges' mindset.

These developments have made enforcement of IP rights most difficult. Unfortunately, there is absolutely no political will to reverse these developments, or even to provide some sort of stability in the area of IP protection. A bill to amend the existing trademark law was introduced in 1994 but it lapsed because of the premature dissolution of the Parliament. The same fate befell the Patent Amendment Bill, which would have amended India's patent law to bring it into conformity with TRIPS.

The Basmati outrage

Two recent developments have exacerbated the situation, giving ammunition to those who argue that IP is a tool used by foreigners to exploit Indians.

First, on December 5, 1997, the WTO ruled that India has to amend its patent system in order to comply with TRIPS.(8) This does not sit well with Indian nationalists.

Then, on February 12, came the Basmati decision. This supposedly granted a U.S. company patent rights to a variety of rice called "basmati," which is grown only in India and Pakistan.

News of this decision was splashed over all the leading newspapers and provoked much public outrage. The government was accused of having sold out the country to the developed nations; by joining agreements such as TRIPS, the government allowed foreigners to walk away with patent rights over something as Indian as basmati rice.

In reality, the decision did not grant the Americans a patent for basmati rice. The patent was for a new variety of rice that had been derived from basmati rice and American long grain rice. The patent acknowledges that basmati rice originates in India or Pakistan, and claims rights only in a new plant which is semi-dwarf, photo-period-insensitive, has rice grains with the peculiar characteristics of traditional basmati, (9) but without some of the negative qualities of basmati. The patent also concerns the seed and the rice grains from such a plant and a method of determining the quality of the rice using a unit of measure known as the starch index.

The Rice Growers Association, comprising basmati growers in India and Pakistan, may have a good case on geographical indications if a third party were to refer to this American rice by the name "basmati." However, this would be a purely private dispute between an association and an individual company. It would be the same as if someone in India were to use the word "Scotch" on an Indian whiskythat would be a private dispute between the Scotch Whisky Association and the Indian wrongdoer.

Unfortunately, this reality has been lost in the public uproar. The hype has left newspapers claiming that the decision is a national tragedy and that the Indian Government should immediately take the U.S. to WTO.

The country needs to create a more balanced system of IP protection that is TRIPS-compliant.

For instance, the courts should be allowed to grant cross-undertakings and award damages against a plaintiff who wrongfully obtains an Anton Piller order. Because there are no such safeguards now, some judges prefer to simply deny Anton Piller relief, even in the most deserving cases.

COSTS AND BENEFITS OF INTELLECTUAL PIRACY
Boris Kargalitsky, The Moscow Times (June 6, 1997).

Several months ago it seemed the market for pirate software was stagnant. Several shipments of Chinese-made disks had been held up at customs and the OMON had raided the Gorbushka market and other selected markets for pirated products. The choice of wares was poorer, and people were gloomy. But not long ago, I once again visited Gorbushka and was simply amazed. The choice was enormous. For $4 or $5, you can buy everything from the latest issue of British Multimedia Encyclopedia to the newest version of IBM and Microsoft operating systems.

Piracy in Russia is not considered an unworthy affair, and the producers themselves are not always interested in defending their rights. Many programming products could not be widely distributed without the help of pirates. Piracy has given rise to not only tens but perhaps hundreds of thousands of new jobs.

Microsoft and other Western corporations complain about multimillion-dollar losses. But the complaints of Western computer monopolies against Russian, Bulgarian and Chinese piracy are, to put it mildly, not entirely sincere. Representatives from the firms estimate the number of their programs that are bought from pirates and count what their profits would be if these programs had been legally obtained. It is on this basis that they calculate their "losses." In fact, most of these programs could simply not be sold at official prices. And this is not only because the consumer does not have the money, but because the firm itself does not have a developed dealer network and market infrastructure in this country.

And Microsoft's leaders understand this full well. It's no accident that this super-monopoly, penetrating the market of a new country, shows relative indifference toward the "pirate" copying of its product. The pirates get hold of a new territory and are the first to generate demand for the product. It is only later, after the pirates have done their work, that Microsoft unexpectedly remembers its losses. In Eastern Europe, the "peaceful coexistence" between Western firms and pirates ended three to four years ago. In Russia, the battle has only begun, since the market is far from mastered.

Attempts have been made to explain to the public that stealing is bad, and by buying pirated material, we become something like fences. The majority of consumers in poor countries, however, don't have any alternative. In Russia or China, families must save up for years to buy a computer. There is no use preaching sermons about morality. It is like trying to forbid a hungry person from taking a piece of bread without asking. Since there is no state money to combat piracy, defending intellectual property inevitably relies on prohibitive legislation. But a conflict arises between defending property rights and human rights. Anyone can become a pirate by simply copying a program for a friend. New technologies allow for sending programs through electronic mail. In order to prevent such uncontrolled and widespread piracy, a system of strict control over the movement of information is needed.

It is not surprising that the Internet has become not only a global information network but a knot of contradictions. Attempts are being made to establish censorship over it. Since last year, the Chinese government has forced its users to send their communications only through special ports and filters that are under the authorities' control. Special systems of filtration and censorship have been worked out by Saudi Arabia, Bahrein, Iran and Vietnam. France is trying to limit the use of English on its "national cyberspace." In the United States, Germany and Japan, legislators are constantly fighting against "indecent" material on the electronic network. Last year, the State Duma drafted a law that contained a detailed list of the "kinds of information that are allowed for export abroad."

Against the background of government attempts at control and filtration, large monopolies in the West—above all Microsoft—continue their attempts to turn the Internet into an arena for their own commercial expansion. All this arouses friendly opposition on the part of its users.

In order to solve the contradictions that are arising from the development of a global information space, what is needed are not prohibitive measures but laws that are set up to defend the interests of users and researchers. But their interests are essentially opposed to those of large Western firms that are monopolizing the information market.

Notes and Questions

1. In addition to the practical problems of expense, training and corruption, enforcement of foreign intellectual property rights may raise the ire of the local populace. Are there steps foreign IP owners can take to reduce these problems, short of ignoring local piracy?

2. Assume that you have been elected to the legislature of a developing country which currently has a limited industrial base, cannot grow enough food to feed its population, and has nearly 60% illiteracy. Your country has adopted TRIPS-compliant intellectual property statutes but has little enforcement of the rights granted under those statutes. What percentage of your national budget would you allocate to alleviating the problem of lack of IPR enforcement? Are there defensible reasons for allocating *any* monies to this problem? For example, what impact could enforcing intellectual property rights have on economic development? On legal systems development? Use your answers to formulate a convincing argument on behalf of a foreign IP owner as to why intellectual property rights should be strongly protected.

3. You represent a foreign manufacturer who desires to build a manufacturing plant in a developing country. In order to build and run this plant your client will be utilizing trade secret know-how and patented technology. What guarantees would you recommend that your client require regarding the enforcement of its intellectual property rights before it agreed to construct and operate such a plant?

4. In addition to pursuing legal remedies against pirates, many companies also use publicity and educational programs to educate people regarding the importance of intellectual property rights. Assume your client is a large software manufacturer who has discovered that its product is being pirated in China. What is the most persuasive argument you can make to convince the local consumer that piracy is harmful to his interests. What methods would you use to spread this message to the public? School programs? Flyers? Concerts?

B. IS THE ENFORCEMENT OF INTELLECTU- AL PROPERTY RIGHTS SOLELY TO BEN- EFIT DEVELOPED COUNTRIES?

THE IMPACT OF FOREIGN INVESTMENT ON INDIGENOUS CULTURE: AN INTELLECTUAL PROPERTY PERSPECTIVE

Doris Estelle Long, 23 N.C. J. Int'l L. & Com. Reg. 229 (1998).

During the late twentieth century, culture has become "big busi-ness." From eco-tourism to cultural tours and souvenir artifacts, culture has been transformed into a commodity that can be merchandised and sold across international borders. This "commodification" of culture is part of a larger trend—the emergence of a global marketplace and the resulting drive by newly industrialized countries to develop an industrial and commercial base in order to participate in this marketplace. These trends impose a growing need for developing countries to seek foreign investment, in both capital and technology, in order to face the economic challenges of the coming century. Increasingly, the ability to attract such foreign investment is tied to the protection of so-called "intellectual property rights," including patents, copyrights, trademarks and trade secrets. Newly industrialized countries are faced with mounting refusals by multinational corporations to enter into joint investment or research-development deals without the assurance of "adequate protection" for the technology the multinational corporations are expected to provide. Such "adequate protection" generally includes the enactment and subse-quent enforcement in the developing countries of laws protecting intel-lectual property rights—laws which are heavily influenced by or modeled on U.S. or European systems. The conflict between developed and developing countries over the enforcement of intellectual property rights is one of the most divisive legal issues of the latter twentieth century. Despite the accession of over 111 countries to the Agreement on Trade–Related Aspects of Intellectual Property Rights (TRIPS), global piracy and the efforts required to eradicate it remain key areas of dispute.

Developing countries cannot survive without becoming active partic-ipants in the global marketplace. Such participation, fueled largely by foreign investment, often places the culture and heritage of developing countries on a collision course with the global consumer culture of the more powerful developed countries. The commodification and de-culturi-zation of native and indigenous culture that results from such a collision is supported, and may even be enhanced, by the intellectual property protection regimes enacted by the developing countries at the behest of foreign investors. Although the purpose of such laws is usually seen through the narrow prism of protecting the technological investment of foreign multinationals, present international protection standards do not require such a view. To the contrary, despite the potential for misuse in supporting the commodification and de-culturization of native and indigenous culture, properly crafted and enforced intellectual property laws may not only meet the protection demands of foreign investors but can actually shield a country's cultural heritage against the leveling forces of globalizing de-culturization. Using the protection norms of the Berne and Paris Conventions, as refined by TRIPS, developing countries can craft a protection regime that would provide protection for such critical cultural elements as folklore, ritual, costumes, and folk medicine. Focusing on copyright as the primary tool for inhibiting unauthorized de-culturization of cultural works, these regimes would recover cultural works by redefining the scope of public domain elements and establishing organizations to administer these newly expanded rights. A careful balance is required to avoid imposing too high a cost for the creation of new works using protected elements and to avoid the threat of harmful censorship. Native culture must not only be protected by such laws, but must also be allowed to flourish. Thus, too strict an application of the laws could destroy (through stagnation) the very culture the law was designed to protect. Appropriately crafted moral rights, trademark, patent, and trade secret laws should be enacted to support these efforts. In addition to serving as a cultural shield, strong intellectual property protection may positively affect the variety of domestically-created products available for consumption. With the assurance of a sufficient economic return granted under such laws, native authors and artists will have greater incentive to spend the time, money and effort to create new products for a growing marketplace. Where legitimate channels of distribution are protected, problems of scarcity and inconsistent supply may be eliminated, further expanding the available pool of products and services. In order to assure that these positive developments are not purchased at the price of the destruction of the country's native and indigenous culture, however, laws must be created with the dual roles of promotion of economic growth and protection of culture firmly in mind. The secret is in creating an acceptable set of intellectual property laws that meet these twin goals. It is not an easy task, but for developing countries, it may well be a matter of cultural survival.

"BOLLYWOOD" CALLS CUT OVER VIDEO PIRACY
Agence France Presse (August 18, 1998).

Production in India's film capital Bombay ground to a halt Tuesday as movie industry workers from stars to clapper boys went on strike over video piracy, shutting down the city's 150 cinemas.

About 1,000 protesting actors, actresses, technicians and studio hands took part in a motorised demonstration through Bombay that ended with a mass rally to demand tough action against video piracy by cable television channels.

The protestors halted outside the offices of two major cable television operators to denounce a practice they said was killing the industry.

"Within a couple of days of the release of a film, it is shown over the cable television network. At this rate cinema houses will have no patrons," said G.P. Shirke, chairman of the Film Makers Combine.

"In some cases, pirated cassettes of the films are in circulation even before the formal release of the movie," Shirke said.

Film industry leaders set up an anti-video piracy organisation several years ago, but have had little success.

One industry spokesman who asked not to be identified said anti-piracy measures had failed because a large number of police were on the payroll of the city's four major cable networks.

Some cable operators hit back at the protestors, complaining that they were being unfairly targeted.

"There are 40,000 cable television operators all over India. If some of them screen pirated cassettes smuggled in from overseas it is unfair to damn the entire cable television industry," said cable television operator Ashok Mansukhani.

India is the world's largest film producer, churning out 900 films a year. The country has 13,000 movie theatres, with a daily audience of around 20 million.

BLOODSHED AND TERROR IN BOLLYWOOD– A TRUE STORY
Manjeet Kripalani, Business Week September 8, 1997.

It had all the ingredients of a Hindi movie blockbuster—religion, glamour, underworld dons, and a rags-to-riches hero—except it was for real. On Aug. 12, Gulshan Kumar, a film producer and millionaire businessman, was assassinated as he was leaving a temple north of Bombay. According to police, he was a victim of extortion by the local mafia led by underworld don Dawood Ibrahim, and he refused to pay. Kumar is the third film personality this year to be killed by an increasingly powerful underworld. His murder has sent producers, financiers, and stars of India's $750 million-a-year film industry scurrying into hiding.

The murders have highlighted the range of problems facing one of India's most dynamic sectors. "Bollywood" produces some 750 films annually, making it one of the major movie industries of the world. But India's tinseltown is increasingly hobbled by bloody relations with mob lenders, runaway production costs, high taxes, and threats from video piracy. "The industry is scared," says Amit Khanna, founder of Plus Channel Ltd., which produces films, music, and TV programs in Bombay.

The most pressing issue is the industry's links to loan sharks and mobsters, who have bankrolled about 60% of Bollywood's production with loans carrying interest rates of around 40%. As a hodgepodge of small independent operators, the industry has found it difficult to find cheaper, legitimate sources of funding. The Indian government's list of officially recognized industries includes steelmaking and textile weaving, but not filmmaking. An industry that wins this recognition requires a license to operate but gets access to cheaper electric rates and institutional lending at 18%. The risky nature of films has made banks reluctant to make loans, leaving the field wide open to the underworld. For the dons, filmmaking became a good place to invest undeclared income and fraternize with starlets.

To compound the industry's woes, the cost of filmmaking is exploding. A star-studded, big-budget film that cost $1 million to produce three years ago now costs twice as much, because Indians increasingly exposed to TV with Western programs are demanding better quality and more exotic locales. Even filmmakers such as Prakash Jha, who makes low-budget art films such as Death by Hanging that have won critical acclaim outside India, find that costs have shot up twentyfold in the past six years, to $200,000 per film. PIRATES, TOO. Yet once a film gets made, it has an 80% chance of flopping at the box office. When that happens, the distributors and cinema owners, who have paid big up-front guarantees to the producers, lose their money. To top it off, grumble distributors, state governments levy taxes on tickets, up to 150% in some states, higher than anywhere in the world.

Ticket prices in major cities have risen tenfold in 10 years, to up to $3—high for a country where movies are normally cheap. The Indian audience is unwilling to be the guinea pig for new, less expensive screen talent. So the demand for superstars is high, with 500 producers chasing the top 25 Indian stars and paying top dollar.

Video piracy is another problem. Cable operators easily and illegally get new films days after their release, killing the film in the theaters. So producers have to go to great lengths to protect copyrights. When Rajshri Productions released its family hit Hum Aap Ke Hain Kaun? ("Who Am I to You?") in 1994, employees kept a 24–hour vigil on the film reels, even sleeping in projection rooms in cinemas throughout India. Since they could only see the movie in theaters, audiences came in droves, making the film a record-breaking $35 million hit at the box office.

COCA-COLA SHARE DEMANDED

Facts on File World News Digest, August 20, 1977.

Industry Minister George Fernandes Aug. 8 demanded that the Coca–Cola Co. of the U.S. transfer the formula of its manufacturing process to India and turn over a 60% share of its wholly-owned American subsidiary to Indian shareholders, or cease operations in the country. The government set April 1978 as the deadline for compliance.

Speaking in Parliament, Fernandes charged that Coca–Cola's operations in India in the past 20 years "furnish a classic example of how a mutinational corporation operating in a low-priority, high-profit area in a developing country attains runaway growth." He said the firm had extracted up to 400% profit from Indian-franchised bottlers.

The government, Fernandes said, had rejected a company offer to reduce the foreign equity share to 40% under certain conditions. The terms called for Coca–Cola to be permitted to retain "quality control" of the beverage and a liaison office in India to protect the "trade secrets" of the formulation of its soft drink.

MULTINATIONALS IN INDIA; NO FIZZ WITHOUT FUSS

The Economist, August 20, 1977.

The Indian government's row with Coca–Cola is one of several it is having with foreign companies. Foreign companies have to reduce their equity stake in their Indian operations to between 40% (in low-priority areas) and 74% (exports and high technology).

Coca–Cola is willing to form an Indian company in which its equity will be reduced to 40%. But it wants to retain 100% of a company controlling quality and guarding the secrets of its formula. The government has said no and threatened to pinch the brand name. There seems little chance of a compromise. Coca–Cola's import licence for raw materials has not been renewed, and its factory has had to shut down.

IBM similarly proposed creating two companies: one would have 40% of its equity foreign-owned and would run IBM data centres in India. The second, fully foreign-owned, would produce $10m-worth of data-processing equipment entirely for export, and also service imported computers.

In theory the government can permit 100% foreign ownership for a project exporting its entire output, but in practice has never done so. The odds are that it will reject IBM's formula, leaving the company to Indianise or quit.

The intention is not to hound multinationals out of the country but to push them into export and high-technology projects. It has yielded mixed results. Union Carbide has shifted from making dry cell batteries for the home market to shrimp fishing for the export market. And India Tobacco, a subsidiary of Imperial Tobacco, has also branched into shrimp fishing, and into luxury hotels (catering for foreign tourists) and paper.

The vast majority of foreign firms are going ahead with equity dilution. But most complain that the state controller of capital issues is forcing them to offer shares to the public at an artificially low rate. Cadbury was permitted a nominal premium of 10% over par value, and its share issue was oversubscribed 15 times.

INTELLECTUAL PROPERTY IN THE DEVELOPING WORLD: CHALLENGES AND OPPORTUNITIES

Economic Perspectives, May 1998.
http://www.usis-israel.org.il/publish/journals/economic/may98/ipclip.htm.

In the wake of the TRIPS agreement and the rapid globalization of the world economy, there is a growing consensus among developed and developing countries alike that intellectual property protection is a vital component of economic development and prosperity. However, the degree to which intellectual property standards are being strengthened in practical terms differs from place to place—and often varies considerably even within a given country.

The editors of Economic Perspectives asked five intellectual property experts with recent experience in the developing world to share their observations and experiences about the challenges and opportunities for promoting intellectual property there. The views they have expressed are their own.

Ralph Oman: Sri Lanka is a very special country with a bright future.

Sri Lanka has a long tradition of folk poetry and authorship, and its contemporary writers have unique stories to tell. I actually met and talked with Romesh Gunesekera, who was a 1994 Booker Prize nominee. He told me that he was both proud and thankful that strong copyright protection for his books already exists in Sri Lanka. Its literature, poetry, architecture, art, and music all represent a high level of artistic achievement. The future of Sri Lanka's ceramics industry is also promising—a future that will depend increasingly on copyright protection. The same is true for the needlework and textile design industry. And Sri Lanka's computer wizards are already writing software for the world market. Some of the best known international companies are waiting in the wings, ready to make major investments in Sri Lanka once it gets its intellectual property laws in order.

Even with these bright spots, however, piracy of software, motion pictures, and music continues, and this activity hurts Sri Lankan creators far more than it hurts foreign companies. While foreigners lose some money to pirating, they always have access to other markets. On the other hand, Sri Lankan creators have fewer alternatives, and piracy destroys their livelihood. Without copyright protection, a Sri Lankan computer programmer has problems on two levels. First, she cannot compete against a cheap, pirated version of an American software package. Second, even if she could get her program published, she could not stop her own countrymen from stealing her work. Just as bad money chases good money out of the marketplace, pirated products displace legitimate products, whatever their nationality. So Sri Lankan creators can't pay the rent and feed their children. That is bad for them, bad for the country, and bad for world trade.

Copyright gives creative men and women—and the companies that hire them—strong incentives to invest time and money in the creation of books, software, movies, art, and music. A copyright expert from Ghana put it this way: "Why plant the field if someone else can harvest the crop?" In an environment of strong copyright protection, music, literature, art, and science can flourish.

A new copyright law in Sri Lanka would recognize that there is no future in piracy. Pirates are low-tech parasites. A Sri Lankan software company that designs custom-tailored programs for the needs of Sri

Lanka and its businesses will give Silicon Valley a run for its money— but only if its software is protected. And this local enterprise will pay taxes, and it will employ far more people, at better pay, and in technologically far more sophisticated and satisfying jobs, than a back-room copy shop whose stock in trade is pirated computer diskettes. In a non-pirate market, the Sri Lankan software will drive down the price of the foreign software. That is how competition works.

One of Sri Lanka's best-known motion picture directors, Vishwaneth Keerthisera, has a real problem competing with pirated videocassettes. At a recent awards ceremony where he was honored for one of his films, he said: "My biggest award will be my ability to show it to a full cinema hall. If I can draw the audience to see my film, that's my real award."

The same is true on the patent side of the shop. Without strong protection, inventors cannot find the financial backing they need to commercialize their innovative ideas. The Sri Lankan inventor P.N. Nandadasa developed an environmentally friendly packaging technique using coconut husks, and, with his patent in hand, he has made it a commercial success. With international patent protection, his idea should really take off.

Sri Lanka has decided to upgrade its intellectual property laws. With these changes, it will establish itself as a leader in intellectual property protection, as an example to its neighbors, and as an avid booster of its own talented people. With a strong regime for protecting authors and inventors, Sri Lanka will stand out as an attractive target for foreign investment in this year of her golden jubilee, and for many years to come.

Salli A. Swartz: While Madagascar has, on paper, one of the most complete intellectual property laws I have ever reviewed, along with an established government office for the protection of artists' rights, there remains a certain level of misunderstanding concerning the concept of ownership of intellectual property rights and the corresponding obligation to obtain authorization and remit payment for the use of music and movie rights.

For example, I learned that certain television stations often purchased videos of well-known American or French movies and played them over the air. An attorney who represented one private television station stated that he was unaware of the obligation to pay royalties and indicated that he did not know to whom such royalties should be paid and how to pay them. I discovered that Madagascar has no movie theaters, and as a result, videotapes of popular movies are often shown in public places. One person I met expressed the concern that if royalties had to be paid, the public videotape showings would stop and children instead would go unattended in the street. Another attorney explained that many judges were unaware of the country's intellectual property law. Even when they were alerted to the law's contents, they hesitated to apply it.

Yet the consequences of lax intellectual property enforcement were already being felt. I was told that several Malagasy recording artists were extremely frustrated over their inability to collect royalties when their songs were played over the radio. Certain had reportedly already left Madagascar, and others were seriously considering leaving the country.

Steven Robinson: Vietnam, in the area of intellectual property rights and in many others areas, is the mass of contradictions I had been told to expect. Still, it was impossible for me to come out of this smart, friendly and industrious country without optimism for it. The current environment for intellectual property and information law in Vietnam is, basically, a demonstration on the national level of why intellectual property rights are also referred to generically as "economic rights." A growing number of entrepreneurs owe their success, in part, to the adoption and use of trademarks, which are legally protected under the law of Vietnam. But infringements of successful and well-known marks are rampant, and enforcement is lacking. There is also a growing software industry in Vietnam. Yet despite legal protection for copyrights in software and in other works, pirated software is everywhere.

One is often told that Vietnam is different and that principles of intellectual property rights that have served the development of other national economies are inapplicable here. But the observation is misleading, and for large sections of the economy, simply untrue.

First, it is worthwhile looking to La Vie, the established brand leader in Vietnam for bottled water and the ongoing target of multiple, flagrant infringements of its trademark and trade dress. In the North, where infringing bottles are ubiquitous, anyone asking for a bottle of La Vie is likely to be given a bottle labeled La Vi, Le Vile, Le Vu, La Vio Le, or the better known La Ville and La Villa, all of which sport carefully detailed imitations of La Vie's label design and bottle decoration. In a class of about 100 law students I taught in mid-April, the entire class, without exception, had at one time or another been sold a bottle of water that infringed La Vie's trademark, trade dress, or both.

La Vie became the market leader because it meets or exceeds the requirements for water purity set by the government of Vietnam. The company places an analysis of the mineral content on the side panel of its bottle. Its competitors are not so detail oriented. Despite the company's ongoing, well-publicized efforts, the enforcement of La Vie's trademark rights has been spotty at best, and often the same group of infringers who stop using one imitation of La Vie will simply start up again using another. As trademark attorneys everywhere will attest, there is nothing like success to inspire infringement. But in this case, the frequency of confusing imitation is not simply a matter of measuring damages for trademark infringement, there are additional, important public health considerations and related public costs.

A second example is a Ho Chi Minh City software developer whose company launched its first mass market application, a Vietnamese language product, and sold 5,000 copies. The CEO also estimates that there are 60,000 pirated copies of the program in circulation in Vietnam. The copyright interest in software, as well as in other forms of work typically protected by copyright, exists under the law of Vietnam. But again, enforcement is lacking.

On this basis, the case for optimism about intellectual property rights in Vietnam may not be obvious. However, these examples show that economic forces that support wider recognition and respect for intellectual property are at work in Vietnam. Notwithstanding an ineffective enforcement environment, La Vie has been able to establish national recognition for its brand of bottled water. Consumers now routinely rely on the La Vie name in making purchasing decisions. In the second case, so many people were willing to pay more for an authorized copy of domestically produced software that the developer could break even, even in the face of widespread piracy.

Enforcement of intellectual property has lagged because it is only now becoming a priority. Less than 10 years ago, there was hunger in Vietnam, and in some areas the memory of that time remains fresh. In those days, most people's economic interests were simply too fundamental to permit considerations of intellectual property rights to be a factor. A sale, any sale, whether of a genuine brand name item or a counterfeit, of an authorized copy of software or a pirated version, meant food for a family. Simply put, in a subsistence economy, intellectual property rights are a luxury.

But that time is now history. Today, Vietnam is one of the largest exporters of rice in the world. In such a climate, intellectual property rights are increasingly recognized as important and, for some, as essential tools for continued development.

In 1996, Vietnam instituted a new Civil Code that provides substantial protections for intellectual property rights. In June 1997, Vietnam signed a bilateral copyright agreement with the United States in which it promised to recognize the rights of copyright owners from the United States whose works were published or distributed in Vietnam. The basic intellectual property rights are now in place, and there is general recognition that Vietnam's next set of intellectual property challenges lies in enforcement.

Substantial reform is needed. Right holders must be assured that there is a regular mechanism, whether through administrative agencies, the courts, or both, to enjoin infringements and award damages, and to resolve ownership disputes and other matters. At present, the press describes officials dealing with infringements as "requesting" that the offending activity cease. Effective enforcement will begin as soon as these "requests" are replaced with lawful orders from the proper authorities requiring that intellectual property rights violations stop on pain of meaningful civil, criminal, and administrative penalties.

The incentive to undertake such reforms seems likely to develop as the consumer goods, media, entertainment, and publishing industries grow and make a greater contribution to Vietnam's economy. In 1994, the courts of Vietnam issued their first judgment ever in favor of a copyright infringement plaintiff, a Ho Chi Minh City composer, arranger, and performer, and the court awarded damages. By the standards of developed economies, the damages were negligible, but a precedent was set. In short, now that intellectual property rights are having greater economic impact, there is reason to think that a consensus for the political, administrative, and legal reforms necessary to improve enforcement will grow. In the programs I taught, participants asked more questions about how the government's enforcement efforts could be improved than about any other single topic.

In sum, Vietnamese experience with intellectual property is beginning to look like that of other market economies. That is good news, because it means that Vietnam can draw on the experience of other countries in developing its system of intellectual property rights protection and enforcement. It also means that the lessons learned in the development of Vietnam's intellectual property rights infrastructure may provide important insights as to how and when this vital area of law can play a part in the economic development of other countries.

Notes and Questions

1. What are the common disadvantages evident in the foregoing articles that a developing country might suffer from protecting intellectual property rights?

2. What benefits might be obtained from protecting intellectual property rights? Has TRIPS been designed to achieve these ends?

3. What is the strongest argument you can make in favor of strong IP enforcement? What is the strongest argument you can make against such enforcement? Select a country other than the United States. Do your arguments address their specialized concerns or are there other political or cultural issues that you need to address? What are they?

4. Despite the strong role that intellectual property protection plays in investment decisions, other factors may also impact a foreign company's decisions to invest in a foreign country including the size of the potential market. In 1993 in a UN sponsored study analyzing the role of IP protection in foreign investment, the author concluded: that decisions to invest abroad are based in part on the strength of IP protection, and in part on the perceived size of the exploitable market. TRANSNATIONAL CORPORATIONS AND MANAGEMENT DIVISIONS OF THE UN DEPARTMENT OF ECONOMIC AND SOCIAL DEVELOPMENT: INTELLECTUAL PROPERTY RIGHTS AND FOREIGN DIRECT INVESTMENT, UN Doc. ST/CTC/SER A/24 (Carlos M. Correa ed, 1993).

C. CAN INTELLECTUAL PROPERTY RIGHTS BE ENFORCED WITHOUT ADOPTING "WESTERN" LEGAL VALUES?

Read the following Articles from TRIPS from the Supplement: 41, 61, 63.

Notes and Questions

1. Does TRIPS require that signatories adopt a common law system where judicial decisions must be based on legal precepts established by previous decisions, and where such previous decisions have a binding, precedential effect?

2. Does TRIPS require that enforcement of rights be ensured through the creation of specialized intellectual property courts? Could a country meet its TRIPS obligations by enforcing IP rights through administrative tribunals where no court or judicial intervention or appeal is allowed or contemplated?

3. You represent Hot Music Company, which produces, manufactures and distributes CDs of the hot new music sensation IP Wright. It is also the sole copyright owner of all music on these CDs, and of Wright's performance. Hot Music has begun to market its CDs in Malaysia and has discovered that pirated versions of Wright's music are already being widely distributed in that country. If you were to attempt to protect the music's (and Wright's) intellectual property rights in Malaysia, what are the minimum procedural rights you would hope were provided to assure effective enforcement of your client's intellectual property rights? What are the minimum remedies you would want to be available under local law?

4. If you were a defendant in any IPR enforcement proceeding, what are the minimum procedural safeguards you would hope to find?

5. *Transparency.* One of the more difficult issues in enforcing intellectual property rights internationally is the problem of "secret" laws or procedures governing the right to relief. One key concept of the "rule of law" is the need for applicable law, statutes and regulations to be "transparent"—in effect, to be publicly available so that the general public can determine what the rules are, and conform their conduct accordingly. Article 63 of TRIPS requires such transparency. How would you define transparency requirements under TRIPS? Is a law transparent if it is kept on file with a government agency so that the public can view the law by visiting such agency? Must a law be "published" to be transparent? Must it be translated into English? Placed on the Internet?

6. *Rule of Man.* Some countries have a political/legal system which is based *not* on "Rule of Law" but on "Rule of Man." Rule of Man systems may vary in their details but they generally share the attribute that determination of rights, and what is lawful, is governed by the sole discretion of one or more individuals who have absolute discretion in deciding such matters.

7. *Rule of Virtue.* Some countries have a political/legal system which is based on the Rule of Virtue. Under such systems, written transparent laws and regulations are not needed because each member of society is presumed to know what conduct qualifies as virtuous (legal) and to conform their conduct accordingly.

8. *Rule by Law.* Some countries have a political/legal system which is governed by laws. Such laws are publicly available, but may not be based on moral authority, since they have been enacted by a few individuals who hold power through the threat of force.

9. *Rule of Law*. Some countries have a political/legal system which is governed by laws that are publicly available (transparent), and which are enforced by unbiased fact-finding in a predictable manner, solely on the basis of evidence, in a proceeding which allows both parties to participate meaningfully in the process, and which grants effective relief in a fair manner.

ENFORCING INTELLECTUAL PROPERTY RIGHTS IN RUSSIA REMAINS PROBLEMATICAL

Michael Solton, Russia and Commonwealth Business
Law Report, January 29, 1997.

It is now generally recognized that in the past four years Russia has succeeded in creating a system of modern intellectual property (IP) laws, which are, for the most part, consistent with that country's multilateral and bilateral international obligations. However, as Russia prepares to join the World Trade Organization (WTO), and as more and more private businesses venture into the vast and dynamic, albeit unruly, Russian market, the issues of adequate enforcement of IP rights become increasingly important.

According to the announcement of the U.S. Trade Representative-designate Charlene Barchefsky made on December 20, 1996, Russia remains on U.S.TR's "watch list" of countries being monitored for failure to provide adequate protection for U.S. IP rights.

Some of the major concerns of U.S. businesses, big and small, with respect to enforcement of IP rights in Russia may be summarized as follows:

The existing civil court and arbitration court systems are inadequate to address complex IP issues. Most Russian judges lack the necessary training and experience, and the resources allocated to the judicial system are extremely limited.

The failure to create the Supreme Patent Chamber, mandated by the Russian patent and trademark statutes, deprives patent and trademark owners of a specialized forum for adjudication of IP disputes.

There is a lack of coordination among various enforcement agencies in implementing enforcement procedures in accordance with IP laws.

Corruption and organized crime are still viewed as a major obstacle to effective enforcement of IP statutes.

Ironically, many IP owners themselves are, in a sense, contributing to the perpetuation of the enforcement vacuum that is so detrimental to their business in Russia. It is quite understandable that an owner of a valuable trademark will likely hesitate to bring an infringement suit in Russia for fear that an adverse decision, which it was impossible to foresee in an untested legal climate, may deprive it of all proprietary rights (the specter of the Smirnoff case is haunting the offices of trademark counsel). But it is also true that if no one brings suit, Russian judges are unlikely to develop the much needed IP expertise in the near future.

The new Russian Criminal Code, effective as of January 1, 1997, was greeted by the international IP community with cautious optimism. While the Criminal Code does provide for stiffer penalties, including prison terms, for various violations of IP rights, the measures are broadly viewed as too mild to serve as an effective deterrent for infringers. In addition, penalties provided for copyright and patent infringement target only those offenders who have caused "significant damages" (a term not defined in the Criminal Code but presumably requiring a higher burden of proof), repeat offenders, conspirators and organized crime rings.

Criminal penalties for trademark infringement are generally lower than penalties for copyright or patent infringement. For example, the maximum penalty for patent infringement is 800 times the minimum monthly wage or imprisonment for up to five years; whereas, the maximum penalty for trademark infringement is 400 times the minimum monthly wage or corrective labor for up to two years. (As of April 1, 1996, the minimum monthly wage was set at 75,900 rubles, or roughly $15.)

General dissatisfaction with existing enforcement practices has led some IP owners to explore another route: filing an unfair competition claim with the Russian Federation State Committee for Anti–Monopoly Policy and Support of New Economic Entities (AMC).

The Russian Federation Law on Competition and on Restricting Monopolistic Activities in Commodities Markets (RF Anti-monopoly Law) defines unfair competition as any action of a business entity that runs afoul of laws, commercial customs, standards of good faith, reasonableness and equity, and that may cause or has caused damages to other competing business entities or has harmed their business reputation (RF Anti–Monopoly Law, Chapter 1, Article 4.7). The list of specific instances of "unfair competition" includes misleading consumers with respect to the nature, method and place of manufacture, consumer properties and quality of a product, and sale of goods "unlawfully incorporating results of intellectual activity and similar means of identification of a legal entity, products or services." (*Id.*, Chapter III, Articles 10.3 and 10.5)

A petition alleging anti-competitive behavior may be filed by Russian federal and local government agencies, business and non-profit entities, including foreign entities, or the proceedings may be initiated by AMC itself. AMC must review the petition and make a determination regarding likelihood of the existence of alleged anti-competitive practices within one month from receipt of the petition. (This term may be extended to up to three months, if AMC requests additional evidence).

If the AMC makes a determination that a violation is likely to exist, then the AMC president, or the head of a local AMC branch refers the dispute for adjudication to a three-person ad hoc commission composed of senior AMC officers. The proceeding, which includes depositions, requests for additional information, expert testimony (if deemed necessary by the commission), hearing, etc., should be completed within three months from the date of determination. After three months, the term may be extended to up to six additional months.

Although the burden of proving anti-competitive practices is on the petitioner, AMC may choose to conduct its own investigation and may enter onto the premises of respondents, both government and private, and upon written notice, examine relevant documents. The police are under the obligation to "provide practical assistance" to AMC officers, which includes ensuring access to the premises.

In the event that the AMC finds a violation of the Anti–Monopoly law, it may grant injunctive relief, impose stiff administrative fines for noncompliance on the infringer (*e.g.*, up to 25,000 minimum monthly wages, or approximately $380,000) and/or on the infringer's officers and directors (e.g., up to 200 minimum monthly wages or approximately $30,000), seek revocation of the infringer's licenses, file criminal charges against the infringer's officers and directors, etc. AMC decisions may be appealed in courts and arbitration courts, both by the alleged infringer and by the petitioner.

In the absence of judicial expertise, well-developed procedures for judicial resolution of intellectual property disputes or efficient mechanisms of enforcement of judicial awards in Russia, the AMC now emerges as a forum for a speedy and relatively inexpensive adjudication of such disputes, providing "built-in" administrative enforcement procedures. (As of January 1, 1996, total AMC fees were 50 minimum monthly wages, or approximately $700).

It is important to note that AMC proceedings do not preclude an aggrieved party from suing. An AMC final decision may be appealed; and even if AMC rules against the petitioner and the unfavorable decision is upheld on appeal, the petitioner may bring an action for intellectual property infringement under Russian patent, trademark and copyright statutes.

Although some companies have successfully used AMC proceedings (e.g., acting on Microsoft's petition, AMC has recently forced the Russian company Firma Visa to stop selling copies of Microsoft software imported from China), others still regard it as an indirect and imperfect means of protecting their IP rights.

It is safe to say that although Russian enforcement procedures are far from perfect, there are numerous signs that Russia is becoming serious about enforcing its IP laws. The adoption of the new Criminal Code brings Russia one step closer to compliance with the provisions of the Agreement on Trade–Related Aspects of Intellectual Property (TRIPS) and to its accession to WTO. Police raids on street vendors offering counterfeit goods are becoming an increasingly familiar sight. A new breed of young judges and lawyers, many Western-trained, is quite capable of understanding and deciding complex IP matters. For some time, however, Russia is likely to remain a land of frustration, pitfalls and defeats for IP owners, but still a huge market impossible to ignore.

Notes and Questions

1. Does the provision of administrative relief by the AMC meet the requirements of TRIPS for the provision of adequate relief for IPR violations?

2. What are the benefits of pursuing administrative relief as opposed to judicial relief? Are there disadvantages to this system of enforcement?

3. *Procedural Advantages.* Proceedings before the AMC are closed to the public which reduces somewhat the risk of disclosure of confidential information. They are also relatively speedy and inexpensive. By contrast, however, the anti-monopoly law expressly excluded intellectual property rights per se from its scope of protection. Instead, claims must demonstrate some form of "unfair competition," such as passing off.

4. Increasingly, countries are developing unfair competition procedures as an alternative or adjunct to "traditional" IP causes of action. Using unfair competition laws how would you challenge the unauthorized reproduction of a copyrighted video game? Of a patented drug? What are the limits of such "alternative" measures?

PIRATES, DRAGONS AND U.S. INTELLECTUAL PROPERTY RIGHTS IN CHINA: PROBLEMS AND PROSPECTS OF CHINESE ENFORCEMENT

Glenn Butterton, 38 Ariz. L. Rev. 1081 (1996).

Are Western style enforcement mechanisms, working in concert with Western-style IPR laws, practical in the Chinese context? Some say they are not, that the whole project is doomed because it is based upon a set of assumptions about law and culture that, being Western, cannot be effectively adopted in the Chinese context. The Chinese, it is argued, have neither a Western concept of private property, nor a Rule of Law tradition, and, therefore, cannot be expected to comprehend fully, much less adhere to, Western-style IPR agreements. Such skeptics argue that even if U.S. pressure tactics are effective in the short term, resulting in well-publicized raids and the closing of a handful of pirate factories, they will not have brought about much needed fundamental changes in Chinese attitudes about property rights, the judiciary or the legal profession—changes substantial enough to survive when there are no U.S. threats in the offing. Moreover, they claim, the U.S. has failed to appreciate the degree to which the Chinese have learned to resent the quasi-colonial meddling of foreign powers in China in the nineteenth and early twentieth centuries, and the fact that for this reason some Chinese are exceptionally wary of pressure exerted by foreign countries who want China to build an elaborate legal apparatus to protect what are in significant part foreign IPR interests. Among ordinary Chinese, there is, say the skeptics, a deep distrust of law rooted both in Confucian tradition and in the bitter knowledge that the Communist Party has exploited law to serve its own often corrupt ends, as well as those of its more powerful members.

In this essay, I would like to ask whether, in fact, Chinese legal and cultural assumptions are today so profoundly non-Western or anti-Western, and whether, in any case, those assumptions adequately explain non-enforcement in China. Alternatively, I want to ask what other factors, particularly economic factors, might be useful in explaining non-enforcement, and whether those factors might be profitably addressed in designing enforcement schemes and practices for IPRs.

There was a disturbing tendency on the part of administrative and judicial bodies to hand out insignificant penalties and damage awards in infringement cases. In the Microsoft trademark case, for example, the Shenzhen Reflective Materials Institute at Shenzhen University was found to have pirated 650,000 holograms specially designed by Microsoft to identify its software products uniquely. The defendant Institute was found to have been filling a fraudulent Microsoft order allegedly placed by a pirate based in Taiwan who then exported thousands of pirated copies of Microsoft software worldwide; the trail of illegal copies has been traced to Canada, Sweden, Italy, Germany, Australia, the United States, the Middle East, the rest of Asia, and even Venezuela. The lost sales for Microsoft have been estimated to be at least U.S. $30 million and possibly as high as U.S. $180 million. Yet a damage award of only U.S. $260 for trademark infringement was rendered against the defendant Institute by the Shenzhen Administration for Industry and Commerce. Clearly, such modest penalties can have little or no deterrent effect on Chinese pirates, be they prime movers or merely co-conspirators in a pirating enterprise, and have raised obvious questions as to China's sincerity in carrying out the terms of the MOU[118] [memorandum of understanding between China and the U.S. regarding IP enforcement]

Some progress has been made in the creation of a judicial mechanism for coping with piracy. Effective August 1993, an intellectual property division was established in Beijing Intermediate People's Court and empowered to hear cases concerning patent, trademark, and copyright (including computer software) infringement, as well as cases concerning licensing agreements and unfair competition law. The Beijing Intellectual Property Trial Division has exclusive jurisdiction for matters arising in the Beijing District, and other analogous trial courts have been established for other geographical areas. By early 1994, courts had been established in Beijing, Shanghai, Fujian, Xiamen, Shenzhen and Haikou, and, as part of a flurry of enforcement activity associated with the April 30, 1994, U.S.TR announcements, the Chinese established additional courts in the cities of Zhuhai, Shantou and Guangzhou, in Guangdong Province. By January 1996, eighteen such courts had been established. In addition, an intellectual property appellate division has been established in the Beijing Municipal Higher People's Court, which has exclu-

---

118. A Chinese firm found guilty of infringing the Walt Disney Company's trademark Mickey Mouse character was fined only U.S.$91. Linus Chua, China Steps Up Enforcement of Piracy Laws, L.A. Times, Apr. 4, 1994, at D3. And a fine for infringement of the rights of the Sino–French joint venture Vie De France (Beijing), Ltd., amounted to only U.S.$1712. Ruth Youngblood, China Fights Trademark Abuse, UPI, Apr. 4, 1994, available in LEXIS, NEWS Library, UPI File.

sive appellate jurisdiction for the whole of China in much the same fashion as the United States Court of Appeals for the Federal Circuit has jurisdiction for the whole of the United States.

In theory, the Chinese have specially trained the judges of these courts in the various disciplines of intellectual property. In practice—on the Chinese view—the judges have fared extraordinarily well. Two senior Chinese judges, Yang Junqi and Jiang Zhipei, speaking on behalf of the intellectual property rights office of the Supreme's People's Court, have asserted that "in fact, China has set up a complete and effective judicial apparatus to protect intellectual property rights" and the Chinese courts have been "offering fair, effective protection of these rights, both domestic and foreign". The West has been less sanguine. There has, in fact, been considerable skepticism regarding the competence of the judges, however well-intentioned they may be.[131]

Technical competence has become an issue because Chinese judges have sometimes appeared puzzled by the technical nature of the IPR facts before them. For example, in a 1994 case, the Hong Kong-based Broad Mind Computer Company sued the Beijing-based Hai Wei Electronic Engineering Company in Beijing Intellectual Property Court for software copyright infringement in making and selling copies of its CT–110 computer terminal. Despite an exceptionally clear demonstration in court that Hai Wei had pirated the Broad Mind software, the court lumbered almost aimlessly and appeared incompetent to deal with the case. More generally, administrative and moral competence have been at issue, too. Chinese judges and court officers do not, it seems, always enjoy sufficient independence such that they are free of the meddling of interested parties, including government and Communist Party authorities; nor are they always free of self-interest.[133]

To date, the Chinese court system has generated a notable, if still modest, number of IPR decisions, involving domestic as well as foreign parties. The more prominent domestic cases have involved patent and copyright infringement matters, some of which have even concerned the indigenous Chinese computer software industry. The first all-Chinese case concerning computer software piracy actually antedated the creation of the first intellectual property court by four months. Weihong Computer Software Institute was awarded Y46,000 (U.S.$8,000) after it was found that Yuanwang Technical had secretly copied and sold translating and editing software created by Weihong. In a later case, the

---

131. "Scepticism over the ability of China's judicial system has been a major reason why many foreign companies have not brought their intellectual property cases to court in China. Foreign companies don't bother because they doubt Chinese courts' ability to try such cases in a fair manner," Dede Nickerson, Progress in Moves to End Copyright Row, So. China Morning Post, Jan. 19, 1995, at 1 (citing anonymous sources).

133. The integrity of Chinese court proceedings has been somewhat tarnished by incidents involving large cash transactions. For example, in one case, American business executives were instructed to pay U.S.$18,000 for a filing fee to have their case heard. The money had to be paid in cash in U.S. currency, and submitted in a suitcase.

Beijing IPR court ruled in favor of a leading Chinese software firm, SunTendy, in its suit against a Chinese pirate. SunTendy makes Chinese Star software which allows Chinese characters to be entered into computers running English language programs. A third case concerned a dispute over the computer input method for Chinese characters known as the five-stroke system. The inventor of the system, Wang Yongmin, won Y500,000 (U.S.$57,500) in compensation when the court supported his claim that Beijing-based China Southeastern Technology and Trading Company had pirated his patented invention.

In a high-profile domestic patent case, Beijing Intermediate People's Court ordered Tangshan Fuhao Company to pay U.S. $120,000 to Sun Yingui, to compensate for lost sales caused by its piracy of a popular mineral water dispenser. In another patent infringement case, the Kangbao Electrical Appliances Factory, which invented a device to sterilize food bowls, filed suit against twenty factories, claiming they were illegally using its invention. On December 26, 1994, the Guangzhou Intermediate People's Court found the factories to be infringing Kangbao's patent and ordered them to cease the infringement, whereupon the twenty factories were closed down by provincial authorities.

Decisions involving U.S. parties have been slow in coming, but the limited results to date have been encouraging for plaintiffs. In the early "M & M's" trademark case, Mars, Inc., sought and won an injunction restraining a Chinese firm from making and selling candies in China that infringed on the "M & M's" trademark. More recently, in the California Beef Noodle case, an unfair competition suit was filed in Beijing Intermediate People's Court by U.S. Hongli International against Beijing West City Xingyan. The Court ordered Xingyan to stop using Hongli's registered name and trademarked red, blue and white color scheme, and to pay Hongli U.S. $11,600 in damages and legal expenses, and U.S. $400 in court costs.

But the most visible of all U.S. suits filed in recent years have been those brought by Disney and by BSA. In the Disney copyright case, the Walt Disney Company filed a civil suit in the Beijing Intellectual Property Trial Court, in January 1994, against two Chinese companies for illegally publishing children's books using Disney cartoon characters. Disney claimed that the books were identical to a series produced under a Disney license with a different party that expired in September 1990, and estimated that 300,000 copies of the books were produced between 1991 and 1993. In July 1994 the court found the two companies liable: Beijing Children's Publishing Press for publishing pirated books, and Beijing Publishing Press for distributing copies. Under Chinese law, Disney could only seek actual damages from lost sales, not punitive damages. Finally, in May 1995, three months after the signing of the 1995 Agreement, a Beijing IPR Court awarded Disney U.S.$27,360 in damages and a public apology.

In February 1994, one month after the Disney suit was filed, BSA, on behalf of Lotus Development Corp., Autodesk, Inc., Microsoft Corp.

and Novell, Inc., filed a suit in the Beijing Intellectual Property Court against five Beijing computer firms (viz., Beijing Gaoli Computer Co., Beijing Sanhua Electronic Control Engineering Corp., Beijing Juren Computer Co., Huili Computer Operations Co., and Huiruan Computer Operator Co.) seeking damages, and claiming illegal copying and selling of software. The suit seemed to show no progress until June 23, 1994, a week before the deadline when China was to be designated a Priority Foreign Country, when the judge suddenly ordered the defendants to produce their financial accounts and other records, and a court-ordered raid was carried out on the defendants' premises to preserve evidence. The police confiscated, inter alia, 300 software programs published by BSA members. The BSA cases then continued to languish until October 1995, when suddenly the Court ruled in favor of BSA, and against Beijing Juren Computer Co. and Beijing Gaoli Computer Co., levying fines of up to U.S. $60,000 and awarding damages as well.

While the Chinese have amended their copyright law in keeping with the letter of the MOU, until July 1994, the law made copyright infringement only a civil, not a criminal, offense. This left a copyright owner who suffered infringement with no recourse but to make use of the administrative fine apparatus overseen by the National Copyright Administration. The copyright law called for fines to be imposed in the range of U.S.$150 to U.S.$11,500 or from two to five times the total fixed price of the lost sales of the legitimate product. But such fines did not appear to be applied broadly enough to act as an effective deterrent; nor were they substantial enough in every case to deter repeat offenses by those pirates whose ill-gotten gains may have made them comparatively affluent. Moreover, NCA could not impose fines itself absent the authority of a court order, nor could it make use of local police for enforcement purposes absent the weapon of criminal penalties. Just as the central government declined to provide the NCA with personnel resources adequate to enforcement needs, so, too, it declined to provide the criminal code resources that might have made for a more effective deterrent.

However, only five days after the U.S. announced its decision to designate China a Priority Foreign Country on June 30, 1994, China's legislature, the National People's Congress, approved new criminal penalties for copyright violators. The new law—the Resolution on Punishing the Crime of Copyright Violations—went into effect on July 5, 1994, and added new provisions to China's 1979 Criminal Law providing for fines and jail terms of up to seven years for violators.[147] The new law is

---

147. The new law calls for confiscation of violators' illegal profits, as well as copied items and materials and tools involved in the piracy. Punishable crimes include the duplication, distribution and marketing of books, fine art, audio-visual products and computer software. If convicted of making "huge profits" for duplicating or distributing, an offender could be sentenced to up to three years in prison and fined; an offender convicted of making "extremely huge profits" could receive up to seven years in prison and fines, though the law does not assign monetary values to the categories "huge" and "extremely huge". Retail sellers are subject to jail sentences of one year less than those for makers and distributors of pirated material. If a company is the

impressive on paper, as are the bulk of domestic IPR reforms initiated by the People's Republic since the 1992 MOU and the 1995 Agreement, and the Chinese have in typical fashion already made dramatic announcements of cases in which criminal penalties have been imposed.[148] However, there is nonetheless abundant skepticism in the international community as to whether the new criminal penalties will be effectively and broadly used to fight piracy.

Why have the Chinese failed to meet their enforcement obligations under the MOU and the Enforcement Agreement? How have they managed to go so far toward satisfying much of the letter of the MOU while seemingly turning a blind eye to its spirit? In its simplest terms, the chief thrust of the explanation from culture is that China has historico-cultural roots that are profoundly different from our own, and that, therefore, we cannot enter into agreements based almost exclusively on our own complex theories of property, with all of the alien economic and cultural baggage they entail, with any reasonable expectation that they will succeed. As Professor William Alford puts it, "laws premised on the values and institutions of an economically advanced capitalist democracy will not generate identical results when transplanted to a different setting. Rules that presume an independent judiciary, a professionalized bar, powerful interest groups and a rights-conscious populace fall chiefly on deaf ears in contemporary China."[158] Put in a somewhat different way, in the words of an official Chinese government spokesman,

> There are historical reasons for such a state of affairs. As the feudal or semifeudal or semicolonial society lasted for a considerably long period in China, people have been confined by feudal ideas for a long time. Compared with Western countries, democracy and a commodity economy developed relatively slowly in China. As IPR is [sic] an outcome of a market economy, China simply did not have the basic conditions for the "IPR" concept before the end of the 19th

violator, top managers could be held responsible and could be sentenced and fined, and the company itself could also be subjected to fines. Intellectual Property Protection in China: New Criminal Penalties for Copyright Violators, E. Asian Exec. Rep., July 15, 1994, available in LEXIS, ASIAPC Library, EASIAN File [hereinafter New Criminal Penalties].

148. For example, on January 6, 1995, the Wuxi Intermediate People's Court sentenced Lu Ping, 31, to a life term in prison for pirating 689,000 volumes of 20 different books since July 1990, and for fraud, falsification of public seals and pimping. Jane Macartney, China Sentences Book Pirate to Life in Jail, Reuters World Service, Jan. 7, 1995, available in LEXIS, ASIAPC Library, REUWLD File. At about the same time,

another Chinese pirate, Wu Wangsheng, was sentenced to seven years in prison for illegally publishing and selling 15,000 copies of the third volume of the selected works of Deng Xiaoping. China Jails Man Who Pirated Deng's Works, Reuters News Service–Far East, Jan. 20, 1995, available in LEXIS, NEWS Library, CURNWS File. In deciding a law suit originally brought by the International Federation of Phonographic Industries, Canton Municipal People's Intermediate Court convicted Su Qiuchun of selling counterfeit CDs. The court ordered him to spend nine months in jail and fined him U.S.$6,024. China Jails Man For Selling Fake CDs, UPI, Aug. 5, 1995, available in LEXIS, NEWS Library, UPI File.

158. William P. Alford, *Pressuring the Pirate*, L.A. Times, Jan. 12, 1992, at M5.

century.[159]

In its purest form, the thesis that China is fundamentally at odds with the Western Rule of Law tradition argues that Chinese society is not and essentially never has been devoted to or guided by the concept of law as it is known in the West. In place of Western-style law, the Chinese rely on a notion of personal relationship associated with the concept of li. The concept, though it is widely identified with the teachings of Confucius (551–479 B.C.), antedated him and appears to have been established in Chinese bureaucratic thought and the larger culture during the Western Zhou Period (1122–771 B.C.), if not before.

What I will call the "Confucian" perspective turns on the concept of li, particularly as it stands in opposition to the concept of fa. But where the concept of li is identified with Confucius' work, the concept of fa is associated with the work of the Chinese Legalist philosophers and the harsh rule of the Qin dynasty in the third century B.C. Put in concise, if misleadingly simple, terms, li is associated with propriety and moral force, while fa is associated with physical force and law, though the concept of law here invoked includes only a limited subset of the meanings of the word "law" in English.

The concept of li, when narrowly construed refers to proper conduct, or politeness or etiquette; more broadly construed, it refers to the whole range of political, social and familial relationships that are the underpinnings of a harmonious Confucian society. Those who are guided by li stand ready to adjust their views and demands in order to accommodate the needs and desires of others, and they demonstrate this by yielding to others for the sake of harmony when confrontation and conflict arise. When all parties to a dispute endeavor to make concessions, the necessity for litigation and the promotion of individual rights are both avoided. Individual interests are subordinated to the interests of the group such that one who, to the contrary, insists on individual rights is very much at odds with li and with the group as well. Li thus tends to lead naturally to compromise and mediation framed not in terms of a legal proposition or requirement but in terms of the circumstances of the participants.

Fa, in contrast to li, is a penal concept; it is associated with punishment, serving to maintain public order through the threat of force and physical violence. The intellectual roots of fa are in the Legalist movement—a group of political philosophers primarily active in the China of the fourth and third century B.C., who held that social order could only be maintained by the use of law as a tool for manipulating society. The Qin dynasty adopted the Legalist philosophy and effectively integrated and centralized the whole of the Chinese Empire in the third century B.C. (221–209 B.C.). The Qin ruled with the aid of a harsh penal law and brutal tactics, and developed a vast administrative law bureaucracy to manage the empire they had created. They thus shaped an image of the "rule of law" as brutal and rigid, and that image endured

159. *China Defends Its Record, supra* note 5 (remarks of Shen Rengan, Deputy Director of the State Copyright Administration) [note from article].

throughout the greatest period of Confucian influence from the first century A.D. to the development of civil-law criminal codes during the late nineteenth-century portion of the Qing dynasty (1644–1912 A.D.) and the beginning of the Republican period following the 1912 revolution, when the last incarnation of those codes was enacted. As for comparing fa to li, the Confucius of the Analects said "govern the people by regulations, keep order among them by chastisements, and they will flee from you, and lose all self-respect. Govern them by moral force, keep order among them by ritual and they will keep their self-respect and come to you of their own accord." [The Analects of Confucius]

Since Confucius has been alternately reviled and embraced in China under the Communists, it is perhaps not surprising that many Confucian habits have not only survived but prospered in the post–1979 China of Deng's reforms. The personal relationship or connection, what the Chinese call guanxi, remains central in interpersonal, bureaucratic and commercial dealings in China today. The Chinese do not necessarily care to be bound by the fetters of law as they appear, for example, in the written language of contract, or in precise codifications of terms or individual rights and responsibilities. They prefer instead to remain flexible, free to adjust their views from time to time as befits unfolding circumstances in light of the needs of their ongoing personal relationships. To many, the shifting sands of "flexibility" and ad hoc adjustments are synonymous with a host of corrupt business practices, and the opportunism, rent-seeking and shirking that are endemic in the state industries and administrative bureaucracies of Communist China. To the extent that the rule of law is antithetical to such practices, fa remains in low esteem, and the concept of li, as regards the centrality of personal relationships, endures as a guiding principle of Chinese social and economic life.

Thus, as regards lax IPR enforcement, the explanation from culture teaches us that the MOU and its attendant domestic law reforms are undermined by a basic Chinese distrust of the formal law upon which enforcement might be predicated, a contempt for the promotion of individual rights of copyright owners at the expense of ongoing personal relationships and "harmony" in the community, and a continuing desire to be able to adjust one's enforcement behavior as regards the rule of law on an ad hoc basis. To the NCA field officer or local proxy, for example, it may be far more worthwhile, and sometimes literally more lucrative, to build a good ongoing relationship with the owner of the local pirate compact disc plant, than to enforce a law whose ultimate effects on the local community may be devastating in terms of loss of jobs and prosperity. This will be all the more true when, as is frequently the case in China, the owner or part-owner of the plant is a government or party official, or the relative of such a person; or a government unit; or a military unit; or even a police unit in charge of raiding pirate factories.

Despite the relative growth of piracy and deep-rooted cynicism about law, there is today reason for optimism. With the creation and ongoing development of Chinese IPR courts, and the acquisition by ordinary

Chinese of intellectual property rights (in addition to other property rights) that may be asserted and defended in those courts, as well as the emergence of a private bar that is more than nominally independent of government, we may have turned not just a "conceptual" but also now a "practical corner" on the road to more vigorous IPR practices and institutions in China. I am inclined to agree with Yu Yingzhong, who, writing about "legal pragmatism" in the PRC, has observed that people's indifference to and mistrust of law can only be reversed with the creation of a true legal consciousness. Creating this legal consciousness necessarily involves bringing citizens into the process of making law and building legal institutions that can be relied upon, which are important components of the transformation from a society ruled by men to a society ruled by law.[200]

Notes and Questions

1. What are the enforcement problems outlined in the above article that intellectual property owners may face in China?

2. What minimum enforcement standards would you require to overcome these problems? Compare your standards to those adopted in TRIPS described in the following section. Does TRIPS resolve all the problems you identified?

3. Do the enforcement standards of Articles 41, 61, and 63 permit legal systems which are based on the concepts of *fa* and *li*? For an interesting discussion of the problems in culture in enforcing intellectual property rights in China, *see* William Alford, *To Steal a Book is an Elegant Offense* (1995).

200. Yu Xingzhong, Legal Pragmatism in the People's Republic of China, 3 J.Chi- nese L. 29 (1989)

Chapter Thirty

CIVIL PROCEDURES UNDER INTERNATIONAL LAW

A. WHAT ARE MINIMUM REQUIREMENTS FOR CIVIL ENFORCEMENT OF INTELLECTUAL PROPERTY RIGHTS INTERNATIONALLY?

Read the following Articles from TRIPS from the Supplement: 42–49.

The Criminal Law Controversy

In many common law countries, such as the United States, Canada, the United Kingdom and Australia, enforcement of intellectual property rights is generally achieved through the mechanism of private lawsuits. Civil relief against infringement includes prompt injunctive relief, seizure of illegal product (and its subsequent destruction if infringement is proven) and hefty monetary penalties, including disgorgement of the defendant's profits earned from its illegal activities. In most civil actions, the major cost of proceeding against infringers is borne by the IP owner, who investigates the alleged infringement, files a complaint seeking civil relief and prosecutes the complaint to termination (whether by judgment or settlement). Because the IP owner prosecutes the action, he is consequently entitled to all the money damages awarded against the infringer. The success of a civil mechanism for intellectual property enforcement, however, requires an adequate tribunal system, with trained judges, who are capable of acting quickly, enforcing their orders, and ensuring prompt and adequate relief to the complaining party. Such civil enforcement systems can be costly to maintain and are generally available in countries whose political system acknowledges the right of private causes of action to enforce personal rights and grievances.

Because of the high cost of establishing and maintaining an effective civil, private-rights, legal system many developing countries have chosen to enforce intellectual property rights under their criminal law procedures. These countries already have highly developed criminal investigative procedures and criminal law tribunals. The adaptation of legal enforcement mechanisms originally designed to protect the State's interest to ones which enforce individual rights has proven to be a difficult one.

Investigative procedures may be slow and unwieldy. Under the legal system of the former Soviet Union, for example, crimes against the State were first investigated by the police, then re-investigated by the procuracy (prosecutor) and potentially re-investigated a third time by the tribunal. Where a citizen's liberty or life interest is impacted, such lengthy procedures might be justified by the need to avoid a hasty (and potentially mistaken) judgment. Where, however, economic crimes (such as the misappropriation or infringement of intellectual property rights) are concerned, such delay may result in unrecompensable harm to the IP owner.

Finally, criminal prosecutions in developing countries do not typically result in monetary compensation to the rights owner. Any fines which are levied are typically paid to the State. While the cost of using government personnel to enforce private rights may justify government recovery of fines, where the IP owner is also required to bear some of the burdens of prosecution, such as the costs of seizures, expert witnesses or the cost of storage of seized items, lack of monetary recovery may be seen as adding insult to injury.

Notes and Questions

1. Even though Article 41 of TRIPS does not facially require the adoption of a particular *system* of enforcement (common law, civil law, judicial, administrative), do Articles 41 through 49 in practice *require* a particular system?

2. You represent the worldwide owner of all copyrights in a new Internet browser software program. This program contains the most sophisticated search engine to date. Your client has licensed the manufacture and distribution of this program to local software companies in Russia, China, Japan and Mexico. You have discovered that pirated copies of your client's program are being sold in each country. What remedies would you seek to protect your client's rights? Are these remedies required to be available under TRIPS?

3. What legal protections would you want in place to protect your client's rights while it was pursuing its legal remedies against the infringers described above? Are they required under TRIPS? What protections, if any, are missing?

4. *Alternative Dispute Resolution.* Although the focus of TRIPS appears to be on judicial or administrative proceedings, arbitration and mediation have become increasingly popular methods for resolving international disputes. For an examination of the availability of such methods, *see* William Grantham, *The Arbitrability of International Intellectual Property Disputes*, 14 Berkeley J. Int'l L. 173 (1996).

B. DO MINIMUM ENFORCEMENT STANDARDS UNDER TRIPS GUARANTEE MINIMUM INFRINGEMENT STANDARDS?

THE ALBUM PHOTOGRAPHY CASE
CREATION RECORDS LTD. v. NEWS GROUP NEWSPAPERS LTD.

Chancery Division, 1997.
16 Tr L 544, The Times 29 April 1997.

LLOYD, J.

This action and the motion before me arise out of arrangements made last week to take photographs intended for the cover of a forthcoming album to be released by the very well-known and popular group, Oasis. This is scheduled to be released later this year and the artwork for the sleeve to the album has been under discussion for some time. These discussions led to a particular idea being favoured and a decision to take the necessary photographs in the grounds of Stocks Country Club Hotel, Hertfordshire, on Wednesday, 16 April. The arrangements commenced the previous day with the draining of the hotel swimming pool and the delivery to the site of a white Rolls Royce which was then lowered by crane into the swimming pool to rest partly on scaffolding at an angle. A number of other objects which were to be or might be used in the photographs were also delivered to the site at that time.

On 16 April the five members of the group arrived at the hotel soon after mid-day. Mr. Noel Gallagher, who it seems has control of the artwork, supervised the placing of various objects around the pool, which by then had been partly refilled with water, until he was satisfied with the scene including the positioning of the members of the group. Photographs were then taken of the scene by Mr. Michael Spencer Jones over a period of time from mid-afternoon to late at night so that the group would have a choice of images in different lights and from different angles and heights. Mr. Gallagher exhibits to his affidavit a photograph which, he says, he envisaged as being used for the front sleeve of the album. This has the swimming pool in the foreground with the Rolls Royce seemingly emerging from the water towards the camera. The hotel is beyond and to the right. In the far distance is a wooded area with a partly clouded sky above. The five members of the group are posed round the pool, one on a scooter, one climbing out of the pool and others with or near other objects seemingly unrelated to each other. The various objects were ordered two days before from a warehouse in London; none of them was made for the purpose.

The plaintiffs' evidence says that it was regarded as essential to keep the group's plans for the photography secret, in particular as regards the new album, and it is said that only a very limited number or people knew about the arrangements. However, the information was not as narrowly restricted as they would have wanted. On 12 April The Sun newspaper booked two rooms at the hotel for the nights of 15 and 16 April, and on 15 April they commissioned a Mr. Seeburg, a freelance photographer, to go to the hotel, stay there and try to take pictures of the shoot. He says in his affidavit that by the time of the shoot another photographer was there, whom he recognized, from The Daily Star, and some local fans who turned up to watch, as well as hotel staff. Some of these people had cameras. He says he remained at the shoot until about 4.30 in the afternoon and took a number of photographs of the scene. One of his photographs shows a version of the scene which is very similar to that of the picture approved by Mr. Gallagher, which I have mentioned, but at a different angle, taken, he says, some 15 to 20 feet to the left of the position of the official photographer.

This photograph and two others taken by him were published in The Sun on 17 April. His main photograph was again published on 18 April with annotations by way of comment on some of the objects in the picture. That article concluded; "See tomorrow's Bizarre to find out how to get a poster version of the cover". Duly on 19 April the Sun carried a feature headed "Get our Oasis poster", showing a further print of the photograph. This invited readers to send in L1.99 at any time up to 28 April to get "a glossy poster of The Sun's world exclusive of the new Oasis album shoot." The Daily Star and other papers also carried photographs taken on this occasion, but I infer that none of them was of the fully composed scene and nor have they threatened publication in poster form.

The plaintiffs contend that Mr. Seeburg's photograph is an infringement of, or is itself the subject of, copyright vested in them or one of them; or, alternatively that it was obtained in circumstances of confidentiality such that any publication without their consent is a breach of copyright or of confidence. They seek an interlocutory injunction restraining such publication. On an application made *ex parte*, though on notice, on Monday of this week I granted an injunction until the inter partes hearing of the motion. I now have to decide whether to continue that until trial or further order.

It is said, first, that the scene itself (the arrangement or composition of the members of the group, the various objects and the site) is a copyright work. I do not see how that can be so. Mr. Merriman argued faintly that it was a dramatic work. Since the scene is inherently static, having no movement, story or action, I cannot accept this. Primarily, he argued that it was an artistic work, as a sculpture or collage within § 4(1)(a) of the Copyright, Designs and Patents Act 1988 or a work of artistic craftsmanship within § 4(1)(c) of that Act.

I do not regard this as seriously arguable. I do not see how the process of assembling these disparate objects together with the members of the group can be regarded as having anything in common with sculpture or with artistic craftsmanship. No element in the composition has been carved, modelled or made in any of the other ways in which sculpture is made. Nor does it seem to me to be the subject or result of the exercise of any craftsmanship (*see George Hensher Limited v. Restawile Upholstery (Lancs) Ltd.* [1976] AC 64, [1974] 2 All ER 420, especially Lord Simon at page 91 of the former report).

I should also mention in this context the case of *Shelley Films Limited v R Features Ltd.* [1994] EMLR 134. In this case Mr. Martin Mann QC, sitting as a deputy judge of this division, held it to be seriously arguable that a film set prepared for the film to be called "Mary Shelley's Frankenstein" was a work of artistic craftsmanship so that an unauthorized photograph taken of an actor on the set was a breach of copyright in the set as well, for different reasons, as of other elements in the photograph. That seems to me quite different on the facts. I can readily accept that a film set does involve craftsmanship. It is not merely an assembly of "objets trouves". I will need to come back to another aspect of that case later.

As for collage, a subject of copyright new to English law in the 1988 Act, the traditional understanding of that word is that it involves the use of glue or some other adhesive in the process of making a work of visual art, being derived from the French. Two Oxford Dictionary definitions were put before me. The Oxford English Dictionary, 2 Edition, 1989 has this:

> "An abstract form of art in which photographs, pieces of paper, newspaper cuttings, string etc are placed in juxtaposition and glued to the pictorial surface; such a work of art".

It then goes on to quote examples which include some loose uses of the word, for example, in relation to poems and music. The Concise Oxford Dictionary, 9 Edition, has a shorter version of these two definitions, but also as its third:

"A collection of unrelated things".

Mr. Merriman submits that it is at least seriously arguable that the composition which Mr. Gallagher put together as the subject of the photography is within the definition of collage in this sense, even though it did not involve the use of any adhesive. More generally, he submitted that this composition is the result of the exercise of artistic creativity and originality and that at a time when the creativity of visual artists is finding outlets in a great variety of novel forms the 1988 Act should not be construed so as to deny such novel works of art the possibility of copyright protection as artistic works within § 4. He asked forensically how it might be found that copyright subsisted in Carl Andre's bricks, in stone circles created by Richard Long, in Rachel Whiteread's house, in the living sculptures of Gilbert and George and in examples of installation art generally. I do not find it necessary or appropriate to answer that question. I would distinguish Mr. Gallagher's composition from all of those examples as being put together solely to be the subject matter of a number of photographs and disassembled as soon as those were taken. This composition was intrinsically ephemeral, or indeed less than ephemeral, in the original sense of that word of living only for one day.

This existed for a few hours on the ground. Its continued existence was to be in the form of a photographic image. Accordingly, it seems to me materially different from all the particular examples put to me in this context by Mr. Merriman.

Even if it were otherwise, I would not accept that it is seriously arguable that this composition is a collage. In my view a collage does indeed involve as an essential element the sticking of two or more things together. It does not suffice to point to the collocation, whether or not with artistic intent, of such random, unrelated and unfixed elements as is seen in the photographs in question.

Accordingly, I am not prepared to regard the plaintiffs' case based on copyright in the subject matter of the shoot as sufficiently arguable to be the basis of an interlocutory injunction.

Next, Mr. Merriman contended that Mr. Seeburg's photograph was itself a copy of the official photograph taken by Mr. Jones, regardless of the order in which the two were taken. I do not see how that can be argued. If the subject matter is not itself copyright, in principle two different photographers can take separate photographs of the same subject without either copying the other. Of course copyright subsists in the official photograph and if it were the only source of the scene it would be an infringement to copy that, either by a direct copying process or by the scene being recreated and a fresh photograph taken of that recreation. But it is a basic proposition of copyright law that two works created from a common source do not by reason of that fact involve copying one of the other, however similar they are.

As a variant on that contention Mr. Merriman submitted that Mr. Gallagher was the owner of the copyright in the Seeburg photograph because he was the author, the person who created it. The basis of this is that Mr. Gallagher created the subject matter and it is therefore said that he created all photographs taken from it. It seems to me that ordinarily the creator of a photograph is the person who takes it. There may be cases where one person sets up the scene to be photographed (the position and angle of the camera and all the necessary settings) and directs a second person to press the shutter release button at a moment chosen by the first, in which case it would be the first, not the second, who creates the photograph. There may also be cases of collaboration between the person behind the camera and one or more others in which the actual photographer has greater input, although no complete control of the creation of the photograph, in which case it may be a work of joint creation and joint authorship.

In the present case, however, it seems to me unarguable that anyone other than Mr. Seeburg is the creator of his photograph. Mr. Gallagher set up the scene and may well have chosen or approved the angle and other details of all or some of the official photographs taken by Mr. Jones, in which case Mr. Gallagher is the creator, or one of the creators, of the official photographs. It seems that Mr. Jones does not claim to own the copyright in any of these. But Mr. Gallagher had nothing to do with the Seeburg photograph except to bring the subject matter into existence and of course to form part of it himself. That does not make him its creator.

In my judgment the scene was set up to be photographed and the plaintiffs' only basis for exclusivity depends primarily on whether they were able to prevent others taking photographs. In fact, of course, as we know, one photograph escaped their attempts.

Accordingly, in the alternative to his claim based on copyright Mr. Merriman submits that there is at least a seriously arguable case, subject to how the facts are found at trial, for saying that Mr. Seeburg took his photographs in circumstances in which he must have realised that it was a breach of confidentiality to do so, or at least it would be such a breach to make the photograph available for publication, and that accordingly publication can be restrained by injunction on the grounds of that breach of confidence.

On balance I am satisfied that the right course is to grant an interim injunction until trial or further order, restraining further publication of the picture on the basis not of copyright but of breach of confidence.

DISPOSITION:

Judgement accordingly.

THE CHERRY RIPE CASE
GROSS v. SELIGMAN

United States Court of Appeals, Second Circuit, 1914.
212 Fed. 930.

LACOMBE, CIRCUIT JUDGE

This cause comes here upon appeal from an order of the District Court, Southern District of New York, enjoining defendant from publishing a photograph. The suit is brought under the provisions of the Copyright Act. One Rochlitz, an artist, posed a model in the nude, and therefrom produced a photograph, which he named the 'Grace of Youth.' A copyright was obtained therefore; all the artist's rights being sold and assigned to complainants. Two years later the same artist placed the same model in the identical pose, with the single exception that the young woman now wears a smile and holds a cherry stem between her teeth. He took a photograph of this pose, which he called 'Cherry Ripe'; this second photograph is published by defendants, and has been enjoined as an infringement of complainant's copyright.

This is not simply the case of taking two separate photographs of the same young woman. When the Grace of Youth was produced a distinctly artistic conception was formed, and was made permanent as a picture in the very method which the Supreme Court indicated in the Oscar Wilde Case (*Burrow-Giles Company v. Sarony*, 111 U.S. 53, 4 Sup.Ct. 279, 28 L.Ed. 349) would entitle the person producing such a picture to a copyright to protect it. It was there held that the artist who used the camera to produce his picture was entitled to copyright just as he would have been had he produced it with a brush on canvas. If the copyrighted picture were produced with colors on canvas, and were then copyrighted and sold by the artist, he would infringe the purchaser's rights if thereafter the same artist, using the same model, repainted the same picture with only trivial variations of detail and offered it for sale.

Of course when the first picture has been produced and copyrighted every other artist is entirely free to form his own conception of the Grace of Youth, or anything else, and to avail of the same young woman's services in making it permanent, whether he works with pigments or a camera. If, by chance, the pose, background, light, and shade, etc., of this new picture were strikingly similar, and if, by reason of the circumstance that the same young woman was the prominent feature in both compositions, it might be very difficult to distinguish the new picture from the old one, the new would still not be an infringement of the old because it is in no true sense a copy of the old. This is a risk which the original artist takes when he merely produces a likeness of an existing face and figure, instead of supplementing its features by the exercise of his own imagination.

It seems to us, however, that we have no such new photograph of the same model. The identity of the artist and the many close identities of pose, light, and shade, etc., indicate very strongly that the first picture was used to produce the second. Whether the model in the second case was posed, and light and shade, etc., arranged with a copy of the first photograph physically present before the artist's eyes, or whether his mental reproduction of the exact combination he had already once effected was so clear and vivid that he did not need the physical reproduction of it, seems to us immaterial. The one thing, viz., the exercise of artistic talent, which made the first photographic picture a subject of copyright, has been used not to produce another picture, but to duplicate the original.

The case is quite similar to those where indirect copying, through the use of living pictures, was held to be an infringement of copyright. *Hanfstaengle v. Baines & Co.* (L.R. 1894) A.C. 20, 30.

The eye of an artist or a connoisseur will, no doubt, find differences between these two photographs. The backgrounds are not identical, the model in one case is sedate, in the other smiling; moreover the young woman was two years older when the later photograph was taken, and some slight changes in the contours of her figure are discoverable. But the identities are much greater than the differences, and it seems to us that the artist was careful to introduce only enough differences to argue about, while undertaking to make what would seem to be a copy to the ordinary purchaser who did not have both photographs before him at the same time. In this undertaking we think he succeeded.

The order is affirmed.

RAVENSCROFT v. HERBERT

High Court Of Justice, Chancery Division, 1979.
[1980] RPC 193.

BRIGHTMAN J.

This is a copyright action brought by the author of a non-fiction book called The Spear of Destiny. The plaintiff alleges that the first defendant, Mr. James Herbert, in writing a novel entitled The Spear, has infringed his copyright. The second defendant is the publisher. A central feature of both books is a spear head which forms part of the Hapsburg treasure exhibited in Vienna. The spear head is described in the museum guide as The Holy Lance. The middle of the spear head has been cut out and the space filled by what is described as the Holy Nail. The guide book (I have been referred to the 1963 edition) records that the spear was carried in important battles as an emblem of the king; that victories were attributed to its power; and that after the 13th century it was venerated as the lance with which the side of Our Lord was pierced at the Crucifixion. The plaintiff's book, which combines historical fact with a great deal of mysticism, purports to tell the story of the spear from the earliest times down to the end of the last war. Mr. Herbert's book is a thriller which weaves an improbable story of neo-Hitler terrorism in England around the supposed post-war exploits of the spear. The fact that the Hofburg Spear, as I will sometimes call it, is harmlessly lying in the Hofburg Museum in Vienna for anyone to see causes Mr. Herbert no problem because, according to the novel, this is only a useless replica. So far, no copyright problem emerges. The reason that battle has been joined is that Mr. Herbert is alleged to have made extensive use of the plaintiff's non-fiction work in order to paint in a backcloth of apparent truth against which his own fiction story can be narrated. The question for decision is whether Mr. Herbert has made a legitimate or illegitimate use of the plaintiff's work.

The Spear of Destiny [written by the plaintiff] is a book of some 350 pages in the paperback edition. It is discursive and disjointed, and demands of the reader considerable effort and concentration. It is packed with an immense amount of historical data which no one suggests are in any way inaccurate. It also contains much philosophical discussion and mysticism. It is divided into a brief prologue, an introduction, 24 chapters and an epilogue.

The prologue introduces the reader to the spear. Its early history is lightly sketched by the plaintiff. Joshua is mentioned as an early holder. It is implied that it helped him to demolish the walls of Jericho. Later it passed to King David, and also into the hands of Herod, before coming into the possession of one of the Roman soldiers present at the Crucifixion. A legend grew up, the plaintiff recounted, that whoever held the spear would have immense power to control the destiny of the world either for good or for evil, as he might choose.

The introduction explains that the book would have been written by Dr. Stein but for his untimely death. The reader is told of the plaintiff's friendship with Dr. Stein, of Dr. Stein's intimate knowledge of Hitler before the 1914 war, and of the way Hitler was attracted to the power of the spear during this period. The first chapter contains a graphic description of Hitler's supposed visit to the Hofburg Museum in 1909 and of his fascination with the guide's description of its supernatural powers.

The book ranges through history, legend and mythology, at times branching into collateral matters, culminating in Hitler's attempt at world domination due to his possession of the spear with its unique properties of good and evil.

The book has a single theme, the identity of the Hofburg Spear with that used at the Crucifixion, and the supernatural qualities of such spear. The book itself is largely a mixture of selected authentic episodes from European history in general, and German history in particular, in the Middle Ages and modern times, derived from the plaintiff's very considerable knowledge as a historian, plus his recollection of what Dr. Stein revealed to him. Authentic recorded history, the personal knowledge of Dr. Stein and the meditations of Dr. Stein, are inextricably mingled and served up to the reader in a highly individualistic and unusual book.

I now turn to the defendant.

Mr. Herbert' novel contains 278 pages. It is divided into seven prologues, twenty-three chapters and an Author's note. The prologues recount the story of the Hofburg Spear from the Crucifixion down to the end of the 1939 war. The chapters record, in the form of a novel, the post-war exploits of the spear.

I will, for the moment, leave aside the prologues and attempt a brief summary of the novel. The time is the present. The hero is a private detective called Steadman, sometimes identified in the story as a modern Parsifal. Steadman is approached by an Israeli Intelligence agent for the purpose of tracing one of their operators who is missing. Steadman turns down the assignment. However, his female business partner thinks that the assignment should be accepted and secretly makes contact with the Israeli agent. She is captured by an enemy and killed in most unpleasant circumstances. Steadman seeks out the Israeli Intelligence agent, thinking that he is the murderer. The agent tells him that the murderer is an arms dealer called Gant. Steadman returns home and finds on the doorstep a man called Pope, who introduces himself as an agent of M15. Pope tells Steadman that Gant is connected with a Nazi secret society called the Thule Gesellschaft operating in England. Pope hints that the society is in possession of a magic spear. [After numerous adventures, Steadman learns that the Hofburg Spear] will be used to slay him in a ritual killing. Fortunately the police, aided by local agents of M15 and the CIA, and a detachment of Marine Commandoes flown from Plymouth, successfully assault the Devonshire. [After numerous other adventures, Steadman is eventually saved and] hurls the spear into the flaming debris.

One must not under-estimate the commercial attraction of the rubbish which I have attempted to describe. The book is written with much inventiveness and a racy flow of language and incident, and the numerous scenes of violence exercise a strong appeal to certain readers. The defendant's novels have enjoyed great financial success.

Mr. Herbert does not dispute that the used the plaintiff's book for the source of much of the material which he recounts in the prologues. He used, he said, the Penthouse article as a sort of card index for identifying the facts which he desired to use, and The Spear of Destiny as a filing cabinet where he could glean the full facts.

There are, in all, fifty alleged instances of language copying. One is to be found on the dust jacket of the defendant's book. Eight in the first prologue, which deals with the Crucifixion. None in the second prologue, which is only concerned with the capture and death of Himmler. Eleven in the third prologue, which deals with Hitler's alleged first visit to the Hofburg Museum in 1909. Eleven in the fourth prologue, which deals with Hitler's alleged historical researches in the Hofburg Library before the First World War. Thirteen in the fifth prologue, which covers the seizure of the spear at the time of the Anschluss. And large scale copying, with particular emphasis on three incidents, in the sixth prologue, which deals with General Patton's visit to the underground store of treasures in Nuremberg. There is no significant copying in the last prologue, which traces the fictional escape of the authentic Hofburg Spear to England.

In the "Author's Note" at the end of the book there is included this sentence:

> "The idea for this book came from Trevor Ravenscroft's extraordinary The Spear of Destiny, a detailed (and unsettling) study of Adolf Hitler's association with the Heilige Lance."

It is quite obvious from a comparison of the two books and from the defendant's evidence that he had the Penthouse article and the plaintiff's book in front of him as he wrote five of the prologues. The first prologue opens with the Roman soldier seated on his horse at the foot of the Cross and ends with the miraculous cure of his defective vision after he had used his spear. All the main facts in the prologue, which extends over two pages, are taken from pages ix to xi of the plaintiff's book. The defendant condenses the story and changes the language to a greater or lesser extent. Where the defendant concedes that the language is the same his answer is:

> "Of course they would be identical words; we are saying the same thing"; or: "Would you think there is another way of putting that?"; or: "I put the same facts down, they have got to appear similar. It would have been very easy for me to disguise all this, but there was no reason to".

The two descriptions of the spear (which Mr. Herbert had never seen for himself) and its mode of display are almost identical.

"(Q) Almost identical words, do you agree? (A) Well, that is what the spear was lying in. Why should I change that? (Q) The one was taken from the other, yes? (A) Of course it is taken from the other, yes.

"(Q) An exact copy, is it not, one from the other? (A) That is the description of the spear, it has got to be exact ... Yes, it is saying the same thing, it must be. (Q) You borrowed it because it was a jolly good description, was it not, that Mr. Ravenscroft used? (A) Of course it was ... yes ... That was how the spear |202Œ looks, why change it? That was the description. (Q) Again, you liked the words, did you, that Mr. Ravenscroft used? (A) They were saying exactly what needed to be said. (Q) Well enough for you to use most of the words yourself? (A) I saw no reason to disguise the words".

In his defence as adumbrated in his affidavit, Mr. Herbert states that the prologues are included as a form of historical background to add credence to the fictional story he was written, and although they are not, he says, central to the story, they form an important part of the structure of the novel. I think that is a fair statement.

As a prelude to a consideration of the opposing arguments I will refer briefly to the nature of copyright protection. Under section 1 of the 1956 Act copyright in relation to a work means (put shortly) "the exclusive right ... to do certain acts in relation to that work". Such acts are "those acts which ... are designated as the acts restricted by the copyright in a work of that description". Under section 2, sub-section (5) the acts restricted by the copyright in (inter alia) a literary or dramatic work include "reproducing the work in any material form". Under section 49 any reference in the Act "to the doing of an act in relation to a work ... shall be taken to include a reference to the doing of that act in relation to a substantial part thereof".

The question with which I have to decide is a question of fact, whether there has been substantial copying of The Spear of Destiny amounting to an infringement of the plaintiff's rights. This raises two issues, first whether there has been copying, and, secondly, whether such copying is substantial within the meaning of section 49. I have read both books. The plaintiff gave evidence before me during a period of over four days, and the defendant for almost three days. It is absolutely plain that in writing five of the prologues that I have mentioned the defendant copied from the plaintiff's book. The next issue, therefore, is whether such copying is in relation to a substantial part of the plaintiff's book and therefore in excess of what is a legitimate degree of copying.

Copyright protects the skill and labour employed by the plaintiff in production of his work. That skill and labour embraces not only language originated and used by the plaintiff, but also such skill and labour as he has employed in selection and compilation. The principles are clear from the cases. There is a helpful summary of the authorities in *Harman*

Pictures N.V. v. Osborne ([1967] 1 W.L.R. 723). For my purposes it is sufficient to cite two passages from that case which are taken from earlier authority:

> "Another person may originate another work in the same general form, provided he does so from his own resources and makes the work he so originates a work of his own by his own labour and industry bestowed upon it. In determining whether an injunction should be ordered, the question, where the matter of the plaintiff's work is not original, is how far an unfair or undue use has been made of the work. If, instead of searching into the common sources and obtaining your subject-matter from thence, you avail yourself of the labour of your predecessor, adopt his arrangements and questions, or adopt them with a colourable variation, it is an illegitimate use". This appears at page 730 of the report. There is also this passage:

> "In the case of works not original in the proper sense of the term, but composed of, or compiled or prepared from materials which are open to all, the fact that one man has produced such a work does not take away from anyone else the right to produce another work of the same kind, and in doing so to use all the materials open to him. But as the law has been precisely stated by Hall V.C. in *Hogg v. Scott*, 'the true principle in all these cases is that the defendant is not at liberty to use or avail himself of the labour which the plaintiff has been at for the purpose of producing his work, that is, in fact, merely to take away the result of another man's labour or, in other words, his property'."

The main thrust of Mr. Laddie's argument was that the plaintiff intended his book to be read as a factual account of historical events, that the defendant accepted it as fact and did no more than repeat certain of those facts. The plaintiff cannot claim a monopoly in historical facts. The law of copyright does not preclude another author from writing upon the same theme. It is perfectly legitimate for another person to contrive a novel about the Hofburg spear, even about its supposed ancestry and supernatural powers. Otherwise one would be driven to the conclusion that the plaintiff has a monopoly of the facts. Members of the public are entitled to use The Spear of Destiny as a historical work of reference. Mr. Laddie conceded that if the plaintiff had researched and selected which facts to use, and had expended substantial labour in making that selection, and a substantial amount of his labour had been taken by the defendant, then there might be infringement. In the present case, he submitted, the plaintiff's facts were selected by history or by Dr. Stein and not by the plaintiff. In the result, there had been no reproduction of the plaintiff's book in relation to a substantial part thereof. In the course of his copying the defendant confined himself to those matters which are represented in the plaintiff's book as historical facts, whether their origin is to be found in documented history or in the meditations of Dr. Stein.

In developing his argument Mr. Laddie drew a distinction between historical works and works of fiction. He said that if any author writes a history book he obtains copyright, but what amounts to an infringement of that copyright, i.e. substantial reproduction, depends to a great extent upon whether all the defendant has taken is historical facts or amounts to more than that. The degree of user which would amount to an infringement is different in the case of a historical work than in the case of a work of fiction. There is more freedom to copy in the case of the historical work.

I am inclined to accept that a historical work is not to be judged by precisely the same standards as a work of fiction. The purpose of a novel is usually to interest the reader and to contribute to his enjoyment of his leisure. A historical work may well have that purpose, but the author of a serious and original historical work may properly be assumed by his readers to have another purpose as well, namely to add to the knowledge possessed by the reader and perhaps in the process to increase the sum |206Œ total of human experience and understanding. The author of a historical work must, I think, have attributed to him an intention that the information thereby imparted may be used by the reader, because knowledge would become sterile if it could not be applied. Therefore, it seems to me reasonable to suppose that the law of copyright will allow a wider use to be made of a historical work than of a novel so that knowledge can be built upon knowledge.

Mr. Laddie referred me to *Oxford Book Co. v. College Entrance Book Co.* 98 Fed. Rep. 688 a decision of the United States Circuit Court of Appeal. The publisher of Visualised American History sued the publisher of Visualised Units of American History alleging breach of copyright. The following passage occurs in one of the judgments: Historical facts are not copyrightable per se nor are errors in fact. The plaintiff's book was designed to convey information to the readers. The defendant authors were as free to read it as anyone else, and to acquire from it such information as they could. They could indeed with equal right obtain such mis-information as it contained for the copyright gave no monopoly of the contents of the book ... and so far as plaintiff's copyright is concerned they could use whatever of either character they gleaned from the book in their own writing provided they did not copy any substantial part of the copyrighted work but created something distinctly their own.

In my judgment, Mr. Laddie's proposition must not be pressed too far. It is, I think, clear from the authorities that an author is not entitled, under the guise of producing an original work, to reproduce the arguments and illustrations of another author so as to appropriate to himself the literary labours of that author.

Mr. Sheridan, for the plaintiff, invites me to view the matter in a different light. He submits that the plaintiff's work is not a historical work of the conventional type, because it is not a chronology. It is not a continuous methodical record of public events (which is the primary dictionary definition of "history"). The plaintiff's book is poles away from history. It is disjointed and unmethodical (no offensive criticism is intended of the literary technique that he employs) being composed of a variety of different events, recollections, quotations, philosophy, meditations and so on, designed to support the theory in which the plaintiff had come to believe. Vast areas of history are left out by the plaintiff in his attempt to persuade the reader that the Hofburg Spear has the ancestry and attributes which the plaintiff believes are to be ascribed to it. The book is a very personal insight into history.

What the plaintiff has done is to select events from history and from his recollection of the meditations of Dr. Stein in order to present to the reader the credentials of the Hofburg Spear.

I accept Mr. Sheridan's analysis of the nature of the plaintiff's work.

Having studied the two books and heard the evidence, I have no shadow of doubt that the defendant has copied from The Spear of Destiny to a substantial extent. In the prologues he has deliberately copied the language of the plaintiff on many occasions. To a more significant extent he has adopted wholesale the identical incidents of documented and occult history which the plaintiff used in support of his theory of the ancestry and attributes of the spear, of Hitler's obsession with it and also General Patton's. He did this in order to give his novel a backbone of truth with the least possible labour to himself. In so doing he annexed for his own purposes the skill and labour of the plaintiff to an extent which is not permissible under the law of copyright. The defendant has clearly infringed the plaintiff's copyright. I am only sorry that so much time, effort and money has had to be spent on the trial of this action.

THE HINDENBERG CASE
GENE MILLER v. UNIVERSAL CITY STUDIOS, INC.

United States Court of Appeals, Fifth Circuit, 1981
650 F.2d 1365.

RONEY, CIRCUIT JUDGE.

A sensational kidnapping, committed over a decade ago, furnishes the factual backdrop for this copyright infringement suit. The issue is whether a made-for-television movie dramatizing the crime infringes upon a copyrighted book depicting the unsuccessful ransom attempt. After careful and lengthy study and consideration, we conclude that the verdict for plaintiff must be reversed and the cause remanded for a new trial because at the request of plaintiff and over defendants' objection, the case was presented and argued to the jury on a false premise: that the labor of research by an author is protected by copyright.

In December 1968 the college-aged daughter of a wealthy Florida land developer was abducted from an Atlanta motel room and buried alive in a plywood and fiberglass capsule. A crude life-support system kept her alive for the five days she was underground before her rescue. Gene Miller, a reporter for the Miami Herald, covered the story and subsequently collaborated with the victim to write a book about the crime. Published in 1971 under the title 83 Hours Till Dawn, the book was copyrighted along with a condensed version in Reader's Digest and a serialization in the Ladies Home Journal. The co-author has assigned her interest in this litigation to Miller.

In January 1972 a Universal City Studios (Universal) producer read the condensed version of the book and thought the story would make a good television movie. He gave a copy of the book to a scriptwriter, who immediately began work on a screenplay. Although negotiations for purchase of the movie rights to 83 Hours Till Dawn were undertaken by Universal, no agreement with Miller was ever reached. The scriptwriter was eventually advised that use of the book in completing the script was "verboten." The movie was completed, however, and aired as an ABC Movie of the Week, The Longest Night.

The evidence at trial was conflicting on whether the scriptwriter relied almost entirely on the book in writing the screenplay or whether he arrived at his version of the kidnapping story independently. Both plaintiff and his expert witness testified to numerous similarities between the works. The jury, which had copies of the book and viewed the movie twice during the trial, found the movie infringed Miller's copyright and awarded him over $200,000 in damages and profits.

The most substantial question presented on appeal is whether the district court erred in instructing the jury that "research is copyrightable."

The district court instructed the jury that if an author engages in research on factual matters, "his research is copyrightable." This instruction, at best confusing, at worst wrong, was given with some reluctance by the trial court over the strenuous objection of defendants on the urging by plaintiff, "That's the heart of the case."

It is well settled that copyright protection extends only to an author's expression of facts and not to the facts themselves. This dichotomy between facts and their expression derives from the concept of originality which is the premise of copyright law. Obviously, a fact does not originate with the author of a book describing the fact. Neither does it originate with one who "discovers" the fact. "The discoverer merely finds and records. He may not claim that the facts are 'original' with him although there may be originality and hence authorship in the manner of reporting, i. e., the 'expression,' of the facts. Thus, since facts do not owe their origin to any individual, they may not be copyrighted and are part of the public domain available to every person."

The court interpreted the copyright law to reward not only the effort and ingenuity involved in giving expression to facts, but also the efforts involved in discovering and exposing facts. In its view, an author could not be expected to expend his time and money in gathering facts if he knew those facts, and the profits to be derived therefrom, could be pirated by one who could then avoid the expense of obtaining the facts himself. Applying this reasoning to the case at bar, the court concluded "(i)n the age of television 'docudrama' to hold other than research is copyrightable is to violate the spirit of the copyright law and to provide to those persons and corporations lacking in requisite diligence and ingenuity a license to steal."

Thus the trial court's explanation of its understanding of its charge undercuts the argument to this Court that the word "research" was intended to mean the original expression by the author of the results of the research, rather than the labor of research.

The issue is not whether granting copyright protection to an author's research would be desirable or beneficial, but whether such protection is intended under the copyright law. In support of its instruction, the district court cited a number of cases, one of which involved the use of another's historical research in writing a literary work. [Among the cases cited by the court were *Hoehling v. Universal City Studios, Inc.*, 618 F.2d 972 (2d Cir.), *cert. denied*, U.S. 101 S.Ct. 121, 66 L.Ed.2d 49 (1980), and *Rosemont Enterprises, Inc. v. Random House, Inc.*, 366 F.2d 303 (2d Cir.1966), *cert. denied*, 385 U.S. 1009, 87 S.Ct. 714, 17 L.Ed.2d 546 (1967).]

Apart from the directory cases, the only decision cited to this Court which lends support for the challenged instruction is *Toksvig v. Bruce Publishing Co.*, 181 F.2d 664 (7th Cir.1950). In *Toksvig*, plaintiff had written a biography of Hans Christian Anderson after extensive research of primary Danish sources. Defendant, who could not read Danish, copied twenty-four specific passages from plaintiff's book in writing her own biography. The Seventh Circuit held the copying of these passages, original translations from Danish separately copyrightable under 17 U.S.C. § 6 (1970), constituted copyright infringement. The court went on to reject defendant's fair use defense, primarily because defendant's use of the translations from Danish had allowed her to write her biography in one-third the time it took plaintiff. The court said the question was not whether defendant could have obtained the same information by going to the sources plaintiff had used, but whether she in fact had done her own independent research. Id. at 667.

Although most circuits apparently have not addressed the question, the idea that historical research is copyrightable was expressly rejected by the Second Circuit in the more soundly reasoned case of *Rosemont Enterprises, Inc. v. Random House, Inc.*, 366 F.2d 303 (2d Cir.1966), cert. denied, 385 U.S. 1009, 87 S.Ct. 714, 17 L.Ed.2d 546 (1967). In Rosemont, it was alleged that defendant's biography of Howard Hughes infringed the copyright on a series of Look articles about Hughes. The district court had asserted in sweeping language that an author is not entitled to utilize the fruits of another's labor in lieu of independent research, relying on *Toksvig*. The Second Circuit reversed. While not challenging the holding of *Toksvig* that substantial copying of specific passages amounted to copyright infringement, it rejected the language regarding independent research: We ... cannot subscribe to the view that an author is absolutely precluded from saving time and effort by referring to and relying upon prior published material. . . . It is just such wasted effort that the proscription against the copyright of ideas and facts, and to a lesser extent the privilege of fair use, are designed to prevent. 366 F.2d at 310 (citations omitted).

The Second Circuit has adhered to its position in the most recent appellate case to address the question, *Hoehling v. Universal City Studios, Inc.*, 618 F.2d 972 (2d Cir.), cert. denied, ___ U.S. ___, 101 S.Ct. 121, 66 L.Ed.2d 49 (1980). *Hoehling* involved various literary accounts of the last voyage and mysterious destruction of the German dirigible Hindenberg. Plaintiff A. A. Hoehling published a book in 1962 entitled, Who Destroyed the Hindenberg? Written as a factual account in an objective, reportorial style, the premise of his extensively researched book was that the Hindenberg had been deliberately sabotaged by a member of its crew to embarrass the Nazi regime. Ten years later, defendant Michael McDonald Mooney published his book, The Hindenberg. While a more literary than historical account, it also hypothesized sabotage. Universal City Studios purchased the movie rights to Mooney's book and produced a movie under the same title, although the movie differed somewhat from the book. During the litigation, Mooney acknowledged he had consulted Hoehling's book and relied on it for some details in writing his own, but he maintained he first discovered the sabotage theory in Dale Titler's Wings of Mystery, also released in 1962.

Hoehling sued Mooney and Universal for copyright infringement. The district court granted defendants' motion for summary judgment and the Second Circuit affirmed, holding that, assuming both copying and substantial similarity, all the similarities pertained to categories of noncopyrightable material. The court noted the sabotage hypothesis espoused in Hoehling's book was based entirely on interpretation of historical fact and was not copyrightable. 618 F.2d at 979. The same reasoning applied to Hoehling's claim that a number of specific facts, ascertained through his personal research, were copied by defendants. Relying on the *Rosemont* case, the court stated that factual information is in the public domain and "each (defendant) had the right to 'avail himself of the facts contained' in Hoehling's book and to 'use such information, whether correct or incorrect, in his own literary work.'" 618 F.2d at 979 (quoting *Greenbie v. Noble*, 151 F.Supp. 45, 67 (S.D.N.Y. 1957)).

We find the approach taken by the Second Circuit in *Hoehling* and *Rosemont* to be more consistent with the purpose and intended scope of protection under the copyright law than that implied by *Toksvig*. The line drawn between uncopyrightable facts and copyrightable expression of facts serves an important purpose in copyright law. It provides a means of balancing the public's interest in stimulating creative activity, as embodied in the Copyright Clause, against the public's need for unrestrained access to information. It allows a subsequent author to build upon and add to prior accomplishments without unnecessary duplication of effort. As expressed by the Second Circuit in *Hoehling* : The copyright provides a financial incentive to those who would add to the corpus of existing knowledge by creating original works. Nevertheless, the protection afforded the copyright holder has never extended to history, be it documented fact or explanatory hypothesis. The rationale for this doctrine is that the cause of knowledge is best served when history is the common property of all, and each generation remains free to draw upon the discoveries and insights of the past. Accordingly, the scope of copyright in historical accounts is narrow indeed, embracing no more than the author's original expression of particular facts and theories already in the public domain.

The valuable distinction in copyright law between facts and the expression of facts cannot be maintained if research is held to be copyrightable. There is no rational basis for distinguishing between facts and the research involved in obtaining facts. To hold that research is copyrightable is no more or no less than to hold that the facts discovered as a result of research are entitled to copyright protection. Plaintiff argues that extending copyright protection to research would not upset the balance because it would not give the researcher/author a monopoly over the facts but would only ensure that later writers obtain the facts independently or follow the guidelines of fair use if the facts are no longer discoverable. But this is precisely the scope of protection given any copyrighted matter, and the law is clear that facts are not entitled to such protection. We conclude that the district court erred in instructing the jury that research is copyrightable.

Notes and Questions

1.   Which test for copyright infringement do you agree with? The one in the *Cherry Ripe* case or the one in the *Album Photography* case? Does copyright infringement of photographs depend on the "artistic nature" of the subject matter of the photograph in either of these cases? For example, if the plaintiff had simply taken an unposed snapshot, would such snapshot be entitled to the same protection against the creation of infringing derivative works as the posed photograph of the album cover? Compare the *Oscar Wilde Photo* case in Chapter Seven. Does the subject matter effect the scope of protection?

2.   Under the reasoning of the *Album Photography* case would the defendant have violated the photographer's rights in the album photograph if he had posed the members of Oasis in the exact pose as the album cover, in the exact location, with the intent to reproduce as closely as possible the original photograph? Would the defendant have violated the photographer's rights under the reasoning of the *Cherry Ripe* case? Which one of these decisions is in accordance with TRIPS standards?

3.   Although both the UK and the U.S. appear to treat photographs as protectable per se without regard to the artistic nature of the craftsmanship that was used to create the photograph, there is some indication that

unposed photographs (i.e. snapshots) are subject to lesser degrees of protection in France due to the lack of artistry in such unposed works. *See generally* Gendreau, *La protection des photographies en droit d'auteur* (1994); W.R. Cornish, INTELLECTUAL PROPERTY: PATENTS, COPYRIGHT, TRADE MARKS AND ALLIED RIGHTS (Sweet & Maxwell 1996).

4. Which of the above decisions meet the enforcement standards of TRIPS? In other words, does TRIPS require a particular test for "violation of an intellectual property right"?

5. In Russia in the late 1990s, no relief for infringement of intellectual property rights was available unless the IP owner could demonstrate a "serious injury." Does this standard violate TRIPS? What evidence would you require before infringement of a trademark resulted in "serious injury"?

6. International conflicts regarding the test for "violation" of an intellectual property right are not limited to cases of patent and copyright infringement. *See* the *Japanese Noodle* case, *supra* Chapter Fifteen, for a discussion of the varying standards that are applied to determine likelihood of confusion for trademarks.

Problem

Your client, Radical Pix, Inc., a New York corporation, has obtained the exclusive right to make digital versions of all of the great 19th Century masterpieces in the Louvre. Its goal is to sell downloadable copies of the digitized masterpieces through its web site—RadPix.com. In order to digitize the paintings, Radical Pix hires a free lance photographer to photograph each individual painting. Using a computerized process that it invented, and for which it has recently filed a U.S. patent application, the photo is turned into a digital database which can be easily downloaded.

Radical Pix began to operate its web site three months ago. Sales relatively slow and then disappeared completely a month ago. Radical Pix has discovered a web site—Museumtour.com—that contains digital versions of paintings from famous art galleries around the world—including 10 of the 19th Century masters from the Louvre that Radical Pix had the exclusive right to digitize and license others to use in a digital environment. Radical Pix has also discovered articles on the London Times web site and the Time Magazine web site that feature pictures of its digitized paintings. The articles deal with a travelling exhibition of French art, including Reviews of the exhibition, and a brief biography of the featured artists. Radical Pix has learned that Museumtown.com is owned by a travel agency based in France. It has no record of having licensed the French travel agency to use its photos. An examination of a download from the Museumtown.com web site indicates that Radical Pix's computer process was used to digitize the picture. What advice would you give Radical Pix about the steps it should take to protect its intellectual property rights? Which, if any, of the parties is guilty of infringement? What further information, if any, would you need to make this determination? How would you obtain any such information?

THE JAPANESE BALL SHAFT CASE

TSUBAKIMOTO SEIKO CO, LTD. v. THK K.K.

Tokyo High Court, 1994.

http://www.softic. or.jp/eng/cases/Tsubakimoto.v.THK.html.

1.   The present case is a suit demanding payment of damages by the appellee on the grounds that the appellant infringed the patent right of the appellee. Summary of the facts of the original appeal is as follows:

(1) The appellee owns a patent right to an invention entitled "Endlessly Sliding Ball Spline Shaft Bearing" (Application date: April 26, 1971; Publication date: July 7, 1978; and Registration date: May 30, 1980; Patent No.999139)(this patent right hereinafter will be referred to as the present patent right, and the invention thereof will be referred to as the present invention).

(3) During the period of January 1983 to October 1988, the appellant had manufactured and sold a product whose features appellee asserted encompass or are equivalent to all of the constituent features of the present invention, and therefore, the appellant's' product falls within the technical scope of the present invention.

In determining whether or not the product made by the other party or the method employed by the other party (hereinafter referred to as "corresponding product etc.") falls within the technical scope of a patented invention in a patent right infringement appeal, the technical scope of the patented invention must be determined based on the description of claims in the specification attached to the application (see Patent Law Section 70 (1)). If there are elements that differ between the constitution described in a patented claim and corresponding product and the like, the corresponding product and the like cannot be said to fall within the technical scope of the patented invention. On the other hand, even if there are elements in the constitution described in a patented claim that differ from the corresponding product and the like, the corresponding product and the like may be equivalent to the constitution described in claim and may appropriately be said to fall within the technical scope of the patented invention if the following conditions are satisfied: (1) the differing elements are not the essential elements in the patented invention; (2) even if the differing elements are interchanged by elements of the corresponding product and the like, the object of the patented invention can be achieved and the same effects can be obtained; (3) by interchanging as above, a person of ordinary skill in the art to which the invention pertains (hereinafter referred to as an artisan) could have easily achieved the corresponding product and the like at the time of manufacture etc. of corresponding product; (4) the corresponding product and the like are not the same as the known art at the time of application for patent or could not have been easily conceived by an artisan at the time of application for patent; and (5) there is not any special circumstances such that the corresponding product and the like are intentionally excluded from the scope of the claim during patent prosecution.

It would be very difficult to write down claims at the finding in anticipation of all type of future infringing situations. Additionally, if enforcement of patent right such as injunction and such by a patentee can be easily circumvented by another party by interchanging a material or a technique-a portion of the constituent features of the claim that is made clear after the filing of the patent application, the drive for invention by the public would be diminished. This not only violates the purpose of patent law to contribute to the development of industries through protection of and encouragement for invention, but also denies social justice, resulting in the breach of the concept of equity. (2) In view of these circumstances, it should be understood that the substantive value of a patented invention should be extended from the claims to cover a technology easily obtainable by a third party, which is substantially identical with the constitution described in the claims, and that this could be anticipated by a third party. (3) On the other hand, since it is not expected for anyone to obtain a patent based on a technology known publicly or easily conceived by an artisan at the time of the filing the patent application (see Patent Law Section 29), such a technology can never be included in the technical scope of a patented claim. (4) once a patentee excludes a technology from the technical scope of a patented invention by intentionally excluding it from the scope of the claim during patent prosecution or committing an act that can be outwardly interpreted as doing so, the patentee cannot substantially make assertions that would contradict this exclusion since such a contradiction would not be permitted in view of the law of prosecution estoppel.

Applying this to the present case, although some differences between the claim of the present specification and the appellant's product were found, the appellant's product was determined in the original appeal to fall within the technical scope of the present invention for the reasons that there was interchangeability as well as ease of interchangeability between the present invention and the appellant's product.

However, it is acknowledged in the original appeal that an endlessly sliding ball spline shaft bearing, constituted by an outer cylinder, a spline shaft and a retainer, was already known prior to the application of the present invention; further, a spline shaft provided with a plurality of ribs extending in the axial direction thereof, the ribs being shaped to conform with a plurality of recessed spaces formed by the balls incorporated between the retainer and the outer cylinder is an ordinary shaft that has been commonly employed for a ball spline bearing: and that (1) the retainer according to the present invention is an integral structure providing the functions of guiding balls to move in endless circulation, retaining balls when the spline shaft is withdrawn, and forming recessed portions for guiding the rib portions of the spline shaft; the retainer according to the appellant's product is a split type structure consisting of three plate-like members, a couple of return caps and the ribs formed between the load bearing ball-guiding grooves of the outer cylinder; and the aforementioned functions of the present invention are effected in the appellant's product by the cooperative action of these members; (2) the retainer of the split type structure consisting of three plate-like members and a couple of return caps according to the appellant's product has already been shown in an endlessly sliding ball spline shaft bearing described in U.S. patent No. 3,360,308, published before the application date of the present invention; and (3) the ribs between the load-bearing ball-guiding grooves of the outer cylinder as being technically necessary in order to retain balls by means of such a slit-type retainer is apparent from a ball spline described in U.S. patent No. 3,398,999, published before the application date of the present invention.

According to the aforementioned Decision in the original appeal, a retainer of the split type structure as well as ribs between the load-bearing ball-guiding grooves of the outer cylinder in the appellant's product were already shown in the known ball spline bearing disclosed prior to the application date of the present invention.

Further, according to the aforementioned to the Decision in the original appeal, the appellant's product is similar to the present invention in that the non-load bearing balls are adapted to circulate in the circumferential direction and that a plural-array type angular contact structure in which both sides of the rib portion of the spline shaft are held between a pair of load bearing balls fitted in the torque-transmitting load-bearing ball-guiding grooves, is utilized. However, since it was acknowledged in the original appeal that both the circulation of the non-load bearing ball in the circumferential direction and the plural-array type angular contact structure were already described in Japanese Patent Publication S/44–2361, in German Federal Republic Patent No. 1,450,060 and in U.S. Patent No. 3,494,148, all published prior to the application date of the present invention, it is deemed that uses of these technologies for a ball spline bearing have been publicly known prior to the application date of the present invention.

Therefore, given that the technologies related to the ball spline bearing provided with the circulation of the non-load bearing ball in the circumferential direction and with the plural-array type angular contact structure, were publicly known prior to the application date of the present invention, the appellant's product is deemed to be simply a combination of a ball spline bearing, which is provided with the known circulation of the non-load bearing ball in the circumferential direction and with the known plural-array type angular contact structure, and a known split type retainer, because it is acknowledged in the original appeal that basically the structure of the retainer cannot be distinguished by the contacting structure of the balls. Given that this combination could have been easily arrived at by an artisan without the disclosure of the present invention, it is deemed that the artisan could have easily conceived the appellant's product at the time of the application date of the present invention from the known art published before the application date of the present invention. Therefore, the appellant's product cannot be said to be equivalent to the constitution set forth in the claim of the present specification, and the appellant's product cannot be said to fall within the technical scope of the present invention.

As described above, it was acknowledged in the original appeal that some of the constituent features set forth in the claim of the present specification differed from those of the appellant's product. However, only the topic of whether or not there exist any interchangeability or ease of interchangeability between the differing elements of the present invention and the constitution of the appellant's product was examined in the original appeal. Then, without discussing the relationship between the appellant's product and the known art at the time of the application of the present invention, a decision was summarily made in the original appeal to the effect that the appellant's product was equivalent to the constitution set forth in the claim of the present specification, and that the appellant's product fell within the technical scope of the present invention.

Therefore, it cannot but be said that the aforementioned Decision made in the original appeal is erroneous in interpretation and application of the Patent Law, thus making it unnecessary to discuss the propriety of the decisions made in the original appeal on other requirements such as equivalence, e.g. interchangeability or ease of interchangeability.

4. As explained above, The Decision of the original appeal is erroneous in interpretation and application of Patent Law. In other words, it is unlawful in terms of premature decision and deficient reasoning. It is apparent that this unlawful interpretation and application has affected the conclusion of the original Decision.

There is a reason for the points of argument as explained above, and original Decision cannot be reversed. Further, since the aforementioned points should be fully reconsidered in the original appeal, this case is thus remanded.

Notes and Questions

1. According to Japan's Patent Law, patent infringement occurs when an unauthorized person directly employs a patented invention for business use or conducts some other activity which constitutes an indirect use of the invention. As in the United States, the most important factor for determining direct infringement is whether an accused device falls within the technical scope of the patented invention (i.e., the claimed invention) under Section 70 of the Japanese Patent Law.

2. Does the court in the *Japanese Ball Shaft* case use an element by element approach (literal infringement) or an invention as a whole approach (essence of the invention) to compare the accused device to the claims at issue. Compare this analysis with the court in the *Epilady* case (below). Does this method of analysis violate the standards of protection required under TRIPS?

3. What prior decisions did the High Court rely on in reaching its decision regarding the scope of the patents? Japan, like many countries, is a

civil law country where courts rely on the wording of the statutes, but the reasoning of previous decisions is not considered binding precedent. Does the lack of *stare decisis* violate the enforcement principles of TRIPS?

4.   What test for equivalence does the court in the *Japanese Ball Shaft* case apply? How does this test compare with the U.S. doctrine of equivalence test used in the *U.S. Doctrine of Equivalence* case (below)?

THE U.S. DOCTRINE OF EQUIVALENCE CASE
GRAVER TANK & MFG. CO. v. LINDE AIR PRODUCTS CO.

Supreme Court Of The United States, 1950.
339 U.S. 605, 70 S.Ct. 854.

MR. JUSTICE JACKSON delivered the opinion of the Court.

Linde Air Products Co., owner of the Jones patent for an electric welding process and for fluxes to be used therewith, brought an action for infringement against Lincoln and the two Graver companies.

At the outset it should be noted that the single issue before us is whether the trial court's holding that the four flux claims have been infringed will be sustained. Any issue as to the validity of these claims was unanimously determined by the previous decision in this Court and attack on their validity cannot be renewed now by reason of limitation on grant of rehearing.

In determining whether an accused device or composition infringes a valid patent, resort must be had in the first instance to the words of the claim. If accused matter falls clearly within the claim, infringement is made out and that is the end of it.

But courts have also recognized that to permit imitation of a patented invention which does not copy every literal detail would be to convert the protection of the patent grant into a hollow and useless thing. Such a limitation would leave room for—indeed encourage—the unscrupulous copyist to make unimportant and insubstantial changes and substitutions in the patent which, though adding nothing, would be enough to take the copied matter outside the claim, and hence outside the reach of law. One who seeks to pirate an invention, like one who seeks to pirate a copyrighted book or play, may be expected to introduce minor variations to conceal and shelter the piracy. Outright and forth-right duplication is a dull and very rare type of infringement. To prohibit no other would place the inventor at the mercy of verbalism and would be subordinating substance to form. It would deprive him of the benefit of his invention and would foster concealment rather than disclosure of inventions, which is one of the primary purposes of the patent system.

The doctrine of equivalents evolved in response to this experience. The essence of the doctrine is that one may not practice a fraud on a patent. Originating almost a century ago in the case of *Winans v. Denmead*, 15 How. 330, it has been consistently applied by this Court and the lower federal courts, and continues today ready and available for utilization when the proper circumstances for its application arise. "To temper unsparing logic and prevent an infringer from stealing the benefit of an invention" a patentee may invoke this doctrine to proceed against the producer of a device "if it performs substantially the same function in substantially the same way to obtain the same result." *Sanitary Refrigerator Co. v. Winters,* 280 U.S. 30, 42. The theory on which it is founded is that "if two devices do the same work in substantially the same way, and accomplish substantially the same result, they are the same, even though they differ in name, form, or shape." *Machine Co. v. Murphy,* 97 U.S. 120, 125. The doctrine operates not only in favor of the patentee of a pioneer or primary invention, but also for the patentee of a secondary invention consisting of a combination of old ingredients which produce new and useful results, although the area of equivalence may vary under the circumstances. The wholesome realism of this doctrine is not always applied in favor of a patentee but is sometimes used against him. Thus, where a device is so far changed in principle from a patented article that it performs the same or a similar function in a substantially different way, but nevertheless falls within the literal words of the claim, the doctrine of equivalents may be used to restrict the claim and defeat the patentee's action for infringement. In its early development, the doctrine was usually applied in cases involving devices where there was equivalence in mechanical components. Subsequently, however, the same principles were also applied to compositions, where there was equivalence between chemical ingredients. Today the doctrine is applied to mechanical or chemical equivalents in compositions or devices.

What constitutes equivalency must be determined against the context of the patent, the prior art, and the particular circumstances of the case. Equivalence, in the patent law, is not the prisoner of a formula and is not an absolute to be considered in a vacuum. It does not require complete identity for every purpose and in every respect. In determining equivalents, things equal to the same thing may not be equal to each other and, by the same token, things for most purposes different may sometimes be equivalents. Consideration must be given to the purpose for which an ingredient is used in a patent, the qualities it has when combined with the other ingredients, and the function which it is intended to perform. An important factor is whether persons reasonably skilled in the art would have known of the interchangeability of an ingredient not contained in the patent with one that was.

A finding of equivalence is a determination of fact. Proof can be made in any form: through testimony of experts or others versed in the technology; by documents, including texts and treatises; and, of course, by the disclosures of the prior art. Like any other issue of fact, final determination requires a balancing of credibility, persuasiveness and weight of evidence. It is to be decided by the trial court and that court's decision, under general principles of appellate review, should not be disturbed unless clearly erroneous. Particularly is this so in a field where so much depends upon familiarity with specific scientific problems and principles not usually contained in the general storehouse of knowledge and experience.

In the case before us, we have two electric welding compositions or fluxes: the patented composition, Unionmelt Grade 20, and the accused composition, Lincolnweld 660. The patent under which Unionmelt is made claims essentially a combination of alkaline earth metal silicate and calcium fluoride; Unionmelt actually contains, however, silicates of calcium and magnesium, two alkaline earth metal silicates. Lincoln-weld's composition is similar to Unionmelt's, except that it substitutes silicates of calcium and manganese—the latter not an alkaline earth metal—for silicates of calcium and magnesium. In all other respects, the two compositions are alike. The mechanical methods in which these compositions are employed are similar. They are identical in operation and produce the same kind and quality of weld.

The question which thus emerges is whether the substitution of the manganese which is not an alkaline earth metal for the magnesium which is, under the circumstances of this case, and in view of the technology and the prior art, is a change of such substance as to make the doctrine of equivalents inapplicable; or conversely, whether under the circumstances the change was so insubstantial that the trial court's invocation of the doctrine of equivalents was justified.

Without attempting to be all-inclusive, we note the following evidence in the record: Chemists familiar with the two fluxes testified that manganese and magnesium were similar in many of their reactions (R. 287, 669). There is testimony by a metallurgist that alkaline earth metals are often found in manganese ores in their natural state and that they serve the same purpose in the fluxes (R. 831–832); and a chemist testified that "in the sense of the patent" manganese could be included as an alkaline earth metal (R. 297). Much of this testimony was corroborated by reference to recognized texts on inorganic chemistry (R. 332). Particularly important, in addition, were the disclosures of the prior art, also contained in the record. The Miller patent, No. 1,754,566, which preceded the patent in suit, taught the use of manganese silicate in welding fluxes (R. 969, 971). Manganese was similarly disclosed in the Armor patent, No. 1,467,825, which also described a welding composition (R. 1346). And the record contains no evidence of any kind to show that Lincolnweld was developed as the result of independent research or experiments.

It is not for this Court to even essay an independent evaluation of this evidence. This is the function of the trial court. And, as we have heretofore observed, "To no type of case is this more appropriately applicable than to the one before us, where the evidence is largely the testimony of experts as to which a trial court may be enlightened by scientific demonstrations. This trial occupied some three weeks, during which, as the record shows, the trial judge visited laboratories with counsel and experts to observe actual demonstrations of welding as taught by the patent and of the welding accused of infringing it, and of various stages of the prior art. He viewed motion pictures of various welding operations and tests and heard many experts and other witnesses." 336 U.S. 271, 274–275.

The trial judge found on the evidence before him that the Lincolnweld flux and the composition of the patent in suit are substantially identical in operation and in result. He found also that Lincolnweld is in all respects equivalent to Unionmelt for welding purposes. And he concluded that "for all practical purposes, manganese silicate can be efficiently and effectually substituted for calcium and magnesium silicates as the major constituent of the welding composition." These conclusions are adequately supported by the record; certainly they are not clearly erroneous.

It is difficult to conceive of a case more appropriate for application of the doctrine of equivalents. The disclosures of the prior art made clear that manganese silicate was a useful ingredient in welding compositions. Specialists familiar with the problems of welding compositions understood that manganese was equivalent to and could be substituted for magnesium in the composition of the patented flux and their observations were confirmed by the literature of chemistry. Without some explanation or indication that Lincolnweld was developed by independent research, the trial court could properly infer that the accused flux is the result of imitation rather than experimentation or invention. Though infringement was not literal, the changes which avoid literal infringement are colorable only. We conclude that the trial court's judgment of infringement respecting the four flux claims was proper, and we adhere to our prior decision on this aspect of the case.

Affirmed.

THE EPILADY CASE

IMPROVER CORPORATION v. REMINGTON CONSUMER PRODUCTS LIMITED

Chancery Division (Patents Court), 1989.
[1990] FSR 181.

HOFFMAN, J.

This is an action for infringement of a European patent for an electrically powered cosmetic device for removing hair. The commercial embodiment of the plaintiff's invention is called "Epilady" and the defendant's device is called "Smooth & Silky." The defences are, first, that Smooth & Silky does not infringe the claims of the patent and secondly, that the patent is invalid for obviousness and insufficiency. In my judgment the patent in suit is valid but the defendant's device does not infringe. The action is therefore dismissed.

Depilation means the removal of hair by the root, as opposed to shaving which leaves the root behind. The advantage of depilation is that the hair takes much longer to regenerate. Various methods have been used in the past for cosmetic depilation, but none was completely satisfactory. An article published in an American marketing journal in 1976 ("Where to look for good product ideas" by Joseph J Montesano in Product Management, August 1976) began as follows:

"If you were seeking a truly new product that meets a genuine consumer need you might start with the women's depilatory market. After many years of looking—ever since ancient Egypt—women still say they have not found the ideal product to remove hair from legs and face.

Pull it off with a hardened wax? It hurts. Use a chemical that dissolves hair? It has an offensive odor. Electrolysis? You need an expert and it's expensive. Use a razor—even a new idea like the disposables? There are still nicks and scratches—at least some women still think so.

It's a huge, waiting market, and the company that comes up with a safe, effective product will hit the jackpot. Everyone knows the market is there and some in the field have been searching for the key to unlock the treasure."

Epilady was invented by two Israelis in 1982. It consists of a small electric motor in a hand-held plastic housing to which is attached a helical steel spring held by its ends and stiffened by a guide wire to form a loop. The arcuate form of the spring causes the gaps between the windings to open on its convex side but to be pressed together on the concave side. When the spring is held close to the skin and rotated by the motor at about 6,000 revolutions per minute, hairs enter the gaps on its convex side and are gripped between the windings as the rotational movement brings them round to the concave side. The effect is to pluck them out of the skin.

Marketing of Epilady began in June 1986. It was an enormous commercial success. In the first two years over 5.8 million devices were made, generating a gross retail turnover in excess of U.S. $340,000,000.

THE PATENT IN SUIT

The basic description of the patent in suit declares that:

"There is thus provided in accordance with an embodiment of the present invention an electrically powered depilatory device including a hand held portable housing, motor apparatus disposed in the housing, and a helical spring composed of a plurality of adjacent windings arranged to be driven by the motor apparatus in rotational sliding motion relative to skin bearing hair to be removed, the helical spring including an arcuate hair engaging portion arranged to define a convex side whereat the windings are spread apart, and a concave side corresponding thereto whereat the windings are pressed together, the rotational motion of the helical spring producing continuous motion of the windings from a spread apart orientation at the convex side to a pressed together orientation at the concave side and for the engagement and plucking of hair from the skin, whereby the surface velocities of the windings relative to the skin greatly exceed the surface velocity of the housing relative thereto."

A preferred embodiment of the invention is said to be one in which the helical spring arcuate hair engaging portion:

"extends along an arc subtending more than 90 degrees and preferably more than 180 degrees, whereby the surface velocities of windings of the helical spring simultaneously include components extending in mutually perpendicular directions, for significantly enhanced hair removal efficiency."

"The looped spring configuration of the present invention is a particular feature thereof in that there are simultaneously present at all times windings of the helical spring whose component of velocity relative to the hair extends in mutually perpendicular directions. The apparatus thus is operative to remove hair oriented in various directions without requiring movement of the housing against the skin in all of these directions."

The description ends, however, with the following general statement, which I shall later refer to as the "equivalents clause":

"It will be evident to those skilled in the art that the invention is not limited to the details of the foregoing illustrative embodiments, and that the present invention may be embodied in other specific forms without departing from the essential attributes thereof, and it is therefore desired that the present embodiments be considered in all respects as illustrative and not restrictive, reference being made to the appended claims, rather than to the foregoing description, and all variations which come within the meaning and range of equivalency of the claims are therefore intended to be embraced therein." (Emphasis supplied.)

Claim 1 reads as follows:

"An electrically powered depilatory device comprising:

a hand held portable housing (2);

motor means (4, 4') disposed in said housing; and

a helical spring (24) comprising a plurality of adjacent windings arranged to be driven by said motor means in rotational sliding motion relative to skin bearing hair to be removed, said helical spring (24) including an arcuate hair engaging portion arranged to define a convex side whereat the windings are spread apart and a concave side corresponding thereto whereat the windings are pressed together, the rotational motion of the helical spring (24) producing continuous motion of the windings from a spread apart orientation at the convex side to a pressed together orientation on the concave side and for the engagement and plucking of hair from the

skin of the subject, whereby the surface velocities of the windings relative to the skin greatly exceed the surface velocity of
the housing relative thereto."

Claims 2, 3 and 4 are for the device according to claim 1 but with
the helical spring respectively subtending more than 90 degrees, more
than 180 degrees and in the looped configuration shown as the preferred
embodiment. Claims 5 to 8 are concerned with variations on the angles
and distances between the windings of the helical spring. Claims 9 to 15
are concerned with various forms and motor and the means by which the
spring may be driven. Claim 16 introduces a stiffening wire which
remains stationary inside the spring. Claims 17 and 18 concern the
spindles to which the spring is attached and Claims 19 and 20 deal with
the speeds at which the helical spring rotates.

Smooth & Silky

Smooth & Silky also consists of a small electric motor in a hand held
housing but the element attached to the motor and used to extract the
hair is not a helical metal spring. Instead it is a cylindrical rod of
elastomerised synthetic rubber held by its ends to form an arc subtending about 60 degrees. I shall for convenience call it "the rubber rod." A
number of parallel radial slits have been cut into the rubber. The
arcuate form of the rod causes the slits to open on its convex side but to
be pressed together on the concave side. When the rod is held close to
the skin and rapidly rotated by the motor, hairs enter the gaps on its
convex side and are gripped between the walls of the slits as the
rotational movement brings them round to the concave side. The effect is
to pluck them out of the skin.

The inventor of Smooth & Silky was Mr. Gross, another Israeli who
gave evidence about how he came to choose the rubber rod. In October
1986 his wife bought an Epilady but found it painful to use. She asked
him to look at it. He is an engineer and inventor by profession and came
to the conclusion that it pulled out too much hair at once. He therefore
looked for a way to reduce the number of slits and had the idea of using
a bendy plastic rod in which he could cut a limited number of slits. After
trying and rejecting a polyurethane tube and ordinary rubber (both of
which tore too easily) he succeeded in developing a suitable synthetic
rubber which can last six or seven hours of use. It is about the same
diameter as the Epilady spring and rotates at about the same speed. Mr.
Gross said that 60 degrees was at present the maximum angle which the
rubber rod could achieve. A tighter angle would cause too much hysteresis (heat generation) and shorten the life of the rubber. The expert
evidence was that for this reason a rubber rod could certainly not be
used in the loop formation of the plaintiff's preferred embodiment.

Mr. Gross has been granted a patent in the United States (U.S.
4,726,375). Claim 1 of this patent is as follows:

"A depilatory device for removing body hair, comprising: a
manually-grippable housing, and a hair-plucker body rotatably
mounted to the housing and having an exposed section formed with

a plurality of gaps in its outer surface which open and close during the rotation of the hair-plucker to receive, pluck and eject body hair growing on a surface over which the hair-plucker body is moved characterised in that the said hair-plucker body is a flexible cylindrical member of plastic material having a smooth outer surface formed with a plurality of slits penetrating only partially through the plastic cylindrical member and extending circumferentially thereof, said plastic cylindrical member being rotated about its longitudinal axis and being supported in an arcuate position such that said slits open at the convex side of the plastic cylindrical member during its rotation to receive the hairs between the open confronting faces of the slits, and close at the concave side of the plastic cylindrical member during its rotation to clamp the hairs between the closed confronting faces of the slits.''

Dr. Laming, a distinguished design engineer called as an expert witness by the defendants, said that Mr. Gross's specification contained nothing which distinguished Smooth & Silky from Epilady by function. The difference lay in their respective forms (Evidence Day 6, p 16A).

Infringement

The question of infringement turns upon a short but undoubtedly difficult point of construction, namely whether the rubber rod is a ''helical spring'' as that expression is used in the claims of the patent in suit.

The proper approach to the interpretation of patents registered under the Patents Act 1949 was explained by Lord Diplock in *Catnic Components Ltd v Hill & Smith Ltd* ([1982] RPC 183, 242). The language should be given a ''purposive'' and not necessarily a literal construction. If the issue was whether a feature embodied in an alleged infringement which fell outside the primary, literal or acontextual meaning of a descriptive word or phrase in the claim (''a variant'') was nevertheless within its language as properly interpreted, the court should ask itself the following three questions:

(1) Does the variant have a material effect upon the way the invention works? If yes, the variant is outside the claim. If no:

(2) Would this (i.e. that the variant had no material effect) have been obvious at the date of publication of the patent to a reader skilled in the art. If no, the variant is outside the claim. If yes:

(3) Would the reader skilled in the art nevertheless have understood from the language of the claim that the patentee intended that strict compliance with the primary meaning was an essential requirement of the invention. If yes, the variant is outside the claim.

On the other hand, a negative answer to the last question would lead to the conclusion that the patentee was intending the word or phrase to have not a literal but a figurative meaning (the figure being a form of synecdoche or metonymy) denoting a class of things which included the variant and the literal meaning, the latter being perhaps the most perfect, best-known or striking example of the class.

Thus in *Catnic* itself the claim of a patent for a lintel of box construction required that the upper plate be supported upon the lower plate by two rigid supports, one in the front and the other "extending vertically" from the one plate to the other at the rear. The defendant's lintel had a rear support which was inclined 6 degrees or 8 degrees from the vertical. The House of Lords decided that this variation had no material effect upon the load-bearing capacity of the lintel or the way it worked and that this would have been obvious to the skilled builder at the date of publication of the patent. It also decided that the skilled reader would not have understood from the language of the claim that the patentee was insisting upon precisely 90 degrees as an essential requirement of his invention. The conclusion was that "extending vertically" meant "extending with the range of angles which give substantially the maximum load-bearing capacity and of which 90 degrees is the perfect example."

In the end, therefore, the question is always whether the alleged infringement is covered by the language of the claim. This, I think, is what Lord Diplock meant in *Catnic* when he said that there was no dichotomy between "textual infringement" and infringement of the "pith and marrow" of the patent and why I respectfully think that Fox LJ put the question with great precision in *Anchor Building Products Ltd. v. Redland Roof Tiles Ltd.* ((CA), unreported, 23 November 1988, transcript at p 18.) when he said the question was whether the absence of a feature mentioned in the claim was "an immaterial variant which a person skilled in the trade would have regarded as being within the ambit of the language" It is worth noticing that Lord Diplock's first two questions, although they cannot sensibly be answered without reference to the patent, do not primarily involve questions of construction: whether the variant would make a material difference to the way the invention worked and whether this would have been obvious to the skilled reader are questions of fact. The answers are used to provide the factual background against which the specification must be construed. It is the third question which raises the question of construction and Lord Diplock's formulation makes it clear that on this question the answers to the first two questions are not conclusive. Even a purposive construction of the language of the patent may lead to the conclusion that although the variant made no material difference and this would have been obvious at the time, the patentee for some reason was confining his claim to the primary meaning and excluding the variant. If this were not the case, there would be no point in asking the third question at all.

(1) Does the variant have a material effect on the way the invention works?

The answer to this question depends upon the level of generality at which one describes the way the invention works. At one extreme, if one says that the invention works by gripping and pulling hair, there is obviously no difference; the same would be true of a pair of tweezers. At the other extreme, if one says that it works by gripping hairs between metal windings of circular cross-section wound in a continuous spiral around a hollow core, there obviously is a difference.

(a) It was accepted by the experts on both sides that a metal spring having windings of circular cross-section which osculate at the point of contact exerts a far greater pressure in pounds per square inch than the plane sides of a slit in the rubber rod. The difference between the pressures exerted by the gripping elements in the two devices is of the order of three magnitudes. The evidence that this made any practical difference to the way the devices worked was in my judgment inconclusive.

It is agreed that both devices can pluck hair to the satisfaction of customers. It seems to me that the right approach is to describe the working of the invention at the level of generality with which it is described in the claim of the patent. As I have said, Dr. Laming agreed that there was no difference between the descriptions in Mr. Gross's patent and the patent in suit of the way the inventions worked. The differences lay entirely in the descriptions of the hardware. In my judgment, at the appropriate level of description, the rubber rod works in the same way as the helical spring and the differences I have mentioned, so far as they exist, are not material.

(2) Would it have been obvious to a man skilled in the art that the variant would work in the same way?

In my view the question supposes that the skilled man is told of both the invention and the variant and asked whether the variant would obviously work in the same way. An affirmative answer would not be inconsistent with the variant being an inventive step. For example, the choice of some material for the bendy rod which was a priori improbable (eg on account of its expense) but had been discovered to give some additional advantage (eg painless extraction) might be a variant which obviously worked in the same way as the invention and yet be an inventive step. Nor would it matter that the material in question, being improbable, would not have suggested itself to the skilled man as an obvious alternative. Questions such as these may be relevant to the question of construction (Lord Diplock's third question) but not at this stage of the inquiry.

Dr. Laming and Dr. Sharp, the eminent engineer called as an expert by the plaintiff, agreed that it would have been obvious to the skilled man that the attributes which enabled the helical spring to function in the way described in the specification were that it was capable of rotating, capable of transmitting torque along its length to resist the forces involved in plucking hairs, bendy (to form an arc) and slitty (to entrap hairs by the opening and closing effect of rotation). They also agreed that it would have been obvious that any rod which had these qualities in sufficient degree and did not have other defects such as overheating or falling to bits would in principle work in the same way and that the rubber rod plainly belonged to that class. On this evidence the second question must in my judgment be answered yes. I express no view on whether the rubber rod was also an inventive step.

On the other hand, the evidence shows that although the rubber rod could be used in a device which would function in the way described in claim 1 of the patent in suit, it would work only in a limited number of embodiments. In particular, it could not be used in the loop formation described as the preferred embodiment.

(3) Would the skilled reader nevertheless have understood that the patentee intended to confine his claim to the primary meaning of a helical spring?

This brings one to the question of construction. The question is what the skilled reader would have understood.

In my judgment the difference between the experts [who testified] depends upon how one construes the equivalents clause. The first part of the clause merely says that the description should not be used to restrict the meaning of the language used in the claims. That is not the question here. What matters is the final words: "and all variations which come within the meaning and range of equivalency of the claims are therefore intended to be embraced therein." If this means: "whatever contrary impression the skilled man may be given by the language of the claims read in the context of the rest of the description, all references in the claims to hardware are deemed to include any other hardware which would in any circumstances function in the same way" then I think Dr. Sharpe must be right. In my judgment, however, the clause does not have so wide an effect. The words I have quoted say that the variation must still come within the meaning of the claims and the reference to "range of equivalency" means in my judgment no more than "don't forget that the claims must be interpreted in accordance with *Catnic* and the [European Patent] Protocol."

Thus interpreted, I do not think that "helical spring" can reasonably be given a wide generic construction and I accept Dr. Laming's reasons for thinking that a skilled man would not understand it in this sense.

The rubber rod is not an approximation to a helical spring. It is a different thing which can in limited circumstances work in the same way. Nor can the spring be regarded as an "inessential" or the change from metal spring to rubber rod as a minor variant. In *Catnic* Lord Diplock asked rhetorically whether there was any reason why the patentee should wish to restrict his invention to a support angled at precisely 90 degrees, thereby making avoidance easy. In this case I think that a similar question would receive a ready answer. It would be obvious that the rubber had problems of hysteresis which might be very difficult to overcome. The plaintiff's inventors had done no work on rubber rods. Certainly the rubber rod cannot be used in the loop configuration which is the plaintiff's preferred embodiment. On the other hand, drafting the claim in wide generic terms to cover alternatives like the rubber rod might be unacceptable to the patent office. I do not think that the hypothetical skilled man is also assumed to be skilled in patent law and he would in my judgment be entitled to think that patentee had good reasons for limiting himself, as he obviously appeared to have done, to a helical coil. To derive a different meaning solely from the equivalents clause would in my view be denying third parties that reasonable degree of certainty to which they are entitled under the Protocol.

THE GERMAN DECISIONS

The patent in suit is being litigated in a number of countries but the only one in which the action has come to trial is in Germany, where the Landgericht of Dusseldorf found in favour of the plaintiff. This naturally causes me concern because the Landgericht was interpreting the same patent according to the same Protocol and came to a different conclusion. It seems to me that the reason for the difference between me and my colleagues in Dusseldorf is that, having answered what I have labelled as Lord Diplock's first two questions in the same way as I have, they treated those answers as concluding the matter in favour of the plaintiff and did not find it necessary to ask the third question at all. The specification, they said, conveyed to the expert "the understanding that the configuration of the hair engaging portion as helical spring has to be understood functionally" (Translation, p 15) and that the expert to whom the patent was directed would have "no difficulties in perceiving and understanding this meaning of the teaching of the invention." This does seem to me with respect to be an interpretation closer to treating the language of the claims as a "guideline" than the median course required by the Protocol. I also detect some difference in approach between the Landgericht and the Oberlandesgericht (Court of Appeal) which had previously discharged an interlocutory injunction granted by the Landgericht. The Court of Appeal placed much more emphasis upon the language of the specification. Its view on the primary meaning of a helical spring was as follows:

> "A spiral or helical shape is characterised by curved lines such as those showing on the level a spiral and, three-dimensionally, more or less the rising turns of a screw. Nothing else is meant by the theory of the [plaintiff's] patent and this is made clear to a person skilled in the art by the state of the art to which the patent refers and on which its proposition is undoubtedly based. A solid roller-shaped hair-engaging part with vertical incisions at a distance from each other can therefore at the most constitute an equivalent means of replacement for the helical spring."

The court went on to say that the rubber rod undoubtedly worked in the same way as the helical spring (i.e. it answered Lord Diplock's first question in the same way as I have). Although it does not specifically say so, I think it may be assumed that it would have regarded this as equally obvious to anyone skilled in the art. But when dealing with the question whether this would affect the question of construction, i.e. whether the skilled man would have regarded the rubber rod as included in the claims of the patent, the Court of Appeal expressed considerable doubt. He could have done so if he had analysed the function of the spring in the invention and then set about thinking of equivalents to perform the same function. But the court doubted whether—"the average person skilled in the art thinks in such a theoretical way. This applies particularly to the present case because there appeared to be no need for theorising in view of the fact that a normal helical spring was known as a perfectly suitable means for plucking."

It may be said that the expert evidence before the Landgericht at the trial was different, but I doubt whether this could have been so. There was no real difference between the views of Dr. Sharpe and Dr. Laming on questions of engineering: the difference lay in the approach to construction, which is really a question of law.

PATENT LITIGATION IN EUROPE

http://www.ladas.com/GUIDES/PATENT/Foreign
PatLit/Europe_Patent_Lit.html

Whatever the merits of the European Union and the European Patent Convention in other matters, they have done little to help rationalize European Patent litigation. At present all questions of infringement and, after the nine month patent opposition term provided for under the European Patent Convention has run, of validity are exclusively matters for the national courts. However, it should be noted that in general European countries have amended their definition of validity to agree with that of the European Patent Convention so that patents granted under national law and by the European Patent Office should be judged by the same standard. Additionally the European Patent Convention does contain, however, one provision which was intended to provide some uniformity in this area. The provision concerns a definition of how a claim in a European patent is to be interpreted. Prior to the coming into effect of the European Patent Convention, the British and Germans maintained opposing views on this. As originally agreed to, the European Patent Convention had a very simple definition of what interpretation the claim should be. Thus, Article 69 read:

> The extent of protection conferred by a European patent or a European patent application shall be determined by the terms of the claims. Nevertheless, the description and drawings shall be used to interpret the claims.

At the diplomatic conference that gave rise to the final form of the European Convention, it was found that this simple wording was interpreted in entirely different ways by the British and the Germans. Rather than reword the article, which had been already incorporated into the draft text, a protocol for explaining what this article meant was agreed upon which reads as follows:

> Article 69 should not be interpreted in the sense that the extent of the protection conferred by a European patent is to be understood

as that defined by the strict, literal meaning of the wording used in the claims, the description and drawings being employed only for the purpose of resolving the ambiguity found in the claims. Neither should it be interpreted in the sense that the claims serve only as a guideline and that the actual protection conferred may extend to what, from a consideration of the description and drawings by a person skilled in the art, the patentee has contemplated. On the contrary, it is to be interpreted as defining a position between these extremes which combines a fair protection for the patentee with a reasonable degree of certainty for third parties.

As a practical matter, the protocol does not yet seem to have helped very much. The celebrated example of this is in respect of the European patent relating to alleged infringement by Remington of Epilady's patent for a hair remover for use on ladies' legs. The British and German courts still came to opposite conclusions as to whether or not a claim calling for a rotating helical spring (which plucked hairs from the legs at one point in its rotation and deposited them at another point when the coils of the spring separated) was infringed by a rotating rubber bar with slits in it, which performed the same function.

There are, however, some steps being taken toward harmonization between countries in the field of patent enforcement. For example, through the influence of the proposed Community Patent Convention, most countries now have more or less the same definition of what acts constitute infringement.

Community Patent Convention; COPAC

Many of these problems will disappear if the Community Patent Convention ever comes into force and significant numbers of patents are granted under it. Under the litigation protocol that is attached to the convention, a number of existing courts throughout the European Union will be designated as Community Patent Courts and will have EU-wide jurisdiction to deal with infringement and validity issues arising from Community Patents. A single appeal court (Community Patent Appeal Court or COPAC for short) will be established having jurisdiction throughout the EU to which all appeals from national courts relating to matters of patent infringement or validity of community patents will be referred. Such rationalization of litigation seems likely to have to wait until a final decision on the Community Convention has been made, although there is some talk of bringing the litigation protocol into effect independently of the full convention and applying the protocol to all patents granted by the European Patent Office, irrespective of whether they are deemed to be Community patents.

Notes and Questions

1. The *Catric* case referred to by the court in the *Epilady* case has been used by other countries in determining patent infringement. *See, e.g., DuPont Cacnada, Inc. v. Glopak Inc.*, 81 C.P.R. 3d 44 (Federal Court, Trial Division 1998).

2. What is the major difference in analysis between the British and German courts in deciding the *Epilady* dispute? Put another way, did they each consider the same questions in deciding how to interpret the relevant claims?

3. Under German law a patent is infringed if the challenged device or process is identical to the invention covered by the patent, *i.e.* if it falls directly under the claims of the patent. However, the protection granted is not limited to the devices and processes covered by the literal terms of the claims. Protection is also extended to equivalents under the theory that no one is in the position to draft claims in a way that will protect against all possible infringing acts. The doctrine of equivalence covers all means that have an effect similar to the means covered by the patent claim, if a person skilled in the art will through his recognition of a specific means used to achieve a specific effect find a different means that achieves the same effect. Again the knowledge at the date of application or the priority date is decisive. To determine whether an equivalent infringement is given is one of the most difficult and disputed issues in practice.

The Federal Supreme Court in Germany has established two requirements for the extension of a patent claim to equivalent means. First, the means used by the infringer must have the same technical function to reach the same technical result. Second, the means are deemed equivalent if a person skilled in the art could derive it—as of the day of the application—as obvious from the claims stated by use of description and drawings contained in the patent. Thus, if the infringer's device is obvious to a person skilled in the art *based on the disclosures in the patent*, then the two devices are equivalents. If, however, the infringer's device would represent a patentable invention at the time of the defendant's patent application (because it is not obvious or requires an inventive step), then the two devices are *not* equivalents.

4. Compare this test with the court's analysis in the *U.S. Doctrine of Equivalence* test. Do they apply the same test for equivalency?

5. Compare the analysis of the court in the *Epilady* case with the analysis of the courts in the *U.S. Doctrine of Equivalence* and *Japanese Ball Shaft* cases regarding the test for equivalency. Are there significant differences between them? Could these differences effect the outcome of a patent dispute? Which court do you believe applied the test required under TRIPS?

C. WHAT REMEDIES MUST BE AVAILABLE INTERNATIONALLY?

Read the following Articles from the Supplement: TRIPS 45, 50; NAFTA 1704, 1714, 1715, 1716.

Notes and Questions

1. *NAFTA.* The North American Free Trade Agreement was first entered into force in 1994. Although NAFTA served primarily as a regional agreement to establish a limited free trading zone between Canada, the United States and Mexico, it also contained numerous substantive provisions

regarding the protection of intellectual property rights in the three signatory countries. Among these provision were several establishing minimum enforcement standards for protecting intellectual property rights. Consequently, NAFTA represented the first multinational effort at establishing enforcement norms for IPR. Compare the NAFTA articles with their counterparts from TRIPS. Which is more extensive? Are there conflicts between the two enforcement regimes?

2.   Like TRIPS, NAFTA represents an attempt to establish agreed-upon standards in countries which do not have the same legal systems. While the United States and Canada contain largely common law systems, Mexico's legal system is a civil law one. Because NAFTA pre-dated TRIPS, it was seen as establishing the floor for TRIPS as far as enforcement standards were concerned. To what extent was this view accurate?

3.   NAFTA remains a model for regional trade agreements. Like the European Union, NAFTA recognized that free trade requires an agreement on IPR protection. It is anticipated that in future years, similar regional trade agreements will develop in Africa and Latin America. The development of these regional trading zones may help stimulate greater harmonization of IPR enforcement standards.

4.   Does TRIPS Article 45 specify the method by which "adequate compensation" must be determined? For example, would the disgorgement of the defendant's profits alone qualify as "adequate"? Would the imposition of a compulsory license fee be "adequate"? Would money damages in a statutorily-mandated amount, based on the average monthly salary of a native worker be "adequate"?

5.   What should the primary focus for monetary relief from infringement be—compensation to the IP owner or elimination of the incentive to infringe IP-protected works? If the goal is elimination of the incentive to infringe, which of the forms of compensation in Question #4 are inadequate to meet that goal? Which forms are required under TRIPS? Under NAFTA?

6.   U.S. copyright law provides for the grant of statutory penalties of $20,000 per act of infringement, up to $100,000 per act of infringement (if such act is wilful). (17 U.S.C. § 504.)

7.   Egyptian copyright law provides that any person who sells an infringing work or causes infringing copies to be brought into Egypt "shall be... punishable with a fine of not less than or more than œ100." (Egyptian Copyright law, Article 47.) In the case of "recidivism," the guilty party "shall be punishable by imprisonment not exceeding three months and by a fine not exceeding œ300, or by one of these penalties only." (*Id.*)

8.   Chinese copyright law provides anyone who infringes a copyrighted work shall be liable for sanctions "in the form of warning, injunction in relation to the production and distribution of infringing copes, confiscation of unlawful gains and seizure of infringing copies and equipments used for making infringing copies, as well as a fine "which shall be as follows:

1) for plagiarism—100 to 5,000 yuan (RMB)

2) for unauthorized reproduction, distribution or publication of a book, sound recording, video or radio or television program—10,000 to

100,000 yuan (RMB) "or an amount of two to five times as much as the prices in total," and

3) for producing or selling a work of fine art where the signature is counterfeited—1,000 to 5,000 yuan (RMB). (China Copyright Law, Article 50.)

9.   Russian law provides that in the event of infringement of a computer software program, the owner is entitled to either "recovery of losses, including sum of earnings unlawfully obtained by offender" or payment of damages "in amount of discretion of court of law, court of arbitration or mediation panel (ranging from 5,000 times to 50,000 times the statutory minimum monthly wage) in cases of infringement of right for profit making purposes." (Computer Software and Database Protection Act, Article 18 (1992).)

10.   Which of the above countries provide "adequate" compensation in accordance with TRIPS? With NAFTA?

DEVELOPING IPR IN THE GULF: CURRENT COVERAGE, PROBLEMS, POST– URUGUAY ROUND TRENDS

Alastair Hirst, 17 Middle East Executive Reports (No. 5) (1994).

As a leisure medium, video-cassettes have come to assume disproportionate importance in the Gulf region because alternative distractions are relatively few, particularly for the large expatriate communities. The inclination of the authorities is to criminalize and repress the production and circulation of video materials, save insofar as specifically authorized by them. The copyright status of such materials will not usually be a foremost concern. Kuwait, Qatar and Oman all regulate the circulation of video materials without having domestic copyright legislation.

The question of alien cultural penetration is more likely to be the paramount concern. This is a seriously viewed, and those engaged in the importation, reproduction and distribution of foreign video materials often operate in gray areas, engaged in a cat-and-mouse game with their regulators and the police.

Against this background, the idea of actually endowing the authors and producers of video materials with monopoly proprietary rights in such materials is not one that readily commends itself locally. Indeed, the authorities might well even feel that a successful and well-publicized copyright action against video piracy could in itself give the wrong signal to the public by suggesting that, but for technical legal defects in the production process, it is in principle acceptable for such articles to circulate freely in the country.

A further factor in the cultural context lies in the pervasive influence of Egypt. Egyptian books, music and films dominate the indigenous entertainment and media world in the Gulf. More than that, Egypt is the prime source of training and expertise in education, law and the civil service, and many of the skilled manpower needs of the GCC countries in these fields cannot be met without the recruitment or secondment of Egyptians. Comparable resources are not really available in any other Arab country.

Clearly, the Egyptian influence has an acceptable pedigree in religious and linguistic terms, and there is not the degree of disquiet aroused by the far more alien cultural penetration from the Indian subcontinent or from western societies. Nonetheless on the personal level there can be a discreet measure of resentment at the necessity for, and the closeness of, Egypt's ample embrace.

As regards the practicalities of antipiracy actions—and these final observations relate to all forms of intellectual property—doubts have been expressed by commentators as to the lack of appropriate procedural rules. While this may be the case in the particular circumstances of Saudi Arabia, the prospects for intending plaintiffs in other GCC territories may not be quite as discouraging as suggested.

Indeed, the modern civil law approach to judicial procedure broadly followed in commercial matters in virtually all Arab countries except Saudi Arabia contains two specific features that are potentially useful in intellectual property actions but that will not usually be familiar to common law country practitioners.

The first is the *partie civile* claim, whereby a party suffering loss or injury as a result of the committing of a criminal offense may become party to the criminal proceedings brought by the state, in effect as a co-plaintiff, and, on conviction of the accused, obtain an award of damages or other relief, including delivery-up of articles used in, or resulting from, the committing of the offense. The penal sanctions are available to procure satisfaction of the *partie civile* award. Given the evident preference of the authorities in the GCC states to deal with intellectual property piracy as a criminal matter, *partie civile* recourse is worth investigation as a potentially useful alternative to protracted and expensive subsequent actions for damages in the civil courts.

The other procedural aspect worth comment is the role of the court expert. It is true that in some Middle Eastern jurisdictions the expert is sometimes seen as a mere fig leaf for judicial sloth. Instances of misuse should not, however, obscure the potential of the expert's role. The expert is the official—or sometimes a private consultant appointed ad hoc by the court—formally deputed to investigate specific issues of fact before the court and to submit a report thereon to the judge. Parties withhold cooperation from the expert at their peril. In fact, they usually put considerable effort into their submissions to him. His report, when submitted, is subject to debate in open court, and his findings are often refined and improved as a result of such debate.

The usefulness of the expert's function lies in that it largely replaces with a much more focused and expeditious inquisitorial procedure the laborious task of leading evidence and establishing factual matters on the sort of adversarial basis that characterizes common law country litigation. Experts are most frequently appointed in cases where the subject matter is technical or specialized, or where significant auditing or computation work is required. If the documentary evidence is voluminous, and in a foreign language, the expert may well be able to save the parties considerable translation costs by dealing with it in its original language. Again, an experienced expert may also have a useful contribution to make on matters of law, in cases where issues of fact and law are intermingled.

At the same time, the judge is not bound to accept the expert's findings, and if he or either of the parties is dissatisfied with the expert, another can be appointed. If properly used, the expert will help the judge to master difficult or unfamiliar subject matter.

As intellectual property litigation becomes more common in the GCC countries, the demand for properly qualified experts will grow. At present, on the panels of experts maintained by the court administrations in the various Gulf states, there are very few individuals capable of acting usefully in international intellectual property cases. On nucleus of such expertise might be developed from within quasi-official bodies like the Industrial Development Centre for Arab States, or private groupings such as the Arab Society for the Protection of Industrial Property. Alternatively, established survey institutes in the maritime or industrial fields might see advantage in developing additional expertise in intellectual property.

Certainly, it is in the interest of international rights-holders having business in the Gulf region to do what they can to ensure that adequate sources of intellectual property expertise are available, and that such availability is known to the local judiciary.

TO BATTLE PIRACY IN CHINA, IP COMPANIES MAY TURN TO SELF-HELP
Konrad L. Trope, IP Worldwide, July/August 1997.

IP rights in China are supposedly protected by a variety of national laws. They are supposedly protected by a variety of international treaties.

They aren't.

The People's Republic of China remains one of the largest infringers of patents, trademarks, and copyrights. China's government remains unable and/or unwilling to protect IP rights, and thus is a haven for bootleggers of videos, audiotapes, CDs, and other forms of high technology.

Other countries have put pressure on China to improve its record in this area. The results have been meager, at best.

Thus, companies doing business in China have little choice. They must protect themselves.

This isn't always easy. It involves planning ahead and hard work, but companies can do much to protect themselves against piracy in

China. They can succeed where the most powerful governments in the world have failed.

Enforcement problems. The problem begins in China. Its laws to protect IP are not truly enforced.

Last summer, for instance, a PRC court found that the IP rights of Microsoft, Autodesk, and WordPerfect Application Group had been infringed by a Chinese software pirate—and the court fined the company a mere U.S.$53,600. That same year, another PRC court awarded the Walt Disney Co. a paltry U.S.$27,360 for unauthorized use of some of its more famous animated characters.

These damage awards are pocket change to the infringers. Such judgments do nothing to deter Chinese pirates or the legitimate licensees who facilitated unauthorized IP transfers to the pirates.

The U.S. has, in recent years, put pressure on China to improve its protection of IP rights. Thus on Feb. 26, 1995, under a threat of U.S. trade sanctions, China signed a bilateral IP agreement with the U.S.. In that agreement, China promised to introduce a series of reforms aimed primarily at halting production of pirated compact disks and permitting U.S. record companies to establish operations in China.

This agreement had little effect. By June 1996, an IP trade war again threatened to erupt between the two countries. In order to avert such a trade war, China and the U.S. signed an eleven point memorandum of understanding, in which China agreed to beef up enforcement of its copyright laws.

In order to show its compliance with these two agreements, China has made sporadic and cosmetic attempts to crack down on piracy of CDs for music, motion picture videos, and computer software. However, since the signing of the June 1996 memorandum, a mere 15 plants making counterfeit CDs have been closed by the PRC. This will do little to stem the flow of pirated goods manufactured in China.

THE KISMET CASE
FRANK MUSIC CORPORATION v. METRO–GOLDWYN–MAYER, INC.

United States Court Of Appeals, Ninth Circuit, 1985
772 F.2d 505.

FLETCHER, CIRCUIT JUDGE:

This copyright infringement suit arises out of defendants' use of five songs from plaintiffs' dramatico-musical play Kismet in a musical revue staged at defendant MGM Grand Hotel in 1974–76. After a bench trial, the district court found infringement and awarded the plaintiffs $22,000 as a share of defendants' profits. Plaintiffs appeal and defendants cross-appeal. We affirm in part, reverse in part, and remand.

The original version of Kismet was a dramatic play, written by Edward Knoblock in 1911. Knoblock copyrighted the play as an unpublished work in that year and again as a published work in 1912. Knoblock's copyright expired in 1967, and the dramatic play Kismet entered the public domain.

In 1952, plaintiff Edwin Lester acquired the right to produce a musical stage production of the dramatic play Kismet. Lester hired plaintiffs Luther Davis and Charles Lederer to write the libretto and plaintiffs Robert Wright and George Forrest to write the music and lyrics for the musical adaptation. In 1953 and 1954, Lederer and Davis copyrighted their dramatico-musical play Kismet, and in 1953, Wright and Forrest assigned to plaintiff Frank Music Corporation the right to copyright all portions of the musical score written for Kismet. Frank Music subsequently obtained copyrights for the entire musical score and for each of the songs in the score.

In 1954, Lederer, Wright, and Forrest entered into a license agreement with Loew's, Inc., a predecessor of Metro–Goldwyn–Mayer, Inc., ("MGM, Inc.") granting to it the right to produce a musical motion picture based on plaintiffs' play. MGM released its motion picture version of Kismet, starring Howard Keel and Ann Blyth, in 1955.

The story presented in the MGM film and in plaintiffs' dramatico-musical play is essentially the same as that told in Knoblock's dramatic play. It is the tale of a day in the life of a poetic beggar named Hajj and his daughter, Marsinah. The story is set in ancient Baghdad, with major scenes in the streets of Baghdad, the Wazir's palace, an enchanted garden, and the Wazir's harem.

On April 26, 1974, defendant MGM Grand Hotel premiered a musical revue entitled Hallelujah Hollywood in the hotel's Ziegfeld Theatre. The show was staged, produced, and directed by defendant Donn Arden. It featured ten acts of singing, dancing, and variety performances. Of the ten acts, four were labeled as "tributes" to MGM motion pictures of the past, and one was a tribute to the "Ziegfeld Follies." The remaining acts were variety numbers, which included performances by a live tiger, a juggler, and the magicians, Siegfried and Roy.

Act IV of Hallelujah Hollywood, the subject of this lawsuit, was entitled "Kismet," and was billed as a tribute to the MGM movie of that name. Comprised of four scenes, it was approximately eleven and one-half minutes in length. It was set in ancient Baghdad, as was plaintiffs' play, and the characters were called by the same or similar names to those used in plaintiffs' play. Five songs were taken in whole or in part from plaintiffs' play. No dialogue was spoken during the act, and, in all, it contained approximately six minutes of music taken directly from plaintiffs' play.

The total running time of Hallelujah Hollywood was approximately 100 minutes, except on Saturday nights when two acts were deleted, shortening the show to 75 minutes. The show was performed three times on Saturday evenings, twice on the other evenings of the week.

On November 1, 1974, plaintiffs informed MGM Grand that they considered Hallelujah Hollywood to infringe their rights in Kismet. MGM Grand responded that it believed its use of plaintiffs' music was covered by its blanket license agreement with the American Society of Composers, Authors and Publishers ("ASCAP"). In 1965, plaintiffs had granted to ASCAP the right to license certain rights in the musical score of their play Kismet.

[The court concluded defendants had infringed plaintiff's copyrights and then considered what monetary damages should be awarded.]

1. ACTUAL DAMAGES

"Actual damages" are the extent to which the market value of a copyrighted work has been injured or destroyed by an infringement. In this circuit, we have stated the test of market value as "what a willing buyer would have been reasonably required to pay to a willing seller for plaintiffs' work." *Krofft I*, 562 F.2d at 1174.

The district court declined to award actual damages. The court stated that it was "unconvinced that the market value of plaintiffs' work was in any way diminished as a result of defendant's infringement." We are obliged to sustain this finding unless we conclude it is clearly erroneous.

Plaintiffs contend the district court's finding is clearly erroneous in light of the evidence they presented concerning the royalties Kismet could have earned in a full Las Vegas production. Plaintiffs did offer evidence of the royalties Kismet had earned in productions around the country. They also introduced opinion testimony, elicited from plaintiff Lester and from Kismet's leasing agent, that a full production of Kismet could have been licensed in Las Vegas for $7,500 per week. And they introduced other opinion testimony to the effect that Hallelujah Hollywood had destroyed the Las Vegas market for a production of plaintiffs' Kismet.

In a copyright action, a trial court is entitled to reject a proffered measure of damages if it is too speculative. Although uncertainty as to the amount of damages will not preclude recovery, uncertainty as to the fact of damages may. It was the fact of damages that concerned the district court. The court found that plaintiffs "failed to establish any damages attributable to the infringement." This finding is not clearly erroneous.

Plaintiffs offered no disinterested testimony showing that Hallelujah Hollywood precluded plaintiffs from presenting Kismet at some other hotel in Las Vegas. It is not implausible to conclude, as the court below apparently did, that a production presenting six minutes of music from Kismet, without telling any of the story of the play, would not significantly impair the prospects for presenting a full production of that play.[7]

---

7. Another panel of this court considered a similar problem recently in *Cream Records, Inc. v. Jos. Schlitz Brewing Co.*, 754 F.2d 826 (9th Cir.1985) (interpreting the 1976 Act). In *Cream Records*, the jury found that Schlitz and its advertising agen-

Based on the record presented, the district court was not clearly erroneous in finding that plaintiffs' theory of damages was uncertain and speculative.[8]

2. INFRINGER'S PROFITS

As an alternative to actual damages, a prevailing plaintiff in an infringement action is entitled to recover the infringer's profits to the extent they are attributable to the infringement. 17 U.S.C. § 101(b). In establishing the infringer's profits, the plaintiff is required to prove only

cy infringed Cream's copyright in "The Theme from Shaft", by using a ten-note ostinato from the song in a television commercial. The district court awarded $12,000 as actual damages for loss of licensing fees. We concluded that the award was insufficient, stating:

The only evidence before the court was that unauthorized use of the Shaft theme music in Schlitz's commercial ended Cream's opportunity to license the music for this purpose. There was no evidence that Schlitz sought, or Cream was willing to grant, a license for use of less than the entire copyrighted work, that a license limited to the portion used in the commercial would have had less value, or that use limited to this portion would have had a less devastating effect upon Cream's opportunity to license to another. Since defendants' unauthorized use destroyed the value of the copyrighted work for this purpose, plaintiff was entitled to recover that value as damages.

Id. at 827–28 (citation omitted).

In *Cream Records,* the evidence showed that another advertiser had approached Cream for a license for the song, but withdrew when the Schlitz commercial was aired. "There was testimony that use of a well-known popular song in a commercial destroys its value to other advertisers for that purpose." 754 F.2d 826, 827. The evidence concerning the effect of defendants' infringement is far less convincing in our case. Plaintiffs did introduce testimony that the infringement had destroyed the Las Vegas market for a full production of Kismet, but that testimony came from Kismet's leasing agent, not a disinterested party. We agree with the district court's characterization of this evidence as "meager," and we cannot conclude that the court clearly erred in discrediting it.

8. Plaintiffs raise several other arguments concerning actual damages, which require only brief discussion.

Plaintiffs suggest that actual damages to the Las Vegas market should be presumed, that such damages are the "natural and

probable result" of an unauthorized performance. Yet, plaintiffs rely for this conclusion on cases in which trial courts found damages merely as a matter of fact, *see, e.g., Metro-Goldwyn–Mayer, Inc. v. Showcase Atlanta Cooperative Productions, Inc.,* 479 F. Supp. 351 (N.D.Ga.1979), or presumed irreparable injury for purposes of issuance of preliminary injunctions, *see, e.g., Uneeda Doll Co. v. Regent Baby Products Corp.,* 355 F. Supp. 438, 445 (E.D.N.Y. 1972). These cases do not suggest, as plaintiffs apparently contend, that a copyright owner is relieved from or aided in proving actual damages by some presumption. *See Shapiro, Bernstein & Co. v. 4636 S. Vermont Ave., Inc.,* 367 F.2d 236, 241 (9th Cir.1966) (plaintiff in copyright action who failed to produce evidence of damages could not complain when trial court determined that no damages were proved).

Plaintiffs further argue that the court accorded so little weight to plaintiff Edwin Lester's testimony concerning the value of Kismet as to be tantamount to excluding it. While *Universal Pictures Co. v. Harold Lloyd Corp.,* 162 F.2d 354, 369 (9th Cir. 1947), held that a copyright owner may testify as to the value of his property, that case did not hold that a court may not consider the self-serving nature of such testimony. *See Runge v. Lee,* 441 F.2d 579, 582 (9th Cir.) ("Credible testimony by the owner of literary property regarding its value can provide an adequate evidentiary basis for an award of damages." (emphasis added)), *cert. denied,* 404 U.S. 887, 30 L. Ed. 2d 169, 92 S. Ct. 197, 171 U.S.P.Q. (BNA) 322 (1971). The district court was entitled to give Mr. Lester's testimony slight weight.

Finally, plaintiffs contend the district court improperly excluded as irrelevant evidence of royalties other Broadway shows had earned in Las Vegas productions. The exclusion was not error. *See Universal Pictures Co. v. Harold Lloyd Corp.,* 162 F.2d at 372, 374–75 (action for violation of motion picture copyright; not error to exclude evidence of value of another movie as not relevant to value of movie involved).

the defendant's sales; the burden then shifts to the defendant to prove the elements of costs to be deducted from sales in arriving at profit. 17 U.S.C. § 101(b). Any doubt as to the computation of costs or profits is to be resolved in favor of the plaintiff. *Shapiro, Bernstein & Co. v. Remington Records, Inc.*, 265 F.2d 263 (2d Cir.1959). If the infringing defendant does not meet its burden of proving costs, the gross figure stands as the defendant's profits. *Russell v. Price*, 612 F.2d 1123, 1130–31 (9th Cir. 1979), *cert. denied*, 446 U.S. 952, 100 S. Ct. 2919, 64 L. Ed. 2d 809 (1980).

The district court, following this approach, found that the gross revenue MGM Grand earned from the presentation of Hallelujah Hollywood during the relevant time period was $24,191,690. From that figure, the court deducted direct costs of $18,060,084 and indirect costs (overhead) of $3,641,960, thus arriving at a net profit of $2,489,646.

Plaintiffs' challenge these computations on a number of grounds.

Plaintiffs challenge the district court's failure to consider MGM Grand's earnings on hotel and gaming operations in arriving at the amount of profits attributable to the infringement. The district court received evidence concerning MGM Grand's total net profit during the relevant time period, totaling approximately $395,000,000, but its memorandum decision does not mention these indirect profits and computes recovery based solely on the revenues and profits earned on the production of Hallelujah Hollywood (approximately $24,000,000 and $2,500,000 respectively). We surmise from this that the district court determined plaintiffs were not entitled to recover indirect profits, but we have no hint as to the district court's reasons.

Whether a copyright proprietor may recover "indirect profits" is one of first impression in this circuit. We conclude that under the 1909 Act indirect profits may be recovered.

The 1909 Act provided that a copyright proprietor is entitled to "all the profits which the infringer shall have made from such infringement." 17 U.S.C. § 101(b). The language of the statute is broad enough to permit recovery of indirect as well as direct profits. At the same time, a court may deny recovery of a defendant's profits if they are only remotely or speculatively attributable to the infringement. *Roy Export Co. v. Columbia Broadcasting System, Inc.*, 503 F. Supp. 1137, 1156–57 (S.D.N.Y.1980) (profits from an infringing unsponsored television broadcast could not be ascertained since benefit received by CBS "consists of unmeasurable good-will with affiliates and increased stature and prestige vis-a-vis competitors."), *aff'd*, 672 F.2d 1095 (2d Cir.), *cert. denied*, 459 U.S. 826, 74 L. Ed. 2d 63, 103 S. Ct. 60 (1982).

The allowance of indirect profits was considered in *Sid & Marty Krofft Television Productions, Inc. v. McDonald's Corp.*, 1983 Copyright L. Rep. (CCH) P25,572 at 18,381 (C.D. Cal. 1983) (Krofft II), a case involving facts analogous to those presented here. The plaintiffs, creators of the "H.R. Pufnstuf" children's television program, alleged that they were entitled to a portion of the profits McDonald's earned on its food sales as damages for the "McDonaldland" television commercials that infringed plaintiffs' copyright. The district court rejected as speculative the plaintiffs' formula for computing profits attributable to the infringement. However, the court's analysis and award of in lieu damages indicate that it considered indirect profits recoverable. The court stated, in awarding $1,044,000 in statutory damages, that "because a significant portion of defendants' profits made from the infringement are not ascertainable, a higher award of [statutory] in lieu damages is warranted." *Id.* at 18,384; *see also Cream Records Inc. v. Jos. Schlitz Brewing Co.*, 754 F.2d 826, 828–29 (9th Cir.1985) (discussed supra note 7) (awarding profits from the sale of malt liquor for Schlitz's infringing use of plaintiff's song in television commercial).

Like the television commercials in Krofft II, Hallelujah Hollywood had promotional value. Defendants maintain that they endeavor to earn profits on all their operations and that Hallelujah Hollywood was a profit center. However, that fact does not detract from the promotional purposes of the show—to draw people to the hotel and the gaming tables. MGM's 1976 annual report states that "the hotel and gaming operations of the MGM Grand—Las Vegas continue to be materially enhanced by the popularity of the hotel's entertainment[, including] 'Hallelujah Hollywood', the spectacularly successful production revue.... " Given the promotional nature of Hallelujah Hollywood, we conclude indirect profits from the hotel and gaming operations, as well as direct profits from the show itself, are recoverable if ascertainable.

3. APPORTIONMENT OF PROFITS

How to apportion profits between the infringers and the plaintiffs is a complex issue in this case. Apportionment of direct profits from the production as well as indirect profits from the hotel and casino operations are involved here, although the district court addressed only the former at the first trial.

When an infringer's profits are attributable to factors in addition to use of plaintiff's work, an apportionment of profits is proper. The burden of proving apportionment, (*i.e.*, the contribution to profits of elements other than the infringed property), is the defendant's. We will not reverse a district court's findings regarding apportionment unless they are clearly erroneous.

After finding that the net profit earned by Hallelujah Hollywood was approximately $2,500,000, the district court offered the following explanation of apportionment:

> While no precise mathematical formula can be applied, the court concludes in light of the evidence presented at trial and the entire record in this case, a fair approximation of the profits of Act IV attributable to the infringement is $22,000.

The district court was correct that mathematical exactness is not required. However, a reasonable and just apportionment of profits is required.

The difficulty in this case is that the district court has not provided us with any reasoned explanation of or formula for its apportionment. We know only the district court's bottom line: that the plaintiffs are entitled to $22,000. Given the nature of the infringement, the character of the infringed property, the success of defendants' show, and the magnitude of the defendants' profits, the amount seems to be grossly inadequate. It amounts to less than one percent of MGM Grand's profits from the show, or roughly $13 for each of the 1700 infringing performances.[11]

On remand, the district court should reconsider its apportionment of profits, and should fully explain on the record its reasons and the resulting method of apportionment it uses. Apportionment of indirect profits may be a part of the calculus. If the court finds that a reasonable, nonspeculative formula cannot be derived, or that the amount of profits a reasonable formula yields is insufficient to serve the purposes underlying the statute, then the court should award statutory damages.

5. STATUTORY "IN LIEU" DAMAGES

Statutory damages are intended as a substitute for profits or actual damage. When injury is proved but neither the infringer's profits nor the copyright holder's actual damages can be ascertained, an award of statutory "in lieu" damages is mandatory. *Russell v. Price*, 612 F.2d at 1131–32. But if either profits or actual damages or both can be ascertained, the trial court has discretion to award statutory damages. Such an award must be in excess of the amount that would have been awarded as profits or actual damages. We review a district court's award or refusal to award statutory damages for abuse of discretion.

A determination as to whether to award statutory damages must abide the district court's reconsideration of whether to award damages based on profits. On remand, the district court should keep in mind the purposes underlying the remedy provisions of the Copyright Act, *i.e.*, to provide adequate compensation to the copyright holder and to discourage wrongful conduct and deter infringements. *See Russell v. Price*, 612 F.2d at 1131. Thus, in determining whether to exercise its discretion to award statutory damages, the district court must consider whether the amount

---

11. The apportionment percentages in similar cases are markedly higher. *See, e.g., Universal Pictures Co. v. Harold Lloyd Corp.*, 162 F.2d at 377 (infringing use of one comedy sketch in motion picture; court affirmed award of 20% of infringing movie's profits); *MCA, Inc. v. Wilson*, 677 F.2d 180, 181–82 (2d Cir.1981) (defendants copied substantial portion plaintiff's song, "Boogie Woogie Bugle Boy", substituted "dirty" lyrics, and performed the song as a portion of an erotic nude show; court affirmed special master's award of approximately $244,000 representing 5% of defendants' total profits from the show); *Lottie Joplin Thomas Trust v. Crown Publishers, Inc.*, 592 F.2d at 657 (infringing songs filled one side of five-record set; court affirmed award of 50% of profits because inclusion of infringing songs made record set the only "complete" collection of Scott Joplin's works); *ABKCO Music, Inc. v. Harrisongs Music, Ltd.*, 508 F. Supp. 798, 800–801 (S.D.N.Y.1981) (infringing song reproduced on one side of single record, "flip side" contained noninfringing song, court awarded 70% of profits from sales of the single because infringing song was more popular than noninfringing song; similarly, court awarded 50% of profits for reproduction of same song on album containing twenty-one other songs).

of profits that have been proved accomplish the purposes of the statute. If not, it should exercise its discretion to award statutory "in lieu" damages that do effectuate the statutory purposes.

The $22,000 awarded by the district court obviously is too little to discourage wrongful conduct or to deter infringement.

III. Conclusion

We affirm the district court's finding that defendants' use of plaintiffs' Kismet exceeded the scope of the ASCAP license. We also affirm the district court's finding that plaintiffs failed to prove actual damages. We vacate the award of defendants' profits derived from the infringement and remand to the district court for further proceedings consistent with this opinion.

Affirmed in part, reversed in part, and remanded with directions.

CONCUR: REINHARDT, CIRCUIT JUDGE, concurring:

I concur fully in the majority opinion, except for Section B.1. I would hold that the district court clearly erred in finding that appellants "failed to establish any damage attributable to the infringement." It seems evident to me that the inclusion of "Kismet" as a part of 1,700 performances of Hallelujah Hollywood served to reduce the market value of appellant's property in the Las Vegas area. The testimony in the record amply supports this proposition. There is no evidence that would support the opposite conclusion. Under these circumstances, I believe the district court clearly erred in disregarding the testimony offered by appellants.

Notes and Questions

1. *Valuation of Rights.* Regardless of the precise method utilized to determine "adequate compensation" (reasonable royalty, lost revenue, profit disgorgement or statutory damages), compensation to be "adequate" should at least have some rational relationship to the harm the IP owner is suffered. Such harm arguably should be measured, at least in part, against the value of the right being used, and any subsequent diminution in value of that right as a result of the unauthorized use. Since intellectual property rights are intangible, unauthorized use does not physically destroy, or whittle down, the right in question. It may, however, harm the economic value of the right. Unauthorized use of a trademark or poorly made products may diminish the reputation (or goodwill) of the mark. Unauthorized production of a patented good may diminish the value of an exclusive license to manufacture the patented invention. Sales of counterfeit CDs reduce the profit earned by the copyright owner.

Part of the problem in determining adequate compensation arises from the difficulty in assessing the value of a unique intellectual property. For example, assume that you have been offered the following deal: You may either buy all of the worldwide physical assets of COCA-COLA®—its plant facilities, bottling agreements, inventory, delivery trucks, production equipment—every item that the Coca-Cola Company owns or legally controls, *except* its trademark and its secret formula, *or* you may buy all rights to the trademark COCA–COLA® world-wide, for the same price. Which offer would you chose? What if instead of the trademark, you could buy the secret formula for Coca–Cola (but *not* its trademark)? Which is more valuable—the trademark or the formula? For articles that discuss the problem of intellectual property valuation *see, e.g.*, Accounting for Brand's—The Practitioner's Perspective in Brand Valuation (John Murphy ed., 2d ed. 1991).

2. How did the court in the *Kismet* case treat the problem of valuation of the copyrighted work involved?

3. *Digital Infringement.* At least in cases of traditional infringement (where the copies have been reproduced in physical medium, the number of unauthorized copies can usually be estimated with some degree of accuracy.) What if the plaintiff's work had been placed on a web-page without authorization? How could the court determine the number of illegal copies produced at the site? For a discussion of the enforcement problems related to the Internet, see Chapter Thirty–Six.

THE RUBBER TYRE CASE
GENERAL TIRE AND RUBBER CO v. FIRESTONE TYRE AND RUBBER CO. LTD

House Of Lords. 1975.
[1975] 2 All ER 173, [1975] 1 WLR 819, [1976] RPC 197, [1975] FSR 273.

LORD WILBERFORCE.

My Lords, the respondents, as patentees of British Letters Patent No 737086, sued the appellants for infringement. The appellants denied infringement and counterclaimed for revocation on the ground that the patent was invalid. After a trial in 1969 before Lloyd Jacob J and a rehearing in 1970 before Graham J (Lloyd Jacob J having died), the patent was held to be valid and infringed, and an enquiry was directed as to damages.

The patent covers an invention relating to synthetic rubber compounds suitable for tyre treads. Essentially it consists of a method of extending tough (high Mooney) synthetic rubbery polymers with large quantities of mineral oil; the mixture so produced (to which the term "oil-extended rubber" or "OER" has come to be applied) may be compounded with, inter alia, carbon black and then becomes "tyre tread stock" ("TTS"), ie a material which can be used for the making of tyres. It is not disputed that this was an important and valuable invention. Graham J described it as a "real breakthrough." It brought about a substantial reduction in the manufacturing costs of tyres and also an improvement in road-holding and durability.

In the enquiry as to damages contentions were filed by each party. The contentions of the respondents as plaintiffs originally claimed damages on the basis of a "fair and reasonable" royalty which it was asserted should be five per cent of the net sales value of all infringing articles, i.e. tyres and compounds containing a substantial portion of oil-extended polymer. This would have resulted in an amount of approximately £7,500,000 plus interest. The contentions filed by the appellants as defendants put forward in order of preference three alternative bases on which damages should be calculated: (i) (the "lump sum basis") a lump sum computed on the basis of existing lump sum licences granted by the respondents: this would produce an amount of £45,357 plus interest; (ii) (the "OER basis") a sum computed on a royalty of three-eighths of a United States cent per lb of oil extended rubber, as therein defined, used by the appellants in infringing tyre treads; this would produce an amount of £215,500 plus interest; (iii) (the "TTS basis") a sum computed on a royalty of three-eights of a United States cent per lb of tread compound containing such oil-extended rubber used by the appellants in infringing tyres. This would produce an amount of £486,-500 plus interest.

Examination of these various bases of computation must necessarily be preceded by some statement of legal principle. This I can do fairly briefly since I do not believe that there is much room for dispute. One who infringes the patent of another commit a tort, the foundation of which is made clear by the terms of the grant. This, after conferring the monopoly of profit and advantage on the patentee, concludes by declaring infringers "answerable to the patentee according to law for his damages thereby occasioned".

As in the case of any other tort (leaving aside cases where exemplary damages can be given) the object of damages is to compensate for loss or injury. The general rule at any rate in relation to "economic" torts is that the measure of damages is to be, so far as possible, that sum of money which will put the injured party in the same position as he would have been in if he had not sustained the wrong.

In the case of infringement of a patent, an alternative remedy at the option of the plaintiff exists by way of an account of profits made by the infringer. The respondents did not elect to claim an account of profits; their claim was only for damages. There are two essential principles in valuing that claim: first, that the plaintiffs have the burden of proving their loss; second, that, the defendants being wrongdoers, damages should be liberally assessed but that the object is to compensate the plaintiffs and not punish the defendants.

These elemental principles have been applied in numerous cases of infringements of patents. Naturally their application varies from case to case.

1. Many patents of inventions belong to manufacturers, who exploit the invention to make articles or products which they sell at a profit. The benefit of the invention in such cases is realised through the sale of the article or product. In these cases, if the invention is infringed, the effect of the infringement will be to divert sales from the owner of the patent to the infringer. The measure of damages will then normally be the profit which would have been realised by the owner of the patent if the sales had been made by him An example of this is *Boyd v. The Tootal Broadhurst Lee Co.* [(1894) 11 RPC 175] where the plaintiff

manufacturers proved that a profit of 7s per spindle would have been made, and settlements of litigation for lesser rates were discarded.

2. Other patents of inventions are exploited through the granting of licences for royalty payments. In these cases, if an infringer uses the invention without a licence, the measure of the damages he must pay will be the sums which he would have paid by way of royalty if instead of acting illegally, he had acted legally. The problem, which is that of the present case—the respondents not being manufacturers in the United Kingdom—is to establish the amount of such royalty. The solution to this problem is essentially and exclusively one of evidence, and as the facts capable of being adduced in evidence are necessarily individual, from case to case, the danger is obvious in referring to a particular case and transferring its conclusions to other situations.

3. In some cases it is not possible to prove either (as in 1) that there is a normal rate of profit, or (as in 2) that there is a normal, or established, licence royalty. Yet clearly damages must be assessed. In such cases it is for the plaintiff to adduce evidence which will guide the court. This evidence may consist of the practice, as regards royalty, in the relevant trade or in analogous trades; perhaps of expert opinion expressed in publications or in the witness box; possibly of the profitability of the invention; and any other factor on which the judge can decide the measure of loss. Since evidence of this kind is in its nature general and also probably hypothetical, it is unlikely to be of relevance, or if relevant of weight, in the face of the more concrete and direct type of evidence referred to under (2). But there is no rule of law which prevents the court, even when it has evidence of licensing practice, from taking these more general considerations into account. The ultimate process is one of judicial estimation of the available indications.

On 9th February 1966 the respondents and Goodyear by agreement settled the litigation pending between them. Goodyear was granted a world-wide licence for a consideration of $2 million. The agreement contained what has come to be called a 'swing' provision by which Goodyear agreed to pay an additional $1 million if the respondents succeeded in their United States litigation against other litigants and were to receive a repayment of $1 million if the respondents failed. The agreement also contained a 'most favoured licensee' clause.

This agreement was followed by the negotiation of a number of lump sum agreements with other companies: these were based on the Goodyear settlement, the capital sum payable being proportionate to the respective manufacturing capacity of the companies concerned as compared with that of Goodyear. Dunlop was one such company. Although one or two of these lump sum agreements contained a "swing" clause the majority did not and this was so whether or not the patent in respect of which the licence was granted was incontestable (as in Japan) or was still the subject of litigation (as in the United States and the United Kingdom). In addition, companies which had agreed to pay a royalty rate of three-eights cent per lb renegotiated their agreements under the "most favoured licensee" clause so as to substitute a capital sum for the royalty rate.

In my opinion there are two conclusions to be drawn from these lump sums agreements. First, they point the contrast between agreements made by way of settlement of litigation concerning the patent on the one hand, and agreements fixing a royalty rate on the basis of a valid patent on the other. The "lump sum" agreements are clearly of the former character. Some of them were not themselves made by way of settlement, but they were based on others which were. The prototype agreement on which they were all modelled—the Goodyear agreement of 1966—was clearly of this kind However all this may be, there is nothing in these agreements which weakens, and much that strengthens, the conclusion that the three-eights cent OER royalty rate was an acceptable and indeed favourable rate for the licensor, based on the assumption of a valid patent.

Secondly, the circumstances and character of these lump sum agreements provide an answer to the question whether the appellants can, as their contentions maintain, settle their liability to pay damages through payment of a capital sum based on them. There are a number of difficulties in their way. First, the Goodyear agreement was not made until 1966 whereas infringement dates from 1958, so that the greater part of the infringement period was anterior to any lump sum settlement. Secondly, I find a difficulty in law in understanding how a lump sum settlement can be worked into the assumptions on which damages must be assessed. Each infringement constitutes a separate tort which is committed de die in diem and seems by its nature to call for damages assessed de die in diem. I should find difficulty in stating a legal basis on which, as at some given date, a new basis should be substituted, and on what assumptions. The only manner in which the appellants' case for a lump sum payment can be put, in my opinion, is to say that there must be assumed a licensing agreement between them and the respondents for the duration of the patent containing a most favoured licensee clause. But a most favoured licensee clause can only find a place in an agreement that licenses use of the patent over an existing period of some time whereas ex hypothesi an infringer must be assumed to be seeking separate licenses from day to day for each infringing use. Thirdly, even if a licensing agreement for the duration of the patent were assumed the factual difficulty arises that the evidence does not disclose a uniform pattern for such clauses. Some (for example those contained in the agreements made with Japanese companies) might permit lump sum settlements to be taken into account, while others, among which is the model form of licence agreement offered to the industry in 1960, exclude lump sum payments from the most favoured licensee provisions. Some took into account licences to other manufacturers under the corresponding patents in other countries; others were confined to licences granted to other manufacturers in the same country as the licensee. I do not think therefore that there is any firm basis for a hypothetical agreement which would enable the respondents to take advantage of the Goodyear settlement.

On all these considerations I find myself unable to accept that the lump sum agreements can be made use of to fix the measure of damages.

I return then to the appellants' second suggested basis—three-eights cent per lb OER. The foregoing analysis satisfies me beyond doubt that this is the right basis on which to assess damages. It was a rate at which the respondents would have been willing from 1960 onwards—and a fortiori before 1960—to license use of the invention. It is supported by strong and concrete evidence of actual bargains. It represents a satisfactory and real measure of the respondents' loss.

THE PROFIT ACCOUNTING CASE
DART INDUSTRIES INC v. DECOR CORP PTY LTD

High Court Of Australia, 1993.
[1994] FSR 567.

MASON CJ, DEANE, DAWSON, TOOHEY JJ:

The appellant (Dart) was the successful plaintiff in an action in the Supreme Court of Victoria against the respondents (Decor and Rian) for infringement of a patent in respect of press-button seals, or lids, used to seal plastic kitchen canisters. Rian manufactured, with tooling provided by Decor, and Decor produced and sold, plastic kitchen canisters with the press-button seals.

Dart having elected between damages and an account of profits, the trial judge, King J, ordered an account of profits by Decor and Rian. In giving directions, King J dealt with two questions, the first of which falls to be determined upon this appeal and the second of which is raised in an application by Decor and Rian for special leave to cross-appeal. The first is whether any part of general overhead costs is allowable as a deduction to Decor or Rian in the determination of the profits made by them from the infringement. The second is whether Decor and Rian must account for profits arising from the manufacture and sale of the composite product, consisting of both the body of the canister and the press-button seal, or merely for those profits attributable to the manufacture and sale of the press-button seal alone, that being the patented invention.

Damages and an account of profits are alternative remedies. An account of profits was a form of relief granted by equity whereas damages were originally a purely common law remedy. As Windeyer J pointed out in *Colbeam Palmer Ltd. v. Stock Affiliates Pty Ltd.* ([1972] RPC 303, (1968) 122 CLR 25 at 34) even now an account of profits retains its equitable characteristics in that a defendant is made to account for, and is then stripped of, profits which it has dishonestly made by the infringement and which it would be unconscionable for it to retain. An account of profits is confined to profits actually made, its purpose being not to punish the defendant but to prevent its unjust enrichment. The ordinary requirement of the principles of unjust enrichment that regard be paid to matters of substance rather than technical form is applicable.

But it is notoriously difficult in some cases, particularly cases involving the manufacture or sale of a range of products, to isolate those costs which are attributable to the infringement from those which are not so attributable. Whilst it is accepted that mathematical exactitude is generally impossible, the exercise is one that must be undertaken, and some assistance may be derived from the principles and practices of commercial accounting. Unfortunately, neither the Australian nor the English authorities contain any precise analysis of the problem.

In calculating an account of profits, the defendant may not deduct the opportunity cost, that is, the profit forgone on the alternative products. But there would be real inequity if a defendant were denied a deduction for the opportunity cost as well as being denied a deduction for the cost of the overheads which sustained the capacity that would have been utilised by an alternative product and that was in fact utilised by the infringing product. If both were denied, the defendant would be in a worse position than if it had made no use of the patented invention. The purpose of an account of profits is not to punish the defendant but to prevent its unjust enrichment.

Where the defendant has forgone the opportunity to manufacture and sell alternative products it will ordinarily be appropriate to attribute to the infringing product a proportion of those general overheads which would have sustained the opportunity. On the other hand, if no opportunity was forgone, and the overheads involved were costs which would have been incurred in any event, then it would not be appropriate to attribute the overheads to the infringing product. Otherwise the defendant would be in a better position than it would have been in if it had not infringed. It is not relevant that the product could not have been manufactured and sold without these overheads. Nor is it relevant that absorption method accounting would attribute a proportion of the overheads to the infringing product. The equitable principle of an account of profits is not to compensate the plaintiff, nor to fix a fair price for the infringing product, but to prevent the unjust enrichment of the defendant.

Of course, further possibilities may in some cases be open on the evidence. Overhead costs might have been increased by the manufacture and sale of the infringing product, or overhead costs might have been reduced had the infringing product not been produced. In either case it may be appropriate to attribute the difference in overhead costs to the infringing product.

It does not appear that in *Leplastrier & Co Ltd. v. Armstrong-Holland Ltd.* the concept of opportunity cost played any part in the reasoning of Harvey CJ in Eq. In allowing the deduction only of expenses "solely referable" to the manufacture of the infringing product, he seems to have intended to exclude overheads except to the extent that they were increased by the manufacture of the infringing product. The examples that he gave indicate such an approach. But this is hardly surprising since the English authorities, even the more recent ones, have not grappled with the concept. Whilst they recognise (*See My Kinda Town Ltd. v. Soll* [1983] RPC at 55) that the purpose of ordering an account of profits is not to inflict punishment, but is limited to compelling the defendant to surrender profits improperly made, there is little examination of the principles to be employed in ascertaining which profits were derived from the infringement (*See also Peter Pan Manufacturing Corp. v. Corsets Silhouette Ltd.* [1963] RPC 45 at 59–60).

In the United States the position is otherwise. It was early recognised in *The Tremolo Patent*, ((1874) 90 U.S. 518) that in the ascertainment of profits arising from the infringement of a patented tremolo attachment to musical instruments, an apportionment of general overheads was required. Strong J in delivering the judgment of the Supreme Court said at pages 528–529:

> We cannot see why the general expenses incurred by the defendants in carrying on their business, such expenses as store rent, clerk hire, fuel, gas, porterage, & c, do not concern one part of their business as much as another. It may be said that the selling [of] a tremolo attachment did not add to their expenses, and therefore that no part of those expenses should be deducted from the price obtained for such an attachment. This is, however, but a partial view. The store rent, the clerk hire, & c, may, it is true, have been the same, if that single attachment had never been bought or sold. So it is true that the general expenses of their business would have been the same, if instead of buying and selling 100 organs, they had bought and sold only 99. But will it be contended that because buying and selling an additional organ involved no increase of the general expenses, the price obtained for that organ above the price paid was all profit? If, therefore, in estimating profits, every part is not chargeable with a proportionate share of the expenses, no part can be. But such a result would be an injustice that no one would defend.

Employing a similar line of reasoning, Decor and Rian contend that in an account of profits, if overheads are disregarded save to the extent that they were increased by the manufacture of the infringing product, then in a case where every product produced by a defendant infringed a patent, there would be no allowance at all for overheads, even though there would clearly be expenses incurred by the defendant in making the total profit from all the infringements. Such a result is, they contend, unacceptable and indicates that a proper allowance for general overheads should be made.

Some caution is to be exercised in the use of United States authorities dealing with accounts of profits because, in some instances, both damages and an account of profits are available, and because a distinction is drawn between wilful and non-wilful infringement which may affect the profits recoverable. Moreover, the approach adopted in the cases varies to some extent. But it is clear enough that the guiding principle in the United States, as here, is that an account of profits aims to have the defendant account for the actual profit, no more and no less, which it has gained from the infringement.

The basis of apportionment may vary from case to case. The guiding principle would seem to be that the onus is on the infringer to provide a reasonably acceptable basis for allocation. This may be the basis of allocation typically used by a manufacturer in that industry.

In the present case, the trial judge accepted that the manufacture and sale of the infringing goods was not a side line. He found that Decor's range of canisters with press-button seals formed part of a much larger range of container systems, storage systems and canisters. On the evidence, the share of sales of the canisters with press-button seals varied from 3.1 per cent to 1.3 per cent over a six-year period after they were added to Decor's existing range, and that percentage was similar to the percentage of sales of other types of containers in Decor's range.

Decor contends that it is possible to identify some overheads as direct costs which may be attributed to the press-button seal canisters as actually incurred in respect of them, namely, the cost of product development/royalty expenses, media advertising, industrial design registration, legal fees and tooling expenses. It seeks to allocate all remaining overheads which are indirect costs by reference to the proportion which sales of canisters with press button seals bear to total sales.

Whether Decor and Rian should succeed in their contentions depends upon whether, as a matter of fact and substance, the overheads which they seek to have deducted are attributable to the manufacture and sale of the infringing product. In arriving at an answer, the court must consider such questions as whether the overheads in any particular category were increased by the manufacture or sale of the product, whether they represent costs which would have been reduced or would have been incurred in any event, and whether they were surplus capacity or would, in the absence of the infringing product, have been used in the manufacture or sale of other products. Dealing with the last of these questions may require the use of the concept of opportunity cost. If any of the categories are to be brought into account, the proportion to be allocated to the infringing product must be determined and it is here that approximation rather than precision may be necessary. But such an approach has long been accepted.

If one man makes profits by the use or sale of some thing, and that whole thing came into existence by reason of his wrongful use of another man's property in a patent, design or copyright, the difficulty disappears and the case is then, generally speaking, simple. In such a case the infringer must account for all the profits which he thus made.

McHugh J.

Are general overheads deductible in an account of profits for a patent infringement?

Dart contends that, in taking an account of profits resulting from a patent infringement, no deduction is allowable for any expenditure "which would have been incurred had infringing manufacture not taken place". It contends that only two categories of costs can be deducted from gross revenue. First, direct costs "solely due" to the manufacture and sale of the product. Secondly, overheads to the extent that they have been increased by the manufacture and sale of the product. Decor and Rian, on the other hand, contend that all general overheads which assist or contribute to the production or sale of the infringing product are deductible.

In my opinion, the correct rule is that, in determining an account of profits in respect of the infringement of a patent, any part of the general overheads of the infringer which assisted in deriving gross revenue from the infringing product is a deductible expense. By general overheads, I mean "those general charges or expenses, collectively, in any business which cannot be charged up as belonging exclusively to any particular part of the work or product [such] as rent, taxes, insurance, lighting, heating, accounting and other office expenses" (Webster's New International Dictionary (2nd ed) unabridged). An expense may be deductible, therefore, although it did not directly increase the cost of producing or distributing the infringing product.

A plaintiff who establishes an infringement of its patent is entitled to an order that the infringer account for the profits derived from the infringement. The object of an account of profits is to make the infringer give up its gains in order to prevent its unjust enrichment. No element of punishment is involved. If an infringer has expended its own money or resources in producing or distributing the infringing product, it is not unjust for it to recoup that expenditure before accounting for the revenue derived from the product. With that general proposition, Dart agrees. But it contends that the case is different when the expenditure would have been incurred "in any event". If the infringer can claim the cost of expenditure which would have been incurred in any event, Dart contends that the infringer will have profited from its wrong. This argument has a certain plausibility. But the answer to it lies in the concept of opportunity cost.

"Opportunity cost" can be defined as "the value of the alternative forgone by adopting a particular strategy or employing resources in a specific manner. (In) economics, the opportunity cost of any designated alternative is the greatest net benefit lost by taking an alternative" (Kohler's Dictionary for Accountants (6th ed, 1983), pp 362–3). The relevance of the concept of opportunity cost in an infringement action was recognised in *Schnadig Corp. v. Gaines Manufacturing Co. Inc.*, ((1980) 620 F 2d 1166 at 1175) where the Court of Appeals for the Sixth Circuit said: "The alternative available uses of the facilities devoted to the infringement must be considered, and these too will vary."

To ignore overheads in the taking of an account of profits can also lead to absurd and unjust results. If all the products of a defendant were infringing products, the defendant would be out of pocket to the extent of its general overheads, even though no product could have been produced or sold without the overheads being incurred. If the infringing product was the first of a range of products, Dart's contention would require that it alone should bear the cost of the overheads. That would be to the detriment of the plaintiff.

The foregoing considerations require the rejection of Dart's contention.

The meaning of the word "profits" is for the courts to determine. But the identification of what in relation to the affairs of a particular company constitutes its profits is determined by the courts with close regard to the views of the accountancy profession. The courts are influenced strongly by the views adopted by professional accountancy bodies and men of business and the evidence of accountants is given great weight by the courts.

Admittedly, the commercial or accounting approach may mean that, in the account of profits, the infringer is credited with an amount of overhead greater than would be the case if no infringement had taken place. But the converse may sometimes be true. Whatever the outcome in a particular case may be, the commercial or accounting approach has one clear advantage over other methods: it deals with historical facts and commercial reality and not hypotheses.

Cases in the United States support the use of the absorption method of accounting in determining the cost of an infringing product in an account of profits. Differences between the intellectual property legislation of this country and the United States mean that the United States cases must be used cautiously in Australia. None the less, as Windeyer J pointed out *in Colbeam Palmer Ltd. v. Stock Affiliates Pty Ltd.*, ((1968) 122 CLR at 44; [1972] RPC at 316) "if used with discrimination, American decisions on the point are illuminating and helpful".

The main idea which runs through the American cases is that the absorption method of accounting should be adopted in relation to general overheads which can reasonably be shown to have assisted in the derivation of revenue from an infringing product. However, the current position in the United States is succinctly and conveniently summarised in Nimmer on Copyright (Vol 3, § 1403 [B]). The learned author declares that the question of which expenses will be regarded as deductible costs:

> will generally turn upon the definition of costs under accepted accounting practices. In general it may be said that only those expenses which are proven with some specificity to relate to the infringing work may be deducted in determining the profits attributable to such work.

A proper allocation of that portion of defendant's overhead attributable to the cost of the said infringing items may be deducted, at least where the infringement was not conscious and deliberate. This determination of overhead presents an issue of fact. The defendant has the burden of proving that each item of general expense contributed to the production of the infringing items, and of further offering a fair and acceptable formula for allocating a given portion of overhead to the particular infringing items in issue. The appropriate formula for allocation may well vary in different industries. For example, it has been held that a music publisher's overhead should be allocated on the basis of the number of songs published in a given period, without reference to the number of copies sold of each such song. This is to be compared with the overhead of a motion picture producer where it has been held that overheads should be allocated according to the direct cost of production of each motion picture.

Whether the overhead did actually assist in the production or sale, etc of the infringing product will be a question of fact in all the circumstances of the case.

The defendant/infringer bears the onus of showing which overheads assisted in the production or sale of the infringing product and of providing a fair basis for allocating the overheads.

THE CHICAGO PIZZA CASE
MY KINDA TOWN LTD. v. SOLL

High Court Of Justice Chancery Division, 1981.
[1983] RPC 15, [1982] FSR 147.

SLADE, J.

This is a passing off action. The plaintiff company runs a restaurant in London under the name "The Chicago Pizza Pie Factory". The two defendants run a restaurant also in London under the name "L.S. Grunts Chicago Pizza Co.". The essence of the plaintiff's complaint is that the defendants have so conducted their business, both by the choice of a name for their restaurant and by the adoption of a number of other features similar to those of the plaintiff's restaurant, as to lead a substantial number of members of the public into supposing that their establishment is a branch of or is otherwise connected with the plaintiff's business.

There are a number of strikingly similar distinctive features of both restaurants. As might be expected in the case of two restaurants which have deliberately chosen to base themselves on a Chicago theme, each has a number of Chicago-type posters and other memorabilia. But the coincidence goes much further than that. Grunts has followed the Chicago Pizza Pie Factory in displaying identical posters of "Elect Mayor Daley" and the Honey Bears sports team, two identical posters of films, "Gangs of Chicago" and "Chicago Syndicate", an identical map of Chicago and the original or a copy of the same front page of a Chicago daily newspaper. It has followed the Chicago Pizza Pie Factory in having pennants of Chicago sports teams, Chicago street signs and in displaying traffic lights, though it uses these lights for rather different purposes. Like the Chicago Pizza Pie Factory, it uses a tannoy-type system to call guests to their tables. Like it also, it offers to customers a bag in which they can take home any of the food which they cannot eat; while the plaintiff calls these bags "doggy-bags", the defendants call them "people bags". Like the plaintiff, the defendants even offer to their customers Trebor Extra Strong Mints as they leave their restaurant. Mr. Soll in cross-examination mentioned several other restaurants which employ tannoy-type systems for the purpose of calling their customers, but was not able to name a single restaurant in London which had adopted a single one of the other common features of the Chicago Pizza Pie Factory and of Grunts to which I have referred. There are other similar features of the decor and get-up of the two restaurants (some trivial and some less trivial) to which I do not think I need refer, though no doubt a discerning eye, such as that of Mr. Dover, would detect numerically many more points of distinction between the two.

The common features in the decor and get-up are by no means the only points of similarity between the two establishments. The defendants follow the plaintiff in playing at their restaurant recorded music from tapes of Chicago radio music. Mr. Soll said in cross-examination that he knew of no other restaurant where this is done.

In my judgment the evidence shows that, when all the features of Grunts, which are common with those of the Chicago Pizza Pie Factory, relating to decor, get-up, music and menu content are taken together, they combine to create a package which is likely to impress many visitors to Grunts, who are already familiar with the plaintiff's restaurant, as being at least strongly reminiscent of that restaurant and in some respects strikingly similar.

Once the phrase "Chicago Pizza" had been removed from the defendants' trading name and logo, then provided that they continued otherwise to conduct their business as at present, any really substantial risk of confusion would in my view disappear.

In the event, the defendants have, I understand, complied with that part of my Order which obliged them to cease to use the name "L.S. Grunts Chicago Pizza Co." within a specified period of time. The form of the Minute has been agreed between counsel, save for the paragraph embodying the order for an account. A subsequent dispute, however, has arisen in regard to the form of this particular part of the Order. The wording which the Plaintiff's Counsel proposes is an order:

> "that it shall be referred to the Master to take an account of the profits made by the business of the second defendants carried on under the name 'L.S. Grunts Chicago Pizza Company' or any other name including the phrase 'Chicago Pizza' from 6 December 1979 down to the date when it ceased to employ such a name (a proper and reasonable allowance to be made for the remuneration of the

working directors thereof) the costs of which account are reserved to the taking thereof and that the defendants do cause to the paid to the plaintiffs the said profits together with such interest thereon as the Master shall think fit."

The defendants' counsel, however, submits that there should be substituted for the phrase "the profits made" the phrase "the net profits improperly made".

In form, therefore, the dispute between the parties centres on the narrow question whether or not the two words "net" and "improperly" should be inserted in the relevant paragraph of the order. In substance the dispute raises the much broader question whether, subject to an allowance being made for the remuneration of the working directors, the defendants should be accountable:

(a) on the one hand (as the plaintiffs contend) for all the profits made by the business of the second defendants carried on under the name "L.S. Grunts Chicago Pizza Co." from 6 December 1979 down to the date when they ceased to employ this name; or

(b) on the other hand (as the defendants contend) only for those additional profits made by the defendants by virtue of their use of this name over this period.

On the evidence which I heard at the trial of this action, I was satisfied that the defendants' use of the name had given rise and was likely to give rise to confusion among a substantial number of people; it was on this basis that I found for the plaintiffs. On the other hand, the evidence showed that many other persons had not been in the least confused by this use. Nevertheless, subject to the proposed allowance for the remuneration of working directors, the plaintiffs now seek to deprive the defendants of all the profits of their business earned over the relevant period, from whomsoever these profits may be derived. If the plaintiffs' claim be correct, no differentiation whatever falls to be made between:

(i) profits made from meals served to customers of the defendants who had been confused into believing that the defendants' restaurant was connected with the plaintiffs' restaurant; and

(ii) profits made from meals served to customers of the defendants who knew of the existence of the plaintiffs' restaurant but had not been confused in any way; and

(iii) profits made from meals served to customers of the defendants who had no knowledge of the existence of the plaintiffs' restaurant.

As I understand the relevant principles, the object of ordering an account in cases such as the present is to deprive the defendants of the profits which they have improperly made by wrongful acts committed in breach of the plaintiffs' rights and to transfer such profits to the plaintiffs. There can, I think, be no doubt that profits falling within the first of the three categories last-mentioned should fall within the ambit of any account ordered. The doubts concern profits falling within the second and third of these categories. Should the profits made by the defendants by the service of meals to customers who were not in the least confused also be treated for present purposes as having been improperly made by wrongful acts of the defendants committed in breach of the plaintiffs' rights?

The purpose of ordering an account of profits in favour of a successful plaintiff in a passing off case is not to inflict punishment on the defendant. It is to prevent an unjust enrichment of the defendant by compelling him to surrender those profits, or those parts of the profits, actually made by him which were improperly made and nothing beyond this. Before specifying the form of the account, the court therefore should, I think, initially ask itself this question: What categories of the relevant profits or parts of such profits ought to be treated as having been improperly made by the defendants? The facts of many particular cases may justify the conclusion that the whole of the relevant profits should be so treated. The facts of the present case, however, do not in my judgment justify such a conclusion.

To ascertain the profits which have been improperly made by the defendants, it is therefore necessary to ascertain how much of the profits made by the defendants over the relevant period are properly attributable to the use of the name "Chicago Pizza Co". Clearly, profits made by the defendants by the sale of meals to customers who were not confused by this name are not attributable to this use.

I cannot accept Mr. Prescott's submission that each and every sale of a meal by the defendants over the relevant period must be treated as tortious merely because of the form of injunction which I have thought it necessary to grant. The matter may be tested by this hypothetical example. Let it be assumed that: (a) on 7 December 1979, 100 persons had eaten meals at the defendants' restaurant; (b) on 8 December 1979, the plaintiffs had issued proceedings claiming damages for passing off against the defendants, exclusively in relation to the defendants' sales of the previous day; (c) the evidence showed clearly that all of the 100 persons concerned were well aware that the defendants' restaurant was not connected with the plaintiffs' restaurant and thus were not in any way misled. On these facts the plaintiffs' action would have wholly failed, because they would have failed to establish that any of the sales in question involved any tort against them. Quite different principles apply where goods are sold, under a misleading get-up, to a middleman. In such a case, as *Lever v. Goodwin* and the other authorities show, the sale itself may constitute a tortious act, even though the middleman is not himself misled.

In all the circumstances, I think that the paragraph of the Order which relates to the account should take substantially the following form:

"AND IT IS ORDERED that it be referred to the Master to take an account of those profits made by the business of the Second Defendants carried on under the name L.S. Grunts Chicago Pizza Co. or any other name including the phrase Chicago Pizza from 6 December 1979 down to the date when the Defendants ceased to employ such name which are properly attributable to the use by the Defendants of such name in the said business AND IT IS ORDERED that the costs of this account are reserved to the taking thereof and that the Defendants do cause to be paid to the Plaintiffs the said profits together with such interest thereon as the Master shall think fit."

An account in this form will, in my judgment, accord with the principles established by cases such as *Cartier v. Carlile* because it will operate to give the plaintiffs that part of the defendants' profits which is attributable to the defendants' wrongful acts, no more and no less. The evidence before me indicated that the defendants' restaurant is a thriving concern and that a considerable part of their profits owes nothing to the plaintiffs or the plaintiffs' reputation. To order an account in the form sought by the plaintiffs would be tantamount to a decision that Mr. Soll and Mr. Jager, whose personal honesty is not in dispute, should be treated as having conducted the whole of the business of the defendants' restaurant throughout the relevant period as trustees for the benefit of the plaintiffs, albeit at a reasonable wage for themselves. In my judgment, any such order on the facts of this case would be quite inequitable. Though the defendants' use of the name "L.S. Grunts Chicago Pizza Co." was, in my judgment, unjustifiable, and correspondingly has had to be restrained by injunction, no other features of their activities, in my opinion, by themselves constituted wrongs against the plaintiffs of which the plaintiffs could complain in law. On the particular facts of some passing off cases, it may be right for the Court to regard the whole of the defendants' business as a parasitical enterprise which has fed itself entirely off the plaintiff's goodwill. The present case is not one of those cases. On the actual taking of the account which I propose to order, the proper comparison will, in my judgment, fall to be one between:

(i) the profits actually made by the Second Defendants' business from 6 December 1979 down to the date when they ceased to use the name "L.S. Grunts Chicago Pizza Company"; and

(ii) the profits which would have been made by that business over that period if that name or any other name including the phrase Chicago Pizza had not been used.

Problem

Your client Lucas Films has just released the ninth episode of its popular science fiction series "Planet Wars" for theatrical release in the United States on September 12. Lucas Films intends to release the movie theatrically in Mexico on December 29th. The film has been widely advertised, its lead characters already the subject of extensive merchandising efforts prior to the release of episode nine. On September 20th, Lucas Films received a report from private investigators in Mexico. A pirated version of the film (in English) is being sold across the border in both video cassette and CD-rom versions. Investigators have also discovered a pirated version of the movie with Spanish subtitles which is being sold in local markets throughout Mexico.

Luca Films is concerned that these pirated versions will undercut box office receipts in Mexico and perhaps other Spanish speaking countries in Central America. Its last movie—Episode Eight—made $100,000,000 gross profits in the U.S. on box office receipts and another $500,000 on videocassette sales. Despite a movie-going population of at least two-thirds of the U.S. movie population, receipts in Mexico for Episode Eight were only one-tenth those of the U.S., due in large part to the problem of video piracy.

Current prices for the pirated videocassettes and CD's in Mexico are $1.00 for the English language versions and $2.00 for the dubbed movies. The investigators have located one of the large distributors in Mexico City of the pirated videocassettes, Distributors, S.A. An informant has told the investigators that Distributors, S.A. has already made about $2,000 gross profits on Episode Nine.

Would you advise Lucas Films to file suit? Where? What relief, if any, would you seek? What evidentiary problems do you foresee? What steps, if any, could Lucas Films take to reduce its piracy problems in Mexico?

Notes and Questions

1. *The Nature of the Right Infringed.* Neither NAFTA nor TRIPS established separate enforcement standards based on the types of intellectual property that was infringed. Since the normal aim of tortious actions such as infringement is to put the victim back to his or her original position before the tort, compensatory relief is generally granted. Similarly, wilful conduct may result in exemplary or punitive damages, regardless of the type of intellectual property right infringed. Although theoretically the same general category of relief is available regardless of the nature of the right infringed—the right to "adequate compensation"—should there be different standards of adequacy depending upon the *nature* of that right? For example, if your client were a publisher of quality, high-end, coffee table books, and her copyrights in those books had been infringed by the unauthorized production of cheap paperback versions, which remedy would be "adequate" to compensate her for the money damages she had suffered? The dependant's profits? A reasonable royalty based on royalties granted by the industry for similar publishing arrangements? A reasonable royalty based on prior licensing agreements entered into by your client with other authorized paperback publishers? Statutory damages? Some other basis for establishing money damages?

2. Which decision(s) above do you believe adequately compensate the IP owner for the money damages incurred as a result of the defendant's infringing acts? Why? On what factors did you base your decision?

3. Draft a proposed treaty article that defines the factors to be considered in determining the "adequacy" of compensation under TRIPS. Prepare to defend your article against attack for economic, political and/or cultural biases. What role do statutory damages play in determining "adequacy" under your draft treaty?

4. As noted above, Chinese law requires that damages for infringement be limited to a maximum award of 5,000 yuan (RMB). In recent cases a

Chinese firm found guilty of infringing the Walt Disney Company's trademark Mickey Mouse character was fined only U.S.$91. Linus Chua, *China Steps Up Enforcement of Piracy Laws*, L.A. Times, Apr. 4, 1994, at D3. A fine for infringement of the rights of the Sino–French joint venture Vie De France (Beijing), Ltd., amounted to only U.S.$1712. Ruth Youngblood, *China Fights Trademark Abuse*, UPI, Apr. 4, 1994. Is the relief granted in these cases "adequate"? Does it comply with your draft treaty definition?

5.   In the *Profit Accounting* case, the court awarded the plaintiff the defendant's profits. How should those profits be determined? On the basis of gross profits? Net profits? What portion of the defendant's cost should be deductible? Would the grant of a reasonable royalty similar to that granted in the *Rubber Tyre* case be a more appropriate remedy?

6.   *Government Use*. What restrictions, if any, should be placed on a government's ability to use intellectual property without the owner's permission? Put another way, when does such unauthorized use violate the protection principles of TRIPS? Under U.S. law, if the U.S. government infringes another's intellectual property rights, no injunction may issue prohibiting such unauthorized use. Instead, the government is required to pay a "reasonable royalty" and receives the continued right to use of the invention. 18 U.S.C. § 1498. Are there instances, other than infringement by governmental institutions, where payment of a reasonable royalty under (in effect) a compulsory licensing arrangement should qualify as "adequate" compensation?

7.   On what basis did the courts decide that compensation should be limited to the defendant's net profits? Does this rationale conflict with the deterrence goals set forth in Article 41 of TRIPS?

8.   Re-examine the statutory damages set forth in Section C above. Do these damages fulfil deterrence or compensation goals?

9.   Which of the cases above meets the "adequate compensation" standard of TRIPS?

THE PICASSO PAINTING CASE
SUCCESSION PICASSO v. PRC INC.

Federal Court, Trial Division, 1996.
70 C.P.R. 3d 313.

McGILLIS, J.

Given the imminent opening of the Modern Art Cafe in Edmonton, Alberta, the application by the plaintiff for interim injunctive relief is urgent and should be determined by the Court. I have reviewed all of the evidence tendered on the application, and have considered the able submissions of counsel. Although the affidavit of the defendant Henri Cynamon did not describe the extent to which the allegedly infringing works are to be used in the decor and the equipment of the restaurant, I accept the statement of counsel that they are prevalent throughout the premises. I further accept his statement that the restaurant would likely not be able to operate without using the equipment consisting of allegedly infringing works. In applying the test for interim injunctive relief, the court must assess the following factors outlined in *RJR-MacDonald Inc. v. Canada (Attorney General)*, [1994] 1 S.C.R. 311, 334, 54 C.P.R. (3d) 114 (S.C.C.):

> "*Metropolitan Stores* adopted a three-stage test for courts to apply when considering an application for either a stay or an interlocutory injunction. First, a preliminary assessment must be made of the merits of the case to ensure that there is a serious question to be tried. Secondly, it must be determined whether the applicant would suffer irreparable harm if the application was refused. Finally, an assessment must be made as to which of the parties would suffer greater harm from the granting or refusal of the remedy pending a decision on the merits."

In my opinion, the evidence clearly establishes that there is a serious issue to be tried in this matter. The evidence also establishes that the plaintiff would suffer irreparable harm, not compensable in damages, as a result of the activities of the defendants. In the circumstances, the balance of convenience lies in favour of the plaintiff.

In making this Order, I am aware that the defendants will suffer serious inconvenience and financial loss. However, the defendants proceeded with this project knowing full well that the plaintiff would assert its intellectual property rights. In that regard, the defendant Cynamon received a letter dated March 15, 1996 which stated as follows:

> "We are the Canadian counsel for the Succession Pablo Picasso, by its duly empowered administrator, Claude Ruiz–Picasso (the Estate). We are aware that you have been duly advised by the Estate's American lawyers by letter dated February 8, 1996 that the Estate has not approved any use of the late Pablo Picasso's name, signature and artwork in connection with the marketing, advertising or operation of cafes, restaurants, or any souvenirs in gift shops associated therewith. If you are proceeding with any plans in that connection, you are doing so at your own peril."

By letter dated March 27, 1996, the defendant Cynamon was informed as follows:

> "Further to our letter to you of March 15, 1996, please be advised that the Estate of Pablo Picasso has secured, in the United States District Court of the Southern District of Florida a preliminary injunction against Cafe Pablo Picasso, Inc. and Patrick Danan, the principal of both First Equity Management Corporation and of Cafe Pablo Picasso, Inc.

> Given that we understand that there are firm plans to open a Picasso cafe at the West Edmonton Mall, we are drawing this injunction to your attention, and we ask that you take appropriate steps to avoid involvement in legal action to enforce our client's rights."

By letter dated March 28, 1996, counsel requested the defendant Cynamon to provide immediate written assurance' that appropriate measures were being taken to avoid infringement of the plaintiff's rights.

On April 4, 1996, counsel for the defendant Cynamon advised that the signage referring to the Picasso name had been removed. By letter dated June 18, 1996, counsel for the plaintiff advised the defendant Cynamon as follows:

> "As you know from [the] previous correspondence, the Estate has secured an order in the United States District Court of the Southern District of Florida which not only prevents the use of a name that includes the word Picasso", but also enjoins the advertising, promotion, displaying or offering for sale any goods or services which bear the Picasso name and/or signautre [sic], and/or the Picasso Artwork or any other goods that are likely to cause confusion or to cause a mistake or to deceive as to the affiliation, connection or association of the defendants or related parties with the Estate or the Picasso Artwork, name or distinct signature.
>
> I have been advised that PRC Inc. is intending to open a restaurant in the West Edmonton Mall under the name 'The Modern Art Café.' While the use of that trade name is not objectionable to my client, I understand that the restaurant will still be making unauthorized use of the late Picasso's name, signature and artwork (Picasso Work), including reproductions of the Picasso Work."

Counsel advised the defendant Cynamon of the steps that could be taken to avoid litigation, and stated that the plaintiff would protect its valuable intellectual property rights to the full extent provided by law. He further indicated that, unless the defendant Cynamon responded by June 20, 1996, action would be taken to protect the plaintiff's rights.

Despite all of the warnings, the defendants proceeded with their plans to open the restaurant. In the circumstances, the defendants cannot claim to be surprised that the plaintiff has instituted an action or moved speedily for injunctive relief.

The application for an interim injunction is granted. Counsel for the plaintiff has indicated his willingness to have the application for an interlocutory injunction argued at the earliest date convenient to counsel and the Court. Application granted.

THE SPOTLIGHT TABLEWARE CASE
ZIVIN v. GILBRO, LTD.

Federal Court, Trial Division, 1988
19 C.P.R. 3d 516.

JOYAL, J.

The plaintiff, the owner of five design registrations under the Industrial Design Act, R.S.C. 1970, c. I–8, applies for an interlocutory injunction, pending the resolution of his infringement action against the defendant, restraining the latter from importing and selling a certain line of plastic tableware called Spotlights manufactured by Novelty Crystal Corporation in the United States and distributed in Canada by the defendant.

In his concurrent statement of claim, the plaintiff alleges that the various items of Spotlights tableware infringe the following registered designs:

(1) Registration No. 59208 "Tumbler" dated August 25, 1987;

(2) Registration No. 59534 "Bowl" dated October 20, 1987;

(3) Registration No. 59561 "Pitchers and Lid" dated October 27, 1987;

(4) Registration No. 59651 "Combined Ice Bucket & Cover" dated November 10, 1987;

(5) Registration No. 59672 "Serving Tray" dated November 17, 1987.

The plaintiff, through his company Zivco Inc., manufactures in the United States and sells in Canada the above-noted items of tableware through an exclusive distributor called Innovations whose head office is in North Vancouver, B.C. The plaintiff alleges that the continuing sale of the Spotlights line of tableware would cause him irreparable harm, the kind of harm that could not be compensable in damages should his infringement action ultimately succeed.

Plaintiff's counsel is aware that in urging the court to grant such interlocutory relief, the well-known tests laid down by the House of Lords in *American Cyanamid Co. v. Ethicon Ltd.*, [1975] 1 All E.R. 504, must be met. The plaintiff must establish:

1. that he has a fair or clear prima facie case or that there is a serious issue to be tried;

2. that permitting the defendant to continue its activities pending trial would cause the plaintiff irreparable harm; and

3. assuming the foregoing tests are met and, on a balance of convenience, the situation favours the court's intervention on the plaintiff's behalf.

The case for the plaintiff, ably put by his counsel, may be summarized as follows:

(1) The registered designs secured by the plaintiff are the result of much research undertaken by him to recapture, perhaps in a more contemporary style, the aesthetic fashion of the Art Deco period of some 50 years ago. This research, as well as the plaintiff's eye for line and form, enabled him at first to design a set of acrylic tumblers of various sizes, all featuring sharply-etched horizontal rings or striations around the body of the tumbler.

(2) From there, the plaintiff proceeded to develop complementary designs for trays, ice buckets, bowls and pitchers so as to create a distinctive line of tableware marketed under the name Images.

(3) The promotion and marketing policy of the plaintiff was to sell these wares in upscale shops and boutiques and to make of them top-of-the-line articles.

(4) In the concept, design, development, production and promotion efforts required of this new line, the plaintiff necessarily had to expend hundreds of thousands of dollars.

(5) Once the plaintiff's full line of tableware was publicized at trade shows and offered for sale, the positive reaction in the market was such that he could hardly meet U.S. demands for the products, let alone penetrate in a meaningful way the Canadian market.

(6) It was on November 19, 1987, that he first delivered to Innovations, his newly-appointed distributor in Canada, some 48 double old-fashioned and 48 highball tumblers together with some 24 photographs of Images wares. It was in early January, 1988, that first production runs of the complementary wares began. It was on January 21, 1988, that the plaintiff was informed of the entry into the Canadian market of the competing Spotlights wares offered by the defendant.

(7) The plaintiff states in his evidence that the two lines of tableware are so similar in appearance and design that the Spotlights line is obviously a knock-off of his own line and evidently constitutes an infringement of the industrial designs he had previously registered in Canada.

(8) Of equal concern to the plaintiff is that the competing products are of lower quality. Some of them are made of styrene instead of acrylic. Their density is lower. There is grave risk that the integrity of the plaintiff's "Images" line would be seriously prejudiced by the entry into the field of these lower-priced, lower-quality products.

(9) And the plaintiff to conclude that what the defendant is effectively doing is piggy-backing on the goodwill, reputation and obvious appeal which his innovative skills have so laboriously created.

The case for the defendant is as ably put by its own counsel. As is usually the case in resisting an interlocutory injunction in infringement actions, counsel bases its defence on several grounds, many of them of course going to the merits of the suit in order to establish that the plaintiff has not made out a strong prima facie case. Defendant's counsel's principal points may be summarized as follows:

(1) The plaintiff's design is not new. Some 50 years earlier, a company called Anchor Hocking had designed its "Manhattan" line of glassware and it was specifically from this old design that the plaintiff has copied its own. The two designs are substantially similar. The Anchor Hocking line had been sold in Canada through Empire Trading Company which had published the line in its own catalogue in 1938.

(2) Furthermore, there is evidence that in about 1987, Anchor Hocking had itself reproduced its earlier 1938 design by fusing what it called its classic line into a more contemporary, revitalized look.

(3) Serious doubts are raised with respect to some if not all of the impugned designs as to whether their registration complies with § 14(1) of the Industrial Design Act which provides that protection under the statute is only available when the registration is effected within one year of the publication of the design in Canada. Counsel argues that according to the chronology of events leading to the registrations, the various items of tableware designed by the plaintiff had been published at a much earlier date.

(5) Finally, counsel contends that notwithstanding the assertions of the plaintiff as to product integrity and quality, i.e., elements relevant to a claim of irreparable injury, the evidence in support is singularly lacking.

Any interlocutory injunction order is by its very nature an exceptional remedy which is why the tests in the *American Cyanamid* case, *supra* have been formulated and why these tests are most often difficult to meet. Especially in matters of patent infringement is there a reluctance on the part of the court to issue such an order. This principle is stated in *Cutter Ltd. v. Baxter Travenol Laboratories Ltd. of Canada, Ltd.* (1980), 47 C.P.R. (2d) 53, where the Chief Justice of this court says as follows at p. 55:

In this Court the grant of an interlocutory injunction in a patent infringement action is not a common occurrence. In most instances, the result of an application for an interlocutory injunction, where infringement and validity are in issue, is that the defendant gives a satisfactory undertaking to keep an account and upon that being done the application is dismissed with costs in the cause.

And further, the Chief Justice says:

The principal reason for this practice is, in my opinion, the fact that in most instances the nature of the patent rights involved is such that damages (provided there is some reasonably accurate way of measuring them) will be an adequate remedy for such infringement of the rights as may occur pending the trial ...

I will concede that the rule might not be as stringently applied when dealing with other fields of intellectual property as in copyright and industrial design. The subject-matter in these instances has often an ephemeral lifespan where market saturation is quickly reached and where the winds of fashion which favour an owner's venture into hopefully exceptional gains will have an equally exceptional fickleness about them. If at the same time, the competing product appears in the eye of the court to be an obvious knock-off and where piggy-back conclusions may be more easily reached, the court will not hesitate for the sake of pure equity, to grant injunctive relief. It means in effect that the plaintiff has not only established a strong prima facie case but has also met the test of irreparable injury of a kind which may not be compensated in damages. It would also follow in such instances that the balance of convenience would tilt in favour of the plaintiff.

In the case at bar, I could perhaps find that the plaintiff has made out a strong prima facie case, a finding consonant with the presumed validity of his industrial design registrations and with an obvious resemblance between the two competing lines of tableware. I might concurrently hesitate to make findings on the numerous challenges as to both validity and infringement raised by the defendant, these being issues which should not be determined in summary proceedings and which should be left to the trial judge.

If I were to assume that this first test imposed on the plaintiff has been met, I should find that he has unfortunately not made out a case for irreparable injury which could not be compensated in damages. With all respect for the plaintiff and for his assertions relating to the integrity of his product, to its top-of-the-line niche in his stable of tableware and to his marketing of it through up-scale shops and boutiques, I fail to find any objective and corroborative evidence of an irreparable harm situation.

I should recall in this respect that there is conflict in the evidence as to the inferior quality of the defendant's product or as to the marketing policies actually carried out by the plaintiff to make of it a more chichi product. There is also evidence that the plaintiff's product is also competing with other products which admittedly owe their own stylistic legitimacy to the same Art Deco period of some 50 years ago. This is similar to the situation facing Rouleau J. in *Windsurfing Int'l Inc. v. Les Entreprises Hermano Ltee* (1982), 69 C.P.R. (2d) 176, where in circumstances where the market already experiences more than two competing products, an injunction against one might be of little benefit to the plaintiff.

In the event, I must conclude that the case falls squarely within accepted doctrine where the rights of the plaintiff may be ultimately confirmed at trial and where monetary compensation for damages sustained may be assessed. In such circumstances, it is unnecessary for me to deal with the matter of balance of convenience.

The application by the plaintiff for an interlocutory injunction is dismissed. The defendant is ordered to keep and maintain full accounting records of his importations, sales and inventory of his complete line of "Spotlights" tableware allegedly infringing on the plaintiff's design registrations which have been cited. Costs shall be in the cause.

Notes and Questions

1. Must injunctive relief be offered under international enforcement standards? What test must be applied to determine if such provisional relief is warranted?

2. Compare the result of the *Picasso Painting* case in Canada with the court's decision in the *Spotlight Tableware* case in Australia regarding the

existence of "irreparable harm". Which standard for determining harm is in accordance with TRIPS? Do you agree that patent infringement may be more readily compensated through money damages alone than either copyright or trademark infringement?

3.   What assumptions did the court in the *Picasso Painting* case make about the harm caused by defendant's unauthorized use? Would such "irreparable" harm be present if the defendant's had *not* used the Picasso name, but had only reproduced his paintings without authorization? Does irreparable harm ever exist absent trademark infringement?

D. DOES "PROMPT RELIEF" INCLUDE THE RIGHT TO *EX PARTE* RELIEF?

THE ANTON PILLER CASE

ANTON PILLER KG v. MANUFACTURING PROCESSES LTD

Court Of Appeal, Civil Division, 1975.
[1976] Ch 55, [1976] 1 All ER 779, [1976] 2 WLR
162, [1976] RPC 719, [1976] FSR 129.

LORD DENNING

During the last 18 months the judges of the Chancery Division have been making orders of a kind not known before. They have some resemblance to search warrants. Under these orders the plaintiff and his solicitors are authorised to enter the defendant's premises so as to inspect papers, provided the defendant gives permission.

Now this is the important point: the court orders the defendant to give them permission. The judges have been making these orders on *ex parte* applications without prior notice to the defendant. None of the cases has been reported. But in the present case Brightman J refused to make such an order.

The plaintiffs are German manufacturers of high repute. They make electric motors and generators. They play an important part in the big new computer industry. They supply equipment for it. They have recently designed a frequency converter specially for supplying the computers of International Business Machines.

Since 1972 the plaintiffs have had, as their agents in the United Kingdom, a company here called Manufacturing Processes Ltd, which is run by Mr. A. H. S. Baker and Mr. B. P. Wallace. These agents are dealers who get machines from the plaintiffs in Germany and sell them to customers in England. The plaintiffs supply the English company with much confidential information about the machines, including a manual showing how they work, and drawings which are the subject of copyright.

Very recently the plaintiffs have found out—so they say—that these English agents have been in secret communication with other German companies called Ferrostaal and Lechmotoren. The object of these communications is that the English company should supply these other German companies with drawings and materials and other confidential information so that they can manufacture power units like the plaintiffs. The plaintiffs got to know of these communications through two 'defectors', if I may call them so. One was the commercial manager of the English company, Mr. Brian Firth; the other was the sales manager, Mr. William Raymond Knight. These two were so upset by what was going on in the English company that on their own initiative, without any approach by the plaintiffs whatever, on 2nd October 1975 one or both flew to Germany. They told the plaintiffs what they knew about the arrangements with Ferrostaal and Lechmotoren. They disclosed also that the English company were negotiating with Canadian and United States firms. In making these disclosures, both Mr. Firth and Mr. Knight were putting themselves in a perilous position, but the plaintiffs assured them that they would safeguard their future employment.

The disclosures—coming from defectors—might have been considered untrustworthy. But they were supported by documents which emanated from both Ferrostaal and Lechmotoren. They showed that the English company were in regular communication with those German companies. They were sending them drawings and arranging for inspection of the plaintiffs' machine, for the express purpose that the Lechmotoren company might manufacture a prototype machine copied from the plaintiffs. One of the most telling communications was a telex from Lechmotoren to Mr. Wallace saying:

> "It is the opinion of Mr. S (of Lechmotoren) that the best way to find a final solution for the prototype is to send Mr. Beck to you as soon as the latest design of [the plaintiffs] has arrived in your factory. In this case it is guaranteed that the Lech prototype will have exactly the same features as the [the plaintiffs'] type. We hope you will agree to this proposal and we ask you to let us have your telex in order to arrange Mr. Beck's visit accordingly."

On getting this information, the plaintiffs were extremely worried. They were about to produce a fine new frequency converter called 'the silent block'. They feared that the English company, in co-operation with the German manufacturers, would make a copy of their 'silent block' and ruin their market.

So, on Wednesday, 26th November 1975 the plaintiffs' solicitor prepared a draft writ of summons and, with an affidavit, they went before Brightman J and asked, first, for an interim injunction to restrain infringement etc, and, secondly, for an order that they might be permitted to enter the premises of the English company so as to inspect the documents of the plaintiffs and remove them, or copies of them. Brightman J granted an interim injunction, but refused to order inspection or removal of documents. He said:

> "There is strong prima facie evidence that the defendant company is now engaged in seeking to copy the plaintiffs' components

for its own financial profit to the great detriment of the plaintiffs and in breach of the plaintiffs' rights."

He realised that the defendants might suppress evidence or misuse documentary material, but he thought that that was a risk which must be accepted in civil matters save in extreme cases. "Otherwise", he said

> "it seems to me that an order on the lines sought might become on instrument of oppression, particularly in a case where a plaintiff of big standing and deep pocket is ranged against a small man who is alleged on the evidence of one side only to have infringed the plaintiff's rights."

Let me say at once that no court in this land has any power to issue a search warrant to enter a man's house so as to see if there are papers or documents there which are of an incriminating nature, whether libels or infringements of copyright or anything else of the kind. No constable or bailiff can knock at the door and demand entry so as to inspect papers or documents. The householder can shut the door in his face and say, "Get out". None of us would wish to whittle down that principle in the slightest. But the order sought in this case is not a search warrant. It does not authorise the plaintiffs' solicitors or anyone else to enter the defendants' premises against their will. It does not authorise the breaking down of any doors, nor the slipping in by a back door, nor getting in by an open door or window. It only authorises entry and inspection by the permission of the defendants. The plaintiffs must get the defendants' permission. But it does do this: it brings pressure on the defendants to give permission. It does more. It actually orders them to give permission—with, I suppose, the result that if they do not give permission, they are guilty of contempt of court.

> This may seem to be a search warrant in disguise. But it was fully considered in the House of Lords 150 years ago in *East India Co. v. Kynaston* [(1821) 3 Bli 153 at 163] and held to be legitimate. Lord Redesdale said:

> "The arguments urged for the Appellants at the Bar are founded upon the supposition, that the Court has directed a forcible inspection. This is an erroneous view of the case. The order is to permit; and if the East India Company should refuse to permit inspection, they will be guilty of a contempt of the Court. It is an order operating on the person requiring the defendants to permit inspection, not giving authority of force, or to break open the doors of their warehouse." That case was not, however, concerned with papers or things. It was only as to the value of a warehouse; and that could not be obtained without an inspection. But the distinction drawn by Lord Redesdale affords ground for thinking that there is jurisdiction to make an order that the defendants 'do permit' when it is necessary in the interests of justice.

> Accepting such to be the case, the question is in what circumstances ought such on order be made. If the defendant is given notice beforehand and is able to argue the pros and cons, it is warranted by that case in the House of Lords. But it is a far stronger thing to make such an order *ex*

parte without giving him notice. This is not covered by the rules of court and must be based on the inherent jurisdiction of the court. There are one or two old precedents which give some colour for it. But they do not go very far. So it falls to us to consider it on principle. It seems to me that such an order can be made by a judge *ex parte*, but it should only be made where it is essential that the plaintiff should have inspection so that justice can be done between the parties; and when, if the defendant were forewarned, there is a grave danger that vital evidence will be destroyed, that papers will be burnt or lost or hidden, or taken beyond the jurisdiction, and so the ends of justice be defeated; and when the inspection would do no real harm to the defendant or his case.

Nevertheless, in the enforcement of this order, the plaintiffs must act with due circumspection. On the service of it, the plaintiffs should be attended by their solicitor, who is an officer of the court. They should give the defendants an opportunity of considering it and of consulting their own solicitor. If the defendants wish to apply to discharge the order as having been improperly obtained, they must be allowed to do so. If the defendants refused permission to enter or to inspect, the plaintiffs must not force their way in. They must accept that refusal, and bring it to the notice of the court afterwards, if need be on application to commit.

One might think that with all these safeguards against abuse, it would be of little use to make such an order. But it can be effective in this way: it serves to tell the defendant that, on the evidence put before it, the court is of opinion that he ought to permit inspection—nay, it orders him to permit—and that he refuses at his peril. It puts him in peril not only of proceedings for contempt, but also of adverse inferences being drawn against him; so much so that his own solicitor may often advise him to comply. We are told that in two at least of the cases such an order has been effective. We are prepared, therefore, to sanction its continuance, but only in an extreme case where there is grave danger of property being smuggled away or of vital evidence being destroyed.

On the evidence in this case, we decided on 2nd December that there was sufficient justification to make an order. It contains an undertaking in damages which is to be supported (as the plaintiffs are overseas) by a bond for £ 10,000. It gives an interim injunction to restrain the infringement of copyright and breach of confidential information, etc. It orders that the defendants do permit one or two of the plaintiffs and one or two of their solicitors to enter the defendants' premises for the purpose of inspecting documents, files or things, and removing those which belong to the plaintiffs. This was, of course, only an interim order pending the return of the summons. It is to be heard, we believe, tomorrow by the judge.

ORMROD, L.J.

I agree with all that Lord Denning MR has said. The proposed order is at the extremity of this court's powers. Such orders, therefore, will rarely be made, and only when there is no alternative way of ensuring that justice is done to the plaintiff.

There are three essential pre-conditions for the making of such an order, in my judgment. First, there must be an extremely strong prima facie case. Secondly, the damage, potential or actual, must be very serious for the plaintiff. Thirdly, there must be clear evidence that the defendants have in their possession incriminating documents or things, and that there is a real possibility that they may destroy such material before any application inter partes can be made.

The form of the order makes it plain that the court is not ordering or granting anything equivalent to a search warrant. The order is an order on the defendant in personam to permit inspection. It is therefore open to him to refuse to comply with such an order, but at his peril either of further proceedings for contempt of court—in which case, of course, the court will have the widest discretion as to how to deal with it, and if it turns out that the order was made improperly in the first place, the contempt will be dealt with accordingly—but more important, of course, the refusal to comply may be the most damning evidence against the defendant at the subsequent trial.

In the circumstances of the present case, all those conditions to my mind are satisfied, and this order is essential in the interests of justice. I agree, therefore, that the appeal should be allowed.

Disposition: Appeal allowed.

THE CRASH DUMMIES CASE
FIRST TECHNOLOGY SAFETY SYSTEMS, INC. v. PAUL DEPINET

United States Court Of Appeals, Sixth Circuit, 1993.
11 F.3d 641.

MILBURN, CIRCUIT JUDGE.

Defendants appeal the district court's order denying their motion to vacate an order granting plaintiff's request for immediate *ex parte* order of inventory and impoundment. On appeal, the issue is whether the district court abused its discretion in refusing to vacate its *ex parte* order, which permitted plaintiff and its counsel, accompanied by the United States Marshal, to enter defendants' business premises and inventory and impound computer programs, computer printouts, and documents bearing the name of plaintiff or its predecessor, and to copy and inventory defendants' business records (purchase orders, invoices, correspondence, customer lists, and customer information materials). For the reasons that follow, we reverse and remand.

On April 3, 1992, plaintiff First Technology Safety Systems, Inc. ("FTSS") filed a verified complaint against defendants for unfair competition, unfair trade practices, conversion, receiving and concealing trade secrets, tortious interference with contract or business advantage, breach of contract, and copyright infringement. At the same time, plaintiff filed an emergency motion for *ex parte* order of seizure and impoundment of evidence, which stated pursuant to 17 U.S.C. @ 503 and [Federal Rule of Civil Procedure] 65, plaintiff FTSS requests the Court to enter an *ex parte* order directing the United States Marshall [sic] to seize and impound certain materials which constitute critical evidence in this litigation, yet are likely to be destroyed or concealed by defendants if an *ex parte* seizure order is not entered.

Within its complaint, brief, and affidavits supporting its motion, plaintiff presented the following information to the district court. Until December 1990, plaintiff was the sole designer and manufacturer of anthropomorphic test devices, more commonly known as crash test dummies. Plaintiff owned various inventions, trademarks, trade secrets, and copyrights on the vehicle crash test dummies and their related calibration software programs, manufacturing processes, component parts, customer lists, contacts, pricing information, and marketing strategy. On December 19, 1990, defendants Stephen Fuhr and Barry Wade, employees of plaintiff, formed defendant Vector Research, Inc. to compete with plaintiff in the design and manufacture of crash test dummies and related calibration software. The day before Vector's incorporation, Fuhr terminated his employment with plaintiff, but Wade continued to be employed as plaintiff's senior project engineer until January 4, 1991. Defendant Paul Depinet continued to be employed as plaintiff's data acquisitions supervisor until March 8, 1991. Plaintiff alleged that Fuhr, Wade, and Depinet violated their fiduciary duty as employees of plaintiff by using plaintiff's trade secrets, proprietary information, and copyrighted materials to build Vector's business.

Eleven days after Vector's incorporation, defendants produced a price list for crash test dummies, calibration equipment, component replacement parts, and data acquisition software effective January 1, 1991. The affidavit of George Pitarra, the former president and CEO of plaintiff, stated that it was "extremely unlikely" that a start-up company could develop and implement computer software for the calibration of crash test dummies in less than one year or could develop and market the full line of crash test dummy equipment described in Vector's price list in less than two years. Plaintiff alleged that information regarding the calibration of the crash test dummies, as well as the software involved, was a trade secret and was prohibited from distribution by former employees as evidenced by the employee proprietary information agreements.

Plaintiff does not seek the impoundment of the defendants' own dummies, or component parts, or business records. The plaintiff does not ask the Court to seize the defendants' inventory and thus stop defendants from continuing to manufacture and sell their product. All the plaintiff seeks is the impoundment of evidentiary materials relevant to the allegation that the defendants built their business using plaintiff's property. Impoundment and destruction of the defendants' computer software and any other infringing material can await a full hearing on the merits, but the critical evidence of defendants' wrongdoing must be seized now.

After considering the materials presented by plaintiff, the district court granted the *ex parte* order of inventory and impoundment and an order to seal the record. The seizure order, which was drafted by plaintiff's counsel, permitted the United States Marshal along with representatives of the plaintiff to inventory and impound certain materials from the business facilities of Vector. The order also provided that plaintiff and its attorneys be allowed to inspect, copy, and photograph all such seized materials.

The order authorized the marshal to impound a variety of items that could be identified as belonging to plaintiff or its predecessors in interest, such as blueprints, computer printouts, computer programs, and documents bearing the name of plaintiff or its predecessor. The order further authorized the copying and inventory of all invoices and purchase orders for parts, customer lists, or other customer information materials held by the defendant, and all correspondence between defendant Vector Research and the plaintiff or the Endevco defendants. The impounded and copied materials were to be retained by the marshal or plaintiff's counsel in trust for the court. The order also required that the plaintiff deposit a cash or surety bond in the amount of $2,000.

On April 8, 1992, at approximately 5:00 p.m., two U.S. Marshals, accompanied by plaintiff's counsel, two FTSS employees, an attorney for plaintiff's local counsel's law firm, two other employees of the law firm, and a computer consultant, accessed Vector's facility to carry out the court's order. Approximately one hour later and after copying machines were set up, the marshals left the premises, leaving the rest of the search party unattended. All parties left the premises at approximately 11:00 p.m. The seized materials were held in trust for the court by plaintiff's local counsel's law firm because the marshals had no space to hold these materials. All individuals involved in the search of the Vector facility signed confidentiality agreements relating to the information viewed. On April 16, 1992, defendant filed a motion to vacate the order of impoundment and inventory and to request an immediate hearing. That same day, the district court held a pretrial conference in response to the hearing request. All counsel were present in chambers. At this conference, the court entertained arguments from defendants' counsel on the motion to vacate and addressed defendants' concerns regarding the execution of the *ex parte* order. At that time, the materials were transferred to the custody of a United States Magistrate Judge, where they remain today.

The parties disagree as to whether the seizure order only preserved the status quo. Plaintiff argues that the order did no more than was necessary to preserve the status quo by taking "an unaltered snapshot of defendants' operation at a particular point in time." Plaintiff notes that the documents authorized for impoundment were all relevant to the merits of the case and were only copied, not taken from defendants, so that defendants' operation would not be affected. Defendants, on the other hand, argue that this order went beyond preserving the status quo. Defendants cite *Warner Bros. Inc. v. Dae Rim Trading, Inc.*, 877 F.2d

1120, 1125 (2d Cir.1989), which stated: "An order issued without notice directing an agent of plaintiff's attorney to search a defendant's premises, seize goods, documents and records and deliver them to the attorney, is not an order aimed at maintaining the status quo."

Regardless of whether the district court's order in this case merely preserved the status quo, plaintiff was required by Fed. R. Civ. P. 65(b) to show that the circumstances were appropriate for *ex parte* relief. The normal circumstance for which the district court would be justified in proceeding *ex parte* is where notice to the adverse party is impossible, as in the cases where the adverse party is unknown or is unable to be found. Plaintiff does not argue that this justification is present in this case. There is, however, another limited circumstance for which the district court may proceed *ex parte*: where notice to the defendant would render fruitless further prosecution of the action.

In order to justify proceeding *ex parte* because notice would render further action fruitless, the applicant must do more than assert that the adverse party would dispose of evidence if given notice. "Where there are no practical obstacles to giving notice to the adverse party, an *ex parte* order is justified only if there is no less drastic means for protecting the plaintiff's interests." *American Can*, 742 F.2d at 323. In this case, the district court could have ordered the defendants not to disturb any of the items listed in the seizure order and held an immediate adversarial hearing to determine whether the seizure order should issue. Therefore, plaintiffs must show that defendants would have disregarded a direct court order and disposed of the goods within the time it would take for a hearing.

The applicant must support such assertions by showing that the adverse party has a history of disposing of evidence or violating court orders or that persons similar to the adverse party have such a history. For example, in *In re Vuitton* [606 F.2d 1 (2d Cir.1979)], a famous manufacturer of expensive luggage explained its need for an *ex parte* restraining order by pointing to its experience in several previous actions it had filed against similar counterfeiters selling luggage unlawfully infringing the manufacturer's trademark. The manufacturer explained that in those previous actions its efforts were foiled because the counterfeiters, after receiving notice of the pending action, simply transferred their inventories to other members of a closely-knit group of counterfeiters. The Second Circuit held that the district court abused its discretion by not issuing the *ex parte* order because the manufacturer had made a sufficient showing of why notice should not be given to the defendants.

However, *American Can*, 742 F.2d at 322–25, a case from the Seventh Circuit, demonstrates the limits of this circumstance. In that trade secrets case, the district court issued an *ex parte* order permitting the plaintiff, accompanied by U.S. Marshals, to enter defendant's business premises and seize samples of the allegedly infringing inks and to copy all documents relating to defendants' sale of jet inks, defendants' production documents, and defendants' correspondence with plaintiff's customers. On appeal from the ensuing preliminary injunction, the Seventh Circuit held that issuing the seizure order *ex parte* was an abuse of discretion because there was no valid reason for proceeding *ex parte* and not complying with Fed. R. Civ. P. 65(b). Plaintiff had supported its argument that notice would have rendered fruitless the further prosecution of the action by asserting that the defendants, after receiving notice, "would have immediately caused [defendants] to alter the inks in their factory and secrete the pertinent documents." The court noted that it "agreed with the Second Circuit that *ex parte* orders of very limited scope and brief duration may be justified in order to preserve evidence where the applicant shows that notice would result in destruction of evidence" but held that plaintiff's unsupported assertions that defendants would destroy evidence were insufficient to show the need for proceeding *ex parte*.

In the present case, the only justification given to the district court for proceeding *ex parte* was that it is current business practice to store many business records electronically on computer tapes, floppy disks and hard disks. Not only is information stored in this manner easier to use than printed materials, it also is easier to destroy. Stated quite simply, if the incriminating evidence which proves the plaintiff's allegations still exists, it can now be seized and impounded but, given the character of the defendants' activities, it is very unlikely that such evidence would ever be produced through normal discovery if *ex parte* impoundment is not ordered.

Showing that the adverse party would have the opportunity to conceal evidence is insufficient to justify proceeding *ex parte*. If it were, courts would be bombarded with such requests in every action filed. The applicant must show that the adverse party is likely to take the opportunity for such deceptive conduct. Plaintiff contends that "the character of defendants' activities" shows that defendants were likely to conceal evidence. Plaintiff was seemingly referring to defendants' having allegedly unlawfully usurped plaintiff's business opportunities and allegedly violating their confidentiality agreements with plaintiff. These allegations are insufficient. Plaintiff did not show that defendants, or persons involved in similar activities, had ever concealed evidence or disregarded court orders in the past.

Plaintiff did not sufficiently show that it was necessary to proceed *ex parte* and that there were no less extreme remedies available. Plaintiff's assertion that defendants would conceal evidence if given notice because defendants allegedly misappropriated trade secrets and infringed plaintiff's copyrights is insufficient to establish that notice to the defendants would have rendered fruitless further prosecution of the action. Because plaintiff failed to comply with Fed. R. Civ. P. 65(b), the district court's *ex parte* order of inventory and impoundment was an abuse of discretion. Therefore, the district court's order denying defendants' motion to vacate that *ex parte* order was, likewise, an abuse of discretion.

THE VUITTON SEIZURE CASE
LOUIS VUITTON v. HELENE WHITE

United States Court of Appeals, Third Circuit, 1991.
945 F.2d 569.

STAPLETON, CIRCUIT JUDGE.

Consistent with their calling, professional counterfeiters and dealers in counterfeit goods generally are not upstanding citizens. This presents a major obstacle to trademark owners trying to protect their marks. As one commentator has described the situation, "Experience in hundreds of cases has shown that it is extremely likely that a counterfeiter, upon being apprised of the institution of a lawsuit by the trademark owner, will conceal his infringing merchandise and either destroy or conceal all records relating to this merchandise, thereby frustrating implementation of the trademark owner's statutory and common law rights." Bainton, *Seizure Orders: An Innovative Judicial Response to the Realities of Trademark Counterfeiting*, 73 Trademark Rep. 459, 464 (1983).

Courts initially responded to these bad faith tactics by granting *ex parte* interim relief. The classic precedent for courts' authority to do so is *In re Vuitton et Fils S.A.*, 606 F.2d 1 (2d Cir.1979). In that case, the Court of Appeals for the Second Circuit granted Vuitton's application for a writ of mandamus directing the district court to enter an *ex parte* temporary restraining order. It found the district court's reluctance to enter the order without notice unjustified:

Vuitton has demonstrated sufficiently why notice should not be required in a case such as this one. If notice is required, that notice all too often appears to serve only to render fruitless further prosecution of the action. This is precisely contrary to the normal and intended role of "notice" ... 606 F.2d at 4–5. Using the Vuitton case as authority, other courts began issuing—not just temporary restraining orders, which are frequently ignored—but seizure orders providing for the seizure of the counterfeit merchandise and related business records by the U.S. marshals or plaintiff's agent.

However, not all courts were persuaded of their authority to enter seizure orders even when they were persuaded that a plaintiff would be denied effective relief in the absence of such an order. At the same time, counterfeiting operations continued to grow and to become increasingly sophisticated. After substantial study, Congress responded to these problems with the Trademark Counterfeiting Act of 1984. That act provided criminal penalties for counterfeiting, mandatory triple damages, and specific authorization for injunctive relief, including *ex parte* seizure orders.

The relevant section, 15 U.S.C. § 1116(d), provides in part that:

(d) Civil actions arising out of use of counterfeit mark

(1)(A) In the case of a civil action [for counterfeiting] the court may, upon *ex parte* application, grant an order under subsection (a) of this section pursuant to this subsection providing for the seizure of goods and counterfeit marks involved in such violation and the means of making such marks, and records documenting the manufacture, sale, or receipt of things involved in such violation.

Further provisions of subsection (d) detail the procedures for applying for a seizure order, what facts must be shown to obtain an order, and what the order must contain. Section 1116(d)(10) provides that a hearing with notice to the defendant must be held no later than fifteen days after the order is issued at which the applicant "shall have the burden of proving that the facts supporting [the seizure] order are still in effect."

The legislative purpose behind § 1116(d) is clear from the Joint Statement of the congressional committees:

> The purpose of the *ex parte* seizure provision is to provide victims of trademark counterfeiting with a means of ensuring that the courts are able to exercise their jurisdiction effectively in counterfeiting cases. Testimony before both the House and Senate Judiciary Committees established that many of those who deal in counterfeits make it a practice to destroy or transfer counterfeit merchandise when a day in court is on the horizon. The *ex parte* seizure procedure is intended to thwart this bad faith tactic, while ensuring ample procedural protections for persons against whom such orders are issued. In essence, both the Senate and House bills permitted issuance of an *ex parte* seizure order if the applicant could show that the defendant would not comply with a lesser court order, such as a temporary restraining order, and that there was no means of protecting the court's authority other than to seize the property in question on an *ex parte* basis. Joint Statement, 130 Cong. Rec. at H12080.

The legislative history thus indicates that Congress considered "*ex parte* seizures, a necessary tool to thwart the bad faith efforts of fly by night defendants to evade the jurisdiction of the court", Joint Statement, 130 Cong. Rec. at H120781, and intended seizure orders to be available whenever a temporary restraining order and the threat of contempt for a violation thereof are unlikely to result in preservation of the evidence and the removal of the counterfeit merchandise from commerce.

We recognize that § 1116(d) requires both a finding that notice will thwart effective relief and a finding that a temporary restraining order would be ineffective. Nevertheless, where, as in this case, the district court finds that notice will cause the defendants to conceal or destroy the counterfeit merchandise and the undisputed facts show that counterfeit merchandise is being sold despite an outstanding permanent injunction against some of the defendants, it is an abuse of discretion for the court to deny § 1116(d) relief without explaining how an *ex parte* restraining order can be expected to effectively alter the defendants' behavior. This record indicates that Vuitton faces precisely the problems that lead Congress to conclude that the traditional remedies of injunction and contempt were inadequate and to supplement them with the § 1116 seizure process. If we were to conclude that a § 1116 seizure order would be inappropriate in this case, we would be hard pressed to image a case in which such an order would be appropriate.

The district court's final reason for not entering the seizure order was a reluctance to employ the U.S. marshals. But the statute specifically calls for the U.S. marshals, or designated law enforcement officers to conduct the seizures. Congress, therefore, fully expected U.S. marshals to conduct these seizures; in fact, the Senate Report notes that having U.S. marshals, rather than private parties, conduct the seizures would be more likely to preserve public order. S. Rep. 526, 98th Cong., 2d Sess. 17 (1984). In the face of this clear Congressional intent, the district court's reluctance to employ the U.S. marshals to make the requested seizures was inappropriate.

Notes and Questions

1. Compare the effect of an *Anton Piller* order with the effect of the seizure order in the *Crash Test Dummies* case. Do they provide the same relief? Does an *Anton Piller* order protect against the loss of evidence? The removal of counterfeit product before its court ordered destruction? Does the order in the *Crash Dummies* case?

2. *Anton Piller* orders have subsequently been extended to permit not only access and copying of material relevant to the alleged infringement, but also to deliver up infringing goods or to maintain such goods and paper to permit their later delivery. For further information on *Anton Piller* requirements, *see* Practice Direction, July 28, 1994. *See generally* W.R. Cornish, *Intellectual Property*, § 2–47 (3d ed Sweet & Maxwell 1998).

3. What power do the courts have to enforce *Anton Piller* orders?

4. *Contempt of Court.* Although both U.S. and U.K. courts have the power to impose fines for the failure to obey their orders, such powers do not currently exist in many countries. Thus, for example, neither in Russia nor China do judges have the ability to enforce injunctions or other orders of relief in civil actions. This makes the effectiveness of such orders extremely problematic.

5. *Civil Seizures.* Compare the personnel required to be present under an *Anton Piller* order with those required under a U.S. seizure order such as in the *Crash Test Dummies* case. In the United States, seizures, even in civil cases, must occur in the company of the U.S. Marshalls—law enforcement personnel. In *Warner Brothers, Inc. v. Dae Rim Trading, Inc.*, 877 F.2d 1120 (2d Cir 1989), the conduct of civil seizures by strictly civil personnel was harshly criticized and specifically rejected the use of attorneys as sufficient to protect the defendant's rights. It stated:

> One obvious reason for the use of a public officer such as a marshal is the likelihood that an attempt by a private person to make a search and seizure will be met with resistance from the person whose privacy is being invaded. The proceedings upon search warrants should be strictly legal, for there is not a description of process known to the law, the execution of which is more distressing to the citizen. Perhaps there is none which excites such intense feeling in consequence of its humiliat-

ing and degrading effects. Not all property owners are as easily cowed as Mrs. Cho, a small, middleaged Oriental woman, who could barely speak English. The Supreme Court undoubtedly had the possibility of resistance in mind when it provided in Rule 5 that the marshal effecting service might use "such force as may be reasonably necessary in the premises."

Another compelling reason for the use of a public officer is that tradition and established law dictate that such drastic acts as seizure and impoundment be conducted by neutral and impartial persons.

Finally, some courts have expressed the belief that when entry upon premises for the purpose of seizing goods and chattels by virtue of a judicial writ such as attachment or execution is made by a sheriff or other officer of the law, many Fourth and Fifth Amendment problems may be avoided.

For all of the foregoing reasons, we agree with Judge Wyatt that the seizure conducted by Warner's attorneys and their agents was improper. We also agree that the "search" conducted by the agents was not authorized by 17 U.S.C. § 503, and that the "discovery" of defendants' documents and records without notice was not authorized by either section 503 or Fed.R.Civ.P. 34.

Compare this language with the *Anton Piller* case. What purpose does the required presence of law enforcement personnel serve?

6. Under U.K. Copyright, Designs and Patents Act of 1988 copyright owners or their authorized agent may seize and detain infringing copies of sound recordings that are "exposed or otherwise immediately available for sale or hire." The local police station must be notified and the seizure must occur in a public place or on public premises from a person who does no have a permanent or regular place of business there. The police have the discretionary power to accompany the copyright owner of the seizure. *See generally* Copyrights Designs and Patents Act of 1988, §§ 100, 196 (1988). As drafted the statute is aimed to a relatively narrow category of offender—the street vendor of counterfeit goods.

7. Despite language in *Anton Piller* indicating that seizure orders should be granted on a limited basis, they have been granted in increasing numbers in intellectual property infringement cases. During the 1980's *Anton Piller* orders were often executed simultaneously with a search warrant produced on suspicion of criminal conduct, such as dealing in obscene material. The practice was challenged as a violation of Article 8 of the European Convention on Human Rights which guarantees respect for private life and the home. In *Chappell v. United Kingdom* [1989] F.S.R. 617, the European Court of Human Rights criticized the practice but ultimately upheld *Anton Piller* orders. To respond to the criticism, a Practice Directive obliges the judge to require a supervising solicitor to serve as a watch-dog for the process or to state why such solicitor is not needed. *See generally* W.R. Cornish, *Intellectual Property*, § 2–47 (3d ed. Sweet & Maxwell 1998).

8. In Russia, seizure of infringing product is not allowed prior to a hearing with notice to the defendant to contest the requested relief. Are there cultural-historical reasons for such reluctance?

9. TRIPS Article 42 requires notice to the defendant and an opportunity to participate. Does an *Anton Piller* order violate Article 42?

10. What potential harm might the plaintiff suffer if the defendant is provided notice of the seizure? Does this harm outweigh the harm to the defendant in all instances? If not, what additional information would you need to know to make your decision? *See* 15 U.S.C. § 1116(d) (factors for consideration of an *ex parte* order in U.S. trademark counterfeiting cases).

11. *Mareva Injunctions.* In addition to obtaining an injunction precluding destruction of evidence, plaintiffs in Great Britain may also obtain an injunction directed to retaining those assets of the defendant required to satisfy money judgments. Referred to as *Mareva* orders, these orders may include the retention of bank accounts and other financial assets.

12. What harm may be caused to the defendant if an *Anton Piller* or *Crash Test Dummies* order is improvidently granted? For a discussion of the rights of defendants in such proceedings, see below.

Problem

Consider the Lucas Film problem set forth above in Section C. What injunctive relief would you seek? Against which parties? Assuming *Anton Piller* orders are available in the relevant jurisdictions, what advice would you give your client regarding its ability to seize the pirated videos and business records of Distributors, S.A.?

E. WHAT SAFEGUARDS MUST THE DEFENDANT RECEIVE UNDER INTERNATIONAL LAW?

Read the following Article from TRIPS from the Supplement: 48.

THE SEIZURE GONE WRONG CASE
UNIVERSAL THERMOSENSORS LTD v. HIBBEN

Chancery Division, 1992.
[1992] 3 All ER 257, [1992] 1 WLR 840, [1992] FSR 361.

Sir Donald Nicholls V–C

This is an unsatisfactory case. The legal costs have mushroomed far beyond anything appropriate to the subject matter. In the end they must have become the item of prime financial importance to the parties. The origin of the action lies in a situation which, regrettably, is not uncommon. A group of employees left their employment to set up a competing business on their own. Dishonestly, they took away with them copies of documents of their erstwhile employer, containing information about customers. The employer found out what had happened and was justifiably angry. So the company launched proceedings, seeking an injunction and damages. An Anton Piller 'search and seize' order was obtained and was executed early in the morning at the homes of three of the defendants, and at the trading premises of two companies in the absence of any representatives of the companies. Documents and components were seized and taken away. An interlocutory injunction was granted. Unfortunately, serious mistakes were made in the execution of the Anton Piller order. It was now the turn for the defendants to be upset and angry. The new business collapsed. So the defendants brought a claim for damages, including exemplary damages, under the plaintiff's undertaking in the Anton Piller order. They claimed that the interlocutory injunction was too wide, and claimed damages under that head also. And a claim was formulated against the plaintiff's solicitors personally, for their role in the faulty execution of the Anton Piller order. The result was a trial with voluminous documentation, which occupied 25 working days.

This case furnishes an illustration of both the virtues and vices of Anton Piller orders. The virtue was that the plaintiff was enabled to recover the item 3 list and the item 4 list and other documents, which, I strongly suspect, would never have seen the light of day if less Draconian steps, such as an order for delivery up of all documents containing confidential information regarding the plaintiff's customer contacts, had been the limit of the relief granted to the plaintiff. In all probability, incriminating evidence of that nature would simply have been destroyed.

But this result was achieved at a very high price. As I have said, the defendants' claims arising out of the faulty execution of the Anton Piller order were disposed of by an agreement reached between the parties during the course of the trial. It would, therefore, be quite wrong for me to say anything which might be understood as criticism of the conduct of those, and in particular the solicitors, who were responsible for the execution of the Anton Piller order in this action. Nevertheless, from the undisputed facts which emerged before me certain lessons are to be learned. I draw attention to these points, in the hope that thereby these problems will not arise again. The Anton Piller procedure lends itself all too readily to abuse. This has been highlighted more than once. My impression is that these warning signals have been heeded, and that Anton Piller orders are, rightly, made much more sparingly than previously. But arising out of the history of what occurred in the present case, the following points may be noted.

Anton Piller orders normally contain a term that before complying with the order the defendant may obtain legal advice, provided this is done forthwith. This is an important safeguard for defendants, not least because Anton Piller orders tend to be long and complicated, and many defendants cannot be expected to understand much of what they are told by the solicitor serving the order. But such a term, if it is to be of use, requires that in general Anton Piller orders should be permitted to be executed only on working days in office hours, when a solicitor can be expected to be available. In the present case Mrs Hibben was alone in her house, with her children in bed. She was brought to the door in her night attire at 7.15 am, and told by a stranger knocking on the door that he had a court order requiring her to permit him to enter, that she could take legal advice forthwith, but otherwise she was not permitted to speak to anyone else at all. But how could she get legal advice at that time in the morning? She rang her solicitor's office but, predictably, there was no response.

There is a further feature of the situation to which I have just alluded which must never be allowed to occur again. If the order is to be executed at a private house, and it is at all likely that a woman may be in the house alone, the solicitor serving the order must be, or must be accompanied by, a woman. A woman should not be subjected to the alarm of being confronted without warning by a solitary strange man, with no recognisable means of identification, waving some unfamiliar papers and claiming an entitlement to enter her house and, what is more, telling her she is not allowed to get in touch with anyone (except a lawyer) about what is happening.

In the present case a dispute arose about which documents were taken away, and from which of the premises visited. Understandably, those who excuse these orders are concerned to search and seize and then get away as quickly as possible so as to minimise the risk of confrontation and physical violence. Nevertheless, in general Anton Piller orders should expressly provide that, unless this is seriously impracticable, a detailed list of the items being removed should be prepared at the premises before they are removed, and that the defendant should be given an opportunity to check this list at the time.

Anton Piller orders frequently contain an injunction restraining those on whom they are served from informing others of the existence of the order for a limited period. This is to prevent one defendant from alerting others to what is happening. There is an exception for communication with a lawyer for the purpose of seeking legal advice. In the present case that injunction was expressed to last for a whole week. That is far too long. I suspect something went awry with the drafting of the order in this case.

In the present case there was no officer or employee of TPL or Emco present when their offices and workshops were searched and documents and components taken away. This is intolerable. Orders should provide that, unless there is good reason for doing otherwise, the order should not be executed at business premises save in the presence of a responsible officer or representative of the company or trader in question.

The making of an Anton Piller order in this case can be seen to be justified by what was discovered. But it is important not to lose sight of the fact that one thing which happened was that Mr. James carried out a thorough search of all the documents of a competitor company. This is most unsatisfactory. When Anton Piller orders are made in this type of case consideration should be given to devising some means, appropriate to the facts of the case, by which this situation can be avoided.

Anton Piller orders invariably provide for service to be effected by a solicitor. The court relies heavily on the solicitor, as an officer of the court, to see that the order is properly executed. Unhappily, the history in the present case, and what has happened in other cases, show that this safeguard is inadequate. The solicitor may be young and have little or no experience of Anton Piller orders. Frequently he is the solicitor acting for the plaintiff in the action, and however diligent and fair minded he may be, he is not the right person to be given a task which to some extent involves protecting the interests of the defendant. When making Anton Piller orders judges should give serious consideration to the desirability of providing, by suitable undertakings and otherwise, (a) that the order should be served, and its execution should be supervised, by a solicitor other than a member of the firm of solicitors acting for the plaintiff in the action, (b) that he or she should be an experienced solicitor having some familiarity with the workings of Anton Piller orders, and with judicial observations on this subject (c) that the solicitor should prepare a written report on what occurred when the order was executed, (d) that a copy of the report should be served on the defendants and (e) that in any event and within the next few days the plaintiff must return to the court and present that report at an inter partes hearing, preferably to the judge who made the order. As to (b), I can see advantages in the plaintiff being required to include in his evidence, put to the judge in support of his application for an Anton Piller order, details of the name of the solicitor of his experience.

Of course this procedure would add considerably to the cost of executing an Anton Piller order. The plaintiff would have to be responsible for paying the fees of the solicitor in question, without prejudice to a decision by the court on whether ultimately those costs should be borne in whole or in part by the defendant. But it must be appreciated, and certainly it is my view, that in suitable and strictly limited cases, Anton Piller orders furnish courts with a valuable aid in their efforts to do justice between two parties. Especially is this so in blatant cases of fraud. It is important therefore that these orders should not be allowed to fall into disrepute. If further steps are necessary to prevent this happening, they should be taken. If plaintiffs wish to take advantage of this truly Draconian type of order, they must be prepared to pay for the safeguards which experience has shown are necessary if the interests of defendants are fairly to be protected.

DISPOSITION: Plaintiff's claim for damages dismissed. Defendants' claim for damages allowed.

PILLERS OF JUSTICE
Sara Lovick, 142 New Law Journal 323, Butterworth & Co. Publishers 1992.

An Anton Piller Order is one of the few mechanisms which offers the dubious privilege of meeting defendants on their home ground. In the wake of growing concern about the dangers of these Orders and their possible abuse, the Vice Chancellor has made some suggestions about service and execution of them which I summarise here—together with some practical tips acquired in the course of duty.

Anton Piller Orders were introduced in the 1970s as a means of allowing solicitors for clients with a strong prima facie case to search for and seize goods and documents which otherwise might be destroyed by defendants if they had prior warning. The field of law in which they are applied is often, but not exclusively, intellectual property.

They soon became highly popular with plaintiffs—so much so that practitioners were growing alarmed at possible abuse. For example, a manufacturer claiming that a business rival was copying his ideas might obtain a Piller Order in order to seize his rival's stock and machinery: this would neatly put the defendant out of business before the courts had had time to resolve the dispute or before the parties had negotiated a settlement.

Another cause for concern is the degree of power given to plaintiffs by the draconian nature of these orders. The average person on the receiving end has not heard of a Piller Order until you arrive on the scene, but once you explain that failure to comply could lead to committal proceedings for contempt of court with the threat of imprisonment and/or a fine, most people open the door.

Before granting an Order, therefore, the court wants to examine the following three issues very closely:

(1) Is there a strong prima facie case?

(2) Is there a genuine risk that the defendant, if put on notice, might destroy goods or documents which he has in his possession and which could be used as evidence?

(3) Is the potential damage to the plaintiff likely to be very serious as a result of the defendant's actions?

In addition the plaintiff must undertake to the court to pay any damages sustained by the defendant if the court decides later that an Order should not have been granted. The plaintiff must show the court that he is good for any such award of damages.

As a result of the judgment of the Vice Chancellor in *Universal Thermosensors Ltd. v. Hibben & Others* (The Times, February 12, 1992) serious consideration must now be given to the desirability of providing by suitable undertakings or otherwise the following:

The Order should be served and its execution supervised by a solicitor other than the one acting for the plaintiff.

It may well be a nuisance to have to instruct another solicitor and to go through the procedure of reporting to the court on the serving of the Order (see below), to say nothing of the additional cost involved—but it may help in the long run to eliminate a degree of argument.

The supervisor should be an experienced solicitor familiar with the operation and judicial decisions of Piller Orders.

There is a strong onus on solicitors to abide by the terms of the Order. If you overstep the mark, you may have to account for your actions but probably only if the case comes to trial. It therefore helps to have an observer who knows the rules—for example, you must not place your foot across the threshold or employ other "doorstepping" techniques which could be construed as forced entry; you cannot enter unless the person on whom you are serving the Order gives you permission, nor can you remove any material which is not clearly covered by the Order.

The Piller service party should include a woman if it is likely that a woman might be alone on the premises where the Order is to be served.

In *Universal Thermosensors Ltd. v. Hibben & Others*, a woman was alone in the house, with her children in bed, when three men knocked on the door at 7.15 am to serve the Order. The Vice Chancellor insists that this type of situation should not be allowed to happen again.

His recommendation was anticipated by a woman who, confronted by several of us serving an Order, announced, "I'm not having men going through my drawers of underwear." The men stood around while I searched upstairs for documents.

Written reports on what happened are to be prepared and presented both to the defendants and to the Court in an inter partes hearing.

To any solicitor who believes he has been falsely accused about his actions by a defendant this suggestion of an independent witness is likely to come as a relief.

These changes take up some of the suggestions made by Professor Dockray and Hugh Laddie QC in Piller Problems (1990) 106 LQR 601. They will undoubtedly add to the cost of obtaining and executing Piller Orders. These are costs which the plaintiff will initially bear and in some cases may end up bearing.

The latest guidelines are additional to earlier safeguards, for example:

Orders should only be served on weekdays during office hours, to give defendants the opportunity to take legal advice before the Order is executed.

The defendant, when served, must be told of his right to take legal advice within a reasonable period of time. If the defendant contacts a solicitor, you are not permitted to enter the premises and carry out the search until after a reasonable period for him to take legal advice.

Simple language must be used by the solicitor serving the Order to explain its terms.

Copies of the affidavits and copyable exhibits forming the evidence on which the court decided to make an Order must be given to the defendant when served.

In case the defendant's solicitor argues that the defendant need not comply with the Order as to do so would be self-incriminating, it is worth noting that s 72 of the Supreme Court Act 1981 has removed this defence in intellectual property cases, although it applies in all other spheres of law (*Rank Film Distributors Ltd. v. Video Information Centre* [1981] 2 All ER 76).

Now it only remains for me to pass on some practical hints of my own, gleaned from my experience in the field:

Case the joint. Do a recce first if possible, to find out roughly what you can expect when you arrive at the premises, and how many people might be there. The Order will normally specify the maximum number of people whom the plaintiff can take to execute the Order.

Co-ordinate service. To reduce the risk of the material disappearing, the Order should usually be served simultaneously at all the defendants' premises.

Cover all exits. On one occasion, a colleague turned up at a private house with a taxi-load of people and rang the bell, but there was no answer. The taxi driver shouted, "I've just seen her drive off—pile in." They went off in pursuit—all except one, who hid in the shrubbery. Sure enough, the woman came back ten minutes later, minus the taxi-load, and walked into the ambush.

Take an escort if necessary. When you feel you might be at risk, contact the police first. If you try to explain the matter down the telephone to a junior policeman who has not heard of a Piller Order you might run into difficulties, so it is better to go to the police station, armed with the Order, and explain.

Get the paperwork right:

(a) Make sure the affidavit setting out the evidence against the defendant is full and frank and discloses all material facts. If in doubt err on the side of excessive disclosure. Failure to disclose a material fact can be a ground for the court to set aside an Order regardless of the merits.

(2) Make sure that the Order goes into sufficient detail—for example, on one occasion documents had been loaded into a vehicle just before the solicitors turned up. They knew fell well where the documents had been taken, but they were helpless as the vehicle was not covered by the Order. However, the Order must not be wider than necessary to achieve the preservation of the material.

(3) Make sure a detailed record of the material taken away is made by the solicitor serving the Order before the material is taken away. Copies of documents seized must be made by the plaintiff's solicitors in accordance with the time limits specified in the Order and then the originals returned to their owner.

In the case of valuable goods, insurance may be a problem: a colleague seized some paintings but did not know whether they were old masters until they had been valued. Practical difficulties about the material cannot always be envisaged in advance. In executing an Order, we were planning to seize some oil-pipe crawlers, expensive devices which are used to check for fractures. Having ascertained that parts were radioactive, we agreed that we would simply take photographs and leave them in situ.

Finally, bear in mind that you can only do what the Order allows. A colleague suffering from an upset stomach was unfortunate enough to encounter a defendant who demanded, "where's the bit in the Order allowing you to use the facilities?" The moral here is that even the most scrupulous attention to detail may be confounded if you meet someone who chooses to exercise a spitefully pedantic interpretation of the rules.

Notes and Questions

1. If the suggestions contained in the Lovick article were followed, would that resolve the problems caused in the *Seizure Gone Wrong* case? Are there additional safeguards which should be taken in the granting of *Anton Piller* orders?

2 Although *Anton Piller* orders are a creature of English common law, similar seizure methods have been adopted or are being considered in various non-common law countries, including Russia and China. How do such orders compare with U.S. seizure orders discussed in the *Vuiton Seizure* case above?

3. Are there additional safeguards that you believe a defendant should receive that are *not* required under Article 48 of TRIPS? Should the defendant have the right of automatic appeal if he is found liable? Should he be entitled to attorneys fees if he has been wrongfully accused?

4. *Costs*. What steps should the court take to ensure the plaintiff can pay damages in the event of a wrongful seizure? In the United States, courts usually require the plaintiff to post a bond in the amount of two times the estimated value of the goods to be seized prior to the issuance of any civil seizure order. *See Louis Vuitton* case, *supra*.

5. What qualified as a "wrongful seizure" in the *Seizure Gone Wrong* case? Could the problem in that case have been solved through a more careful drafting of the seizure order?

F.   WHAT ADDITIONAL ENFORCEMENT MEASURES MUST BE USED TO PROHIBIT COUNTERFEITING AND PIRACY?

Read the following Article from TRIPS from the Supplement: 61.

KILLER-LIQUOR MAKERS EXECUTED
China Daily (December 21, 1994).

Four people convicted of selling adulterated liquor have been executed in three Chinese provinces.

More than 120 people were alcohol or methanol for industrial use. Of these, 15 people died and three were seriously injured.

Cheng Yingzhi, 40, a farmer from Sichuan's Yibin County, added water to 75 kilograms of methanol he bought from a local chemical plant. He made 350 kilograms of poisonous, fake spirits for sale to the public.

Over the next few weeks several cases of poisoning were reported in surrounding townships, and traced to Cheng's liquor.

Of the victims, eight people died and one was blinded.

Meanwhile, in Hubei Province, Pi Chenggang sold liquor made from industrial alcohol, poisoning 46 people, three of whom died.

The other two executed on Monday on the orders of the Supreme People's Court were Chen Xinguo and Li Jianhai, from Zhoukou City in Central China's Henan Provcal plant, bought 3,800 kilograms of methanol from a private businessman in June last year, and resold it as potable alcohol to local retailers.

Li Jianhai, a local farmer, bought 600 kilograms of the alcohol to make liquor, knowing that the alcohol was dangerous.

Liu Jiachen, vice-president of the Supreme People's Court, said the production and sale of poisonous food and drink can cause severe damage to society, and the court will spare no efforts to crack down on the criminals involved.

ILLEGAL, OBSCENE WORKS UNDER FIRE
China Daily (October 13, 1994).

The State is drafting rules and regulations to control the printing and marketing of illegal and obscene publications, the Beijing-based Guangming Daily reported yesterday.

The promise of huge profits has lured many traders into defying laws and State policies. Currently there are more than 100,000 printing houses in China, while only about 5,000 have official approval from the State Press and Publication Administration.

The article said that in the first half of this year, China seized more than 5.94 million illegal books and magazines. Among the confiscated materials were 660,000 obscene books and magazines and 20,000 illegal reactionary publications. In addition, there were more than 45,000 pirated CD and LD discs and 1.15 million audio and video tapes forbidden by the State.

The number of seized materials in the first half of this year amounted to nearly twice that of 1993.

At the same time, 7,091 violators were arrested. Some of them have been sentenced to death for the serious nature of their activities, according to the newspaper.

Despite progress that has been made against pornographic publications, the variety appears to be increasing.

Official statistics show that in the past there were about 40 types of x-rated publications available per year.

This year, however, more than 300 kinds of obscene books have been confiscated in Hubei and Gansu provinces alone.

Responsibility for the problem falls on a variety of causes including loopholes in the printing industry, the distribution system, lack of a complete legal system, weak legal enforcement and loose control by local governments.

Notes and Questions

1. What guarantees must a defendant accused of trademark counterfeiting under criminal laws be afforded under TRIPS?

2. Which of the following qualifies as an "equivalent" crime to copyright piracy:

theft of a car

theft of a painting

espionage

burglary

What factors would you consider to determine which crimes were equivalent to piracy and counterfeiting?

3. *The Element of Willfulness.* Many countries include an element of willfulness in defining criminal piracy or counterfeiting. The defendant must have some knowledge that his actions are unlawful before criminal penalties attach. Although including a *mens rea* element may make criminal prosecution "fairer," is such an element required under TRIPS?

4. Which intellectual property forms do not require the availability of criminal relief under TRIPS? What argument would you use to support the exclusion of protection to the forms? What argument would you use to challenge such exclusion?

THE COMPUTER HACKER CASE
UNITED STATES v. DAVID LAMACCHIA

United States District Court for Massachusetts, 1994.
871 F.Supp. 535.

STEARNS, DISTRICT JUDGE.

This case presents the issue of whether new wine can be poured into an old bottle. The facts, as seen in the light most favorable to the government, are these. The defendant, David LaMacchia, is a twentyone year old student at the Massachusetts Institute of Technology (MIT). LaMacchia, a computer hacker, used MIT's computer network to gain entry to the Internet. Using pseudonyms and an encrypted address, LaMacchia set up an electronic bulletin board which he named Cynosure. He encouraged his correspondents to upload popular software applications (Excel 5.0 and WordPerfect 6.0) and computer games (Sim City 2000). These he transferred to a second encrypted address (Cynosure II) where they could be downloaded by other users with access to the Cynosure password. Although LaMacchia was at pains to impress the need for circumspection on the part of his subscribers, the worldwide traffic generated by the offer of free software attracted the notice of university and federal authorities.

On April 7, 1994, a federal grand jury returned a one count indictment charging LaMacchia with conspiring with "persons unknown" to violate 18 U.S.C. § 1343, the wire fraud statute. According to the indictment, LaMacchia devised a scheme to defraud that had as its object the facilitation "on an international scale" of the "illegal copying and distribution of copyrighted software" without payment of licensing fees and royalties to software manufacturers and vendors. The indictment alleges that LaMacchia's scheme caused losses of more than one million dollars to software copyright holders. The indictment does not allege that LaMacchia sought or derived any personal benefit from the scheme to defraud.

On September 30, 1994, the defendant brought a motion to dismiss, arguing that the government had improperly resorted to the wire fraud statute as a copyright enforcement tool in defiance of the Supreme Court's decision in *Dowling v. United States*, 473 U.S. 207, 105 S.Ct. 3127, 87 L.Ed.2d 152 (1985).

Paul Edmond Dowling was convicted of conspiracy, interstate transportation of stolen property [ITSP], copyright violations and mail fraud in the Central District of California. Dowling and his co-conspirators sold bootleg Elvis Presley recordings by soliciting catalogue orders from post office boxes in Glendale, California. The infringing recordings were shipped in interstate commerce to Maryland and Florida. The eight ITSP counts on which Dowling was convicted involved thousands of phonograph albums. Dowling appealed his convictions (except those involving copyright infringement). The Ninth Circuit Court of Appeals affirmed. The Supreme Court granted certiorari only as to Dowling's convictions for interstate transportation of stolen property. The Court, in an opinion by Justice Blackmun, held that a copyrighted musical composition impressed on a bootleg phonograph record is not property that is "stolen, converted, or taken by fraud" within the meaning of the Stolen Property Act. Justice Blackmun emphasized that cases prosecuted under § 2314 had traditionally involved "physical 'goods, wares [or] merchandise.'" The statute "seems clearly to contemplate a physical identity between the items unlawfully obtained and those eventually transported, and hence some prior physical taking of the subject goods" *Id*. at 216, 105 S.Ct. at 3133. In Dowling's case there was no evidence "that Dowling wrongfully came by the phonorecords actually shipped or the physical materials from which they were made.".

Justice Blackmun felt compelled, however, to answer the government's argument that the unauthorized use of the underlying musical compositions was itself sufficient to render the offending phonorecords property "stolen, converted or taken by fraud." The Government's theory here would make theft, conversion, or fraud equivalent to wrongful appropriation of statutorily protected rights in copyright. The copyright owner, however, holds no ordinary chattel. A copyright, like other intellectual property, comprises a series of carefully defined and carefully delimited interests to which the law affords correspondingly exact protections. *Id.* at 216, 105 S.Ct. at 3133.

A copyright, as Justice Blackmun explained, is unlike an ordinary chattel because the holder does not acquire exclusive dominion over the thing owned. The limited nature of the property interest conferred by copyright stems from an overriding First Amendment concern for the free dissemination of ideas.

It follows that interference with copyright does not easily equate with theft, conversion or fraud.

In 1976, Congress revamped the Copyright Act by eliminating the crime of aiding and abetting copyright infringement. It also eased the mens rea requirement for criminal copyright infringement by eliminating the burden of proving that an infringer acted "for profit," requiring instead only that the infringement be conducted "willfully and for purposes of commercial advantage or private financial gain." 17 U.S.C. § 506(a). Criminal infringement under the 1976 Act was a misdemeanor except in the case of repeat offenders (who could be sentenced to a maximum of two years and a fine of $50,000).

After lobbying by the Motion Picture Association and the Recording Industry Association, Congress increased the penalties for criminal infringement in 1982. Certain types of first-time criminal infringement were punishable as felonies depending on the time period involved and the number of copies reproduced or distributed. *See* 18 U.S.C. § 2319. The mens rea element, however, remained unchanged, requiring proof of "commercial advantage or private financial gain." 17 U.S.C. § 506(a). Most criminal infringements remained misdemeanor offenses despite the new penalty structure.

In the decade following the 1982 revisions to the Copyright Act, the home computing and software industry underwent a period of explosive growth paralleling the expansion in the 1960's and 1970's of the recording and motion picture industries. "Rather than adopting a piecemeal approach to copyright legislation and simply adding computer programs to audiovisual works, and sound recordings to the list of works whose infringement can give rise to felony penalties under [18 U.S.C.] § 2319," Congress passed the Copyright Felony Act. The Act amended § 2319 by extending its felony provisions to the criminal infringement of all copyrighted works including computer software. The mens rea for criminal infringement remained unchanged, requiring prosecutors to prove that the defendant infringed a copyright "willfully and for purpose of commercial advantage or private financial gain." 17 U.S.C. § 506(a).

The wire fraud statute, 18 U.S.C. § 1343, was enacted in 1952. In its entirety, the statute reads as follows: Whoever, having devised or intending to devise any scheme or artifice to defraud, or for obtaining money or property by means of false or fraudulent pretenses, representations, or promises, transmits or causes to be transmitted by means of wire, radio, or television communication in interstate or foreign commerce, any writings, signs, signals, pictures, or sounds for the purpose of executing such scheme or artifice, shall be fined not more than $1,000 or imprisoned not more than five years, or both. If the violation affects a financial institution, such person shall be fined not more than $1,000,000 or imprisoned not more than 30 years, or both.

The wire fraud statute was enacted to cure a jurisdictional defect that Congress perceived was created by the growth of radio and television as commercial media.

The issue thus is whether the "bundle of rights" conferred by copyright is unique and distinguishable from the indisputably broad range of property interests protected by the mail and wire fraud statutes. I find it difficult, if not impossible, to read *Dowling* as saying anything but that it is. "A copyright, like other intellectual property, comprises a series of carefully defined and carefully delimited interests to which the law affords correspondingly exact protections." *Dowling, supra* 473 U.S. at 216, 105 S.Ct. at 3133.

What the government is seeking to do is to punish conduct that reasonable people might agree deserves the sanctions of the criminal law. But as Justice Blackmun observed in Dowling, copyright is an area in which Congress has chosen to tread cautiously, relying "chiefly . . . on an array of civil remedies to provide copyright holders protection against infringement," while mandating "studiously graded penalties" in those instances where Congress has concluded that the deterrent effect of criminal sanctions are required. *Dowling, supra* at 221, 225, 105 S.Ct. at 3135, 3137. "This step-by-step, carefully considered approach is consistent with Congress' traditional sensitivity to the special concerns implicated by the copyright laws." *Id.* at 225, 105 S.Ct. at 3137.

While the government's objective is a laudable one, particularly when the facts alleged in this case are considered, its interpretation of the wire fraud statute would serve to criminalize the conduct of not only persons like LaMacchia, but also the myriad of home computer users who succumb to the temptation to copy even a single software program for private use. It is not clear that making criminals of a large number of consumers of computer software is a result that even the software industry would consider desirable.

In sum, I agree with Professor Nimmer that: The *Dowling* decision establishes that Congress has finely calibrated the reach of criminal liability [in the Copyright Act], and therefore absent clear indication of Congressional intent, the criminal laws of the United States do not reach copyright-related conduct. Thus copyright prosecutions should be limited to Section 506 of the Act, and other incidental statutes that explicitly refer to copyright and copyrighted works. 3 Nimmer on Copyright, § 15.05 at 15–20 (1993).

Accordingly, I rule that the decision of the Supreme Court in *Dowling v. United States* precludes LaMacchia's prosecution for criminal copyright infringement under the wire fraud statute.

This is not, of course, to suggest that there is anything edifying about what LaMacchia is alleged to have done. If the indictment is to be believed, one might at best describe his actions as heedlessly irresponsible, and at worst as nihilistic, self-indulgent, and lacking in any fundamental sense of values. Criminal as well as civil penalties should probably attach to willful, multiple infringements of copyrighted software even absent a commercial motive on the part of the infringer. One can envision ways that the copyright law could be modified to permit such prosecution. But, " '[i]t is the legislature, not the Court which is to define a crime, and ordain its punishment.' "*Dowling, supra*, 473 U.S. at 214, 105 S.Ct. at 3131.

For the foregoing reasons, defendant LaMacchia's motion to dismiss is ALLOWED.

Notes and Questions

1.   Should an element of commercial gain or financial advantage to the defendant be required before criminal penalties attach?

2.   In 1998 U.S. law was changed to remove the requirement of commercial advantage in the instance of criminal copyright infringement. According to the House Report, the reason for the change was as follows:

NO ELECTRONIC THEFT (NET) ACT
Committee Report—House Rpt. 105–339.

Section 106 of the Copyright Act (Title 17 of the U.S. Code) gives the owner of a copyright the exclusive rights to reproduce and distribute copies of the copyrighted work. An individual who otherwise violates any of these exclusive rights is an infringer, and may be subject to criminal penalties set forth in Section 506 of the Act and section 2319 of Title 18. Current penalties include fines of $250,000 per individual ($500,000 per organization) and imprisonment of up to five years (10 years for second or subsequent offenses).

Notwithstanding these penalties, copyright piracy flourishes in the software world. Industry groups estimate that counterfeiting and piracy of intellectual property—especially computer software, compact discs, and movies—cost the affected copyright holders more than $11 billion last year (others believe the figure is closer to $20 billion). In some countries, software piracy rates are as high as 90% of all sales. The U.S. rate is far lower (27%), but the dollar losses ($2.3 billion) are the highest worldwide. The effect of this volume of theft is substantial: 130,000 lost U.S. jobs, $5.6 billion in corresponding lost wages, $1 billion in lower tax revenue, and higher prices for honest purchasers of copyrighted software.

Unfortunately, the potential for this problem to worsen is great. By the turn of the century the Internet is projected to have more than 200 million users, and the development of new technology will create additional incentive for copyright thieves to steal protected works. The advent of digital video discs, for example, will enable individuals to store far more material on conventional discs and, at the same time, produce perfect secondhand copies. The extension of an audio-compression technique, commonly referred to as MP–3, now permits infringers to transmit large volumes of CD-quality music over the Internet. As long as the relevant technology evolves in this way, more piracy will ensue. Many computer users are either ignorant that copyright laws apply to Internet activity, or they simply believe that they will not be caught or prosecuted for their conduct.

In light of this disturbing trend, it is manifest that Congress must respond appropriately with additional penalties to dissuade such conduct. In effect, H.R. 2265 does just that: it criminalizes computer theft of copyrighted works, whether or not the defendant derives a direct financial benefit from the act(s) of misappropriation, thereby preventing such willful conduct from destroying businesses, especially small businesses, that depend on licensing agreements and royalties for survival.

3.   Do you agree with Congress's reasoning? Does the removal of any requirement of commercial gain threaten to criminalize innocent infringement?

4.   If copyright does not qualify as the equivalent of tangible property, what types of crimes can be considered "equivalent" to copyright infringement? How harsh should criminal penalties be for infringing intellectual property rights? What factors would you consider in establishing the amount of fines? Prison terms? Other forms of punishment?

G.   WHAT ROLE DOES EDUCATION AND SELF–HELP PLAY IN PROTECTING INTELLECTUAL PROPERTY RIGHTS INTERNATIONALLY?

TO BATTLE PIRACY IN CHINA, IP COMPANIES MAY TURN TO SELF–HELP

Konrad L. Trope, IP Worldwide (July/ August 1997).

If companies doing business in China want to protect their IP rights, they need to take special precautions. They need to create their own protections.

Four key provisions High technology companies and other companies licensing IP rights should make sure to include four key provisions in their Chinese licensing agreements.

First, the agreement should have a choice-of-law provision that mandates all contractual disputes be resolved in an appropriate court in a jurisdiction that protects IP rights. If a potential licensee refuses to accept such a choice-of-law provision, the licensor should reevaluate the desirability of the completing the deal. Because of the time and expense needed to pursue a foreign licensee for lost revenue, it is probably not worth the risk of doing business without this contractual provision.

Second, the agreement should contain a covenant that requires the licensee to designate, in a jurisdiction with strong IP protections, an authorized representative to receive service of process for any breach of the license agreement. Proof of this designation should be annexed to the contract by the time the deal is to be signed.

This designation will allow a licensor to effect quick service of process on a breaching licensee who operates from China (or any other jurisdiction that offers weak IP protections). The absence of such an authorized representative may otherwise allow a licensee to claim it is not doing business in the jurisdiction where enforcement is sought, and thereby escape enforcement efforts.

Failure to insist on this provision can force companies to incur the expensive and time-consuming. task of making service abroad under the Hague Convention. And this is available only if the foreign licensee is based in a country that has signed the Hague Convention for international service of process.

Third, the licensing agreement should contain a covenant mandating that the licensee will require all sublicensees to be bound by the terms of the main licensing agreement and to subject themselves to the jurisdiction of the courts specified in the main licensing agreement. This provision is critical for protecting IP rights against sublicensees.

The failure of any sublicensee to ratify the main licensing agreement creates additional enforcement opportunities for the licensor and liability for the original licensee. A licensee's failure to contractually compel sublicensees to sign the original licensing agreement should constitute a material breach that is addressable in the designated courts.

In other words, a licensee should be held strictly liable for any harm that results to the licensor when a sublicensee fails to ratify the original licensing agreement. This concept of strict liability should be spelled out in the agreement.

Such a strict-liability provision forces the licensee to be careful with the IP rights that have been placed in its care. This provision will cause licensees to think twice before freely transferring IP without making sure that the proper copyright, trademark and patent protections are adhered to.

Fourth, the license should contain a clause that holds the licensee and its executives strictly liable for any infringement of IP rights committed by a sublicensee. This provision should be broad enough to hold a licensee liable for a sublicensee's breach of any laws or regulations concerning technology transfers. Again, this provides a licensee with a real incentive to protect the licensed IP rights.

Technological protections could significantly reduce unauthorized pirating of CDs.

Many of the current CD-duplication devices, also known as "read-write devices," cannot copy CDs made with enhanced recording technology. Using this new technology would at least temporarily interfere with piracy, until the pirates acquire new read-write devices.

Another way to technologically foil bootleggers is to implant a pass code on CDs. A pass code can be designed so that the CD can be played on a "read-only device," such as a CD player, but on a duplication device, the pass code will prevent duplication from directly occurring.

A pirate would thus have to record the original CD onto audio cassette, and then transfer that onto a blank CD. The resulting sound quality will be noticeably diminished from a CD-to-CD duplication. Moreover, pirating the CD will be more costly.

Legitimate companies would be well-advised to engage in direct economic warfare against pirates. Companies should set up retail outlets in China that carry the latest products priced at or below the price at which such goods are sold by pirates. Eventually, the Chinese public will flock to the legitimate stores, and the lost sales will drive many, if not all, of the pirates out of business.

What happens when the legitimate stores start to raise their prices? Won't the pirates start to flourish again? Yes, but far fewer of them will come back if the Chinese government is given a real economic incentive to crack down on

Notes and Questions

1   You represent Eli Lilly who has discovered that its patented drugs are being infringed in China, Saudi Arabia and Chile. Your client does not want to pursue litigation in these countries because it believes such efforts would be too costly, and would ultimately result in too little relief. What steps could you take short of litigation to resolve the problem? What U.S. government agencies could you contact to help you?

Chapter Thirty–One

BILATERAL ENFORCEMENT EFFORTS

A. WHAT ROLE DO BILATERAL EFFORTS PLAY IN RESOLVING INTERNATIONAL IP DISPUTES?

Read the following Sections from the TRADE ACT of 1974 from the Supplement: 2101, 2411, 2413.

REPORT TO CONGRESS ON SECTION 301 DEVELOPMENTS
(June 1996–January 1998).

D. China Intellectual Property Enforcement and Market Access for Persons That Rely on Intellectual Property Protection (301–92)

On June 30, 1994, the U.S.T.R. designated China a Priority Foreign Country (PFC) under the Special 301 provisions of the Omnibus Trade and Competitiveness Act of 1988, and pursuant to § 302(b) (2) (a) of the Trade Act, initiated an investigation of the acts and practices that formed the basis for its designation as a PFC. The reason for the designation was because China had failed to create an effective intellectual property enforcement regime. Specifically, the U.S.T.R. found problems with: copyright piracy and trademark infringement, the implementation of China's new patent law and administrative protection program for pharmaceuticals and agricultural chemicals, and the failure to provide fair and equitable market access for persons who rely on intellectual property protection. Negotiations reached no agreement on the issues that were the subject of the investigation. On December 31, 1994, the U.S.T.R. extended the investigation until February 4, 1995, and sought public comment on proposed determinations. On February 4, 1995, the U.S.T.R. determined that the acts, policies and practices of the Chinese Government at issue in the investigation were unreasonable and constitute a burden or restriction on U.S. commerce. The U.S.T.R. also determined that the appropriate action in response was to impose 100 percent ad valorem duties on certain Chinese-origin products that were entered, or withdrawn from warehouse for consumption, on or after February 26, 1995.

Following an exchange of letters, China committed to protecting intellectual property, improving market access, border enforcement, and legal system transparency. On the basis of the measures that China undertook in the agreement, the U.S.T.R. terminated the sanctions announced on February 4, 1995, and revoked China's designation as a PFC. In response to these assurances, on March 7, 1995 the U.S.T.R. terminated this investigation pursuant to § 301 of the Trade Act. However, the U.S.T.R. monitored China's implementation of the agreement, holding more than thirty consultations and meetings on intellectual property rights enforcement (IPR) and market access issues and making three general high-level trips to China.

On April 29, 1996, the United States again designated China as a PFC because of IPR and market access problems. On May 20, 1996, the U.S.T.R. determined that China was not satisfactorily implementing the 1995 agreement and requested public comment on a proposed action in the form of the imposition of increased tariffs on selected Chinese products under § 301(a) of the Trade Act. In discussions held in June 1996, Chinese officials explained steps that had been taken and future actions to ensure effective enforcement of IPRs and market access. On June 17, 1996, China and the United States confirmed these steps and future actions that will be taken to implement the 1995 agreement and resolve the issues raised in the § 301 investigation. The discussions of June 1996 confirmed that China has taken action in some key areas. In addition, China will undertake verification and inspections to ensure compliance. Since China confirmed the steps it has taken, and will take in the future, to address the matters raised in the § 301 agreement, the United States decided not to impose increased duties on imports from China and to revoke China's designation as a PFC. Although further Chinese progress was also noted in the 1997 Special 301 Annual Review, the U.S.T.R. continues to vigorously monitor and enforce China's commitments under the 1995 IPR Enforcement Agreement and the June 17, 1996 IPR Accord pursuant to § 306 of the Trade Act.

E.   Brazil Intellectual Property (301–91)

On April 30, 1993, Brazil was identified as a Priority Foreign Country (PFC) under the Special 301 provisions in § 182(a) of the Trade Act. On May 28, 1993, the U.S.T.R. initiated an investigation under § 302(b)(2)(A) of the Trade Act with respect to certain acts, policies, and practices of the Government of the Republic of Brazil that deny adequate and effective protection of intellectual property rights, and consultations were requested. During consultations, Brazil indicated that it had undertaken a number of actions to improve the protection of intellectual property in Brazil, and to provide greater market access for products relying on the protection of intellectual property. Based on these representations, the U.S.T.R. terminated this investigation on February 28,

1994, and decided that the information received warranted revocation of Brazil's identification as a PFC.

Due to its lack of progress, however, Brazil was placed on the Priority Watch List in April 1995. On April 17, 1996, the Brazilian Congress passed a new patent law that provides product patent protection for pharmaceutical products after a short, one-year transition period. While the law contains some problematic provisions, it represents a significant improvement in the level of protection available in Brazil. Due to Brazil's progress on the patent law, Brazil was moved from the Special 301 Priority Watch List to the Watch List during the April, 1996 Special 301 review. Subsequently, legislation on computer software, copyrights and semiconductor mask works were introduced into the Brazilian Congress, but have not been passed. As a result, in the 1997 Special 301 review, Brazil was kept on the Watch List, pending completion of the IPR reforms outlined in 1994. In May, 1997, the Government of Brazil passed a law protecting plant varieties. However, further compliance is still required. The U.S.T.R. continues to press for full Brazilian compliance in this case and is monitoring Brazil's implementation of these measures under § 306 of the Trade Act.

"SPECIAL 301" ON INTELLECTUAL PROPERTY RIGHTS FACT SHEET

http://www.ustr.gov/reports/301report/factsheets.html#special301.

ACTIONS TAKEN

Acting United States Trade Representative Charlene Barshefsky today announced the Administration's decision with respect to this year's review under the so-called "special 301" provisions of the Trade Act of 1974, as amended (Trade Act).

This decision reflects the Administration's continued commitment to aggressive enforcement of protection for intellectual property, which has been improving in part as a result of accelerated implementation of the WTO Agreement on Trade–Related Aspects of Intellectual Property Rights (the TRIPs Agreement). The decision also reflects progress made over the course of 1995 in resolving many longstanding problems.

The Administration reiterates its commitment to ensure full and effective implementation of the "special 301" provisions of the Trade Act and rapid implementation of the WTO TRIPs Agreement. The Administration will continue to encourage other countries to accelerate implementation of the WTO TRIPs agreement and move to even higher levels of IPR protection. To these ends, the Administration will continue to engage countries in dialogues not only aimed at resolving the problems that brought about their inclusion on the "special 301" lists, but also seeking an improvement in the overall level of intellectual property protection.

STATUTORY AUTHORITY

The "special 301" provisions of the Trade Act of 1974, as amended, require the U.S.T.R. to determine whether the acts, policies and practices of foreign countries deny adequate and effective protection of intellectual property rights or fair and equitable market access for U.S. persons who rely on intellectual property protection. "Special 301" was amended in the Uruguay Round Agreements Act to clarify that a country can be found to deny adequate and effective intellectual property protection even if it is in compliance with its obligations under the TRIPS Agreement. It was also amended to direct the U.S.T.R. to take into account a country's prior status and behavior under "special 301."

Once this pool of countries has been determined, the U.S.T.R. is required to designate which, if any, of these countries should be designated "priority foreign countries." "Priority foreign countries" are those countries that:

(1) have the most onerous and egregious acts, policies and practices which have the greatest adverse impact (actual or potential) on the relevant U.S. products; and,

(2) are not engaged in good faith negotiations or making significant progress in negotiations to address these problems.

If a trading partner is identified as a "priority foreign country", the U.S.T.R. must decide within 30 days whether to initiate an investigation of those acts, policies and practices that were the basis for identifying the country as a "priority foreign country". A "special 301" investigation is similar to an investigation initiated in response to an industry Section 301 petition, except that the maximum time for an investigation under Section 301 is shorter in some circumstances (i.e., where the issues do not involve a violation of the Agreement on TRIPS) than are other Section 301 investigations.

The U.S.T.R. undertakes a review of foreign practices each year within 30 days after the issuance of the National Trade Estimate (NTE) Report. Today's announcement follows a lengthy information gathering and negotiation process. The interagency Trade Policy Staff Committee that advises the U.S.T.R. on implementation of "special 301," obtains information from the private sector, American embassies abroad, the United States' trading partners, and the NTE report.

This Administration is determined to ensure the adequate and effective protection of intellectual property rights and fair and equitable market access for U.S. products. The measures announced today result from close consultations with affected industry groups and Congressional leaders, and demonstrate the Administration's commitment to utilize all available avenues to pursue resolution of intellectual property rights issues. In issuing the announcement, Ambassador Barshefsky is expressing the Administration's resolve to take consistently strong actions under the "special 301" provisions of the Trade Act.

DESCRIPTION BY COUNTRY OF EXISTING SITUATION AND
MEASURES TAKEN PRIORITY FOREIGN COUNTRY

China remains the site of extensive piracy of intellectual property, particularly copyrighted sound recordings, music, videos and business and entertainment software. Despite signing a bilateral IPR Enforcement Agreement with the United States in February 1995, in which China promised to substantially improve enforcement efforts and grant market access for legitimate audiovisual and computer software products, piracy remains rampant, and economic damage to U.S. industries continues to rise. Overall, China has made some progress in halting the retail trade in infringing goods, but has failed to stop illegal CD, video and CD–ROM production at some 31 plants operating in China to prevent the export of infringing goods, or to honor its promise to grant market access for legitimate audiovisual products. No new investigation will be initiated following this designation; rather, the focus of further efforts will be on China's compliance with the current Agreement. Trade sanctions for noncompliance could be imposed at any time pursuant to a decision by U.S.TR that China is not satisfactorily implementing the Agreement.

PRIORITY WATCH LIST

The Administration has decided to place eight trading partners on the priority watch list because the lack of adequate and effective intellectual property protection or market access in these countries is especially significant for U.S. interests. The trading partners are:

Argentina recently enacted new patent legislation and an implementing decree that fall far short of adequate and effective protection and fail to achieve earlier Argentine assurances. As a result, Argentina is being placed back on the priority watch list. This regressive movement on Argentina's part is particularly striking in comparison to the positive direction of patent protection in its MERCOSUR partner Brazil. The United States will continue to seek further improvements, monitor this situation and review Argentina's status as appropriate. The United States will continue to seek further improvements, monitor this situation and review Argentina's status through an out-of-cycle review no later than December 1.

The *European Union's* patent fees and those of its member-states are extraordinarily expensive; fees associated with filing, issuance and maintenance of a patent over its life far exceed those in the United States and other countries. The EU's new single trademark system raises concerns as does the reciprocity requirement in the recently approved data base directive. The availability of *ex parte* relief in civil cases remains uncertain in some member-states. Denial of national treatment with respect to audio and video levies remains a problem in certain member-states. Certain provisions in the patent laws of some member-states appear to be inconsistent with the provisions of the WTO's TRIPS Agreement. In this context, the United States is invoking

WTO dispute settlement procedures against Portugal with respect to its patent law.

Greece has not yet acted to stop motion picture, software and sound recording piracy, including widespread unauthorized broadcasts of protected films and T.V. programs by unlicensed television stations. U.S.T.R. moved Greece to the priority watch list in November, 1994 and maintained this designation in 1995. In August, 1995, Greece took the potentially significant step of enacting a new Broadcast Law—apparently with strong enforcement provisions—which could have addressed been used to address the unauthorized broadcasting and re-transmission of U.S. programming on Greek television. However, the Greek Government has chosen not to use the new law to move against T.V. piracy. The United States will press Greece to honor its TRIPS obligation to provide for the effective enforcement of intellectual property rights and will consider available remedies if conditions warrant. An out-of-cycle review will be conducted in September.

India was a "priority foreign country" from 1991–1993. India has failed to implement its obligations under Articles 70.8 and 70.9 of TRIPS Agreement. These articles require developing countries not yet providing patent protection for pharmaceutical and agricultural chemical products to provide a "mailbox" in which to file patent applications, and the possibility of up to five years of exclusive marketing rights for these products until patent protection is provided. India has affirmed its intention to pass legislation implementing its TRIPs obligations. India established TRIPS provisions administratively (which have subsequently lapsed) and has introduced legislation but has not provided a legal basis for the filing of such patent applications for these products. As a result, the Administration will initiate formal consultations with India under WTO dispute settlement procedures in the near future. Moreover, India's industrial property laws continue to fall well short of providing adequate and effective protection. In particular, the Administration looks to India to enact and enforce modern patent and trademark legislation. India has modern copyright legislation but improvements continue to be necessary in the enforcement area.

Indonesia: Enforcement, including the imposition of deterrent penalties for computer software and book piracy, needs to be improved. In April 1995 the Indonesian Government announced an action plan to intensify its enforcement efforts against copyright piracy and to require Government Ministries to purchase only licensed software. This plan needs to be implemented fully and aggressively. U.S. owners of well-known marks encounter serious problems with trademark infringement, which also must be addressed. Although Indonesia has taken some steps this year to improve IPR protection, the efforts have not been adequate given the magnitude of the problems. Consequently, Indonesia is being elevated to the priority watch list.

Japan: Despite conclusion of two patent-related agreements in 1994, patent-related problems continue, particularly with respect to the uneven and overly narrow interpretation of patent claims in Japanese courts and concerns among American industry about patent "flooding" practices in Japan. These practices have limited the ability of U.S. patent holders in a range of industries to acquire exclusive rights comparable to those available to Japanese patent holders in the United States. Concerns also remain about the inadequate protection of trademarks and trade secrets, as well as end-user software piracy. The United States continues to pursue a WTO dispute settlement proceeding regarding Japan's failure to provide an adequate term of protection for pre-existing sound recordings.

Korea: While progress has been made over the past year, major problems from last year's review remain, including lack of adequate protection for trade secrets, software, textile designs and trade dress. Administrative measures were taken in early 1996 to enhance the protection of well-known U.S. trademarks, but the effectiveness of that system is uncertain at this time and we will continue to monitor it closely. Large end-user piracy of software continues to be a problem. A particularly serious problem with Korea's legal system is its failure to provide full retroactive copyright protection for pre–1957 works as required under the TRIPS Agreement.

Turkey has been on the priority watch list since 1992 largely because it has had inadequate intellectual property laws and its enforcement efforts have been ineffective. Copyright and patent piracy are widespread. As part of Turkey's entry into a customs union with the EU, Turkey has agreed to continue to improve its intellectual property protection. Turkey also maintains a discriminatory 25 percent municipality tax only on receipts from the showing of foreign films in a manner inconsistent with the national treatment obligations of Article III of the GATT 1994. The Administration will invoke formal consultations with Turkey under WTO's dispute settlement procedures in the near future with respect to this matter.

WATCH LIST

In reviewing the practices of our trading partners, the U.S.T.R. has decided that 26 countries should be placed on the "watch list". The Administration uses the "watch list" as a means of monitoring progress in implementing commitments with regard to the protection of intellectual property rights and for providing comparable market access for U.S. intellectual property products.

Countries placed on the watch list are:

Australia: The Government of Australia does not provide adequate protection for test data submitted to regulatory authorities for the marketing approval of pharmaceuticals and agricultural chemicals. Such data are developed at great expense to the originating company. Australia allows competing companies to rely indirectly on such data to support their own later-filed applications. In addition to concerns about WTO consistency, permitting this to occur unfairly allows later applicants to free-ride on the first applicant's significant investment in developing the data and puts the first applicant at a competitive disadvantage. Australia very recently has taken some steps to address our concerns. The Administration would be prepared to reconsider this listing when Australia provides adequate and effective protection for test data.

Bahrain expressed its intent to join international intellectual property conventions in February 1995. The U.S. urges Bahrain to bring its copyright regime into line with its obligations under the Berne Convention and the WTO, and to begin to take effective enforcement action against widespread piracy of copyrighted works of all types.

Brazil has recently taken the admirable step of enacting a modern patent law that comes into effect one year after its publication. Among other things, the new law will provide pharmaceutical patent protection and pipeline protection. As a result, the Administration is moving Brazil from the priority watch list to the watch list. Beyond the above-mentioned patent legislation, the U.S. Administration looks to Brazil to fulfill its longstanding commitments to enact outstanding legislation on computer software and semi-conductor layout designs, and to introduce much-needed amendments to its copyright law.

Canada: In 1995, the Government of Canada implemented the proposed 80% tax on split-run editions of U.S. magazines, specifically Sports Illustrated Canada. The Administration has initiated WTO dispute settlement procedures on this matter. Because this issue is already subject to action under the section 301 provisions of our Trade Act, initiation of an additional section 301 investigation is not warranted. See 19 U.S.C. 2242(f) and 19 U.S.C. 2412(b)(2)(A)(ii). In December 1995 the Canadian Radio-television Telecommunications Commission announced discriminatory direct-to-home satellite television licensing conditions of serious concern to U.S. industry. U.S.T.R. is continuing to collect information on the new licensing system with the goal of determining whether it is actionable under article 2106 of the NAFTA and Canada's WTO obligations. On April 25, 1996, Canada introduced copyright law amendments that could discriminate against U.S. right holders. A stated objective of the reforms is to help strengthen Canadian identity and contribute to the cultural sector. The Administration wants to ensure that these amendments are not at the expense of U.S. copyright interests.

Chile: Chile's patent term is TRIPS-inconsistent, pipeline protection remains unavailable, and there is inadequate protection for plant varieties and animal breeds. Additional problems are computer software piracy and the absence of protection for semi-conductor mask works and encrypted satellite signals. Copyright protection for computer software and the existence of rental and importation rights remain unclear.

Colombia: Enforcement efforts against copyright piracy have increased; however, piracy continues to be a significant problem. Colombia joined the Paris Convention and has not yet fully implemented the WTO TRIPS Agreement. Deficiencies in its patent and trademark regime include insufficiently restrictive compulsory licensing provisions, working requirements, inadequate protection of pharmaceutical patents, and lack of protection against parallel imports. Also, in the copyright area, a 1994 Broadcast Law increased restrictions on foreign content, including imposition of a complicated, burdensome system of subquotas for different hours of the day.

Costa Rica: Costa Rica's patent law is deficient in several key areas. The term of patent coverage is a non-extendable 12 year term from the date of grant. In the case of products deemed to be in the "public interest", such as pharmaceuticals, chemicals and agro-chemicals, fertilizers, and beverage/food products, the term of protection is only one year from date of grant. The U.S. looks to the Government of Costa Rica, as it implements its WTO obligations, to adopt a term of patent protection of 20 years from filing as required by TRIPS.

Ecuador has not yet ratified and implemented the 1993 U.S.-Ecuador Intellectual Property Rights Agreement. Furthermore, Ecuador has not yet repealed a GATT-inconsistent law, the Dealers' Act, which denies national treatment and protection to U.S. investment and U.S. trademarks. In the context of WTO accession, the GOE has committed to fully implement TRIPS by July 1996. We look to the GOE to implement fully our bilateral IPR Agreement and its TRIPS commitments, and to repeal the Dealers' Act.

Egypt has taken significant steps in improving the legal framework for protection of copyright works and has devoted resources to enforcing its copyright law. The United States remains seriously concerned, however, about the lack of effective patent protection in Egypt. The United States urges Egypt to enact promptly a modern patent law that provides immediate patent protection for all types of products, including pharmaceuticals, agricultural chemicals and foodstuffs.

El Salvador's copyright law went into force in June 1994 but implementation and enforcement of the law has been extremely lax. Despite widespread piracy, there were no seizures of pirate materials by government officials until late February 1996, when police raided more than 20 establishments and seized 43,000 cassettes and videos, as well as duplication equipment, and other materials. No arrests were made as a result of these raids. The Government of El Salvador has promised additional raids in 1996, as well as instructions to judges on the proper handling of IPR cases. Salvadoran laws protecting patents and trademarks are deficient and their enforcement remains weak. The United States supports efforts by the Government of El Salvador to implement and enforce its laws and will conduct an "out-of-cycle" review of these efforts in July 1996.

Guatemala does not adequately protect pharmaceuticals and its copyright law is deficient. The United States urges Guatemala to give priority to moving copyright law reform through its legislature and to offer better patent and trademark protection. The United States remains concerned about the interception and unauthorized retransmission of

U.S. satellite-carried programming by cable and multichannel microwave distribution systems.

Italy: The Italian Government stepped-up enforcement efforts over the past year, including several large well-publicized raids, particularly against copyright piracy. Nevertheless, losses due to piracy remain high. A major impediment to reducing video piracy has been the inadequacy of criminal penalties. Italy's failure to enact pending anti-piracy legislation that would significantly increase criminal penalties is a significant problem. Counterfeiting of trademark products is also a major concern for U.S. industry. The degree to which Italy provides TRIPS-mandated protection against "bootleg" sound recordings (i.e., protection of live performances) is unclear. An "out-of-cycle" review will be conducted to evaluate Italy's progress in addressing these issues. The United States will press Italy to honor its TRIPs obligation to provide for the effective enforcement of intellectual property rights.

Kuwait: Enforcement efforts by the Government of Kuwait to combat piracy of software and audiovisual products have improved following an April 1995 decree issued by the Ministry of Information. However, unauthorized duplication of software, especially in government agencies continues to be a major problem. Kuwait has been slow to move ahead on adopting copyright legislation. Pharmaceutical patents are not protected under the existing 1962 law, which is deficient in numerous other regards as well.

Oman: Modernization of Oman's intellectual property regime is lagging with review of draft patent and copyright legislation extending to over a year. Legal protection for pharmaceutical product patents is also absent. Because its protection of intellectual property remains minimal and stagnant, while neighbors strengthen their regimes, Oman increasingly appears to be a haven for pirates. The United States will continue to monitor levels of piracy in Oman and efforts to improve intellectual property protection, including the status of draft legislation to update copyright and patent regimes.

Pakistan: Pakistan's patent law provides process but not product protection for pharmaceutical and agricultural chemicals. Proving infringement of a process patent is difficult and such patents are easily circumvented. The United States seeks the prompt revision of this law. Of a more immediate nature, Pakistan has failed to implement its obligations under Articles 70.8 and 70.9 of TRIPS Agreement. These articles require developing countries not yet providing patent protection for pharmaceutical and agricultural chemical products to provide a "mailbox" in which to file patent applications, and the possibility of up to five years of exclusive marketing rights for these products until patent protection is provided. Pakistan's cabinet on April 8 approved an amendment to its patent law that includes a "mailbox" provision to take effect upon passage and other broadened patent protections to take effect in 2005. The amendment must now go to the National Assembly before becoming law. To encourage quick passage, the Administration will initiate formal consultations with Pakistan under WTO dispute settlement procedures.

Paraguay increasingly has become a piracy center in South America, particularly in production of sound recordings and entertainment software. Pirate production centers have been built on the Brazilian and Argentine borders. Paraguay also has become a transshipment center for pirate goods originating in China bound for larger South American markets. Enforcement actions against these activities are urgently needed in Paraguay. In addition, Paraguay's patent, trademark and copyright laws are in need of significant revision to bring them into conformity with international obligations. An out-of-cycle review will be conducted in September to evaluate whether sufficient progress toward addressing these problems has occurred.

Peru: INDECOPI's actions and decisions over the last year have demonstrated progress in the protection of intellectual property rights in Peru. However, while enforcement efforts against copyright piracy have increased, piracy continues to be a significant problem. The Peruvian Government needs to intensify its anti-piracy efforts, particularly to combat sound recording and book piracy. Deficiencies in its patent and trademark regime include compulsory licensing provisions, working requirements, inadequate protection of pharmaceutical patents, and lack of protection from parallel imports.

Philippines: The Philippines has made progress improving its enforcement efforts against intellectual property piracy, as promised in our 1993 bilateral IPR agreement. While the legislative commitments of that agreement have not yet been fulfilled, the Philippines Congress is currently considering legislation that would go beyond the 1993 commitments and make its major IPR laws TRIPS consistent. The Administration looks to the Government of the Philippines to 1) enact this legislation quickly and 2) continue progress in eliminating the use of pirated software in government agencies. In anticipation of progress in both of these areas, an out-of-cycle review will occur in October.

Poland: The United States continues to monitor implementation and enforcement of rights provided under the copyright law enacted in February 1994. The United States notes that the national treatment obligations of the TRIPS Agreement now obligate Poland to provide full protection for foreign sound recordings. The Administration will monitor carefully to ensure that such protection is now provided.

The *Russian Federation* has fulfilled some of its obligations under the 1992 U.S.-Russia Trade Agreement, namely passage of intellectual property protection laws and adherence to the Berne and Geneva Conventions. However, extensive piracy of U.S. video cassettes, films, music, recordings, books, and computer software considerably overshadows these legislative developments. Initial real enforcement efforts have begun only recently. Russia's failure to combat aggressively the rampant and increasing piracy of U.S. intellectual property must be remedied immediately. An "out-of-cycle" review in December will monitor Russia's effort to (1) put in place meaningful criminal penalties and (2) provide retroactive protection for artistic and literary works and sound recordings. Other issues to be reviewed for progress include improved trademark protection for well-known marks. Finally, a side letter to our bilateral trade agreement on compulsory licensing of patents is long overdue for signature.

Saudi Arabia has made progress in improving its enforcement activities against copyright piracy, particularly for motion pictures and sound recordings. However, serious copyright problems remain particularly regarding computer software piracy, including end-user piracy. Saudi Arabia's copyright law contains deficiencies making it incompatible with international standards, including an inadequate term of protection. It is important that existing efforts be maintained and that further improvements occur, particularly in terms of software enforcement. To ensure that such progress is maintained, an out-of-cycle review will occur in September.

Singapore: Although Singapore has a good record of protecting intellectual property, its copyright law is not TRIPS consistent. Outstanding issues include lack of rental rights for sound recordings and software, inadequate protection against making bootleg copies of musical performances, the scope of copyright protection for cinematographic works and overly broad exceptions from copyright protection. Singapore's level of economic development is sufficiently advanced to expect TRIPS implementation as a developed country.

Thailand: Despite progress in providing more effective intellectual property protection, including the entry into force of a modern copyright law in March 1995, certain concerns remain. These include: a falling off of enforcement activity in 1995; the lack of a TRIPS-consistent patent law; and the need to ensure that deterrent penalties are imposed on convicted pirates. To better monitor this situation, an out-of-cycle review will occur in October.

UAE (*United Arab Emirates*): Piracy of motion pictures and sound recordings has been largely eliminated in the UAE. However, a 1995 "out-of-cycle" review confirmed that software piracy remains a serious problem. While the pace of enforcement activity against business software piracy picked up in 1995, efforts have not been sufficiently aggressive or penalties severe enough to significantly reduce the level of illegal activity. The UAE's copyright law omits specific protection for sound recordings and is deficient in a number of other areas. UAE patent law exempts medicines and pharmaceutical compounds from protection and contains onerous compulsory licensing provisions. Concerns remain about reports of the unauthorized production of pharmaceutical products.

Venezuela: While Venezuela's copyright law establishes a generally effective and Berne-consistent system, the GOV's enforcement efforts against copyright piracy continue to be modest. Piracy and lack of border enforcement continue to be a significant problem. Deficiencies in its patent and trademark regime include compulsory licensing provisions, working requirements, inadequate protection of pharmaceutical patents, and lack of protection against parallel imports. The United States will continue to monitor the implementation and enforcement of IPR laws, as well as proceedings for patent and trademark applications. Venezuela has not yet fully implemented the WTO TRIPs Agreement.

OTHER OBSERVATIONS

This year, the U.S.TR wishes to draw attention to a number of countries where the lack of adequate and effective protection of intellectual property rights also is a concern. These countries are the Dominican Republic, Lebanon, Nicaragua and Qatar. The U.S.TR expects these countries to take steps to address the shortcomings in their intellectual property regimes. In the case of Nicaragua, the United States and Nicaragua continue their negotiations on a bilateral IPR Agreement to help resolve these problems. The U.S.TR will monitor developments in all of these countries and, in next year's Special 301 review, will assess the extent to which they have made progress in providing better protection for intellectual property.

In addition, the U.S.TR wishes to note developments in the following countries.

Bolivia has made some efforts to enforce its antipiracy laws. However, TV, book, and sound recording piracy continues to be a significant problem. In addition, Bolivian copyright law is unclear as to the protection of software. The United States notes that the national treatment obligations of the TRIPS Agreement now require Bolivia to provide full copyright protection for sound recordings. The Administration will monitor carefully to ensure that such protection is provided. Finally, legislation has not been passed either to enact the national 1992 copyright law or to implement the Andean Pact copyright Decision 351. An "out-of-cycle" review will be conducted in September to evaluate continued antipiracy efforts in all areas as well as revisions in the copyright law that are consistent with international standards.

Bulgaria: The Government of Bulgaria has implemented a substantial portion of its commitments under an April 1995 exchange of letters by adhering to the Geneva Phonograms Convention and publishing a statement in its official gazette confirming copyright protection for U.S. and other foreign sound recordings. Another positive step was the recent passage of a decree establishing a title verification system aimed at preventing and detecting unlicensed production at the CD plants and other facilities. However, Bulgarian enforcement efforts have waned recently. As a result, exports of pirated product appear to have increased significantly. An "out-of-cycle" review will be conducted in September to ensure implementation of the title verification system and that enforcement efforts are improved. Special attention will be paid to the level of production of pirated CDs and CD-roms carrying computer software, as well as the export of illegitimate CDs and CD-roms from Bulgaria throughout the region and to other markets.

Cyprus has made progress on piracy since passage of is copyright law in January 1994. The United States will be monitoring efforts by the Government of Cyprus to continue to act aggressively against piracy of software and of video and audio recordings. The current patent regime in Cyprus is inadequate as well as inconsistent with TRIPS. We expect that the Government of Cyprus will act expeditiously to implement fully its TRIPS obligations, especially with regard to patent protection for pharmaceuticals and enforcement against piracy.

Germany: Efforts by U.S. firms to combat high levels of computer software piracy are undercut by the apparent unavailability of *ex parte* search and seizure procedures in civil court cases. The Administration will consider the TRIPS-consistency of this situation after establishing more definitively the unavailability of these procedures in Germany.

Honduras: The Government of Honduras has drafted and submitted to the Honduran Assembly amendments intended to address shortcomings found in Honduras' 1993 copyright law. The United States continues to work with the Government of Honduras to improve patent and trademark laws and better its enforcement, particularly through negotiations on a bilateral IPR agreement and implementation of the TRIPS Agreement.

Hong Kong has taken steps to combat the flood of pirated compact discs entering its territory from China, and to draft legislation to enable local prosecutors to pursue Hong Kong investors in pirate plants on the mainland. Despite these efforts, however, the problem is growing, as evidenced by the ubiquity of pirated CDs and software throughout Hong Kong. The United States urges the Hong Kong Government to act decisively against the retailers, wholesalers and investors who have made Hong Kong a center for pirated goods. U.S.TR will review Hong Kong's performance in six months to determine whether Hong Kong's status on Special 301 should be modified or terminated.

Ireland's patent law is not in conformity with the patent compulsory licensing provisions of the TRIPS Agreement. The law appears to violate the discrimination and "working requirement" limitations under Article 27.1 of the TRIPS Agreement and the limitations on the grant of compulsory licenses under Article 31 of the TRIPS Agreement. The Administration expects that Ireland will comply promptly with its TRIPS obligations.

Israel has an inadequate copyright law which, combined with poor enforcement, has led to widespread cable and software piracy. The Administration seeks revision of the copyright law and improved enforcement and passage of a law governing licensing of satellite signals by cable operators. The Administration remains concerned about the potential passage of troubling modifications to Israel's patent law.

Jordan's 1992 copyright law is cumbersome and falls far short of international standards in most respects. Jordan intends to revise its copyright law as part of its economic liberalization program and accession to the WTO. The inadequacies of the patent law, which dates from

1953, have led to a growing problem of patent infringement for pharmaceuticals which are manufactured for both domestic and export markets. Trademark protection is unavailable absent extreme vigilance by U.S. rights holders and revisions in the law are necessary to expand the definition of "trademark" to include services and goods.

Mexico is experiencing significant problems with copyright piracy and, to a lesser extent, trademark counterfeiting. As a result, a bilateral working group on intellectual property has been established which has already begun to make progress. The Administration looks for increased efforts by the Government of Mexico to amend its copyright law and to improve copyright and trademark enforcement.

Panama has become a major transshipment and assembly point for pirated and counterfeited products. The Government of Panama has only recently begun to enforce its customs and IPR laws, particularly in the Colon Free Zone, where most of this activity occurs. The United States welcomes the recent passage of Panama's new industrial property law and looks to Panama to continue improving its intellectual property laws and their enforcement, particularly in the context of its WTO accession.

Portugal: Portuguese patent law does not comport with the TRIPS requirement that the term of a patent be 20 years from filing and that this term apply to new patents granted as well as to those that are still in effect. Portugal has chosen to interpret TRIPS as requiring that the 20-year term apply only to new patents granted after June 1, 1995, not to existing patents. As a result, the Administration will initiate formal consultations with Portugal under WTO dispute settlement procedures.

Romania provides no pipeline patent protection for pharmaceuticals despite assurances under the U.S.-Romania Trade Agreement to "exert best efforts" to enact such legislation by December 1993. However, the Romanian Government passed a new copyright law on March 13, 1996 which appears to meet international standards. We will monitor developments over the coming year to ensure that the new law is effectively implemented and enforced in order to end (1) the piracy of U.S. motion pictures by TV stations in Romania, (2) the production of pirated audio cassettes and (3) piracy of American books.

South Africa is provisionally removed from the Watch List. In September 1996, an out-of-cycle review will be conducted to confirm that (1) the legislative changes to which South Africa committed itself in December 1995 are being expeditiously accomplished; and (2) legislation has been introduced into Parliament and other appropriate measures have been undertaken which would bring South Africa into compliance with its international obligations and resolve outstanding trademark concerns.

Taiwan has continued to make significant strides in improving the protection of intellectual property in Taiwan. As a result, Taiwan is being removed from the watch list. However, concerns remain about certain aspects of IPR protection and enforcement in Taiwan. As result, an 18 point action plan was concluded in late April. The plan outlines improvements to be made in such areas as cross-strait piracy, enforcement, education and the export monitoring system. To monitor implementation, an out-of-cycle review will be conducted in October.

Vietnam U.S. works do not receive copyright protection in Vietnam unless published in Vietnam within 30 days of their first publication elsewhere, basically leaving all U.S. works without protection in Vietnam. Discussions have begun to conclude a bilateral agreement with Vietnam which would establish bilateral copyright relations, and in doing so, bring Vietnam into closer conformity with Berne Convention requirements. Other issues must be addressed in the context of the broader bilateral trade agreement that is being negotiated to allow Vietnam to receive MFN status.

Notes and Questions

1.   Section 301 has served as a primary mechanism for initiating bilateral efforts by the U.S. to assure enforcement of intellectual property rights internationally. Are there benefits in utilizing bilateral efforts to enforce IP rights as opposed to private lawsuits?

2.   What are the potentially harmful effects that arise from the use of bilateral enforcement efforts such as those under Section 301? Are these different in nature from the potentially harmful effects of a multilateral treaty regime where a country's position is not adopted?

3.   How effective are bilateral enforcement efforts? Pick one of the countries listed on the Watch List. Are the complaints described in the Watch List still of concern today? For an example of some of the problems which arise through bilateral negotiations, compare the U.S.-China memorandum of understanding (MOU) of 1995 with the China–U.S. MOU of 1993. The 1995 MOU was established after a threatened trade war between China and the U.S. based on China's purported failure to enforce IP rights.

OVERVIEW OF THE STATE-OF-PLAY OF WTO DISPUTES
http:www.wto.org/wto/dispute/bulletin.htm.
Implementation of Adopted Reports.

APPELLATE AND PANEL REPORTS ADOPTED SINCE 1 SEPTEMBER 1998

(1) *India—Patent Protection for Pharmaceutical and Agricultural Chemical Products*, complaint by the European Communities (WT/DS79/1). This request, dated 28 April 1997, is in respect of the alleged absence in India of patent protection for pharmaceutical and agricultural chemical products, and the absence of formal systems that permit the filing of patent applications of and provide exclusive marketing rights for such products. The EC contends that this is inconsistent with India's obligations under Article 70, paragraphs 8 and 9, of the TRIPS Agreement (see similar U.S. complaint in DS50, where the Panel and Appellate Body reports were adopted on 16 January 1998). On 9 September 1997, the EC requested the establishment of a panel. At its meeting on 16 October 1997, the DSB established a panel. The U.S.

reserved its third-party rights. The Panel found that India has not complied with its obligations under Article 70.8(a) of the TRIPS Agreement by failing to establish a legal basis that adequately preserves novelty and priority in respect of applications for product patents for pharmaceutical and agricultural chemical inventions, and was also not in compliance with Article 70.9 of the TRIPS Agreement by failing to establish a system for the grant of exclusive marketing rights. The report of the Panel was circulated to Members on 24 August 1998. At its meeting on 2 September;1998, the DSB adopted the Panel Report.

Completed Cases

(8) *India—Patent Protection for Pharmaceutical and Agricultural Chemical Products*, complaint by the United States (WT/DS50). This request, dated 2 July 1996, concerns the alleged absence of patent protection for pharmaceutical and agricultural chemical products in India. Violations of the TRIPS Agreement Articles 27, 65 and 70 are claimed. The United States requested the establishment of a panel on 7 November 1996. The DSB established a panel at its meeting on 20 November 1996. The Panel found that India has not complied with its obligations under Article 70.8(a) or Article 63(1) and (2) of the TRIPS Agreement by failing to establish a mechanism that adequately preserves novelty and priority in respect of applications for product patents for pharmaceutical and agricultural chemical inventions, and was also not in compliance with Article 70.9 of the TRIPS Agreement by failing to establish a system for the grant of exclusive marketing rights. The report of the Panel was circulated on 5 September 1997. On 15 October 1997, India notified its intention to appeal certain issues of law and legal interpretations developed by the Panel. The Appellate Body upheld, with modifications, the Panel's findings on Articles 70.8 and 70.9, but ruled that Article 63(1) was not within the Panel's terms of reference. The report of the Appellate Body was circulated to Members on 19 December 1997. The Appellate Body report and the Panel report, as modified by the Appellate Body, were adopted by the DSB on 16 January 1998. At the DSB meeting of 22 April 1998, the parties announced that they had agreed on an implementation period of 15 months.

Notes and Questions

1.   The Use of Section 301 has led to international challenges regarding its legality in light of the WTO's requirement of use of the WTO dispute mechanism for issues arising under TRIPS. In November 1998 a complaint was filed by the European Communities challenging the legality of Section 301. As reported by the WTO: "This dispute, dated 25 November 1998, is in respect of Title III, chapter 1 (sections 301–310) of the U.S. Trade Act of 1974 (the Trade Act), as amended, and in particular sections 306 and 305 of this Act. The EC contends that by imposing strict time limits within which unilateral determinations must be made and trade sanctions taken, sections 306 and 305 of the Trade Act do not allow the U.S. to comply with the rules of the DSU in situations where a prior multilateral ruling under the DSU on conformity of measures taken pursuant to implementation of DSB recom-

mendations has not been adopted by the DSB. The EC further contends, that the DSU procedure resulting in a multilateral finding, even if initiated immediately after the end of the reasonable period of time for implementation, cannot be finalized, nor can subsequent DSU procedure for seeking compensation or suspension of concessions be complied with, within the time limits of sections 306 and 305. The EC alleges that Title III, chapter 1 (sections 301–310) of the Trade Act, as amended, and in particular sections 306 and 305 of the Act, are inconsistent with Articles 3, 21, 22 and 23 of the DSU; Article XVI:4 of the WTO Agreement; and Articles I, II, III, VIII and XI of GATT 1994. The EC also alleges that the Trade Act nullifies and impairs benefits accruing, directly or indirectly, to it under GATT 1994, and also impedes the objectives of GATT 1994 and of the WTO. The EC is also seeking consultations in respect of announcements by the U.S., which are unilateral determinations under section 306 of the Trade Act, on retaliatory actions being prepared by the U.S. for what it considers non-implementation by the EC of the recommendations of the DSB in the dispute. *European Communities—Regime for the Importation, Sale and Distribution of Bananas.* Overview of the State-of-play of WTO Disputes, http://www.wto.org/wto/dispute/bulletin.htm (1998). For a discussion regarding the potential conflict between TRIPS and Section 301, see Nicole Telecki, *The Role of Special 301 in the Development of International Protection of Intellectual Property Rights After the Uruguay Round,* 14 B.U. Int'l L. J. 187 (1996).

2. As demonstrated above, and in Chapter Twenty-Two various claims have been filed in front of the WTO in connection with intellectual property violations under TRIPS. Out of the claims listed above, most are settled by negotiation. In light of this track record of dispute resolution, what role should bilateral efforts (such as Section 301) continue to play in international enforcement?

3. Select one of the disputes before the WTO listed above or in Chapter Twenty-Two. How was the dispute resolved? Is the subject of the complaint still a problem today?

*

Part IX

GOVERNMENT "TAKINGS"
AND OTHER STATE–
BASED CONTROLS

In a well-known U.S. Supreme Court decision *Pennsylvania Coal Co. v. Mahon*, 260 U.S. 393 (1922), Justice Holmes recognized that government regulation could result in a taking of property, even if "ownership" remained with the purported property owner. In the area of international intellectual property, fair use exclusions and compulsory licenses are the most frequent "takings" which appear to be sanctioned to some degree by the international community. As countries, however, seek to expand the scope of compulsory licenses and other restrictions on an owner's ability to control the use of his intellectual property, such legal "takings" may pose a serious threat to the "private rights" regime which TRIPS seems to require. Although certain "fair uses" of copyrighted works have been recognized internationally, (such as for education and news reporting purposes), the scope of such uses has been the subject of heated debate. As you examine the materials in this chapter ask yourself if there are legitimate national goals to be furthered in a compulsory licensing scheme. If so, how should such a scheme be structured to assure adequate compensation to the IP owner while maintaining a relatively effective and easily administered system? Short of compulsory licenses, are there additional restrictions governments may legitimately impose on the exercise of recognized intellectual property rights? Where should the balance be struck between an owner's right to exploit her intellectual property and society's interest in directing the methods in which the property may be used?

Chapter Thirty–Two

COMPULSORY LICENSES

A. CAN DOMESTIC GOVERNMENTS COMPEL THE EXPLOITATION OF AN INTELLECTUAL PROPERTY RIGHT?

Read the following Articles from TRIPS from the Supplement: 11,13, 30, 31.

Notes and Questions

1. What types of intellectual property are *excluded* from compulsory licenses under TRIPS? Is there something unique about these forms of intellectual property which warrant their exclusion from compulsory licensing potential?

2. What are the limitations which TRIPS places upon the grant of a compulsory license? Compare the language of Articles 13 and 30 of TRIPS with Article 9 of Berne and Article 5 of Paris. Are these limitations equivalent? Or does TRIPS impose an additional or different burden on the exercise of compulsory license rights?

Read the following Articles from the Supplement: Berne Convention 9, Paris Convention 5, TRIPS 21.

Notes and Questions

1. *Special Problems in Trademark Licensing.* The compulsory licensing of trademarks permitted under Article 5C of Paris was strongly contested by IP owners. Under these provisions, numerous countries, including Canada, imposed registered user requirements on the registration and protection of trademarks under domestic law. Some of these registered user provisions, such as those under Brazilian law, included the requirement that the mark be licensed to a local company for use domestically. Because of the special nature of trademarks, in particular their role as a quality and source designator, owners were concerned over their inability to control the use of their marks by third party users under a compulsory license. As a result of the controversy, TRIPS specifically precludes the grant of compulsory licenses for trademarks under Article 21.

741

2. What are the limits which are placed internationally on a country's ability to compel the licensing of a patent?

3. Could a country require a patentee to grant an exclusive compulsory license to a third party, thereby precluding the patentee from further exploiting his incentive?

4. What is the harm caused by a compulsory patent licensing scheme? What are the benefits?

5. What are the limits which are placed internationally on a country's ability to compel the licensing of a copyrighted work?

6. Are the harms and benefits of a compulsory licensing scheme for a copyrighted work different from those caused by a compulsory licensing scheme for a patented invention?

7. If you were an IP owner, what protections would you want if your property were subject to a compulsory licensing scheme?

THE TRIPS LICENSE CASE
ALLEN & HANBURYS LTD v. CONTROLLER OF PATENTS, DESIGNS & TRADEMARKS

The High Court (Ireland), 1996.
[1997] FSR 1.

MELLA CARROLL, J.

This is an appeal under section 75 of the Patents Act 1964 against an Order of the Controller of Patents, Designs and Trademarks (the Controller) made on June 2, 1995. The Order provided for compulsory licences in respect of two patents for the life of the patents to come into force with effect from the date they were executed by the parties.

The preliminary issue of law is in the following terms:

1. Do the provisions of the Agreement on Trade Related Aspects of Intellectual Property Rights oblige the Controller of Patents or the Court to refuse the grant of compulsory licences pursuant to section 42 of the Patents Act 1964 to the second named defendant on any date after the aforementioned agreement became known to the State?

2. In the event that the Controller had jurisdiction to grant such licences, can the licences have any validity after the date of application of the aforesaid agreement to the State?

The facts on which the case is based are as follows:

On November 8, 1991 and February 13, 1992 respectively the second defendants ("Clonmel") applied under section 42 of the Patents Act 1964 (the 1964 Act) for patent licences in respect of Patent No 45456 and patent No 51604 owned respectively by the first plaintiff and the second plaintiff.

On June 2, 1995 the Controller made an order granting compulsory licences to Clonmel. The written grounds for his decision were delivered on July 3, 1995. He held that TRIPs had no application in the internal legal system of the state as it had not been enacted into domestic law.

On January 1, 1996 the transitional year provided for by Article 65(1) of TRIPS expired.

Section 42(1) of the 1964 Act provides:

(1) Without prejudice to the foregoing provisions of this Act, where a patent is in force in respect of

(a) a substance capable of being used as food or medicine or in the production of food or medicine; or

(b) a process for producing such a substance as aforesaid; or

(c) any invention capable of being used as, or as part of a medical, surgical or other remedial device.

The Controller shall, on application made to him by any person interested, order the grant to the applicant of a licence under the patent on such terms as he thinks fit, unless it appears to him that having regard to the desirability of encouraging inventors and the growth and development of industry and to such other matters as he considers relevant, there are good reasons for refusing the application.

It is not contested that section 42 does permit discrimination as to the field of technology in respect of enjoyment of patent rights contrary to Article 27(1) of TRIPS. What is in issue is whether Article 27(1) applied at the time of the Controller's decision so as to prevent a grant of licences under section 42 or alternatively whether it applies now.

The date the Controller made the Order was July 3, 1995 which was after the signing of the Treaty on April 15, 1994. Therefore , the Controller's order was made long after TRIPs became known.

According to Article 65(1) [of TRIPS], no member is obliged to apply TRIPS before the expiration of one year following the date of entry into force of the WTO Agreement. In order to give a sensible interpretation to Article 65(1), it seems to me that the controller being under the direct control of the Minister could not grant licences under section 42 in breach of Article 27(1) after the date TRIPs became known. He granted them after the date of signing which was April 15, 1994. Since he could not grant them after the draft became known, Article 65(1) is subservient and does not apply and Article 65(5) is irrelevant. Therefore, the answer to question 1 of the preliminary issue of law is "yes" and the second question does not arise.

Since the plaintiffs succeed on the interpretation of section 46(3) it is not necessary to deal with the further arguments raised by the plaintiffs.

DISPOSITION:

Judgment accordingly.

THE DIVING SUIT CASE

HARVEY'S SKINDIVING SUITS OF CANADA
v. POSEIDON INDUSTRI AB

Commissioner of Patents, 1984.
5 C.P.R. 3d 154.

Application for a compulsory licence for abuse of patent.

THE COMMISSIONER:

This decision is made on the allegations of abuse of patent rights under paras. 67(2)(a) and (b) of the Patent Act, R.S.C. 1970, c. P–4, brought by Harvey's Skindiving Suits of Canada (hereinafter Harvey's), regarding Canadian patent No. 910,001, owned by Poseidon Industri AB (hereinafter Poseidon) and exclusively licensed to Parkway Fabricators Inc. (hereinafter Parkway).

In order that an abuse under § 67(2)(a) may be proven to my satisfaction, it is necessary that the following things be shown:

(a) that the patent is over three years old;

(b) that the patented invention is capable of being worked in Canada;

(c) that it is not being worked in Canada on a commercial scale;

and once these three have been shown, it is then necessary to establish that no satisfactory reason exists for such non-working.

Canadian patent No. 910,001 issued on September 19, 1972, and thus the three year limit of § 67(1) expired in 1975. It contains five claims, each of which is to a diving suit. Under §§ 2 and 72(2) of the Patent Act, it is this suit which is to be manufactured in Canada in order for the invention to be worked as required by para. 67(2)(a). Harvey's has alleged that it can manufacture the diving suit of the patent, and requires only the making of a testing tank to complete its facilities. Harvey's witness, Mr. Singer, testifies that he has a factory that is capable of making the suit, that he has repaired them, and that repair is more difficult than original manufacture. This testimony is uncontradicted, and satisfies me that Harvey's is a person interested.

There is only one fact alleged in the application to show abuse under para. 67(2)(a), this is the statement in the declaration by Mr. Singer, that the diving suit of the patent is not manufactured in Canada. It is this fact which must be proven in order for abuse to be shown.

TESTIMONY

Mr. Singer, pp. 28–30

Well, there are, I think, one or two companies in Canada that are doing nothing but dry suits.

There is one of them in Victoria and I think there is one in Vancouver.

I have been in one factory for sure . . . two years ago he did nothing but dry suits.

And he made a good one.

There is also testimony by Mr. Sanger, witness for the opponents, that neither Poseidon nor Parkway have manufactured the diving suit in Canada and that they are not willing to establish such manufacture themselves in Canada.

Mr. Sanger, page 185

Q. "And you admit that it has not been manufactured by the patentee or any representative of the patentee in Canada?

A. "Yes."

Mr. Sanger, page 100

Q. "Would Parkway Fabricators be willing today to set up a dry suit manufacturing business in Canada knowing that it could sell 500 units?"

A. "No."

Considering the above, the facts proven to my satisfaction are

(1) the patented invention is manufactured in Canada, but, not by, nor with the authorization of, the patentee

(2) the patentee is unwilling to manufacture itself, in Canada

(3) the manufacture that is being done is infringing manufacture.

While Mr. Singer, in his declaration, alleges that the invention has not been manufactured in Canada, and while the facts show that manufacture has occurred, such manufacture having been conducted by infringers, I am satisfied Section 67(3) requires that the manufacture to be considered must be secure manufacture. It is plainly stated that it is an object of the Act to secure working of inventions on a commercial scale in Canada, and proceedings under § 67(2)(a) are to be interpreted with that in mind.

Working or manufacture by an alleged infringer is not secure, for it may be stopped by injunction at the instance of the patentee. Infringing manufacture is wrongful and illicit, and therefore, in my opinion, it is not to be taken into account for the purpose of determining whether a patentee has fulfilled its duty to manufacture, but may only be considered as to whether there is satisfactory reason why the patentee has not fulfilled its duty.

On this basis, then, the statement of fact by Harvey's that there is no manufacture of the diving suit in Canada must be read as if it included the word "secure" taken from § 67(3). When so read, it is correct and proven to my satisfaction.

It remains to be seen if the opponents have put forward any satisfactory reason for the failure to achieve secure working in Canada. Parkway has specifically stated that it has no intention of working in

Canada, but has referred to licensing negotiations with one of the alleged infringers, Rowands, since 1980 (before the date of the application) as a defence. Evidence and testimony were presented that Rowands seeks a licence and that the opponents intend to grant one, a draft licence has resulted which both Rowands and Parkway appear to be willing to sign.

However, I consider that these negotiations do not constitute satisfactory reason. The opponents have known of Rowands' alleged infringement for five years according to the counterstatement, have bargained for three years, and even now 11 years after grant of patent, the opponents knowing of this proceeding have not managed to yet achieve secure working of the invention in Canada. I am satisfied that this failure constitutes undue delay in the circumstances, and the defence based on a possible licence to Rowands must be dismissed.

In summary, the patent is over three years old, the invention is shown to be capable of being worked on a commercial scale in Canada, the patentee has failed to secure manufacture in Canada, and no satisfactory reason for this has been shown. This satisfies me that there is an abuse of patent rights as alleged under para. 67(2)(a) of the Patent Act.

Regarding the abuse alleged under para. 67(2)(b), the counterstatement admits importation of 100 suits yearly as authorized by the opponents, and it has been found that there is no authorized or secure working in Canada.

Where all of a market is satisfied by importation, with no willingness to establish manufacture in Canada, I am of the opinion that the import operates to hinder or prevent manufacture in Canada. As that is the case here, I am satisfied that an abuse under para. 67(2)(b) has been established.

Abuse having been found as alleged, it remains for me to consider if a licence should issue, and if so upon what terms. Opponents have pointed out that it is not mandatory that a licence issue if abuse is found. Section 68(e) of the Patent Act clearly relates the ordering of a licence to attainment of the objects of the Act, and these must be considered before deciding whether to order licence or refusal of the application.

Again, I refer to the express wording of the Patent Act at § 67(3). The purpose of grant of a patent is, *inter alia*, to secure working in Canada. The opponents expressly repudiate their willingness to work, and by advancing an alleged infringer as one to satisfy their duties propose to render licit what is presently illicit to satisfy their duties under the Patent Act. Yet, even with all persons knowing of this proceeding, due to the advertisements in the C.P.O.R. and the Canada Gazette since October 5, 1982, over 10 years after date of grant of the patent, the opponents have been unable to secure working in Canada. The applicant, Harvey's, was shown on cross-examination to have everything it needs to manufacture except a licence and a water-testing-tank which, it was stated, could be made within a week. Consequently, I am satisfied that, in order to secure working of the invention in Canada, a licence should issue.

Having decided that a licence will issue, the Patent Act directs that I am to settle the terms of such licence.

The terms set by the commissioner must,

(a) secure manufacture in Canada § 67(3)

(b) cure the abuses found by granting relief § 70(2)

(c) secure widest user of the invention § 68(a)(i)

(d) secure maximum advantage to the patentee § 68(a)(ii) with reasonable profit to the licensee

(e) secure equality of advantage among licensees § 68(a) (iii).

Argument on terms was heard at the hearing. Pages 335–44 are concerned with a request by Harvey's for an exclusive licence. Section 68(b) of the Patent Act gives me explicit authority to order such an exclusive licence but under the condition that I am satisfied that it is necessary to rely upon the exclusive rights in order to raise the capital necessary to work on a commercial scale. At p. 33 of the transcript, Harvey's witness states that the only capital equipment that is missing is a water tank for testing having a capital cost of between $300 to $500. As I am not satisfied that it will be necessary to rely upon the exclusive rights to raise this amount of capital, there will be no order that the licence be exclusive.

Harvey's also requested that a term be settled barring it from importing the diving suits, which by § 68(a) would also bar such import by the opponents and any other licensees. As an abuse by importation has been proven, and it is an object of the Act to cure any abuse by the terms ordered, I am satisfied that such a term should be ordered.

Harvey's has objected to terms being ordered regarding quality control, while the opponents argued for such terms relying upon the evidence of their own witness that for nuclear power plant use it is essential that not one drop of water enter, that integrity of the suit is essential to diving under ice, and that the suit is used in the military and coast guard. The water tank, referred to by Harvey's witness as something necessary for production, is to be used to test the quality of the suit. Where Harvey's has referred to this as necessary thus indicating that it will conduct quality testing of its own accord, and is aware of the consequences to users of faulty suits, I am not satisfied that it is necessary that I order a term regarding quality when that term will be carried out voluntarily in any event.

Harvey's agrees that it take a sublicence from Parkway and report quarterly to Parkway, and it also agrees that a proper consideration regarding royalty is that amount (5%) which was negotiated with Rowands as prospective voluntary licensee.

The royalty rate, having been negotiated at arm's length with a party not directly interested in this proceeding but dealing with the subject-matter of the licence, would appear to represent a proper market valuation as agreed to by an outside party, and falls between the extremes urged by Harvey's of 0.5% and by the opponents of 10%. Accordingly, I am satisfied that a royalty of 5% on wholesale price will achieve advantage to the patentee and profitability to the licensee, and a term to this effect will be ordered.

As to minimum manufacture, opponents have indicated that they intend to grant a licence to Rowands, "whether there is or is not an order" for grant of a licence in this proceeding. Where there will be more than one manufacturer in Canada, I am satisfied that there should not be any term ordered requiring a minimum manufacture by one of them.

ORDER

WHEREAS in my decision regarding the abuses of patent rights alleged to have occurred under Canadian Patent 910,001, issued simultaneously with this order, I have found the abuses to be proven to my satisfaction;

AND WHEREAS I have also determined that a licence should be ordered to secure working of the invention in Canada and to grant relief from the abuses found;

AND WHEREAS the terms to be included in the licence are considered in my decision;

NOW THEREFORE be it known that pursuant to the powers conferred upon me by Section 68 of the Patent Act I do hereby order the grant of a non-exclusive licence to Harvey's Skindiving Suits of Canada of 30 Duncan Street, Toronto, Ontario under Canadian Patent 910,001 under the terms and conditions set out below.

(a) This licence shall be interpreted according to the laws of Ontario and shall not extend to any action done outside of Canada.

(b) This licence shall operate as a sub-licence between Harvey's Skindiving Suits of Canada (Harvey's) and Parkway Fabricators Inc., (Parkway) for so long a period of time as Parkway retains its exclusive licence of manufacture and a licence of use and sale under Canadian Patent 910,001 from Poseidon Industri AB (Poseidon), and shall in any other case operate as a direct licence between Harvey's and Poseidon.

(c) This licence does not extend to any property rights other than those in Canadian Patent 910,001, nor shall it impose any marking requirements or quality requirements other than those of the Patent Act.

2. (a) Harvey's shall have freedom from suit of infringement, for itself and its customers, under Canadian Patent 910,001 for the manufacture, use, and sale of diving suits made by Harvey's under that patent, in return for payment of a royalty of five (5) percent of the net wholesale selling price received by Harvey's for the sale of each such suit.

(b) "Net wholesale selling price" as used above shall mean that price at which ownership of the diving suit is first transferred from Harvey's to another person who deals at arm's length with Harvey's, less sales tax and any allowance for returns or refunds.

(c) The royalties of clause 2(a) shall be paid in Canadian dollars by Harvey's to Parkway for so long as it retains its licence as set out in clause 1(b), and in any other case to Poseidon.

3. (a) Harvey's shall keep an accurate record of all matters pertaining to this ordered licence and shall furnish Parkway with quarterly statements showing the descriptions, quantities, and selling prices of all suits manufactured and sold under this order during the preceding quarter, including any sold by persons not dealing at arm's length with Harvey's.

(b) In view of Parkway's obligation to report to Poseidon, the first statement by Harvey's shall be mailed by registered mail to Parkway 30 days before the first day of June 1984 and shall include all matters between that date and the date of this order, and subsequent statements shall be mailed by registered mail quarterly thereafter, and Poseidon shall accept receipt of copies of such statements from Parkway as fulfillment of its quarterly reporting obligation under their existing exclusive licence as regards any actions taken by Harvey's under this licence.

(c) Any royalties payable, shall accompany the quarterly statements.

(d) Should Parkway lose its status as exclusive licensee under Canadian Patent 910,001, then royalties and statements shall be sent directly to Poseidon by Harvey's.

4. This ordered licence may only be terminated under one of the following conditions:

(a) if the patent expires, or is impeached or held invalid in court;

(b) if Harvey's is shown to have imported diving suits made under the patent during the life of this licence;

(c) if Harvey's fails to commence manufacture in Canada of the patented article within one year from the date of this order, or fails for any period of one year thereafter to continue to manufacture the patented article in Canada;

(d) if Harvey's is shown to have willfully and knowingly failed to carry out any other of its obligations under this order, and not to have attempted to correct such failure upon being given 30 days notice by registered mail of such failure, or and not to have raised a bona fide dispute within such period as to whether or not it has so failed.

5. Any party may apply to a court, or, if the parties agree, to a mutually agreeable arbitrator, for a determination under 4 above, and the winning party shall register the determination in the Patent Office.

6. Harvey's shall at all reasonable times but after forty-eight hours' notice and until complete settlement of all transactions which

have taken place during the existence of this licence permit an independent chartered accountant (a non-employee of the company) acting on behalf of Parkway (or Poseidon if the licence becomes a direct one), but approved of by Harvey's, to inspect and take copies of its records or books pertaining to its operations pursuant to this ordered licence, but not otherwise, and such accountant shall only be entitled to report as to whether the statements furnished pursuant to clause 3 of this licence are correct or not.

7.   This licence is not transferrable and Harvey's is precluded from granting any sub-licence to manufacture.

8.   Notices, statements, payments or any documents dealing with this licence shall be sent to the parties at their last known address notified by each party to the others.

9.   Harvey's is precluded from importing into Canada any goods the importation of which, if made by persons other than the patentee or persons claiming under him, would be an infringement of the patent.

10.   Upon termination of this licence, Harvey's shall provide a full statement of account to Parkway (or Poseidon as the case may be) and a full settlement of all royalties due, including a royalty on all suits manufactured to date of termination but not sold, at the average royalty per suit paid during the last quarter in which sales occurred.

11.   This licence shall take effect immediately.

12.   Parkway and Poseidon shall notify Harvey's of any change to their existing licence which would affect clauses 1(b), 2(c), 3(d), 6, and 10 of this licence, and Harvey's shall not be bound by any such change until it is confirmed by each of them. 85–8293/CPR

Notes and Questions

1.   Are there any legitimate reasons for a patent owner's refusing to work an invention in a particular country?

2.   What legitimate purposes are served by requiring that a patent be worked in a country that grants patent protection to the invention at issue?

3.   Is the court's decision in the *Skin-diving* case in violation of Canada's treaty obligations under TRIPS? What standard should be used to determine what qualifies as sufficient compensation for the patent owner?

4.   Even if a patent owner is required to grant a compulsory license to a third party, can the Government require the patent owner to also disclose any information she has regarding the best method for practicing the patented invention without violating international standards?

5.   Are there clauses in the order that you would exclude or alter? Are there clauses you would add?

6.   *United States.* The United States does not currently have a provision which requires the compulsory licensing for any patented invention which is not worked in the country. Under 28 U.S.C. § 1498, however, the Government is entitled to a type of compulsory licensing since it is only required to pay compensation for its unauthorized use of a patented invention. It cannot

be enjoined from such unauthorized use. Does the absence of procedures for approving the Government's use of a particular invention under this "compulsory license" violate TRIPS or Paris obligations? Should such review procedures be imposed internationally for granting compulsory patent licenses?

THE MAGILL TV GUIDE CASE

RADIO TELEFIS EIREANN v. EC COMMISSION (MAGILL TV GUIDE LIMITED INTERVENING)

Court Of First Instance Of The European Communities (2nd Chamber), 1991.
[1991] 4 CMLR 586.

By application lodged at the Registry of the Court of Justice on 10 March 1989, Radio Telefis Eireann (hereinafter referred to as "RTE") sought the annulment of the Commission Decision of 21 December 1988 (hereinafter referred to as "the decision") in which the Commission found that RTE's policies and practices, at the material time, in relation to publication of its advance weekly listings for television and radio programmes which may be received in Ireland and Northern Ireland constituted infringements of Article 86 EEC in so far as they prevented the publication and sale of comprehensive weekly television guides in Ireland and Northern Ireland.

The background to the decision may be summarised as follows. Most homes in Ireland and between 30 and 40 per cent of homes in Northern Ireland can receive at least six television channels: RTE1 and RTE2, provided by RTE, which enjoys a statutory monopoly for the provision of a national radio and television broadcasting service in Ireland, BBC1 and BBC2, provided by the BBC, and ITV and Channel 4, provided at the material time by the companies franchised by the Independent Broadcasting Authority ('the IBA') to supply independent television programmes. In the United Kingdom, the BBC and IBA enjoyed a duopoly for the provision of national television broadcasting services. In addition, many television viewers in Great Britain and Ireland could receive several satellite channels either directly or through cable networks. There was, however, no cable television in Northern Ireland.

At the material time, no comprehensive weekly television guide was available on the market in Ireland or Northern Ireland owing to the policy of the organisations to which the decision was addressed regarding the dissemination of information on the programmes of the six channels referred to above. Each of those organisations published a specialised television guide containing only its own programmes and, under the United Kingdom Copyright Act 1956 and the Irish Copyright Act 1963, claimed copyright in its weekly programme listings, preventing their reproduction by third parties.

Those listings indicate programme content and specify the broadcasting channel, together with the date, time and title of each programme. They go through a series of drafts, which become increasingly detailed and precise at each stage, until a weekly schedule is finalised approximately two weeks before transmission. At that stage, as the decision states the programme schedules become a marketable product. With particular reference to the present case, it is to be noted that RTE reserved the exclusive right to publish the weekly programme schedules for RTE1 and RTE2 in the RTE Guide, its own magazine for presenting its programmes.

In 1988 the RTE Guide sold about 123,000 copies in Ireland and 6,500 in Northern Ireland, the prices being LIrl 0.40 and L0.50 respectively. Those figures indicate inter alia, according to the applicant, that in the Irish Republic only 11.5 per cent of households or other establishments with television, that is to say 3.7 per cent of viewers, bought the RTE Guide.

At the time of the adoption of the decision, the RTE Guide published the television programme listings for RTE1 and RTE2 only, supplemented by cast lists and synopses. It also contained short comments or articles, in Irish and English, concerning certain programmes, feature articles, background information, readers' letters and a considerable amount of advertising space.

At the material time, RTE's policy towards third parties with regard to information concerning its programmes was as follows: it provided daily and periodical newspapers with its programme schedules free on request, accompanied by a licence for which no fee was charged, setting out the terms on which that information might be reproduced. Daily newspapers could thus publish the daily listings or, if the following day was a public holiday, the listings for two days, subject to certain conditions as to the format of publication. Weekly and Sunday newspapers were also permitted to publish "highlights" of the week's television programmes. RTE ensured strict compliance with the licence conditions, by taking legal proceedings, where necessary, against publications which failed to comply with them.

The publisher Magill TV Guide Limited (hereinafter referred to as "Magill"), a company governed by Irish law, is a wholly owned subsidiary of Magill Publications Holding Ltd. It was established in order to publish in Ireland and Northern Ireland a weekly magazine containing information on the television programmes available to viewers in that area, the Magill TV Guide. After the publication on 28 May 1986 of an issue of the Magill TV Guide containing all the weekly listings for all the television channels available in Ireland—including RTE1 and RTE2—an Irish court, in response to an application from RTE, the BBC and ITP, issued an interim injunction restraining Magill from publishing weekly lsitings for those organisations' programmes. Following that injunction, Magill ceased its publishing activities. The substance of the case was considered in part by the High Court which, in a judgment of 26 July 1989 delivered by Lardner J, gave its ruling on the scope of the copyright in the programme listings under Irish law. The judge stated: "I am satisfied that each weekly schedule is the result of a great deal of preliminary consideration and work and the exercise of skill and judgment. It is the creation of RTE. I am satisfied by the evidence that RTE's weekly programme schedules as published in RTE Guide are literary works and compilations in the ordinary sense of the latter word within section 8 and section 2 of the Copyright Act 1963, that RTE have shown that they are entitled to copyright in these schedules and that the defendants by the publication of their TV Guide for the week 31 May to 6 June 1986, have breached that copyright by reproducing a substantial part of RTE's copyright material".

The Commission finds that because of the factual monopoly enjoyed by the broadcasting organisations over their respective weekly listings, third parties interested in publishing a weekly television guide are "in a position of economic dependence which is characteristic of the existence of a dominant position." Furthermore, the Commission adds, that monopoly is strengthened into a legal monopoly in so far as those organisations claim copyright protection for their respective listings. In those circumstances, the Commission observes, "no competition from third parties is permitted to exist on [the relevant] markets". From that it infers that "ITP, BBC and RTE each hold a dominant position within the meaning of Article 86."

The Commission rejects the argument that the conduct to which it objects is justified by copyright protection and states that in the present case ITP, the BBC and RTE "use copyright as an instrument of the abuse, in a manner which falls outside the scope of the specific subject-matter of that intellectual property right."

In the third part of its plea based on infringement of Article 86, the applicant denies that its programme information policy constituted an abuse within the meaning of Article 86. Essentially, it claims that by acting in the manner complained of in the decision, it was merely protecting the specific subject-matter of its copyright in its own programme listings, which cannot constitute an abuse within the meaning of Article 86.

The applicant relies on the judgment in Case 238/87, *VOLVO v. VENG* to maintain that the conduct complained of is covered by the protection afforded by Community law to the very subject-matter of its copyright in its listings. It claims that the only distinguishing feature in this case is that Magill is prevented from making a product for which it sees a market because of RTE's refusal to grant it a licence to publish its weekly listings, in which copyright subsists. The Court of Justice has accepted that such a refusal is lawful, holding in the aforementioned *VOLVO v. VENG* case, which concerned exclusive rights in registered designs, although its terms may also be applied to copyright, that "the right of the proprietor of a protected design to prevent third parties from manufacturing and selling or importing, without its consent, products incorporating the design constitutes the very subject-matter of his exclusive right. It follows that a refusal to grant such a licence cannot in itself constitute an abuse of a dominant position." Consequently, the applicant considers that the condemnation of its policy regarding its listings deprives it of the very substance of its copyright, in breach of the Community rules.

As regards the possibility, to which the Court of Justice drew attention in *VOLVO v. VENG*, of the abuse, within the meaning of Article 86 of an intellectual property right by its proprietor, the applicant states that no such conduct has been found by the Commission in this instance. It emphasises that the practices at issue were described as abusive in the decision, firstly on the ground that they prevented "the meeting of a substantial potential demand existing on the market for comprehensive TV guides" and, secondly, that their purpose was to protect the position of the RTE Guide on the market. The applicant observes that the Commission has not proved that there is a demand among consumers for a comprehensive guide. Moreover, in any event the circumstances just referred to do not justify undermining the very substance of its copyright by virtue of which "only RTE has the power to decide whether [the] schedules are published and if so by whom, in what form, etc." The refusal to grant a licence cannot therefore in any way be regarded as an abuse of a dominant position, even if there were a strong demand for the product which could have been produced under such a licence. The applicant also claims that, in the present case, its conduct cannot be regarded as abusive, in so far as it authorises and encourages the publication of complete daily television listings.

Similarly, the applicant rejects the Commission's argument that it sought to expand its licence to broadcast radio and television programmes to include a monopoly in the subsidiary market of publications. The applicant claims that its copyright in its listings and the exercise of that right are totally unrelated to its licence to broadcast. In the applicant's view, the copyright protection of its listings, as literary worked and compilations within the meaning of sections 2 and 8 of the Irish Copyright Act 1963, is itself sufficient to justify the conduct complained of, regardless of any consideration concerning its legal monopoly in national broadcasting.

The Commission further contends that the conduct for which RTE is criticised is different from that which the Court held to be lawful in the *VOLVO* judgment. It is apparent from that judgment that the fact that a car manufacturer who holds protective rights in a design reserves for himself the right to manufacture all spare parts for his cars does not in itself constitute an abuse. In the present case the Commission draws attention to the fact that the market in spare parts was within the area of Volvo's main business activity. By contrast, RTE was exploiting a dominant position in one market (the market in information on its programmes) which is within the area of its main activity—broadcasting—in order to obtain advantages in the publishing market, a separate economic activity, downstream. Moreover, the prejudice to consumers, who were denied access to a new product, namely a general television magazine for which there was a strong demand, is an aggravating factor which renders the applicant's policy as regards information on its weekly programmes abusive. On the other hand, the Commission emphasises, in the VOLVO case consumers were able to obtain the spare parts and competition was possible between independent repairers, and indeed between the various manufacturers themselves, since customers could opt for other makes if spare parts became too costly or difficult to obtain.

The Commission further states that its analysis of the abuse of copyright applies also to situations different from that at issue in this case, in the area of computer software for example.

In the absence of harmonisation of national rules or Community standardisation, the determination of the conditions and procedures under which copyright is protected is a matter for national rules.

The relationship between national intellectual property rights and the general rules of Community law is governed expressly by Article 36 of the Treaty, which provides for the possibility of derogating from the rules relating to the free movement of goods on grounds of the protection of industrial or commercial property. However, that derogation is explicitly made subject to certain reservations. The protection of intellectual property rights conferred by national law is recognised, in Community law, only subject to the conditions set out in the second sentence of Article 36. Under that provision, restrictions on free movement arising out of the protection of intellectual property "shall not constitute a means of arbitrary discrimination or a disguised restriction on trade between member-States." Article 36 thus emphasises that the reconciliation between the requirements of the free movement of goods and the respect to which intellectual property rights are entitled must be achieved in such a way as to protect the legitimate exercise of such rights, which alone is justified within the meaning of that article, and to preclude any improper exercise thereof likely to create artificial partitions within the market or pervert the rules governing competition within the Community. The exercise of intellectual property rights conferred by national legislation must consequently be restricted as far as is necessary for that reconciliation.

Under Article 36, only those restrictions on freedom of competition, free movement of goods or freedom to provide services which are inherent in the protection of the actual substance of the intellectual property right are permitted in Community law. In Case 78/70, DEUTSCHE GRAMMOPHON, which concerned a right similar to copyright, the Court of Justice held.

Although it permits prohibitions or restrictions on the free movement of products, which are justified for the purpose of protecting industrial and commercial property, Article 36 only admits derogations from that freedom to the extent to which they are justified for the purpose of safeguarding rights which constitute the specific subject-matter of such property.

It is common ground that in principle the protection of the specific subject-matter of a copyright entitles the copyright-holder to reserve the exclusive right to reproduce the protected work. The Court of Justice expressly recognised that in Case 158/86, *WARNER BROTHERS v. CHRISTIANSEN*, in which it held that "(the) two essential rights of the author, namely the exclusive right of performance and the exclusive right or reproduction, are not called in question by the rules of the Treaty."

However, while it is plain that the exercise of the exclusive right to reproduce a protected work is not in itself an abuse, that does not apply when, in the light of the details of each individual case, it is apparent that that right is exercised in such ways and circumstances as in fact to pursue an aim manifestly contrary to the objectives of Article 86. In that event, the copyright is no longer exercised in a manner which corresponds to its essential function, within the meaning of Article 36 of the Treaty, which is to protect the moral rights in the work and ensure a reward for the creative effort, while respecting the aims of, in particular, Article 86. In that case, the primacy of Community law, particularly as regards principles as fundamental as those of the free movement of goods and freedom of competition, prevails over any use of a rule of national intellectual property law in a manner contrary to those principles.

In the present case, it must be noted that the applicant, by reserving the exclusive right to publish its weekly television programme listings, was preventing the emergence on the market of a new product, namely a general television magazine likely to compete with its own magazine, the RTE Guide. The applicant was thus using its copyright in the programme listings which it produced as part of its broadcasting activity in order to secure a monopoly in the derivative market of weekly television guides. It appears significant, in that connection, that the applicant also authorised, free of charge, the publication of its daily listings and of highlights of its weekly programmes in the press in both Ireland and United Kingdom. Moreover, it authorised the publication of its weekly listings in other member-States, without charging royalties.

Conduct of that type—characterised by preventing the production and marketing of a new product, for which there is potential consumer demand, on the ancillary market of television magazines and thereby excluding all competition from that market solely in order to secure the applicant's monopoly—clearly goes beyond what is necessary to fulfil the essential function of the copyright as permitted in Community law. The applicant's refusal to authorise third parties to publish its weekly listings was, in this case, arbitrary in so far as it was not justified either by the specific needs of the broadcasting sector, with which the present case is not concerned, or by those peculiar to the activity of publishing television magazines. It was thus possible for the applicant to adapt to the conditions of a television magazine market which was open to competition in order to ensure the commercial viability of its weekly publication, the RTE Guide. The applicant's conduct cannot, therefore, be covered in Community law by the protection conferred by its copyright in the programme listings.

In the light of the foregoing considerations, the Court finds that, although the programme listings were at the material time protected by copyright as laid down by national law, which still determines the rules governing that protection, the conduct at issue could not qualify for such protection within the framework of the necessary reconciliation between intellectual property rights and the fundamental principles of the Treaty concerning the free movement of goods and freedom of competition. The aim of that conduct was clearly incompatible with the objectives of Article 86.

The applicant maintains that the granting of compulsory licences is incompatible with the Berne Convention. It considers that, since all the member-States of the Community are parties to the Berne Convention, that convention must be regarded as forming part of Community law and reflecting the relevant principles thereof, pursuant to Article 234 of the Treaty.

The applicant points out that Article 9(1) of the Convention confers on the author of a literary or artistic work the exclusive right of reproducing the protected work. Article 9(2), introduced by the Paris revision of 1971, it claims, allows a signatory State to permit the reproduction of literary and artistic works in certain special cases, provided that such reproduction does not conflict with a normal exploitation of the work and does not unreasonably prejudice the legitimate interests of the author.

The applicant infers that the decision is incompatible with the Berne Convention inasmuch as it conflicts with the normal exploitation of its copyright in the programme listings and seriously prejudices its legitimate interests.

The Commission contends, however, that the Berne Convention does not apply to the present case. The Community is not a party to the Convention, the Commission explains, and it has consistently been held that "in matters governed by the EEC Treaty, that Treaty takes precedence over agreements concluded between member-States before its entry into force." Moreover, the Berne Convention is not applicable in any event because, in the Commission's view, copyright within the meaning of that Convention cannot subsist in programme listings. However, even if the decision did cover information in which copyright subsisted, the Commission contends in the alternative that the fact that the information was provided free of charge to certain third parties for publication shows that compulsory licensing for a reasonable fee would not prejudice the legitimate interests of the applicant and would therefore be in conformity with the Berne Convention.

Logically, consideration must first be given to the problem of the applicability to the present case of the Berne Convention and to the Commission's argument that Community law takes precedence over the provisions of that Convention. In that regard, the Court observes, first of all, that the Community—to which, as Community law now stands, powers have not been transferred in the field of intellectual and commercial property—is not a party to the Berne Convention, which has been ratified by all the member-States. As regards conventions concluded by member-States, it must be noted that Article 234 of the Treaty governs the relationship between the provisions of the Treaty and international agreements concluded by the member-States before its entry into force. It provides: "The rights and obligations arising from agreements concluded before the entry into force of this Treaty between one or more member-States on the one hand, and one or more third countries on the other, shall not be affected by the provisions of this Treaty." Agreements concluded prior to the entry into force of the Treaty may not therefore be relied upon in relations between member-States in order to justify restrictions on trade within the Community.

In the present case concerning Ireland and the United Kingdom, it must be pointed out that, under Article 5 of the Act of Accession, Article 234 EEC applies to agreements or conventions concluded before their accession to the Community on 1 January 1973. In intra-Community relations, therefore, the provisions of the Berne Convention, ratified by Ireland and the United Kingdom before 1 January 1973, cannot affect the provisions of the Treaty. The applicant may not rely on them to justify restrictions on the system of freedom of competition established and implemented within the Community pursuant to the Treaty and, in particular, Article 86 thereof.

THE COURT (Second Chamber), HEREBY

1.   Dismisses the application;

2.   Orders the applicant to pay the costs, including those of the intervener.

THE SOFTWARE APPLICATION CONTROVERSY

"MAGILL" AND COMPUTER SOFTWARE.

Liam McNeive and Cyrus Mehta, Nabarro Nathanson,
89 Law Society's Gazette 27 (4 March 1992).

The decision of the EC Court of First Instance in *RTE, BBC and ITP v. EC Commission* [1991] 4 CMLR 586 (Magill) last July indicates that holders of copyright in a dominant position may be in breach of Art 86 of the Treaty of Rome if they refuse to license their copyright material to suppliers in downstream derivative markets. This decision has generated considerable debate in relation to the licensing of intellectual property rights (IRPs).

Under the Copyright Designs and Patents Act 1988, computer programs are accorded copyright protection as literary works. The right to reproduce, as well as to translate, adapt and distribute a copyright program, is reserved to the copyright owner. Consequently the use of any computer program without the licence of the owner will infringe the owner's copyright, since use necessarily entails reproduction of the program in the computer into which it is loaded.

Generally computer hardware cannot be operated without an operating system. The operating system causes computer hardware to carry out the instructions given by the application program (which provides the functions used by the computer operator, such as spread-sheet or word-processing). Application programs are often created by an entity other than the owner of the IRPs in the operating system. Where an application program is successful, downstream software suppliers may wish to create compatible application programs which provide further functions when used with the original application program.

There are four principal ways in which a downstream software supplier may be enabled to create these new application programs.

Decompilation. In decompiling (or reverse engineering) a program, a skilled person attempts by analytical and translation techniques to gain access to the source language instructions in which the program is written. The machine code which is processed by the computer is generated from this source code. The current position under UK law is that unauthorised decompilation is most likely to infringe the owner's copyright in the program decompiled, although some commentators disagree on the point.

Supply of interface information. This involves specifying the communicating elements of the original program sufficient for a new connecting program to be created. By comparison with decompilation, supply of interface information has the advantage that it does not require expensive and time-consuming engineering effort. However, it has the disadvantage that the person supplying the information is able to control the quality and quantity of the information disclosed.

Direct licensing of source code. This method is sometimes used in the markets for developmental and "building-block" software.

Copying of interface source code. The copying into a new program by a downstream software supplier of the source code comprised in a program's interface would, if that code were a "substantial part" of the original program, infringe copyright. However, a recent decision of the High Court on a preliminary issue casts doubt on whether interface source code will always satisfy the test of substantiality (*Total Information Processing Systems Ltd. v. Daman Ltd.*, 25 June 1991, unreported).

Except in cases where the supply of interface information or the licensing of source code are granted by the program's owner, the downstream software supplier must resort to decompilation or direct copying of source code in (probable) breach of the owner's copyright.

DOWNSTREAM SOFTWARE SUPPLIERS

A recital to the Software Directive states that the Directive's provisions are to be without prejudice to the application of Art 86 "if a dominant supplier refuses to make information available which is necessary for interoperability".

The Software Directive goes on, in its most controversial provision (art 6), to allow a person having a right to use a program to decompile it, but only to the extent necessary to create another program which communicates and interacts ('interoperates') with, but does not substantially replicate, the program decompiled. This right may not be excluded by contract.

The problem for the downstream software supplier is that to benefit from art 6, he or she must either have a right to use the program in question (in most relevant cases through a direct licence from the program's owner) or otherwise be authorised (although authorised by whom is not clear) and acting on behalf of a rightful user. It is likely that many downstream software suppliers will not fall into either of these categories, as dominant manufacturers may avoid granting licences to or "authorising" them.

Art 6 goes on to provide that the decompilation right may not be interpreted to unreasonably prejudice the "legitimate interests" of the program's owner or to conflict with the "normal exploitation" of that program. It remains to be seen whether the creation by a decompiler of an interoperable program for the use of others (rather than for the decompiler's own use) will be considered unreasonably prejudicial to the rights of the original program's owner. The owner would argue that the normal exploitation of a program legitimately entails the exploitation of its derivative markets—including the market for interoperating programs.

It is precisely because of these limitations and uncertainties in the Software Directive that downstream software suppliers may need to have recourse to remedies under art 86 to obtain the material necessary to create interoperable software.

Magill

The Court of First Instance's controversial decision in *Magill* (one of a number of recent competition law rulings which have tested the mettle of the new EC court) raises important questions about the extent to which dominant software manufacturers may be required to license copyright material in computer programs to downstream suppliers.

In *Magill*, the CFI had little difficulty in identifying additional extraneous factors which rendered the behaviour of the broadcasters abusive within the context of the supply of programme listings information. In the first place, it was considered that the broadcasters had already opened the door to the production and marketing of programme information by authorising publication of daily listings and weekly highlights (and indeed, by granting licences to print full weekly listings in other member states). In this context, their refusal to license weekly listings, having already generated a clear consumer demand for them, was unreasonably restrictive.

Secondly, the court regarded the broadcasters' restrictive licensing policy as an arbitrary measure designed to protect and preserve the monopoly position of their own individual weekly listings magazines. Thirdly, and perhaps most importantly, the refusal to authorise third parties to publish weekly listings had in the court's view artificially prevented the emergence and growth of a new product—a comprehensive weekly TV guide covering all channels—for which there was a large potential consumer demand, as evidenced by the success of similar publications in other member states. Indeed, the limiting of market growth is specifically warned against in sub-para (b) of Art 86, which states that abusive behaviour consists in particular in "limiting production markets or technical development to the prejudice of consumers".

These factors, in other contexts, have often been regarded as the classic ingredients of abusive conduct.

The decision raises three issues which are of immediate relevance to the computer software industry. First, *Magill* confirms the trend of the EC competition authorities towards very narrow product market definitions for the purposes of assessing dominance under Art 86. The relevant market in which RTE, BBC and ITP were found to be dominant was that for weekly (as opposed to daily) programme listings.

As much of the computer software industry comprises licensors with large shares of niche markets (such as software controlling clothing manufacture and for weapons guidance), the deployment of such narrow market definitions will make it hard to avoid the establishment of dominance.

Secondly, *Magill* may give some hope to third party maintainers of computer software (who at the least require access to the source code of the software to be maintained) that there may be circumstances in which they are entitled to compulsory licences of software from dominant software manufacturers. After all, in *Volvo* the ECJ accepted that a dominant car manufacturer may be in breach of Art 86 if it refuses to supply spare parts to an independent repairer. This situation may be (at least superficially) analogous in the software industry to the refusal of a dominant software manufacturer to license a program (or its source code) to a third party maintainer of that program.

Thirdly, *Magill* suggests that additional remedies may be available to the downstream software supplier prevented from creating an interoperable software product by a dominant manufacturer. IBM had previously indicated that timeous provision of interface information is one potential remedy available under Art 86. However, the downstream software supplier may wish to press for the right to decompile in these circumstances as an alternative (or possibly in addition) to the provision of interface information. The argument would be that it is incongruous that the downstream software supplier should be denied the right to decompile accorded to ordinary licensees of a program (under art 6 of the Software Directive), and therefore that it should have the right to be granted a licence (on payment of the normal fee).

Magill serves as a reminder to the software manufacturer that the Software Directive is not conclusive as to the rights of others who wish to create interoperable programs. The downstream software supplier and third party maintainer who are denied necessary information or a licence by the manufacturer may choose to take action under Art 86. A refusal to license in breach of Art 86 could expose the producer to the risk of a claim for third party damages and fines imposed by the EC Commission. It remains to be seen, however, whether the decision increases the vulnerability of dominant software manufacturers (or indeed other dominant holders of IPRS) to third-party complaints and proceedings—and indeed whether the appeal of the Magill judgment to the ECJ is successful.

Notes and Questions

1. Does the court's decision in the *Magill TV Guide* case qualify as a "taking" for which compensation should be provided?

2. Under Section 712 of the Restatement (Third) of the Foreign Relations Law of the United States "a state is responsible under international law for injury resulting from a taking by the state of the property of a national of another state that is not for a public purpose, or is discriminatory, or is not accompanied by provision for just compensation." The Restatement goes on to define "just compensation" as "in the absence of exceptional circumstances, an amount equivalent to the value of the property taken paid at the time of taking, or within a reasonable time thereafter with interest from the date of taking, and in a form economically usable by the foreign national." Has the court in the *Magill TV Guide* case provided for "just compensation" for the use being granted competitors of plaintiff's copyright protected work?

3. Has the court granted the defendants a compulsory license to use plaintiff's work, or have they said such uncompensated use is a "fair" one which requires *no* compensation?

4. TV directories are not the only form of copyrighted work that the law may require to be licensed in order to improve competition. As the above article demonstrates, computer software also presents unique problems of access and competitive need. One way of resolving the problem is through the grant of fair use rights to use the work in question to create competitive, *non-infringing* works. *See* Chapter Thirty–Seven. Can you distinguish the TV listings in the *Magill TV Guide* case from computer software to avoid the application of *Magill's* principles to such software?

5. In addition to granting compulsory licenses for categories of works (*i.e.,* patents that have not been worked in the country), some countries grant compulsory licenses for categories of *uses,* such as public or private performances. Thus, for example, numerous countries, such as Japan, Sweden and Denmark, have established statutory compulsory licenses for the rental of video tapes or sound recordings for private use. Others, such as the United States have established a compulsory license system for the production and distribution of sound recordings in non-dramatic musical works. *See, e.g.,* 17 U.S.C. § 115.

6. One of the biggest problems in establishing a statutory compulsory licensing system is establishing the amount and method for distribution of

the royalty to be paid under the license system. Assume that you were establishing a compulsory licensing system for the right to rent video tapes for home use. How would you determine the rate to be paid? Should it be a specified amount or should it vary depending on the fame of the licensed work? Who should collect the royalty and distribute it? The IP owner? A private collective rights organization? A government royalty tribunal? How should the royalty be levied? As an extra charge for every recorded video cassette? As an extra charge on every blank tape? How should the royalty be distributed? On what basis should the copyright owner of a recorded film be entitled to royalties? For a discussion of some of the problems in administering collective licenses, *see generally*, Gary S. Lutzker, *Dat's All Folks: Cahn v. Sony and the Audio Home Recording Act of 1991, Merrie Melodies or Looney Tunes?*, 11 Cardozo Arts & Ent. L.J. 145 (1992); Jane c. Ginsburg, *Reproduction of Protected Works for University Research or Teaching*, 39 U. Copyright Soc'y U.S.A. 181 (1992).

B. WHAT ARE THE PROBLEMS IN ADMINISTERING A COMPULSORY LICENSING SCHEME?

THE RENTAL RIGHTS CONTROVERSY

COPYRIGHT AND THE URUGUAY ROUND AGREEMENTS: A NEW ERA OF PROTECTION OR AN ILLUSORY PROMISE?

Doris Estelle Long, 22 AIPLA Quarterly Journal 531 (1995).

Compulsory Licensing And Rental Rights. Many countries require copyright owners to enter into compulsory licensing as a compromise between a copyright owner's economic interest in compensation and a public policy that allows unrestricted use of such works as an incentive to industrial growth. Essentially, the copyright owner receives an established royalty in exchange for a compelled license of the work. The collection of royalties required under a compulsory licensing system is often managed by collective licensing societies. On its face, such a collective licensing system may provide an acceptable balance between a copyright owner's economic interests and a nation's public policy interests. Restrictions on the ability of a copyright owner to receive the designated royalty, however, can undermine the benefits otherwise available under such a system. None of the developed countries seriously challenged the right of any country to provide for compulsory licensing agreements. The United States, however, objected to certain compulsory licensing schemes such as the French video levy which restricted recovery by foreign owners for a levy on blank videocassettes (to compensate copyright owners from losses due to home taping) to monies collected solely for authors. French companies, by contrast, could recover from the author's fund, the fund for performers, and the fund for French videogram producers. The United States objected to any exception to national treatment that would allow such discriminatory licensing schemes to remain unchallenged. The United States also objected to any provision that would allow for the rental of copyrighted phonorecords. Under U.S. copyright law, phonorecords may not be rented or otherwise distributed without the permission of the copyright owner. By contrast, Japan permits the unrestricted rental of phonorecords. Japanese law allows Japanese companies to ban rentals during the first year but allows no such ban by foreign record companies. The United States sought a standard in TRIPS identical to its own laws, which would prohibit commercial rental of phonorecords without the copyright owner's permission.

Commercial Rental Rights. TRIPS requires member countries to provide authors and their successors in title with the right to control the commercial rental to the public of both originals and copies of computer programs, cinematographic works, and phonograms. [In connection with the rental of cinematographic works, TRIPS allows countries to avoid granting such rental rights unless the rental of these works "has led to widespread copying of such works," which is "materially impairing the exclusive right of reproduction conferred in that member" country or their authors]. TRIPS does not exempt computer software or phonograms. However, exclusive rental rights are avoided for computer software rentals "where the program itself is not the essential object of the rental." With regard to the commercial rental of phonograms, any system for equitable remuneration or right holders in force as of April 15, 1994 (the date of the Ministerial Meeting concluding the Uruguay Round) may be maintained so long as such system "is not giving rise to the material impairment of the exclusive rights of reproduction of right holders."

Notes and Questions

1. The problem of administering rental rights programs for video tapes and sound recordings has been exacerbated by its international treatment as a subject for reciprocity. Does a reciprocal system, one which allows payment to foreign owners of a royalty for rentals of sound recordings or video tapes only if the foreign country grants similar rights, violate the national treatment provisions of TRIPS or Berne?

2. How would you demonstrate that rental materially impairs the exclusive right of reproduction? Does any rental of a copyrighted work have the necessary potential for unauthorized copying sufficient to trigger the prohibitions of TRIPS? Is there a greater or lesser possibility for unauthorized reproduction if a person rents a video game as opposed to a computer program?

THE GREY MARKET DRUG PATENT CASE
MERCK & CO. INC. v. PRIMECROWN LTD.

Court of Justice of the European Communities, 1996.
1996 ECJ CELEX LEXIS 4496.

FENNELLY, J.

The plaintiffs, Merck & Co. Inc. (hereinafter 'Merck'), claim that the defendants Primecrown Ltd and Others (hereinafter 'Primecrown') infringed their patents for a hypertension drug (known by the trade mark 'Innovace' in the United Kingdom and that of 'Renitec' elsewhere), for a prostate drug known by the trade mark 'Proscar' and for a glaucoma drug known by the trade mark Timoptol. The plaintiffs challenged the legality of importing into the United Kingdom Renitec and Proscar were from Spain and Timoptol from Portugal. Although Merck has patents in the United Kingdom for these products, it has no such patents in Spain or Portugal. The issue before the court was whether plaintiffs could prevent the parallel importation of patented products from countries in the European Union where no such patent protection existed.

Essentially the Court is asked to renounce or, alternatively, revise its 1981 judgment in *Merck v. Stephar*, [Case 187/80 1981 ECR 2063] that the rules contained in the Treaty [of Rome] concerning the free movement of goods prevent the proprietor of a patent for a medicinal product who has voluntarily marketed the product in one Member State which does not recognize the patentability of the product from invoking his national patent rights in other Member States to prohibit parallel imports of that product from the first Member State.

In *Merck v. Stephar* the Court held that the rules contained in the EEC Treaty concerning the free movement of goods, including the provisions of Article 36, must be interpreted as preventing the proprietor of a patent for a medicinal preparation who sells the preparation in one Member State where patent protection exists, and then markets it himself in another Member State where there is no such protection, from availing himself of the right conferred by the legislation of the first Member State to prevent the marketing in that State of the said preparation imported from the other Member State.

Merck filed for its British product patent covering Proscar (EP0155096) on 20 February 1985. This patent is due to expire on 20 February 2005 but, pursuant to Council Regulation (EEC) No 1768/92 of 18 June 1992 (13) concerning the creation of a supplementary protection certificate for medicinal products (hereinafter the SPC 'Regulation'), effective patent protection will last until 26 May 2007. The registration papers relating to Proscar were submitted in Spain in July 1991. Marketing authorization was granted in September 1993, whereupon the product was launched in Spain. Merck filed for its British product patent covering Renitec (0012401) on 10 December 1979. It will expire on 10 December 1999.

The national court explains that the problems in the main proceedings arise firstly because the patentees do not have, and never could have obtained, patent protection in Spain or Portugal for the products concerned. In addition, it says that prices in those countries are much lower than elsewhere in the European Union so that medicines sold by the patentees to wholesalers there are, instead of going to Spanish or Portuguese patients, immediately exported to other Member States.

Merck's primary argument is that the rule adopted by the Court in *Merck v Stephar* should be reconsidered so that a patentee will be deemed not to have exhausted his patent right in respect of a product only when he has had the opportunity of first marketing it in the Community with the protection of the patent and with the concomitant guarantee of absence of competition from unauthorized copies. It advances [several] principal arguments in support of this submission.

Firstly, at the time of *Merck v. Stephar*, the patentability of pharmaceuticals in Europe was the exception rather than the rule, whereas it is now recognized by most industrialized nations. Pharmaceuticals are now patentable in all EEA countries except Iceland.

The Community has in recent years emphasized the importance of patents to the pharmaceutical sector.

Moreover, the negative repercussions of the continued application of the *Merck v. Stephar* rule will be magnified following the entry into force of association agreements with the countries of central and Eastern Europe, as a result of the permanent non-patentability—due to lack of novelty—of pharmaceuticals first put on the market in those countries before pharmaceuticals became patentable there during the early 1990s. Merck submits that, when these countries join the EC, the *Merck v. Stephar* rule will apply to all pharmaceuticals originating or put on the market in these countries (where prices are on average up to 33% lower than in the EC).

Secondly, *Merck v. Stephar* significantly reduces the value of patents granted in the EC. Merck claims that the presence of unauthorized copies on the Spanish and Portuguese markets has enabled the authorities to use national price regulations to fix prices below the average level in the EC. Such copies can be launched before, at the same time as, or, in any event, within 12 months of, the launch of the original. At the hearing Merck submitted that the link between non-patentability and price levels was clearly demonstrated by the effect of the appearance of generic products once patents in Member States where patent protection is recognized have expired. A very rapid fall in price occurs both in contemplation of and in the aftermath of the end of the period of patent protection. Furthermore, Merck submitted at the hearing that the presence or absence of patent protection affects the bargaining position of pharmaceutical companies when negotiating with national authorities; if a generic alternative has been or is about to be launched, the price negotiating position of those authorities is strengthened vis-a-vis the patentee.

Merck maintains that parallel imports from Spain and Portugal generally work to the benefit of parallel traders rather than patients or national health authorities in the importing Member States, while exposing the proprietors of pharmaceutical patents to large losses by reducing the value and, thus, effectively shortening the patent life of affected products. It submits that, in the absence of common Community rules concerning the marketing of patentable products, obstacles to free movement within the Community designed to encourage research for pharmaceutical products should be accepted as necessary. In its third and fourth arguments, Merck submits that there can be no exhaustion of patent rights where such rights do not exist. In *Merck v. Stephar* the Court held that the specific subject-matter of a patent right does not guarantee that the patentholder will always obtain a reward for his creative effort, while Advocate General Reischl stated that it merely presented the patentee with an opportunity to obtain a recompense for his creative effort. Merck, on the other hand, submits that a reasonable reward for the patentee's creative effort is crucial to the pharmaceutical industry, given that the average cost of researching and developing a new medicinal product is now estimated at ECU 200 million. The survival of pharmaceutical companies depends on the profitability of a small number of successful products and on the regular renewal of portfolios of patents on new medicinal products. On average, out of every 10 000 substances synthesized by the pharmaceutical industry, only one or two will become marketable medicines. The huge risks involved make individual companies very vulnerable, not least because 90% of the cost of research is financed by the industry itself. The return on research investment depends on numerous market factors, including the commercial potential of the patented product and the early presence of substitute products. Substitute products include fast follower products which are therapeutically similar to the initial product but sufficiently differentiated to avoid patent infringement.

In these circumstances, Merck submits that a patent should be deemed to be exhausted only where the patentee consents to the use of that patent's essential and constant characteristic, namely the right to put the patented product on the market for the first time with the assurance that no unauthorized copies will be put on the market for the duration of the patent. Thus, the financial value of the product is protected from the competition of unauthorized cheaper copies. The mere receipt of a financial reward should not be regarded as exhausting the patent where the commercial potential of the product was limited by the absence of patentability. Merck relies upon *Pharmon v. Hoechst* where, in the context of a compulsory licence, the acceptance of royalties by the patentee was held not to have exhausted the patent, because they were not received in return for the voluntary exercise of the guaranteed property right. Merck cites the view of Advocate General Warner in his Opinion in *Musik-Vertrieb Membran v. GEMA* that there can be no exhaustion of rights where no rights exist'.

Fifthly, in *Warner Brothers v. Christiansen* (copyright) and *IHT Internationale Heiztechnik v. Ideal–Standard* (trade marks), Merck submits that the Court accepted that, in the absence of parallel levels of protection in both the exporting and importing Member States, Community law should not export the legislative policy of the former to the latter. Merck submits that this reasoning should apply a fortiori in respect of patents.

The *Merck v. Stephar* rule provides legal certainty to traders, the public and holders of industrial property rights because, according to Primecrown, national courts can normally readily assess whether the necessary consent exists. To accept Merck's argument, which is based on the need for the exhaustion of a parallel patent, would require national courts to determine whether the patent rights in the country of first marketing were equivalent to the patent rights in the country of importation. This could lead to fragmentation of the Common Market caused by major pharmaceutical companies, backed by their considerable financial resources, pursuing litigation against smaller parallel importers.

Finally, Primecrown claims that losses caused by parallel imports will not damage future research and development in the pharmaceutical industry. Firstly, it would be irrational to reduce prospective research on future patentable drugs by reason of losses on earlier unpatentable ones. Secondly, research is a worldwide activity; a product, once developed, can then be marketed worldwide in a climate which is increasingly favourable to pharmaceutical companies as a result of the progressive extension of patent protection flowing, *inter alia*, from Annex 19 to the Agreement on Trade–Related Aspects of Intellectual Property (hereinafter 'TRIPS') concluded as part of the Uruguay Round of GATT negotiations.

The plaintiffs have perhaps placed the greatest reliance on the judgment in *Warner Brothers v. Christiansen*. Danish law confers on the holder of copyright in video-cassette recordings the additional right to oppose the rental of the video-cassette even when it has been sold with the copyright holder's consent. The law of the United Kingdom, at the material time, did not grant any equivalent right. The voluntary sale by or on behalf of the holder of the copyright exhausted his rights in United Kingdom but not in Danish law. Mr. Christiansen purchased in London, for the express purpose of hiring it out at his video shop in Copenhagen, a video-cassette of a film the copyright of which was owned by Warner Brothers and which at the material time was not available in Denmark. Warner Brothers and its Danish assignee (Metronome Video ApS) obtained an injunction at first instance restraining the envisaged hiring-out but, on appeal, a reference was made to the Court asking essentially whether the legislative provisions permitting such a prohibition were compatible with Community law.

Mr. Christiansen argued that Warner Brothers had chosen to market the video-cassette in the United Kingdom. If it had been marketed in Denmark or Germany the authors' remuneration would have been appreciably lower than it was in the United Kingdom 'since the high

(British) sale-price of the cassette included a component to cover the intellectual property rights represented by the possibility of hiring it out'. [Thus, having chosen to market its product, Christiansen contended Warner Brothers could not thereafter control its subsequent distribution in the European Union.]

In its observations the Commission pointed out the serious potential loss of revenue for copyright owners in view of the increased popularity of renting as opposed to purchasing video-cassettes. In its view, the fact that not all Member States recognize such a right should not prevent copyright owners from relying on the laws of those which do.

The Court, taking account of the evolution in market conditions, endorsed the Commission's submission that a specific market for the hiring-out of video-cassette recordings had emerged, stating that laws designed to guarantee to makers of films a remuneration which reflects the number of occasions on which the video-cassettes are actually hired out and which secures for them a satisfactory share of the rental market are justified on grounds of the protection of industrial and commercial property pursuant to Article 36 of the Treaty. It followed that: it cannot therefore be accepted that the marketing by a film-maker of a video-cassette containing one of his works, in a Member State which does not provide specific protection for the right to hire it out, should have repercussions on the right conferred on that same film-maker by the legislation of another Member State to restrain, in that State, the hiring-out of that video-cassette.

In my opinion the decision in *Warner Brothers v. Christiansen* amounts to a fundamental departure in the Court's approach to the relationship between copyright and the free movement of goods. Warner Brothers undoubtedly profited from the voluntary sale of the video-cassette to Mr. Christiansen in the United Kingdom, but the Court nevertheless ruled that it could still invoke its Danish copyright to restrict the further exploitation by Mr. Christiansen of that cassette. Applying this approach to *Merck v. Stephar*, I cannot but conclude that the exploitation by Merck in Italy of its patented products, where no patent right whatsoever was recognized by Italian law, should not have been viewed as exhausting its exclusive patent right in the Netherlands. To paraphrase slightly the language used by the Court at paragraph 18 (quoted at paragraph 132 above) of its judgment in *Warner Brothers v. Christiansen*, it cannot therefore be accepted that the marketing by a patentee of a patented product, in a Member State which does not recognize the patent right, should have repercussions on the right conferred on that same patentee by the legislation of another Member State to restrain, in that State, the parallel importation of that product. In plain terms, the patentee should not have to bear the consequences of marketing in a Member State where its patent right is not recognized.

The exhaustion doctrine is based on the availability of parallel prerogatives in both the country of exportation and that of importation; a decision applying the doctrine in the absence of such parallelism would be tantamount to lowering the protection available in the country of importation to the level of the less protective legislation of the country of exportation, thus operating a choice of legislative policy which must be left to the Member States. In my opinion, there is no convincing reason associated with the freedom of movement of goods why the previous Spanish and Portuguese policies of refusing to recognize the patentability of pharmaceutical products should be imposed upon other Member States, who abandoned that particular policy many years before the Act of Accession required Spain and Portugal to follow suit.

I believe that the Court incorrectly emphasized the requirements of free trade at the expense of national patent rights in *Merck v. Stephar*. While I am led to believe that the balance struck in that judgment should no longer be applied, I also think that the Court should carefully consider the need to limit the retroactive effect of a new judgment which rejects the reasoning underlying *Merck v. Stephar*.

I recommend that the questions referred to the Court should be answered as follows:

(3) The rules contained in the EC Treaty concerning the free movement of goods, including the provisions of Article 36, should be interpreted as not preventing the proprietor of a patent for a pharmaceutical product who sells that product in one Member State where patent protection exists, and who also markets it in another Member State at a time when that proprietor is unable to obtain such protection for that product, from availing himself of the right conferred by the law of the first Member State to prevent the marketing in that State of units of the said product imported from the other Member State. This interpretation should have effect only from the date of the Court's judgment in the present cases.

Notes and Questions

1. *Exhaustion of Rights.* Where nations join in regional affiliations to eliminate trade barriers and create free trade zones (such as with NAFTA and the European Union), the issue of the scope of protection to be afforded intellectual property rights—particularly the ability to control grey market imports—becomes problematic. Grey market goods are those goods which are lawfully produced in one country and then imported into another country without the consent of the intellectual property owner. "Exhaustion" means that once an IP-protected good has been sold the IP owner has no further right to control its distribution—he has "exhausted" his rights. In *Warner Brothers* (discussed in the case above) the concern was over the ability to assert video rental rights; *Stephar* (also discussed in the case above) the ability to prohibit the importation of a domestically patented product from a state where no patent rights existed. Is there a fundamental difference in the nature of copyrights and patents that would warrant different treatment under exhaustion of rights principles?

2. Based on the court's discussion in the *Grey Market Drug* case regarding the Danish rental royalty system, what are some of the problems

in administering a compulsory licensing system? What solutions would you propose to resolve these problems?

3.   For a further discussion of European Union issues in international IP protection, including grey market and exhaustion issues, see Part XI.

Problem

You represent the Internet Protection League, a trade association which represents the interests of authors of various copyrighted works, including books, photographs and music, who are concerned about protecting their rights in the new digital environment. They have hired you to draft proposed legislation that would establish a compulsory licensing system for copyrighted materials used on the Internet. In drafting the proposed legislation, consider the issues raised in the following criticism of such compulsory licensing systems:

While legislatively determined licensing of this sort does appear to reduce certain transaction costs, a compulsory license involves costs and problems of its own. First, Congress would have to devise a schedule of royalties, thus encouraging lobbying. Rights holders would spend money to persuade Congress to set high rates for each type of content (music, text, photographs, etc.), while potential buyers would argue for low royalties to stimulate growth in the industry. Congress is as likely to be influenced by lobbying as by underlying economic logic. Even if Congress gets it right, the money spent to educate Congress is wasted. The industry could get the same deal without many of these costs. Even if the royalties made sense when enacted, there is a good chance that conditions in the industry will change over time. Indeed, if past experience with compulsory licenses is any guide, the royalty rates might well become "locked in," and therefore subject to only very modest changes over time.

Industry participants faced with the need to transact over and over again could probably work out something much more in tune with their needs than a congressional scheme of one-size-fits-all transactions. The necessity of coming together to negotiate would produce pressure to come up with some system for handling these transactions. It might be a simple system, such as some basic "rules of thumb," widely shared in the industry, about how much each piece of content should cost. Or it could be more elaborate—maybe even entailing some administrative structure for setting royalties and settling disputes about the proper royalty rate. Whatever institutional structures the content owners and users devised, they would reflect the expertise of these industry insiders. Even more important, they could be changed over time by industry participants. For these reasons, private, voluntary organizations of this kind would be superior to state-mandated compulsory licenses. (Robert P. Merger, *Contracting Into Liability Rules: Intellectual Property Rights and Collective Organizations*, § 4 Calif. L. Rev. 1293 (1996)).

How would you deal with these criticisms? Who would oversee your compulsory licensing system—an agency of the U.S. government or a private licensing society such as ASCAP (American Society for Composers, Authors and Publishers)(U.S.), GEMA (Gesellschaft für Musikalische Aufführungs und Mechanische Verviel fältigungsrechte) (Germany) or SACEM (Société des Auteurs, Composteurs et Editeurs de Musique) (France). How would the royalty rate be established in your licensing system? What other problems do you anticipate?

PROPOSAL FOR A WORLDWIDE INTERNET COLLECTING SOCIETY: MARK TWAIN AND SAMUEL JOHNSON LICENSES

Alan R. Kabat, 45 J. Copyright Soc'y U.S.A. 329 (1998).

A.   COLLECTING SOCIETIES AS THEY EXIST TODAY.

Collecting societies, which trace their origins to the 1850s, arose from the inability of musical authors and publishers to monitor the transient performances of the numerous musical works in their repertoire. At the present, there are over 240 collecting societies and related organizations, the majority covering performance and/or reproduction rights in musical works. Many of these collecting societies operate under the principle of blanket licensing: the user, invariably a commercial establishment, pays the collecting society one fee, typically a fixed percentage of the user's gross revenues, which allows the user access to all of the works in the society's repertoire. [Instead of the cumbersome individual monitoring and metering of each use of each work, the blanket license represents a new "product" which significantly reduces the transaction costs for all parties.] Musical works societies are both the oldest and the best developed of all collecting societies. I shall describe and differentiate their licenses and rights protected, since they provide a useful starting point . First, none of these societies licenses all possible rights in a single musical work, although many will license some of the diverse bundle of rights inherent in copyright. The best known right to be licensed is the public performance right. This allows a musical work to be played or sung in a public forum, traditionally a restaurant or nightclub, and in this century by radio, television, motion picture (*i.e.*, the synchronization license, separate from a performing license), and most recently online through the Internet. The United States alone has three performing rights collecting societies—ASCAP, BMI, and SESAC—and most developed countries have their own such societies.

However, in order to perform a musical work (as opposed to a sound recording), it is often necessary to reproduce and/or distribute the underlying lyrics and notes, either to the performers (so that they may learn the music), or, more recently, to the public (as transmitted through the Internet). This invokes the reproduction and distribution rights, which are distinct from the public performance right. In the United States, the Harry Fox Agency is the best known of these "mechanical" rights collectives, which is a compulsory license, as opposed to the nonexclusive (voluntary) performing rights license. Thus, separate licenses may have to be obtained in order for a commercial enterprise to use a single musical work.

The traditional justification for collective blanket licensing—the difficulty of monitoring, let alone metering, uses of a musical work—

becomes less and less compelling in the online world. In the 1850s, or even the 1980s, a musical copyright owner could scarcely be expected to keep track of the thousands of public fora (physical or broadcast) where her works could be performed. However, the Internet eventually will offer copyright owners the potential to use comparatively inexpensive electronic means to survey the online world to determine who is performing their works, how often, and whether for revenue or gratis. Indeed, the U.S. Supreme Court noted that "of course changes brought about by new technology or new marketing techniques might also undercut the justification for the practice [of blanket licensing]." Although written nearly two decades ago, these judicial musings surely apply with full force to cyberspace.

NEED FOR A WORLDWIDE INTERNET COLLECTING SOCIETY.

The foregoing discussion may lead some to conclude that the preexisting collecting societies are sufficient for the Internet world—all we need is an extension of their licenses into cyberspace, with requisite fine-tuning of the contractual terms. I reject this assumption, for three reasons: (1) none of these societies license all possible uses of all possible works which a single web site may want to use, thus forcing a web operator to obtain a multitude of disproportionately expensive licenses in order to use multimedia works on her web site; (2) even for a single category of works, a web operator may have to obtain several licenses for a single right (*i.e.*, ASCAP, BMI, and SESAC, merely to perform a variety of musical works), and yet another license for another right in these same works (*i.e.*, Harry Fox, merely to distribute or reproduce the musical works); (3) none of these licenses recognize the fair use doctrine, as all expect that even a de minimis use must be licensed; and (4) the effectively compulsory nature of these licenses is not necessarily in the copyright owners' best interests.

A. SINGLE SET OF STANDARDS.

First and foremost, a [Worldwide Internet Collecting Agency] WICS would operate under a single set of contractual standards, rather than the current balkanized situation, where not only are there separate standards from country to country, but even among similar collecting societies within the same country. This uniformity would significantly reduce transaction costs: instead of using the reciprocal arrangements with the collecting societies in (potentially) some 180+ countries (and usually requiring more than one license per country), a web site operator can sign one agreement to cover the entire borderless cyberspace. This is essential because not only can the Internet, in theory, be accessed from each country of the world, but also because many lesser-developed countries have no mechanisms available for the collective licensing of copyrighted works, thus requiring individual transactions for each work.

However, I recognize several problems in this realm which cut against having uniform standards. One is the fact that neither contract law nor the scope and duration of copyright protections are uniform from country to country. Despite the harmonization and minimum standards required by the Berne Convention and (more recently) the 1994 TRIPS [agreement] countries remain free to provide more than the minimum baselines. This results in the "copyright gulf" whereby a work that is in the public domain in one country, which has a short term of protection, remains protected in another country, which has a longer term of protection. Similarly, one country may choose to protect a category of rights (e.g., moral rights) or works (e.g., databases) which other countries do not recognize, or protect at low levels.

It would be needlessly cumbersome for a WICS to have to track the divergent copyright laws of 180+ countries in order to determine the extent of protection available for each work in its repertoire. This would significantly increase the transaction costs of Internet licensing, which cuts against the *raison d'etre* for the Internet—its low cost and rapid responsiveness in contrast to traditional media. I can foresee no ready resolution for this problem, other than to suggest that the WICS be somehow treated as extraterritorial and subject only to meeting the minimum Berne/TRIPS requirements, but not any greater protections provided by individual countries. As demanded by the Berne Convention and TRIPS, it will be essential to agree upon a single set of standards-rights and works protected-in order for the WICS to operate so as to provide the greatest economic and intellectual benefits to all parties involved: authors, publishers, and the general public.

B.   Elimination of Piracy and Rogue Countries

Second, the WICS should serve as an effective mechanism for protecting authors and publishers (collectively, copyright owners), from the economic losses resulting from piracy and from those countries which do not provide adequate copyright protections.

TWO PROPOSALS FOR STRUCTURING A WORLDWIDE INTERNET COLLECTING SOCIETY.

Specifically, the Mark Twain Blanket License is a modified compulsory, blanket license which represents a quantum improvement upon the present collecting society systems. The Samuel Johnson Object License is a modified transactional, object-specific license, which also represents a quantum improvement upon the present systems for using works (or rights) not encompassed by present-day collecting societies.

A.   Common Issues.

There are eight common issues which must be resolved for any licensing system, Internet-based, or otherwise. I will describe my resolution for these issues with regard to the proposed WICS and will contrast these resolutions with the present systems.

1.   Management.

The Internet is respected for, or notorious because of, its seeming anarchy: it has the apparent or actual freedom of being able to disregard the present legal regimes, largely because no one governmental authority has legal control over its borderless operations. Indeed, much of the reluctance of the traditional print/broadcast media towards moving on-line has stemmed from their difficulty in monitoring or metering the online uses of their copyrighted materials. In order to facilitate the maximum online availability of intellectual property without destroying the author's economic interests, it will be desirable to have a central legal authority capable of enforcing intellectual property rights in cyber-space. Although national collecting societies and copyright owners using anti copying protection techniques may be able to protect their works in most situations, there will inevitably be pirate users or rogue nations, which can be reached, if at all, by such a central legal body.

2. Enforcement Mechanisms.

I then propose that enforcement mechanisms would be provided through a multi-tier system. If a copyright owner had an infringement claim—or a user had a defense that an owner was claiming protection where none was legally warranted—then as a first remedy, WIPO [the proposed administrative body] would provide a dispute resolution mecha-nism, through a form of non-binding arbitration which could rapidly resolve the problem at low litigation expenses. If arbitration was not successful for both parties (as would assuredly happen with pirates!), then they could proceed to litigation. To avoid "forum-shopping" by either party, I would stipulate a choice-of-law provision that specifies not only that the courts of one country would be used, but also that the court be limited to applying the contractual terms and rights recognized under the WICS. Thus, a complainant could not use the more generous copyright provisions of her own country (*e.g.*, on copyright term or moral rights), but would be limited to the WICS minima. Finally, if multiple user entities in one country were not in compliance, and the country's government was "protecting" these rogue entities, then I would consider proposing that WIPO be allowed to impose trade sanctions on behalf of all other member countries through the World Trade Organization, as part of the 1994 TRIPS Agreement (although this last proposal may prove too impractical at the present time).

3. Metes and Bounds of the Copyright Rights.

As should be obvious, I believe that the current collecting societies are severely and needlessly restricted by their fragmentation in terms of the rights protected. This historical schism arose from the divergent interests of copyright owners: *e.g.*, songwriters (authors) and musicians (performers) are competing for royalties from musical performances. There are separate collecting societies for cable retransmission rights and other audiovisual rights, dramatic staged works and screenplays, pictorial, graphical and sculptural works, translation, performance and lending of literary works, performance, reproduction, and distribution of musical works, performance of phonograms, and copying of literary works. Thus, a multimedia web site faces a panoply of licenses merely to be in compliance with the copyright laws of one country; additional expenses are necessary in order to comply with those of all other countries where each web site can be accessed. Even if a web site is limited to a single category of works, its operator may need to get separate licenses for distributing and performing those works.

Therefore, the proposed WICS will encompass all copyright rights which are widely recognized on an international basis, other than the moral right of integrity. Thus, the WICS will provide one-stop licensing to cover (1) reproduction onto the web site, (2) preparation of derivative works; (3) distribution of the works over the Internet; (4) performance of the work on the web site; and (5) passive displaying of the work. Although this "bundle of rights" is obviously derived from the exclusive rights under Section 106 of the U.S. Copyright Act, I believe that it meaningfully encompasses the rights inherent in the online use by one person of another's copyrighted works. In particular, for multimedia works, it will not be necessary to separately license individual "sticks"— one can license the entire bundle in a single transaction.

4. Moral Rights.

The WICS should have little difficulty enforcing the first two moral rights—those of publication and attribution, since the user's use of a copyrighted work can be made conditional upon the original authorship being credited on the user's web site, and an author would not make her work accessible in an online format until she was ready to disclose it to the public. The WICS, ironically, could be a quite easy mechanism for enforcing the fourth and least recognized right, that of withdrawal, since technological measures could be taken to not only remove a work from its original posted site but also to retrieve it from all its licensed users, perhaps with compensation for termination of the license.

It is the third moral right—that of integrity—which is most problematic for the WICS. Consider the present day collecting societies: the copyright owners invariably have no control over who can license their works, as long as the licensees are willing to pay the requisite license fees. Thus, for example, an American gospel songwriter cannot stipulate that her works can only be sung on religious occasions: if an unsavory nightclub singer or rapper wants to sing her song in what she perceives to be a blasphemous setting, she will have no recourse under the copyright statute or the terms of her license to a musical collective society. Even if her work is parodied by another so that its integrity is assuredly harmed, she may still have no cause of action. Although some other countries, notably France, provide broader protections through their copyright law of the right to integrity, the significant international disparities in this area mean that there is no one generally accepted level of protection. I believe that the Internet only magnifies the problems inherent in protecting the right to integrity, since it can be all too easy for a user to take another's work and place it into an online context which, while not necessarily defamatory, severely comprises the integrity of the author's original work. For example, one organization might set up a "fake" web site that misuses copyrighted materials from another "enemy" organization, thus damaging the integrity of those works.

5. Fair Use.

I have already alluded to the problems of fair use in a licensing regime, contrasting the views of the copyright minimalists (and moderates, for that matter) with the collecting societies. Obviously a line has to be drawn, and I propose a pragmatic compromise that will optimize the balance between the public interests and the economic interests of the author/copyright owners. My modest compromise is based on an analogy with bookstores and record outlets. Anyone can enter any bookstore (other than "adult") and can browse through any printed item in their stock. Similarly, many record stores offer a media-wall where one can listen to a number of top hits or sale titles on individual headsets. In neither case is the browser or listener under any obligation to purchase the copyrighted works, unless perchance they should damage the item. However, if the browser or listener wants to have a copy of the work, then she must purchase it; to take the work otherwise is theft.

As a first approximation, I propose that the WICS should allow an individual user to merely "view" or "listen" to a copyrighted work, on a one-time basis, at no charge. If the user wants to use the work a second time, or if the user wants to download a copy (either to her printer or to her computer or website), then she will be charged an appropriate license fee. However, if the user only wants to download an excerpt of the copyrighted work, then she would be able to do so, under the fair use doctrine, without having to pay a license fee. I would still require that she respect the author's moral rights of attribution and withdrawal.

6. Monitoring and Metering of Use: Copyright Management Systems.

The essential technological component for the WICS is the ability for copyright owners and the WICS itself to monitor and meter the online uses of copyrighted works. The aforementioned baseline estimate of 320 million web pages is a sobering reminder of the vastly increased number of public fora presented by the Internet, and suggests that current monitoring and metering techniques will have to be modified or replaced by more sophisticated protocols.

Fortunately, inventors have come up with devices that, taken together, encompass several attributes essential to the WICS: (1) each copyrighted work, or copyrighted segment thereof, is electronically "tagged" with a unique digital object identifier (DOI) that identifies the copyright owner; (2) this DOI is linked to a transactional database that allows the user to enter into a transaction for her choice of a number of potential uses (corresponding to the various exclusive rights of the copyright owner) for that copyrighted work; (3) both the copyright owner and the user can readily tailor the transaction to the desired level of compensation and use, and (4) any attempt by the user to circumvent the DOI or the transaction process automatically destroys the computer file containing the copyrighted work itself, which remains encrypted until the user receives authorization from the collecting society or copyright owner.

Indeed, even copyright minimalists and moderates have recognized that licensing combined with an encryption-based management system is probably the best approach for using copyrighted works in cyberspace, although some of the minimalists might not want to recognize copyright interests in the underlying print work itself. One criticism which most have overlooked is the potential "Big Brother" nature of DOIs—if the copyright owner itself is allowed to "know" who is using each of its works, and how its works are being used, then we will have entered a world vastly different from today's world, where copyright owners have relatively little or no specific information about their users. For example, a magazine publisher currently will know a little about its subscribers, but essentially nothing about third parties whom the subscriber allows to read the copy, let alone the newsstand purchasers. Similarly, bookstore owners record the purchases made by credit card (but not cash) customers; such records can even be subject to prosecutorial subpoenas. Although privacy issues are beyond the scope of copyright law, I recognize their importance in cyberspace, and note that the interposition of the WICS between the copyright owner and the user can shield the latter from the former. This would occur if specific identifying information about the user is not transferred from the WICS to the copyright owner; instead the owner learns only about the general nature of the uses of her work. Thus, the WICS should serve to enhance anonymity in the online world. Indeed, the WICS itself could be shielded from users who use anonymous "cybercash" as opposed to an individual charge account.

Another potential criticism is that DOIs may be overused, since a copyright owner, instead of using one DOI for an entire work, will be tempted to divide up her work into numerous subcomponents (e.g., chapters or even paragraphs of a literary work; individual photographs in a newsmagazine; perhaps even the verses of a multi-verse song) and attach a separately chargeable DOI to each fragment of her overall work, even though most works have intellectual value in their entirety but not as chopped-up segments. Ultimately, I believe that the marketplace will sort out the overzealous chargers from those who recognize a more rational approach in making their works available to the public in an intellectually meaningful fashion.

Although there are competing technological mechanisms available, some tailored to a specific medium, it will be necessary to adopt a uniform system applicable to all copyrightable works. Not only will this reduce transaction costs, but also it will eliminate any conflicts of licensing terms as applied to multimedia works. I do not advocate that any one of the currently existing or proposed systems be adopted in too, but recommend that computer and copyright experts make a careful comparison of all such systems, perhaps as a part of an industry-wide team effort to produce a single system that combines the best features from each mechanism. Most importantly, the system as ultimately used must be able to accommodate the fair use doctrine based upon my aforementioned pragmatic proposal to adapt fair use to cyberspace.

To ensure the effectiveness of these technological measures, it will be necessary for each country to enact effective anticircumvention measures to prevent hackers from disabling the measure in order to use the copyrighted work in an infringing manner. Even if the DOI is linked with a "disabler" that destroys the computer file once it is tampered with, I am confident that some hackers will be able to circumvent the disabler function. Thus, meaningful legal remedies for copyright owners and the WICS are needed, and indeed the 1996 WIPO Copyright Treaty requires such legislation which should suffice for the WICS.

7. *Licensing Mechanism: Uploader Pays or Downloader Pays?*

Another issue, often overlooked by commentators, concerns the relative role of the various online parties. Let us suppose that User A, on his computer, downloads several songs as sung by the Beatles, together with copyrighted photos of the Beatles, and several John Lennon obituaries in their entirety, all of which he then uploads to his web server in order to create a Beatle fan web site. User B, on several occasions, visits this web site, and downloads, in their entirety, several of the works to her own web site. Who pays, and when? Under one hypothetical scenario, User A would have to pay not only for downloading, then uploading these works to his web site, but also for each time other users download from his web site. This scenario shifts all the costs to the first user, and transforms secondary users into free riders. A more precisely crafted scenario would charge User A only for downloading, then uploading these works to his web site, with subsequent users being charged for their own downloading, and further uses of works, from A's web site. This latter scenario would continue, ad infinitum, as each work is copied and recopied (or transmitted and retransmitted) through the online world. Although it would require sophisticated technological linking to ensure that the WICS maintains "contact" with each copy of the work throughout its downstream peregrinations, this latter scenario better allocates the costs among the users, and ensures that copyright owners will continue to receive economic benefits throughout the term of protection of their works.

8. *Compulsory or Conditional Licensing?*

The final common issue, and one which in fact leads to the essential difference between my two proposed WICS licenses, concerns whether the license is to be a blanket license, or a conditional, transactional license. As discussed previously, most collecting societies, especially those for musical performance rights, operate under the former paradigm: the user pays a set fee which covers an unlimited number of performances of all the works in the collecting society's repertoire. The individual copyright owners have no say over the license fee or uses for their works, although they do have a choice of performing rights collecting societies (which are voluntary, unlike the compulsory mechanical rights licenses). In contrast, a conditional, transactional license would be object-specific, and could also allow the parties to individually negotiate a fee based upon the nature of the use of the copyrighted work.

I recognize that the former system has its advantages for a user who wants to use a diverse number of works, such as a web site that performs, on a rotating basis, numerous musical videos (analogous to MTV). However, the "one-size-fits-all" blanket license is poorly adapted to the majority of web sites, which usually only want to use a few copyrighted works, and perhaps only extracts thereof. Thus, the latter transactional system would better serve the needs of the majority of web sites, and would also return some measure of control to the copyright owners themselves, as opposed to the collecting societies. Therefore, instead of mandating that the proposed WICS adopt a single licensing system, I recommend that both systems be adapted for the online world.

B.   MARK TWAIN BLANKET LICENSE.

The first WICS license system that I propose is a modified blanket license, derived in its general principles from those used by musical performing rights collective societies such as ASCAP, BMI, and SESAC. This license would be of greatest interest to commercial web site operators—those who desire to use large numbers of diverse copyrighted works, and who expect to generate revenue from the users of their web sites, either directly through subscriptions or indirectly through framed advertising. Thus, the web site operator would pay a fee, based not merely upon the web site revenues, but also upon the proportion of the web site occupied by licensed works, as opposed to the operator's own intellectual property. A subscription web site which comprised nothing but musical videos would pay a higher fee than a web site (generating the same revenue) for which musical videos comprised only a small portion of the total informational content. Similarly, the ASCAP and BMI Internet licenses do adjust the license fee based on the extent to which the copyrighted works comprise the overall web site.

Another modification is that the blanket license for WICS should allow for some level of price discrimination according to the nature of the copyrighted work or rights thereof. There could be one "global" license fee to cover all uses of all works, with proportionately smaller licenses for (a) uses of some kinds of works but not others (*e.g.*, musical works but not PGS works), and/or (b) uses of some rights but not others (*e.g.*, performance but not preparation of derivative works). Nonetheless, in keeping with the need to minimize transaction costs for a blanket license, I would still retain a uniform license fee for each category of works or rights, instead of engaging in variable pricing according to the economic demand for individual works. Thus, I recognize the inapplicability of the fair use doctrine on behalf of the potential users of a blanket license: their commercial uses are so pervasive on their web site, that none of the traditional fair use factors would be available to exculpate unlicensed uses by these entities.

One limitation of traditional blanket licensing systems needs to be addressed before entering the online world: that prices are set by the collecting society itself, and not as a function of economic supply and demand. Even where there is, in theory, competition between collecting societies (*e.g.*, ASCAP vs. BMI vs. SESAC), the present perception among some is that their pricing reflects cartelization of the market. I suggest that a way to avoid this problem, instead of having the WICS unilaterally set prices, is to establish a coordinating committee, analogous to the Copyright Clearance Center, composed of both users and authors (not just publishers, but also the individual creators themselves!) to agree, through a process of collective bargaining or negotiation (moderated by the WICS), on the licensing fees for the various components of the blanket license. These fees can be periodically adjusted, either for inflation, or to reflect changes in the supply and demand for various works or rights thereof.

C.   SAMUEL JOHNSON OBJECT LICENSE.

The second WICS license system that I propose is a modified object-specific, or transactional license, in which each object, or right thereof, has its own set of license fees. These license fees are individually calibrated not only according to the extent to which the object is used and the exclusive rights invoked, but also according to the nature of the user's web site (commercial revenue generating or personal). This license would be advantageous to the personal user or the small-time commercial user, either of whom would typically use only a few copyrighted works, as a small component of their web sites. For the commercial user, it is expected that the use of the copyrighted works would contribute but a small fraction of the revenue generated from the web site itself.

For either commercial or personal user, I recognize the applicability of the statutory fair use doctrine (in contrast to the blanket licensees), based on my aforementioned pragmatic resolution of this doctrine to the online world. However, I would expect that a web site which continuously displays/performs an excerpt from a single copyrighted work would be less likely to qualify than one that uses a series of such excerpts, on a nonrepetitive basis. The full resolution of the fair use problem in the online world is beyond the scope of this paper; I can only suggest some approaches towards this difficult issue.

At present, some collecting societies allow for such individualized licenses; the best examples are those for PGS works, for which there is individualized demand: *e.g.*, a typical user will want to use only one photograph, not the entire repertoire of a society. The traditional obstacle towards such systems has been their high transaction costs (typically 15% for performing rights societies), since each use must be individually licensed and negotiated. The online world can only succeed if these costs are driven downwards to the absolute minimum, so that both user and copyright owner can obtain the maximum economic benefit from their transaction, as opposed to the middleman (= collecting society). Fortunately, the use of DOIs will facilitate the reduction of transaction costs, as their electronic mechanisms will minimize online transaction costs. This will allow object-specific transactional online licenses for not only PGS works, but also any and all copyrighted works.

Notes and Questions

1.   Which of the proposed licensing systems—Mark Twain or Samuel Johnson—do you believe is the better system? Why?

2.   Based on the above article, what changes, if any, would you make in your proposed Internet licensing legislation?

3.   The Internet poses the most recent challenge to the development of a workable collective rights administrative system. Do the proposals contained in the above excerpt resolve the problems which you identified in developing a workable collective rights organization?

4.   Are there additional problems in administration which are not resolved by the author's proposal?

5.   For an excellent examination of the problems that arise in determining what qualifies as a "reasonable royalty" under a compulsory licensing scheme, *see British Sky Broadcasting Ltd. v. The Performing Right Society Ltd.*, [1998] RPC 467 (UK Copyright Tribunal).

Chapter Thirty-Three

COPYRIGHTS AND FAIR USE

A. WHAT QUALIFIES AS A "FAIR USE"?

Read the following Articles from the Supplement: Berne Convention 10, 10bis, TRIPS, 17.

Notes and Questions

1. Are there specific categories of uses that automatically qualify as a "fair use" under the Berne Convention? Under TRIPS? What are they?

2. What limitations, if any, are placed on the exercise of fair use rights internationally?

3. Must a copyright owner be compensated for a "fair use" of his work under international law? How should the level of such compensation be established?

THE DUCHESS OF WINDSOR LETTERS CASE
ASSOCIATED NEWSPAPERS GROUP PLC v. NEWS GROUP NEWSPAPERS LIMITED

Chancery Division (Patents Court), 1986.
[1986] RPC 515.

WALTON J.

[The plaintiffs were the owners of the Daily Mail who had for a limited time obtained the exclusive rights in an exchange of letters between the late Duke and Duchess of Windsor. They printed a series of these in their newspaper. The defendants were the owners, editors and printers of The Sun who printed one such letter and a portion of another in their newspaper. The plaintiffs obtained an injunction to restrain copyright infringement and sought a further injunction to last until their rights in the correspondence expired.]

The situation of the parties is that the plaintiffs are the proprietors of the Daily Mail newspaper, and incidentally of the Evening Standard . The first defendants are the proprietors of the Sun newspaper, Mr.

McKenzie is its editor and London Post (Printers) Limited are its printers.

The situation is that the plaintiffs have, but only for a limited time, until 19 May, certain rights in the nature of copyright in a collection of letters written by the late Duchess of Windsor to her husband, the late Duke of Windsor, formerly King Edward VIII. Having acquired those rights, the Daily Mail naturally exploited them, and it is running, as I understand it, in its day to day publication, starting last Monday, a series of these letters.

Somehow the Sun newspaper appears to have got hold of the letters and in its publication earlier this week it printed a very much shorter piece than the Daily Mail was printing, but in it it reproduced one whole letter of the letters published by the Daily Mail up to that point, and a portion of another such letter. Consequently, the plaintiffs have moved, first *ex parte*, for an order that the defendants and each of them be restrained from reproducing or permitting to be reproduced in the Sun newspaper or any other newspaper the publication, direction or printing of which is under their respective control, either of the letters or extracts from letters quoted on page 4 of the Sun newspaper for 28 April 1986 or any other substantial part of the material (including letters or parts of letters) forming part of the works "Wallis and Edward: Letters 1931–1937: The Intimate Correspondence" edited by Michael Bloch or "The Obituary" by Michael Bloch, and from distributing or permitting to be distributed copies of newspapers containing any such substantial part. There is in force at the moment an interlocutory injunction down to today. The notice of motion asks for an interlocutory injunction until judgment in this action or further order in the meantime, but having regard to the limits upon the rights which the plaintiffs have, if granted it would be until 19 May or further order in the meantime.

I agree with Mr. Gray, who appeared for the Sun newspaper, that this is not the kind of case in which the principles enshrined in *American Cyanamid Co v. Ethicon Ltd* [1975] AC 396 are apposite. The reason is that for all practical purposes the granting of an interlocutory injunction must settle one way or other the rights of the parties. It is totally unrealistic to think there could, even with the speed with which matters now move in the Chancery Division, be a full-scale trial before 19 May of this year. Therefore (and this of course applies to a great many actions besides the present type of action) it is necessary for the court to consider in some detail what the actual chances of success by the plaintiffs in the action when it comes to trial will be.

Mr. Gray, forensically, has tried to make a great deal of play on the lines that to grant the injunction would be to interfere with the press's freedom of speech or publication. It seems to me that that is total nonsense. A person is not in any way prohibited from saying exactly what he likes, or publishing exactly what he likes, if he cannot publish it in the precise words which somebody else has used, which is the essence of copyright. Freedom of speech is interfered with when somebody is not allowed to say what is the truth: and the truth here is that the Duchess wrote a large number of letters to the Duke and the Duke wrote a large number of letters to the Duchess and anybody is free to say that and also to say, on the one hand, that they are the most tender love letters they have ever read or, on the other hand, that they consider them about the most banal letters they have ever read. There is no interference of any description in the present application with freedom of speech.

It being conceded that a substantial portion of the work in which the plaintiffs have this temporary copyright has been utilised in the Sun newspaper, how do the defendants justify what they have done? Basically they justify it under the terms of section 6 of the Copyright Act of 1956, subsections (2) and (3). Subsection (2) says:

> "No fair dealing with a literary, dramatic or musical work shall constitute an infringement of the copyright in the work if it is for purposes of criticism or review, whether of that work or of another work, and is accompanied by a sufficient acknowledgement.

(3) No fair dealing with a literary, dramatic or musical work shall constitute an infringement of the copyright in the work if it is for the purpose of reporting current events—(a) in a newspaper, magazine or similar periodical, or ... and, in a case falling within paragraph (a) of this subsection, if accompanied by a sufficient acknowledgement."

There is no doubt there has been in this case a sufficient acknowledgement.

Let us just see what might be fair, I do not think it depends upon any one criterion, that is to say, whether large chunks of the copyright material have been used as opposed to small chunks; probably it does not depend upon the precise ratio of the chunks used to the surrounding material, although I must point out that in the present case the matters of which complaint is made represent no less than one-third of the totality of the material that the Sun has put out relating to the letters. The question of fairness must at bottom depend upon the motive with which the material has been copied. I can imagine (I do not think that this has happened but as I do not read The Times I may be wrong) that The Times could have had a long article devoted to commenting on the education afforded to monarchs of the House of Windsor utilising a great many extracts from the letters to demonstrate how, or how not, they have received adequate instruction in English grammar, spelling, orthography, and modes of expressing themselves. That would be a perfectly fair use of the material. It really would be a perfectly fair use of the material because the material would not be used to attract readers to The Times. The article itself might of course enhance the reputation of The Times for printing material of that nature and quality; but the extracts which would be taken from the letters, however extensive and they might well be very extensive indeed, would merely be as illustrations of the theme.

I can similarly imagine that an extreme left-wing paper might print large extracts from the letters to make it perfectly plain to their readers that those who are Dukes and Duchesses are at bottom exactly the same as members of the proletariat. Once again the aim would not be to attract readers by means of the extracts from the letters; it would be to ram home a political message.

In the present case it is clear beyond a peradventure, even without Mr. Gray having told us, that the whole case is about attracting readers and the reason that the Sun is printing these letters or extracts from these letters is in order to attract readers. That being the case, I think that the matter lies within a nutshell because Lord Denning, MR, in the well-known case of *Hubbard v. Vosper* [1972] 2 QB 84, said at page 93:

> "The question is, therefore, whether Mr. Vosper's treatment of Mr. Hubbard's books was a 'fair dealing' with them 'for the purposes of criticism or review'. There is very little in our law books to help on this. Some cases can be used to illustrate what is not 'fair dealing'. It is not fair dealing for a rival in the trade to take copyright material and use it to his own benefit, such as when The Times published a letter on America by Rudyard Kipling. The St James' Gazette took out half-a-dozen passages and published them as extracts. This was held to be an infringement: see *Walter v. Steinkopff* [1892] 3 Ch 489".

That seems to me to be exactly what has happened in the present case. There is no blinking the fact that the Sun is trying to attract readers by means of printing these letters or extracts from these letters. That seems to me not to be fair.

However, that is not the end of the matter because subsection (3) says:

> "No fair dealing with a literary, dramatic or musical work shall constitute an infringement of the copyright in the work if it is for the purpose of reporting current events—(a) in a newspaper ... and, in a case falling within paragraph (a) of this subsection, is accompanied by a sufficient acknowledgement."

What here are the current events? Is such dealing as there has been by the Sun with the Daily Mail's copyrights for the purpose of reporting current events? Mr. Gray for the Sun submitted to me that the current events are the death of the Duchess, her motives and intentions in seeking publication of her letters, and the fact that the undisclosed letters themselves have been published casting, as he says, light on matters of historical interest. The death of the Duchess is a current event. Whether her motives and intention in wanting publication is a current event seems to be dubious, but one will let that pass. It does not seem to me that the actual publication of the letters is the sort of current event of which subsection (3) is speaking. It seems to me that there may well have been cases where the publication of historical material, material that is strictly historical, may nevertheless be of urgent necessity in reporting current events. One has only to think, for example, of correspondence dealing with nuclear reactors which have just blown up or have had a core melt-down: that might date from a very considerable period previous to the event happening, but would be of a topical nature in order to enable a report on what had actually happened to be properly prepared.

It seems to me that although of course there is no requirement, as Mr. Jacob for the plaintiffs has freely admitted, of necessity in subsection (3), that at any rate is a good start. If one asks the question: is it reasonably necessary to refer to these matters in order to deal with current events? It seems to me that the answer is no. The death of the Duchess does not require the publication of the contents of the letters. Her motive and intention in wanting publication, still less so. The mere fact that undisclosed letters have now been published do not require that one should go further and go into those matters by breaching the plaintiffs' copyright.

It seems to me that the defendants fail in establishing, and fail beyond all question, that there has here been by them any fair dealing with this copyright material; they would also fail, even assuming they could get over that, when one looks at the actual use they have made of it, because it is not necessary in any shape or form and is not incidental to reporting any current events. It must be borne in mind, as Mr. Jacob forcibly pointed out to me, that it is in each of these letters that copyright subsists and therefore reproducing the one whole letter, short though it is, that the defendants did reproduce they have hardly dealt with that letter as a matter of criticism or review for the purposes of reporting current events: they have taken the whole of it. Although that may for various reasons be permissible in other circumstances, it seems to me in the circumstances of the present case it would not.

At the end of the day I come to the unhesitating conclusion that the plaintiffs have made out a very strong case for success at trial and that, of course limited in the way I have already indicated so that the injunction expires on 19 May, they are entitled to the order sought by the notice of motion.

Review the *World Cup Case* from Chapter 13.

Notes and Questions

1. Is the problem with the use of the letters in the *Duchess of Windsor* case based on the amount of materials reproduced without permission or the type of materials?

2. Compare the British court's decision in the *Duchess of Windsor* case with the U.S. court's decision in *Religious Technology Center v. Lerma*, 908 F.Supp. 1362 (E.D.Va.1995), where the unauthorized publication of copyrighted religious documents in news articles qualified as a "fair use."

3. Applying the courts rationale in the *World Cup* case, would the broadcast of the finals of the World Cup, without permission of the copyright owner, as a year end sports retrospective have qualified as fair dealing? How would you define the news event that you are covering?

4.   Your client is a television documentary producer who has decided to create a on hour documentary about "check book journalism." As part of the documentary your client includes a 30 second sequence of film showing a woman and her partner in a toy shop selecting eight teddy bears. This film sequence was taken from a report about the woman included in a daily magazine program called TAFF made by another television producer. In order to obtain the report, your client had reproduced the entire program and then copied the shopping sequence from it. The TAFF producer has threatened your client with copyright infringement. Does his use of the shopping segment from the interview program qualify as "fair dealing?" In formulating your response, consider your definition of the news event you are covering. Is the shopping segment part of that news event? *See Pro Sieben Media AG v. Carlton UK Television LTD.*, [1998] FSR 43 (July 18, 1997).

5.   Do the fair dealing provisions of British law in connection with news reporting violate the United Kingdom's obligations under TRIPS?

6.   What effect, if any, should the legality of the reporter or producer's actions in obtaining the copyrighted materials to be included in their news report be considered in determining if such use is fair?

7.   In *Queensland v. TCN Channel Nine Pty Ltd.*, 25 IPR 58 (August 19, 1992), the Supreme Court of Queensland Australia rejected a fair dealing defense by the plaintiff for its broadcast of tapes recording hypnotic sessions between a person accused of murder and her defense attorneys. The tapes had been entered in evidence before the Queensland Mental Health Tribueal to determine if the woman were fit to stand trial on the charge of murder. Copies had been leaked to the defendant by a police officer engaged in the murder investigation. Australian law provides for a defense of fair dealing if the use of the work is "for the purpete of , or is associated with, the reporting of news in a newspaper, magazine or similar periodical [or] by means of broadcasting or in cinematograph film." Section 103B of the 1968 Australian Copyright Act. The court found that the use of the interview did not qualify as a fair one, stating: "There is a difficulty in saying that a publication of leaked documents, which could not without the leak have been published at all, is a 'fair dealing' with unpublished works in the circumstances to which I have referred. . ." *Compare Lynda Fletcher Gordon, et al v. Southam Inc, et al*, 1997 ACWSJ LEXIS 85491 (January 29, 1997)(British Columbia Supreme Court)(Canada)(qualified privilege to publish documents obtained under Freedom of Information Act) *and Harper & Row Publishers, Inc. v. Nation Enterprises*, 471 U.S. 539 (1985)(United States)(unauthorized publication of former President's memoirs outside scope of fair use).

THE TRIPLE X CASE
PRODUCTIONS AVANTI CINE–VIDEO INC. v. FAVREAU
Quebec Superior Court, 1997.
79 C.P.R. 3d 385.

COTE J.

The plaintiff ("Avanti"), exclusive owner of a series of broadcasts created for television entitled La Petite Vie, for which it holds a registered copyright, claims that its rights have been infringed by the defendants ("Favreau", "DeFavreau Productions", and "B.A.I." respectively, and collectively, "Favreau and his businesses"), based on the production and sales of a pastiche of its broadcast entitled La Petite Vie, or La Petite Vite—Reflexologie erotique, for viewing by erotic cinema buffs. Avanti accordingly seeks the following relief: to have its seizure before judgment declared valid; an order declaring it to be owner of the copyright in La Petite Vie, its characters, set and costumes; declaratory relief that the defendants infringed its copyright, and lastly, a permanent injunction to prohibit any further production of La Petite Vite, its distribution or sales as well as ordering destruction of all copies and related materials.

Avanti contends that La Petite Vie is an original work in which it holds the copyright; this right is admitted by the defendants. The issue in dispute is whether the production, marketing and eventual distribution of La Petite Vite infringes its copyright insofar as it unlawfully copies it.

Favreau is the owner and president of B.A.I., which carries on the business of selling "adult" videocassettes by mail order. DeFavreau Productions has had only one production to date: the making of La Petite Vite. In view of the fact that in the United States, erotic films which parody or appear to parody well-known films were frequently produced, it occurred to him to do the same. The suggestion of a client led him to La Petite Vie as his first subject, if not victim.

Favreau maintains nevertheless that La Petite Vite does not ridicule La Petite Vie nor are the characters shown in an unfavourable light, although it is admittedly a caricature of it. For purposes of the caricature, he reproduces the characters from La Petite Vie in La Petite Vite as well as on the advertising for the production, including the box in which the video-cassette is sold.

The script of La Petite Vite is thin: a few minutes of exposition in which the characters who are clearly copied from La Petite Vie are developed, which is quickly followed by sexual activity of all types under the transparent pretext of a trance in which the character enters (the "Reflexologie erotique" of the title) which permits him to live out his fantasies. Favreau readily admits that the erotic scenes are the main if not the only purpose of his work which seeks to provoke sexual arousal in those who watch it, having borrowed neither script nor set from La Petite Vie.

A large number of comparisons were made between the titles of dramatic works and erotic productions which more or less parody them. This evidence was intended to show that such use was wide-spread.

The claim which the court must adjudicate seeks to prevent La Petite Vite from being sold or rented in the erotic video market known as triple X-rated, on the grounds that it is the result of an unauthorized copy of La Petite Vie. Avanti's obvious goal is to protect the product on which it holds rights such that it can not be used for purposes other than those intended by its rightful owner.

The court has to consider the matter strictly from the point of view of violation of copyright held by Avanti in La Petite Vie, without regard to the good or bad taste involved in the impugned use. *Campbell v. Acuff–Rose Music Inc.*, 114 S.Ct. 1164 (1994) (United States Supreme Court).

For those who watch La Petite Vite and who are familiar with La Petite Vie (which includes more than four million Quebeckers), the borrowing of ideas is obvious. Favreau admits it without hesitation, and in fact, the defendants count on the identification of their production with Claude Meunier's original work, in order to exploit the original and to arouse the interest of the public in what they maintain is a parody of it.

If it is a parody, it becomes necessary to engage in a certain amount of borrowing from the original work in order to make it recognizable by the audience (the conjure up standard of American law). In that respect, the defendants invoke the parody defence and quote an article taken from the Harvard Law Review3 (1983–84) 97 Harvard Law Review, at p. 1395 and following.3, which sets out the theory (p. 1395):

> Parody, in its purest form, is the art of creating a new literary, musical, or other artistic work that both mimics and renders ludicrous the style and thought of an original.

In order to ridicule a work, the parodist must recall it to the minds of his audience. Because some parodists achieve this effect through extensive use of the original, parodists have occasionally come into conflict with the law of copyright.

The author in examining the sources of current legal theory specifies later in the article that (p. 1401):

> The key determination in each case was whether the mimicry had the effect of substituting itself for actual or potential commercial use of the original. The courts clearly felt that, in the absence of such direct competition, copyright law should not restrict socially valuable uses.

Accordingly, our American neighbours have adopted as part of their praetorian law a three step approach with which to examine the typical problems posed by parody, in order to arrive at acceptable uses. The above-noted writer expresses it as follows (p. 1409):

> Although fair use doctrine must continue to allow for some degree of judicial discretion, courts should reorient their discretion—indeed, their entire method of analyzing productive fair use—to conform to the utilitarian basis of copyright law. Courts could achieve this goal by adopting a three-part approach to productive fair use. First, if the plaintiff proves substantial similarity between use and original, the defendant should have the burden of showing that his use is "productive"—that it falls into one of the recognized

categories of productive fair use or that in some way it adds to and alters the function of the original work. Second, if the defendant establishes that his use is productive, the inquiry should shift to whether there is a substantial possibility that the use will compete significantly for the market of the original. If the plaintiff cannot prove such a possibility, the court should protect the use. Third, if there is a substantial possibility of substitution, the court should weigh the social value of the use against the countervailing economic disincentive to the author.

This approach, taken from an analysis dating from 1984, is taken up 10 years later in the oft-cited judgment in *Acuff-Rose Music* in which the United States Supreme Court applied the provisions of American law as they stood in Copyright Act of 1976, 17 U.S.C. § 107 which provisions read as follows:

107. Limitations on exclusive rights—Fair use

Notwithstanding the provisions of sections 106 and 106A, the fair use of a copyrighted work, including such use by reproduction in copies or phonorecords or by any other means specified by that section, for purposes such as criticism, comment, news reporting, teaching (including multiple copies for classroom use), scholarship, or research, is not an infringement of copyright. In determining whether the use made of a work in any particular case is a fair use the factors to be considered shall include–

(1) the purpose and character of the use, including whether such use is of a commercial nature or is for nonprofit educational purposes;

(2) the nature of the copyrighted work;

(3) the amount and substantiality of the portion used in relation to the copyrighted work as a whole; and

(4) the effect of the use upon the potential market for or value of the copyrighted work.

The fact that a work is unpublished shall not itself bar a finding of fair use if such finding is made upon consideration of all the above factors.

In Canadian law, the judgment of *Acuff-Rose Music* is discussed in *Les Cahiers* de propriete intellectuelle "L'affaire Campbell c. Acuff–Rose Music, Inc. et la defense du 'fair use' " by Professor Todd H. Shuster, of Northeastern University, Boston, Massachusetts, in (January 1995), 7 Cahiers prop. intel. 287.6 in 1994. In that case, it was a question of a rap song (Pretty Woman) which took a limited number of musical themes and verses7 *Op. cit.*: page 299.7 from a rock song (Oh, Pretty Woman) which was composed in an entirely different style. The writer says the following:

> In carrying out a precise comparison of the words of the two songs, the court noticed that 2 Live Crew had for the most part written new words, which described a rather vulgar woman who was

not particularly seductive, whereas the words of the original song described a rather perfect, sexy woman.

The following year, in 1995, the judgment in *Campbell v. Acuff–Rose* is once again discussed in Canada Zegers, James, "Parody and Fair Use in Canada after Campbell v. Acuff–Rose" (February 1995), 11 C.I.P. Rev. 205.8 in an article dated August 11, 1994. The author invites the adoption in Canada of American law on the subject, by prefacing his article as follows:

> The legal status of parody and the fair use of copyright in Canada is uncertain at best, largely because there are so few decided cases. In the United States copyright law pertaining to parody is considerably more developed. Over the last forty years American courts have gradually recognized the importance and legitimacy of parody and have accorded it special privileges as far as the use of copyrighted work is concerned. Recently the United States Supreme Court, in *Campbell v. Acuff–Rose,* ruled that parody may constitute fair use of copyrighted work. *Campbell* is an important decision for parodists in both the United States and Canada. For American parodists, it provides certain reassurances that they may practice their satirical trade in peace. For Canadian parodists, it provides a model for the future development of Canadian copyright law.

In comparing the two systems of North American law, the author has the following to say (pp. 207–208):

> The closest the Canadian copyright law comes to providing a fair use defence for parody is in paragraph 27(2)(a) of the Canadian Copyright Act in which "fair dealing with any work for the purposes of private study, research, criticism, review or newspaper summary" is recognized as not constituting infringement of copyright. Despite the fact that parody could be included within this exception as a fair dealing for the purpose of criticism, paragraph 27(2)(a) has not been invoked as a defence to a copyright infringement in parody cases. Parody in Canada is protected mainly by its dissimilarity to the original work. Under § 3(1) of the Canadian Copyright Act the owner of copyright has "the sole right to reproduce the work or any substantial part thereof". As long as there is no reproduction of a substantial part of the original work, there is no infringement of copyright. While this grants sufficient protection for written parody, song parodies are at a disadvantage, for the reason that parodies of songs must stick closely to the music of the original in order to be recognizable as parodies. In using the music of the original, the song parody invariably infringes copyright. In the United States, song parodies have recourse to the fair use provisions of § 107. Under Canadian law, recourse to comparable "fair dealing" provisions has yet to be attempted.

[The author] concludes his examination of the issue with the following (p. 210):

Parody is entitled to protection under § 107 of the United States Copyright Act and should be entitled to similar protection under paragraph 27(2)(a) of the Canadian Act. That such protection has not yet been recognized in Canada is more a result of a lack of opportunity than anything else. Certainly there are no barriers to adopting the American jurisprudence on parody directly into Canadian law. Future Canadian copyright cases dealing with the issue of parody would do well to consider the American law in this area and adopt the reasoning of the United States Supreme Court.

If such ought to be the approach in our law in the absence of a distinct Canadian authority on the exact issue, the following questions must be answered:

1. If the plaintiff has discharged the burden of proving a significant similarity between the original work and the defendant's use of it, has the defendant established that its use is productive, allowing one to classify it as a reasonable and permitted use, or to find that this use adds to or modifies the function of the original?

2. If the defendant proves the use to be productive, the court should then decide whether it is probable that the use constitutes significant competition in the market for the original work. In the absence of such competition, the use should be protected by the court.

3. Finally, if such competition exists, the court must weigh the sociocultural value of the use against the economic disincentive to the original author.

In this case, Avanti has proven that there are, at least in brief moments of the production of short scenes of which La Petite Vite is composed, a similarity of set, costumes, and general appearance of characters, as well as more or less disguised copies of their names, mannerisms, and manner of expressing themselves, which deliberately makes them resemble characters found in La Petite Vie. In that regard there is a significant similarity, although it does not extend to the scripts of La Petite Vie from which nothing has been borrowed, except for the imperfect copies of characters' names, such that "popa" becomes "peupa", "moman" becomes "meuman" and so forth. It becomes important then to determine whether such similarities, as extensive or as limited as they may be, are protected by copyright.

The characters in La Petite Vie, themselves instruments of caricature of daily life as conceived of by the author, do not present characteristics sufficiently original that they could, standing alone without script or direction, be said to be subject to copyright protection. It is what they are involved in, the words they speak, the staging of their actions, which give them life, that animate them and confer upon them their personality. La Petite Vite borrows little or nothing of the words, the text or the plot of La Petite Vie, at least nothing of any importance. Artistic works such as cartoon characters ought not to be confused with characters taken from literary works, the latter generally having no independent life from that of the work itself. The case at bar is no exception to this rule.

La Petite Vie is most certainly an original dramatic work protected by the Act, but Avanti has failed in its efforts to prove that La Petite Vite constitutes a use in which the similarity to La Petite Vie is substantial. Consequently, it does not violate the plaintiff's copyright. Having reached this conclusion the remaining issues need not be dealt with.

FOR THESE REASONS, the court:

UPHOLDS the position of the defendants;

QUASHES and NULLIFIES the seizure effected before judgment;

DISMISSES the application by the plaintiff for a permanent injunction;

ORDERS the plaintiff and the guardian named in the seizure order as well as any subsequent guardian if there is one, to return to the parties or persons from whom the following list of objects were seized before judgment within 72 hours of notice of the judgment: all advertising material and packaging, as well as drawing boards, masters, prints, cassette tapes, photographs, negatives, cassettes, videodiscs, video-cassettes, and any other goods seized;

DECLARES vacated the order for an injunction issued as security, on November 21, 1997;

ORDERS that the copies of the videocassette sealed on November 22, 1996 be sent back to one or the other of the parties or persons who may establish their ownership over it, after the appeal period has expired, if no appeal has been taken;

ORDERS costs payable by the plaintiff.

Application dismissed.

Notes and Questions

1. *Use of Precedents From Other Countries to Determine Standards.* Note in the *Triple X* case, the Canadian court considered the treatment of parody in a well-known U.S. case, *Campbell v. Acuff–Rose*. What is the value of considering the laws of other countries?

2. Do TRIPS or the Berne Convention establish an international standard for deciding fair use in cases of alleged parody or pastiche? What factors must a court consider in deciding a fair use parody claim in accordance with these treaties?

3. In the *Triple X* case, the court found no copyright infringement. This finding in essence eliminated the need to determine whether the defendant's use was a fair one. Under most countries laws, a fair use or fair dealing defense is only available once copyright infringement has been found. By contrast in *Campbell v. Acuff–Rose Music, Inc.*, 510 U.S. 569 (1994), examined by the Canadian court in the *Triple X* case, the court

actually determined whether the parody in question qualified as a fair use under U.S. law.

4. In *Campbell,* the plaintiff had challenged the unauthorized recording of a rap version parody of a well-known copyrighted rock ballad called "Pretty Woman" on the grounds that any use of plaintiff's song (including music and lyrics) qualified as a fair use. In upholding the defendant's claim, the court reasoned:

> The germ of parody lies in the definition of the Greek *parodeia* as "a song sung alongside another." Modern dictionaries accordingly describe a parody as a "literary or artistic work that imitates the characteristic style of an author or a work for comic effect or ridicule," or as a "composition in prose or verse in which the characteristic turns of thought and phrase in an author or class of authors are imitated in such a way as to make them appear ridiculous." For the purposes of copyright law, the nub of the definitions, and the heart of any parodist's claim to quote from existing material, is the use of some elements of a prior author's composition to create a new one that, at least in part, comments on that author's works. If, on the contrary, the commentary has no critical bearing on the substance or style of the original composition, which the alleged infringer merely uses to get attention or to avoid the drudgery in working up something fresh, the claim to fairness in borrowing from another's work diminishes accordingly (if it does not vanish), and other factors, like the extent of its commerciality, loom larger. Parody needs to mimic an original to make its point, and so has some claim to use the creation of its victim's (or collective victims') imagination, whereas satire can stand on its own two feet and so requires justification for the very act of borrowing.

> The fact that parody can claim legitimacy for some appropriation does not, of course, tell either parodist or judge much about where to draw the line. Like a book review quoting the copyrighted material criticized, parody may or may not be fair use, and petitioners' suggestion that any parodic use is presumptively fair has no more justification in law or fact than the equally hopeful claim that any use for news reporting should be presumed fair, *see Harper & Row,* 471 U.S., at 561, 105 S.Ct., at 2230. The Act has no hint of an evidentiary preference for parodists over their victims, and no workable presumption for parody could take account of the fact that parody often shades into satire when society is lampooned through its creative artifacts, or that a work may contain both parodic and nonparodic elements. Accordingly, parody, like any other use, has to work its way through the relevant factors, and be judged case by case, in light of the ends of the copyright law.

> While we might not assign a high rank to the parodic element here, we think it fair to say that 2 Live Crew's song reasonably could be perceived as commenting on the original or criticizing it, to some degree. 2 Live Crew juxtaposes the romantic musings of a man whose fantasy comes true, with degrading taunts, a bawdy demand for sex, and a sigh of relief from paternal responsibility. The later words can be taken as a comment on the naivete of the original of an earlier day, as a rejection of its sentiment that ignores the ugliness of street life and the debasement

that it signifies. It is this joinder of reference and ridicule that marks off the author's choice of parody from the other types of comment and criticism that traditionally have had a claim to fair use protection as transformative works.

We think the Court of Appeals was insufficiently appreciative of parody's need for the recognizable sight or sound when it ruled 2 Live Crew's use unreasonable as a matter of law. It is true, of course, that 2 Live Crew copied the characteristic opening bass riff (or musical phrase) of the original, and true that the words of the first line copy the Orbison lyrics. But if quotation of the opening riff and the first line may be said to go to the "heart" of the original, the heart is also what most readily conjures up the song for parody, and it is the heart at which parody takes aim. Copying does not become excessive in relation to parodic purpose merely because the portion taken was the original's heart. If 2 Live Crew had copied a significantly less memorable part of the original, it is difficult to see how its parodic character would have come through. This is not, of course, to say that anyone who calls himself a parodist can skim the cream and get away scot free. In parody, as in news reporting, context is everything, and the question of fairness asks what else the parodist did besides go to the heart of the original. It is significant that 2 Live Crew not only copied the first line of the original, but thereafter departed markedly from the Orbison lyrics for its own ends. 2 Live Crew not only copied the bass riff and repeated it, but also produced otherwise distinctive sounds, interposing "scraper" noise, overlaying the music with solos in different keys, and altering the drum beat. This is not a case, then, where "a substantial portion" of the parody itself is composed of a "verbatim" copying of the original.

We do not, of course, suggest that a parody may not harm the market at all, but when a lethal parody, like a scathing theater review, kills demand for the original, it does not produce a harm cognizable under the Copyright Act. Because "parody may quite legitimately aim at garroting the original, destroying it commercially as well as artistically," B. Kaplan, *An Unhurried View of Copyright* 69 (1967), the role of the courts is to distinguish between "[b]iting criticism [that merely] suppresses demand [and] copyright infringement[, which] usurps it." *Fisher v. Dees*, 794 F.2d, at 438. This distinction between potentially remediable displacement and unremediable disparagement is reflected in the rule that there is no protectible derivative market for criticism. The market for potential derivative uses includes only those that creators of original works would in general develop or license others to develop. Yet the unlikelihood that creators of imaginative works will license critical reviews or lampoons of their own productions removes such uses from the very notion of a potential licensing market. "People ask ... for criticism, but they only want praise."

JUSTICE KENNEDY (concur)

Parody may qualify as fair use only if it draws upon the original composition to make humorous or ironic commentary about that same composition. It is not enough that the parody use the original in a humorous fashion, however creative that humor may be. The parody must target the original, and not just its general style, the genre of art to which it belongs, or society as a whole (although if it targets the original, it may target those features as well). *See Rogers v. Koons*, 960 F.2d 301, 310 (C.A.2 1992) ("[T]hough the satire need not be only of the copied work and may ... also be a parody of modern society, the copied work must be, at least in part, an object of the parody"); *Fisher v. Dees*, 794 F.2d 432, 436 (C.A.9 1986) ("[A] humorous or satiric work deserves protection under the fair-use doctrine only if the copied work is at least partly the target of the work in question"). This prerequisite confines fair use protection to works whose very subject is the original composition and so necessitates some borrowing from it. *See MCA, Inc. v. Wilson*, 677 F.2d 180, 185 (C.A.2 1981) ("[I]f the copyrighted song is not at least in part an object of the parody, there is no need to conjure it up").

5. If the court in the *Triple X* case had found that defendant's use was infringing, would such use have been privileged under the reasoning of *Campbell*? What limitations should be put on the right of an unauthorized party to parody or criticize another's work by reproducing that work in whole or in part without compensation to the copyright owner?

THE MARLBORO MAN CASE
Bundesgerichtshof (German Federal Supreme Court), 1984.
[1986] ECC 1.

The defendant markets the "Marlboro" brand of cigarettes in Germany. For years it has advertised them with illustrations from cowboy life and the slogan: 'Marlboro—the taste of freedom and adventure'.

In 1972 it organised a competition with prizes, which it advertised in the same style. The simple coloured drawing showed a cowboy holding playing cards, a "royal flush", in one hand and a cigarette in the other, under the heading "Great Marlboro Poker!" and the prizes. On the right hand side of the poster, beneath a "Marlboro" cigarette packet, appeared the prize question relating to the fifth card of the royal flush and the conditions for taking part. The slogan which has already been described appeared at the bottom of the poster.

The poster was altered by a doctor by means of photo-montage. The heading as replaced by the words: "Great Mordoro (Murder) Poker!" At the level of the cowboy's chest the following text was inserted:

"1st Prize: Gastric Ulcer

2nd Prize: Coronary Thrombosis

3rd Prize: Lung Cancer"

The prizes shown in the original and the advertising slogan were removed.

A black and white photograph of the montage was included as the page for November in a "Heidelberg Calendar for non-smokers 1981"

The plaintiff, which describes itself in its bye-laws as a non-profit-making association for the promotion of public health by educational measures against smoking, nevertheless wishes to use the calendar sheet in question with the parody of the defendant's advertising slogan in connection with its anti-smoking campaign.

After the defendant had explained that it still regarded the parody of its advertising slogan as unlawful the plaintiff instituted proceedings for a declaration which was originally to the general effect that it was not infringing any rights of the defendant by selling the parody of the advertisement.

The Landgericht (Regional Court) dismissed the application as inadmissible in the absence of any interest in a declaration. In the appeal proceedings the plaintiff limited its application for a declaration to the effect that it sought authorisation to distribute the parody of the advertisement only in a calendar for non-smokers.

The appeal court granted this application. In this further appeal on a point of law the defendant seeks dismissal of the plaintiff's application.

In pursuit of its aim as an association, the plaintiff wishes to offer enlightenment, by means of the calendar sheet, concerning the harmfulness of smoking, *i.e,* wishes to serve the public interest. Precisely because the defendant tries, in its advertising, to divert attention from the dangers of smoking, it must put up with the plaintiff in return setting to work on its advertising slogan as intended and turning it round by satirical parody, so as to point to these dangers. Furthermore anyone looking at the calendar sheet would not misunderstand the play on words "Marlboro–Mordoro" to mean that the defendant had drawn close to criminal activity or that it and its "Marlboro" brand of cigarettes were intended to be offered as a target for criticism. The court added that it must be presumed that the calendar sheet was to be used in a calendar for non-smokers. This would show anyone looking at it that it was intended to be only part of a campaign directed against smoking generally. There was nothing to indicate that the plaintiff intended to use it in any other way, and the onus of this was on the defendant because it had to show the requirements for a claim to an injunction.

In the final analysis this reasoning stands up to the appellant's attacks.

The protection of names under section 12 of the Civil Code aims only to prevent the confusion of identity arising from unauthorised use of a name and to prevent the right of the bearer of a name to use it from being disputed by another person. This does not arise here either. The distortion of the mark "Marlboro" as "Mordoro" and the references to the defendant which are created in the mind of anyone looking at the calendar sheet do not violate its interest in identity which is protected by its right to the name. On the contrary, the calendar uses the cigarette mark "Marlboro" precisely as a reference to market recognition of these tobacco products of the defendant and the style of advertising which it has linked with this brand, for the effect aimed at by ridiculing the brand, which is to create resistance to such products.

The calendar affects the defendant's interests relating to its enter-prise, which are protected by its personality rights and the right in the business which it has established and carries on. The importance of the calendar for the defendant is not simply that it is a warning against the health risks of smoking, which would have only reflex effects for ciga-rette manufacturers and which they would be unable to resist, on this ground alone, with an action for an injunction. The dangers to health touched upon in the calendar are not the subject of its application for an injunction. The defendant complains of the use of its trade mark and the image it has created by advertising for an anti-smoking campaign, particularly by ridicule in a way which causes it to consider itself disparaged and discriminated against. It is resisting the injury to its reputation thereby caused, the parodying of its image in anti-advertising, and the adverse effect on its advertising appeal. In this respect the calendar which is construed to refer to the defendant does indeed directly encroach upon its protected interests. However, it cannot pro-hibit the plaintiff's use of the calendar sheet in a calendar for non-smokers on these grounds either. For this purpose the plaintiff also can invoke interests which merit protection and which the appeal court, after weighing up the respective interests as it was required to do, found to be the stronger. This finding is correct in law.

The appeal court presumes correctly that the plaintiff can claim the basic right of freedom of expression (Art 5(1) of the Constitution) for criticising the consumption of cigarettes, which it wishes to campaign against by publishing calendars for non-smokers. Public debate on the risks of smoking to health is in the general interest. Campaigns which—as here—aim to make people aware of these risks must be tolerated by the tobacco industry even if it considers that the emphasis on the negative side of smoking is all too one-sided and it must therefore expect reduced sales. Article 5(1) of the Constitution allows critics to state their viewpoint on this question in an over-emphatic way: it is not confined to balanced or even lenient treatment. The special limits to which consum-er information on the quality of consumer goods is subject, particularly by means of comparative tests do not apply to information campaigns such as those in question here. In the former case they must continue to exist because the consumer expects a fair comparison of products, for which the authority of scientific investigation and appraisal is claimed. The plaintiff's criticism makes no comparable claim to objectivity.

This does not mean that the plaintiff could promote its cause among the public without regard to the defendant, whose interests also merit protection. Indeed there is no question here of untrue allegations by the plaintiff for which no critic can claim the guarantee given by article 5(1) of the Constitution. The defendant is not complaining of the plaintiff's statement concerning the risks of smoking to health, but only of the design of the calendar, which is derogatory to it, *i.e.*, the form in which the plaintiff wishes to promote its cause. Although for the sake of the freedom of expression, the plaintiff must be granted wide scope in the way it presents its criticism and, above all, must be allowed to advocate its viewpoint as effectively as possible, it must keep its statements, in the formal respect too, in justifiable proportion to its substantive cause and the damaging effects on the defendant. It must not, without substantive reference to its own cause, make the defendant a target for its criticism in a way which defames or discriminates against it in public, nor may it "personalise" its criticism, which is primarily directed at general consumer habits, in respect of the defendant's enterprise merely in order to take advantage of its popularity and advertising appeal at the defendant's own expense. The plaintiff may place the defendant at the forefront of its criticism only if this appears materially justified when weighed against the defendant's economic interests also.

However, in the final outcome this was correctly assumed by the appeal court.

Contrary to the appellant's opinion, the calendar sheet does not expose the defendant to ridicule in a discriminating manner or even disparage it in a defamatory manner.

Even for an uncritical observer the calendar's message is not directed against the "Marlboro" brand of cigarette, but against the consumption of cigarettes in general. It is true that the advertising image of the "Marlboro" cigarette is seized upon, together with its brand name which offers itself to the play on words (Marlboro–Mordoro), but clearly it is taken only as a prototype of the kind of cigarette advertising which, according to the findings of the appeal court which have not been challenged, associates mainly for young smokers ideas of freedom, adventure and romance, virility and toughness with the enjoyment of cigarettes. In this satirical reversal of the value references of smoking which are suggested by the advertising, to the health risks associated with it, the observer's attention is taken away from the "Marlboro" brand of cigarette and the defendant as its manufacturer, and is directed to the imaginary brand "Mordoro" as a "brand" which stands for cigarettes in general and the health risks generally attributed to them. The aim of "exposing" the advertising image of "Marlboro" at this general level merely as representing all kinds of cigarettes is so clearly the main purpose that there is no room for any misunderstanding that the criticism is directed at the defendant as the manufacturer specifically of "Marlboro". Neither is this altered by the fact that a cigarette packet with "Marlboro" printed on it appears as an embellishment on the calendar, nor by the mental connection which an observer familiar with the defendant's advertising makes with the defendant. For that observer, these features do not cast any doubt on the direction of the attack in the calendar against the smoking of cigarettes in general.

For this reason alone it is impossible to accept the argument in the appeal that the defendant is singled out arbitrarily among cigarettes manufacturers, and thereby discriminated against, simply because it is accidentally open to the play on words "Marlboro–Mordoro". The calendar does not bring the "Marlboro" brand into the firing line of criticism in a discriminating manner by this means because this would contradict the symbolic force of the treatment which must be taken into account in assessing such stylistic resources. It may be that smokers of the "Marlboro" cigarette are reminded more strongly of the calendar's warning than smokers of other brands, because of the mental connection between the calendar and their brand. This would be attributable primarily to a special advertising image of the brand which the calendar adopts for the "Mordoro" brand. In view however, of the plaintiffs' cause, there would be nothing arbitrary in singling out this advertisement but this would remain within the material context of its warning. From the plaintiff's viewpoint the warning about the health risks of smoking is closely related to criticism of cigarette advertising which converts these risks into value concepts. This Court upholds the appeal court's view that cigarette manufacturers who advertise their products in this way must put up with even harsh criticism of their advertising by committed opponents of cigarette smoking. This alone does not involve discrimination.

Nor does it result in defamation of the defendant. In view of the message which is directed generally at the risks of smoking cigarettes, there can be no question of the defendant being bound to regard itself, as the appeal states, as classified by advertising for the "Mordoro" brand as more or less a criminal because of the significance of its advertising image. The calendar does not aim to expose to scorn any criminal acts by the defendant but to draw attention to the risks of smoking, although in a drastic form. It tries to demonstrate to the observer that smoking amounts to a game of poker for which the prize is health. The fact that the cigarette manufacturer, his products and his advertising are included in this "murderous game" follows necessarily from the viewpoint of critics who condemn smoking. In this respect also the defendant runs no risk that the observer will misunderstand the calendar.

Moreover, the fact that the plaintiff wishes to present its criticism in such a way that the defendant's advertising appears to be hoist with its own petard because of the parodying of its own advertisements does not result in the criticism degenerating into vilification of the defendant. Providing that such "anti-advertising" is unmistakably at the service of material criticism, as here, the risk that the advertiser will be exposed to ridicule as a result takes second place to the critic's cause, for which he wishes to be taken seriously. This applies especially where the aim of the "anti-advertising" is, for material reasons, precisely to "expose" advertising methods. The use of "anti-advertising" which campaigns against the criticised advertising with its own methods is perfectly appropriate for the plaintiff's objective of pointing out the risks of cigarette advertising at the same time as the health risks of smoking.

Again, the fact that the defendant fears a reduction in the advertising appeal of its "Marlboro" brand and encroachment upon its enterprise due to use of the calendar is no reason why the plaintiff's protectable interest in giving free form to its criticism should take second place. The usual reasons why, for the purpose of protecting the advertising image, it is unlawful to use trade marks belonging to others because of the risk of confusion or dilution, do not apply to cases of "anti-advertising" for the simple reason that the "borrowed" mark is not being used as a distinguishing feature, as the defendant uses it. The only adverse effects which this may produce for the defendant are that its mark bears the burden of the reversal effect of the "anti-advertising". This burden, however, is only the effect of the criticism of the advertising method which the defendant, as already stated, must put up with because of the plaintiff's cause which underlies that criticism and which pursues general interests.

Moreover, the defendant cannot object that the plaintiff wishes to use the "anti-advertising" for its criticism solely in order to make its criticism more cogent by means of the advertising appeal of the defendant's name. Of course the reversal effect created by the disputed calendar is produced by the popularity of the "Marlboro" brand and its advertising image. This is normally the case with regard to "anti-advertising". It must also be conceded that, as the defendant says, a course of action which "tacks on" to another person's advertising expenditure in this way does not have to be simply tolerated. If this is disputed however the plaintiff can as already stated claim material reasons for linking its "anti-advertising" with the defendant's cigarette advertising. There is no justification for assuming that the plaintiff's main purpose is to harness the defendant's financial resources in an improper manner for pursuing its own interests because here the purpose of the "anti-advertising" is to criticise the methods of cigarette advertising and their importance for the dangers of smoking.

(c) Since the appeal court's judgment otherwise shows no mistakes in law to the defendant's disadvantage its appeal should be dismissed.

Notes and Questions

1.   Do you believe the court would have reached a different result if the anti-smoking campaign had been connected to the sale of a product designed to reduce the craving for nicotine? What role, if any, should the commercial use of a parody have on the determination of whether such use qualifies as a "fair" one?

2.   In a copyright infringement action which concerned the music and lyrics of the song "There is Nothin' Like a Dame" from the Rodgers and Hammerstein musical "South Pacific", the plaintiffs were the exclusive licencees in the United Kingdom of the copyrights in this musical. One defendant was an advertising agency having among their clients a bus company. The first defendants had created a television advertisement for the bus company that made use of words and music which the plaintiffs claimed infringed their copyrights in the above mentioned song. Plaintiffs moved for appropriate interlocutory relief after this advertisement had been seen on television. Defendants admitted that the lyrics and music had deliberately been created so as to parody the Rogers and Hammerstein number. Assuming the evidence demonstrates that a substantial portion of the Rogers and Hammerstein song is contained in the advertisement and that a survey

indicated that five out of one hundred and thirty who heard the piano recording of defendant's song and had not seen the commercial expressly identified the song as "There is Nothing Like a Dame," would you consider the defendant's use a fair one. *See Williamson Music Ltd. v. The Pearson Partnership Ltd.,* [1987] FSR 97 (Chancery Division July 29, 1986)(United Kingdom).

3. *Right to Use versus Right to Compensation.* Even if a court were to determine that a defendant is entitled to use a copyrighted work without the copyright owner's permission because her proposed use is a "fair one," should the parodist still be required to compensate the copyright owner for such use? Is there something in the nature of a copyrighted work that allows the grant of a compulsory license in the form of fair use, for which no compensation should be required? Should such uncompensated use qualify as a taking?

4. *Parody, Satire and Pastiche.* The *Triple X* and *Marlboro Man* cases entail the unauthorized use of a copyrighted work to create a parody. Should the same fair use treatment be afforded a satire or a pastiche?

5. In *Clark v. Associated Newspapers Ltd.,* [1998] 1 All ER 959, [1998] RPC 261 (Chancery Division January 21, 1998)(United Kingdom), the court in considering publication of a series of newspaper articles in the form of a diary, parodying published diaries of a former cabinet minister, defined a parody as follows:

Parodies date back as far as Greek antiquity. "Parody or satire, as we understand it, is when one artist, for comic effect or social commentary, closely imitates the style of another artist and in so doing creates a new art work which makes ridiculous the style and expression of the original". But parodies have a legal hurdle to overcome. Federal law prohibits copies or imitations that confuse consumers. This protects trademarks as a form of intellectual property and guards against confusion, deception or mistake by the consuming public. Whether a customer is confused is the ultimate question. If the defendant employs a successful parody, the customer would not be confused, but amused. Thus we agree with the district court that parody is not an affirmative defence, but an additional factor in the analysis. "The keystone of parody is imitation. It is hard to imagine, for example, a successful parody of Time magazine that did not reproduce Time's trade-marked red border. A parody must convey two simultaneous—and contradictory—messages: that it is the original, but also that is not the original and is instead a parody. To the extent that it does only the former but not the latter, it is not only a poor parody, but also vulnerable under trademark law, since the customer will be confused." Thus the parody has to be a take-off, not a rip-off.' (quoting *Nike Inc. v. "Just Did It" Enteprises,* 6F.3d 1225 (7th Cir. 1993))

6. By contrast in *Dr. Seuss Enterprises L.P. v. Penguin Books U.S.A Inc.,* 109 F.3d 1394 (9th Cir. 1997), the court declined fair use protection to a "parody" of a children's work that made a biting comment about the O.J. Simpson case because it was a "satire" and not a parody. The court indicated that a parody is directed toward commenting on a particular work while a satire comments or criticizes an event or societal trend.

7. A "patische" has been defined as an imitation of "a particular manner" (as opposed to a caricature of a particular work). *Jacques Dezandre v. SA Musidisc*, [199] ECC 495 (Cour D'Appel, Paris 1990)(France). Would a "patische" be protectable under the rationale of *Campbell*?

8. In *Dezandre,* the Cour d'Appel held that a music disc which imitated the front page layout of a daily periodical entitled "Liberation" did not qualify as a fair use parody of the newspaper. "It should be observed that pastiche, which imitates a particular manner, and parody, which imitates a serious work by caricaturing it, are the products of creative work which aims to cause laughter. In the present case, the text and illustrations on the sleeve have no obvious connection with what Liberation offers its readers. Although the variety of coarse expressions used [on the music disc] is clearly aimed to shock and no doubt does so, they have no comic virtue whatever. In the absence of pastiche or parody, SNPC is right to complain of infringement of its copyright...."

9. Are the distinctions between parody, satire and pastiche required under TRIPS or Berne? Are they defensible?

10. Although many fair use or fair dealing cases arise as a result of new reporting are there other categories of use which ought to qualify as fair?

THE PRINCESS CAROLINE PHOTO CASE
BANIER v. NEWS GROUP NEWSPAPERS LIMITED

Chancery Division, 1997.
[1997] FSR 812.

LIGHTMAN, J.

Mr. Banier is a photographer of international repute. He has brought two actions for infringement of copyright in a distinctive photograph of the head and shoulders of Princess Caroline of Monaco ("the photograph"). The first is against Times Newspapers Limited ("TN"), the publishers of The Times. The second is against News Group Newspapers Limited ("NGN") the publishers of the Sun.

Princess Caroline is reported to have suffered from alopecia. In September 1996, apparently having come to terms with this condition courageously she posed for the photograph and it is included in a collection of Mr. Banier's photographs entitled "Past Present".

TN applied to Mr. Banier's agent for a licence to publish the photograph in The Times. There is an issue in the action against TN whether such a licence was granted: TN contend that Mr. Banier's agent granted a licence on terms that no fee need be paid but TN should acknowledge Mr. Banier as the photographer and refer to the collection. The Times thereafter published the photograph.

NGN decided that it wished to publish the photograph in the Sun. NGN tried to obtain the necessary licence from the agent, but the agent could not be contacted in time. Having regard to the terms on which TN obtained its licence and the practice of newspapers to publish copyright photographs ahead of obtaining the necessary licence from the copyright owner once another newspaper has published it, NGN went ahead and published the photograph with an article underneath headed "The courage of Caroline—royal bald for photos". The article reads as follows:

Tragic Princess Caroline of Monaco faces up to the world and bravely shows how she is now totally bald.

The 39–year-old suffers alopecia brought on by stress and has only appeared in public in hats and scarves.

Now she has come to terms with her illness and allowed French photographer Francois–Marie Banier to use her as a model. She is included in a collection of his photos in a stunning pose.

Caroline has had her fair share of pain. She and first husband Phillipe Junot parted after a year. Her second husband died in a boat accident and last year she was dumped by lover Vincent Lindon.

NGN cannot and does not dispute that it reproduced the photograph in the Sun. There is no evidence to support any contention that Mr. Banier granted any licence to NGN and there is accordingly no arguable case of the existence of such a licence. But NGN maintain that there are arguable defences of fair dealing and estoppel.

NGN contend that it is common press practice, after one newspaper has published a copyright photograph, that other newspapers without waiting for the grant of a licence by the copyright owner themselves publish copies of the photograph. The relevant evidence is contained in paragraph 4 of the affidavit of Mr. Lennox, the Picture Editor for the Sun. It reads as follows:

In my experience it is common practice when one paper publishes a picture first for another newspaper to contact it with regard to the circumstances of the permission the first paper was given to publish the picture. While the paper will always then try to obtain its own specific licence, if for any reason it is not possible (within the often very tight time table of a daily newspaper) it will often publish without permission, with the confidence of the knowledge of what they have learnt about the circumstances of the first publication and in keeping with that knowledge. It will also, where appropriate, expect to pay retrospectively, an appropriate licence fee. I would say that this happens several times a day almost every day, in every newspaper.

This may be common newspaper practice and one which newspapers normally get away with. The risk of infringement proceedings may from a business and circulation point of view be worth taking: it may be economic to "publish and be damned". But it is plainly unjustified and unlawful and the sooner this is recognized the better for all concerned. The adoption of this practice is not a passport to infringe copyright.

Section 30(1) of the 1988 Act provides that fair dealing with a work for the purpose of criticism or review does not infringe any copyright in the work or another work provided that it is accompanied by a sufficient acknowledgement. This defence is available in the case where the copyright work is a photograph. By way of contrast, section 30(2) provides that (subject to certain conditions) fair dealing with a work (other than a photograph) for the purpose of reporting current events does not infringe copyright. This latter provision cannot apply in this case as the work in question is a photograph. To invoke the defence of fair dealing in this case, NGN must establish that the article of which the photograph was part was a fair dealing for the purposes of criticism or review.

What amounts to fair dealing must depend on the facts of the particular case and must to a degree be a matter of impression. What is of prime importance is to consider the real objective of the party using the copyright work. Section 30 is designed to protect a critic or reviewer who may bona fide wish to use the copyright material to illustrate his review or criticism. To ascertain the objective in the present case it is necessary to examine the article as a whole.

It is in my view totally unreal to suggest in this case that the objective in the publication of the photograph in the Sun was to illustrate any review or criticism of any copyright work, whether the photograph or the collection. The article is a news story namely that Princess Caroline after a period of stress and pain has bravely posed for the photograph. The photograph has a prominent place above the article to make the news story come to life. It is true that reference is made to her stunning pose, but that is merely an aspect of the news story. The heading to the article highlights the real point of the article, namely the courage of a princess.

I accordingly hold that there is no conceivable defence to this action for infringement of copyright in the photograph. Mr. Banier is prima facie entitled to a declaration of his ownership of the copyright in the photograph, an injunction to restrain infringement and an inquiry as to damages.

Notes and Questions

1.   Compare the court's decision in the *Princess Caroline* case under the "criticism" branch of fair use, with the decision in the *Duchess of Windsor* case above under "news reporting." Does the category of use make a difference in the analysis? In the outcome?

2.   If, instead of fair use, the law imposed a compulsory license for newsreporting would such license requirement be in violation of Berne or TRIPS?

THE PAROLE CASE
HINDLEY v. HIGGINS
Court of Appeal (Civil Division), 1983.

GRIFFITHS, LJ.

This is an appeal by Mr. Stuart Higgins, who is a journalist employed by News Group Newspapers Limited, and that company, the publishers of The Sun newspaper, from the refusal of Mr. Justice Mervyn Davies to lift an interlocutory injunction obtained by Miss Myra Hindley preventing the further publication of a series of articles which The Sun newspaper proposed to publish during the course of this week.

The matter arises against the following background of fact. Miss Myra Hindley, as is common knowledge, was in 1966 convicted with a man named Brady of the murder of children, commonly known as the Moors murders. In August 1978 she wrote a very lengthy submission in support of her application to be considered for parole. The statement is headed as follows: "Statement, for Mr. P. J. Donnelly, Solicitor, for eventual perusal by the Home Secretary and members of the Parole Board, including the Chairman. Dated 31.8.78." The statement was written wholly in the handwriting of Miss Hindley herself. She is prepared to depose upon affidavit (but because of her present confinement in prison it has not yet been possible to swear the affidavit) that she intended a very limited number of persons to see that document. They were limited to those members of the parole board before whom her application might come; to Lord Longford, who was interested in supporting her plea for parole; and to one other lady, a psychiatrist. In some manner which is not explained to the court but referred to in an affidavit of the first defendant, Mr. Stuart Higgins, a copy of that application came into his hands. He has sworn an affidavit which reads as follows: "I ... have been for four and a half years a journalist with The Sun, which is published by the Second Defendants. On Monday of this week the Sun began publishing a series of articles relating to the Plaintiff which is intended to run over a number of days. 2. I was responsible for researching and writing this series. I am unable to reveal from whom I obtained a copy of the letter ... It was made available to me by a source whom I believe to be reputable and whom I believe was legitimately in possession of it." He then exhibits to his affidavit certain newspaper articles to which I shall have to refer hereafter.

It is to be observed that in that affidavit Mr. Higgins does not assert that whoever gave him the parole submission of Miss Myra Hindley had her permission to give it to him or that Miss Hindley at any stage gave permission to anybody to part with that statement to anyone other than the parole board and the two or three other people she intended to have it to support her application for parole.

The copyright in that long statement is clearly in Miss Hindley. The Sun newspaper, after an advertising campaign both in the newspapers and on the television, then proceeded to publish a series of articles beginning this week about Miss Myra Hindley and her hopes of obtaining parole. The first article in the series merited a very large headline on the front page of The Sun on Monday 22nd August. It is headed: "MYRA—How Moors killer fights for freedom", and there is a large picture of Miss Hindley on the front page with the comment: "Myra Hindley ... this is how the Moors killer's looks have changed". On the second page, which is a continuation of the text of the article that begins on the first page there appears under "EMOTIONS" the following passage: "The Sun's file on the nation's most-hated woman is a compelling story that will arouse strong emotions in everyone—ranging from outrage and hatred to sheer surprise. In her own words and neat handwriting, Hindley pleads her case for release on parole. The Sun's amazing series will reveal for the first time the full inside story of what life is really like for Hindley in prison at Cookham Wood, Kent."

Then on the Tuesday, again on the front page, there is this heading: "World Exclusive"—"WHY I SHOULD BE FREE By Moors murderess MYRA HINDLEY—Centre Pages". When one turns to the Centre pages there is a very large headline: "WHY I SHOULD BE SET FREE—BY MYRA"—" 'I was a victim of Brady's evil influence' ". The introductory text reads as follows: "EVIL child-killer Myra Hindley wants to be set free because she feels that after 18 years in jail she has paid her debt to society. She has poured her heart out in a remarkable 22,000–word statement to the Parole Board which she hopes will help secure her release and explode the 'myth' of Myra The Monster. Her case for freedom will arouse emotions all over Britain, ranging from anger and horror to amazement and surprise. In her passionate plea for parole, Hindley, 41, portrays herself as the helpless—almost innocent—victim of the evil influence of her lover, Ian Brady."

Thereafter, the remainder of this two-page spread is devoted almost entirely to long excerpts in inverted commas from the text of her submission written to the parole board in 1978. There is very little comment on the text itself, but in an editorial appearing in the same copy at page 6 under the heading "THE SUN SAYS" there is a sub-heading "For life!": "Myra Hindley has a different hairstyle. She has had her nose fixed. She says she is a changed person and a suitable candidate for probation. But we—and, we imagine, decent, caring people everywhere—cannot erase the ghastly memory of the helpless little children she and her vile partner, Ian Brady, tortured and killed for pleasure. At present, the country is outraged over a sexual assault on a boy of just six years old." Then, in black type, underlined: "Rather than face the remotest risk of another child suffering, we would wish Myra Hindley to be kept in prison for the rest of her days."

It was following that publication of The Sun and with the intimation through the advertisement that this series of articles was to be continued throughout this week, with, as the plaintiff believed, the likelihood of further very substantial quotations from her parole submissions, that she applied to the High Court for an injunction to restrain further publication, both on the ground of breach of confidence, in that her submission to the parole board was a confidential publication and it was a breach of The Sun newspaper to publish it, and also on the ground that it was a breach of copyright.

The learned judge granted the injunction limited to Friday. The Sun newspaper immediately appealed because this series of articles is planned, as I understand it, to run through this week, terminating on Saturday, and we have had the advantage of seeing the copy that it was intended to publish today, but for the injunction, which contains further substantial quotation from her submission. As they were not able to publish it, they published on the front page, in even larger headlines than appeared on Tuesday, the following heading: "EVIL MYRA GAGS THE SUN"—"Judge halts parole story", and there then follows a factual account of the proceedings before Mr. Justice Mervyn Davies resulting in the temporary injunction.

That is the background upon which this matter comes before the court. On the face of it, the copyright being in Miss Hindley in respect of her parole submissions, there is in this case a clear breach of copyright which the plaintiff would be entitled to ask should be restrained by an injunction unless the defendants can bring themselves within the special defences provided by section 6 of the Copyright Act of 1956. They rely upon the exceptions contained in section 6 subsection (2) and subsection (3). Subsection (2) reads as follows: "No fair dealing with a literary, dramatic or musical work shall constitute an infringement of the copyright in the work if it is for purposes of criticism or review, whether of that work or of another work, and is accompanied by a sufficient acknowledgment." Subsection (3) provides: "No fair dealing with a literary, dramatic or musical work shall constitute an infringement of the copyright in the work if it is for the purpose of reporting current events—(a) in a newspaper, magazine or similar periodical, or (b) by means of broadcasting, or in a cinematograph film, and, in a case falling within paragraph (a) of this subsection, is accompanied by a sufficient acknowledgment."

For myself, having read the articles, I have very considerable doubt whether The Sun's articles are a criticism of her parole submissions within the meaning of section 6(2). It seems to me that they are no more than setting out for the readership of The Sun extensive passages that she wrote on her own behalf to the parole board. I see little, if any, detailed criticism of any of the reasons that she puts forward or any of her thinking in those submissions, but what is said is that, by including an editorial in which The Sun expressed their view that, whatever was in the submissions, the risk of releasing her should not be taken, that amounts to a criticism of the material that she placed before the parole board. I very much doubt if anybody, applying the ordinary meaning of the word "criticism", would regard that as a criticism of her submissions. However, I can see that the matter is at least arguable and, this being an interlocutory stage, it is not for this to finally make up its mind on issues but to examine whether or not they are arguable.

The next question that arises is whether in all the circumstances it is a fair dealing for a public newspaper, who has obtained by unknown means, so far as this court is concerned, a parole submission by a prisoner, to publish and criticise that parole submission without either the knowledge and certainly without the consent of the prisoner and against the prisoner's wishes. I can think of nothing more damaging to the parole system and more inimical to the public interest than that prisoners should fear that what they might write to the parole board in confidence in support of their applications for parole may be leaked to the press and become published in national newspapers and publicly attacked. I do not think that any prisoner, if he felt that there was a real risk of that happening, would write with the freedom that is desirable when the parole board are considering this submission. The parole board want, so far as they can, to understand from the prisoner himself the reasons why he wishes to have parole and why he thinks he deserves parole. They raise many highly confidential matters and it would be corrosive and destructive of any confidence between board and prisoner if it was felt that such documents were to be leaked and receive general publication.

In fairness to The Sun newspaper, Mr. Hoffmann on their behalf has freely acknowledged that if The Sun had come into possession of this document without the consent of Miss Hindley it would, as a general rule, be unfair dealing for them to publish it, particularly when, as they say, they are publishing it for the purpose of criticising it, that is, undermining the reasons given by the prisoner in support of his application for parole. But, as I understand the argument, it is submitted that because of previous publications in the press there are in this case special circumstances that make The Sun's publication against Miss Hindley's wishes fair dealing. That brings me back to Mr. Higgins' affidavit and the article to which he refers in that affidavit.

Miss Hindley is prepared to swear an affidavit to the effect that she had never given permission for that statement to be revealed to any of those newspapers.

I arrive at this decision: I cannot say for myself that there is no arguable case that it might be fair dealing to criticise this parole submission, because, if Miss Hindley had chosen to make it public through one national newspaper in the hope of enlisting support, I am very doubtful if it could be said that it was not fair dealing for another newspaper to answer on the same material stating their view of the matter. But, as I say, as the matter rests at the moment, all one can say is that there may be the beginnings of an arguable case.

Even if there is an arguable case, how does the matter lie upon a balance of convenience? So far as The Sun newspaper is concerned, this is not a matter of instant news: this is an ongoing situation. It is public knowledge that Miss Hindley's further application for parole is not to be considered until the year 1985. If The Sun newspaper wishes to interest their readers in the contents of her parole statement and to criticise it, there are still years ahead in which the matter may be of lively interest to their readers. It is not suggested that they are going to suffer any financial loss if they cannot in their next two issues print extracts from the submissions. It is quite apparent that these proceedings are providing exceedingly newsworthy material, meriting, as I have already observed, one of the largest headlines I have ever seen, and I look forward with interest to tomorrow. It therefore appears to me that The Sun newspaper is neither going to be damaged in its pocket, nor in its circulation, and nor will their readers be deprived of any matter of really compelling interest if this case goes for the moment against them. If they fight the action out and it is held that they make good their defence under section 6 subsection (2), then they will be free to run this series of articles if they wish.

So far as the plaintiff, Miss Hindley, is concerned, if an injunction is not granted, then the damage is done. "But", say The Sun, "what damage? She does not suffer any damage." I cannot agree. I think that a prisoner who finds his or her confidential outpourings to the parole board published in great detail in a national newspaper with, I believe, the largest circulation in the country and criticised and undermined will naturally suffer great anguish of mind during the course of her imprisonment pending the next parole review. Of course one would not in fact expect the members of the parole board to be affected by such a series of articles when they came to consider her case, but those in prison, awaiting with mounting anxiety the result of their parole application, cannot be expected to consider these matters with rational detachment; they are deeply emotionally involved in their applications, and I think it very understandable that, if they see their applications being torn apart and rejected by a great newspaper, they will consider that it does great damage to their parole prospects and the anguish of mind will be great. "That can all be compensated for in damages", say The Sun: "She can have damages for it." I do not think any money, in the situation in which this woman finds herself, would be an adequate compensation for that sort of tribulation. Accordingly, I have no doubt in my mind that in this case, even if there is just an arguable case, the balance of convenience comes down heavily in favour of the judge's decision to grant an injunction.

KERR, L.J.

In this case there is no doubt that the copyright in the plaintiff's lengthy submission to the secretary of the parole board is in her. What is quite clear, however, is that, but for any previous publications of extracts from the submissions to the parole board with Miss Myra Hindley's consent, so as to place the contents of that long submission into the public domain, any defence of fair dealing must be out of the question. It cannot be fair to publish confidential submissions from a prisoner to the parole board and then to express the view that they are without substance and that parole ought not to be granted. Mr. Hoffman fairly conceded that if it were not for the previous publications, he could not begin to say that there is any arguable case of fair dealing within section 6.

As regards the earlier publications, the only one of these in relation to which it is suggested, though not on affidavit, that the plaintiff co-operated in any way is the one which appeared in The Sunday Times. I am prepared to infer from the material before the court, from the article in The Sunday Times, and from what Mr. Hoffmann said on behalf of The Sun, that there may well have been a disclosure by Miss Hindley of that document to The Sunday Times. But what she swears, which is at present uncontradicted on behalf of the defendants, is that "the document has never been published with my consent or acquiescence. Nor have I ever licensed the publication of parts." That is quoted from her second affidavit. In her first affidavit she said: "As appears from its title", (this document) "was of a confidential nature and it has never been published with my consent or acquiescence."

The fact that she may have disclosed it to a reporter of The Sunday Times is in no way inconsistent, as I see it, with her statement that she never agreed to the publication of any parts of the statement, let alone to what we have in the present case, which is the reproduction of long extracts with some linking passages. These were published yesterday, and other extracts would have appeared today but for the injunction.

On the state of the evidence before the court at present, even allowing for the inferences to be drawn from The Sunday Times article and from what Mr. Hoffmann has said, there is no reason to infer that Myra Hindley is inaccurate when she says that she never authorised the publication of this statement or of extracts from it. However, there is a triable issue on that point, and therefore I say no more about it.

When one then comes to consider the relative damage that would be done to the two parties to this litigation if the injunction is maintained or lifted, there can, as I see it, only be one answer. She, the prisoner, is bound to see this campaign of a week, in which her submission to the parole board is in effect being torn to shreds, as extremely damaging and as prejudicing her chances of obtaining parole in 1985; and indeed that is what she says in her affidavit. On the other hand, so far as The Sun is concerned, no financial damage is suggested, and the series can clearly go on, and no doubt will go on, but without—if the injunction stays— infringing her copyright any further. In this connection it is very important to bear in mind that there is no defense of public interest raised on behalf of The Sun in this case; no doubt for good reason.

So it seems to me that the balance of convenience is all one way. Let there be a trial if the defendants wish it, and then, if they succeed, despite all the difficulties, in showing that this is a case of fair dealing and that the infringement of the prisoner's copyright is permitted by law, then let them publish the statement thereafter to any extent that they may wish.

I agree that this appeal should be dismissed.

Notes and Questions

1.   To what extent should a court be allowed to second guess a reporter's determination of the newsworthy nature of a particular copyrighted work? On the trial below, assuming that the evidence demonstrates that Ms. Hindley had actually showed the reporter the confidential statement, should the subsequent publication of the statement without her consent qualify as "fair dealing"?

2. Does the publication of this statement conflict with a "normal exploitation of the work" or "unreasonably prejudice the legitimate interests of the right holder"?

3. In December 1996, the WIPO Copyright Treaty was adopted which dealt largely, although not exclusively, with copyright issues related to the digital media. Similar to TRIPS and Berne, its Article 10 outlined the acceptable limitations and exceptions which may be placed on copyright protected works:

WIPO Copyright Treaty

Article 10

(1) Contracting Parties may, in their national legislation, provide for limitations of or exceptions to the rights granted to authors of literary and artistic works under this Treaty in certain special cases that do not conflict with a normal exploitation of the work and do not unreasonably prejudice the legitimate interests of the author.

(2) Contracting Parties shall, when applying the Berne Convention, confine any limitations of or exceptions to rights provided for therein to certain special cases that do not conflict with a normal exploitation of the work and do not unreasonably prejudice the legitimate interests of the author.

Compare this language with Article 10 of Berne and Article 13 of TRIPS. What appears to be the international standard for determining not only fair use but also compulsory licenses of copyrighted materials after the WIPO Copyright Treaty? Are the cases you read in accordance with WIPO obligations under this "new" standard?

4. Are the rights of the copyright owners adequately protected under the present international standards? For example, does the grant of a fair use exemption under copyright laws adequately consider the moral rights which certain countries grant creators? Are there other concerns which the TRIPS/WIPO standard fails to consider?

Chapter Thirty–Four

TRADEMARKS

A. WHY LIMITATIONS MAY BE PLACED ON INTERNATIONAL TRADEMARK LICENSES

HAMBURGERS ABROAD: CULTURAL VARIATIONS AFFECTING FRANCHISING ABROAD

Michael Wallace Gordon, 9 Conn. J. Int'l L. 165 (1994).

The franchise is especially useful to illustrate that its cultural impact tends not to be very specifically governed by written law, but is likely to draw into the governance scheme the unwritten law. I use the franchise predominantly because it is such an openly expressed symbol of culture, from golden arches to "finger lickin' good." It is essential to maintain consistency in selling the franchise's product abroad, and maintaining that consistency may create conflicts with local culture.

The consistency has several facets. It is a consistency in architectural style, expressed in golden arches above Route 44 in Hartford, Connecticut, or on a street in Kensington in London, or around the corner from the Piazza di Spagna (Spanish Steps) in Rome. That consistency in style is maintained no matter how those arches may conflict with local architectural tastes. It is also a consistency in name recognition, as seen by a Big Mac being on essentially every menu in every McDonald's throughout the world. That consistency in name recognition is maintained regardless of what that name means in the local language. It is a consistency in menu, expressed by the availability of essentially the same products in every nation. That consistency in menu is maintained no matter what the local preferences or mores might suggest is more suitable. It is a consistency in advertising as expressed by the same slogans used around the globe. Consistency in advertising is maintained whether or not it makes any sense if in English in the foreign country, or in translated form in the local language. It is a consistency in taste as expressed by a uniformity of taste (or absence of identifiable taste). That consistency in taste is maintained no matter what the taste buds of local persons are attuned to recognize and deem pleasurable. And finally, it is a consistency in price as expressed by a kind of equivalency in value under different currencies. That consistency in price is maintained even if the goods are priced out of the mass market most franchises seek to serve.

Consistency may be critical to protecting the trademark, but it may be carried to such extremes that it creates an inertia of its own as new franchise outlets are opened in country after country. One important element of success in operating a franchise abroad is to be able to make deviations from this demand for consistency to satisfy local standards. Many of those deviations will be undertaken to adjust to local culture.

A trademark must be protected to be retained. Part of the trademark may be the building and/or the symbols, such as the McDonalds's golden arches, or the Kentucky Fried Chicken red and white striped buildings. These symbols, identified with United States culture, may not be acceptable in other nations in all their size and color, and visually attracting (or distracting) impact. Unless subdued or altered to meet local norms, the franchise may be rejected by a local planning commission or a national foreign investment review agency. The reasons for rejection may not be clearly stated, but may clearly be because the United States cultural symbolism may be too prominent. Two examples will illustrate this concern. The first is where the foreign franchise was accepted at least partly because it was believed the foreign cultural symbolism could be controlled, and the second is where the idea was rejected because there was fear that it could not be controlled. A third situation may appear, however, where the foreign cultural symbolism may be accepted in all its foreign splendor as a welcome symbol of a market economy.

In Heidleberg, Germany, on a small square near the center of the attractive old town, is a McDonald's. It is in a four story red stone building, the façade expressing an old world ornateness and elegance repeated in most other adjacent buildings, at least those which escaped World War II damage. No golden arches reach above the building. Above the door is the word "McDonalds" in white letters perhaps 8 inches high. The word is 3–4 feet long. Over each of two Paladian windows aside the door is a gold "M" arch, perhaps two feet high each at the most, and affixed flatly to the window ledge. At the corner of the building is the only sign visible from other than standing in front of the building, another two foot high gold "M" in a black metal frame, jutting out perhaps two feet from the building in much the same manner as the trade symbols which appear in signs in many old European towns, such as a shoe for a shoe store, a mortar and pestle for a pharmacy, etc. The overall presentation of this McDonalds is as subdued as any of the adjacent local stores. The McDonalds in Heidleburg is representative of the acceptance of foreign culture when presented in a manner consistent with and respectful of its surroundings. It exists in a successful format perhaps less due to company planning, where consistency would demand that the arches soar, than to local planning councils clearly dictating the conditions of appearance and of style under which it may function. In this case there are written rules, at least planning guidelines. Where such written rules do exist, such as the regulation of architectural style, there seems to be less public objection than where the method of control is less clearly expressed.

Foreign franchises may be allowed with little if any restraint on their cultural symbolism, because the host nation wishes to make a statement regarding its status as a free market economy. McDonalds in a number of such nations, Costa Rica, Hong Kong, and more recently some former non-market economy nations including such as Russia, appear in much the same U.S. cultural clothing as any McDonalds franchise in the United States. They speak of market economy freedoms. Costa Rica is a small nation in need of foreign investment; McDonalds symbolizes the nation's unrestrictive investment policy.

In addition to how the foreign franchise entity appears to the eye, what it is called may also be misunderstood or objected to abroad. The name of the franchise, as well as the product, may make little sense, or too much sense, abroad. Advertisements referring to "Colonel" Sanders of Kentucky Fried Chicken met with objection in Germany where "Colonel" suggests reference to the less than loved United States military. Chevrolet certainly gave little thought to selling the Nova in Latin America, where "no va" means "it does not go."

In Mexico in the 1976 Tradenames and Inventions Law's infamous articles 127 and 128, these provisions mandated foreign businesses to link Mexican origin names with foreign names, and constituted one of the first attempts by developing nations during the nationalistic and restrictive 1970s to reduce the dominance of foreign brand names, and to attempt to create local names for familiar foreign origin products. There was considerable urging to require the foreign name be dropped after the linked name gained local recognition. Thus, Cristal–Gleem toothpaste would ultimately become Cristal toothpaste. The response from foreign producers was so negative that the implementation of these articles was delayed a year, and the following year annually delayed year after year until the provisions were repealed. The problems associated with linking names were considerable. For example, Coca–Cola was, at the time, mainly sold in the familiar green molded glass bottle, which would have to be totally replaced with new bottles with the linked name.

While I am not aware of many other attempts in other nations to mandate by written law the adoption of local names for the names of foreign businesses or their products, there have been local language laws which have affected various aspects of business, such as the language of the menu and the language used in advertising.

Moreover, it is not only the language which must be considered, but pictorial elements intended to convey a meaning. For example, baby food in the familiar small jars with photos of babies on the label did not sell well on the shelves of some African nations. Illiterate mothers wondered why anyone would buy jars containing ground up babies.

Product names also create confusion. Products may be known by a different name even in another English speaking nation, such as chips rather than french fries in England. Translated product names may also create confusion or rejection of the product, as when a company sold its big burrito as a burrada, the colloquial meaning in Spanish being "big mistake."

Where there is no pressure to use the host nation language, good sense may suggest translating English advertising into the foreign language. Attempted translations, however, can create the most embarrassing situations. Obscenities are obviously not intended by foreign multinationals, and they are often accepted abroad as unintended blunders. Some translations are not offensive, but simply convey unintended meanings. For example: (1) A toy Taiwanese made bear which sang such Christmas carols as "Oh Little Town of Birmingham"; (2) KFC's "finger lickin' good" in Chinese as "eat your fingers off"; and (3) Coor's Light beer sold with the slogan "Turn it loose" translated into Spanish to mean "Drink Coors and get diarrhea."

Additionally, not all nations read from left to right. Obvious confusion was created in a nation which reads from right to left in a three picture advertising display of dirty clothes on the left, the suggested washing soap in the middle and the clean clothes on the right. Even the order of word translations may cause trouble, Bud Lite's "delicious, less filling" slogan was translated into Spanish to read "filling, less delicious."

Notes and Questions

1. Are there legitimate reasons why a foreign government would want to require the use of local brand names on all products sold within the country? Should any of these reasons be accorded the status of an internationally accepted exclusion to the national treatment obligations of the Paris Convention and TRIPS?

2. Are there legitimate reasons why a country would want to require a trademark to be licensed on a compulsory basis to a local company?

3. *Registered User Requirements.* Prior to the adoption of TRIPS, several countries, such as Canada, enacted registered user provisions that required the filing of a license to use by a domestic entity prior to the grant of a trademark registration based on a foreign mark. What policy is furthered by such requirements?

4. What are the problems that are posed by the compulsory licensing of a trademark? Are such problems different from those that arise from the compulsory licensing of a patent or a copyright?

5. You represent Burger Pride, one of the fastest growing U.S. franchises for organic foods and healthy alternatives to red meat and fat. Burger Pride's logo contains a smiling clown's face on a background of blue skies and green grass, surrounded by white script lettering which proclaims "All Natural, All Organic, All the Best." Burger Pride had a distinctive interior featuring all natural furniture made out of wood and rattan, and paintings of green farm land in the style of Grandma Moses. In addition to operating fast food franchises, Burger Pride has begun to sell take-home versions of All Soy Burgers and Non–Fat Fries. Burger Pride has decided to open its first

international franchise restaurants in New Delhi, India and Mexico City, Mexico. What advice would you give Burger Pride about the potential problems it might confront in expanding into these countries? What steps should it take to protect its IP rights in these countries? What major provisions should be included in its franchise agreement to protect its trademarks and corporate symbols?

COMPULSORY LICENSING OF A TRADEMARK: REMEDY OR PENALTY?
Thomas McCarthy, 67 TMR 197 (1977).

The propriety of compulsory licensing of a trademark has been receiving considerable publicity because it has been suggested as a remedy for a variety of social and economic ills. Some nations recently have adopted laws controlling the use of trademarks owned by foreigners in order to promote domestic political and economic programs and to favor domestic producers over foreign importers or trademark licensors. Such laws range from virtual prohibition of trademark licenses to domestic producers, to "dual use" requirements which mandate use of domestic trademarks in equal prominence with foreign licensed marks. While the effect of such foreign laws regulating trademark usage is similar to that proposed by United States advocates for compulsory licensing, the underlying legal and economic theories are quite divergent.

The specter of compulsory trademark licensing also has made an appearance on the legislative front. In January, 1977, Representative Rosenthal introduced H. R. 46, which, among other things, allows the Federal Trade Commission (F.T.C.), if it finds that the producer of a prescription drug is charging more than five times the "cost of production," to order the grant of a patent license and "if necessary to open the relevant market to competition, and if in the public interest, an unrestricted trademark license." An "unrestricted trademark license" is defined in the bill as a license "containing no condition, limitation, or restriction on the use or transfer of all trademarks owned or used by the patentee relevant to the patented product."

The Federal Trade Commission, which has for several years been seeking compulsory trademark licensing as a remedy for antitrust violations, recently met with success when an F.T.C. administrative law judge granted an unprecedented order of compulsory licensing of a trademark ("ReaLemon") as a remedy for illegal monopolization. The remedy was granted upon the premise that it "is not essentially different from a requirement of compulsory licensing of a patent."

Through all of these orders, litigations, laws and bills runs a common thread. It is that trademarks are somehow inherently antisocial and are fair game in the promotion of various other economic and political concerns.

While one could identify dozens of important differences between patents and trademarks, the following differences appear to be the most critical.

(1) The Differing Scope of Exclusionary Rights

Compare the scope of the exclusionary right of a patent vis-a-vis a trademark. The exclusive right defined by a patent is the right to make, use and sell devices defined by the patent claims. Compulsory licensing of a patent as an antitrust remedy is designed to diffuse any economic power or barriers to entry created by the patent by putting the right to use the patented technology into the hands of competitors. This is based upon the theory that the more licenses granted under a patent, the less the possible monopolistic barriers to entry created by the patent. On the other hand, the scope of the exclusionary right of a trademark is defined by the likelihood of customer confusion. That is, the only competition excluded by a trademark is "unfair competition." The exclusionary scope of a trademark (the range of similar marks and types of products on which another's mark is likely to cause customer confusion) turns upon the amount and kind of use of that mark by the owner or controlled licensees.

This difference in exclusionary scope of a patent compared to a trademark appears to create a paradox when compulsory trademark licensing is ordered. When compulsory licensing of a trademark is ordered, assuming arguendo adequate quality control, the more users in more territories of the trademark under license, then the greater is the exclusionary power of that trademark likely to be. The paradox would appear to be that at the end of the term of compulsory license, the power of the trademark has increased in proportion to the increased scope of usage by properly controlled licensees. Thus, as a long-term competitive remedy to diffuse undue power of a trademark, compulsory licensing seems to be a self-defeating remedy.

(2) Quality Control in Trademark Licensing

The above-mentioned paradox may be merely theoretical, since the assumption of proper quality control will probably be difficult, if not impossible, in the real world. Forced quality control in a compulsory trademark license is a unique element which is not necessary in a compulsory patent license. A patent license is primarily merely a waiver of the right to sue for infringement, with the main obligation of the patent licensee being merely regularly to pay royalties in order to buy immunity from an infringement suit.

The required element of quality control in a trademark license is the main distinguishing characteristic as compared to a patent license. It is black letter law that any license of a trademark must provide for adequate controls exercised by the trademark licensor over the quality of goods and services sold by licensees under the mark. If adequate quality control is not exercised, the license is "naked" and can result in partial or total abandonment of the mark, since it is in danger of becoming a weapon of deception to the public which relies upon the mark as an indicia of equal quality. If forced quality control is not realistically possible, then a compulsory trademark license may be merely a euphemism for judicially-ordered confiscation of the trademark, since when quality standards are not observed by licensees, the trademark ceases to have meaning and becomes either generic or deceptive.

Whereas in a voluntary trademark licensing plan, licensees have a vital economic interest in keeping quality levels up to par so as to preserve the "image" of the licensing program, in a forced licensing scheme, competitor-licensees would seem to have an exactly opposite incentive. The possibility that a licensee under a compulsory license could cut corners on quality standards would be tempting indeed. In connection with the practicality of forced quality control, it is interesting to note in the ReaLemon case that the ALJ found that Borden's major competitor had been adulterating its lemon juice with citric acid and sugar without disclosing that fact on its labels. If one of the prime candidates for a compulsory license has been in the habit of routinely adulterating its product, it would not seem too speculative to wonder what the product will contain if that producer operates under a loosely administered quality control system overseen by a third party. Also, the appointment of a third-party "quality control czar" would take inspection and termination powers out of the hands of the trademark owner, and introduce an insulating layer of bureaucracy between trademark owner and licensee which makes quality supervision just that much more difficult.

(3) Consumer Perception in a Forced Trademark License

It would not seem proper to say that a compulsory trademark license will result in consumer perception being the same as that in a voluntary licensing program. There is an important difference between impact on the public mind in a forced license as compared with a voluntary licensing program. In a voluntary licensing plan, the trademark owner carefully chooses licensees such that the licensed trademark is a symbol of equal quality in the inter-brand competitive struggle with other brands of competing products. But in a compulsory licensing scheme, by definition, all sellers in a competitive market are able to, and probably will, obtain a license. When a trademark is licensed by compulsion, all competitors in a relevant market will be using the same trademark. What will the ordinary consumer think the trademark signifies then? When we think of a term used by all sellers in a market, we think of a generic term which signifies not one source or one level of quality, but which signifies the very name of the product itself. When the public sees a word or design appearing on products sold by all sellers of an article, it seems reasonable that they will assume that the term is the name of that product. If this, in fact, happens, then what had been a trademark now becomes a generic term and any exclusivity and property rights are lost.

At the very least, one must admit that under a compulsory license order, the trademark which is licensed ceases to serve as a symbol of differentiation among competing sellers. If this is so, then the trademark owner and the licensees will use some other symbol to differentiate their product. What will probably happen is that each competitor will use its own house mark along with the licensed mark. Intra-brand competition will soon break down again into inter-brand competition as each seller will feature its own house brand as the best. Certainly, the trademark owner will have little incentive to spend money to advertise the licensed mark if all competitors can use it for a small royalty fee. The trademark owner, like the licensees, will feature its own house mark in advertising. The original trademark owner now starts from whatever brand recognition its own house mark already had. Thus, when the licensed mark is made available to all sellers, it becomes useless as a symbol of differentiation, so other marks will be developed and promoted. When consumers see the licensed term used in conjunction with various house marks, they are more likely to think of the licensed term as the generic name of the product.

> "Preservation of the trademark as a means of identifying the trademark owner's products serves an important public purpose. It makes effective competition possible in a complex, impersonal marketplace by providing a means through which the consumer can identify products which please him and reward the producer with continued patronage. Without some such method of product identification, informed consumer choice, and hence meaningful competition in quality, could not exist. [*Smith v. Chanel, Inc.*, 402 F2d 562, 566, 159 U.S.PQ 388, 391 (9th Cir 1968).]"

Even if one does not accept the argument that compulsory trademark licensing is an inherently punitive and confiscatory device, it would seem beyond dispute that compulsory trademark licensing is a drastic remedy of last resort, to be properly invoked only after seriously considering and rejecting less restrictive alternatives. Some other less restrictive remedies are suggested here. For example:

(2) Impose limits on the amount of money that may be used to advertise the mark for a time. This would tend to cool off a too powerful mark and allow others in the market to catch up or over any barriers to entry.

(3) Require modifications of size of the trademark on labels. The impact of a trademark may be lessened by requiring additional material to appear on the defendant's label along with the trademark or to require that such additional material be of a size so as to predominate over the trademark in visual impact. Since trademark power is often a direct result of visual impact on the consumer, that power could be lessened by reducing its impact without impinging on the use of the mark *per se*.

(4) Enjoin exclusionary behavior. If the trademark has been artificially "pumped up" with market power because of illegal conduct by the owner, that power can be most easily diluted and diffused by enjoining such illegal conduct.

Notes and Questions

1. In *In re Borden Inc.* 92 FTC 669 (1978) (the "ReaLemon" case referred to above), the Federal Trade Commission found that Borden's mark

"ReaLemon" was "virtually synonymous with bottled lemon juice itself" and, as relief for alleged violations of U.S. antitrust laws involving claims of attempted monopolization of the lemon juice market, ordered Borden to grant licenses to anyone engaged in or desiring to engage in the production and marketing of processed lemon juice. Quality control was to be administered by an independent third party acceptable to Borden and the licensee. The decision was strongly criticized.

2.   Although the above article focuses primarily on the appropriateness of compulsory licensing as relief for antitrust violations, its criticisms appear applicable to any compulsory trademark license. Do you agree with the criticisms raised? Could you devise a compulsory trademark license that would meet these criticisms? Under what circumstances should such a license be required?

3.   As a result of the outcry that efforts such as Mexico's linking laws caused internationally, compulsory licensing of trademarks is now expressly prohibited by international law. Article 21 of TRIPS expressly provides:

> Members may determine conditions on the licensing and assignment of trademarks, it being understood that the compulsory licensing of trademarks shall not be permitted and that the owner of a registered trademark shall have the right to assign the trademark with or without the transfer of the business to which the trademark belongs.

As a result of the enactment of TRIPS, Canada and other countries have since rescinded their registered user and linking laws.

4.   Although Article 21 prohibits the compulsory licensing of trademarks, it continues to allow governments to regulate the licensing of such marks. Among the types of requirements that may be imposed are quality control, registration (except for famous marks under Article 6bis of the Paris Convention) and actual use.

THE COCA–COLA EXPORT CASE
COCA–COLA LTD. v. PARDHAN
Federal Court, Trial Division, 1997.

WETSTON J.

By statement of claim filed December 19, 1995, the plaintiffs, Coca–Cola Ltd. ("CCL") and Coca–Cola Bottling Ltd. ("CCBL"), commenced an action against the defendants, alleging that they infringed the plaintiffs' trade-marks, and depreciated the value of the plaintiffs' goodwill in them, by selling Coca–Cola, made for sale and consumption only in Canada, abroad. On January 8, 1996, the plaintiffs obtained an interlocutory injunction and an Anton Piller Order against the defendants.

The defendants argue that the plaintiffs' two primary claims cannot stand, i.e., that the defendants' export of Coca–Cola products purchased in Canada is an unauthorized use of the plaintiffs' trade-marks in those products, under the Trade-marks Act, R.S.C. 1985, c. T–13, and that the effect of the defendants' activities constitutes a devaluation of the plaintiffs' goodwill in those marks, in breach of § 22(1) of the Act. They contend that mere export of trade-marked products does not constitute "use" within the definition provided in § 4(3) of the Act. Moreover, if there has been any devaluation of goodwill in the subject marks, which is denied, that can be attributed to the activities of the defendants, it occurred outside Canada, and is thus not subject to any determination under § 22 of the Act. If it can be established that the defendants' purchase and subsequent re-sale of Coca–Cola products abroad violated the plaintiffs' policy that such products may be purchased for domestic consumption only, which is enforced by CCL through licensing agreements, such a violation is a matter of common law of contract and, therefore, beyond the jurisdiction of this Court.

The plaintiffs also submit that § 8 of the Act provides the trade-mark owner with the right to attach binding limitations to the use of a mark, so long as such limitations are expressly set out prior to the transfer of trade-marked wares. Accordingly, since the defendants were aware that CCL strictly prohibited export of its trade-marked products for resale abroad, their sales for export constitute infringement under the Act. Moreover, the defendants' unauthorized sales-for-export have diminished the goodwill enjoyed by the plaintiffs in the marks, and as such, the plaintiffs are entitled to pursue a cause of action under § 22(1) of the Act against them.

The defendants argue that they did not use the plaintiffs' marks because they were not the first to have purchased the products with which such marks are associated, *i.e.*, the "doctrine of first use". The plaintiffs submit that, although a purchaser of goods in Canada bearing a trade-mark is entitled to resell those goods without incurring liability for infringement, this entitlement is subject to the right of a trade-mark holder, under § 8 of the Act, to place a limitation on how the mark may not be used in connection with the goods. The plaintiffs limit the re-sale of products which bear their trade-marks to the Canadian market only. As such, any sale for export of such products would violate the plaintiffs' "warranty of lawful use" and constitute infringement under the Act.

If goods have been placed into trade channels by the owner of a trade-mark, and have subsequently been acquired by another party in the ordinary course of business, it is not an infringement for those same goods to be re-sold by that party in association with the trade-mark: *Wilkinson Sword (Canada) Ltd. v. Juda* (1966), 51 C.P.R. 55 (Ex. Ct.). In other words, the defendants are entitled to purchase and re-sell trade-marked products in Canada and such activity does not per se, constitute "use" under the Act: *Wella Canada Inc. v. Pearlon Products Ltd.* (1984), 4 C.P.R. (3d) 287 (Ont. H.C.J.) at 288.

The plaintiffs contend that they may dictate the destination of the markets in which the goods they produce may be sold and resold by virtue of the trade-marks they hold in association with such goods and § 8 of the Act. The plaintiffs also argue that the export of trade-marked products is deemed to be a "use in Canada" under § 4(3) of the Act.

Therefore, any unauthorized export by the defendants would also constitute infringement under the Act.

I am unable to accept this argument. In enacting section 4(3) of the Act, Parliament cannot be said to have intended that the provision should apply to every carriage of goods between Canada and another country, whether personal or commercial. Nor can section 4(3) be interpreted as being limited to exports which constitute commercial transactions only. It is clear that for an export to be deemed a "use in Canada" under § 4(3), it need not take place in the normal course of trade: *Molson Companies Ltd. v. Moosehead Breweries Ltd.* (1990), 32 C.P.R. (3d) 363 (F.C.T.D.) at 373.

In my opinion, § 4(3) is intended to ensure that what would constitute infringement under the Act if done in Canada, will also constitute infringement if done abroad. For example, if a person in one province produced counterfeit Coca–Cola products, replete with trade-marks it was not authorized to use, and sold such goods in another province, it would be deemed to have used the plaintiffs' marks under § 4(1), and would be liable for infringement under the Act. With respect to § 4(3), that same person could export the counterfeit products to the United States, and incur no liability in Canada. By enacting § 4(3), Parliament closed this loophole.

In the present case, there has been no allegation of actual use of the plaintiffs' trade-marks by the defendants. The defendants have not produced counterfeit Coca–Cola products for sale locally or abroad. They have not used a confusing mark on similar cola products which they sold in Canada or exported for sale abroad. If the facts alleged by the plaintiffs are taken as proved, the defendants have merely purchased large quantities of genuine Coca–Cola products from a third-party retailer, and then exported them for sale abroad, against the obvious wishes of the plaintiffs. "Goods which originate in the stream of commerce with the owner of a trade mark are not counterfeit or infringing goods simply because they may have arrived in a particular geographical market where the trade mark owner does not wish them to be distributed": *Smith & Nephew Inc. v. Glen Oak Inc.* (1996), 68 C.P.R. (3d) 153 (F.C.A.) at 158. The plaintiffs also submit that the activities of the defendants have resulted in a depreciation of the value of the goodwill attached to its marks, contrary to section 22(1) of the Act. Section 22(1) provides:

> 22(1) No person shall use a trade-mark registered by another person in a manner that is likely to have the effect of depreciating the value of the goodwill attaching thereto.

[Once again, assuming the alleged facts as proved, the defendants have not violated § 22(1) of the Act. They have not engaged in activities which constitute "use" under the Act, such as the unauthorized use of a trade-mark or the use of a confusing mark on a product it produces. If the defendants have not used the trade-marks in question, it is plain and obvious that their activities cannot be said to have violated § 22(1) of the Act.]

The plaintiffs cite a U.S. decision, *Warner-Lambert Co. v. Northside Development Corp.*, an unreported decision of Winter C.J., 29 May 1966 (C.A. 2nd Cir.) at 5, for the proposition that failure to meet quality control standards set by the holder of a registered trade-mark for its associated products can vitiate the doctrine of first use, and give rise to a claim under American trade-mark law for depreciation of goodwill. Whether this decision also represents the law in Canada does not need to be answered here. It is clear that, if the defendants have failed to observe quality control standards set by the plaintiffs for the shipment and sale of Coca–Cola products, the activity took place abroad, and only involved the sale of Coca–Cola products abroad.

Generally, evidence of confusion or depreciation of the value of goodwill in foreign jurisdictions is not evidence of confusion or depreciation of the value of goodwill in Canada. Moreover, "the nature of goodwill as legal property with no physical existence means that where a business is carried on in more than one country or jurisdiction there must be a separate goodwill in each": C. Wadlow, *The Law of Passing– Off* (London: Sweet & Maxwell, 1990), at 62. I agree with this principle. In a case such as this, the jurisdiction of this Court to determine claims under the Trade-marks Act should be considered in the context that the Act applies only in Canada.

The allegations contained within paragraph 17 are the basis only for causes of action which are beyond the jurisdiction of this Court to adjudicate. If the sale-for-export of trade-marked products constitutes infringement under the trade-mark laws of foreign jurisdictions, it is for the court of those jurisdictions to adjudicate. Similarly, if the sale-for-export of trade-marked products somehow constitutes a breach of a contractual relationship between the plaintiffs and the defendants, remedy for such breach must be found in another court because the statement of claim in such a case would not be founded on existing federal law.

It is not for this Court to adjudicate whether the defendants have failed to ensure that the Coca–Cola product in question is labelled in accordance with the laws of the country where the product is to be delivered, or whether the defendants have failed to obtain the necessary licences to sell such products abroad.

Export of trade-marked products by a secondary purchaser cannot constitute "use" as defined in § 4(3) of the Act. The defendants have not used the marks associated with the Coca–Cola products they purchased and resold simply by virtue of their having resold the products abroad, in violation of the plaintiffs' express intent that export should not take place.

The plaintiffs have failed to plead the facts necessary to establish "use" under the Act, and as such, § 22(1) of the Act cannot be engaged by their conduct. Further, any depreciation of the value of goodwill in the trade-marks in question which may have taken place, would have taken place outside Canada, and is therefore beyond the jurisdiction of this Court to adjudicate.

Notes and Questions

1. *Grey Market Goods.* Goods which have been legitimately manufactured in a particular country but which are then exported to another are referred to as "grey market" or "parallel imports." Such goods are not illegal per se (they are not counterfeit), but their unauthorized exportation may create problems in the trademark owners global marketing plans. The ability of countries to preclude the importation of copyrighted or trademarked goods remains a hotly debated international topic.

Current U.S. law grants a domestic rights holder only limited rights to preclude the importation of grey market goods. Where the good contains a trademark, under *K Mart Corp. v. Cartier, Inc.*, 486 U.S. 281 (1988), its parallel importation may only be prohibited if the domestic and foreign mark owners are *not* subject to common ownership or control. Where the good contains a copyright, its parallel importation may not be prohibited where the goods have been manufactured lawfully in the United States. Whether the importation of copyrighted goods manufactured lawfully abroad can be prohibited under U.S. law remains unclear. *See, e.g., Quality King Distributors, Inc. v. L'Anza Research International, Inc.*, 523 U.S. 135 (1998).

In the European Union, the ability to import grey market goods similarly depends upon the type of right being exercised and the site of manufacture of the product in question. Thus, goods which have been manufactured within the European Union can be imported through-out the Union. Once the good has been sold, the rights holder's ability to control its subsequent distribution by prohibiting importation of the good, is exhausted. *See generally Musik–Vertrieb Membran GmbH v. Gema*, [1982]1 CMLF 630 (German Federal Supreme Court)(copyrighted works); *Centrafarm BV v. Sterling Drug, Inc.*, [1974] ECR 1147 (European Court of Justice)(trademarked works); *Merck & Co., Inc. v. Stephar BV*, [1981] ECR 2063 (European Court of Justice)(patented goods). For a more detailed discussion of exhaustion rights in the European Union, see Chapter Forty.

2. Does the court's refusal in the *Coca-Cola Export* case to permit the trademark owner to control the use of its mark on exported products qualify as an unauthorized "taking" of the mark?

3. Since the Coca–Cola products in this case were lawfully produced in Canada, would they qualify as infringing products in the United States where they were being imported without the consent of either the U.S. or Canadian trade-mark owners? *See K Mart Corp. v. Cartier, Inc.*, 486 U.S. 281 (1988). Should trademark owners be able to control the unauthorized exportation of their goods in order to protect their global distribution plans? For example, could such control help the owner reduce global counterfeiting by permitting differential pricing of its products without risking a flood of low-priced grey market goods in markets which could support higher prices due to higher standards of living?

Chapter Thirty–Five

"PROPERTY" REVISITED

A. WHEN DO UNPROTECTED EXPRESSIONS QUALIFY AS PROTECTED PROPERTY?

THE CIA BOOK CASE

JACK B. PFEIFFER v. CENTRAL INTELLIGENCE AGENCY

United States Court Of Appeals, District of Columbia Circuit, 1995.
60 F.3d 861.

GINSBURG, CIRCUIT JUDGE.

As part of his duties as an historian employed by the CIA, Dr. Jack B. Pfeiffer wrote a report dealing with the Agency's internal investigation of the Bay of Pigs Operation. When he left the CIA Pfeiffer took a copy of that report, which he later asked the Agency to review and clear for publication. When the CIA declined, Pfeiffer brought suit in district court claiming that the Agency's refusal to undertake such a review operated as a prior restraint upon his right to speak, in violation of the First Amendment to the Constitution of the United States. The United States intervened and counterclaimed for return of Pfeiffer's copy of the report. The district court granted summary judgment in favor of the Government on both Pfeiffer's claim and the Government's counterclaim. Because Pfeiffer has no right to a copy of the document and the CIA's conduct in this case does not implicate the first amendment, we affirm the judgment of the district court.

Pfeiffer joined the CIA in 1955. At that time he signed a "Secrecy Agreement" stating:

I do not now, nor shall I ever possess any right, interest, title or claim, in or to any of the information or intelligence which has come or shall come to my attention by virtue of my connection with the [CIA], but shall always recognize the property right of the United States of America, in and to such matters.

Pfeiffer worked for the CIA for nearly 30 years. During his last ten years there he worked on a series of historical reports on the Bay of Pigs

Operation. The report at issue here deals with the Agency's internal investigation of that Operation.

On his last day at the Agency (December 28, 1984) Pfeiffer sent a memorandum to the Information and Privacy Coordinator asking him to declassify an edited version of the report pursuant to Executive Order No. 12,356, which establishes a procedure whereby a federal agency is required to declassify material unless the agency identifies some legal ground for nondisclosure. Also on his last day at the Agency, Pfeiffer signed a "Security Reminder" that states, in part:

I have also been reminded that I am not permitted to retain any documents or other materials which are the property of the CIA or the custodial responsibility of CIA, and I affirm that I do not have in my possession, nor am I taking away from CIA any such documents or materials.

Nevertheless, Pfeiffer admits, he took a copy of the unedited version of the Bay of Pigs report with him when he left the Agency.

Pfeiffer asked the Agency to undertake a "prepublication review" of the report. Every current and former CIA employee is required to get Agency approval before publishing any writing that may contain or be based upon classified information that the employee obtained as a result of his service with the Agency.

The Agency responded to Pfeiffer's request by stating that its prepublication review procedure does not apply to a work created in the course of an employee's official duties, as opposed to a work that, while "prepared for nonofficial publication in [the former employee's] personal capacity," might reflect information acquired though his CIA employment. In addition, the CIA warned Pfeiffer that if he had a copy of the report, his possession of it "could be a violation of criminal statutes regarding theft of Government property and/or retention of information relating to the national defense."

Pfeiffer then brought this action in district—court claiming, among other things, that the CIA's refusal to review the report for publication is an unconstitutional prior restraint of his first amendment right to speak.

The report at issue in this casein both its original form and in the form of Pfeiffer's copy—is indisputably the property of the Government. It was created at government expense, *i.e.*, with government materials and on government time. *See Reporters Committee for Freedom of the Press v. Vance*, 442 F.Supp. 383, 387 (D.D.C.1977), *aff'd*, 191 U.S. App. D.C. 213, 589 F.2d 1116 (1978), *aff'd in part, rev'd in part* as *Kissinger v. Reporters Committee for Freedom of the Press*, 445 U.S. 136, 63 L.Ed.2d 267, 100 S.Ct. 960 (1980). If more is needed to establish the Government's ownership, it may be found in Pfeiffer's agreement with the Agency disclaiming any personal property interest in information coming to his attention "by virtue of [his] connection with the [CIA]" and in the

CIA regulation expressly asserting the Government's property interest in any report prepared by an employee as part of his official duties.

Pfeiffer asserts nonetheless that the Copyright Act of 1976 precludes the Government's assertion of any property interest because he took only a copy of the report—albeit one made at government expense. Here he points to *17 U.S.C. § 105,* which provides that "copyright protection . . . is not available for any work of the United States Government." See also *17 U.S.C. § 101* (defining a "work of the United States Government" as "a work prepared by an officer or employee of the United States Government as part of that person's official duties"). The "copyright protection" denied to the Government is quintessentially the exclusive right "to reproduce the copyrighted work." *17 U.S.C. § 106.* Moreover, Pfeiffer states that the Copyright Act "abolished all common law protections . . . tantamount to copyright," see *17 U.S.C. § 301*(a), thereby leaving the Government with no source of protection for "a work prepared by an officer or employee."

That the Government generally cannot prevent the reproduction of its works (classified information apart) seems a fair enough interpretation; by no stretch of the interpretive imagination, however, do the cited provisions mean that a copy of a government work cannot be the Government's property. And what the Government asserts here is not a copyright but a possessory interest in the copy Pfeiffer took with him when he left the CIA. Not only is there no inconsistency between the Government's asserted interest and the Copyright Act, the Act specifically provides: "Ownership of a copyright . . . is distinct from ownership of any material object in which the work is embodied." *17 U.S.C. § 202;* see also H.R. Rep. No. 1476, 94th Cong., 2d Sess. 133 (1976) (this section does not "preclude[ ] the owner of a material embodiment of a copy . . . from enforcing a claim of conversion against one who takes possession of the copy . . . without consent"). So far as the Copyright Act is concerned, therefore, Pfeiffer has no more legal right to the copy of the report that he took from the Agency than he has to take a book from the bookstore of the Government Printing Office without paying for it.

That Pfeiffer must return his copy of the report is compelled also as a matter of equity; for he obtained it only by violating his fiduciary duty to the CIA. *See generally Snepp v. United States*, 444 U.S. 507, 510, 62 L.Ed.2d 704, 100 S. Ct. 763 (1980). Even if he had reproduced the report at his own expense, that is, he was still bound by his agreements not to do so. Of course, we express no view upon the question whether a third-party who copies a government document, such as a journalist presumably unencumbered by the "extremely high degree of trust" invested in an employee of the CIA, *id.* at 507, could likewise be required to relinquish it. *Cf. New York Times Co. v. United States*, 403 U.S. 713, 29 L.Ed.2d 822, 91 S. Ct. 2140 (1971) (Government failed to make sufficient showing to enjoin newspapers' publication of "Pentagon Papers").

For the foregoing reasons, the judgment of the district court is, in all respects, affirmed.

THE THREE STOOGES CASE
COMEDY III PRODUCTIONS, INC.
v. NEW LINE CINEMA

United States District Court, C.D. California, 1998.
46 U.S.P.Q.2D 1930.

B. COLLINS, J.

Plaintiff's Complaint alleges, in pertinent part, as follows:

Plaintiff, a California corporation, is the exclusive owner of all rights, title, and interest in the world-famous comedy team known as "The Three Stooges." Defendant is a Delaware corporation, with its principal place of business in California. From about 1934 to 1970, various performers played the parts of the famous comedy team known as "The Three Stooges." These performers included Larry Fine, Moe Howard and Joe DeRita.

In or about June, 1993, heirs of Larry Fine and Joe DeRita filed suit against heirs of Moe Howard in the Los Angeles Superior Court ("the DeRita lawsuit."). The plaintiffs in the DeRita lawsuit contended, among other things, that all rights, title and interest to The Three Stooges rightfully belonged to Comedy III. Pursuant to a unanimous jury verdict, the Court issued a verdict in favor of plaintiffs on all counts. Among other things, the Court issued a judicial declaration which determined that the rights in and to The Three Stooges belong, in total, to Comedy III. The judgment declared, in part:

All of the right, [sic] title and interest arising out of or relating to The Three Stooges and its members . . . , including but not limited to any Civil Code Section 990 rights (faces, voices, photographs, names, likenesses, signatures, and characters of The Three Stooges), rights to licensing, merchandising and production, the rights to the name The Three Stooges or variations thereof, the Act including tricks, antics, dialogue, sobriquets, routines, or mannerisms, copyright, licenses, authorizations, trademarks, tradenames, or such other rights, were transferred to and belong exclusively to Comedy III Productions, Inc.

Plaintiff, therefore, owns all rights, of every kind or nature, (referred to by Plaintiff as "proprietary rights") in and to The Three Stooges. Plaintiff, as owner of the proprietary rights, has over fifty (50) licensees and is engaged in the business of merchandising products bearing The Three Stooges brand trademark, as well as producing new productions featuring the mannerisms, antics and act that have become to be associated with The Three Stooges.

On or about January 11, 1995, Plaintiff's representatives met with Michael De Luca ("De Luca") of Defendant. At that meeting, Plaintiff's representatives discussed with De Luca a proposal to enter into an arrangement pursuant to which Plaintiff and Defendant would produce a new theatrical motion picture based on Plaintiff's exclusive rights in and to The Three Stooges. During that meeting, Plaintiff's representatives explained the history of The Three Stooges, Comedy III, and the lawsuit which vested all proprietary rights in Plaintiff.

Thereafter, with full knowledge of the rights vested in Plaintiff, Defendant utilized, exploited, and misappropriated Plaintiff's proprietary rights by incorporating an approximately 30–second film clip of The Three Stooges from a Three Stooges feature (the "Clip") entitled "Disorder in the Court" into a full-length theatrical motion picture feature film entitled "The Long Kiss Goodnight." Produced by Defendant, "The Long Kiss Goodnight" was released and distributed for exhibition to the general public. At no time was Plaintiff advised, consulted or requested to consent, and Plaintiff did not consent to, authorize or license use of its proprietary rights by Defendant. Defendant has falsely designated itself as a licensor of the proprietary rights in The Three Stooges and Defendant has falsely claimed that Plaintiff is associated with, has endorsed or otherwise is affiliated with Defendant or "The Long Kiss Goodnight."

Plaintiff promptly notified Defendant in writing of Defendant's wrongful acts. Defendant has refused, and continues to refuse, to cease and desist from its conduct.

Part of Plaintiff's business consists of film clip licensing. The act, mannerisms, and characters of The Three Stooges have acquired secondary meaning and the public associates such characters with Plaintiff. Plaintiff licenses public domain film clips such as "Disorder in the Court" to film and television producers in exchange for a license fee. For years, Plaintiff has licensed major studios for the use of film clips using The Three Stooges characters, virtually none of which involve copyrights currently recognized to be owned by Plaintiff. For example, Plaintiff received a license fee from 20th Century Fox film corporation in 1991 for the use of a few seconds from The Three Stooges' film "Disorder in the Court" for use in a television series. This is the same feature that was inappropriately used by Defendant in "The Long Kiss Goodnight."

Plaintiff's proprietary rights in and to The Three Stooges and its members, including tradenames, trade dress and trademarks of The Three Stooges' names, acts, characters, characterizations, mannerisms, antics and other depictions by reason of their creation thereof and by their public performances over a long period of time as The Three Stooges, have acquired distinctiveness and/or a secondary meaning. Plaintiff's proprietary rights include the right to license others to utilize the names, faces, likenesses, characters, acts or routines of The Three Stooges in theatrical and television films and derivatives of those rights.

Defendant's use of the names, faces, likenesses, characters, acts or routines of The Three Stooges in connection with "The Long Kiss Goodnight" constitutes a violation of Section 43(a) of The Federal Trademark Act of 1946, 15 U.S.C § 1125(a) because it (1) constitutes a false designation of origin of Defendant's goods and services or a false description or representation of Defendant's goods and services, and (2) creates a likelihood of confusion among prospective purchasers and because it induces purchasers and others to believe, contrary to fact, that Defendant's services and products are performed, manufactured, approved by or otherwise connected in some way to Plaintiff and The Three Stooges.

As a direct result of Defendant's violation of the Lanham Act and acts of unfair competition, Plaintiff has suffered and continues to suffer great financial harm, including but not limited to, the loss of past and prospective income from those and other similar projects, and the devaluation and dilution of Plaintiff's rights. If not enjoined by this Court, Defendant's acts will continue to cause Plaintiff immediate and irreparable harm. If permitted to continue, Defendant's conduct will result in Defendant's misappropriation of the valuable and unique goodwill and persona which Plaintiff's predecessors, The Three Stooges, have created in the proprietary rights. Plaintiff is without legal remedy because the amount of damages cannot be readily ascertained.

Defendant initially seeks to dismiss Plaintiff's [complaint] because "plaintiff is attempting to invoke the Lanham Act to protect copyright rights." Based on Defendant's assertion, the Court ordered Plaintiff to provide further briefing explaining "the nature of the plaintiff's" enforceable trademark interest in the Clip used by Defendant in "The Long Kiss Goodnight." In response to the Court's Order, Plaintiff contends that it is not claiming a legally protected right in the Clip, but in the "name, the characters, the likeness, and overall 'act' of The Three Stooges." Thus, Plaintiff asserts that it seeks to enforce its trademark rights in the "characters and images appearing in the Clip," which are not affected by the fact that the Clip itself is in the public domain.

Plaintiff cites to several cases to support its contention that the name, characters, likeness, and overall act of The Three Stooges may be protected by trademark law separately from copyright law. [S]ee, e.g., *Waits v. Frito–Lay, Inc.*, 978 F.2d 1093, 1107 (concluding that unauthorized use of singer's voice in an advertisement is cognizable under Lanham Act); *Frederick Warne & Co. v. Book Sales, Inc.*, 481 F.Supp. 1191, 1196 (S.D.N.Y.1979) (finding protection under trademark laws of copyrightable character that has fallen into the public domain possible if character has "acquired independent trademark significance"); *Wyatt Earp Ent., Inc. v. Sackman, Inc.*, 157 F. Supp. 621 (S.D.N.Y.1958) (holding that plaintiff could have invested the name, mark, and symbol "Wyatt Earp", although a historical figure, with commercial significance such that defendant's use "Wyatt Earp" in its products could constitute trademark infringement). The Court does not dispute that trademark rights can be enforced separately from copyright interests or that characters, such as The Three Stooges, may be protected under trademark law. However, Plaintiff has failed to articulate how Defendant's use of the 30–second Clip implicates the trademark right that Plaintiff alleges it holds with regard to The Three Stooges' name, characters, likeness, and overall act. The Court finds the cases that Plaintiff relies on to establish its protectable trademark interest in the Clip distinguishable.

Plaintiff relies heavily on the facts and holding of *Warne* as authority for Plaintiff's claim against New Line Cinema. The Court in *Warne* held that the plaintiff may have a legally protectable trademark interest in the cover illustrations of the well-known Beatrix Potter Peter Rabbit Books ("Books") despite the fact that the Books' copyright had entered the public domain. The court found that, although the defendant had a right to copy the Books themselves, defendant's creation of a new book "with plaintiff's character illustrations [used] in a way in which those illustrations were never used in the public domain books," raised a question of fact as to whether the defendant had infringed plaintiff's mark in the Books' characters. Based on the foregoing, Plaintiff argues that the characters of The Three Stooges are protectable under the Lanham Act requiring "the proper inquiry in the present case [to be] whether the image of The Three Stooges has acquired a secondary meaning, identifying Comedy III as the sponsor of goods bearing that image."

Although the characters of The Three Stooges may indeed have acquired a secondary meaning, this does not necessarily imply that Defendant's use of the Clip implicates any trademark interest in The Three Stooges that Plaintiff might have. Unlike Comedy III, the Court does not find the Warne defendant's use of the characters at issue analogous to New Line Cinema's use of the characters of The Three Stooges via the Clip in the instant action. Distinct from the defendant in *Warne*, New Line Cinema has not used the characters of The Three Stooges in a "way in which [they] were never used in the public domain [film]." Plaintiff does not allege that New Line Cinema has used the characters from The Three Stooges to create a new and different Three Stooges film or an original "clip" of The Three Stooges. Nor does Plaintiff allege that Defendant has removed the characters of The Three Stooges from the Clip and superimposed those characters onto a product, such as a t-shirt or any other marketing paraphernalia to sell to the public in association with New Line Cinema's "The Long Kiss Goodnight." Thus, the Court finds that Plaintiff has not pled sufficient facts to establish that New Line Cinema, by showing the Clip in "The Long Kiss Goodnight," has used the characters or act of The Three Stooges in a manner different from the way in which the characters have been used in the public domain.

Furthermore, the court in *Warne* acknowledged that the defendant had a right to copy the Books that were in the public domain. Only if the defendant went "beyond mere copying" such that the defendant's use of the illustrations "may lead the public to believe that defendant's different, and allegedly inferior publication has been published or is somehow associated with plaintiff" would the defendant have infringed on the plaintiff's trademark rights. In the instant action, Plaintiff has not alleged facts to indicate that New Line Cinema's use of the Clip has gone beyond "mere copying" of the public domain work, so that it can state a claim for trademark infringement. Again, unlike the defendant in *Warne*, New Line Cinema has copied the Clip as it was originally published, rather than exploited the Three Stooges' characters or act apart from the Clip.

Plaintiff continuously states that it does not assert a trademark interest in the Clip itself, yet it is the Clip itself that the Defendant has used. Thus, the Court finds that it is the Clip which Defendants have incorporated into their film, not the character, likeness, or overall act of The Three Stooges. Plaintiff concedes that it does not claim a legally protected right in the Clip; therefore the Court finds that Plaintiff has failed to articulate a legally protectable trademark interest for purposes of this action. Absent a legally protectable trademark interest, Plaintiff cannot survive Defendant's motion to dismiss Plaintiff's Lanham Act claim. Furthermore, because the Court finds that Plaintiff has failed to articulate a legally protected right in the Clip, Plaintiff's state law claims for unfair competition—passing off, unfair competition—misappropriation, and unfair competition must also be dismissed.

For all of the reasons set forth above, the Court hereby ORDERS that Defendant's motion to dismiss is GRANTED with prejudice.

Notes and Questions

1. Before a claim for "taking" can arise, a party must have a property right that the government has taken without adequate compensation. Do you agree with the courts that no such taking occurred in either the *Three Stooges* or the *CIA Book* cases? Could you frame the party's claims in terms that would implicate on their intellectual property rights?

2. Would the defendant in the *CIA Book* case have succeeded if he had sought to use the information contained in the documents in question under an allegation of fair use?

3. Compare the court's decision in the *Three Stooges* case with the court's decision in the *World Cup Case*. Would the plaintiff have had a better chance in the *Three Stooges* case if it had worded its claim in terms of unauthorized copyright use?

*

Part X

IN–DEPTH TOPICS: FACING THE TECHNOLOGY CHALLENGE

The history of intellectual property law has been a series of legal advances designed to take into account the latest technological advances in science, communications media and/or marketing. Thus, copyright law became necessary after movable type made books accessible as a commercial commodity. Subsequent developments in communications media, including photography, motion pictures, and radio broadcast, resulted in subsequent expansions of copyright law to assure protection for works in these new media. Similarly, international protection issues arose as a European market for literary works developed in the 17th and 18th Centuries. Improvements in communications and transportation led to a global marketplace for copyrighted works which, in turn, gave greater impetus to the need to develop *international* standards for protection for these works.

Scientific and medical advances have similarly pushed the boundaries of patent laws. From the mechanical developments of the Eighteenth Century through the biogenetic breakthroughs of the Twentieth Century, patent laws have expanded to permit protection of such diverse new inventions as genetically-engineered living organisms, asexually reproducing plants and computer software.

Technology continues to advance at a dizzying pace, creating new problems in protection that the international marketplace is struggling to resolve. Widely available personal computers, with the subsequent demand for a great variety of software programs, bio-genetic engineering, robotics and computerized design and manufacturing processes have stretched intellectual property protection doctrines, perhaps to their breaking point. The rapid development of the Internet as both a medium of communication and a marketing device has raised new problems that serve as a microcosm for international protection issues in the Twenty–First Century. As the international community struggles to develop new standards of protection, the role of law in the face of technology is increasingly placed at issue. As you read the following, ask yourself whether the protection problems caused by technology can or should be

836

resolved through multinational treaty initiatives. Should key technological advances in medicine be subject to protection, or should they be available to all mankind without charge or reservation? What impact does international protection have on the impetus to research, develop and commercialize new technologies? Where should the line be drawn between ownership and public need?

Chapter Thirty–Six

THE INTERNET

A. WHO HAS THE RIGHT TO CONTROL THE CONTENT OF WORKS ON THE INTERNET?

One of the most legal-norm-shattering technological advances in communications at the latter part of the Twentieth Century was the development, and widespread availability, of digital communications via the Internet. Originally developed as an army defense communications network, the Internet revolutionized global communications, and increasingly, global commerce. It also became one of the primary areas of international concern as intellectual property standards–developed to regulate the creation of physical copies–struggled to protect content in a digital, non-physical, universe.

THE U.S. CYBERSQUATTER CASE
INTERMATIC INCORPORATED
v. DENNIS TOEPPEN

United States District Court, N.D. Illinois, 1996.
947 F.Supp. 1227.

REPORT AND RECOMMENDATION

DENLOW, UNITED STATES MAGISTRATE JUDGE.

The Internet is a vast and expanding network of computers and other devices linked together by various telecommunications media, enabling all the computers and other devices on the Internet to exchange and share data.

The Internet provides information about a myriad of corporations and products, as well as educational, research and entertainment information and services. An estimated 30 million people worldwide use the Internet with 100 million predicted to be on the "net" in a matter of years. A computer or device that is attached to the Internet is often referred to as a "host." In order to facilitate communications between hosts, each host has a numerical IP (Internet protocol) address. The IP address is comprised of four groups of numbers separated by decimals. For example, the IP address of one of Toeppen's host computers is 206.139.80.66. Each host also has a unique "fully qualified domain name." The "fully qualified domain name" may not be repeated in the Internet. In the case of 206.139.80.66, the "fully qualified domain name" is "winslow.net66.com".

In its most generic form, a fully qualified domain name consists of three elements. Taking "winslow.net66.com" as an example, the three elements are the hostname ("winslow"), a domain name ("net66") and a top level domain ("com"). A given host looks up the IP addresses of other hosts on the Internet through a system known as domain name service.

Domain name service is accomplished as follows: The Internet is divided into several "top level" domains. For example, "edu" is a domain reserved for educational institutions, "gov" is a domain reserved for government entities and "net" is reserved to networks. Although "com" is short for "commercial," it is a catchall domain and the only one generally available to Internet users that have no special attributes i.e., they are not a school or a government office or a network. Each domain name active in a given top-level domain is registered with the top level server which contains certain hostname and IP address information.

In order to access the Internet, most users rely on programs called "web browsers." Commercially available web browsers include such well-known programs as Netscape and Mosaic. If an Internet user desires to establish a connection with a web page hosted at winslow.net66.com, the Internet user might enter into a web browser program the URL "http: www.net66.com." (URL stands for uniform resource locator.) The first element of the URL is a transfer protocol (most commonly, "http"—standing for hypertext transfer protocol). The remaining elements of this URL (in this case, "www"—standing for World Wide Web—and "net66.-com") are an alias for the fully qualified domain name of the host winslow.net66.com. Once a URL is entered into the browser, the corresponding IP address is looked up in a process facilitated by a "top-level server." In other words, all queries for addresses are routed to certain computers, the so-called "top level servers". The top level server matches the domain name to an IP address of a domain name server capable of directing the inquiry to the computer hosting the web page. Thus, domain name service ultimately matches an alphanumeric name such as www.net66.com with its numeric IP address 206.139.80.66.

Domain names using the suffix ".com" are established by registration with an organization called Network Solutions, Inc. ("NSI"). Registration of the other available top-level domain names, "edu," "gov" and "net", is handled by other organizations. With some limitations, NSI will register any combination of up to 24 alphanumeric characters as a domain name on a first-come, first-served basis to anyone who has access to at least two domain name servers. A domain name server is a host computer with software capable of responding to domain name inquiries and accessible on a full-time basis to other computers on the Internet.

Registering a domain name is the step that allows the top-level servers within the Internet to know where the domain name servers or hosts associated with those domain names are located in the Internet. The cost for a domain name registration is currently $100. Domain name service can be operated by the domain name holder or obtained from any entity with the proper computer equipment, including hundreds of Internet service providers.

One way to establish a presence on the Internet is by placing a web page, which is, ultimately, a computer data file on a host operating a web server within a given domain name. When the web server receives an inquiry from the Internet, it returns the web page data in the file to the computer making the inquiry. The web page may comprise a single line or multiple pages of information and may include any message, name, word, sound or picture, or combination of such elements. Most web browsers will show somewhere on the screen the domain name of the web page being shown and will automatically include the domain name in any printout of the web page. There is no technical connection or relationship between a domain name and the contents of the corresponding web page.

There are a number of ways for an Internet user to find a web page. Web browsers feature access to various indexes, commonly referred to as search engines. Well-known indexes include InfoSeek Guide, Lycos, Magellan, ExCite and Yahoo. These indexes will allow the user to enter a name or a word or a combination of words, much like a Lexis or WestLaw search, and will return the results of the search as a list of "hyperlinks" to web pages that have information within or associated with the document comprising the page responding to the search.

A hyperlink is a link from one site on the Internet to a second site on the Internet. "Clicking" on a designated space on the initial page which references the subsequent site by a picture, by some highlighted text or by some other indication will take a person viewing the initial web page to a second page. In addition to their use in indexes, hyperlinks are commonly placed on existing web pages, thus allowing Internet users to move from web page to web page at the click of a button, without having to type in URLs.

Hyperlinks can be and commonly are established without reference to the domain name of the second site. A hyperlink for the Champaign–Urbana map page might be a picture of a map or a statement such as "a map of Champaign–Urbana" or, more simply, "Champaign–Urbana." A hyperlink is not technically related to a domain name and therefore it can be identical to an existing domain name without conflicting with that domain name. For example, were Intermatic to establish an Intermatic home page at http: www.xyz.com, any number of indexes could be employed and hyperlinks could be established to bring up the page through use of the word INTERMATIC.

[For the remainder of this case, discussing a cybersquatter's right to register a purported famous mark as his domain name, see below]

THE ELECTRONIC FREELANCE AUTHORS CASE

JONATHAN TASINI v. THE NEW YORK TIMES CO.

United States District Court, S.D. New York, 1997.
972 F.Supp. 804.

JUDGE SOTOMAYOR

In this action, the Court is called upon to determine whether publishers are entitled to place the contents of their periodicals into electronic data bases and onto CD–ROMs without first securing the permission of the freelance writers whose contributions are included in those periodicals. According to the Complaint, filed by a group of freelance journalists, this practice infringes the copyright that each writer holds in his or her individual articles. The defendant publishers and electronic service providers respond by invoking the "revision" privilege of the "collective works" provision of the Copyright Act of 1976, 17 U.S.C. § 201(c). Defendants maintain that they have not improperly exploited plaintiffs' individual contributions, but that they have permissibly reproduced plaintiffs' articles as part of electronic revisions of the newspapers and magazines in which those articles first appeared.

Plaintiffs are six freelance writers who have sold articles for publication in a variety of popular newspapers and magazines, including The New York Times, Newsday, and Sports Illustrated.

The defendant publishers deliver or electronically transmit to NEXIS the full text of all of the articles appearing in each daily or weekly edition of their periodicals. The publishers provide NEXIS with a complete copy of computer text files which the publishers use during the process of producing the hard copy versions of their periodicals. Coded instructions as to page lay out added to these files permit typesetters working for the publishers to produce "mechanicals"—which resemble full pages as they will appear at publication—copies of which are transmitted to printing facilities for mass production. NEXIS does not use the electronic files to create "mechanicals" or to emulate the physical lay out of each periodical issue: such things as photographs, advertisements, and the column format of the newspapers are lost. NEXIS instead uses the electronic files to input the contents of each article on-line along with such information as the author's name, and the publication and page in which each article appeared. The articles appearing in The New York Times and Newsday are available within twenty-four hours after they first appear in print, and the articles from an issue of Sports Illustrated appear on-line within forty-five days of the initial hard copy publication.

Customers enter NEXIS by using a telecommunications package that enables them to access NEXIS' mainframe computers. Once on-line, customers enter "libraries" consisting of the articles from particular publications, or groups of publications. Customers can then conduct a "Boolean search" by inputting desired search terms and connectors from which the system generates a number of "hits." These "hits," the articles in the library corresponding to the selected search terms, can be reviewed either individually or within a citation list. A citation list identifies each article by the publication in which it appeared, by number of words, and by author. When a particular article is selected for full-text review, the entire content of the article appears on screen with a heading providing the same basic information reported within a citation list. Although articles are reviewed individually, it is possible for a user to input a search that will generate all of the articles—and only those articles–appearing in a particular periodical on a particular day.

All of the parties recognize that the defendant publications constitute "collective works" under the terms of the Copyright Act of 1976. A collective work is one "in which a number of contributions, constituting separate and independent works in themselves, are assembled into a collective whole." 17 U.S.C. § 101. The rights which exist in such works are delineated in 17 U.S.C. § 201(c):

> Copyright in each separate contribution to a collective work is distinct from copyright in the collective work as a whole, and vests initially in the author of the contribution. In the absence of an express transfer of the copyright or of any rights under it, the owner of copyright in the collective work is presumed to have acquired only the privilege of reproducing and distributing the contribution as part of that particular collective work, any revision of that collective work, and any later collective work in the same series.

Plaintiffs maintain that the publisher defendants have exceeded their narrow "privileges" under this provision by selling plaintiffs' articles for reproduction by the electronic defendants. In particular, plaintiffs complain that the disputed technologies do not revise the publisher defendants'.

Plaintiffs liken the "privileges" which Section 201(c) extends to "the owner of copyright in the collective work" to narrowly circumscribed nonexclusive licenses. Unlike assignments or exclusive licenses or most other conveyances under copyright law, such limited grants are not transferable. See 17 U.S.C. § 101 (defining "transfer of copyright ownership"). Because the publisher defendants own the copyrights in their collective works, plaintiffs reason that the electronic defendants are guilty of infringement even in the event that they are creating revisions—authorized by the publisher defendants—of the disputed periodicals.

One of the defining original aspects of the publisher defendants' periodicals is the selection of articles included in those works. Indeed, newspapers and magazines are quite unlike phone books. Far more so even than books of terminology or baseball card guides, selecting materials to be included in a newspaper or magazine is a highly creative endeavor. The New York Times perhaps even represents the paradigm, the epitome of a publication in which selection alone reflects sufficient originality to merit copyright protection. Identifying "all the news that's fit to print" is not nearly as mechanical (or noncontroversial) a task as gathering all of the phone numbers from a particular region. Indeed, recognizing matters of interest to readers is a highly subjective undertaking, one that different editors and different periodicals undoubtedly perform with varying degrees of success.

The defendant publishers' protected original selection of articles, a defining element of their periodicals, is preserved electronically.

According to plaintiffs, the electronic reproductions cannot reasonably be considered revisions of the publisher defendants' periodicals because significant elements of each disputed periodical are not preserved electronically. Put differently, plaintiffs object to the Court's approach because it focuses upon that which is retained electronically, as opposed to that which is lost. Most notably, aside from the image-based CD–ROM, the disputed technologies do not reproduce the photographs, captions, and page lay-out of the defendant publications. With these significant differences between the technological reproductions and the defendant publications, plaintiffs' position has a certain appeal. There is no avoiding that much of what is original about the disputed publications is not evident online or on disc. Ultimately, however, these changes to the defendant publishers' hard copy periodicals are of only peripheral concern to the "revision" analysis.

By its very nature, a "revision" is necessarily a changed version of the work that preceded it. Section 201(c) permits even major changes to collective works. The critical question for the Court, then, is not whether the electronic reproductions are different from the publisher defendants' collective works; it is inevitable that a revision will be different from the work upon which it is based. The question for the Court is whether the electronic reproductions retain enough of defendants' periodicals to be recognizable as versions of those periodicals.

Because a collective work typically possesses originality only in its selection and arrangement of materials, it is to be expected that, in a revised version of such a work, either the selection or arrangement will be changed or perhaps even lost. This is precisely what has happened here. Lacking the photographs and page lay out of the disputed periodicals, NEXIS plainly fails to reproduce the original arrangement of materials included in the publisher defendants' periodicals. By retaining the publisher defendants' original selection of articles, however, the electronic defendants have managed to retain one of the few defining original elements of the publishers' collective works. In other words, NEXIS [carries] recognizable versions of the publisher defendants' newspapers and magazines. For the purposes of Section 201(c), then, defendants have succeeded at creating "any revision[s]" of those collective works.

Plaintiffs are adamant that a ruling for defendants in this case leaves freelance authors without any significant protection under the 1976 Act. This result, according to plaintiffs, cannot be reconciled with the fact that the passage of Section 201(c)—and the dismantling of indivisibility—represented an important victory for individual authors.

As an initial matter, plaintiffs exaggerate the repercussions of this decision. The electronic data bases retain a significant creative element of the publisher defendants' collective works. In numerous other conceivable circumstances, Section 201(c) would apply to prevent the exploitation, by publishers, of individual articles. And publishers cannot create television or film versions of individual freelance contributions to their periodicals. Though these scenarios are perhaps overshadowed by the seeming omnipresence of NEXIS and CD–ROM technology, authors remain protected under Section 201(c).

The Court does not take lightly that its holding deprives plaintiffs of certain important economic benefits associated with their creations. This does not result from any misapplication of Section 201(c), however, but from modern developments which have changed the financial landscape in publishing. In particular, on-line technologies and CD–ROMs did not begin to flourish commercially until the early to mid 1980s. Thus, when the Copyright Act was formulated, during the 1960s and early 1970s, the most immediate economic threat to freelance writers was not posed by computer technology, but by the sort of transactions described in the preceding paragraph—e.g., the sale of articles between magazines, television adaptations of stories, etc. Congress responded with a provision targeted to prevent such exploitation. Publishers were left with the right to revise their collective works; a right then perceived to have only limited economic value, but a right that time and technology have since made precious.

In sum, plaintiffs insist that the framers of Section 201(c) never intended the windfall for publishers permitted under this Court's ruling. This may well be. If today's result was unintended, it is only because Congress could not have fully anticipated the ways in which modern technology would create such lucrative markets for revisions; it is not because Congress intended for the term revision to apply any less broadly than the Court applies it today. In other words, though plaintiffs contend mightily that the disputed electronic reproductions do not produce revisions of defendants' collective works, plaintiffs' real complaint lies in the fact that modern technology has created a situation in which revision rights are much more valuable than anticipated as of the time that the specific terms of the Copyright Act were being negotiated. If Congress agrees with plaintiffs that, in today's world of pricey electronic information systems, Section 201(c) no longer serves its intended purposes, Congress is of course free to revise that provision to achieve a more equitable result. Until and unless this happens, however, the courts must apply Section 201(c) according to its terms, and not on the basis of speculation as to how Congress might have done things differently had it known then what it knows now.

For the reasons set forth above, defendants' motion for summary judgment is GRANTED.

Notes and Questions

1. The court rejected the plaintiffs' claim that loss of the "individuality" of the article, in other words its ability to be called up separately from the other articles in the collected work, places the "revision" beyond the scope of the rights granted under Section 201 to collective work copyright owners. What is the court's rationale for rejecting this argument? Are there any limits placed on a collective work copyright owner's ability to revise collective works to place them into an electronic database format? For example, could the collective work copyright owner remove the citation information from such format? Does such citation alone qualify as an original contribution by the collective rights owner?

2. Does the revision of a hard copy work, such as a magazine article, qualify as a derivative work under international copyright standards? Would the changes made to such an article to put it in a digital format qualify as a derivative work under these standards? If so, without the special language of Section 201(c), granting creators of collective works the right to revise such works, would the plaintiffs claim of copyright infringement succeeded? Should it?

THE BRITISH ART WORKS CASE

THE BRIDGEMAN ART LIBRARY, LTD. v. COREL CORPORATION, ET AL.

United States District Court, S.D. New York, 1999.
36 F. Supp. 2d 191.

KAPLAN, DISTRICT JUDGE.

[United Kingdom-based company, which marketed transparencies and CD–ROMs of reproductions of public domain works of art brought suit alleging copyright infringement.]

On November 13, 1998, this Court granted defendant's motion for summary judgment dismissing plaintiff's copyright infringement claim on the alternative grounds that the allegedly infringed works—color transparencies of paintings which themselves are in the public domain— were not original and therefore not permissible subjects of valid copyright and, in any case, were not infringed. It applied United Kingdom law in determining whether plaintiff's transparencies were copyrightable. The Court noted, however, that it would have reached the same result under United States law.

On November 23, 1998, plaintiff moved for reargument and reconsideration, arguing that the Court erred on the issue of originality. It asserted that the Court had misconstrued British copyright law in that it failed to follow *Graves' Case*, L.R. 4 Q.B. 715 (1869), which was decided in the Court of Queens Bench in 1869.

[T]he ability of Congress to extend the protection of copyright is limited by the Copyright Clause. Bridgeman claims that the infringed works are protected by United Kingdom copyrights and that the United States, by acceding to the Convention for the Protection of Literary and Artistic Works, popularly known as the Berne Convention, and by enacting the Berne Convention Implementation Act of 1988 (the "BCIA"), [Pub. L. 100–568, 102 Srar. 2853 (1988)], agreed to give effect to its United Kingdom copyrights.

The fact that plaintiff's rights allegedly derive from its claimed British copyrights arguably is material. Granting that Congress, in light of the originality requirement of the Copyright Clause, in ordinary circumstances may not extend copyright protection to works that are not original, the questions remain whether (1) the United States constitutionally may obligate itself by treaty to permit enforcement of a foreign copyright where that copyright originates under the law of a signatory nation which does not limit copyright protection to works that are original in the sense required by the United States Constitution and, if so, (2) the United States in fact has done so.

Article II, Section 2, of the Constitution provides that the President "shall have Power, by and with the Advice and Consent of the Senate, to make Treaties, provided two thirds of the Senators present concur." Treaties, by virtue of the Supremacy Clause, join the Constitution and federal statutes as "supreme law of the land."

The Copyright Clause and the Copyright Act both recognize that the United States has an important interest in protecting the intellectual property of its citizens and of those whose creative efforts enrich our. lives. In this increasingly interconnected world, securing appropriate protection abroad also is important.

Decades ago, the Supreme Court held in *Missouri v. Holland,* 252 U.S. 416, 432, 40 S.Ct. 382, 64 L.Ed. 641 (1920), that Congress could enact legislation necessary and proper to the implementation of a treaty which, absent the treaty, would have been beyond its powers. [T]he case suggests that the Conventions, if their purported effect actually is to permit enforcement in the United States of foreign copyrights which do not meet U.S. standards of originality—in other words, if they require enforcement here of any copyright valid under the law of the signatory nation in which copyright attached, even if that copyright does not meet U.S. standards of validity—would not be obviously invalid.

In view of these considerations, the proposition advanced by Professor William Patry [who filed a micus brief]—that the Copyright Clause forecloses any choice of law issue with respect to the validity of a foreign Berne Convention work, is not free from doubt. It is necessary to decide that question, however, only if the Conventions require application of foreign law in determining the existence of copyright and, if so, whether there is any true conflict of law in this case on that point.

In most circumstances, choice of law issues do not arise under the Berne and Universal Copyright Conventions. Each adopts a rule of national treatment. Article 5 of the Berne Convention, for example, provides that "authors shall enjoy, in respect of works for which they are protected under this Convention, in countries of the Union other than the country of origin, the rights which their respective laws do now or may hereafter grant to their nationals, as well as the rights specially granted by this convention" and that "the extent of protection, as well as the means of redress afforded to the author to protect his rights, shall be governed exclusively by the laws of the country where protection is claimed." [Berne Convention art. 5(1)–5(2).] Hence, the Conventions make clear that the holder of, for example, a British copyright who sues for infringement in a United States court is entitled to the same remedies as holders of United States copyrights and, as this Court previously held, to the determination of infringement under the same rule of law.

While the nature of the protection accorded to foreign copyrights in signatory countries thus is spelled out in the Conventions, the position of the subject matter of copyright thereunder is less certain. Do the Conventions purport to require signatory nations to extend national treatment with respect to such enforcement-related subjects as remedies for infringement only where the copyright for which protection is sought would be valid under the law of the nation in which enforcement is sought? Or do they purport to require also that a signatory nation in which enforcement is sought enforce a foreign copyright even if that copyright would not be valid under its own law?

Although the Supreme Court has not yet decided the point, it seems quite clear at this point that the Berne Convention is not self-executing. Section 3(a) of the BCIA confirms this view, stating that:

"The provisions of the Berne Convention—

"(1) shall be given effect under title 17, as amended by this Act, and any other relevant provision of Federal or State law, including the common law, and

"(2) shall not be enforceable in any action brought pursuant to the provisions of the Berne Convention itself."

Section 4(c), now codified at 17 U.S.C. @ 104(c), states in relevant part that "no right or interest in a work eligible for protection under this title may be claimed by virtue of, or in reliance upon, the provisions of the Berne Convention or the adherence of the United States thereto." Thus, while the Copyright Act, as amended by the BCIA, extends certain protection to the holders of copyright in Berne Convention works as there defined, the Copyright Act is the exclusive source of that protection.

The statutory basis of the protection of published Berne Convention works such as the photographs here at issue is Section 104(b), which states in relevant part that:

"The works specified by sections 102 and 103, when published, are subject to protection under this title if—

"(4) the work is a Berne Convention work ..." [17 U.S.C, § 104(B).]

Section 102(a) limits copyright protection in relevant part to "original works of authorship...." Accordingly, Congress has made it quite clear that the United States' adherence to the Berne Convention has no such effect in the courts of this country.

There is little doubt that many photographs, probably the overwhelming majority, reflect at least the modest amount of originality required for copyright protection. "Elements of originality ... may include posing the subjects, lighting, angle, selection of film and camera, evoking the desired expression, and almost any other variant involved."[39] But "slavish copying," although doubtless requiring technical skill and effort, does not qualify.[40] As the Supreme Court indicated in *Feist*, "sweat of the brow" alone is not the "creative spark" which is the sine qua non of originality.[41] It therefore is not entirely surprising that an attorney for the Museum of Modern Art, an entity with interests comparable to plaintiff's and its clients, not long ago presented a paper acknowledging that a photograph of a two-dimensional public domain work of art "might not have enough originality to be eligible for its own copyright."[42]

In this case, plaintiff by its own admission has labored to create "slavish copies" of public domain works of art. While it may be assumed that this required both skill and effort, there was no spark of originality—indeed, the point of the exercise was to reproduce the underlying works with absolute fidelity. Copyright is not available in these circumstances.

UNITED KINGDOM LAW

While the Court's conclusion as to the law governing copyrightability renders the point moot, the Court is persuaded that plaintiff's copyright claim would fail even if the governing law were that of the United Kingdom.

39. *Rogers v. Koons*, 960 F.2d 301, 307 (2d Cir.), *cert. denied*, 506 U.S. 934, 121 L. Ed. 2d 278, 113 S. Ct. 365 (1992); *accord*, *Leibovitz v. Paramount Pictures Corp.*, 137 F.3d 109, 116 (2d Cir.1998).

40. In *Hearn v. Meyer*, 664 F. Supp. 832 (S.D.N.Y.1987), Judge Leisure held on the authority of Batlin that "slavish copies" of public domain reproductions of public domain original works of art were not copyrightable despite the great skill and effort involved in the copying process, and minor but unintentional variations between the copies and the works copied.

41. 499 U.S. 340, 111 S. Ct. 1282, 113 L. Ed. 2d 358.

42. Beverly Wolff, *Copyright, in ALI–ABA Course of Study, Legal Problems of Museum Administration*, C989 ALI–ABA 27, at *48 (available on Westlaw). See also Lynne A. Greenburg, *the Art of Appropriation: Puppies, Piracy, and Post–Modernism*, 11 CARDOZO ARTS & ENT. L.J. 1, 20–21 (1992) (photographic copies of original art photographs taken by the famous photographer, Edward Weston, which were made to "deconstruct the myth of the masterpiece" not copyrightable).

Plaintiff's attack on the Court's previous conclusion that its color transparencies are not original and therefore not copyrightable under British law depends primarily on its claim that the Court failed to apply *Graves' Case*.

Graves' Case in relevant part involved an application to cancel entries on the no longer extant Register of Proprietors of Copyright in Paintings, Drawings and Photographs for three photographs of engravings. In rejecting the contention that the photographs were not copyrightable because they were copies of the engravings, Justice Blackburn wrote:

> "The distinction between an original painting and its copy is well understood, but it is difficult to say what can be meant by an original photograph. All photographs are copies of some object, such as a painting or statue. And it seems to me that a photograph taken from a picture is an original photograph, in so far that to copy it is an infringement of the statute." [L.R. 4 Q.B. at 722.]

Plaintiff and the amicus therefore argue that plaintiff's photographs of public domain paintings are copyrightable under British law. But they overlook the antiquity of *Graves' Case* and the subsequent development of the law of originality in the United Kingdom.

Laddie, a modern British copyright treatise the author of which now is a distinguished British judge, discusses the issue at Bar in a helpful manner:

> "It is obvious that although a man may get a copyright by taking a photograph of some well-known object like Westminster Abbey, he does not get a monopoly in representing Westminister Abbey as such, any more than an artist would who painted or drew that building. What, then, is the scope of photographic copyright? As always with artistic works, this depends on what makes his photograph original. Under the 1988 Act the author is the person who made the original contribution and it will be evident that this person need not be he who pressed the trigger, who might be a mere assistant. Originality presupposes the exercise of substantial independent skill, labour, judgment and so forth. For this reason it is submitted that a person who makes a photograph merely by placing a drawing or painting on the glass of a photocopying machine and pressing the button gets no copyright at all; but he might get a copyright if he employed skill and labour in assembling the thing to be photocopied, as where he made a montage. It will be evident that in photography there is room for originality in three respects. First, there may be originality which does not depend on creation of the scene or object to be photographed or anything remarkable about its capture, and which resides in such specialties as angle of shot, light and shade, exposure, effects achieved by means of filters, developing techniques etc: in such manner does one photograph of Westminster Abbey differ from another, at least potentially. Secondly, there may be creation of the scene or subject to be photographed. We have

already mentioned photo-montage, but a more common instance would be arrangement or posing of a group ... Thirdly, a person may create a worthwhile photograph by being at the right place at the right time. Here his merit consists of capturing and recording a scene unlikely to recur, e.g. a battle between an elephant and a tiger...."[45]

Moreover, the authors go on to question the continued authority of Graves' Case under just this analysis:

"It is submitted that *Graves' Case* (1869) LR 4 QB 715 (photograph of an engraving), a case under the Fine Arts Copyright Act 1862, does not decide the contrary, since there may have been special skill or labour in setting up the equipment to get a good photograph, especially with the rather primitive materials available in those days. Although the judgments do not discuss this aspect it may have been self-evident to any contemporary so as not to require any discussion. If this is wrong it is submitted that *Graves' Case* is no longer good law and in that case is to be explained as a decision made before the subject of originality had been fully developed by the courts. [Id. at 239 n. 3]

Most photographs are "original" in one if not more of the three respects set out in the treatise and therefore are copyrightable. Plaintiff's problem here is that it seeks protection for the exception that proves the rule: photographs of existing two-dimensional articles (in this case works of art), each of which reproduces the article in the photographic medium as precisely as technology permits. Its transparencies stand in the same relation to the original works of art as a photocopy stands to a page of typescript, a doodle, or a Michelangelo drawing.

Plaintiff nevertheless argues that the photocopier analogy is inapt because taking a photograph requires greater skill than making a photocopy and because these transparencies involved a change in medium. But the argument is as unpersuasive under British as under U.S. law.

The allegedly greater skill required to make an exact photographic, as opposed to Xerographic or comparable, copy is immaterial. As the Privy Council wrote in *Interlego AG v. Tyco Industries, Inc.*, [1 A.C. 217 (P.C.1989), 3 All E.R. 949, 970 (1988)], "skill, labor or judgment merely in the process of copying cannot confer originality...." [Id. 3 All.E.R. at 971–72.] The point is exactly the same as the unprotectibility under U.S. law of a "slavish copy."

Nor is the change in medium, standing alone, significant. The treatise relied upon by plaintiff for the contrary proposition does not support it.

---

45. Hugh Laddie, Peter Prescott, & Mary Vitoria, The Modern Law of Copyright and Designs § 3.56, at 238 (1995).

Rather, a copy in a new medium is copyrightable only where, as often but not always is the case, the copier makes some identifiable original contribution.

Here, as the Court noted in its earlier opinion, "it is uncontested that Bridgeman's images are substantially exact reproductions of public domain works, albeit in a different medium." There has been no suggestion that they vary significantly from the underlying works. In consequence, the change of medium is immaterial.

For all of the foregoing reasons, the Court is persuaded that its original conclusion that Bridgeman's transparencies are not copyrightable under British law was correct.

Notes and Questions

1. Who is the author of the works at issue–the original painter or the one who created the transparencies? Whose law would you consider to decide this issue—the United States or the United Kingdom?

2. What if the works in question were digitized versions of public domain works? Would the effects required to create digitized versions be sufficient to qualify as protected works under either U.S. or British law?

3. Whose law should apply to determine whether the work is copyright protectable—the law where the work was created or the law where the work was allegedly infringed? *Compare* the *British Art Works* case with *Mecklermedia Corp. v. DC CongressGmbH*, [1998] 1 All ER 148 [1997] and *Itar— Tass Russian News Agency v. Russian Kurier, Inc.*, 153 F.3d 82 (2d Cir. 1998).

4. How did the court in the *British Art Works* case decide whose law should govern the decision regarding the copyright protectable nature of the work? Do you concur with its decision? Compare the court's discussion of British copyright law with the *Princess Caroline Photo* case in Chapter Thirty–Three. Did the court get the law right?

5. In the *British Art Works* case, the court concluded that British law actually supported its conclusion. What if under British law the photos were copyright protectable? What impact, if any, should this fact have on the court's decision?

THE GEORGIA TECH CONTROVERSY

[In 1994 France enacted the Toubon Law (Loi Toubon) which required that all advertisements be in French. Although the law did not refer specifically to the Internet, two organizations dedicated to the preservation of the French language sued Georgia Tech University for violating the Toubon Law by offering an English-only web site. The plaintiffs claimed the law was violated each time the web site was accessed.]

A Paris court on Monday delayed a ruling on the extent of France's reach into cyberspace, ordering more hearings on whether the French campus of a U.S. university violated French law by using English alone on its Internet site.

The court set further arguments for April 28 on procedural aspects of France's 1994 Toubon law promoting the French language—a move suggesting the court may be trying to throw out the case on technical grounds, officials on both sides said.

"This would be a pity because the fundamental question in the case is an important one," said attorney Marc Jobert, representing the private French culture watchdog groups who brought the case against the French campus of the Georgia Institute of Technology.

"It is very important that we prevail in this case, or a large number of (Internet) sites in France will be quickly disconnected and set up in other countries, a development which would be inconsistent with France's economic development hopes," countered Hans Puttgen, director of Georgia Tech Lorraine in the eastern city of Metz.

The legal debate is part of a long-running battle by France to protect the language of Moliere and Racine against the growing global grip of English.

The ruling is likely to have wide implications for the reach of national laws over the Internet. While Internet champions argue the network should operate free of local restraint, many national governments have asserted authority over it, often to restrict pornography or stifle political dissent.

The Paris court asked for additional debate specifically on the Toubon law's procedures for bringing complaints. Lawyers predicted a judgment before the end of June.

Georgia Tech argued in the January 6 trial that communications on the Internet were like telephone calls and outside the reach of the Toubon law, which requires that all advertising in France be in French.

The two watchdog groups, Defence of the French Language and Future of the French Language, said the Internet was public in nature rather than private like a phone call.

They urged the court to force Georgia Tech Lorraine to pay a fine and damages of 20,000 francs ($4,000) and oblige it to translate the Internet site into French.

"You cannot legislate language," Puttgen told reporters on Monday. "People must want to learn that language."

He argued that numerous other French Internet sites including some under state control were in English alone and said he regretted that Georgia Tech had been singled out since it sought to promote multicultural integration.

But Jobert dismissed as "paranoia" Puttgen's argument that Georgia Tech had been made into a scapegoat by his clients.

"We are entirely prepared to pursue all offenders," he said, denying any anti-American bias. "All we want is a French version of the site."

The Georgia Tech Lorraine site—whose Internet address is www.georgiatech-metz.fr—offers course descriptions, a guide to the campus and other information for current and potential students.

Georgia Tech Lorraine, most of whose students are French, has argued that the site is in English because all its courses are taught in English and all its students are required to be fluent English-speakers.

But Puttgen said the site might be revised in the future to add material in other languages including German as well as French though it would not be revised until the current lawsuit had been decided.

Notes and Questions

1. The court originally dismissed the complaint against Georgia Tech on procedural grounds. On its eventual retrial, the court held that the university could have an English-only Internet web site. The decision, however, was handed down *after* Georgia Tech had added a French and German version of the cite. The cite itself may be found at http://www.georgiatech-metz.fr/. Is the French language requirement of the Loi Toubon a content regulation or a labelling requirement? What right, if any, should countries have to require that information on the Internet that enters their borders be in the local language?

2. Should countries be allowed to control the content of the Internet for other purposes, such as prohibiting the distribution of pornographic materials or restricting the dissemination of harmful or scatalogical information? What types of content restrictions would you consider lawful?

3. *The German Pornography Case.* In *Germany v. CompuServe Deutschland*, the former head of CompuServe Germany—a German subsidiary of a U.S. Internet provider—was convicted of child pornography under German law for failing to block third party postings of pornographic pictures. There was no evidence that CompuServe was aware of the existence of the pornographic materials. The conviction was appealed and CompuServe blocked the offending site from entering Germany.

THE IRISH FRAMING CASE
SHETLAND TIMES LIMITED v. DR. JONATHAN WILLS

Court of Sessions (Outer House), 1996.
[1997] FSR 604.

Lord Hamilton:

The pursuers own and publish The Shetland Times, a newspaper which carries local, national and international news. The second defenders provide a news reporting service and trade under the name "The Shetland News". The first defender is the managing director of the second defenders.

In The Shetland Times there appear news items comprising texts under relative headlines. Photographs also appear.

In the Issue of The Shetland Times printed on Friday, October 11, 1996, there appeared an item, running to several paragraphs, concerning financial difficulties about the Fraser Peterson Centre in Shetland. It appeared under the headline "Bid to save centre after council funding 'cock up'". A number of other items also appeared in that issue, each under a relative headline.

The Internet is a world-wide electronic system used for the exchange of information. Such information may include advertising material. Information is accessed through computers in conjunction with the telephone system. Persons wishing to impart information or to advertise on the Internet can do so by establishing for themselves a "web site". Access to the information available at a web site is gained by callers accessing a relative "web address".

The pursuers have recently established such a web site. By this means they make available on the Internet items, including photographs, which appear in printed editions of The Shetland Times. Such items are stored electronically by reference to an index of relative headlines, being the headlines which appear above those items in the printed issues. Access to the text of the printed items is gained by the caller clicking on the relative headline which appears on a "front page". The front page is the display which first appears on access being gained to the pursuers' web site. The pursuers' front page bears the heading "The Shetland Times". On an item being accessed there appears below the text a note in the following terms:

CONTACTING THE SHETLAND TIMES

Comments or suggestions on this server [sic] please to webmaster@shetland-times.co.uk.

The pursuers have expended resources in establishing this web site. It is their expectation that, once this information service becomes known to and is used by Internet users, the pursuers will be able to sell advertising space on the front page on their web site.

The defenders also operate a web site with a relative web address. The front page accessed by callers at that web address is headed "The Shetland News" and sub-headed "Main Headline Page". A number of advertisements appear on that page. Beneath those are a number of news headlines.

Since about October 14, 1996 the defenders have included among the headlines on their front page a number of headlines appearing in recent issues of The Shetland Times as reproduced on the pursuers' web site. These headline are verbatim reproductions of the pursuers' headlines as so reproduced. A caller accessing the defenders' web site may, by clicking on one of those headlines appearing on the defenders' front page, gain access to the relative text as published and reproduced by the pursuers. Access is so gained and subsequent access to other such headlines also gained without the caller requiring at any stage to access the pursuers' front page. Thus, access to the pursuers' items (as published in printed editions and reproduced by them on their web site) can be obtained by by-passing the pursuers' front page and accordingly missing any advertising material which may appear on it.

In this action the pursuers seek a declaration that the defenders' acts constitute an infringement of copyright owned by them.

The grounds of action are twofold. The pursuers maintain that the headlines made available by them on their web site are cable programmes within the meaning of section 7 of the Copyright, Designs and Patents Act 1988 ("the Act"), that the facility made available by the defenders on their web site is a cable programme service within the meaning of section 7 and that the inclusion of those items in that service constitutes an infringement of copyright under section 20 of the Act. The pursuers also maintain that the headlines are literary works owned by them and that the defenders' activities constitute infringement by copying under section 17 of the Act, the copying being in the form of storing the works by electronic means.

Section 7, by subsection (1), defines "cable programme" as meaning "any item included in a cable programme service" and defines "cable programme service" as meaning—a service which consists wholly or mainly in sending visual images, sounds or other information by means of a telecommunications system, otherwise than by wireless telegraphy, for reception–at two or more places (whether for simultaneous reception or at different times in responses to requests by different users), or

(b) for presentation to members of the public,

and which is not, or so far as it is not, excepted by or under the following provisions of this section.

Subsection (2) provides:

The following are excepted from the definition of "cable programme service"

(a) a service or part of a service of which it is an essential feature that while visual images, sounds or other information are being conveyed by the person providing the service there will or may be sent from each place of reception, by means of the same system or (as the case may be) the same part of it, information (other than signals sent for the operation or control of the service) for reception by the person providing the service or other persons receiving it . . .

In my view the pursuers' contention that the service provided by them involves the sending of information is prima facie well founded. Although in a sense the information, it seems, passively awaits access being had to it by callers, that does not, at least prima facie, preclude the notion that the information, on such access being taken, is conveyed to and received by the caller. If that is so, the process may arguably be said to involve the sending of that information.

If the information is being sent, it prima facie is being sent by the pursuers on whose web site it has been established. The fact that the information is provided to the caller by his accessing it through the defenders' web site does not, in my view, result in the defenders being the persons sending the information.

On the information that was available and on the basis of the arguments presented, the pursuers have, in my opinion, a prima facie case that the incorporation by the defenders in their web site of the headlines provided at the pursuers' web site constitutes an infringement of section 20 of the Act by the inclusion in a cable programme service of protected cable programmes.

As to section 17, Mr. MacLeod submitted that headlines such as "Bid to save centre after council funding 'cock up'" and the other headlines complained of in the Summons were not original literary works within the meaning of the Act and that accordingly there was no infringement in copying them by any means. It was submitted that there was not such expenditure of skill or labour as to make any of them original literary works; they were "ordinary in the extreme". Mr. MacLeod did not go so far as to submit that no newspaper headline could ever attract copyright. His position was that those complained of did not.

While literary merit is not a necessary element of a literary work, there may be a question whether headlines, which are essentially brief indicators of the subject matter of the items to which they relate, are protected by copyright. However, in light of the concession that a headline could be a literary work and since the headlines at issue (or at least some of them) involve eight or so words designedly put together for the purpose of imparting information, it appeared to me to be arguable that there was an infringement, at least in some instances, of section 17.

The balance of convenience clearly, in my view, favoured the grant of interim interdict subject to certain amendments in the formulation of the conclusion. The defenders' activities of which complaint is made have just begun. It was not suggested that they would sustain any loss if prevented ad interim from making use of the pursuers' material in this way. It was fundamental to the setting up by the pursuers of their web site that access to their material should be gained only by accessing their web directly. While there has been no loss to date, there is a clear prospect of loss of potential advertising revenue in the foreseeable future. The extent of any loss will be difficult to quantify. There was, in the circumstances, no substance, in my view, in the suggestion that the pursuers were gaining an advantage by their newspaper items being made available more readily through the defenders' web site.

Certain amendments having been made to the second conclusion, I granted interim interdict in terms of that conclusion as amended.
DISPOSITION:

Judgment accordingly.

Notes and Questions

1. What is the harm that was caused by framing the news items on the Shetland Times web page with the defendant's web frames? Would the same

harm have occurred if the defendant's had simply provided a hyperlink to the Shetland Times web page? Why or why not?

2. Do you agree with the court's conclusion that the plaintiff's headlines may be copyright protectable? Is there another intellectual property based claim under which defendant's unauthorized framing could be challenged? For example, does the framing of plaintiff's articles qualify as an unauthorized derivative work under TRIPS? A fair use?

3. In the *Irish Framing* case the plaintiffs attempted to analogize Internet communications to cable programming. Other parties have analogized such communications to the telephone, others to browsing in a bookstore. Which do you think is most appropriate? Why?

4. Is the plaintiff's claim merely an attempt to censor defendant's content?

THE ENCRYPTION DEBATE

CHRISTIAN R. WHITE, DECRYPTING THE POLITICS: WHY THE CLINTON ADMINISTRATION'S NATIONAL CRYPTOGRAPHY POLICY WILL CONTINUE TO BE DICTATED BY NATIONAL ECONOMIC INTEREST

7 CommLaw Conspectus 193 (1999).

Encryption is one component of the art and science of cryptography. Cryptography is a method of hiding and storing information by using a code or cipher. The process of encryption involves transforming an original text to an unintelligible form, unreadable by anyone except the intended recipient. Information which has not yet been encrypted is referred to as plaintext. Once encrypted, the text is known as ciphertext. Simply, encryption is the process of securing communications and decryption is the way in which ciphertext becomes legible to the intended recipient.

In order for a message to be encrypted, a mathematical function called an algorithm must be applied to the intended text. Basically, an algorithm is a "set of rules or series of mathematical steps" used in the encrypting and decrypting process; it will scramble the text until the recipient applies the corresponding key to unscramble the message. The algorithm is not what allows the text to become secure; rather, security occurs when the user of encryption technology selects an individual key. Similar to a traditional lock box and key, a cryptographic algorithm implements a key to encrypt and decrypt a message. Once the sender encrypts the message and sends it, the recipient must use the same algorithm to decrypt the message.

The length of the key and the complexity of the algorithm determines the strength of the encryption algorithm. The key is measured in bits, and for every bit the number of possible key sequences is doubled, resulting in dramatically stronger encryption as the number of bits increases. For example, over one trillion potential combinations exist for a 40–bit key and more than seventy-two quadrillion potential combinations exist for a 56–bit key. Today, the most advanced forms of encryption software have a key length of 1,052–bits.

As technology advances and the need for security persists, businesses utilize encryption software products as a primary form of security for three main purposes: (1) confidentiality; (2) authentication; and (3) integrity. Confidentiality allows communications between individuals to become and remain private. Preserving confidential communications is vital to securing business plans, intellectual property, and other private communications. Authentication ensures that a particular message was sent by the stated sender. By authenticating a message, the probability of forgery and repudiation is significantly diminished. Certifying the integrity of a message confirms that a message has not been altered in any way during transit.

The Clinton Administration proposed a key recovery or key escrow system as a way to balance the "needs for information security against the needs of law enforcement and to a lesser extent national security." Key escrow encryption systems provide encryption key codes to a trusted third party that stores the keys for the users of such technology. These codes allow the holder of the keys to decrypt any encrypted message. Under this law, encryption key codes on all encryption software shipped internationally would be provided to the trusted third parties. These third parties could release the codes to predetermined authorized parties or to law enforcement officials who have obtained a valid court order.

The NSA is strongly opposed to any relaxation of export controls on encryption software because such encryption technology may facilitate terrorists' efforts in conducting targeted attacks against U.S. interests. The Aldrich Ames case and Ramzi Yousef case are often cited as examples of criminals who have used encryption technology as a means to avoid revealing their criminal activity.

The FBI firmly believes that criminals will increasingly use encryption technology as a tool in perpetrating their crimes. Therefore, in order to fulfill its "responsibility for protecting public safety and national security," the FBI argues for key recovery technology that allows "immediate access to the plaintext of encrypted criminal-related data" provided they have obtained a lawful court order.

The FBI is not only interested in obtaining the keys to encryption codes to monitor international criminal activity, but it also wants to monitor domestic criminal activity. Presently, domestic use of the strongest encryption technology is permitted without any key recovery system in place. The FBI is pressuring the Clinton Administration to mandate such systems for both domestic and international users of encryption software.

In its inception, the Clinton Administration's policy towards encryption was largely shaped by law enforcement organizations and agencies responsible for national security. Though the Administration does not support domestic controls on the use of encryption technology, it did attempt to steer policy towards the use of key recovery systems by "using the indirect route of export controls to influence what types of encryption products are available."

In April 1994, the first initiative, known as the "Clipper Chip" policy, encouraged the software industry to voluntarily use key recovery systems and governmental key recovery agents. The industry strongly objected, primarily based on the fact that the government would hold the keys. The Clinton Administration eventually abandoned this policy and agreed to discuss other options with industry leaders.

In July 1994, the second Administration policy encouraged the industry to develop key recovery systems voluntarily; this policy created the "trusted third party" concept, thereby removing the keys from government entities. The software industry continued to object to a key-recovery system as well as the export controls, because the government did not relax the controls to their satisfaction.

After the two unsuccessful attempts at reaching a compromise, Vice President Gore released a statement on May 20, 1996, detailing the particular changes to encryption policy under consideration by the Administration. These changes include: the replacement of the term "key escrow" with the term "key recovery." The concept of a "trusted third party" was also expanded to allow an organization or the company itself to hold the key or rather "self escrow." These proposed changes were eventually implemented through President Clinton's November 15, 1996, Executive Order.

On May 8, 1997, one of the first changes in policy by the Administration was directed toward banks and other financial institutions. Banks that conduct international transactions are now allowed to use the most powerful encryption technology available without a key recovery system in place. The Clinton Administration reasoned that such institutions are "subject to explicit legal requirements and have shown a consistent ability to provide appropriate access to transaction information in response to an authorized enforcement request...." In July 1998, this policy was extended to include securities firms. These financial institutions are allowed to use advanced encryption technology in the forty-five countries which have acceptable money-laundering laws according to U.S. standards.

One of the most dramatic policy changes occurred on September 16, 1998. Vice President Gore announced that the licensing requirements implemented only two years ago by the BXA had been totally restructured. In a significant policy shift, the government, after a one-time initial review, now allows the mass marketing of 56–bit encryption technology, as opposed to only 40–bit. Surprisingly, the Administration also eliminated the requirement that companies create and implement a key recovery system. For those companies that do choose to export key recovery technology, it is no longer necessary to report information to a key recovery agent.

Numerous U.S. international companies, discouraged by government regulations, are attempting to skirt U.S. encryption policy by forming foreign ventures. Such ventures will allow them to develop, manufacture and export powerful data scrambling technology without regard to the U.S. export policy. Network Associates Inc., a data-security software retailer based in Santa Clara, California, for example, is conducting business through a Dutch subsidiary in order to sell their data security software. As a result of this outsourcing, it is estimated that the United States could forfeit 200,000 jobs to foreign competition by year 2000.

Encryption technology is also widely distributed through illegal means. A personal use exemption exists that allows U.S. citizens and permanent residents to travel abroad with encryption hardware and software. Although guidelines are in place for travel with such equipment, no definitive means exist to determine if a product is illegally exported or not, thereby enabling the illicit transportation of the software. This is also easily accomplished by sending the software to foreign countries via a modem. For the government to assert that regulating the export of encryption technology will prevent foreign nations or individuals from acquiring these products is clearly unrealistic.

Though the battle to loosen encryption regulations has been fought mainly between the government and the actual software industry, many in the computer industry are now trying to increase public awareness in order to assert political pressure on the Clinton Administration.

The Clinton Administration is experiencing political pressures from international organizations like the Organization for Economic Cooperation and Development and the European Union (EU). The EU expressed disapproval of the Clinton Administration's desire to implement a key escrow system. In fact, some foreign governments view the U.S. policy as a potential method of committing industrial espionage, though the main EU argument is that it is opposed to "imposing a specific technological approach," (i.e. key escrow systems). Even members of President Clinton's own party are openly opposing the Administration's policy and believe that the EU policy will influence the United States. As on-line transactions become increasingly more commonplace, a standardized encryption policy will provide the security demanded by foreign nations if they are to expand their international transactions with U.S. businesses.

The original encryption policy implemented through President Clinton's Executive Order will continue to undergo significant modifications. The software industry will continue to maintain constant political pressure on the Clinton Administration to further deregulate the encryption technology serving commercial purposes. As encryption becomes more ubiquitous, law enforcement and national security entities will be forced to adapt to changing technology. Prohibiting such beneficial technology is not and will not be a viable option for the Administration to pursue. Law enforcement organizations have managed to respond to rapid technological change in the past, and should be encouraged to continue to adapt to new technologies, but should not be allowed to impede on the development of a profitable U.S. based market in advanced encryption technology. These changes will provide the business community and the software industry with more than mere profits. It will provide them with the security needed to flourish in a competitive global market place.

Notes and Questions

1. *Technological Fixes and Legal Regimes.* The encryption debate discussed above is only one of a number of debates occurring internationally regarding the method to control copyright and other content issues on the Internet. At the heart of the debate is a question over the methodology to be used. Should legal regimes, including multinational treaties, be established to regulate the Internet content or should any problems be solved through technological measures? Since technology created the problem, should it be the sole method used to resolve it?

B. HOW SHOULD CONTROL BE EXERCISED?

TO NET OR NOT TO NET: SINGAPORE'S REGULATION OF THE INTERNET

Sarah B. Hogan, 51 Fed. Comm. L.J. 429 (1999).

In the modern information age, technology is a double-edged sword. As new uses for the Internet rapidly emerge, it is clear that this particular technology is at the forefront of the information age, becoming almost necessary in order for individual nations to promote development and to remain competitive. But with this development comes the proliferation of human vices. For nations like Singapore and the People's Republic of China (China) that wish to control the exchange of ideas, particularly those of Western origin, the desire to advance technologically is tempered by the desire to maintain censorship powers. For example, in 1991, Singapore's National Computer Board directed a study of the advantages of nationwide information technology development. Coinciding with that study was an examination of Singapore's censorship laws by the Ministry of Information and the Arts. A review of the two studies reaffirmed that modern technology, particularly the Internet, and censorship may not coexist in an entirely peaceful manner. The government's desire to become the Asian "information-technology hub" comes into conflict with the oft-practiced control over the amount and type of information entering the nation

The Internet is an international system that knows no boundaries and has no centralized control over the content transmitted. It began in the late 1960s when the U.S. Defense Department commissioned the Advanced Research Projects Agency (ARPA) to create a computer network that could survive a nuclear attack. ARPANET was created, a decentralized network that utilized a process known as "packet-switching." In packet-switching, a message sent from one computer to another is divided into separate pieces of data that are called packets. The packets each follow separate routes, using different networks until they reach their final destination, where a computer reassembles the original message. The utilization of this technology ensures that if a portion of the network becomes inoperable due to a catastrophe such as nuclear attack, the other computers on the network will automatically reroute the packets so that the information will arrive at its destination. Soon after the U.S. Defense Department developed this system, other institutions became interested in the decentralized system of computer communication. Commercial and educational institutions began adding their own networks to the ARPANET. By 1982, the term "Internet" described the former ARPANET along with the additional networks. Because of its conception as a decentralized system of computer communication designed to withstand nuclear attack, the Internet is not an entity capable of being controlled by any one government or organization. As such, problems arise when governments seek to control access to materials deemed to be undesirable. Even the most fleeting study of international cultures will indicate that values of a similar nature do not span the globe. The problem with control arises because of the truly international nature of the Internet. Any computer linked to the Internet is capable of being connected with any other computer linked to the Internet. In fact, the most valuable characteristic of the Internet is the ability to establish almost instantaneous international communication through the use of its network. Yet, this characteristic may also promote the proliferation of human vices across international borders. Although a country may control the exchange of information within its borders, it cannot control an individual in another country from making that same information available on the Internet where it may readily be available to all users.

There are various technological means of protecting Internet users from "undesirable content." A government may either prevent transmission of the undesirable material, remove the material once it arrives, or prevent users from accessing such content.

1. Preventing Transmission of Undesirable Content

To prevent the transmission of content determined by the government to be undesirable, the government must stall the content in transit. Censors may then scan the content of the message for any terms or displays that have previously been defined as undesirable. Certain difficulties arise with this means of censorship. In order for this process to be successful, the senders of the content scanned must send their messages via the government computers. In addition, any message sent in code frustrates the purpose of the censorship. Perhaps the greatest problem posed by this means of censorship, however, is the significant delays caused by the amount of time necessary to scan every single message for undesirable content. This method impedes access to and the flow of information from the Internet, creating a significant stumbling block to any nation wishing to harness the Internet for its technological advantages.

2. Removal of Undesirable Content

A government may hold users responsible for all content that they provide and force those individuals to remove any undesirable content.

Difficulties also arise with this means of censorship. Governments may only force removal of content that was physically posted within their borders. Governments may not exert control over Internet service providers (ISPs) located in other countries. In addition, should a government determine that a particular content is undesirable for only some members of society, removal of that content withholds that information from everyone, not merely the group to be protected.

3. PREVENTING ACCESS TO UNDESIRABLE CONTENT

There are several ways to prevent users from retrieving content that a government has deemed undesirable.

a. *Blacklisting*

Blacklisting is the prevention of user access to sites that have been determined by the government to contain undesirable content. A government may also blacklist a site by forming laws that order ISPs to prevent their users from accessing any site containing undesirable content. This has been one method selected by the Singapore government to monitor the content of the Internet. Another method of blacklisting involves the proxy server, which is a computer that screens user requests and prevents access to sites considered undesirable by the government. However, those countries that have attempted the proxy server method of control have experienced prohibitive time delays in accessing the Internet. As with most means of censoring Internet content, blacklisting falls prey to certain difficulties. The undesirable material may easily be moved to another site or may even be transferred via e-mail. As such, blacklisting is not an effective means of Internet control.

b. *Whitelisting*

Whitelisting allows access only to those sites approved by the government and known not to contain undesirable content. A government may also require ISPs to only allow access to those sites containing approved content. However, limiting user access to a preapproved list of sites defeats one purpose of the Internet, which is to provide a vast and international source of information.

c. *Word and Character Search*

A third method of controlling access to undesirable content is through certain software that blocks access to sites by using a list of criteria selected by the user. The difficulty involved with this type of Internet control, however, is that certain words have both sexual and nonsexual meanings. As such, a vast amount of helpful or non objectionable information may not be made available simply because the software cannot differentiate among the many connotations of certain words.

Singapore has lofty goals for its use of the Internet. The government would like to make Singapore the "information-technology hub" for Asia. At the same time, however, the government would like to "rid the Net of content that 'threaten[s] public order and national security, religious and racial harmony, and morality.'" The chosen method, of course, is through attempted regulation of Internet content.

The Singapore Broadcasting Authority (SBA) is charged with the regulation of the Internet. The Internet is subject to Singapore's traditionally strict laws that apply to all other media, including the Defamation Act, Sedition Act, and Maintenance of Religious Harmony Acts. However, Singapore has gone a step further in its regulation of the Internet, encompassing a wide variety of subjects in its definition of "undesirable content."

On March 5, 1996, Brigadier General George Yeo, the Minister for Information and the Arts, introduced new Internet regulations for Singapore. Under the powers created for the SBA under section 21 of the Singapore Broadcasting Authority Act, the SBA issued the Singapore Broadcasting Authority (Class Licence) Notification 1996. The new regulation established broad categories of proscribed contents that were not to be accessed by any Internet user in Singapore.

The first category of proscribed communications include any that could be considered to jeopardize public safety or the national defense. Included in this vast category are the following communications: Contents which undermine the public confidence in the administration of justice; Contents which present information or events in such a way that alarms or misleads all or any of the public; Contents which tend to bring the Government [of Singapore] into hatred or contempt, or which excite disaffection against the Government [of Singapore]. Those in favor of the regulation believe that this measure protects the public from unsubstantiated allegations that are used to assassinate the character of the government.

The second category of proscribed communications is those that weaken racial and religious harmony. Such communications have been construed by the government to include the following: "(i) Contents which denigrate or satirise any race or religious group; (ii) Contents which bring any race or religious group into hatred or resentment; (iii) Contents which promote religious deviations or occult practices such as Satanism."

Contents that are proscribed under section (iii) include astrology, fortune-telling, and palm-reading. These would appear to be prohibited merely because they may be described as "deviations" from the norm.

The third category of proscribed content under the SBA's regulations consists of communications that are thought to promote immorality, as defined by Singapore's value system. Such communications include the following: "(i) Contents which are pornographic or otherwise obscene; (ii) Contents which propagate permissiveness or promiscuity; (iii) Contents which depict or propagate gross exploitation of violence, nudity, sex or horror; (iv) Contents which depict or propagate sexual perversions such as homosexuality, lesbianism, and paedophilia."

This material has been banned for quite some time from all books, periodicals, newspapers, and films in Singapore. The SBA has indicated that no access is to be given to certain sites perceived to be obscene, including the Playboy homepage on the World Wide Web (WWW).

A perfect form of censorship does not seem to exist. Governments and individuals alike have tried different methods of regulating access to the Internet. The Internet is a global network of computers designed to be reliable. Therefore, it stands to reason that any attempt to control information transmitted on the Internet must do more than merely attempt to block such information. Computer data on the Internet is broken into packets that are independently routed to the destination computer; there is no end-to-end connection to be broken. Therefore, if one connection is broken, or blocked, the packets along that link are rerouted to arrive at their destination via a different path. Indeed, the Internet perceives censorship attempts to be "damage" that necessitates rerouting of information.

As such, an attempt to regulate the flow of information must account for this characteristic of the Internet. There are many different means of regulation, from preventing the transmission of certain content to preventing user access to that content. Internet service providers in Singapore have selected proxy servers as the procedural means of complying with the SBA's Class Licence Scheme. All censorship, however, involves some cost. With the use of proxy servers, there is a concession to the loss of some access speed and reliability.

Proxy servers may be used to actually improve user access to certain popular sites by storing copies of the sites locally and thereby reducing traffic elsewhere on the Internet. Used as a tool for censorship, proxy servers will have little detrimental effect on the speed of access unless the list of forbidden sites is long.

The use of proxy servers in Singapore may be seen as the introduction of congestion to the network system there. The proxy servers must check every outgoing user request for information that is blacklisted by the Singapore government. This action necessarily increases the amount of time between the request for and receipt of information. However, with the number of users and user requests increasing, the proxy servers will become flooded with demands that must be checked against the government-supplied blacklist. As ISPs are required to procedurally implement the Class Licence Scheme, they will have to delay network traffic to allow the proxy servers to screen user requests. This procedure results in congestion, which will cause delayed and dropped packets of information. In the end, this defeats one purpose of the Internet—the almost instantaneous global transmission of information.

Considering the sacrifices of speed and reliability required, the proxy server is a remarkably ineffective means of censorship. The SBA has compiled a list of forbidden sites, identified by Internet address. The primary weakness of a proxy server is that it identifies Internet sites by address, not by content. The provider of the unwelcome content need only change the address in order to make the content accessible to users.

If Singapore truly wishes to harness the power and potential of the Internet for national economic growth, it must be willing to sacrifice a measure of its control over Internet content. The current system, as established by the SBA and implemented by the ISPs, provides a relatively full measure of control over Internet content. However, it also involves heavy costs, namely speed and reliability.

Singapore is not unusual in its desire to control Internet access to undesirable content. Nations worldwide are trying to protect their citizens from pornography, deviant materials, and, in some cases, conflicting cultural values. The methods of censorship used vary, but in most cases, the lesson is the same. Complete control over Internet content simply cannot coexist with a desire to harness the technology for its economic potential. Studies of individual nations' attempts to do so are informative for the rest of the world, since all may learn from others' successes and mistakes. Singapore may very well possess the potential to become the Asian "information technology hub," but to do so, the government must first compromise its position on Internet censorship.

Notes and Questions

1. What methods have been proposed for controlling Internet content domestically? Which of these methods, if any, do you believe provide a potentially workable solution to content control.

2. Is it possible to reach an international agreement regarding what content should be considered undesirable and therefore subject to exclusion or content regulation on the Internet? *See East Asian Censors Want to Net the Internet*, Christian Sci. Monitor, Nov. 12, 1996, at 19 (noting that China has determined that certain Western publications, including the New York Times, Wall Street Journal, and Washington Post are harmful and a threat to national security, and that Burma prohibits sending or receiving any information concerning the national culture, the economy, or state security) (cited in the excerpted article above).

3. *The Technological Problems of Content Regulation.* In January 1996, the French government banned a book, which subsequently appeared on a Web page found on a French server. The government forced the server to eliminate the Web page. The book, however, soon appeared on Web pages on servers located outside of France, thus, appearing to circumvent French control of such content. *See* Robert Uhlig, *Lords of the Net to Patrol Their Creation*, Daily Telegraph (London), Sept. 24, 1996, at 8. Should France be able to prohibit the circulation of illegal information from web servers beyond its jurisdiction? What limitations would you place on one country's ability to regulate the content available to its citizens?

4. The concern of Singapore to allow the benefits of Internet communication while controlling what are perceived to be its detriments is shared by all countries to some degree or another. While the control of obscene or culturally unacceptable materials forms a large part of the global concern over Internet content, the Internet's role as an engine of political criticism

and potential destabilization raises equally great concerns among certain countries. Thus, for example, in Malaysia in 1997, four people who circulated a purportedly erroneous report on the Internet of a riot in a city due to the government's failure to grant work permits, resulted in their arrest and led the Malaysian government to question the benefits of Internet connectivity. *See,* Shareem Amry, *Yes, Malaysia, you definitely can!,* New Straits Times (12/31/98).

5. Given the technological nature of the problem of Internet censorship, is it more desirable to permit technology to resolve these problems, as opposed to any national or multinational legal regime?

AGAINST CYBERANARCHY
JACK L. GOLDSMITH
65 U. Chi. L. Rev. 1199 (1998).

People transacting in cyberspace do things that would be regulated by state, national, or international law if they occurred in person or by telephone or mail. They defame, invade privacy, harass, and commit business torts. They make and breach contracts. They distribute pornography and swap bombmaking tips. They infringe trademarks, violate copyrights, and steal data. They issue fraudulent securities and restrict competition. And so on.

Are these and other cyberspace activities governed by the same laws that govern similar transnational activities mediated in person, or by phone, or by mail? If so, which jurisdiction's law governs? If not, what governs instead?

The regulation skeptics' analysis of these questions makes two sets of assumptions. The first concerns the nature of legal regulation of non cyberspace events. The skeptics tend to conceptualize a nation's legal authority as extending to its territorial borders and not beyond. This conception makes them skeptical about the legitimacy of one nation regulating activities that take place in another. And it leads them to believe that transnational disputes must be resolved by choice-of-law rules that select a unique governing law on the basis of where an event occurs or where transacting parties are located. On this view, tort liability is governed by the law of the place where the tort occurred and the validity of a contract is governed by the law of the place where the contract was made. Such choice-of-law rules are thought to promote rule-of-law values like uniformity (that is, every forum will apply the same law in a given case), predictability, and certainty. And they are supposed to give the parties to transnational transactions reasonable notice of governing law.

The skeptics' second set of assumptions concerns the architecture of cyberspace. They view cyberspace as a unique "boundary-destroying" means of communication. Internet protocol addresses do not necessarily correlate with a physical location. As a result, the skeptics assert, persons transacting in cyberspace often do not, and cannot, know each other's physical location. In addition, information mediated by certain cyberspace services appears "simultaneously and equally in all jurisdictions" around the world. A web page in Illinois can be accessed from and thus appear in any geographical jurisdiction that is plugged in to the World Wide Web. When I participate in an online discussion group, my messages can appear simultaneously in every geographical jurisdiction where persons participate in the group. In neither case can I control, or even know about, the geographical flow of the information that I upload or transmit.

It is against this background that the skeptics make their descriptive and normative claims. Descriptively, they claim that cyberspace is a borderless medium that resists regulation conceived in geographical terms. One reason is that information transmitted via cyberspace can easily flow across national borders without detection. Another reason is that it is senseless to apply geographically configured choice-of-law rules to a geographical cyberspace activities. A third reason is that regulation of the local effects of cyberspace information flows permits all nations simultaneously to regulate all web-based transactions. The result is multiple and inconsistent regulation of the same activity. A final reason is that the architecture of cyberspace enables its users to route around or otherwise evade territorial regulation

The skeptics' normative arguments build on these assumptions. Their essential normative claim is that it is illegitimate for any particular nation to regulate the local effects of multijurisdictional cyberspace activity. This is so for three reasons. First, such regulation will often apply to acts abroad, and will thus be impermissibly extraterritorial. Second, because cyberspace information flows appear in every jurisdiction simultaneously, unilateral regulation of these flows will illegitimately affect the regulatory efforts of other nations and the cyberspace activities of parties in other jurisdictions. Third is the problem of notice. The skeptics argue that because a person transacting in cyberspace does not know when or whether her activity produces effects in a particular jurisdiction, she lacks notice about governing law and therefore cannot conform her behavior to it. They claim that under these conditions, it is unfair to apply law to her cyberspace activities. The skeptics believe that all three of these problems can be avoided by cyberspace self-regulation.

To make these claims more concrete, consider the predicament of one of the scores of companies that offer, sell, and deliver products on the World Wide Web. Assume that the web page of a fictional Seattle-based company, Digitalbook.com, offers digital books for sale and delivery over the Web. One book it offers for sale is Lady Chatterley's Lover. This offer extends to, and can be accepted by, computer users in every country with access to the Web. Assume that in Singapore the sale and distribution of pornography is criminal, and that Singapore deems Lady Chatterley's Lover to be pornographic. Assume further that Digitalbook.com's terms of sale contain a term that violates English consumer protection laws, and that the publication of Digitalbook.com's Lady Chatterley's Lover in England would infringe upon the rights of the novel's English copyright owner. Digitalbook.com sells and sends copies of Lady Chatterley's Lover to two people whose addresses (say, anonymous@aol.com and anonymous@msn.com) do not reveal their physical location but who, unbeknownst to Digitalbook.com, live and receive the book in Singapore and London, respectively.

The skeptics claim that it is difficult for courts in Singapore or England to regulate disputes involving these transactions in accordance with geographical choice-of-law rules. In addition, they argue that English and Singaporean regulations will expose Digitalbook.com to potentially inconsistent obligations. Finally, the skeptics claim that Digitalbook.com can easily evade the Singaporean and English regulations by sending unstoppable digital information into these countries from a locale beyond their enforcement jurisdiction.

On the normative side, the skeptics are concerned that the application of English and Singaporean law to regulate Digitalbook.com's transactions constitutes an impermissible extraterritorial regulation of a U.S. corporation. Because Digitalbook.com might bow to the English and Singaporean regulations, and because the company cannot limit its cyberspace information flows by geography, the English and Singaporean regulations might cause it to withdraw Lady Chatterley's Lover everywhere or to raise its price. The English and Singaporean regulations would thus affect Digitalbook.com's behavior in the United States and adversely affect the purchasing opportunities of parties in other countries. The skeptics believe these negative spillover effects of the national regulations are illegitimate. They also think it is unfair for England and Singapore to apply their laws in this situation because Digitalbook.com had no way of knowing that it sold and delivered a book to consumers in these countries.

The skeptics are in the grip of a nineteenth century territorialist conception of how "real space" is regulated and how "real space" conflicts of law are resolved. This conception was repudiated in the middle of this century. The skeptics' first mistake, therefore, is to measure the feasibility and legitimacy of national regulation of cyberspace against a repudiated yardstick.

Three factors led to the overthrow of the traditional approach to choice of law. The first was significant changes in the world. Changes in transportation, communication, and in the scope of corporate activity led to an unprecedented increase in multijurisdictional activity. These changes put pressure on the rigid territorialist conception, which purported to identify a single legitimate governing law for transborder activity based on discrete territorial contacts. So too did the rise of the regulatory state, which led to more caustic public policy differences among jurisdictions, and which pressured the interested forum to apply local regulations whenever possible.

A second factor, legal realism, contributed to the demise of hermetic territorialism. All conflict-of-laws problems by definition have connections to two or more territorial jurisdictions. The legal realists showed that nothing in the logic of territorialism justified legal regulation by any one of these territories rather than another. They also argued that a forum's decision to apply foreign law was always determined by local domestic policies. This established the theoretical foundation for the lex fori orientation that has dominated choice of law ever since.

A third factor, legal positivism, exacerbated the problem of finding a unique governing law in transactional cases. Courts avoided many choice-of-law problems in such cases by applying universal customary laws tied to no particular sovereign authority, such as the law merchant, the law maritime, and the law of nations.

These factors did not completely undermine traditional views about territorial regulation. But they did lead to an expansion of the permissible bases for territorial jurisdiction. Both the Constitution and international law permit a nation or state to regulate the extraterritorial conduct of a citizen or domiciliary. In short, in modern times a transaction can legitimately be regulated by the jurisdiction where the transaction occurs, the jurisdictions where significant effects of the transaction are felt, and the jurisdictions where the parties burdened by the regulation are from.

This expansion of the permissible bases for the application of local law has revolutionized conflict of laws in the second half of this century. Any number of choice-of-law regimes are now consistent with constitutional and international law. The earlier belief in a unique governing law for all transnational activities has given way to the view that more than one jurisdiction can legitimately apply its law to the same transnational activity.

Cyberspace transactions are subject to private legal ordering. At the most basic level, private ordering is facilitated by the technical standards that define and limit cyberspace. To participate in the Internet function known as the World Wide Web, users must consent to the TCP/IP standards that define the Internet as well as to the HTML standards that more particularly define the Web. Similarly, sending e-mail over the Internet requires the sender to use TCP/IP standards and particular e-mail protocols. One's experience of cyberspace is further defined and limited by the more particular communication standards embedded in software. For example, within the range of what TCP/IP and HTML permit, an individual's communication via the World Wide Web will be shaped and limited by (among many other things) her choice of browsers and search engines. These and countless other technical standard choices order behavior in cyberspace. In this sense, access to different cyberspace networks and communities is always conditioned on the accessors' consent to the array of technical standards that define these networks and communities.

Technical standards cannot comprehensively specify acceptable behavior in cyberspace. Within the range of what these standards permit, information flows might violate network norms or territorial laws. Many network norms are promulgated and enforced informally. A more formal method to establish private legal orders in cyberspace is to condition access to particular networks on consent to a particular legal regime.

This regime could take several forms. It could be a local, national, or international law. When you buy a Dell computer through the company's web page from anywhere in the world, you agree that "(a)ny claim relating to, and the use of, this Site and the materials contained herein is governed by the laws of the state of Texas." Alternatively, the chosen law could be a free standing model law attached to no particular sovereign but available to be incorporated by contract. For example, parties to a commercial transaction over the Internet could agree that their transaction is governed by UNIDROIT Principles or the Uniform Customs and Practice for Documentary Credits. Or the governing law could be the contractual terms themselves. Waivers and exclusions operate as private law in this way. So too do chat rooms, discussion lists, and local area networks that condition participation on the user's consent to community norms specified in a contract.

Cyberspace architecture can also help to establish other aspects of a private legal order. Through conditioned access, cyberspace users can consent to have subsequent disputes resolved by courts, arbitrators, systems operators, or even "virtual magistrates." They can also establish private enforcement regimes. Technical standards operate as an enforcer of sorts by defining and limiting cyberspace activity. For example, software filters can block or condition access to certain information, and various technologies perform compliance monitoring functions. In addition, the gatekeeper of each cyberspace community can cut off entry for noncompliance with the community rules, or punish a user for bad acts by drawing on a bond (perhaps simply a credit card) put up as a condition on the user's entry.

But the possibility of extraterritorial and multiple regulations remains. Consider the Bavarian Justice Ministry's threat in December of 1995 to prosecute CompuServe for carrying online discussion groups containing material that violated German antipornography laws. CompuServe responded by blocking access to these discussion groups in Germany. Because of the state of thenavailable technology, this action had the effect of blocking access to these discussion groups for all CompuServe users worldwide. This is precisely what the skeptics fear from unilateral regulation of cyberspace. Germany enforced a mandatory law against an international access provider with a presence (office, staff, servers, etc.) in Germany. Faced with multiple regulatory regimes in the many places where it did business, CompuServe bowed to the most restrictive. The consequence was massive extraterritorial regulation, for the German regulation interrupted the flow and availability of the discussion groups for CompuServe clients everywhere in the world.

The skeptics frequently recount this story to show how unilateral national regulation of cyberspace can have multijurisdictional consequences. But the rest of the story suggests a somewhat different lesson. After closing down transmission of the offending discussions, Compu-

Serve offered its German users software that enabled them to block access to the offending discussion groups. The company then began to search for a more centralized way to filter the illegal newsgroups in Germany alone. German prosecutors subsequently indicted a Compu-Serve executive, alleging that the company failed to implement such national-level filtering technology to prevent dissemination of other illegal information in Germany. At about the same time, the German parliament enacted a law clarifying that cyberspace access providers are liable "if they are aware of the content" and fail to use "technically possible and reasonable" means to block it.

The subsequent events of the CompuServe controversy make clear the growing importance of information discrimination technology to the cyberspace regulation debate. Many jurisdictional challenges presented by cyberspace result from the purported inability of content providers to prevent information flows from appearing simultaneously in every juris-diction. Thus far I have assumed, with the skeptics, that this is a necessary (and accurate) feature of cyberspace architecture. But it is not. Cyberspace information can only appear in a geographical jurisdiction by virtue of hardware and software physically present in the jurisdiction. Available technology already permits governments and private entities to regulate the design and function of hardware and software to facilitate discrimination of cyberspace information flows along a variety of dimensions, including geography, network, and content. This technology is relatively new and still relatively crude, but it is growing very quickly in both sophistication and effectiveness. This technology facilitates discrim-ination and control of information flows at any of several junctures along the cyberspace information stream.

At the most basic level, the content provider can take steps to control the flow of the information. This happens, for example, whenever a web page operator conditions access to the page on the users' presenta-tion of information. Consider the many precautions taken by adult web pages. Some pages simply warn minors or persons from certain geo-graphical locations not to view or enter, and disclaim legal liability if they do. Others condition access on proof of age or on membership in one of dozens of private age-verification services. Others require potential end-users to send by fax or telephone information specifying age and geographical location. Still others label or rate their pages in order to accommodate end-use filtering software, as described below. Finally, digital identification technology developed for Internet commerce pro-vides a way to authenticate the identity of a party in a cyberspace transaction. Although digital identification is usually used to verify who someone is, it can also be used to verify other facts about cyberspace users, such as their nationality, domicile, or permanent address.

At the other end of the distribution chain, end-users can employ software filters to block out or discriminate among information flows. Parental control software is the most prominent example of an end-user filter, but many businesses and other local area networks also employ these technologies. Content filters also can be imposed at junctures along the cyberspace information stream between content providers and end-users. They can be imposed, for example, at the network level or at the level of the Internet service provider. They can also assist governments in filtering information at the national level. A government can choose to have no Internet links whatsoever and to regulate telephone and other communication lines to access providers in other countries. China, Singapore, and the United Arab Emirates have taken the somewhat less severe steps of (i) regulating access to the Net through centralized filtered servers, and (ii) requiring filters for instate Internet service providers and end-users. We have seen that Germany has chosen to hold liable Internet access providers who have knowledge of illegal content and fail to use "technically possible and reasonable" means to filter it. The Federal Communications Commission recently required V-chip blocking technology to be placed in computers capable of receiving video broadcasting, and pending antispam[10] legislation would impose identification requirements on commercial e-mail senders and filtering requirements on Internet service providers.

An additional reason that techniques for controlling cyberspace information flows are likely to be at least moderately successful is that so many participants in the cyberspace regulation debate—parents, businesses, content suppliers, service providers, governments, and even some anticensorship civil libertarians—desire such control.

Many commentators are skeptical about these filtering and identification technologies. They argue that content filters invariably both over- and under-filter; that identification technologies sometimes misidentify; and that some hackers will access prohibited information. These worries are to some degree well-founded. What is not well-founded, however, is the belief that imperfect regulation means ineffective regulation. Real space is filled with similarly imperfect filtering and identification techniques: criminals crack safes and escape from jail, fifteen year olds visit bars with fake IDs, secret information is leaked to the press, and so on. In cyberspace as in real space, imperfections in filtering and identification regimes do not render the regimes ineffective. Although the ultimate accuracy of cyberspace filtering and identification technologies remains an open question, there is little doubt that such technologies will contribute significantly to cyberspace regulation by enabling governments, content providers, end-users, and service providers to raise significantly the cost of accessing certain information. Indeed, this has already happened throughout cyberspace, where content filtering, conditioned access, and identification codes are pervasive.

The skeptics argue that unilateral extraterritorial regulation of cyberspace differs from similar regulation of real-space activities because of the regulation's spillover effects in other jurisdictions. These effects are inevitable, they think, because information flows in cyberspace appear simultaneously in all territorial jurisdictions. As a result, unilateral territorial regulation of the local effects of cyberspace transmission

---

10.   [Authors' note: Spam is e-mail *]

flows will sometimes affect the flow and regulation of web information in other countries. This is especially true when the regulation is directed at a multijurisdictional access provider, as was the case with Germany's regulation of CompuServe.

There is nothing extraordinary or illegitimate about unilateral regulation of transnational activity that affects activity and regulation in other countries. Germany's regulation of CompuServe is no less legitimate than the United States' regulation of the competitiveness of the English reinsurance market, which has worldwide effects on the availability and price of reinsurance. Nor is it any different in this regard from national regulation of transborder pollution, or from national consumer protection regulation of transnational contracts, or from national criminal prohibitions on transnational drug activities, all of which produce spillovers. In many contexts, there are powerful reasons for nations to surrender their regulatory prerogatives in order to reduce spillover and other costs. But at least under our current conceptions of territorial sovereignty, such reforms must proceed by national consent. The need for such consent begins from the premise that in its absence, national regulation of local effects is a legitimate incident of sovereignty, even if such regulation produces spillover effects.

Germany's regulation of CompuServe is not just a legitimate incident of territorial sovereignty. It is also fair to CompuServe under a straightforward reciprocal benefits rationale. CompuServe reaps financial and other benefits from its presence in Germany. Without this presence, German enforcement threats would be largely empty. CompuServe need not remain in Germany; it could close its shop there. Its decision to stay in Germany and comply with German regulations might increase the price of its services in Germany and elsewhere. For CompuServe this is a cost of doing business via a new communication medium. The desire to reduce this and related costs is driving the development of technology that permits geographical and other forms of discrimination on the Internet. But even in the absence of such technologies, Germany's local regulation of CompuServe remains within traditional reciprocity-based justifications for regulating local effects.

What about CompuServe users in other countries who are affected by the German regulation? It is hard to see how the German regulation unfairly burdens them. They remain free to choose among dozens of Internet access services that are not affected by the German regulation. Consider further the German perspective. Germany bans certain forms of pornography within its borders. If the medium of this pornography were paper, there would be no fairness-based jurisdictional objection to a German prohibition on the pornography's entry at the border or to German punishment of those who are later discovered to have smuggled it in. From Germany's perspective, it makes no difference whether the pornography enters the nation via cyberspace or the postal service. The rationale for the regulation is the same in both cases: something is happening within Germany that implicates the government's paternalistic concerns or that harms third parties within its borders. The fact that the local regulation might affect the cost or availability of pornography in other countries is, from this perspective, irrelevant. Fairness does not require Germany to yield local control over its territory in order to accommodate the users of a new communication technology in other countries. Nor does it require Germany to absorb the local costs of foreign activity because of the costs that the German regulation might impose on such activity.

Regulation sceptics] take it as an article of faith that cyberspace participants form a self-contained group that can internalize the costs of its activity. But this assumption is false. Cyberspace participants are no more self-contained than telephone users, members of the Catholic Church, corporations, and other private groups with activities that transcend jurisdictional borders. They are real people in real space transacting in a fashion that produces realworld effects on cyberspace participants and non participants alike. Cyberspace users solicit and deliver kiddie porn, launder money, sexually harass, defraud, and so on. It is these and many other real-space costs—costs that cyberspace communities cannot effectively internalize—that national regulatory regimes worry about and aim to regulate.

So the spillover argument runs in both directions. Cyberspace activity outside of Germany produces spillovers in Germany, and German regulation produces spillovers on cyberspace activity beyond its borders. The legitimacy and fairness of Germany's territorial regulation does not depend on minimization of these costs.

The skeptics' final normative argument against mandatory law regulation of cyberspace concerns notice. They worry that cyberspace participants therefore lack notice about governing mandatory law and hence cannot conform their behavior to it. The skeptics claim this lack of notice violates basic norms of fairness.

A manufacturer that pollutes in one state is not immune from the antipollution laws of other states where the pollution causes harm just because it cannot predict which way the wind blows. Similarly, a cyberspace content provider cannot necessarily claim ignorance about the geographical flow of information as a defense to the application of the law of the place where the information appears. At first glance it appears unfair to expose Digitalbook.com to the antipornography laws of Singapore. But it would not seem unfair if Digitalbook.com could at a small cost prevent its information from entering Singapore. Nor would it seem unfair to expose Digitalbook.com to liability for the damage caused in Singapore by a virus that it released into cyberspace that destroyed every Apple computer hard drive connected to the Internet.

Cyberspace transactions are no different from "real-space" transnational transactions. They involve people in real space in one jurisdiction communicating with people in real space in other jurisdictions in a way that often does good but sometimes causes harm. There is no general normative argument that supports the immunization of cyberspace activities from territorial regulation. And there is every reason to believe that nations can exercise territorial authority to achieve significant regulatory control over cyberspace transactions. Resolution of the choice-of-law problems presented by cyberspace transactions will be challenging, but no more challenging than similar problems raised in other transnational contexts.

Notes and Questions

1. According to the above article, what is the strongest argument you can make against any effort to control the content of Internet communications? What is the strongest argument you can make in favor of attempting to control such communications?

2. The two articles above appear to disagree on whether or not content control can be exercised through technological measures. Which side do you believe has the better argument?

3. *The Spill-over Effect.* Scholars and practitioners have disagreed over whether national laws controlling content will have an adverse impact on the content viewed by other countries. Professor Goldsmith appears to believe that such controls will not generally have a great effect on the materials allowed to be circulated in other countries. Do you agree? If he is wrong, whose laws or culture will control the Internet? Will it be the country with the most stringent laws?

Read the following Articles from the WIPO Copyright Treaty from the Supplement: 1, 8, 11, 12.

Notes and Questions

1. What method(s) does the WIPO Copyright Treaty establish for governing the unauthorized distribution of copyright protected works on the Internet or in other digital media?

2. Does the WIPO Copyright Treaty establish international standards for content regulation? What technological measures does it *require*? What technological measures does it *support*?

3. One of the most difficult issues regarding content regulation on the Internet is what acts should subject a party to liability. For example, should the person who uploads (copies onto the Internet) a copyrighted work without authorization be held liable? Should a person who has downloaded that work? What if the person only downloaded the work in order to read it? Should that act be sufficient to qualify as an act of infringement? What answers does the WIPO Copyright Treaty provide to these questions?

4. For an interesting article that contends that reading material off the Internet should be considered a fair use, *see* Jessica Litman, *The Exclusive Right To Read*, 13 Cardozo Arts & Ent. L.J. 29 (1994). Do you concur? Under what circumstances should end users be liable for their use of unauthorized or illegal content from the Internet?

5. In addition to deciding which acts should qualify as infringement, countries have also struggled to decide what burden, if any, should be placed on Internet service providers to police the acts of their users. In 1998, under the Digital Millenium Copyright Act (DCMA), the United States Title II of the DMCA adds a new section 512 to the 1976 Copyright Act to create four

new limitations on liability for copyright infringement by online service providers. The limitations are based on four categories of conduct by a service provider:

1) Transitory communications;

2) System caching;

3) Storage of information on systems or networks at direction of users; and

4) Information location tools.

To qualify for a safe harbor, the Internet Service Provider (ISP) must also meet various reporting and policing requirements when a complaint is filed.

6. Not all parties agree that Internet Service Providers should be immune from liability. In comparing certain ISP's to newspaper publishers, Jack Goldsmith insisted that such publishers should be held to the same liability standards. He stated:

> It is relatively uncontroversial that a newspaper publisher is liable for harms caused wherever the newspaper is published or distributed. This seems appropriate because, among other reasons, we think the publisher can control the geographical locus of publication and distribution. Requiring such control imposes modest costs on the publisher; she must, for example, keep abreast of regulatory developments in different jurisdictions and take steps to exclude publication and distribution in places where she wants to avoid liability.

> Now consider the cyberspace content provider. Many have an intuition that such content providers should not be liable for harms caused wherever the content appears. The primary basis for this intuition is that the content provider cannot control the geographical and network distribution of his information flows. But this latter point is groundless. Content providers already have several means to control information flows. As the cost of such control continues to drop, and the accuracy and ease of this control increases, cyberspace content providers will come to occupy the same position as the newspaper publisher. It will thus be appropriate in cyberspace, as in real space, for the law to impose small costs on both types of publisher to ensure that content does not appear in jurisdictions and networks where it is illegal. (Jack L. Goldsmith, *Against Cyberanarchy*, 65 U. Chi. L. Rev. 1199 (1998)). Do you agree?

C. HOW SHOULD DOMAIN NAMES BE ALLOCATED?

As you know from the *U.S. Cybersquatter* case, above, domain names serve as the web address for a given site. In certain instances, where the domain name is used as a source identifier for goods or services, it may also fill a trademark function. In certain instances the same trademark may be used by various companies for different goods without violating trademark laws. Thus, Allied Van Lines, Allied Toys and Allied Computers may all use the dominant term "Allied" without infringing the others' rights, so long as no likely confusion occurs. By contrast, however, due to the nature of a domain name, only one company can own "Allied.com" for its domain name. Determining how to allocate these precious resources and avoid public confusion is a subject of continued international debate.

THE BRITISH CYBERSQUATTER CASE
BRITISH TELECOMMUNICATIONS PLC v. ONE IN A MILLION LTD AND OTHERS

Court Of Appeal (Civil Division), 1998.
[1998] 4 All ER 476.

ALDOUS LJ

There are before this court appeals in five actions. Those actions came before Mr. Jonathan Sumption QC sitting as a deputy judge of the High Court. On 28 November 1997 he granted summary judgment under RSC Ord 14 as the defendants had threatened to pass off and infringe the registered trade marks of the plaintiffs (see [1998] FSR 265).

In each case the first defendant was One In A Million Ltd, a company owned and controlled by its two directors, Mr. Conway and Mr. Nicholson. They are the second and third defendants. The fourth defendant, Global Media, and fifth defendant, Junic, are firms through which Mr. Conway and Mr. Nicholson trade. Each of the defendants has done acts alleged to infringe the rights of a plaintiff, but resolution of the issues in this appeal does not depend upon the identity of any particular defendant. I will refer to them generally as the appellants except where it is necessary to differentiate between them.

The appellants are dealers in Internet domain names. They register them and sell them. They have made a speciality of registering domain names for use on the Internet comprising well-known names and trade marks without the consent of the person or company owning the goodwill in the name or trade mark. Examples are the registration and subsequent offer for sale to Burger King by the second defendant of the domain name burgerking.co.uk for L25,000 plus value added tax and of bt.org to British Telecommunications plc for L4,700 plus value added tax.

The plaintiffs Marks & Spencer plc, J Sainsbury plc, Virgin Enterprises Ltd, British Telecommunications plc, Telecom Securicor Cellular Radio Ltd, Ladbrokes plc are well-known companies. In the actions brought by them, they allege that the activities of the appellants amount to passing off, to infringement of their well-known registered trade marks, to threats of passing off and infringement, and to wrongful acts such as to entitle them to injunctive relief. Their complaints stem from the registration by One In A Million Ltd of ladbrokes.com; sainsbury.com; sainsburys.com; j-sainsbury.com; marksandspencer.com; cellnet.net; bt.org and virgin.org: by Global Media Communications of marksandspencer.co.uk; britishtelecom.co.uk; britishtelecom.net; and by Junic of britishtelecom.com.

At its simplest the Internet is a collection of computers which are connected through the telephone network to communicate with each other. As explained by the judge ([1998] FSR 265 at 267):

"The Internet is increasingly used by commercial organisations to promote themselves and their products and in some cases to buy and sell. For these purposes they need a domain name identifying the computer which they are using. A domain name comprises groups of alphanumeric characters separated by dots. A first group commonly comprises the name of the enterprise or a brand name or trading name associated with it, followed by a 'top level' name identifying the nature and sometimes the location of the organisation. Marks & Spencer, for example, have a number of domain names, including marks-and-spencer.co.uk, marks-and-spencer.com and stmichael.com. The domain name marks-and-spencer.co.uk, for example, will enable them to have an e-mail address in the form johnsmith@marks-and-spencer.co.uk and a web site address in the form http://www.marks-and-spencer.co.uk. The top level suffix co.uk indicates a United Kingdom company. Other top level names bear conventional meanings as follows:

- com   International commercial organisations
- edu   Educational organisation
- gov   Government organisation
- org   Miscellaneous organisations

There is no central authority regulating the Internet, which is almost entirely governed by convention. But registration services in respect of domain names are provided by a number of organisations. Network Solutions Inc of Virginia in the United States is the organisation generally recognised as responsible for allocating domain names with the top level suffixes 'com' and 'edu'. In the United Kingdom a company called Nominet UK provides a registration service in respect of domain names ending with the geographical suffix uk preceded by functional suffixes such as co, org, gov or edu."

Nominet UK applied to intervene in this appeal. It is a "not for profit" limited company, which is registered with the Internet Assigned Numbers Authority. It operates what is known as the Register Database, which contains the domain names and IP addresses for .co.uk, .net.uk, .ltd.uk and plc.uk and full details of the registrant of the domain name and its registration agent. It charges a fee for its service. From time to time (eg every two hours or so) the information on the database is extracted to a number of domain name servers. Domain name servers are computers which hold the index of names which map to particular numbers used in intercomputer transactions. For example, if I wanted to contact Marks & Spencer plc, I can use the domain name marks-and-spencer.co.uk. The domain name server will recognise the domain name and provide the appropriate sequence of numbers, called the IP address. It is that address which identifies the computer owned by Marks & Spencer plc, thereby enabling my computer to contact that owned by Marks & Spencer plc.

As part of its service Nominet offers a "Whois" service to the public. Thus the public can type in a domain name on Nominet's website and press the appropriate button to execute the "Whois" search. The answer sets out the recorded information on the organisation or person who has registered the domain name. This is useful if, for example, a person wishes to contact the owner of a domain name.

Members of the public would not ordinarily have a domain name. They would subscribe to a service provider and have an e-mail address. That enables a subscriber to send messages to another computer through the service provider, which forwards the message when requested to the appropriate computer. The subscriber can also browse around the world wide web and seek web pages associated with a particular domain name. Thus if he transmits a domain name to his service provider, it will contact the domain name and the web pages sought and provide the information obtained.

Web sites are used for many activities such as advertising, selling, requesting information, criticism and the promotion of hobbies.

The basic facts are not in dispute. The appellants accept that the trade names Marks & Spencer, Ladbroke, Sainsbury, Virgin, BT and Cellnet are well-known brand names used by the respective respondents in the course of their businesses. Their use in this country is such that the respondents have built up and own a substantial goodwill attaching to them. The appellants also accept that the respondents are the registered proprietors of the pleaded trade marks which embody the trade names and that such trade marks are valid and subsisting. The dispute concerns the liability of the appellants for what they have done and whether they have threatened to do anything which is unlawful. The appellants are dealers in internet domain names and as part of their business, they secure registrations of prestigious names as domain names without the consent of the enterprise owning the goodwill in those names. Their case is that they register the domain names with a view to making a profit either by selling them to the owners of the goodwill, using the blocking effect of the registration to obtain a reasonable price, or, in some cases, selling them to collectors or to other persons who could have a legitimate reason for using them. That, they submitted, could not amount to passing off or a threat to pass off or render them liable as joint tortfeasors or as being persons equipped with or who are likely to equip others with instruments of fraud.

The true attitude of the appellants can be seen from what they have said and done in the past. In 1996 British Telecommunications plc became aware of the activities of Mr. Conway who had registered domain names which included the word, britishtelecom. They wrote threatening proceedings. The dispute between them and Mr. Conway was settled upon Mr. Conway giving written undertakings in a document dated 3 November 1996. The first two undertakings were in this form:

"1. To immediately cease all use of the domain names britishtele-com.co.uk and britishtelecom.net and forthwith to take all necessary steps to have the registrations of these domain names transferred to the ownership and control of BT by the relevant registration authority in each case.

2. Not at any time in the future to register on the internet any domain name or to host or operate on the internet any site using a domain name containing the words 'British Telecom' or the letters 'BT' (where the use of the letters might reasonably be taken to refer to BT) or any name containing any confusingly similar variation of those words, whether or not in conjunction with any other letters, numbers or symbols."

Pursuant to the first undertaking Mr. Conway cancelled the domain names and they were transferred by reregistration at the cost of British Telecommunications plc.

Despite Mr. Conway's capitulation and the provision of undertakings at the end of 1996, the domain name britishtelecom.com was registered by Junic, the firm name used by Mr. Nicholson on 20 March 1997. On 16 May 1997 BT wrote to Mr. Nicholson complaining about the registration. That did not end the matter. One In A Million Ltd, the company owned and controlled by Mr. Nicholson and Mr. Conway registered bt.org on 28 May 1997. BT complained about this in their letter of 12 August 1997. The reply dated 18 August 1997 accepted that the domain name had been registered by One In A Million. It stated:

"The domain name bt.org was registered on behalf of a client of One In A Million Ltd, who requires the domain for his personal use, with his initials being BT ... As a computer and telecommunications consultant and journalist myself, I am fully aware that British Telecommunications plc have a habit of suddenly requiring domain names that are already registered to third parties. This is despite the fact that British Telecommunications plc has had ample opportunity to register such domain names previously had they required use of them. Should you take up your threats of legal action then this will be most welcome as it will make the situation substantially more appealing to the media. Additionally, if the sale to my client of the bt.org domain is hindered in any way due to any actions you may have taken, or will take in the future, then we shall immediately be taking all necessary and appropriate action against British Telecommunications plc for the resulting loss of business."

J. Sainsbury plc also complained to One in a Million Ltd about registration of domain names using the mark Sainsbury. The reply dated 26 September 1997 accepted that the registrations had been completed and made it quite clear that they would not be relinquished. It said:

"We are not trading under the name Sainsbury nor do we intend to trade under the name Sainsbury. We have merely purchased the Internet domain names j-sainsbury.com, sainsbury.com and sainsburys.com as part of our personal collection."

In my view there was clear evidence of systematic registration by the appellants of well-known trade names as blocking registrations and a threat to sell them to others. No doubt the primary purpose of registration was to block registration by the owner of the goodwill. There was, according to Mr. Wilson nothing unlawful in doing that. The truth is different. The registration only blocks registration of the identical domain name and therefore does not act as a block to registration of a domain name that can be used by the owner of the goodwill in the name. The purpose of the so-called blocking registration was to extract money from the owners of the goodwill in the name chosen. Its ability to do so was in the main dependent upon the threat, expressed or implied, that the appellants would exploit the goodwill by either trading under the name or equipping another with the name so he could do so.

I believe that domain names comprising the name Marks & Spencer are instruments of fraud. Any realistic use of them as domain names would result in passing off and there was ample evidence to justify the injunctive relief granted by the judge to prevent them being used for a fraudulent purpose and to prevent them being transferred to others.

I also believe that the names registered by the appellants were instruments of fraud and that injunctive relief was appropriate upon this basis as well.

Mr. Wilson submitted that to infringe there had to be use of the trade mark as a trade mark and that the use had to be a trade mark use in relation to goods or services, in the sense that it had to denote origin. He also submitted that the use had to be confusing use.

I am not satisfied that the law's requirement of use for infringement to occur does require the use to be trade mark use nor that it must be confusing use, but I am prepared to assume that it does. Upon that basis I am of the view that threats to infringe have been established. The appellants seek to sell the domain names which are confusingly similar to registered trade marks. The domain names indicate origin. That is the purpose for which they were registered. Further they will be used in relation to the services provided by the registrant who trades in domain names.

Mr. Wilson also submitted that it had not been established that the contemplated use would take unfair advantage of, or was detrimental to the distinctive character or reputation of the respondents' trade marks. He is wrong. The domain names were registered to take advantage of the distinctive character and reputation of the marks. That is unfair and detrimental.

I conclude that the judge came to the right conclusion on this part of the case for the right reasons.

For the reasons given I would dismiss this appeal.

THE U.S. CYBERSQUATTER CASE
INTERMATIC INCORPORATED
v. DENNIS TOEPPEN

United States District Court, N.D. Illinois, 1996.
947 F.Supp. 1227.

WILLIAMS, DISTRICT JUDGE.

The court has carefully reviewed Magistrate Judge Denlow's report and recommendation ("R & R"), the objections of defendant Toeppen, and the responses of plaintiff Intermatic Inc. By applying the law of trademarks to the internet, Magistrate Judge Denlow strikes an appropriate balance between trademark law and the attendant policy concerns raised by the defendant.

REPORT AND RECOMMENDATION

DENLOW, UNITED STATES MAGISTRATE JUDGE.

Welcome to cyberspace! This case presents the Court with the increasingly important issue of whether and how federal and state trademark laws apply to govern names selected by users for their Internet website. As the Internet grows in prominence as a venue for business, the courts will be called upon to apply traditional legal principles to new avenues of commerce. This is such a case.

Intermatic is a Delaware corporation having a place of business in Spring Grove, Illinois. Intermatic has been doing business under the name INTERMATIC since 1941. Intermatic has 37 offices throughout the United States and has been in business in Illinois since 1892. Intermatic is a manufacturer and distributor of a wide variety of electrical and electronic products, including computerized and programmable timers and other devices which are sold under the name and trademark INTERMATIC.

Intermatic's sales and advertising of INTERMATIC labeled products have been continuous since the 1940's. In the last 8 years, its sales in the U.S. have exceeded $850 million. Id. Intermatic's products prominently bear the INTERMATIC name and trademark, and well over 100 million units have been installed in homes and businesses throughout the United States.

Advertising and promotional expenditures for products bearing the INTERMATIC mark for the last 8 years have exceeded $16 million ... Intermatic's coop advertising consists of approximately 700 print ads per year, with each displaying the INTERMATIC mark. Intermatic also advertises and promotes its INTERMATIC products, mark and name by way of trade shows throughout the United States, magazines, point-of-purchase displays, brochures, radio, and television.

Defendant Toeppen resides in Champaign, Illinois, where he operates an Internet service provider business known as Net66. Toeppen has registered approximately 240 Internet domain names without seeking the permission from any entity that has previously used the names he registered, because he contends that no permission was or is necessary. Among the domain names which he has registered are the following well known business names:

deltaairlines.com	greatamerica.com
britishairways.com	neimanmarcus.com
crateandbarrel.com	northwest airlines.com
ramadainn.com	ussteel.com
eddiebauer.com	unionpacific.com

One of Toeppen's business objectives is to profit by the resale or licensing of these domain names, presumably to the entities who conduct business under these names.

In December of 1995, Toeppen applied for registration of the domain name http: www.intermatic.com ("intermatic.com") and NSI registered the domain name to Toeppen's domain name servers. A given domain name, the exact alphanumeric combination in the same network and using the same suffix, can only be registered to one entity. Intermatic subsequently attempted to register the same domain name and was prevented from registering "intermatic.com" as its domain name because of Toeppen's prior registration of that domain name.

Intermatic also became aware that Toeppen was using the mark "Intermatic" in connection with the sale of a computer software program. Upon discovery of Toeppen's prior registration and use of the Intermatic mark, Intermatic made a written demand on Toeppen that he relinquish or assign the "intermatic.com" domain name registration and discontinue use of the Intermatic mark. Toeppen agreed to discontinue using the Intermatic mark for his software product but refused to give up the "intermatic.com" domain name registration. In response to a formal request by Intermatic, NSI put Toeppen's registration on hold in April of 1996.

As long as Mr. Toeppen is allowed to retain the "intermatic.com" registration, Intermatic will be unable to acquire "intermatic.com" as an Internet domain name or use "intermatic.com" as an email address on the Internet. However, Intermatic is technically capable of establishing its web page at another domain name, including, for example, "intermaticinc.com" and it is technically capable of establishing at any available domain name a web page featuring the INTERMATIC mark and any other Internet-related marketing or business information. To date, Intermatic has not chosen to reserve any other domain name or to take any other action to establish a presence on the Internet. However, some of its distributors have placed Intermatic information on the Internet.

Until NSI placed the intermatic.com domain name on hold, Toeppen maintained intermatic.com as an active domain name on the Internet. Although he initially set up a web page regarding a software program he was developing and intended to call "Intermatic," Toeppen removed that page (which was available for less than a week) and dropped the proposed name for his software in response to demand from Intermatic. No software programs were ever sold. He then instituted as a web page a map of ChampaignUrbana, the community where Toeppen resides.

When Toeppen became aware of Intermatic's efforts to have the intermatic.com domain name placed on hold, he changed the web page associated with intermatic.com to bear the caption "ChampaignUrbana Map Page/has Moved To www.cu.com." Toeppen moved the map and put the forwarding address on the intermatic.com page so that Internet users could update relevant hyperlinks before the NSI freeze simply locked them out of the page, as is now the case. Presently, entering intermatic.com will return a message that there is no functional domain name server at that domain name.

At no time did Toeppen use intermatic.com in connection with the sale of any available goods or services. At no time has Toeppen advertised the intermatic.com domain name in association with any goods or services. Presently, the intermatic.com domain name is not available for use by any party. Toeppen did not seek permission from Intermatic to use the intermatic.com domain name because he believes that no permission was or is necessary. Intermatic disagrees. This litigation ensued.

This case involves a dispute over the ownership of a highly prized Internet address. The issue is whether the owner of the Intermatic trademark may preclude the use of the trademark as an Internet domain name by defendant Toeppen, who had made no prior use of the Intermatic name prior to registering it as an Internet domain name. This case does not involve competing claims to the same name by parties who have actively used the same name in their business, such as the use of the term "United" by United Airlines, United Van Lines, United Mineworkers Union and the United Way.

Toeppen is what is commonly referred to as a cybersquatter. These individuals attempt to profit from the Internet by reserving and later reselling or licensing domain names back to the companies that spent millions of dollars developing the goodwill of the trademark. While many may find patently offensive the practice of reserving the name or mark of a federally registered trademark as a domain name and then attempting to sell the name back to the holder of the trademark, others may view it as a service. Regardless of one's views as to the morality of such conduct, the legal issue is whether such conduct is illegal. Cybersquatters such as Toeppen contend that because they were the first to register the domain name through NSI it is theirs. Intermatic argues that it is entitled to protect its valuable trademark by preventing Toeppen from using "intermatic.com" as a domain name.

The practical effect of Toeppen's conduct is to enjoin Intermatic from using its trademark as its domain name on the Internet. Unlike the typical trademark dispute, where both parties are using the name simultaneously and arguing whether confusion exists, the current configuration of the Internet allows only one party to use the "intermatic.com" domain name. Because the Internet assigns the toplevel domain name .com to commercial and noncommercial users, there does not currently appear to be a way in which both Intermatic and Toeppen can both use the intermatic.com name.

Congress and the states have been slow to respond to the activities of the cybersquatters.

Intermatic's name and prior rights over Toeppen to use the INTERMATIC name are clear. Intermatic's first use of the INTERMATIC name and mark predates Toeppen's first use of "intermatic.com" by more than fifty years. Also, it is undisputed that Intermatic holds a valid registration for the trademark INTERMATIC.

Toeppen does not contest the fact that Intermatic's mark is strong. The Court finds that the mark is strong and entitled to broad protection as a matter of law.

Intermatic argues that Toeppen's registration of more than 200 domain names is indicia of willful intent. However, Toeppen argues that he was motivated in part to test the legality of arbitraging domain names. This is a relatively new area of law and Toeppen is free to test the waters. There has been no evidence that Toeppen intended to pass off any of his products or services as Intermatic's. Neither the software nor the map of Urbana are in any way similar to Intermatic's products. He immediately ceased to market the software under the Intermatic name when contacted by Intermatic's counsel. Whether Toeppen's registration of several domain names is sufficient to rise to the level of willful intent is also a question of fact. Id. at 123132.

Therefore the Court recommends that since there are questions of fact as to a likelihood of confusion, the parties' cross motions for summary judgment should be denied.

The Federal Trademark Dilution Act provides that: the owner of a famous mark shall be entitled, subject to the principles of equity and upon such terms as the court deems reasonable, to an injunction against another person's commercial use in commerce of a mark or trade name, if such use begins after the mark has become famous and causes dilution of the distinctive quality of the mark ... 15 U.S.C. § 1125(c)

Factors considered in determining the distinctiveness and fame of the mark are: a) degree of inherent or acquired distinctiveness of the mark; b) duration and extent of use of the mark; c) duration and extent of advertising and publicity of the mark; d) geographical extent of the trading area in which the mark is used; e) channels of trade for the goods or services; f) degree of recognition of the mark in the trading area; g) use of the same or similar marks by third parties; and h) whether the mark was federally registered. 15 U.S.C. § 1125(c)(1)(A)(H).

In order to state a cause of action under the Act a party must show that the mark is famous and that the complainant's use is commercial and in commerce which is likely to cause dilution. The statute defines the term "dilution" to mean "the lessening of the capacity of a famous mark to identify and distinguish goods or services, regardless of the presence or absence of (1) competition between the owner of the famous mark and other parties, or (2) likelihood of confusion, mistake, or deception." 15 U.S.C. § 1127. "The definition is designed to encompass all forms of dilution recognized by the courts, including dilution by blurring, by tarnishment and disparagement, and by diminishment. In an effort to clarify the law on the subject, the definition also recognizes that a cause of action for dilution may exist whether or not the parties market the same or related goods or whether or not a likelihood of confusion exists. Thus, a mark protected against dilution can have acquired its fame in connection with one type of good or service and, as a result, be so famous as to be entitled to protection against dilution when used on or in connection with an unrelated good or service." H.R.Rep. No. 374, 104th Cong., 1st Sess.1995, 1995 WL 709280, pg. 3 (Leg.Hist.).

Under the Act, the owner of a famous mark is only entitled to injunctive relief unless the person against whom the injunction is sought willfully intended to trade on the owner's reputation or to cause dilution of the famous mark. The Act does not preempt state dilution claims. The Act specifically provides that noncommercial use of the mark is not actionable. 15 U.S.C. § 1125(c)(4)(B).

As a matter of law the Court finds that the Intermatic mark is famous within the meaning of 15 U.S.C. § 1125(c). The Intermatic mark is a strong fanciful federally registered mark, which has been exclusively used by Intermatic for over 50 years. Therefore since Intermatic has established that its mark is famous, it need only show that Toeppen's use is a commercial use in commerce and that by his use dilution will likely occur.

Toeppen argues that there has been no violation of the Federal Trademark Dilution Act because his use of the Intermatic mark is not a commercial use.

Toeppen's intention to arbitrage the "intermatic.com" domain name constitutes a commercial use. At oral argument Toeppen's counsel candidly conceded that one of Toeppen's intended uses for registering the Intermatic mark was to eventually sell it back to Intermatic or to some other party. Toeppen's desire to resell the domain name is sufficient to meet the "commercial use" requirement of the Lanham Act.

Toeppen's use of "intermatic.com" is likely to cause dilution of its mark. For purposes of the Act, the "term 'dilution' means the lessening of the capacity of a famous mark to identify and distinguish goods or services, regardless of the presence or absence of (1) competition between the owner of the famous mark and other parties, or (2) likelihood of confusion, mistake or deception." 15 U.S.C. § 1127. Toeppen's conduct has caused dilution in at least two respects. First, Toeppen's registration of the intermatic.com domain name lessens the capacity of Intermatic to identify and distinguish its goods and services by means of the Internet. Intermatic is not currently free to use its mark as its domain name. This is not a situation where there were competing users of the same name by competing parties and a race to the Internet between them. This case involves one party, Intermatic, with a long history of trademark use, and a second, Toeppen, who has effectively enjoined Intermatic from using its trademark by the payment of $100 to register the "intermatic.com" domain name. This activity clearly violates the Congressional intent of encouraging the registration and development of trademarks to assist the public in differentiating products ... Such conduct lessens the capacity of Intermatic to identify its goods to potential consumers who would expect to locate Intermatic on the Internet through the "intermatic.com" domain name.

Second, Toeppen's conduct dilutes the Intermatic mark by using the Intermatic name on its web page. As the Seventh Circuit explained in *Polaroid Corp. v. Polaraid, Inc.*, 319 F.2d 830, 836 (7th Cir.1963), The gravamen of a dilution complaint is that the continuous use of a mark similar to plaintiff's works an inexorably adverse effect upon the distinctiveness of the plaintiff's mark, and that, if he is powerless to prevent such use, his mark will lose its distinctiveness entirely ... dilution is an infection which, if allowed to spread, will inevitably destroy the advertising value of the mark. "The harm caused by dilution is, for example, that the distinctiveness of the name [Intermatic] and the favorable association that accrued to it by virtue of [Intermatic's] commercial success would be undermined by the use of similar names in connection with other noncompeting and nonconfusing products." *Ringling Bros.– Barnum & Bailey Combined Shows, Inc. v. Celozzi–Ettelson Chevrolet, Inc.*, 855 F.2d 480, 485 (7th Cir.1988). If Toeppen were allowed to use "intermatic.com", Intermatic's name and reputation would be at Toeppen's mercy and could be associated with an unimaginable amount of messages on Toeppen's web page. "It is the same dissonance that would be produced by selling cat food under the name 'Romanoff,' or baby carriages under the name 'Aston Martin' " *Exxon Corp. v. Exxene Corp.*, 696 F.2d 544, 550 (7th Cir.1982).

Dilution of Intermatic's mark is likely to occur because the domain name appears on the web page and is included on every page that is printed from the web page. At oral argument counsel agreed that almost all web pages will include the domain name on the computer screen as well as printing the name on any and all pages that are printed. The all inclusive nature of the domain name all but guarantees that "intermatic.com" will appear on the web page and any printouts. Attaching Intermatic's name to a myriad of possible messages, even something as innocuous as a map of Urbana, Illinois, is something that the Act does not permit. The fact that "intermatic.com" will be displayed on every aspect of the web page is sufficient to show that Intermatic's mark will likely be diluted.

Notes and Questions

1. Compare the court's decisions in the *British* and *U.S. Cybersquatter* cases. What rationale(s) do they find persuasive? Are they the same?

2. What "evidence" would you require to determine if a person were a "cybersquatter"? Should it be sufficient to prove they were aware of the mark? What if the mark were not being used in the "cybersquatter's" home country? Would his registration of the domain name still be unlawful?

3. Can any company register as a domain name a trademark of a foreign entity without being accused of being a cybersquatter? Under what circumstances, if any?

THE BRITISH REGISTRATION CASE
PITMAN TRAINING LIMITED v. NOMINET UK

Chancery Division, 1997, [1997].
FSR 797, 17 Tr L 173.

SIR RICHARD SCOTT

This case raises questions about the rights acquired by someone who registers an Internet domain name and it has required me to try to understand the way in which the Internet system operates.

The Internet is a network of computer networks. A computer which is attached to an appropriate network can use appropriate software to communicate and exchange information quickly with any other computer on the network. In order to receive or to make available information on the Internet a domain name is needed. A domain name can be likened to an address. It identifies a particular Internet site. A particular domain name will only be allocated to one company or individual. It represents that company's computer site and is the means by which that company's customers can find it on the Internet. Electronic messages (e-mail) can be transmitted and received on the Internet. These messages are directed to e-mail addresses which will include the domain names of the addressees. A web site address, too, will include the main name of the owner of the web site. A web site is a series of files on a computer on the Internet that can be accessed by anyone via the Internet.

It will be apparent, therefore, that in order to receive e-mail on the Internet and in order to establish a web site on the Internet a domain name is needed. Domain names appear as words. The name in issue in the present case, for example, is "pitman.co.uk". However, when a domain name is used on the Internet it is translated into numbers known as IP numbers. The translation is carried out by a series of computer software packages known as domain name servers. An IP number is required both to send and to receive e-mail. Besides translating domain names into IP numbers the name servers provide services to the software on clients' computers.

Co.uk and com. are two of the most common domain name suffixes. They connote respectively United Kingdom companies and international companies. The Internet system has grown up informally and without statutory regulation. It was originally established and run, as I understand it, by academic bodies. The Internet Assigned Numbers Authority ("IANA") is operated by the Information Sciences Institute of Southern California and is the body which has become, for historical reasons, responsible for the allocation of top level domains. In the domain name "pitman.co.uk", "uk" is the top level domain designating the United Kingdom. In about 1985 IANA authorised an academic organisation in the United Kingdom, known as the United Kingdom Education and Research Networking Association (UKERNA) to administer the domain name system for the United Kingdom under the "uk" top level domain.

Initially the Internet was only used by academics and UKERNA gave domain names to universities and to other academic bodies. From about 1992, however, the Internet began to be used commercially and the business transacted on the Internet began to increase dramatically. Arrangements became necessary to deal, inter alia, with the allocation of domain names to companies and individuals desirous of using the Internet. In September 1985 a committee, the United Kingdom Naming Committee, was formed as an off-shoot of UKERNA to administer the United Kingdom domain. The Naming Committee consisted of United Kingdom Internet Service Providers. A service provider is a company whose business it is to arrange access to the Internet for its customers. A charge is naturally made for this service. The service provider can provide the customer with the facilities the customer needs in order to get connected to the Internet. It can obtain for the customer a domain name and e-mail facilities and set up a web site for the customer.

The United Kingdom Naming Committee, at its inaugural meeting on September 30, 1995, agreed on rules to be followed in dealing with applications for co.uk domain names. It may seem a matter of some surprise that it had operated from 1985 to 1995 apparently without rules. Be that as it may, in September 1995 it decided to have rules.

One of the rules was that if more than one application for the same domain name should be received, a first come/first served rule would be applied. On August 1, 1996 a company, Nominet UK, which is the first defendant in this action, took over from the United Kingdom Naming Committee the responsibility for allocating United Kingdom domain names.

When on August 1, 1996 Nominet UK took over the allocation of domain names from the Naming Committee, the first come/first served rule was maintained. Nominet adopted a rule that "where two applications are for the same name then the one which is received first shall have prior claim."

The problem in the present case has arisen out of the circumstance that both the plaintiffs, Pitman Training Ltd and PTC Oxford Ltd, and the second defendant, Pearson Professional Ltd, are entitled to use for their respective trading purposes the name or style "Pitman". One of the divisions of Pearson Professional Ltd, which is a wholly owned subsidiary of Pearson Plc, is Pitman Publishing, whose main business is the publication of books and electronic publications for university or college students. The managing director of Pitman Publishing, Mr. Bristow, has described it in his affidavit as "Europe's largest publisher of business management, education and development materials in the English language in paper based and screen formats." Pitman Publishing has an annual turnover in excess of L20 million. Its United Kingdom annual turnover is in excess of L10 million. The Pitman name has been associated with the publishing business since 1849. The Pitman business, founded as I understand it by Sir Isaac Pitman, originally included not only publishing but also a training business and an examination business. Of course the Pitman name was associated with each of these businesses. The businesses were sold in 1985. The publishing business was acquired by Pearsons. The training business was acquired by Pitman Training Ltd, the first plaintiff. The examination business was sold off to another party.

The continued use of the Pitman style, the Pitman name, for trading purposes by each of these purchasers of parts of the previous Pitman business was regulated by an agreement to which Pitman Training Ltd and, as I understand it, the predecessors of Pearson Professional Ltd were parties. It was dated June 28, 1985. Under the agreement Pitman Trading Ltd covenanted for itself and its successors in title to the training business:

that none of them will at any time hereafter carry on or be directly or indirectly engaged or concerned or interested in carrying on in any part of the world, whether on its own account or as the agent, partner or associate of any other person, firm or company or to any subsidiary company:

> (1) the publishing of books, periodicals or magazines with the exception of publications ancillary to the training business including correspondence courses under the name or imprint of Pitman or which includes the name Pitman, or

> (2) any trade or business under the name Pitman or any name likely to cause confusion therewith but so that Pitman Training Ltd shall be authorised by virtue of this agreement to carry on and conduct training and correspondence courses under the following names,

and then a number of names are set out:

and such other names including the name Pitman which clearly indicate that the use is in connection with training or correspondence courses.

It would seem that this covenant would bar Pitman Training Ltd from using for its business purposes the domain name "pitman.co.uk".

It is said that the use by Pitman Publishing of the domain name "pitman.co.uk" would constitute passing off. This strikes me as a strange proposition, bearing in mind that Pitman Publishing has traded under the style Pitman for nearly 150 years and that in 1985 when the Pitman businesses were sold off separately it was agreed that the purchaser of the publishing business would continue to trade under the style Pitman. Indeed, it was agreed that the purchaser of the training business would not trade under that style unless the name "Pitman" was accompanied by the word "training". The use by PTC of the "pitman.co.uk" domain name seems to me to be in breach of the 1985 agreement. Be that as it may, it is not Pitman Publishing that is suing PTC. It is the other way around. PTC contends that its, PTC's, use of the domain name in the period March 1996 to date has led the public to associate that domain name (as opposed to the style Pitman per se) with it, PTC. So the use of the domain name "pitman.co.uk" by Pitman Publishing would, it is contended, constitute passing off by Pitman Publishing. The evidence does not even begin to support the contention that the public associates the domain name "pitman.co.uk" with PTC. PTC has had only two e-mail responses to the advertisements it has put out. During the time PTC has been using the "pitman.co.uk" domain name in its advertisements so too has Pitman Publishing been using the domain name in its advertisements. Both have been using the domain name in their respective advertisements. Not only is there no evidence that the public has come to associate the domain name exclusively with PTC, but it is in my opinion highly improbable that that could have happened. That there may be some confusion experienced by some members of the public is undoubtedly so. But that confusion results from the use by both companies, PTC and Pitman Publishing, of the style Pitman for their respective trading purposes. No viable passing off claim against Pitman Publishing arising out of the future or past use by Pitman Publishing of the "pitman.co.uk" domain name has, in my judgment, been shown.

I have come to the conclusion that the plaintiffs have no viable or reasonably arguable cause of action against the second defendant. Accordingly, I must dismiss this application for interlocutory relief and I do so.

DISPOSITION:

Application dismissed.

Notes and Questions

1. On what basis should conflicting domain names be awarded–first to file, longest use as a trademark, most famous? What is the strongest argument you can make in favor of each system? What are the biggest problems caused by each system?

2. On December 4, 1998, the Paris Court of Appeal struck down an interim decision ordering cancellation of the registration of the domain name "alice.fr." The domain name registrant–Alice 5A–was created in 1996 and was a software company. It registered the mark "Alice d'ISOFT" and the

domain name "alice.fr" under which it operated a web site since December 1996. The challenger–Alice SNC–was an advertising company, established since 1957, with a registered trademark "Alice" since 1975 for advertising services. There was no evidence of fraudulent behavior or any attempt to trade in on the senior user's goodwill. The lower court declined to enforce the first-come, first-served rule of the domain name system and found that Alice SA's registration would "prejudice the elder company because it would deprive it of its corporate name and identity on the Internet whereas it owns a true property right in such name." The appellant court reversed, finding no intent to defraud and that Alice SA had followed Nic France's rules for registration of the domain name. *See, e.g.,* Richard Raysman & Peter Brown, *Developments in Trademarks and Domain Name Disputes*, 221 New York Law Journal 3 (col 1) (March 9, 1999). Which decision do you agree with? Why? What domain name can Alice SN use now for its web page?

3. *U.S. Registration System.* The U.S. equivalent to Nominet UK was Network Solutions Inc. (NSI). NSI was the sole U.S. organization authorized to register domain names under a contract with the U.S. government. NSI registered domain names on a first-come first-served basis. It made no effort to determine whether a particular domain name infringed another's rights and conducted no examination of registration applications. After severe criticism of its operating procedures, NSI initiated a policy of putting a disputed domain name on hold while the interested parties resolved the dispute but took no further actions, contending it had no responsibility to do so. The Internet has grown exponentially. In 1995, there were about 100,000 domain names. By early 1999, there were 4.8 million names. The increase in the number of domain names has necessarily led to increased disputes over the rights to such names, particularly when the domain name owner is not the trademark owner. As a result of these problems, numerous international organizations have attempted to resolve the problem of domain name trademark disputes. Among those organizations which are studying the problem are the U.S. Department of Commerce, the World Intellectual Property Organization, the International Trademark Association and the Internet Corporation for Assigned Names and Numbers ("ICANN").

4. *Generic and Toplevel Domains.* A domain name is composed of a second-level domain and a top-level domain. The second-and top-level domains are separated by a period. Thus, in the domain name Westlaw.com, "Westlaw" is the second-level domain and "com" is the top-level domain. There are currently seven generic top-level domains (gTLDs): ".com," ".org," ".net," ".edu," ".gov," ".mil," and "int." Three of these generic top-level domains are open, meaning anyone can apply for domain names using the .com, .org, and .net domains. There are also 249 country-code top-level domains which appear at the end of the domain name, as in "Amazon.com.uk." One suggestion for resolving trademark disputes recommended the establishment of five new top-level generic domains—.firm; .shop; .web; .arts; .rec; .info; .nom.

5. *Proposed Resolutions–U.S.* On January 30, 1998 the U.S. Department of Commerce issued "A Proposal to Improve the Technical Management of Internet Names and Addresses" (the Green Paper) that proposed that NSI lose its monopoly status as a registry for the .com, .net, .org and .edu gLTDs and that five new domain name registrars and a non-profit

U.S. corporation take over management of the domain name system. The Green Paper failed to treat the problem of trademark conflicts.

In June 1998, the U.S. Department of Commerce issued a "Statement of Policy on the Management of Internet Names and Addresses" (known as the "White Paper") which called for the creation of a private-sector, non-profit organization to manage the domain name system. In addition to privitizing the domain name system, the White Paper sought to expand domain name registration procedures by establishing additional registrants. It also called upon the WIPO to develop recommendations for a uniform approach to resolving domain name disputes. On October 2, 1998, the Internet Assigned Numbers Authority and NSI proposed establishing a new corporation named the Internet Corporation for Assigned Names and Numbers (ICANN) which would conduct the policy and supervising functions proposed in the White Paper. ICANN would have three supporting organizations: Address Supporting Organization, Domain Name Supporting Organization (DNSO) (name registries and TLD recommendations) and a Protocol Supporting Organization. In November 1998, the United States officially recognized ICANN in a memorandum of Understanding and began to phase out NSI's monopoly.

6. *Proposed Resolutions–WIPO.* In its interim report, WIPO recommended that applicants provide reliable contact information and a representation of non-infringement. It further proposed that disputes be resolved through Alternative Dispute Resolution (ADR) conducted on-line and limited to the sole issue of the status of the domain registration. This ADR would not be bending in any court or other proceeding, and would not prohibit future litigation. In deciding disputes, WIPO recommended permitting the owners of famous and well-known marks to obtain an exclusion which would give rise to an evidentiary presumption in favor of the exclusion holder.

THE PLANNED PARENTHOOD CASE
PLANNED PARENTHOOD FEDERATION OF AMERICA INC. v. BUCCI

United States District Court, S.D. New York, 1997.
42 U.S.P.Q.2d 1430.

WOOD, J.

Plaintiff Planned Parenthood Federation of America, Inc. ("Planned Parenthood") has moved to preliminarily enjoin defendant Richard Bucci ("Bucci"), doing business as Catholic Radio, from using the domain name "plannedparenthood.com," and from identifying his web site on the Internet under the name "www.plannedparenthood.com."

The parties do not dispute the following facts. Plaintiff Planned Parenthood, founded in 1922, is a nonprofit, reproductive health care organization that has used its present name since 1942. Plaintiff registered the stylized service mark "Planned Parenthood" on the Principal Register of the United States Patent and Trademark Office on June 28, 1955, and registered the block service mark "Planned Parenthood" on the Principal Register of the United States Patent and Trademark Office on September 9, 1975. Plaintiff's 146 separately incorporated affiliates, in 48 states and the District of Columbia, are licensed to use the mark "Planned Parenthood." Plaintiff expends a considerable sum of money in promoting and advertising its services. The mark "Planned Parenthood" is strong and incontestable.

Plaintiff operates a web site at "www.ppfa.org," using the domain name "ppfa.org." Plaintiff's home page offers Internet users resources regarding sexual and reproductive health, contraception and family planning, pregnancy, sexually transmitted diseases, and abortion, as well as providing links to other relevant web sites. In addition, plaintiff's home page offers Internet users suggestions on how to get involved with plaintiff's mission and solicits contributions.[2]

Defendant Bucci is the host of "Catholic Radio," a daily radio program broadcast on the WVOA radio station in Syracuse, New York. Bucci is an active participant in the anti-abortion movement. Bucci operates web sites at "www.catholicradio.com" and at "lambsofchrist.com." On August 28, 1996, Bucci registered the domain name "plannedparenthood.com" with Network Solutions, Inc. ("NSI"), a corporation that administers the assignment of domain names on the Internet. After registering the domain name, Bucci set up a web site and home page on the Internet at the address "www. plannedparenthood.com."

Internet users who type in the address "www.plannedparenthood.com," or who use a search engine such as Yahoo or Lycos to find web sites containing the term "planned parenthood," can reach Bucci's web site and home page. Once a user accesses Bucci's home page, she sees on the computer screen the words "Welcome to the PLANNED PARENTHOOD HOME PAGE!" These words appear on the screen first, because the text of a home page downloads from top to bottom. Once the whole home page has loaded, the user sees a scanned image of the cover of a book entitled The Cost of Abortion, by Lawrence Roberge ("Roberge"), under which appear several links: "Foreword," "Afterword," "About the Author," "Book Review," and "Biography."

After clicking on a link, the user accesses text related to that link. By clicking on "Foreword" or "Afterword," the Internet user simply accesses the foreword or afterword of the book The Cost of Abortion. That text eventually reveals that The Cost of Abortion is an antiabortion book. The text entitled "About the Author" contains the curriculum vitae of author Roberge. It also notes that "Mr. Roberge is available for interview and speaking engagements," and provides his telephone number. The "Book Review" link brings the Internet user to a selection of quotations by various people endorsing The Cost of Abortion. Those quotations include exhortations to read the book and obtain the book. "Biography" offers more information about Roberge's background.

The parties dispute defendant's motive in choosing plaintiff's mark as his domain name. Plaintiff alleges that defendant used plaintiff's

---

2. Plaintiff's Houston affiliate owns the domain name "plannedparenthood.org," and is in the process of transferring that domain name to plaintiff.

mark with the "specific intent to damage Planned Parenthood's reputation and to confuse unwitting users of the Internet." Discussing the difference between the domain name at issue here and defendant's other web sites, defendant's counsel states that "[t]he WWW.PLANNEDPARENTHOOD.COM [sic] website ... enables Defendant's message to reach a broader audience."

Defendant stated that his motive in using plaintiff's mark as his domain name was "to reach, primarily, Catholics that are disobedient to the natural law." In an affidavit submitted to the Court, defendant stated that he wanted his "antiabortion message to reach as many people as possible, and particularly the people who do not think that abortion has an inimical effect on society." Defendant conceded that he was aware that by using plaintiff's mark to identify his web site, he was likely to draw in Internet users who are "proabortion." Defendant demonstrated full knowledge of plaintiff's name and activities, and admitted to an understanding that using plaintiff's mark as his domain name would attract "proabortion" Internet users to his web site because of their misapprehension as to the site's origin. I therefore now make the factual finding that defendant's motive in choosing plaintiff's mark as his domain name was, at least in part, to attract to his home page Internet users who sought plaintiff's home page.

Defendant argues that his use of plaintiff's mark cannot be reached under the Lanham Act because it is noncommercial speech. Planned Parenthood has brought suit under Sections 1114, 1125(a), and 1125(c) of the Lanham Act, Title 15, United States Code. Section 1114 of the Lanham Act forbids a party to "use in commerce any reproduction, counterfeit, copy, or colorable imitation of a registered mark in connection with the sale, offering for sale, distribution, or advertising of any goods or services on or in connection with which such use is likely to cause confusion, or to cause mistake, or to deceive." (Emphasis added). An injunction under Section 1125(c) is proper to stop "commercial use in commerce of a mark or trade name" if that use causes dilution of a famous mark. (Emphasis added). Finally, with respect to Section 1125(a), defendant may be liable if he has used the plaintiff's mark "in commerce" in a way that either "is likely to cause confusion, or to cause mistake, or to deceive as to the affiliation, connection, or association of such person with another person, or as to the origin, sponsorship, or approval of his or her goods, services, or commercial activities by another person," Section 1125(a)(1)(A), or "in commercial advertising or promotion, misrepresents the nature, characteristics, qualities, or geographic origin of his or her or another person's goods, services, or commercial activities," Section 1125(a)(1)(B). (Emphasis added). Section 1125(c)(4)(B) specifically exempts from the scope of all provisions of Section 1125 the "noncommercial use of a mark." (Emphasis added).

Defendant argues that his use of the "planned parenthood" mark is not likely to confuse because it is similar to a parody. A parody "depends on a lack of confusion to make its point," and " 'must convey two simultaneous and contradictory messages: that it is the original, but also that it is not the original and is instead a parody.' " *Hormel Foods Corp. v. Jim Henson Productions, Inc.*, 73 F.3d 497, 503 [37 U.S.PQ2d 1516] (2d Cir.1996). Here, an Internet user may either find the defendant's web site through a search engine or may simply enter the words "planned parenthood" in the expectation that she will find the plaintiff's web site. Seeing or typing the "planned parenthood" mark and accessing the web site are two separate and nonsimultaneous activities. Furthermore, the greeting "Welcome to the Planned Parenthood Home Page!" does not immediately contradict an Internet user's assumption that she has accessed the plaintiff's home page. Only when an Internet user actually "clicks" on one of the topics and accesses commentary on The Cost of Abortion does she encounter defendant's message.

I am not persuaded by defendant's argument that the message of the home page provides an ironic and contrasting allusion to plaintiff, nor do I find convincing his argument that the banner heading of the home page is sarcastic. Similarly, I do not conclude that defendant's use of the term "planned parenthood" in the context described above is intended not to confuse the user into an association with plaintiff, but rather "to reference Plaintiff as the 'enemy.' " Because defendant's use of "planned parenthood" does not convey the simultaneous message that the home page and web site are those of plaintiff and those of defendant, defendant's argument that his use of the mark is a parody fails. Thus, I have found that the Polaroid factors demonstrate that there is a likelihood of confusion that arises from defendant's use of the domain name "plannedparenthood.com," the home page address "www.plannedparenthood.com," and the banner at the top of the home page stating, "Welcome to the Planned Parenthood Home Page!"

Defendant also argues that his use of the "planned parenthood" mark is protected by the First Amendment. As defendant argues, trademark infringement law does not curtail or prohibit the exercise of the First Amendment right to free speech. I note that plaintiff has not sought, in any way, to restrain defendant from speech that criticizes Planned Parenthood or its mission, or that discusses defendant's beliefs regarding reproduction, family, and religion. The sole purpose of the Court's inquiry has been to determine whether the use of the "planned parenthood" mark as defendant's domain name and home page address constitutes an infringement of plaintiff's trademark. Defendant's use of another entity's mark is entitled to First Amendment protection when his use of that mark is part of a communicative message, not when it is used to identify the source of a product. *Yankee Publishing, Inc. v. News America Publishing, Inc.*, 809 F. Supp. 267, 275 [25 U.S.PQ2d 1752] (S.D.N.Y.1992). By using the mark as a domain name and home page address and by welcoming Internet users to the home page with the message "Welcome to the Planned Parenthood Home Page!" defendant identifies the web site and home page as being the product, or forum, of plaintiff. I therefore determine that, because defendant's use of the term "planned parenthood" is not part of a communicative message, his infringement on plaintiff's mark is not protected by the First Amendment.

Defendant argues that his use of the "Planned Parenthood" name for his web site is entitled to First Amendment protection. . . .

Defendant offers no argument in his papers as to why the Court should determine that defendant's use of "plannedparenthood.com" is a communicative message rather than a source identifier. His use of "plannedparenthood.com" as a domain name to identify his web site is on its face more analogous to source identification than to a communicative message; in essence, the name identifies the web site, which contains defendant's home page. The statement that greets Internet users who access defendant's web site, "Welcome to the Planned Parenthood Home Page," is also more analogous to an identifier than to a communication. For those reasons, defendant's use of the trademarked term "planned parenthood" is not part of a communicative message, but rather, serves to identify a product or item, defendant's web site and home page, as originating from Planned Parenthood.

Defendant's use of plaintiff's mark is not protected as a title under *Rogers v. Grimaldi*, 875 F.2d 994, 998 [10 U.S.PQ2d 1825] (2d Cir.1989). There, the Court of Appeals determined that the title of the film "Ginger and Fred" was not a misleading infringement, despite the fact that the film was not about Ginger Rogers and Fred Astaire, because of the artistic implications of a title. The Court of Appeals noted that "[f]ilmmakers and authors frequently rely on word-play, ambiguity, irony, and allusion in titling their works." *Id*. The Court of Appeals found that the use of a title such as the one at issue in Rogers was acceptable "unless the title has no artistic relevance to the underlying work"; even when the title has artistic relevance, it may not be used to "explicitly mislead[ ] [the consumer] as to the source or content of the work." *Id*. Here, even treating defendant's domain name and home page address as titles, rather than as source identifiers, I find that the title "plannedparenthood.com" has no artistic implications, and that the title is being used to attract some consumers by misleading them as to the web site's source or content. Given defendant's testimony indicating that he knew, and intended, that his use of the domain name "planned parenthood.com" would cause some "proabortion" Internet users to access his web site, he cannot demonstrate that his use of "planned parenthood" is entitled to First Amendment protection.

Defendant argues that a disclaimer, rather than an injunction, is the appropriate remedy here. I disagree. Due to the nature of Internet use, defendant's appropriation of plaintiff's mark as a domain name and home page address cannot adequately be remedied by a disclaimer. Defendant's domain name and home page address are external labels that, on their face, cause confusion among Internet users and may cause Internet users who seek plaintiff's web site to expend time and energy accessing defendant's web site. Therefore, I determine that a disclaimer on defendant's home page would not be sufficient to dispel the confusion induced by his home page address and domain name.

Notes and Questions

1. Would the web page in question have been infringing if it were "plannedparenthoodnot.com"? If it was "plannedparenthoodsucks.com"? What if the web page criticized Planned Parenthood's activities as part of its web page? Would this fact require a different result?

2. Your client Gore, Inc. is a start-up company that intends to specialize in adult-oriented virtual reality video games with a strong violence, gore and sex content. Gore, Inc. wants to set up a web page advertising its games but is concerned about criticism of its adult oriented video game by various anti-violence, anti-pornography organizations. What domain names should it consider registering internationally to protect its interests?

D.   WHOSE LAWS DETERMINE INTERNET CONTROL?

THE PASSIVE SITE CASE

THE HEARST CORPORATION v. ARI GOLDBERGER

United States District Court, S.D. New York, 1997.
1997 WL 97097.

PECK, UNITED STATES MAGISTRATE JUDGE:

The issue before the Court is whether the Court has personal jurisdiction over defendant because his Internet web site is accessible to, and has been electronically "visited" by, computer users in New York. Defendant has not contracted to sell or sold any products or services to anyone in New York (or elsewhere for that matter—his "business" is not yet operational).

Hearst Corporation, owner and publisher of ESQUIRE Magazine, brought this trademark infringement action against defendant Ari Goldberger, who has established an Internet domain name and web site, "ESQWIRE.COM." Goldberger's web site exists to offer law office infrastructure network services for attorneys, but such services are not yet available, and also to provide legal information services, so far limited to information about this lawsuit. Goldberger lives in Cherry Hill, New Jersey and works in Philadelphia.

The Internet is "a decentralized, global medium of communications—or 'cyber space'—that links people, institutions, corporations and governments around the world.... These communications can occur almost instantaneously, and can be directed either to specific individuals, to a broader group of people interested in a particular subject, or to the world as a whole."

"Individuals have a wide variety of avenues to access cyberspace in general, and the Internet in particular. In terms of physical access, there are two common methods to establish an actual link to the Internet.

First, one can use a computer or computer terminal that is directly (and usually permanently) connected to a computer network that is itself directly or indirectly connected to the Internet. Second, one can use a 'personal computer' with a 'modem' to connect over a telephone line to a larger computer or computer network that is itself directly or indirectly connected to the Internet. . . . Individuals can also access the Internet through commercial and noncommercial 'Internet service providers' that typically offer modem telephone access to a computer or computer network linked to the Internet." *ACLU v. Reno*, 929 F.Supp. at 832–33.

"One method of communication on the Internet is via electronic mail, or 'e-mail,' comparable in principle to sending a first-class letter." Another method of communicating over the Internet, "and fast becoming the most well-known on the Internet, is the 'World Wide Web.' . . . Though information on the Web is contained in individual computers, the fact that each of the computers is connected to the Internet. allows all of the information to become a part of a single body of knowledge."

Each host computer providing Internet services ("site") has a unique Internet address. Users seeking to exchange digital information (electronic mail ("email"), computer programs, images, music) with a particular Internet host require the host's address in order to establish a connection. Hosts actually possess two fungible addresses: a numeric "IP" address such as 123.456.123.12, and an alphanumeric "domain name" such as microsoft.com, with greater mnemonic potential. . . . Internet domain names are similar to telephone number mnemonics, but they are of greater importance, since there is no satisfactory Internet equivalent to a telephone company white pages or directory assistance, and domain names can often be guessed.

"When information is made available, it is said to be 'published' on the Web. Publishing on the Web simply requires that the publisher, has a computer connected to the Internet. . . ." *ACLU v. Reno*, 929 F.Supp. at 837. "Once a provider posts content on the Internet, it is available to all other Internet users worldwide. . . . Once a provider posts its content on the Internet, it cannot prevent that content from entering any community. . . . Internet technology gives a speaker a potential worldwide audience." *Id*. at 844.

Plaintiff The Hearst Corporation and its predecessors-in-interest (collectively "Hearst") have published the well-known monthly, ESQUIRE Magazine, since 1933. Hearst owns the trademark registration for the mark ESQUIRE for such goods. Hearst also has used the marks ESQUIRE or ESQ. or marks incorporating those terms on a variety of products and services.

"Hearst has been involved in computer related activities under the ESQUIRE mark. Since approximately June, 1995, selections from Hearst's ESQUIRE magazine have been available on-line. Hearst's collateral products have also been promoted and sold via the computer in 1995." "Hearst is the owner of the domain names viaesquire.com, esquiremag.com and esquireb2b.com which are registered with" Internic.

Defendant Goldberger resides in Cherry Hill, New Jersey and works as an associate at the Pepper, Hamilton & Scheetz law firm in Philadelphia.

In 1992, Goldberger came up with the idea to "create an electronic law office infrastructure network that would provide individual attorneys, via computer, with legal support services equivalent to those available to lawyers practicing in large law firms." The scope of Goldberger's idea subsequently expanded to possibly include information services such as the provision of reporting and commentary on legal issues, but so far this has been limited to his own case.

Goldberger decided to call his service "ESQ.WIRE1" and, on September 16, 1994, applied to register that service mark with the Patent and Trademark Office. Hearst opposed Goldberger's application. The Trademark Office suspended its proceedings pending disposition of this lawsuit.

In September 1995, Goldberger registered the Internet domain name ESQWIRE.COM with Internic. In June 1996, Goldberger published a worldwide web site on the Internet at the address http://www.esqwire.com. Goldberger has published his web site through an Internet provider, Voice Net of Ivyland, Pennsylvania. Goldberger's web site consists of a "home page" that briefly describes the services Goldberger plans to offer, and also contains a summary of Hearst's activities against Goldberger in this lawsuit, along with computer "links" to court filings and other documents related to this action.

Although Goldberger has established his ESQWIRE web site, it is undisputed that he does not yet have any services or products to sell, and that he has not sold any products or services in New York, or anywhere else for that matter.

It is further undisputed that New Yorkers have accessed Goldberger's ESQWIRE. com web site. Goldberger's web site also has been accessed by people from at least 20 other states and 34 foreign countries.

The issue of personal jurisdiction and the Internet has split the federal district courts that have addressed the issue to date. Unless and until Congress or the New York legislature enacts Internet specific jurisdictional legislation, however, the Court must employ New York's existing jurisdictional statutes.

New York "long-arm" jurisdiction is codified in CPLR § 302(a). CPLR § 302(a) provides:

(a) Acts which are the basis of jurisdiction. As to a cause of action arising from any of the acts enumerated in this section, a court may exercise personal jurisdiction over any nondomiciliary . . . who in person or through an agent:

1. transacts any business within the state or contracts anywhere to supply goods or services in the state; or

2. commits a tortious act within the state. or 3. commits a tortious act without the state causing injury to person or property within the state . . . if he

> (i) regularly does or solicits business, or engages in any other persistent course of conduct, or derives substantial revenue from goods used or consumed or services rendered, in the state, or

> (ii) expects or should reasonably expect the act to have consequences in the state and derives substantial revenue from interstate or international commerce. . . .

CPLR § 302 does not extend New York's long-arm jurisdiction to the full extent of constitutional limits. " '[I]n order for personal jurisdiction over [Goldberger] to lie in New York [under CPLR § 302(a)(1), Goldberger] must have transacted business in this state and the cause of action must arise out of such transaction.' " *Rolls–Royce Motors, Inc. v. Charles Schmitt & Co.*, 657 F.Supp. 1040, 1050 (S.D.N.Y.1987) (Leisure, J.). As Judge Leisure further explained in *Rolls-Royce*:

> The test [under CPLR § 302(a)(1)] is hardly a precise one; the court must look at the aggregation of defendant's activities, coupled with the selective weighing of the various actions. . . . Moreover, it is the "nature and quality, and not the amount of New York contacts [which] must be considered by the court." . . . Primary factors to consider include the physical presence of defendant in New York, the risk of loss as it effects the New York transaction, and the extent to which the contract is performed in New York.

The present case does not involve a contract, but rather a tort (trademark infringement) in the course of a commercial activity, i.e., Goldberger's Internet web site. It is undisputed that Goldberger created and "published" his ESQWIRE web site from the Cherry Hill, NJPhiladelphia area, not New York. It is also undisputed that people located in New York have accessed ("visited") Goldberger's web site. Further, it is undisputed that Goldberger has not sold any product or services. His Internet web site is, at most, an announcement of the future availability of his services for attorneys.

Goldberger's ESQWIRE Internet web site thus is most analogous to an advertisement in a national magazine. Like such an ad, Goldberger's Internet web site may be viewed by people in all fifty states (and all over the world too for that matter), but it is not targeted at the residents of New York or any other particular state.

New York law is clear, however, that advertisements in national publications are not sufficient to provide personal jurisdiction under Section 302(a)(1). Even advertisements targeted at the New York market have been found to be insufficient for CPLR 302(a)(1) transaction of business jurisdiction.

The courts that already have addressed Internet personal jurisdiction have reached conflicting results.

A. Cases Finding No Jurisdiction

In this District, in *Bensusan Restaurant Corp. v. King*, 937 F.Supp. 295 (S.D.N.Y.1996), Judge Stein reached the same conclusion as I do here—that an Internet web page is not sufficient to establish long-arm jurisdiction in New York. Bensusan was a trademark infringement suit by the owner of the famous New York jazz club (and of the federally registered trademark) "The Blue Note" against King, owner of a small Missouri jazz club with the same name, over King's Internet web site. 937 F.Supp. at 297. Judge Stein found personal jurisdiction over King lacking under both CPLR § 302 and constitutional due process. As to CPLR § 302(a)(2), Judge Stein held that "the mere fact that a person can gain information on the allegedly infringing product is not the equivalent of a person advertising, promoting, selling or otherwise making an effort to target its product in New York." 937 F.Supp. at 299. As to CPLR § 302(a)(3), King did not derive substantial revenue from interstate commerce, nor was the "foreseeability" requirement met based on King's knowledge that plaintiff's club was in New York. 937 F.Supp. at 300. "That prong of [CPLR § 302(a)(3)(ii)] requires that a defendant make a discernable effort ... to serve, directly or indirectly, a market in the forum state." 937 F.Supp. at 300. Plaintiff in Bensusan, as does Hearst here, argued that the accessibility of the defendant's web site in New York should be sufficient to establish jurisdiction. As does this Court, Judge Stein disagreed, holding that "mere foreseeability of an instate consequence and a failure to avert that consequence [by restricting New Yorkers' access to the web site] is not sufficient to establish personal jurisdiction." 937 F.Supp. at 300. Finally, Judge Stein held that even if jurisdiction were proper under New York's long-arm statute, asserting jurisdiction would violate constitutional due process. Judge Stein explained:

> King has done nothing to purposefully avail himself of the benefits of New York. King, like numerous others, simply created a Web site and permitted anyone who could find it to access it. Creating a site, like placing a product into the stream of commerce, may be felt nationwide—or even worldwide—but, without more, it is not an act purposefully directed towards the forum state. There are no allegations that King actively sought to encourage New Yorkers to access his site, or that he conducted any business—let alone a continuous and systematic part of its business—in New York. There is in fact no suggestion that King has any presence of any kind in New York other than the Web site that can be accessed worldwide.
> *Id.* at 301 (citations omitted).

Similarly, Goldberger has "simply created a Web site and permitted anyone who could find it to access it." *Id.* This Court, like Judge Stein in *Bensusan*, does not find the mere creation of a web site, without more, to constitute sufficient contacts to provide this Court with personal jurisdiction over Goldberger.

The Court declines to follow the decisions in *Maritz, Inc. v. Cybergold, Inc.*, 947 F.Supp. 1328 (E.D.Mo.1996), *Inset Systems, Inc. v. Instruction Set, Inc.*, 937 F.Supp. 161 (D.Conn.1996), and *Heroes, Inc. v. Heroes Foundation*, No. 961260, slip op., available on BNA's Electronic Info. Policy & Law Report (D.D.C. Dec. 12, 1996).

In *Maritz*, defendant's only contact with Missouri was a web site, "published" on a computer in California, that "provide[d] information about CyberGold's new upcoming [Internet] service." Defendant's web site was accessible to any Internet user, including those in Missouri, and in fact had been accessed by people in Missouri.

In *Inset*, defendant's only contacts with Connecticut were an Internet web site and an 800 telephone number, both of which advertised defendant's services. The web site and 800 number were accessible to anyone with Internet access or a telephone, respectively, including Connecticut residents.

In *Heroes*, the defendant charity had placed an ad seeking donations in the Washington Post and also had an Internet web page that was nationally accessible. The Court found transacting business and causing tortious injury (trademark infringement) in the forum jurisdiction based on the combination of the local newspaper ad and the Internet site. While the Court held that because of the newspaper ad it need not decide if the Internet web site alone would support jurisdiction, the opinion left little doubt that it would.

The courts in these three cases *Maritz*, *Inset* and *Heroes*chose to exercise personal jurisdiction for similar reasons, which can be summarized as follows: through their web sites, defendants consciously decided to transmit advertising information to all Internet users, including those in the forum state, thereby (allegedly) committing trademark infringement in the forum state and purposefully availing themselves of the privilege of doing business within the forum state.

The Court recognizes that there is some truth in the *Maritz* court's statement that "while modern technology has made nationwide commercial transactions simpler and more feasible, . . . it must broaden correspondingly the permissible scope of jurisdiction exercisable by the courts." *Maritz, Inc. v. Cybergold*, 947 F.Supp. at 1334. This Court, however, agrees with the sentiments expressed by Judge Scheindlin in a slightly different context, that to allow personal jurisdiction based on an Internet web site "would be tantamount to a declaration that this Court, and every other court throughout the world, may assert [personal] jurisdiction over all information providers on the global World Wide Web. Such a holding would have a devastating impact on those who use this global service." *Playboy Enterprises, Inc. v. Chuckleberry Pub., Inc.*, 939 F.Supp. 1032, 1039–40 (S.D.N.Y.1996). Upholding personal jurisdiction over Goldberger in the present case would, in effect, create national (or even worldwide) jurisdiction, so that every plaintiff could sue in plaintiff's home court every out-of-state defendant who established an Internet web site. The Court declines to reach such a far-reaching result in the absence of a Congressional enactment of Internet specific trademark infringement personal jurisdictional legislation.

For the reasons set forth above, I recommend that the Court hold that Goldberger's out-of-state creation of an Internet web site that is accessible in New York, standing alone, does not provide personal jurisdiction over defendant in New York. Pursuant to the parties' agreement, the case thus should be transferred to the United States District Court for the District of New Jersey, Camden Division.

THE INTERNET WORLD CASE

MECKLERMEDIA CORPORATION
v. DC CONGRESS GmbH

Chancery Division, 1997.
[1998] Ch 40, [1998] 1 All ER 148, [1997] 3 WLR 479, [1997] FSR 627.

JACOB, J.

[Plaintiffs, Mecklermedia Corporation, a company incorporated in Delaware, U.S.A, and Mecklermedia Ltd, its English subsidiary, alleged that the defendant, DC Congress GmbH, a German company, was committing the English tort of passing off in respect of the use of the words "Internet World," in which the plaintiffs claimed to have established an extensive goodwill in England. The writ was served in Germany. By a summons dated 22 January 1997 the defendant applied to have the writ and service of it in Germany struck out on the ground that the High Court of England and Wales did not have jurisdiction under the Civil Jurisdiction and Judgments Act 1982 to hear and determine the claim. Alternatively the defendant claimed that the action should be stayed on the ground that the Landgericht Munchen I was seised of a related action in which the defendant was plaintiff and Messe Berlin GmbH was defendant and that the Landgericht was the court first seised within the meaning of the Act. The defendant's summons further alleged, alternatively, that the plaintiffs' statement of claim should be struck out on the grounds that (i) it disclosed no reasonable cause of action, (ii) was scandalous, frivolous or vexatious, (iii) that it might prejudice, embarrass or delay the fair trial of the action and/or (iv) that it was an abuse of the process of the court.]

The plaintiffs allege that DC is committing the English tort of passing off. The relief sought is in relation to the activities of DC in and from Germany said to lead to that tort being committed. It is said that the plaintiffs have a goodwill in England and Wales, that DC is making a misrepresentation within the jurisdiction and that that misrepresentation has caused and will cause the plaintiffs damage within the jurisdiction—the trinity of elements constituting passing off.

The first plaintiff, Mecklermedia Corporation, is incorporated in Delaware. The second plaintiff, Mecklermedia Ltd, is its English subsidiary. The second plaintiff has, since 1994, been involved in the organisation of three trade shows in the United Kingdom. These were called "Internet World and Document Delivery World" (1994) and "Internet World International" (1995–96). It is said that these trade shows were widely advertised and attended. The trade shows were organised in conjunction with a licensee company. It is said that it was specifically agreed that all goodwill in the name "Internet World" should vest in the first plaintiff, which I will henceforth call "Mecklermedia."

Mecklermedia has, since 1993, published in the United States a magazine called "Internet World." This is claimed to have some circulation within the UK, but this must be essentially of the "spillover" variety. In the autumn of 1996 an English version of the magazine was launched under the same name. It is published by VNU Business Publications but claims association, correctly, with the U.S. magazine by saying: "Internet World is already the most popular Internet magazine in the U.S.. Now Internet World is to be published in the UK by the people who bring you Personal Computer World."

The first edition was given away free with "Personal Computer World" and there was no dispute but that that magazine has a substantial UK circulation. It is claimed that VNU publishes the English edition under licence from Mecklermedia and that it is specifically agreed by VNU that the goodwill in the name "Internet World" should belong to Mecklermedia.

Finally it is claimed that Mecklermedia owns two web sites having the addresses "http://www.internet-world.com" and "http://www.iworld.com." It is said that anyone "visiting" these sites would see prominent use of the name "Internet World" and promotion of the plaintiff's trade shows and magazines. [The court found "serious questions" existed regarding each of the three elements. It then considered whether service could properly be extended to the defendants.]

The Convention

Article 2 of the [Brussels] Convention sets out the basic rule: "Subject to the provisions of this Convention, persons domiciled in a contracting state shall, whatever their nationality, be sued in the courts of that state." In footballing terms the plaintiff must "play away." Section 2 of the Convention provides for "Special Jurisdiction," under which a plaintiff is given a choice of other forums in the circumstances defined. The relevant provision here is article 5(3):

"A person domiciled in a contracting state may, in another contracting state, be sued ... 3. In matters relating to tort, delict or quasi-delict, in the courts for the place where the harmful event occurred."

It is settled, and self-evident from the Convention, that where article 5(3) applies the plaintiff is given an option to sue either in the forum of the defendant's domicile or forum (or forums) of the place (or places) where the harmful event occurred. For the present I will assume that article 2 would permit an action in Germany in respect of the passing off in England (though as to this see below). That does not prevent an action in England if the "harmful event" occurs here.

It is well settled that a plaintiff cannot rely upon mere indirect or consequential loss as a "harmful event:" *see Dumez France v. Hessische Landesbank (Helaba)* (Case C–220/88) [1990] ECR I–49. In that case the French parent company tried to sue in France in respect of losses suffered by its German subsidiaries in Germany. Not surprisingly France was held not to be the place where the harmful event occurred. The court had already held in *Handelskwekerij GJ Bier BV v. Mines de Potasse d'Alsace SA* (Case 21/76) [1978] QB 708 that the "place where the damage occurred" may be interpreted as referring to the place where the indirect victims of the damage ascertain the repercussions on their own assets. That case was concerned with discharge of a saline waste into the Rhine in France which affected crops in the Netherlands. There the court held that the plaintiffs could sue in the Netherlands because that was the place where the damage occurred, even though the wrongful act of discharge was in France.

DC asserts that in this case Germany is the place of the harmful event. I do not accept that submission. So far as the English tort of passing off is concerned, the harm is to the goodwill in England, and is the effect on the reputation in England. That is a direct effect on the plaintiffs' claimed English property.

All the components of liability of the tort take place in England. A trial would require proof of goodwill, misrepresentation and damage in England. It would not matter whether or not what DC was doing in Germany was, so far as German law and facts were concerned, lawful or not.

I find further support for the proposition that in relation to the English law claim it is in England that the harmful event is occurring from the decision of Knox J in *Modus Vivendi Ltd v. British Products Sanmex Co Ltd* [1996] FSR 790. Knox J had to consider the Convention in the context of a choice between England and Scotland as the appropriate forum. The defendants were in Scotland, where they filled butane containers. These were transported through England to Hong Kong and China. The artwork was deceptive in the ultimate markets. An argument that the harmful event occurred in England failed. Knox J said that the place where the damage occurred was the place where the deception occurred, namely Hong Kong and China. Knox J said, at p 802:

"If one supposes that the passing off in the present case was effected in a Convention country, say, for example, France ... there would in my view be seen to be close connecting factors with France where, to put it neutrally, the illicit incursion into the plaintiff's goodwill ... occurred."

In this case the deception alleged is in England. On that reasoning there are close connecting factors with England.

DC puts its case in an alternative way. Assume, it says, that the German court is prepared to consider the English passing off claim.

Then there would be a risk of inconsistent judgments, the very thing that the *Dumez France* case says it is an object of the Convention to avoid.

[I]t is clear that each of the derogations from article 2 gives the plaintiff the possibility of an alternative forum from that of the defendant's domicile. If the argument were right, then there would never be alternatives. Putting the point another way, implicit in the argument is that there is only one possible forum. Once that is made explicit one can see it is fallacious. The fallacy is even more apparent when one considers the important case of *Shevill v. Presse Alliance SA* (Case C–68/93) [1995] 2 AC 18. The plaintiffs, an individual and some companies, sued in England in respect of an alleged libel in daily newspaper "France Soir." "France Soir" had a limited circulation here and in several other European countries, but its main distribution was in France. The court accepted that there was a possible multiplicity of jurisdictions. The "place where the harmful event occurred" was any place where damage was directly caused, namely the place where the publisher was established, ie France, and the place where the publication was distributed, i.e. England, and possibly other countries too. If the action was brought in a state where the publisher was established, the courts of that state had jurisdiction to award damages in respect of all the harm caused by the publication. If the action was brought "locally" the courts of the state concerned had jurisdiction to award damages for the publication in that state. The case is of great importance if it also governs parallel infringements of intellectual property rights and governs the grant of injunctions as well as damages. It would mean that a plaintiff could not forum-shop around Europe for a Europe-wide injunction. He could only seek such an injunction in the state of the source of the allegedly infringing goods or piratical activity. I say no more here. For present purposes *Shevill's* case is as clear a case as one could find that article 5(3) does not exclude the possibility of action in several states.

I think the plaintiffs are within article 5(3).

It is submitted that it would be better if all questions were decided by a single court and that multiple litigation should be avoided. That, as a generality, is of course always true, but on the other hand when an enterprise wants to use a mark or word throughout the world—and that may include an Internet address or domain name—it must take into account that in some places, if not others, there may be confusion. Here it is clear that DC knew that Mecklermedia used the name "Internet World" and I do not think it is surprising that it is met with actions in places where confusion is considered likely. So I decline to set aside service.

DISPOSITION

Application dismissed.

Notes and Questions

1. Compare the test for jurisdiction under U.S. law (as represented by the *Passive Site* Case) and under the Brussels Convention (which establishes

jurisdictional rules for commercial and civil procedures between member countries of the European Union) according to the *Internet World* case. What principles do they share in common in deciding whether external acts can subject a party to jurisdiction in a particular country or location?

2. What role did the existence of an Internet site play in the *Passive Site* and *Internet World* cases? What role, if any, should the ability to receive an Internet web site uploaded from another country play in deciding jurisdictional?

3. In the *Internet World* case, the court appears to accept that different countries decide infringement issues differently, even where the same mark or domain name is involved. What are the problems that may be caused by these differences? Would you support a multinational treaty establishing a single site for Internet disputes? Should such site be where the site is uploaded? Where it is downloaded? Where the harm (infringement) occurs?

THE FIRST STRIKE CASE
DEF LEPP MUSIC v. STUART–BROWN

Chancery Division, 1986.
[1986] RPC 273.

Sir Nicholas Browne-Wilkinson V–C:

This is an application by two defendants to set aside service on them outside the jurisdiction of the writ in this action.

The eight plaintiffs are members of a pop group known as DEF LEPPARD and their associates. They claim to be the owners of the United Kingdom copyright in a tape recording "First Strike". In the action they claim that that recording has been pirated by the defendants who have copied the tape and sold the copies on the market. Some of the defendants are resident in the United Kingdom, others are resident outside the United Kingdom. The sixth defendant, Music Services SARL, is a company incorporated and resident in Luxembourg. It is common ground that the sixth defendant manufactured copies of the tape in Luxembourg and then sold such copies to the eighth defendant. The eighth defendant is a company incorporated and resident in Holland. The copies of the tape acquired from the sixth defendant were sold by the eighth defendant in Holland. It is alleged by the plaintiff that some of the copies of the tape manufactured by the sixth defendant and sold by the eighth defendant have been imported into the United Kingdom, but there is no allegation that either the sixth defendant or the eighth defendant themselves did the importing.

Leave to serve the sixth and eighth defendants outside the jurisdiction was obtained and service was in due course effected. The sixth and eighth defendants now apply to set aside such service.

It became clear at an early stage that the central question in the case was whether the writ, statement of claim, and affidavits in support disclosed any reasonable cause of action against the sixth and eighth defendants.

The statement of claim alleges that the copyright in the tape of "First Strike" was vested in the plaintiffs or some of them and that various of the defendants had purported to authorise the making of copies by the sixth defendant. Paragraph 20 then alleges that the sixth defendant had manufactured at least 7,000 copies of "First Strike". The statement of claim does not allege where such manufacture took place but the only evidence is that the manufacture took place outside the United Kingdom. Paragraph 21 alleges, inter alia, that the sixth defendant sold a number of copies to the eighth defendant and that the eighth defendant sold a number of records to the ninth defendant. Paragraph 11 then alleges that the ninth defendant imported a number of the copies into the United Kingdom. The statement of claim does not allege where such sale by the eighth to ninth defendants took place but there is uncontroverted sworn evidence that the sale took place in Holland and that the eighth defendant did not import the records into the United Kingdom. Paragraph 25 alleges that the first to sixth defendants inclusive infringed the copyright in the tape of "First Strike" and had converted the tape to their own use. Paragraph 26 alleged in the alternative that each of the nine defendants had separately or together caused the sale or exposing for sale of the "First Strike" copies which they knew to be infringing copies or had caused the importation of infringing copies into the United Kingdom. Paragraph 28 alleges that each of the defendants knew that the making of the copies "would have constituted an infringement if these had been made in the United Kingdom". Paragraph 29 alleges that "these acts and each of them were not justifiable in Luxembourg ... (or) Holland".

Accordingly, the claim on its face is a claim for infringement of the United Kingdom copyright in "First Strike" by acts done by the sixth and eighth defendants wholly outside the United Kingdom. The sixth and eighth defendants claim that acts done by them outside the United Kingdom cannot constitute breaches of the United Kingdom copyright in the tapes. Accordingly, no cause of action is disclosed against them.

The draughtsman of the Copyright Act 1956 scrupulously ensures that at no stage does the Act have any application outside the United Kingdom and the other countries to which the Act extends (which do not include Holland or Luxembourg). Thus in section 1 "copyright" is defined as meaning "the exclusive right ... to do, and to authorise other persons to do, certain acts in relation to that work in the United Kingdom ...". It then defines such acts as being the acts restricted by the copyright. Section 1(2) provides that "the copyright in a work is infringed by any person who (without authority) does, or authorises another person to do, any of the said acts in relation to the work in the United Kingdom ...". Section 5 deals with infringement by importation sale and other dealings, but expressly limits such infringement to cases of importation "into the United Kingdom" or sale and other dealings "in the United Kingdom". So far as copyright in sound recordings is concerned, copyright is created by section 12, and section 16 sub section (2) and (3) deal with the importation of, and dealings with, copies of such recordings, again in both cases the importation and dealing being expressly limited to acts done in the United Kingdom.

It is therefore clear that copyright under the English Act is strictly defined in terms of territory. The intangible right which is copyright is merely a right to do certain acts exclusively in the United Kingdom: only acts done in the United Kingdom constitute infringement either direct or indirect of such right.

In the circumstances, it is not surprising that, with one exception, the text books have taken the view that acts done outside the United Kingdom cannot be the subject matter of an action for infringement in the English courts.

However, Mr. Rubin, for the plaintiffs, contends that the law is otherwise. He relies on the principle set out as rule 172 in Dicey [& Morris on Conflict of laws 10th Ed] as approved by the House of Lords in *Chaplin v. Boys* [1971] AC 356. Rule 172 reads as follows:

"1. As a general rule, an act done in a foreign country is a tort and actionable as such in England only if it is both

(a) actionable as a tort according to English law, or in other words is an act which, if done in England, would be a tort: and

(b) actionable according to the law of the foreign country where it was done."

Mr. Rubin says that it is common ground that under the law of Luxembourg and Holland the making of the records and their sale constitute legal wrongs.

Further the manufacture and sale of the copies if done in England would have constituted infringements under the English Copyright Act. Therefore, he says, the acts although done outside the United Kingdom are actionable in the English courts.

I reject Mr. Rubin's submissions. The only wrong under English law that he can rely on for this purpose is breach of the statutory rights conferred by the Copyright Act 1956 and particularly section 1(1). Those rights do not extend to render unlawful anything done outside the United Kingdom. His right under English law is a statutory right not a tort at common law. No common law rule of international law can confer on a litigant a right under English law that he would not otherwise possess.

In my judgment, this conclusion is supported by considering what would happen if the action were to proceed in the English courts. The majority decision in *Chaplin v. Boys (supra)* seems to me to show that rule 172 is a rule for regulating the choice of law to be applied to the tort. In cases brought in England under rule 172, the court generally gives effect to the substantive law of England (*lex fori*) as opposed to the law of the place where the act is committed (*lex delicti*). Having once applied rule 172 to establish which law is applicable and found that the applicable law is the law of England, the question must be whether under English law those acts constitute an actionable wrong. For that purpose, if under English law the plaintiff's right is to complain of acts done in England alone (the place of the doing of the act being of the very essence of the claim) it could not be right for the trial judge to proceed on the footing that acts in fact done abroad were done in the United Kingdom. In other words, although for the purpose of establishing what is the appropriate law the acts may have to be deemed to have been done in England, on the trial of the substantive case the court must be bound to have regard to the actual facts not to any deemed facts.

In my judgment, therefore, a successful action cannot be brought in England for alleged infringement of United Kingdom copyright by acts done outside the United Kingdom.

For those reasons, in my judgment the plaintiffs have not shown to my satisfaction that they have any case which was a proper one for service out of the jurisdiction within the meaning of RSC Order 11 rule 4(2). I accordingly set aside service on the sixth and eighth defendants.

Notes and Questions

1. *Personal Jurisdiction.* One of the practical problems in determining which country's laws should apply to determine if a particular use violates the IP owner's right is obtaining jurisdiction over the alleged violator. Would the issue have been clearer in this case if the sixth and eighth defendants had placed copies of the records on their web sites, without permission of the copyright owner, and those websites were available in the UK?

2. To resolve the problem of obtaining personal jurisdiction over domain name users, in a recent case brought by Porsche AG in the United States, the plaintiff brought an *in rem* proceeding against 130 domain names. By bringing suit against the property itself, Porsche avoided the need for obtaining personal jurisdiction over the diverse domain name owners. Its claims of dilution and federal infringement were directed against the domain names, eliminating even the need to find the actual domain name owner. For relief, Porsche sought transfer of the domain names so that it could have them permanently cancelled. The court, however, ultimately rejected the effort on the grounds that the statute in question did not permit in rem proceedings for trademark and dilution claims.

Problem

You represent Healthy Eats Corporation, a Delaware based company which operates a chain of franchised fast food restaurants in the United States. These restaurants specialize in low cost, healthy snack food. They feature a neon red outline of an apple in their roofs with the slogan "Because Your Health Deserves It" across the center. Healthy Eats has decided to develop a web cite advertising its healthier menus. It has registered the domain name HealthyEats.com and hired an independent consultant to create an attractive web cite. On the web cite it plans to advertise the restaurants in its chain, offer franchise opportunities to the public, and include articles about the importance of healthy eating. These articles will be excerpted from various medical and nutrition magazines. The day before Healthy Eats launches its new web page, it discovers another web page at HealthyEatsSucks.com. The page contains a parody of the Healthy Eats apple logo and slogan and numerous articles that criticize the fat content of Healthy Eats menu. An investigation discloses that the web cite is run by a former franchisee of Healthy Eats, who is currently living in Canada. The metatags for this web cite include "healthy eats," "health food," and "franchise" and "Because Your Health Deserves It." Among the articles included on the web cite are excerpts from British and Canadian medical journals. What steps should your client take to challenge this web cite?

Assume that some of the articles on the web cite contain personal medical data which is illegal to distribute in Germany without the permission of the individuals identified in the study. What risk of liability, if any, does your client run if it does not enjoin this web cite? What steps should your client take to minimize such risk?

Chapter Thirty–Seven

COMPUTER SOFTWARE AND INTERNET BUSINESS METHODS

If the Internet provides the best paradigm for international law problems caused by technological advances in the communications media, computer software is the best representation of international law problems when technology itself outpaces domestic and international law standards. The industrial (and to a certain extent, political) advances of the latter part of the Twentieth Century have been driven, in large part, by the technological advances of the computer/robotics industry. Many of the international fights over intellectual property law have focused on the need for developing countries to obtain free, or at least in-expensive, access to computer technology to permit industrial development and, concurrently, a better standard of living. From video games, to word processing systems, from robotized industrial technology to the Internet, computer programming has revolutionized the global economy. It has also lead to bitter trade disputes over the scope of protection to be afforded such advances when they are so closely tied to perceived industrial advances.

Part of the problem in determining the scope of both domestic and international protection for computer software is created by the unique nature of the goods. Modern computer systems generally include a central processing unit (CPU), internal memory storage, disk drives (or other forms of external memory) and network connections to connect the computer to other computers, including local area networks (LAN) and the Internet. The internal memory of a computer typically features three types of information storage: random access memory (RAM), read only memory (ROM) and data storage memory (disk space). Computer software programs are basically detailed sets of instruction that direct the use of the various computer components. Such computer programs may be either operating systems (designed to direct the internal functions of a computer) or applications programs (designed to perform specific data processing tasks, such as word processing, spread sheets, or video game programs). As computer processing speeds have increased, more computers use microprograms or microcodes (also referred to as firmware) "wired" into computer chips.

Most computer programs use arithmetic statements or algorithms. If the program contains significant end user elements, such as the visual displays for video games, it may at least produce screen displays that resemble traditional works protected under copyright laws. The program that produced those user displays, however, is usually composed of a series of arithmetic instructions that in machine readable code (also referred to as object code) are nothing more than binary instructions. In this form, such programs more closely resemble industrial applications governed by patent laws.

Like most intellectual property goods in today's technological era, computer programs suffer from the "public goods" problem. Basically, a "public good" is one from which the public is not easily excluded and for which additional users do not deplete the available supply to the rest of the public. A classic "public good" is military defense. Computer programs appear closely related to this classic example. Once the program is distributed, given the ease and ready availability of low cost copying, it is difficult to exclude nonpurchasers from the benefits of the program. Furthermore, use by one person does not detract from another person's ability to use or enjoy the program. And their use in turn does not diminish the original, since the program can be copied without affecting the quality or content of the original program. This public goods nature has made enforcement of any agreed-upon international protection standards problematic in both the domestic and international arena.

Computer programs also are subject to network externalities. The greater the number of consumers that use a particular program, the more popular that program becomes. The more popular a program, the more valuable it appears to be. Such externalities are particularly true for operating systems. For example, the more programs that a particular operating system supports, the more popular that system becomes. Conversely, the more popular a particular operating system becomes, the more programmers want to create programs that are compatible with that particular system, and the more valuable (from a property stand point) the compatibility features of the operating language of that program become.

Externalities are not limited to compatibility issues. Instead, the manner in which users interface with the program itself creates marketing externalities. Theoretically keyboards for computers could use any arrangement of keys. In fact some have suggested that an arrangement other than the standard QWERTY may be more ergonomically sound. Nevertheless, more computer keyboards use the standard QWERTY board. Use of the identical "standard" thus assures that all typists need only learn one keyboard system. This problem of "user friendliness" is not limited to keyboards, but applies to virtually any issue of user interface. Because standards appear necessary to permit maximum utilization, one of the early areas of dispute over the scope of protection to be afforded computer software was the extent of protection, if any, to grant the language impacted by such externalities.

The early fight over computer software appeared limited to the basic of question of whether such programs should be protected, and under what laws. Internationally, however, the fight over technology has questioned the desirability of protection for a technological advance that is considered so critical it should qualify as a "common heritage of mankind" available for all to use. As you consider the following cases, ask yourself to what extent, if any, computer software should be protected under intellectual property laws. Should they be protected under patent laws, because they are connected with the use of machines? Should they be protected under copyright laws because they are based on a written "script"? Or, are they unique public goods, with a unique role in industrialized society that requires special international treatment? If so, what kind? What about new computerized techniques that are used in connection with electronic commerce (e-commerce) on the Internet? Should these "methods" be subject to intellectual property protection?

A. IS COMPUTER SOFTWARE ANALOGOUS TO A PATENTED MACHINE, A COPYRIGHTED LITERARY WORK OR AN UNPROTECTED IDEA?

[For additional cases on computer software protection, see the *Rasterizer* case in Chapter Eight and the *Apple Software* case in Chapter Nine.]

THE MENU COMMAND HIERARCHY CASE
LOTUS DEVELOPMENT CORP. v. BORLAND INTERNATIONAL INC.

United States Court of Appeals, First Circuit, 1995.
49 F.3d 807, 34 U.S.P.Q. 2d 1014.

STAHL, J.

This appeal requires us to decide whether a computer menu command hierarchy is copyrightable subject matter. In particular, we must decide whether, as the district court held, plaintiff-appellee Lotus Development Corporation's copyright in Lotus 1–2–3, a computer spreadsheet program, was infringed by defendant-appellant Borland International, Inc., when Borland copied the Lotus 1–2–3 menu command hierarchy into its Quattro and Quattro Pro computer spreadsheet programs.

Lotus 1–2–3 is a spreadsheet program that enables users to perform accounting functions electronically on a computer. Users manipulate and control the program via a series of menu commands, such as "Copy," "Print," and "Quit." Users choose commands either by highlighting them on the screen or by typing their first letter. In all, Lotus 1–2–3 has 469 commands arranged into more than 50 menus and submenus.

Lotus 1–2–3, like many computer programs, allows users to write what are called "macros." By writing a macro, a user can designate a series of command choices with a single macro keystroke. Then, to execute that series of commands in multiple parts of the spreadsheet, rather than typing the whole series each time, the user only needs to type the single pre-programmed macro keystroke, causing the program to recall and perform the designated series of commands automatically. Thus, Lotus 1–2–3 macros shorten the time needed to set up and operate the program.

The district court found, and Borland does not now contest, that Borland included in its Quattro and Quattro Pro version 1.0 programs "a virtually identical copy of the entire 1–2–3 menu tree." In so doing, Borland did not copy any of Lotus's underlying computer code; it copied only the words and structure of Lotus's menu command hierarchy. Borland included the Lotus menu command hierarchy in its programs to make them compatible with Lotus 1–2–3 so that spreadsheet users who were already familiar with Lotus 1–2–3 would be able to switch to the Borland programs without having to learn new commands or rewrite their Lotus macros.

The district court ruled that the Lotus menu command hierarchy was copyrightable expression because [a] very satisfactory spreadsheet menu tree can be constructed using different commands and a different command structure from those of Lotus 1–2–3. In fact, Borland has constructed just such an alternate tree for use in Quattro Pro's native mode. Even if one holds the arrangement of menu commands constant, it is possible to generate literally millions of satisfactory menu trees by varying the menu commands employed.

On appeal, Borland does not dispute that it factually copied the words and arrangement of the Lotus menu command hierarchy. Rather, Borland argues that it "lawfully copied the unprotectable menus of Lotus 1–2–3." Borland contends that the Lotus menu command hierarchy is not copyrightable because it is a system, method of operation, process, or procedure foreclosed from protection by 17 U.S.C. Section 102(b).

Whether a computer menu command hierarchy constitutes copyrightable subject matter is a matter of first impression in this court. While some other courts appear to have touched on it briefly in dicta, we know of no cases that deal with the copyrightability of a menu command hierarchy standing on its own (i.e., without other elements of the user interface, such as screen displays, in issue). Thus we are navigating in uncharted waters.

Borland vigorously argues, however, that the Supreme Court charted our course more than 100 years ago when it decided *Baker v. Selden*, 101 U.S. 99 (1879). In *Baker v. Selden*, the Court held that Selden's copyright over the textbook in which he explained his new way to do accounting did not grant him a monopoly on the use of his accounting system.[6] Borland argues:

The facts of *Baker v. Selden*, and even the arguments advanced by the parties in that case, are identical to those in this case. The only difference is that the "user interface" of Selden's system was implemented by pen and paper rather than by computer. To demonstrate that *Baker v. Selden* and this appeal both involve accounting systems, Borland even supplied this court with a video that, with special effects, shows Selden's paper forms "melting" into a computer screen and transforming into Lotus 1–2–3.

We do not think that *Baker v. Selden* is nearly as analogous to this appeal as Borland claims. Of course, Lotus 1–2–3 is a computer spreadsheet, and as such its grid of horizontal rows and vertical columns certainly resembles an accounting ledger or any other paper spreadsheet. Those grids, however, are not at issue in this appeal for, unlike Selden, Lotus does not claim to have a monopoly over its accounting system. Rather, this appeal involves Lotus's monopoly over the commands it uses to operate the computer. Accordingly, this appeal is not, as Borland contends, "identical" to *Baker v. Selden*.

Borland argues that the Lotus menu command hierarchy is uncopyrightable because it is a system, method of operation, process, or procedure foreclosed from copyright protection by 17 U.S.C. Section 102(b). Section 102(b) states: "In no case does copyright protection for an original work of authorship extend to any idea, procedure, process, system, method of operation, concept, principle, or discovery, regardless of the form in which it is described, explained, illustrated, or embodied in such work." Because we conclude that the Lotus menu command hierarchy is a method of operation, we do not consider whether it could also be a system, process, or procedure.

We think that "method of operation," as that term is used in Section 102(b), refers to the means by which a person operates something, whether it be a car, a food processor, or a computer. Thus a text describing how to operate something would not extend copyright protection to the method of operation itself; other people would be free to employ that method and to describe it in their own words. Similarly, if a new method of operation is used rather than described, other people would still be free to employ or describe that method.

We hold that the Lotus menu command hierarchy is an uncopyrightable "method of operation." The Lotus menu command hierarchy provides the means by which users control and operate Lotus 1–2–3. If users wish to copy material, for example, they use the "Copy" command. If users wish to print material, they use the "Print" command. Users must use the command terms to tell the computer what to do. Without the

---

6. Selden's system of double-entry bookkeeping is the now almost-universal T-accounts system.

menu command hierarchy, users would not be able to access and control, or indeed make use of, Lotus 1–2–3's functional capabilities.

The fact that Lotus developers could have designed the Lotus menu command hierarchy differently is immaterial to the question of whether it is a "method of operation." Our initial inquiry is not whether the Lotus menu command hierarchy incorporates any expression. Rather, our initial inquiry is whether the Lotus menu command hierarchy is a "method of operation." Concluding, as we do, that users operate Lotus 1–2–3 by using the Lotus menu command hierarchy, and that the entire Lotus menu command hierarchy is essential to operating Lotus 1–2–3, we do not inquire further whether that method of operation could have been designed differently. The "expressive" choices of what to name the command terms and how to arrange them do not magically change the uncopyrightable menu command hierarchy into copyrightable subject matter.

In many ways, the Lotus menu command hierarchy is like the buttons used to control, say, a video cassette recorder ("VCR"). A VCR is a machine that enables one to watch and record video tapes. Users operate VCRs by pressing a series of buttons that are typically labelled "Record, Play, Reverse, Fast Forward, Pause, Stop/Eject." That the buttons are arranged and labeled does not make them a "literary work," nor does it make them an "expression" of the abstract "method of operating" a VCR via a set of labeled buttons. Instead, the buttons are themselves the "method of operating" the VCR.

When a Lotus 1–2–3 user chooses a command, either by highlighting it on the screen or by typing its first letter, he or she effectively pushes a button. Highlighting the "Print" command on the screen, or typing the letter "P," is analogous to pressing a VCR button labeled "Play."

Just as one could not operate a buttonless VCR, it would be impossible to operate Lotus 1–2–3 without employing its menu command hierarchy. Thus the Lotus command terms are not equivalent to the labels on the VCR's buttons, but are instead equivalent to the buttons themselves. Unlike the labels on a VCR's buttons, which merely make operating a VCR easier by indicating the buttons' functions, the Lotus menu commands are essential to operating Lotus 1–2–3. Without the menu commands, there would be no way to "push" the Lotus buttons, as one could push unlabeled VCR buttons. While Lotus could probably have designed a user interface for which the command terms were mere labels, it did not do so here. Lotus 1–2–3 depends for its operation on use of the precise command terms that make up the Lotus menu command hierarchy.

One might argue that the buttons for operating a VCR are not analogous to the commands for operating a computer program because VCRs are not copyrightable, whereas computer programs are. VCRs may not be copyrighted because they do not fit within any of the Section 102(a) categories of copyrightable works; the closest they come is "sculptural work." Sculptural works, however, are subject to a "useful-article" exception whereby "the design of a useful article ... shall be considered a pictorial, graphic, or sculptural work only if, and only to the extent that, such design incorporates pictorial, graphic, or sculptural features that can be identified separately from, and are capable of existing independently of, the utilitarian aspects of the article." 17 U.S.C. Section 101. A "useful article" is "an article having an intrinsic utilitarian function that is not merely to portray the appearance of the article or to convey information." *Id.* Whatever expression there may be in the arrangement of the parts of a VCR is not capable of existing separately from the VCR itself, so an ordinary VCR would not be copyrightable.

Computer programs, unlike VCRs, are copyrightable as "literary works." 17 U.S.C. Section 102(a). Accordingly, one might argue, the "buttons" used to operate a computer program are not like the buttons used to operate a VCR, for they are not subject to a useful-article exception. The response, of course, is that the arrangement of buttons on a VCR would not be copyrightable even without a useful-article exception, because the buttons are an uncopyrightable "method of operation." Similarly, the "buttons" of a computer program are also an uncopyrightable "method of operation."

Because we hold that the Lotus menu command hierarchy is uncopyrightable subject matter, we further hold that Borland did not infringe Lotus's copyright by copying it. The judgment of the district court is Reversed.

BOUDIN, J., concurring.

The importance of this case, and a slightly different emphasis in my view of the underlying problem, prompt me to add a few words to the majority's tightly focused discussion.

Most of the law of copyright and the "tools" of analysis have developed in the context of literary works such as novels, plays, and films. In this milieu, the principal problem—simply stated, if difficult to resolve—is to stimulate creative expression without unduly limiting access by others to the broader themes and concepts deployed by the author. The middle of the spectrum presents close cases; but a "mistake" in providing too much protection involves a small cost: subsequent authors treating the same themes must take a few more steps away from the original expression.

The problem presented by computer programs is fundamentally different in one respect. The computer program is a means for causing something to happen; it has a mechanical utility, an instrumental role, in accomplishing the world's work. Granting protection, in other words, can have some of the consequences of patent protection in limiting other people's ability to perform a task in the most efficient manner. Utility does not bar copyright (dictionaries may be copyrighted), but it alters the calculus.

Of course, the argument for protection is undiminished, perhaps even enhanced, by utility: if we want more of an intellectual product, a temporary monopoly for the creator provides incentives for others to create other, different items in this class. But the "cost" side of the equation may be different where one places a very high value on public access to a useful innovation that may be the most efficient means of performing a given task. Thus, the argument for extending protection may be the same; but the stakes on the other side are much higher.

It is no accident that patent protection has preconditions that copyright protection does not—notably, the requirements of novelty and non-obviousness—and that patents are granted for a shorter period than copyrights. This problem of utility has sometimes manifested itself in copyright cases, such as *Baker v. Selden*, 101 U.S. 99 (1879), and been dealt with through various formulations that limit copyright or create limited rights to copy. But the case law and doctrine addressed to utility in copyright have been brief detours in the general march of copyright law.

Requests for the protection of computer menus present the concern with fencing off access to the commons in an acute form. A new menu may be a creative work, but over time its importance may come to reside more in the investment that has been made by users in learning the menu and in building their own mini-programs—macros—in reliance upon the menu. Better typewriter keyboard layouts may exist, but the familiar QWERTY keyboard dominates the market because that is what everyone has learned to use. The QWERTY keyboard is nothing other than a menu of letters.

Thus, to assume that computer programs are just one more new means of expression, like a filmed play, may be quite wrong. The "form"—the written source code or the menu structure depicted on the screen—look hauntingly like the familiar stuff of copyright; but the "substance" probably has more to do with problems presented in patent law or, as already noted, in those rare cases where copyright law has confronted industrially useful expressions. Applying copyright law to computer programs is like assembling a jigsaw puzzle whose pieces do not quite fit.

If Lotus is granted a monopoly, users who have learned the command structure of Lotus 1-2-3 or devised their own macros are locked into Lotus, just as a typist who has learned the QWERTY keyboard would be the captive of anyone who had a monopoly on the production of such a keyboard. Apparently, for a period Lotus 1-2-3 has had such sway in the market that it has represented the de facto standard for electronic spreadsheet commands. So long as Lotus is the superior spreadsheet—either in quality or in price—there may be nothing wrong with this advantage.

But if a better spreadsheet comes along, it is hard to see why customers who have learned the Lotus menu and devised macros for it should remain captives of Lotus because of an investment in learning made by the users and not by Lotus. Lotus has already reaped a substantial reward for being first; assuming that the Borland program is now better, good reasons exist for freeing it to attract old Lotus customers: to enable the old customers to take advantage of a new advance, and to reward Borland in turn for making a better product. If Borland has not made a better product, then customers will remain with Lotus anyway.

Thus, for me the question is not whether Borland should prevail but on what basis. To call the menu a "method of operation" is, in the common use of those words, a defensible position. After all, the purpose of the menu is not to be admired as a work of literary or pictorial art. It is to transmit directions from the user to the computer, i.e., to operate the computer. The menu is also a "method" in the dictionary sense because it is a "planned way of doing something," an "order or system," and (aptly here) an "orderly or systematic arrangement, sequence or the like." RANDOM HOUSE WEBSTER'S COLLEGE DICTIONARY 853 (1991).

A different approach would be to say that Borland's use is privileged because, in the context already described, it is not seeking to appropriate the advances made by Lotus' menu; rather, having provided an arguably more attractive menu of its own, Borland is merely trying to give former Lotus users an option to exploit their own prior investment in learning or in macros. The difference is that such a privileged use approach would not automatically protect Borland if it had simply copied the Lotus menu (using different codes), contributed nothing of its own, and resold Lotus under the Borland label.

The closest analogue in conventional copyright is the fair use doctrine.

But a privileged use doctrine would certainly involve problems of its own. It might more closely tailor the limits on copyright protection to the reasons for limiting that protection; but it would entail a host of administrative problems that would cause cost and delay, and would also reduce the ability of the industry to predict outcomes. Indeed, to the extent that Lotus' menu is an important standard in the industry, it might be argued that any use ought to be deemed privileged.

In sum, the majority's result persuades me and its formulation is as good, if not better, than any other that occurs to me now as within the reach of courts. Some solutions (e.g., a very short copyright period for menus) are not options at all for courts but might be for Congress. In all events, the choices are important ones of policy, not linguistics, and they should be made with the underlying considerations in view.

Notes and Questions

1. *The Limits of Literary Works.* Under U.S. law computer programs receive copyright protection as "literary works." 17 U.S.C. Section 102(a)(1) (granting protection to "literary works") and 17 U.S.C. Section 101 (defining "literary works" as "works . . . expressed in words, numbers, or other verbal or numerical symbols or indicia, regardless of the nature of the material objects, such as books, periodicals, phonorecords, film, tapes, disks , or cards, in which they are embodied." *See also* H.R. Rep. No. 1476, 94th Cong., 2d

Sess. 54 (1976), *reprinted in* 1976 U.S.C.C.A.N. 5659, 5667 ("The term 'literary works' . . . includes computer data bases, and computer programs to the extent that they incorporate authorship in the programmer's expression of original ideas, as distinguished from the ideas themselves."). Article 10 of TRIPS similarly defined computer programs as a literary work under the Berne Convention. This addition was similarly reflected in Article 4 of the WIPO Copyright Treaty. What are the problems that the definition of computer programs as a literary work may present according to the court in the *Menu Command Hierarchy* case?

2. The decision in the *Menu Command Hierarchy* case has been both hailed and criticized. What is the definition of a "method of operation" that falls outside of the confines of copyright protection according to the court in? Are methods of operation protectable under the Berne Convention?

3. Is the court's decision in the *Menu Command Hierarchy* case motivated by a realistic definition of a copyright protectable work or by economic considerations caused by market externalities? Do you agree with the court's decision? With its rationale?

4. Is the source code for the menu hierarchy protectable under copyright? Should it be? What impact would protection of the source code have upon the ability of programmers to utilize Lotus Borland's menu hierarchy?

5. The language "method of operation" appears to refer to machines, which are more often the subject of patent protection. Would the menu hierarchy in *Lotus Borland* qualify for patent protection under TRIPS? Assuming that it meets the requirements of novelty and non-obviousness, would these hierarchies fall within the scope of patentable subject matter under Article 27 of TRIPS?

6. Because of its importance as a potential industry standard should the menu command hierarchy be considered the "common heritage of mankind," available for use by all?

THE U.S. BUSINESS METHODS CASE
STATE STREET BANK & TRUST CO. v. SIGNATURE FINANCIAL GROUP, INC.

United States Court of Appeals, Federal Circuit, 1998.
149 F.3d 1368.

RICH, CIRCUIT JUDGE.

Signature Financial Group, Inc. (Signature) appeals from the decision of the United States District Court for the District of Massachusetts granting a motion for summary judgment in favor of State Street Bank & Trust Co. (State Street), finding U.S. Patent No. 5,193,056 (the '056 patent) invalid on the ground that the claimed subject matter is not encompassed by 35 U.S.C. s 101 (1994).

Signature is the assignee of the '056 patent which is entitled "Data Processing System for Hub and Spoke Financial Services Configuration." The '056 patent issued to Signature on 9 March 1993, naming R.

Todd Boes as the inventor. The '056 patent is generally directed to a data processing system (the system) for implementing an investment structure which was developed for use in Signature's business as an administrator and accounting agent for mutual funds. In essence, the system, identified by the proprietary name Hub and Spoke (R), facilitates a structure whereby mutual funds (Spokes) pool their assets in an investment portfolio (Hub) organized as a partnership. This investment configuration provides the administrator of a mutual fund with the advantageous combination of economies of scale in administering investments coupled with the tax advantages of a partnership.

State Street and Signature are both in the business of acting as custodians and accounting agents for multitiered partnership fund financial services. State Street negotiated with Signature for a license to use its patented data processing system described and claimed in the '056 patent. When negotiations broke down, State Street brought a declaratory judgment action asserting invalidity, unenforceability, and noninfringement in Massachusetts district court, and then filed a motion for partial summary judgment of patent invalidity for failure to claim statutory subject matter under s 101. The motion was granted and this appeal followed.

The patented invention relates generally to a system that allows an administrator to monitor and record the financial information flow and make all calculations necessary for maintaining a partner fund financial services configuration. As previously mentioned, a partner fund financial services configuration essentially allows several mutual funds, or "Spokes," to pool their investment funds into a single portfolio, or "Hub," allowing for consolidation of, *inter alia*, the costs of administering the fund combined with the tax advantages of a partnership. In particular, this system provides means for a daily allocation of assets for two or more Spokes that are invested in the same Hub. The system determines the percentage share that each Spoke maintains in the Hub, while taking into consideration daily changes both in the value of the Hub's investment securities and in the concomitant amount of each Spoke's assets.

In determining daily changes, the system also allows for the allocation among the Spokes of the Hub's daily income, expenses, and net realized and unrealized gain or loss, calculating each day's total investments based on the concept of a book capital account. This enables the determination of a true asset value of each Spoke and accurate calculation of allocation ratios between or among the Spokes. The system additionally tracks all the relevant data determined on a daily basis for the Hub and each Spoke, so that aggregate year end income, expenses, and capital gain or loss can be determined for accounting and for tax purposes for the Hub and, as a result, for each publicly traded Spoke.

It is essential that these calculations are quickly and accurately performed. In large part this is required because each Spoke sells shares to the public and the price of those shares is substantially based on the

Spoke's percentage interest in the portfolio. In some instances, a mutual fund administrator is required to calculate the value of the shares to the nearest penny within as little as an hour and a half after the market closes. Given the complexity of the calculations, a computer or equivalent device is a virtual necessity to perform the task.

[C]laim 1, properly construed, claims a machine, namely, a data processing system for managing a financial services configuration of a portfolio established as a partnership, which machine is made up of, at the very least, the specific structures disclosed in the written description and corresponding to the means-plus-function elements (a)(g) recited in the claim. A "machine" is proper statutory subject matter under s 101. We note that, for the purposes of a s 101 analysis, it is of little relevance whether claim 1 is directed to a "machine" or a "process," as long as it falls within at least one of the four enumerated categories of patentable subject matter, "machine" and "process" being such categories.

This does not end our analysis, however, because the court concluded that the claimed subject matter fell into one of two alternative judicially created exceptions to statutory subject matter. The court refers to the first exception as the "mathematical algorithm" exception and the second exception as the "business method" exception. Section 101 reads:

Whoever invents or discovers any new and useful process, machine, manufacture, or composition of matter, or any new and useful improvement thereof, may obtain a patent therefor, subject to the conditions and requirements of this title.

The plain and unambiguous meaning of § 101 is that any invention falling within one of the four stated categories of statutory subject matter may be patented, provided it meets the other requirements for patentability set forth in Title 35, i.e., those found in §§ 102, 103, and 112, P 2.[2]

The repetitive use of the expansive term "any" in § 101 shows Congress's intent not to place any restrictions on the subject matter for which a patent may be obtained beyond those specifically recited in § 101. Indeed, the Supreme Court has acknowledged that Congress intended § 101 to extend to "anything under the sun that is made by

---

2. As explained in *In re Bergy*, 596 F.2d 952, 960, 201 U.S.PQ 352, 360 (CCPA 1979) (emphases and footnote omitted): The first door which must be opened on the difficult path to patentability is s 101.... The person approaching that door is an inventor, whether his invention is patentable or not.... Being an inventor or having an invention, however, is no guarantee of opening even the first door. What kind of an invention or discovery is it? In dealing with the question of kind, as distinguished from the qualitative conditions which make the invention patentable, s 101 is broad and general; its language is: "any process, machine, manufacture, or composition of mat-

ter, or any improvement thereof." Section 100(b) further expands "process" to include "art or method, and a new use of a known process, machine, manufacture, composition of matter, or material." If the invention, as the inventor defines it in his claims (pursuant to s 112, second paragraph), falls into any one of the named categories, he is allowed to pass through to the second door, which is s 102; "novelty and loss of right to patent" is the sign on it. Notwithstanding the words "new and useful" in s 101, the invention is not examined under that statute for novelty because that is not the statutory scheme of things or the long-established administrative practice.

man." *Diamond v. Chakrabarty*, 447 U.S. 303, 309, 100 S.Ct. 2204, 65 L.Ed.2d 144 (1980); see also *Diamond v. Diehr*, 450 U.S. 175, 182, 101 S.Ct. 1048, 67 L.Ed.2d 155 (1981). Thus, it is improper to read limitations into § 101 on the subject matter that may be patented where the legislative history indicates that Congress clearly did not intend such limitations.

THE "MATHEMATICAL ALGORITHM" EXCEPTION

The Supreme Court has identified three categories of subject matter that are unpatentable, namely "laws of nature, natural phenomena, and abstract ideas." *Diehr*, 450 U.S. at 185, 101 S.Ct. 1048. Of particular relevance to this case, the Court has held that mathematical algorithms are not patentable subject matter to the extent that they are merely abstract ideas. See *Diehr*, 450 U.S. 175, 101 S.Ct. 1048; *Parker v. Flook*, 437 U.S. 584, 98 S.Ct. 2522, 57 L.Ed.2d 451 (1978); *Gottschalk v. Benson*, 409 U.S. 63, 93 S.Ct. 253, 34 L.Ed.2d 273 (1972). In *Diehr*, the Court explained that certain types of mathematical subject matter, standing alone, represent nothing more than abstract ideas until reduced to some type of practical application, i.e., "a useful, concrete and tangible result." *Alappat*, 33 F.3d at 1544, 31 U.S.PQ2d at 1557.

Unpatentable mathematical algorithms are identifiable by showing they are merely abstract ideas constituting disembodied concepts or truths that are not "useful." From a practical standpoint, this means that to be patentable an algorithm must be applied in a "useful" way. In *Alappat*, we held that data, transformed by a machine through a series of mathematical calculations to produce a smooth waveform display on a rasterizer monitor, constituted a practical application of an abstract idea (a mathematical algorithm, formula, or calculation), because it produced "a useful, concrete and tangible result"—the smooth waveform.

Today, we hold that the transformation of data, representing discrete dollar amounts, by a machine through a series of mathematical calculations into a final share price, constitutes a practical application of a mathematical algorithm, formula, or calculation, because it produces "a useful, concrete and tangible result"—a final share price momentarily fixed for recording and reporting purposes and even accepted and relied upon by regulatory authorities and in subsequent trades.

However, after *Diehr* and *Alappat*, the mere fact that a claimed invention involves inputting numbers, calculating numbers, outputting numbers, and storing numbers, in and of itself, would not render it nonstatutory subject matter, unless, of course, its operation does not produce a "useful, concrete and tangible result." *Alappat*, 33 F.3d at 1544, 31 U.S.PQ2d at 1557. After all, as we have repeatedly stated,

> every step-by-step process, be it electronic or chemical or mechanical, involves an algorithm in the broad sense of the term. Since § 101 expressly includes processes as a category of inventions which may be patented and § 100(b) further defines the word "process" as meaning "process, art or method, and includes a new use of a known process, machine, manufacture, composition of matter, or material,"

it follows that it is no ground for holding a claim is directed to nonstatutory subject matter to say it includes or is directed to an algorithm. This is why the proscription against patenting has been limited to mathematical algorithms.... *In re Iwahashi*, 888 F.2d 1370, 1374, 12 U.S.PQ2d 1908, 1911 (Fed.Cir.1989).

The question of whether a claim encompasses statutory subject matter should not focus on which of the four categories of subject matter a claim is directed to—process, machine, manufacture, or composition of matter—but rather on the essential characteristics of the subject matter, in particular, its practical utility. Section 101 specifies that statutory subject matter must also satisfy the other "conditions and requirements" of Title 35, including novelty, nonobviousness, and adequacy of disclosure and notice. For purpose of our analysis, as noted above, claim 1 is directed to a machine programmed with the Hub and Spoke software and admittedly produces a "useful, concrete, and tangible result." *Alappat*, 33 F.3d at 1544, 31 U.S.PQ2d at 1557. This renders it statutory subject matter, even if the useful result is expressed in numbers, such as price, profit, percentage, cost, or loss.

The Business Method Exception

As an alternative ground for invalidating the '056 patent under § 101, the court relied on the judicially-created, so-called "business method" exception to statutory subject matter. We take this opportunity to lay this ill-conceived exception to rest.

The business method exception has never been invoked by this court to deem an invention unpatentable. Application of this particular exception has always been preceded by a ruling based on some clearer concept of Title 35 or, more commonly, application of the abstract idea exception based on finding a mathematical algorithm.

[Thus], *In re Schrader*, 22 F.3d 290, 30 U.S.PQ2d 1455 (Fed.Cir. 1994), while making reference to the business method exception, turned on the fact that the claims implicitly recited an abstract idea in the form of a mathematical algorithm and there was no "transformation or conversion of subject matter representative of or constituting physical activity or objects." 22 F.3d at 294, 30 U.S.PQ2d at 1459.[13]

In view of this background, it comes as no surprise that in the most recent edition of the Manual of Patent Examining Procedures (MPEP) (1996), a paragraph of § 706.03(a) was deleted. In past editions it read:

> Though seemingly within the category of process or method, a method of doing business can be rejected as not being within the statutory classes. *See Hotel Security Checking Co. v. Lorraine Co.*, 160 F. 467 (2d Cir.1908) and *In re Wait*, 24 U.S.PQ 88, 22 C.C.P.A. 822, 73 F.2d 982 (1934).

---

13. Any historical distinctions between a method of "doing" business and the means of carrying it out blur in the complexity of modern business systems. *See Paine, Webber, Jackson & Curtis v. Merrill* *Lynch*, 564 F.Supp. 1358, 218 U.S.PQ 212 (D.Del.1983), (holding a computerized system of cash management was held to be statutory subject matter.)

MPEP § 706.03(a) (1994). This acknowledgment is buttressed by the U.S. Patent and Trademark 1996 Examination Guidelines for Computer Related Inventions which now read: Office personnel have had difficulty in properly treating claims directed to methods of doing business. Claims should not be categorized as methods of doing business. Instead such claims should be treated like any other process claims. Examination Guidelines, 61 Fed.Reg. 7478, 7479 (1996). We agree that this is precisely the manner in which this type of claim should be treated. Whether the claims are directed to subject matter within § 101 should not turn on whether the claimed subject matter does "business" instead of something else.

The appealed decision is reversed and the case is remanded to the district court for further proceedings consistent with this opinion.

THE UK BUSINESS METHODS CASE
MERRILL LYNCH'S APPLICATION

Court of Appeal (Civil Division), 1989.
[1989] RPC 561.

Fox, LJ

This is an appeal by the applicant from a decision of Falconer J, upholding the determination of the examiner and the principal examiner that the subject matter of the application was unpatentable by virtue of the provisions of section 1(2)(c) of the Patents Act 1977. The case concerns computer-program-related inventions.

The application describes the invention as follows:

"This invention relates to business systems and, more specifically, to an improved data processing based system for implementing an automated trading market for one or more securities. The system retrieves and stores the best current bid and asked prices; qualifies customers buy/sell orders for execution; executes the orders; and reports the trade particulars to customers and to national stock price reporting systems. The system apparatus also determines and monitors stock inventory and profit for the market maker."

As regards the objects of the invention, the application states:

"It is an object of the present invention to provide an improved data processing apparatus for making an automated market for one or more securities.

"More specifically, it is an object of the present invention to provide an automated market making system for qualifying and executing orders for securities transactions.

"It is a further object of the present invention to provide automated market making program controlled apparatus which monitors the securities position of the market maker, and which develops and provides information characterising the market maker's trading profits".

The specification then goes on to state:

"The above and other objects of the present invention are realised in specific, illustrative data processing based apparatus which makes an automated trading market for one or more securities".

Claim 1 is in the following terms:

"In combination in a data processing system for making a trading market in at least one security in which the system proprietor is acting, as principal; said system including means for receiving trade orders for said at least one security from system customers, said trade orders including fields identifying the stock to be traded and characterisation of the trade as a customer purchase or sale, and the number of shares for the transaction; means for retrieving and for storing operative bid and asked prices for said at least one security; means for entering and for storing order qualification parameters, said parameters and said stored prices determining which received orders and qualified for execution; means for storing data characterising position, cost and profit for said at least one security; qualifying means responsive to said received trade orders and said stored prices and order qualification parameters for qualifying a trade order for execution when the received trade order fields do not violate the stored prices and qualification parameters; means for executing each trade order qualified by said qualification means; and post-execution updating means for updating said position and at least one of said stored parameters upon execution of a trade order."

The system can be implemented by any data-processing equipment of the kind familiar to those skilled in the art.

I come to the statutory provisions. They are in section 1 subsections (1) and (2) of the Patents Act 1977, and are as follows:

"(1) A patent may be granted for an invention in respect of which the following conditions are satisfied, that is to say—

(a) the invention is new;

(b) it involves an inventive step;

(c) it is capable of industrial application;

(d) the grant of a patent for it is not excluded by subsections (2) and (3) below;

and references in this Act to a patentable invention shall be construed accordingly.

"(2) It is hereby declared that the following (among other things) are not inventions for the purposes of this Act, that is to say, anything which consists of—

(a) a discovery, scientific theory or mathematical method;

(b) a literary, dramatic, musical or artistic work or any other aesthetic creation whatsoever;

(c) a scheme, rule or method for performing a mental act, playing a game or doing business, or a program for a computer;

(d) the presentation of information;

but the foregoing provision shall prevent anything from being treated as an invention for the purposes of this Act only to the extent that a patent or application for a patent relates to that thing as such".

I should also refer to the European Patent Convention, Article 52, of which is as follows:

"Patentable inventions

(1) European patents shall be granted for any inventions which are susceptible of industrial application, which are new and which involve an inventive step.

(2) The following in particular shall not be regarded as inventions within the meaning of paragraph 1:

(a) discoveries, scientific theories and mathematical methods;

(b) aesthetic creations;

(c) schemes, rules and methods for performing mental acts, playing games or doing business, and programs for computers;

(d) presentations of information.

(3) The provision of paragraph 2 shall exclude patentability of the subject-matter or activities referred to in that provision only to the extent to which a European patent application patent relates to such subject-matter or activities as such.

(4) Methods for treatment of the human or animal body by surgery or therapy and diagnostic methods practised on the human or animal body shall not be regarded as inventions which are susceptible of industrial application within the meaning of paragraph 1. This provision shall not apply to products, in particular substances or compositions, for use in any of these methods".

The issue is whether the present case falls within the prohibition in section 1(2)(c) of the Patents Act 1977.

[T]he Guidelines for Examination in the European Patent Office (which have no binding effect in law) provide, *inter alia*, in part C, Chapter IV, as follows:

"2.2 In considering whether the subject-matter of an application is an invention within the meaning of Article 52, paragraph 1, there are two general points the examiner must bear in mind. Firstly, any exclusion from patentability under Article 52, paragraph 2, applies only to the extent to which the application relates to the excluded subject-matter as such. Secondly, the examiner should disregard the form or kind of claim and concentrate on its content in order to identify the real contribution which the subject-matter claimed, considered as a whole, adds to the known art. If this contribution is not of a technical character, there is no invention within the meaning of Article 52, paragraph 1. Thus, for example, if the claim is for a known manufactured article having a painted design or certain written information on its surface, the contribution to the art is as a general rule merely an aesthetic creation or presentation of information. Similarly, if a computer program is claimed in the form of a physical record, e.g. on a conventional tape or disc, the contribution to the art is still no more than a computer program. In these instances the claim relates to excluded subject-matter as such as is therefore not allowable. If, on the other hand, a computer program in combination with a computer causes the computer to operate in a different way from a technical point of view, the combination might be patentable".

The contention of the applicant (appellant) in the present appeal is that the question to be addressed is: "Is the subject matter of the claim a computer program?" If it is, then it is not patentable. If it is not, then the invention is not excluded from patentability by section 1(2) provided, of course, that the requirements of section 1(1) are satisfied. Thus it is said that a piece of machinery (a computer) which follows the instructions of a novel computer program is patentable although the program itself would be excluded from patentability by section 1(2).

Section 1(2), it is said, only excludes the specified matters "as such". A computer program is a text which, when loaded into a computer, directs the matter in which the computer is to operate. A computer when programmed with a novel program is itself a novel piece of apparatus which, directed by the program, operates in a new way. The view of Falconer J was that if the novelty of the claim was in matter excluded by section 1(2), then you ignore that and look only at what is left, i.e., a conventional computer which is not patentable. That approach was held to be wrong in *Genentech* and the present claim (it is said) can properly be regarded as a claim to a novel piece of apparatus or machinery which is patentable.

I should now refer to the decision, dated 5 July 1986, of the Technical Board of Appeal of the European Patents Office in the case of *Vicom Systems Inc's Application* (Decision T208/84), [1987] Official Journal EPO 14. The decision of the Board is a matter of which we are required, by section 91(1) of the Patents Act 1977, to take "judicial notice". In *Vicom* it appears (at page 15(IV)), that the Examining Division regarded the claim as being concerned with mathematical operations which would be carried out on a conventional general-purpose computer, and, since there was no detailed discussion of the circuitry of special-purpose hardware, there was no basis for claiming the apparatus as being anything other than a suitably programmed conventional computer. The appellants asserted, however, that the claim related to special-purpose hardware which was to be put into practice by the skilled man designing circuitry which would perform specific operations detailed in the specification.

As I have already indicated, Article 53 of the Convention, like section 1(2), excludes from patentability mathematical methods as such.

The Board held (paragraph 6) that even if the idea underlying an invention is considered to reside in a mathematical method, a claim directed to a technical process in which the method is used does not seek protection for the mathematical method as such.

The Board went on to consider the Examining Division's argument that the implementation of the claimed methods for image processing by a program run on a computer could not be regarded as an invention under Article 52(2)(c) and (3) of the Convention. In paragraph 12 the Board stated:

"The Board of Appeal is of the opinion that a claim directed to a technical process which process is carried out under the control of a program (be this implemented in hardware or in software) cannot be regarded as relating to a computer program as such within the meaning of Article 52(3) EPC, as it is the application of the program for determining the sequence of steps in the process for which in effect protection is sought. Consequently, such a claim is allowable under Article 52(2)(c) and (3) EPC".

Generally, claims which can be considered as being directed to a computer set up to operate in accordance with a specified program (whether by means of hardware or software) for controlling or carrying out a technical process cannot be regarded as relating to a computer program as such and thus are not objectionable under Article 52(2)(c) and (3) EPC".

Finally, the Board expressed the view, in paragraph 16, that:

"Generally speaking, an invention which would be patentable in accordance with conventional patentability criteria should not be excluded from protection by the mere fact that, for its implementation, modern technical means in the form of a computer program are used. Decisive is what technical contribution the invention as defined in the claim when considered as a whole makes to the known art".

There must, I think, be some technical advance on the prior art in the form of a new result (e.g., a substantial increase in processing speed as in *Vicom*).

Now let it be supposed that claim 1 can be regarded as producing a new result in the form of a technical contribution to the prior art. That result, whatever the technical advance may be, is simply the production of a trading system. It is a data-processing system for doing a specific business, that is to say, making a trading market in securities. The end result, therefore, is simply "a method ... of doing business", and is excluded by section 1(2)(c). The fact that the method of doing business may be an improvement on previous methods of doing business does not seem to me to be material. The prohibition in section 1(2)(c) is generic; qualitative considerations do not enter into the matter. The section draws no distinction between the method by which the mode of doing business is achieved. If what is produced in the end is itself an item excluded from patentability by section 1(2), the matter can go no further.

Claim 1, after all, is directed to "a data processing system for making a trading market". That is simply a method of doing business. A data processing system operating to produce a novel technical result would normally be patentable. But it cannot, it seems to me, be patentable if the result itself is a prohibited item under section 1(2). In the present case it is such a prohibited item.

In the end, therefore, for the reasons which I have indicated, I reach the result that there is not a patentable invention here.

I would dismiss the appeal.

Notes and Questions

1.   What requirements were imposed by TRIPS for patent protection? Does the software in either the *U.S.* or *UK Business* Methods cases meet these requirements? Must countries protect computerized "methods of doing business" under patent laws under TRIPS? Can they protect such methods without violating TRIPS?

2.   Compare the courts' analyses in the *U.S.* and *UK Business Methods* cases. If the *UK case* were analyzed under U.S. law, would the invention be patentable?

3.   What is the economic benefit of extending patent protection to the methods of doing business discussed in the *U.S. Business Methods* case? What about the externality concerns expressed in the *Menu Command Hierarchy* case? Do they have any application to computerized methods of doing business? Does the court's decision in the *U.S. Business Methods* case adequately reflect these decisions?

4.   *European Treatment of Computerized Inventions:* The original European Patent Office Guidelines for Article 52 (regarding the protection of computer programs) stated:

"If the contribution to the known art resides solely in a computer program then the subject matter is not patentable in whatever manner it may be presented in the claims. For example, a claim to a computer characterized by having the particular program stored in its memory or to a process for operating a computer under control of the program would be as objectionable as a claim to the program per se or the program when recorded on magnetic tape."

This interpretation led to the rejection of a number of applications for patent protection for various computerized inventions until the Guidelines were revised in 1985 so that they now state that, although "computer programs per se are unpatentable and this situation is not" normally changed when a program is loaded into a known computer, "if" the subject matter as claimed makes a technical contribution to the known art, patentability should not be denied merely on the ground that a computer program is involved in its implementation." Among the examples of patentable inventions included in the Guidelines were: "program-controlled machines and program-controlled manufacturing and control processes."

This change in approach was reflected in the Vicom decision mentioned above, *Vicom Systems' Application*, [1987] OJ EPO 14. The invention in

Vicom related to a method of digitally processing images using a computer. The Board reversed the rejection by the Examining Division maintaining that even if the idea underlying an invention may be considered to reside in a mathematical method, a claim directed to a technical process in which the method is used is not an attempt to obtain protection for the mathematical method as such. Basically, after *Vicom*, the Board upholds patentability if after the program element has been removed from the claim, there is still left a "technical problem" to be solved.

Exactly what constitutes a "technical problem," however, is still not entirely clear. For example a method of translating the printer control features in a word processing program to another program has been held to constitute the solution of a technical problem. *See IBM/Editable Document Form*, T110/90, [1994] OJ EPO 557. Similarly in *General Purpose Management System/Soler*, T 769/92, [1995] OJ EPO 525, the claim in question was for a computer system for plural types of independent management including at least financial and inventory management. This was held to be patentable as being the application of specified processing steps to various files in a computer's memory and the organization required to permit use of a single "transfer slip" which together constituted a sufficient "technical problem: to justify holding that the invention was neither a computer program as such nor a method of doing business. On the other hand, in *IBM/Text Processing*, T 65/86, [1990] EPOR 181, it was held that the only problem solved by a program to detect and correct contextual homophone errors (e.g. "there" instead of "their") was an essentially mental one; consequently, the invention was not patentable. Similarly, in *Character Form/Siemens*, T 158/88, [1991] OJ EPO 566, it was held that the problem was merely a mental one in a case dealing with the form that a letter may take in different parts of a word. In some languages (e.g. Arabic) the form of a letter depends upon whether the letter appears at the beginning, middle, or end of a word. An invention relating to the display of the correct form of the letter on a visual display screen by control of the display by a computer program was held to be unpatentable because the problem solved by the computer program was not a technical one but merely "the making of the mental registering" of the letters easier. U.S. distinctions between patentable and unpatentable computer related inventions have been no less clear. *See* the *Rasterizer* case in Chapter Eight and the *State Street Bank* case, *supra*.

5. *Methods of Doing Business*. Under Article 52, methods of doing business are presumably unpatentable. Despite this apparent blanket prohibition, the EPO has permitted the patenting of inventions so long as the method relates to the solution of a technical problem. Thus, for example, in *IBM/Card Reader*, T 854/90, [1993] OJ EPO 669., a claim for an "electronic application form" to determine whether the user was entitled to access to, for example a cash dispensing machine was considered unpatentable as essentially a business operation. Even though a technical means was used to perform the process, this was not sufficient to make it more than an unpatentable mental process.

However, in *Queuing System/Petterson*, T 1002/92, [1995] OJ EPO 605, a system for determining the queue sequence for serving customers at a plurality of service points was held to be patentable, notwithstanding the rejection of a corresponding Swedish national application after an appeal to the Swedish Supreme Administrative Court. The system in question consisted of a turn-number allocating unit, an information unit, a selection unit and a computing means which *inter alia* decided which particular turn-number is to be served at a particular free service point. The Swedish application had been rejected on the ground that the problem solved by the invention was not a technical one. The EPO Appeal board disagreed, holding that the problem to be solved was the means of interaction of the components of the system which was a technical problem whose solution (the invention in question) was therefore patentable.

6. *The Problem of Innocence.* Under patent law, innocent infringement or independent creation is no defense. Thus, patent protection prevents others from practicing the claimed invention, regardless of the innocence of their actions. What impact, if any, should this distinction play on whether patent or copyright protection should be extended to computer software programs?

7. *The Novelty Question.* Aside from the problems of determining whether a claimed computer-related invention qualifies as patentable subject matter, scholars and practitioners have severely criticized the ability of patent examiners to determine the novelty or non-obviousness of a claimed computerized invention. Thus, for example, in the United States a patent originally granted for multimedia database allowing users to simultaneously search for text, graphics, and sounds to Compton's New Media was later reexamined and revoked when public outcries established that the program was based on widespread practices in the computer industry. The problem of adequately determining appropriate prior art in a constantly changing technological environment remains a domestic and international problem.

8. If the United States grants what appears to be broader patent protection for methods of doing business than that required under TRIPS or supported by the European Union, does such broad protection make sense from an international point of view? In other words, if such patents cannot be protected internationally, how much value does such a territorially limited patent have, other than to suppress competition domestically?

9. Based on the foregoing cases and information, would the following patents qualify as protectable subject matter under the EPO? Under the *State Street Bank* case?

a) Method and apparatus for determining behavioral profile of a computer user. A Computer network method and apparatus that provides targeting of the appropriate audience based on psychographic or behavioral profiles of end users. The psychographic profile is formed by recording computer activity and viewing habits of the end user. Using the profile (with or without additional user demographics), advertisements are displayed to appropriately selected users. Based on regression analysis of recorded responses of a first set of users viewing the advertisements, the target user profile is refined. Viewing by and regression analysis of recorded responses of subsequent sets of users continually auto-targets and customizes ads for the optimal end user audience.

b) Method and apparatus for a cryptographically assisted commercial network system designed to facilitate buyer-driven conditional purchase offers. A method and apparatus for effectuating bilateral buyer-driven commerce. The invention allows prospective buyers of goods and services to communicate a binding purchase offer globally to potential sellers, for sellers conveniently to search for relevant buyer purchase offers, and for sellers potentially to bind a buyer to a contract based on the buyer's purchase offer. In a preferred embodiment, the apparatus of the present invention includes a controller which receives binding purchase offers from prospective buyers. The controller makes purchase offers available globally to potential sellers. Potential sellers then have the option to accept a purchase offer and thus bind the corresponding buyer to a contract. The method and apparatus of the present invention have applications on the Internet as well as conventional communications systems such as voice telephony.

10. *Patents and the Internet.* A great number of both U.S. and international patent applications have as their subject matter technology and methods of doing business. Consider, for example, the following:

"You're an Internet merchant ramping up for the holiday shopping season. Your store uses a "shopping cart" for buyers to select purchases, accepts credit card payments, and offers airline frequent flyer miles for purchases.

"You pay people who click on your banner ads and send e-mail to notify regular customers of promotions, including a URL so they can go directly to the right page. For close-out items, you let shoppers name their price for an item, letting consumers say how much they'll pay.

"Call your patent attorney, because you may be violating six e-commerce patents, all issued since March." Tim Clark, *Will patents help e-commerce?*, http://www.CNETnews.com (August, 1998).

If such patents are enforceable internationally, they may serve to establish industry standards for the Internet. They may also serve to limit growth by establishing monopolies over such potential standards. How should the problems be solved? By declining to find such inventions patentable under international standards? By establishing an internationally recognized exception to protection for inventions which concern methods of doing business on the Internet? How would you draft such an exception?

B. DOES THE SPECIAL NATURE OF SOFTWARE REQUIRE SPECIALIZED TREATMENT?

PATENTLY ABSURD

SIMON GARFINKEL

http://www.wired.com/wired/archive/2.07.

Both fans and critics of software patents have a tendency to quote from the U.S. Constitution, which states that the purpose of the patent system is "to promote the progress of science and useful arts, by securing for limited times to authors and inventors the exclusive right to their respective writings and discoveries." Is this in fact what patents are doing for the world of computer science?

Patents may be less justified in the world of software, where major application programs can be developed by a few people working in somebody's living room over just a few months. While copyright protection for a program prevents software pirates from handing out illegal copies, patent protection prevents other developers from writing their own version of a program and trying to sell it—or even give it away.

A less drastic solution is favored by John Preston, who headed MIT's patent office for nearly ten years. Preston would set up a system of mandatory licensing, in which patent holders would be legally required to license any software patent at a preset fixed fee. Such a scheme would prevent large companies from cross-licensing patents among themselves and then using patent pools to shut out upstart competitors, a practice common in other industries. "After a technology has been introduced, it should be made available to everyone," says MIT's Preston.

LEAGUE FOR PROGRAMMING FREEDOM— AGAINST SOFTWARE PATENTS

February 28, 1991

Software patents threaten to devastate America's computer industry. Patents granted in the past decade are now being used to attack companies such as the Lotus Development Corporation for selling programs that they have independently developed. Soon new companies will often be barred from the software arena—most major programs will require licenses for dozens of patents, and this will make them infeasible. This problem has only one solution: software patents must be eliminated.

Until recently, patents were not used in the software field. Software developers copyrighted individual programs or made them trade secrets. Copyright was traditionally understood to cover the implementation details of a particular program; it did not cover the features of the program, or the general methods used. And trade secrecy, by definition, could not prohibit any development work by someone who did not know the secret.

On this basis, software development was extremely profitable, and received considerable investment, without any prohibition on independent software development. But this scheme of things is no more. A change in U.S. government policy in the early 1980's stimulated a flood of applications. Now many have been approved, and the rate is accelerating.

The Patent Office and the courts have had a difficult time with computer software. Patent examiners are often ill-prepared to evaluate software patent applications to determine if they represent techniques that are widely known or obvious—both of which are grounds for rejection.

Their task is made more difficult because many commonly-used software techniques do not appear in the scientific literature of computer science. Some seemed too obvious to publish while others seemed insufficiently general; some were open secrets.

Computer scientists know many techniques that can be generalized to widely varying circumstances. But the Patent Office seems to believe that each separate use of a technique is a candidate for a new patent. For example, Apple was sued because the Hypercard program allegedly violates patent number 4,736,308, a patent that covers displaying portions of two or more strings together on the screen—effectively, scrolling with multiple subwindows. Scrolling and subwindows are well-known techniques, but combining them is now apparently illegal.

For example, the technique of using exclusive-or to write a cursor onto a screen is both well known and obvious. (Its advantage is that another identical exclusive-or operation can be used to erase the cursor without damaging the other data on the screen.) This technique can be implemented in a few lines of a program, and a clever high school student might well reinvent it. But it is covered by patent number 4,197,590, which has been upheld twice in court even though the technique was used at least five years before the patent application. Cadtrak, the company that owns this patent, collects millions of dollars from large computer manufacturers.

English patents covering customary graphics techniques, including airbrushing, stenciling, and combination of two images under control of a third one, were recently upheld in court, despite the testimony of the pioneers of the field that they had developed these techniques years before. (The corresponding United States patents, including 4,633,416 and 4,602,286, have not yet been tested in court, but they probably will be soon.)

Nothing protects programmers from accidentally using a technique that is patented, and then being sued for it. Computer programming is fundamentally different from the other fields that the patent system previously covered.

Patent examiners and judges are accustomed to considering even small, incremental changes as deserving new patents. For example, the famous *Polaroid vs. Kodak* case hinged on differences in the number and order of layers of chemicals in a film—differences between the technique Kodak was using and those described by previous, expired patents. The court ruled that these differences were unobvious.

Computer scientists solve problems quickly because the medium of programming is tractable. They are trained to generalize solution principles from one problem to another. One such generalization is that a procedure can be repeated or subdivided. Programmers consider this obvious—but the Patent Office did not think that it was obvious when it granted the patent on scrolling multiple strings, described above.

Cases such as this cannot be considered errors. The patent system is functioning as it was designed to do—but with software, it produces outrageous results.

Sometimes it is possible to patent a technique that is not new precisely because it is obvious—so obvious that no one would have published a paper about it.

For example, computer companies distributing the free X Window System developed by MIT are now being threatened with lawsuits by AT & T over patent number 4,555,775, covering the use of "backing store" in a window system that lets multiple programs have windows. Backing store means that the contents of a window that is temporarily partly hidden are saved in off-screen memory, so they can be restored quickly if the obscuring window disappears.

Early window systems were developed on computers that could not run two programs at once. These computers had small memories, so saving window contents was obviously a waste of scarce memory space. Later, larger multiprocessing computers led to the use of backing store, and to permitting each program to have its own windows. The combination was inevitable.

The technique of backing store was used at MIT in the Lisp Machine System before AT & T applied for a patent. (By coincidence, the Lisp Machine also supported multiprocessing.) The Lisp Machine developers published nothing about backing store at the time, considering it too obvious. It was mentioned when a programmers' manual explained how to turn it on and off.

But this manual was published one week after the AT & T patent application—too late to count as prior art to defeat the patent. So the AT & T patent may stand, and MIT may be forbidden to continue using a method that MIT used before AT & T.

The result is that the dozens of companies and hundreds of thousands of users who accepted the software from MIT on the understanding that it was free are now faced with possible lawsuits. (They are also being threatened with Cadtrak's exclusive-or patent.) The X Window System project was intended to develop a window system that all developers could use freely. This public service goal seems to have been thwarted by patents.

Why Software Is Different

Software systems are much easier to design than hardware systems of the same number of components. For example, a program of 100,000 components might be 50,000 lines long and could be written by two good programmers in a year. The equipment needed for this costs less than $10,000; the only other cost would be the programmers' own living expenses while doing the job. The total investment would be less than a

$100,000. If done commercially in a large company, it might cost twice that. By contrast, an automobile typically contains under 100,000 components; it requires a large team and costs tens of millions of dollars to design.

And software is also much cheaper to manufacture: copies can be made easily on an ordinary workstation costing under ten thousand dollars. To produce a complex hardware system often requires a factory costing tens of millions of dollars.

There will be little benefit to society from software patents because invention in software was already flourishing before software patents, and inventions were normally published in journals for everyone to use. Invention flourished so strongly, in fact, that the same inventions were often found again and again.

The field of software is one of constant reinvention; as some people say, programmers throw away more "inventions" each week than other people develop in a year. And the comparative ease of designing large software systems makes it easy for many people to do work in the field. A programmer solves many problems in developing each program. These solutions are likely to be reinvented frequently as other programmers tackle similar problems.

The prevalence of independent reinvention negates the usual purpose of patents. Patents are intended to encourage inventions and, above all, the disclosure of inventions. If a technique will be reinvented frequently, there is no need to encourage more people to invent it; since some of the developers will choose to publish it (if publication is merited), there is no point in encouraging a particular inventor to publish it—not at the cost of inhibiting use of the technique.

Much software innovation comes from programmers solving problems while developing software, not from projects whose specific purpose is to make inventions and obtain patents. When patents make development more difficult, and cut down on development projects, they will also cut down on the byproducts of development—new techniques.

Although software patents in general are harmful to society as a whole, we do not claim that every single software patent is necessarily harmful. Careful study might show that under certain specific and narrow conditions (necessarily excluding the vast majority of cases) it is beneficial to grant software patents.

Nonetheless, the right thing to do now is to eliminate all software patents as soon as possible, before more damage is done. The careful study can come afterward.

If it is ever shown that software patents are beneficial in certain exceptional cases, the law can be changed again at that time—if it is important enough. There is no reason to continue the present catastrophic situation until that day.

Notes and Questions

1. Consider the *U.S.* and *UK Business Methods* cases in light of the above articles. Given your earlier analysis of these cases, and the problems they present, should patent protection be extended to software? What is the strongest argument you can make that patent protection should be extended? What is the strongest argument against such protection?

2. What if patent protection for software were left to each country's discretion? What would be the economic impact of this decision? Would investment in research and development in the field continue? At the same rate?

3. What response would you make to the foregoing articles if you represented Microsoft?

THE VIRTUAL COP CASE

SEGA ENTERPRISES LTD v. GALAXY ELECTRONICS PTY LTD

Federal Court of Australia, New South Wales
District Registry, General Division, 1996.

BURCHETT, J.

Each of these proceedings raises, as a separate question, a problem of the meaning and possible application of the definition of "cinematograph film" in § 10(1) of the Copyright Act 1968, as amplified by § 24. Are the applicants' video games, involving computer-generated images, cinematograph films within the definition? The answer to this question is vital because, if they are not, it is accepted that the applicants' cases meet an insuperable obstacle in *Avel Pty Ltd. v. Wells* (1992) 36 FCR 340.

There are two video games with which the cases are concerned, one entitled "Virtua Cop" and the other "Daytona U.S.A". Each presents on the video screen a series of images resembling, more or less, a traditional movie film. In the case of Virtua Cop, an extremely simple but violent tale is told of assaults by police upon a criminal organisation. In the case of Daytona U.S.A, what is involved is car racing. The parties were agreed that it is sufficient to concentrate upon Virtua Cop, since the two video games are constructed upon the same principle. In Virtua Cop, the protagonists are two police officers (with whom the players of the game identify) whose investigations are resisted, first, at a cargo wharf, next, at a construction site, and finally at their antagonists' evil headquarters. To begin with, there is a brief introduction, followed by the main part of the game in which the player must keep shooting quickly and accurately, with a make-believe weapon or "input" device, at the correct villainous targets, so that the various assaults will progress according to the script. At the end, there is a triumphant finale, when the police congratulate each other and the dastards are led away in handcuffed defeat. Only the successful player will reach this denouement, and only the very skilled can possibly do so without numerous setbacks along the way, caused by misdirected responses, or failures to respond, to the actions depicted on the screen. For example, if the player's shot misses a criminal, the player may himself be shot by the criminal; and if this happens a predetermined number of times, the assault fails, and the game ends. Also, each time a criminal is merely winged, he may react differently, depending on where he has been hit. Thus, except for the opening and closing sequences, the events represented on the screen will show differences from screening to screening, except where the player's responses are all correct.

What this means, it will be appreciated, is that the apparatus is designed to screen the simple story only when the correct responses to a series of cues are fed into it by the player; and when incorrect responses are given, a number of variations will result.

I was provided with a considerable amount of evidence concerning the manner in which Virtua Cop was created. Sega Enterprises Ltd formed a team to do this. Graphic designers developed the scenes, and representations of the characters. In doing so, they made drawings and models, and decided, for instance, how a particular character would walk. Sets were made up. A "test version" was prepared on a computer and copied onto a video tape. Further detailed sketches of scenes to be depicted on the screen were prepared by hand. These sketches were used as the basis for the preparation of the computer programme, according to which particular scenes were ultimately enabled to be depicted on the screen. The programme itself was extremely sophisticated. It calculated the three-dimensional position of each part of each object and character at each stage of all movements. An example of the sophistication involved is the windscreen of a car, which is shown three-dimensionally, with a superimposed two-dimensional image of a reflection of the sky appearing on it.

Sound effects, music, and very simple dialogue were also required. Over eighty sound effects were selected from a sound library or created, and then manipulated, for inclusion in the programme. Dialogue was recorded, and that recording was also manipulated and included in the programme. Music was added after composition on a synthesiser.

When all the work had been completed and was brought together, it was represented by a highly specialised piece of computer equipment, suitable, and suitable only, for bringing Virtua Cop to the screen. Although, as I have said, sketches, models and video tape were used in the course of the creation of the programme, in the finished product, the screen images were not represented by anything comparable to the tiny translucent images which characterise the original technology of cinematograph film. A closer analogy could be drawn to video tape, containing magnetic fields that may be transformed into visual images upon a screen. But the respondents argue that even this analogy misses the mark. According to their contention, Virtua Cop is not represented in any form until it is born on the screen out of the union between the player's input and the computer programme that calculates the three-dimensional reference points, not images, by reference to which the images themselves are made to appear on the screen. The respondents say that the visual images were not stored in any manner; mathematical co-ordinates of models of objects, together with animation and texture mapping data, were stored in digital form, and are used by the controlling programme to create images on the screen. In doing so, the respondents say, the "microcomputer controls the sequence of visual displays and aural effects in response to a player's actions and this generates a different game play for each player within the overall limitations of objects and scenes available to be generated by the controlling program". Thus, they contend, "the visual imagery ... is an artifact of real-time computer graphics in that the images on the screen are synthesised on the fly by the controlling program". On this basis, their argument asserts it is "not correct to say that the 2–dimensional screen images themselves are stored in the computer like some form of 'digital movie' and simply played back during the game".

The provisions of the Copyright Act 1968 with which this case is centrally concerned are the definition of "cinematograph film" in § 10(1), and the amplification of that definition which is to be found in § 24. Section 10(1) provides:

"In this Act, unless the contrary intention appears— ... 'cinematograph film' means the aggregate of the visual images embodied in an article or thing so as to be capable by the use of that article or thing–

(a) of being shown as a moving picture; or

(b) of being embodied in another article or thing by the use of which it can be so shown, and includes the aggregate of the sounds embodied in a sound-track associated with such visual images". § 24 provides:

"For the purposes of this Act, sounds or visual images shall be taken to have been embodied in an article or thing if the article or thing has been so treated in relation to those sounds or visual images that those sounds or visual images are capable, with or without the aid of some other device, of being reproduced from the article or thing."

The expert evidence adduced by the respondents appeared to seize upon the expression "the visual images embodied in an article or thing". Plainly enough, what is seen by the viewer is shown as a moving picture; but the point made was "that there does not exist inside the computer anywhere a 2–dimensional image [of what appears on the screen]. That 2–dimensional image is simply computed from looking at all the three-dimensional vertices of the polygon model [this is a reference to the way in which the computer apprehends objects] and doing what is a clever arithmetic on it".

To narrow the sense of the word so as to confine an embodiment of a visual image to something in the nature of a frame, of which the image on the screen is a reflection, would be to introduce a limiting concept not inherent in the language. The phonetic symbols on paper to which Lord Cranworth alluded did not directly reflect words. Sumerian cuneiform or

Egyptian hieroglyphics would have come closer to doing so. But, in reality, writing is a code which the brain interprets, just as the computer in the present case interprets coded co-ordinates and input data which it "reads" as visual images on the screen.

In the case of copyright in a film, the legislative history shows plainly that Parliament did intend to take a broad view, and not to tie the copyright to any particular technology. The often cited Gregory Report of 1952, presented to the Parliament of the United Kingdom, attests this. By para 93, attention was drawn to developments in recording technology. The committee commented:

"Further, it can no longer be assumed that the reproduction of visual effects must be preceded by photographs, and we are given to understand that even now it is possible to record on a magnetic tape a spectacle which can be reproduced visually as a television programme. Accordingly, in drafting provisions relating to records, cinematograph films and such matters, we consider that the wording adopted should have regard to the end-product (e.g. sound or visual representation) rather than to the means whereby these effects are produced."

Similarly, in Australia, the second reading speech of the Attorney–General, Mr. NH Bowen QC (as he then was), in relation to the Copyright Bill 1968 includes the following (Hansard (1968), House of Representatives, 1534):

"For many purposes, ordinary cinematograph film and videotape are interchangeable. Thus a scene may be recorded by a television camera on videotape and the videotape later copied on to [an] ordinary cinematograph film. The incidents recorded may be seen either by viewing the videotape on a television screen or by viewing the cinematograph film on a cinema screen. The Bill therefore assimilates videotape to ordinary cinematograph film for the purposes of copyright protection and the term 'cinematograph film' appearing in the Bill is defined as including videotape."

An important additional matter of context, bearing on the construction of the definition of "cinematograph film", is the definition in § 10(1) of "copy". For this, "in relation to a cinematograph film, means any article or thing in which the visual images or sounds comprising the film are embodied". It cannot have been intended that the word "embodied" should, in this definition, have a meaning which would allow computer technology, of the kind employed in the present case, to be utilised to mimic with impunity, for example, a new animated film of the "Mickey Mouse" variety. Dr. Lambert, a suitably qualified expert called on behalf of the applicants, gave evidence that some existing movies could be reproduced by object based encoding, and I can see no reason to doubt the feasibility of this being done, now or at least at some time in the expanding future of the technology. An "infringing copy" of a cinematograph film, as defined in § 10(1), must be "a copy of the film". It would be strange indeed if Parliament intended the definition of "copy" to be construed so narrowly that a representation of an animated film, which looked just like the film, would not constitute an infringement, simply because it was produced by the computer technology involved in the present case.

But the respondents refer to the provisions of the Copyright Act and of the Circuit Layouts Act 1989 which were in question in *Avel Pty Ltd. v. Wells* (1991) 105 ALR 635; and on appeal, (1992) 36 FCR 340, to argue that the integrated circuits involved in this case must find their protection, if at all, in those provisions. I do not accept this argument. The fact that there are here integrated circuits, and that these give rise to the application of particular statutory provisions, does not subtract from the further, and relevant, fact that the use of the integrated circuits is capable of bringing to the screen, so as to be shown as a moving picture, the aggregate of visual images making up Virtua Cop. That attracts the operation of the provisions of the Copyright Act in respect of cinematograph films.

Then the respondents return to the proposition that a cinematograph film must utilize frames, as, of course, the original moving pictures produced by photographic processes did. But it seems to me that this involves the fallacy of confusing the means with the ends. A cinematograph film is "shown as a moving picture". That is how it appears to the viewer. But the means by which the effect is produced are not the effect, and it may be accepted that the frames involved in the original technology may not be essential to the production of the effect by other technologies, such as computer graphics.

Although the Acts in force in the United Kingdom and South Africa today differ from the Australian legislation, it is interesting to note that *Joynson-Hicks on UK Copyright Law* (1989) at para 1.49 states:

"As with sound recordings, neither the medium from which the moving image may be produced, nor the means of producing the image is relevant. For that reason again, computer programs and in particular many computer games, could be protected as films, as well as in their own right."

And the Supreme Court of South Africa has held in *Nintendo Co Ltd. v. Golden China TV–Game Centre* (1993) 28 IPR 313 that a computer generated video game is, within the meaning of the South African legislation, a cinematograph film.

I have concluded that the applicants are entitled to succeed on the separate question, but the only order I make at this stage is to direct them to bring in, on a date to be fixed, short minutes of appropriate orders. The respondents must bear the costs.

Notes and Questions

1.   Under Australian copyright law, the term "literary work" in Section 10 specifically includes "a computer program or compilation of computer programs". This definition, however, does not apply in the *Virtua Cop* case

because it does not cover moving images that are generated by integrated circuits. Under Section 24(2) of the Circuit Layouts Act of 1989, the protection of such images are excluded from copyright protection. Thus, if the video game at issue in *Galaxy Electronics* did not qualify as a cinematographic film, the unauthorized reproductions of the graphics would not be challengeable under Australia's copyright laws.

2. One of the problems in treating computer software under "traditional" copyright analysis is the unique nature of the program. The "cinematographic" work in the *Virtua Cop* case is actually the video output of the underlying code. This output is generated by the code itself (which also generates the non-literal aspects of the program). This code is closer to a "literary work" even though in object code form it is not capable of being read by a human agent. Theoretically, identical screen displays can be generated by codes that are *not* identical. What impact, if any should these differences have upon a party's liability for copyright infringement? What if the screen displays generated by the video game program were not action oriented, but a simple display of a tic-tac-toe board? Would this board also qualify as a "cinematographic" work?

3. Because of the uneasy fit between computer software programs and "traditional" categories of copyrighted works, many countries protected software under sui generis regimes. *See* for example, South Africa, Russia, Korea, Brazil. Are these regimes in violation of TRIPS or the WIPO Copyright Treaty?

4. Judge Burchett's decision was ultimately upheld on appeal, *Galaxy Electronics Pty (Ltd) v. Sega Enterprises*, 1997 Aust. Fed Ct LEXIS 241 (1997).

5. Who is the author of the "cinematographic work" in the *Virtua Cop* case? The programmer? The player? Both? What if the program at issue were created by artificial intelligence? Does the Berne Convention establish the test for deciding authorship in these cases?

Read the following Articles from the Software Directive from the Supplement: 1, 2, 4, 5, 6, 9.

Notes and Questions

1. Does this Directive establish an appropriate balance between protection and access? What changes, if any, would you make if this Directive were instead the language of a draft multinational treaty?

2. The Software Directive reflects the intense lobbying efforts of various members of the international computer industry. Do you agree with the guidelines it established for permissible reverse engineering?

3. Why is reverse engineering precluded under patent law and generally permitted under trade secret law? Should it be permitted in all cases regardless of whether the work is otherwise IP-protected?

THE U.S. REVERSE ENGINEERING CASE
SEGA ENTERPRISES LTD. v. ACCOLADE, INC.

United States Court of Appeals, Ninth Circuit, 1992.
977 F.2d 1510.

REINHARDT, CIRCUIT JUDGE:

This case presents several difficult questions of first impression involving our copyright laws. We are asked determine whether the Copyright Act permits persons who are neither copyright holders nor licensees to disassemble a copyrighted computer program in order to gain an understanding of the unprotected functional elements of the program.

Plaintiff-appellee Sega Enterprises, Ltd. ("Sega"), a Japanese corporation, and its subsidiary, Sega of America, develop and market video entertainment systems, including the "Genesis" console (distributed in Asia under the name "Mega-Drive") and video game cartridges. Defendant-appellant Accolade, Inc., is an independent developer, manufacturer, and marketer of computer entertainment software, including game cartridges that are compatible with the Genesis console, as well as game cartridges that are compatible with other computer systems.

Sega licenses its copyrighted computer code and its "SEGA" trademark to a number of independent developers of computer game software. Those licensees develop and sell Genesis-compatible video games in competition with Sega. Accolade is not and never has been a licensee of Sega. Prior to rendering its own games compatible with the Genesis console, Accolade explored the possibility of entering into a licensing agreement with Sega, but abandoned the effort because the agreement would have required that Sega be the exclusive manufacturer of all games produced by Accolade.

Accolade used a two-step process to render its video games compatible with the Genesis console. First, it "reverse engineered" Sega's video game programs in order to discover the requirements for compatibility with the Genesis console. As part of the reverse engineering process, Accolade transformed the machine-readable object code contained in commercially available copies of Sega's game cartridges into human-readable source code using a process called "disassembly" or "decompilation".[2] Accolade purchased a Genesis console and three Sega game

---

2. Computer programs are written in specialized alphanumeric languages, or "source code". In order to operate a computer, source code must be translated into computer readable form, or "object code". Object code uses only two symbols, 0 and 1, in combinations which represent the alphanumeric characters of the source code. A program written in source code is translated into object code using a computer program called an "assembler" or "compiler", and then imprinted onto a silicon chip for commercial distribution. Devices called "disassemblers" or "decompilers" can reverse this process by "reading" the electronic signals for "0" and "1" that are produced while the program is being run, storing the resulting object code in computer memory, and translating the object code into source code. Both assembly and disas-

cartridges, wired a decompiler into the console circuitry, and generated printouts of the resulting source code. Accolade engineers studied and annotated the printouts in order to identify areas of commonality among the three game programs. They then loaded the disassembled code back into a computer, and experimented to discover the interface specifications for the Genesis console by modifying the programs and studying the results. At the end of the reverse engineering process, Accolade created a development manual that incorporated the information it had discovered about the requirements for a Genesis-compatible game. According to the Accolade employees who created the manual, the manual contained only functional descriptions of the interface requirements and did not include any of Sega's code.

In the second stage, Accolade created its own games for the Genesis. According to Accolade, at this stage it did not copy Sega's programs, but relied only on the information concerning interface specifications for the Genesis that was contained in its development manual. Accolade maintains that with the exception of the interface specifications, none of the code in its own games is derived in any way from its examination of Sega's code.

We have previously held that the Copyright Act does not distinguish between unauthorized copies of a copyrighted work on the basis of what stage of the alleged infringer's work the unauthorized copies represent. *Walker v. University Books*, 602 F.2d 859, 864 (9th Cir.1979) ("[T]he fact that an allegedly infringing copy of a protected work may itself be only an inchoate representation of some final product to be marketed commercially does not in itself negate the possibility of infringement."). Our holding in *Walker* was based on the plain language of the Act. Section 106 grants to the copyright owner the exclusive rights "to reproduce the work in copies", "to prepare derivative works based upon the copyrighted work", and to authorize the preparation of copies and derivative works. 17 U.S.C. s 106(1)(2). Section 501 provides that "[a]nyone who violates any of the exclusive rights of the copyright owner as provided by sections 106 through 118 is an infringer of the copyright." Id. § 501(a). On its face, that language unambiguously encompasses and proscribes "intermediate copying". *Walker*, 602 F.2d at 86364.

In order to constitute a "copy" for purposes of the Act, the allegedly infringing work must be fixed in some tangible form, "from which the work can be perceived, reproduced, or otherwise communicated, either directly or with the aid of a machine or device." 17 U.S.C. § 101. The computer file generated by the disassembly program, the printouts of the disassembled code, and the computer files containing Accolade's modifications of the code that were generated during the reverse engineering process all satisfy that requirement. The intermediate copying done by

sembly devices are commercially available, and both types of devices are widely used within the software industry.

Accolade therefore falls squarely within the category of acts that are prohibited by the statute.

In light of the unambiguous language of the Act, we decline to depart from the rule set forth in *Walker* for copyrighted works generally. Accordingly, we hold that intermediate copying of computer object code may infringe the exclusive rights granted to the copyright owner in section 106 of the Copyright Act regardless of whether the end product of the copying also infringes those rights. If intermediate copying is permissible under the Act, authority for such copying must be found in one of the statutory provisions to which the rights granted in section 106 are subject.

Accolade contends, that its disassembly of copyrighted object code as a necessary step in its examination of the unprotected ideas and functional concepts embodied in the code is a fair use that is privileged by section 107 of the Act. Because, in the case before us, disassembly is the only means of gaining access to those unprotected aspects of the program, and because Accolade has a legitimate interest in gaining such access (in order to determine how to make its cartridges compatible with the Genesis console), we agree with Accolade. Where there is good reason for studying or examining the unprotected aspects of a copyrighted computer program, disassembly for purposes of such study or examination constitutes a fair use.

Section 107 lists the factors to be considered in determining whether a particular use is a fair one. Those factors include: (1) the purpose and character of the use, including whether such use is of a commercial nature or is for nonprofit educational purposes; (2) the nature of the copyrighted work; (3) the amount and substantiality of the portion used in relation to the copyrighted work as a whole; and (4) the effect of the use upon the potential market for or value of the copyrighted work. 17 U.S.C. § 107. The statutory factors are not exclusive. Rather, the doctrine of fair use is in essence "an equitable rule of reason." *Harper & Row, Publishers, Inc. v. Nation Enterprises,* 471 U.S. 539, 560, 105 S.Ct. 2218, 2230, 85 L.Ed.2d 588 (1985) (quoting H.R.Rep. No. 1476, 94th Cong., 2d Sess. 65, *reprinted in* 1976 U.S.C.C.A.N. 5659, 5679).

Unlike the defendant in *Harper & Row,* which printed excerpts from President Ford's memoirs verbatim with the stated purpose of "scooping" a Time magazine review of the book, 471 U.S. at 562, 105 S.Ct. at 2231, Accolade did not attempt to "scoop" Sega's release of any particular game or games, but sought only to become a legitimate competitor in the field of Genesis-compatible video games. Within that market, it is the characteristics of the game program as experienced by the user that determine the program's commercial success. As we have noted, there is nothing in the record that suggests that Accolade copied any of those elements.

By facilitating the entry of a new competitor, the first lawful one that is not a Sega licensee, Accolade's disassembly of Sega's software undoubtedly "affected" the market for Genesis-compatible games in an indirect fashion. We note, however, that while no consumer except the most avid devotee of President Ford's regime might be expected to buy more than one version of the President's memoirs, video game users typically purchase more than one game. There is no basis for assuming that Accolade's "Ishido" has significantly affected the market for Sega's "Altered Beast", since a consumer might easily purchase both; nor does it seem unlikely that a consumer particularly interested in sports might purchase both Accolade's "Mike Ditka Power Football" and Sega's "Joe Montana Football", particularly if the games are, as Accolade contends, not substantially similar. In any event, an attempt to monopolize the market by making it impossible for others to compete runs counter to the statutory purpose of promoting creative expression and cannot constitute a strong equitable basis for resisting the invocation of the fair use doctrine. Thus, we conclude that the fourth statutory factor weighs in Accolade's, not Sega's, favor, notwithstanding the minor economic loss Sega may suffer.

The second statutory factor, the nature of the copyrighted work, reflects the fact that not all copyrighted works are entitled to the same level of protection. The protection established by the Copyright Act for original works of authorship does not extend to the ideas underlying a work or to the functional or factual aspects of the work. 17 U.S.C. § 102(b). To the extent that a work is functional or factual, it may be copied, as may those expressive elements of the work that "must necessarily be used as incident to" expression of the underlying ideas, functional concepts, or facts.

Computer programs pose unique problems for the application of the "idea/expression distinction" that determines the extent of copyright protection. To the extent that there are many possible ways of accomplishing a given task or fulfilling a particular market demand, the programmer's choice of program structure and design may be highly creative and idiosyncratic. However, computer programs are, in essence, utilitarian articles—articles that accomplish tasks. As such, they contain many logical, structural, and visual display elements that are dictated by the function to be performed, by considerations of efficiency, or by external factors such as compatibility requirements and industry demands. In some circumstances, even the exact set of commands used by the programmer is deemed functional rather than creative for purposes of copyright. "[W]hen specific instructions, even though previously copyrighted, are the only and essential means of accomplishing a given task, their later use by another will not amount to infringement." CONTU Report at 20; see CAI, 23 U.S.P.Q.2d at 1254.

Because of the hybrid nature of computer programs, there is no settled standard for identifying what is protected expression and what is unprotected idea in a case involving the alleged infringement of a copyright in computer software.

Because Sega's video game programs contain unprotected aspects that cannot be examined without copying, we afford them a lower degree of protection than more traditional literary works. We conclude that the second statutory factor also weighs in favor of Accolade.

As to the third statutory factor, Accolade disassembled entire programs written by Sega. Accordingly, the third factor weighs against Accolade. The fact that an entire work was copied does not, however, preclude a finding a fair use. In fact, where the ultimate (as opposed to direct) use is as limited as it was here, the factor is of very little weight.

In summary, careful analysis of the purpose and characteristics of Accolade's use of Sega's video game programs, the nature of the computer programs involved, and the nature of the market for video game cartridges yields the conclusion that the first, second, and fourth statutory fair use factors weigh in favor of Accolade, while only the third weighs in favor of Sega, and even then only slightly. Accordingly, Accolade clearly has by far the better case on the fair use issue.

When technological change has rendered an aspect or application of the Copyright Act ambiguous, "the Copyright Act must be construed in light of this basic purpose." As discussed above, the fact that computer programs are distributed for public use in object code form often precludes public access to the ideas and functional concepts contained in those programs, and thus confers on the copyright owner a de facto monopoly over those ideas and functional concepts. That result defeats the fundamental purpose of the Copyright Act—to encourage the production of original works by protecting the expressive elements of those works while leaving the ideas, facts, and functional concepts in the public domain for others to build on.

We conclude that where disassembly is the only way to gain access to the ideas and functional elements embodied in a copyrighted computer program and where there is a legitimate reason for seeking such access, disassembly is a fair use of the copyrighted work, as a matter of law. Our conclusion does not, of course, insulate Accolade from a claim of copyright infringement with respect to its finished products. Sega has reserved the right to raise such a claim, and it may do so on remand.

THE SINGAPORE REVERSE
ENGINEERING CASE

CREATIVE TECHNOLOGY LTD. v.
AZTECH SYSTEMS PTE LTD.

Court of Appeal of the Republic of Singapore, 1996.
[1997] FSR 491.

THE COURT OF APPEAL OF THE REPUBLIC OF SINGAPORE:

This is an appeal from the judgment of the Judicial Commissioner Lim Teong Qwee sitting in the High Court, dated October 24, 1994. In those proceedings, the appellants ("Creative") counterclaimed, *inter alia*, that the respondents ("Aztech") had disassembled and copied a substantial portion of the firmware which is housed in the microprocessor of the

Creative Sound Blaster Card; and that their copyright in TEST.SBC (a program ancillary to and supplied with the Sound Blaster package) was infringed when it was unlawfully copied for the purpose of effecting assembly through the running of the DEBUG program. Aztech in turn denied disassembling the firmware and argued that such copying of the TEST.SBC program was a fair dealing for the purpose of research or private study under section 35(1) Singapore Copyright Act (Cap 63) ("SCA"). Furthermore it was argued by Aztech that being the lawful owners of TEST.SBC they were entitled to use it for any reasonable purpose, including the purpose of investigating how it interacted with the Sound Blaster card, relying principally on *Betts v. Willmott* (1871) LC 6 Ch App 239.

It was held by the Judicial Commissioner that, in relation to the firmware, Aztech had not been shown to have had access to the firmware program which is usually secured by way of a fuse, and that they had successfully explained away apparent similarities in both programs. He further held that the copying of TEST.SBC by Aztech constituted fair dealing for the purpose of private study under section 35 SCA, and that such use for experimentation was one of the rights of ownership implied in the software licence.

Creative manufacture and sell "Sound Blaster" sound cards. The sound card is an "add-on" product, a circuit board that can be inserted into a personal computer ("PC"). The sound card generates sounds through a speaker system by means of a digital signal processor ("DSP") and a digital-to-analog converter ("DAC"). When an applications program runs on a PC and requires sound, it sends commands to a software program in a driver for conversion into low-level commands. These commands are sent to the DSP, and subsequently on to the DAC where the data are converted into sound through the speaker system. For the DSP, Creative used an Intel 8051 chip. The firmware program was burnt into the ROM of this chip. The other program of significance is TEST. SBC, which formed part of the ancillary executable software that was supplied with every purchase of the Soundblaster sound card.

Aztech, who are also commercial developers of sound cards, developed a sound card, "Sound Galaxy" (in three versions, "Sound Galaxy BX", "Sound Galaxy NX" and "Sound galaxy NX PRO"), which was compatible or interoperable with the application programs that have been developed to operate with Sound Blaster. Sound Galaxy is thus a competing product, providing the same functionality as Creative's Sound Blaster card, with additional capabilities. Like the Sound Blaster sound card, Sound Galaxy sound cards also make use of the Intel 8051 chip, a DAC and a FM synthesizer. It also has its own firmware burned into the ROM by the manufacturer of the chip.

Creative developed two versions for their Sound Blaster sound card, and this was matched by Aztech. Version 1 ("Sound Galaxy BX" and "Sound Galaxy NX") of Aztech's card was available by March 1992.

Creative launched the second version of their firmware on or about March 1992. Aztech released their second version by August 1992. To this version Aztech added two more test commands. At the end of phase 2 Aztech's card was capable of responding in a sophisticated way to a full range of Creative's undocumented commands. Creative further asserted that it was during this phase that Aztech most likely had access to and disassembled its sound blaster firmware.

It is Creative's contention that most of the evidence of disassembly occurred in the six months, during which Aztech significantly modified their sound card firmware and moved from partial to full sound blaster compatibility and which was the period described as "phase 2" above. It was submitted that in this phase, the "fingerprints" of disassembly could clearly be seen. The attention of the Court was specifically directed at five undocumented commands (instructions which are sent to operate the micro-controller) that were fully implemented for the first time in phase 2.

We have considered all the evidence adduced in the court below, and form the view, after consultation with the appointed assessor that the similarities between Creative's and Aztech's firmwares are such that the chance of independent development is low. We have accordingly come to the conclusion that it was highly probable that disassembly had taken place. Aztech did infringe the copyright of Creative.

It is our view that Aztech had the means and sufficient time to extract the relevant program from the Sound Blaster card, to disassemble raw data, and to analyse the commands of interest. They had at least four months to perform the acts of extraction and disassembly.

With disassembly, raw numbers from the firmware will be converted into text, which reveals the instructions specified by the numbers. It should be noted that disassembly does not present a copy-perfect source code complete with names and helpful comments. Even with disassembly the functionality of the program in question is not immediately clear. The numbers are primarily converted into commands, which then have to be analysed by a programmer to understand what the program does. Much of this depends on the size and complexity of the program.

The evidence suggests that the computer program underlying the Sound Blaster card is not complex, but is highly structured in that there is a separate set of instructions for each command which the card can perform.

Contrary to evidence produced by Aztech that it is necessary to analyse the entire program to obtain useful information, Dr. Nichols has expressed the view that the four primary commands at issue in these proceedings are independent of each other and any other routine in the program. They can be analysed independently; and this exercise would, according to Dr. Nichols, take the average programmer less than a week for all four commands. In his opinion, if Aztech had obtained a Sound Blaster board with a Matra part, they could have extracted the code and analysed the commands of interest in about one month.

We now turn to the substantial issues of law in this appeal. Creative alleged that, when investigating the E2 command, Aztech copied the whole of the TEST.SBC program, through running it with the DEBUG program, for the purpose, they claim, of "understanding functionality in order to make a non-infringing, compatible product." This was admitted by Aztech at trial. The Judicial Commissioner said: "To run a program it has to be downloaded to the PC, *i.e.* copied to its memory. There can be no doubt that the software program in TEST–SBC has been copied by running it with DEBUG when investigating the E2H command and I so find."

Such copying was found to be lawful by the Judicial Commissioner, on two grounds; (a) fair dealing for the purposes of research and private study under section 35(1) SCA; and (b) use of copyrighted software for a reasonable purpose as implied by licence: *Betts v. Willmott* (1871) LC 6 Ch App 239.

It is useful to set out an overview of software copyright protection in Singapore. Computer programs are protectable under the SCA as a type of "literary work". Section 7(1) defines a computer program as:

an expression, in any language, code or notation, of a set of instructions (whether with or without related information) intended, either directly or after either or both of the following:

(a) conversion to another language, code or notation;

(b) reproduction in a different material form,

to cause a device having information processing capabilities to perform a particular function.

The above definition, which is *in pari materia* with the definition found in the Australian Copyright Act 1968 (as amended), removes any doubt that might remain as to whether the source code and object code of a computer program are both protected by copyright in Singapore. Under section 26 SCA, generally the exclusive rights granted to the software copyright owner include, *inter alia*, the right to reproduce the computer program in a material form. By section 17 of the SCA, a reproduction of a computer program includes storage thereof in a computer, and the right to make an adaptation thereof. By section 7(1) of the SCA, an "adaptation" means a version of the computer program, not being a reproduction thereof, whether or not in the language, code or notation in which the computer program was originally expressed.

The scope of software copyright protection is limited by certain defences contained in the SCA. [S]ection 39(3) provides that it is not an infringement for the owner of a computer program to make or authorise the making of another copy or adaptation of that computer program provided that such a new copy or adaptation is created as an essential step in the utilisation of the program in conjunction with a machine. The other important defence, for the purposes of this appeal is the defence of "fair dealing for the purpose of research or private study", under section 35 of the SCA. It is this issue to which we now turn.

The Judicial Commissioner accepted that although the running of TEST.SBC involved copying, such an act did not constitute copyright infringement under section 35 SCA, which provides so far as it is relevant as follows:

35(1) A fair dealing with a literary work ... for the purpose of research or private study shall not constitute an infringement of copyright.

(2) For the purposes of this Act, the matters to which regard shall be had, in determining whether a dealing with a literary ... work ... constitutes a fair dealing with the work ... for the purpose of research or private study shall include—

(a) the purpose and character of the dealing, including whether such dealing is of a commercial nature or is for non-profit educational purposes;

(b) the nature of the work or adaptation;

(c) the amount and substantiality of the part copied taken in relation to the whole work or adaptation; and

(d) the effect of the dealing upon the potential market for, or value of, the work ...

. . .

(5) In this section, "research" shall not include commercial research, research carried out by bodies corporate (not being bodies corporate owned or controlled by the Government), companies, associations or bodies of persons carrying on a business.

We agree with the Judicial Commissioner that this section involves two separate questions. First, was the use for the purpose of research or private study? Second, was the use fair?

RESEARCH OR PRIVATE STUDY

Despite the statutory exclusion of "commercial research" in section 35(5) SCA the Judicial Commissioner held that the copying of TEST.SBC could be brought under the wording of section 35(1) SCA, since some private study for commercial purposes may yet count as a defence to a claim for infringement. Moreover, "research" and "study" are qualified differently; the two qualifications being that "research" should exclude that undertaken by companies and bodies corporate; and "study" should be private. The Judicial Commissioner said: "Mr. Loh and his colleagues in the R & D department might have been engaged in research but that does not rule out the possibility that the purpose might also have been 'study' ".

The Judicial Commissioner was influenced by the argument that since the court is required, when deciding whether the research or private study was "fair" to have regard, *inter alia*, to whether the dealing was "of a commercial nature or was for non-profit educational purposes": section 35(2)(a) of the SCA.

Much of the tenability of this construction, for the purposes of this appeal, turns on the interpretation of "private study".

Having considered all the arguments, including parliamentary debates, which provide limited assistance on this point, we take the view that section 35(1) excludes commercial research, as well as private study for commercial purposes. The exception is, of course, any research undertaken by "bodies corporate owned or controlled by the Government."

"Private study" should be construed to refer only to individuals actually performing a study. In order to come within the "private study" exception, the dealing (usually copying) must be undertaken by the student himself.

If one were to adopt a broader construction of "private study" to extend to "private study for commercial purposes", this interpretation would render otiose the specific exclusion of commercial research under section 35(5), in that all commercial research will almost inevitably be private study as well. It could not have been the intention of Parliament to propagate this non-distinction.

Let us take, for example, the difference between a university researcher undertaking private study for a project commissioned by an external commercial enterprise on the one hand and a person who undertakes private study in the pursuit of academic edification. The latter dealing, which falls under the rubric of "research and private study", arguably has a better prospect in arguing that such dealing is "fair" under section 35(2).

For the reasons stated above, it is our view that Aztech's admitted copying of TEST.SBC does not even qualify as "research or private study", and it follows that they may not avail themselves of the copyright defence offered by section 35(1). This is the result of a construction based on the plain, ordinary meaning of the words contained in section 35. Having answered the first question in the negative, it is therefore unnecessary to consider the second question on whether the dealing was "fair".

Judgment accordingly.

Notes and Questions

1. Compare the decisions in the *U.S.* and *Singapore* Reverse Engineering cases. Which decision do you think establishes the appropriate balance between protection and competitive necessity?

2. Consider the economic factors cited by the concurrence in the *Menu Command Hierarchy* case. Which of the above decisions reflects these concerns?

3. Should "fair use" include use to creating a competing product? How do you draw the line between property rights that encourage innovation and access to necessary technology to permit innovation? Are they mutually exclusive?

4. Should copying to achieve compatibility be justified? Compare the *U.S. Reverse Engineering* case with the *Apple Software* case in Chapter Nine.

5. Given the problems with patent and copyright protection for computer software, how should software be protected internationally? How should such protection handle the concerns of innovation, compatibility and access to technology for developing countries?

Chapter Thirty–Eight

FUTURE TECHNOLOGY PROBLEMS

A. DO DATABASES REQUIRE SUI GENERIS PROTECTION?

[Review the *Telephone Directory* case in Chapter One.]

TRIPS,
ARTICLE 10

2. Compilations of data or other material, whether in machine readable or other form, which by reason of the selection or arrangement of their contents constitute intellectual creations shall be protected as such. Such protection, which shall not extend to the data or material itself, shall be without prejudice to any copyright subsisting in the data or material itself.

Read the following Articles from the Database Directive in the Supplement: 1–5, 7–14.

Notes and Questions

1. Does the Directive violate Article 10 of TRIPS?

2. Which of the following works are governed by the Directive:

a) a collection of factual information about the buying habits of a grocery store's customers

b) a videotape composed of two movie trailers, a feature film and an FBI warning label

c) U.S. census data

d) A collection of financial information about the top 1,000 companies in the world

e) Formulas used to produce the drug AZT

f) A history book on the development of the Internet.

3. If database protection were limited to copyright protectable works, which of the above works would *not* qualify for protection?

4. Would the "database" in the *Telephone Directory* case qualify for protection under the EC directive?

5. You represent B + D who collects, analyzes and distributes over the Internet financial information about the top 5,000 UK companies, ranked by gross annual profits. Access is provided only to dues paying subscribers. What steps should your client take to protect its financial information under the Directive?

6. You represent a non-profit, educational institution that conducts research on weather and methods for predicting future meteorological events. What problems, if any, do you foresee for your client under the Directive?

Read the following Articles from the WTO Draft Database Treaty from the Supplement: 1–10.

IS A SUI GENERIS APPROACH TO DATABASE PROTECTION NECESSARY?

by Doris Estelle Long.

Despite claims to the contrary,[2] the "substantial investment" standard in the EC Database Directive and in the WIPO Draft Treaty are not as high as proponents would have one believe.[3] "Substantiality" in both cases is based on an unspecified amount of resources used in the preparation of the database.[4] Although the Directive does not specify what types of "investment" may be considered, the WIPO Draft Treaty expressly provides that significant investments in "human, financial, technical or other resources" qualify.[5]

Under both the EC and Draft Treaty standards, substantiality of investment may be demonstrated through "quantity" (numbers matter) *or* through "quality" (presumably based on the difficulty of the task although the factors in deciding such difficulty remain unspecified). I do not mean to suggest that "substantiality" has no meaning. Clearly some modicum of investment in time, money *or* effort is required. The problem is——"substantial" may not be so "substantial" after all. Does a database composed of three entries qualify for protection, if the cost for obtaining those entries is "substantial"? Does a database composed of

---

2. G.M. Hunsucker, *The European Database Directive: Regional Stepping Stone to an International Model?*, 7 FORDHAM INTELL. PROP. MEDIA & ENT. L.J. 697, 704 (1997); Jane C. Ginsburg, *No Sweat? Copyright and Other Protection of Works of Information After Feist v. Rural Telephone*, 92 COLUM. L. REV. 338, 383—84 (1992).

3. The low *protection* threshold posed by a "substantial investment" standard remains problematic under the recently proposed Collections of Information Antipiracy Act (HR 2652) which similarly limits its sui generis protection to collections of informa-

tion "gathered, organized, or maintained by another person through the investment of *substantial* monetary or other resources ..." HR 2652, 105th Cong. 1201 (1997)(emphasis added).

4. The EC Directive requires substantiality in "the obtaining, verification or presentation of the contents." Directive at Article 7 (1). The Draft Treaty requires substantiality in the collection, assembly, verification, organization or presentation of the contents of the database. Draft Treaty at Article 1(1).

5. Draft Treaty at Article 2 (iv).

the white pages of a telephone directory qualify for protection if "substantial time" is spent verifying those entries? I suspect that the answer may be "yes" under both the EC Directive and the WIPO Draft Treaty. Whether such databases *should* be protected as a policy matter however, is far from clear.

The adoption of a relatively low threshold for protection under the EC Directive and the WIPO Draft Treaty must be balanced against the scope of rights granted database creators and owners, including most importantly, control over the use of the information contained in the database, to determine if such protection is warranted.

Under current U.S. law, facts are not protected under copyright law. A database owner cannot restrict the use of factual information contained in an otherwise protectable database. Admittedly, the owner can control access to the database as a whole by refusing distribution of, or access to, her creation, but once access is obtained in a lawful manner, a database user may extract factual information from that database, and use such factual information without the database creator's permission and without paying a compulsory license or similar fee.[6]

The rights granted a database creator under the sui generis proposals of the EC Directive and the WIPO Draft Treaty are not so narrowly circumscribed.

Under Article 7 of the EC Directive, a qualifying database maker is granted the right "to prevent extraction and/or reutilization of the whole or of a substantial part . . . of the contents of the database."[7] Once again "substantiality" is measured quantitatively or qualitatively.[8] The right of extraction under the Directive includes "the permanent or temporary transfer of all or a substantial part of the contents to another medium by any means."[9] Thus, transferring pure facts from a database requires the permission of the database maker. Moreover, the substantiality requirement under the extraction right can be met by the "repeated and systematic extraction . . . of unsubstantial parts of the contents of the database."[10] The intention is apparently to prohibit acts "which conflict with a normal exploitation of the database"[11] or "which unreasonably prejudice the legitimate interests" of the database maker.[12]

Since the "legitimate interests" of the database maker include the right to control the use of its database, including its compiled materials, regardless of their nature, I am hard pressed to see how repeated extractions of factual data would somehow escape the strictures of the Directive. Thus, under the sui generis system established by the EC

---

6. Contractual arrangements which alter this scheme of protection and require payment of extraction fees for unprotected factual data may be unenforceable as a misuse of copyright. *See Lasercomb America Inc. v. Reynolds*, 911 F.2d 970 (4th Cir. 1990).

7. Directive at Article 7(1).

8. *Id.*

9. *Id.* at Article 7 (2).

10. *Id.* at Article 7 (2)(a).

11. *Id.* at 7 (5).

12. *Id.*

Directive, there is a real threat that data base compilers will be able to control the subsequent use of the factual information contained in their databases. This potential monopolization of facts has no U.S. equivalent, and is in fact directly contrary to the Constitutional underpinnings of most U.S. intellectual property laws. The potential harm of such broad protection is mitigated somewhat in the EC Directive by permissible exceptions set forth in Article 9. These exceptions permit uncompensated extraction in the following situations:

1) for teaching or scientific research so long as the source is indicated;[13]

2) for "purposes of public security;"[14]

3) for purposes of "an administrative or judicial procedure;"[15] and

4) for "private purposes" but only if the extraction is made from a "non-electronic database."[16]

These exceptions it should be noted are not mandatory, but permissive.

The WIPO Draft Treaty establishes the same right of extraction as the Directive with the same potential for monopolization of compiled facts. Consequently, both the EC Directive and the WIPO Draft Treaty pose the very real threat that database compilers will be able to monopolize the facts contained in their databases.[17]

There is no question that the creation of databases, in general, often, if not always, requires a substantial investment in time, labor and/or capital. Even databases which are composed of nothing more than a collection of factual information may require significant expenditures to obtain, compile and verify the information. It is equally indisputable that society often benefits from the creation of such databases and that their creation should largely be encouraged.

Such encouragement, however, must be carefully circumscribed to assure the appropriate balance between the proprietor's and the public's interests. The goal of database protection should be to encourage the compilation of materials in a usable format. What should be protected is the act of compilation, *not* the underlying materials themselves. Protec-

---

13. *Id.* at Article 9 (b). The use is further limited so that such extraction is proper "to the extent justified by the non-commercial purpose to be achieved." *Id.*

14. *Id.* at Art. 9 (c).

15. *Id.*

16. *Id* at Art. 9 (a).

17. The Database Investment Antipiracy Act (HR 3531) poses a similar threat since it grants the same extraction and reutilization rights to database compilers. HR 3531, 104th Cong. 2 (1996). The Collections of Information Antipiracy Act (HR 2652)

also poses a threat of monopolization since it grants database compilers a right of control over extraction of facts. HR 2652, 105th Cong. 1201 (1996). Unlike HR 3531, however, HR 2652 excludes certain uses from protection, including using or extracting the information "for not-for-profit educational, scientific and research purposes in a manner that does not harm the actual or potential market for the product ..." or for "news reporting." *Id.* at 1202. The effectiveness of such exceptions remains uncertain.

tion standards which grant database owners exclusive control over the facts contained in their databases may well harm the public.

In an era when developing countries are wrestling with the problems of transparency of laws, it is counterproductive to support a measure which has the realistic potential for removing facts from the public. Factual databases are compiled and used for a variety of scientific research, educational and governmental purposes. Many such databases, including the compilation of, for example, weather data, census information, and the like, are based on access to government-gathered information. If the first compiler of this information is granted the exclusive control over such government-developed data, the public could be denied access to information gathered by government officials, using the public's money, simply because the database is created by a non-governmental agency. The public, in effect, would not be able to use such data without paying for the privilege![18]

The sui generis approaches posited in the EC Directive, the WIPO Draft Database Treaty and the Database Investment Antipiracy Act (HR 3531) all present the very real potential that a database maker may be granted a perpetual monopoly over the facts contained in his database.[19]

If a sui generis approach is to be adopted the rejection of any intellectual creativity requirement in such a scheme should be carefully considered. The protection of factual compilations which contain no intellectual creativity should not be considered an international norm. Although the recent European Community Directive on the Legal Protection of Databases provides protection for databases which lack any originality or similar intellectual creativity component, this norm is not, and should *not* be automatically adopted as, an international standard. To the extent an international standard exists, that standard is represented by the Agreement on Trade Related Aspects of Intellectual Property Rights (TRIPS). Article 10 of TRIPS protects compilations of data or other material ... which by reason of the selection or arrangement of their contents constitute intellectual creations."[20] Such protection under TRIPS, however, is restricted to the compilation and [does] not extend to the data or material itself."[21] At least an intellectual creativity requirement assures that facts *per se* are not removed from the public's unfettered use. Protection regimes that require users to pay as they go for access to unprotected facts ignores centuries of careful

18. The Collections of Information Antipiracy Act (HR 2652) at least attempts to avoid this absurd result by excluding protection to collections of information "gathered, organized, or maintained" by a "governmental entity ..., including any employee or agent," or by "any person exclusively licensed by such entity." HR 2652, 105th Cong. 1203 (a)(1997).

19. The Collections of Information Antipiracy Act (HR 2652) may pose a similar threat since it uses the same low threshold of protection—substantial investment—and grants database compilers *rights* over the extraction of factual data. HR 2652, 105th Cong. 1201 (1997). Even worse, unlike the EC Directive, the WIPO Draft Treaty or the Database Investment Antipiracy Act (HR 3531), HR 2652 does not place a term limit on the rights granted a database compiler. Thus, the threat of perpetual monopolization seems even greater than in previous proposed sui generis regimes.

20. TRIPS at Article 10 (2).

21. *Id.*

balance between creators' and the public's rights represented by copyright law. The solution is to correct existing law—not march head-long into a new legal quagmire. Database protection is far too critical an issue to trust to legal prestidigitation. Before we kick over a two-centuries-old regime simply because we are dazzled by the potential problems of "technology," we should remember that technology is a continuing process. Copyright has always dealt with the problems of technology. From photography, to sound recordings, to motion pictures, copyright has had to cope with technological advances. There is no reason to abandon this approach now simply because the technology at issue (digitization) appears difficult to control. Any effort to develop a sui generis scheme outside copyright analogies raises serious policy issues. Competitive harm caused by the unauthorized copying and/or distribution of a database (in whole or in part) is already covered by copyright law. Such laws clearly prohibit the scope of protection envisioned by WIPO and the EC Directive. Any "special protection" of a sui generis regime that ignores this competition policy should be accepted only after clear and convincing evidence that such policy is no longer desirable.

Any grant of a one-sided monopoly over facts—the fundamental building block of scientific and historic research, of educational instruction, and news reporting and business prognostication—must be rejected. The easy answer to this criticism is to provide a "fair use" loophole so that certain users will be excluded from protection, similar to Article 9 of the EC Directive.[22] Experience with "fair use" to date under copyright analogues demonstrates that fair uses are not so broad as we might hope. Since U.S. law has yet to recognize an absolute right of fair use, I doubt such will be developed for databases. Instead, users will be subjected to a case-by-case investigation which will no doubt find that the database maker's economic interests outweigh most potentially fair uses. Such lack of clarity might be acceptable if sui generis protection of otherwise unprotectable contents were required. But it is not.

Notes and Questions

1. What response would you make to the author's criticisms? What changes would you make to the suggested draft treaty to respond to the criticisms that you consider valid?

2. *Draft Database Treaty.* The WIPO Draft Database Treaty was tabled in December 1996 for further study. Efforts remain on going by WIPO to study the question of database protection and develop an acceptable international model.

COLLECTIONS OF INFORMATION
ANTIPIRACY ACT

1201. Definitions

"As used in this chapter:

"(1) Collection of information.—The term 'collection of information' means information that has been collected and has been organized for

---

22. *See* notes 55–58 *supra* and accompanying text.

the purpose of bringing discrete items of information together in one place or through one source so that users may access them.

"(2) Information.—The term 'information' means facts, data, works of authorship, or any other intangible material capable of being collected and organized in a systematic way.

"(3) Potential market.—The term 'potential market' means any market that a person claiming protection under section 1202 has current and demonstrable plans to exploit or that is commonly exploited by persons offering similar products or services incorporating collections of information.

"(4) Commerce.—The term 'commerce' means all commerce which may be lawfully regulated by the Congress.

"1202. Prohibition against misappropriation

"Any person who extracts, or uses in commerce, all or a substantial part, measured either quantitatively or qualitatively, of a collection of information gathered, organized, or maintained by another person through the investment of substantial monetary or other resources, so as to cause harm to the actual or potential market of that other person, or a successor in interest of that other person, for a product or service that incorporates that collection of information and is offered or intended to be offered for sale or otherwise in commerce by that other person, or a successor in interest of that person, shall be liable to that person or successor in interest for the remedies set forth in section 1206.

"1203. Permitted acts

"(a) Individual Items of Information and Other Insubstantial Parts.—Nothing in this chapter shall prevent the extraction or use of an individual item of information, or other insubstantial part of a collection of information, in itself. An individual item of information, including a work of authorship, shall not itself be considered a substantial part of a collection of information under section 1202. Nothing in this subsection shall permit the repeated or systematic extraction or use of individual items or insubstantial parts of a collection of information so as to circumvent the prohibition contained in section 1202.

"(b) Gathering or Use of Information Obtained Through Other Means.—Nothing in this chapter shall restrict any person from independently gathering information or using information obtained by means other than extracting it from a collection of information gathered, organized, or maintained by another person through the investment of substantial monetary or other resources.

"(c) Use of Information for Verification.—Nothing in this chapter shall restrict any person from extracting information, or from using information within any entity or organization, for the sole purpose of verifying the accuracy of information independently gathered, organized, or maintained by that person. Under no circumstances shall the information so extracted or used be made available to others in a manner that harms the actual or potential market for the collection of information from which it is extracted or used.

"(d) Nonprofit Educational, Scientific, or Research Uses.—Nothing in this chapter shall restrict any person from extracting or using information for nonprofit educational, scientific, or research purposes in a manner that does not harm the actual or potential market for the product or service referred to in section 1202.

"(e) News Reporting.—Nothing in this chapter shall restrict any person from extracting or using information for the sole purpose of news reporting, including news gathering, dissemination, and comment, unless the information so extracted or used is time sensitive, has been gathered by a news reporting entity for distribution to a particular market, and has not yet been distributed to that market, and the extraction or use is part of a consistent pattern engaged in for the purpose of direct competition in that market.

"(f) Transfer of Copy.—Nothing in this chapter shall restrict the owner of a particular lawfully made copy of all or part of a collection of information from selling or otherwise disposing of the possession of that copy.

"1204. Exclusions

"(a) Government Collections of Information.—

"(1) Exclusion.—Protection under this chapter shall not extend to collections of information gathered, organized, or maintained by or for a government entity, whether Federal, State, or local, including any employee or agent of such entity, or any person exclusively licensed by such entity, within the scope of the employment, agency, or license. Nothing in this subsection shall preclude protection under this chapter for information gathered, organized, or maintained by such an agent or licensee that is not within the scope of such agency or license, or by a Federal or State educational institution in the course of engaging in education or scholarship.

"(2) Exception.—The exclusion under paragraph (1) does not apply to any information required to be collected and disseminated by either a national securities exchange under the Securities Exchange Act of 1934 or a contract market under the Commodity Exchange Act.

"(b) Computer Programs.—

"(1) Protection not extended.—Subject to paragraph (2), protection under this chapter shall not extend to computer programs, including, but not limited to, any computer program used in the manufacture, production, operation, or maintenance of a collection of information, or any component of a computer program necessary to its operation.

"(2) Incorporated collections of information.—A collection of information that is otherwise subject to protection under this chapter is not disqualified from such protection solely because it is incorporated into a computer program.

"1207. Criminal offenses and penalties

"(a) Violation.—

"(1) In general.—Any person who violates section 1202 willfully, and—

"(A) does so for direct or indirect commercial advantage or financial gain, or

"(B) causes loss or damage aggregating $10,000 or more in any 1–year period to the person who gathered, organized, or maintained the information concerned, shall be punished as provided in subsection (b).

"(2) Inapplicability.—This section shall not apply to an employee or agent of a nonprofit educational, scientific, or research institution, library, or archives acting within the scope of his or her employment.

"(b) Penalties.—An offense under subsection (a) shall be punishable by a fine of not more than $250,000 or imprisonment for not more than 5 years, or both. A second or subsequent offense under subsection (a) shall be punishable by a fine of not more than $500,000 or imprisonment for not more than 10 years, or both."

Notes and Questions

1. Does the above language respond to the concerns raised about the Draft Database Treaty? What problems do you foresee if this language were incorporated into a multinational treaty?

2. Would the "databases" listed above be protected under the above proposal?

3. If you represented the government of a developing country would you support the above proposal? Why or why not?

*

Part XI

IN-DEPTH TOPIC: THE EUROPEAN UNION

The European Union was originally created as a trade union, designed to reduce the commercial trade barriers between the member states. Under the Treaty of Rome, one of the primary purposes of the European Union is to promote the "free movement of goods" within the Union. To assure such "free movement" the Union has dealt extensively with the trade impact of diverse domestic intellectual property laws. Recognizing that inconsistent domestic IP laws could create unintended barriers to trade, the Union has created an extensive network of harmonization directives, regulations and court decisions designed to balance the interests of intellectual property owners with the goals of a barrier-free regional trading zone.

Currently the European Union contains 15 members–Austria, Belgium, Denmark, Finland, France, Germany, Greece, Ireland, Italy, Luxembourg, the Netherlands, Portugal, Spain, Sweden, and the United Kingdom. Like the rest of the world, these 15 countries represent differing legal, political and economic systems. Although located in the same geographic region, they contain different histories, different cultures, even different languages. As a result of these differences, the regulations and directives of the EU governing intellectual property represent the accord of a diverse group of nations. They have consequently served as a guideline for other countries in developing their own domestic intellectual property regimes. EU regulations have also served as a guide for other regional trading organizations, such as Mercosur and NAFTA who recognize that any trading region must deal with IP issues on a harmonized basis. As you read the following materials, ask yourself what special problems are posed by establishing a supra-national structure for regulating intellectual property rights. Who should have the right to determine individual rights for citizens in various countries–the domestic courts or a supra-national court? How would such rights be balanced? What limits would you place on each body to decide the rights of individual companies?

Chapter Thirty–Nine

INTRODUCTION

A. DOES THE EUROPEAN UNION REQUIRE IDENTICAL TREATMENT OF INTELLECTUAL PROPERTY RIGHTS THROUGHOUT THE UNION?

TREATY OF ROME

Article 30

Quantitative restrictions on imports and all measures having equivalent effect shall, without prejudice to the following provisions, be prohibited between Member States.

Article 31

Member States shall refrain from introducing between themselves any new quantitative restrictions or measures having equivalent effect.

Article 32

In their trade with one another Member States shall refrain from making more restrictive the quotas and measures having equivalent effect existing at the date of the entry into force of this Treaty.

Article 34

1. Quantitative restrictions on exports, and all measures having equivalent effect, shall be prohibited between Member States.

2. Member States shall, by the end of the first stage at the latest, abolish all quantitative restrictions on exports and any measures having equivalent effect which are in existence when this Treaty enters into force.

Article 36

The provisions of Articles 30 to 34 shall not preclude prohibitions or restrictions on imports, exports or goods in transit justified on grounds of public morality, public policy or public security; the protection of health and life of humans, animals or plants; the protection of national treasures possessing artistic, historic or archaeological value; or the protection of industrial and commercial property. Such prohibitions or restrictions shall not, however, constitute a means of arbitrary discrimination or a disguised restriction on trade between Member States.

Article 85

1. The following shall be prohibited as incompatible with the common market: all agreements between undertakings, decisions by associations of undertakings and concerted practices which may affect trade between Member States and which have as their object or effect the prevention, restriction or distortion of competition within the common market, and in particular those which:

   a.   directly or indirectly fix purchase or selling prices or any other trading conditions;

   b.   limit or control production, markets, technical development, or investment;

   c.   share markets or sources of supply;

   d.   apply dissimilar conditions to equivalent transactions with other trading parties, thereby placing them at a competitive disadvantage;

   e.   make the conclusion of contracts subject to acceptance by the other parties of supplementary obligations which, by their nature or according to commercial usage, have no connection with the subject of such contracts.

2. Any agreements or decisions prohibited pursuant to this Article shall be automatically void.

Article 177

The Court of Justice shall have jurisdiction to give preliminary rulings concerning:

   a.   the interpretation of this Treaty;

   b.   the validity and interpretation of acts of the institutions of the Community and of the ECB;

   c.   the interpretation of the statutes of bodies established by an act of the Council, where those statutes so provide.

Where such a question is raised before any court or tribunal of a Member State, that court or tribunal may, if it considers that a decision on the question is necessary to enable it to give judgment, request the Court of Justice to give a ruling thereon.

Where any such question is raised in a case pending before a court or tribunal of a Member State against whose decisions there is no judicial remedy under national law, that court or tribunal shall bring the matter before the Court of Justice.

Article 222

This Treaty shall in no way prejudice the rules in Member States governing the system of property ownership.

Read the following articles from the Trademark Harmonization Directive from the Supplement: Articles 2, 3, 4, 7, 8, and 16.

Notes and Questions

1. Does the Trademark Directive require EU members to enact identical domestic trademark laws?

2. Consider the definitions of a trademark set forth in Chapter Ten in the Notes and Questions. Which of those definitions comply with the EU Directive?

3. Does the Directive require complete harmonization of trademark laws? Which areas have been left out? For example, does the Directive establish a test for likelihood of confusion? Does it establish whether similar marks on non-similar goods qualify as trademark infringement? Should it, given the goals of harmonization set forth in the the preamble?

4. *Treaty of Rome.* The European Union (originally called the "Common Market") was established by the Treaty of Rome in 1957. This Treaty did not directly address the protection of intellectual property in the Union. To the contrary, court decisions, directives and regulations regarding intellectual property have been enacted as part of the Union's effort to promote the "free movement of goods" within its borders.

5. *The Legislative Process in the European Union.* Most directives and laws begin with a proposal by the European Commission. This proposal is generally the result of widespread consultation. Such proposal is then submitted to the Council of Ministers for action. Under the original Treaty of Rome, only the Council of Ministers could decide legislation. Subsequent treaties, however, have required consultation with the European Parliament and have even granted the Parliament power to amend and/or adopt legislation. Under present consultation procedures Parliament must provide an opinion before the Council can adopt a Commission Proposal. Under present cooperation procedures, Parliament is given two readings of Commission proposals during which they may amend such proposals. All Community legislation are published in the *Official Journal.*

6. *The Role of the European Court of Justice.* Until September 1, 1989, the European Court of Justice (ECJ) was the sole judicial body of the EU. In 1989, the Court of First Instance was established to enable the ECJ to concentrate on the task of ensuring uniform interpretation of Community law.

The court of First Instance has jurisdiction to deal with all actions brought by individuals and companies against decisions of Community institutions and agencies. Its judgments may be subject to an appeal brought before the Court of Justice but only on a point of law. Broadly speaking two types of cases may be brought before the Court of Justice:

1. Direct actions may be brought directly before the ECJ by the Commission, by other Community institutions or a Member State. Cases

brought by individuals or companies challenging the legality of a Community act are brought directly before the Court of First Instance. If an appeal is lodged against a decision of the Court of First Instance it is dealt with by the Court of Justice according to a procedure similar to that of other direct actions;

2. Preliminary rulings may also be requested from the ECJ by courts or tribunals in the Member States when they need a decision on a question of Community law in order to be able to give a judgment. The Court of Justice is not a court of appeal from the decisions of national courts and can only rule on matters of Community law. Having given its decision the national court is bound to apply the principles of Community law as laid down by the Court in deciding the case before it.

The ECJ is not bound by its previous decisions (such as under the common law doctrine of precedent), but in practice it does not often depart from them. *See, e.g.*, Anthony Arnull, *Owning up to Faillability: Precedent and the Court of Justice*, 30 C.M.L.R 247 (1993).

7. *The Binding Nature of European Union Law.* Regulations are directly applied without the need for national (domestic) measures to implement them. By contrast, directives bind member states regarding their stated objectives but leave each nation free to choose the form to be used to achieve those ends. Thus, the Trademark Harmonization Directive is *not* legislation to be enacted, but standards to be achieved. Compare the role of the EC Trademark Harmonization Directive with Articles 15 to 21 of TRIPS. Do they have the same effect on domestic legislation?

8. In *Becker v. Finanzami Münster-Innenstadt*, [1988] 3 C.M.C.R. 301, the Court was faced with the question of whether an individual can rely upon the terms of a directive against a member state that failed to implement it. The court responded as follows:

According to Article 189(3) of the Treaty, 'a directive shall be binding, as to the result to be achieved, upon each member-State to which it is addressed, but shall leave to the national authorities the choice of form and methods.'

It is clear from that provision that States to which a directive is addressed are under an obligation to achieve a result, which must be fulfilled before the expiry of the period laid down by the directive itself.

It follows that wherever a directive is correctly implemented, its effects extend to individuals through the medium of the implementing measures adopted by the member-State concerned (judgment of 6 May 1980 in Case 102/79 *E.C. Commission v. Belgium* [1980] E.C.R. 1473, [1981] 1 C.M.L.R. 282 (Re Type Approval Directives)).

However, special problems arise where a member-State has failed to implement a directive correctly and, more particularly, where the provisions of the directive have not been implemented by the end of the period prescribed for that purpose.

It follows from well-established case law of the Court and, most recently, from the judgment of 5 April 1979 in Case 148/78 *Pubblico Ministero v. Ratti* [1979] E.C.R. 1629, [1980] 1 C.M.L.R. 96, that whilst under Article 189 regulations are directly applicable and, consequently, by their nature capable of producing direct effects, that does not mean that other categories of measures covered by that Article can never produce similar effects.

It would be incompatible with the binding effect which Article 189 ascribes to directives to exclude in principle the possibility of the obligations imposed by them being relied on by persons concerned.

Particularly in cases in which the Community authorities have, by means of a directive, placed member-States under a duty to adopt a certain course of action, the effectiveness of such a measure would be diminished if persons were prevented from relying upon it in proceedings before a court and national courts were prevented from taking it into consideration as an element of Community law.

Consequently, a member-State which has not adopted the implementing measures required by the directive within the prescribed period may not plead, as against individuals, its own failure to perform the obligations which the directive entails.

Thus, wherever the provisions of a directive appear, as far as their subject-matter is concerned, to be unconditional and sufficiently precise, those provisions may, in the absence of implementing measures adopted within the prescribed period, be relied upon as against any national provision which is incompatible with the directive or in so far as the provisions define rights which individuals are able to assert against the State.

9. The EU has enacted numerous Directives regarding intellectual property issues. You have already seen portions of the Directives relating to Software, to Trademark Harmonization and to Database Protection. Other directives cover such diverse topics as Topographies of Semiconductor Products, Rental Rights, Biotech Inventions and Designs. *See* Council Directive 87/54/EEC of 16 December 1986 on the legal protection of topographies of semiconductor products, OJ L 024 27.01.87 p.36; First Council Directive 89/104/EEC of 21 December 1988 to approximate the laws of the Member States relating to trade marks, OJ L 040 11.02.89 p.1; Council Directive 91/250/EEC of 14 May 1991 on the legal protection of computer programs, OJ L 122 17.05.91 p.42; Council Directive 92/100/EEC of 19 November 1992 on rental right and lending right and on certain rights related to copyright in the field of intellectual property, OJ L 346 27.11.92 p.61; Council Directive 93/83/EEC of 27 September 1993 on the coordination of certain rules concerning copyright and rights related to copyright applicable to satellite broadcasting and cable retransmission, OJ L 248 06.10.93 p.15; Council Directive 93/98/EEC of 29 October 1993 harmonizing the term of protection of copyright and certain related rights, OJ L 290 24.11.93 p.9; Council Regulation (EC) No 40/94 of 20 December 1993 on the Community trade mark, OJ L 011 14.01.94 p.1; Council Regulation (EC) No 2100/94 of 27 July 1994 on Community plant variety rights, OJ L 227 01.09.94 p.1; Directive 96/9/EC of the European Parliament and of the Council of 11 March 1996 on the legal protection of databases, OJ L 077 27.03.96 p.20; Regulation (EC) No 1610/96 of the European Parliament and of the Council of 23 July 1996 concerning the creation of a supplementary protection certificate for plant protection products, OJ L 198 08.08.96 p.30; Directive 98/44/EC of the European Parliament and of the Council of 6 July 1998 on the legal protection of biotechnological inventions, OJ L 213 30.07.98 p.13;

Directive 98/71/EC of the European Parliament and of the Council of 13 October1998 on the legal protection of designs, OJ L 289 28.10.98 p.28.

To date, the EU has not yet enacted a directive aimed at harmonizing European patent law.

10.   In the absence of harmonization rules at the Community level, national laws establish whether, and under what conditions, intellectual property rights exist. Such laws, of course, must come within the permissible exceptions to Article 30's prohibition against import prohibitions recognized under Article 36. On this basis, the ECJ has regarded as justified the following:

- the uniform Benelux law which, on the subject of designs, grants an exclusive right to the first person to file a design, but without requiring that he should be the originator of the design or should have obtained a licence from him (*Keurkoop v. Nancy Kean Gifts*, [1982] E.C.R. 2853);

- British legislation which, on the basis of the principle of "relative novelty", allows the grant of a patent for inventions which have already been the subject of a previous patent filed more than 50 years previously and not subsequently used or published (*Thetford Corporation v. Fiamma* [1988] E.C.R. 3585, [1988] 3 C.M.L.R. 549);

- Italian and British legislation which recognise an exclusive right in an ornamental design in respect not only of the whole bodywork of a motor car but also of the individual bodywork components, thus preventing the marketing of spare parts by unauthorised independent manufacturers (*Volvo* [1988] E.C.R. 6211, [1989] 4 C.M.L.R. 122).

B.   WHEN DOES DOMESTIC LAW GOVERN INTELLECTUAL PROPERTY ISSUES IN THE EUROPEAN UNION?

THE QUATTRO CASE
DEUTSCHE RENAULT AG v. AUDI AG.

Court of Justice of the European Communities, 1993.
[1995] 1 C.M.L.R. 461.

This question arises in a dispute between Deutsche Renault AG (hereinafter "Renault"), the German subsidiary of a French motor-vehicle manufacturer, and AUDI AG (hereinafter "AUDI"), a German motor-vehicle manufacturer, regarding the use by Renault of the designation "Quadra".

According to the Warenzeichengesetz (Law on Trade Marks, hereinafter "the WZG"), numerals cannot be registered as trade marks unless the mark in question has gained acceptance in the trade as a distinctive feature of the products to which it is applied.[19]

---

19.   Section 4 WZG. Section 4 states in pertinent part:

(1) Freely available marks (*Freizeichen,* e.g. generic names) shall not be registered in the trade mark register.

Moreover, the proprietor of a trade mark cannot prevent a competitor from applying to his products particulars of their special characteristics as long as such particulars are not used by way of a trade mark.[20] Finally, a get-up ("Ausstattung") which is regarded in the trade circles concerned as sufficiently distinctive is also protected, essentially in the same way as a registered trade mark.[21]

AUDI has had the trade mark "Quattro" registered twice in the German trade-mark register. Since 1980 it has been marketing under that designation motor-cars with four-wheel drive. In mid-March 1988 Renault introduced on to the German market a motor-car with four-wheel drive manufactured in France and already marketed in other European countries under the designation "Espace Quadra".

In March 1988 Renault applied to the German Patent Office to have the two trade marks registered by AUDI removed from the register. By decisions of 9 August and 11 October 1990 the Trade-Mark Division of the German Patent Office removed both "Quattro" trade marks from the register on the ground that a numeral could not be registered even as a foreign word and that moreover at the time of registration the designation in question had not gained the necessary acceptance in the trade. An action brought by AUDI against those decisions was dismissed by the Bundespatentgericht, which, however, gave leave to appeal ("Rechtsbeschwerde") . It stated *inter alia* that the word "Quattro", as the Italian word for the number 4, must be left free for national trade but above all for purposes of the import and export trade in the motor-vehicle sector and that in any event in that sector the figure 4 had an importance in advertising or for designating models which could not be compared with that of any other figure.

In the litigation giving rise to this reference for a preliminary ruling AUDI claims that Renault should be ordered to cease to use the designation "Quadra" and to pay compensation. It contends that there is a risk

(2) In addition the following marks shall not be registered:

(i) those which are devoid of any distinctive character or contain exclusively numerals, letters or words designating the kind, time, or place of production, quality, intended purpose, price, quantity or weight of the goods.

(3) Registration shall however be permitted in cases referred to in subsection (2)1 where the mark has gained acceptance in the trade as a distinctive symbol of the applicant's products.

20. § 16 WZG. Section 16 states: The registration of a trade mark shall not affect the right of any person to apply to goods, their packaging or wrapping, even in an abbreviated form, his name, trade name, address or indications regarding the kind, time or place of production, quality, intend-

ed purpose, price, quantity or weight of goods or to use similar indications in trade, provided that such use is not made by way of a trade mark.

21. § 25 WZG. Section 25 states:

(1) Where any person, in the course of trade activities, unlawfully provides goods, their packaging, wrapping, prospectuses, price lists, business letters, advertisements, invoices or similar documents with a get-up regarded in the trade circles concerned as the distinctive sign of the same or the like goods of another person, or who sells such goods so marked or offers them for sake, proceedings may be brought against him by that other person, requiring him to desist from such conduct.

(2) Any person who knowingly of negligently acts in the manner aforesaid shall be required to compensate the person injured for the injury caused thereby.

of confusion between the designations "Quattro" and "Quadra" and bases its claim on its rights derived from the registration of the trade mark.

AUDI was successful at first instance. In its decision of 30 November 1988 the Landgericht Muenchen I (Seventh Chamber for Commercial Cases) referred *inter alia* to the risk of phonetic as well as conceptual confusion between "Quattro" and "Quadra"; both concepts referred to the figure 4 for the same goods, namely motor vehicles with four-wheel drive.

The Oberlandesgericht Muenchen (Sixth Civil Senate), by a judgment of 21 September 1989 (that is, before the decisions of the German Patent Office referred to in paragraph 6 above) dismissed Renault's appeal. It based its decision essentially on the protection of get-up and decided in particular that AUDI's claims based thereon were justified and that there was no need for the designation to be kept free for competitors.

Renault appealed on a point of law to the Bundesgerichtshof (hereinafter "the BGH"), which came to the conclusion, contrary to the appeal court, that specialist circles in motor-vehicle manufacturing had a considerable interest in ensuring that the figure 4, which was of importance for that sector in many respects, should be kept free for general use, even in the Italian version in its verbal form, which was widely understood in Germany.

Since the defendant regards such a prohibition as an unlawful restriction of intra-Community trade, the court making the reference has decided to refer a question to the Court of Justice for a preliminary ruling. Its question is worded as follows:

"Is there an unlawful restriction of intra-Community trade for the purposes of Articles 30 and 36 of the EEC Treaty if a subsidiary trading in Member State A of an automobile manufacturer established in Member State B is prohibited from using as a mark in Member State A the designation 'Quadra', which the manufacturer has hitherto used without restriction for a four-wheel-drive motor vehicle, both in its own State and elsewhere, on the ground that another automobile manufacturer in Member State A claims validly under the internal law of Member State A a trade-mark right ('Warenzeichenrecht') and/or a right to a get-up ('Ausstattungsrecht') in the word 'Quattro', even though that word denotes a numeral in another Member State and that meaning is clearly discernible in yet other Member States, and even though the number 4 thereby designated plays a significant and varied role in automobile manufacturing and the automobile trade?"

According to the provisions of the EEC Treaty on the free movement of goods, one of which is Article 30, quantitative restrictions on imports and all measures having equivalent effect are prohibited between Member States. However, according to the first sentence of Article 36, those

provisions do not preclude prohibitions or restrictions on imports justified on grounds of the protection of industrial and commercial property.

According to the second sentence of Article 36, the prohibitions and
restrictions mentioned in the first sentence "shall not constitute a
means of arbitrary discrimination or a disguised restriction on trade
between Member States".

As the Court decided in the judgment in Case 238/87 Volvo 1988
ECR 6211 with regard to designs and in Case 35/87 Thetford 1988 ECR
3585 with regard to patents, in the present state of Community law and
in the absence of Community standardization or harmonization of laws,
the conditions and procedures for the protection of an intellectual
property right are a matter for national law.

Consequently, the conditions for the protection of a designation such
as "Quattro" are, subject to the limits imposed by the second sentence of
Article 36, a matter for national law.

The first point to be made in this regard is that the national
legislation at issue, in the interpretation given by the court making the
reference, lays down very strict conditions for the protection under
trade-mark law of a designation such as "Quattro".

Apart from the statutory limitations on the registration of a numeral as a trade mark, an unregistered trade mark is in general protected
only if it has gained acceptance in trade, that is, if the mark is perceived
by the German public as an indication that the goods to which it is
applied come from a particular undertaking. That is the position only if
the great majority of consumers have that impression.

This degree of recognition, which is called for by the court making
the reference, must be all the higher if, as with the figure 4 in the
automobile sector, the symbol is one which ought to remain available for
use. In view of the importance of keeping the symbol available, the court
making the reference regards the degree of recognition hitherto demonstrated as insufficient.

Secondly, it should be noted that it does not appear from the
documents before the Court that a manufacturer from another Member
State is precluded from claiming under the same conditions the protection granted under German law to a registered or unregistered trade
mark or that such protection varies according to whether or not the
goods bearing that trade mark are of national or foreign origin.

It follows that national legal provisions such as those at issue in the
main proceedings, which permit the establishment under the aforementioned conditions of an exclusive right to the use of a designation such as
"Quattro", represent neither arbitrary discrimination nor a disguised
restriction on intra-Community trade.

With regard to the exercise of the right, the Commission states that
the concept of actual risk of confusion must be strictly interpreted in
order to avoid obstructing the free movement of goods further than is
necessary for the protection of trade marks. As an exception to a basic

principle of the common market Article 36 allows restrictions to the free movement of goods only in so far as they are justified by the protection of the rights which constitute the specific subject-matter of the industrial or commercial property at issue.

Community law does not lay down any strict interpretative criterion for the concept of risk of confusion.

However, national law is subject to the restrictions set out in the second sentence of Article 36 of the Treaty. As it is, there is nothing in the documents before the Court to indicate that those restrictions have been exceeded. In particular, there is nothing to suggest that the German courts interpret the concept of confusion broadly where the protection of the trade mark of a German producer is at issue, but interpret the same concept strictly where the protection of the trade mark of a producer established in another Member State is concerned.

In these circumstances, national laws such as those in question here, under which an exclusive right to use a designation such as "Quattro" may be exercised in order to prevent the use of a designation such as "Quadra", which is assumed to be capable of creating a risk of confusion with the former designation, constitute neither arbitrary discrimination nor a disguised restriction on intra-Community trade.

It is for the national court to decide whether the use of the words "Quattro" and "Quadra" in composite designations such as "AUDI Quattro" and "Espace Quadra" is sufficient to exclude the risk of confusion, even if it be established that the designation "Quattro" has achieved a high degree of recognition.

In view of all the foregoing considerations, the answer to the question referred to the Court must be that it does not represent an unlawful restriction of intra-Community trade for the purposes of Articles 30 and 36 of the EEC Treaty if a subsidiary trading in Member State A of an automobile manufacturer established in Member State B is prohibited from using as a mark in Member State A the designation "Quadra", which the manufacturer has hitherto used without restriction for a four-wheel-drive motor vehicle, both in its own State and elsewhere, on the ground that another automobile manufacturer in Member State A claims validly under the internal law of Member State A a trademark right ("Warenzeichenrecht") and/or a right to a get-up ("Ausstattungsrecht") in the word "Quattro", even though that word denotes a numeral in another Member State and that meaning is clearly discernible in other Member States, and even though the number 4 thereby designated plays a significant and varied role in automobile manufacturing and the automobile trade.

Notes and Questions

1. Do the German Trademark law provisions conform to the requirements of the EC Trademark Harmonization Directive? Do these provisions violate TRIPS?

2. Does inconsistent treatment of numerals as trademarks distort trade any more than any territorial-based, domestic intellectual property protection regime?

3. How much deference did the ECJ accord the German Court's interpretation of its national law?

4. Did the Trademark Harmonization Directive establish a clear rule on which marks must be protected in the European Union, or is the protection of marks still left to the individual vagaries of local law? For example, which of the following marks must be protected under the Trademark Harmonization Directive:

- The sound of a Harley–Davidson motorcycle

- An animated logo consisting of an animated version of the Venus De Milo statue of Venus walking across the sea for travel services

- Edom as a mark for cheese

- Queso (which means "cheese" in Spanish) as a mark for cheese products

- 475 as a mark for eyeglasses

- Jasmine as a scent mark for motor oil

5. For an example of the problems of harmonization of trademark standards in the EU, see the *Japanese Noodle* case, *supra*, Chapter Fifteen.

THE PATENT TERM EXTENSION CASE
KINGDOM OF SPAIN v. COUNCIL OF THE EUROPEAN UNION

Court Of Justice Of The European Communities, 1995.
[1996] 1 C.M.L.R. 415.

OPINION OF THE ADVOCATE GENERAL (MR FRANCIS JACOBS)

In these proceedings Spain seeks the annulment of Council Regulation 1768/92 concerning the creation of a supplementary protection certificate for medicinal products (hereafter referred to as "the Regulation"). The Regulation provides for a longer period of patent protection in the case of medicinal products which require authorisation prior to being placed on the market. Spain claims, first, that the Community has no competence to act in the area of patent law. Greece has intervened in support of Spain, France and the Commission have intervened in support of the Council.

The Regulation

According to its preamble, the Regulation has a number of different objectives. The preamble refers first to the fact that the development of medicines requires long and costly research, and that therefore a sufficient level of protection is necessary in order to encourage such research. The implication is that there may be a risk of research centres relocation to third countries thus undermining the development of medicines in Europe. Before the adoption of the Regulation, according to the French

Government, the laws of Japan and the United States offered better protection than the laws of most Member States. The problem lies in the lapse of time between the filing of an application for a patent and the marketing authorisation, making the period of effective protection under the patent insufficient to cover the investment put into the research.

The preamble also states that a uniform solution at Community level should be provided for, since disparities in national law would be likely to create obstacles to the free movement of medicinal products and thus directly affect the establishment and functioning of the internal market. That explains the choice of a regulation as the most appropriate legal instrument for laying down rules regarding:

> ... the creation of a supplementary protection certificate granted, under the same conditions, by each of the Member States at the request of the holder of a national or European patent relating to a medicinal product for which marketing authorisation has been granted ...

The subject-matter of the protection afforded by the certificate is defined in Article 4:

> Within the limits of the protection conferred by the basic patent, the protection conferred by a certificate shall extend only to the product covered by the authorisation to place the corresponding medicinal product on the market and for any use of the product as a medicinal product that has been authorised before the expiry of the certificate.

The effects of the certificate are specified in Article 5:

> Subject to the provisions of Article 4, the certificate shall confer the same rights as conferred by the basic patent and shall be subject to the same limitations and the same obligations.

Article 6 confirms that only the holder of the basic patent or his successor in title is entitled to a certificate.

Article 13 determines the duration of the certificate. It takes effect at the end of the lawful term of the basic patent, and is valid for a certain period, calculated by reference to the period which elapsed between the date on which the application for a basic patent was lodged and the date of the first authorisation to place the product on the market in the Community: the latter period, reduced by five years, is the duration of the certificate, with a maximum of five years.

A hypothetical example (confined to a single Member State) may illustrate how the system operates. Suppose an application for a basic patent was lodged in 1990, the patent expiring in 2010. If the marketing authorisation is given in 1997, the certificate takes effect in 2010 for a period of seven minus five years, and will therefore lapse in 2012.

Spain claims that the Community has no competence whatsoever in relation to the substance of patent law. That is said to follow from Articles 36 and 222 of the Treaty, and to be confirmed by the Court's case law, which distinguishes between the existence and the exercise of intellectual property rights.

In that respect, Spain refers to the judgment in *Parke, Davis v. Centrafarm*, where the Court drew a distinction, in the context of Articles 85 and 86 of the Treaty, between the existence and the exercise of patent rights.

Similarly, in *Deutsche Grammophon v. Metro* the Court stated that it was clear from Article 36 that:

> ... although the Treaty does not affect the existence of rights recognised by the legislation of a Member State with regard to industrial and commercial property, the exercise of such rights may nevertheless fall within the prohibition laid down by the Treaty.

Spain deduces from that case law that the Community is not competent to regulate what the applicant calls substantive patent law, but may only harmonise those aspects relating to the exercise of industrial property rights which are capable of having some influence on the realisation of the general objectives of the Treaty. The adoption of the Regulation is said to go beyond the Community's competence, since in effect it extends the duration of patent protection, which is considered to be part of the substance of patent law.

In Spain's view patent law has a status under Community law which is different from that of other intellectual property rights, such as trade marks. In the field of patents, the Community had not yet acted, and the Regulation is said to constitute a grave infringement of the sovereignty of the Member States, which have never agreed to a transfer of competence to the Community in that area.

JUDGMENT:

By application lodged at the Court Registry on 4 September 1992, the Kingdom of Spain brought an action for the annulment of Council Regulation (EEC) No 1768/92 of 18 June 1992 concerning the creation of a supplementary protection certificate for medicinal products (OJ 1992 L 182, p. 1).

The Kingdom of Spain, supported by the Hellenic Republic, argues first that, in the allocation of powers between the Community and the Member States, the latter have not surrendered their sovereignty in industrial property matters, as is demonstrated by the combined provisions of Articles 36 and 222 of the Treaty.

Citing the case-law of the Court Spain argues that the Community has no power to regulate substantive patent law, and may harmonize only those aspects relating to the exercise of industrial property rights which are capable of having an effect upon the achievement of the general objectives laid down in the Treaty. Such action may not take the form of a new industrial property right which, by its nature, content and effects, alters the basic concept in force under the national legal systems of each of the Member States. The duration of a patent is its most important feature, since it intrinsically affects the balance in time between the rights and obligations of its holder, whether legal or economic in character.

The case-law has not excluded the possibility of the Community determining by legislation the conditions and rules regarding the protection conferred by industrial property rights, should such action prove necessary in pursuing its objectives. In any event, the creation of the supplementary certificate does not in any way affect the substance of the rights of the holder of the basic patent. It is a mechanism for correcting the shortcomings of the system for protecting pharmaceutical research, which arise from the need to obtain marketing authorization in order to make use of the innovation.

In the light of those arguments, the Court must examine whether Articles 222 and 36 of the EEC Treaty reserve the power to regulate substantive patent law for the national legislature, thereby excluding any Community action in the matter.

In that respect, the Court held in its judgment in *Commission v United Kingdom*, cited above (paragraphs 16 and 17), that, as Community law stands, the provisions on patents have not yet been the subject of unification at Community level or in the context of approximation of laws, and that, in those circumstances, it is for the national legislature to determine the conditions and rules regarding the protection conferred by patents.

However, it added that the provisions of the Treaty—and in particular Article 222, which provides that the Treaty does not in any way prejudice the rules in Member States governing the system of property ownership—cannot be interpreted as reserving to the national legislature, in relation to industrial and commercial property, the power to adopt measures which would adversely affect the principle of free movement of goods within the common market as provided for and regulated by the Treaty.

Thus, far from endorsing the argument that rules concerning the very existence of industrial property rights fall within the sole jurisdiction of the national legislature, the Court was anticipating the unification of patent provisions or harmonization of the relevant national legislation.

The Court followed similar reasoning in relation to Article 36 of the Treaty. That provides, in particular, that the provisions of Articles 30 to 34 shall not preclude prohibitions or restrictions justified on grounds of the protection of industrial and commercial property, but that such prohibitions or restrictions shall not constitute a means of arbitrary discrimination or a disguised restriction on trade between Member States.

In its judgment in Case 35/76 *Simmenthal v Italian Minister for Finance* 1976 ECR 1871, paragraph 14, the Court held that Article 36 is not designed to reserve certain matters to the exclusive jurisdiction of Member States but permits national laws to derogate from the principle of the free movement of goods to the extent to which such derogation is and continues to be justified for the attainment of the objectives referred to in that article.

It follows that neither Article 222 nor Article 36 of the Treaty reserves a power to regulate substantive patent law to the national legislature, to the exclusion of any Community action in the matter.

In this case, the Council has pointed out that, at the time the contested regulation was adopted, provisions concerning the creation of a supplementary protection certificate for medicinal products existed in two Member States and were at the draft stage in another State. The contested regulation is intended precisely to establish a uniform Community approach by creating a supplementary certificate which may be obtained by the holder of a national or European patent under the same conditions in each Member State, and by providing, in particular, for a uniform duration of protection (Article 13).

The regulation thus aims to prevent the heterogeneous development of national laws leading to further disparities which would be likely to create obstacles to the free movement of medicinal products within the Community and thus directly affect the establishment and the functioning of the internal market (sixth recital).

The Council rightly emphasizes that differences in the protection given in the Community to one and the same medicine would give rise to a fragmentation of the market, whereby the medicine would still be protected in some national markets but no longer protected in others. Such differences in protection would mean that the marketing conditions for the medicines would themselves be different in each of the Member States.

The Kingdom of Spain rightly argues that the objectives set out in Article 8a of the EEC Treaty require that a balance be struck in this case between the interests of undertakings which hold patents and the interests of undertakings which manufacture generic medicines.

Nevertheless, the regulation recognizes the necessity, in a sector as complex as the pharmaceutical sector, to take all the interests at stake into account, including those of public health (ninth recital). In that regard, Article 13(2) of the regulation provides that the certificate may not be issued for a period longer than five years.

In those circumstances, it does not appear that the Council has disregarded the interests of consumers or of the generic medicines industry.

It follows from the above that the regulation was validly adopted.

The plea challenging the regulation for lack of a legal basis is therefore without foundation.

Since both the applicant's pleas have failed, the action must be dismissed.

Notes and Questions

1. Article 8a mentioned in the *Patent Term Extension* case provides for the free movement of citizens within the Union and for their right to reside freely within the territory of the member states.

2. Assume you represent a generic drug company doing business in Greece. Your client has located a manufacturing facility there because Greece (for purposes of the hypothetical) provides limited patent protection for pharmaceutical products. This allows your client to manufacture and sell generic products sooner than in other EU countries. Does the Patent Term Extension Regulation have an adverse impact on your client's substantive rights under Greek patent law? Is it contrary to Greek governmental policy in establishing minimal patent terms for pharmaceutical products in Greece?

3. Should your client be allowed to distribute its lawfully manufactured generic products to other EU countries who continue to protect the subject patents for a longer period of time? If not, wouldn't such limits have a harmful effect on the free movement of goods within the EU?

4. Could the EU enact a regulation that established a maximum term of patent protection for pharmaceutical products of 20 years from the date of application without violating Community law?

Chapter Forty

REGULATING IP–PROTECTED GOODS IN THE EU

A. WHO HAS THE RIGHT TO CONTROL THE PROTECTION/DISTRIBUTION OF COPY-RIGHTED WORKS IN THE EU?

THE GERMAN SOUND RECORDING CASE
DEUTSCHE GRAMMOPHON GESELLSCHAFT GMBH v. METRO–SB–GROSSMARKTE GMBH & CO. KG.

Court Of Justice Of The European Communities, 1971.
[1971] ECR 487, [1971] CMLR 631.

The company Deutsche Grammophon Gesellschaft (hereinafter re-ferred to as 'DG') is a subsidiary of the company Philips Gloeilampen–Fabrieken, Eindhoven (Netherlands), and of the company Siemens AG, Berlin and Munich.

Its principal products are gramophone records which it distributes directly or through its subsidiaries established in several EEC States. Amongst its 99.55% owned subsidiaries is the company Polydor SA, Paris (hereinafter referred to as 'Polydor') with places of business in Paris and Strasbourg.

In Germany the records are sold directly through retailers and through two wholesale booksellers. DG sells records to those dealers at a price of DM 12.33 (plus VAT) and the controlled retail selling price is DM 19. The records are only supplied to dealers who have signed a written undertaking ('Revers') to observe the agreement on prices.

In the other EEC countries, DG distributes its records by means of licensing agreements concluded with its own subsidiaries or with the subsidiaries of the company NV Philips Phonografische Industrie of Baarn (Netherlands), which is a subsidiary of Philips Gloeilampen–Fabrieken and of Siemens AG. In paragraph (1) these licensing agree-ments state in particular that DG assigns to the licensee the exclusive right to exploit its recordings in the territory covered by the agreement in a manner in accordance with normal commercial usage.

DG concluded such an agreement with its subsidiary Polydor of Paris.

From April to the end of October 1969 the undertaking Metro–SB–Grossmarkte GmbH & Co. KG (hereinafter referred to as 'Metro') was supplied with Polydor records by DG and, since it was not bound by a pricing agreement, it sold those records to its customers at the price (plus VAT) of DM 41.85 in May 1969 and DM 13.50 in August 1969. In October 1969 DG discovered that it did not possess a written undertaking to observe the controlled prices. Since Metro refused to sign such an undertaking DG severed commercial relations. As a result of this, Metro obtained supplies of Polydor records through the undertaking Rosner & Co. of Hamburg, selling them to its customers for DM 11.95 plus VAT in January 1970 and for DM 12.95 plus VAT in February 1970.

The records in question had been pressed by DG in Germany and supplied to its subsidiary Polydor in Paris. Polydor had disposed of a number of those records to an undertaking operating in a third country which had supplied a proportion of them to the undertaking Rosner & Co. The latter in its turn resold those records to the undertaking Metro–SB–Grossmarkte GmbH of Hamburg, which has a controlling interest in Metro.

DG considered that the sale of its records by the said undertaking constitutes an infringement of Article 85 of the Urheberrechtsgesetz (the German Copyright Law) and thereby of its right of exclusive distribution in the Federal Republic. It also considered that its right was not 'exhausted' since the goods were marketed abroad and not on the national territory. On 20 March 1970 it obtained an injunction from the Landgericht Hamburg prohibiting Metro–SB–Grossmarkte from selling or from marketing in any other manner DG records bearing the designation 'Polydor' and having specific catalogue numbers.

On 7 April 1970 the undertaking Metro–SB–Grossmarkte GmbH & Co. KG requested the Bundeskartellamt (the Federal Cartel Office) to review the system of controlled prices operated by DG and requested it to annul as an abuse the clause controlling prices and to prohibit the application of any such clause. At the same time Metro made an application to the Commission of the European Communities requesting it to find that there was an infringement of Articles 85 and 86 of the Treaty and to require DG, Polydor Nederland NV and Plydor France to bring such infringement to an end.

Metro appealed to the Hanseatisches Oberlandesgerichy which, by an order of 8 October 1970, decided to stay proceedings and put the following questions to the Court of Justice:

"(a) Is it contrary to the second paragraph of Article 5 or Article 85(1) of the EEC Treaty to interpret Articles 97 and 85 of the Federal law of 9 September 1965 on copyright and related rights to mean that a

German undertaking manufacturing sound recordings may rely on its distribution rights to prohibit the marketing in the Federal Republic of Germany of sound recordings which it has itself supplied to its French subsidiary which, although independent at law, is wholly subordinate to it commercially?''

OPINION: K. Roemer, The Advocate General

The Landgericht, Hamburg, drew upon Articles 85 and 97 of the German Law, which provide as follows:

Article 85

'The manufacturer of a sound recording shall have the exclusive right of reproducing and distributing the recording.'

Article 97

'Any person unlawfully infringing a copyright or any other right protected in accordance with this law may be required by the injured party to put an end to the infringement and, if there is a likelihood of repetition, to desist therefrom and if the infringement occurs deliberately or negligently, to pay damages.'

Furthermore, that court clearly found that DG's exclusive right to distribute its records in Germany was not exhausted as provided in the following terms in Article 17 of the Copyright Law which is applicable by analogy:

'If the original or reproductions of a work are marketed with the consent of the person entitled to distribute them within the territory governed by this law, their further distribution shall be lawful'. In the view of the court this provision would only apply if distribution had taken place in the Federal Republic of Germany. Thus the sale of reimported records in Germany could be considered unlawful.

[T]he present case is chiefly concerned with the problem of the so-called 'exhaustion' of national industrial property rights related to copyright as laid down in Article 17 of the German Copyright Law. The Oberlandesgericht has declared that the wording of that provision leaves open the question whether placing goods on the market abroad with the consent of the holder of the right also exhausts the latter's distribution rights in Germany. Apparently, in view of the principle of territoriality as it is widely understood in this field, the court is inclined to hold that the right is not thereby exhausted. On the other hand, however, because of the unclear wording of the Law in question, the lack of unanimity in the legislative provisions and the fact that the Law was enacted after the entry into force of the EEC Treaty, the court considered it necessary to pose the question in the light of the principles of the Treaty relating to this field. In my opinion, this can only mean that the court intends to seek an interpretation of the national law that will conform to Community law, if necessary at the expense of the principle of territoriality.

[F]ree, unhindered movement of goods must be regarded as a fundamental principle of the common market. Furthermore, one must bear in mind the concept of the unity of the common market and its system of competition, which is intended to achieve the comprehensive prevention of distortions of competition and in particular to maintain competition between Member States.

Obviously, national industrial property rights, that is to say, including copyright and related protection rights, appropriately formulated or interpreted, may operate against this objective since, as the argument of DG shows, they permit, under certain circumstances, a market to be partitioned at all levels of the economy, that is, the absolute control and blocking of trade between Member States. [A]lthough the Treaty leaves the existence and substance of industrial property untouched (the national legislature decides these questions) their exercise is completely subject to Community law.

Consequently, the main problem in the present case also is to differentiate between the existence of rights and the exercise of rights. As the Commission rightly stresses, the capacity to manufacture and to effect the initial distribution of the protected product certainly comes within the sphere of the existence of the right, since it ensures for the holder the benefit to which he is entitled. On the other hand, it seems doubtful whether the principle of territoriality, to which reference is constantly made in connexion with industrial property rights, also forms part of the substance and is of the essence of such rights. In my view, it is significant that here we are faced with an ambiguous concept the contours of which cannot be discerned with absolute clarity, and on which there is clearly no unanimity. It is occasionally said that the principle of territoriality states (in accordance with the Paris Convention) that the protection granted in one State is independent of protection rights conferred in other States. Moreover, it is also formulated to mean that the effects of protection rights are restricted to the territory of the State in which the rights are granted, although the national legislature may make the legal effects dependent on facts which occur abroad. In any event this permits it to be said that in spite of the principle of territoriality the holder of trade-mark rights who uses the same trade-mark internally and abroad cannot prohibit the import of a product by virtue of his domestic trade-mark if he has supplied the product with the trade-mark and placed it on the market abroad. With regard to copyright, reference may be made in this context to a recent decision of the Austrian Oberster Gerichtshof according to which the right of a manufacturer of sound recordings is exhausted (that is, it is not possible to prohibit imports) if the holder of the right has placed the product on the market or if it has been placed on the market abroad by an authorized exporter or by a licensee.

Here it should be decisive that the objective of the industrial property right was attained when the goods were first placed on the market, since it was possible to use the monopolistic opportunity for gain. On the other hand, it would undoubtedly go beyond the objective of that right if the holder was permitted to control further marketing, in particular to prohibit re-importation, and the free movement of goods was impeded. Thus in view of the reservation contained in Article 36, the fundamental aims of the Treaty and the principles of the common market, and in spite of the guarantee of the subsistence of industrial property rights, in a situation such as that in the present case it may be held that the right has been exhausted, and the exercise of the distribution right is thus precluded.

JUDGMENT:

The court is asked to rule whether it is contrary to the EEC Treaty to interpret Articles 97 and 85 of the German Law of 9 September 1965 on copyright And related rights to mean that a German undertaking manufacturing sound recordings may rely on its exclusive right of distribution to prohibit the marketing in the federal republic of Germany of sound recordings which it has itself supplied to its French subsidiary which, although independent at law, is Wholly subordinate to it commercially.

It is clear from the facts recorded by the Hanseatisches Oberlandesgericht, Hamburg, that what it asks may be reduced in essentials to the question whether the exclusive right of distributing the protected articles which is conferred by a national law on the manufacturer of sound recordings may, without infringing community provisions, prevent the marketing on national territory of products lawfully distributed by such manufacturer or with his consent on the territory of another Member State. The Court of Justice is asked to define the tenor and the scope of the relevant community provisions, with particular reference to the second paragraph of Article 5 or Article 85 (1).

According to the second paragraph of Article 5 of the treaty, member states "shall abstain from any measure which could jeopardize the attainment of the objective of this Treaty". This provision lays down a general duty for the Member States, the actual tenor of which depends in each individual case on the provisions of the Treaty or on the rules derived from its general scheme.

According to Article 85 (1) of the Treaty "the following shall be prohibited as incompatible with the common market : all agreements between undertakings, decisions by associations of undertakings and concerted practices which may affect trade between Member States and which effect the prevention, restriction or distortion of competition within the Common Market". The exercise of the exclusive right referred to in the question might fall under the prohibition set out by this provision each time it manifests itself as the subject, the means or the result of an agreement which, by preventing imports from other Member States of products lawfully distributed there, has as its effect the partitioning of the market.

If, however, the exercise of the right does not exhibit those elements of contract or concerted practice referred to in Article 85 (1) it is necessary, in order to answer the question referred, further to consider whether the exercise of the right in question is compatible with other provisions of the Treaty, in particular those relating to the free movement of goods.

Amongst the prohibitions or restrictions on the free movement of goods which it concedes Article 36 refers to industrial and commercial property. On the assumption that those provisions may be relevant to a right related to copyright, it is nevertheless clear from that article that, although the Treaty does not affect the existence of rights recognized by the legislation of a Member State with regard to industrial and commercial property, the exercise of such rights may nevertheless fall within the prohibitions laid down by the Treaty. Although it permits prohibitions or restrictions on the free movement of products, which are justified for the purpose of protecting industrial and commercial property, Article 36 only admits derogations from that Freedom to the extent to which they are justified for the purpose of safeguarding rights which constitute the specific subject-matter of such property.

If a right related to copyright is relied upon to prevent the marketing in a Member State of products distributed by the holder of the right or with his consent on the territory of another Member State on the sole ground that such distribution did not take place on the national territory, such a prohibition, which would legitimize the isolation of national markets, would be repugnant to the essential purpose of the Treaty, which is to unite national markets into a single market.

That purpose could not be attained if, under the various legal systems of the Member States, nationals of those States were able to partition the market and bring about arbitrary discrimination or disguised restrictions on trade between Member States.

Consequently, it would be in conflict with the provisions prescribing the free movement of products within the common market for a manufacturer of sound recordings to exercise the exclusive right to distribute the protected articles, conferred upon him by the legislation of a Member State, in such a way as to prohibit the sale in that state of products placed on the market by him or with his consent in another member state solely because such distribution did not occur within the territory of the first member state.

Notes and Questions

1.   The exhaustion of rights principle discussed in the *German Sound Recording* case is also referred to as grey market or parallel imports. These principles only apply where the imported goods have been lawfully produced. Were the goods at issue lawfully produced? Where–in Germany or Great Britain? Should it matter for purposes of balancing IP rights and the goals of barrier-free intra-market circulation of goods where the goods were first manufactured?

2.   What is the strongest argument you can make in favor of permitting the copyright owner to prevent the importation of grey market goods? What is the strongest argument against permitting such importation?

3. What commercial harm is caused by the unauthorized importation of grey market goods? Are there any benefits from such importation?

4. In the *German Sound Recording* case the sound recordings at issue also contained a DG trademark. Should DG be able to preclude the importation of grey market trademarked goods? Is there a difference in the nature of the intellectual property right that would require a different treatment for trademarks as opposed to copyrights?

THE GERMAN LICENSING CASE
MUSIK–VERTRIEB MEMBRAN GMBH v. GEMA

Bundesgerichtshof (German Federal Supreme Court), 1981.
[1982] 1 CMLF 630.

The plaintiffs is the Germany performing right society, Gesellschaft fur Musikalische Auffuhrungs-und Mechanische Vervielfaltigungsrechte (GEMA), which has concluded reciprocal agreements with foreign performing right societies, and represents almost the entire world repertoire of protected music.

It trades in various special products, mainly records, and other articles of everyday use. In March 1974 [the defendant] imported 100,-000 copies of the long-playing record '25 Rockin' Greats' from Great Britain into the Federal German Republic. It a cquired these records from its sister company, K-tel international Ltd which had obtained a licence from the Mechanical Copyright Protection society Ltd (MCPS) to distribute the records in Great Britain. Between the MCPS and the plaintiff there is an agreement whereby the MCPS has the right and obligation, if it is planned to export records to the Federal Republic, to grant licences at the rates applying in the Federal Republic.

The licences are related basically to the retail selling prices of the records. The retail selling prices and licence fees in the Federal Republic are higher than those in Great Britain.

After the MCPS had unsuccessfully claimed the difference between the German and English rates of remuneration from the defendant's English sister company, the plaintiff demanded payment of this sum from the defendant.

The Landgericht granted the plaintiff's claim. [The] Bundesgerichtshof stayed a decision on the appeal and submitted the following question to the European Court of Justice for a preliminary ruling pursuant to Article 177(3) of the EEC Treaty:

Is it compatible with the provisions concerning the free movement of goods (Article 30 et seq of the EEC Treaty) for a management company entrusted with the exploitation of copyrights to exercise the exclusive rights held by the composer in member-State A to the transcription of his musical works onto sound recordings, their reproduction and marketing in such a way as to require, in respect of the marketing in member-State A of sound recordings which have been produced and placed on the market in member-State B–the composer's licence fee which is calculated on the quantity and final selling price relevant to that member-State–a payment which is equal to the customary licence fee in respect of production and marketing in member-State A, but which takes into account the (lower) licence fee which has already been paid in respect of production and marketing in member-State B?

DECISION:

. [T]he defendant cannot refuse payment of the royalty for utilisation of the copyright work in the Federal German Republic by pleading exhaustion of copyright under section 17(2) of the Copyright Act. Even the lawful marketing in a foreign country of records protected by copyright does not lead to exhaustion of the publication right in the Federal Republic if the copyright exploitation rights have been assigned to the foreign holder with a territorial limitation to foreign countries. The principle of exhaustion of copyright is a consequence of the idea that the owner of the right has, by his own acts of utilisation, taken advantage of the exclusive right of exploitation granted to him by law and has consequently exhausted it, so that further acts of exploitation in the course of utilisation are no longer covered by copyright protection. The national publication right can only be said to be exhausted when the owner has himself published in the Federal Republic or has consented to the publication by a third party in the Federal Republic. Otherwise the comprehensive protection granted by law would not be guaranteed. The creator of a work has exclusive right to exploit his work economically. It is also open to him to divide up his right in such a way that he grants licences only for certain States or grants licences in different States for which he grants no licences. Since, according to the findings of the appeal court, the defendant or its seller was granted a marketing right for Great Britain only, publication in the Federal Republic is an unlawful infringement of the publication right for territory.

According to the judgment of the European Court of Justice dated 20 January 1981 which is cited above ([1981] 2 CMLR 44 (GEMA)), on the other hand, the claim for the difference in royalties is precluded by the provisions of Article 30 et seq of the EEC Treaty on the free movement of goods if the records in question have already been marketed in another member-State (in casu Great Britain) by the copyright owner or with his consent. On this point the European Court of Justice emphasised that sound recordings, even if incorporating protected musical works, are products to which the system of free movement of goods provided for by the Treaty applies, and it followed that national legislation whose application results in obstructing trade in sound recordings between member-States must be regarded as a measure having an effect equivalent to a quantitative restriction within the meaning of Article 30 of the Treaty. The Court added that this was the case where such legislation permits a copyright management society to object to the distribution of sound recordings originating in another member-State on the basis of the exclusive exploitation right which it exercises in the name of the copyright owner. The owner or the copyright management society cannot invoke Article 36 of the Treaty because, in the event of a dispute, it is the economic aspect of copyright which is in issue and, in this regard, in the application of Article 36 of the Treaty there is no reason, according to the Court of Justice, to make a distinction between copyright and other industrial and commercial property rights. The Court pointed out that it was apparent from its own well-established case law that the proprietor of an industrial or commercial right protected by the law of a member-State could not rely on that law to prevent the importation of a product which has been lawfully marketed in another member-State by the proprietor himself or with his consent.

Arguing against this, the plaintiff is wrong in saying that it depends on the question, which has not yet been clarified, whether the consent for manufacture and distribution obtained for Great Britain is based on a contract or on the statutory system applying in Great Britain. The statutory system, as the European Court of Justice pointed out in paragraph [22] of the above-mentioned judgment, has the practical result that the royalty in Great Britain for the manufacture and distribution of sound recordings is always 6.25 per cent of the retail selling price and no licensee would be willing to agree on a higher rate with the author of the work, because he only needs to wait until the record has been manufactured by someone else to be able to copy and distribute the protected work on payment of the statutory fee of 6.25 per cent. When the European Court of Justice refers, in its judgment, to licences in return for payment of remuneration, this includes both possibilities–contractual agreement and statutory system. Therefore it is not a question of whether the licence for Great Britain was obtained by contract or by fulfilling the statutory requirements.

However, as against the prohibition of any restriction on the free movement of goods in the Common Market (Article 30 EEC) which the Court of Justice emphasises in its judgment, the plaintiff is right to question whether the records concerned were "put into circulation" in Great Britain at all–with the consent of the copyright owner. In the plaintiff's opinion this cannot be the case where the records were delivered–as here–by the English licensee direct to a financially dependent sister company in the Federal German Republic.

[I]t cannot automatically be accepted that the records in question were put into circulation in Great Britain for the purpose of the provisions of the EEC Treaty on free movement of goods and for the purpose of the case law of the European Court of Justice. The position is rather that there may have been a movement of goods purely within the group, which should be regarded economically as an internal process because no commercial transaction with genuine outsiders took place, and the movement of goods within the group constitutes an internal distribution of goods, notwithstanding the fact that the group enterprises are legally independent. In this case the records would not have been purchased in the course of free trade for the purpose of the case law of the European Court of Justice.

[I]n its earlier decision of 8 June 1971 (Case 78/70 *Deutsche Gram-mophon*) ([1971] ECR 487, [1971] CMLR 631, [19711] NJW 1533) the Court stated that it would be incompatible with the rules on the free circulation of goods if an exclusive right existing in one member-State were used to prevent the marketing of products which had been sold by the owner of the right in another member-State merely because this had not taken place in the first member-State. This also accords with the principle of protecting the free movement of goods, as repeatedly empha-sised by the Court, and which only arises when the goods are actually in circulation, i.e. in the (Common) Market.

However, there is no question of such protection of the free move-ment of goods in the case of mere movements of goods within a group of enterprises where the goods have not yet left the group's internal field of operation and have not come into free circulation, *ie* have entered the (Common) Market.

Notes and Questions

1. Do the *German Sound Recording* and *German Licensing* cases contradict each other regarding the copyright owner's ability to control the distribution of her works?

2. What is the critical difference between these two cases? Would it make a difference if the intra-company transfers were treated as a sales of goods, as opposed to a license arrangement?

3. If your client were to establish a publishing house in France for tax reasons, what advice would you give him regarding his ability to control the distribution of his copyrighted works in the European Union?

4. What if the records obtained by the UK company in the *German Licensing* case were first manufactured in the United States (a country that is *not* a member of the EU)? Would this fact require a different result regarding the duty of the U.S. company to pay the potentially higher compulsory licensing fees in the U.S. for sound recordings? Should it? What if the U.S. manufacturers were a wholly-owned subsidiary of the German company? Would that fact require a different result with regard to the application of EU structures on grey market goods? Where should the boundary of copyright "exhaustion" be established?

B. WHO HAS THE RIGHT TO CONTROL THE PROTECTION/DISTRIBUTION OF PATENTED GOODS IN THE EU?
THE ITALIAN PHARMACEUTICAL PATENT CASE
MERCK & CO. INC. v. STEPHAR BV

Court Of Justice Of The European Communities, 1981.
[1981] ECR 2063, [1981] 3 CMLR 463, [1982] FSR 57.

The American company Merck & Co. Inc., which is established in Rahway (New Jersey), and which I shall call "Merck", is the proprietor of two Netherlands patents taken out in 1973 and 1974 to protect a drug known as "Moduretic" and the process for manufacturing it. Similar parallel patents identical with at least one of those patents exist in all the Member States of the Community with the exception of Luxembourg and Italy. The preparation, which is used in the treatment of high blood pressure, amongst other things, is manufactured and marketed together with other products by a wholly-owned subsidiary of the American company established in the Netherlands. In particular the product is also put on the market in Italy where by virtue of Article 14(1) of the Italian Patent Law (Regio Decreto) ([Royal Decree] No. 1127 of 29 June 1939) patents were not available for drugs and the processes for manufacturing them. Although that provision was declared unconstitutional by Decision No. 20 of the Italian Constitutional Court of 20 March 1978 (Official Gazette of the Italian Republic of 29 March 1978) Merck was unable even subsequently to obtain patent protection in Italy because until now there have been no corresponding transitional provisions with retroactive effect.

Stephar B.V. of Rotterdam, a company of which Mr. Exler is the shareholder and director (I shall refer to it simply as "Staphar") purchased supplies of the preparation described above and placed by Merck on the market in Italy from wholesalers in that country and imported them into the Netherlands for the purpose of marketing the product there. In carrying out this parallel import it benefits from a considerable difference in price because the preparation is sold in Italy at a lower price.

In an application for an interim injunction heard by the Arrondissementsrechtbank [District Court] Rotterdam, Merck opposed the imports on the ground that they infringed its Netherlands patents. It based its application on Article 30 of the Netherlands Patent Law (Rijksctrooiwet) which gives the proprietor of a patent exclusive rights to manufacture and exploit the protected product and according to which the acquirer or later proprietor does not infringe the patent if he exploits the product which has been lawfully put on the market in the Netherlands.

On the basis of those facts the President of the Arrondissementsrechtbank Rotterdam by order of 2 July 1980 suspended the proceedings and referred the following questions to the Court of Justice for a preliminary ruling under Article 177 of the EEC Treaty:

"In a case where:

1.   an undertaking is the proprietor of a patent in a Member State of the European Communities for a drug and the processes for manufacturing it;

2.   by or with the consent of that undertaking that drug is marketed in Italy where the undertaking could not by law acquire a patent for that drug by virtue of Article 14(1) of the Italian Patent Law (Regio Decreto of 29 June 1939 No. 1127), later declared unconstitutional by the Italian Constitutional Court in its judgment of 20

March 1978, which prohibited the grant of patents for drugs and processes for manufacturing them;

3.   a third party imports the drug referred to in paragraph 2 above from Italy into the Member State referred to in paragraph 1 above and deals in them there;

4.   and the patent legislation in that country gives the proprietor of the patent the right to oppose by legal action the marketing there by others of the products protected by the patent even if previously they had been lawfully marketed in another country by or with the consent of the proprietor of the patent or with his consent;

do the rules contained in the EEC Treaty concerning the free movement of goods, notwithstanding the provisions of Article 36, then prevent the proprietor of the patent from availing himself of the right referred to in paragraph 4 above?''

The question is essentially whether and to what extent Articles 30 and 36 of the EEC Treaty prevent the proprietor of a national patent from relying on that patent to prevent the product protected by the patent from being imported from another Member State, in which no patent protection is available and in which the product had been place on the market by the proprietor of the patent himself or with his consent, and from being subsequently marketed.

The Court takes as its starting point the premise that the relevant national protective rights must be considered in the light of the provisions in the Treaty concerning the free movement of goods, in particular Article 30 et seq., according to which quantitative restrictions on imports and all measures having equivalent effect are prohibited between Member States. Under Article 36 those provisions nevertheless do not preclude prohibitions or restrictions on imports justified on the ground of protection of industrial and commercial property. However, it is clear from that article, in particular the second sentence, as well as from the context, that whilst the Treaty does not affect the existence of rights recognized by the legislation of a Member State in matters of industrial property, the exercise of those rights may nevertheless, depending on the circumstances, be restricted by the prohibitions contained in the Treaty. Inasmuch as it creates an exception to one of the fundamental principles of the Common Market, Article 36 in fact admits of exceptions to the rules on the free movement of goods only to the extent to which such exceptions are justified for the purpose of safeguarding the rights which constitute the specific subject-matter of that property. That statement is complemented in the relevant decisions by a definition of what constitutes the specific subject-matter of individual property rights and, based on that, which trade barriers may be accepted under Community law and which may not. What is clear is that the Court has consistently held that an exclusive right guaranteed by the legislation on industrial and commercial property is exhausted when a product has been lawfully distributed by the actual proprietor of the right or with his consent, on the market in another Member State.

In its judgment in Case 24/67 (*Parke, Davis & Co. v. Probel, Reese, Beintema–Interpharm and Centrafarm,* judgment of 29 February 1968 [1968] ECR 55) the Court had the occasion for the first time, albeit in the context of competition law, to state its views in regard to the exercise of national patent rights in relation to parallel imports of pharmaceutical products from Italy, which did not recognize any exclusive right to the manufacture and marketing of such products. Although it did not state so clearly, the Court appears to have proceeded on the assumption that the proprietor of a Netherlands patent was entitled, notwithstanding Article 30 et seq. of the EEC Treaty, to prohibit parallel imports of pharmaceutical products from Italy, but the Court did not on that occasion consider whether those products had been manufactured or put on the market in Italy by the Netherlands proprietor of the patent or with its consent.

On the other hand that factor was held to be of decisive importance in the Court's judgment of 8 June 1971 in Case 78/70 (*Deutsche Grammophon Gesellschaft GmbH v. Metro–SB–Grossmarkte GmbH & Co.* KG [1971] ECR 487) which is also pertinent to the judgment of the issues in the present case. The *Deutsche Grammoophon Gesellschaft* case concerned a right analogous to a copyright, connected with the reproduction of sound recordings. The Court was called upon to decide whether a German manufacturer of sound recording was able on the basis of such a right to prevent the marketing in the Federal Republic of Germany of sound recordings which it had itself delivered to its legally independent but economically wholly dependent subsidiary in France. It is noteworthy that at the time in question, despite the existence in France of a certain degree of protection against unfair competition, there was no parallel right of exclusivity for manufacturers of sound recordings comparable to German protective rights. That was not considered by the Court to be relevant to the decision, however, as it confined itself upon a consideration of the specific subject-matter of the exclusive right in question, to holding that such an exclusive right might not be used to prohibit parallel imports of products which have been put on the market in the territory of another Member State by the proprietor of the right or with his consent.

In the field of patent law the specific subject-matter of industrial property has been described by the Court in the *Sterling Drug* judgment (Case 15/74) as the guarantee "that the patentee, to reward the creative effort of the inventor, has the exclusive right to use an invention with a view to manufacturing industrial products and putting them into circulation for the first time, either directly or by the grant of licences to third parties, as well as the right to oppose infringements". In that definition the Court made it plain, as Stephar and the Commission observe, rightly in my view, that the essence of a patent right lies primarily in the fact that the inventor is guaranteed an exclusive right to manufacture and market the product in question. That exclusive right necessarily also embraces the right to oppose the marketing of the patented product where it is manufactured by third parties or put on the market without the consent of the proprietor of the patent. These rights are not an end in themselves, however, but are designed, as the Court noted in the definition cited above, to provide the proprietor of patent rights with the possibility of obtaining a recompense for his creative effort of invention. However, whilst that is one of the objectives of a patent right it is not, in my view, inherent in that right but must be seen as being separate from it, for it is open to any proprietor of a patent to put his invention on the market without seeking the recompense described above. Furthermore, it should not be forgotten that the return on research investment is merely a possibility, the realization of which depends on numerous market factors such as the presence of substitute products, commercial exploitability and similar conditions.

But there is a further conclusion to be drawn, at least indirectly, from the definition given by the Court, namely that the purpose of an industrial property right is achieved when the product is first lawfully put on the market because that is when the opportunity for making a monopoly profit may be exploited and it would exceed the purpose of the protection were the patentee to be given control over subsequent marketing. That is why in most of the Member States, too, the concept of the exhaustion of patent rights is recognized as embracing the principle that the rights flowing from the patent may no longer be exercised within the territory in which the patent has effect once the product has been put on the market there by the proprietor of the patent himself or with his consent, for the proprietor of the patent has then enjoyed the advantages conferred on him by the patent and has thus exhausted his right. Although that doctrine, which is based on the national patent, cannot be directly applied as far as the Community rules are concerned, as Mr. Advocate General Trabucchi stated in his opinion of 18 September 1974 in Case 15/74 (*Sterling Drug* [1974] ECR 1147, at p. 1169), it must still be acknowledged that even that theory is posited on the putting on the market of the patented product. Thus the Court of Justice, too, stated in Case 15/74 (*Sterling Drug*) that when a patentee has put the patented product on the market in one Member State the product is "released" for further sale on that market and that the product thus released must be permitted to circulate freely on the other markets within the Community too, in accordance with the principle of the free movement of goods.

DECISION:

The parties to the proceedings commenced their discussion of the question by emphasizing that the Court has already stated, in its judgment of 31 October 1974 (*Sterling Drug*, Case 15/74 (1974) ECR 1147), that inasmuch as it provides an exception, for reasons concerned with the protection of industrial and commercial property rights, to one of the fundamental principles of the Common Market, Article 36 admits of such a derogation only in so far as it is justified for the purpose of safeguarding rights which constitute the specific subject-matter of that property, which as far as patents are concerned is in particular to guarantee "that the patentee , to reward the creative effort of the inventor, has the exclusive right to use an invention with a view to manufacturing industrial products and putting them into circulation for the first time, either directly or by the grant of licences to third parties, as well as the right to oppose infringements''.

In the same judgment the court declared that an obstacle to the free movement of goods may be justified on the ground of protection of industrial property where such protection is invoked against a product coming from a Member State where it is not patentable and has been manufactured by third parties without the consent of the patentee.

The parties are in agreement as to the fact that the situation under consideration in the present instance differs from that which was the subject of that decision because, although it concerns a Member State where the product in question is not patentable, that product has been marketed not by third parties but by the proprietor of the patent and manufacturer of the product himself; however, from that statement they draw opposite conclusions.

Stephar and the commission conclude that once the proprietor of the patent has himself placed the product in question on the open market in a Member State in which it is not patentable, the importation of such goods into the Member State in which the product is protected may not be prohibited because the proprietor of the patent has placed it on the market of his own free will.

In contrast Merck , supported by the French government and the government of the United Kingdom, maintains that the purpose of the patent, which is to reward the inventor, is not safeguarded if owing to the fact that the patent right is not recognized by law in the country in which the proprietor of the patent has marketed his product he is unable to collect the reward for his creative effort because he does not enjoy a monopoly in first placing the product on the market.

In the light of that conflict of views, it must be stated that in accordance with the definition of the specific purpose of the patent, which has been described above, the substance of a patent right lies essentially in according the inventor an exclusive right of first placing the product on the market.

That right of first placing a product on the market enables the inventor, by allowing him a monopoly in exploiting his product, to obtain the reward for his creative effort without, however, guaranteeing that he will obtain such a reward in all circumstances.

It is for the proprietor of the patent to decide, in the light of all the circumstances, under what conditions he will market his product, including the possibility of marketing it in a member state where the law does not provide patent protection for the product in question. If he decides to do so he must then accept the consequences of his choice as regards the free movement of the product within the Common Market, which is a fundamental principle forming part of the legal and economic circumstances which must be taken into account by the proprietor of the patent in determining the manner in which his exclusive right will be exercised.

That is borne out, moreover, by the statements of the Court in its judgments of 22 June 1976 (*Terrapin*, Case 119/75 (1976) ECR 1039) and 20 January 1981 (*Musik-Vertrieb Membran and K–Tel*, Joined Cases 55 and 57/80 (not yet published)) inasmuch as the "proprietor of an industrial or commercial property right protected by the law of a Member State cannot rely on that law to prevent the importation of a product which has been lawfully marketed in another Member State by the proprietor himself or with his consent".

Under those conditions to permit an inventor, or one claiming under him, to invoke a patent held by him in one member state in order to prevent the importation of the product freely marketed by him in another member state where that product is not patentable would bring about a partitioning of the national markets which would be contrary to the aims of the Treaty.

The reply to the question which has been raised therefore should be that the rules contained in the EEC Treaty concerning the free movement of goods, including the provisions of Article 36, must be interpreted as preventing the proprietor of a patent for a medicinal preparation who sells the preparation in one member state where patent protection exists, and then markets it himself in another Member State where there is no such protection, from availing himself of the right conferred by the legislation of the first Member State to prevent the marketing in that State of the said preparation imported from the other Member State.

Notes and Questions

1.   The court in the *Italian Pharmaceutical* case emphasized the need to avoid "partitioning" of the market by permitting Merck to prohibit the importation of drugs it had already marketed in Italy. To what extent has the marketplace already been partitioned by the differing treatment of pharmaceutical products under Italian and Netherlands law? Is this "partitioning" different in market/trade impact than that caused by prohibiting the importation of grey market goods?

2.   The European Union currently has no specific harmonization standards for patents and no European Community Patent. Given this lack of treatment, should national decisions regarding protection (or the decision to deny protection) be given greater weight than under, for example, trademarks where the Union has, at least, enacted some Union-wide protection standards?

3.   Once Merck failed to obtain patent protection under Italian law, what realistic commercial options remained for it in regard to its pharmaceutical products if it could not prohibit the importation of grey market goods from Italy?

4.   Your client, a British citizen, has obtained patent protection for its method of conducting an auction on the Internet utilizing a claimed algorithm. She has patented her invention in the United States, the UK, France and Germany. Her patent applications have been rejected in all other countries of the EU. If she licenses her invention for use on the Internet to a

French company, what risk, if any, does she run that she will be unable to protect her invention from unauthorized use throughout the EU?

5.   Assume for purposes of this hypothetical only that the following countries grant the following terms of protection for computer software:

United Kingdom–20 years from issuance of patent

France–20 years from filing

Italy–no patent protection

Germany–10 years from filing

Your client has obtained a patent for its software in the UK, France and Germany. It begins to sell its software in all four countries. As a practical matter, how long will your client's patented invention actually be protected in the EU? *See Centrafarm BV v. Sterling Drugs, Inc.* [1974] ECR 1147, [1975] FSR 161, [1974] 2 CMLR 480.

C. WHO HAS THE RIGHT TO CONTROL THE PROTECTION/DISTRIBUTION TRADE-MARKED GOODS IN THE EC?

THE HAG II CASE

SA CNL–SUCAL NV v. HAG GF AG

Court of Justice of the European Communities, 1989.
[1990] 3 C.M.L.R. 571.

OPINION OF THE ADVOCATE GENERAL

This case comes before the Court by way of a reference for a preliminary ruling from the Bundesgerichtshof (German Federal Supreme Court). It is concerned primarily with the relationship between the principle of the free movement of goods laid down in Articles 30 to 34 of the EEC Treaty and the exception to that principle laid down in Article 36 thereof with regard to restrictions "justified on grounds of . . . the protection of industrial and commercial property". The present case constitutes a sequel to Case 192/73 *Van Zuylen v HAG* 1974 ECR 731. Inevitably, that case and the present one will become known as HAG I and HAG II respectively. These are convenient epithets and I shall use them myself.

The plaintiff in the main proceedings, HAG GF AG (hereafter "HAG Bremen"), is a German company based in Bremen. It has been in existence since 1906 and its main activities, arising from the invention of the first process for decaffeinating coffee, have long been the production and distribution of such coffee. In 1907 it had the trade mark "HAG" registered in its name in Germany. The following year the same mark was registered in its name in Belgium and Luxembourg. In 1927 it set up a subsidiary company in Belgium, trading as "Cafe HAG SA", which was wholly owned and controlled by it. In 1935 it transferred the Belgian and Luxembourg trade marks to the subsidiary. In 1944 the entire assets of the subsidiary, including the trade marks for Belgium and Luxembourg, were sequestrated as enemy property. The company was sold en bloc to the Van Oevelen family. In 1971 the trade marks, which had at some stage been converted into Benelux marks, were assigned to Van Zuylen Freres, a firm based in Liege.

When in 1972 HAG Bremen began exporting coffee to Luxembourg under the mark "Kaffee HAG", Van Zuylen Freres commenced infringement proceedings before a Luxembourg court. Those proceedings led to the preliminary ruling in HAG I, in which the Court held that:

"To prohibit the marketing in one Member State of a product legally bearing a trade mark in another Member State for the sole reason that an identical trade mark, having the same origin, exists in the first State, is incompatible with the provisions for the free movement of goods within the common market."

The implications of that ruling seem clear. It was drafted in such wide terms as to give the impression that, if Van Zuylen could not rely on their Benelux trade mark to prevent HAG Bremen from selling coffee under that mark in Luxembourg (and indeed Belgium), neither could HAG Bremen rely on their German trade mark to prevent Van Zuylen from supplying the German market under the same mark. Van Zuylen did not, however, attempt to do that. For the next decade HAG Bremen continued to enjoy undisturbed use of the HAG trade mark in Germany.

In 1979 the firm Van Zuylen Freres was purchased by a Swiss company now called Jacobs Suchard AG, which is the market leader in coffee products in Germany. According to HAG Bremen's observations, Jacobs Suchard AG disposed of the bulk of Van Zuylen's coffee business, retaining only the shell of the firm and the HAG trade marks. The firm was transformed into a wholly owned subsidiary of Jacobs Suchard AG trading under the name SA CNL–SUCAL NV (hereafter "HAG Belgium").

In 1985 HAG Belgium began to supply decaffeinated coffee under the HAG trade mark to the German market. HAG Bremen, which maintains that "Kaffee HAG" has acquired the status of a famous brand in Germany and that its product is, by virtue of a new manufacturing process, superior in quality to the coffee supplied by HAG Belgium, applied to the competent German court for an injunction restraining HAG Belgium from infringing its trade mark. HAG Bremen succeeded before the Landgericht Hamburg and, on appeal, before the Hanseatisches Oberlandesgericht. HAG Belgium appealed to the Bundesgerichtshof, which referred the following question to the Court for a preliminary ruling.

"(1) Is it compatible with the provisions on the free movement of goods (Articles 30 and 36 of the EEC Treaty)—having regard also to Article 222—that an undertaking established in Member State A should, by virtue of its national rights in trade names and trade marks, oppose the importation of similar goods of an undertaking established in Member State B if, in State B, those goods have legally received a mark which:

(a) may be confused with the trade name and trade mark reserved in State A to the undertaking established there, and

(b) had originally existed in State B—albeit registered later than a mark protected in State A—for the benefit of the undertaking established in State A and had been transferred by that undertaking to a subsidiary undertaking set up in State B and forming part of the same concern, and © was, as a consequence of the expropriation in State B of that subsidiary, transferred as an asset of the sequestrated subsidiary (together with that undertaking as a whole) to a third party which, in turn, assigned the mark to the legal precursor of the undertaking which now exports the goods bearing that mark to State A?

III.   The relevant Treaty provisions and Community legislation

Article 30 of the Treaty provides that:

"Quantitative restrictions on imports and all measures having equivalent effect shall, without prejudice to the following provisions, be prohibited between Member States."

Article 36 of the Treaty provides in pertinent part that:

"The provisions of Articles 30 to 34 shall not preclude prohibitions or restrictions on imports, exports or goods in transit justified on grounds of . . . the protection of industrial and commercial property. Such prohibitions or restrictions shall not, however, constitute a means of arbitrary discrimination or a disguised restriction on trade between Member States."

Article 222 of the Treaty provides that:

"This Treaty shall in no way prejudice the rules in Member States governing the system of property ownership."

Finally, Article 85(1) of the Treaty—which is not directly relevant to the present case but which still needs to be borne in mind because it contains one of the essential yardsticks for judging whether a particular course of conduct is acceptable under Community law—provides that:

"The following shall be prohibited as incompatible with the common market: all agreements between undertakings, decisions by associations of undertakings and concerted practices which may affect trade between Member States and which have as their object or effect the prevention, restriction or distortion of competition within the common market."

Articles 30 and 36 articulate a conflict between two competing interests. On the one hand, Article 30, together with the succeeding articles, lays down the fundamental principle of the free movement of goods. On the other hand, Article 36 safeguards, amongst other things, intellectual property rights, which, owing to their territorial nature, inevitably create obstacles to the free movement of goods. Article 36 itself goes some of the way towards explaining how that conflict is to be resolved. It is clear from the wording of the article that not all restrictions on trade created by intellectual property rights are excluded from the prohibition laid down by Article 30. In order to be excluded from the prohibition, a restriction must, in the first place, be "justified" within the meaning of the first sentence of Article 36. Secondly, it must not constitute a "means of arbitrary discrimination or a disguised restriction on trade between Member States" within the meaning of the second sentence of Article 36.

In keeping with its nature as a *traité-cadre*, the EEC Treaty does not purport to lay down an exhaustive code of rules governing the status of intellectual property rights in Community law. It merely provides a skeleton. The task of putting flesh on the bones falls to the Community legislature and to the Court of Justice. In the field of trade mark law the legislature has not been as active as it might have been, having undertaken only two major initiatives, one of which—the proposed Council Regulation on the Community trade mark (Official Journal 1984 C 230, p. 1)—has not yet come to fruition. The one measure that has so far been adopted is Council Directive 89/104/EEC of 21 December 1988 approximating the legislation of Member States on trade marks (Official Journal 1989 L 40, p. 1), hereafter "the trade mark directive". [The CTM was finally established in 1993.]

IV.   The principles established by the Court' s case-law

In view of the modest scale of legislative activity in relation to trade marks and to intellectual property in general, the task of reconciling the competing interests enshrined in Articles 30 and 36 of the Treaty has fallen mainly to the Court. It has worked out three fundamental principles, which have played a central part in the entire field of intellectual property, and all of which have their origin in Case 78/70 *Deutsche Grammophon v Metro* 1971 ECR 487.

(i) While the Treaty does not affect the existence of intellectual property rights, there are none the less circumstances in which the exercise of such rights may be restricted by the prohibitions laid down in the Treaty (see, for example, *Deutsche Grammophon*, paragraph 11).

(ii) Article 36 permits exceptions to the free movement of goods only to the extent to which such exceptions are necessary for the purpose of safeguarding the rights that constitute the specific subject-matter of the type of intellectual property in question (Deutsche Grammophon). Perhaps the main advantage of this formula, apart from the fact that it narrows the scope of the exceptions permitted by Article 36, is that it allows subtle distinctions to be made depending on the type of intellectual property in issue.

(iii) The exclusive right conferred on the owner of intellectual property is exhausted in relation to the products in question when he puts them into circulation anywhere within the common market. Spelt out more fully, "the proprietor of an industrial or commercial property right protected by the legislation of a Member State may not rely on that legislation in order to oppose the importation of a product which has lawfully been marketed in another Member State by, or with the consent of, the proprietor of the right himself or a person legally or economically dependent on him" (see, for example, Case 144/81 *Keurkoop v Nancy Kean Gifts* 1982 ECR 2853, at p. 2873, one of many cases confirming a principle first developed in the *Deutsche Grammophon* case).

In addition, the Court has developed the principle that the rights conferred under national law by a trade mark (or presumably by any other form of intellectual property) cannot be exercised in such a way as to frustrate the competition rules of the Treaty. The exercise of such rights must not result from agreements or concerted practices that have as their object or effect the isolation or partitioning of the common market, contrary to the terms of Article 85 of the Treaty. In particular, the proprietor of a trade mark may not use it to erect "impenetrable frontiers between the Member States" by assigning the mark to different persons in different Member States.

It is against that background that there falls to be considered the doctrine of common origin, under which, where similar or identical trade marks that have a common origin are owned by different persons in different Member States, the proprietor of one of the marks cannot rely on it to prevent the importation of goods lawfully marketed under the other mark by its proprietor in another Member State. The doctrine of common origin was laid down by the Court in HAG I and confirmed in Case 119/75 *Terrapin v Terranova* 1976 ECR 1039. To a large extent, the outcome of *HAG II* will depend on whether that doctrine is to be recognized as a legitimate child of Community law.

Like patents, trade marks find their justification in a harmonious dovetailing between public and private interests. Whereas patents reward the creativity of the inventor and thus stimulate scientific progress, trade marks reward the manufacturer who consistently produces high-quality goods and they thus stimulate economic progress. Without trade mark protection there would be little incentive for manufacturers to develop new products or to maintain the quality of existing ones. Trade marks are able to achieve that effect because they act as a guarantee, to the consumer, that all goods bearing a particular mark have been produced by, or under the control of, the same manufacturer and are therefore likely to be of similar quality. The guarantee of quality offered by a trade mark is not of course absolute, for the manufacturer is at liberty to vary the quality; however, he does so at his own risk and he—not his competitors—will suffer the consequences if he allows the quality to decline. Thus, although trade marks do not provide any form of legal guarantee of quality—the absence of which may have misled some to underestimate their significance—they do in economic terms provide such a guarantee, which is acted upon daily by consumers.

A trade mark can only fulfil that role if it is exclusive. Once the proprietor is forced to share the mark with a competitor, he loses control over the goodwill associated with the mark. The reputation of his own goods will be harmed if the competitor sells inferior goods. From the consumer' s point of view, equally undesirable consequences will ensue, because the clarity of the signal transmitted by the trade mark will be impaired. The consumer will be confused and misled.

With the first question the national court in essence asks whether Articles 30 and 36 EEC preclude national legislation from enabling an enterprise owning a trade mark right in a Member State to prevent the importation from another Member State of similar products to which an identical mark or a mark which may cause confusion with the protected mark has lawfully been affixed in the latter State, even though the mark under which the disputed products are imported originally belonged to a subsidiary of the enterprise which is resisting importation and was acquired by a third enterprise following the expropriation of that subsidiary.

According to settled case law, Article 36 allows exceptions to the fundamental principle of freedom of movement of goods in the Common Market only in so far as such exceptions are justified for safeguarding the rights which are the specific subject matter of that property and, consequently, an owner of an industrial and commercial right protected by the law of a State cannot rely on that law in order to prevent the importation or marketing of a State by the owner of the right himself or with his consent, or by a person connected with him by ties of legal or economic dependence: *see* Case 78/70, *Deutsche Grammophon*.

With regard to trade mark rights, it should be observed that such rights constitute an essential element of the system of undistorted competition which the Treaty aims to establish and maintain. In such a system enterprises must be able to gain customers by the quality of their products or services, which can be done only by virtue of the existence of distinctive signs permitting identification of those products and services. For a trade mark to be able to play this part, it must constitute a guarantee that all the products bearing it have been manufactured under the supervision of a single enterprise to which responsibility for their quality may be attributed.

Consequently, as the Court has stated on many occasions, the specific subject-matter of a trade mark right is to grant the owner the right to use the mark for the first marketing of a product and, in this way, to protect him against competitors who would like to abuse the position and reputation of the mark by selling products to which the mark has been improperly affixed. To determine the exact effect of this exclusive right which is granted essential function of the mark, which is to give the consumer or final user a guarantee of the identity of the origin of the marked product by enabling him to distinguish, without any possible confusion, that product from others of a different provenance.

In assessing in the light of the foregoing considerations a situation such as that described by the national court, the decisive fact is the absence of any element of consent, on the part of the owner of the trade mark right protected by national legislation, to the marketing in another Member State, under a mark which is identical or may cause confusion, of a similar product manufactured and marketed by an enterprise which has no tie of legal or economic dependence with that owner.

Under these circumstances the essential function of the mark would be compromised if the owner of the right could not exercise his option under national law to prevent the importation of the similar product under a name likely to be confused with his own mark because, in this situation, consumers would no longer be able to identify with certainty the origin of the marked product and the bad quality of a product for which he is no way responsible could be attributed to the owner of the right.

This conclusion cannot be altered by the fact that the mark protected by national legislation and the similar mark borne by the imported product pursuant to the legislation of the Member State of provenance originally belonged to the same owner, which was dispossessed of one of the marks as a result of expropriation by one of the two States in question before the Community was established.

In fact, since the date of expropriation and in spite of their common origin, each of the marks has independently fulfilled, within its own territorial limits, its function of guaranteeing that the marked products come from a single source.

It follows from what has been said that, in a situation like the present, where the mark originally had one owner and where single ownership ended as a result of expropriation, each of the owners of the trade mark right must be able to prevent the importation and marketing, in the Member State where the mark belongs to him, of products originating from the other owner, if they are similar products bearing a mark which is identical or which may cause confusion.

Therefore the reply to the first question should be that Articles 30 and 36 of the EEC Treaty do not preclude national legislation from allowing an enterprise which in the holder of a trade mark in a Member State from opposing the importation from another Member State of similar products lawfully bearing an identical trade mark in the latter State or liable to confusion with the protected mark, even though the mark under which the disputed products are imported originally belonged to a subsidiary of the enterprise which opposes the importation and was acquired by a third enterprise as a result of the expropriation of that subsidiary.

On those grounds the Court, in answer to the questions referred to it by the Budesgerichtshof by order of 24 November 1988,

HEREBY RULES:

> Articles 30 and 36 of the EEC Treaty do not preclude national legislation from allowing an undertaking which is the holder of a trademark in a Member State from opposing the importation from another Member State of similar products lawfully bearing an identical trade mark in the latter State or liable to confusion with the protected mark even though the mark under which the contest-

ed products are imported originally belonged to a subsidiary of the undertaking which opposes the importation and was acquired by a third undertaking as a result of the expropriation of that subsidiary.

Notes and Questions

1. If a trademark owner cannot prohibit the importation of legitimately produced grey market goods, should she be able to prohibit the importation of goods bearing a confusingly similar trademark which have been legitimately manufactured abroad? In *Van Zuylen v. HAG*, [1974] ECR 731, [1976] 2 CMLR 482, referred to as "HAG I," both parties had rights to the mark HAG for coffee in their respective countries. As noted in the HAG II case above, originally the marks had been owned by the same company. In HAG I, the court held that the importation of products bearing marks of "common origin" could not be prohibited without violating Community law. The court stated in pertinent part:

> The exercise of a trade mark right tends to contribute to the partitioning off of the markets and thus to affect the free movement of goods between Member States, all the more so since—unlike other rights of industrial and commercial property—it is not subject to limitations in point of time.

> Accordingly, one cannot allow the holder of a trade mark to rely upon the exclusiveness of a trade mark right—which may be the consequence of the territorial limitation of national legislations—with a view to prohibiting the marketing in a Member State of goods legally produced in another Member State under an identical trade mark having the same origin.

> Such a prohibition, which would legitimize the isolation of national markets, would collide with one of the essential objects of the Treaty, which is to unite national markets in a single market.

> Whilst in such a market the indication of origin of a product covered by a trade mark is useful, information to consumers on this point may be ensured by means other than such as would affect the free movement of goods.

> Accordingly, to prohibit the marketing in a Member State of a product legally bearing a trade mark in another Member State, for the sole reason that an identical trade mark having the same origin exists in the first state, is incompatible with the provisions providing for free movement of goods within the common market.

For similar treatment of marks in the United States, *see K Mart Corp. v. Cartier, Inc.*, 486 U.S. 281 (1988).

> Does this common origin rule survive HAG II?

2. Does the application of national laws regarding trademark infringement have an adverse impact upon "free trade"? For example, if a German plaintiff who owns rights to the mark TERRANOVA for building materials in Germany sues a British manufacturer of pre-fabricated houses for houses in Germany under the mark TERRAPIN, does this implicate EC trade policy? The court in *Terrapin (Overseas) Limited v. Terranova Industrie CA*

Kapferer & Co., [1978] 3 CMLR 102, decided the answer was a qualified yes. It stated:

The rules of the EEC Treaty on the free movement of goods do not prevent the plaintiff company from restraining, on the basis of its trade name and trade mark rights established under German law, the use in the Federal Republic of Germany by the Defendant of a good designation capable of confusion, even though the defendant company is thereby hindered in the import of its goods, lawfully marked in Great Britain.

The Commission [has] expressed reservations about the view that the principles governing the danger of confusion and the similarity of goods in trade name and trade mark law are determined exclusively according to the law of the Member States. Danger of confusion and similarity of goods, the Commission argued, are central concepts of trade name law and trade mark law, which constitute their essence. [The Commission's argument was as follows:] The principles which are applied in the national systems of law of the Member States in order to determine the scope of protection under national trade mark rights have direct repercussions on the free movement of goods. In so far as they affect the movement of goods inside the Community, they are accessible to an evaluation by Community law. Unreserved recourse to national rights, which differ substantially from one another, cannot enter into consideration, for this would be tantamount to relinquishing the guarantee of protection rights according with the objective and the legal principles of the Common Market. The laying down and evaluation of these principles is not at the disposal of the legislator, the courts or authorities of any Member State, but must take place on the basis of the criteria of Community law, on which, in the framework of the interpretation of Article 36 of the EEC Treaty, the European Court of Justice has to rule. While the European Court of Justice does not have to assess whether, in the particular case, trade names or trade marks are to be regarded as capable of confusion or not, it does have to determine the principles on which this assessment must be undertaken. In this connection, it must be borne in mind that the question of whether trade marks are capable of confusion and whether they relate to similar goods acquires a new dimension at Community level, and conflicts on a major scale could arise in a Common Market which is characterised by the movement of goods between several Member States and by the fact that nine different systems of trade mark law exist side by side. Under Community law, the principles governing the capability of confusion must be reduced to the strict minimum which is necessary to guarantee the protection of national trade mark rights. [Such was the argument advanced by the Commission].

The European Court of Justice stated [that] the national court, if it affirms the similarity of the goods and the danger of confusion, has to examine further whether the exercise of industrial and commercial property rights does not constitute a means of arbitrary discrimination or a veiled restraint on trade between Member States. In this context, it must in particular examine whether the disputed rights would be exercised with the same strictness by the owner without regard to the national citizenship of any person infringing them.

With this, the European Court of Justice did not associate itself with the Commission's more far-reaching view, according to which concepts, central to trade mark law and its protective scope, of the danger of confusion and of similarity of goods–and correspondingly also of proximity of sector in trade name law–must, in the interest of free movement of goods in the Common Market, be reduced to the strict minimum which is necessary to guarantee national trade mark protection. The present Court concurs with this. The provisions of the EEC Treaty on the removal of quantitative restrictions between the Member States (Articles 30 et seq) offer no basis for such a limitation of the scope of protection, accorded by the national system of law, of the characterisation rights recognised and guaranteed in their continued existence by Article 36(1) of the EEC Treaty. As the European Court of Justice stated, the provisions of the EEC Treaty on the removal of quantitative restrictions between the Member States do not prevent import prohibitions or restrictions which are justified for the protection of industrial or commercial property; Article 36 of the EEC Treaty allows restrictions on the free movement of goods in so far as they are justified for the preservation of the rights which form the object of this property.

The specific object of characterisation rights, however, includes–regardless of the partly differing systems of protection rights and regardless of the individually different form of the characterisation rights accorded by the national system of law–their character as exclusion rights of a nature at least akin to property, with a protective scope extending over objects of territory. The EEC Treaty, which leaves untouched the system of property in the Member States (Article 22 of the EEC Treaty), did not interfere with this existing law, as the European Court of Justice acknowledged. Nor in particular does any such inference result from Article 36(2) of the EEC Treaty. In the view of the European Court of Justice, the national court, if it affirms similarity of goods and danger of confusion, has admittedly under this provision to examine whether the exercise of the industrial and commercial property rights does not constitute a means of arbitrary discrimination or a veiled restraint on trade between Member States: for this reason, the European Court of Justice in particular regarded as necessary the further examination as to whether the disputed rights are exercised with the same strictness by the owner without regard to the national citizenship of any person infringing them. On the other hand, the European Court of Justice obviously did not regard it as justified to reduce to a minimum, as the Commission proposed, the protection scope, accorded by the national system of law, of the characterisation rights, a scope which is delimited by the inclusion of characterisations capable of confusion (in the sphere of similarity of goods or, as the case may be, in proximity of sector in trade name law); for, by this, the content of the characterisation rights, themselves and thus their continued existence, which is accepted by the EEC Treaty, would be affected, and not merely their exercise.

Terranova was decided prior to the Trademark Harmonization Directive. Has the Community now interjected itself more completely into the infringement issue? Is every decision regarding potential trademark infringement one that impacts EU trade? If not, which infringement cases implicate such trade?

3. Is there a difference between trademarks and patents that would warrant greater concern over the potential adverse trade effect of broad protection under national laws?

4. Article 7 of the Trademark Harmonization Directive provided that a trademark owner's rights are "exhausted" when such goods are placed on sale with the trademark owner's consent anywhere in the EU. Does this Article violate Article 36 of the Treaty of Rome? In *Eurim-Pharm Arzneimittel GmbH v. Biersdorf*, the ECJ maintained that Article 7 and Article 36 must be interpreted in the same way because "Article 7 of the Directive, like Article 36 of the Treaty, is intended to reconcile the fundamental interest in protecting trade mark rights with the fundamental interest in the free movement of goods with the Common Market."

5. Could national laws provide for international exhaustion without violating Article 36? In other words, could a member state deny to trade mark owners the right to prohibit the importation of goods sold with the owner's permission anywhere in the world? *See* the *Silhouette* case, below.

THE EDAM CHEESE CASE
MINISTERE PUBLIC v. GERARD DESERBAIS

Court of Justice of the European Communities, 1988.
[1988] ECR 4907, [1989] 1 CMLR 516.

Opinion By Advocate General:

Pursuant to the International Convention on the Use of Designations of Origin and Names for Cheeses, "the Stresa Convention", of 1 June 1951, to which inter alia France and the Netherlands are parties but to which the Federal Republic of Germany is not, French legislation prohibits the marketing of cheese under the appellation "Edam" unless it has a minimum dry-matter content of 52% and a fat content of 40%. Gerard Deserbais, the manager of the French company Fromex SARL imported into France cheese originating in the Federal Republic of Germany which had a dry-matter content of 50.4% and a fat content of 34.3%. That cheese was prepacked and labelled (in French):

"German Edam cheese

Fat content 30%

Imported by Fromex, Strasbourg"

In respect of that importation, he was prosecuted and convicted of passing off ("usurpation d' une denomination") liable to mislead the buyer as to the nature and inherent qualities of the goods concerned. He appealed to the Court of Appeal, Colmar, on the basis that Community law allowed him to import the cheese into France under the appellation "Edam" because it was lawfully manufactured and marketed under that name in the Federal Republic of Germany.

To resolve the issue, the Court of Appeal, Colmar, referred the following question to the Court of Justice for a preliminary ruling by an order of 30 October 1986:

"Must Article 30 et seq of the EEC Treaty be interpreted as meaning that national legislation which, for the purpose of protecting a trade name,

(1) restricts that trade name to national products or those of another State, to the exclusion of the products of other Member States;

(2) makes the right to use the trade name of a cheese imported from a Member State conditional on the observance of a minimum fat content, even though the imported cheese is lawfully and traditionally produced and marketed in its country of origin in accordance with different technical and quality requirements constitutes a quantitative restriction on imports or a measure having equivalent effect thereto?"

The Netherlands Government contends that, although the appellation "Edam" is now applicable to cheese manufactured outside the Edam region of the Netherlands it must be confined to cheese complying with a certain technical description and in particular having a fat content of at least 40%. It contends that respect for the traditional production techniques fixed and accepted at the international level for Edam cheese requires the Member States of the EEC to be able to prohibit imports from other Member States of cheese not complying with such techniques, even if the consumer is informed of the difference of composition of the product. It therefore proposes that the question should be answered along the lines that Community law does not prohibit national provisions which allow a name to be used for cheese only if certain characteristics are complied with such as those stipulated inter alia in the Stresa Convention and the Codex Alimentarius.

It is well established in the case-law of the Court that a marketing restriction which operates by way of a restriction on the use of a name, rather than directly on the product, can none the less be a restriction for the purposes of Article 30 of the EEC Treaty.

National legislation such as the French legislation in issue in the present case does restrict or may restrict the sale of goods imported from other Member States, which brings it within the definition of a measure having an effect equivalent to a quantitative restriction on imports laid down by the Court in its case-law. Accordingly, it is prohibited by Article 30 of the EEC Treaty unless it falls within one of the exceptions in Article 36.

As the Netherlands Government admits, "Edam" long ago ceased to be reserved for cheese made in the Edam region of the Netherlands, and so it cannot be regarded as a designation of origin. Indeed in the Stresa Convention "Edam" is not classified among the "designations of origin" but only among the "names" of cheeses for which a lesser degree of protection is provided. It is now a name for a type of cheese but no longer with any geographical limitation on its place of production.

Decisions of the Court have laid down that Member States are not allowed to restrict a generic term to one national variety alone to the detriment of other varieties lawfully produced in other Member States.

It is difficult to say when a name which was originally specific to an area becomes a generic name, but it seems on all the evidence that "Edam" has now become a generic name and falls within the rule just stated. In any event as I see it "Edam" does not fall within the provisions of Article 36 of the EEC Treaty relating to the protection of industrial and commercial property.

In the present state of Community law there are no Community rules governing the names or designations of origin of different types of cheese within the Community. As the Court held at paragraph 8 of "CASSIS DE DIJON", in the absence of such common rules, "it is for the Member States to regulate all matters relating to the production and marketing of [the product] on their own territory. Obstacles to movement within the Community resulting from disparities between the national laws relating to the marketing of the products in question must be accepted in so far as those provisions may be recognized as being necessary in order to satisfy mandatory requirements relating in particular to ... the fairness of commercial transactions and the defence of the consumer".

The Stresa Convention, with its specifications *inter alia* for "Edam" cheese, has been signed by Denmark, France, Italy and the Netherlands but not by the other Member States. In the Federal Republic of Germany in particular it appears that the legislation allowing "Edam" cheese to be manufactured with a fat content as low as 30% dates back to 1934: 54 years ago. Moreover, it appears that in recent years Edam with a 30% fat content has represented one third of German production of Edam cheese. In such circumstances I do not consider that any mandatory requirement as to the fairness of commercial transactions can justify one Member State in banning the sale of Edam with a 30% fat content from another Member State.

As regards the defence of the consumer, it is well-established in the Court' s case-law that such a total ban is disproportionate to the purpose of protecting the consumer from deception if the same purpose can be achieved by less restrictive means such as labelling . That rule seems to me to apply in the present case, and it appears from the order for reference that the cheese in question was adequately labelled. Furthermore, the need to protect consumers from fraud must be set against the rule that national legislation "must not crystallize given consumer habits so as to consolidate an advantage acquired by national industries concerned to comply with them": judgment in the "beer" Case, [1988] 1 CMLR 780.

Mere labelling would not be sufficient if the product proposed was something radically different from the product usually recognized as "Edam" in the importing Member State, e.g. blue cheese or cream cheese . That, however, is not this case.

JUDGMENT:

In order to reply to the question submitted by the national court, it must be observed in the first place, as is apparent from the order for reference, that the designation "Edam" is not an appellation of origin or an indication of origin, terms which, as has been held by the Court, describe products coming from a specific geographical area. It is merely the name under which a type of cheese is sold. Moreover, in the Stresa Convention, the word "Edam" does not appear among the appellations of origin but among the "names" of cheeses.

In that connection, the national court starts from the premise that the cheese in question, containing 34% fat, has been lawfully and traditionally produced in the Federal Republic of Germany under the name "Edam" in accordance with the laws and regulations applicable to it there, and that consumers' attention is adequately drawn to that fact by the labelling.

It must also be stated that at the present stage of development of Community law there are no common rules governing the names of the various types of cheeses in the Community. Accordingly, it cannot be stated in principle that a Member State may not lay down rules making the use by national producers of a name for a cheese subject to the observance of a traditional minimum fat content.

However, it would be incompatible with Article 30 of the Treaty and the objectives of a common market to apply such rules to imported cheeses of the same type where those cheeses have been lawfully produced and marketed in another Member State under the same generic name but with a different minimum fat content. The Member State into which they are imported cannot prevent the importation and marketing of such cheeses where adequate information for the consumer is ensured.

The question may arise whether the same rule must be applied where a product presented under a particular name is so different, as regards its composition or production, from the products generally known by that name in the Community that it cannot be regarded as falling within the same category. However, no situation of that kind arises in the circumstances described by the national court in this case.

The Netherlands Government points out in this regard that consumer protection and fair trading require observance of international agreements concerning the use of the name of a particular product. Consequently, each Member State could make the right to use the name "Edam" subject to compliance with the requirements laid down by the Stresa Convention and the Codex Alimentarius, drawn up jointly by the Food and Agriculture Organization and the World Health Organization, both of which instruments lay down a minimum fat content of 40% for that type of cheese.

In reply to the question submitted, Article 30 et seq of the Treaty must be interpreted as precluding a Member State from applying national legislation making the right to use the trade name of a type of cheese subject to the observance of a minimum fat content to products of the same type imported from another Member State when those products have been lawfully manufactured and marketed under that name in that Member State and consumers are provided with proper information.

Notes and Questions

1. Does the refusal to protect "Edam" as a source designator violate the Trademark Harmonization Directive? Does it violate obligations under TRIPS?

2. Although TRIPS only requires protection for certain indicators of geographic origin relating to certain liquors and wines, other categories of foods and beverages, including cheese, are the source of continuing international debate.

3. Would it violate European Union law if Italy, for example, declared that "Swiss chocolate" was generic, and Switzerland declared the term a protectable geographic indicator and prohibited the importation of products bearing the term "Swiss Chocolate" unless they were made in Switzerland?

4. *Community Trademark.* Unlike patents, there is a supranational trademark regime in the EU. The Community Trademark (CTM) provides protection throughout the EU with a single registration in the Community Trademark Office in Alicante, Spain. Such CTM, however, remains subject to prior rise rights based on nationally registered/used marks in the member states. See Council Regulation (EC) No 40/94 of December 20, 1993 on the Community Trade Mark, OJL 011 (14/1/1994).

D. ARE INTELLECTUAL PROPERTY RIGHTS EXHAUSTED UPON A SALE ANYWHERE IN THE WORLD?

Read the following Articles from TRIPS from the Supplement: 3, 4, 6.

THE SILHOUETTE CASE

SILHOUETTE INTERNATIONAL SCHMIED GMBH & CO. KG v. HARTLAUER HANDELSGESELLSCHAFT MBH

Court Of Justice Of The European Communities, 1998.
1998 ECJ Celex Lexis 3682.

JACOBS, J.

The Court's case-law on Articles 30 and 36 of the EC Treaty established for trade marks, as well as for other forms of intellectual property, a principle of Community-wide exhaustion: thus the sale in the Community of the trade-marked goods, by or with the consent of the trade-mark owner, exhausts the trade-mark rights throughout the Community, and he cannot, other than in exceptional circumstances, oppose the use of the mark by others in subsequent transactions anywhere in the Community.

Article 7(1) of the Trade Marks Directive gives effect to the principle of Community exhaustion as developed by the Court's case-law. It provides that a trade mark does not entitle the proprietor to prohibit its use in relation to goods which have been put on the market in the Community under that trade mark by the proprietor or with his consent. Subsequently the principle was extended, by virtue of the Agreement on the European Economic Area (the EEA), to the territory of the EEA, now consisting of the Community on the one hand and Iceland, Liechtenstein and Norway on the other hand. But can the trade-mark owner prevent a third party from using the mark in the Community or in the EEA for goods which have been put on the market under that mark, by or with the consent of the owner, outside the EEA? The question comes by way of a request for a preliminary ruling from the Oberster Gerichtshof (Supreme Court), Austria.

The issue therefore is whether Community law requires Member States to provide for exhaustion only when the goods have been marketed in the EEA, or whether Member States may (or perhaps even must) provide for exhaustion when the goods have been marketed in a third country—a principle of international (i.e. worldwide) exhaustion.

The plaintiff, Silhouette International Schmied Gesellschaft mbH & Co. KG (Silhouette), is an Austrian company which produces fashion spectacles in the higher price ranges. It distributes the spectacles worldwide under the word and picture trade mark Silhouette', which is registered in Austria and in most countries of the world, as well as internationally. In Austria Silhouette supplies the spectacles to specialist opticians; in other countries it has subsidiary companies or distributors.

The defendant, Hartlauer Handelsgesellschaft mbH ('Hartlauer'), sells spectacles in numerous branches in Austria and solicits customers mainly by its low prices. It is not supplied by Silhouette because Silhouette considers sales by Hartlauer to be harmful to the image which Silhouette has created for its products as fashionable spectacles of special quality.

In October 1995 Silhouette sold 21 000 spectacle frames of an outdated model which had expired to a firm called Union Trading for U.S.D 261 450. The transaction was arranged by Silhouette's sales representative for the Middle East. Silhouette directed him to instruct the purchaser to sell the frames in Bulgaria or the States of the former Soviet Union only and not to export them to other countries. The sales representative informed Silhouette that he had instructed the purchaser accordingly. The Oberster Gerichtshof observes that it has not been possible to ascertain whether that actually happened.

Silhouette delivered the goods to Union Trading in Sofia in November 1995. Hartlauer subsequently acquired the goods (according to the Oberster Gerichtshof, it has not been possible to ascertain from whom) and offered them for sale in Austria from December 1995. It announced in a press campaign that, although it had not been supplied by Silhouette, it had succeeded in purchasing 21 000 Silhouette frames from abroad. In its observations, Hartlauer maintains that when it acquired the products it was assured that there would be no obstacle to importing them into Austria.

Silhouette objects to the sale of its frames by Hartlauer in Austria and seeks an order prohibiting Hartlauer from marketing under its trade mark spectacles or spectacle frames which were not put on the market in the EEA by it or with its consent. It argues that it has not exhausted its trade-mark rights because the Directive provides that such rights can be exhausted only by reason of marketing within the EEA by the trade-mark owner or with his consent.

The Oberster Gerichtshof (German Court of Appeal) has submitted the following question to this Court:

Is Article 7(1) of the First Council Directive 89/104/EEC of 21 December 1988 to Approximate the laws of the Member States relating to trade marks (OJ 1989 L 40, p. 1, "the Trade Marks Directive") to be interpreted as meaning that the trade mark entitles its proprietor to prohibit a third party from using the mark for goods which have been put on the market under that mark in a State which is not a Contracting State?

It should also be assumed for present purposes that Silhouette did not consent to its products being resold within the EEA. That is so even though the national court expresses some doubt as to whether the restrictions upon resale were passed on to the purchaser. If Silhouette had consented to marketing in the EEA, the answer to the first question referred would clearly be that Silhouette could not oppose the import of its products into Austria.

Article 7(1) of the Directive provides for exhaustion only where the goods have been put on the market in the Community: it provides therefore only for Community-wide, not for international exhaustion.

It is accepted on all sides, and with good reason in my view, that the Directive does not require Member States to provide for international exhaustion: at most, it leaves that open as an option for Member States. If the Directive had sought to impose international exhaustion, Article 7(1) would not have referred only to marketing in the Community.

Since the terms of the Directive are not conclusive, the aims and scope of the Directive are of crucial significance in interpreting its provisions. The indications in the preamble, however, do not all point in the same direction. On the one hand, the Directive does not purport to undertake full-scale approximation of the trade-mark laws of the Member States but aims to approximate those national provisions of law which most directly affect the functioning of the common market. On the other hand, the Directive seeks to ensure, with certain limited exceptions, that trade marks enjoy the same protection under the legal systems of all the Member States.

Those who favour international exhaustion point to the limited nature of the harmonisation attempted by the Directive and contend that the reference to Community exhaustion in Article 7(1) should be regarded only as a minimum standard.

Moreover, they argue that the intention of Article 7 was simply to codify the Court's existing case-law on the exhaustion of rights since the Court has stressed that Article 7 is to be interpreted in the same way as the Court's case-law on Articles 30 and 36. They contend that, prior to implementation of the Directive, Member States had a discretion as to whether or not to adopt the principle of international exhaustion; and that, in the absence of express language to the contrary, that should remain the position under the Directive.

The opponents of international exhaustion, relying on the wording of the third recital of the preamble to the Directive, argue that, whilst it is true that the Directive is not a measure of total harmonisation, the application by a Member State of the principle of international exhaustion is one of the provisions which most directly affect the functioning of the internal market and is accordingly the type of issue which the Directive sought to harmonise. Moreover, the purpose of the Directive was to ensure that trade marks enjoy the same protection under the legal systems of all the Member States. Although the protection afforded by the Directive does not impose a totally uniform system since certain areas are left to the discretion of the Member States, those areas are very limited and the choice carefully specified.

As regards the scope and effects of the Directive, it can in my view be argued that the Directive has transformed the impact of Community law on trade-mark protection. Previously the only issue under Community law was that of the impact of Articles 30 to 36 of the Treaty on national trade-mark law. The Directive harmonises the essential conditions and consequences of trade-mark protection. Although in an internal Community context the Court has treated Article 7 of the Directive as codifying the previous case-law, it cannot be assumed that that is the sole function of Article 7. The Directive regulates the substance of trade-mark rights, and its provisions are designed to be substituted for the diverse national laws across the whole range of its provisions.

If the Directive is seen as establishing the essential terms and effects of trade-mark protection, it is difficult to argue that it leaves Member States free to opt for international exhaustion. The scope of the exhaustion principle is after all central to the content of trade-mark rights.

But even if one takes a narrower view of the character of the Directive, it seems clear that international exhaustion is one of the matters which most directly affect the functioning of the internal market' and which the Directive therefore seeks to harmonise. If some Member States practise international exhaustion while others do not, there will be barriers to trade within the internal market which it is precisely the object of the Directive to remove.

In the present case the Swedish Government contends that the Directive leaves the issue of international exhaustion to be resolved by national law.

It seems to me that a distinction has to be made between measures of commercial policy on the one hand and provisions governing the effects of trade-mark rights within the Community on the other. Although to preclude international exhaustion clearly has an effect on external trade, it is less clear that it actually regulates such trade: contrary to the suggestion of the Swedish Government, the Directive, if interpreted as precluding international exhaustion, would not regulate relations between Member States and third States. Rather, the Directive lays down the rights of trade-mark owners in the Community. It provides for the conditions under which the trade-mark owner can take action against the marketing of certain goods, which may or may not be imported from third countries. Moreover it is inevitable that internal market measures will affect imports from third countries. Thus measures harmonising technical standards will affect goods from third countries, but can properly be based on Article 100a of the Treaty.

The Swedish Government also relies on the Court's case-law on the function of trade marks. That function is essentially to guarantee the consumer the possibility of identifying the origin of the product. It is no part of the function of a trade mark to enable the owner to divide up the market and to exploit price differentials. The adoption of international exhaustion would bring substantial advantages to consumers, and would promote price competition.

I confess to finding those arguments extremely attractive. However it must be remembered that the Court's case-law on the function of trade marks was developed in the context of the Community, not the world market.

There is of course a powerful argument based on the concern for free trade at the international level. To some commentators the exclusion of international exhaustion will appear protectionist and therefore harmful. Commercial policy considerations may however be more complex than they allow for. I have already alluded to concern about the possible lack of reciprocity if the Community were unilaterally to provide for international exhaustion. In any event it is no part of the Court's function to seek to evaluate such policy considerations.

As regards price competition and the benefit to consumers, such benefits again have to be set against the threat to the integrity of the internal market. That integrity would be severely prejudiced if one Member State provided for international exhaustion while another did not. Only consumers in the first State would benefit from the lower prices of imports from third countries. Price competition within the internal market would be distorted.

Finally, it should be recalled that some Member States, and some third countries, do not practise international exhaustion, and that that has not been held to be contrary to the General Agreement on Tariffs and Trade (the GATT). The situation is not changed in that respect by the WTO Agreement. Annex 1C, the Agreement on Trade-related aspects of Intellectual Property Rights (the TRIPS) provides by Article 6 that, for the purposes of dispute settlement under that Agreement, nothing in the Agreement (subject to certain provisions) shall be used to address the issue of the exhaustion of intellectual property rights.

I accordingly conclude, having regard to the wording and purpose of the Directive, its legislative history, and the undesirable effects of leaving the question to the discretion of the Member States, that Article 7(1) of the Directive precludes Member States from adopting the principle of international exhaustion.

Thus, Article 7(1) of the Directive is to be interpreted as meaning that the proprietor of a trade mark is entitled to prevent a third party from using the mark for goods which have been put on the market under that mark outside the territory of the EEA. Member States are accordingly precluded from adopting the principle of international exhaustion.

By its first question the Oberster Gerichtshof is in substance asking whether national rules providing for exhaustion of trade-mark rights in respect of products put on the market outside the EEA under that mark by the proprietor or with his consent are contrary to Article 7(1) of the Directive.

It is to be noted at the outset that Article 5 of the Directive defines the rights conferred by a trade mark and Article 7 contains the rule concerning exhaustion of the rights conferred by a trade mark.

According to Article 5(1) of the Directive, the registered trade mark confers on the proprietor exclusive rights therein. In addition, Article 5(1)(a) provides that those exclusive rights entitle the proprietor to prevent all third parties not having his consent from use in the course of trade of, *inter alia*, any sign identical with the trade mark in relation to goods or services which are identical to those for which the trade mark is registered. Article 5(3) sets out a non-exhaustive list of the kinds of practice which the proprietor is entitled to prohibit under paragraph 1, including, in particular, importing or exporting goods under the trade mark concerned.

Like the rules laid down in Article 6 of the Directive, which set certain limits to the effects of a trade mark, Article 7 states that, in the circumstances which it specifies, the exclusive rights conferred by the trade mark are exhausted, with the result that the proprietor is no longer entitled to prohibit use of the mark. Exhaustion is subject first of all to the condition that the goods have been put on the market by the proprietor or with his consent. According to the text of the Directive itself, exhaustion occurs only where the products have been put on the market in the Community (in the EEA since the EEA Agreement entered into force).

No argument has been presented to the Court that the Directive could be interpreted as providing for the exhaustion of the rights conferred by a trade mark in respect of goods put on the market by the proprietor or with his consent irrespective of where they were put on the market.

On the contrary, Hartlauer and the Swedish Government have maintained that the Directive left the Member States free to provide in their national law for exhaustion, not only in respect of products put on the market in the EEA but also of those put on the market in non-member countries.

The interpretation of the Directive proposed by Hartlauer and the Swedish Government assumes, having regard to the wording of Article 7, that the Directive, like the Court's case-law concerning Articles 30 and 36 of the EC Treaty, is limited to requiring the Member States to provide for exhaustion within the Community, but that Article 7 does not comprehensively resolve the question of exhaustion of rights conferred by the trade mark, thus leaving it open to the Member States to adopt rules on exhaustion going further than those explicitly laid down in Article 7 of the Directive.

As Silhouette, the Austrian, French, German, Italian and United Kingdom Governments and the Commission have all argued, such an interpretation is contrary to the wording of Article 7 and to the scheme and purpose of the rules of the Directive concerning the rights which a trade mark confers on its proprietor.

Articles 5 to 7 of the Directive must be construed as embodying a complete harmonisation of the rules relating to the rights conferred by a trade mark. That interpretation, it may be added, is borne out by the fact that Article 5 expressly leaves it open to the Member States to maintain or introduce certain rules specifically defined by the Community legislature. Thus, in accordance with Article 5(2), to which the ninth recital refers, the Member States have the option to grant more extensive protection to trade marks with a reputation.

Accordingly, the Directive cannot be interpreted as leaving it open to the Member States to provide in their domestic law for exhaustion of the rights conferred by a trade mark in respect of products put on the market in non-member countries.

This, moreover, is the only interpretation which is fully capable of ensuring that the purpose of the Directive is achieved, namely to safeguard the functioning of the internal market. A situation in which some Member States could provide for international exhaustion while others provided for Community exhaustion only would inevitably give rise to barriers to the free movement of goods and the freedom to provide services.

The Community authorities could always extend the exhaustion provided for by Article 7 to products put on the market in non-member countries by entering into international agreements in that sphere, as was done in the context of the EEA Agreement.

In the light of the foregoing, the answer must be that national rules providing for exhaustion of trade-mark rights in respect of products put on the market outside the EEA under that mark by the proprietor or with his consent are contrary to Article 7(1) of the Directive, as amended by the EEA Agreement.

Notes and Questions

1.   Earlier drafts of Trademark Harmonization Directive specifically permitted a doctrine of international exhaustion. The final version, however, was limited to EU wide exhaustion. What is the strongest argument you can make in favor of international exhaustion? What is the strongest argument you can make against such an extension?

2.   Do you agree with the court's decision in the *Silhouette* case? Is it in accordance with EU Member States' obligations under TRIPS?

3.   On what basis does the court in the *Silhouette* case justify requiring EU-wide exhaustion but *not* requiring global exhaustion? Do you find its reasoning persuasive? Would you permit global exhaustion for copyrights–which appear less territorial in nature–but deny such exhaustion for patents or trademarks?

4.   Compare the treatment of intellectual property issues under the Treaty of Rome and NAFTA–which established a regional free trade zone between the U.S., Canada and Mexico. Which do you believe is the more appropriate device to deal with IP matters–through extensive treaty provisions such as in NAFTA? Or by directives and case law such as the EU? Why?

*

Part XII

THE IMPACT OF CULTURAL RIGHTS ON INTELLECTUAL PROPERTY

When the first multinational accords regarding intellectual property protection were adopted, the participating nations shared the Western European "Romantic" view of creation. Solitary artists, authors, and inventors labored to create new works that would advance the scientific, technological or artistic fields of endeavor. Such solitary creators were entitled to a "property" right over the products of their individual intellectual labor. The underlying assumptions of individual ownership and private rights were shared by all the participants in these early multilateral conferences.

Such uniformity is no longer possible in the multicultural, global, intellectual property environment of the latter part of the Twentieth Century. To the contrary, indigenous peoples who share a communal view of property are challenging these assumptions and demanding recognition of their views on the international stage.

At the same time that the underlying assumptions regarding the nature of intellectual property are being debated internationally, the need for heightened protection of cultural patrimony is growing. Even as this book is being written, in Bosnia fears about the survival of the 13 century Sarajevo Haggadah codex are being raised in the face of plans to subject such codex to a revolving exhibition by the Bosnian–Serb museum. At one time threats to the continued existence of the Great Sphinx in Egypt, the repatriation of the "Elgin" Marbles to Greece, or scholarly access to the Dead Sea Scrolls was considered the sole province of antiquities or cultural patrimony laws. Gradually, however, the boundaries between "cultural patrimony" and "intellectual property" are blurring. As you will see in the materials below, the issues remain hotly debated, with no easy solutions. As you read these materials, ask yourself what role, if any, intellectual property regimes should play in the problems disclosed. What assumptions must be altered to take account of these new problems? Most importantly, what are the logical limits that intellectual property law can play in resolving these problems?

Chapter Forty-One

INTRODUCTION

A. WHAT ROLE DO COMMUNAL RIGHTS HAVE IN INTERNATIONAL INTELLECTUAL PROPERTY LAW DISPUTES?

THE BELLAGIO DECLARATION
March 1993.

We, the participants at the Bellagio Conference on intellectual property, come from many nations, professions and disciplines. We lawyers and literary critics, computer scientists and publishers, teachers and writers, environmentalists and scholars of cultural heritage.

Sharing a common concern about the effects of the international regime of intellectual property law on our communities, on scientific progress and international development, on our environment, on the culture of indigenous peoples. In particular,

Applauding the increasing attention by the world community to such previously ignored issues as preservation of the environment, of cultural heritage, and biodiversity. But

Convinced that the role of intellectual property in these areas has been neglected for too long, we therefore convened a conference of academics, activists and practitioners diverse in geographical and cultural background as well as professional area of interest.

Discovering that many of the different concerns faced in each of these diverse areas could be traced back to the same oversights and injustices in the current intellectual property system, we hereby

Declare the following:

First, intellectual property laws have profound effects on issues as disparate as scientific and artistic progress, biodiversity, access to information, and the cultures of indigenous and tribal peoples. Yet all too often those laws are constructed without taking such effects into account, constructed around a paradigm that is selectively blind to the scientific and artistic contributions of many of the world's cultures and constructed in *fora* where those who will be most directly affected have no representation.

Second, many of these problems are built into the basic structure and assumptions of intellectual property. Contemporary intellectual property law is constructed around a notion of the author as an individual, solitary and original creator, and it is for this figure that its protections are reserved. Those who do not fit this model–custodians of tribal culture and medical knowledge, collectives practicing traditional artistic and musical forms, or peasant cultivators of valuable seed varieties, for example–are denied intellectual property protection.

Third, a system based on such premises has real negative consequences. Increasingly, traditional knowledge, folklore, genetic material and native medical knowledge flow *out* of their countries of origin unprotected by intellectual property, while works from developed countries flow *in*, well protected by international intellectual property agreements, backed by the threat of trade sanctions.

Fourth, in general, systems built around the author paradigm tend to obscure or undervalue the importance of "the public domain," the intellectual and cultural commons from which future works will be constructed. Each intellectual property right, in effect fences off some portion of the public domain, making it unavailable to future creators. In striking respects, the current situation raises the same concerns raised twenty years ago by the impeding privatization of the deep sea bed. The aggressive expansion of intellectual property rights have the potential to inhibit development and future creation by fencing off "the commons," and yet–in striking contrast to the reaction over the deep sea bed–the international community seems unaware of the fact.

Fifth, we deplore these tendencies, deplore them as not merely unjust but unwise, and entreat the international community to reconsider the assumptions on which and the procedure by which the international intellectual property regime is shaped.

In general, we favor increased recognition and protection of the public domain. We call on the international community to expand the public domain through expansive application of concepts of "fair use," compulsory licensing, and narrower initial coverage of property rights in the first place. But since existing author-focused regimes are blind to the interests of non-authorial producers as well as to the importance of the commons, the main exception to this expansion of the public domain should be in favor of those who have been excluded by the authorial biases of current law.

Specifically, we advocate consideration of special regimes, possibly in the form of "neighboring" or "related" rights regimes, for the following areas:

    Protection of folkloric works.

    Protection of works of cultural heritage.

Protection of the biological and ecological "know-how" of traditional peoples.

In addition, we support systematic reconsideration of the basis on which new kinds of works related to digital technology, such as computer programs and electronic data bases, are protected under national and international intellectual property regimes. We recognize the economic importance of works falling into these categories, and the significant investments made in their production. Nevertheless, given the importance of the various concerns raised by any such a regime–concerns about public access, international development and technological innovation–we believe that choices about how and how much to protect databases should be made with a view to the specific policy objectives such protection is designed to achieve, rather than as a reflexive response to their categorization as "works of authorship."

On a systemic level, we call upon states and non-governmental organizations to move towards democratization of the fora in which the international intellectual property regime is debated and decided.

In conclusion, we declare that in an era in which information is among the most precious of all resources, intellectual property rights cannot be framed by the few to be applied to the many. They cannot be framed on assumptions that disproportionately exclude the contributions of important parts of the world community. They can no longer be constructed without reference to their ecological, cultural and scientific effects. We must reimagine the international regime of intellectual property. It is to that task this Declaration calls its readers.

Notes and Questions

1. The Bellagio Declaration is not a multinational treaty but a declaration of principles by a group of scholars, practitioners and other interested parties. Do you agree with their declaration regarding the nature of presently-recognized intellectual property rights? What assumptions does the Declaration make regarding the nature of intellectual property that it believes should be protected?

2. Does the Declaration propose workable standards for determining what works of indigenous cultures are to be protected? If not, what standards would you propose?

3. Compare the Bellagio Declaration with the Preamble of TRIPS. Do the two represent irreconcilable philosophies regarding the nature of intellectual property rights?

4. *Human Rights and Intellectual Property*. Numerous international human rights instruments affirm the right of indigenous peoples to enjoy and protect their own culture and traditions. For example, the International Covenant on Civil and Political Rights (ICCR) provides:

"In those States in which ethnic, religious or linguistic minorities exist, persons belonging to such minorities shall not be deprived of the right, in community with the other members of their group, to enjoy their own culture, to profess and practice their own religion or to use their own language."

See also treaties discussed in the Notes and Questions in Chapter Six.

5. *Cultural Exemptions.* Concern over the protection of indigenous or national culture is not restricted to developing countries or aboriginal peoples. To the contrary, such industrialized countries as France and Canada have erected trade and/or language barriers to protect their cultural industries from the intrusions of American consumer pop culture. Thus, for example, the North American Free Trade Agreement states:

> "Notwithstanding any other provision of this Agreement, as between the United States and Canada, any measure adopted or maintained with respect to cultural industries and any measure of equivalent commercial effect taken in response, shall be governed exclusively in accordance with the terms of the Canada–United States Free Trade Agreement. The rights and obligations between Canada and any other Party with respect to such measures shall be identical to those applying between Canada and the United States." NAFTA, Annex 2106. The Canada–United States Free Trade Agreement provides that "cultural industries are exempt from the provisions of this Agreement, except as specifically provided in Article 401 (Tariff Elimination), paragraph 4 of Article 1607 (divestiture of an indirect acquisition) and Articles 2006 [Retransmission Rights] and 2007 [Print–In–Canada Requirement] of this Chapter". U.S.-Canada Free Trade Agreement Implementation Act of 1988, Pub.L. No. 100–449, 102 Stat. 1851 (1988), *reprinted in* 27 I.L.M. 281 (1988).

"Cultural industries" are generally considered to include motion picture and video production, distribution, and exhibition; production, distribution and sale of music, audio recordings, and books; radio, television and cable services, and other printed material. *See, e.g.,* Amy Lehmann, *The Canadian Cultural Exemption Clause and the Fight to Maintain An Identity,* 23 Syracuse J. Int'l & Com. 187 (1997); Stephen R. Konigsberg, *Think Globally, Act Locally: North American Free Trade, Canadian Cultural Industry Exemption, And the Liberation of the Broadcast Ownership Laws,* 12 Cardozo Arts & Ent. L. J. 281 (1994).

THE MORNING STAR POLE CASE
YUMBULUL v. RESERVE BANK OF AUSTRALIA

Federal Court Of Australia–General Division, 1991.
21 I.P.R. 481.

FRENCH J.

In 1988, the Reserve Bank of Australia released a special $10 bank note to commemorate the first European settlement of this country. The note incorporated elements of Aboriginal artworks including, in part, a reproduction of the design of a "Morning Star Pole" made by Mr. Terry Yumbulul in 1986. The reproduction was made under a sub-licence of the copyright in the work granted to the bank by the Aboriginal Artists Agency Limited. That company, in turn, had an exclusive licence from Mr. Yumbulul. He now contends that he was induced to sign the licence by misleading or deceptive conduct on the part of the agency. His action against the bank for infringement of his copyright has been settled by a consent order made earlier in these proceedings. He has continued the proceedings against the agency and its director, Anthony Wallis, seeking injunctive and declaratory relief and damages. The action was heard over the last two days on the issue of liability only. It demonstrates difficulties that arise in the interaction of traditional Aboriginal culture and the Australian legal system relating to the protection of copyright and the commercial exploitation of artistic works by Aboriginal people.

Factual Background

Terry Yumbulul is an Aboriginal artist of considerable skill and reputation. He was born on Wessel Island on the north-east coast of Arnhem Land on 11 September 1950. Mr. Yumbulul began his career as an artist by producing paintings depicting traditional Aboriginal stories which he learnt as part of his schooling in Aboriginal culture. Since he began painting about ten years ago, he has been selling his works. They have been exhibited in the Northern Territory Museum and some have been purchased by the Northern Territory Government as official gifts for visiting foreign dignitaries. He has had a number of exhibitions of his works at private galleries.

Mr. Yumbulul has authority within his own clan to paint certain sacred designs. He has passed through various levels of initiation and revelatory ceremonies in which he has gradually learnt the designs and their meanings. The authority to paint them derives from his father. During the last initiation rite in which he participated, he was presented by the elders of his clan with two sacred bags. Their presentation reflected the power and title he has been given to paint the sacred objects of his people. It is from his mother's clan group, however, that Mr. Yumbulul has inherited the right to make Morning Star Poles, one of which is the subject of these proceedings.

The poles have a central role in Aboriginal ceremonies commemorating the deaths of important persons, and in inter-clan relationships. They are wooden, decorated with painted designs, feathers and string. Different clan groups make them in different ways, and the identifying attributes of the Morning Star Pole of a particular group may be maintained jealously. Traditional belief has it that the Morning Star Pole is imbued with the power to take the spirits of the dead to the Morning Star, which will return them to their ancestral home. According to the evidence of Dr. Ian Keen, an anthropologist who is a senior lecturer at the Australian National University, the pole and banyan fibre string that goes with it, is made as a gift. A Morning Star ceremony is commissioned by one group who may send various objects belonging to, or associated with particular persons, to be incorporated in the pole or string. The ceremony is said to be a way of establishing ties of friendship and gift exchange between groups which are geographically, and in kin terms, distant. While a pole intended for ceremonial use is displayed in public as part of the ceremony, it is made in secret in a men's ceremonial shelter.

According to Dr Keen, the making of the pole must be done in accordance with religious rules. There is nothing inconsistent with this tradition and the making of a Morning Star Pole specifically for public display in a museum. Aboriginal people often believe that it does not matter if some such designs or objects are revealed to non-Aboriginal people because they will not know their meanings. This evidence was borne out by that of Roy Marika, the senior male member of the Rirratjingu clan, who has been a leader among Aboriginal people in north east Arnhem Land for many years. He said that some traditional objects, such as the Morning Star Pole, can be made for sale to a museum or craft shop. It is regarded as important that white people learn to respect the Aboriginal people and their land. He understood that Mr. Yumbulul had the right to make the Morning Star Pole for ceremonial purposes and also for sale to places such as museums in order to educate people. However, to do this he would need to make sure that the clan people involved, that is, the traditional owners and managers of the rights to the pole and the ceremony, knew what he was doing. Mr. Marika said that the subject of mass production of paintings and important objects is very sensitive because it takes the ability and right to produce and supervise the production of these objects out of the hands of the Aboriginal people. He said:

Objects such as the Morning Star Pole are only meant to be made in a sacred camp by men who have been properly taught the rules relating to their production. It is not right for such objects to be made by children, women or men who do not understand their meaning and power and who have not been given the right to make such things.

Another witness, Mandawuy Yunupingu, of Yirkala in the Northern Territory, said of the Morning Star Pole and ceremony that it brings together people of different areas and clans to perform rituals relating to the remembrance of important people who have died.

The ceremony is always concerned with groups of people coming together usually from different clans and an important part of the ceremony involves the presentation of a ceremonial pole, the Morning Star Pole to the family of the dead person who is being commemorated. It is a very important ritual which reinforces the mutual respect between clan groups. It also serves to diffuse (sic) any tension or disharmony between clans.

And further:

The attainment of the right to make such a pole is a matter of great honour, and accordingly abuses of rights in relation to the careful protection of images on such poles is a subject of great sensitivity amongst people who believe in the Morning Star Ceremony and of the ceremonial Morning Star Pole.

None of this or other similar evidence was challenged, and I accept the inference that flows from it that the Morning Star Pole, whether made specifically for ceremonial use or for public display in museums or other places in wider Australian society, is of considerable significance to the clans who are concerned with the rights to its creation and use. I accept also, that the maker of such poles for public display, other than in a ceremonial context, has a cultural obligation to those clans to ensure that it is not used or reproduced in a way that offends against their perceptions of its significance. This is reflected in Mr. Yumbulul's evidence on affidavit. In 1985 he created five Morning Star Poles, on commission from a company called Inada Holdings Pty. Ltd. They were sold to five different museums, one of which was the Australian Museum in Sydney. He had previously created other poles for ceremonial use which were not appropriate for public display. He said, however, that those made for public display were examples of poles used in ceremonies. Although made for public exhibition, they have sacred power deriving in part from the images they bear which embody the creative spirits which he believes created the land of his mother's people.

Mr. Yumbulul created the pole the subject to this proceeding in 1986. I accept the description in Mr. Yumbulul's affidavit evidence, which says that the feather work on the pole is intricate, and the design complex and unique to him. I also accept his affidavit evidence, which was not disputed, that he made the pole without assistance from any other person and that its creation was the subject of considerable care and attention on his part. In the sense relevant to the Copyright Act (1968 (Cth)), there is no doubt that the pole was an original artistic work, and that he was its author, in whom copyright subsisted. Mr. Yumbulul sold the pole to Inada Holdings Pty. Ltd. in 1986 for about $500. He said that he was entitled to sell it because the eventual destination, the Australian Museum, was, in his opinion, an appropriate place for its display. It is nevertheless the fact that he sold the pole without imposing any restriction on its subsequent use. I should add that Mr. Yumbulul's reputation as an artist long preceded this sale. In January 1983, the Curator of Anthropology of the Australian Museum, wrote a memorandum recommending the purchase of two of his bark paintings and a pole with the comment that:

The works are excellent, well documented examples of the output of a young artist who is rapidly becoming famous.

The business of the Aboriginal Artists Agency Ltd. is essentially to act as a collecting society for Aboriginal artists. It acquires exclusive licences to their works, which it then sub-licences to commercial users. In 1985, Mr. Wallis was approached by the Reserve Bank of Australia to assist it in locating suitable Aboriginal artwork for use in the design of a $10 note to be produced as part of the Australian Bicentennial celebrations in 1988.

On 14 May 1987, Bridget Tang, the executive officer of the agency, wrote to Mr. and Mrs. Yumbulul attaching a standard form licence agreement. The covering letter was in the following terms:

Dear Terry and Clely,

Re: Copyright Agreement

It would be appreciated if you would sign and return as soon as possible the attached copyright agreement.

Once I have received this I will be able to collect $850.00 for you on one particular clearance for an important government · organisation.

Copyright payments are very useful for an artist because they are received on top of the money you can earn for the actual works.

Yours sincerely,

Bridget Tang,

Executive Officer

Mr. Yumbulul said in evidence that he did not understand the letter and telephoned Mr. Wallis to find out what it was all about. Mr. Wallis, he said, told him not to worry, and that the agreement that he was being asked to sign was just a legal document. Mr. Wallis, he said, told him that he would look after him and send him money. When he asked Mr. Wallis what he was signing the agreement for, Mr. Wallis told him that it would be giving the agency authority for an important government agency to look at his work. The document that was being sent was just a usual document, and a further agreement would be sent which properly reflected what was going on. If the government agency were interested in reproducing any of the work, there would be another contract sent which would specifically permit such reproduction.

Mr. Yumbulul said he read the form of licence and it did not make a great deal of sense to him. There was, he said, no mention at the time of the Morning Star Pole, and no mention of the Reserve Bank or the use of his work on the currency. He said that he trusted Mr. Wallis to tell him all of what was going on. Initially, he was not happy about simply signing the form, but Mr. Wallis rang him again and again and said he should sign the form, and he did so.

I am satisfied on the evidence, that Mr. Yumbulul understood the general nature of the licence he was signing, and that it went beyond merely conferring the right to inspect his works. While his evidence indicated that he had some difficulty with particular words of the English language, he showed a grasp of the concept of royalty and the general notion of a licence.

Subsequently, the agency signed an agreement with the Reserve Bank of Australia granting it a non-exclusive licence to reproduce the Morning Star Pole as a design element on a bank note. The licence fee agreed was $1,000. A cheque for that amount was sent to the agency by the bank on 30 June 1987 with a request that the matter be treated "with the utmost confidentiality". A fee of $850 was paid to Mr. Yumbulul in advance of this receipt, by telegraphic transfer to his account on 22 June. The Morning Star Pole was ultimately embodied in the Bicentennial bank note which was made available to the public in 1988.

THE CAUSES OF ACTION

There was evidence that Mr. Yumbulul came under considerable criticism from within the Aboriginal community for permitting the reproduction of the pole by the bank. It may well be that when he executed the agreement he did not fully appreciate the implications of what he was doing in terms of his own cultural obligations. Certainly, it appears to be the case that neither Mr. Wallis, nor anyone else at the agency, felt a need to explore these ramifications with him. Mr. Wallis saw that as a matter which was Mr. Yumbulul's responsibility. It may be that greater care could have been taken in this case. And it may also be that Australia's copyright law does not provide adequate recognition of Aboriginal community claims to regulate the reproduction and use of works which are essentially communal in origin. But to say this is not to say that there has been established in the case any cause of action.

[I]t may be the case that some Aboriginal artists have laboured under a serious misapprehension as to the effect of public display upon their copyright in certain classes of works. This question and the question of statutory recognition of Aboriginal communal interests in the reproduction of sacred objects is a matter for consideration by law reformers and legislators. For what it is worth, I would add that it would be most unfortunate if Mr. Yumbulul were to be the subject of continued criticism within the Aboriginal community for allowing the reproduction of the Morning Star Pole design on the commemorative banknote. The reproduction was, and should be seen, as a mark of the high respect that has all too slowly developed in Australian society for the beauty and richness of Aboriginal culture.

For the reasons which I have given I will order that:

The application is dismissed.

THE ABORIGINAL CARPET CASE
MILPURRURRU v. INDOFURM

Federal Court Of Australia, Northern Territory, 1994.
30 I.P.R. 209.

VON DOUSSA, J.

This is a claim for remedies under the Copyright Act 1968 (Cth) for copyright infringement and under the Trade Practices Act 1974 (Cth) for alleged contraventions of §§ 52, 53(c) and (d) and 55.

The first three applicants are Aboriginal artists. The fourth applicant, the Public Trustee, represents the estates of five deceased Aboriginal artists. The skill of each of the artists is recognised nationally and internationally as exceptional; their works are represented in national, state and other major collections of Australian artworks. The pleadings allege that since about October 1992 the respondents have manufactured, imported into Australia, offered for sale and sold woollen carpets which reproduce artwork, or substantial parts thereof, of each of the artists without the licence of the owners of the copyright.

In accordance with Aboriginal custom, and out of respect for the deceased artists, their names have not been spoken in the course of the trial. They have been referred to throughout by their appropriate skin names. It is, however, necessary to adequately identify the artworks in question to refer once in the judgment to these artists by name, but having done so, the skin names will be used thereafter. Particulars of the art works and the artists are as follows:

Artist Skin name Artwork

1. George Milpurrurru Goose Egg Hunt

2. George Garrawun Ngaritj Freshwater Fish

(died August 1993)

3. Paddy Dhatangu Gamarang Wititj (olive python)

(died 23 March 1993)

4. Fred Nanganaralil Wamut Crow and Praying-mantis

(died 28 August 1993)

5. Banduk Marika Tjapaltjarri Djanda and the Sacred Waterhole

6. Tim Leura Tjapaltjarri The Seven Sisters Dreaming

(died 18 June 1984)

7. Uta Uta Tjangala Jangala Emu

(died 8 December 1990)

8. Tim Payunka Kangaroo and Shield People Dreaming

The first four artists are from Central Arnhem Land. The artworks in question are bark paintings. The first three paintings are presently owned by the Australian National Gallery (the ANG). In 1993, in recognition of the International Year for the World's Indigenous People, the ANG held the first solo exhibition of the works of an Aboriginal artist. The exhibition was a retrospective look at the works of Mr. Milpurrurru, and included the Goose Egg Hunt which is also featured in the publication, The Art of George Milpurrurru, which was published by the ANG at the same time. As part of the program for the 1993 International Year for the World's Indigenous People, Goose Egg Hunt was adopted as the design for the 85 cent Australian stamp issued on 4 February 1993. A large number of these stamps were put into circulation, perhaps as many as two to three million.

Freshwater Fish is recognised as one of the major works of Gamarang, and was one of two paintings hung in the foyer of the ANG when it was opened by Her Majesty the Queen.

The first three paintings, together with the work of Ms. Marika were included in a portfolio of 12 Aboriginal artworks which was published by the ANG in 1988 under the auspices of the ANG's education staff. One of the purposes of the portfolio was to provide a resource item for teachers and students. The portfolio was intended to be representative of the best Aboriginal artworks in the ANG collection. The artwork of Wamut is in the National Museum of Australia collection, and was reproduced in a portfolio of Aboriginal art published for the Australian Information Service (AIS) by the Australian Government Printer. It was also reproduced in a calendar for the month of June 1982 similarly published for the AIS.

Ms. Marika's work is a six colour lino cut, ink on paper, that was created by her on a special commission for the Australian National University for the Bicentenary. Her father is recognised as a great bark painter whose work is also in the ANG. She was the first Aboriginal person appointed to the Board of the ANG. More recently she has been appointed to the Board of the Northern Territory Museum and Art Gallery. She is and was at the time of the events the subject of these proceedings heavily involved in community groups mainly as a consultant for arts related cross-cultural exchange, and as an educator in Aboriginal culture.

The remaining three artists are from the western desert areas of central Australia. The artworks are "Papunya" style paintings in acrylic paint on canvas. Each work is recognised as one of the major works of a very important artist. The works have been exhibited nationally and internationally and have also been reproduced in a portfolio of Aboriginal art by the AIS, and in a calendar produced by that body for the months of January, March and November of 1986.

In both the ANG portfolio, and the AIS publications the reproduction of the artworks were published over the name of the artist. Among the carpets the subject of this action, seven of the eight artworks were reproduced in virtually identical form and colour. It is common ground that the source of the artwork reproduced was these publications.

The reproduction of the artworks in the ANG and AIS portfolios, and on the postage stamp, followed formal approval and royalty agreements with the artists or their representatives. The evidence is to the effect that reproductions of this kind are permitted by Aboriginal artists, including those involved in this case, and by traditional owners, where the reproduction is in a prestigious publication for the purposes of educating members of the white community about Aboriginal culture. In each of the ANG and AIS publications the artworks were accompanied by brief descriptions of the subject matter of the artist's work. With one qualification, the descriptions made it plain that the subject matter concerned creation stories of spiritual and sacred significance to the artist. The one qualification is in respect of the Seven Sisters Dreaming where the description at the foot of the AIS reproduction does not spell that out expressly. However, the introduction page to the 1986 calendar makes the following clear statement about the significance of the works in that publication:

The paintings have been acclaimed as "statements of great value to the people who made them". They express concepts that are intensely personal. These are very often private expressions concerned with ownership, ownership of land, ownership of stories, stories of the Dreamtime, that indefinable period of past time which to the Aboriginals is the source of all knowledge and of all living things.

Sacred ceremonies, generally restricted to the initiated members of the tribe or those undergoing initiation, and their related celebrations in dance, song and design, form the basis of what may seem nothing more than complex abstract patterns in the paintings. The patterns in fact represent explicit visual descriptions, stylised maps of identifiable locations and myths, though the full meaning of each painting may not be clear to non-Aboriginal viewers.

Nevertheless, the paintings are eloquent witnesses to the rich and enduring nature of Aboriginal culture.

The evidence led at trial, including the evidence of an Aboriginal artist, Mr. Bruce Wangurra, called by the respondents, explained the importance of the creation stories and dreamings in the cultures of the clans to which they relate. Those stories are represented in ceremonies of deep significance, and are often secret or sacred, known only to a few senior members of the clan chosen according to age, descendence, sex, initiation, experience in the learning of the dreamings and ceremonies, and the attainment of skills which permit the faithful reproduction of the stories in accordance with Aboriginal law and custom. Painting techniques, and the use of totemic and other images and symbols are in many instances, and almost invariably in the case of important creation stories, strictly controlled by Aboriginal law and custom. Artworks are an important means of recording these stories, and for teaching future generations. Accuracy in the portrayal of the story is of great importance. Inaccuracy, or error in the faithful reproduction of an artwork, can cause deep offence to those familiar with the dreaming.

The right to create paintings and other artworks depicting creation and dreaming stories, and to use pre-existing designs and well recognised totems of the clan, resides in the traditional owners (or custodians) of the stories or images. Usually that right will not be with only one person, but with a group of people who together have the authority to determine whether the story and images may be used in an artwork, by whom the artwork may be created, to whom it may be published, and the terms, if any, on which the artwork may be reproduced. The evidence in this case about these aspects of traditional collective ownership was similar to the account recently published in "Unauthorised Reproductions of Traditional Aboriginal Art", Dean A. Ellinson, (1994) 17 UNSW Law Journal 327.

If unauthorised reproduction of a story or imagery occurs, under Aboriginal law it is the responsibility of the traditional owners to take action to preserve the dreaming, and to punish those considered responsible for the breach. Notions of responsibility under Aboriginal law differ from those of the English common law. If permission has been given by the traditional owners to a particular artist to create a picture of the dreaming, and that artwork is later inappropriately used or reproduced by a third party, the artist is held responsible for the breach which has occurred, even if the artist had no control over, or knowledge of, what occurred. The evidence of Ms Marika, which I accept without hesitation, illustrates the severe consequences which may occur even in a case where plainly the misuse of the artwork was without permission, and contrary to Australian statute law. In times past the "offender" could be put to death. Now other forms of punishment are more likely such as preclusion from the right to participate in ceremonies, removal of the right to reproduce paintings of that or any other story of the clan, being outcast from the community, or being required to make a payment of money; but the possibility of spearing was mentioned by Mr Wangurra as a continuing sanction in serious cases.

Ms. Marika has endeavoured to conceal the unauthorised reproduction on carpets of Djanda and the Sacred Waterhole from her community as she will be held responsible. Her artwork expresses pictorially the creation when her ancestral creator Djang'Kawu and his two sisters, the Wagilag sisters, at the end of their journey from Burralku, landed at Yelangbara, south of Port Bradshaw, the site of their first journey. The image which she utilised in the artwork is associated with this place. Her rights to use the image arise by virtue of her membership of the landowner group in that area, and is an incident arising out of land ownership. She explained in an affidavit:

As an artist, while I may own the copyright in a particular artwork under western law, under Aboriginal law I must not use an image or story in such a way as to undermine the rights of all the other Yolngu (her clan) who have an interest whether direct or indirect in it. In this way I hold the image on trust for all the other Yolngu with an interest in the story.

Her creation of the artwork contemplated that it would be displayed with appropriate sensitivity in art galleries and for education purposes to help bring about a greater awareness of Aboriginal culture. The reproduction of the artwork, in circumstances where the dreaming would be walked on, is totally opposed to the cultural use of the imagery employed in her artwork.

This misuse of her artwork has caused her great upset. If it had become widely known in her community at the time, she believes that her family could have ordered her to stop producing any works of art; they might have stopped her participating in ceremonies; they might have outcast her, and they may have sought recompense from her—nowadays in money terms. So far these possibilities have not eventuated—and now that she has taken action to prevent further misuse and to seek a public recognition of the past misuse through the courts, she is hopeful that the community reaction, when it learns what has happened, will be more forgiving. I note, in passing, the observation in the paper "Aboriginal Designs and Copyright", Stephen Gray, Copyright Reporter vol. 9, No. 4, p. 8 at 11 that punishment of the Aboriginal law breaker may to a large extent be determined by the success or failure of action in the Anglo–Australian courts.

It is a feature of the style of the artworks in question that the artist will encode into the artwork secret parts of the dreaming that will be recognised and understood only by those who are initiated into the relevant ceremonies, or at least have a close knowledge of the cultural significance of the story. This adds to the sensitivity and risk of offending the traditional owners involved in the reproduction of Aboriginal artwork, unless the reproduction is accurate in every respect and done with full and proper permission.

The extent to which Aboriginal law and culture imposes limitations on the reproduction of Aboriginal artwork will vary according to the clans concerned and the significance of the imagery and dreaming which is reflected in the particular artwork. Where the artwork concerns a public story or ceremony there may be few restrictions on reproduction. This is plain from the quantity and variety of artwork presently produced by Aborigines for the commercial market. Again, depending on the subject of the artwork there may be no restriction on an artist creating a work for use under appropriate copyright licence in the mass productions of items such as clothing and wall-hangings. The licence agreement which the respondents have with Mr. Wangurra and other artists provide examples. Evidence in this case indicates that there is continuing uncertainty in some sections of the Aboriginal community as to the appropriateness of the use of traditional images on products which utilise non-traditional mediums, and on carpets designed to be walked upon.

The reproduction of paintings which depict dreaming stories and designs of cultural significance has been a matter of great concern to the Aboriginal community. Pirating of Aboriginal designs and paintings for commercial use without the consent of the artist or the traditional owners was common for a long time. The recognition of the sacred and religious significance of these paintings, and the restrictions which Aboriginal law and culture imposes on their reproduction is only now being understood by the white community.

Carpet weaving is an age-old Vietnamese skill. Carpets are made in a cottage industry environment. They are made by outworkers one at a time in their homes. The "carpet factory" acts as a clearing house through which orders are distributed to individual carpet markets, and later collected and packed for shipment to Australia.

At a visit to the carpet factory [in Hanoi] on about 17 October 1991, Mr. Bethune says he was shown the ANG and AIS portfolios and calendars. These he says were part of the "material" which the factory already held. He looked through these reproductions and ordered several carpets which would reproduce certain of the prints in full. He indicated others that he told the factory manager were too complicated, and asked that they make something along the same lines, utilising the same colours, but which were "less busy". The orders placed at this time were packed and shipped on 21 December 1991 and 11 January 1992.

The samples arrived in Australia on 20 March 1992. They were favourably received by those to whom they were shown, and Mr. Bethune decided to place larger orders. He did so in about early April 1992. The carpets were shipped under cover of packing slips dated 30 April 1992, 12 May and 1 June 1992 indicating that the carpets had been woven in the meantime. These orders were for a further 70 carpets, each the subject of these proceedings. When the orders were placed it was anticipated that the carpets would arrive in Australia in about September or October 1992.

Mr. Bethune says that when he returned to Australia after placing these orders he found that there were "lots and lots of National Gallery posters for sale everywhere" and it was no trouble to obtain copies of those which had been copied into the carpet designs. A number of his friends told him he should be careful reproducing Aboriginal art because of copyright. He says that he and his wife decided it would be prudent to investigate the copyright implications. Through his local doctor he was introduced to Mr. Ian Horrocks, who had considerable experience with Aboriginal affairs. Mr. Horrocks was at the time the office manager of the Aboriginal Legal Service of Western Australia Inc. He was not a lawyer. By arrangement Mr. and Mrs. Bethune visited Mr. Horrocks at his home one evening in June 1992. Mr. Bethune discussed his proposal to import carpets. Different versions of this and later discussions between them have been given by Mr. Bethune on the one hand and Mr. Horrocks on the other. Where their evidence differs I prefer the evidence of Mr. Horrocks. It is common ground that Mr. Horrocks confirmed that there was a copyright issue to be addressed. He expressed his view that the importation of carpets into Australia which reproduced the artwork constituted a breach of copyright. He suggested that the appropriate body through which to seek copyright permission would be the Aboriginal Arts Management Association (AAMA), a body which had recently been set up under the auspices of the Aboriginal Arts Unit of the Australia Council with funding from that body to provide advice to Aborigines on copyright matters and to seek remedies where infringements were detected. Mr. Horrocks knew that this body had been established following The Aboriginal Arts and Crafts Industry Report of the Review Committee in 1989.

Mr. Horrocks was asked to make a very general inquiry with AAMA regarding copyright permission from the artists, but not to mention that some carpets had already been imported.

Mr. Horrocks says he informed Mr. Bethune that as it would probably be necessary for AAMA to contact the artists there could be significant delay before a reply was received, and that there was no certainty that copyright approval would be granted.

Unfortunately the letter [requesting permission to import carpets bearing the designs in question] was never received by AAMA.

Agreement was not reached with any artist, and these proceedings were commenced on 8 April 1993. The exhibition held on 23 October

1992 established that there was a viable market for carpets of this kind in Australia and in the 2 years since the exhibition the respondents have extended the importation and distribution of Vietnamese carpets to many centres in Australia. For the most part it appears that from 10 December 1992 carpets that are exact reproductions of the subject artworks have not been distributed or displayed for sale, although there has been at least one and possibly more isolated sales on inquiry to an agent who held consignment stock, and the importation of two Freshwater Fish.

Wititj

According to the information which accompanies the ANG portfolio this artwork is a representation of an olive python and its young. It is the final painting in a series of 15 by the artist which depicted aspects of the story of the Wagilag Sisters (to whom reference has already been made in relation to Ms Marika's artwork). The artist, an old man at the time that the artwork was created, knew both the "inside" and "outside" meanings of the story. Only the "outside" version can be told to women and children. In the painting the artist has used a stylised representation of an olive python to symbolise the mythical rainbow serpent. The artwork is rectangular in shape, and in the particular representation an adult python is curled closely around two baby pythons. The body of the python is shown lying in "square coils", i.e. the body, commencing with the tail located at one corner of the bark, follows the border of the bark for one complete circuit, and then makes three more circuits, each inside of, but parallel to, the previous one. In this way the painting depicts four curls of the body before the head reaches the centre portion of the painting. Encompassed within the four coils is a rectangle containing the two baby pythons and the head of the adult. The depiction of the adult python's vent, the cross-hatching or rarrk which infills the body sections, and the shape of the head are distinctive. One of the baby pythons is black, and the other a dark ochre. The painting is predominantly in white, yellow and ochre colours.

The snake carpet reproduces the same basic colours and hues. The predominant feature of the carpet is one snake which follows a course parallel to the edges of the carpet so as to create a broad border image. The major area of the carpet, lying within that border is a plain ochre colour closely similar to the background of the Wititj artwork. The unusual depiction of the vent of the snake and the particular cross-hatching which infills the body of the python on the Wititj is reproduced in almost identical form on the carpet. The difference in the body of the snake reproduced in the carpet is mainly in the number of curls of its body. The shape of the head of the snake on the carpet bears some similarity to that of the adult in the Wititj artwork, but whereas the artwork shows the python with an ochre head and white neck, the neck and head on the snake on the carpet is black. There are therefore differences. The carpet has only one snake, the body of that snake while closely similar in pattern to the adult python on the Wititj, has a different coloured head, and the body travels only once round the border of the carpet. It should be added that both the Wititj and the carpet have a thin white line as an extreme outer border.

In determining whether the copying is substantial Brightman, J. accepted the submissions of counsel for the defendants that there are four principal matters to be taken into account in deciding whether copying is substantial (at 203):

First, the volume of the material taken, bearing in mind that quality is more important than quantity; secondly, how much of such material is the subject matter of copyright and how much is not; thirdly, whether there has been an animus furandi on the part of the defendant; fourthly, the extent to which the plaintiff's and the defendant's books are competing works.

Brightman, J. also cited with approval passages from *Harman Pictures NV v. Osborne* [1967] 1 WLR 723, one of which is material to the present case where part of the respondent's case is that the image of the Wititj is common in many Aboriginal artworks and involves no originality. That passage from *Harman Pictures NV v. Osborne* at 732 reads:

In the case of works not original in the proper sense of the term, but composed of, or compiled or prepared from, materials which are open to all, the fact that one man has produced such a work does not take away from anyone else the right to produce another work of the same kind, and in doing so to use all the materials open to him. But as the law has been precisely stated by Hall VC in *Hogg v. Scott*: "the true principle in all these cases is that the defendant is not at liberty to use or avail himself of the labour which the plaintiff has been at for the purpose of producing his work, that is, in fact, merely to take away the result of another man's labour or, in other words, his property".

Applying these principles to the snake carpet, I am in no doubt that it constitutes a reproduction of a substantial part of the artwork. There are striking similarities on a visual comparison of the artwork with the carpet. While the dreaming of the Wititj is often told in Aboriginal artwork, the particular depiction of the tail and the rarrk used in this artwork is original and distinctive. There is, in any view, a substantial use of that part of the artwork in the carpet. I reject the arguments of the respondents that the particular depiction of the Wititj on the carpet is common to many Aboriginal artworks and involves no originality. I have looked through the several recognised texts on Aboriginal art which have been tendered by the respondents. In my view the artworks that they have identified to support this argument establishes that the contrary is the case. None of the other artworks show anything which closely resembles the main features of the snake carpet. The most important consideration however concerns the existence of an "animus furandi" on the part of the designers of the carpets, that is to say, an intention on the part of these people to take from the Wititj artwork for the purpose of saving themselves labour. The evidence of Mr. Bethune is revealing. The artwork was before him and the factory manager. Mr. Bethune said it was too complicated (otherwise, by inference, the artwork without modification would have been copied), so he instructed that it be simplified. This was achieved by an uncomplicated elimination of part of the body of the adult Wititj, the removal of the babies, and a transfer of the striking colour from one of the baby pythons to the head of the adult. The complex parts of the design and artwork in the tail and body colouring was copied exactly to form the predominant feature of the carpet. It is also revealing that the carpet factory then assigned the carpet the code 4A, 4 being the number of the ANG portfolio print, and also coded three of the exact copies from other prints according to the ANG numbers, viz 5A, 6A and 9A.

It is surprising in light of the evidence, that the argument that the snake carpet does not substantially reproduce the artwork has been maintained to the last, and even more surprising that the respondents have maintained that they are not in breach of the assurance they gave to AAMA following its letter of 10 December 1992 that carpets "which may bear some resemblance to artworks by your clients have been withdrawn from sale and manufacture".

[The court found copyright infringement and turned to the question of damages.]

The statutory remedies do not recognise the infringement of owner-ship rights of the kind which reside under Aboriginal law in the traditional owners of the dreaming stories and the imagery such as that used in the artworks of the present applicants. That is a matter which has been commented on in the course of the trial, as the evidence discloses the likelihood that the unauthorised reproduction of the art-works has caused anger and offence to those owners, and the potential for them to suffer humiliation and repercussions in their cultural envi-ronment. It will be necessary to return to that topic.

On express instructions from the applicants, counsel has informed the court that Aboriginal law and custom would treat each of the applicants in a case like the present one equally so that the fruits of the action would be shared equally between the named parties. Counsel for the applicants acknowledged that to treat the invasion of the rights of each artist (or those of his estate) on the basis of equality would not be in accordance with the principles of assessment of damages for infringe-ment under the Copyright Act. While not suggesting that the court should assess the liabilities of each respondent otherwise than according to those principles, counsel invited the court to express its judgment in terms which defined the aggregate liability of each respondent to the applicants as a group, rather than as individual judgments in favour of each applicant. A judgment so expressed would enable the applicants, including the Public Trustee in consultation with those entitled by Aboriginal law and custom to the proceeds of each estate, to agree upon a division of the damages which met with their cultural and other wishes. Under Pt. III, Div. 4A, of the Administration and Probate Act 1969 (NT), the estate of an intestate Aboriginal may, on order of the Supreme Court of the Northern Territory, be distributed in accordance with the traditions of the community or group to which the intestate Aboriginal belonged. While the Copyright Act only recognises the rights of the copyright owner, in a practical way it appears that there may be scope, even in the case of the estates administered by the Public Trustee, for the distribution of the proceeds of the action to those traditional owners who have legitimate entitlements according to Aboriginal law to share compensation paid by someone who has without permission reproduced the artwork of an Aboriginal artist.

So far as the procedural rules and practice of the court permit I consider this court should accommodate the applicants' request. In so doing, the reasons for judgment must indicate the basis of assessment according to the established requirements of copyright law so that the respondents' liability is patently established according to the municipal law of Australia. In what follows, I have had regard both to this need, and to the request of the applicants.

In the present case, insofar as the exploitation by the copyright owners of their copyright might be productive of monetary or other commercial return, that exploitation was likely to involve the reproduction of the artworks for educational purposes or portfolios and posters similar to those produced by the ANG and AIS, or through use by some other public authority in connection with the promotion of Aboriginal culture, as in the case of Goose Egg Hunt on the Australian postage stamp. The evidence led on behalf of the applicants indicates that the prospect of the artworks being commercially exploited in the carpet or other fabric market was extremely remote. Insofar as a loss in commercial potential resulted from the infringement, that loss would most likely be one arising from diminution in the value of the copyright for the purposes identified because the artwork had been degraded by the commercial use to which it had been put by the respondents. Fortunately, the speedy action by AAMA reduced that potential as the exact copies most likely to have that result were for practical purposes withdrawn from the market within approximately 6 weeks of being introduced.

[The court determined that under copyright law, minimal money damages should be awarded.]

Principles discussed in the authorities on the assessment of damages under [Australian copyright law]concentrate upon aspects of monetary loss likely to flow from the impaired commercial potential of the copyright. That is hardly surprising as infringement actions usually arise in the commercial context of our market economy. In the circumstances of this case the damages sustained, at least by the living artists, extend beyond the commercial potential for monetary return from the copyright. In the present case the infringements have caused personal distress and, potentially at least, have exposed the artists to embarrassment and contempt within their communities if not to the risk of diminished earning potential and physical harm. The losses arising from these risks are a reflection of the cultural environment in which the artists reside and conduct their daily affairs. Losses resulting from tortious wrongdoing experienced by Aborigines in their particular environments are properly to be brought to account.

The applicants contend that the unauthorised use of the artwork was in effect the pirating of cultural heritage. That is so, but under copyright law damages can be awarded only insofar as the "pirating" causes a loss to the copyright owner resulting from infringement of copyright. Nevertheless, in the cultural environment of the artists the infringement of those rights has, or is likely to have, far reaching effects upon the copyright owner. Anger and distress suffered by those around the copyright owner constitute part of that person's injury and suffering.

If these matters of personal and cultural hurt are to be the subject of compensatory damages assessed under [the compensatory damage provision of Australian law], the damages awarded would vary from artist to artist. In the case of the artists who died before the infringement occurred I do not think the copyright owner, the Public Trustee, has suffered any losses beyond the commercial considerations arising from the depreciation in the value of the copyright. In the case of the artists who were alive when the infringement occurred but died at about the time that the proceedings were commenced or shortly thereafter, the damages would cover the harm actually suffered by them up to the date of death. In the case of the other applicants the damages would be considerably higher, covering harm already suffered and the potential for further harm in the future. Assessments along these lines, artist by artist, would not be in accordance with the principles of equality which the court has been invited by the applicants to follow.

If an award of additional damages under § 115(4) is made to reflect culturally based harm, the particular losses of the artists who were alive at the time of the infringement which might otherwise be assessed under [Australian copyright law] can be subsumed within the additional damages [awarded based on the flagrancy of the defendant's conduct]. Upon an assessment of the cultural aspects of the harm as additional damages a position of equality between the artists can more easily be rationalised. Nevertheless there is a plain distinction between the living artists and those who are deceased. In the case of the latter some died before the infringement and some after, but those that died after the infringement did so only shortly after they became aware of the infringement and probably before their communities did so. In these circumstances I see force in the applicants' submission that all the deceased artists should be treated equally but that there must be some differential between them and the first three applicants.

Notes and Questions

1. Under Aboriginal law, rights in artistic works are owned collectively. Only certain artists are permitted to depict certain designs within the tribe and are granted a license to reproduce them. *See*, Colin Golvan, *Aboriginal Art and the Protection of Indigenous Cultural Rights*, [1992] 7 E.I.P.R. 229–230. Under Aboriginal law, did Yumbulul own the rights to the morning pole design? If not, did he have the right to license its reproduction?

2. Were designs at issue in the *Aboriginal Carpet* case owned by the painters or the tribe? What interest, if any, did the tribe have in the designs at issue?

3. Was the design of the morning star pole copyright protectable? Was it a "traditional" design whose elements were owned by the tribe? By the public?

4. Were the designs in the *Aboriginal Carpet* case copyright protectable? How did the court treat the totemic elements in the paintings at issue? As original works? As part of the public domain?

5. What relevance did the court in the *Morning Star Pole* case place on aboriginal law in deciding the validity of the assignment in the *Morning Star Pole* case? How did the court treat Aboriginal law and customs in the *Aboriginal Carpet* case?

6. In the *Aboriginal Carpet* case, copyright infringement was clear because the entire work had been reproduced. What if the carpets had merely reproduced the totemic symbols and painting techniques? Would such "derivative works" qualify as an infringing work under the Berne Convention? Who owns the infringed elements–the artist or the tribe?

7. The *Aboriginal Carpet* case focused on the harm to the individual artists. Does the tribe have a cause of action under current international copyright standards? Would they under the Bellagio Declaration?

8. Does the definition of a protectable work under the Berne Convention permit communal ownership of protected works? Communal authorship? Would it recognize Aboriginal rights to control the folkloric elements of the works in question in the above cases?

9. What is the strongest argument you can make *against* extending copyright protection to communal-owned works such as Aboriginal art or folklore?

Chapter Forty-Two

APPLICATIONS

A. SHOULD FOLKLORE AND OTHER ASPECTS OF TRADITIONAL CULTURE BE PROTECTABLE UNDER INTERNATIONAL INTELLECTUAL PROPERTY REGIMES?

TOWARD MORE UNIVERSAL PROTECTION OF INTANGIBLE CULTURAL PROPERTY

Cathryn A. Berryman, 1 J Intell. Prop. L. 293 (1994).

BACKGROUND INFORMATION ON FOLKLORE

The term "folklore" literally means "wisdom of the people," but obtaining a more explanatory definition is difficult due to folklore's amorphous and inclusive nature. A general understanding can be gleaned from reading folklorist Kanwal Puri's explication: Folklore is a living phenomenon which evolves over time. It is a basic element of our culture which reflects the human spirit. Folklore is thus a window to a community's cultural and social identity, its standards and values. Folklore is usually transmitted orally, by imitation or by other means. Its forms include language, literature, music, dance, games, mythology, rituals, customs, handicrafts and other arts. Folklore comprises a great many manifestations which are both extremely various and constantly evolving. Because it is group-oriented and tradition-based, it is sometimes described as traditional and popular folk culture. This passage touches upon folklore's basic traits: namely, that (i) it is passed from generation to generation by unfixed forms; (ii) it is a community-oriented creation in that its expression is dictated by local standards and traditions; (iii) its creations generally are not attributable to individual authors; and (iv) it is being continually utilized and developed by the society in which it lives. Folklore perpetually identifies a nation's cultural history and is considered a fundamental element of a nation's cultural patrimony. Because of its evolutionary and unfixed form, external sources subject folklore to substantial threats. Folklore, especially within developing countries, is being consumed by mass communication and importation of

1046

foreign cultural works. The risk of total dissolution of folkloric culture is prevalent if preservation actions are not taken. Economic exploitation of folkloric works has also been usurped by outside forces to the point that, even within a nation's own territory, nationals pay foreign publishers for reproductions of their own cultural works. Those publishers reap a substantial profit without providing any compensation to the nation's culture as creator. Folkloric works also are victims of integrity violations in that they suffer mutilation, distortion, and misappropriation, particularly when recreated outside their natural habitat or without authorization. For example, an American production company could capture an African tribal ritual on film or tape and, upon return to America, incorporate the recording into a television documentary, movie, radio program, or advertisement without any obligation to remunerate the African performers for exploiting the ritual and without any obligation to accurately attribute the ritual to its creating tribe.

Notes and Questions

1. Do traditional notions of copyright law as reflected in Berne permit the protection of folklore as defined in the above excerpt? What is the greatest impediment to copyright protection for folklore?

2. What is the strongest argument you can make for extending copyright protection to folklore? What problems are caused by such extension?

3. In 1998, the Walt Disney Company released an animated motion picture called *Mulan*, based on an old Chinese folk tale about a young girl who passes as a man to serve in her elderly father's place as a warrior in the Emperor's army. Some Chinese criticized certain aspects of the film as being contrary to the folk tale. Among the aspects criticized were the introduction of a romantic subplot between Mulan and her commanding officer, use of an animated dragon for comic effect, and the threat of execution should Mulan's disguise be discovered. Critics contend that these elements harmed the integral meaning of the tale as a story of filial loyalty. Is the harm to the folk tale created by these changes actionable under copyright law as set forth in the Berne Convention?

4. A Chinese film company creates an animated film called "Mulan" based on the traditional folk tale. The main characters of Mulan's family, army companions, commanding officer, and Mulan herself bear a strong resemblance to the characters in the Disney film. Does Walt Disney have a viable copyright claim based on international standards in Berne and TRIPS?

5. Who owns the rights to the folk tale which formed the basis of the two films? The Chinese people? The Chinese government? The public at large? Who suffers "harm" if the folk tale is used in a manner that alters its teachings? Should this harm be cognizable under international intellectual property law?

THE IMPACT OF FOREIGN INVESTMENT ON INDIGENOUS CULTURE: AN INTELLECTUAL PROPERTY PERSPECTIVE

Doris Estelle Long, 23 North Carol J. Int'l & Comm. Reg. 229 (1998).

[I]n reality not all aspects of such "culture" need specially crafted intellectual property laws to protect them from deculturization. "Traditional" artistic, literary and musical forms are already amply supported by "traditional" Western views of protected rights represented in the intellectual property laws sought by foreign multinationals. Instead, it is those forms of "culture" that do not readily conform to such traditional views that are most in need of a new approach to assure their protection. Such "nontraditional" forms lack an identifiable creator. They cannot be considered within the type of "products of the mind" protected due to individual effort or by the need to protect a particular creator's personality value. They are most often forms which are currently considered part of the public domain because of their long existence or their current identification as part of a nation's cultural patrimony. Such forms include, but are not be limited to, fables, stories, myths, rituals, costumes, folk medicine and other elements of preliterate society that combine to form cultural "expression" or heritage. Since most folklore and ritual lack identifiable creators or holders of rights, their protection pose unique problems for intellectual property regimes.

There is no question that one of the most difficult issues regarding the protection of works of folklore is the adverse effect such protection would presumably have on the scope of works available from the public domain. Virtual elimination of the public domain through the wholesale protection of all cultural elements of a society would do untold harm to the creation of future works. At a minimum, such control would impose derivation costs not currently present by requiring the payment of license fees for use of protected elements. Where control over the formerly public domain elements is exercised by a governmental agency, there is also a serious threat of censorship. Selective use of protection of cultural works that might otherwise be considered part of the public domain, creating a limited "domain public payant," should reduce harmful derivation costs by removing only those elements of the nation's culture from unfettered use which the nation itself believes to be either more vulnerable to deculturization or more valuable to the maintenance of the country's cultural heritage.

Censorship is a more problematic issue, but the refusal to protect cultural elements from the harm of deculturization solely on the basis that such protection might result in censorship is to ignore the concrete problem of deculturization for the potential problem of harmful censorship. Moreover, the threat of uncontrolled censorship can be reduced through careful delineation of the types of elements to be protected and the acts or uses that qualify as "unauthorized." The purpose of the protection regime proposed in this Article is to prevent the creation and distribution of deculturized products. Only those uses that remove the significant cultural meaning of works, rituals and the like should be prohibited. Thus, for example, parody and satire should not generally be prohibited since they are not based on de culturization but, in fact, rely upon the acknowledged existence of the cultural traditions being parodied.

It is the author's contention that copyright laws can form the first line of defense in protecting indigenous culture and still comply with TRIPS standards. There is no requirement under TRIPS that protected works be recorded or fixed in some tangible medium of expression. Oral works and performances, such as fables, storytelling, and folkloric dances and rituals, may thus be protected despite the absence of a fixed record of such performances. Since there is no requirement of originality or intellectual creativity under TRIPS for copyright-protected works, the fact that such folklore has been in existence for centuries—and may therefore lack present day "originality"—should not preclude its protection.

Similarly, the absence of an identifiable "author" for such folklore should not preclude protection. U.S. and European intellectual property laws reflect the "romantic" view of the author as creative genius and appear on their face to require a natural person to be at the heart of the creative experience. No such international requirement exists, however. Furthermore, the growth of doctrines such as "work for hire," which grant copyright ownership to the employer for works created by employees within the scope of their employment, and the protection of collective works have already seriously eroded the view that "authorship" requires a sole human agent as the focus for copyright protection.

As a practical matter, the absence of an identifiable author may make the enforcement of granted rights difficult because no one person would have the standing to assert the protected right. Where there is no identifiable author, as in the case of a folkloric fable or traditional ritual, copyright ownership could reside in a private or governmental rights organization charged with licensing the use of such works. Such organizations could assure that commercialization of protected works does not result in deculturization.

Developing countries are already using copyright law to protect their folkloric traditions. For example, Russian copyright law protects oral works, including folklore. Chinese copyright law protects quyia form of unfixed ritual dance and pantomime. Cuban copyright law protects "works of folklore" that apparently are "of an original character," and "involve creative activity on the part of their authors." These laws could form useful study models for other countries to consider in developing protection standards for their own folkloric and ritual traditions. However, when crafting protection for "folklore," the scope of the protected work should be clearly defined so that enforcement is predictable in accordance with international standards. Similarly, a finite term of protection needs to be established. The term of protection should be no greater than required to protect the cultural element at issue from the threat of deculturization. This period of protection could be limited by a specified term measured from the date of creation (if such a date can be determined), or from the date of first efforts to produce or market deculturized products.

The integrity of costumes, rituals, literature and artwork can be further protected through carefully drafted moral rights and trademark laws. Moral rights are noneconomic rights granted to the author of a protected work. Because they protect reputational rights and the creative value of the work, moral rights generally survive the transfer of the author's copyright interest, and are usually nontransferable and non-waivable. Moral rights are not required under TRIPS. They are, however, required under Article 6 bis of the Berne Convention, which provides: Independently of the author's economic rights, and even after the transfer of said rights, the author shall have the right to claim authorship of the work and to object to any distortion, mutilation or other modification of or other derogatory action in relation to, the said work, which would be prejudicial to his honor or reputation.

One of the rights included among an author's moral rights is the right of integrity. This right prohibits the alteration of a protected work without the author's permission. Thus, for example, films in the United States may be colorized without the director's permission because the director has no recognized moral rights in the film. By contrast, in France, the director's moral rights preclude such unauthorized mutilation of the film's integrity. Moral rights laws may similarly be used to maintain the cultural integrity of native works. Such laws could grant the creator of the work the legal right to protect the work against unauthorized alterations. These laws should specify that such rights exist separate from any copyright transfers. Where the work has no identifiable creator, a designated rights organization could be granted moral rights over the work. However, where moral rights are not exercised by a natural person, who has a finite lifespan and, therefore, a finite right to control the moral rights contained in a work, it may be desirable to establish a measurable period of time during which moral rights exist. Care should be exercised to limit control over integrity to deculturizing uses. Thus, for example, while a parody may, on its face, appear to violate the integrity of a work, such uses should generally qualify as permissible exceptions since, as noted earlier, parodies do not usually qualify as a deculturizing use.

Notes and Questions

1. Who should make the determination that a particular use is a deculturizing one? What is to prevent a governmental authority from decreeing that all traditional folk works are protected and therefore subject to a licensing fee or some other form of compensation?

2. How do you determine what uses of folklore qualify as fair uses? Who makes the decision–the courts or the same governmental authority that licenses the works?

3. *Public domain "payant."* Works in the public domain are generally unprotected under international intellectual property law. Some have advocated the development of a licensing system for works in the public domain, particularly where the work is one of folklore (thus, the term "payant"). What are the advantages of such a system? What are its disadvantages?

4. Consider the problems discussed in Chapter Thirty–Two regarding compulsory licenses. Which of these problems would be applicable to a public domain payant system? Would they require the same solutions?

Read the following Articles from the TUNIS Model Code from the Supplement: 2, 4, 5, 6, 17, 18, and Note 39.

Notes and Questions

1. What test should be applied to determine if a work qualifies as one of "national folklore"?

2. Would the following qualify as a "work of national folklore" under the Tunis model code?

    a. A religious dance by Hopi Indians;

    b. An oral folktale handed down by the Cossacks;

    c. An ancient Indian cure against infection using turmeric;

    d. An ancient Chaci mool statue from Mexico;

    e. A Han dynasty scroll;

    f. A frieze from the Parthenon;

    g. A nursery rhyme;

    h. A story from the Bhahagevad–Gita;

    i. A parable from the New Testament;

    j. A 13th Century Haggadah codex;

    k. The Dead Sea Scrolls.

3. Which of the above works should be protected against unauthorized uses? Against deculturizing uses?

4. Does the public domain payant system proposed under Article 17 of the Tunis model code resolve the problems you listed above? What additional problems does it pose?

5. In 1982, UNESCO/WIPO developed "Model Provisions for National Laws on the Protection of Expressions of Folklore Against Illicit Exploitation and Other Prejudicial Actions". It does not define "expressions of folklore" but provides for protection for verbal expressions such as folk tales, folk poetry and riddles; for musical expressions, such as folk songs and instrumental music; and for expressions by action, such as folk dances, plays, and artistic forms or rituals. (Section 2). Protection is not limited in time. Commercial use is permitted by prior authorization of the "competent authority" who represents the community's interests. Would the works listed in Question #2 qualify for protection under the Model Provisions?

6. WIPO is attempting to draft a sui generis form of protection for folklore. How would you define protectable folklore?

B. WHAT PROTECTION IS AVAILABLE UNDER INTERNATIONAL INTELLECTUAL PROPERTY LAW FOR FLORA, FAUNA AND MEDICAL CURES?

DOUBLESPEAK AND THE NEW BIOLOGICAL COLONIALISM

by S. M. Mohamed Idris.
"Third World Network Features".

On 2 October [1997] half a million Indian farmers held a rally in Bangalore to make known their strong feelings about the looming threats to their future caused by the patenting of seeds and other biological materials. These hundreds of thousands of farmers have made it known to the world that the ordinary people, the local communities of Third World countries, are becoming very much aware of the new kind of colonialism that the rich countries are trying to impose.

Unlike the colonialism of the past, this new colonialism is more subtle, more invisible and therefore more dangerous. The rich countries and their corporations have already taken most of the Third World's natural resources, minerals, trees, and soils, as raw materials for their industries. Now that these resources are almost gone, they want to take away the Third World's rich and diverse biological materials, seeds and genetic resources.

They are trying to do this by defining to their own advantage what is the meaning of 'knowledge'. Through a very tricky use of words and language, they are saying that the knowledge of Third World farmers and communities to grow food, to live in harmony with Nature and with one another, does not count as knowledge. They say it is not knowledge because this is what has developed 'naturally' and so no one is responsible for it and no one should be rewarded for it.

On the other hand, if a company in the rich countries were to 'invent' something in a laboratory, then this is taken to be the creation of 'new knowledge' and that company must be rewarded with a patent. Having this patent means that no one else can make use of the company's product, unless they pay a higher price to that company, this price being higher because of the monopoly enjoyed by the company because of the patent protection granted to it.

This double standard of what is the meaning of knowledge and who should be rewarded, and who will lose out, is most clearly seen in the case of agriculture and genetic materials. When Third World farmers through thousands of years evolve and develop sophisticated and scientific ways of producing food, with such a diverse range of seeds, and without harming the environment, this was not considered scientific agriculture but was instead looked down upon as primitive.

The so-called Green Revolution, which is not green at all, wiped out a huge range of farmers' seeds, whilst making profits for the big companies. Having realised that these seeds are after all very important, the companies are taking them, even stealing them from Third World farmers.

In the laboratory they alter the seeds through biotechnology. The modification may often be slight, just so as to meet the legal requirement that they must invent something 'new' to get a patent. The gene taken from a good plant variety evolved by generations of farmers, is inserted into another seed, and as if by magic the seed with the good gene now belongs to the company.

Now we are entering a new and dangerous phase. Through the Uruguay Round negotiations, the Northern governments want Third World governments to accept TRIPS, or a new intellectual property rights law. This will require Third World countries to allow for 'intellectual protection' of the seed companies through patenting or some other form of intellectual protection. Eventually the farmers will not be allowed to save their seeds but must buy seeds from the companies, from those same companies that took away the seeds from the farmers.

The whole affair is very devious. It is the basis for the new genetic colonialism which will be even worse than the old-type colonialism. Through a use of double standards in language, Third World farmers' deep knowledge of seeds and sustainable agriculture is cast aside as 'folklore' or 'naturally occurring'; the companies' manipulation of genes is worshipped as 'scientific invention' and rewarded with a patent. The farmer who evolved and used the seed is forced to buy back the seed. It is like the robber entering your house and taking away your possessions, and then the same robber charging you in court for theft.

It is now time to turn around the language that they are using to dominate us. The traditional agricultural practices of Third World farmers are not 'folklore' and 'naturally occurring', but the result of sophisticated science which embodies deep ecological and agricultural knowledge. The Green Revolution is not green but environmentally destructive. The new biotechnologies are not a saviour but the channel for greater ecological catastrophe as well as for economically devastating Third World farmers' livelihood and our food supplies.

The companies are not 'inventing' new seeds but have stolen them from Third World farmers. They did not create 'intellectual property' but committed 'intellectual piracy'. They are given 'patent protection' not to rightfully protect what they invented, but to legally protect them from what is morally indefensible, and that is the theft of the farmers' seeds.

AMAZON INDIANS ASK 'BIOPIRATES' TO PAY FOR RAIN–FOREST RICHES

Howard La Franchi, November 20, 1997.

The dozen tropical plants growing in dappled sunlight under the thick Amazon canopy hardly look like the focus of a controversy with global impact.

But the plants, part of a modest nursery on a Kaxinawa Indian reserve in southwestern Brazil, stand center stage in a brewing battle over what Brazilians call "biopiracy."

Indians and state officials accuse an Austrian-born Brazilian of using a nonprofit charity, Living Jungle, to trick the Indians of Acre State into sharing their knowledge of plants and their traditional uses. The Indians helped catalog more than 300 species and searched for new ones. With the Kaxinawas' help, Living Jungle began developing a nursery of potentially exportable plants for development by international pharmaceutical companies. Officials further claim that while the potential profits from development of newly discovered plants are huge, the Indians received only a few baseball caps and an occasional box of aspirin as compensation.

In growing numbers, pharmaceutical and cosmetics companies are turning to the Amazon to find the plants, barks, and seeds that might provide tomorrow's medical and beauty products. And officials are responding with measures designed to protect Brazil from the kind of biological theft it has experienced in the past.

Brazilians still have bad memories of perhaps one of the first biopiracy cases. Last century, British interests smuggled rubber tree seeds to Malaysia, ending the Amazon's lucrative monopoly on the rubber trade. Not surprisingly, the Kaxinawa case has sparked substantial interest.

"Our gold, our oil, is our biodiversity," says Edvaldo Magalhaes, a state legislator who sponsored Acre's recently approved biopiracy legislation. "But while ... big companies are already heavily involved in developing uses for jungle plants, we are only starting to demand a share of the benefit," he says. "We have to protect our wealth."

Brazil has a congressional investigative commission looking into the issue, and a federal biopiracy law is in the works. Brazil passed a biodiversity law in 1993, but the existing law is very general and lacks regulations.

Acre's new law makes plant researchers sign a contract detailing what they are looking for and whom they are working with. The law also requires them to work with a national research institute and to pay royalties to the state for the information they use.

The legislation is being criticized by some as a xenophobic reaction that showers cold water on the open research environment that promotes progress, and by others as simply ineffectual.

Pharmaceutical companies say they test about 10,000 plant species for every one that is used and marketed. So laws requiring contracts and compensation would put new financial restraints on an already slow and costly process, they say.

"I don't see this as a nationalist impulse, I see it in terms of establishing an equilibrium," says Patricia Rego, a public prosecutor in the Acre attorney general's environmental protection office.

"What we learned from our investigation is that many Indians ... and other forest dwellers are being used by all kinds of ... company representatives," Ms. Rego says. "We discovered that plants and other materials ... were being carried away in suitcases, without any control. The point of the law is that there has to be interchange and mutual benefit as the riches of our forest are put to use."

Investigations have turned up dozens of cases where foreign companies have patented materials from the rain forest and gone on to develop products, sometimes even using the original Indian name. But the Indians whose knowledge led to the particular plant being used usually receive no compensation. In one case, a U.S. company was even found to be selling Amazon Indians' blood for DNA research.

HUMANITY'S HERITAGE?

The criticism that the rain forest is a natural wealth that should be accessible to all mankind draws bitter smiles from Acre officials. "Isn't it ironic how ... the companies that want to benefit from the jungle and the Indians living there plead the case that the jungle's genetic riches are the 'heritage of all humanity,' " Mr. Magalhaes says. "But then when they turn a plant into a product, they want all the ... profits for themselves."

But other officials say that, while the issue of biopiracy is serious, legislation alone cannot regulate the problem. Too-rigid laws could hurt Brazil by discouraging the technology transfers it needs to participate more fully in product development.

"A plant's genetic properties can be carried out of the jungle with one leaf in a pocket, so simple interdiction will never be enough," says Eduardo Martins, president of Brazil's environmental protection agency. He also notes that the Amazon's vastness makes attempts to geographically limit researchers almost meaningless. "You approve their work in one place, then you find they've ended up someplace else," he says. The growth of ecotourism also complicates attempts to regulate access to the rain forest.

But a clampdown can drive research, once relatively open, underground. Officials say they are now encountering clandestine research sites operating much like illegal drug laboratories.

COOPERATION ONLY SOLUTION

Given these factors, Mr. Martins says the only long-term solution is cooperation: "Cooperation on genetic transfers and access to the rain forest is part of a two-way street that also includes compensation ... and technology transfer, so that newly discovered materials will increasingly be used here in Brazil."

Some Indians say past experiences will make them wary about cooperating with outsiders. "If they come again with the idea of getting something for nothing in return, then we'll say 'No, we've already learned that lesson,' " says Valdir Ferreira, a Kaxinawa leader. Meanwhile, he says the nursery on the Muru River "will be used for our own research."

WELCOME TO BIOCOLONIAL TIMES: AYAHUASCA

Http://www.web.net/c̄sc/text

Ayahuasca is a traditional medicine central to the lives of indigenous peoples throughout the Amazon river basin. Almost a decade ago, Loren Miller of the International Plant Medicine Corporation applied to the U.S. government to be recognized as the "inventor" of ayahuasca. Although ayahuasca has been produced and used by Amazonian peoples since time immemorial, the U.S. Patent and Trademark Office agreed to grant Miler, a patent, a form of intellectual property that conveys exclusive rights to produce and trade the patented item, at least within the country where the patent is granted.

Currently, the patent on ayahuasca applies only to a few Northern states, including the U.S.. However, when Amazonian peoples first learned about the patent in the summer of 1996, the Ecuadorian government was considering entering into a trade agreement with the U.S. that would have led to patent granted in the U.S. being extended to Ecuador. Although popular organizing by indigenous peoples and environmentalists temporarily defeated that trade deal, the threat remains that some day the patent on ayahuasca may be recognized and enforced in the Amazon, leading to restrictions on indigenous peoples' use of their sacred plant.

And regardless of whether or not this threat ever turns into reality, granting a foreign corporation intellectual property rights over ayahuasca represents direct denial of indigenous peoples' rights over their own knowledge and innovation.

The patenting of ayahuasca is not an isolated case. In fact, it is only one example of the increasingly frequent assault on indigenous people's knowledge and the richness and variety of living things that we steward. In 1994, for example, a U.S. university patented a variety of the indigenous grain quinoa, a vital subsistence food crop grow throughout the Andes. The university also patented all other quinoa bred from this variety now and in the future. Similar, U.S. plant breeder Sally Fox has been awarded patent-like rights over coloured cotton derived from virtually identical varieties long grown by indigenous peoples through-out America. And the U.S. government itself patented, and later released into the public domain, the gene code of an indigenous Hagahai man from Papula, New Guinea, without evidence of proper informed consent on the part of the man or his people.

Notes and Questions

1. *Turmeric Patent.* In 1995 the U.S. Patent Office granted a patent on the medicinal properties of turmeric powder in promoting blood vessel growth in wound healing. The outcry from the Indian nation was loud, challenging the propriety of granting a patent for a use that represented the

traditional knowledge base of the Indian people. The Indian Council of Scientific and Industrial Research filed a written challenge to the patentability of such claims. This challenge was ultimately accepted and the patent was rejected. The refusal to grant patent protection for medicinal uses of turmeric marks a rare instance where traditional knowledge of a third country has been used to prevent patent protection by foreign inventors.

2. Most patents based on traditional knowledge of indigenous peoples are not based on the plant itself. Instead, they patent an extraction or manufacturing process that increases the effectiveness of the active ingredient. Thus, for example, the controversy over the patenting of the neem seed did not involve a plant patent. Instead, W.R. Grace & Co. obtained a U.S. patent for an extraction process that significantly increased the shelf-life of the fertilizing ingredient. It was alleged that the extraction process was widely known to Indian farmers and that patent protection for this process represented "genetic colonialism."

3. On what basis, if any, could patent protection be extended to the Indian people's knowledge about the use of turmeric and neem seed. Does such knowledge qualify for protection under TRIPS? If not, what is their fatal flaw?

4. An explorer discovers a plant on the banks of the Amazon that is previously unknown to the rest of the world. She discovers from the indigenous tribe living near the discovery site that the plant has the power to cure "the wasting diseases"—cancer. Can she obtain a patent for her discovery under TRIPS?

5. Assume that the plant discoverer in Question #4 obtains a patent on the extraction process. As a result of global demand for the drug, she becomes a billionaire. Under present intellectual property regimes does she owe the Native tribe any portion of her income for exploiting the plant and knowledge they disclosed to her?

6. Short of enacting intellectual property laws that specifically protect indigenous knowledge, what steps could the government of the country where the plant was found take to assure itself a share of the earnings from the exploitation of the indigenous knowledge? What are the problems posed by such laws? See Thais move to patent Hom Mali jasmine rice, Bangkok Post (June 27, 1998).

7. What if instead of an indigenous plant, the discoverer in Question #4 obtained body tissue from a native man that contained in his cells, a cure for cancer. Would this discovery be patentable under TRIPS? Would the human donor of the cells have a right to any monies earned by exploiting the tissue under current intellectual property laws? Should he? On what legal grounds?

Read The COICA Statement from the Supplement.

Read the Julayinbul Statement on Indigenous Intellectual Property Rights from the Supplement.

SUVA DECLARATION (1995)

FINAL STATEMENT FROM THE UNDP CONSULTATION ON INDIGENOUS PEOPLES' KNOWLEDGE AND INTELLECTUAL PROPERTY RIGHTS

Suva, Fiji (April 1995).

The participants at a regional consultation on Indigenous peoples knowledge and intellectual property rights held in Suva in 1995 made a Statement which, among other things, reaffirms that "imperialism is perpetuated through intellectual property rights systems, science and modern technology to control and exploit the lands, territories and resources of Indigenous peoples" and condemns "those who use Indigenous biological diversity for commercial and other purposes without our full knowledge and consent." To this end, the Statement proposes and seeks support for the following plan of action:

Initiate the establishment of a treaty declaring the Pacific Regions to be life forms Patent–Free Zone.

Call for a moratorium on bioprospecting in the Pacific and urge Indigenous peoples not to cooperate in bioprospecting activities until appropriate protection mechanisms are in place. Commit ourselves towards raising the public awareness as to the danger of expropriation of Indigenous knowledge and resources.

Recognise the urgent need to identify the extent of expropriation which has already occurs and continues to occur.

Urges Pacific Governments who have not signed GATT to refuse to do so and encourage those Governments who have already signed to protect against provisions which facilitate the expropriation of Indigenous peoples' knowledge and resources and patenting of life forms

Encourage the South Pacific Forum to amend its rules of Procedure to enable accreditation of Indigenous Peoples and NGOs as observers to future forum officials meetings

Strengthen Indigenous networks, encourage the United Nation's Development Program (UNDP) and regional donor to continue to support discussions on Indigenous Peoples' knowledge and intellectual property rights.

Strengthen the capacities of Indigenous peoples to maintain their oral traditions, and encourage initiatives by Indigenous peoples to record their knowledge in a permanent form according to their customary access procedures.

Urge universities, churches, governments, NGOs and other institutions to reconsider their roles in the expropriation of Indigenous Peoples' knowledge and resources and to assist in their return to their rightful owners.

Call on the government and corporate bodies responsible for the destruction of Pacific biodiversity to stop their destructive practices and to compensate the affected communities and rehabilitate the affected environment.

Notes and Questions

1. The Coordinating Body of Indigenous Organizations of the Amazon Basin (COICA) co-hosted a regional meeting in Bolivia in 1994 to debate intellectual property rights and biodiversity. The foregoing statement represents the consensus of the conference.

2. Compare the COICA, Julayinbul and Suva Statements. Do they share the same approach to resolving the conflict over the use of intellectual property laws to protect indigenous heritages? What is their underlying philosophy? Can it be reconciled with TRIPS?

3. Do these statements resolve the problems posed by the earlier materials? Do they present workable guidelines?

4. What areas remain to be clarified under these declarations?

C. CAN NATIVE CULTURE BE PROTECTED FROM DE–CULTURIZING USES UNDER INTELLECTUAL PROPERTY LAWS?

FOR TUSCANS, HOW CAN YOU COPYRIGHT PARADISE?

Bohlen, Celestine, New York Times (August 7, 1997)(section A, page 3).

The ocher hills, patchwork vineyards and olive groves of Tuscany, lorded over by medieval towns and elegant villas shielded by clumps of pine, are probably among the most familiar of the world's backdrops, used to felicitous effect in Renaissance paintings, 19th-century novels and innumerable Italian movies. So now Tuscany is striking back, with a proposal to effectively copyright the region's natural landscape. Local officials, aware that such a notion could never have the force of law, hesitate to use words like copyright, license or trademark. But they are quite serious about trying to stop non-Tuscan brand names from flitting across Tuscan scenes. "We are simply trying not to let our landscape be trivialized by ugly advertising," said Vannino Chiti, president of the Tuscan region.

For centuries, Tuscans have been fiercely protective of a countryside that is a harmonious blend of man-made and natural beauty.

"We feel that our landscape and cultural heritage are the oil of Tuscany," Mr. Chiti said. "People have worked nature for centuries, so it is up to us not to destroy it."

But there are always threats, like a 380,000–watt power line, strung across giant orange and white pylons 220 feet high, that recently sprang across the hills to the southeast of Florence like a huge ski lift.

Aghast at the prospect of losing views that had remained virtually untouched since the Middle Ages, neighbors in the hilly area known as the Colleramole mounted a vigorous campaign, joined by historical societies and consumer groups.

The protesters insisted that they had nothing against progress, or the benefits of electricity. But in a country where eagle-eyed state inspectors are ready to swoop down with fines and denunciations for the slightest alteration to historic and artistic monuments, it seemed ludicrous that the state should deliberately bring ugliness to one of Italy's most precious spots.

At a time when the marketing of Tuscany, its image and its products, is enjoying a boom overseas—particularly in New York, where Tuscan Square, an emporium featuring the regions' products, is to open in Rockefeller Center soon—the region is more sensitive than ever to the preservation and protection of its natural assets.

The main target of a new regional law, now under review, is the protection of Tuscany's agricultural products—its olive oils, cheeses and wines, which include the Chianti region. To protect Tuscan producers, the region is proposing its own voluntary "made in Tuscany" trademark that would guarantee the quality it wants to maintain for local products.

But the other aim is to weed out those products—agricultural and other—that try to associate and sell themselves with images of Tuscany.

"There are so many ads that give the impression that the products they are promoting are Tuscan when they are not," Mr. Chiti said. "That makes it false advertising."

"We would like to insure that if Tuscan landscape is used, that it be credited," Mr. Chiti said. "You would have to specify that you are looking at a Tuscan countryside, because we feel this would have positive implications for the region. For example, a contribution could be given that could be put in a fund for the protection of the landscape and monuments."

Predictably, the region's proposal has been met with outrage and scorn from advertisers, and photographers.

"If ad agencies choose to make their advertisements in Tuscany, they do it because it is a very beautiful region that no one has succeeded in ruining," said Oliviero Toscani, the celebrated image-maker for Benetton, told an Italian newspaper.

"Now they are trying to defend themselves, but against whom? Advertisers? Advertisers aren't a threat, they are simply a link between producers and consumers."

THE WASHINGTON REDSKINS CASE
HARJO v. PRO–FOOTBALL

Trademark Trial and Appeal Board, 1999.
50 U.S.P.Q.2d 1705.

WALTERS, ADMINISTRATIVE TRADEMARK JUDGE.

Petitioners allege that they are Native American persons and enrolled members of federally recognized Indian tribes. As grounds for cancellation, petitioners assert that the word "redskin(s)" or a form of that word appears in the mark in each of the registrations sought to be canceled; that the word "redskin(s)" "was and is a pejorative, derogatory, denigrating, offensive, scandalous, contemptuous, disreputable, disparaging and racist designation for a Native American person"; that the marks in Registration Nos. 986,668 and 987,127 "also include additional matter that, in the context used by registrant, is offensive, disparaging and scandalous"; and that registrant's use of the marks in the identified registrations "offends" petitioners and other Native Americans. Petitioners assert, further, that the marks in the identified registrations "consist of or comprise matter which disparages Native American persons, and brings them into contempt, ridicule, and disrepute" and "consist of or comprise scandalous matter"; and that, therefore, under Section 2(a) of the Trademark Act, 15 U.S.C. 1052(a), the identified registrations should be canceled.

Respondent, in its answer, denies the salient allegations of the petition to cancel and asserts that "through long, substantial and widespread use, advertising and promotion in support thereof and media coverage, said marks have acquired a strong secondary meaning identifying the entertainment services provided by respondent in the form of professional games in the National Football League"; and that "the marks sought to be canceled herein cannot reasonably be understood to refer to the Petitioners or to any of the groups or organizations to which they belong [as] the marks refer to the Washington Redskins football team which is owned by Respondent and thus cannot be interpreted as disparaging any of the Petitioners or as bringing them into contempt or disrepute."

Petitioners contend that the subject registrations are void ab initio and that the word "redskin(s)" "is today and always has been a deeply offensive, humiliating, and degrading racial slur." Petitioners contend that "a substantial composite of the general public considers 'redskin(s)' to be offensive" and that "the inherent nature of the word 'redskin(s)' and Respondent's use of [its marks involved herein] perpetuate the devastating and harmful effects of negative ethnic stereotyping." Petitioners contend, further, that Native Americans "have understood and still understand" the word "redskin(s)" to be a disparaging "racial epithet" that brings them into contempt, ridicule and disrepute.

Petitioners contend that the Board must consider "the historical setting in which the word 'redskin(s)' has been used." In this regard, petitioners allege that "the history of the relationship between EuroAmericans and Native Americans in the United States has generally been one of conflict and domination by the EuroAmericans"; that "[b]eneath this socioeconomic system lay an important cultural belief, namely, that Indians were 'savages' who must be separated from the AngloAmerican colonies and that AngloAmerican expansion would come at the expense of Native Americans"; that, in the 1930's, government policies towards Native Americans began to be more respectful of Native American culture; that, however, these policies were not reflected in the activities and attitudes of the general public, who continued to view and portray Native Americans as "simple 'savages' whose culture was treated mainly as a source of amusement for white culture"; and that it was during this time that respondent first adopted the name "Redskins" for its football team.

Petitioners presented the testimony of its linguistics expert, Dr. Geoffrey Nunberg, regarding the usage of the word "redskin(s)." Petitioners contend that the primary denotation of "redskin(s)" is Native American people; that, only with the addition of the word "Washington," has "redskin(s)" acquired a secondary denotation in the sports world, denoting the NFL Football club; that the "offensive and disparaging qualities" of "redskin(s)" arise from its connotations; and that these negative connotations pertain to the word "redskin(s)" in the context of the team name "Washington Redskins." Regarding whether the negative connotations of "redskin(s)" are inherent or arise from the context of its usage, petitioners contend that "redskin(s)" is inherently offensive and disparaging.

Respondent contends that the word "redskin(s) has throughout history, been a purely denotative term, used interchangeably with 'Indian'." In this regard, respondent argues that "redskin(s)" is "an entirely neutral and ordinary term of reference" from the relevant time period to the present; and that, as such, "redskin(s)" is "[synonymous] with ethnic identifiers such as 'American Indian,' 'Indian,' and 'Native American'." Respondent also states that, through its long and extensive use of "Redskins" in connection with professional football, the word has developed a meaning, "separate and distinct from the core, ethnic meaning" of the word "redskin(s)," denoting the "Washington Redskins" football team; and that such use by respondent "has absolutely no negative effect on the word's neutrality and, indeed, serves to enhance the word's already positive associations as football is neither of questionable morality nor per se offensive to or prohibited by American Indian religious or cultural practices."

Respondent states that while "the term 'redskin,' used in singular, lower case form references an ethnic group, [this] does not automatically render it disparaging when employed as a proper noun in the context of sports."

In response to petitioners' contentions, respondent argues that while " 'redskin' may be employed in connection with warfare, [this] is but a reflection of the troubled history of American Indians, not of any negative connotation inherent in the term itself." Respondent argues that " 'redskin' is not always employed in connection with violence"; that, when "redskin" appears in a violent context, the neutrality of the word "redskin" is apparent from the fact that, as it appears in the evidence of record, the word "Indian" or "Native American" can be substituted therefore without any change in meaning; and, further, that it is often the negative adjective added to this neutral term that renders the entire phrase pejorative.

Respondent contends, further, that its evidence establishes that Native Americans support respondent's use of the name "Washington Redskins"; and that Native Americans "regularly employ the term 'redskin' within their communities."

Respondent concludes that its marks "do not rise to the level of crudeness and vulgarity that the Board has required before deeming the marks scandalous," nor do its marks disparage or bring Native Americans into contempt or disrepute. Respondent argues that disparagement requires intent on the part of the speaker and that its "intent in adopting the team name was entirely positive" as the team name has, over its history, "reflected positive attributes of the American Indian such as dedication, courage and pride." Similarly, respondent notes that third-party registrations portraying Native Americans and the United States nickel, previously in circulation for many years, portraying a Native American are similar to respondent's "respectful depiction in the team's logo"; and that petitioners have not established that this logo is scandalous, disparaging, or brings Native Americans into contempt or disrepute.

Section 2(a)

The relevant portions of Section 2 of the Trademark Act (15 U.S.C. 1052) provide as follows:

No trademark by which the goods of the applicant may be distinguished from the goods of others shall be refused registration on the principal register on account of its nature unless it

(a) Consists of or comprises immoral, deceptive, or scandalous matter; or matter which may disparage or falsely suggest a connection with persons, living or dead, institutions, beliefs, or national symbols, or bring them into contempt, or disrepute;

Scandalous Matter

The vast majority of the relevant reported cases involving that part of Section 2(a) with which we are concerned in this case were decided principally on the basis of whether the marks consisted of scandalous matter. We begin with a review of this precedent.

Faced with a "paucity of legislative history," to aid in interpreting the term "scandalous" in Section 2(a), one of the predecessor courts of our primary reviewing court found that it must look to the "ordinary and common meaning" of that term, which meaning could be established by reference to court and Board decisions, and to dictionary definitions. In particular, the Court looked to dictionary definitions extant at the time of the enactment of the Trademark Act in 1946, and noted that "scandalous" was defined as " 'Giving offense to the conscience or moral feelings; exciting reprobation, calling out condemnation. Disgraceful to reputation.' [and] 'shocking to the sense of truth, decency, or propriety; disgraceful, offensive; disreputable, as scandalous conduct.' " *In re McGinley*, 660 F.2d 481, 211 U.S.PQ 668, 673 (CCPA 1981).

"In determining whether or not a mark is disparaging, the perceptions of the general public are irrelevant. Rather, because the portion of Section 2(a) proscribing disparaging marks targets certain persons, institutions or beliefs, only the perceptions of those referred to, identified or implicated in some recognizable manner by the involved mark are relevant to this determination." *In re Hines*, 31 U.S.PQ2d 1685, 1688 (TTAB 1994), *vacated on other grounds*, 32 U.S.PQ2d 1376 (TTAB 1994).

We agree that there is a substantial amount of evidence in the record establishing that, since at least the 1960's and continuing to the present, the term "Redskins" has been used widely in print and other media to identify respondent's professional football team and its entertainment services. But our inquiry does not stop here. Our precedent also requires us to consider the manner in which respondent's marks appear and are used in the marketplace. In this regard, while petitioners concede that, from at least the 1960's to the present, the word "Redskins," in the context of professional sports, identifies respondent's football team, petitioners contend, essentially, that all professional football teams have themes that are carried through in their logos, mascots, nicknames, uniforms and various paraphernalia sold or used in connection with their entertainment services. Petitioners point to the Native American theme evident in respondent's logos and the imagery and themes used by respondent in connection with its football team and games. This imagery is also evident in the writings and activities of the media and in the activities and writings of the team's fans. Petitioners contend that, in view of the team's Native American theme, one cannot separate the connotation of "redskin(s)" as a reference to Native Americans from the connotation of that word as it identifies respondent's football team and is used in connection with respondent's entertainment services.

We conclude from the evidence of record that the word "redskin(s)" does not appear during the second half of this century in written or spoken language, formal or informal, as a synonym for "Indian" or "Native American" because it is, and has been since at least the 1960's, perceived by the general population, which includes Native Americans, as a pejorative term for Native Americans.

We find the context provided by Dr. Hoxie's historical account, which respondent does not dispute, of the often acrimonious AngloAmerican/Native American relations from the early Colonial period to the present to provide a useful historical perspective from which to view the writings, cartoons and other references to Native Americans in evidence from the late 19th century and throughout this century.

Finally, we note petitioners' telephone survey, as described herein, purporting to measure the views, at the time of the survey in 1996, of the general population and, separately, of Native Americans towards the word "redskin" as a reference to Native Americans. When read a list of seven words referring to Native Americans, 46.2% of participants in the general population sample (139 of 301 participants) and 36.6% of participants in the Native American sample (131 of 358 participants) indicated that they found the word "redskin" offensive as a reference to Native Americans. We have discussed, supra, several of the flaws in the survey that limit its probative value. [T]he survey is of limited applicability to the issues in this case as it sought to measure the participants' views only as of 1996, when the survey was conducted, and its scope is limited to the connotation of the word "redskin" as a term of Native Americans, without any reference to respondent's football team. However, considering these limitations, we find that the percentage of participants in each sample who responded positively, i.e., stated they were offended by the word "redskin(s)" for Native Americans, to be significant. We conclude that the marks in each of the challenged registrations consist of or comprise matter, namely, the word or root word, "Redskin," which may bring Native Americans into contempt or disrepute.

Notes and Questions

1. *De-culturizing Uses.* In the Marvel comic book *The Kachinas Sing of Doom*, published in 1992, the villains are white members of a local gambling cartel who wear Kachina masks and costumes as disguises. The use of such imagery was directly contrary to the transformative power represented by the masks in the Hopi religion. The Kachina mask does not serve as a disguise. Instead, the wearer is transformed into the spirit represented by the mask. One scholar, David Howes, posits that the harm caused by such a deculturizing use is actually twofold. The first he calls "the dilution of tradition," which results in the undermining of the culture's fundamental beliefs by incorporating the misconceptions derived from the deculturization. In the case of the Marvel Comics, the misconception would be that masks are for disguise, not revelation. The second harm he calls "the dissemination of tradition," which is the loss of control over public dissemination of "culturally sensitive information." Where, as in the Hopi culture, the ritual or information is considered sacred, or restricted only to initiates, its uncontrolled public dissemination is directly contrary to the cultural precepts in which it arises. David Howes, Cultural Appropriation and Resistance in the American Southwest: Decomodifying 'Indianness,' in CrossCultural Consumption: Global Markets, Local Realities (1996).

2. *Ceremonial Rituals.* In New Zealand the traditional hangi–Maori greeting–by law can only be performed in marae or meeting places. It can no

longer be performed in hotels. Maoris are also developing a hall mark of authenticity to endure product quality. What other intellectual property related steps can indigenous peoples take to protect their native ceremonies and rituals?

3. Can the scenery of Tuscan be protected from use on posters, in plays or paintings under current international intellectual property standards? Does the scenery represent a work of national folklore that could be protected under the Tunis Model Law?

4. Could the Grand Canyon be protected from unauthorized use on posters, plays or paintings? Should such works of natural beauty be protected from unauthorized commercial reproductions? From disparaging uses? What about works of constructed beauty such as the Eiffel Tower? Could reproductions of such works be controlled?

5. How should the concerns of indigenous people's over the protection of their indigenous knowledge, folklore and rituals be balanced against the property rights of intellectual property owners? Did the court in the *Washington Redskins* case strike the appropriate balance?

D. WHO HAS THE RIGHT TO CONTROL THE PROTECTION OF WORKS THAT CONSTITUTE THE COMMON HERITAGE OF MANKIND?

THE ELGIN MARBLES CONTROVERSY

In 1799, Thomas Bruce, the seventh Earl of Elgin, was the British ambassador to the Ottoman Empire when he received a permit from the Sultan to remove some of the famous marble sculptures from the Parthenon. The permit was granted in extraordinary circumstances since the Ottomans were urgently seeking British help against Napoleon. The language did not clearly indicate that Elgin could remove the Marbles from Greece. More importantly, no under asked the Greeks, who were then under Turkish domination if they objected to the removal of the Marbles. In 1806 Elgin removed the Marbles to London. Eventually, the Marbles were displayed in the British Museum.

The return of the so-called "Elgin Marbles", has become a cause celebre in the arena of cultural patrimony. Poems by Lord George Byron, impassioned pleas by Melina Mercouri, even a petition signed by various member nations of the European Union have all contributed to the demand to return the Marbles to their "home."

There is no question the Marbles have been safeguarded from potential harm during Greece's various wars. They have also been safeguarded from potential harm caused by Athens' pollution and automotive fumes. Such concerns, it is claimed, are no longer relevant in view of Greece's plans to establish an Acropolis Museum where they could be safely stored.

Greece claims a right to the return of its cultural patrimony. Britain claims the continued right to safeguard this important work of cultural significance, a work that represents the "common heritage of mankind."

Such disputes are not limited to the return of Greek marbles. The Mexican government has requested the return of diverse Aztec and Mayan artifacts; the Irish have sought the return of codices containing ancient sagas of their ancestors.

But in the absence of international rules, determinations remain a matter of individual choice.

COMMON CULTURAL PROPERTY: THE SEARCH FOR RIGHTS OF PROTECTIVE INTERVENTION

M. Catherine Vernon, 26 Case. W. Res. J. Int'l L. 435 (1994).

MORE ARGUMENTS AGAINST INTERVENTION: NATIONAL PATRIMONY VS. COMMON CULTURAL PROPERTY

In addition to claims of territorial sovereignty as an argument against protective intervention, many nations claim that treasures located within their boundaries are part of their national patrimony rather than the common heritage of mankind. Cultural heritage takes on particular significance in this manner with the lessor economically and politically developed states. In its purest form, the concept of national cultural patrimony views cultural objects produced, or first discovered, within a state as belonging to that state based on the special relationship between that state's people and their cultural artifacts. In fact, a basic principle of cultural property preservation is that cultural objects, as basic elements of civilization and national culture, can only be fully appreciated in close connection with accurate information as to their origin, history, and traditional status. But often these claims are based on the mere physical presence of a work in the claiming country, without exclusive cultural attachment. As in the case of the Acropolis of Greece or the Great Pyramids of Egypt, for example, or any other internationally significant sites within a given state, the weaknesses of the doctrine of national patrimony come to light: it could effectively cut off the bulk of humanity from exposure to that great civilization. Under the national patrimony doctrine, and its reliance on the law of the situs to govern access and protection of cultural property, other states cannot influence the fate of commonly significant property, despite the property's importance to the common heritage of mankind. This was painfully shown by the Chinese Cultural Revolution and its destructive effects on cultural property within the People's Republic.

Further support for national patrimony claims of control over cultural property comes from those politicians and historians who argue that pride in past achievements can increase the attachment of citizens to current social and political structures associated with that tradition. Experience shows that politically motivated cultural associations may be argued from racial descent, territorial coincidence, or even from mere cultural sympathy. Some observable examples in this century include Iran under the Shah, Kampuchea as heir to the Khmer culture, Israel as heir to Hebrew culture, and many modern African States. Cultural association as a nationalistic medium can take on deep significance for the people of a country in terms of identification and unification.

To these ends, unfortunately, national patrimony is sometimes manipulated, its stories and history rewritten in efforts to use the past as propaganda for a current regime. The National Socialist Regime in Germany under Hitler's Third Reich was notorious for its use and abuse of the past for imperialist and racist purposes, invoking the concept of Kulturkreis, the identification of ethnic regions based on excavated cultural materials, and then using this theory to support Nazi expansionist aims in central and eastern Europe. The flaws inherent in basing cultural property rights on national patrimony arguments become even more evident in the context of such abusive examples as the Third Reich.

Notes and Questions

1. What standards should be used to determine ownership of works of global cultural significance? Should the domiciliary country of the creator of such works have the exclusive right to determine how such works will be preserved?

2. Should the possessor of an ancient manuscript of international cultural significance have the right to control access to the manuscript? Could the possessor decide to destroy the manuscript because it was determined to be culturally disparaging?

3. Do the "Elgin Marbles" qualify as a work of national folklore? Do the Irish sagas?

4. What standards should be applied internationally to determine ownership and control of works of global cultural significance? How should such works even be identified? Can such works be parodied or altered without violating international norms? Who decides?

5. For a further discussion on the problems of cultural patrimony, see D'Amato & Long, International Intellectual Property Anthology, Chapters 5 & 6 (Anderson Publishing Co. 1995).

Index